History of the
U.S. NAVY

History of the
U.S.
NAVY

1942–1991

Robert W. Love, Jr.

Stackpole Books

Published by
STACKPOLE BOOKS
Cameron and Kelker Streets
P.O. Box 1831
Harrisburg, PA 17105

Interior design by Marcia Lee Dobbs

Maps by Chris Jung

Printed in the United States of America

10 9 8 7 6 5 4 3 2 1

Library of Congress Cataloging-in-Publication Data
Love, Robert William, 1944–
   History of the U.S. Navy.

   Includes bibliographical references and indexes.
   Contents: v. 1. 1775–1941 — v. 2. 1942–1991
   1. United States. Navy—History. 2. United States—History, Naval.
   I. Title. II. Title: History of the United States Navy.
VA55.L68 1991   359'.00973—dc20   91-27510
ISBN 0-8117-1862-X (v. 1)
ISBN 0-8117-1863-8 (v. 2)

Contents

Chapter One

From Pearl Harbor to the Java Sea

1942

"What a holocaust!" Winston Churchill exclaimed on hearing of the Japanese attack on Pearl Harbor on 7 December 1941. At 0355 that Sunday, the coastal minecraft *Condor* on patrol off the entrance to Pearl Harbor had sighted the periscope of a Japanese midget submarine and issued a report to Captain William Outerbridge, who was directing the harbor patrol in the nearby destroyer *Ward*, but at the time, Outerbrige did not act on this news. Less than three hours later, Commander Lawrence C. Grannis in the storeship *Antares* sighted another midget submarine trailing him into Pearl Harbor and he also alerted Outerbridge, who then reacted quickly by launching a depth-charge attack that sank the hostile boat at 0645. The commander in chief of the Pacific Fleet, Admiral Husband Kimmel, was apprised of this incident at 0710, but owing to "so many . . . false reports of submarines in the outlying area, I thought . . . I would wait for verification," and so he failed to order that an alarm be sounded throughout the fleet. Unbeknownst to Kimmel, yet another Japanese midget submarine was being attacked at the time by a harbor patrol PBY Catalina. This incident was not reported to Kimmel's fleet headquarters but to the naval district commander, Rear Admiral Claude Bloch, who did not deem it urgent. Two of the three new mobile Army radar sets on northern Oahu were tracking incoming flights of unidentified aircraft at roughly the same time, but the duty officers at Wheeler airbase dismissed these two last-minute warnings without further investigation.

To attack Pearl Harbor, Admiral Isoroku Yamamoto, Commander of the Japanese Combined Fleet, had organized a Striking Force composed of 6 carriers and 6 cruisers operating 370 planes under the command of Vice Admiral Chuichi Nagumo. He had been steaming unobserved in bad weather through the North Pacific for nearly two weeks. At 0600 on 7 December Nagumo reached a point about 240 miles north of Oahu from which he launched a first wave of 183 aircraft, a flight that arrived over Pearl Harbor at 0755. The battle began when Japanese dive bombers destroyed the Navy's patrol planes and fighters on Ford Island while Zero fighters smashed the Marine air wing at Ewa Airfield. A flight of Japanese Val dive bombers attacked the PBY Catalinas at the Kaneohe Naval Air Station and destroyed or damaged nearly all the aircraft there. The Japanese also destroyed most of the Army Air Corps planes at Hickham, Bellows, and Wheeler fields.

These successful strikes gave the Japanese air superiority for the rest of the operation. From intelligence provided by Japan's consul in Honolulu, Nagumo thought he knew Kimmel's berthing arrangements for the Pacific Fleet, and this led his planners to assign sixteen Kate torpedo bombers to attack the seven American battleships moored at Ford Island opposite the Navy yard. The *West Virginia* was hit by several torpedoes, but an alert crew saved her from sinking. The *Oklahoma* capsized after being struck by three torpedoes, and the *Arizona*, blown apart by torpedo and bomb explosions, sank so quickly that more than one thousand sailors were trapped below. Two Japanese torpedoes punctured the hull of the *California* and she settled to her superstructure. Moments later low-flying Kate level-bombers came in and seriously damaged the inboard battleships *Tennessee* and *Maryland.* The old battleship *Nevada*, hit by a torpedo and two bombs, got under way nonetheless and was heading down the channel for open water when Kimmel reached his headquarters at the Submarine Base and ordered her not to leave the harbor. This gallant ship was about to anchor off Hospital Point when she was struck again by three Val dive bombers and ran gently aground.

By 0825, the first flight of Japanese planes was returning to the carriers, but fifteen minutes later a second wave of 171 fighters, dive bombers, and level-bombers appeared over Oahu. By

this time the American antiaircraft batteries had recovered, however, and the second wave did relatively little damage. After crippling the *Nevada*, the enemy planes turned their attention to the
fleet flagship *Pennsylvania*, which they soon located in the drydock across from Ford Island. Captain Charles M. Cooke and his
well-trained gunners had put up a withering antiaircraft fire during the first phase of the battle, but at 0905 the *Pennsylvania* suffered moderate damage from a bomb hit, and the destroyers
Cassin and *Downes*, also wedged in the drydock, were consumed
by fires. "There were always too many ships in Pearl Harbor to
take an air attack," Admiral Leahy observed, but Kimmel had
done nothing to reduce the risk. Kimmel later claimed that it was
lucky that the Battle Force was not caught at sea and that the confines of Pearl Harbor had saved many lives. However, had he sent
the battleships out for the weekend—or at least rotated the battleship divisions in and out of Pearl Harbor every few days—the
Japanese would not have known where to find those that were at
sea. Japan's aircraft were not equipped with radar, and Nagumo's
purpose was to launch a lightning strike and retire, not to loiter
off Hawaii and conduct long-range searches.

When the last enemy plane flew away from Pearl Harbor,
Rear Admiral Patrick Bellinger, the patrol wing commander who
had warned Kimmel of just such an attack in March 1941, assumed that "they probably would . . . refuel and come back." Damage reports told Nagumo that he faced no threat to his task force.
Most of Hawaii's aircraft were destroyed or inoperable, the airfields were damaged, and it would take days or weeks for reinforcements to arrive from the mainland. Nagumo's planes had
sunk or damaged all of the battleships in Pearl Harbor. He was
surprised not to find the American carriers in Pearl Harbor but
knew that only two or three flattops, at most, might be at sea, half
the number in his task force. He had lost only twenty-nine planes,
his ships were unharmed, and his oilers were well positioned a
short distance to the north. "Stay in the area for several days and
run down the enemy carriers," advised Commander Minoru Gen-
da, the author of Operation Hawaii's air plan. There were many
targets on Oahu that had not been attacked, and the younger air
officers urged Nagumo to launch at least one more strike. He declined. Like most Japanese admirals, he often talked about winning battles of annihilation but refused to risk his ships when
these opportunities arose. "The objective of the Pearl Harbor op-

eration has been achieved," Rear Admiral Ryunosuke Kusaka announced decisively. The carriers recovered their aircraft, turned to the west, and headed for home. Nagumo's planes had not touched the Pacific Fleet's vital fuel farms, its submarine pens, or the large ammunition dump foolishly situated at the entrance to Pearl Harbor, but Nagumo's attack on Pearl Harbor, however incomplete, was a major tactical victory for Japan. Inasmuch as the old American battleships posed no threat whatsoever to Japan's upcoming western Pacific and Southeast Asia offensives, however, it had no long-lasting strategic significance. And it was a political blunder without parallel in modern history.[1]

Returning from Wake Island in the *Enterprise*, the commander of the Pacific Fleet carriers, Vice Admiral William Halsey, got word of the attack when he was 200 miles west of Oahu. His search for the Japanese carriers was frustrated, however, because, on the advice of Lieutenant Commander Edwin Layton, the Pearl Harbor–based Pacific Fleet intelligence officer, Kimmel sent the *Enterprise*'s search planes south of Hawaii to find the Japanese Striking Force. This decision was surprising inasmuch as all prewar exercises demonstrated that the enemy would most likely launch an attack from a position to the north. Owing to the great disparity of the opposing carrier forces, however, Halsey was fortunate that he did not locate Nagumo's ships that day.

An aroused president went before an enraged joint session of Congress on 8 December, and in a stirring, patriotic address denounced the "day of infamy" and called for a declaration of war against Japan, correctly anticipating the disastrous decisions by Hitler and Mussolini three days later to honor the Tripartite Pact and declare war on the United States. A few days later, Kimmel's anguished, hounded features were painted on the cover of *Time* magazine against a background of burning ships. FDR soon announced that the Pearl Harbor attack would be investigated by a presidential commission chaired by his partisan, Associate Supreme Court Justice Owen Roberts. The Roberts Commission Report, though based on incomplete evidence, nonetheless drew the correct conclusion: Kimmel and, to a lesser extent, Army Lieutenant General Walter Short, the Hawaiian Department commander, were largely responsible for the tragedy. "If the Navy Department had in any way condoned the conduct of the officials it considered responsible for Pearl Harbor," wrote Captain W. D. Puleston, a former director of ONI, "it would have fatally

lowered the standard of conduct expected of its high commanders." Admiral King, who had been surprised when Kimmel had
been named to command the Pacific Fleet in early 1941, thought
him to be unfit for such an important job. King later concluded
that Kimmel had a plan, and the means, to defend his base but
failed to implement it. Pearl Harbor, thereafter synonymous with
a sneak attack on an unprepared enemy, stunned all Americans.
Most had expected the country to enter the war soon, but a siz-
able minority, most of whom opposed assisting Stalin's Russia,
were still resisting Roosevelt's pro-Soviet policy. Pearl Harbor instantly unified public opinion behind the war effort.[2]

Admiral Harold Stark, the CNO, now tried to reorganize
America's position in the Pacific, but it was crumbling everywhere under the weight of Japan's offensive. The Yangtze Patrol
gunboat *Wake* was captured on 8 December, Britain's crown
colony of Hong Kong fell, and two days later the Marines at
Peking and Tientsin surrendered. Guam was overrun on the
10th. Stark expected to give up these forward outposts, but he
wanted to prevent the enemy from moving into the South Pacific
and to hold Midway Island, now menaced by a Japanese movement into the Gilberts. To defend Hawaii, Kimmel had recalled
the *Lexington* task force from Midway, and Stark directed Rear
Admiral Frank Jack Fletcher in the carrier *Saratoga* to steam from
San Diego to Oahu as quickly as possible. On 11 December, before Fletcher stood into Pearl Harbor, a Japanese amphibious
landing was repulsed by 500 Marines defending Wake Island.
Their heroic stand moved Kimmel to organize an operation intended both to obstruct an enemy thrust against Midway and reinforce Wake with more Marines and a fighter squadron. Also in
the back of Kimmel's mind may have been his prewar plan to
lure the enemy fleet into the central Pacific. Halsey in the *Enterprise* was to cover the Hawaii-Midway axis, Vice Admiral Wilson
Brown with the *Lexington* task force was to raid Jaluit in the Marshalls as a diversion, and Fletcher in the *Saratoga* was to deliver
the reinforcements to Wake.

The day before the Wake Island plan went into effect, Navy
Secretary Frank Knox arrived in Hawaii to investigate the Pearl
Harbor attack and fix some preliminary blame. Kimmel con-
fessed to Knox that he had been caught unawares, and after
Knox returned to Washington on 14 December he and Roosevelt
agreed to instruct Vice Admiral William Pye to take Kimmel's

place until the newly appointed Pacific Fleet commander, Admiral Chester Nimitz, the former chief of the Bureau of Navigation, reached Oahu at the end of the month. Soon after Pye took command, Commander Joseph Rochefort, who directed the Navy's radio intelligence center in Hawaii, warned him that his code breakers had just located some Japanese carriers in the Marshalls. Pye therefore canceled Brown's raid on Jaluit and ordered him to rendezvous with Fletcher and reinforce the Wake relief expedition.

To everyone's distress, Fletcher's progress was agonizingly slow. The only fleet oiler available to support the *Saratoga* was the old *Neches*, and Fletcher allowed her 12-knot speed to dictate the movement of his entire task force. When the weather turned bad on 21 December, he decided to refuel his destroyers, but saltwater contamination of the *Saratoga*'s fuel tanks caused an additional delay. Two days later the Japanese unexpectedly landed on Wake and overcame the gallant American defenders. Pye, alarmed by the reported presence of two Japanese carriers in the area, now asked for Stark's permission to abandon the Wake Island relief operation and recall both Brown and Fletcher to Hawaiian waters. This difficult decision led to the discredit of just about everyone involved in the affair. When an embarrassed Stark explained the withdrawal to Roosevelt, he was subjected to a sarcastic condemnation of the fiasco. Confidence in Washington in the Pacific Fleet's eagerness to engage the enemy sought a new low. The admirals were "very crusty and bigoted and arrogant," FDR complained to General Marshall a few weeks later.[3]

Pearl Harbor not only galvanized American determination to defeat the Axis but also put pressure on Roosevelt to reorganize his chaotic administration and revamp his military command. He had no confidence in the State Department but refused to replace Secretary Hull. Instead, he continued conducting his own form of intuitive diplomacy from the White House with a small personal staff consisting solely of longtime political aides and cronies. His closest adviser was Harry Hopkins, but he had no training in foreign affairs. Like FDR, Hopkins consistently espoused pro-Soviet measures. Roosevelt created a number of new civilian agencies to deal with industrial matters, but he hampered their work by refusing to appoint strong figures to oversee the war economy or to clearly delegate authority.

The Pacific Ocean in World War II

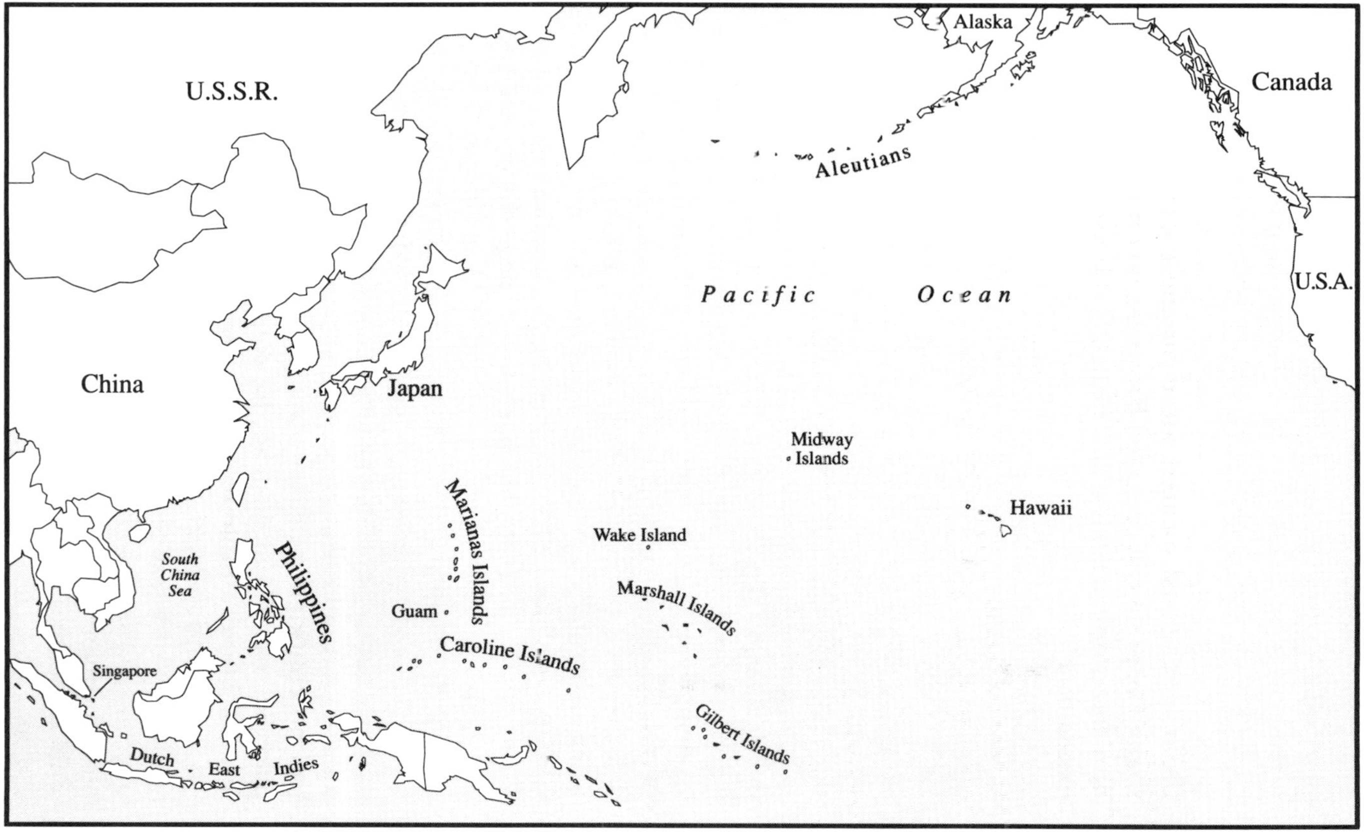

Canada

U.S.A.

Alaska

Aleutians

Hawaii

Pacific   Ocean

Midway
Islands

Wake Island

Marshall Islands

Gilbert Islands

Marianas Islands

Caroline Islands

Guam

Japan

Philippines

U.S.S.R.

China

South
China
Sea

Singapore

East Indies

Dutch

Nonetheless, the huge American industrial base, spurred by enormous wartime deficit spending, converted to military production with astounding results. The president was opposed to reorganizing the War or Navy departments, although he did agree to General Marshall's purge of the Army's bureaucracy in March 1942. Roosevelt was more resistant to Navy reform, however, either because he was familiar with the status quo or because administrative tidiness held no appeal for him. He was probably upset with the CNO, Stark, over the Pearl Harbor disaster, and a week after the attack, he approved Secretary Knox's plan to name the commander in chief of the Atlantic Fleet, Admiral Ernest J. King, as the Washington-based commander in chief of the U.S. Fleet. Since King's relationship to Stark was unclear, both men asked Roosevelt to clarify their responsibilities, but he refused to do so and tolerated this absurd, confusing arrangement until March 1942. On his own, Stark at last brought matters to a head by announcing that he intended to resign, and in mid-March Roosevelt reacted by naming him to the command of all American naval forces in Europe. In this way, King became both commander in chief of the U.S. Fleet and CNO, the most powerful naval leader in American history.

The need to reorganize the rest of the American high military command became evident soon after Prime Minister Churchill and the British chiefs of staff arrived in Washington on Christmas Day 1941 to discuss grand strategy during the month-long Arcadia Conference. Comfortable with familiar faces, FDR decided simply to transform the old Joint Army-Navy Board into the Joint Chiefs of Staff, a body that at first included Admirals Stark and King, General Marshall, and Marshall's deputy, Lieutenant General Henry H. Arnold, the chief of staff of the Army Air Forces. In July 1942, when political pressure mounted to name General MacArthur the global commander of all American military forces, Roosevelt, who regarded MacArthur as "dangerous," handled the problem by selecting Admiral William D. Leahy as his military chief of staff. Shrewd, intelligent, and blunt, Leahy was an intense nationalist who despised the Axis and distrusted America's foremost allies, Britain and Russia, but he could never get FDR to share his concern about Stalin's war aims. A former CNO, he kept his hands off Navy affairs so as not to antagonize King, and much of his time was spent mediating military-civilian and military-industrial disputes. Leahy apparently had no strong views on strategy, nor did he feel that it was his duty to impose his opinions on others. By reason of his seniority, Leahy became chairman of the JCS. When they met together during wartime conferences, the JCS and the British Chiefs of Staff Committee assumed the title of the Combined Chiefs of Staff. Because FDR refused to coordinate policy through his cabinet, and because the JCS negotiated strategy with the British, Navy Secretary Knox and Secretary of War Stimson were effectively isolated and prevented from influencing high policy or strategy. When, in April 1942, Knox asked plaintively to be given copies of JCS minutes and informed of their decisions, King brusquely told his flag aide that the secretary was only "to see my copies from time to time." Nor was Knox given access to the heavily guarded plot room where King's flag traffic was maintained, and soon after King became CominCh-CNO, Knox was fighting a rearguard action to maintain Undersecretary James Forrestal's influence over procurement, one of the few bureaucratic battles he eventually won.[4]

Days after the attack on Pearl Harbor, it was clear in Washington that the Allied forces in the western Pacific were facing ruin at the hands of the Japanese. In March 1941, Stark had suggested that Admiral Thomas Hart, who commanded the small Asiatic Fleet, create a cruiser-destroyer task force to operate with the British and Dutch navies after war broke out. Several prewar attempts to coordinate Allied strategy in the Far East failed, however. In short, when Japan invaded the Philippines, Hart intended to use his submarines to defend Luzon and to assemble his cruisers and destroyers into a striking arm that would operate between Mindanao and the Dutch East Indies. In November 1941, Hart sent a destroyer division to the Dutch port of Balikpapan. He fully expected the Japanese to attack the Philippines any day, and he understood that the islands could not be held.

Earlier in the year, Stark had toyed with a plan to send the cruiser *Houston*'s task force to support Singapore, a scheme that Hart opposed, both because it might put him under British command and because it diluted his ability to conduct even a perfunctory defense of the Philippines. Therefore Stark postponed creating the multinational Eastern Allied Naval Force until the British were ready to send a fleet to the Far East sufficient to hold the seaward approaches to Singapore and the Malay Peninsula. This caused Churchill to name Vice Admiral Sir Tom Phillips to the command of the Royal Navy's Far Eastern Fleet in November 1941 and to direct him to defend Singapore with the battleship *Prince of Wales* and the battlecruiser *Repulse*, thus meeting Stark's precondition for more American support for Britain's position in Asia. Combat air patrol for these ships was to have been provided by the British carrier *Indomitable*, but she could not join Phillips after her captain ran her aground in the West Indies late that month.

On 6 December, Hart conferred with Phillips in Manila. No opponent of Anglo-American cooperation, Hart did dislike the Englishman's plan to use the Asiatic Fleet's destroyers to escort convoys between the Dutch East Indies and Singapore rather than attack the Japanese invasion convoys he already knew to be at sea. However, he approved Phillips' suggestion that the American destroyer division at Balikpapan head to Singapore and operate there for the time being under British command. These ships were at sea steaming for Malaya when the war broke out. Although Hart and Phillips were agreed on the rudiments of a strategy to delay the Japanese storm, Hart had in the meantime become involved in a nasty, personal feud with his old friend, General Douglas MacArthur, the Army's new Far Eastern commander. At the root of this quarrel was MacArthur's obvious disinterest in Hart's intentions and MacArthur's bizarre plan to defend the entire Philippine archipelago instead of carefully withdrawing to entrenched lines on the Bataan Peninsula once the enemy landed. Hart, predicting that MacArthur's strategy would fail, was preparing for the day that Stark would order the Navy to evacuate the islands.

When Hart learned about the attack on Pearl Harbor, his Asiatic Fleet was ready for war, but MacArthur, the most bellicose commander in the Pacific, seemed paralyzed. During that first morning of war, both Hart and MacArthur received news of the Hawaiian disaster several hours before any Japanese airplanes appeared over the Philippines. The Asiatic Fleet was on full alert. MacArthur's Army Air Force took to the skies to reconnoiter, while he mulled over whether and how he should implement prewar orders from General Marshall to bomb enemy airfields on Formosa. At noon, while MacArthur was still deliberating with himself, a flight of Army Air Force B-17 bombers landed at Clark Airfield on Luzon and their P-40 pursuit plane escorts returned to the fighter base at Iba; the pilots went to lunch, leaving no aircraft on patrol overhead. Within moments, two waves of Mitsubishi bombers escorted by Zero fighters struck both Clark and Iba, destroying nearly half of MacArthur's front-line planes, most of which were hit on the ground. Although a few vessels were damaged and two PBY Catalinas were splashed, the Asiatic Fleet's losses were few, but Hart warned Stark later that day that the Army had been thoroughly "mauled."[5]

"We have to do our best and we shall," Hart bravely told his men, although his "grand little air force" consisted of only one Navy patrol wing of twenty-eight PBY Catalinas. On 8 December, the seaplane tender *Langley*, two oilers, and two destroyers left Manila Bay and, on the following day, rendezvoused south of Luzon with Rear Admiral William Glassford's task force of two cruisers and four destroyers. Then, on the 10th, Hart learned that Admiral Phillips had been killed when the *Prince of Wales* and *Repulse*, on a sortie to obstruct an enemy landing on the Kra Peninsula, were caught without air cover and sunk by Japanese torpedo bombers. While reading this message, Hart heard aircraft overhead, and he looked out of his office window just in time to see the approach of the first wave of Japanese planes to bring Cavite under attack. Fifty-four bombers pummelled the yard for two hours, sinking the old submarine *Sealion* and shooting up the destroyer *Pillsbury* and the minesweeper *Bittern*. The yard was in flames and little could be saved. Six days later, a Japanese task force put assault troops ashore on northern Luzon. Although Manila was now "untenable as a base on account of the air situation," Glassford's cruiser-destroyer task force was by this time well on its way to the Dutch East Indies, owing to Hart's careful prewar preparations. Rear Admiral William Purnell's small destroyer group was escorting a freighter convoy and survived a harrowing voyage to reach the Asiatic Fleet's new base at Surabaja on 17 December. Stark was now worried that Hart had stayed too long in Manila, and on that same day he directed Hart to abandon the Philippines "when in your judgment you can from elsewhere more effectively direct operations."[6]

With MacArthur's air force shattered, only Hart's submarines could now contest Japanese movements in Philippine waters. However, the Navy's newer S-class fleet submarines were not designed to operate in the shallow coastal waters off Luzon, and, unless they were careful, submarine skippers found themselves easy targets for the enemy's air patrols. Hart wanted to disrupt the busy Japanese anchorage off the main invasion beach on Lingayen Gulf, but this water was only 120 feet deep and when American submarines were spotted by the enemy they had little room to maneuver to escape depth-charge counterattacks. "We were under aerial surveillance all the time," recalled Hart's aide, Lieutenant Commander Robert Dennison. "The submarines had to sit on the bottom during daylight when they came off patrol and then surface at night for replenishment." Moreover, Hart had only two destroyers, one of which was damaged, six PT boats, and a handful of yard patrol craft to defend the *Canopus*, his lone submarine tender. The Asiatic Fleet's powerful Submarine Force included twenty-three modern fleet-class and six over-age *S*-class submarines, but Hart was frustrated that they accomplished very little. A veteran submariner, he did not fully realize that many of his skippers were too old, too timid, and too devoted to a tactical doctrine that emphasized attacks on warships rather than transports or freighters. And, unbeknownst to Hart, the Navy's new Mark XIV steam torpedo repeatedly malfunctioned.[7]

Angered and confused by the lack of results, Hart relieved several skippers after unsuccessful patrols and instructed his submariners to attack any Japanese ship, but these measures made little difference. On 12 December, Lieutenant Commander Wreford G. Chapple in the *S-38* closed on a Japanese transport, maneuvered into a perfect attack angle, and fired a brace of torpedoes at close range, but to no avail. Either the Mark XIV torpedoes ran under the ship or the Mark VI exploders went off prematurely. Nine days later, Lieutenant Commander David A. Hurt in the *Permit* fired two torpedoes at a Japanese destroyer at point-blank range, but neither weapon did any damage. Then, on Christmas Day, Lieutenant Commander Charles L. Freeman in the *Skipjack* located an enemy cruiser, surfaced to attack, and drilled her with three torpedoes. Again, the torpedoes malfunctioned. By this time the Japanese had taken the precaution of providing powerful escort groups to defend the Lingayen Gulf transport anchorage, a force so active that only Chapple in the *S-38* managed to reenter the Gulf, where he finally bagged a transport riding at anchor.

On 22 December, General Nasaharu Homma landed two understrength divisions on the shores of Lingayen Gulf and quickly advanced on Manila. MacArthur's plan to defend the Philippine beaches was now in shambles. That day Hart and

MacArthur, very old friends, met for the last time in their lives. The stormy farewell was charged with emotion. MacArthur, bitter over his impending defeat, condemned the Navy for not supporting his operations. "What in the world is the matter with your submarines?" he asked spitefully. Hart's boats had fired sixty-six torpedoes during thirty-one attacks but had sunk only two Japanese ships. Hart, knowing that MacArthur was looking for a scapegoat, offered no answer to the charges. He also understood that it would be futile to point out MacArthur's many mistakes. The "submarines and I must hang on from here as long as we can," he wrote that night. "We have to guard the Navy's white plume." Then, without warning Hart, MacArthur announced on 25 December that he was declaring Manila an "open city" and ordered his troops to withdraw to the Bataan Peninsula. According to Dennison, Hart "couldn't believe it." Hart had earlier assembled several oil barges and support craft in Manila Bay and planned to withdraw them to the southern Philippines and continue submarine operations from there, but with no timely warning that MacArthur was about to abandon the capital this well conceived strategy now had to be abandoned. The veteran 5,900-ton tender *Canopus* had escaped harm during the air raids over Cavite, but when MacArthur declared Manila an "open city," Hart had to order her to retire to Mariveles Bay at the tip of Bataan. On the 29th, and again two days later, she was badly damaged by enemy planes and could no longer support the Asiatic Fleet's submarines. Three days earlier, before dawn on the 26th, Hart had boarded the submarine *Shark* and sailed for the Dutch East Indies. Six days later, MacArthur was boated over to his tunnel bunker on Corregidor Island in the middle of Manila Bay.[8]

MacArthur had made no attempt to prepare Bataan for a long siege or to stock his positions there with ammunition, food, spares, and medicine. On 9 January 1942, he was taken by a PT boat from Corregidor to visit the Bataan battlefield, assured everyone there that he could hold the peninsula for "several months," and retired to his tunnel command post. This was his only visit to Bataan during the entire campaign. His press releases, badly distorting reality, soon made MacArthur a national hero for directing the defense of Bataan. This performance sickened Hart, who was forced to leave behind a scratch force of naval infantry with the Bataan garrison. In the meantime, MacArthur was trying to pin the blame for the loss of the Philippines on Hart, whom he denounced as a "defeatist."[9]

The unexpectedly sudden collapse of Luzon and the threat to the Malay Peninsula led the Anglo-American Combined Chiefs at the Arcadia Conference to make several major decisions that affected the Far East command. They divided the world into several operational theaters. India and the Middle East were exclusively British spheres of influence; and Churchill readily agreed that the Pacific, Southwest Pacific, and South Atlantic should become American commands. Thus, for the first time, the United States assumed the responsibility for defending New Zealand and Australia. This alone undermined the old Orange Plan strategy for dealing with Japan. The North Atlantic, Europe, and the Mediterranean were regions of shared interests. King rejected Churchill's scheme for a combined Atlantic naval command, but General Marshall was eager to set a precedent for multiservice, multinational, unified geographic commands and so persuaded the British to establish a supreme headquarters for a new Australian-British-Dutch-American area running from Singapore to New Zealand. Hart assumed nominal command of all naval forces in this theater under the supine direction of Field Marshal Sir Archibald Wavell, whom Churchill had recently sacked from Britain's Middle East command. For reasons that defy comprehension, King rejected the advice of his staff and unexpectedly agreed to this unsound if temporary arrangement. He realized that unity of command was "not a panacea for all military difficulties" and knew that it was a favorite of a clique of "amateur strategists" led by the aged Secretary of War Stimson. Moreover, King's experience in the North Atlantic in 1941 had resulted in his stalwart opposition to "mixing" Allied ships in combat formations.[10]

En route to Java, Hart was entrusted with an Allied naval command consisting of nine cruisers, twenty-six destroyers, and thirty-nine submarines belonging to three navies, each of which took great pride in its own maritime traditions, battle doctrine, strategy, tactics, and means of communication. Supreme national interests also divided the Allied commanders. The Dutch were interested solely in holding on to the East Indies, while the British wanted to protect Burma and India. The dim prospect of slowing down the Japanese advance with this small force depressed Stark, who reckoned that MacArthur could not hold the Philippines and that it would be foolish to risk ships in those waters. When the enemy outflanked the Philippines and established a base on Borneo on 28 December, the CNO understood that the end was also near for the Dutch East Indies. Hart wanted to concentrate the Asiatic Fleet and inflict as much damage as possible on the Japanese, but Stark, who had to provide every theater with ships, was more willing to concede territory and save the Asiatic Fleet for another day. As a result, he told Hart to withdraw his auxiliaries to Darwin on the Australian coast, where Hart had already established a new American submarine base under Captain John Wilkes.

During the first week of January, Hart organized his new multinational command at Surabaja. The British unwisely allowed their worst generals to dominate the ABDA command, while the Dutch, whose home government was ruling its empire from exile in London, smarted over the Anglo-American decision to deprive them of the Allied naval command. Hart's mission was to deal with a three-pronged enemy offensive. The western arm was slamming into Southeast Asia, the central arm was moving south from the Philippines to oil-rich Borneo, and the eastern arm was plunging toward the Molucca Sea, poking at weak spots on Hart's right flank. Hart's job was also complicated once King took over operational command of all American fleets because King swiftly told both Hart and Nimitz at Pearl Harbor that their primary mission was to defend the sea line of communications linking Hawaii, Australia, and New Zealand. The Dutch cared not a fig about Australia, and the Dutch Navy commander, Admiral Conrad Helfrich, made it plain to Hart that he was angry at not being selected for the ABDA naval command. Helfrich and his fleet commander, Rear Admiral Karel Doorman, wanted to conserve their forces so as to strengthen the defenses of the Dutch East Indies. Wavell's first priority was to snatch away Dutch and American ships and men to save Singapore without committing British ships or troops to their doom in the Dutch East Indies. All this became clear to Hart when the Allied commanders met at Batavia on 10 January. In addition, while Wavell could not move American or Dutch forces without Hart's or Helfrich's approval, neither could Hart conduct ABDA fleet operations without the agreement of his British and Dutch counterparts.

Hart was tired of the bickering and wanted to fight. When he learned on the 13th that a Japanese task force was steaming along the coast of Borneo, he sent out a powerful cruiser-destroyer formation to intercept it, but after sweeeping the area, the Americans reported that the "game had flown." A week later Hart was warned by Dutch radio intelligence that the Japanese were about to penetrate the Makassar Strait, so he sent out his entire cruiser-destroyer Striking Force to ambush them, but the Japanese never appeared and the charts of those waters were so poor that the cruiser *Boise* scraped her bottom and the submarine *S-36* ran aground on a coral reef. Pleading "for a little luck," Hart next ordered his Striking Force out again to attack another Japanese invasion fleet off Balikpapan. The American ships were low on fuel and the recent sweeps had exhausted the crews, but the old 7,000-ton cruiser *Marblehead* and four destroyers drew blood when they caught a large enemy convoy at anchor on the night of 24 January. The gallant, World War I era four-stackers charged the Japanese convoy with a violent gunfire and torpedo attack, sank four ships and three transports, and retired safely into the darkness.[11]

The Battle of Balikpapan momentarily boosted American morale but entirely failed to stem the Japanese tide, so Hart decided to bring up some of his smaller ships from Darwin to cover the line from Java to Australia. He was furious with Wavell for wasting ships in useless convoys that shuffled men and material from one defeat to another. "Exhausting our ships in that purely defensive work," he told Wavell, was robbing the command "of the power of offensive work, by Cruisers and Destroyers, just at the time when a good chance for it arrived." Hart kept trying. He ordered Doorman's Dutch-American cruiser-destroyer force into the Makassar Strait on 2 February, but the Dutch ships were so poorly handled that it took two days before the formation put to sea. Within hours, Doorman's task force was spotted by Japanese reconnaissance aircraft, and the cruisers *Marblehead* and *Houston* and the Dutch cruiser *De Ruyter* were badly damaged. Hart was furious about Doorman's decision to retire, and Hart's impolitic attitude undermined Allied unity. Behind Hart's back, Wavell had already convinced Churchill to get Roosevelt to relieve Hart and to award the ABDA naval command to Admiral Helfrich.[12]

The Japanese were likewise dumbfounded by the weak resistance that Wavell's ABDA command threw up against their armies and navies. The enemy landed on the Kra Peninsula in northern Malaya, then descended on Singapore, and that stronghold fell after a brief siege on 15 February. Another Japanese army rampaged across British Burma, chasing the defenders up to the border with India. Beset by these and other calamities, Wavell paid little heed to his southern flank. In a last, desperate bid to hold the Dutch East Indies, Doorman assembled a multinational Striking Force of five cruisers and nine destroyers, which sortied from Surabaja into the Java Sea on 27 February to intercept a Japanese troop convoy escorted by four cruisers and fourteen destroyers. According to Dennison, bitter over Hart's relief, the Dutch "didn't have any concept of how to handle task forces."[13]

When the opponents engaged in the Java Sea, the *Houston* drew first blood at 30,000 yards by knocking an enemy cruiser out of the line, but the Japanese crippled the British cruiser *Exeter* and forced her to flee. At nightfall, the two sides exchanged destroyer torpedo attacks. The cruisers *Java* and *De Ruyter* sank, but the *Houston* and the Australian cruiser *Perth* escaped into the darkness. The next day, they blundered upon the main Japanese invasion force in the Sunda Strait, and a melee ensued in which the Allied cruisers shot up four Japanese transports before they were both sunk by enemy torpedoes and gunfire. When four Japanese cruisers and a section of carrier-based bombers found the destroyer *John Pope* and the *Exeter* off Surabaja on 1 March, both ships went down. So did the old seaplane tender *Langley*, which was hit that same day by Japanese bombers while she was ferrying planes to Australia. This left the Japanese with undisputed control of the East Indies, and the Dutch government formally surrendered a week later. "The Japanese have demonstrated a capacity for powerful mobility beyond anything we are prepared to offer," warned Rear Admiral Charles M. Cooke, the Navy's new chief strategic planner. "They have moved from one thing to another with a continuous . . . tempo contemplated in some of our plans but declared impossible by practically all the planners and by external criticizers."[14]

After the ABDA command collapsed, the JCS agreed to divide the Pacific basin into two commands, the Southwest Pacific Theater under General MacArthur, and the Pacific Ocean Area under Admiral Nimitz. For a few weeks, King tried to direct South Pacific operations from Washington, but this clearly was unworkable, so he decided to transfer control of this area to Nimitz' supervision. He also named Vice Admiral Robert L.

Ghormley, then serving in London, a sub-theater commander and ordered him to establish his headquarters in French New Caledonia. By now the American position in the Philippines was untenable, and General Marshall convinced FDR to order MacArthur to leave the islands and withdraw to Australia. On the night of 11 March, Lieutenant Commander John Buckeley's PT boat squadron sped into Corregidor, embarked MacArthur, his family, and Rear Admiral Francis Rockwell, the commander of the Philippine naval district, and headed south for Mindanao, where the passengers boarded Army Air Force B-17s for the flight to Australia. When MacArthur reached Darwin, he made a dramatic, public vow "to return" to the Philippines, a pledge that captured the American public's imagination at the lowest point in the war.

The curtain quickly came down on the forces remaining in the Philippines. The gallant tender *Canopus* fought to the end. Her launches were converted into small gunboats, which harassed the enemy's flanks, and her crew joined the improvised naval infantry battalion that held the neck of the Bataan Peninsula until it was overrun. When Bataan surrendered on 9 April, however, her position was hopeless, and the following day the *Canopus* proudly backed into deep water in Manila Bay where she was scuttled by her crew. Three weeks later, organized resistance on the outlying islands was crushed by the Japanese, and the Army command in the Philippines agreed to an unconditional surrender on 5 May. At that very moment, however, the Navy was about to strike back.

Chapter Two

From the Marshalls Raid to the Battle off Midway
1942

Weeks before the collapse of the ABDA command and months before the fall of the Philippines, Admiral King had crafted an overall strategy for containing the Japanese advance in the Pacific. To dislocate the enemy's offensive balance, he intended to launch a series of raids against weakly defended points along Japan's Pacific front. At the same time, King wanted to garrison a line of island bases in the South Pacific to secure the sea line of communications from Hawaii to New Zealand and Australia. This became all the more important in April when the United States formally assumed responsibility for the strategic defense of Australia and New Zealand within the new South Pacific area. "The Navy wants to take all the islands in the Pacific," complained Brigadier General Dwight D. Eisenhower, the new head of the Army War Plans Division, and "have them held by Army troops, to become bases for Army pursuit planes and bombers. Then the Navy will have a safe place to sail its vessels." This pejorative description of King's concept illustrated the continual opposition he faced from the War Department in obtaining garrison troops for the South Pacific bases and Army Air Force aircraft to support the movements of the fleet.[1]

If the Japanese fleet ventured beyond the protection of its land-based aircraft, then King intended to challenge it in battles of attrition with his few carrier task forces. King's ruthless logic was that the United States could afford losses in ships and aircraft but Japan could not, owing to its comparative lack of industrial strength. Admiral Nimitz, who took command of the Pacific Fleet at the end of 1941, was uneasy about this ambitious plan and acutely aware of the constant threat to Hawaii from another Japanese attack. However, in January 1942 Nimitz found himself under unremitting pressure from King for "some aggressive action for effect on general morale." Early that month, American naval intelligence placed the Japanese carriers in the southwestern Pacific, so King decided to relieve some of the burden on the ABDA command by mounting a series of diversionary raids into the central Pacific. On 20 January, he instructed Nimitz to send a task force to raid Wake Island, and Nimitz assigned this mission to Vice Admiral Brown in the *Lexington*. However, the plan was aborted after fleet oiler *Neches*, which had been allowed to leave Pearl Harbor without an escort, was sunk on the early morning of 23 January by the Japanese submarine *I-72* about 135 miles off Oahu.[2]

At the same time, King had persuaded Marshall to reinforce the Army garrison on Samoa. To this end, a troop convoy was organized on the West Coast, and in late January 1942 it steamed into the South Pacific escorted by a task force commanded by Rear Admiral Fletcher in the carrier *Yorktown*. After the transports reached Samoa, Nimitz decided to send Fletcher north to rendezvous with Admiral Halsey in the *Enterprise*. Together they were to raid Japanese positions in the Gilberts and Marshalls. The cancellation of Brown's raid on Wake made it especially imperative that Halsey's raid on the Marshalls be "driven home." And Roosevelt told Churchill on 10 February that "we must at all costs maintain our two flanks—the right based in Australia and New Zealand and the left in Burma, India, and China . . . and plan for a more southerly permanent base to strike back from."[3]

A few days later, Admiral Halsey sailed into the South Pacific and rendezvoused with Fletcher. The two-carrier task force steamed northward toward the Marshalls and, undetected, approached the islands on the morning of 1 February. Dive bombers and torpedo planes from the *Enterprise* attacked enemy airfields, damaged nine ships, and sank one transport in a series of attacks on Wotje, Roi-Namur, and Kwajalein. A section of five Japanese twin-engine land-based bombers in glide formation appeared over the *Enterprise*, but the carrier's well-trained antiaircraft batteries forced the enemy planes to pull up, and a pattern of fifteen bombs just missed hitting the ship on the port side. Hours later the Japanese made a second ineffective high-level bombing run. After the American air strikes, a cruiser group under Rear Admiral Raymond Spruance was brought up for offshore gunfire bombardment. As a result of the extraordinary publicity that followed this daring raid, "Bull" Halsey became one of the first American heroes of World War II. Meanwhile, Fletcher in the *Yorktown* repeatedly assaulted Japanese targets in the Gilberts. On 21 February, Admiral Brown in the *Lexington* arrived in the South Pacific and prepared to attack the large enemy airbase at Rabaul, but he was detected 350 miles from his objective and had to abort the mission. Before he retired, however, his air group handily defeated several Japanese flights. Joined by the *Yorktown*, Brown next entered the Coral Sea and steamed northward to a position off Port Moresby, where he launched air strikes against the Japanese bastions at Lae and Salamaua on the northern coast of New Guinea. On 24 February, Halsey in the *Enterprise* hit Wake Island and on 4 March raided Marcus Island, only 1,000 miles from Japan.

Admiral King's raiding strategy came to a spectacular climax in April 1942. The notion of retaliating against Japan's Home Islands had adorned some of the earliest Allied discussions of Pacific strategy after Pearl Harbor. In January 1942 Captain Francis S. Low prepared a plan for a carrier attack against Tokyo, but King considered it impractical inasmuch as the range of the best American carrier bombers was less than that of the patrol planes that defended the Japanese homeland. Low then suggested launching a group of Army Air Force medium bombers from a carrier deck for a one-way mission from the North Pacific over Tokyo and on to airfields in China. "Two carriers should be used," said Captain Donald B. Duncan, who planned the operation, "one to carry the bombers and one to carry . . . fighters . . . for the protection of the task force." General Arnold agreed to Low's plan and assigned the mission to Colonel James Doolittle, a distinguished aviator. In late March, after a specially trained bombardment group of sixteen B-25 Mitchell bombers were lifted onto the *Hornet*'s deck in San Francisco, the new carrier steamed into the North Pacific, rendezvoused with Vice Admiral Halsey in the *Enterprise* on 13 April, and headed toward a position about 450 miles from Tokyo where Halsey planned to launch the raid. However, Lieutenant G. M. Slonin's shipboard radio intelligence unit told Halsey that it had deciphered a contact report broadcast by a Japanese picket boat, which had spotted the task force about 700 miles east of Japan, a warning that forced Halsey to launch the raid ahead of schedule so that his ships might retire safely to the east.[4]

At 0824 on the morning of 18 April, Doolittle's bombers took off from the *Hornet*'s flight deck, reached Tokyo by noon, dropped their bomb loads—which did little damage—and then escaped to the west. The Japanese were alert to the presence of the American task force in the North Pacific, but they expected Halsey to close to within 200 miles of the Home Islands before launching his aircraft and, as a result, their patrol planes failed to locate his carriers. Soon after the raid, the enemy dispatched a

Fleet Admiral Ernest J. King. Commander in Chief, Atlantic Fleet, 1941; Commander in Chief, U.S. Fleet, and Chief of Naval Operations, 1942–1945.

Admiral Charles M. "Savvy" Cooke. Assistan Chief of Staff and later Chief of Staff to the Commander in Chief, U.S. Fleet, 1942–1945 Commander, U.S. Naval Forces, Western Pa cific, 1946–1948.

U.S. Naval Institute

U.S. Navy Department

powerful task force to conduct a vain pursuit of the Americans into the North Pacific. Although most of the B-25s reached friendly Nationalist Chinese airfields, a few crashed off the coast, several men were killed, and two captured American pilots were executed by the Japanese Army. The Tokyo raid was an enormous boost to American morale and a devastating blow to the prestige of Japan's military leadership, humiliated by their inability to defend the Home Islands. When FDR was asked during a press conference where the raid had originated, he replied jauntily, "Shangri-La," the name of a fictional paradise in the Himalayas. Neither the Tokyo raid nor Pacific Fleet's earlier carrier raids inflicted much damage, but these bold strikes unnerved the Japanese high command, induced them to divert a large number of pursuit and patrol planes on a permanent basis for territorial air defense, and dislocated their overall strategic plan. In the near term, this meant hastening the entry of the Japanese Fleet into the Coral Sea, moving ahead the planning date for the invasion of Port Moresby, and preparing to take Midway.

The Japanese had in the meantime mounted a raid of their own into the Indian Ocean, conducted by Admiral Kondo's task force of five carriers and four *Kong*-class battleships against the British Far Eastern Fleet, which included Admiral James Sommerville's four old *R*-class battleships and three understrength carriers. During this early April operation, the Royal Navy lost two heavy cruisers and the old carrier *Hermes*. Kondo's raid brought the entire British position in the Indian Ocean to its nadir, and only three weeks later the Japanese Army entered the British stronghold of Lashio, Burma, thus cutting the last road link between China and British India and isolating Chiang Kai-shek's Chungking regime from outside military assistance. Within a week after Kondo withdrew from the Indian Ocean, Churchill, whose unrelenting insistence on the primacy of the North Atlantic and Mediterranean theaters colored every British move, admitted to FDR that "a proportion of our combined resources must, for the moment, be set aside to halt the Japanese advance."[5]

The first chance to do this began to unfold on 15 April when Captain John Redman of Naval Communications in Washington presented King with a deciphered Japanese message revealing that an enemy carrier division was to arrive at Truk in the Carolines later that month. Days after Pearl Harbor, Navy code breakers had abandonded their concentration on Japan's flag officers' code and turned their attention instead to a more vulnerable operational naval code labeled JN25. Only in February 1942 were most of the new keys to this machine cipher solved, initially by Lieutenant Commander Rudolph Fabian's Corregidor-based unit, and within a few weeks it was on occasion being read concurrently. Redman's message led King to warn Nimitz on 18 April that the Japanese intended to move during the first week in May against Port Moresby, an Australian stronghold on the southern coast of New Guinea's Papuan Peninsula. Once the Japanese controlled the Coral Sea, they would be well positioned to move on Fiji and Samoa via New Caledonia and thereby sever the sea line of communications between Australia and Hawaii. King immediately understood that he could not allow the Port Moresby operation to proceed without check. The next day, Nimitz' staff recorded in the Pacific Fleet war diary that "an offensive in the Southwest Pacific is shaping up." Although Admiral Fletcher's *Yorktown* task force had been in the South Pacific since February, Nimitz now directed him to remain there during April, and he also ordered Rear Admiral Aubrey Fitch in the carrier *Lexington* to join Fletcher at the end of the month. However, King's earlier decision to send Halsey with both the *Enterprise* and the *Hornet* into the North Pacific on the Tokyo raid had inadvertently resulted in a division of Nimitz' carriers precisely at the time when he needed to concentrate them. Prodded by King to defend Port Moresby and the Coral Sea, Nimitz reluctantly decided on the 22nd that, a day or two after Halsey returned to Pearl Harbor, he was to put to sea again, steam into the South Pacific, and join Fletcher to help him deal with the Japanese offensive, although it seemed clear that these ships would not arrive in the Coral Sea on time.[6]

On 5 May, Navy cryptanalysts provided King with more details of Yamamoto's plan to move into the Coral Sea and occupy Port Moresby. Yamamoto had ordered Rear Admiral Shima with the light carrier *Shoho* and four cruisers to cover the assault shipping and to land troops on the island of Tulagi near Guadalcanal. From Tulagi, Japanese seaplanes were to search to the west and south and warn of any attempt by the American fleet to enter the Coral Sea. Rear Admiral Takeo Takagi's newly constructed heavy carriers *Shokaku* and *Zuikaku* were to steam from Truk to the Coral Sea and cover a landing near Port Moresby by the Invasion Force then assembling at Rabaul. This plan assumed a high degree of coordination among the three forces and utterly ignored the need to establish unchallenged air superiority over the Coral Sea before invading Port Moresby. Nevertheless, after Shima occupied Tulagi on 3 May, the *Shoho* sped north to Rabaul to cover the Port Moresby Invasion Force. Fletcher in the *Yorktown* had already rendezvoused with the *Lexington* two days earlier, and while she was refueling, the *Yorktown* steamed to a position to the north; from there she launched ineffective air strikes against Tulagi on 4 May, turned back, and rejoined the *Lexington* one day later. This alerted the Japanese to Fletcher's presence, but they unwisely failed to adjust their plans to meet this threat.

Fletcher's mission was to support Port Moresby's defenses, so General MacArthur was willing to provide aerial reconnaissance over the Coral Sea. Lieutenant General George Brett, his new Army Air Force chief, sent air raids against Rabaul and search planes into the Solomon Sea, but he was unable to cover either the eastern Solomon or the central or eastern Coral Sea, and he failed to apprise Fletcher of this. For his part, Fletcher had learned some more details of Yamamoto's battle plan from the American code breakers, and he reorganized his ships accordingly. He integrated his two carriers into a single task force, sent the fleet oiler *Neosho* and the destroyer *Sims* to the south where he thought they would be safe, and assembled an independent force of three cruisers and three destroyers under Australian Rear Admiral Sir John Crace, who was to station his ships south of the Louisiade Archipelago. Fletcher instructed Crace to hold that position in case the American carriers were overwhelmed in the Coral Sea, heedless of the facts that Crace's unsupported cruiser-destroyer force was too weak to stop the Japanese carriers and that detaching Crace's ships reduced the American carriers' antiaircraft defenses. Fletcher next turned to the problem of locating the enemy. Having learned nothing from the Army Air Force, he sent out search planes on 6 May, but they did not find Takagi's carriers, then only about seventy miles from the American position in the central Coral Sea.

Takagi learned where Admiral Fletcher was that afternoon, but he decided against attacking because of bad weather. As a result, at dawn on 7 May, when both admirals sent out a large number of scout planes to find each other, their task forces were steaming in opposite directions. By 0900, however, both Fletcher and Takagi had received contact reports from their respective dawn patrols, all of which were wrong in some important detail. Mistaking the *Neosho* and *Sims* for a carrier task force, Takagi committed his entire air striking group against them, a step that resulted in the destruction of both American ships but left the Japanese carriers without much protection. Fletcher was unable to exploit this opportunity, however, because an American scout plane mistook the Port Moresby Invasion Force transports for the Japanese carriers. Acting on this erroneous report, Fletcher sped north to close on the enemy and launched ninety-three fighters and bombers, which chanced upon the small carrier *Shoho* at 1100, put thirteen bomb and torpedo holes in her, and then returned to the American carriers while the enemy flattop sank. The *Shoho*'s loss not only caused the Port Moresby Invasion Force to retire from the Jomard Passage but also alarmed Admiral Takagi. He steamed north with the *Shokaku* and *Zuikaku* to challenge the Americans late that afternoon and lost twenty-three aircraft during the desperate search-attack mission.

After spending three frustrating days trying to locate the enemy's heavy carriers, Fletcher's dawn patrols finally found them on the morning of the 8th and reported their location at 0800, about the same time that Fletcher's ships were again discovered by Takagi's scouts. An hour later Admiral Fitch, who directed task force air operations, sent strikes from the *Yorktown* and the *Lexington* against the enemy. Takagi had hidden his task force under a storm front; Fletcher failed to take advantage of the weather, however, and was steaming about under clear skies. The *Yorktown*'s attackers could not find the carrier *Zuikaku*, which was hidden under a rain squall, and concentrated instead on the carrier *Shokaku*, which was visible. A TBD Devastator torpedo bomber attack on this carrier failed, but soon thereafter the SDB Dauntless dive bombers scored two hits, which so badly damaged her flight deck that she could no longer operate aircraft. She suffered another hit when the attackers from the *Lexington* appeared on the scene, and Takagi was forced to order the *Shokaku* to withdraw from the Coral Sea.

Simultaneously, Takagi launched his own powerful strike of seventy aircraft against the American carriers, which were poorly defended owing to Fletcher's decision to detach Crace's cruiser-destroyer force, uneven coordination of the remaining antiaircraft batteries, and poor direction of the protective combat air patrol. Admiral Fitch had kept only fifteen fighters to defend the carriers, and they were stationed close in to the task force where they were easily overwhelmed by the incoming enemy planes. In addition, Fitch had not positioned his fighters at an altitude high enough to attack the Japanese dive bombers, and a flight of SDB Devastators, assigned to intercept the enemy torpedo bombers, had been sent out in the wrong direction. Control of the antiaircraft fire was so poor, claimed Lieutenant John Greenbacker, a gunnery officer in the *Yorktown*, that the Americans "started and ended our engagement by shooting at our own planes." The agile *Yorktown*'s short turning radius allowed Captain Elliott Buckmaster, a superb shiphandler, to execute a series of violent maneuvers, which forced the Japanese to fly into a crosswind to attack his ship, and she escaped the battle with only one minor bomb hit. The *Lexington* was less fortunate, taking two bomb and two torpedo hits. Captain Frederick Sherman, a brilliant fighter, kept his carrier operating and recovered his remaining aircraft, but at 1445 the second of two gasoline line explosions forced him to shift some of his planes to the *Yorktown* and, soon after, to abandon ship.[7]

Reports from the Japanese pilots misled Admiral Takagi into believing that he had sunk both American carriers, but he was unable to seize this supposed advantage because of the withdrawal of the *Shokaku* and the losses to the *Zuikaku*'s air group, which was now too depleted to cover the invasion of Port Moresby. He was unwilling to risk his remaining aircraft against the Allied land-based forces there and so withdrew from the Coral Sea. Fletcher, aware that the Japanese had been bloodied, also decided to retire on 9 May, having lost the *Lexington* and over half of his aircraft.

Although the Japanese sank more tonnage than did the Americans at the Battle of the Coral Sea, the Americans won a strategic victory by thwarting the invasion of Port Moresby. And, while the Japanese air groups deployed a higher proportion of modern fighters and torpedo planes than the Americans, they lost more aircraft in attacks on the enemy's ships than did their opponents. King was bitterly discouraged nonetheless by Fletcher's poor dispositions, his failure to use the storm front to hide his carriers, and the "lack of aggressive tactics of his force." Nimitz stoutly defended Fletcher, telling King that these faults "can be charged partly to the lack of sufficiently reliable combat intelligence" and "the necessity for replenishment of fuel and provisions." Expecting another Japanese stroke to fall on the Americans in the immediate future, King decided not to over-rule Nimitz for the moment, and Fletcher kept his command. Although "we seem to have stopped the advance on Port Moresby for the time being," King told Britain's First Sea Lord, Admiral Sir Dudley Pound, the "Battle of the Coral Sea was merely the first round of an engagement which will continue."[8]

On the day after Fletcher entered the Coral Sea, the Tokyo raid forced the humiliated Japanese naval staff to agree to Admiral Yamamoto's bold plan to attack Midway Atoll, an operation he had advocated ever since Halsey's first raid on the Marshalls. Yamamoto believed that if he seized Midway it would force King to send Nimitz' carriers into the central Pacific and so expose them to destruction by the Combined Fleet. Yamamoto reckoned that he would be challenged by only two American carriers at most, but the naval staff in Tokyo had less faith in Japan's intelligence estimates. The staff raised other objections. The seizure of Midway might prove to be a futile gesture unless the Americans were willing to accept the bait. Midway was unsuitable either for use as a fleet anchorage or as a base from which to conduct bombing operations against Hawaii, and it was far beyond the range of effective protection by Japan's land-based air forces in the central Pacific. Furthermore, the Japanese had no long-range strategic bombers or fighter escorts capable of penetrating Hawaii's bristling air defenses, and any attempt to hold Midway would tie down the Combined Fleet to the defense of a new, vulnerable, extended sea line of communications. These arguments gave way to Yamamoto's insistence that the American carriers would be lured out to defend Midway and that they had to be destroyed before Japan could resume her South Pacific offensive.[9]

Yamamoto's Midway plan reflected the addiction of Japan's admirals to complexity. Both strategically and tactically, he divided his forces. Under Vice Admiral Hosogaya, the Northern Force, composed of the light carriers *Ryujo* and *Junyo*, three heavy cruisers, and their escorts, was to steam into the North Pacific, attack the American base at Dutch Harbor on the island of Unalaska in the eastern Aleutians, and then cover the landing of Japanese troops on Attu, Adak, and Kiska in the western Aleutians. A submarine task force was to rendezvous off French Frigate Shoals in late May to report on and interdict the movement of any American warships bound for Midway. Even at this early stage of the war, however, Japan's industrial inferiority was beginning to impede her operations. The *Zuikaku*'s and *Shokaku*'s air groups had been shattered in the Coral Sea, and the Japanese did not have enough planes or pilots to reconstitute them before the Midway plan went into effect. This left Nagumo with only the two large carriers *Akagi* and *Kaga* and the medium carriers *Hiryu* and *Soryu* in his Carrier Force. He was to steam for Midway ahead of the Main Body, attack the naval station there, and cover the invasion. The separate Main Body was led by the superbattleship *Yamato*, five smaller battleships, ten powerful heavy and light cruisers, and twenty destroyers. Should the American carriers appear, Nagumo's planes were to destroy their air groups and Yamamoto's battleships would then pursue and sink them with 18-inch gunfire. Positioned to the south of the Main Body, a separate Invasion Force was to occupy Midway before the fleet action began.

This formidable fleet stood out of Japanese waters in late May and began its menacing progression into the central Pacific. On 3 June, Yamamoto detached a Guard Force of four battleships and two cruisers from the Main Body and created a strategic reserve that was to support either the invasion of the Aleutians or the Midway operation. He also kept two light carriers with the Main Body to provide some air defense for the battleships, which remained about 350 miles behind Nagumo's Carrier Force. In short, despite the experience of Pearl Harbor and the Coral Sea, he expected that the upcoming battle would evolve into a gun duel in which the *Yamato*'s speed and 18-inch guns would give him the decisive edge. However, Yamamoto's dedication to overrunning Midway and converting it into a Japanese air base had led him to use about one-third of the space on his carrier decks for land-based aircraft, thus reducing the number of fighters for defensive combat air patrols by the same fraction. Because of this fundamental misunderstanding of the function of the heavy carrier, Yamamoto unwittingly diminished his fleet's enormous offensive and defensive potential at the very moment he needed it most.

On 5 May, Yamamoto had broadcast a preliminary order to begin assembling ships for the Midway operation. The importance of this unusually long message was first realized by Lieutenant Commander Fabian's code-breaking team in Melbourne, a small group that had been evacuated from Corregidor in February. Using loud, cumbersome IBM tabulators, Navy code breakers in Melbourne, Hawaii, and Washington were able to decipher several parts of the critical 5 May message, enciphered in JN25, over the next few days. The product of this and related work on other deciphered messages contained contradictory clues about the upcoming Japanese strategy. Captain Redman in Washington and his counterpart in Hawaii, Commander Joseph Rochefort, both directed their efforts against the JN25 naval code, but Rochefort's attention was diverted from this work by a bitter personal struggle with Redman involving their respective prerogatives and status in Pacific intelligence matters.

At first Redman predicted that the Japanese intended to renew the South Pacific offensive in the late summer, and on 12 May King warned General Marshall that a powerful Japanese "force is training for another campaign or large operation to be initiated the last of May or the first part of June." There was as yet no "information as to the nature or direction" of the thrust, but King was "inclined to believe that the enemy will first proceed with the Moresby operation," although he admitted that "between June 1st and 5th it could arrive near Alaska, the West Coast, Hawaii, or any of the island positions on the line to Australia, New Guinea, or Australia itself." Rochefort, however, was convinced that Yamamoto intended to overrun Midway Atoll, and Nimitz agreed with this assessment. King thus faced two contradictory conclusions prepared by two capable intelligence analysts, and he had to decide which option the Japanese were likely to choose. His view was colored by Nimitz' continued opposition to the deployment of the American carriers in the South Pacific and by King's own determination to resist Japan's offensive against the Hawaii-Australia line of communications.[10]

Before the *Yorktown* limped back to Pearl Harbor after the Battle of the Coral Sea, King instructed Nimitz to have Halsey in the *Enterprise* attack a convoy heading for Ocean and Nauru islands on 16 May so as to unsettle Yamamoto once again. His more specific purpose was to alert Yamamoto that there were still American carriers within a few days' steaming time of the Coral Sea. Citing Rochefort's intelligence, Nimitz tried to cancel this raid, but King overruled him. Nimitz decided to circumvent King's orders, and he broadcast a secret message to Halsey on the 16th, instructing him to send out scout planes as he approached the Marshalls and to make certain that they were spotted by the Japanese. Inasmuch as King had just warned Nimitz not to risk his carriers against land-based bombers, this gave Nimitz an excuse to give to King when Halsey began to retire to Hawaii. Unclear about Nimitz' purposes, Halsey obeyed. His planes were sighted, and he duly informed Nimitz and King that the *Enterprise* was withdrawing to Oahu.

When King received this message he faced a frightful decision. If he allowed Nimitz to position the carriers *Hornet, Enterprise,* and *Yorktown* to defend Midway, then Yamamoto might exploit this American concentration, reenter the Coral Sea, and renew the drive against Port Moresby. Something akin to this was what Redman's code breakers in Washington were predicting. "The majority of our effective forces had been operating in the South Pacific," King wrote, "and the primary question was whether some should be left there . . . or whether all our carriers should be concentrated at Pearl Harbor." King checked with Admiral Pound, but he replied that British intelligence expected no major Japanese operations in the Pacific in the near future. Because "Nimitz was certain that they were going after Midway and Hawaii," King agreed, on 17 May, to Nimitz' plan to concentrate the American carriers under Admiral Halsey, who was to command the task force and ambush the Japanese if and when they appeared off Midway Atoll. Although King's eye was always on the main chance, he was under no illusion as to the great risk his strategy entailed.[11]

Nimitz was elated at this news, and he immediately prepared his battle plan. When the *Enterprise* and the *Hornet* arrived in Pearl Harbor on 26 May, however, Halsey was so ill with dermatitis that he had to be hospitalized, thus depriving the Americans of their most able tactician and leaving Fletcher, whom King did not trust, in command of the Midway ambush. Nimitz nominated Rear Admiral Raymond Spruance as Fletcher's second in command. An extraordinarily talented leader, Spruance had served under King in the Atlantic Fleet in 1941 and had commanded Halsey's cruisers during the Marshalls, Wake, Marcus, and Tokyo raids. With a screen consisting of five fast cruisers and nine destroyers, Spruance with the carriers *Enterprise* and *Hornet* steamed from Hawaiian waters into the central Pacific in late May. The *Yorktown* was in need of hurried repairs after being damaged in the Coral Sea, but she was nearly ready two days later when Fletcher stood out of Pearl Harbor. Spruance and Fletcher rendezvoused on 2 June; Fletcher assumed command and sped toward a hiding position several hundred miles north of Midway. Unbeknownst to the Americans, the arrival on the scene of the *Yorktown* endowed them with numerical superiority in the air. In the upcoming battle, 261 Japanese carrier-based planes were about to face 233 American carrier-based and 119 Midway-based aircraft. In addition, Nimitz told Rear Admiral Patrick Bellinger to use his Hawaii-based long-range patrol bombers to neutralize Japan's forward-deployed submarines at French Frigate Shoals and directed Rear Admiral Robert English to deploy his nineteen Pacific Fleet submarines to stations along an arc west of Midway, where they were to intercept the Japanese Fleet and provide an early warning of enemy movements to Admiral Fletcher's task force.

The Battle of Midway opened with a Japanese stroke against Dutch Harbor, which was part of Major General Simon Bolivar Buckner's Alaskan command. Nimitz had only recently established an adjacent North Pacific naval area and he now assigned it to Rear Admiral Robert Theobald, who arrived in Alaskan waters in late May. Theobald quickly reached the conclusion that his cruiser-destroyer group was too weak to challenge a forceful Japanese thrust without the assistance of the Army Air Force's land-based aircraft, but the testy admiral neither worked to achieve good relations with Buckner nor acted quickly to improve the obviously imperfect coordination among the American forces in the area. On 28 May, Nimitz alerted Theobald that Rochefort's code breakers were predicting that Admiral Hosogaya's Northern Force was about to occupy Adak, Attu, and Kiska, but Theobald reckoned that this was a feint intended to induce him to send his cruisers into the western Aleutians while the Japanese hit Dutch Harbor. For reasons that defy comprehension, Theobald now decided to defend his area mostly with passive measures. Not only did he fail to exploit the substantial Army Air Forces in the area, but also he instructed his naval air squadrons at Kodiak, Cold Bay, and Umnak to take only defensive actions. Instead of trying to defend the western Aleutians, Theobald concentrated five cruisers and four destroyers 400 miles south of Kodiak, stationed nine destroyers off Unalaska to interdict any landing force advancing on Dutch Harbor, and instructed the twenty PBY Catalina patrol bombers there to provide an early warning patrol. Then he divided his submarines between Dutch Harbor and the Bering Sea.

The result was to weaken a force already thought to be inferior to the approaching enemy.

To deceive Nimitz into believing that the Combined Fleet intended to descend on Alaska, Admiral Yamamoto began his offensive on 2 June by ordering Hosogaya's Northern Force to close on the Aleutians. Theobald was already at sea in the light cruiser *Nashville* searching for the Northern Force, but in the fog and darkness Rear Admiral Kakuta with the carriers *Ryujo* and *Junyo* evaded a handful of American pickets, steamed to a position within 170 miles of Dutch Harbor, and launched air strikes on the morning of the 3rd that damaged installations at that base. Alarmed by this news, Theobald sped toward the Bering Sea while Kakuta unexpectedly retired to the southwest. Bad weather prevented Kakuta from invading Adak as planned, so he decided to hit Dutch Harbor once again. As his carriers were steaming back toward Unalaska on 4 June, a PBY Catalina appeared overhead and reported the position of the Japanese ships to the nearby American airbase. In spite of this, an attack by Army Air Force level-bombers and Navy PBY Catalinas did little damage to the enemy vessels, and Kakuta had already launched his own strike against Dutch Harbor, inflicting additional destruction.

Kakuta withdrew once more after this strike was recovered, intending next to invade Adak, but one of his search planes discovered the existence of a secret Army Air Force base at Otter Point on nearby Umnak. Since this was within range of Adak, Admiral Hosogaya abandoned the original plan to land on that island and shaped a course for the western Aleutians, leaving Theobald in complete confusion. On 6 June, Japanese troops occupied Kiska, and the following day, another landing force went ashore on Attu. Theobald was unaware of these steps until a few days later when the presence of the Japanese was discovered by a PBY Catalina. The Japanese had won the opening round of the Battle of Midway, but Yamamoto had nonetheless failed to deceive Nimitz as to his true intentions. Moreover, Hosogaya's first attack on Dutch Harbor disclosed to the Americans that Yamamoto had not only divided his fleet but also that he was willing to split up his powerful carrier forces.

Once Theobald's misadventure began to evolve, Nimitz turned his attention to the progression toward Midway of Nagumo's Carrier Force and Yamamoto's Main Body. Just after

Nimitz learned of Hosogaya's presence in the Aleutians on 3 June, Ensign Jack Reid flying a PBY Catalina patrol bomber sighted the enemy Invasion Force about 700 miles west of Midway and reported his contact to Captain Cyril Simard, who commanded the Midway garrison. Simard sent out nine B-17 Flying Fortresses to molest the Japanese formation, but neither this attack nor subsequent sorties by the heavy Army Air Force bombers inflicted any damage on the enemy ships. An evening torpedo attack by PBY Catalinas was also unsuccessful. On the other hand, the Flying Fortresses' long-range, heavy bomb loads and high-level immunity scared the Japanese, who often allowed this unwarranted fear to dictate their movements. The important report from Reid reaffirmed Nimitz' faith in the prediction that Nagumo's carriers would approach Midway from the northwest and launch their attack the following day. Expecting Nagumo to appear at a position about 200 miles northwest of Midway on the morning of the 4th, Fletcher steamed southward on the night of 3 June with the intention of reaching a point roughly 200 miles to the north of the island by dawn. When the Japanese air groups were busy attacking Midway, he intended to ambush their defenseless carriers.

At 0507 on the morning of 4 June, an Army Air Force B-17 reported that Nagumo's carriers were closing on Midway, but the American bomber pilot failed to correctly identify his coordinates; he put the enemy on the American plot about forty miles to the south of the actual Japanese position. Next, at 0534, a PBY Catalina on dawn patrol reported that Nagumo was about 200 miles to the northwest of Midway. Nimitz, who was listening for such a report, now ordered Captain Simard to "go all out for the carriers," and Simard sent out an unescorted flight of fifteen B-17 Flying Fortresses, four medium Marine Marauder bombers, and six TBF Avenger torpedo planes, which reached the enemy carriers after 0700 but were crushed by defending Zeroes and failed to inflict any damage. In the meantime, Nagumo had struck Midway at 0630 with a flight of about 108 Val dive bombers, Kate torpedo bombers, and Zero fighters and seriously damaged the naval station. The unsuccessful strike by the Midway aircraft against the Carrier Force was not in vain, however, inasmuch as it unnerved Nagumo and caused him to order half of his aircraft to be armed for a second strike on the atoll.

By 0730, the Japanese had in fact nearly destroyed the shore defenses on Midway and had shot down about seventy-five American aircraft. Nonetheless, Japanese tactics had already brought the Americans to the brink of victory even before the Americans had launched their first flight of carrier-based bombers. Japan's fleet doctrine told Yamamoto to rely on his battleship and cruiser float planes for reconnaissance, and he discouraged active patrolling by his carrier air groups. His scouting crews were largely inexperienced, however, and almost invariably their reports came in late. Nor did Yamamoto pay much attention to the deployment of his submarine pickets at French Frigate Shoals or to the fact that they had been dispersed earlier by Bellinger's Hawaii-based patrol planes. This was a sure sign that the Americans knew that something was afoot in the central Pacific.

The result of all this was that, until 0728 when the cruiser *Tone*'s float plane reported sighting Spruance's formation about 240 miles north of Midway, neither Yamamoto nor Nagumo knew that Fletcher's three-carrier task force was almost within striking range of Nagumo's four carriers. At this moment, however, the Japanese ordnance crews were removing the armor-piercing anti-ship bombs and torpedoes from their naval bombers and replacing them with land-attack fragmentation bombs, in compliance with Nagumo's order to prepare for a second strike against Midway. Unsettled and confused by the *Tone*'s report and paralyzed by indecision, Nagumo toyed with the idea of hitting Midway again, dithered for fifteen minutes, and finally decided to suspend rearming his bombers, ordering them instead to be readied to attack the approaching American carriers. He directed a change in course to the northeast to approach the American carriers but was unhinged again at 0820 when a flight of eleven Marine Vindicators from Midway conducted yet another attack on the Carrier Force. These old, slow American dive bombers suffered heavy losses, however, and were easily driven off. This attack was not in vain in that it contributed to Nagumo's overall confusion.

At 0603 on 4 June, a PBY Catalina reported to Admiral Fletcher sighting two Japanese carriers. Subsequent reports established that a huge gap separated these ships from Yamamoto's powerful Main Body. Indeed, Yamamoto had so poorly positioned his ships that when Fletcher learned this news he suspected a trap. Admiral Spruance, who expected Nagumo to mass his carriers, had already decided to launch his entire air strength of 116 planes once the enemy was located. At 0700, when he believed his task force to be within 155 miles of the enemy carriers,

Spruance gave the order to begin the attack. Launching all these aircraft took so long, however, that Spruance finally decided to allow the first planes in the sky, the *Enterprise*'s SDB Dauntless dive bombers, to proceed with the attack without waiting for their fighter escorts. By 0800 five separate air groups had been launched against the Japanese carriers, but the disorganization of this strike virtually guaranteed that it would be totally uncoordinated. Fletcher, meanwhile, was waiting on events. At 0808, he received another contact report on two enemy carriers. He then directed Spruance to speed to the southwest with the *Enterprise* and *Hornet*, but the *Yorktown* remained behind, steaming into the wind to recover her search planes. When this was accomplished, Fletcher also turned southward, and at 0838 he launched a partial attack composed of his TBD Devastator torpedo bombers escorted by six F4F Wildcat fighters. He held seventeen SDB Dauntless dive bombers in reserve, however.

By this time the American attack on the Japanese carrier task force had already begun. The *Hornet*'s dive bombers, flying above cloud cover, missed Nagumo's ships completely, while the *Hornet*'s torpedo planes came in at such a low altitude that they were destroyed by a combat air patrol of Zeroes. These defenders then turned on the *Enterprise*'s torpedo planes, which lost ten of fourteen aircraft in short order. Next, Lieutenant Commander John Thach with the *Yorktown*'s well-trained F4F Wildcat fighters arrived on the scene, drew the defending Zeroes away from the ships like a magnet, and decimated part of Nagumo's combat air patrol. At the same time, Lieutenant Commander Wade McClusky, leading the *Enterprise*'s thirty-three SDB dive bombers, reached the end of his search pattern without finding the enemy carriers. Then, instead of following a flight of *Hornet* dive bombers, which was heading southward, he decided to trail a lone enemy destroyer that he had sighted steaming to the north.

At 1022 his planes appeared over the four enemy carriers, which seemed to be arranged in a diamond formation. Unmolested by hostile fighter opposition—the Zeroes had been drawn down earlier to deal with the fighters and Avenger torpedo bombers—McClusky's dive bombers left the carriers *Kaga* and *Akagi* in flames within minutes. Thach called it a "classic coordinated attack, with the torpedo planes going in low and the dive bombers coming in high." The *Akagi* was struck only twice, but the vessel was doomed when the resulting fires reached the flight deck and exploded carelessly stacked ordnance, rupturing the ship's gasoline lines. Just moments before, to the east, Zeroes had shot down the *Yorktown*'s torpedo bombers, which came in at low level. This action, too, drew down the carrier *Soryu*'s defending combat air cover, and the Zeroes were therefore unable to ascend and contest a second attack on the ship, which developed high overhead by Lieutenant Commander Maxwell Leslie's SDB Dauntless dive bombers from the *Yorktown*. Arriving over the Japanese task force at exactly the same moment as McClusky's planes, Leslie's seventeen SDBs hit the *Soryu* three times with 1,000-pound bombs. One of the carriers "was burning with bright pink flames sometimes blue flames," Thach recalled. "I remember gauging the height of the those flames by the length of the ship. The distance was about the same." A total of 125 bombers escorted by 26 fighters had flown against the 4 enemy carriers, of which now only the *Hiryu* survived. The Japanese were paying a heavy price for their failure to emphasize damage control in their peacetime training.[12]

The victorious Americans flew back to their carriers, but Fletcher still had to worry about an enemy counterattack. At about 1000, he launched search planes to scout ahead of the *Enterprise*, at roughly the same time that the *Hiryu* launched two flights of eighteen bombers and ten torpedo planes escorted by twelve fighters to find and attack the American carriers. The Japanese followed some American planes back to the *Yorktown*. Her combat air patrol splashed most of the attackers, but three Val dive bombers put two bombs onto the flight deck and another into the side of the ship. "That explosion blew out all the fires in the boilers and *Yorktown* soon lost power, speed, and came dead in the water," recalled Ensign William D. Owen, a turret officer. "We were dead in the water." Although her engineers repaired the boilers and the ship got under way soon after, the Japanese torpedo bombers next took their turn, approaching the vessel from two opposite directions, with the result that "no matter which way we turned we would be vulnerable." Two torpedoes entered the carrier's port side and exploded, and the ship began to list. Captain Buckmaster had "never had an abandon ship drill" on the grounds that such drills were "destructive of morale and confidence," so at 1500, when the *Yorktown*'s crew was ordered to abandon ship, chaos ensued. Badly damaged, the *Yorktown* remained afloat for two more days. Nimitz sent the minesweeper *Hamman* out to try to save the crippled carrier, and she was taken under tow by the minesweeper *Vireo* and protected by a destroyer screen. Shortly after noon on 6 June, however, the Japanese submarine *I-168* found the two American ships and sank them both with a salvo of four torpedoes.[13]

When the *Yorktown* was first hit on the early afternoon of 4 June, Admiral Fletcher shifted his flag to a cruiser and wisely transferred tactical command of the rest of the battle to Spruance. Spruance now decided to husband his fighters for combat air patrols and to launch a powerful flight of twenty-four dive bombers and torpedo bombers at 1600 from all three American carriers, which were to bring to book the *Hiryu*. These aircraft closed on the enemy within an hour, met shallow resistance, and put four large holes in the ship. Now all four of Nagumo's carriers were destroyed. The *Soryu* sank before 2000, but Japanese destroyers had to fire torpedoes into the *Akagi* and *Hiryu* to send them under the next morning.

Yamamoto lost four carriers on 4 June, but he waited until 0300 the following morning before calling off another attack on Midway Island and ordering a general retreat. That night, the Japanese battleships had chased the American carriers to the east, and the following day Spruance chased Yamamoto to the west. Spruance could not catch up with the Main Body in daylight when his carriers gave him superiority, however, although some carrier-based aircraft did sink the cruiser *Mikuma* that day, and the cruiser *Mogami* was successfully located and attacked on the 6th. Spruance decided to retire to Hawaii on 7 June, while Yamamoto was limping back to Japan.

In spite of this extraordinary victory, the U.S. Navy was not prepared to reenter the central Pacific for another year, but the battle thoroughly reversed the long-term balance of power in the Pacific. Japan's aircraft losses, including float planes, were about 300, but for a modern belligerent this figure seemed fairly small, even at the time. Japan's shipbuilding industry could not replace two medium and two heavy carriers, however, and such losses were by any standard a very high price to pay for merely sinking the *Yorktown*. American aircraft losses, including land-based aircraft, were about 150. Few Japanese aviators survived the battle. The *Hiryu*, for instance, lost 130 out of 150 pilots. The Japanese Navy had put most of its experienced pilots into operational squadrons, and the aircrew losses at Midway caused a disproportionately disruptive effect on Japan's poorly organized wartime pilot-training program.

Whereas the Japanese did not possess the shipbuilding capacity to replace the four lost carriers for six years or the means to create equally lethal carrier air groups, Admiral King told Nimitz, shortly after the Battle of Midway, that the first of twenty-four new 27,000-ton *Essex*-class heavy carriers would enter the Pacific Fleet before the year was out. Japan's prewar and wartime strategic planning, bereft of the most elementary and easily available economic intelligence, never truly came to grips with the preponderant influence of the American economy on the battles of the Pacific. And, after the crushing defeat off Midway, Japan's search for solutions came altogether too late. Japan no longer stood among the Great Powers. Tens of thousands of American men who fought later in the war would owe their lives to the gallant victors at Midway, for once the last of those four big flattops sank, the menace of the Imperial Navy to the Pacific Fleet was diminished considerably. Midway ended Japan's rampage in the Pacific, and Admiral King was sharp-eyed enough to see that now was the moment for the U.S. Navy to get under way.

Chapter Three

Guadalcanal
1942–1943

On 10 June, after confirming the Japanese losses off Midway, Admiral King went to the White House and obtained FDR's agreement to mount a counteroffensive in the South Pacific. "Since the Japanese had gotten a rude shock at the Battle of Midway," he recalled, "here was a good chance to get the enemy off balance and *keep* them off balance." Although King later stressed that the Guadalcanal campaign was simply "an immediate result of the Battle of Midway," the greater strategic issue was in reality far more complex. His most immediate problem was how to deal with the fact that defending the American position in the Pacific now, and for the foreseeable future, rested almost wholly on the Navy, owing to the agreed upon Allied grand strategy of "Europe first." Having heard from Admiral Mountbatten only a few days earlier that Churchill was objecting to a 1942 cross-Channel invasion, King faced the likelihood that the Allies would conduct no major operation in the Atlantic theater that fall or winter. So, in June, he allocated some of the new LSTs and other landing craft to the Pacific Fleet. This would allow Nimitz to mount a minor stroke so as to increase the military pressure on the Japanese and, indirectly, put some diplomatic pressure on the British—who were worried that the Americans might adopt a Pacific-first grand strategy—to agree to a 1943 cross-Channel operation. King was keenly aware that Churchill was fearful that the JCS would abandon Europe first.[1]

King's plan was to land forces below the Solomon Islands, at the outermost edge of Japan's strategic perimeter, and so test the enemy's shipping and logistics capacity to the full. Getting Marshall to agree to the occupation of his first objectives, Guadalcanal and Tulagi islands, was not easy, however. Captain Low of the CominCh staff recalled that in return for the Army's cooperation in the South Pacific, King "was forced to make commitments to Marshall for subsequent transfers of naval units to the Atlantic" to support the invasion of North Africa. As Roosevelt had just declared it "unwise to attempt a major offensive in the Pacific area" during 1942, King disingenuously portrayed the expensive counterstroke against Guadalcanal as merely a shift from the "defensive" to the "defensive-offensive" phase of the war against Japan.[2]

The object of the invasion of Guadalcanal, codenamed Watchtower, was to begin a drive against Rabaul in New Britain, the hub of Japan's air power in the South Pacific, and to attrite enemy ships and planes in the area. King supposed that, with his vastly greater resources, he would be able to resupply and build up the battlefield more quickly than the enemy. He vested overall direction of the campaign in Vice Admiral Robert Ghormley, who arrived from London at his new headquarters at Nouméa, French New Caledonia, in June 1942. King had been inclined to remove Rear Admiral Fletcher from command of the Pacific Fleet carriers after the Battle of the Coral Sea in May, but Nimitz had defended him stoutly, and Fletcher's handling of the Midway battle seemed to justify this vote of confidence. After that engagement, Nimitz nominated Fletcher for promotion to vice admiral and proposed that he command the carriers for Watchtower. King winced and dallied. On 14 July, the carriers, with Fletcher in command, sailed for a rendezvous with the Guadalcanal-bound transports off Fiji. The next day, King relented, promoted Fletcher, and agreed to allow him to remain in the carrier command.

King was unaware that confusion and discord were already pervading the South Pacific command. Before the invasion, Ghormley arranged for his principal subordinates to confer, but he did not attend this important meeting, sending his chief of staff, Rear Admiral Daniel Callaghan, in his stead. There, Fletcher announced that he would not risk his carriers within range of Japanese land-based aircraft for more than forty-eight hours.

The American high command in World War II. Admiral Ernest J. King (*left*), Admiral William D. Leahy (*center*), and the Chief of Staff of the Army, General George C. Marshall, leaving the Oval Study on 28 July 1942. The White House had just announced that Leahy would be Chief of Staff to the Commander in Chief of the Army and the Navy; this made him, in effect, the first Chairman of the Joint Chiefs of Staff.

This position angered Rear Admiral Richmond Kelly Turner, the intelligent but volatile commander of the amphibious forces, but Turner was unable to shake Fletcher's resolve. Ghormley, overwhelmed by his new burdens, refused to intervene. This was a harbinger of trouble ahead.

Although King later labeled the invasion of Guadalcanal "Operation Shoestring," the Invasion Force of eighty-two ships that he cobbled and sent into the South Pacific was formidable, including three carriers, one powerful fast battleship, eleven heavy cruisers, two light cruisers, thirty destroyers, four minesweepers, and various oilers, transports, freighters, and landing craft. Despite this impressive array of power and clear indications that the Japanese did not expect an invasion, Ghormley begged King to postpone the landing, but King stiffly refused. Nimitz also had tried to suspend the landing once before, and he now tried again, but King, his eye always on the main chance, insisted that it proceed on schedule.

On 7 August 1942, Fletcher's task force, composed of the three carriers *Enterprise, Saratoga,* and *Wasp,* steamed into position off Guadalcanal and launched sweeps that covered the landing of Major General Archer Vandegrift's 1st Marine Division on that island and nearby Tulagi. Tulagi was quickly overrun. On Guadalcanal, about 2,000 Japanese support troops and workers fled into the jungle, and an incomplete airstrip, later named Henderson Field, quickly fell to the invaders. That day, Turner's transports and escorts were attacked by twenty-five Japanese land-based bombers, but the American fighters were ready and, supported by highly accurate antiaircraft gunfire, successfully repulsed this first strike. Neither side fully realized at this time that seizing Henderson Field endowed the Americans with daytime air superiority over the Lower Solomons and the whiphand in the upcoming struggle. The Japanese could still run nighttime reinforcement convoys to Guadalcanal, but the Americans always reasserted their grip at dawn, and Japanese cargo ships could not offload munitions and supplies for more than a few hours.

In spite of this considerable advantage, the Battle of Savo Island, northwest of Guadalcanal, was about to prove that the Japanese could make the cost of holding Guadalcanal prodigious. Fletcher's air plan called for Rear Admiral John S. McCain's land-based PBY Catalinas to conduct long-range patrols over the Lower Solomons, but when it came time to launch the search planes on 8 August great confusion arose owing to the boundary of the adjacent Southwest Pacific theater. MacArthur controlled air operations in this theater, and as usual, he was reluctant to cooperate with the Navy and difficult to deal with. Although normal practice was to launch the carriers' search planes at dawn each day, Fletcher sent out no aircraft on the morning of 8 August to cover the Slot, the name for passages on either side

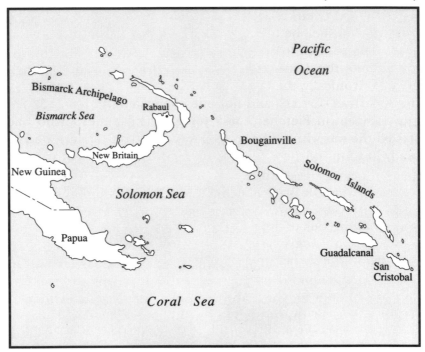

Guadalcanal

of Savo Island, where Japanese battleships or cruisers heading for
the Marine lodgment on Guadalcanal might have been expected
to appear at night. Later that morning, Fletcher decided to concentrate his Wildcat fighters over Savo Island to prevent another
Japanese air attack from reaching the American beachhead, but
the enemy reacted by sending forty twin-engine torpedo
bombers in over Florida Island to strike the landing ships. Nevertheless, American antiaircraft gunfire again exacted a heavy toll
on this flight, although one transport was lost and the destroyer
Jarvis sustained some damage. At the close of two days of brisk
enemy air attacks, the Navy's casualties totalled only one transport sunk, eighteen carrier aircraft downed, and two damaged
destroyers.

Nevertheless, Fletcher announced on the afternoon of
8 August that he intended to withdraw his carriers at once on the
grounds that there were a "large number of enemy torpedo
planes and bombers in this area" and that his own "fighter

strength [had been] reduced from 99 to 78." His ships were "running low" on fuel, he told Ghormley, although each of the carriers had oil enough to steam for at least ten days, and neither the cruisers nor the destroyers would need to be refueled for another week. Ironically, the Japanese had been as yet unable to locate the American carriers, and not one enemy aircraft had inflicted any damage on Fletcher's task force. The Japanese, who had started the war with six heavy and medium fleet carriers, had already lost four of these ships at Midway. Only the heavy carriers *Zuikaku* and the *Shokaku* were prepared for action, but neither of these ships was in the South Pacific at the time. And, although Fletcher did not know this, by 8 August the Japanese at Rabaul were running out of aircraft and Rabaul's air base commander was calling on Tokyo to send out replacements. Not only did Fletcher withdraw his carriers from the waters off Guadalcanal earlier than planned, but also he took with him the new fast battleship *North Carolina*, the most powerful surface combatant then in the South Pacific, and a screen of six heavy cruisers and sixteen destroyers. From his headquarters in Nouméa, Ghormley belatedly agreed with Fletcher's decision, and at 1810 the carrier-battleship task force steamed away from Guadalcanal to a position about 100 miles to the southwest.[3]

Both Ghormley and Fletcher assumed that the beachhead and the transports were in no danger because there had been no alarm from MacArthur's Southwest Pacific air force or Admiral McCain, who had been given the job of providing an early warning of enemy movements in the Solomons to Fletcher and Turner. McCain commanded a force of 300 PBY Catalina seaplanes, land-based observation planes, and Army Air Force bombers. Half of these aircraft were based to the rear on Fiji, Tonga, and the Samoan Islands, but Ghormley had earlier instructed McCain to move the remainder forward to Espíritu Santo to support the invasion of Guadalcanal. These aircraft were active during the first day of the invasion, but bad weather compelled McCain to restrict his northern searches on the afternoon of 8 August. Unfortunately, he failed to relay this decision to Fletcher, who had previously agreed to "fill in for short range scouting" whenever McCain's effort was incomplete.[4]

Unbeknownst to Ghormley, the Japanese had already reacted to the American landing. On 7 August, only hours after the Marines waded ashore on Guadalcanal, Vice Admiral Gunichi

Mikawa stood out of Rabaul with a task force composed of five heavy cruisers, two light cruisers, and one destroyer and headed south for Guadalcanal about 600 miles away. At 1026 on the 8th, he was 340 miles northeast of Guadalcanal when his ships were sighted by the pilot of a Royal Australian Air Force Hudson bomber flying out of Milne Bay, New Guinea, which was within MacArthur's Southwest Pacific theater. The pilot, without any excuse, not only failed to keep contact with the Japanese force but also decided to maintain radio silence and so did not report his sighting until he returned to his airfield. As a result, his alarm did not reach Turner until about 2100 that evening. A pair of McCain's Army Air Force B-17 bombers from Espíritu Santo searching to the north of Choiseul Island approached Mikawa's task force at 1215, but the Americans cut short their mission and turned back just as they were about to come upon the enemy. And at 1630, an Australian coast watcher on Vella Lavella Island broadcast a sighting of Mikawa's ships. Fletcher received this message soon after, but it was not conveyed to Turner or to the commander of his Screening Group.

Based on the coast watcher's message, Commander John Crommelin in the *Enterprise* estimated that Mikawa would arrive off Savo Island at about 0100 on 9 August, and he was concerned for the safety of Turner's amphibious ships, many of which had yet to be unloaded. Crommelin wanted Rear Admiral Thomas Kinkaid to ask Fletcher for permission to launch a dawn air strike against Mikawa's cruisers, but Kinkaid told him that Fletcher was certain to veto it, and there the matter ended. About the time that Fletcher had decided to withdraw his carriers, Turner had learned that a flight of forty Japanese bombers was heading toward Guadalcanal, and he ordered some of the transports to get under way, but a number still remained in the sound when darkness fell. British Rear Admiral V. A. C. Crutchley, who was commanding the cruiser-destroyer Screening Group and was responsible for defending the transport anchorage, believed "heavy ships in groups of more than four to be unwieldy at night" and so he divided his force into three formations. One group of three cruisers was to block the southern passage into the sound between Savo Island and Guadalcanal. Another three cruisers were to guard the northern passage between Savo and Florida Island. About twenty miles to the south, Rear Admiral Norman Scott's two cruisers were to steam back and forth across the sound between Tulagi and Lunga Point to prevent any Japanese submarines from entering the sound from the south and attacking the transports. For a close-in antisubmarine screen, Turner had positioned several destroyers close by the transports, leaving Crutchley only two destroyers to stand radar picket duty abreast of Savo Island.

When Turner learned that Fletcher had withdrawn the carriers, he told Crutchley to come ashore later on to decide what they should do at dawn. Thus, at 2315, the cruiser *Australia*, Crutchley's flagship, steamed away from the southern blocking station, leaving Captain Howard Bode in the cruiser *Chicago* in tactical command of that group. Bode knew that Crutchley had departed, but Crutchley had failed to alert Captain Frederick Riefkohl in the cruiser *Vincennes* that he was now in tactical command of the northern group. The crews in both groups were released from general quarters and a Condition Two alert was set, during which half the men were on watch while the rest slept. Shortly after midnight the radar picket destroyer *Blue* announced over the TBS talk-between-ships radio that an unidentified aircraft was overhead. Because her running lights were lit, however, Bode assumed her to be friendly, and he sounded no alarm. A few minutes later, he retired to his sea cabin to get some sleep.

Unaware of the danger to his force from the American radar pickets, Mikawa expected the upcoming battle to be decided by the superior night-fighting training of the Japanese cruisers and the oxygen-breathing Long Lance torpedo, a lethal weapon that carried a 1,345-pound warhead and could run toward a target eight miles away at a speed of 50 knots. The Americans, on the other hand, believing that cruisers would never fight at such close ranges, had not fitted their post–World War I–era cruisers with torpedo tubes, although all Japanese cruisers had torpedo tubes and the Japanese had trained for years in their use in night engagements. Mikawa also hoped to achieve tactical surprise, but he nearly lost this advantage just after midnight when his cruisers came upon the *Blue*. The Japanese gunners prepared to open fire on her, but the *Blue*'s surface search radar was malfunctioning and her lookouts were not alert, so Mikawa withheld his fire and his task force steamed quietly past the American picket in the middle of the dark night.

The Battle of Savo Island began at 0136 when Mikawa launched a torpedo attack against the southern group of Allied cruisers, a blow that was quickly followed by a devastating gunfire barrage delivered at close range. The Australian cruiser *Canberra* was hit by two torpedoes and destroyed by gunfire, while Bode in the *Chicago* unwittingly escaped from the battle by turning to the west to chase the lone Japanese destroyer *Yunagi*, which he soon sank. In an inexplicable decision, Bode not only continued to steam westward, but he also did not alert Captain Riefkohl, whose northern cruiser group was at the time encased by a rain squall, and who was still unaware that the Japanese had passed Savo Island and launched an attack. Dividing his cruisers into two columns to envelop Riefkohl's northern group, Mikawa passed Savo Island, closed on the American ships, and launched a torpedo and gunfire attack that mortally wounded the cruiser *Astoria* and sank the cruiser *Quincy*. Stunned, Riefkohl in the *Vincennes* scored only one hit against the enemy before his own ship went under.

Mikawa, after costing the Allies four cruisers in slightly over thirty minutes, now feared that his formation was about to be exposed to an American air attack at dawn. His ships had fired most of their torpedoes, and gunfire from the American cruisers had damaged the flagship cruiser *Chokai*'s chartroom. He did not know that only Scott's two light cruisers stood between his ships and the American transports. So, instead of brushing Scott aside, attacking the transports, and shelling the beachhead, Mikawa retired from the sound and steamed northward at full speed, leaving behind four Allied cruisers sunk, 1,024 dead, and 709 wounded. At about the same time, Rear Admiral Noyes rejected a plan put forth by Captain Forest Sherman of the *Wasp* to turn north and launch an air strike against the Japanese cruisers. The action was a thorough defeat for the Americans, who, perhaps, had been overly confident after the victory off Midway. After the engagement, the Navy found slight consolation in the fact that Lieutenant Commander John R. Moore in the fleet submarine *S-44* sank the heavy cruiser *Kako* on her return to Kavieng from the Battle of Savo Island.

Nimitz bore much of the blame for the disaster. He possessed considerable intelligence about Japanese night-fighting tactics and the Long Lance torpedo but had done nothing to revise Pacific Fleet tactical doctrine to accommodate these threats. Japanese doctrine called for their ships to form up in columns abreast, close the distance between the opposing formations at high speed, and open the battle by firing torpedo barrages to shock and maim the enemy. The Americans, on the other hand, intended to stick to the simple, tightly spaced line-ahead, to rely on their radars to warn them of approaching Japanese ships, and to decide the battle with gunfire at ranges of about 10,000 yards, a distance at which they believed torpedoes would not come into play. The use of search radars was imperfectly understood, however, and the effective range of the Long Lance was only slightly less than that of cruiser gunfire. The Americans were bound to be caught up short once the Japanese elected to close at high speed and accept a melee because the line-ahead formation exposed the length of every ship to torpedoes.

The next morning, Turner unloaded as much material as he could before standing out to sea with his transports at 1600, leaving behind about 15,000 Marines on Guadalcanal. They had only four days' worth of ammunition, few rations, and no heavy construction equipment to complete Henderson Field. Ghormley believed that the Marines' lodgment was in jeopardy, and he warned Nimitz to expect the Japanese to "try to land an expedition against our positions in the Tulagi area." Apart from Mikawa's sortie, however, the Japanese were generally slow to react. Dedicated to ejecting MacArthur from Port Moresby and unaware—owing to an almost complete absence of interservice collaboration—that the Combined Fleet had lost four carriers at Midway, the Japanese Army in August misjudged the balance of power in the South Pacific and assumed that a small counterstroke would dislodge the Marines from Guadalcanal.[5]

Yamamoto still expected Nimitz to attack the outer Japanese defensive perimeter in the central Pacific. In order to thwart such a move, he had stationed the remaining Japanese carriers at the fleet base at Truk in the Carolines. In the first attempt to reinforce Guadalcanal, 1,000 Japanese troops boarded destroyers that put them ashore east of Henderson Field on 18 August, but they were annihilated during a hastily planned assault against the Marine defenses on the Ilu River. Meanwhile, other Marines were working furiously with captured equipment to finish the airstrip at Henderson Field. By this time, Ghormley had organized a task group of four fast destroyers laden with aviation fuel, munitions, and technicians, and these ships slipped into Guadalcanal on the 15th. Five days later, the new escort carrier *Long Island* launched a flight of nineteen fighters and twelve dive bombers, which landed at Henderson Field that afternoon. The arrival of these planes gave the Americans daytime air superiority in the Lower Solomons, although at night Japan's battleships and cruisers still ruled Ironbottom Sound between Guadalcanal and Tulagi.

Yamamoto responded to the defeat on the Ilu River and the opening of Henderson Field by shifting his heavy carriers to Rabaul and instructing Vice Admiral Nobutake Kondo to form two carrier task forces to escort Rear Admiral Raizo Tanaka's Guadalcanal-bound reinforcement convoy of transports carrying 1,500 troops. The light carrier *Ryujo*, positioned in the van of this formation, was assigned to attack Henderson Field. In the center, separated from the van by at least fifty miles, were the heavy carriers *Shokaku* and *Zuikaku*. To the west, Tanaka's transports and the light cruiser *Jintsu* brought up the rear. Ghormley, alerted by radio intelligence and Australian coast watchers to Kondo's movements, wanted to obstruct the enemy's progress, so he ordered Fletcher to bring up his carriers from the south and block the flanking approaches to the Lower Solomons.

Inasmuch as Fletcher mistakenly believed that the Japanese carriers were still at Truk, he did not expect a fleet engagement and, therefore, on the evening of 23 August, detached the *Wasp* to go south to refuel. The need to do this is unclear since he had previously refueled the *Wasp* and the *Enterprise* and the *Wasp* still had over half her fuel left, but he was always concerned about running low. The result was to reduce the American air strength by one third. Fletcher was caught off guard when an American scout plane sighted the *Ryujo* advancing on Santa Isabella Island, but he decided to attack and sent thirty dive bombers and eight torpedo planes against the small Japanese carrier, which was mortally wounded and sank that night. Although Fletcher now knew that Kondo's carriers might be in the area, he had chosen, nonetheless, to attack precipitously, thus exposing his depleted task force to a frontal assault from the enemy. Taking another curious step, Fletcher divided his carriers, leaving Admiral Kinkaid in the *Enterprise* to direct air operations while he withdrew the *Saratoga* and the new fast battleship *North Carolina* ten miles to the south.

In spite of these disadvantages, the Americans successfully repulsed Kondo's counterattack, which was poorly coordinated. The first flight of enemy aircraft was battered by the F4F Wildcat fighters flying combat air patrol, and only a few of the second group of Japanese planes reached the *Enterprise*, whose lethal antiaircraft batteries alone accounted for fifteen enemy aircraft. The attackers managed to drop three bombs on the deck of the *Enterprise*, but they were unable to penetrate the American defenses and approach the *Saratoga*. In the meantime, Fletcher's search planes were locating Kondo's heavy carriers, and he launched a flight of bombers and torpedo planes from the *Saratoga* against them, but a weather front shielded the Japanese task force from discovery and the Americans were able to find and sink only the seaplane tender *Chitose*. Although Fletcher had lost only seventeen aircraft, he was moved to withdraw to the south owing to the damage to the *Enterprise*, his ever constant concern about refueling, and the fear that Kondo would close for a night engagement. Kondo did bring up his battleships and cruisers to challenge the Americans, but he had lost ninety aircraft and one small carrier already and did not want to fight the next day, so at midnight he decided to retire to the northeast. This stripped Tanaka of his air cover, but his transports continued to steam toward Guadalcanal. At dawn, Army Air Force B-17 Flying Fortresses from Espiritu Santo and naval bombers from Henderson Field damaged the cruiser *Jintsu*, sank a destroyer, and finally compelled Tanaka to withdraw.

Although the Battle of the Eastern Solomons ended in a tactical draw, the Americans had at least succeeded in preventing the Japanese reinforcements from reaching Guadalcanal. The temporary loss of the *Enterprise* shook Ghormley, inasmuch as he had only one carrier left. To reinforce the South Pacific, King directed Nimitz to deploy the *Hornet* to Ghormley's area, and until the *Hornet* could reach the South Pacific, Ghormley instructed Fletcher to hold the *Saratoga* at least 200 miles south of Guadalcanal, to avoid exposing her once again to Kondo's pair of heavy carriers. Thus, Fletcher was patrolling off San Cristóbal Island about 260 miles southeast of Guadalcanal on 31 August when the Japanese submarine *I-26* approached the task force and put a torpedo into the side of the *Saratoga*. Good damage control once again saved an American ship, but the *Saratoga* had to limp back to the West Coast for repairs, carrying Fletcher, who had been slightly wounded. Despite his many accomplishments, Fletcher left the South Pacific with a string of disasters behind him. Nimitz, ever charitable, held this to be the result of bad luck. King, less forgiving, thought Fletcher to be error-prone, and in late 1943 he exiled Fletcher to the North Pacific command for the rest of the war. On the other hand, King ignored Navy Secretary Knox's demand that he hold Turner responsible for the disaster off Savo Island and relieve him also. King understood that Turner was a fighter, and fighting admirals were what the Navy badly needed.

Set back in the Battle of the Eastern Solomons, the Japanese were still bent on ejecting the Marines from Guadalcanal. By the end of the month, the "Tokyo Express" of nighttime destroyer-transports to Guadalcanal had landed nearly 6,000 troops who were concentrated south of Henderson Field. General Vandegrift repulsed the enemy's ill-conceived frontal assault on Bloody Ridge on the night of 13 September, and the next day Turner sailed from Espíritu Santo with a convoy of seven transports carrying reinforcements from the 7th Marine Regiment, escorted by Rear Admiral Leigh Noyes' task force composed of the carriers *Wasp* and *Hornet* and the fast battleship *North Carolina*. Captain Forest P. Sherman in the *Wasp* was 250 miles southwest of Guadalcanal at noon on 15 September when Noyes decided to turn into the wind and launch a flight of SDB Dauntless dive bombers to search ahead of the convoy. After these planes took off, Sherman ordered that the carrier resume her previous course and speed, and her escorts swiftly conformed, but this increased the noise produced by their engines to a level that overwhelmed their rudimentary sonar listening systems.

At 1444, the Japanese submarine *I-119*, having approached the task force without being detected, fired six torpedoes at the *Wasp*. A lookout spotted one of the wakes and Sherman immediately tried to swerve, but it was too late and the weapon slammed into the carrier's starboard side. The resulting explosion engulfed the area in flames. More fires erupted when the second and third torpedoes hit the ship, detonating the ready ammunition for the forward antiaircraft guns and buckling the forward flight deck. The timing of the attack proved catastrophic. The aircraft had just been refueled, so the gasoline system was in operation, the fuel lines were full, and the fire quickly spread to the main gas tank below. After Sherman's crew had abandoned ship, Noyes instructed the destroyer *Landsdowne* to sink the *Wasp* with five torpedoes. In the meantime, the escorting destroyer *O'Brien* was hit by a Japanese torpedo. Then, at 1452, another torpedo struck the port bow of the *North Carolina*. She listed to port, but her thorough underwater protection and superb damage-control parties saved the battleship and allowed her to maintain her station even though Noyes increased the task force's speed to 25 knots. The destroyer *Mustin* made sonar contact with the *I-119* and dropped nine depth charges, but after an attack lasting twenty minutes the Japanese submarine eluded the pursuit.[6]

After the battle, the *North Carolina* had to return to Pearl Harbor for repairs. The sinking of the *Wasp* left Ghormley with the recently arrived *Hornet* as the only aircraft carrier available to support the Marines' lodgment on Guadalcanal. When these losses—still kept from the public—became known in Washington, the struggle for Guadalcanal assumed a domestic political importance that neither FDR nor the JCS had anticipated. When the *Wasp* was sunk, Roosevelt confessed to the Allied Pacific War Council that he was "frankly . . . pessimistic at the moment about the whole situation" and warned that the loss of Guadalcanal would devastate American public opinion. His administration was already discredited by Pearl Harbor and the loss of the Philippines, and he was openly worried that the Democrats would lose control of Congress in the upcoming November 1942 elections. Nimitz, who had wanted to postpone the descent on the Solomons, now increased his demands for more ships and aircraft, and on 7 September—during one of their bimonthly conferences in San Francisco—complained to King that the South Pacific badly needed reinforcements. When Nimitz met with General Arnold, the chief of the Army Air Force, on 21 September, he insisted that Guadalcanal could be held. "Nimitz' idea is that Japanese shipping losses are so great that they cannot keep up operations indefinitely," Arnold recorded.[7]

While he was planning the offensive against Guadalcanal in July, King thought that the Americans might overrun Rabaul by the end of the year. He later confessed that he was thoroughly "surprised by the violence and persistence of the Japanese reaction to our movement into the Solomons." Pointing out to General Marshall that the Navy had "gone much beyond our commitments" toward meeting the needs of Operation Torch, the forthcoming invasion of North Africa, King now insisted that more Army Air Force pursuit planes and bombers be sent to Ghormley's command in the South Pacific. However, Arnold had opposed the Guadalcanal operation from the start, as had Marshall, who now told King that "the reinforcements which you propose can only be effected by diversions from Torch," a step the Army chief of staff would not take. Despite King's badgering, FDR refused for over a month to intervene to resolve this impasse and did so only when it became evident that the crisis in the South Pacific might adversely effect the upcoming midterm elections. In late October, prompted by reports of a renewed Japanese counteroffensive, Roosevelt directed Marshall and King "to make sure that every possible weapon gets in that area to hold Guadalcanal . . . even though it means delay in our other commitments."[8]

Nimitz, aware that the American position was eroding—and not just for lack of reinforcements—flew down to Nouméa to confer with Ghormley and order him to provide more support to the Marines on Guadalcanal. Ghormley resisted this at first; he was more concerned with the need to establish a secure air base on Ndeni, one of the Santa Cruz Islands about 325 miles south of Guadalcanal. Under Nimitz' pressure, however, he finally relented and directed Turner to organize a convoy of two transports carrying an Army regiment, which stood out of Nouméa on 9 October. The covering force for this convoy included the carrier *Hornet*, the new fast battleship *Washington* with her 16-inch guns, and a Scouting Force of four cruisers and five destroyers under Admiral Scott. He appeared off Guadalcanal on the 11th and deployed his ships in a line-ahead west of Savo Island, thoroughly prepared to disrupt the nighttime Tokyo Express. In the afternoon, an American search plane reported sighting Rear Admiral Aritomo Goto's three heavy cruisers and two destroyers, an escort force for two seaplane tenders and six transport destroyers ferrying Japanese troops and equipment to Guadalcanal. At 2330, Scott reversed his course and began to steam toward the Florida Island passage when the cruiser *Helena*'s radar picked up Goto's escorts, although this news was not relayed to Scott for another ten minutes.

When the enemy appeared out of the night, the *Helena*'s alert crew immediately opened fire, followed shortly by the rest of the ships on both sides. Scott tried in vain to cross Goto's "tee," but the American admiral could not keep control of his line. During the ensuing gunnery duel, the American cruisers blew up the destroyer *Fubuki* and crippled the heavy cruiser *Furutaka* so badly that she went down while trying to withdraw. Scott, attempting to reorganize his formation, ordered his ships to cease firing for a few minutes, but this gave the Japanese an unwarranted opportunity to retire to the north before Scott could resume fighting. Not one American destroyer had launched a torpedo, and Scott apparently gave no thought to pursuing and annihilating Goto's crippled and outnumbered force. Although the destroyer *Duncan* was sunk and the cruiser *Boise* badly damaged, and the enemy transports reached Guadalcanal, Scott's poorly conducted action off Cape Esperance was the Navy's first night surface victory in the South Pacific.

At dawn two days later, Turner's transports appeared off Guadalcanal once again, and by 1200 he had put ashore a large number of Army troops, trucks, ammunition, and rations. That night, however, two Japanese battleships took station in Ironbottom Sound and fired 900 14-inch high-explosive shells at Henderson Field, putting the main runway out of commission and damaging half of the Marine aircraft parked there. Heavy enemy cruisers took up this work the next two nights, and the Japanese shipped 4,000 more troops to Guadalcanal, prompting Vandegrift to warn Ghormley that it was "urgently necessary that" the Marines "receive maximum support of air and surface units" if they were to hold the lodgment. Clearly, something had to be done.[9]

For several weeks, word had been leaching out of the South Pacific to Pearl Harbor and back to Washington that Ghormley was unsuited for the heavy burdens of high command. General Arnold visited Nouméa in September and returned to Washington convinced that the Navy in the South Pacific needed "new leaders who know and understand modern warfare; men who are aggressive and not afraid to fight their ships." Part of the problem arose from Ghormley's confusion about his orders. King had instructed Ghormley to run the South Pacific Area from his headquarters at Nouméa, whereas Nimitz expected Ghormley to put to sea and personally direct the battles around Guadalcanal. Nimitz also faulted Ghormley for allowing the logistics and shipping situation in his area to reach crisis proportions and for misusing the scarce, large LSTs as floating warehouses. "We are unable to control the sea in the Guadalcanal area, thus our supply of the positions will only be done at great expense to us," Nimitz warned King. "The situation is not hopeless, but it is certainly critical." On 17 October, Nimitz suggested to King that Admiral Halsey be named to replace Ghormley, and King, impatient with the blunders and lack of progress in the South Pacific, quickly agreed to this important step.[10]

Backed by Roosevelt's increased commitment to the South Pacific theater, Halsey arrived like a storm in Nouméa on 20 October. First, he bullied the coven of arrogant French officials in New Caledonia into cooperating with the Americans; then he attended to the considerable friction existing between Turner and Vandegrift. At the root of this problem was Turner's violent personality and the inexperience of most Navy line officers with logistics, a field of activity that had been left to the Supply Corps' procurement staff during the austere interwar years. Although Halsey did not understand why, he realized that Vandegrift was not receiving supplies and munitions he knew to be in the South Pacific. One reason was that Turner had held a large body of Marines in reserve to occupy Ndeni, but Halsey now ordered him to cancel that operation and concentrate all his resources in support of Vandegrift's position on Guadalcanal. To reduce Vandegrift's blistering criticism of Turner, Halsey divorced him from Turner's Navy chain of command, decreeing that once a Marine or Army landing-force headquarters was established ashore, command of the ground forces was to shift from the admiral afloat to the general on the beach. Vandegrift was also heartened by Halsey's decision to station Rear Admiral Willis Lee in the fast battleship *Washington* in Ironbottom Sound to prevent further nighttime bombardments of Henderson Field by Japanese surface forces. And to relieve Fletcher in command of the carriers, Halsey selected Kinkaid, whom he told to take station north of the Santa Cruz Islands with a powerful task force built around the *Hornet* and *Enterprise* and the new fast battleship *South Dakota*. Once established, Kinkaid was to make ready to ambush any Japanese forces that appeared to the northeast of Guadalcanal during the day.

While Halsey was reorganizing his command, Yamamoto prepared another counteroffensive to retake Henderson Field. In mid-September, the 11,000 Marines on Guadalcanal had outnumbered the 5,000 Japanese defenders, but the Japanese sent in more reinforcements over the next month. This left Vandegrift and the Japanese Army commander, Major General Haruyoshi Hyakutake, with about 22,000 men each by the third week in October. Expecting that Hyakutake would soon overrun Henderson Field, Yamamoto planned to send land-based aircraft from Rabaul to Guadalcanal and use them to support naval operations aimed at reestablishing Japanese control south of the Lower Solomons. To this end, on 23 October, Vice Admiral Kondo brought a task force of four carriers and four battleships down to a position to the northeast of Guadalcanal. However, an enemy air code recovered from a downed Japanese plane on Guadalcanal enabled Marine Major B. T. Holcomb's shipboard-based radio intelligence unit to provide Halsey and Kinkaid with several vital enemy messages, which gave them insight into Kondo's battle plan. That same day, Hyakutake hurled the first of a succession of poorly coordinated assaults against the Marines' perimeter around Henderson Field. In bloody fighting over the next seventy-two hours, this attack was thoroughly repulsed and American defenses never threatened.

When news of the Marines' victory in the land Battle of Guadalcanal reached Yamamoto on the morning of 26 October, he directed Kondo to withdraw his carriers from the area. But when Kondo began to retire to the northwest, his ships were spotted by a PBY Catalina from Espíritu Santo, which broadcast a contact report to Halsey. Halsey immediately ordered Kinkaid to "Strike. Repeat. Strike!" Within hours, American planes located Kondo's formation and destroyed the light carrier *Zuiho*'s flight deck with two 500-pound bombs. The Japanese had launched their own attack aircraft before Kinkaid had, however, and the next phase of the Battle off the Santa Cruz Islands was waged over the American task force. The direction of the combat air patrol was so flawed that the defending F4F Wildcat fighters could not gain enough altitude before the Japanese attackers appeared over the carrier *Hornet*, with the result that she was mortally wounded by two torpedoes and five bombs, one delivered by a crippled bomber that crashed against the ship. The *Enterprise*, ten miles away, was more stoutly defended by her experienced antiaircraft batteries and by the battleship *South Dakota*'s furious antiaircraft fire. Meanwhile, American torpedo and dive bombers from the *Hornet* were damaging the heavy cruiser *Chikuma* and crippling the heavy carrier *Shokaku*. When Kinkaid retired that evening, he counted the loss of one carrier, the destroyer *Porter*, and seventy-four aircraft. Only two American carriers were left in the Pacific. Attrition was also working against the Japanese. They lost 113 naval aircraft between 16 and 25 October around Guadalcanal, whereas the Americans lost only 14, and several of Japan's larger ships had been roughly handled. Though Yamamoto still had three undamaged carriers in the South Pacific, he had few naval aircraft left and was forced to return his carriers to Japan to reconstitute their air groups. In the Battle off the Santa Cruz Islands, the Japanese had again won a slight tactical victory at the cost of a major strategic setback.

When the Japanese ground offensive against Henderson Field collapsed on 26 October, Vandegrift expanded his perimeter enough to move his opponent's heavy artillery out of range of the runway. To support him, Halsey stripped troops from many of his outlying bases and deployed them to Guadalcanal. In addition, Turner shipped elements of the 2nd Marine Division and more soldiers from the Army's American Division to Guadalcanal in early November in a convoy defended by Rear Admiral Callaghan's hastily organized task group of five cruisers and eight destroyers. Despite recent Japanese losses, Yamamoto was still determined to eject the Americans from the Lower Solomons. In early November, eleven transports embarked 13,000 fresh Japanese troops and sped south to the Slot under the protection of eleven destroyers commanded by Rear Admiral Tanaka. An escorting force under Vice Admiral Hirosaki Abe, who commanded the battleships *Hiei* and *Kirishima*, was to steam into Ironbottom Sound at night, cover Tanaka's landing, and shell Henderson Field.

Turner was withdrawing his transports and cargo ships from Guadalcanal when he learned of the enemy's plan, and he ordered Callaghan to remain behind with his cruiser-destroyer force and challenge Abe's approaching battleships. Supporting Callaghan was a separate formation of five American cruisers under Admiral Scott in the *Atlanta*. On the evening of 12 November, Callaghan's ships entered Ironbottom Sound and sailed north to the Slot to meet Abe, who was at the time steaming to the southeast and closing on the American formation. Inasmuch as the Americans had surface-search radar sets and knew that the Japanese did not, Callaghan planned to exploit the element of surprise to make up for his numerical inferiority, but his battle plan quickly went awry.

The naval Battle of Guadalcanal opened when the *Helena*'s radar detected the Japanese at 0124 on 13 November; the two fleets were only fourteen miles apart at the time. Intent on capping Abe's "tee," Callaghan now ordered his ships to turn to the north, but when the destroyer *Cushing* sighted an enemy vessel, she broke from the line, advanced toward it, and disrupted the entire American movement. The cruisers turned to the southwest to avoid colliding with their own screening destroyers, and just at this moment Abe ordered his ships to open fire. A melee of confusing gun duels ensued. Because their magazines were loaded with high-explosive shells for bombarding the airfield, rather than armor-piercing anti-ship ordnance, the Japanese battleships' 14-inch guns could not dominate the action. Indeed, fifty American hits crippled the *Hiei* and she was sunk the next day by aircraft from Henderson Field. In addition, two Japanese destroyers went down. The Americans paid dearly for their poor tactics, however. The cruisers *Atlanta* and *Juneau* were lost that night, along with four destroyers. All but one of the surviving American ships were badly damaged. Both Callaghan and Scott perished during the naval Battle of Guadalcanal, but at least in the end they had forced the Japanese to retire, saving Henderson Field from the agony of another nighttime bombardment.

When dawn broke on the morning of 14 November, Kinkaid's task force, including the carrier *Enterprise* and the new fast battleships *Washington* and *South Dakota*, steamed into range south of Guadalcanal. Air attacks from the *Enterprise*, Henderson Field, and Army Air Force B-17 bombers from Espíritu Santo struck Abe's cruisers during their withdrawal to New Georgia Island and hit several enemy transports in the Slot. One cruiser sank and three others were damaged. Three of Mikawa's seven transports went down too, but he grittily forged southward toward the coast of Guadalcanal. By this time Kondo in the battleship *Kirishima*, screened by four cruisers and nine destroyers, was steaming south to Guadalcanal to shell Henderson Field. Under orders from Halsey to parry this thrust, Kinkaid sent Lee's powerful battleships into Ironbottom Sound. Kondo, who had divided his task force into three separate formations, dodged about Savo Island, movements that cluttered the Americans' radar screens and confused them momentarily. He then pounced on the battleship *South Dakota* and pummeled her so furiously that she had to retire for the moment. Reacting quickly, Lee used his radar fire control to train the *Washington*'s 16-inch guns on the lesser battleship *Kirishima*, and she had to be scuttled after taking fifty punishing hits. Mikawa tenaciously guided his four stricken transports to the beach, but these vessels were attacked the next morning by American aircraft and blown apart by ships' gunfire. Once more the enemy paid dearly to put a few men ashore on Guadalcanal.

The Battle of Tassafaronga on 30 November 1942 was anti-climactic, a result largely of the inability of the Japanese high command to agree upon a new strategy. Not only had Japan's leaders failed to dislodge the Marines from Guadalcanal, but they also had suffered a reversal on New Guinea when General MacArthur belatedly took the offensive and pushed the Japanese Army back over the Owen Stanley Mountains and up against Buna on the coast of the Solomon Sea. Prime Minister Tojo then shifted his focus from New Guinea to Guadalcanal, rejecting Yamamoto's plan to abandon that position and insisting that the Japanese Army there be supported at least until a new airfield could be established on Kolombangara Island in the Central Solomons. Unwilling to risk any more heavy ships south of Savo Island, Yamamoto instructed Tanaka in late November to run into Ironbottom Sound with eight destroyer-transports and land troops and provisions at the village of Tassafaronga. Tanaka was to retire before dawn exposed his ships to the American air forces.

Soon after he had assumed command, Halsey realized that the Americans needed different night surface tactics, and so in early November he formed a different task force of five cruisers and six destroyers under Kinkaid, giving him one month to drill his ships off Espíritu Santo before they would be committed to disrupting the Tokyo Express. Kinkaid realized the inadequacy of line-ahead tactics in gunfire-torpedo battles, and so he decided to hold his cruisers out of range of the enemy's Long Lance torpedoes and to divide his destroyers into columns to launch fast, well-coordinated torpedo attacks. On 28 November, however, King told Kinkaid to fly to Alaska to relieve Admiral Theobald in command of the North Pacific Area, and a new arrival in the South Pacific, Rear Admiral Carleton H. Wright, took over the cruiser-destroyer force at Espíritu Santo. The following evening, reports of a concentration of Japanese shipping in the southern Bougainville area convinced Halsey that Yamamoto was preparing another major resupply operation, and he ordered Wright to steam into Ironbottom Sound to thwart this move. Tanaka's eight destroyers passed to the west of Savo Island on the night of 30 November, at about the same time that Wright's task force was steaming north to challenge them. Owing to a dead calm, Wright's float planes could not take off, so he depended wholly on his radars to locate the enemy.

The Battle of Tassafaronga opened when, at 2316, the destroyer *Fletcher*'s radar found the opposing ships, then hugging the coastline. Wright was urged to launch a quick torpedo attack, but he debated with himself about this for four minutes, just enough time for Tanaka to reverse course and open up the distance between the two formations. When Wright finally ordered his destroyers to attack, none of the American torpedoes could overtake the enemy ships. He directed his cruisers to open fire at about the same time, and this devastating barrage sank the destroyer *Takanami*, but it also unintentionally betrayed the position of every American cruiser to the enemy. Tanaka, reacting promptly, formed his destroyers into three columns and launched a determined torpedo counterattack that damaged the heavy cruisers *Minneapolis*, *New Orleans*, and *Pensacola* and sank the heavy cruiser *Northampton*. "For an enemy force of eight destroyers . . . to inflict such damage on a more powerful force at so little cost is something less than a credit to our command," Halsey snorted.[11]

Tanaka's victory off Tassafaronga notwithstanding, he was unable to land any men or equipment on Guadalcanal. As a result, Yamamoto refused to send any more ships into the sound during December, relying instead that month on transport submarines to carry provisions to the stranded Japanese troops. Meanwhile, the 1st Marine Division was relieved in December by the rest of the 2nd Marine Division and by Army Major General Alexander Patch's Americal Division. Before he left Guadalcanal, General Vandegrift finally launched an offensive to reduce the Japanese garrison, and the Army continued this operation into the new year. As Yamamoto could no longer reinforce or supply the Japanese Army on Guadalcanal, Tojo instructed him on 4 January 1943 to evacuate the defenders from the island and ready a secondary defensive line in the Central Solomons. On the outer perimeter of this northern line of defenses was a new airstrip at Munda, which Rear Admiral Walden Ainsworth's new cruiser-destroyer task force shelled on the night of 4 January.

Misreading Yamamoto's intentions, Halsey reckoned that the Japanese were about to make "a final, supreme effort" to retake Guadalcanal, a conviction reinforced by reports from American search planes that enemy carriers and battleships were congregating off Rabaul. He reacted by assigning Rear Admiral Robert C. Giffen's cruiser-destroyer task force to escort four reinforcement transports to Guadalcanal, thus tempting Yamamoto into exposing his heavy ships once again to American air power. To ambush Kondo's carriers, Halsey also sent two fast carriers to the waters south of Guadalcanal and instructed the new escort carriers *Chenango* and *Suwannee* to provide air cover for Giffen's cruisers. Giffen was impatient with the slow escort carriers, however, and he left them en route from Espíritu Santo to Guadalcanal and sped north to rendezvous with the American transport group. He was thus without any combat air patrol when his formation was caught by land-based Japanese bombers off Rennell Island on the night of 29 January, and two enemy torpedoes so damaged the cruiser *Chicago* that she had to be taken in tow by the cruiser *Louisville*. Fighters from the nearby *Enterprise* defended the crippled ship for most of the next day, but at 1600 four Betty torpedo bombers attacked the formation and sank the *Chicago*. Although Giffen's losses off Rennell Island were heavy, the American transports nevertheless reached Guadalcanal intact.[12]

Still convinced that the Japanese intended to reinforce their garrison, Halsey held his carriers south of Guadalcanal and sent another convoy to the island. But Yamamoto, discouraged by the costly battles of attrition, decided at last on 1 February to cut his losses. He assigned twenty destroyers to evacuate the Japanese troops from Guadalcanal, and north of the Solomons, he stationed a large force of cruisers and destroyers, ready to pounce on any surface opposition during the night. The Evacuation Force came under attack by aircraft from Henderson Field and by American patrol torpedo boats, but during the next week the Japanese saved nearly 12,000 soldiers from Guadalcanal, which was thereafter firmly in American hands.

This confusing series of battles not only exposed the inability of some American commanders to deal with the complexity and stress of combat but also illuminated the superiority of Japan's torpedoes and night surface tactics, the fanaticism and tenacity of the individual Japanese sailor and soldier, and the grim determination of his leaders. At every level, the U.S. Navy now began to realize that it would have to devise new night-fighting tactics to deal with Japan's ferocious Long Lance torpedoes. On the other hand, the successful occupation of Guadalcanal highlighted the greater resourcefulness and overall flexibility of the Americans, the technological superiority of just about everything they brought to the battlefield, and the overwhelming material resources of the American industrial base, advantages that were about to be fully exploited by Halsey, Turner, Kinkaid, and a newly emerging cadre of truly exceptional fighting admirals. The slogging match for Guadalcanal, which left King thoroughly unhappy with Nimitz' conduct of the campaign, led to a recasting of Pacific theater strategy. "The concept that it was necessary to drive the Japanese from Guadalcanal before doing anything else was unsound," King lectured Nimitz and Cooke at a meeting in San Francisco on 23 February 1943. "In the six months that this operation has required, the enemy has materially strengthened his positions elsewhere. The best method is to reach around and outflank [him]." Exploiting American superiority in aircraft carriers, submarines, and amphibious forces, King intended in short order to put this concept into practice on a grand scale in the Pacific.[13]

Chapter Four

The Atlantic Front
1942

One of the Allies' major strategic premises in World War II was that Germany could not be defeated unless the Soviet Union, ill prepared for war in 1941 and badly bruised thereafter, held the German Army on the Eastern Front. While Russia bled Germany, the Allies would harry the Axis at sea, bomb Germany's cities and industry, and, someday, invade Europe and face Hitler with a two-front war. Without trying to extract political concessions from Stalin, FDR decided in late 1941 to ship Lend Lease material to Russia to strengthen her ability to resist. He believed, quite innocently, that Stalin would express his gratitude at the peace table. Churchill recognized the dangers in this openhanded policy, but Britain nonetheless followed suit. The North Russia PQ convoys were organized by the Admiralty in the fall of 1941 to carry Lend Lease material shipped from the East Coast to a midocean meeting point off Iceland and cargo ships from Britain to Murmansk and Archangel, but during the segment of the voyage off the North Cape they were prey to attacks by Norway-based German air and naval forces. This danger appeared to increase when, despite considerable British surveillance, on 11 February 1942, the German cruisers *Prince Eugen*, *Scharnhorst*, and *Gneisenau* stood out of Brest, passed up the English Channel at night, and arrived safely in Norwegian waters. The Channel dash was another blow to British pride and the Royal Navy's much heralded ability to exploit Ultra, the radio intelligence operation.

The Admiralty was overly concerned, Admiral King believed, that a German task force led by the battleship *Tirpitz* might break out of the North Sea into the North Atlantic, but the Channel dash so humiliated London that he generously agreed to Admiral Pound's mid-March plea for American capital ship reinforcements of the Home Fleet. This led King to order Rear Admiral Robert Giffen to assemble a powerful Atlantic Fleet task force built around the carrier *Wasp* and the new fast battleship *Washington* and steam for British waters. Giffen reached Scapa Flow on 3 April 1942, thus allowing Pound to shift some British capital ships to Gibraltar and reinforce the Royal Navy's understrength Indian Ocean Fleet. The purpose of strengthening Gibraltar was to create a powerful covering force to protect a convoy that was to ferry fighters to Malta, and Pound asked King if the *Wasp* could help out. Though unhappy with Britain's Mediterranean strategy, King allowed the carrier to ferry one deckload of fighters to Malta, but this operation was so poorly handled that most of the planes were splashed upon arrival by Axis air forces. King reluctantly authorized the *Wasp* to ferry more fighters to Malta in May, and even ordered the small carrier *Ranger* to ferry an Army Air Force fighter group to Egypt to reinforce Britain's hard-pressed 8th Army, which was trying to prevent the Afrika Korps from reaching Cairo. Things went from bad to worse for the Royal Navy in the Mediterranean when Churchill, in an attempt to duplicate the Midway operation, ordered Pound to use the British Mediterranean Fleet at Alexandria to open up a secure supply line to Malta. This desperate gamble failed entirely when the German air forces pounced on the Malta-bound convoys and inflicted unbearable losses, leaving Malta no more secure and the Admiralty once again distressed over Churchill's management of the war.

Pound also asked King to assist with the North Russia PQ convoys. On 28 June, Admiral Giffen in the *Washington* stood out of Scapa Flow, accompanied by two heavy cruisers and four destroyers, and rendezvoused with the Home Fleet, which included a carrier and another battleship. This Covering Force steamed into the Norwegian Sea to defend the passage of PQ.17, a Murmansk-bound Lend Lease convoy that had departed Reykjavik one day earlier with a close escort of two American and two British cruisers and over twenty destroyers, corvettes, and minesweepers. Things started to go awry on 3 July when Ultra intercepts alerted Pound that the heavy cruisers *Admiral Sheer* and *Lutzow* from Narvik and the *Tirpitz* and the cruiser *Hipper* from Trondheim had put to sea with the intention of rendezvousing at Altafiord to the north. Pound was panicked by the news that the Germans had located the convoy, that Dönitz was concentrating U-boats along its route, and that PQ.17 was within range of German airbases in northern Norway. Instead of welcoming a general action between the powerful Home Fleet and the *Tirpitz* task force, he pulled back the battleship-carrier Covering Force, ordered the cruiser escorts to retire, and instructed the helpless freighters to scatter. Owing to Pound's bungling, convoy PQ.17 lost twenty-four ships and two-thirds of its cargo. Giffen's consternation was matched by King's fury, and on 12 July King hastily ordered Giffen's task force back to New York, ignoring Pound's request that the *Washington* and her four destroyers be held in British waters to provide distant cover for Murmansk-bound PQ.18 later that month. The slaughter of PQ.17 ultimately led to the suspension of the North Russia convoys until the fall, by which time King had sent the *Washington* and *Wasp* into the Pacific where their offensive power would not be wasted.

Congress' declaration of war on 8 December 1941 had instantly exposed all U.S. Navy vessels, Army troop transports, and Allied merchant shipping around the world to Axis submarine attacks. The areas of greatest danger, owing to their inadequate defenses, outside of the Alaska-Hawaii-Panama strategic triangle, were the western Atlantic, the Caribbean, and the Gulf of Mexico. Soon after Pearl Harbor, King decided that the Navy's first priority would be to defend American overseas troop shipping. Late in December 1941, Roosevelt, Churchill, and the Combined Chiefs decided to send roughly five U.S. Army divisions and a large Army Air Force to Britain, movements that demanded King's immediate attention. Two British and one American fast 26-knot passenger liners, converted into troop transports, could speed across the Atlantic in five days and outrun the swiftest 17-knot U-boat, needing neither convoys nor escorts. While the liners transported nearly one million Americans overseas during the war, most troops shipped out in much smaller vessels, a large fraction in slow, converted 10,000-ton *Liberty*-class cargo ships. For reasons that defy understanding, soon after Pearl Harbor, Admiral Stark allowed the Army to assume the Navy's World War I–era job of transporting troops, with the result that during

World War II, the War Department purchased and built an immense fleet of troopships over which the Navy had little control. The Navy was still responsible for providing strong oceangoing escorts for this shipping, however, and for transporting its own personnel and the Marines in both the Atlantic and Pacific.

The first large American troop convoy to Britain, AT.10, stood out of New York on 10 January 1942, escorted by the old battleship *Texas*, a pair of heavy cruisers, and a screen of four destroyers. When it arrived at the midocean meeting point south of Iceland, four decrepit British trawlers relieved the powerful American escort task group. On another occasion, a single British cruiser escorted a convoy of transports carrying 40,000 troops through U-boat–infested waters from Britain to South Africa. King was furious at the Admiralty's callous disregard for the safety of American troops, and he complained angrily about this to Admiral Pound, who responded that the Admiralty "simply cannot afford the scale of escort" that King was providing. Not only did Britain not have enough destroyers deployed to the North Atlantic theater to defend the great circle merchant convoys, but most of her destroyers lacked the endurance to provide an adequate defense for troop shipping during a transatlantic passage. AT.12, an even larger troop convoy consisting of fifteen transports defended by an Atlantic Fleet escort task group composed of eighteen battleships, cruisers, and destroyers, stood out of New York on 19 February bound for Britain. Large-scale transatlantic troop movements continued throughout the war. King and General Marshall were insistent that escorting troop shipping should be the U.S. Navy's highest priority and warned London that the Royal Navy's "escort protection provided troop convoys . . . would be unacceptable."

The result was that King had to accept responsibility for escorting all transatlantic troop shipping in April 1942, and this forced him to redistribute the Atlantic Fleet's ocean escort groups by withdrawing escorts from the great circle merchant convoys to Britain and denying destroyers to the Eastern Sea Frontier, which was responsible for protecting merchant shipping along the Atlantic coast.

The entire problem of defending troop shipping both in the western Atlantic and eastern Pacific was greatly complicated by General Marshall's thoughtless practice of ordering small bodies of troops, antiaircraft elements, and Army Air Force units to strengthen various outlying Army garrisons without providing the Navy Department with more than a few days' notice of the embarkation and sailing schedules. Admiral King often had only three or four days to assemble an escort for these troop movements. On one occasion, when King could provide no escort for a hastily scheduled sailing, Marshall was ready to allow the transports to steam into submarine-infested waters without any protection. The anomalous command relationship Roosevelt created by having Stark as CNO and King as CominCh between December 1941 and March 1942 prevented King from dealing effectively with this problem. In mid-March, however, upon succeeding Stark as CNO, King brusquely told Marshall to suspend all "emergency" troop shipments until the Army was prepared to provide the Navy with advance notice of its embarkation schedules. This solved that problem, but the drain on the escorting forces was still acute. Overall, however, the Navy's defense of American troop shipping was one of the unalloyed victories of World War II inasmuch as few troopships under escort were lost, and only a handful were attacked while steaming in areas the Navy deemed safe. Even the British understood at the time the unprecedented scope of the troop shipping dilemma. "The U. S. commitments for escorting troop carriers are heavier than expected," Admiral Pound told Churchill in March 1942. King never wavered from the soundness of this strategy, although it spawned a host of troubles.[1]

Before Japan attacked Pearl Harbor, the Navy expected German U-boats to descend on East Coast shipping, but in late 1941 and early 1942 neither the Atlantic Fleet nor the Eastern Sea Frontier's understrength coastal command was prepared to check these enemy raiders. This lamentable state of affairs was wholly a result of the slow pace of American rearmament in the 1930s and Roosevelt's decisions to transfer fifty American escort destroyers to the Royal Navy in 1940, ship Lend Lease material to Britain and Russia in 1941, and dedicate the Atlantic Fleet temporarily to the defense of Iceland and British merchant shipping in the North Atlantic in September of that year. Protection of East Coast shipping was further hampered after Pearl Harbor by the need to reinforce the Pacific Fleet, strengthen the local American sea frontier forces in the Pacific from Alaska to Panama, and escort troop transports and cargo-bearing convoys sailing from Panama and the West Coast into the South Pacific. An additional drain on the

Atlantic theater was the ruinous decision taken by Roosevelt and Churchill at the White House on 13 January 1942 not to reduce the Lend Lease convoys to the Soviet Union. Owing to the ineptitude of Japanese strategists, however, the threat from the I-boats to the eastern Pacific never materialized, but this was not evident until mid-1942. These many demands compelled King in January to begin to withdraw some American destroyers from the North Atlantic ocean escort groups, although in March so many Royal Navy and Canadian escorts were under repair that King had to revise this policy. To correct the problem, Admiral Pound wanted to reduce the number of escorts per convoy, but King insisted on decreasing the number of convoy crossings per month to maintain the defensive strength of the escort groups while releasing American destroyers for the Eastern Sea Frontier. In April, the British finally agreed to stretch out the convoy cycle, and King responded by shutting down the Iceland-based Support Force and withdrawing most of the American destroyers from the ocean escort groups defending the great circle Lend Lease convoys. King fully understood, however, that this arrangement was by no means a final solution to the problems of strategy and command and control of the Allied escort and antisubmarine campaign.

A few days after Pearl Harbor, King warned Roosevelt to expect the first wave of U-boat attacks on the East Coast within a month, and on 29 December the Admiralty alerted Washington that several German submarines were heading toward the eastern seaboard, where about 8.5 million tons of American merchant shipping were concentrated. This was an offspring of Dönitz' strategy of tonnage warfare. "In 1940 the British and American shipyards . . . could build about 200,000 tons per month," he explained. "This figure would be increased in the years ahead," he realized, but "the increase . . . could only be achieved step by step, and the effects of it would therefore take some time to make themselves felt. Equally, the enemy's shipping requirements would be growing progressively greater." Dönitz reckoned that monthly sinkings of about 700,000 tons would crimp Anglo-American military operations, undermine Britain's ability to wage war, and eventually "make Britain . . . come to terms" with Germany.[2]

Dönitz discounted as propaganda Roosevelt's call on 19 February 1942 for the construction of 24 million tons of new merchant shipping in American yards alone by the end of the year and 50 million tons in 1943, an increase of one cargo ship or tanker launched to three each day. In early 1942, before the Navy's defensive measures came into play, U-boats were sinking about three Allied cargo ships every two days. In short, merely increasing the rate of American ship construction would deal a lethal blow to German naval strategy. Moreover, Dönitz' political objective was unrealistic. U-boats sank 452 Allied ships totaling over 2 million tons in 1941, but Britain spurned negotiations, and once the United States entered the war, even the Germans realized that a negotiated peace was an illusory goal. Dönitz ascribed the failure of the 1941 offensive to a shortage of U-boats and persuaded Hitler to increase submarine construction; by the end of the year the German Fleet had a front-line strength of about 100 boats. Dönitz' strategy had little chance of succeeding, however, because he failed to take into account the enemy's highly collaborative politics, shipping pool increases resulting from American mobilization, or the effect of new Allied countermeasures. His strategy also did not account for marginal improvements in the strength, equipment, or tactics of the Allied escort and antisubmarine forces. However, the ferocious 1942 U-boat offensive did succeed in upsetting Allied strategic planning, harming relations between the Navy Department and the Admiralty, and straining the resources of the Atlantic Fleet.

Dönitz indeed had moved quickly. Soon after Pearl Harbor he inaugurated Operation Roll of Drums by sending five submarines to North American waters, a number limited mostly by Hitler's decision to station several U-boats in Norway to guard against an expected Allied invasion and to concentrate the rest off Gibraltar. Hoping that the U.S. Navy's few escorts would be overtaxed by competing demands and that America's coastal shipping would therefore be poorly defended, Dönitz eschewed wolfpack tactics and instructed his U-boat captains to conduct independent antishipping patrols off the American coast. The result was a hidden—but significant—collateral advantage for the Germans inasmuch as the low volume of radio message traffic between Roll of Drums submarines and Dönitz' headquarters mitigated the role of Ultra and radio direction-finding in determining the outcome of the campaign. And, in February, the Germans adopted a new naval cipher for U-boat operations, blinding the Allies almost completely to this valuable source of intelligence for the remainder of the year.

To defend a 3,000-mile-long coastal shipping zone from Maine to Key West, Florida, Admiral Stark had in early 1941 established the North Atlantic Coastal Frontier—later renamed the Eastern Sea Frontier—under Vice Admiral Adolphus E. Andrews, who was also responsible in part for organizing troop transports and for supporting the easternmost leg of the transatlantic merchant convoy route. Complicating Andrews' job was the fact that he exercised command of his operating forces via the commandants of the coastal naval districts, commands organized to handle their traditional shipyard, industrial, and training activities. To protect coastal shipping, Andrews had at his disposal in December 20 small Coast Guard cutters, patrol craft, and gunboats, none of which could outrun a U-boat, and 108 aircraft, mostly trainers unfit for antisubmarine operations manned by aircrews who had no special training to operate against submarines. In its entire inventory, the Eastern Sea Frontier had only six PBY Catalinas properly equipped for antisubmarine operations. "Should the enemy submarines operate off the coast," Andrews dourly warned King, "this command has no forces available to take effective action against them, either offensive or defensive."[3]

Admiral Leahy had recognized the need for new mass-produced ocean escorts for convoy and antisubmarine operations when the Five Power Treaty expired in 1937, but the availability of large numbers of World War I–era four-stack destroyers in the reserve fleet relieved this requirement of any urgency. Some Navy men strongly opposed constructing large numbers of single-purpose escorts that had only minimal antiaircraft defenses and could not participate in fleet operations. When confronted with a specific proposal to lay down a class of fast, large aluminum-hulled torpedo boat escorts to succeed the old World War I–era Eagle-class patrol boats, the General Board declared that a small ocean escort "has no place in our Fleet . . . which cannot be better filled by the current type of 1,630-ton destroyer."[4]

Two years later, Commander Robert Carney challenged this view on the grounds that American industry could not be expected to build enough of these full-sized, multipurpose destroyers even at the peak of military mobilization. "Whatever else a destroyer may be called upon to do in war-time," he pointed out, "it is certain that some sort of [antisubmarine] screening duty will be a major requirement." Owing to the "immediate need" for ocean escorts, Carney claimed that "a simplified type can be produced quicker and in greater volume" than "our most modern" destroyer. The War Plans Division agreed in 1939 that a "special type . . . could relieve our new destroyers," and favored building a 1,200-ton ocean escort capable of cruising for 6,000 miles without refueling, but the planners were fearful that such ships might someday have to operate within range of enemy planes and insisted that the vessel had to incorporate the "maximum power against submarines and effective anti-aircraft armament . . . to justify the development of the type at all."[5]

The problem became acute soon after Roosevelt delivered a large fraction of the American force of war reserve escorts to the Royal Navy in the August 1940 Destroyer Deal. A few weeks later, Admiral Stark finally persuaded FDR of the need to lay down a new type of light, austere antisubmarine escorts for wartime mass production, but these ships would not be available for at least two years. The function of the ocean escort was becoming increasingly narrow, as explained by the General Board on 28 February 1941 when it set a requirement for "an escort designed to protect convoys against submarines in the western part of the North Atlantic where extreme opposition from the air is not expected." King, who had served on the General Board in 1940, claimed that FDR was still "convinced that the Navy should be able to counter the U-boat with small patrol craft," which could be acquired "hastily at the last moment." For these reasons, the president "insisted [in 1941] that projects for the construction of antisubmarine vessels be kept in the background so as not to interfere with the capital-ship program." Roosevelt may also have held up the escort program that year in the fear that it would provide his domestic political opponents with unmistakable evidence that he intended to involve the United States in a war against Germany. Nonetheless, pressure to produce an oceangoing escort mounted. The destroyer escort's preliminary design was the work of Captain E. L. Cochrane of the Bureau of Ships. Because he had just returned in the spring of 1941 from a tour in London, Cochrane's views about escorts were profoundly colored by British experience. He devised a plan to lay down fifty light destroyer escorts, but Stark now took the position that this scheme would compete with and subvert the Navy's plan to construct several hundred general-purpose destroyers, and he vetoed the fifty-ship plan on 16 May 1941.[6]

Scarcely a month elapsed, however, before the British unwittingly saved Cochrane's plan by placing an order for 250 of the 1,150-ton destroyer escorts from the Navy under the Lend Lease Act. Two or three destroyer escorts cost about the same as one general-purpose destroyer, explained Rear Admiral J. W. S. Dorling, the Admiralty's agent in Washington, but "vessels of less than 1,500 tons . . . are not able to fulfill their functions in the Atlantic." This effectively settled the displacement of the destroyer escort. This request was approved by FDR eight weeks later, over the strident objections of Admiral Samuel Robison, the able chief of the Bureau of Ships, whose shipbuilding schedules were now in disarray. The general-purpose destroyer had grown in size and cost so much that not enough of them could be built to fill out the burgeoning number of ocean escort groups, but the destroyer escort, a frigate-type vessel, was designed almost exclusively for antisubmarine operations, although she might be armed with antiaircraft guns and some torpedo tubes with which to conduct a surface action. However, the destroyer escort could neither deliver a surface torpedo attack nor defend against one by opposing cruisers or destroyers—traditionally the main function of destroyers. When King moved to Washington in December 1941, he established an initial requirement of 250 destroyer escorts—later increased to 1,000—in an effort to strengthen the sea frontiers and the ocean escort groups, and placed this building program at the top of the president's priority list for materials and manpower in January 1942.

Several new shipyards had to be constructed to build these vessels, and priority conflicts between the destroyer escort program and the First Landing Craft program, which was developed in May, had to be resolved. After the April 1942 Anglo-American decision to invade France either that September or in the spring of 1943, Roosevelt ordered the Navy and the War Production Board to accelerate the production of large landing craft and *Liberty*-class cargo ships at the expense of the destroyer escorts. "The antisubmarine vessel program must be given the highest priority and must be maintained in that priority," King warned, "even if it is necessary to reduce or postpone the construction of *Liberty* ships or similar vessels to accomplish this end." FDR turned aside this argument with the result that the escort program slowed down. The first destroyer escort keel was laid in February 1942, but none of these invaluable ships would enter the fleet for at least another year. "We need modified DEs . . . at the earliest possible moment," King pleaded with Roosevelt in June. "If we cannot get them soon it will be necessary to put some important [shipping] routes 'out of bounds' in order to prevent prohibitive losses." He failed to persuade FDR to change his mind until December of that year, after the invasion of France had been postponed.[7]

Admiral Stark had already decided to substantially increase the number of subchasers and patrol craft to be built, owing to strong White House support for these programs. In December 1941, the Navy ordered sixty subchasers of the SC-435-class, a 110-foot wooden-hulled vessel armed with depth-charge racks and light guns. With U-boat sinkings off the East Coast escalating in April 1942, Navy Secretary Knox put this program on a "crash" basis, a step necessitated by shortages of machine tools, skilled manpower, and materials that were disrupting scheduled construction. The War Production Board, responsible for much of the program, told the Navy in early May that the "production of submarine chasers has been discouragingly slow," and that "less than half of the ships scheduled for completion by May 1st are actually completed." These patrol craft were to make up the backbone of the coastal escort groups, and such inevitable delays, rooted in Roosevelt's Lend Lease program and his chaotic industrial mobilization effort, retarded the creation of an effective coastal convoy system. Some within Roosevelt's circle even believed that cargo-ship construction should have a higher priority than warship building. War Shipping Administrator Lewis Douglas claimed in June that the only way to defeat the U-boats was to postpone escort construction until 1943 and build more merchant ship tonnage in 1942. Such a policy would be "fatal," King exclaimed in fury. Roosevelt was unable to make a choice between these conflicting policies and allowed King and Douglas to continue their squabbling. King not only pressed ahead with subchaser construction in early 1942 but also let contracts for 173 steel-hulled PC-452-class patrol craft, vessels armed with depth-charge racks and twin 3-inch guns. Over the next two years, more than 350 patrol craft were delivered to the fleet.[8]

The subchaser, patrol craft, and destroyer escort programs promised to greatly strengthen the coastal patrol forces, ocean escort groups, and antisubmarine forces over the next eighteen months, and King spent a great deal of time pushing these programs. The sorry state of American tactical doctrine in early 1942 also demanded King's immediate attention. Between the wars, little had been done to improve escort or antisubmarine doctrine, owing to the success of the Navy's World War I convoy operations—although work by the Naval Research Laboratory's Sound Division was discovering the basic scientific principles of underwater acoustics. The invention of echo-ranging sonar and its introduction into the fleet beginning in 1937 reinforced a widespread satisfaction with older escort and convoy tactics and with antisubmarine tactics to defend capital ship formations, something that the interwar Navy considered on the whole to be more important inasmuch as the Japanese operated a very large number of submarines.

The interwar Navy had lavished talent and money on sonar but had virtually ignored improving other weapons and equipment for escort and antisubmarine operations. In 1939, the most effective antisubmarine weapon was the ashcan depth charge, but it had not been substantially improved since 1918. Also, escort and antisubmarine tactics and the operational capability of antisubmarine weapons and radar were poorly understood by both the Americans and the British at the time of Pearl Harbor, despite the Royal Navy's considerable experience in dealing with U-boats over the previous two years. The result was that the U.S. Navy's tactical doctrine was sadly deficient, the product of lessons learned by Admiral King's Atlantic Fleet in the latter months of 1941. He fully understood the problem, but it was Captain Carney of the Atlantic Fleet Support Force who proposed a solution. In March 1942 he suggested establishing an independent operations analysis group to study the tactical problems of escorting convoys and conducting antisubmarine warfare. King turned this task over to an experienced Atlantic Fleet ocean escort group commander, Captain Wilder Baker, who assembled a team of civilian scientists and Navy officers in Boston. In July 1942 they issued the first wartime manual for ocean escort group tactics and a month later published the first manual on convoy defense and antisubmarine search and attack tactics.

None of these measures insulated the Navy from the public's outraged reaction to the hideous results of the German U-boat campaign in early January 1942. The *U-123* appeared in Canadian waters on 12 January and sank the steamer *Cyclops* about 300 miles east of Cape Cod. A total of about twenty U-boats operated at one time or another off Nova Scotia and Newfoundland that month, attacking Allied shipping bound to and from Halifax and overwhelming Canada's poorly equipped local escort groups. No help could be expected from the Royal Canadian Navy, which had participated in the transatlantic convoy operations in 1941 but was now virtually exhausted. Ottawa had expanded its fleet from a few ships in 1939 to a large corvette escort force within two years, but these vessels were ill trained, poorly equipped, and badly administered. Losses to a December 1941 eastbound convoy defended by Canada's Newfoundland Escort Force were so great that the merchantmen were forced to return to Halifax, the only occasion during the entire war when U-boats forced a convoy to turn back. The influence of this setback on King's views on poorly defended convoys was profound. In early 1942, the Germans found better hunting farther south, however. Off the East Coast in January, U-boats sank fourteen Allied merchantmen, nine of which were oil tankers, in especially short supply at the time, and the German skippers reported that American defensive measures were weak. Shipping was independently routed and many targets were brightly lit with running lights. Many coastal cities resisted putting blackout regulations into effect. The commander of the *U-66*, for example, joked that he had watched couples dancing atop the Empire State Building while sinking the tanker *Allen Jackson* just off New York harbor. FDR foolishly allowed several months to pass before imposing a partial blackout by presidential fiat.

Vice Admiral Andrews seemed to be helpless to prevent these depredations. During January and February 1942, a daily average of twelve U-boats operating in American waters sank twenty-eight freighters and tankers. A German submarine usually approached a coastal shipping lane at periscope depth during the day, surfaced at night, located landward ships silhouetted against the coastline, and attacked them with gunfire or torpedoes. The horrendous losses increased during March and April. Meanwhile, in late February Dönitz inaugurated Operation Neuland by dispatching a dozen U-boats to prey on Allied shipping in the Caribbean Sea and the Gulf of Mexico. Between 16 and 28 February, German submarines sank seventeen ships in these waters, a figure that climbed in March and again in April. Other than formations about to join the transatlantic convoys, troop shipping, and a few special convoys, cargo ships on the

East Coast were not organized into convoys because Andrews' Eastern Sea Frontier did not have enough vessels to create effective escort groups.

Early in the western Atlantic U-boat campaign, King decided to forswear antisubmarine operations in order to concentrate on establishing coastal convoy escort groups and air coverage off the East Coast. He stood firmly opposed to instituting a convoy system until adequate coastal escort groups were available. Andrews did not disagree, drawing on Canada's recent experience with losses in poorly defended transatlantic convoys off Newfoundland in late 1941. Because coastal traffic used established shipping channels, it could not be defended by resorting to evasive routing or offensive surface antisubmarine operations. Andrews told King in late February that "an improperly escorted convoy is more vulnerable, and subject to greater losses, than ships proceeding singly, particularly when routed close inshore." This view was affirmed by an independent Navy board that studied the problem in March. "Effective convoying depends on the escort being in sufficient strength to permit their taking offensive action against attacking submarines," it reported. Also, the cause of many losses was unclear. Under a 1941 agreement, the Canadian Navy routed all shipping in North American waters until CominCh assumed this duty in June 1942. The efficiency of the Canadian routing unit is questionable. Moreover, merchantmen often ignored routing orders or Sea Frontier sailing directives. King therefore had no alternative but to accept fairly high merchant ship losses for a few months until the subchaser, patrol craft, and Navy patrol bomber building programs produced enough vessels and aircraft to allow Admiral Andrews to inaugurate a fully protected convoy system. In the meantime, the Navy was deluged by criticism from the press, the White House, Congress, and the British. Matters looked grim. From January through April, U-boats sank 198 ships totaling 1.1 million tons in American waters, but only two U-boats were sunk by American naval forces.[9]

Andrews realized that the way to defeat the U-boat was to introduce a coastal convoy system and establish effective antisubmarine air patrols, but until he could do this he took some interim steps to reduce the effect of the U-boat offensive. He correctly put the highest priority on defending the approaches to the most congested harbors: Norfolk, New York, Philadelphia, Narragansett Bay, and Portland, Maine. "It is absolutely essential that these approaches be guarded," he told King, although this reduced the number of escorts available for inshore patrols. Andrews also improved shipping security, organized antisubmarine sweeps along critical shipping channels, and established an effective rescue service for stricken vessels. And when Atlantic Fleet destroyers entered the Eastern Sea Frontier, he assigned them to hastily assembled convoys before they were recalled to the North Atlantic ocean escort groups. One of these ships was Lieutenant Commander Hugh Black's destroyer *Jacob Jones*, which was withdrawn from an Argentia-based ocean escort group and ordered to sweep the entrance to the Delaware Bay for U-boats in late February. The *U-578* chanced upon the old four-stacker on the evening of the 28th, surfaced, and drilled her with two torpedoes that broke her in half and sent her under with most of her crew.

Andrews tried other interim measures, such as adjusting the shipping lanes. During the first two months of the war, he had attempted to push shipping away from the coast so as to give the vessels more sea room, but this failed so he decided on 31 January to bring shipping in "as close to shore as safe navigation" might allow. He directed that all cargo ships were to sail at night without navigation lights along these new routes. This reduced losses, but it so increased the fear of collisions that the merchant masters refused to follow the Navy's orders. In March, Andrews took the first step in establishing a complete convoy system by instituting the "bucket brigade," daylight convoys that protected a fraction of the endangered coastal shipping. Lightly defended convoys were told to hug the coast during the day and anchor at night at preselected, well-defended inlets or harbors. He could not even provide these anchorages with continuous air cover, although he understood that this was an essential to good escort operations. In December 1941, he had no aircraft capable of operating at sea for more than three hours or of delivering a depth-charge attack. Andrews quickly grasped the need for effective maritime air coverage and established a large force of Navy blimps operating from the naval air station at Lakehurst, New Jersey. King assigned more Navy aircraft to the Eastern Sea Frontier over the next few months, and more Army Air Force bombers arrived, but the shortage of trained aircrews severely restricted air escorts or antisubmarine sweeps.[10]

FDR badgered the Navy without cause over the issue. "I still do not understand the long delay in taking all ships under escort," he complained. "It has taken an unconscionable time to get things going." Congress put tremendous pressure on the White House and the Navy to act quickly. Overly fond of small craft and blind to their unsuitability for open-ocean antisubmarine operations, FDR directed Admiral King in February 1942 to commission thousands of civilian yachts and larger fishing craft into the Coast Guard and ordered Andrews to organize a huge civilian coastal patrol. These wasteful measures had no effect whatsoever on U-boat operations, subtracted manpower and weapons from other, more important tasks, and delayed the inauguration of effective coastal convoys. FDR also bowed to Churchill's demand that the Navy commission some Q-ships, antisubmarine vessels disguised as unarmed merchantmen, which were assigned to endangered waters to lure U-boats into surfacing and attack them with gunfire. FDR instructed King to convert four merchantmen into Q-ships, but the entire scheme was discredited when the *U-123* sank the mystery ship *Atik* on 26 March 1942 leaving no survivors. King was furious and demanded that FDR tell Churchill that the Navy was abandoning the prime minister's bizarre, wasteful project.

The British also tried to discredit the Navy by exploiting the losses on the Eastern Sea Frontier in an attempt to persuade Roosevelt to agree to the establishment of a single Atlantic theater under the Admiralty's control. Overlooking the other calls on the American fleet, Churchill subjected FDR to a din of complaints about King's management of the anti–U-boat campaign in the western Atlantic. While Churchill laid siege to Roosevelt, Pound hounded King with gratuitous advice. Many of his schemes reflected a British affinity for exotic, complex small-unit operations, which drained skilled personnel from regular forces and showed few results. One of Pound's more unusual proposals was to erect a gigantic mine, net, and boom barrier stretching 3,000 miles along the Atlantic coast from Maine to Florida. Such silly ideas undermined the Admiralty's plea for a unified command, and King repeatedly pointed out that the British had no record of accomplishment to point to in arguing for a unified Atlantic command. The Canadians, whose Newfoundland Escort Force operated under the strategic direction of Admiral Royal Ingersoll's Atlantic Fleet, were also opposed to the scheme. Moreover, King was furious over the affront to admirals Andrews and Ingersoll. It even annoyed Roosevelt, for when the issue came to a head he rejected the British plan with uncharacteristic brusqueness, one of the few occasions in 1942 that he refused to cater to British interests.

Britain's major contribution to defeating the German Roll of Drums offensive came in late January 1942 when Admiral Pound offered to lend the Eastern Sea Frontier twenty-four old, converted fishing trawlers for work as coastal escorts. Although this reverse Lend Lease did not in any way begin to compensate the Atlantic Fleet for the 1940 Destroyer Deal or the huge number of American warships transferred to the British under Lend Lease, the trawler loan did permit admirals King and Andrews to begin to consider the adoption of a full-fledged, twenty-four-hour convoy system for the Eastern Sea Frontier.

On 2 February, King had suspended a CominCh staff proposal to inaugurate coastal convoys. Owing to the demands of the transatlantic merchant convoys, the AT troop convoys to Britain, "emergency" War Department troop movements, and several other theaters, all of which were short of ships, King was desperately short of destroyers, Andrews still could not defend the major ports, and no major East Coast port, including New York, was prepared to handle the simultaneous assemblage and receipt of such a large number of freighters. A minimum of thirty-one destroyers and forty-seven subchasers, trawlers, corvettes, and patrol craft would be needed to institute coastal convoys, Andrews estimated. Although the number of aircraft assigned to the Eastern Sea Frontier increased to 167 in March, only half of these planes were medium-range bombers and most of them had yet to be converted for antisubmarine work. Furthermore, the Army Air Force had yet to send Andrews any aircrews trained in ocean navigation.

The arrival on the East Coast of the converted British trawlers in March and the concurrent commissioning of a dozen new patrol craft and subchasers paved the way for King to name a Convoy Board on 27 March. This board prepared a plan for what was to become the extremely complex Interlocking Convoy System. With only twenty-three escorts over 90 feet long and forty-two small craft under 75 feet long, Andrews implemented his Daylight Convoy System on 1 April. The addition of more patrol craft that month finally permitted him to organize six coastal escort groups and introduce the first two sections of unrestricted day-and-night convoying between New York and Halifax and between Hampton Roads and Key West in mid-May. Andrews provided each coastal convoy of forty-five merchantmen with continuous air coverage and an escort group consisting of two destroyers, one subchaser, two patrol craft, and two British trawlers. Two out of every three convoys were fast convoys consisting of ships that could make 10 knots from Hampton Roads to Key West, while one-third were slated for slower vessels. The Eastern Sea Frontier War Diary recorded the results. "April, when ships had gone down at the rate of one a day, was the worst month within the Frontier since the submarine first invaded the coast." However, during "the first seventeen days of May not one ship was lost in the Eastern Sea Frontier" and during "the 14 days that remained [in the month] only four vessels were sunk." More U-boats operated between Halifax and Key West in June than ever before, but as the month wore on American losses plunged. Adolphus Andrews, a marvelously enterprising commander, had soundly defeated Dönitz in their contest for control of the Atlantic seaboard.[11]

The establishment of the Halifax–Key West coastal convoys caused Dönitz to shift his U-boats southward to the Gulf of Mexico and the Caribbean, an operation codenamed Neuland, which had begun back in February. Fifteen merchant vessels and valuable oil tankers were sunk in these waters in April, and this figure skyrocketed to eighty in May. Owing to this loss of shipping, the Puerto Ricans could not export their crops during June. To patrol these waters, the newly established Gulf and Caribbean Sea Frontier command at Key West could call on only a handful of Army and Navy patrol bombers, a few miscellaneous yard craft, and two old destroyers. "We must get every ship that sails the seas under constant close protection," King told General Marshall in reply to an unprecedented, ill-informed attack in June on the Navy's escort operations by the usually courteous Army chief of staff. In fact, as Marshall well knew, the Army had done precious little to assist in antisubmarine work in early 1942. For patrol, escort, or antisubmarine operations, old-style Navy observation planes were useful, but the task truly demanded large numbers of long-range Navy patrol planes or Army medium bombers. King told General Arnold on 14 February that the Atlantic theater needed 200 B-24 and 400 B-25 medium bombers by mid-1943 to handle the U-boats, but the Army Air Force chief responded tartly, "There are no heavy or medium bombers available for diversion to the Navy," owing to the Army's plan to build up a strategic bomber force in Britain. Marshall belatedly established the 1st Bomber Command on the East Coast, later renamed the 1st Anti-Submarine Command, but this was more a bid to take over all escort and antisubmarine air operations than to support the Eastern Sea Frontier. The Army Air Force built up this command to a total of 200 aircraft in July, but by October 1942, once the opportunity to transfer them to Britain arose, Arnold allowed the number to drop to 150, only 25 of which were equipped with radar. Not until the following year was the Army willing to abandon its campaign to take over antisubmarine air operations.[12]

To deal with the summer 1942 problem in the Caribbean, King shifted sixteen Coast Guard cutters, five new subchasers and patrol craft, and a squadron of patrol bombers to the Gulf and Caribbean Sea Frontier and then established an Interlocking Convoy System by linking new Caribbean and Gulf convoys to the system already in place within the Eastern Sea Frontier. The first escorted convoy sailed from Key West to Panama on 6 July. Soon another leg was added for Jamaica-bound shipping, and King had the complete Interlocking Convoy System in place from Cuba to Halifax one month later. Feeder convoys were later added to allow ships from smaller ports to join up with and break off from the larger movements without disrupting the regular five-day convoy cycle. King also decided to bring transatlantic evasive routing operations under his direct scrutiny by transferring them from Naval Operations to the CominCh staff. The practical effect of this was to link the strategic routing and intelligence functions of the troop convoys, transatlantic merchant convoys, and the Interlocking Convoy System.

The result of the introduction of the Interlocking Convoy System was instantaneous. Alarmed that U-boat losses were increasing while sinkings declined, Dönitz decided on 26 July to withdraw most of his submarines from the American sea frontiers, concentrate them in the mid-Atlantic, and resume attacks in the air gap south of Greenland. By this time, the Allied fleets were ready to roll back Germany's U-boat offensive either by strengthening their ocean escort groups and deploying powerful, hunter-killer antisubmarine task forces or by landing an Anglo-American army in France. King understood that one obvious result of a cross-Channel invasion would be to shut down the U-boat bases on the Bay of Biscay. The disastrous July decision to invade North Africa, however, led to the wasteful diversion of these ships and planes and the unnecessary continuance of the Battle of the Atlantic into 1943.

Where to land in the Atlantic theater was first discussed at the Arcadia Conference from late December 1941 to January 1942, when the Allies reached several fundamental agreements on the conduct of the war. Roosevelt reaffirmed his commitment to a strategy of Europe first and agreed to underwrite Britain's war effort through Lend Lease, although Britain's utter dependence on American ships, arms, and planes was already retarding the growth of America's armed forces. Roosevelt and Churchill were guided by a shared concern for Russia's fate. Although the German offensive had stalled in the Moscow suburbs in early December 1941, Allied strategists believed that their armies would have to engage the German Army during 1942 to prevent either a Soviet collapse or another separate Nazi-Soviet peace. FDR also favored quick action to boost American morale in the wake of Pearl Harbor, and Churchill badly needed American support for his faltering North African campaign. To achieve both ends, Roosevelt proposed to order the Marines then garrisoning Iceland to seize Dakar in French West Africa and Casablanca in French Morocco, a stroke intended to provide the Navy with bases on West Africa's coast and pressure Axis forces in North Africa to defend their rear areas at Tunis. Churchill readily agreed to this plan, codenamed Gymnast, and the Combined Chiefs were instructed in January 1942 to prepare to mount it that spring. King opposed direct American participation in the Desert War, however, because the Atlantic Fleet did not have enough escorts to defend East Coast shipping, protect the transatlantic troop convoys, or support the great circle merchant convoys to Britain, let alone establish and defend a new line of communications into the Mediterranean.

Navy strategists, long unhappy with Britain's Mediterranean diversion, had examined an African campaign as early as May 1941 when Roosevelt toyed with the idea of landing an American expeditionary force at French Dakar. Admiral Stark agreed then with Captain Oscar Smith's assessment that the Dakar operation "would contribute little or nothing towards winning the present war" and might "delay our capacity to . . . strike directly at Germany." This dark forecast was reflected in King's dim view in the winter of 1941 that Gymnast, too, would be an expensive diversion, but he did not object when Marshall asked General Joseph Stilwell to head an Army-Navy board charged with studying the operation. Stilwell's group concluded that there probably was not enough shipping to support a landing. Then, on 4 March, Churchill asked FDR if the Americans would assume the responsibility for the defense of Australia and New Zealand, to prevent those governments from withdrawing more troops from the 8th Army in the western desert. This was a huge, unforeseen drain on American resources. The result, King recalled, was that "Gymnast could not be undertaken." Thus, three months after Pearl Harbor, the Allies were bereft of a strategy to deal with their foremost enemy.[13]

Marshall's spring 1942 proposal to invade France that fall came about as a result of the abandonment of Gymnast and in reaction to King's persistent demands that the Army send its freshly trained divisions to the South Pacific to garrison a string of island bases between Hawaii and Australia, obligations that the Army chief of staff believed were undermining the Europe-first strategy. To reverse this trend, he proposed that the Allies invest more of their assets in Operation Sledgehammer, the codename for an invasion of the Normandy coast of France to be mounted from southern England in mid-September 1942. Two British divisions would land, secure a lodgment, and be reinforced by three American divisions. They would hold the Cherbourg Peninsula over the winter, forcing Hitler to divert German forces from the Eastern Front and relieving the pressure on Russia. Even at this early date the JCS were worried that, if Germany were to collapse suddenly, then the Red Army would overrun Europe. To avoid this they wanted American troops to be ready to occupy western Europe from the Channel to the Elbe. Work on a plan to accomplish this, codenamed Rankin, continued until late 1943. The second phase of Marshall's strategy was to follow up Sledgehammer in the spring of 1943 with Operation Roundup, an invasion of France by at least thirty Allied divisions that would cross into Germany, occupy central Europe, and end the war in the west. The Army now possessed enough troops and aircraft to execute either Sledgehammer or Roundup, even though there were few large landing craft and severe shortages of troop shipping, escorts, and attack transports. On the other hand, the bulk of Germany's army and air force personnel were in Russia and the defenses of occupied France were known to be quite weak.[14]

King liked the concept of a single, bold, concentrated stroke that took advantage of the principle of economy of force and halted the continuing dispersion of Allied assets. "Even at the cost of taking extensive risks in the Pacific," he told FDR, "we should be concentrating to the maximum on one front." And Sledgehammer's success would result in a swift victory over the U-boats by shutting down Germany's naval bases on the Bay of Biscay. For these reasons, King agreed to the Sledgehammer and Roundup plans, FDR blessed them, and Marshall flew to London in April 1942 to discuss them with the British.[15]

In 1942, Stalin, who was fully informed of Allied policy via the machinery of the international socialist community and his considerable network of spies in the Western governments, pressured Roosevelt and Churchill to establish in Europe a "second front"—a phrase of communist origins that described an Allied cross-Channel invasion and carried the inaccurate, sneering implication that Russia alone was fighting the Axis. FDR, wrongly viewing the war as a common cause, seemed willing to tolerate any abuse from Moscow. The British chiefs of staff, led by the brilliant General Alan Brooke, were uniformly against invading France that year on the grounds that the Allies lacked enough troops to hold on to a lodgment. Admiral Pound told Churchill that the Allied navies did not operate enough landing craft to land on the French coast, while Brooke pressed unceasingly for a Mediterranean offensive. Churchill, who had little faith in Britain's generals, opposed an early return to the Continent, preferring instead to wage war on the periphery by defeating the U-boat, bombing Germany, and taking the offensive in North Africa. Only when Germany was gravely weakened would the British be willing to send their army across the English Channel. He worried nonetheless that the Americans might abandon the grand strategy of Europe first unless the British appeared eager to fight. Thus, in April 1942 Churchill met with Marshall in London and agreed to the Sledgehammer and Roundup plans, but he conditioned his assent on several improbable assumptions. After Marshall's return to Washington, the first calls on Allied resources for Sledgehammer were made. When Soviet Foreign Minister V. Molotov met with Roosevelt in Washington at the end of May, he was told to "expect the formation of a second front this year."

The cross-Channel strategy came unraveled in June. Early that month, Vice Admiral Lord Louis Mountbatten, the chief of British combined operations, brought to Washington a catalog of Churchill's many reservations about the operation. According to Robert Sherwood, a White House assistant, Churchill's complaints were "the first danger signal" received by the Americans "that British thinking was beginning to veer toward diversionary operations far removed from the main point of frontal attack across the Channel." At about the same time, it became evident that the First Landing Craft Program would not produce enough vessels to allow the Allies to execute Sledgehammer in the fall, a point that the Americans were unwilling to concede openly to the British. From the start this was a problem. The Navy's landing craft program, and the competing destroyer escort building program, had to be superimposed over the existing 1940 Two-Ocean Navy Act shipbuilding schedule. If Marshall and King had to cancel Sledgehammer, they wanted at least to get the British to agree to conduct Roundup in the spring of 1943.[16]

Churchill cabled Roosevelt on 8 July and told him that the British chiefs of staff had concluded that no lodgment could be established in France that fall. Marshall and King were furious at the British for reneging on their earlier promise and, at the same time, desperate to get them to agree to a cross-Channel operation the following year. To this end, the JCS went so far as to threaten the British with a "Pacific alternative" to the Europe-first strategy, upon which rested all Anglo-American strategic understandings. King considered this to be a bluff and never gave it much credence, but he agreed on the basis that it might just get the British in line behind the cross-Channel plans. Roosevelt, not fully realizing that the United States held the upper hand, rejected this gesture on the basis that "success against Japan in one year or two years would not win the war if Germany beats Russia." He repeated Admiral Stark's formulation that "an offensive in 1943 has a good chance of forcing Germany out of the war, in which case Japan could not conduct war in the Pacific alone for more than a few months." FDR refused to force Churchill to accept Sledgehammer or Roundup, which left the central issue of Allied grand strategy in limbo.[17]

To conciliate the Americans, Churchill adjusted his views, agreeing to an offensive in the Atlantic in 1942 and arguing that the revival of Gymnast would not doom the prospects for Operation Roundup in 1943. To settle the question, the president sent Marshall and King to London in late July; they found the British ruggedly opposed to a cross-Channel operation that year or the next. For instance, Pound claimed that the British Fleet was totally occupied in escorting convoys and in preventing a breakout of the German battleships and battlecruisers and could not provide a bombardment force for the landing. Moreover, Pound asserted that the British Fleet could not prevent German U-boats from disrupting communications between Britain and an invasion beach in nearby Pas de Calais. Churchill then resurrected his plan to invade French North Africa, a move the JCS had anticipated when they warned Roosevelt in June that "the occupation of Northwest Africa . . . [should] not be attempted." Owing to FDR's insistence on offensive ground operations in 1942, however, they had no choice but to refer the question to the president, who, eager to maintain Allied harmony at any cost, overrode Marshall's and King's objections and directed them on 23 July to agree to Gymnast, which was soon renamed Torch. In desperation, the JCS asserted that if the Allies occupied North Africa in 1942, they could not invade France in 1943. Churchill protested that he still favored an invasion of France in the future, but he quietly agreed to this formulation.

Admiral Mountbatten's bungled raid on the French port of Dieppe in August, which took place weeks after the decision to mount Torch, persuaded King and Marshall that the British misunderstood how to conduct shore-to-shore amphibious operations but did not dampen the American conviction that only a cross-Channel operation, like Sledgehammer or Roundup, would lead to Germany's defeat. In effect, Churchill's opposition to Sledgehammer, combined with Roosevelt's vacillation, condemned the Allies to a wasteful, peripheral strategy in the Mediterranean for two years. It unwittingly allowed the Soviets to so improve their position on the Eastern Front that they were poised to overrun central Europe in 1944, when the Americans finally invaded France, and gave the Germans another twenty-four months to construct the formidable defenses found on the Normandy coast on D-Day.[18]

Because relations between Britain and Vichy France, which governed all French colonial territories in North Africa, were poor, Churchill wanted the British troops assigned to Torch to land under American command, and General Marshall readily agreed to Admiral King's suggestion that General Dwight D. Eisenhower, then commanding the U.S. Army in Britain, be named supreme commander of Operation Torch. Eisenhower in turn named British officers to command his air, ground, and naval components. Admiral Andrew B. Cunningham, the most capable Royal Navy figure of the war, became the overall Allied naval commander for Torch. Admiral H. Kent Hewitt, who commanded the Atlantic Fleet's Amphibious Force, would direct the Western Task Force, the American landings in French Morocco. King admired Cunningham but disliked Eisenhower's command arrangements, and he paid less attention to Torch then he might have. He failed to assign enough Navy planners to Eisenhower's staff in London in August, when the general decided to divide the operation into three parts. Staging from Hampton Roads, the American-led Western Task Force was to take Casablanca. The Center Task Force, which was to assemble in Britain, would enter the Mediterranean and land at Oran, Algeria, while the Eastern Task Force, also staged from Britain, would seize Algiers and Bône.

Admiral H. Kent Hewitt's Atlantic Amphibious Command was transformed into the Western Task Force and hastily made ready to land in Northwest Africa. The magnitude, timing, and unprecedented complexity of this shore-to-shore operation caused Hewitt more than his share of problems. Above all, there was a shortage of attack transports for Major General George Patton's troops, and "not until very late was it possible to determine just how many would be available, and some reported barely in time for the final rehearsal." Eisenhower was trying to persuade the Vichy French in North Africa not to contest the Torch landings, but for planning purposes Hewitt assumed that they would resist. This was an important assumption inasmuch as the presence of the French fleet in the harbor, strong fixed batteries, and the absence of suitable nearby landing beaches ruled out a direct attack on Casablanca. Hewitt instead decided to land at Fedala, a small port fifteen miles up the coast at the extreme range of Casablanca's coastal defense batteries, which offered good landing beaches and was weakly defended. Since the only air cover for the Western Task Force was to be provided by the *Ranger*'s air group until Army Air Force aircraft could be ferried ashore, Hewitt also decided to seize the airfield and seaplane base at Port Lyautey on the Sebou River, eighty miles up the coast from Casablanca.

The concept of "mutual cooperation" during amphibious operations embodied in the "Joint Action of the Army and Navy" document, first issued in 1927 and revised again eight years later, was clearly unworkable for Torch because of the Army's lack of training in forced landings. Patton's plan provided that once he was ashore he would send his 2nd Armored Division toward Casablanca, but to do this he needed at least fifty medium tanks. Delays in the First Landing Craft Program meant that none of the new large LSTs would be available for Operation Torch, and the small LCT tank landing craft could handle only old light tanks. Hewitt devised an ingenious solution to the problem. He

Vice Admiral H. Kent Hewitt, Commander, 8th Fleet, and Commander G. J. Dyff of his staff, on board the flagship *Ancon* en route to the invasion of Salerno, Italy, in September 1943.

discovered that there was a large dock at the phosphate port of Safi, about 160 miles south of Casablanca, which could accommodate a converted Florida car ferry that was assigned to carry the tanks. Inside Safi's breakwater there were no beaches, however, so Hewitt prepared to seize the port by a daring maneuver. He selected two World War I–era destroyers, cut down their stacks and masts, thus reducing their silhouettes, and equipped them with scaling ladders adjusted to the level of the Safi docks at high tide. The destroyers were to dash into the harbor, tie up at the docks, and quickly disembark Army Rangers, who would then take over the town before the defenders could destroy the port installations.[19]

Hewitt divided his command of over 100 warships, transports, and auxiliaries into five groups. On 24 October 1942, the first detachment of the Western Naval Task Force under Rear Admiral Monroe Kelly stood out of Hampton Roads, steamed single-file through the swept channel, and sailed into the Atlantic for its rendezvous with the rest of Admiral Hewitt's forces. Rear Admiral Robert C. Giffen commanded the Support Group, which included the old battleships *Massachusetts* and the heavy cruisers *Wichita* and *Tuscaloosa*, and Rear Admiral E. D. McWhorter's Air Group was composed of the *Ranger* and four auxiliary carriers. The Northern and Southern Attack Groups steamed southward, while the Center Attack Group, which departed the next day, headed to the northwest. On 26 October, the supporting groups began to join up with the main Western Task Force, which changed course repeatedly to confuse the large number of U-boats that Dönitz had positioned in the mid-Atlantic to intercept the American movement.

Hewitt planned to refuel his ships at sea on 3 November, but a storm played havoc with this schedule for three days. Although the weather improved on 6 November and the task force refueled, the Army forecast for 8 November was "uniformly unfavorable" and "the Navy report was slightly more optimistic, but not too encouraging." Advised by his meteorological officer that "the landing would be practicable" on 8 November but that "conditions would be much less suitable on the following day," Hewitt grasped the nettle at 0700 on the 7th and ordered the Northern and Southern Attack Groups to detach and steam to prearranged positions off Port Lyautey and Safi, respectively. When the fleet neared North Africa, Hewitt attached one escort carrier to the Northern Group, which now broke off and steamed for Mehdia, only a few miles from the French airbase at Port Lyautey. Two escort carriers sailed in company with the Southern Group for Safi, while the light carrier *Ranger* and the remaining escort carriers covered the Center Group as it closed on Fedala. In an extraordinary example of careful planning and skillful execution, each of the three invasion formations appeared at its assigned station within fifteen minutes of midnight.[20]

Operation Torch began when dawn broke over Safi on 8 November 1942 and the destroyers *Bernadou* and *Cole* charged into the protected harbor, suppressed light French resistance, and landed Army Rangers on the docks. Meanwhile, the cruiser *Philadelphia* and the battleship *New York* destroyed most of the nearby coastal batteries while aircraft from the escort carriers shot up a handful of decrepit French warplanes before they got off the ground. Once Safi was in American hands, the ferry *Lakehurst* landed thirty tanks, which drove north along the coastal road to Casablanca, their movement covered by the guns of the *Philadelphia*, following them up the coast.

In contrast to the swift, almost flawless seizure of Safi, the Battle for Port Lyautey was marked by confusion and mistakes. Army Brigadier General Lucien Truscott, who had studied amphibious operations with Admiral Mountbatten in London in the spring of 1942, accepted the British view that naval gunfire could not suppress a well-commanded shore battery. He persuaded Patton to tell Admiral Hewitt that the Army intended to storm the ancient fort at Kasba, an important stronghold that guarded the Sebou River leading to Port Lyautey. Moreover, the Navy's boat plan was so poorly devised and executed that most of the assault troops were put ashore on the wrong beaches, and the beaches were so widely separated that the troops could not provide each other with mutual support. As a result, the Army failed to take the Kasba fortress. The cruiser *Savannah* came up and brought the French artillery under fire, and the four-stack destroyer *Dallas* tried to ram a boom that obstructed the mouth of the Sebou, but both measures failed. Not until 10 November was the *Dallas* able to steam up the Sebou and land troops at the airfield, but the fighting there did not end until all French forces in North Africa surrendered.

The Center Group, whose mission was to take Casablanca, faced the greatest French opposition. During the planning phase of the invasion, Hewitt and Patton disagreed about when to land. Patton went to see Admiral Cooke about the issue, complaining that "a daylight landing would be suicidal." He proposed to land at night. Patton had no faith in offshore naval gunfire, Cooke discovered, nor any grasp as to how difficult the movement from the anchorage to the beach would be. Cooke persuaded Patton to consider "the naval point of view," reminding him that Hewitt was in command of the invasion until Patton established his headquarters ashore. Hewitt decided that the amphibious ships would anchor offshore at 2400 when the first wave of assault troops would start to move toward the beaches, an evolution that he estimated would take about four hours.

In the dark early morning hours of 8 November, the cruisers *Augusta* and *Brooklyn* and ten destroyers escorted fifteen transports to a rendezvous five miles offshore, but maladroit shiphandling and swift currents set up a chain of errors. Overburdened with their packs, troops failed to fill up the landing boats before the craft headed for the beach—so the first wave to hit the beach was 50 percent of the planned strength. By this time, the storm was piling 15-foot breakers on the shore. Not only did the boats scouting the beaches turn on their guiding lights too early, thus drawing fire from the French shore batteries, but the poorly trained Navy boat crews allowed their craft to crash into one another, ground on the reefs, or miss their designated beach segments entirely. Nearly half of the landing craft were damaged, but the Western Task Force had no means available to perform emergency repairs. The Army insisted on bringing its heavy equipment ashore as quickly as possible despite the fact that Navy planners, drawing on two decades of working out these problems with the Marines, preferred that the assault troops be lightly armed. As a result, many of the overburdened troops drowned and many others abandoned their gear in the surf. Also, vehicles, heavy guns, rations, ammunition, and garrison equipment were all brought ashore simultaneously, congesting the beachhead; and the Navy beach parties were too few and too small to quickly resolve the problem.[21]

Following this night of blunders, at dawn 3,500 American troops were ashore and Fedala was secure. At about this time, however, Admiral François Michelier, who commanded the forces defending Morocco, ordered his shore batteries to fire on the American fleet, French fighters attacked naval aircraft flying over Casablanca from the carrier *Ranger*, and the battleship *Jean Bart* in the harbor shelled Hewitt's Covering Force. A salvo from the *Massachusetts* destroyed one of the *Jean Bart's* turrets, but the El Hank battery to the southwest of the harbor entrance continued the duel and Hewitt ordered Giffen's Covering Force westward to reduce this hostile position.

Michelier rapidly recovered from these setbacks and instructed Rear Admiral Gervais de la Fond to organize a torpedo counterattack against the transport anchorage with his seven destroyers and eight submarines. Shortly thereafter, an American scout plane reported to Hewitt that the French destroyers were advancing along the coast under the cover of a smokescreen in the direction of the helpless transports. Wary of just such a problem, Hewitt had held the *Augusta* and the *Brooklyn* and two destroyers in reserve off Fedala and now directed them to break up the French sortie. Firing into the smoke with bearings and ranges provided by their scout planes, the American ships forced de la Fond's destroyers to retire. Michelier tried again at 0930. A French cruiser led another formation of destroyers and submarines up the coast, but they never threatened the American transports because Hewitt quickly recalled the Covering Force and it broke up the French attack, sank several French ships, and damaged all the rest. The French Navy was unable to inflict even minor damage on an American combatant.

Not even half of the Army troops were ashore on 9 November and little of their equipment was available. The batteries at Fedala were taken and an armored column, moving south along the coast from the beachhead to Casablanca, was stopped momentarily by gunfire from two French corvettes. Shells from the *Augusta* forced these vessels to retreat, but the cruiser then came under fire from the repaired turret of the *Jean Bart*. Doing what he should have done much earlier, Hewitt ordered an attack by dive bombers from the *Ranger*, which sank the battleship in the harbor. Because of poor communications among the gunfire support ships, their spotting aircraft, and the shore-based fire control parties, and because the battleships, cruisers, and destroyers maneuvered at high speed and fired at long range, the naval gunfire support for these landings was relatively ineffective. "Naval gunfire support is a very weak reed on which to lean," Patton complained afterward. "It is too inaccurate and they will not get close enough."[22]

Despite the confusion during the landings, by 10 November Patton's ground forces were converging on Casablanca, and the Royal Navy had landed troops inside the Mediterranean at Oran and Algiers and headed eastward. That evening, Hewitt assembled a Bombardment Force consisting of the battleship *New York,* the cruisers *Augusta* and *Cleveland,* and four destroyers and directed them to open fire on the French defenses at Casablanca at 0715 the next morning. Fifteen minutes before this shelling was to begin, he received a message from Patton that the French had agreed to a ceasefire. "It was in the nick of time," Hewitt recorded, "for fingers were already on firing keys and bomb releases." Admiral Jean F. Darlan, the commander of the French Navy, had found himself by chance in North Africa and, by reason of seniority, in command of all forces there when the Allies came ashore. After negotiating an agreement with Eisenhower that guaranteed his survival and that of other French collaborationists, he ordered Michelier to stop fighting on 10 November. Within three months of the decision to land in Northwest Africa, the Allies were now safely ashore. Michelier grandly surrendered and offered to help Admiral Hewitt clear the debris out of the Casablanca harbor and prepare for Allied operations against the Axis army in Tunis. Thanks to Churchill's strategy of dispersion and Roosevelt's refusal to back up his military leaders, the Allies were now stuck in the Mediterranean.[23]

Chapter Five

Winning the Battle of the Atlantic
1943–1945

Roosevelt, Churchill, and the Combined Chiefs of Staff met at the Casablanca Conference in January 1943 to decide what to do in the European theater after General Eisenhower's forces evicted the Axis armies from Tripoli. At the end of the conference, FDR unexpectedly announced to the press that the Allies sought as a war aim the "unconditional surrender" of Germany, Italy, and Japan, a declaration intended to bolster Soviet morale and assure Stalin that the Allies would not make a separate peace. He also wanted to assert American primacy as the senior partner in the Anglo-American Grand Alliance and reassure the public that Eisenhower's dealings in November 1942 with Admiral Darlan—a Vichy collaborationist whose command over French forces in Africa had been recognized by Eisenhower in a controversial decision—augured nothing less than the destruction of unified Germany and Japan's East Asia Co-prosperity Sphere.

The complex negotiations at Casablanca set Britain's preference for a peripheral grand strategy in the Mediterranean in sharp relief against the Americans' advocacy of strategic concentration and a cross-Channel invasion of France. Both Allies agreed to increase Lend Lease support to the Soviets after learning that the Red Army intended to mount a counteroffensive in the summer after they had reduced the Germans at Stalingrad. The Allies also formulated plans to conduct a Combined Bomber Offensive against Germany's industries and cities. But they were sharply divided about where and when their armies should reenter Europe. United in their opposition to Operation Roundup, the plan for a cross-Channel invasion of France in the fall of 1943, the British chiefs of staff instead backed General Alan Brooke's plan to overrun Sicily, cross the Straits of Messina, and advance up the Italian peninsula to Rome and beyond to the Po Valley. This stroke promised to exploit bases acquired during the Allied conquest of North Africa and keep employed the large British and American fleets already deployed in the Mediterranean. It was also intended to open up the Mediterranean to British shipping, drive Italy from the war, and encourage the neutral Turks to declare against Germany.

The JCS saw Italy as a defender's paradise and an invader's nightmare. When the British refused to invade France in 1943, however, the Americans could not agree among themselves on an alternative, and FDR did not demand that they do so. Whereas General Marshall stood behind the Roundup plan, Admiral King calculated that the shipping would not be available that year to transport Eisenhower's armies from North Africa to England. And even should the shipping be found, King believed that Churchill, regardless of his protestations of good faith, would still refuse to consent to the cross-Channel invasion in 1943. Although no firm decision was reached on European strategy at Casablanca, thus making it difficult to assign objectives for any campaign against Sicily and Italy, by the end of the conference the JCS reckoned that their forces were destined to be stranded in the Mediterranean for at least another year. Since the invasion of France had once more been postponed and Dönitz could continue to operate U-boats from his Bay of Biscay bases without fearing a landward attack, the Battle of the Atlantic assumed a larger place in overall Allied grand strategy, and Admirals King and Pound persuaded their colleagues to agree to a declaration that "the defeat of the U-boat must remain a first charge on the resources of the United Nations."[1]

The renewal of the Battle of the Atlantic in early 1943 was due in part to the Allies' decision to invade North Africa the previous November. The introduction of the Navy's Interlocking Convoy System in the summer of 1942 had almost ended freighter and tanker sinkings off the East Coast and in the Gulf of Mexico and the Caribbean. Dönitz reacted that fall by deploying his U-boats back to the mid-Atlantic, just south of Greenland, where they were beyond the range of Allied patrol aircraft coverage. King warned FDR in the autumn of 1942 that losses to North Atlantic merchant convoys would increase if an Allied army were landed in North Africa. "The U.S., by employing every available escort vessel in the Atlantic, could not establish a new escort route without either serious effect on the movement of ships to the U.K. and elsewhere in the Atlantic or the transfer of escorting ships from the Pacific." Paradoxically, Churchill's success in persuading Roosevelt to overrule Marshall and King and settle on Operation Torch directly resulted in reduced imports of American foodstuffs and Lend Lease to Britain in 1943. Torch would "require the use of naval escorts now engaged in escorting vessels to outlying stations all over the world. The result of our thinning out of resources of this kind may bring disaster in the North Atlantic," King told FDR on the eve of his decision to invade North Africa.[2]

While the Allies braced for the next stage of the U-boat campaign, Admiral Dönitz reassessed his situation. From July through December 1942, the Allies lost 575 ships totaling about 3 million tons. Since the start of the war, over 14 million tons of shipping had been sunk. During these months, however, the Germans had lost only sixty-six U-boats in combat. Although King's Interlocking Convoy System had forced the Germans to begin to shift submarines back into the North Atlantic, Allied shipping losses remained high in August 1942 when 102 ships totaling over 500,000 tons were sunk. An important fraction of this figure included unescorted shipping plying the Caribbean and South Atlantic, which King intended to soon bring under the convoy.

During November these figures climbed to 106 ships totaling nearly 640,000 tons—a wartime high. However, the strength of the Allied ocean escort groups defending the North Atlantic convoys had been reduced because Admiral Ingersoll had to create a new pool of Atlantic Fleet ocean escort groups to defend shipping between Norfolk and Gibraltar to support Torch. In December, losses again declined dramatically, owing to the North Atlantic's bad winter weather, the release of some Allied escorts that had been assigned to the Torch invasion forces, and Hitler's vain attempt to use his U-boats to thwart the North Africa landings. Dönitz' U-boats sank only sixty-one ships that month, of which seven were stragglers and nineteen were steaming in convoys. The number of North Atlantic escorts increased in January

1943, and U-boat operations were hampered by the storms, with the result that the Germans claimed only fifteen convoyed ships that month. In February, however, the weather in the North Atlantic improved somewhat, and 9 convoys containing 242 ships were attacked by U-boats; 34 ships were lost, provoking unnecessary alarm in Washington and London. And on the 5th of that month, King was stunned to learn that the *U-456* had chanced upon the 5,200-ton transport *Dorchester*, then en route from St. Johns, Newfoundland, carrying U.S. Army troops and supplies to the garrison at Skovfjord, Greenland, penetrated the ocean escort group of three Coast Guard cutters, and sent her under. Of the 906 men on board, only 229 were saved. Clearly something had to be done to improve the defense of American transatlantic troop and merchant shipping.

Hitler, angered that his balanced fleet had done little to its credit, sacked the commander of the German Navy, Admiral Raeder, in January 1943 and named Dönitz in his place. Dönitz paid off most of his big ships and bent his resources to the U-boat campaign. He had several obstacles to overcome but believed in early 1943 that he was on the brink of a great victory. In October 1942, Dönitz had counted 196 front-line U-boats. He had lost about eleven boats each month in 1942, but twenty new submarines had entered the fleet each month as well. On the strength of the successful campaign in early 1942, Dönitz had persuaded Hitler to increase U-boat construction, and by 1 March 1943 there were 400 German submarines in commission and nearly 300 more in the shipyards. After Russia's victory at Stalingrad, however, Hitler increased Germany's tank production at the expense of the U-boat program. Dönitz was able nevertheless in early 1943 to concentrate a great fraction of his fleet in the North Atlantic. Of 222 front-line boats, 18 were positioned in Arctic waters to attack the North Russia Lend Lease convoys, 19 were on station in the Mediterranean and the Black Sea, and 182 were assigned to bases in the Bay of Biscay for operations in the Atlantic. Two-thirds of these vessels were in French harbors or in transit to or from the operating areas, and one-seventh were deployed to the South or central Atlantic, leaving Dönitz with roughly forty-five U-boats on station in the North Atlantic at the end of February 1943.[3]

By the time that the Combined Chiefs formally recognized this formidable threat at the Casablanca Conference, the means to overcome it were already in hand. For one thing, by January 1943 the Americans alone were building new cargo ships faster than the Axis could sink older ones. During the first three months of that year—allegedly the most critical period in the Battle of the Atlantic—American shipyards constructed 1.5 million more tons of shipping than the combined Axis air and naval forces sank. For the rest of the war this quarterly figure never fell below 2 million tons.

This good news was offset by FDR's nearly disastrous decision to allocate a large percentage of American shipping to the British import program. When the British first created the transatlantic merchant convoys in 1941, they established a six-day convoy cycle, which thereafter formed the basis for a large number of their vital production and rationing schedules. However, various calls on both Allied fleets and the need to provide escorts for the Torch invasion forces moved Admiral King in the spring of 1942 to ask Roosevelt to insist that Churchill agree to stretch out the convoy cycle to seven days. Churchill accepted this disruptive step only after FDR promised to increase Lend Lease shipping to Britain in 1943. King, who believed that Churchill's strategy of dispersion was squandering Britain's limited resources, loudly protested Roosevelt's decision. To abate the acrimony, Roosevelt removed the issue from the JCS and handed it over to an ad hoc commission headed by his closest adviser, Harry Hopkins. Hopkins conceded every point to the British and agreed to a further monthly transfer of twenty freighters to Britain from new American construction. This decision, however, threatened to exhaust American shipping in short order and paralyze operations in the Pacific and elsewhere, unless U-boat sinkings could somehow be reduced.

Once the Western Hemisphere's Interlocking Convoy System was established, Admiral King's first priority had been to strengthen the individual Atlantic Fleet ocean escort groups and then to increase their overall number. The 1940 Two-Ocean Navy Act and the early 1942 Navy Small Craft Act led to the mass construction of hundreds of 110-foot SC coastal subchasers and 180-foot PC oceangoing patrol escort craft. At the end of 1942 these vessels began to meet the needs of the Gulf and Caribbean and Eastern sea frontiers. King could therefore divide new destroyer and minelayer construction between the Atlantic and Pacific fleets, and in early 1943 allow Admiral Ingersoll to organize sev-

eral new Atlantic Fleet ocean escort groups. Moreover, the first of
nearly 500 destroyer escorts, the mainstay of the Allied ocean escort groups after mid-1943, entered the Atlantic Fleet in January
1943. Despite King's protests, FDR had delayed destroyer escort
production in early 1942 in favor of the First Landing Craft Program, a decision that retarded the expansion of the ocean escort
groups since these two building programs competed directly for
tools, workers, machines, and common parts. After the British
torpedoed the Sledgehammer and Roundup plans, King convinced Roosevelt to suspend the First Landing Craft Program
temporarily in favor of destroyer escort construction. Although
King transferred many of these vessels to the Royal Navy and sent
some of them into the Pacific, the greatest number were dedicated to escort operations in the Atlantic.

With the appearance of more escorts, the Atlantic Fleet
could also adopt a more aggressive battle doctrine in 1943. Admiral King increased the authority of ocean escort commodores to
change course, pursue and hunt down attacking U-boats, and
call in nearby ships and aircraft. He reasoned that both land-
based patrol planes and carrier-based aircraft would be needed
to provide a second layer of protection to the transatlantic merchant convoys. Five fast escorts took six days to search an area of
100 square miles, but an aircraft could do this in about four
hours. Owing to extraordinary increases in American military
aircraft production, the Navy was able not only to transfer a large
number of patrol bombers and other types to the Royal Navy under Lend Lease but also to strengthen the Eastern and Gulf and
Caribbean Sea Frontiers' patrol wings. In addition, the marriage
of radar to aircraft made the antisubmarine patrol bomber an especially lethal foe of the U-boat. By late 1941, the Royal Navy had
fitted about forty destroyers with radar, and these vessels were deployed to the western approaches to the British Isles, but ship-
borne radar could detect a U-boat on the surface at a range of
only three miles, whereas airborne radar operating overhead
from an altitude of 2,500 feet could locate the same enemy out to
about fifteen miles. Britain's success using airborne radars to
suppress German submarines led the British and American
navies in 1942 to equip all patrol aircraft with more sophisticated
radars and to get them out on patrols for the German enemy.

This technicians' battle of measures and countermeasures
continued throughout the war. In 1942, the Allies developed a

crude magnetic anomaly detector, a device that recorded slight distortions in the earth's magnetic field caused by the presence of a nearby submarine in the ocean. Functional only at short range, these detectors nevertheless could be used to erect barriers across straits or other restricted waters. In May 1943, the Navy's Moroccan Sea Frontier command established a barrier using magnetic anomaly detectors, radar-equipped planes, and destroyers to seal off the Strait of Gibraltar and close off the Mediterranean to U-boats for the rest of the war. Lastly, the introduction of radar-equipped sonobuoys, dropped in patterns by patrol aircraft in the vicinity of a contact, helped keep the U-boats down in the Atlantic and enhanced the lethality of land-based patrol aircraft.

By early 1943, transatlantic merchant convoys enjoyed some form of Allied air protection everywhere along the great circle route except for one segment known as the Greenland Air Gap. American PBY Catalinas based in Newfoundland had an operational range of 900 miles; so did Royal Air Force Coastal Command B-24 Liberators operating from the British Isles. Less capable patrol bombers could fly south about 500 miles from their bases in Greenland and Iceland. Beyond these patrol boundaries, however, lay a considerable area of the mid-Atlantic where Dönitz now decided to concentrate his U-boat wolfpacks. Several factors prevented an earlier extension of Allied air coverage over the Greenland Air Gap. Foremost was the reluctance of the Army Air Force to allow the Navy to operate long-range land-based bombers. The Royal Air Force adopted a parallel stance with respect to the Royal Navy. Both air forces were dominated by men so strongly prejudiced in favor of the Combined Bomber Offensive that they assumed any other use of bomber-type aircraft was wasteful. Only in June 1942, when the crisis in the Eastern Sea Frontier had come and gone, was King able to persuade General Marshall to instruct the 1st Bomber Command on the Atlantic Coast to respond promptly to requests from Admiral Andrews to undertake patrol missions.

The success of the Interlocking Convoy System and the establishment of continuous antisubmarine air patrols in the Eastern and Gulf and Caribbean Sea Frontiers paradoxically worked against the extension of air coverage over the Greenland Air Gap. During February 1943, American maritime patrol aircraft flew over 26,000 hours of antisubmarine patrols in these waters without sighting one U-boat, and the Admiralty believed that this lack of enemy activity justified shifting these aircraft to Greenland and the British Isles, but King reckoned that he had finally achieved a satisfactory level of protection for shipping in American waters and objected to reducing it. At the same time, the British Coastal Command had only fifteen B-24 Liberators, of which only eight were operational. Not until March 1943 was King able to persuade Marshall or the British chiefs of staff to agree to divert long-range Army Air Force bombers to the British Coastal Command or the Atlantic Fleet Patrol Force, and not until the summer did he finally prevail in a silly struggle with Secretary of War Stimson over Navy command and control of all antisubmarine warfare.

Complicating a coordinated Allied response to Dönitz' mid-Atlantic campaign was the overly complex multinational command structure, which had evolved after the 1941 Argentia Conference. Four separate headquarters shared command of the transatlantic merchant convoys: the Navy's Eastern Sea Frontier and Atlantic Fleet, Canada's coastal and Newfoundland forces, and Britain's Western Approaches command. Admiral Ingersoll's Atlantic Fleet conducted all troop convoys and most merchant convoys in the central Atlantic, while Vice Admiral Jonas Ingram's Brazil-based South Atlantic Force provided escorts for convoys off South America. Organizing and routing the transatlantic convoys was the responsibility of Rear Admiral M. K. Metcalf, the director of Convoy and Routing, an office that King brought under the CominCh staff in June 1942.

Eight days before an eastbound convoy was to sail, Metcalf arranged its composition and route with the Admiralty in London and Canadian Naval Headquarters in Ottawa and requested the assignment of an ocean escort group from Vice Admiral Brainard at Argentia, who commanded all American and Canadian ocean escort groups in the western North Atlantic. Metcalf then arranged for support from the Canadian Newfoundland Force at St. Johns and the Atlantic Coast Force at Halifax and from Admiral Andrews' Eastern Sea Frontier Force at New York. On the morning of his departure, the convoy commodore, usually a retired admiral or captain recalled to active duty, convened a meeting of his merchant masters with the local ocean escort group commander, during which the convoy route, discipline, and defensive tactics were explained.

The freighters and tankers stood out to sea in the afternoon so as to be in convoy formation before darkness fell. They formed up into columns of three ships each, with seven to fourteen columns per convoy. Ideally, about 800 yards fore and aft separated the vessels within a column, and each column advanced about 1,500 yards apart. In the event of an attack on the convoy, the escort force commodore took charge of all Allied naval and merchant vessels and aircraft within a radius of thirty-five miles, altered the convoy's route if necessary, and directed its defense. Captain Kenneth Knowles, who handled Ultra for the CominCh staff in Washington, attempted to maintain overall strategic direction of each convoy in the western Atlantic, as he alone had access not only to Ultra intelligence and direction-finding reports but also to reports of the movements of other convoys in the vicinity and the availability of nearby escorts and aircraft. At this time, however, Knowles was not empowered to order an escort group commodore to change course—another defect in the system that occasionally led to tragic results.

Locating German submarines and predicting their movements played an essential role in the conduct of successful Allied escort and antisubmarine operations. The most accurate means of doing this available to the Allies in 1941 was Ultra radio intercepts. Hitler "may make me an admiral," Dönitz once remarked, "but communications can put me in command." German cryptanalysts cracked the Anglo-American merchant convoy code in 1941, and Dönitz skillfully exploited this intelligence to establish picket lines, concentrate U-boats into wolfpacks against convoys, and regroup his forces for new assaults. Once a wolfpack was concentrated, each submarine skipper could communicate with the nearby U-boats over special frequencies, but the Germans nonetheless never achieved any tactical coordination during their attacks. And the product of their constant communications was a steady steam of fleet broadcasts from German transmitters in occupied France and a regular patter of required reports back from every U-boat at sea to Dönitz' headquarters in France and Berlin. Whenever the Admiralty or the Navy Department conducted an evasive routing operation, there was a corresponding increase in the volume of German message traffic. During the summer and fall of 1941, the British deciphered these messages with growing regularity, but in February 1942, the Germans adopted a new, complex submarine code, Triton, which took Britain's code breakers nearly a year to understand.

The British provided the Navy Department with partial information derived from intercepted Ultra messages as early as 1940, and in the spring of the following year a small joint Army-Navy team arrived in London to work with the War Office and Admiralty intelligence branches. Before Pearl Harbor, however, Ultra was not fully exchanged, partly because the United States was still neutral and partly because Britain's intelligence officials wrongheadedly worried about American security precautions rather than their own—Britain's entire intelligence organization was at the time thoroughly compromised by Soviet spies. Churchill broke a segment of this logjam in June 1941 by directing that Ultra messages about U-boats be shared with the U.S. Navy once the Atlantic Fleet began convoy operations. Soon after Pearl Harbor, however, the Americans charged that the British were withholding intercepts, and talks the following spring between ONI and the Admiralty did not resolve the problem. "Our cipher experts of the . . . navies were in close touch," Roosevelt claimed in July 1942, but Admiral King was still so dissatisfied that he sent Captain Kenneth Knowles to London that summer to report on the British organization and improve the exchanges. Knowles learned that Bletchley Park deciphered Ultra messages with a Bombe, a British-made machine that duplicated the functions of the German Enigma, and the British promised to ship a Bombe to Washington later that summer, but they failed to do so.

Britain's reluctance to share her secrets, plus Bletchley Park's inability to break the new Triton U-boat code, caused King to tell the Admiralty in 1942 that he was about to order Naval Communications to build its own version of the Bombe and conduct an independent attack on the German codes, unless the British cooperated more fully. The British wanted Ultra for their own, but in September King's blunt talk forced them to negotiate a complete, secret sharing arrangement between the respective naval headquarters. Two months later, Alan Turing, Britain's foremost code breaker, was sent to Washington to provide technical advice, but King's continued dissatisfaction with the sharing agreement led him in 1943 to order the construction of a monster data processing computer designed to provide the U.S. Navy with an independent means of deciphering German radio traffic. Years later, Knowles bristled at the notion that the British "succeeded in breaking the German U-boat cipher . . . and sort of spoon-fed the Americans with its tremendous benefits throughout the Battle of the Atlantic." The Navy was "ever grateful for [Britain's] . . . more experienced counsel and advice," he recalled, but "once we got into the war, the American contribution to Ultra was at least equal to the British effort."[4]

The absence of timely radio intelligence in 1942 meant that the Allies had to depend heavily on direction-finding reports from their network of shore stations on both sides of the Atlantic and on high-frequency direction-finding sets carried by their escorts. Tactical high-frequency direction finding was so success ful that many U-boat captains, lacking good frequency data on Allied radars, suspected that their own passive radar detectors were emitting radio waves and often turned them off to prevent their vessels from being located by Allied aircraft. Between September 1942 and April 1943, over half of the U-boat attacks on convoys were thwarted by Allied surface escort groups assisted by direction finding. When a U-boat picket located a convoy, she surfaced and transmitted frequent contact reports to Berlin. Allied shore stations or sea-based direction finding in turn located the U-boat, which was then forced to submerge and take evasive action to avoid the escorts. By the time the submarine resurfaced, the convoy had been rerouted and was steaming away over the horizon. Direction-finding results formed the basis for most successful evasive routing operations in 1942, although the shortage of ocean escorts, the lack of sea-based air cover, and the existence of the Greenland Air Gap limited the application of this strategy to both ends of the great circle route.

For the Allies, March 1943 began on an especially grim note. A slow eastbound convoy, SC.118, defended by a powerful ocean escort force with air cover during most of its voyage, was intercepted by a U-boat wolfpack and lost ten ships. American escort skippers were now raining complaints on the Navy Department about British antisubmarine routines. Among other things, they complained that British crews unnecessarily jammed their communications circuits during a battle, and they asked for more high-frequency radios. They also pressed for more efficient underway refueling methods.[5]

Captain Paul R. Heineman, a brilliant tactician who commanded an ocean escort group consisting of two Coast Guard cutters, five British and Canadian corvettes, and a Polish destroyer, defended the westward movement of ON.166 to the prearranged midocean meeting point south of Iceland where he turned the convoy over to the British. Then Heineman rendezvoused with the destroyer *Greer* at Argentia and steamed south to protect SC.121, an eastbound convoy consisting of fifty-six ships. Between 6 and 9 March, Heineman's escorts fought their way through three separate wolfpack attacks with a loss of six freighters and tankers. The next slow eastbound convoy, SC.122, also courageously defended, lost nine ships. The losses for even well-defended convoys were clearly too high.

The passage of convoy HX.229 from Halifax, Nova Scotia, to Londonderry, Northern Ireland, illustrated most of the problems that the attacking U-boats encountered once the Allied ocean escort forces were properly equipped. The ships that constituted HX.229 stood out of Halifax at 2000 on the evening of 8 March, after receiving last-minute routing directions from Admiral Metcalf to steam northeast off Argentia, turn eastward into the mid-Atlantic, and then head to the northeast to reach Londonderry, Northern Ireland. Based on the latest radio intelligence from London about German U-boat barrier patrols, this course was updated frequently during the voyage, often once or twice every few hours, depending on new Allied intercepts of Dönitz' broadcasts. Captain Knowles had to divert the convoy not only around the U-boat pickets but also around a severe storm that was gathering force south of Iceland. At the same time, the storm hampered the U-boat skippers attempting to locate and maintain contact with convoy HX.229. Although an evasive routing strategy allowed the convoy to steam through a gap between the storm and the first U-boat patrol line at 0725 on 16 March, the Allied ships were sighted by *U-653* only three hours later. The skipper alerted Dönitz, and he rapidly concentrated twenty U-boats against HX.229.

In the midocean air gap, a 600-mile-long segment of the transatlantic voyage, two separate German wolfpacks mounted a total of seven attacks against convoy HX.229 over the next three days and nights. Now German tactics were to infiltrate the convoy, identify the best targets, and not waste torpedoes. Faulty German torpedoes, fragile American radars and high-frequency direction-finding equipment, inexperienced skippers and crews on both sides, and storms undid both the attackers and defenders, however. The weather was so violent at the height of the battle on the night of 18 March that all radar screens were thoroughly cluttered. Eight U-boats tried to enter the convoy's perimeter that night, and three maneuvered into firing positions within about 2,200 yards of the Allied formation. The first was driven off by depth charges and hedgehogs, but two-thirds of these charges were duds. The next U-boat charged a destroyer and fired three torpedoes at her, but they all misfired, and an American destroyer then brought the U-boat under attack, firing hedgehogs and thirty-eight depth charges, most of which failed to detonate. The third and final U-boat surfaced and attacked without being detected by the escorts, but all five of her torpedoes missed their targets because of faulty settings. Forced to dive, she easily rode out an assault by a corvette, which dropped only six depth charges.

Later that evening, another trio of U-boats closed to within 1,250 yards of the convoy, but rain squalls had so reduced visibility that the Germans were unable locate targets to fire at. The Allied counterattacks were equally ineffective. Only one U-boat sustained minor damage when a depth-charge attack forced it to submerge rapidly and withdraw. On the morning of the fourth day of the battle, sixteen Allied aircraft appeared over the convoy, compelling the Germans to adopt more conservative tactics. Unable to surface when they got close to the convoy, the U-boats stood off, and the aerial escorts recorded only one confirmed sighting that day. Twice this U-boat was counterattacked, but several of the depth charges got stuck in the racks and she escaped with only minor damage.

Although nineteen direction-finding bearings were made from U-boat signals on the fifth day, the Germans were by now at such a distance from the convoy that the escorts could not counterattack. Convoy HX.229 reached Londonderry a few days later, having lost a dozen merchantmen while its escorts had sunk only one U-boat, but at least three or four submarines had been so badly damaged that they had to cut short their war patrols and return home. Moreover, good German tactics had not accounted for the Allied losses. Instead, they resulted from the fact that on 17 March only four escorts were guarding the entire convoy. This figure doubled the following day when the ocean escort group was augmented by a handful of aircraft, and Allied losses ended once these reinforcements appeared on the scene. Nonetheless, the loss of nearly 87,000 tons of shipping was a major tactical

German victory. German radio intelligence, observed Captain Knowles, "probably cost us the worst convoy defeat" of the war. Dönitz had concentrated forty U-boats against convoys HX.229 and SC.122, sinking a total of twenty-one Allied ships while losing only one U-boat.[6]

The defeat of the U-boat was almost at hand, however. The Allies lost 108 ships totaling 627,000 tons in March 1943, but a high percentage of these vessels went down to unexpectedly large concentrations of U-boats in the Greenland Air Gap. Dönitz simply could not sustain this tempo of operations in the coming months. Moreover, the Allies had found evasive routing operations especially difficult to conduct during March because of the unusually high number of escorts undergoing repairs and the resultant reduction in their ocean escort groups. For example, in early 1943, the Canadian Navy's entire midocean escort force was withdrawn from the convoy routes to be retrained and reequipped at the insistence of the Admiralty. This would not recur for the rest of the war. On the other hand, the transatlantic ocean escort groups were strengthened when, in February 1943, Churchill at long last agreed to again suspend the costly North Russia Lend Lease convoys—although the Allies failed to demand political concessions from Stalin when the convoys resumed in November. This released nearly thirty cruisers and destroyers, mostly British, for the great circle convoys in the spring and summer months. Although a new means of underway refueling of escorts was yet to be perfected because there were not enough oilers to provide one to each ocean escort group, the addition of more American-built oilers to the Allied ocean escort groups in April allowed both navies to lessen their dependence on the great circle route, send some convoys farther north, and increase the flexibility of evasive routing operations. The three naval headquarters also agreed about this time to increase the size of each North Atlantic merchant convoy. Although seventy-three ships were lost in convoys in March, only one-tenth of the total number of convoyed vessels even came under attack, whereas nearly four-fifths of the independently routed vessels brought under attack were sunk. These figures revealed that enlarging each convoy did not risk the loss of more ships and that strengthening the ocean escort groups and air patrols reduced losses.

The tide of the Battle of the Atlantic turned at the end of March 1943. During the previous month, Allied ocean escort groups sank only twelve U-boats. In March the Germans lost thirty-eight U-boats, however, while only twenty-six new submarines entered their fleet. Attrition, the bearing beam of Dönitz' strategy of tonnage warfare, worked thereafter in favor of the Allies and demonstrated in short order just how feeble the entire German naval effort really was. This outcome surely was not evident at the time of the Atlantic Convoy Conference in March 1943, a high-level meeting that came about as a result of pressure from the Canadian Navy to release its Newfoundland Force from American naval command and because of a general agreement among the navies that simplifying command arrangements was long overdue. The Canadians were chafing because their Newfoundland Force was still under Vice Admiral Brainard's Argentia Task Force, although the number of Canadian ocean escort groups defending Britain-bound convoys in the North Atlantic now greatly exceeded the American contribution. Shifting escort responsibilities for each convoy in midocean off Iceland was awkward and time-consuming for the convoy commodores, the merchantmen, the ocean escort group commanders, and the various shore-based commands. Air Marshal Philip Joubert de la Ferté, head of Coastal Command, had put forth a British proposal in September 1942 to create a "single supreme control for the whole anti–U-boat war" to overcome "the separate and often conflicting policies of the British, Canadian, and American naval and air authorities." King's attention to this problem was underscored by the endorsement of Joubert's plan by Captain L.H. Thebaud, who commanded the American escort task group at Londonderry.[7]

King convened the Atlantic Convoy Conference in Washington to address these problems. He bluntly dismissed Joubert's plan for a unified Atlantic naval command and suggested that the conferees reorganize their areas of operation. It was decided that the Atlantic Fleet would entirely withdraw its escort groups from the North Atlantic merchant convoys, leaving the Admiralty in charge of these operations and the Canadians in command of their own fleet. Admiral Ingersoll's Atlantic Fleet was to assume responsibility for all central Atlantic convoys to Gibraltar and for the defense of shipping in the Caribbean and the South Atlantic. Of course, Ingersoll continued to be responsible for the defense of all American troop shipping in the Atlantic theater. In addition, it was decided to enlarge each convoy, a move made on the basis of studies done by Allied operations analysts who pointed out that Dönitz was rarely able to concentrate more than ten U-boats in one wolfpack to attack a single convoy. Large Allied convoys sailing between January 1941 and April 1943 with more than forty-five ships lost an average of only 1.7 ships per voyage, whereas smaller convoys over the same time period lost an average of 2.6 ships. The decision to enlarge the size of each convoy to sixty or more ships resulted in the more rapid movement of Lend Lease goods across the Atlantic without risking greater losses. No overall strategic plan was devised by the Atlantic Convoy Conference, but restructuring the areas of operation and reducing the incidence of mixing Allied forces clearly improved the defenses of the overall shipping effort.

One other outcome of the Atlantic Convoy Conference was noteworthy from a purely American perspective. On 6 April 1943, King brought all the Navy's Atlantic ocean escort and anti-submarine warfare operations under his immediate strategic control, and on 20 May he established the 10th Fleet. Although he named himself to command this new organization, the 10th Fleet chief of staff, Rear Admiral Francis S. Low, directed daily operations. Evasive routing and escort and convoy movements had previously been divided up among the CominCh Convoy and Routing, the Atlantic Fleet, the sea frontiers, and the Canadian and British shore-based commands. King abandoned this arrangement and put in its place a new command with ready, unfettered access to Ultra, knowledge of the availability of escorts and the whereabouts of all convoys, and authority to issue routing orders to any element in the central Atlantic without first getting approval from another chain of command. The creation of the 10th Fleet proved to be important not only to the prosecution of a more vigorous evasive routing strategy but also to an aggressive antisubmarine campaign conducted by the newly assembled escort carrier hunter-killer formations.

Evidence that the Germans were losing the war in the North Atlantic surfaced in May 1943. That month, British Commander Peter Gretton with an ocean escort group of nine Allied vessels conducted a brilliant operation in which he successfully repelled fifty-one U-boat attacks by the largest multi-wolfpack concentration of the war. Although Convoy ONS.5 lost thirteen of forty-two ships between 28 April and 5 May, Gretton's escort group sank five enemy submarines, and supporting PBY Catalina patrol planes accounted for two more. Strengthened ocean escort groups, more air coverage, the introduction of underway refueling for escorts, and better intelligence about German movements resulted thereafter in an increasing number of successful evasive routing operations. While Dönitz was finding convoys harder to locate, the number of independently routed freighters and tankers was declining as a growing percentage of Allied shipping came under the protection of one or another convoy system. And, once a German picket located a convoy, the scale of effort just to maintain and prosecute the contact was becoming prohibitive. During April and May, the Germans lost fifty-six U-boats, forty-one in May alone. This was a level of attrition Dönitz reckoned he could not sustain. On 24 May 1943, he announced that the "superiority of enemy location instruments" and their ability to achieve "surprise from the air . . . now forces a temporary shift of operations." He ordered a general withdrawal from the North Atlantic. Dönitz also reviewed his communications security and decided that it was adequate, even though it was not. Instead, he wrongly deduced that the source of his trouble lay with unaccountable emissions of radio waves by German equipment that allowed the Allied direction finders to identify U-boat movements. As a result, over the next two years the Germans wasted considerable talent and time trying to overcome a problem that did not exist.[8]

The introduction of the escort carrier task group into the Atlantic Fleet not only allowed Admiral King to assist the British in closing the Greenland Air Gap, but also permitted him to inaugurate a new, aggressive antisubmarine campaign. The Navy had long understood that a wartime emergency would require the conversion of merchantmen or liners to auxiliary or escort aircraft carriers; the few heavy attack carriers were thought to be too important to risk as scouts, escorts, and submarine hunters or in attacks against enemy bases. Converting cruisers to carriers had been considered in the 1920s, and in 1935 the Bureau of Construction and Repair had drafted a plan to convert ten fast passenger liners to carriers "for quick action when the war emergency required the conversion of merchant type vessels to auxiliary aircraft carriers." Liners seemed an ideal choice in that they could fulfill the Navy's size and speed requirements for carriers. However, little work was done on this until October 1940 when, acting on a British suggestion, FDR ordered Admiral Stark to obtain a 6,000- to 8,000-ton merchant ship, convert it to a carrier, and transfer it to the Royal Navy. Stark was told by the Maritime Commission in early 1941 that the diesel-powered, 13,500-ton, 17-knot cargo ship *Mormacmail* was available, and in three months that summer, she was converted into the escort carrier *Long Island.* She was turned over to the British, who had completed their first conversion about the same time. Following the *Long Island* model, five more C-3 Maritime Commission hulls were converted in 1941 and early 1942 .

King arranged for the program to be accelerated in December 1941 when a plan to convert twenty more C-3 hulls into 15,000-ton, 18-knot escort carriers was approved. He also persuaded Secretary Knox to agree to convert four 23,500-ton *Cimmaron*-class oilers to escort carriers. These four ships became the *Sangamon*-class escort carriers, which were rushed to completion to provide additional air forces for Admiral McWhorter's task force during the November 1942 landings in North Africa. Meanwhile, shipbuilder Henry J. Kaiser had become interested in the program, and proposed in 1942 to use prefabricated sections to mass-produce fifty highly maneuverable 10,900-ton, 19-knot *Casablanca*-class escort carriers. This remarkable shipbuilding effort was completed within two years.

The Allies' first escort carrier, the *Audacity*, had been commissioned into the Royal Navy in 1941 and assigned to provide close-in air support to the ocean escort groups. In mid-December, she was attached to HG.76, a Gibraltar-to-Britain convoy, to deal with Bordeaux-based German FW-200 bombers. While only two cargo ships were lost during its passage and the defenders claimed four U-boats, the Germans badly mauled the escort force and torpedoed the poorly screened *Audacity.* A large number of the American-built escort carriers were given to the Royal Navy, but the British wasted considerable time trying to improve these emergency vessels by adding ballast, installing fighter directors needed only for heavy carrier operations, and unnecessarily lengthening the flight decks—with the result that many British escort carriers spent the war in the shipyards. Moreover, Britain's archaic carrier doctrine was anathema to the Americans, especially to Admiral King. "The inability of the [Royal Navy's] officers to efficiently operate the carriers is deplorable," reported one American investigator, Captain Marshall R. Green, in October 1943. "I can now better understand why it is necessary to run the carriers from headquarters ashore [the Admiralty] like a puppet show instead of giving them complete freedom of action which we are successfully employing." In his opinion, the Navy Department would have to "accept the unpleasant truth that we cannot expect much from British CVEs in antisubmarine warfare in the near future."

The Americans used a few escort carriers to defend a handful of convoys in 1942, and this experience provided valuable information from which a new tactical doctrine was developed. The most important lesson was that few attempts by naval aircraft to hunt down U-boats located by sightings in midocean or during attacks on convoys succeeded because the submarine could outlast and exhaust the hunting aircraft. On the other hand, Navy operations analysis demonstrated that escort carrier-based aircraft were most effective in attacking a U-boat the moment it was located, rather than waiting for it to come to the convoy. In 1943, Navy aircraft began flying search and attack patterns that kept them out of the visual range of the U-boats they were stalking, thus reducing the number of evasive maneuvers made by the Germans and even encouraging the submarine skipper to surface again, thereby subjecting himself to renewed air attacks.[9]

The need to ferry aircraft into the South Pacific in late 1942 compelled King to send many of the new escort carriers to the Pacific Fleet, and he attached seven Atlantic Fleet escort carriers to the Western Naval Task Force for the invasion of North Africa. At the same time, however, he instructed Admiral Ingersoll to prepare to assemble the first four escort carrier antisubmarine hunter-killer task groups. Each new vessel embarked an air group of twenty-four planes, mostly TBF and TBM Avenger torpedo bombers equipped with a variety of devices unique to antisubmarine operations. A screen consisting of a destroyer and a handful of destroyer escorts supported the air group, and this combination was so lethal that only one escort carrier was lost in the Atlantic during the war. In early 1943, admirals King and Pound agreed on a plan to deploy hunter-killer carrier task groups to the United Kingdom, Iceland, and Newfoundland, locations from which they could be called upon to cover the Greenland Air Gap or to reinforce or support land-based patrol bombers defending threatened convoys. The utility of continuous air coverage was demonstrated in late March 1943 when the *Bogue* task group successfully escorted the slow eastbound convoy SC.123 through a U-boat concentration in the Greenland Air Gap and lost only a handful of ships.

Admiral King had never been happy with the existing evasive routing strategy and intended at some point to create ocean escort and hunter-killer groups so powerful that they could reinforce convoys and fight their way through the strongest U-boat concentrations. Now the chance to do just that was at hand. With the new escorts, Ingersoll adopted different tactics for his ocean escort groups to use in attacking U-boats. Examination of destroyer attacks against U-boats during 1942 disclosed that a U-boat could usually evade a single pursuing destroyer, but the chances for a successful attack increased disproportionately to the increased escort strength when three destroyers advanced in line abreast against the submarine. By June 1943, after the first forty-two destroyer escorts were launched, and the hunter-killer escort carriers were ready, more aggressive antisubmarine tactics became possible for the first time.

Dönitz was also now rethinking his strategy. When the central Atlantic offensive failed, he gave up on wolfpack tactics and dispersed his U-boats against Allied shipping in the South and Southeast Atlantic, the Caribbean, and the Indian Ocean. This desperate move was not carefully considered, however. For the 700-ton U-boats to operate beyond the North Atlantic, they needed to be refueled by large submarine tankers, and the German Navy deployed few such tankers. The Allies responded to Dönitz' strategic dispersion by concentrating their attacks on the submarine tankers—a strategy that was so successful that by the end of the year the Germans had to contract the scope of their campaign considerably. One of the escort carriers' first objects were the German U-boat tankers. Four Atlantic Fleet antisubmarine hunter-killer task groups built around the new escort carriers *Card*, *Bogue*, *Core*, and *Santee* were established between May and December 1943, and during those months they sank twenty-seven U-boats in the central Atlantic.

Shortly after Dönitz had withdrawn his U-boats from the North Atlantic, he inaugurated a new campaign in the central Atlantic, a direct challenge to the Atlantic Fleet under the new convoy arrangement. On 26 May 1943, Dönitz created a barrier force of U-boats across the route taken by American troop and munitions shipping from Norfolk to Gibraltar. Captain Knowles routed convoy GUS.7A around these U-boats, then asked Ingersoll to send an escort carrier task group charging directly into the enemy line. Ingersoll ordered Captain Giles E. Short's *Bogue* task group

The escort carrier *Bogue* (CVE-9), built on a Maritime Commission C-3 hull, was launched on 15 January 1942 and completed in September. Fitted with an HFDF sensor and SC surface search radar, she entered the Atlantic Fleet in February 1943 and became the main element of one of the first hunter-killer task groups. These austere 18-knot escort carriers made possible the inauguration of an antisubmarine offensive against the U-boat and served in a variety of roles in the Pacific.

to steam from Argentia into the central Atlantic and attack the enemy U-boat picket line. One week later, Short's patrols located the Germans, and aircraft from the *Bogue* sank the supply submarine *U-118* and forced the U-boat wolfpacks to disperse, utterly disrupting their concentrations south of the Azores and allowing convoy USG.9 to proceed with impunity. Then, in late June, Captain Marshall Green in the escort carrier *Core* sailed into the central Atlantic to protect the slow westbound convoy GUS.9. Within a few days, Wildcats and Avengers flying off the *Core* sank one German submarine tanker and two U-boats and caused a number of others to withdraw in panic. And later in July another American hunter-killer task group, composed of the escort carrier *Santee* and three destroyers, sank four U-boats and one submarine tanker south of the Azores. During a cruise in the same waters in August, the escort carrier *Card*'s task group left two more German picket lines in shambles. Within a span of slightly more than three months, Ingersoll's intrepid hunter-killers had sunk sixteen U-boats and eight tankers, while only one ship in a convoy defended by the lethal escort carriers was lost.[10]

King's adoption of an offensive antisubmarine strategy now began to pay off. Attrition was working against the Germans. Losses to Allied ocean escorts and land- and sea-based aircraft during July 1943 totaled forty-six U-boats, of which thirty-seven sank in the Atlantic. As a result, Dönitz canceled the central Atlantic offensive and decided to disperse his submarines into the Caribbean, South Atlantic, Indian Ocean, and southwest of the Azores, areas not yet under Allied air cover. Not only was the U-boat concentration off the Azores hounded by the unexpected appearance of an escort carrier task group, but also this finally moved Churchill and Roosevelt to force Antonio Salazar, Portugal's dictator, to allow the Royal Air Force to establish an air base in the islands from which very long-range patrol bombers began to operate in October 1943. The hunter-killer escort carrier task groups provided the only air coverage over the Greenland Air Gap until the Azores were available to the Allied fleets in late 1943.

Dönitz had decided by this time to resume the North Atlantic offensive, but he now faced a far stronger force of British and Canadian ocean escort groups stiffened with newly constructed American destroyer escorts transferred to the Allies under Lend Lease. He also confronted the growing menace of the offensive Allied hunter-killer task groups. Banking on a new German acoustic torpedo that he hoped would fend off the surface escorts, he concentrated a wolfpack of sixteen U-boats south of Greenland and instructed them to descend on two successive westbound convoys. The defending ocean escort group overpowered the U-boats, however, the Germans' acoustic torpedo proved to be a resounding failure, and the convoys steamed safely around the flank of the enemy picket line. Next, two hunter-killer carrier task groups appeared on the scene and scattered the German concentration. During September and October 1943, Dönitz sustained an average of about sixty U-boats on patrol, but they sank only nineteen Allied ships at a cost of fifty-two submarines. Then, in late 1943 Dönitz sent several U-boat formations back into the Caribbean, but this was quickly thwarted by the Navy's dense aircraft patrols and the strong escort groups that defended the southernmost legs of the Interlocking Convoy System. And, when Dönitz deployed a handful of U-boats into the South Atlantic, Vice Admiral Ingram's small but aggressive 4th Fleet prevented the enemy from accomplishing much. Dönitz was aware that, faced with a lack of overseas bases and friendly neutrals and declining numbers of supply submarines, he could not conduct long-range operations like this for very long.

During 1944, the Germans continued limited U-boat operations, but they failed utterly to prevent the enormous buildup of U.S. Army and Army Air Force formations in England for the cross-Channel operation or the continuous flow of Lend Lease to Britain. U-boat losses that year were so high that Dönitz considered suspending operations altogether, but he decided to continue "guerrilla war" at sea to keep Allied naval and air forces occupied and to challenge their redeployment against northwestern Europe. In August 1944 the entire U-boat campaign ground to a virtual halt when General Patton's 3rd Army isolated the Brittany coast, forcing Dönitz to evacuate his bases there and shift his U-boats to bases in Norway, where they were easily bottled up by the Royal Navy. German submarine operations on the high seas were also about to collapse. By the end of the year, Captain Knowles' skilled use of Ultra decrypts to direct Atlantic Fleet hunter-killer groups had resulted in the destruction of a total of fifty-one U-boats.

Although Germany's submarine offensive cost the Allies 2,775 merchant ships and the Germans 784 U-boats, Dönitz' strategy of tonnage warfare had little chance of succeeding. Indeed, the Germans lost the Battle of the Atlantic for many of the same reasons that they lost the entire war. Hitler and his admirals viewed the world from a European perspective, assumed that the relative balance of power existing in 1939 would remain largely unchanged except by reason of their conquests, and greatly underestimated both the economic potential and latent military strength of the United States. Dönitz also grossly miscalculated the skill of British and American naval men to recover from savage losses and reverse the tide of the campaign. The expensive U-boat campaign served no justifiable German purpose other than to diminish or eliminate Britain's military contribution to the Grand Alliance, but once the United States was committed to defend the transatlantic lines of communication and to the Lend Lease program in 1941, reaching this goal was beyond Germany's grasp. Nonetheless, Dönitz persisted—and Hitler supported him, albeit with declining enthusiasm. Dönitz, a fine tactician, had little understanding of military policy or grand strategy. He failed to examine the economic premises upon which tonnage warfare was based and assumed wrongly that it would be more difficult for the Allies to improve their relatively primitive early defensive measures than for Germany to increase its rate of submarine construction and perfect its U-boats' tactics. And, since the German Air Force controlled most German military aircraft, Dönitz had had little opportunity to study the importance of air forces to escort-of-convoy or offensive antisubmarine operations. He completely misread the potential of American-built carrier aviation to operate successfully against his U-boats.

The defects of Britain's grand strategy, more than the weight of Dönitz' offensive, accounted for the pseudo-crises in the Battle of the Atlantic in 1942 and early 1943. Churchill refused to instruct the Royal Air Force to bomb the U-boat bases on the Bay of Biscay until it was far too late. King pointed this out as early as 1941, but he was ignored. At a time when bombers were in short supply, Churchill permitted Britain's Bomber Command to conduct a nighttime area strategic bombing campaign over Germany to sap the enemy's will, but this produced few demonstrable results and consumed an immoderate fraction of Allied resources. He refused to take a stand on the diversion of bombers from strategic bombing to the Royal Navy's Coastal Command until the decisive moment in the North Atlantic had passed by. He also allowed the Admiralty to needlessly antagonize Admiral King, its most important patron. And he virtually created the problems of March 1943 by persuading FDR to agree to the wasteful, diversionary invasions of North Africa and Italy. This allowed the U-boats to operate from the Bay of Biscay with no threat to their landward flank until mid-1944. The Royal Navy, which bore the greatest burden in the Battle of the Atlantic, developed a superb force of ocean escort groups, destroyer support groups, and hunter-killer task groups, and did so almost in spite of Churchill's misguided and overbearing leadership and Admiral Pound's feeble subservience. Pound's death in late 1943 and the appointment of a far more able figure as First Sea Lord, Admiral Arthur B. Cunningham, improved the picture greatly, but by that time the U-boat had already been handed a sound defeat.

The U.S. Navy's record in the Battle of the Atlantic was also mixed. Roosevelt gave away America's reserve escorts in the 1940 Destroyer Deal and a year later committed the United States to the defense of Britain's war policy, Churchill's grand strategy, and Lend Lease to Russia, without much thought as to the consequences—other than thinking that it would contribute somehow to Germany's defeat. Admiral King erred in agreeing to hastily arranged Army troop movements in the Atlantic right after Pearl Harbor, and this partly limited his ability to support the Eastern Sea Frontier during the U-boat campaign off the East Coast in early 1942. When the JCS tried to concentrate Allied forces and invade occupied France in the fall of 1942 or early 1943, FDR refused to support them and allowed the British to dictate Allied strategy for a full two years. Admiral King contributed greatly to the defeat of the U boat, but he was an intense nationalist, ill suited by reason of personality and prejudice to conduct such a coalition campaign. He did, however, understand the basic strategy, technology, and tactics needed to defeat the U-boat better than any other leader on either side. He supported the subchaser and patrol escort craft building programs and adopted the Navy's immense, costly destroyer escort program as his own and, despite many obstacles, saw it to fruition.

King was also largely responsible for the success of the huge escort carrier building program and, to a lesser extent, for the establishment of the successful American hunter-killer escort carrier task groups. He believed that the Navy's first responsibility was to defend American troop shipping and that this took precedence over any other demand. As a result, he took a beating during the early 1942 German campaign on the East Coast and he was bitterly criticized by his Allies in 1943. It is, however, hard to argue with the outcome. The U.S. Army and Army Air Force arrived in Europe safely and the U-boat was thrashed by the time the liberation of Europe began on the shores of Normandy in June 1944.

Chapter Six

The Invasion of Sicily and Italy
1943–1944

At the Casablanca Conference in January 1943 the British persuaded the Americans to continue operations in the Mediterranean for the rest of the year on the understanding that the Americans would mount a new offensive in the central Pacific. Faced with a choice of invading Sardinia or Sicily, the Combined Chiefs tentatively settled on Sicily, according to King, "because the occupation of Sicily would at the enemy's expense furnish the Allies with a useful air base at a narrow point in the Mediterranean" and "raised the possibility of eliminating Italy from the war." The Allied high command for this operation remained essentially intact: Eisenhower as supreme commander, British Admiral Cunningham as the Allied naval commander, and Vice Admiral Hewitt as the American naval commander.[1]

Eisenhower, distracted by problems dealing with French General Charles de Gaulle, spent little time on the Husky plan, the codename for the invasion of Sicily. As a result there was uneven cooperation between the air forces, commanded by Army Air Force General Carl Spaatz, and the naval forces. Spaatz insisted on throwing his bombers and fighters against the Axis airbases on Sicily and refused to provide Admiral Hewitt's task force with any tactical air support during the landings. On the other hand, the U.S. Navy's forces in the Mediterranean were far better prepared for the landing on Sicily than for the 1942 Northwest Africa operation. Hewitt's 8th Fleet had grown considerably since the North African invasion, and by June 1943 included 580 cruisers, destroyers, minecraft, submarines, and landing ships and craft. For the Sicily operation, several new large landing vessels had been produced by the First Landing Craft Program, including the large 1,500-ton LST tank landing ship, the 550-ton LCT tank landing craft, and the 200-ton LCI(L) large infantry landing craft. LSTs and LCTs were to run up onto the beach and lower ramps over which tanks and trucks could drive ashore; the LCI(L) was to beach, lower her gangways, and allow infantry to walk or run onto the beach. Also available for the first time were a large number of Army DUKW amphibious trucks, which could carry twenty-five men or over two tons of cargo directly from a ship offshore over the beach to a supply dump nearby.

Preparing for Husky posed particular problems for Rear Admiral John Hall, who was put in charge of all Navy amphibious training. Not only had King thoughtlessly neglected to inform his Mediterranean commanders about the number and arrival dates of new ships and landing craft in the theater, but also Admiral Cooke and the CominCh staff had failed to protest Eisenhower's decision to construct an amphibious training center at Arzew to train boat crews under Army command. Inasmuch as the Army had no landing doctrine or any experienced instructors, the scheme created unnecessary confusion. Only when the Arzew experiment—and similar army facilities elsewhere—were proven to be ineffective and redundant did General Marshall agree to transfer all amphibious training to the Navy.

The ill-considered system of unified command caused other problems. Owing to his experience at Casablanca, General Patton rejected Hewitt's call for at least a few hours of preliminary naval gunfire off Sicily, and Eisenhower's staff supported him. Patton believed naval gunfire to be ineffective and wanted his assault troops to benefit from the element of surprise. This reasoning was flawed, however, inasmuch as Patton also intended to drop Major General Matthew Ridgway's 82nd Airborne Division onto the island to secure important inland points before the landing, and their presence ashore was certain to alert the Axis defenders to the imminence of an invasion. Whereas Hewitt and his admirals preferred to approach the hostile shore on as dark a night as possible, Patton persuaded British Admiral Cunningham to land on 10 July 1943, when a full moon would illuminate the paratroopers' drop zones. Despite this excessive concern for the paratroop-

President Franklin D. Roosevelt and Prime Minister Winston Churchill at Marrakesh, French Morocco, January 1943.

ers at the expense of the assault troops, Cunningham could not prevail upon Eisenhower to insist that the generals take into account the naval leaders' views or that the air forces cooperate with the combined planning staffs. This allowed General Spaatz to prepare his air plan almost in isolation. Only at the end of June, for instance, did Admiral Hall learn that airborne troops would be dropped near Gela to capture the Point Olivo airfield and light beacon fires in the vicinity of the landing beaches, and Hall did not receive Spaatz' complete plan for the parachute drops and his tactical air support until after the invasion force had put to sea.

Departing from several widely scattered North African ports, the Western Task Force rendezvoused on schedule and steamed toward Sicily, only to run into a storm on the evening of 9 July, the third day at sea. Hewitt again called on Commander Steele, his brilliant aerological officer, who predicted that the winds would die down by the evening and that the ships and landing craft would find calmer waters on the leeward side of the Sicilian coast. For a while, the storm threatened the invasion, and handling the smaller landing vessels tested the seamanship of the crews, but the bad weather ultimately worked to the Allies' advantage. The Axis commanders were braced for the operation, but when the storm arose they reduced their alert and allowed their troops to stand down. Guided by three submarines that flashed infrared blinker beacons from stations about five miles off each of the three invasion beaches, the invasion force was in place shortly after midnight.

At 0245 on 10 July, Rear Admiral Richard Conolly's Joss Force, supported by Rear Admiral Laurence Dubose's Bombardment Group of two cruisers and two destroyers, landed assault

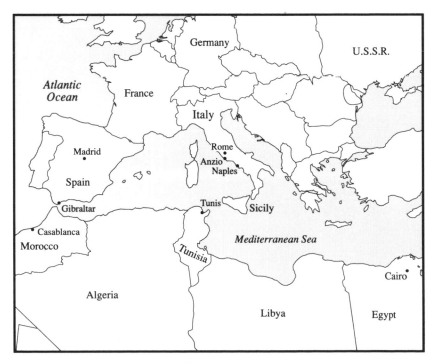

Mediterranean

troops from Major General Truscott's 3rd Division on the left flank of the American beachhead. Despite a pounding surf, the larger landing craft had made it over the reefs and bars that troubled the smaller vessels. Truscott thrashed the light opposition on the beach, established his headquarters ashore, and took nearby Licata the next day. On the right flank, Rear Admiral Alan G. Kirk's Cent Force landed Major General Troy Middleton's 45th Infantry Division at Scoglitti on the southwestern coast, and the assault troops secured their early objectives without too much trouble.

Also on schedule was Admiral Hall's Dime Force. Colonel William O. Darby's Army Rangers hit the beaches at exactly 0245, but at just that moment enemy spotlights lit up and the opposing shore batteries opened up. Hall ordered the destroyers *Shubrick* and *Jeffers* to fire at the searchlights and then concentrate on the opposing gun emplacements, and at 0400 the cruisers *Savannah* and *Boise* appeared and joined the fray. When dawn broke the assault troops had established a beachhead, but now two columns of Italian tanks drove onto the Gela Plain, converged near the town, and prepared to advance on the American position. Responding quickly, Hall directed his Gunfire Support Group to close the beach and disrupt the Italian counterattack. The cruiser-destroyer force hit several of the leading enemy tanks, damaged others, and turned back the Italian armored column. Hall also employed his cruiser float planes to direct and control gunfire from the Gunfire Support Group, an improvisation that turned his duels with a succession of Axis tank formations into the stuff of minor legends. "First Division Artillery recognizes superior gunnery when it sees it," wrote Major General Terry Allen, the commander of the assault troops.[2]

Owing to the presence of large Allied land-based air forces in North Africa, the fear of Axis air power in southern Europe, and the need to establish hunter-killer antisubmarine task forces in the Atlantic, Admiral King could provide Hewitt with no escort carriers for Operation Husky. This left the Western Task Force entirely dependent on the Army Air Force for combat air patrol coverage, but General Spaatz refused to make adequate provisions to defend the invasion force despite a determined German air attack against offshore shipping. During one raid, thirty-two enemy aircraft operated with impunity over the American task force. Spaatz had assigned less than half a dozen fighters to protect Admiral Hall's Center Force, but Hall had no say in their employment, an issue that mattered little at the time since these planes seldom appeared over the anchorages or the beaches when they were needed.

The Germans reacted to the invasion by sending flights of dive bombers from Sicily and southern Italy to attack the Western Task Force. One enemy aircraft hit the destroyer *Maddox*, which sank within a few minutes. On 11 July, the German dive bombers flew more than 300 sorties against the Western Task Force, sinking the *Liberty* ship *Robert Rowan*. Several other vessels were damaged over the next few days. Spaatz' failure to heed Admiral Hewitt's calls for support resulted in another tragedy. Soon after the ammunition-laden *Liberty* ship blew up, a flight of unidentified Army Air Force C-47 transport planes carrying reinforcements for the 82nd Airborne got off course and inadvertently flew over the anchorage off Gela while the ships and the Army's antiaircraft batteries ashore were still fighting off a heavy attack by German dive bombers. Unable to distinguish friend from foe, American gunners shot down 22 of 144 helpless transport planes. A subsequent Navy investigation traced the root of this tragedy to Spaatz' doorstep and to Eisenhower's refusal to insist on truly collaborative planning for the invasion.

The flawed strategic thinking that had drawn the Americans into the Mediterranean in the first place was replicated in the overly cautious strategy that the British persuaded Eisenhower to adopt to overrun Sicily. About 300,000 Italians—stiffened by 50,000 Germans—defended Sicily. Instead of using the British Mediterranean Fleet to boldly seize the Straits of Messina and prevent the enemy from escaping to the mainland of Italy, Admiral Cunningham convinced Eisenhower to land Patton's 7th Army and Montgomery's 8th Army on the southern coast of Sicily. This allowed the Germans plenty of time to prepare their retreat. While Patton's troops took Gela and Licata and moved rapidly westward toward Palermo, Montgomery advanced to the north toward Messina over more difficult terrain against determined opposition. Thus Montgomery, who refused to employ amphibious forces during his ascent up the eastern coast, fell behind schedule in capturing the ports of Augusta and Syracuse. Meanwhile, Patton swung to the east after taking Palermo and pressed along the northwestern coastal road. Rear Admiral Lyal Davidson's cruiser-destroyer Gunfire Support Group, built around the cruiser *Philadelphia*, provided mobile offshore artillery for this movement, while Patton used the 8th Fleet's amphibious forces remaining off Sicily to make a series of landings to outflank and unbalance his opponents. By the time Montgomery and Patton converged on Messina on 17 August, however, most of the Germans had crossed the straits to the Calabrian peninsula on the mainland. Eisenhower had done nothing to prevent this, despite the fact that the Allies were already committed to exploiting their new position in Sicily by invading Italy and digging themselves even deeper into the Mediterranean morass.

The British used the successful invasion of Sicily and the collapse of Mussolini's regime to draw the Americans into a series of costly, wasteful landings on the Italian peninsula. The generally high quality of Allied military intelligence during World War II—most of it derived from code breaking—was often inversely proportional to the low caliber of Allied political intelligence. For instance, both Roosevelt and Churchill were greatly surprised when, during the battle for Sicily, the Fascist Council ousted Mussolini, allowed him to be jailed, and replaced him with Marshall Pietro Badoglio, the aged conqueror of Ethiopia. Badoglio publicly reaffirmed the Axis Pact while privately sending an envoy to Lisbon, where he put forth an astounding offer to a team of British and American diplomats. Italy did not propose to surrender—she wanted to change sides. In effect, Badoglio was asking the Allies to save Italy from the German reinforcements that had begun to flood the country after the invasion of Sicily. Churchill, who intended to move from Sicily to the mainland anyway, promptly agreed to Badoglio's offer. So did FDR, who trimmed his sails on unconditional surrender with such unseemly haste that many wondered why he had raised it as a war aim in the first place. On 3 September, Badoglio agreed to the terms of an armistice requiring him to announce Italy's surrender and simultaneously issue a call to arms against the Germans just before the Allies invaded the peninsula.

Eisenhower was in the meantime preparing to conduct operations Goblet and Avalanche in Italy. On 3 September 1943, Admiral Cunningham's British Mediterranean Fleet covered the movement of Montgomery's British 8th Army from Messina across the straits to Calabria. Goblet was virtually unopposed, and Montgomery moved promptly to overrun the large Italian airbase at Foggia and the Italian fleet base at Taranto. However, 300 miles separated the British lodgment from Naples, the object of the American Operation Avalanche, and only one narrow highway ran from Calabria northward up the western coast of southern Italy.

Eisenhower wanted to overrun Naples quickly to provide a major port for shipping to support his advance against Rome. He told Montgomery that he was to support the American landings near Naples, not by racing to link up with the west coast lodgment but by drawing German forces southward into the heel of the Italian boot. Once Montgomery was established in Calabria and working his way up the single road along the Adriatic coast, Eisenhower intended to send Hewitt's Western Naval Task Force to take Salerno, a small port about thirty miles south of Naples. He assigned command of the ground forces for Operation Avalanche to Lieutenant General Mark Clark, an irresolute figure who understood little about amphibious landings. When Clark first examined the Avalanche plan, he proposed to substitute Gaeta, a port north of Naples, for Salerno, but Eisenhower's staff pointed out that Salerno had been chosen because it was at the outer edge of operational range of the short-range, land-based British Spitfires on Sicily.

Admiral Hewitt's Western Task Force was to lift Clark's newly established 5th Army onto the beaches at Salerno. He divided his command into two elements. The Northern Attack Force, mostly British, under British Commodore G. N. Oliver and Rear Admiral Conolly, was to land the British X Corps north of the Sele River, which divided the Salerno beachhead. Rear Admiral Hall's Southern Attack Force was to land the U.S. Army's VI Corps on a beach south of the river, about eight miles from the northern landing. Field Marshal Albert Kesselring, who commanded German forces in Italy, knew that Allied fighters based in Sicily could not operate north of Naples and that to the south of Naples, the beaches at Salerno constituted the only possible landing site. During July and August, German aircraft raided Bizerte, where many of the Allied landing craft were assembled, and German intelligence soon guessed that another major operation was afoot.

Kesselring poured formidable reinforcements into the hills surrounding Salerno, made certain that the waters offshore were thoroughly mined, and instructed his armored columns to throw the Allied invaders back into the sea. Alert to some of these measures, Hewitt discounted the possibility of achieving a strategic surprise and argued strongly that the beach defenses be reduced by a substantial preinvasion naval bombardment. Admiral Hall, on the other hand, believed that a nighttime bombardment would be ineffective and that a day-long bombardment would give the enemy too much time to bring more reinforcements up to the Salerno beachhead. Hewitt received little support from Admiral Cunningham, and Eisenhower endorsed General Clark's rejection of the Navy's bombardment plan.

At 1815 on 8 September, while the Western Task Force was steaming from North Africa toward Salerno, Eisenhower broadcast the announcement of the surrender of the Italian government. Upon hearing this news, the Germans rapidly disarmed over fifty divisions of the Italian Army and completely occupied the country. Eisenhower's ill-timed broadcast also had the perverse result of leading the troops and sailors who were about to invade Salerno to believe that the Italians would welcome their arrival, whereas for some days it had been evident that the Germans intended to fiercely resist Operation Avalanche. It was, Hall later remarked, "a damn fool performance all around."[3]

In the meantime, Hewitt's task force picked up some landing craft at Palermo and proceeded north along the southwestern Italian coast. Around midnight on 9 September, the ships and invasion craft arrived off Salerno under a clear, moonlit sky. Two weeks earlier, Admiral Hall had learned that the Germans had planted several minefields off Salerno, so he had altered his landing plan, moving the Southern Attack Force's transport anchorage out to a position about eight to ten miles offshore. This was possible since the Navy boat crews had become quite proficient in handling their craft in deep water and the confusion that had marred earlier landings no longer bothered the commanders. Owing to Clark's insistence on achieving tactical surprise, however, during the long run from the transport anchorage to the beaches the first waves of landing craft—which got under way at 0330—were provided with no close fire support by gunboats or rocket-firing landing craft. The German gunners held their fire until the Americans closed the beach, but when the troops entered the surf the defenders raked their lines with a deadly fire. Alert German machine gunners and light artillery took an unnecessarily heavy toll of the assault troops. Moreover, enemy gun emplacements prevented many tank-carrying LSTs from beaching and there were few American tanks ashore that day to support the hard-pressed infantry.

German armor reacted quickly to the invasion, and by 0700 enemy tanks appeared on the scene and began to thrust toward the fragile beachhead. To check these tank movements, Hall had sent over 100 Army DUKWs racing toward the beach, many carrying 105mm howitzers. Their timely arrival broke up this first major enemy counterattack. Admiral Davidson's Gunfire Support Group, comprising the cruisers *Philadelphia* and *Savannah* and four destroyers, provided long-range naval gunfire against preselected targets inland until 0900, when spotting reports belatedly began to arrive from the beaches and the ships could begin firing at targets of immediate tactical importance. With spotting by the cruisers' float planes and specially trained Army Air Force P-51 Mustangs from Sicily, Davidson's gun batteries succeeded in preventing several German armored concentrations from reaching the American beaches. The British Northern Attack Force also ran into fierce resistance, but Admiral Conolly's daring decision to station three destroyers one mile off the beaches to provide more intense gunfire support for the assault troops prevented the Germans from organizing a successful armored counterattack. Many parts of the landings were flawed, however. Ship-to-shore communication circuits were overloaded, for instance, and handling the congestion on the beaches had yet to be mastered. At the end of the first day ashore, moreover, neither of the landing forces had secured their inland objectives. The British occupied a thin beachhead north of the Sele, but a gap of seven miles separated this enclave from the American beachhead to the south of the river.

Kesselring moved against the Sele River gap on 10 September. He shifted German fighter aircraft to airfields in southern Italy in an attempt to achieve air superiority over Salerno. He sent German fighters to bring down Allied combat air patrols over the anchorage and deployed waves of level-bombers armed with radio-controlled glide bombs to attack Allied shipping. Crude devices, the glide bombs usually created more disruption than damage. On 11 September, however, one glide bomb hit the cruiser *Savannah* and inflicted sufficient damage to force her to withdraw. Hewitt quickly replaced her with the cruiser *Boise*. However, on the 12th, the escort carriers had to steam away to refuel at Palermo. That same day, Kesselring massed nearly 600 tanks and self-propelled guns for an assault intended to cut the beachhead in two by moving into the Sele River gap, which separated the British and American sectors. General Clark panicked, relieved his corps commander, and begged Hewitt to prepare to withdraw the troops to the transports.

Cooler heads, Hewitt's included, prevailed. Assuring Clark that the escort carriers would soon return to provide the beachhead with air cover, Hewitt proposed that he ask Eisenhower for reinforcements to expand the lodgment. Clark radioed Eisenhower for assistance, and a parachute division arrived at Salerno on 14 September. One day earlier, Allied naval gunfire had disrupted the major German armored thrust against the Allied lodgment. Hewitt thereafter regrouped his cruisers and destroyers to pound enemy assembly areas. They were joined by the British battleships *Valiant* and *Warspite*, but the latter was damaged by a German glide bomb and forced to retire. Meanwhile, Eisenhower had directed Montgomery to swing over to the western coastal highway, fight his way northward, and relieve Clark at the Salerno enclave. Montgomery slowly moved north over poor roads, but by 16 September he had reached Salerno beachhead; this compelled the Germans to abandon their attacks on Salerno and retreat to the north to prepare defensive positions along the Volturno River. While Montgomery pursued the Germans, Hewitt's 8th Fleet salvage crews opened up the port of Salerno, landed more reinforcements, and supported a landward siege of Naples, which ended when the city fell on 1 October 1943. Naples was available to American shipping soon after.

The plan to land at Anzio was part of the British strategy of continuing to pressure Germany on her strong Mediterranean flank while trying to delay the invasion of France. Following the American seizure of Naples, the Germans skillfully exploited the mountainous terrain of the Italian peninsula to delay an Allied advance against Rome. Kesselring's troops were ejected from the Volturno Line in the fall, but they merely retired to stronger prepared defensive positions along the Gustav Line, which stretched across the waist of the country from Gaeta Gulf in the west to Ortona on the Adriatic. General Clark's 5th Army was unable to penetrate this barrier.

To outflank the enemy, Clark proposed in November 1943 that Admiral Hewitt's 8th Amphibious Force lift an American infantry division north to Anzio, a small port not far from the Alban Hills, only thirty-five miles from Rome. Anzio seemed to be an ideal landing site. Its sandy beaches emerged from a flat coastal plain covered with pine scrub, an area quite unlike the rocky, cliff-lined coast the Allies had previously encountered in Italy. In addition, Allied intelligence insisted that the Anzio beaches were lightly defended. Clark intended to mount an offensive against the Gustav Line simultaneous to the Anzio landing, thus allowing the beachhead to quickly link up with the advance elements of the 5th Army. Eisenhower approved this plan, and Admiral Hewitt began to prepare for the landing shortly thereafter. However, on 2 December over 100 German Ju-88 bombers conducted a daring night raid on the port of Bari, destroying sixteen large Allied cargo ships and damaging eight others. Soon after this blow, Field Marshal Kesselring repulsed Clark's offensive against the Gustav Line. This led Eisenhower to cancel the Anzio plan on 22 December, a few days before he planned to leave the Mediterranean and fly to London to assume command of the cross-Channel invasion.

The cancellation of the Anzio landing disturbed Churchill, who summoned Eisenhower and his designated successor, British Field Marshal Henry M. Wilson, to an impromptu conference at Tunis on Christmas Day. Without the Anzio operation, the prime minister protested, "the Italian battle will stagnate and fester" and would delay the cross-Channel operation in 1944. Although Eisenhower ultimately objected, Wilson buckled under the weight of Churchill's rhetoric and agreed to conduct Operation Shingle, a two-division amphibious assault on Anzio set for January 1944. The objective of this landing was not to put a force ashore that would quickly link up with the 5th Army, but instead to establish a threat to the German flank that would compel Kesselring to withdraw troops from the Gustav Line. Nonetheless, British General Harold Alexander, the new ground commander in Italy, instructed Clark to "make as strong a thrust as possible towards" the Gustav Line "shortly prior to the assault landing." This would, in Alexander's view, "create a breach in his front through which every opportunity would be taken to link up rapidly with the seaborne operation."[4]

Rear Admiral Frank J. Lowry, a dynamic figure who had relieved Admiral Hall in command of the 8th Fleet Amphibious Force, was assigned command of the naval phase of Operation Shingle. Clark named Major General John Lucas, who was oddly unassertive for a high-ranking Army commander, to direct the ground forces. Lowry immediately pointed out that the withdrawal of large numbers of LSTs from the Mediterranean to

Britain would limit his ability to support the Anzio landing. The Combined Chiefs soon solved this problem by scaling back operations in Burma and by delaying the movement of a handful of LSTs out of the Mediterranean theater. The resulting lift schedule left Lowry with enough large landing ships to support a lodgment over the beach at Anzio for about twelve days.

Planning for the Shingle operation was accomplished at breakneck speed, but the final detailed operational order was not finished until 12 January 1944, less than two weeks before the invasion force was to put to sea. Meanwhile, Lowry conducted a rehearsal for both divisions on the Salerno beaches. The British phase went well, but the American phase "not only was bad," according to General Clark, "it was almost fatal. Everything went wrong." Admiral Lowry did not disagree. The transports were positioned so far offshore that the landing craft took over four hours to reach the beach, none of the assault troops were put ashore on the correct beach, communications between the landing craft and the beaches broke down, and a large number of howitzers, antitank guns, and Army DUKW landing craft were lost. Clark attributed this to "the overwhelming mismanagement of the naval phase of the operation," an ungenerous and inaccurate criticism of Admiral Lowry's performance.

While Lowry was revising his plans, General Alexander directed Lieutenant General Ira Eaker's 5th Air Force to isolate the Anzio beachhead from outside support by bombing roads and rail lines leading to the vicinity of the landing site. On 19 January Eaker reported to Admiral Hewitt that this had been accomplished. In fact, few German movements had been hindered; moreover, the German Air Force was active over the Anzio area before, during, and after the Allied landings. In the meantime, Clark's 5th Army had once again gone on the offensive against the formidable Gustav Line, and on the 20th American infantry established a bridgehead on the northern bank of the Rapido River, but Kesselring committed his reserves and forced Clark's men to retreat after two days of bitter fighting. The Gustav Line had held.

On 21 January, the two main elements of Lowry's Anzio Task Force—a thorough mix of British and American cruisers, destroyers, minesweepers, landing ships, and beaching craft—stood out of Salerno and the port of Pozzuoli. Despite the clear, mild weather, the Germans did not spot these formations as they sailed up the Italian coast, and Lowry's ships arrived safely off Anzio before midnight. The Army and the Royal Navy commanders had once again objected to a U.S. Navy plan for a preliminary naval gunfire bombardment, but—for once—a surprise nighttime landing proved to be the better strategy because the German defenses at Anzio were so weak. Off X-ray Beach, the codename for the site where the 3rd Infantry Division would land, minesweepers began to clear channels shortly before midnight, and at 0153 on 22 January rocket-firing LCTs sped toward the beaches and opened fire on the defenders. Only a handful of Germans were guarding this area, and they were so completely overwhelmed that by 0634 eight waves of assault troops had come ashore with much of their equipment intact. One mile from Anzio harbor, Colonel Darby's Rangers were all ashore by 0645, and their transports had already begun to withdraw. Shore fire-control parties had also landed, and at 0748 Captain Robert W. Cary's Gunfire Support Group consisting of two light cruisers and a destroyer squadron opened fire.

By contrast, British Rear Admiral T. H. Troubridge, who was in charge of putting ashore the 1st British Infantry Division, ran into considerable difficulty on Peter Beach. Troubridge had failed to properly rehearse his minesweeping force, and its commander even complained that the admiral had not provided him with a minesweeping plan much in advance of the landing. As a result, the minesweeping operation was so slow that immense congestion developed between Troubridge's transport anchorage and Peter Beach and prevented the large LSTs from unloading until 1045. In addition, the planners had erred in selecting Peter Beach where, among other problems, the sand was altogether too soft for vehicles to quickly drive off the dunes onto the exit lanes. As a consequence, once both divisions were safely ashore, Admiral Lowry decided to abandon Peter Beach and divert his follow-up convoys to X-ray Beach.

Although German artillery fire had been minimal and the harbor at Anzio was taken with only slight opposition, at dawn on January 22, the German Air Force appeared over the beachhead and a flight of Folke-Wulf bombers attacked and damaged the pontoon causeways off X-ray Beach and sank the *LCI-20*. Soon after, the nearby minesweeper *Portent* struck a mine and sank within three minutes. Nevertheless, by the end of the day Lowry's task force had put more than 36,000 men and 3,000 vehicles on the beach, and the admiral had transferred command of the ground forces to General Lucas, who had established his headquarters ashore.

The German counterattack gained momentum on the 23rd when Kesselring sent a flight of fifty-five aircraft against the Allied lodgment. Although Army Air Force fighters drove off most of these planes, more than twenty penetrated the air defenses and attacked the beaches and the nearby shipping anchorages. A German radio-guided bomb sank the British destroyer *Jervis,* while another British destroyer, the *Janus,* was damaged by an air-dropped torpedo and forced to withdraw. British Rear Admiral J. M. Mansfield relieved Captain Cary in command of the Gunfire Support Group that morning. After the *Jervis* sank, Mansfield instructed all three British cruisers to withdraw from Anzio and steam south to Naples, an order that would leave only the cruiser *Brooklyn* and a handful of destroyers and gunboats to support the divisional artillery already ashore. Admiral Lowry grimly told Mansfield to countermand this order and remain on station, but after a long and bitter exchange Lowry relented and, in the name of Allied unity, allowed Mansfield and the British cruisers to retire after the evening air raid. This considerably lessened the antiaircraft defenses of the Anzio Task Force and reduced the Gunfire Support Group's ability to respond to German armored thrusts against the lodgment. Lowry also decided that the twilight and nighttime guide-bomb attacks so imperiled his ships that the remaining cruisers and destroyers would have to move farther off shore after 1600 each day to gain sea room to maneuver. The price for this was paid the next day when over 100 enemy fighter-bombers conducted three separate strikes against the beachhead, lasting from afternoon into the evening. One German bomb crippled the destroyer *Plunkett,* which had to retire, while a near miss put the minesweeper *Prevail* out of action. During one of these strikes, the Germans bombed and sank one clearly marked British hospital ship and damaged two others.

After the second day of Operation Shingle, Lowry and several of his fellow commanders realized that the Allied lodgment at Anzio was in trouble. Instead of aggressively striking toward the Alban Hills or up the road to Rome, Lucas had consolidated his position, an excessively cautious strategy that entirely forfeited the advantage of the surprise landing. Hitler, on the other hand, had responded swiftly, issuing orders that transferred reinforcements to Italy from as far away as France, Yugoslavia, and Greece. With fresh divisions on the way, Kesselring organized a counterattack against the Anzio beachhead, which began when German artillery observers set up posts in the Alban Hills shortly after the landing. On 24 January, a German armored column started down the Mussolini Canal on the left flank of the Allied lodgment to the south of Anzio, but Commander A. D. Kaplan in the destroyer *Mayo* kept up such an accurate, incessant shelling of the canal that the enemy was unable to cross it. At 1945 when more than two miles offshore, however, the *Mayo* struck a mine, which damaged her propeller shaft and flooded the engine room. Kaplan and his well-trained crew saved their ship, but she had to be taken under tow back to Naples for repairs. Lowry then ordered the destroyers *Trippe* and *Edison* to take station off the canal and prevent the Germans from menacing the southern flank of the lodgment.

The next day, 25 January, a storm blew over Anzio, driving many of the ships out to sea while the rest of the force rode it out at anchor. When the weather improved on the following morning, all of the pontoon causeways used to unload the LSTs had been damaged. "Had not the port of Anzio been operated at three or four times its expected capacity," Lowry reported, "the loss of the pontoon causeways would have doomed the beachhead." While Lowry had tolerated unnecessary confusion on the beach and had not prepared a good salvage plan, his brilliant decision to strain his resources to get the small port functioning quickly after the landing saved the entire operation. The day after the storm subsided, Lucas' troops began to move inland beyond the range of the 5-inch destroyer gunfire. When they met stiff German resistance Lowry asked Admiral Hewitt to deploy a heavy cruiser to reinforce the Gunfire Support Group; unfortunately, none was available.[5]

By this time, Churchill had become aggravated about the hapless Anzio lodgment. "I had hoped we were hurling a wildcat onto the shore," he remarked colorfully, "but all we got was a stranded whale." By allowing the Germans to block the road to Rome and establish artillery in the Alban Hills within range of every square yard of the lodgment, Lucas condemned his men to several months of savage fighting along static lines. Both Generals Alexander and Clark repeatedly visited Anzio, but neither man objected to Lucas' strategy until Clark suddenly relieved him on 22 February, only two days after Lucas had conducted a stout defense of the Allied lodgment. Major General Truscott, the new ground commander, fared little better, however. And Captain Harry Sanders, who had already relieved Admiral Lowry in command of the remaining destroyers and landing craft, discovered that his shipping resources were so strained by March that a determined breakout by Truscott's divisions was impossible. "There could be no hope now of a break-out from the Anzio beachhead," Churchill later wrote in his memoirs, "and no prospect of an early link-up between our separated forces." The JCS were less worried than the British about this ignominious but temporary collapse of the Italian offensive, because the Americans had long held that the entire campaign led to nowhere. Clark's 5th Army finally cleared the hills around the enemy strongpoint of Monte Cassino on 23 May 1944, and two days later linked arms with patrols from Anzio. Together, they advanced on Rome. On 4 June Rome fell to the Allies, an anticlimax that brought down the curtain on Churchill's majestic yet wasteful four-year long Mediterranean diversion.[6]

Chapter Seven

Advancing on the Flanks in the Pacific

1943–1944

Operations in the North Pacific in 1943 resulted from domestic political pressure to evict the Japanese from Attu and Kiska, two strategically worthless islands in the western Aleutians occupied during the Midway campaign. Although the North Pacific commander, Rear Admiral Robert Theobald, had bungled the Alaskan aspect of the June 1942 Midway battle, Admiral King, an old drinking companion, ignored pleas by Admiral Cooke, among others, to give him the boot. Relations between Theobald and his Army counterpart, General Simon Bolivar Buckner, soured that autumn, owing in part to Theobald's lack of aggressiveness. Theobald had sent a cruiser-destroyer force to bombard Attu and Kiska, but it was unable to locate the islands in the dense fog. A subsequent bombardment force did no more than pound holes in the tundra. Theobald was "as tender of his [ship's] bottoms as a teenage girl," Buckner complained hotly. Theobald's profane reply generated even more tension. General Marshall suggested that both men be replaced, but Navy Inspector General Admiral Peck Snyder convinced King that Theobald was at fault, and in late 1942 he was relieved by Admiral Kinkaid, a combat-tested veteran who was hastily called out of the South Pacific at the height of the fighting there.[1]

Both Kinkaid and Buckner chafed at the inactivity in the North Pacific and together urged the JCS to allow them to move against Attu and Kiska. The Army had garrisoned Adak and

Amchitka islands, only fifty miles from Kiska, Army Air Force bases were built there to extend American air operations over the western Aleutians, and by early 1943, land-based fighters were interrupting enemy communications between Japan and Kiska, but not with Attu. The Japanese, expecting an American invasion, hurried work on the two incomplete airfields and tried to reinforce their garrisons. Kinkaid was determined to prevent the enemy from reinforcing the islands. After his task group of two cruisers and four destroyers bombarded Attu on 18 February 1943, Rear Admiral Charles McMorris divided his force into two formations and ordered his skippers to attack Japanese shipping in the area. The cruiser *Indianapolis* sank an enemy ammunition ship, and two Japanese transports heading for Attu were forced to turn back to Paramushiro in the Kuriles. Japan's North Pacific commander, Admiral Boshiro Hosogaya, organized another convoy of transports and, with a powerful escort of two heavy and two light cruisers and four destroyers, reached Attu without incident in early March. When Hosogaya put to sea with yet another convoy later that month, however, McMorris and a task group composed of the cruisers *Salt Lake City* and *Richmond* and five destroyers were already on patrol west of Attu. When radio intelligence told McMorris that an enemy convoy was heading his way on the morning of 26 March, he steamed north to intercept it.

At 0730, the destroyer *Coghlan*'s surface search radar located the enemy transports about 500 miles south of Russia's Komandorski Islands. Unaware that Hosogaya's escorts were nearby, McMorris charged ahead for another hour. He ordered his cruiser scout planes to take off, then changed his mind for no apparent reason, and as a result he had no clear picture of what he faced. At 0840, the cruiser *Nachi* unexpectedly appeared on the horizon and opened fire on the *Richmond* at a range of 21,000 yards, disrupting the entire American advance. McMorris, who had prepared no battle plan, was so stunned that he allowed a full, agonizing two minutes to elapse before ordering his ships to return fire. "Both sides were shooting well," he observed three minutes later, but "the odds were too great against us to continue," thus making it "expedient to retire."

McMorris increased speed, withdrew to the east, and radioed Kinkaid to send aircraft to the scene. At that moment, an Adak-based Army Air Force bomber squadron, armed with general-purpose bombs, was about to take off and bomb Kiska, but they now had to be rearmed with armor-piercing bombs to attack ships and this work consumed half a day. Meanwhile, Hosogaya was pursuing McMorris, trying to prevent him from escaping eastward to the security of land-based air cover. Hosogaya was not terribly aggressive during this three-hour stern chase, however. He zigzagged continuously and so was unable to reduce the distance between the opposing formations and exploit his guns' superior throwweight. He was also plagued by bad luck. The Japanese fired forty-two Long Lance torpedoes during this action, but they were uncommonly ineffective. Also preventing Hosogaya from narrowing the gap was the *Salt Lake City*'s superbly controlled long-range gunfire.[2]

Just as it appeared that McMorris might escape in a cloud of smoke laid down by his intrepid destroyers, the tide of battle again turned. A seaman in the *Salt Lake City*'s engineering department mistakenly opened a valve that sent salt water rushing into all eight of her boilers, dousing their fires and leaving the ship

Invasion scene off Pacific beaches in World War II.

dead in the water—and without electricity—at 1150. Though apprised of the plight of the *Salt Lake City*, McMorris continued to steam away in the *Richmond*, ignoring the need to regroup his ships to protect the crippled cruiser. While his engineers worked to restore her power, Captain Bertram Rodgers finally persuaded McMorris to detach the destroyer *Dale* to shield the *Salt Lake City* with smoke and to agree to a desperate torpedo attack by the other three destroyers. Captain Ralph Riggs in the *Bailey* skillfully led this suicidal charge, chasing and dodging a hailstorm of Japanese shells that straddled the small ships as they tried to steam within torpedo range of the enemy. At 9,500 yards, the *Bailey*, badly damaged, prematurely launched a salvo of five torpedoes and then turned away to escape the rain of fire. To the Americans' astonishment, at that moment Hosogaya also turned away and retreated. After power was restored to the *Salt Lake City*, McMorris' task group limped back to Dutch Harbor. Nimitz, assuming that the decision to launch the torpedo attack had saved the day, rewarded McMorris by asking him to succeed Admiral Spruance as the Pacific Fleet chief of staff. Unbeknownst to the Americans, however, when Hosogaya reached Paramushiro, he reported that he had retired because of his fear that American bombers would soon arrive over the battle. For forfeiting a near certain victory, Hosogaya was retired in disgrace.

The Battle of the Komandorski Islands strengthened Kinkaid's conviction that he had to retake Attu before he landed on Kiska. Recent Army Air Force reconnaissance flights over Attu had sighted only a few Japanese defenders and the unfinished airstrip. For the Attu operation, General Marshall shipped a division from the training camp in the hot Nevada desert to a cold and dreary staging point in Alaska. Tactical command of the invasion force was vested in Rear Admiral Francis Rockwell, who one year earlier had escaped from the Philippines. His Covering Force included three old battleships and nineteen destroyers, but the nearest Army Air Force base was 250 miles to the east and only a single escort carrier was available to provide air cover for the task force, the shipping anchorage, and the beachhead.

The Attu operation began on 11 May 1943 when five transports put an Army battalion ashore near Holtz Bay and landed two battalions at Massacre Bay on the other side of the island. Rockwell expected the enemy to retire to the east coast, but instead the Japanese lodged themselves in the mountains and used their camouflaged artillery to prevent the junction of the slowly converging American troops. Fearful that his battleships might be hit by Japanese artillery, Rockwell held them seven miles off-shore, too far away to effectively support the Army's advance. Rockwell was, nonetheless, angry over the slow progress on the island, and he badly misinterpreted a poorly worded message from the Army ground commander, Major General Albert E. Brown, about the need for reinforcements. This led to Kinkaid's precipitous decision to relieve Brown, a serious error that did nothing to improve interservice relations.

Owing to the limited air cover for the unloaded transports, Kinkaid and Rockwell were constantly worried that Japanese aircraft based on Paramushiro would attack the task force, and they relied heavily on their shipboard radio intelligence units to provide them with an early warning. The code breakers failed to predict one strike that developed at 1100 on 24 May, but that attack fortunately did little damage. Two days later, however, the code breakers redeemed themselves by deciphering a noontime message from a nearby enemy weather plane indicating that an attack would develop that afternoon. Kinkaid put up a strong combat air patrol and called on Amchitka-based Army Air Force P-38s to cover the beachhead and anchorage for a short time. When the flight of Betty bombers appeared at 1600, it fell victim to an ambush. By this time, Kinkaid had already committed his reserves and the two landing forces had at last converged. On the 29th, 1,000 Japanese defenders, wielding only swords and knives, made a last, suicidal charge against the American lines. Less than three dozen Japanese prisoners were alive after the Attu bloodbath, which cost the Americans 600 dead and 2,700 other casualties.

Not content to simply isolate and occasionally bomb Kiska, over whose skies the Army Air Force now roamed at will, Kinkaid persuaded the JCS to commit more than 35,000 men and a naval task force of battleships, cruisers, and over 100 landing craft and auxiliaries to the 15 August invasion of that island. King was in Navy Secretary Frank Knox's office when the first message after the landing was received from Kinkaid, announcing that no Japanese remained on Kiska, only dogs and hot coffee. "What does this mean?" Knox asked. "The Japanese are very clever," King shot back. "Their dogs can brew coffee." King later learned that two weeks before the invasion a Japanese relief force, hidden by cloud cover, had eluded the American patrols, embarked the defenders, and escaped. With the western Aleutians now back in American hands, King sent Kinkaid, who could fight, to the Southwest Pacific, and ordered Admiral Fletcher to take his place in Alaska. For the rest of the war, the North Pacific remained what it always should have been: a diversion of no strategic consequence.

In the meantime, Halsey's campaign in the central and northern Solomons was proceeding apace. Despite King's best efforts to revise the July 1942 JCS directive covering Pacific operations, General Marshall insisted that when the fighting moved out of the Navy-dominated South Pacific area and into the Southwest Pacific, an Army theater, MacArthur was to assume overall command. Then, in late 1942, MacArthur asked King to replace Vice Admiral Fairfax Leary, the Southwest Pacific naval commander, and King, disappointed with Leary, agreed. This coincided with King's decision to establish the 3rd Fleet under Halsey in the South Pacific. Halsey looked to Nimitz for administrative and logistical support, but fell under MacArthur's operational command once the campaign in the Solomons moved northward. King also established the 7th Fleet, assigned it to the Southwest Pacific theater, and named Vice Admiral Arthur S. Carpender to this command. The intended outcome of these moves was to keep the command of the Fast Carrier Force and Admiral Turner's growing 3rd Fleet Amphibious Force out of MacArthur's hands.

For the moment this hardly mattered inasmuch as MacArthur was unwilling to budge. MacArthur's strategic opinions were, at best, eccentric. In late September 1942, when General Arnold had visited Australia, he was told that the "Japs can take New Guinea at will, can take Fijis, [and] will then control Pacific for one hundred years." Rather than investing more resources in the Pacific theater, MacArthur felt that "our plan should be to give more aid to Russia, put troops in there, [and] work from interior lines against Germany and Japan." It was not surprising that Marshall and King seldom took MacArthur seriously, and King was doubly dismayed when, on 27 January 1943, just as the Japanese were abandoning the struggle for Guadalcanal, MacArthur announced that he found it "not now immediately possible to undertake a further offensive in the Southwest Pacific" owing to the shortage of land-based Army Air Force aircraft.[3]

Nimitz, whose assessments of the situation more closely resembled reality, was also inclined to move slowly. He was badly shaken by the losses in the Watchtower campaign. Following Halsey's seizure of the Russell Islands thirty miles northwest of Guadalcanal on 21 February 1943, there was a lull in the offensive while the American air forces established superiority in the central Solomons and Halsey readied a drive that would form the eastern arm of the pincer around Rabaul. King was furious that Nimitz had failed to keep up the pressure and urged him at every opportunity to get moving, but Nimitz refused to spur Halsey to action until the American air forces in the South Pacific were considerably strengthened. Thus, the grim attritional battles continued to gnaw away at the enemy's front-line inventory. Finally, on 16 June, the Japanese sent ninety-four aircraft to attack American shipping off Guadalcanal, but the defenders were now so powerful that only one plane returned to Rabaul. Then, five days later, a Marine raider battalion was put ashore by the converted destroyer transports *Dant* and *Waters* at Segi Point, New Georgia, a preliminary to the invasion of Rendova nine days later.

MacArthur launched a concurrent attack on the northern coast of New Guinea supported by PT boats and other small craft, while Rear Admiral Anson S. Merrill's cruiser-destroyer force bombarded Kolombangara and Bougainville islands in order to divide and confuse the Japanese air forces. In addition, an American destroyer force shelled nearby Munda to silence its shore batteries. The destroyer *Gwinn* was hit and forced to retire, but Munda's guns could no longer disrupt the upcoming landings. Under the cover of Guadalcanal-based aircraft, Turner landed troops on Rendova Island, to the southwest of New Georgia. The whole plan was so well orchestrated that Japanese aircraft did not appear over the American beachhead until the attack transports had been withdrawn at 1500, and then the attacking flight was driven away. This put American artillery within range of vital enemy positions on nearby New Georgia.

MacArthur was still clearly in no mood to boldly outflank the enemy. "Like a good many Army officers of his time," Commander Robert Dennison observed, MacArthur "looked on a Navy as a seaward extension of the Army's flank and that's all." On 2 July, Rear Admiral Theodore Wilkinson, who had just relieved Turner in command of the South Pacific Amphibious

Force, put Marines and troops from two Army divisions ashore near Munda, now the strongest Japanese airbase in the central Solomons. Reckoning that the loss of Munda would expose Rabaul's southern flank, the enemy on the scene responded with renewed determination, although Tokyo refused to recognize the crisis and support the campaign with reinforcements. On the night of the 6th, the Japanese cruiser *Yubari* and nine destroyers closed on Rendova and began to shell the island, which also came under attack by Japanese land-based aircraft from Rabaul. Halsey responded by striking back quickly.[4]

The Battle of Kula Gulf developed when Rear Admiral Walden L. Ainsworth, who commanded a light cruiser-destroyer task group, bombarded Vila, Bougainville, and Bairoko Harbour on nearby New Georgia. A Japanese force emerged to defend these positions and Ainsworth lost the destroyer *Strong* to a Japanese torpedo attack. This bombardment did, however, pave the way for landings near Vila by 2,600 Marines and soldiers, who cut off enemy communications to Munda. Shortly after midnight on 6 July, Rear Admiral Akiyuma's ten destroyers were escorting troop transports to Munda when they came upon Ainsworth's Bombardment Group of four cruisers and four destroyers. Once the battle began, the cruiser *Helena*, which had used up most of her flashless powder the day before, was so brightly lit up by her own gunfire that she was a perfect target for a Japanese torpedo attack. In short order, five Long Lance torpedoes struck the *Helena* and she went down at 0200. However, when the destroyer *Nizuki* was hit and sunk, Akiyuma, realizing that he was out-gunned, formed his ships into two columns and tried to escape. Ainsworth now saw his chance and rearranged his own ships into a line ahead and capped Akiyuma's "tee." The two leading Japanese destroyers were shot up so badly that they turned away, laid down smoke, and retired at 0220. Although a few Japanese transport destroyers were still in the area, Ainsworth's gunners were nearly out of ammunition and he too withdrew before dawn's early light brought the rival air forces into play. Though possessing radar and superior armor and gunnery, Ainsworth had lost the battle to Japan's torpedoes and superior night-fighting tactics. The fighting continued ashore on Munda even after the Americans overran the vital airstrip on 5 August.

The last Japanese attempt to reinforce the central Solomons provoked the battle off the island of Kolombangara. On the night of 13 July, Rear Admiral Izaki's force of one cruiser and five destroyers, which was screening a convoy of destroyer transports, closed on Ainsworth's group of three cruisers and ten destroyers. Alerted by radar to Izaki's movements, Ainsworth wasted no time and launched a fast destroyer attack. The Americans fired fifty torpedoes, which quickly disabled the Japanese cruiser *Jintsu*; she went down under a hail of American gunfire, taking with her Izaki and her entire crew. The Japanese started to retire and Ainsworth closed to keep gunfire range, but the enemy suddenly turned and loosed his own torpedo attack, which put the New Zealand cruiser *Leander* out of action. Charging north with his cruisers and half of his destroyers, Ainsworth spotted a destroyer but refused to open fire until she was positively identified. This delay allowed the Japanese to strike back again with another devastating torpedo attack, which sank the *Gwinn*, damaged the cruisers *Honolulu* and *St. Louis,* and caused the destroyers *Woodworth* and *Buchanan* to collide with each other. Izaki's tactics had bested Ainsworth, and the enemy transports landed their troops at Vella Gulf, although aircraft from Henderson Field covered the retirement of the crippled American vessels the next day. It was now evident to Halsey that his ships needed new night-fighting tactics.

The Battle of Vella Gulf developed when the Americans learned through radio intelligence that the Japanese intended to send four destroyers to resupply Kolombangara on the night of 6 August. Halsey reacted by dispatching Commander Frederick Moosbrugger's division of six destroyers to Vella Gulf to intercept the convoy, although he now had no cruisers to support Moosbrugger. By this time, the Americans had thoroughly revised their night-fighting tactics by abandoning the line-ahead in favor of columns, perfecting their use of radars, and coordinating the sequence of their torpedo and gunfire attacks. And before this battle, Moosbrugger and Captain Arleigh Burke, two superb fighters, had prepared a coherent tactical plan and made certain that their subordinates clearly understood it. The plan called for Moosbrugger's six destroyers to divide into two equal columns, to close rapidly on the enemy, but to withhold their gunfire so as to mask their line of approach. Once the Japanese ships were within range, the American destroyers would fire their torpedoes and then separate and wheel away at high speed in opposite directions, and in this way avoid the enemy's torpedo counterattack. Next, one column would use gunfire to crush the Japanese van while the other column would charge the enemy's center.

The plan worked perfectly in Vella Gulf. At 2330 on the 6th, American radar located the Japanese destroyers heading for Kolombangara, Moosbrugger closed, launched his torpedo barrage at 2347, and followed this up with a blistering gunfire attack. Within thirteen minutes, the destroyers *Kawakaze*, *Hagikaze*, and *Arashi* were sunk and the rest of the Japanese ships were withdrawing. Moosbrugger sank three of four enemy ships without taking a single casualty, the most one-sided naval victory between two evenly matched forces in the twentieth century.

The Japanese, expecting Halsey to invade Kolombangara, built up impressive forces to defend that bastion. As a result, Halsey decided to outflank Kolombangara. He instructed Wilkinson to land 6,000 men of the 3rd Amphibious Force on Vella Lavella Island, a large island on the northeast side of the Vella Gulf about ten miles from Kolombangara, on 15 August 1943. This operation was risky owing to the proximity of Japanese air forces, but Vella Lavella was not defended and the Seabees soon built airstrips there, enabling Halsey to establish American air superiority in the area within a few weeks. After Kolombangara was effectively surrounded, the Japanese turned to small ship convoys to evacuate their isolated positions in the area during September and early October. Over 12,000 enemy soldiers were saved from Kolombangara alone, just enough to completely overburden Japanese logistics in the northern Solomons.

The enemy's high command, now determined to obstruct the central Solomons offensive, inflicted a stinging reverse on the Americans off Vella Lavella. On 6 October, American patrol planes reported that Rear Admiral M. Ijuin's nine destroyers were covering the evacuation of troops from Vella Lavella, and this led Admiral Wilkinson to order Captain Frank R. Walker's destroyer task group to disrupt the operation. Three of the six American destroyers were trailing Walker's lead destroyer by ten miles when his radar located Ijuin's force, itself divided into six destroyers in the van and three destroyers several miles to the rear. Walker, impatient to attack, did not wait to concentrate his ships, and at 2255 the destroyers *Chevalier* and *Selfridge* launched a spread of fourteen torpedoes at a range of 7,000 yards. So far so good, but Walker then exposed his awkward position by prematurely ordering his main batteries to open fire. Before the

Yugumo was sunk by the American torpedoes, she had time to launch her own torpedo counterattack, which badly damaged the *Chevalier* and caused her to collide with the destroyer *O'Bannon*. Both ships had to retire. Walker in the *Selfridge* continued to chase Ijuin, but the Japanese admiral opened the distance separating the two forces to about 10,000 yards. This was beyond the range of the Americans' torpedoes but just within range for the Long Lance. Ijuin now fired a brace of torpedoes, causing so much damage to the *Selfridge* that she was later scuttled. The Americans could afford an occasional reverse, like the one at Vella Lavella, but the Japanese, who had lost forty destroyers since Pearl Harbor, could not stand much more attrition.

Halsey now faced a dispirited enemy whose only remaining strongpoints south of Rabaul were Choiseul and Bougainville. As a distraction, he had a Marine raider team go ashore on Choiseul on 27 October and quickly withdraw. On the same day, he landed troops in the Treasury Islands, thus giving him a staging area for the move against Bougainville. And on 1 November, Wilkinson landed the 3rd Marine Division at Cape Torokino near Empress Augusta Bay. Although "both our naval bombardment and our air strikes missed most of the enemy fortifications," according to Major John Brody, the Marines quickly overcame light Japanese resistance and established a secure beachhead. Meanwhile, Rear Admiral Frederick Sherman's Pacific Fleet Carrier Force composed of the *Saratoga* and the new light carrier *Princeton* hit airstrips guarding the neighboring Buka Passage.[5]

The action off Empress Augusta Bay took shape on the evening of 1 November 1943 when Merrill's task group of four light cruisers and eight destroyers, which had bombarded the Buka Passage airfields that day, turned to the south to meet Rear Admiral Sentaro Omori's approaching formation of four cruisers and six destroyers. Omori had been sent from Rabaul to attack American shipping off Bougainville. Merrill's object was to interpose his ships between Omori's force and the Marines on the beach, so he held his cruisers about 16,000 yards away from the Japanese to avoid a torpedo attack. One division of destroyers commanded by Captain Burke and another led by Captain Bernard Austin were to conduct fast torpedo attacks.

When they came upon Omori that night off Cape Torokino, Austin smashed at the Japanese flank, but Burke lost control of his ships, wasted his time trying to regroup, and ended the battle by firing at Austin's vessels. Although the American cruisers' 6-inch guns could not reach the enemy, their radar-controlled 8-inch main batteries fired more than 4,000 shells, which rained down on the Japanese ships during the battle. Hit several times, the light cruiser *Sendaii* began to steam around in circles, the *Samidare* and *Shiratsugu* collided with each other, and the destroyer *Hatsukazu* sank. Omori was thoroughly shocked and quickly retired. Merrill declined to pursue, however, knowing that he had to reorganize his formation and fend off an enemy air strike at dawn. By steaming clockwise and firing every gun except the 8-inch batteries, the task group put up such a stiff antiaircraft fire when the Japanese aircraft appeared that the enemy lost several planes and managed only to inflict two bomb hits on the light cruiser *Montpelier.*

Merrill's victory at Empress Augusta Bay led the Japanese to shift cruisers and aircraft from Truk to Rabaul, but Halsey was apprised of this and ordered Sherman's carrier task force to coordinate a strike against Rabaul with New Georgia-based Navy aircraft. At Halsey's request, Nimitz sent carriers from the central Pacific to join Sherman's task force, and the reinforced formation appeared off Rabaul on 11 November. Of the 173 planes that the Japanese had shifted from Truk to Rabaul, 121 were destroyed during the ensuing air battle, and the Japanese now had to withdraw their cruisers from the area. While Rabaul-based aircraft no longer threatened Halsey's ships, the enemy did not abandon his Cape Torokino garrison. On the night of 23 November, off Cape St. George, Burke's five-destroyer formation came upon two enemy destroyers, which were leading three transport destroyers by about 13,000 yards. Again splitting his ships into two columns separated by 5,000 yards, he waited until he was within three miles of the enemy before launching his torpedo attack. Upon learning that both of the enemy's lead destroyers were damaged, he pursued the transports for another two hours and sank one more ship. The vast improvement in American night surface tactics illustrated in the battles of Empress Augusta Bay and Cape St. George meant the end to such engagements in the South Pacific; the Japanese simply could not replace the ships they were losing through attrition.

The western arm of the pincers reaching around Rabaul moved more slowly. Admiral Carpender, the 7th Fleet commander, was unable to stand up to MacArthur's foul-tempered chief of staff, Lieutenant General Richard Sutherland, so King replaced Carpender in July 1943 with Vice Admiral Kinkaid, a far more resolute figure. Kinkaid served under MacArthur as the theater's naval commander, but he reported to King on purely naval issues. King later admitted that he "didn't like the idea of leaving Navy forces under . . . MacArthur, who neither knew nor liked to work with the Navy or Marines," but Kinkaid was one of the Navy's most successful admirals and King trusted him completely. Kinkaid soon discovered that MacArthur's megalomaniacal ego was being nourished at his Australian headquarters by Sutherland's sycophantic praetorian guard. He effectively ignored Sutherland, tried to deal directly with MacArthur as much as possible, and insisted that in the future the Navy admiral command landing operations until the Army or Marine general established his headquarters ashore. Kinkaid was fortunate that his principal subordinate, Rear Admiral Daniel E. Barbey, who commanded the 7th Amphibious Force, was an extremely bright organizer and a gallant combat leader, and that he got along surprisingly well with MacArthur. Barbey directed more than fifty joint amphibious operations over the next two years, although he was invariably short of landing craft and other essential beaching equipment.[6]

With the Papuan Peninsula in Allied hands after the seizure of Buna in November 1942, the JCS on 29 March 1943 instructed MacArthur to dislodge the Japanese from strongpoints astride the Vitiaz Strait, which divided New Britain and New Guinea. In June, Barbey's amphibious vessels put ashore elements of Lieutenant General Walter Krueger's newly organized 6th Army on the Woodlark and Kiriwina islands to the southwest of Huon Gulf, and airfields were built there to support sweeps and bombing raids by General George C. Kenney's Southwest Pacific Army Air Force against Japanese bases at Madang, Wewak, and Rabaul.

With Rabaul now within easy range of American land-based aircraft, King proposed that the JCS reconsider the entire South Pacific campaign with a view toward shifting the weight of the advance into the central Pacific. Cooke pointed out that the Japanese on Rabaul would be enfeebled by the proposed movement of the new 5th Fleet into the Gilberts and Marshalls, thus alleviating the need for a frontal assault on New Britain. MacArthur protested that Rabaul was "a prerequisite to a move in force along the north coast of New Guinea," but his progress had been so slow that for the moment his strategic argument carried little weight in Washington. On the other hand, Roosevelt was worried that MacArthur might be a candidate for the presidency in 1944, and the last thing Marshall and King wanted was for MacArthur to return to Washington, so the JCS could never ignore him entirely. Because Marshall needed King's backing for a cross-Channel invasion of France, the Army chief of staff agreed with the Navy's plan to inaugurate the central Pacific offensive and encircle, rather than assault, the Rabaul stronghold.[7]

The JCS decision to open the central Pacific campaign caused MacArthur to fear that the Southwest Pacific route leading back to the Philippines via New Guinea would be passed by, and this concern energized his offensive. On 4 September 1943, Admiral Barbey, with eight destroyers, thirty-nine LSTs, and over fifty supporting vessels, landed Australian and American troops east of Lae. Gunfire from the American destroyers drove the Japanese defenders inland, while land-based Army Air Force pursuit planes covered the beachhead and the movements of the 7th Fleet. During the landing, two LSTs were struck by enemy bombs, but these vessels proved to be far sturdier than anyone expected and neither of them sank. After the lodgment to the east of Lae was secured on the 8th, Barbey sent his destroyers north to bombard Lae and so support the advance toward the town of the Australian troops. The Allied forces laying siege to nearby Salamaua finally took the offensive, and both Lae and Salamaua fell within the week. Moving with unaccustomed swiftness to exploit this enemy collapse, MacArthur told Barbey to take six destroyers and a task group of landing craft and put ashore an Australian brigade on Finschhafen before dawn on 22 October.

MacArthur now had the 1st Marine Division in Australia—reequipped after the victory on Guadalcanal—to send onto the western edge of New Britain to establish a bridge over the passages between New Guinea and New Britain. He intended to do this by taking Cape Gloucester, which commanded the Dampier Strait between Rooke Island and New Britain. On 15 December, Barbey's 7th Amphibious Force landed an Army brigade at Arawa Harbor on southern New Britain, and an airbase was quickly constructed there. Then, on the day after Christmas, the 1st Marine Division stormed ashore on the northwestern coast of New Guinea at Cape Gloucester. One new feature of this operation was the appearance of two LCI infantry landing craft fitted with launching rails, which were used to fire rockets at enemy positions ashore. This was an experiment that King assessed to be so successful that he ordered over 100 rocket-launching LCIs to be built and deployed to the Pacific. It took the Marines over two weeks to overcome fierce Japanese resistance to the Cape Gloucester landing, and the American lodgment was not secured until 16 January 1944. One of Barbey's major problems at Cape Gloucester was that Kenney's Army Air Force seldom provided combat air cover for his assault shipping anchorage. As a result, the destroyer *Brownson* was sunk there and three destroyers and two LSTs were badly damaged.

To complete the encirclement of Rabaul, MacArthur now decided to seize airfields in the Admiralty Islands in April 1944, but the date for this invasion was rashly advanced when an Army Air Force B-25 flew over the islands and reported that the Japanese garrisons there had been evacuated. Based on this fragmentary and incorrect intelligence, MacArthur instructed Barbey to land the 1st Cavalry Division on Los Negros Island on 29 February. However, the Americans ran into unexpectedly stiff resistance, which took nearly a month and very heavy casualties to overcome. Once Los Negros was secure, Kinkaid landed troops on Manus Island, the largest of the Admiralties, which was overrun on 3 April 1944. From the large natural harbor there, the 7th Fleet would stage its remaining operations along the northwest coast of New Guinea and prepare to move north to the Philippine Islands.

The encirclement of Rabaul and MacArthur's movements up the New Guinea coast convinced Admiral Soemu Toyoda, an aggressive strategist who had succeeded Koga in command of the Combined Fleet, that the Americans intended to concentrate their forces against New Guinea. Eager for another decisive battle, this time near Japanese airbases in the Palaus, Toyoda instructed Rear Admiral Naomasa Sakonju to take command of a task force composed of a battleship, two heavy cruisers, and five destroyers and escort a cruiser-destroyer formation that was to carry 2,500 troops from Mindanao to Biak. The order for this movement was translated by the code breakers in Hawaii, and the progress of Sakonju's task force was also reported to Pearl Harbor by the American picket submarines *Cabrilla* and *Bluefish*. Ironically, when the submarine *Rasher* sent off her own contact report on 3 June, the message was intercepted by a Japanese signal intelligence unit, and this caused Toyoda to order Sakonju to retire. Sakonju directed his transports to carry the troops to northern New Guinea, but the screening Japanese destroyers returned to Davao, where Commander John C. Roach in the submarine *Hake* was on station and waiting for their arrival. When the destroyer *Kazagumo* approached the harbor, Roach fired a salvo of torpedoes and sank her.

Stunned by this setback, Toyoda shifted a large number of land-based aircraft from the Marianas to the Carolines and the Palaus and reinforced the Japanese base at Hollandia on the New Guinea coast. He also ordered Admiral Sakonju to form a new task force consisting of two cruisers and six destroyers and to escort a second relief expedition to Biak. Kinkaid, apprised of this plan by radio intelligence, moved to block Sakonju by sending Rear Admiral Victor Crutchley's Allied cruiser-destroyer task group to a station northeast of Biak and by asking General Kenney to dispatch a land-based fighter-bomber flight to attack the enemy column at sea. Kenney's aircraft sighted Sakonju's ships before they reached the island and, using new skip-bombing tactics, damaged three destroyers and sank the destroyer *Harusame*. Sakonju pressed on nonetheless, only to run into Crutchley's superior formation, which shot up two more Japanese destroyers and compelled the relief expedition to withdraw once again.

At the same time, Commander Samuel D. Dealey in the submarine *Harder* was entering the Sibutu Passage just south of Tawitawi, and there he happened upon a supporting Japanese convoy of three transports and two destroyers. He decided not to take any chances with malfunctioning torpedoes, a problem that had plagued American submarine operations since the withdrawal from the Philippines. After being spotted by the destroyer *Minazuki*, Dealey allowed her to close to within 1,100 yards of his boat before sending her under with a brace of three torpedoes from the *Harder*'s stern tubes. He then waited until the *Hayanami* was within 650 yards of his submarine before firing a salvo of three torpedoes, which broke this enemy destroyer leader in half and sank her. Escaping through the Sibutu Passage, Dealey next took station off Tawitawi. The next evening, he sighted a pair of enemy destroyers and fired a four-torpedo spread, which sank the *Tanikaze*.

Admiral Toyoda was more than ever convinced by these actions that the Allies' main line of advance was against New Guinea and that he had to relieve Biak. The third relief force was escorted by the superbattleships *Yamato* and *Musashi*, five cruisers, and several minelayers, but it was screened by only seven destroyers—attrition having already reduced Japan's escort pool. Dealey in the *Harder* had returned to his station off Tawitawi on 10 June 1944 when the third Biak relief task force put to sea. The *Harder*'s attack against these ships was unsuccessful, but Dealey reported their movements to Pearl Harbor. Afraid that the Americans now knew that the superbattleships were steaming for Biak, Toyoda was stunned once more by the news on the evening of 12 June that American naval aircraft had attacked Japan's airbases on Saipan and Guam. This confounded his strategy. He canceled the Biak relief operation and started to shift forces to the central Pacific.[8]

MacArthur had already decided to advance on Hollandia, but it was 500 miles to the west of Saidor and 150 miles beyond the range of Kenney's land-based fighters. Since jumping to Hollandia meant bypassing enemy strongpoints at Madang and Wewak, MacArthur needed the support of Nimitz' Fast Carrier Task Force to give air cover to the Hollandia invasion. Nimitz was willing to support the operation but warned MacArthur that the carriers could not safely remain in the vicinity of Japan's airfields in the Southwest Pacific for more than four days. As a result, MacArthur chose to mount a simultaneous invasion of the island of Aitape, about 125 miles from Hollandia, from which the Army Air Force could support the main landings. B-25 bombers hit Hollandia on 30 March, destroying nearly 500 enemy planes, and on 22 April Americans landed on Aitape and easily overran it. That same day Rear Admiral Marc Mitscher's Fast Carrier Task Force provided air cover for Barbey's 7th Amphibious Force, which landed one Army division east of Hollandia and another division twenty-five miles to the west. Mitscher's carriers withdrew on 26 April, one day before Hollandia fell.

With no fast carrier task force dedicated to the Southwest Pacific, MacArthur had to move in measured paces dictated by the availability of flanking air bases. On 17 May, the 7th Amphibious Force landed a regimental combat team on the Toem-Wakde Islands, and Wakde's airstrip was soon readied to support the next stroke, the seizure of Biak. Early on the 27th, Rear Admiral William M. Fechteler's heavy cruiser-destroyer task group conducted a ferocious bombardment of Biak on Schouten Island off New Guinea's northcentral coast, and Fechteler put an Army division ashore later that morning. Ten thousand enemy troops opposed the invasion, and a full month of bitter fighting elapsed before American aircraft could operate from the Biak airstrips. With the seizure of Hollandia and Biak, and the unopposed landing in July on the Vogelkop Peninsula on the northwestern tip of New Guinea, the second phase of the campaign in the Southwest Pacific drew to a close. MacArthur was now only 500 miles south of Mindanao and his long-awaited return to the Philippines.

Chapter Eight

The Invasion of France and Germany
1944–1945

The invasion of France in 1944 grew out of Admiral Stark's Plan Dog concept of a Germany-first strategy; that strategy was embodied in the Rainbow Five, Sledgehammer, and Roundup war plans. Because of the defeat of the U-boat, the Allied invasion of Italy, and the Russian victory over the German Army at Kursk, "the tide of war has changed in our favor," wrote Admiral Leahy in the summer of 1943. "Unless we make some stupid tactical or strategic error, the Axis is certain to be defeated." As a result, the JCS were anxious to liberate France, enter Germany, and prevent the Red Army from overrunning central and western Europe. "The British seem to favor . . . an 'opportunist war,' that is, striking where and when the circumstances seem to dictate at a given moment," King mused. "Americans, on the other hand, like to plan and fight by that plan and not run a hit or miss war." In late 1943, for the first time in over a year, General Marshall and Admiral King agreed on a unified negotiating strategy and persuaded Roosevelt at last to insist that the British support a cross-Channel invasion in the spring of 1944.[1]

The decision to invade France was made at the Tehran Conference. Roosevelt and Churchill had tried more than once to convince Stalin to meet them at a summit conference, but he had refused until the Red Army took the offensive and so improved his bargaining position. In November 1943 the Big Three and their military staffs met in Tehran, the capital of occupied Iran.

There the Americans discovered that Stalin apparently believed that his army could defeat Germany only if the Allies invaded northern France. Playing on FDR's belief that the Soviet Union had to be appeased, the Russian dictator denounced the Allies for not establishing a second front earlier in the war. "It became apparent," King wrote, "that Stalin had no real understanding of the magnitude of operations that would be involved in crossing the English Channel [which] he thought . . . would be very much like crossing a large river, which the Russians had done many times." The Americans bridled at Stalin's accusations. But at the same time the JCS were, Leahy recorded, delighted that he was "insisting on a fixed, early date, Churchill [was] asking for delay, and the President [was] favorably inclined toward the Soviet proposal." Either Roosevelt used Stalin to lever Churchill into agreeing to a cross-Channel invasion, or he simply continued to cater to Soviet policy. In any case, before the Allies left Tehran, the British and Americans settled on Operation Overlord for May or June 1944. Only an invasion of France, they agreed at long last, would bring Hitler to book.[2]

Bypassing General Marshall, FDR selected General Eisenhower for the supreme command of all Allied forces in northwestern Europe—except those dedicated to the Combined Bomber Offensive—and Eisenhower in turn named British officers to Overlord's major tactical commands. General Montgomery, the most talented field commander in Europe, was to direct the land campaign, and Admiral Sir Bertram Ramsay, an unfortunate choice, was given overall command of the naval phase of the campaign, Operation Neptune. In 1943, the Admiralty had informed Admiral King that the Royal Navy could handle the Neptune operation by itself so long as the U.S. Navy provided all the large landing ships and most of the beaching craft, but when Eisenhower increased the landing force from three to five divisions in January 1944 the picture changed entirely.

Admiral King was not entirely pleased with these developments. He rightly believed that mixing multinational naval forces was a recipe for confusion and so proposed to establish an independent command, under Admiral Stark, to handle the American aspects of the Neptune landing. The Admiralty and the U.S. Army generals opposed this, however, so King decided that Stark's 12th Fleet would be responsible for logistical support for Overlord and that Rear Admiral Alan G. Kirk, a veteran of several

Rear Admiral Alan G. Kirk (*left*), Commander, U.S. Naval Forces, Overlord, confers with Lieutenant General Omar Bradley (*right*) and others soon after the D-Day landing, June 1944. Kirk later served as U.S. Ambassador to Belgium, the Soviet Union, and Taiwan.

amphibious operations, would be the U.S. Navy's operational commander. Kirk had visited Nimitz in Hawaii to study the South and Southwest Pacific landings in late 1943, but none of them had been conducted against beaches so heavily defended as he would find on Normandy's coast. Studying the Tarawa, Sicily, and Salerno operations did convince Kirk of the need for a massive, preinvasion bombardment, but Admiral Ramsay disagreed and foolishly refused to pass Kirk's proposals on to Eisenhower for consideration by the JCS. Eisenhower, a shameless devotee of Allied unity, would not overrule his British subordinate, the very situation King had feared. King was also annoyed that the Admiralty still had a large number of heavy carriers and modern battleships positioned at the Royal Navy's main northern fleet base at Scapa Flow and refused to assign them to Overlord, in spite of the fact that none of the major German ships could put to sea. According to Lieutenant George Elsey, neither King nor Kirk understood "why the British were so intimidated by the remnants of the German fleet." Admiral Cooke visited London in February to straighten things out, discussed the touchy bombardment problem with Churchill, Stark, and Kirk, and reported back to King that the Atlantic Fleet would have to provide a powerful battleship-cruiser gunfire support group for the landings. Cooke also enumerated other, unexpected calls on the Navy's resources. Eisenhower's agreement with Montgomery's plan to increase the size of the initial landing meant that King had to send two months of LST production to Europe that he had already scheduled for the Pacific theater.[3]

The Germans were constructing a strong Atlantic wall to defend northwest France, but a confusing chain of command and unresolved strategic conflicts played havoc with their plans. Field Marshal Gerd von Rundstedt, the overall German commander in France, wanted to defend the French coast with a powerful mobile reserve; Field Marshal Erwin Rommel, responsible for the Atlantic wall, intended to turn back an invasion on the beaches. The German Air Force, though crippled by the Combined Bomber Offensive, had its own independent headquarters in France. Admiral Theodor Krancke, the German Navy's coastal commander at Cherbourg, had at his disposal a handful of E-boats, a crude but effective radar network covering the eastern English Channel, and a few maritime patrol planes. Rommel expected the Allies to land in the vicinity of Calais—the landing site nearest to England's southern ports—but he did not neglect the Cotentin Peninsula. He posted some of his best troops and heaviest artillery at Le Havre and Cherbourg, and between these mooring points erected a thin crust consisting of mutually supporting heavy and medium artillery batteries and machine gun pillboxes. Normandy's tidal range and gradually sloping beaches led Rommel to reason that the assault troops would debark far from the shore, so he ordered the erection of three rows of mined, underwater obstacles parallel to the coast. Manpower and material shortages meant that he did not have time to finish his Atlantic wall, but it was nonetheless a formidable barrier to a successful invasion.

Overlord's success rested first and foremost on the Allied navies achieving strategic surprise in the English Channel on D-Day. Eisenhower accomplished this by landing near Cherbourg rather than Calais—although farther from England than Calais, the Cherbourg Peninsula was more lightly defended—and by crafting an elaborate deception that led the Germans to believe that the Allies were assembling a large army in southeastern England across from Calais. The Neptune plan called for landings at five beaches, from the base of Normandy's Cotentin Peninsula to a point fifty miles to the east. The British Eastern Naval Task Force under Rear Admiral Philip Vian would land three assault divisions on beaches designated Juno, Gold, and Sword, and to defend the northern flank of this lodgment from a German counterattack, two parachute divisions would be dropped around Caen to sever vital bridges. On the same day, Kirk's Western Naval Task Force was to land two U.S. Army divisions on beaches designated Omaha and Utah. In addition, two airborne divisions under Major General Matthew Ridgway were to drop inland from Utah Beach and cover the right flank of the American beachhead.

When it came to devising the landing plans, Kirk decided to assemble his transports 23,000 yards offshore, beyond the range of the coastal batteries. Vian chose to send his transports as close as 13,000 yards to the shore batteries—despite the fact that his battleships' counterbattery fire was less powerful than that of the U.S. Navy's Bombardment Group. Inshore from the assembly areas, Kirk planned to arrange his battleship and cruiser formation in two firing lines through which the American landing craft were to charge toward the beaches along channels that had been cleared and marked by minesweepers. Navy underwater demolition teams were trained for the dangerous job of clearing the beaches of obstacles before the assault troops reached the far shore. Admiral John Hall, the commander of the Omaha Force, established an immense training command on the English coast to prepare for the invasion, a herculean task he accomplished with unusual efficiency. Rear Admiral Don P. Moon, another veteran, arrived in England in the spring of 1944 to take command of the Utah Force.

The training for Overlord was marked by a great tragedy that exposed the utter folly of mixing the British and American navies in combat. Exercise Tiger, one of several large-scale rehearsals, was intended to train Moon's Utah Force by landing troops at Slapton Sands on Lyme Bay, a site that closely resembled Utah Beach. The initial landings took place on 27 April. That night Commodore Bernard Skahill's convoy of nine American LSTs stood out of Plymouth and steamed for Slapton Sands, where he was to land tanks, artillery, and a pair of floating causeways designed to span the lagoon and permit vehicles to drive off the LSTs directly onto the beach. The Royal Navy assigned two British escorts, one fast, one slow, to screen the LST convoy's movement, but the faster vessel collided with an LST one day before Exercise Tiger began and no replacement for her was found, even though the second escort, the old corvette *Azalea*, could make only 16 knots. Skahill in the *LST-515*, unaware of the reduced escort, unwittingly compounded the danger to his ships by issuing an operational order containing an error about the radio frequency the LSTs were to use to communicate with Plymouth naval headquarters and the screening *Azalea*.

In the early hours of 28 April, Skahill's formation was heading south toward Slapton Sands when the British destroyer *Onslow* reported to Plymouth that three fast German E-class patrol torpedo boats from Cherbourg were entering nearby Lyme Bay. Plymouth broadcast this report to the *Azalea*, but the corvette's skipper, wrongly assuming that Commodore Skahill was also listening, failed to relay it to the LST convoy. At 0200 one E-boat torpedoed the *LST-507* and her crew was forced to abandon ship before she sank. Skahill quickly ordered his ships to return fire and zigzag, but these measures were largely ineffective. Seventeen minutes later another E-boat torpedo hit the *LST-531*. She went down in ten minutes and took with her over 400 men. Very reluctantly Skahill now decided that the remaining LSTs should head for port. This order was ignored by Lieutenant John Doyle in the *LST-515*, who bravely remained behind to rescue some of the hundreds of American soldiers who were trying to stay afloat in the 40-degree water. The *Onslow* and several British motor torpedo boats hounded the E-boats back to Cherbourg, while the Americans counted a toll for the massacre of nearly 800 men. A Royal Navy inquiry into the tragedy cited poor communications and the *Azalea*'s lack of aggressiveness, but Rear

Admiral Arthur D. Struble, Kirk's chief of staff, held Moon to be at fault, and a few weeks later Struble loudly denounced Moon in the presence of Moon's staff. Moon became so depressed over the whole affair that he committed suicide later in the year. Moon was less to blame for the disaster in Lyme Bay, however, than the Royal Navy's wrongheaded policy of mixing national navies under combat conditions.

Other rehearsals went well, and General Eisenhower recorded in his diary in mid-May that "the smell of victory was in the air." Admirals Ramsay and Kirk had assembled "the greatest armada . . . the world had ever seen," and the invasion was to be covered by over 11,000 Allied warplanes. Three weeks later, however, storm clouds covered the French coast and grounded aircraft, and the waves tossed seasick soldiers about in their ships, so on 4 June when Kirk boarded his flagship, the cruiser *Augusta*, he was not certain when the invasion would get under way. Weather forecasts for the Channel were poor, and Eisenhower decided to delay the invasion for one day. He was tempted to postpone Overlord again on the morning of the 5th, but the admirals warned him that because the landing had to take place at low tide, for this was the only time when most of the beach obstacles would be visible, the invasion would have to be suspended for at least another two weeks should the Neptune Task Force not sail that day. Luckily, the Overlord chief meteorologist accurately predicted a break in the storm for the 6th. Eisenhower took a calculated risk and issued the fateful order to invade France.

It was ironic that this storm, which caused the Allies such great distress, worked to their advantage on D-Day. "The same foul weather that had tied knots in the Overlord schedule had put the enemy to sleep," wrote Rear Admiral Edward Ellsberg, one of Stark's most able subordinates. The storm forced the Germans to shut down their own routine air patrols and to cancel planned sweeps into the English Channel on the 5th, and it completely masked the southward movement of the invasion ships from England's ports that day. And when the German shore-based radars malfunctioned, it was attributed to the weather and they were not properly tended.[4]

Vian's British Eastern Task Force landed on Gold, Sword, and Juno beaches along a twenty-five-mile front to the east of the Cotentin Peninsula in the early hours of 6 June 1944. He created a forward bombardment group consisting of the battleships *Warspite* and *Ramillies*, twelve cruisers, and thirty-seven destroyers, and held the battleships *Nelson* and *Rodney* and three cruisers in strategic reserve. A British parachute division had been dropped inland from the invasion site the night before, and it took the Caen Canal and several bridges crossing the Orne River. The following morning the British landings proceeded without disruption for three reasons. First, Vian's Bombardment Group did not face a concentration of long-range coastal artillery, so he could station his battleships close to the beaches and provide the assault troops with highly accurate naval gunfire. Second, the British miscalculated the flood tide in their area. This error forced Vian to postpone the British landings for almost ninety minutes, a fortunate delay that allowed the Bombardment Group additional time to reduce the opposing German gun emplacements. Finally, only one German coastal defense division was in place in the British sector, and these tired, dispirited troops retired rapidly. On the other hand, Montgomery had intended to take Caen a day or two after landing, but the Germans encircled his lodgment and another month of bitter fighting elapsed before he entered this important inland stronghold.

The American landings encountered far greater resistance. At 0200 on 6 June, the Western Naval Task Force arrived at a position several miles off the Normandy coast without being sighted by the enemy. Kirk's Bombardment Groups consisted of three old battleships, nine cruisers, and twenty destroyers. The landing forces included 4 attack transports, 93 mine vessels, 175 LCTs, 55 LSTs, and over 100 other assorted supporting craft. The closer he got to the French coast, the more Kirk worried about straying into an enemy minefield. The Allies knew that the Germans had sown sixteen minefields in the Channel in 1943, but they were unaware that these mines' detonating mechanisms had badly deteriorated and that British air and naval patrols in the English Channel had prevented Admiral Krancke from conducting more minelaying operations in early 1944. "So to the incredulous amazement of all hands in the naval convoy, the invasion squadrons stood on across the Channel, undetected and unmolested in any way, either by torpedoes or by mines," Admiral Ellsberg recorded. As it neared the French coast, the invasion fleet steamed through channels in the offshore German minefields that Admiral Krancke had kept open for his own ships.

Moreover, the German Air Force on the French coast, consisting of fewer than 100 planes, was prevented from molesting the Allied task forces inasmuch as the Germans had to contend with over 11,000 front-line Allied aircraft, which easily established air superiority over the Channel, the beaches, and the landward approaches to the Allied lodgment. U.S. Navy B-24 Liberators based in Devon and Royal Air Force patrol bombers provided antisubmarine coverage over the Channel during the crossing and the following days over the Normandy shipping anchorages.[5]

Upon arriving off Utah Beach, Kirk divided the task force into Hall's Omaha Force, which steered due south, and the Utah Force under Moon, which headed to the southwest. Moon anchored his transports about 11,000 yards offshore and put his landing plan into effect. The first Americans to reach the shore were specially trained Navy underwater demolition teams whose job it was to clear paths through the dangerous beach obstacles. Thirty-four American and British minesweepers began to sweep narrow transit lanes from the transport anchorage to within one

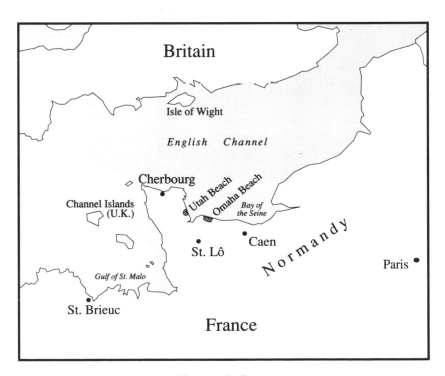

Normandy Coast

mile of two landing beaches, which Moon had designated Red and Green. Rear Admiral Morton Deyo in the battleship *Nevada* stationed his Bombardment Group between the transports and the shore batteries to cover the minesweepers and screen the transports from the German's long-range artillery. The *Nevada* and the heavy cruisers *Tuscaloosa* and *Quincy* took station about 11,000 yards from the beaches, while the destroyers formed a line about 5,000 yards opposite the nearest German strongpoints.

The battle for Utah Beach began at 0505 when the Germans sighted the minesweeping force and opened fire, forcing Moon to adjust his landing schedule and to commence firing half an hour later. The smoke-laying support aircraft had not arrived on time, so the destroyer *Corry*, riding at anchor in the narrow swept channel and unable to maneuver, came under concentrated fire from the Saint-Marcouf battery. She exploded and sank just before 0700, the victim of either enemy gunfire or a floating mine. The alertness of the crew and a heroic rescue effort by nearby ships and landing craft resulted in only thirteen men being lost. Already the assault troops had begun to climb down from the transports into their landing craft. To increase the firepower deployed by the assault waves as they advanced on the beach, the British had invented a special amphibious tank that was to be carried to a point about 5,000 yards offshore where it would be launched into the water. A canvas bloomer float was attached to prevent the tank from sinking on its run to the beach. At Utah Beach, twenty-eight British amphibious tanks were launched into calm water. All made it onto the beach and immediately opened fire in support of the first wave of assault troops. After the underwater demolition teams had punched pathways through the relatively modest beach obstacles, the first wave of assault troops waded ashore at 0630.

The swift and successful landings on Utah Beach were made possible in large measure by the highly accurate offshore gunfire support of Deyo's Bombardment Group. A direct hit around 0630 knocked out three powerful 210mm German guns near Saint-Marcouf, and the *Nevada* and the heavy cruisers suppressed the German batteries around Saint-Vaast-la-Hougue during a bombardment lasting fifty minutes. Nevertheless the "direct hits . . . did not permanently disable the batteries, which within a few hours or days were able to resume fire," Deyo admitted. Indeed, Moon later commented that "no battery could be considered destroyed unless captured." Despite considerable confusion when the troops were landed on the wrong beaches, the German defenders at Utah Beach were so weak and disorganized that, by the end of D-Day, elements of the 4th Division had cleared almost the entire six-mile-wide beachhead and had moved several miles inland. At 0200 that morning, the paratroopers had dropped inland, often up to fifty miles behind the German lines at Utah Beach, and on the evening of 6 June they linked up with the assault troops and effectively secured the beachhead's perimeter.

When the Western Task Force had parted at 0300, Admiral Hall continued a few miles southward until he reached a point slightly more than twelve miles off Omaha Beach. Although the invasion force had encountered no U-boats or E-boats in the English Channel, the storm meant that station-keeping in the convoy formations was difficult for the flat-bottomed, keelless landing craft, and when Hall's task force arrived off Omaha there were many stragglers. "We chased landing craft all over the coast of Normandy," recalled Captain Lorenzo Sabin. "Many of those landing craft were loaded with the most important personnel and equipment." Hall intended to remain just out of range of Pointe du Hoe, a promontory that jutted out into the Bay of Seine between Omaha and Utah beaches, where the Germans were thought to have positioned six 155mm guns. The minesweepers now steamed ahead of the main body and began to sweep an anchorage parallel to the coast for the Bombardment Group. Next, the minesweepers moved inshore to establish a cleared channel for the destroyers and the landing craft. Rear Admiral Carleton F. Bryant's Bombardment Group, consisting of the battleships *Texas* and *Arkansas*, three British light cruisers, one French light cruiser, nine American destroyers, and three British escorts, took station ahead of the transports about nine miles offshore. Along the 7,000-yard expanse of Omaha Beach, the Germans had established twelve strongpoints composed of mixed batteries totaling more than sixty light artillery guns. From four positions in the open field and eight thick concrete casemates, the Germans intended to cover the beach with a withering field of fire. Concrete pillboxes, tunnels, and an underground command post supported these strongholds. Moreover, concrete wing walls had been poured around the casemates to conceal the flashes of the larger guns, thus making them difficult to spot from the sea.[6]

The battleship *Texas*, sporting 14-inch guns, took station off Point du Hoe. The *Arkansas*, armed with 12-inch guns, took station off the less menacing Port-en-Bessin battery on the eastern side of Omaha Beach between the American and British beachheads. Kirk positioned the *Augusta* so that she stood opposite the middle of the American invasion beaches. A nearby Escort Force included six destroyers, two destroyer escorts, three French frigates, and thirty-six trawlers, mine vessels, and patrol craft. Once the Bombardment Group was in place, Kirk assembled a formation of eight destroyers and directed it to close to within 5,000 yards of Omaha Beach where they were to suppress fire against the landing craft from the German guns that sat on the cliffs above the landing sites. Blacked out in the darkness, it took about two hours for all these ships to reach their stations.

At 0550, when Piper Cubs from England appeared over the beaches to spot for the naval gunners, Bryant's Bombardment Group opened fire. The concern about gunfire support notwithstanding, the eleven destroyers fired only the equivalent of one full destroyer load before the troops hit Omaha Beach, and in short order heavy smoke and dust obscured the beach targets from the spotters overhead. Hall had anticipated this, and he ordered a halt to the firing at 0625 and waited for a wave of Army Air Force B-24 bombers to arrive on the scene and bomb the German defenses. To protect the assault troops from the German batteries, Lieutenant General Carl Spaatz, who commanded the Army Air Forces, promised Kirk that his bombers would appear over Omaha Beach at exactly 0630. The night before the invasion, however, Spaatz learned that low clouds were covering the beach, and, to avoid hitting the troops, he ordered his bombardiers to drop their 13,000 bombs inland instead. Eisenhower backed this decision. Unfortunately, Spaatz neglected to tell either Admiral Kirk or General Omar Bradley, who commanded the U.S. Army troops participating in the invasion, of this important change in his air plan. Kirk and Hall were counting on the Liberators to disrupt the German defenses, but "they didn't drop a bomb within three miles of my beaches," Hall complained bitterly.[7]

When the battleship fire was lifted around 0630, Hall established a line of rocket-firing LCTs about 3,000 yards offshore. While heavy seas and wakes from the surrounding landing craft made it difficult for these vessels to keep station, the LCTs launched 9,000 high-explosive 105mm rockets. They made a tremendous racket but overshot the beach defenses and caused little harm. The *Texas* then began to fire the first of 250 rounds at Pointe du Hoe to cover the landing of the Army Rangers, who were to scale the cliffs and overcome the German battery. While it was under fire from the *Texas*, the Pointe du Hoe battery never fired a round at the invasion force. To allow the Rangers to land, the *Texas* lifted her gunfire from Pointe du Hoe, but the strong tidal current pushed the landing craft to the left toward Pointe de la Percee, and the Rangers nearly landed there before discovering their mistake. As a result, the Rangers did not get ashore at Pointe du Hoe until 0710, but they discovered that Rommel had situated the larger guns inland and that the danger to the heavy ships from this long-range artillery had been exaggerated owing to poor tactical intelligence. Within moments, the Germans isolated the Rangers on the cliff, but the destroyers *Talybont* and *Satterlee* closed on the beach and fired at the defenders with their 5-inch main batteries and antiaircraft guns. After the Rangers took Pointe du Hoe, the destroyers *Barton* and *Thompson* took station nearby and assisted the Rangers in repulsing several German counterattacks.

Meanwhile, the fourteen Navy demolition teams were running into trouble on Omaha Beach. Hall had wanted to advance the assault troops' landing from 0630 to 0400 to give the teams more time in the darkness to neutralize the beach obstacles, but Ramsay vetoed this suggestion. Hall then ordered a section of LCTs to carry sixteen bulldozers up to the obstacles so that the engineer teams might use them and explosives to drive gaps through the obstacle rows. In this way the landing craft could penetrate the obstacle barrier and reach the beach safely on the flood tide. At 0630, Lieutenant Philip Bucklew, leading a column of LCTs, closed on his beach in the western sector and ordered his men to launch their British amphibious tanks. Most of them in this area reached the beach, but confusion reigned in both sectors. The LCTs got scattered, the bulldozers were late, and German artillery and machine gun fire decimated the underwater demolition teams, half of whom were casualties by 0630. The survivors managed to blow a total of six gaps to the beach in both sectors, but these openings were unmarked and many of the mined obstacles were intact when the first troop carriers began their run inshore.

Choppy water created more difficulties. Hall thoroughly distrusted the floating British amphibious tanks, but, recognizing the need for early close-in artillery ashore, he arranged for the LCTs to launch their tanks about three miles from the beach. Of sixty-four amphibious tank carriers, however, only twenty-nine launched their tanks; all but two of these were swamped, and the remaining LCTs had to run up as close as 1,000 yards from the beach before launching their tanks. Moreover, a large fraction of the heavily laden DUKWs—the small, unstable, Army-built landing craft—could not make the beach because of the high seas.

The first line of assault troops had boarded their small LCVP landing craft by this time, and the boat waves assembled about 4,000 yards offshore. A large number of LCVPs became misaligned, however, and many headed toward the wrong beaches. Closing the beach under intense German cannon, artillery, and machine gun fire, which they first encountered about 1,700 yards offshore, the landing craft grounded on sandbars 100 yards from the low-water mark, and it was here that the assault troops suffered their worst casualties. At 0630, although the presence of some of the unexploded underwater obstacles disrupted the movements of the landing craft, eight assault battalions were ready to hit the beach. Owing to an adverse current, however, the assault troops landed well to the east of their assigned areas, many of the small units were widely dispersed, and fewer than half of their ninety-six tanks scheduled to land were still running. At 0700, the second wave of assault troops arrived at the beach, and boat waves were expected every thirty minutes thereafter. By 0730, the landing on Omaha Beach was paralyzed in desperate confusion, and thirty minutes later the German command post reported that the defenders had stopped the invasion at the waterline.

By 0800, disabled LCVPs, wrecked tanks, crippled bulldozers, and dead and wounded soldiers were cluttering the beaches, just as the larger landing craft—the LCTs and the self-propelled Rhino Ferries—began to arrive. Thirty minutes later, the confusion had become so great that the Navy beachmaster, to prevent matters from deteriorating, suspended the landing of any more vehicle-bearing craft. With nowhere to go, over fifty LCTs and LCSs began to turn around in circles, trying to locate gaps in the beach obstacles, "just like a herd of stampeded cattle," according to Colonel Benjamin Talley, the assistant chief of staff of V Corps. Navy fire-control parties attached to the infantry units ashore were in an awful quandary because of the failure of communications with their ships and because many of these men got separated from the infantry commanders they were supposed to assist. Helpless to do anything without proper instructions from the fire-control parties, one destroyer division commander offshore recorded how "galling and depressing" it was "to lie idly a few hundred yards off the beaches and watch our troops . . . being heavily shelled and not be able to fire a shot to help them." But he had "no information as to what to shoot at" and could not see the German defenses ashore.[8]

The landing was in jeopardy. At 0930, Admiral Bryant warned Captain Harry Sanders, the commander of the destroyers, that the Germans were "raising hell with men on the beach," and this caused Sanders to instruct his ships to risk their bottoms by closing on the beach and providing more intense gunfire support to the assault troops. Within minutes, the destroyer *Carmick* closed the shore, swung broadside, opened fire, and turned the German emplacements at Les Moulins into rubble. The rest of the destroyers followed, often firing from less than 900 yards offshore, their shells whizzing just a few feet over the heads of the troops on the beach. It felt as though the "destroyers were almost on the beach themselves, firing away at pillboxes and strongpoints," recalled Lieutenant William Wade. Although the destroyers soon knocked out a large number of machine gun pillboxes, they had trouble registering their fires against the deadly, well-concealed German mortars, whose positions were not exposed when they lobbed their explosives at the American assault troops. Despite the gallant destroyers' heroic effort, at 1030 General Bradley asked Hall if the issue was still in doubt and began to discuss shutting down Omaha Beach and shifting all of the American forces to Utah. Admiral Kirk dismissed Bradley's idea as the product of unreasoned panic, and Admiral Hall, a battered veteran of several landings, assured the general that some confusion on the beach was almost inevitable.[9]

At 1030, when the battle for the western sector of Omaha Beach hung in the balance, Lieutenant Sidney W. Brinker in the *LCT-30* closed the beach and saw that other landing craft nearby were paralyzed. Two waves of LCTs were languishing off the beach, unable to disgorge their tanks in the rough seas. Turning his landing craft toward the beach, Brinker drove at full speed directly into the dangerous obstacles at the head of one of the cleared channels. With all weapons firing from the front, the *LCT-30* beached, disembarked its troops, and continued to fire. Within minutes, all the German guns within range were silenced. Brinker's heroic maneuver illustrated that the American landing craft could successfully ram the obstacles, beach, and cover the infantry, and other landing craft soon followed his example.

At 1137, Hall received word from the Omaha beachmaster that German guncrews were beginning to surrender. The battle continued throughout the morning until all the German guns up one western draw were captured. This then became the main funnel for movements of troops from the landing craft to the beach. Breakout from the beach areas was achieved under the cover of gunfire from destroyers, which created exit lanes through which the soldiers could storm. Although German artillery fires still covered all the exits from the beach, these guns were slowly being disrupted or silenced. However, at 1200 the assault troops were still bottled up at Villeneuve Draw. The *Texas* was nine miles out, having just lifted her fire from Pointe du Hoe, while the destroyer *McCook* was just offshore. A desperate Navy shore fire-control party called for gunfire from the *Texas* against the German battery covering the Villeneuve Draw, and in response four salvoes of high, plunging fire forced the German gunners to stumble out of their emplacements and surrender. One hour later, the *Texas* brought her guns to bear on the casemated Pointe de la Percee battery on the western flank of Omaha Beach, a bombardment so furious that it blasted off the face of the cliff and sent all the German guns tumbling into the ocean. As a result of these well coordinated combined-arms actions, when night fell over Omaha Beach the Americans clung by a toehold to a cramped position out of which the troops would have to fight the next day. The British, who provided most of the Allied intelligence on German defenses in France for Overlord, had badly underestimated the enemy's strength on Omaha Beach. "All of our intelligence indicated that we would run into static troops who had been stationed there for a long time," Hall recalled, and he was therefore surprised to discover that "they had moved the 352nd German division, . . . a very fine division, and it had been sent in there [for maneuvers] a few weeks or a few days before the attack, and we ran head-on into them." [10]

The invasion of Normandy surprised Hitler. It also led him to the erroneous conclusion that Eisenhower had executed a feint by landing at the base of the Cotentin Peninsula and that the Allies still intended their major blow to fall near Calais. As a result, Hitler refused for far too long to shift a powerful Panzer corps from Calais to Normandy, thus weakening Rommel's attempt to organize a counteroffensive against Montgomery's lodgment. Hitler did admit early on that the "only way possible" to throw back the Allies was "to eliminate or neutralize the enemies' naval forces, particularly his battleships," but the Germans simply did not possess the means to do this. In spite of Hitler's analysis, Admiral Dönitz reacted with unusual lethargy to the invasion. It was now clear that the German Navy had invested far too much in offensive capital ships and U-boats and not nearly enough in prosaic, defensive minelaying craft. Three Le Havre–based E-boats dashed toward the Bay of the Seine and sank the Norwegian destroyer *Svenner*, the only Allied ship lost to naval action on the 6th. Fifteen Cherbourg-based E-boats sortied for the invasion anchorage, but the poor weather forced these small craft to turn back, and the E-boats based in Brittany and on the Bay of Biscay did not have enough cruising range to reach the Cotentin Peninsula. British, Canadian, and Polish destroyers sank or damaged four German destroyers off Brest on the night of the 9th, the largest purely naval action of the entire event. In an act of desperation, Dönitz dispatched suicide torpedo boats against the Bombardment Group, but they inflicted only minor damage on four cruisers. And none of these operations disrupted the landings or interfered with the Allied navies' logistical support.[11]

Supporting inland operations now became the Allied navies' main task. Quite belatedly, Admiral Ramsay asked the British Bomber Command on 14 June to raid the nearby German naval base at Le Havre. This operation and one the next day against Boulogne destroyed most of the German fleet in the vicinity of the Allied lodgment. Dönitz recalled a number of U-boats from the North Atlantic and other stations, organized a counteroffensive, and over the next few weeks flung a total of fifty-eight submarines against the Allied invasion force, but land-based patrol bombers over the Bay of Biscay and naval aircraft and escorts assigned to antisubmarine patrols in the English Channel successfully barred German access to the waters off the Normandy coast. The menace of German mines, however, was constant, and the

Western Task Force did not operate nearly enough minesweepers. On 7 June, a delayed-action sonic mine sank the destroyer *Susan B. Anthony* off Omaha Beach, and the following day a collision with a German mine sent under the destroyer escort *Rich*. Although the German Air Force did not distinguish itself during the invasion, Berlin did transfer over 1,000 planes from Germany and Italy to France. On the night of the 7th, an enemy attacker appeared over the Allied anchorage and delivered a glide bomb that sank the destroyer *Meredith*. Another sortie the following day sent a *Liberty* ship under. Fortunately, after this the Army Air Force paid greater attention to maintaining constant air coverage over the invasion anchorages.

The Neptune forces put 132,000 men ashore in less than thirteen hours on 6 June. Within a week, this figure increased to 250,000. Montgomery's subsequent advance into the deep hedgerow country around Caen was slowed by strong German resistance, but in the west General Bradley sent a corps across the base of the Cotentin Peninsula and laid siege to Cherbourg on 18 June. Deyo's battleships and cruisers assisted with these operations, providing naval gunfire support to the advancing troops and preventing the Germans from establishing defensive strongholds near the coast. American battleships and heavy cruisers exchanged fires with German tanks, artillery, and, on occasion, enemy infantry. Naval gunfire against armored formations was especially successful, not because it destroyed a large number of German tanks but because it stripped the tanks of their supporting infantry, repair crews, communications, and engineers, and made it hazardous for the vehicles to concentrate for a counterattack.

Von Rundstedt understood that Germany's coastal defenses had to contain and annihilate the beachhead inasmuch as the battleships' gunfire could halt the movement of his tanks and field artillery toward the Allied lodgment, but the Germans no longer possessed the resources to prevent an enemy breakout. "The guns of most enemy warships have so powerful an effect on areas within their range that any advance into this zone dominated by fire from the sea is impossible," he and Rommel told Hitler on 10 June. Five days later, however, the American drive inland had progressed beyond the range of the large naval guns. To the north at Caen, where the Germans concentrated most of their tanks, offshore naval gunfire was so intense that von Rundstedt asked Hitler for permission to withdraw beyond the range of the battleships. Hitler instructed Rundstedt that a "tenacious defense" would prevent "further breakthrough by the enemy," but the German troops were finally forced to pull back and all Allied ground forces had advanced out of the range of the heavy naval guns in mid-July.[12]

One of Admiral King's contributions to the original Overlord plan was to call for the early seizure of Cherbourg and three other French ports—Brest, L'Orient, and St. Nazaire—all of which had been in French hands during World War I. The capture of these German naval bases would not only shut down U-boat operations in the Bay of Biscay but also provide important ports for Allied shipping. King also envisioned the use of Quiberon Bay, situated between Brest and L'Orient, as a vast anchorage for Admiral Stark's 12th Fleet. Kirk had created a bombardment group of three battleships, four cruisers, and eleven destroyers, and at 1200 on the 25th, they blasted an 11-inch enemy coastal battery near Cherbourg and reduced other isolated enemy pockets. The Germans scored one hit on the *Texas* and one hit against a screening destroyer, but they inflicted little damage. After bitter fighting, Cherbourg fell to the U.S. Army the following day, while Montgomery's British and Canadian troops took Caen on 9 July. However, the Germans had so successfully mined the harbor and destroyed the docks, piers, and warehouses before surrendering Cherbourg that, although unloading over the beach began immediately and the first freighter entered the harbor on 16 July, Rear Admiral John Wilkes' Navy and Coast Guard salvage crews and Seabees could not clear the port completely for Allied shipping until 7 August.

To support Montgomery's drive inland, Admiral Ramsay had put in motion Operation Mulberry, a scheme to create two large artificial ports, one at Gold Beach, the other at Omaha. Churchill had lent his support to the Mulberry project. So had Roosevelt, who was fond of eccentric ideas and who later enjoyed regaling the White House press corps with details of the contraptions. The 1.5-million-ton, 400-section Mulberries arrived off the French coast at dawn on 7 June. Old merchantmen, called Gooseberries, were lined up offshore and sunk, thus creating an artificial breakwater. Ten massive concrete caissons were sunk closer to the shore, but their top sections remained above the water so that an LST could tie up and unload the tank deck and main deck simultaneously. When Hall "first saw the plans for these monstrosities," he told Ramsay that the Mulberry concept was "poorly conceived . . . and unnecessary and completely useless." Ramsay ignored his objections and unstintingly poured resources into the project. On 17 June, after ten days had been spent erecting these harbors, they were ready to function. After only two days, however, a storm ripped down from the northeast. By English Channel standards it was mild, with the winds never even reaching gale force. Mulberry B, off Gold Beach, was sheltered by the cape to the north and had a good lee against the wind, but off Omaha Beach, Mulberry A, wholly exposed, was nearly destroyed. Not only was it abandoned, Hall complained, but "the wreckage cluttered up the beaches tremendously." He "could never see the use [for the Mulberries] when you could beach an LST, dry it out, lower the ramp, let them drive off; then float the LST on the incoming tide and withdraw it. That's what LSTs were built for, and they [the British] had to go into this other scheme." Indeed, "the Normandy beaches were so flat," according to Lieutenant George Elsey, that "it was not necessary to use lighters or barges." More supplies actually came over the beach using LSTs than the Mulberries could have handled.[13]

With the seizure and reconstruction of Cherbourg under way, General Bradley's American Army group broke out of the Cotentin Peninsula and reached St. Lô on 18 July. A week later, he pierced German resistance at Avranches, and by 1 August enemy resistance in the area had crumbled. The road to Paris was open, thus menacing Germany's grip on Belgium and the gateway to the Rhine. As a result of the development of the port of Cherbourg and the rapid movement of the Allied armies in France, however, King's plan to exploit several other French coastal ports was abandoned.

Knowing there was a shortage of landing craft for Overlord, Eisenhower had convinced the JCS in February 1944 to delay the invasion of southern France, codenamed Anvil-Dragoon, until the late summer. Before and after the landing in Normandy, Churchill tried by persuasion and bluster to convince Eisenhower to cancel the Anvil landings and instead to press north in Italy up to the Po River Valley. He also wanted to land near Trieste at the head of the Adriatic and send an Anglo-American army north through the Balkans to liberate southeastern Europe in advance of the Russians. Britain's chiefs of staff were upset with Churchill's Trieste scheme, although they also disliked the Anvil plan. Their preference was to batter up the rugged, well-defended Italian peninsula. General Marshall and Admiral King had long secretly suspected that postwar international politics would be greatly influenced by the boundaries of the respective Allied and Soviet occupation zones, although Roosevelt insisted that he could manage Stalin through personal diplomacy and clung to his unthinking pro-Soviet policy to the end. Nonetheless, King and Marshall wanted American and British troops to occupy as much of industrial northwest Europe as possible before the Germans collpased. United against getting American forces immersed in the Balkans and disenchanted with the futile Italian campaign, the JCS vetoed both projects, thus allowing the invasion of southern France to proceed according to Eisenhower's timetable. Marshall intended to establish a third army group under General Jacob Devers on Eisenhower's right, or southern, flank and so support the main Allied drive into Germany. King stressed the need to seize the port of Marseilles to supply the Allied army in France and reasoned that it would be some time before Montgomery's army wrested control of the large Belgian and Dutch ports from the Germans.

Admiral H. Kent Hewitt, the master of shore-to-shore landings, commanded Anvil-Dragoon. His Western Naval Task Force was composed mostly of American ships and landing craft from his 8th Fleet, in addition to a large number of British, French, and Canadian vessels. To secure his objectives, Marseilles and Toulon, Hewitt selected five beaches along the coast of Provence between the Gulf of Fréjus and St. Tropez. The Germans had long feared an Allied invasion of southern France, and the beach defenses, although not so formidable as those of Normandy, were not to be taken lightly. In this general area, the German garrison included 30,000 troops near the landing zone, and another 200,000 men stationed in neighboring provinces, but the German collapse in northern France acted as a suction pump on these forces. Along the beaches the Germans had buried thousands of land mines, and the landing zone was defended by light and heavy artillery protected by concrete casemates, batteries that included some large naval guns the Germans had removed from captured French warships in nearby Toulon. To suppress the Germans' heavy artillery, Admiral Deyo organized a Gunfire Support Group consisting of the veteran battleships *Nevada*, *Texas*, and *Arkansas*, the British battleship *Ramillies*, and the French battleship *Lorraine*. In addition, Deyo could call on fires from the three heavy cruisers *Augusta*, *Quincy*, and *Tuscaloosa* and an assortment of various Allied destroyers, escorts, and gunboats.

At 0315 on 15 August, one American parachute division was dropped by 400 Army Air Force transport planes behind the German lines to isolate the Anvil beachhead. Soon after, Rear Admiral Lyal Davidson's Sitka Force landed American and French commandos who seized the small island of Iles d'Hyères and established a position on the road from Toulon that blocked enemy movements to the main beachhead. Then, at 0600, Deyo's Gunfire Group opened up on the German beach defenses, an Escort Carrier Force under Rear Admiral Calvin Durgin in the carrier *Tulagi* sent aircraft aloft to spot the fall of the shells, and Navy aircraft bombed and strafed several key German inland positions. At about 0730, the air strikes ended, the fire support destroyers closed on the coast and opened up, and the landing craft started their run down the boat lanes to the beaches. The Alpha Force landed over 16,000 men and 2,150 vehicles and took Cap Camarat in a nearly flawless exercise of amphibious skill. With about the same number of men attacking the more heavily defended beaches from Pointe des Issambres to the Golfe de la Napoule, Rear Admiral Spencer S. Lewis' Camel Force stormed ashore under the withering covering fire of Deyo's battleships, fire that continued until 0800. Twice, nearby, Rear Admiral Bertram J. Rodgers' Delta Force put ashore those numbers of Allied men and vehicles without mishap.

Stunned by the ferocity of this textbook landing, the German defenses soon gave way, and by the end of the first day of operations, Hewitt had accomplished all his objectives. Lieutenant General Alexander Patch's 7th Army was reunited within a week with General DeLattre de Tassigny's French corps into an independent army group that came under General Devers on 2 September. Devers took Marseilles and Toulon, then stormed north up the Rhone Valley, rolling up the German defenders and soon linking up with the right flank of General Bradley's Army group. Eisenhower, now in overall command of three great Army groups, decided to advance on Germany along a broad front stretching from Belgium in the north to Alsace-Lorraine in the south. The success of Overlord, Anvil-Dragoon, and a punishing Soviet summer offensive meant that the days of Hitler's Third Reich were clearly numbered. The Navy had once again played a vital role in upsetting Europe's balance of power.

Chapter Nine

The Pacific Submarine Offensive
1942–1945

Submarines operating independently played an important role in the Pacific war. As part of the sweeping offensive that initiated the battles in the Pacific, the Japanese brought their submarines into action quickly but could neither sustain nor exploit an early momentum. Before the attack on Pearl Harbor, nine large, oceangoing I-type Japanese submarines were positioned along the Pacific coast from the mouth of the Strait of Juan de Fuca to San Diego. I-boats also transported to Oahu five converted midget boats that were to attack any ships that tried to escape from Pearl Harbor, but these small raiders accomplished nothing and nearly gave away the Japanese plan on the morning of 7 December 1941. When the Japanese carriers retired, they left behind one oceangoing submarine off Hawaii, and before the year was out I-boats in the eastern Pacific sank five American merchantmen and damaged five more. In early 1942, an I-boat shelled Vancouver Island off the coast of British Columbia, and another shot up a Santa Barbara, California, oil refinery. This served to convince Americans that resident Japanese aliens and Japanese-Americans on the West Coast had committed espionage and contributed to Roosevelt's decision that spring to have the Army intern them in large inland relocation camps. Admiral Nimitz wanted to expel all Japanese-Americans from Hawaii, but King told him that this was impractical.

The Navy's understrength Western Sea Frontier—a backwater of the 1941 Europe-first strategy—responded slowly to Japan's submarine challenge. Like other naval commands, the Western Sea Frontier was short of destroyers and other escorts and hamstrung by the lack of reliable radio intelligence about enemy submarine deployments and strategy. Radio direction finding was equally inefficient. In addition, King had ordered the Sea Frontier and the Pacific Fleet to organize ocean escort groups on the West Coast and establish convoys for all troop and other shipping bound to and from Hawaii and the South Pacific, an enormous drain on Navy resources from San Diego to Bremerton to Hawaii. One slow convoy, codenamed Bobcat, consisting of two transports and four cargo ships carrying troops and equipment to Bora-Bora, where they were to establish an important fueling station, was escorted from Panama into the South Pacific in late January by two cruisers and four destroyers. The escorts did not return to Pearl Harbor until mid-February. Because of the U-boat campaign on the East Coast and troop movements to Britain, King had few destroyers to transfer from the Atlantic to the Pacific, with the result that a large fraction of American cargo shipping in the eastern Pacific was completely exposed to enemy submarines for many months.

The Japanese failed entirely to exploit this rare opportunity. Unprepared to operate several thousand miles from their nearest base at Kwajalein in the Marshalls, Japan's submarine skippers soon found that neither their peacetime training nor their battle doctrine had prepared them for long-range antishipping patrols. Aggressive escorts and antisubmarine sweeps found the I-boats extremely vulnerable because Japanese submarines were not fitted with radars and operated primitive sonars. Nor did the I-boats receive much attention or support from Admiral Yamamoto and his battleship-oriented subordinates, who failed to appreciate that their small submarine arm was fully capable of attacking cargo shipping in the eastern Pacific. Instead, the Japanese, like some U.S. Navy men, wanted their submarines to sink only battleships, carriers, and cruisers, but when the I-boats could not locate or hunt down any American warships in the eastern Pacific during the first few months of the war, Japan's high command resignedly ordered them to reconnoiter and harass the enemy. As a result, the volume of radio transmissions to and from each Japanese submarine increased substantially and provided U.S. Navy cryptanalysts and radio direction-finding stations with an intelligence cornucopia. Following a brief and unsuccessful campaign, the Japanese were forced to retire from the eastern Pacific.[1]

Before they went to war, the Japanese had neglected to consider seriously the enormous strains that a protracted American antishipping campaign might impose on their economy. Japan's industry depended on iron ore and coal from Manchuria, rubber from Indochina, and oil from the Dutch East Indies, but prewar Japan exported few manufactured goods to Southeast Asia or the South Pacific. As a result, Tokyo could devise no satisfactory shipping system to prevent the inevitable movement of a large number of empty freighters and tankers between these points. The establishment of important, far-flung military outposts in China, Southeast Asia, the South Pacific, and the central Pacific tested Japan's limited shipping pool and increased the exposure of her undefended shipping routes. Nor did the Japanese bring their freighters and tankers under an organized escort-of-convoy system until April 1942, when minor losses prodded the Navy minister into assembling an escort fleet to cover the movement of convoys between Japan and China and Formosa and, later, between the Home Islands and the Philippines, Vietnam, and Thailand. The Combined Fleet could spare few destroyers for ocean escort duty, however, and the new escort command made the wrong decision to stick to large numbers of small convoys consisting of fewer than ten ships defended by one or two escorts. This was an utterly inefficient way to distribute scarce escorts. Moreover, the U.S. Navy's ciphers confounded the skills of enemy code breakers, and so Japan's escort command was unable to respond to the Pacific Fleet's antishipping campaign with a counterstrategy of evasive routing. The entire Japanese escorted convoy system represented only a modest improvement over independent routing and brought with it a new merchant shipping code, known as the Maru code, used to broadcast instructions to convoys and vessels sailing independently. This code, containing transit routes and destinations and alterations to cruising schedules, was one of the weaker components of a frail, vulnerable shipping system.

American submarine doctrine and strategy—theretofore largely dedicated to supporting fleet operations—was overhauled in 1941 by Admiral Stark, the prewar CNO. Though he expected the Pacific Fleet Battle Force to remain on the defensive as required by Plan Dog, he intended that "as many United States submarines as possible shall be used on the strategic offensive, and be operated in far distant waters where the greatest density of enemy naval operations will occur." In the Rainbow Five War Plan issued later that year, Admiral Ingersoll, the Assistant CNO, laid down for the first time the notion that "offensive tasks against Japanese commerce and shipping" were "largely tasks for submarines," and the British were told in early 1942, after Admiral King became CNO, that he did not intend to have his attack submarines tied down to fleet operations. Compunctions about attacking defenseless transports and cargo shipping had attended interwar American diplomacy and naval policy, but outrage over Pearl Harbor was a liberating balm for a wartime Navy that cast these scruples overboard with the other luxuries of peace.[2]

FDR alluded to the Navy's new antishipping strategy in his State of the Union address on 7 January 1943 when he announced that the United States had, after Pearl Harbor, "set as a primary task in the war of the Pacific a day-by-day and week-by-week destruction of more Japanese war material than Japanese industry could replace." Lamentably, from the withdrawal from the Philippines in late 1941 through the Battle of Midway, the Pacific Fleet's submarines accomplished very little. The tide did not turn until later that year. Japan's high command had anticipated the loss of the 800,000 tons of shipping that American submarines and aircraft sank during 1942, and the effects of this attrition did not influence Tokyo's strategy until Yamamoto discovered late that year that he did not possess enough transports or freighters to continue offensive operations in the Lower Solomons and would, therefore, have to withdraw from Guadalcanal.[3]

The Pacific Fleet's submarines found their best hunting grounds in 1942 in Japan's Empire waters, the East China Sea, and the shipping lanes around Formosa, areas where fifty-four American war patrols accounted for eighty-one Japanese ships, half the total sunk that year. "A large part of this task has been accomplished by . . . our American submarines who strike on the other side of the Pacific at Japanese ships—right at the very mouth of Yokohama," Roosevelt told Congress. Admiral Cooke, the Navy's chief planner and one of its earliest submariners, predicted in 1942 that his beloved boats would account for at least

4 million tons of Japanese shipping within two years, but he was bitterly disappointed by their dismal performance in 1942. Although frustrated by setbacks for a year after Pearl Harbor, the Pacific Fleet's submariners were prepared in early 1943 to lash back at the Japanese with a staccato of savage blows.[4]

Recovering from the Japanese offensive after Pearl Harbor, reorganizing the Submarine Force, and commencing a campaign against enemy shipping tested the Navy's resources in 1942. The Asiatic Fleet's submarines, operating from Manila when the war broke out, were unable to prevent or disrupt the Japanese invasion of Luzon, and in December 1941 Admiral Hart ordered Rear Admiral William Purnell to pull back his submarines to Surabaja and harry the enemy's movement into the Dutch East Indies. With the collapse of the American–British–Dutch Area command after the Battle of the Java Sea, King might have withdrawn the Asiatic Fleet's submarines to Pearl Harbor, but he decided instead to shift Purnell's nineteen boats to a new base at Fremantle on Australia's west coast, from where they were to attack Japanese shipping in the Tonkin Gulf, the Dutch East Indies, and the southern Philippines. King's immediate purpose was to slow down the velocity of Japan's offensive, not to interdict shipping between Japan and her imperial outposts. For several reasons, this strategy failed. Malfunctioning torpedoes and inexperienced, unaggressive skippers were in part responsible for the poor performance. The distances between Fremantle and Pearl Harbor and the West Coast were so great that supporting these operations greatly strained the Pacific Fleet's resources. And with only nineteen submarines, Purnell could maintain no more than five or six on all of the various distant patrol stations at one time.

The reorganization of the Pacific theaters in April 1942 forced King to rearrange his submarine commands concurrently. Purnell returned to Washington to serve as Assistant CNO, one of the most important billets in the wartime Navy, and King selected Vice Admiral Fairfax Leary to take command of the newly created Southwest Pacific Naval Forces and Rear Admiral Charles Lockwood, a talented submariner, to direct operations from Fremantle. Soon after arriving in Australia, Lockwood decided that the reason the Asiatic Fleet's submarines "didn't get more enemy ships" could be ascribed to a "bad choice of stations . . . , bad torpedo performance, in that they evidently ran much too deep and had numerous prematures . . . , [and] lack of or misunderstanding of aggressiveness." One skipper reported that "he thought a sub should never 'pick a fight with a destroyer.'" Lockwood would change all that. King also established a second Southwest Pacific submarine command at Brisbane, on Australia's east coast, to reassure the Australians of American support and punish Japanese shipping in the South Pacific. For this command he selected Rear Admiral Ralph Christie, who arrived in Brisbane with eleven S-class submarines on 15 April. It was perhaps natural that Lockwood and Christie would wrangle over resources, but neither Leary nor his successor in the Southwest Pacific naval command, Rear Admiral Arthur S. Carpender, seemed able to resolve these disputes. Admiral Kimmel's relief hard upon the Pearl Harbor fiasco brought out to the Pacific theater Admiral Nimitz, another veteran submariner. The early war patrols from Pearl Harbor were as unproductive as those in the Southwest Pacific, however, so in April 1942, Nimitz reorganized the Submarine Force and selected Rear Admiral Robert English, an experienced submariner, for this command.[5]

Sorting out effective skippers was a more dogged problem. The number of submarines based in Australia and Pearl Harbor doubled in 1942, and again in 1943, an expansion that moved up many of the best submarine skippers to squadron commands, training billets, and vital staff positions. Of those who remained in command, many were too old, too timid, or very unlucky. The earliest example of the "skipper problem" involved Commander Morton C. Mumma, who brought the *Sailfish*—the ex-*Squalus*, which had gone down off Cape Cod in 1939 and had been refloated, repaired, and renamed—out to the Asiatic Fleet in the Philippines in 1941. She was patrolling off Vigan on 13 December when Mumma sighted two Japanese destroyers, dived to 100 feet, fired two torpedoes, and rode out a ferocious counterattack of upward of twenty depth charges. Captain John Wilkes at Asiatic Fleet headquarters in Manila was astounded when he received a message from the *Sailfish* announcing that Lieutenant Commander Hiram Cassedy, the executive officer, had taken command of the submarine because Mumma was "breaking down." Although extreme, Mumma's crackup was by no means unique. Most U.S. Navy submarine skippers had never heard a close depth charge, knew little about Japanese antisubmarine tactics, and worried excessively about enemy aircraft. Some younger submariners have claimed that interwar training was unrealistic, but no evidence supports this view.

There were other problems. The radar installed in prewar submarines was so primitive that Lieutenant Richard Laning claimed that early in the war it acted as "a most effective beacon to attract Japanese planes while we charged batteries [on the surface] at night."

The appearance of advanced radar sets for the Submarine Force coincided with the arrival of a new sonar system that considerably improved underwater evasive maneuvers. Sonar was the eyes of the submariner, as well as of his opponents, and had evolved considerably from the primitive hydrophones used during World War I. Even with this early passive listening gear, two or three escorts could, using triangulation, often pinpoint the location of a U-boat lurking between them. The first echo-ranging sonar—which issued a sound impulse and measured the time it took to return to its source—might be found in a few American submarines by 1930. Perfecting active sonar had to await the subsequent discovery by Woods Hole Oceanographic Institute scientists that the sea was divided by thermoclines, layers of water with varying temperatures, and that sound often bounced off thermo-

The 1,526-ton *Harder* (SS-257), a typical 312-foot-long *Gato*-class fleet submarine of World War II, enters Mare Island Navy Yard, California, on 19 February 1944. Laid down only days before the attack on Pearl Harbor, she entered the fleet exactly one year later under the command of Commander Samuel D. Dealy. The *Harder* distinguished herself during five unusually successful war patrols in the western Pacific. On 23 August 1944, while on her sixth patrol, she was sunk with the loss of all hands, after a depth charge attack by a two-ship Japanese escort force.

U.S. Naval Institute

clines much as it did off solid objects. Simple guesswork had dictated underwater evasion maneuvers until the arrival later in the war of the new bathythermograph. This device, which measured the temperature of the surrounding seawater, was originally intended to help the diving officer maintain the boat's trim. However, the bathythermograph also identified thermoclines, which deflected echo-ranging sonar and so could be used to mask the submarine's presence from an attacker's pings. "Submariners soon learned to go deep and get below a [thermal] layer to screen their movements while evading a surface pursuer," recalled Lieutenant Commander Paul R. Schratz.[6]

An important result of these observations was the invention of the Fathometer, a sonic depth finder, a device that was necessary if submarines were to survive depth-charge attacks by sonar-guided enemy ships. The Navy had equipped only about 170 destroyers and submarines with sonar in 1941, but within four years sonar was installed in all American warships, including submarines. In short, the development of modern echo-ranging sonars on the eve of World War II enhanced the submarine's lethality but also endangered it, since the enemy had access to sonar as well.

The introduction of improved sonar and radar sets coincided with a vast increase in the number and quality of vessels comprising the Submarine Force. This resulted from construction begun under the 1940 Two-Ocean Navy Act and accelerated by congressional enactment in early 1942 of a separate Submarine Act. These measures led to the early 1942 arrival in the Pacific Fleet of the first 1,500-ton *Gato*-class fleet-type submarines and, later in the war, their closely related successors, the *Balao*s and *Tench*s. Capable of surface speeds of 20 knots and 9 knots underwater, these extremely rugged 311-foot-long diesel-driven fleet submarines possessed enough endurance to steam at 10 knots for over 11,000 miles during war patrols that averaged about seventy-five days and often found them in just about every corner of the Pacific. The *Gato*s' torpedo data control, which automated many firing calculations, and a new gray wartime camouflage paint job, gave them the flexibility they needed to conduct daytime or night surface attacks. Recently installed air conditioning and a new high-capacity, fresh-water distiller greatly improved habitability and made possible extended, long-range war patrolling. Air conditioning also reduced the incidence of electrical malfunctions and machinery breakdowns. All three fleet-type classes were armed with six torpedo tubes fore and aft, but the *Gato*s and *Balao*s carried twenty-four torpedoes whereas the newer *Tench*s carried twenty-eight.

Ruggedness was the main feature of these new vessels. The *Gato*, for instance, which was commissioned only three weeks after Pearl Harbor, participated in the action off Midway, steamed into the North Pacific on two different patrols, supported several operations in and around the Bismarcks barrier, and performed reconnaissance missions and lifeguard duty—standing off Japanese-held islands during carrier air strikes to rescue American pilots who had ditched their planes—during the Battle of the Philippine Sea. After attacking cargo shipping in the Yellow Sea, she ended the war on patrol off Honshu. Altogether, she completed a total of thirteen long-range war patrols, interrupted by only one brief overhaul. King protected the costly *Gato*-class building program from slowdowns threatened by sporadic labor disruptions, industrial shortages, and competing Navy projects. This policy allowed him to rapidly withdraw the older, less rugged 800-ton *S*-class boats as the new *Gato*-class vessels entered the Pacific Submarine Force. By the end of 1943, he had established a force of thirty submarines operating from two bases in Australia and nearly seventy-five from the Pacific Fleet's submarine base at Midway.

In spite of an occasional successful war patrol, American submarines contributed little to reversing the tide of the Pacific war in 1942. The Australia-based submarines played no role in the Battle of the Coral Sea. Admiral English at Pearl Harbor deployed nineteen Pacific Fleet submarines to reinforce Nimitz's ambush of Yamamoto's Combined Fleet off Midway, but they neither provided good reconnaissance nor sank any hostile vessels. The submariner who most actively participated in the battle, Lieutenant Commander John Murphy, maneuvered the *Tambor* into the midst of a Japanese formation and broadcast an ambiguous contact report that led Spruance to wrongly deploy his carriers on 5 June. Murphy did, on the other hand, unwittingly cause the heavy cruisers *Mogami* and *Mikuma* to collide with one another. He refused to quibble when he was relieved after the battle.

English, now afraid that he too would be sacked, ordered Lieutenant Commander William Brockman in the old 2,730-ton *Nautilus*, a notoriously unmanageable vessel, to steam into the western Pacific, penetrate Tokyo Bay, and shell the emperor's palace with his two 6-inch deck guns. When the *Nautilus* reached the heavily defended mouth of Tokyo Bay, Brockman forsook English's bizarre plan and instead conducted successful attacks against two convoys bound for the Marshalls. And on 25 June, he surprised the destroyer *Yamakaze*, sank her with two torpedoes, and survived an aggressive depth-charge counterattack. News of the *Nautilus'* spectacular patrol not only saved English's job but also exposed the weakness of Japan's antisubmarine defenses in Empire waters and led English to send out more boats on very deep penetration patrols in the second half of 1942. This episode also made it clear that Nimitz had erred in selecting English, who ignored the problem of malfunctioning torpedoes, allowed his boats to be diverted on missions of minimal importance, and re-fused to settle on a firm war patrol strategy.

To support the invasion of Guadalcanal, Captain Christie sent his eleven old Brisbane-based S-class boats to stations off enemy bases in the Upper Solomons and the Bismarck Archipelago. The most important result of this strategy was that it placed Lieutenant Commander John R. Moore in the *S-44* off Kavieng on 10 August 1942. The victorious Japanese cruisers, which had just sunk four Allied cruisers off Savo Island and were on their way back to base, suddenly steamed into Moore's view. He backed off to improve his firing position, then launched four torpedoes at a range of 700 yards. They hit the last ship in the line, the heavy cruiser *Kako*. "Evidently her boilers blew up," Moore recalled. "You could hear hideous noises that sounded like steam hissing through water. These noises were more terrifying to the crew than the actual depth charges that followed."[7]

In 1942, admirals King, Cooke, and Nimitz, all former submariners, were distressed with the Pacific Fleet's submarines. Sending slow submarines chasing after fast, well-defended enemy carriers, battleships, and cruisers was not producing substantial results. "There was a general belief that the proportion of torpedo failures in attacks on Japanese heavy warships was greater than it was in attacks on the slower and lighter-built" freighters and tankers, recalled Captain Holmes, a Pearl Harbor code breaker. But by June of that year Lockwood had discovered that a large fraction of the problem could be laid at the doorstep of the Bureau of Ordnance and its wildly defective Mark XIV torpedo and its unpredictable Mark VI magnetic exploder.

Soon after Lockwood arrived in Fremantle in May 1942, he received incredible reports of torpedo failures. Lieutenant Commander Tyrell Jacobs in the *Sargo* had fired thirteen torpedoes from close range at a perfect target, but each of them missed. This cast more suspicion on the torpedo. Jacobs proposed that Lockwood ignore the Bureau of Ordnance's claim that the Mark XIV functioned properly and conduct his own tests instead, which Lockwood and Captain James Fife did on 20 June. Lockwood, convinced that these tests demonstrated that the Mark XIV ran at least ten to fifteen feet deeper than set, was outraged when the bureau, "instead of thanking us . . . scorned our inaccurate approach to obtain these findings." He alerted King to the problem, and King—who later put the blame squarely on Blandy's predecessor, Admiral William Furlong—issued a blistering order to Rear Admiral William Blandy, the bureau chief, that he was "to take steps to restore . . . confidence in the reliability and accuracy" of the torpedoes. Meanwhile, Lockwood had issued his own directive warning his skippers that the Mark XIV ran at least ten feet deeper than its setting. Although torpedo performance improved slightly in late 1942, he realized that many undiscovered flaws still plagued the weapon.[8]

In January 1943, a plane crash took Admiral English's life, thus providing King with an opportunity to shuffle figures once again. He chose Lockwood to command the Pearl Harbor submarines instead of the more senior Rear Admiral Christie, who replaced Lockwood at Perth-Fremantle. Admiral Carpender remained in command of the Brisbane Submarine Force until King replaced him later that year with Rear Admiral Fife. Lockwood's first move was to transfer the Pacific Fleet's submarine base from Oahu to Midway, thus saving each submarine about 2,400 miles per patrol. Then he immersed himself in the daunting problem of the faulty Mark XIV steam torpedoes, which still did not work well.

Owing to the complexity of the weapon, ridding the Mark XIV of its many flaws proved to be a laborious task. On 10 April, Lieutenant Commander John A. Scott in the newly commissioned fleet submarine *Tunny* had received from Pearl Harbor an Ultra message that allowed him to intercept a large Japanese task force consisting of the auxiliary carrier *Taiyo* and two destroyers south of Truk. Scott, who distrusted the Mark VI exploder, set his torpedoes to run at ten feet so that they would explode on contact. He fired ten torpedoes against the enemy ships at close range, escaped, and reported to Pearl Harbor that he had sunk two carriers. Within a few hours, however, Commander Edwin Layton, the Pacific Fleet's intelligence officer, learned from a deciphered radio message that Truk's port director had just reported to Tokyo the *Taiyo* and her formation had arrived safely.

Then, on 19 July, Lieutenant Commander Lawrence R. Daspit in the *Tinosa*, on patrol in the vicinity of Truk, maneuvered into a short-range firing position with his submarine at a right angle to a slow-moving 19,000-ton Japanese tanker. Although he fired fifteen successive torpedoes, he could not hit the enemy vessel. Enraged, Daspit returned his one remaining torpedo to Pearl Harbor for examination. "We quickly found that every 90-degree impact resulted in a dud," Lockwood recalled. He now told his skippers "to fire their torpedoes at sharp or oblique angles to the path of the target—anything but a 90-degree tack." This correction unfortunately did not end the problem of unaccountable misses, since the faulty Mark VI magnetic exploder reacted differently in each patrol area, the result of variations in the pull of the earth's magnetic field. Often the Mark VI's magnetic mechanism exploded when the torpedo was more than 100 feet from its target. Lockwood ordered his Pacific Fleet skippers to inactivate the magnetic exploder, but the torpedo still did not perform properly. Christie in Brisbane resisted many of the improvements that Lockwood advanced. "Christie was one of the fathers or godfathers of this [Mark VI] exploder and was determined to make it work," Lockwood observed. "Therefore, the submarines 'down under' struggled along with it for about another year" with the result that the Australia-based submarines performed poorly when compared to those operating out of Midway.[9]

Soon after Lockwood was satisfied that the faults of the fast Mark XIV 46-knot steam torpedo had largely been corrected, the Bureau of Ordnance introduced a new, slow 27-knot Mark XVIII electric torpedo. The wakeless electric torpedo was an improvement over the steam-driven weapon inasmuch as it did not announce its presence to the enemy, but the Mark XVIII also contained an inexplicable number of bugs. However, Lockwood convinced Commander Dudley Morton, one of the great aces of the Submarine Force, to carry a mixed arsenal of Mark XIVs and XVIIIs when Morton put to sea in the *Wahoo* on 10 September 1943 on his fifth war patrol. He steamed into the Japan Sea in early October, sank an 8,000-ton cargo ship near the Tsushima Strait on the 5th, and sent under three more enemy vessels totaling 5,300 tons during the next few days. However, on 11 October a Japanese antisubmarine patrol bomber located the *Wahoo* near the narrow La Perouse passage and sank her with three depth charges; all hands were lost. A few weeks later, Commander Eugene Sands in the *Sawfish*, who had accompanied Morton into Empire waters, returned to Pearl Harbor and reported that he had sighted eighteen enemy ships and had conducted seven attacks with Mark XVIII electric torpedoes but could not sink any of his targets. Lockwood now ordered another cycle of tests and improvements for the Mark XVIII; these enhanced its lethality and led to its eventual adoption as the Pacific Fleet's standard torpedo. The electric-drive torpedo was never completely reliable, however. In late October 1944, Commander Richard H. O'Kane was off the China coast in the *Tang* conducting an attack on two large freighters when he fired a Mark XVIII. The torpedo exited the tube, completed a full circle, slammed into the submarine, and sank the vessel. Only O'Kane and three of his men survived.

Correcting the torpedo problems came in tandem with a change in Submarine Force strategy occasioned by a startling intelligence coup. "American submarine operations had forced the Japanese to organize freighters, tankers, and transports . . . in convoys, which were formed at the points of departure and routed to their destinations by divergent tracks," wrote Captain Wilfred J. Holmes, who served in the Pacific Fleet's Ultra radio intelligence unit. "The escort commander, the convoy commander, the port director at the port of arrival, and other interested parties were informed by radio of the route and schedule of each convoy." Under the direction of Captain William B. Goggins, who had replaced Commander Joseph Rochefort, Pacific Fleet cryptanalysts broke this relatively simple four-digit Maru convoy code in early 1943. "Our ability to read the 'Maru' code allowed us to plot the Japanese convoy routes from their daily position reports," Layton recalled.[10]

Holmes arranged for daily meetings with Captain Richard Voge, Lockwood's chief of staff, during which he passed on the latest Ultra intercepts of the Maru code. During 1943 and 1944, Holmes recalled, there "were nights when nearly every American submarine on patrol in the central Pacific was working on the basis of information derived from cryptanalysis." Ultra did not completely account for the success of the Submarine Force against Japan's tankers and freighters, however. During the last nine months of 1943, the Pearl Harbor code breakers deciphered over 800 Japanese convoy messages, which were relayed to patrolling submarines, but these vessels located only two out of five targets, attacked only a third of those ships, and sank a mere 14 percent of targets they attacked. Owing largely to incomplete or inaccurate message deciphering—Layton's intelligence staff graded only 13 percent of the intercepts as positive and only 4 percent as probable—and to local conditions, an American submarine enjoyed only a 2 percent chance of intercepting, attacking, and sinking an enemy freighter or tanker identified by Ultra in 1943. Of the 300 Japanese vessels sunk between January and October of that year, at most about fifteen sinkings resulted from Ultra messages, and one postwar Navy study concluded that without being assisted by Ultra "American submarines sank almost as many, if not just as many, Japanese ships as when the Japanese messages were being read." Moreover, Ultra may well have been used unwittingly to divert submarines from some highly productive patrol stations. The record improved the following year, but the massacre of Japan's shipping in 1944 was largely the result of the concurrent amphibious campaign, the greater number of Pacific Fleet submarines, a significant increase in the number of war patrols against well-known Japanese convoy routes and destinations, fewer faulty torpedoes, and more experienced, aggressive American skippers and better trained crews.[11]

The Submarine Force's antishipping offensive in 1944 sapped the strength of the Combined Fleet, reduced Japan's ability to support besieged strongpoints, and undermined her eroding industrial production. In short, American submarines directly and indirectly softened up enemy resistance to the Pacific Fleet's grand progression across the central Pacific that year. At the same time, however, the carrier raids, the constant pressure in the South Pacific, and the landings in the central Pacific prevented the Japanese from diverting escorts to defend their cargo shipping. While both admirals Lockwood and Christie had to support the fleet's amphibious operations and provide long-range reconnaissance of enemy movements, the timing of Nimitz' offensive campaign made these demands intermittent and allowed the Submarine Force to increase the tempo of its antishipping campaign. When the 5th Fleet invaded the Gilberts in November 1943, Nimitz expected the Combined Fleet to rendezvous at Truk and steam for the Marshalls to counterattack. Lockwood's submarines were stationed along this line of approach, but because of a shortage of air groups and screening ships, the Japanese battleships and carriers could not challenge the American advance.

When the Combined Fleet entered the Philippine Sea to contest Spruance's invasion of the Marianas in June 1944, the Submarine Force was an invaluable adjunct to the 5th Fleet. At Spruance's request, Christie stationed submarines east of the enemy's base at Tawitawi and one of them, Commander Samuel Dealey's *Harder*, sank three Japanese destroyers and damaged two more. Before the fleets joined in battle, Lockwood established patrols to watch the Luzon, San Bernardino, and Surigao straits, passages from which he expected the Combined Fleet might emerge. He also created a patrol line across the Philippine Sea to report on the enemy's advance and disrupt his movements and sent into the area a roving three-boat submarine tactical wolfpack under Captain Leon N. Blair. Late in May, Lieutenant Commander John Coye in the submarine *Silversides* came upon the first of a string of seven convoys transporting Japanese troops and supplies to Saipan. Coye sank six ships and summoned Blair's nearby wolfpack to the scene. Between them, Lieutenant Commanders Chick Clarey in the *Pintado* and Edwin N. Blakey in the *Shark II* accounted for 35,000 tons of enemy shipping, destroyed one entire inbound convoy, and thwarted Japanese plans to reinforce their garrisons in the Marianas. The Navy's submarines also provided Spruance with invaluable contact reports on Admiral Ozawa's movements, sank the heavy carriers *Shokaku* and *Taiho*, and harassed the enemy when he retired.

Following the fleet engagement in the Philippine Sea, Lockwood surged submarines into the Luzon Strait and dispatched a three-boat formation into the East China Sea. On the night of 24 June 1944, Commander O'Kane in the *Tang* sighted sixteen Japanese escorts screening a six-ship convoy heading toward Nagasaki. Upon summoning the rest of the wolfpack, O'Kane discovered that they were too far away, so he closed the convoy on his own and fired six torpedoes, which sank two large transports and two freighters. After rendezvousing with the *Sealion* and *Tinosa* in the Yellow Sea, O'Kane took station off the coast of

Korea, where on 4 July he sank two more 7,000-ton freighters. By the time the *Tang* returned to Midway, O'Kane, the leading American submarine ace in the Pacific, had sunk ten ships totaling 39,100 tons during the most successful submarine patrol of the entire war.

During the Battle of Leyte Gulf in October 1944, American submarines issued the first report on the Japanese fleet's counteroffensive and sank three cruisers and so badly damaged two more that they had to withdraw. Halsey's advance into the Philippines forced the Japanese to move reinforcements to Formosa and Luzon, thus providing additional shipping targets for both the 7th Fleet and Pacific Fleet submarines. On 21 November, Commander Eli Reich in the *Sealion II* was on patrol off Formosa when he came upon the battleships *Kongo* and *Haruna* en route from Brunei Bay to the Inland Sea. Reich surfaced, turned on his search radar, and closed on the formation at flank speed. Only 3,000 yards separated the *Sealion II* and the enemy at 0256 when Reich fired six electric torpedoes at the leading battleship and three more at her companion. The destroyer escort *Urakaze* intercepted the second salvo, but the *Sealion II*'s sonar recorded three hits from the first shots against the hull of the 31,000-ton *Kongo*. Reich was therefore dumbfounded when the Japanese task force continued on its way at 16 knots. The *Sealion II* was soon in hot pursuit. Three hours later, after overtaking the enemy, Reich was ready to attack again when he saw a "tremendous explosion dead ahead" so bright that the sky "looked like a sunset at midnight." The *Kongo*'s magazine was exploding, and she slid under the waves moments later, the only battleship to be sunk by a submarine in the Pacific war.[12]

The heightened tempo of the Submarine Force's antishipping offensive combined with the movements of Kinkaid's 7th Fleet, Halsey's 3rd Fleet, and Spruance's 5th Fleet to create a synergy of pressure on Japan's shrinking escort pool. Lieutenant Commander George Grider in the *Flasher*, a member of a three-boat wolfpack, took station west of Mindoro to interdict any Japanese ships that tried to interrupt the Leyte invasion force and on 4 December chanced upon an enemy convoy. Maneuvering to attain a good submerged attack position, Grider was alarmed when his executive officer, Lieutenant Commander Philip Glennon, warned that one of the escorting destroyers had discovered their presence and was bearing down on the *Flasher* at

high speed. Grider reacted by shooting a spread of four torpedoes in blazing succession, which sank the destroyer *Kishinami*
and a 10,000-ton tanker. The *Flasher* then dove down to 250 feet,
where she survived a furious enemy counterattack with sixteen
depth charges. When the *Flasher* rose again to periscope depth
ninety minutes later, Grider sighted the nearby destroyer *Iwana-
mi* and swiftly dispatched her with another deadly brace of four
torpedoes. This was one of thirty-one destroyers, ten cruisers,
and seven aircraft carriers of various sizes lost by Japan in 1944
alone to American submarines, a blow so devastating that, combined with the losses to the 3rd, 5th, and 7th fleets, the Japanese
Navy did not have enough ships left to conduct another fleet
action.

In January 1945, when preparations for the invasion of
Japan got under way, Nimitz moved his Pacific Fleet headquarters
to Guam, and Lockwood followed. After the Leyte invasion, both
Admiral Lockwood and Admiral Fife, who had relieved Ralph
Christie as commander of the Southwest Pacific Submarine Force
in December 1944, flooded the South China Sea with submarines
to cut off the flow of oil from the Dutch East Indies to Japan's
Home Islands. "Frequently aided by radio intelligence in finding
convoys, the submarines sent more tankers to the bottom of the
sea than got through to Japan," wrote Captain Holmes. In March,
the Combined Fleet abandoned its effort to transport oil to Japan,
and American submarines on deep-penetration war patrols started to run out of victims. By this time, they had forced the
Japanese to abandon thirty-five of their forty-seven convoy routes.
In June, Lockwood initiated Operation Barney, which aimed at
cutting the lifeline from Japan to China by infesting the Sea of
Japan with submarines. "We believed [from radio intercepts] that
mines had been laid to watch for submarines at the surface, at
periscope depth, and at a depth of 100 feet, but that the Japanese
had no magnetic bottom mines," Holmes recalled. "The information probably was responsible for the happy decision to run
through at a depth of 150 feet." Armed with short-range FM
sonars, which could detect underwater mines and therefore allow
the submarines to feel their way safely through the hostile minefields, nine Pacific Fleet boats entered the Inland Sea that month.
One of these submarines was lost, but the patrol sank twenty-eight
Japanese ships totaling 55,000 tons before escaping back through
the minefields to safety.[13]

In the Pacific war, American submarines sank over 1,300 enemy vessels, and probably accounted for the loss of another 78, a total of more than 5.3 million tons of Japanese merchant and naval shipping. The collapse of Japan's shipping meant the loss of fuels, lubricants, iron ore, rubber, and other vital imports without which Japan's industry could not produce war goods. By the summer of 1945, Japanese industrial output had almost ground to a halt. The authors of the postwar *U. S. Strategic Bombing Survey*, a vast compilation of Axis losses, summed up this extraordinary accomplishment of the Submarine Forces: Their "war against shipping was perhaps the most decisive single factor in the collapse of the Japanese economy and logistic support of Japanese military and naval power."[14]

Chapter Ten

Beginning the Central Pacific Offensive
1943–1944

Referring to the early South Pacific and Southwest Pacific operations, President Roosevelt declared in January 1943 that "these actions were essentially defensive. They were part of the delaying strategy that characterized this phase of the war." With Japan's withdrawal from Guadalcanal, the strategic landscape of the Pacific began to change once more. King had repeatedly expressed his unhappiness with the high cost and slow pace of the South Pacific campaign in late 1942 and wanted to curtail operations in the South and Southwest Pacific before they became too expensive. On a regular basis throughout the war he met with a group of reporters in secret to explain American strategy, and on 29 November he told them that "once the Japanese have been expelled from Rabaul" he did not "think it desirable to press north from Australia into the Dutch East Indies." King believed that "the best idea is to drive straight north from Rabaul, attacking Truk in the Carolines and Guam and Saipan in the Marianas" since this would "cut off the whole Mandated archipelago from Japan and open the way to get back into the Philippines, which in turn would cut off the Dutch East Indies and make it impossible for the Japs to hang on there." Nimitz demurred. A central Pacific offensive "might be the reverse of Midway," he told King at a conference on 13 December. Owing to the proximity of land-based enemy aircraft to an invasion fleet, "it would constitute a frontal attack, which would not be as profitable as a continuation

of the campaigns where we are now in contact with the Japs."
King dismissed this argument, however, and instructed Nimitz to
begin planning to shift the weight of his offensive the following
year.[1]

At the Casablanca Conference in January 1943 King announced to the Combined Chiefs of Staff that the North Pacific
and South Pacific routes from Hawaii to Japan were inferior to a
direct thrust across the central Pacific via the Gilberts and the
Carolines or Marianas. The British opposed diverting American
resources from the Atlantic to the Pacific, however, a view supported by General Arnold, while General Marshall loyally backed
MacArthur's plan to drive north from New Guinea to the Philippines. Not only did the British view diversions to the Pacific with
alarm, they also did not believe that King's strategy, which depended upon using the Pacific Fleet's fast carriers to defeat
Japan's land-based air forces, would succeed. "Too much importance should not be attached to the idea of advancing step by
step through the Japanese islands," Admiral Pound told
Churchill. "The battle fleets would have to fight a fleet action in
which the whole area was supported by Japanese shore-based air."
Nonetheless, on 9 February 1943, King instructed Nimitz to prepare for an invasion of the Gilberts, which the Japanese had fortified the previous September. To overcome the opposition in
Washington and London, King shrewdly traded his agreement
for continued Mediterranean operations in return for a statement by the Combined Chiefs approving his new drive in the
central Pacific.[2]

When representatives from Nimitz' and MacArthur's commands met with the JCS in Washington in March 1943 at the
Pacific Military Conference, however, the resulting directive approved only the continuance of the two converging South and
Southwest Pacific offensives against Rabaul. Nevertheless, when
the British chiefs of staff appeared in Washington in May for the
Trident Conference, Admiral Leahy sided with King's arguments
in favor of a new front in the central Pacific. King told Halsey
that he was "appalled at the slowness of the progress in the area
[Southwest Pacific] where you are working," and had rounded
up support for the central Pacific campaign from General
Arnold, who now wanted to establish bombardment groups of
new B-29 Superfortress long-range bombers in the Marianas to
begin the strategic bombing of Japan. Inasmuch as MacArthur's

Attack carrier *Essex* (CV-9), the workhorse of the carrier war in the Pacific, in 1943. Authorized by the 1938 Second Vinson Act, ordered in 1940, and completed on 31 December 1942, the *Essex* was the lead vessel in the largest capital ship-building program in history. Although the *Essex*-class ships were the U.S. Navy's first post–treaty-class carriers, a provision in the 1936 London Naval Treaty limited American and British carriers to 23,000 tons displacement, which fixed this ship's initial design size. Demands from the fleet for higher speed, more protection against enemy cruiser shellfire, and a five-squadron air group, as well as the Roosevelt administration's denunciation of the London Treaty in late 1939, resulted in raising the displacement from 20,400 to 27,100 tons and delayed laying down the lead ship until April 1941. While the deck had some protection against bombing and shelling, the carrier still could not accommodate an armored flight deck. Nonetheless, the *Essex*-class carriers operated the largest possible air group that could satisfactorily be managed during the deck-load strike tactics used by the Pacific Fleet against Japan in World War II. The June 1940 Naval Appropriations Act provided for three additional ships, and the August 1940 Two-Ocean Navy Act provided for seven more that were ordered immediately, two ordered eight days after Pearl Harbor, ten ordered in August 1942, and the final three ordered in mid-1943. With a view to mass production, Admiral King agreed to only a few changes in the basic design, the most important and controversial being a slight shortening of the flight deck. During the war, the Navy ordered twenty-six *Essex*-class carriers; twenty-four were completed and entered the fleet, with only one, the *Oriskany*, being built to a modified design. The Navy turned these ships into antisubmarine carriers in the 1950s, and a hunter-killer task force built around the *Essex* successfully located and brought to the surface several diesel-powered Soviet submarines during the October 1962 Cuban Missile Crisis.

advance had been so cautious, King insisted that Nimitz' Pacific Fleet be allowed to move in a separate offensive in the central Pacific. In June 1943, Nimitz, invariably conservative, made the case for taking the Gilbert Islands before venturing into the Marshalls, but this did not appreciably delay the decision to unleash his newly powerful forces. To paper over the quarrel between MacArthur and Nimitz, the JCS on 6 August 1943 issued a directive calling for a dual offensive from the central and Southwest Pacific theaters, which was to converge on the Philippines in 1944. In short, Pacific strategy reflected a series of grudging compromises about objectives because of interservice rivalries and the refusal by both King and Marshall to anoint a single supreme Pacific commander from the rival service. Competition rather than collaboration decided grand strategy and higher command on the American side in the Pacific War.[3]

Strung across the equator 2,000 miles southwest of Hawaii, the Gilbert Islands were the target of the first amphibious operation of the great central Pacific campaign. Japanese troops defending the Gilberts were supported by air forces based on Roi and Namur islands in the Kwajalein Atoll in the Marshall Islands, 600 miles to the northwest of the Gilberts, and on Nauru to the west. Truk in the Carolines, the major Japanese fleet base in the Pacific, lay 1,500 miles to the northwest. Admiral Cooke's original plan to invade the Gilberts instructed Nimitz to seize not only Tarawa Island, but also Ocean and Nauru, which lay 380 miles from Tarawa and fairly close to Truk. Spruance objected that he could not cover Nauru and Tarawa at the same time, and the Marines' commander, Major General Holland M. Smith, believed that the steep bluffs on Nauru's atolls would make an amphibious assault excessively dangerous. He also claimed not to have enough assault troops to overcome the large Japanese garrison defending Nauru. As a result, when King conferred with Nimitz at Pearl Harbor on 25 September 1943, King agreed to the substitution of Makin for Nauru. However, overall intelligence about Japanese defenses in the Gilberts, Smith admitted, "wasn't too good."[4]

In June 1943 the first 27,100-ton *Essex*-class carrier, the product of the 1940 Two-Ocean Navy Act, arrived in Pearl Harbor. This ushered in the era of large-scale fast carrier bombing strikes and made possible the inauguration of the central Pacific offensive. By the end of the year the striking arm of the 5th Fleet's Fast

Carrier Force would include over 700 aircraft operated by the old carriers *Saratoga* and *Enterprise,* the new *Essex*-class carriers *Essex, Yorktown,* and *Bunker Hill,* and the 11,000-ton light carriers *Princeton, Independence, Monterey, Belleau Wood,* and *Cowpens.* Moreover, King had just recently assigned several of the new 7,800-ton escort carriers to the Pacific Fleet. Originally intended to provide some air coverage to ocean escort groups in the Atlantic, the escort carrier proved her worth in the Pacific as a plane ferry and as a provider of air cover for invasions and close ground support for troops ashore. Industrialist Henry J. Kaiser designed these small ships and eventually built fifty of them for the Navy, many of which were turned over to the British; seventeen others were cargo ship conversions and an additional nineteen represented new construction modeled after the conversion class. Indeed, in the summer of 1943, over half of all the ships of the Pacific Fleet were new.

Nimitz not only possessed more ships but also a vastly strengthened carrier air arm. Combat experience in the Coral Sea and off Midway had led King to decide that each new *Essex*-class heavy carrier would embark five squadrons—thirty-six fighters, eighteen torpedo planes, and thirty-six dive bombers. The recently organized fighter squadrons, which arrived in the Pacific beginning in November 1942, flew the new Grumman F6F Hellcat, a faster, more rugged, and more heavily armed fighter than the Japanese Zero, and an aircraft whose operational ceiling of 23,000 feet exceeded that of the Zero. And to counter Japan's superior night surface tactics, Captain Arthur Radford of the Bureau of Aeronautics had worked with Commander W. J. Widhelm to assemble the first squadron of radar-equipped Chance-Vought F4U Corsairs for night fighting. Other new Corsairs did not fare so well, however, and soon after one squadron was qualified the Navy declared them all unfit for carrier landings. As a result the shore-based Marine air squadrons got the heavy Corsairs until late in the war when these planes were again accepted for carrier duty. Improved naval bombers were slower to reach the fleet. As the old SDB Dauntless dive bomber lacked the speed and range to keep up with its new escort, the Hellcat fighter, Rear Admiral John Towers, the chief of the Bureau of Aeronautics, arranged with Curtis Wright in early 1942 for the mass production of the new, fast SB2C Helldiver, but the first of these planes to reach the Pacific Fleet repeatedly malfunctioned and it was not until 1944 that they were accepted by the Navy in large numbers. On the other hand, the aircraft and spares shortages that plagued American operations in 1942 had, by the summer of the following year, nearly vanished.

The Pacific Fleet was also immeasurably strengthened in 1943 by the introduction of a number of new radar and communications devices. The *Essex*-class carriers had new four-channel, short-range VHF radios, which allowed communicators to dedicate each channel to a specific function—fighter direction, attack operations, scouting, and so forth. Before the war, the Bureau of Ordnance intended radar to be a vital component of its advanced antiaircraft fire-control system, but as it turned out radar proved to be relatively more important in providing the carrier with an early warning of approaching enemy aircraft and in directing the fighter defenses of the task group. The Mark IV air search radar, introduced in 1943 and modified one year later, vastly improved the fleet's air defenses because it was able to fix the composition and vertical formation of approaching enemy aircraft at a distance of about 75 miles out. The new Position Plan Indicator system solved the perennial debate over single-versus multi-carrier task groups in favor of the latter by allowing a ship within a high-speed formation to maintain station at night or in bad weather. Finally, the addition to the *Essex*-class carriers of a combat information center, which fed radar, radio, and visual observations to the flag plot, bridge, gun director, and air plot, enabled the entire carrier task group to conduct defensive and offensive operations more effectively.[5]

To prepare the new carriers and air groups for the invasion of the Gilberts, Nimitz ordered Rear Admiral Charles A. Pownall to assemble a task force built around the heavy carriers *Yorktown* and *Essex* and the light carrier *Independence* and to raid the enemy line in the central Pacific. On 29 August, Pownall began to follow a weather front that was heading toward the Gilberts, and when he arrived at a position 110 miles from Marcus Island two days later, his radar located a Japanese patrol plane returning to base. Pownall reacted quickly. At 1622 the first F6F Hellcat to fight in the Pacific War lifted off the deck of the *Yorktown*, followed by TBF Avenger torpedo planes carrying 2,000-pound blockbuster bombs and SDB Dauntless dive bombers armed with 1,000-pound fragmentation bombs. Five deckload strikes pounded the enemy airstrip and adjacent buildings on Marcus and destroyed seven Betty torpedo bombers on the runway. Then, on 18 September, Pownall put to sea again with a task group composed of the newly commissioned heavy carrier *Lexington* and the light carriers *Princeton* and *Belleau Wood* and closed on the Japanese airstrip on Tarawa Atoll in the Gilberts, preceded by a flight of Army Air Force bombers from the Southwest Pacific. Only three enemy aircraft from Kwajalein in the Marshalls even approached the American ships, and these intruders were splashed by a ferocious combat air patrol of F6F Hellcat fighters. After his bombers had destroyed several planes and small boats at Tarawa, Pownall turned his attention to nearby Makin and Apamama.

Next, Rear Admiral Alfred E. Montgomery with a six-carrier task force, the largest to operate in the Pacific since Pearl Harbor, appeared off Wake Island during the predawn hours of 5 October. Thirty Zero fighters arose to defend this Japanese base, but they were splashed by a much larger flight of incoming F6F Hellcats, thus confirming the Americans' faith in the superiority of that aircraft. The raid on Tarawa convinced the Japanese that the Gilberts were immediately threatened, and the Mobile Fleet, consisting of three carriers and two battleships, stood out of Truk, steamed into the northern Marshalls, and appeared off Wake Island, withdrawing back to the Carolines only upon discovering that the American carriers had already retired from the central Pacific. This led Nimitz to anticipate a fleet action when the 5th Fleet entered the Gilberts in force.

To command the 5th Fleet for the upcoming invasion, King and Nimitz agreed to the selection of the Pacific Fleet's chief of staff, Vice Admiral Raymond Spruance, who had worked for King in the Atlantic Fleet in 1941 and had received most of the credit for the victory off Midway. Pownall would be in command of the Fast Carrier Force, while Vice Admiral Turner, who had just been shifted out of the South Pacific, was to direct the Amphibious Force. King had discovered in 1942 that his operational control of the Marines provided him with tremendous leverage in the struggle in Washington over Pacific strategy, so he persuaded FDR during the crisis on Guadalcanal to agree to such a vast increase in the size of the Marine Corps that within two years it totaled nearly half a million men. The first of these newly trained amphibious divisions were ready in late 1943 to begin the central Pacific offensive under General Holland M. Smith, an extremely able, mercurial figure for whom King had great respect. In addition, General Marshall had organized a large Army amphibious training command for all theaters, and he provided the 27th Infantry Division for the Gilberts invasion. Last, Nimitz expanded the old patrol bomber command into a large Shore-based Air Force consisting of a variety of Navy patrol aircraft and Army medium-range bombers under Rear Admiral John Hoover, a dour but competent aviator. Hoover's first step was to revive the long neglected American base on Funafuti Atoll, which was within 700 miles of the Gilberts archipelago, so that land-based reconnaissance and bombers might be brought into play for the landings.

Spruance, uncertain how the Japanese might react to the invasion of the Gilberts, reasoned that he had to achieve tactical surprise before the troops went ashore and then prevent the enemy carriers from coming within striking range of the landing beaches or shipping anchorages. This assessment resulted in three major decisions. First, Spruance decided that Makin had to be taken within a day, since it was only 175 miles from the nearest opposing air base in the Marshalls. Second, he ruled that the preliminary offshore naval gunfire bombardment was to be accomplished on the morning of the landing so as to minimize the time available to the Japanese to organize their reinforcements. Finally, he dedicated the Fast Carrier Force to the close-in defense of the Amphibious Force rather than to the pursuit of an enemy fleet that might appear on the scene.

Pownall complained that tying the heavy carriers to the defense of the beachhead was "dangerous," but Spruance refused to revise his plan. In effect, Spruance chose to absorb a Japanese air strike rather than risk the security of the landing force. He also believed that the Japanese might bring on a surface engagement with their *Yamato*-class superbattleships. He attached his new *South Dakota*-class fast battleships to the carrier groups to strengthen the task force's antiaircraft defenses, but if the Japanese fleet sortied he intended to send the carriers to the rear and form his battleships and cruisers into a classic battle line-ahead. Spruance also faced such a serious shortage of destroyers that he was unable to attach two to each carrier as a screen, the minimal requirement of the Navy's then current battle doctrine. Furthermore, although the Fast Carrier Force would be exposed to nighttime attacks by Japanese land-based aircraft, the only night fighters in the entire task force were Commander Butch O'Hare's special section, which was part of Radford's *Enterprise* air group.[6]

Pownall organized his carriers into four task groups. Rear Admiral Frederick Sherman's Relief Carrier Group with the *Saratoga* and the light carrier *Princeton* was to hit the Japanese airfield at Nauru and then place itself in strategic reserve. Rear Admiral Radford's Northern Carrier Group was to act as an intercepting force while also covering the landing of the Northern Attack Force on Makin Island. Montgomery's Southern Carrier Group was to cover the main landing of the Southern Attack Force on Tarawa Atoll. Pownall stationed his own Central Carrier Group between the Gilberts and Marshalls to intercept Japanese air attacks from the north and to attack Japanese airfields on Mili and Jaluit in the southern Marshalls.

On 21 October, the first elements of Turner's huge Amphibious Force, which staged from the South Pacific, Pearl Harbor, and the West Coast, set sail for the central Pacific. Over 200 ships carrying more than 100,000 men were to converge west of Hawaii and steam to the west in mid-November. Pownall put to sea with two carrier task groups early that month and rendezvoused with two more carrier task groups from the South Pacific a few days later. The carriers sent reconnaissance flights over the Gilberts, launched air strikes against Tarawa and Makin atolls, and flung diversionary attacks against enemy bases on Wake and Marcus islands. Starting on 13 November, Hoover sent the first level-bombing raid, composed of Army Air Force and Navy B-24 Liberators, over Tarawa and Makin, and he continued these operations for a week. Meanwhile, the Attack Forces made contact and, steaming along parallel courses, headed into the central Pacific. Defended by an Escort Force of eight new escort carriers embarking a total of 216 aircraft and a Bombardment Group of seven old battleships, eight heavy and light cruisers, and thirty-eight destroyers, the Attack Forces included twenty troop carriers and cargo supply ships and two new large landing ship docks.

During the opening phase of the central Pacific offensive, the Navy discovered that the Japanese airbase at Rabaul was no longer immune to American attacks. On 5 November 1943, Sherman's task force attacked Japanese shipping at that erstwhile bastion and damaged six cruisers and two destroyers, a stroke that finally ended the threat to the Southwest Pacific theater from Japanese surface forces in the Solomons. This large-scale raid, conducted by ninety-seven planes, was made possible because land-based Navy aircraft from Barakoma provided Sherman's ships with combat air patrol during the operation. Six days later, Sherman's air groups returned to the skies over Rabaul, as did planes from Admiral Montgomery's task group built around the heavy carriers *Essex* and *Bunker Hill* and the light carrier *Independence*. Over fifty enemy aircraft were shot down, forcing the Japanese to withdraw their front-line aircraft from the area. The second air strike on Rabaul also compelled the Japanese to summon weak replacements from the Marshall Islands to the South Pacific. These raids, and the menace of Halsey's operations around Bougainville, also convinced the Japanese to evacuate their shipping from Rabaul. On the 13th, Admiral Koga withdrew most of his aircraft from Rabaul, but so many planes had been lost that he now needed entirely new air groups to operate his carriers. Moreover, having lost seven cruisers, he now could not assemble an effective screen for his battleships and, therefore, was unable to send the Combined Fleet north to defend the Gilberts and the Marshalls later that month.

The invasion of the Gilberts opened at 0620 on 20 November 1943 with a preliminary naval gunfire bombardment of Tarawa that lasted two and one-half hours. Rear Admiral Harry Hill's old battleship bombardment force fired almost 3,000 high-explosive, fragmentation, and airburst shells against enemy defenses on small Betio Island, destroying most of the enemy's buildings, communications, and antiaircraft guns. This failed to damage the Japanese blockhouses, pillboxes, or major artillery emplacements, however, and when the first wave of Marines waded ashore they confronted machine guns that raked the beaches. "So strong was Betio that our naval gunfire did not materially reduce resistance," Holland Smith recorded angrily. The landing on Butaritari Island in Makin Atoll went much more smoothly, although it took the Army four days to overcome only 300 enemy troops and 500 laborers.[7]

Even after the Marines got ashore on Betio Island, Admiral Keiji Shibasaki's 4,500 elite defenders stiffly resisted by taking advantage of prepared positions and by establishing new strongholds in the rubble created by the dawn bombardment. Poor communications between the flagship *Maryland* and the other ships led to confusion during the assault wave, disrupted the bombardment schedule, and allowed the defenders too much time to brace for the landing. The first wave of assault troops, carried over the coral reef in ninety-three new alligator LVT amphibian tractors, hit the beach at 0913. The two dozen Higgins-type landing boats could not cross the reef, however, and when the tank-loaded mechanized landing craft from the LSD *Ashland* tried to cross at low tide they stranded, forcing the Marines to offload their Sherman tanks while standing in several feet of water. Inasmuch as the landing craft could not make it over the reef, subsequent assault waves had to wade ashore over a distance of 400 yards under enemy machine gun fire. Turner improvised a shuttle between the anchorage and the beach using the LVT tractors, but this did not entirely solve the problem. In some of the heaviest fighting of the war, Major General Julian Smith's 2nd Marine Division established a beachhead and began to push the Japanese into several isolated pockets on the edge of the island. Air operations from the captured airstrip finally began at noon on 23 November, and Betio was secure that evening. Almost the entire Japanese garrison died at Tarawa, as did over 1,000 Marines. Holland Smith condemned this slaughter as useless. Tarawa was a costly but nonetheless useful training ground, and by studying it commanders of all echelons were able to perfect the evolving doctrine of amphibious operations.

As a result of the slow advance on Makin and the bitter resistance on Tarawa, Spruance had to hold the carriers in the Gilberts for several days. Owing to the shortage of destroyers, he could spare for each task group only one radar picket, which was deployed about twenty-five miles ahead of the carriers. On 20 November, as a result of this weak early-warning line, a flight of long-range Betty torpedo bombers from Kwajalein and Maloelap evaded radar detection and attacked the Southern Carrier Group off Tarawa, damaging the *Independence* so badly that she had to retire to the West Coast for repairs. Although the Japanese were completely surprised by the move into the Gilberts, they had reacted with the most thoroughly coordinated torpedo plane attacks that they conducted during the entire war, and the American commanders were clearly worried. The Japanese used plain-language signals to position their aircraft for an attack, however, and these messages often provided the American shipboard radio intelligence units with advance notice of an upcoming attack. One pitch-black night, a formation of Japanese bombers was approaching a task group at an altitude of 500 feet when they were overheard by a shipboard radio intelligence unit that was eavesdropping on the enemy frequency. The admiral ordered his antiaircraft batteries to remain silent, and the enemy flew directly over the darkened ships, unaware of their presence in the black waters below. In spite of considerable success in fending off Japanese attacks, the loss of the *Independence* clearly concerned Nimitz, and he was persuaded by Rear Admiral Forrest Sherman to instruct Spruance to detach some carriers from the covering forces and send them to attack enemy air concentrations in the northern Marshalls. For the moment, however, Spruance kept all his attack carriers on station in the Gilberts to provide close air support to the Marines until the stubborn resistance on Betio ended on 23 November.

Turner now began to withdraw his Attack Forces. Early the following day Rear Admiral Henry M. Mullinnix's Northern Attack Force task group of three newly constructed escort carriers was steaming about twenty miles south of Butaritari Island en route to Pearl Harbor. At 0510, just as Mullinnix was about to launch his dawn patrols, the Japanese submarine *I-175* closed on the *Liscome Bay* and fired two torpedoes, which struck the escort carrier in the bomb storage spaces. Twenty-three minutes later she sank, taking with her the admiral and over half her crew. Two days earlier, a flight of about twenty Japanese Betty bombers had attacked Radford's Northern Carrier Group, but this strike was broken up by O'Hare's night-fighter section during an action in which he was killed. The Marines overran the remaining defenders, and the Gilberts were declared secure on 28 November. In the aftermath, however, Rear Admiral J. J. Clark expressed his outrage at Spruance's decision to hold the carriers close to the Gilberts, claiming that the Fast Carrier Force had become "a stationary target for enemy submarines and aircraft."[8]

King had insisted in September that the movement into the Gilberts be followed by a rapid stroke into the nearby Marshalls. To seize the Marshalls, Spruance divided the 5th Fleet into three task forces and planned to launch the operation on 1 January 1944 when his forces would invade Wotje and Maloelap, the two well-defended atolls nearest to Hawaii, and Kwajalein, the central atoll where the Japanese headquarters was located. Kwajalein Atoll was composed of Roi, Namur, and Kwajalein islands. Holland Smith, sobered by what he believed to have been the unnecessary slaughter at Tarawa, persuaded Spruance to take the outposts first, then move against the enemy headquarters. Although Smith believed that the fleet "should take Maloelap and Wotje first, and then move on to Kwajalein," at a minimum he wanted to "abandon the idea of taking the three objectives selected in the Marshalls and concentrate on one." Again King intervened, urging Nimitz not to worry about the losses at Tarawa but instead to increase the pace of the offensive. At the same time, Commander Layton, the fleet intelligence officer, was convincing Nimitz that the Japanese "were moving army units and artillery away from their Kwajalein headquarters to the out atolls," and Rear Admiral Forrest Sherman, whom Nimitz trusted completely, was urging him to invade Kwajalein. Although this was opposed by Spruance, Smith, and Turner, on 14 December 1943 Nimitz directed them to bypass the outlying atolls and concentrate on capturing Kwajalein and Majuro, a poorly defended atoll with the best anchorage in the Marshalls.[9]

Spruance now ordered Pownall to take his six-carrier Interceptor Group north, attack enemy airbases on Kwajalein, and conduct photo reconnaissance of that atoll's fortifications. The Japanese, expecting a raid, presumed that Pownall would approach from the south, and thus were surprised on 4 December when the carriers descended from the north. Pownall had planned to conduct two successive air strikes, but the first flight of attackers failed to destroy a squadron of Betty torpedo bombers at Kwajalein. This made Pownall worry that the Japanese would counterattack, so he canceled the second strike and began to withdraw. At 2000 that night, the American carriers were found by a flight of about forty Wotje-based Japanese torpedo bombers.

The poorly coordinated strike that ensued resulted in only minor damage to the *Lexington*, but it exposed Pownall to critics, led by Clark, who charged that Pownall, plagued by "undue anxiety," had unwisely failed to press home the attack, and in so doing had needlessly exposed the carriers. Clark's indictment was supported by Forrest Sherman and his immediate boss, Nimitz' foul-tempered chief of staff, Rear Admiral Charles H. McMorris. Mildly annoyed by his ever feuding air admirals, Nimitz sent Pownall ashore. Later in the war Pownall performed one more service for naval aviation by helping Vice Admiral Lockwood devise the submarine lifeguard system to rescue downed pilots during amphibious operations. Pownall was replaced in command of the Fast Carrier Force not by the volatile Frederick Sherman, the most able

The 1,400-ton *England* (DE-635), a *Buckley*-class destroyer escort commissioned on 10 December 1943, compiled an unmatched record in wartime antisubmarine operations by sinking six Japanese picket submarines in twelve days in May 1944. Early in World War II, the U.S. Navy turned to mass-produced, austere destroyer escorts because the nation's shipyards could not concurrently build enough general-purpose destroyers and large landing ships to provide for simultaneous offensives in both the Atlantic and Pacific theaters. Even so, the entire destroyer escort program was slowed until late 1942 owing to President Roosevelt's insistence that large landing ships and high-octane aviation fuel deserved a higher priority. Nearly 500 destroyer escorts were built during the war, and these sturdy, unexpectedly versatile ships proved to be superb convoy escorts as well as lethal submarine killers.

task group commander in the Pacific, but by Rear Admiral Marc Mitscher—a move Nimitz made over Spruance's objections.[10]

Nimitz' bold decision to drive into the Marshalls and take Kwajalein before overrunning the outlying islands rested on the assumption that the Pacific Fleet could defeat the Japanese air forces in the Marshalls before the Amphibious Force entered the archipelago. In early January 1944, Admiral Hoover established airbases in the Gilberts and inaugurated daily reconnaissance flights and level-bombing raids against enemy airfields in the Marshalls. Mitscher's basic air plan was for three of his carrier task groups to neutralize enemy air forces on Truk and in the Marianas while the fourth supplied close air cover for the invasion forces. On the morning of 29 January, the Fast Carrier Force reappeared in the central Pacific. Its fighters swept over Kwajalein, establishing air superiority by noon. Soon after, an escort carrier task group arrived, attacked Japanese defenses on Kwajalein, and prepared to provide the assault troops with close air support. Sherman's carrier task group was detached and assigned to hit targets on Eniwetok for three days to prevent the enemy from staging any more aircraft into the Marshalls. Two days later, Rear Admiral Richard Conolly's Northern Attack Group put the untested 4th Marine Division ashore on Roi and Namur islands, forty-four miles to the north of Kwajalein Atoll. This uncoordinated assault against relatively weak opposition resulted in 750 casualties. Resistance ended on Roi on 1 February and on Namur one day later.

When Major General Charles H. Corlett's 7th Infantry Division landed on Kwajalein on 1 February, they found that Turner had chosen to lift them onto an exposed beach at the thinnest portion of the western edge of the island. With no room to maneuver, Corlett's men slogged forward in a series of plodding frontal attacks against an ill-trained, poorly equipped 8,000-man Japanese field force. With absolute air superiority and precise offshore gunfire support, this slow but relentless advance overran the defenders at a cost of nearly 1,200 American casualties. On 4 February, the last enemy commanders committed suicide and Spruance declared the islands secure.

With Kwajalein in American hands, Spruance steamed for the fleet anchorage at Majuro Atoll, which was to serve as an advance base for the next phase of the central Pacific offensive. Under pressure from King to strike more deeply into the central Pacific, Nimitz now ordered Spruance to take Eniwetok, which would deprive the Japanese of an outpost that guarded their major fleet base at Truk, 750 miles distant in the Caroline Islands and less than 1,000 miles from the Marianas. Evidence of the weak Japanese resistance on Kwajalein had convinced Nimitz to direct Spruance to move ahead the date for seizing Eniwetok, which was assaulted on 17 February by Army troops and the 22nd

Marines and overrun after five days of heavy fighting. Owing to the confusion sown by the carrier attacks against Truk and enemy bases in the Marianas, the Eniwetok task groups were never even bothered by Japanese aircraft. In the process of taking Eniwetok, Spruance had bypassed Jaluit, Mili, Maloelap, and Wotje atolls, which meant that these once powerful enemy airbases were now isolated and could be ignored for the rest of the war.

By this time, Nimitz had instructed Spruance to lead the fleet in a raid against Truk, which he still supposed to be the main Japanese strongpoint in the central Pacific. On the morning of 17 February, Mitscher's Fast Carrier Force arrived at position ninety miles northeast of Truk and launched a predawn sweep of F6F Hellcat fighters that shot down fifty Zero fighters at a cost of four American planes, thus clearing the airspace over the enemy fleet base and making way for the naval bombers. They appeared over Truk at noon, destroying or damaging about 150 aircraft that were parked on the three airstrips there. To the Americans' surprise, Admiral Koga had already withdrawn most of his combatants from the lagoon, but over 200,000 tons of Japanese transport and cargo shipping were sunk during the raid, along with one luckless light cruiser and a destroyer.

The raid on Truk emboldened Spruance, and he sent Mitscher and the Fast Carrier Force on another raid into the Marianas. While closing on the islands on the night of 21 February, the nine American carriers were sighted by a lone Betty torpedo bomber on patrol, but, instead of retiring, Mitscher, perhaps recalling Pownall's unhappy experience, announced they would "fight our way in." A flight of Japanese torpedo bombers attacked Admiral Montgomery's task group at 2200, but a furious antiaircraft fire splashed about ten of these planes and drove off the rest before dawn. Then, Mitscher launched a sunrise sweep of Hellcats, which shot down most of the seventy-five Zero fighters that took off to defend the Japanese airfields on Guam, Saipan, and Tinian islands. After destroying 45,000 tons of shipping and 168 aircraft, he retired that afternoon back to the fleet anchorage at Majuro. The seizure of the Gilberts and Marshalls, and the daring raids on Truk and the Marianas, left the Americans perfectly positioned to accelerate the pace of the great central Pacific campaign.[11]

Chapter Eleven

The Battle
of the Philippine Sea
1944

Admiral King viewed the Marianas as the linchpin of his entire Pacific strategy and had explained in detail why they were important to the Japanese as early as the December 1941 Arcadia Conference. In the spring of 1943, Admiral Cooke won over General Arnold to the Navy's view by pointing out that the Army Air Force's new long-range B-29 bombers might mount a strategic bombing campaign against Japan's Home Islands from bases on Guam, Saipan, and Tinian. General MacArthur vigorously opposed this strategy, insisting instead on an advance in the Southwest Pacific from New Guinea north to Mindanao and Luzon in the Philippines, and General Marshall half-heartedly backed him. King, as always, rested his case on the ruthless logic of the master strategist.

MacArthur relied on hyperbole and hysterics and totally misunderstood the principle of economy of force. "These frontal attacks by the Navy, as at Tarawa, are tragic and unnecessary massacres of American lives," he told Secretary of War Stimson. "The Navy fails to recognize that the first phase is an Army phase to establish land-based air protection so the Navy can move in. . . . Give me central direction of the war in the Pacific, and I will be in the Philippines in ten months." Roosevelt was eager to please MacArthur so that the popular general would not return home and run for the presidency in 1944. At the November 1943 Cairo Conference, the JCS tried to satisfy both Nimitz and MacArthur by agreeing to a dual offensive with two fronts: north from New Guinea to Mindanao and west from Hawaii into the central Pacific. Nimitz had begun to vacillate, pressured by the new administrator of the Pacific Fleet's air forces, Vice Admiral John Towers, who proposed instead to seize the Admiralties and the Palaus, bypass Truk, and converge with MacArthur's offensive in the Philippines. King rejected this idea in a blistering message to Nimitz characterizing Towers' plan as not only "absurd" but also "not in accordance with the decisions of the Joint Chiefs."[1]

Advancing into the Marianas was made considerably easier by Mitscher's reconnaissance-in-force against Truk on 17 February, which revealed not only that the Combined Fleet had nearly abandoned that base but also that Japan's defensive perimeter was cracking under unbearable stress. The light resistance in the Marshalls, overrun far more easily than Nimitz had expected, supported a new appreciation of the frailty of Japan's overall position. After several options were explored at a conference in Washington in March 1944, King instructed Nimitz to move ahead his invasion of the Marianas to June. At the same time he warned that this would in all likelihood provoke a general naval action and strongly urged Nimitz to go after the Japanese fleet. King had applauded Spruance's conservative handling of the 5th Fleet in the Gilberts-Marshalls invasions. By the spring of 1944, however, fearing that King believed the Pacific Fleet insufficiently aggressive, Nimitz felt it necessary to give reassurance that the "destruction of the enemy fleet is always the primary objective of our Naval forces."[2]

While Turner prepared his Pacific Amphibious Force for the invasion of the Marianas, Mitscher's Fast Carrier Task Force conducted several lethal raids against Japan's remaining air strength in the central Pacific. The first blow landed in the Carolines on the morning of 30 March 1944 when Admiral Frederick Sherman's carrier task group closed on the Palau Islands and launched the first of two days of air strikes that sank three oilers and twenty-six merchantmen and left the harbor thoroughly mined. The old Japanese base at Yap was also struck on the same day. Then, on April Fools' Day, Mitscher's Fast Carrier Force appeared off Woleai in a new formation. In the van were Vice Admiral Willis Lee's Screening Force, composed of *Iowa-* and *South Dakota*-class fast battleships, which was to provide a daytime antiaircraft gunfire shield for the carriers and to be ready for a night surface action. The American carriers again attacked Japanese shipping, fuel depots, supply dumps, and air facilities at Truk on 29 April, an operation similar to the one conducted a month earlier. By this time Spruance had enough escorts to establish a separate Heavy Bombardment Group composed of nine heavy cruisers and eight destroyers under Rear Admiral Jesse B. Oldendorf, and he detached these ships from the carriers to bombard Satawan Island. On May Day, Lee's Screening Force shelled Ponape. Rear Admiral Montgomery with two carriers, five cruisers, and twelve destroyers raided Marcus Island on 19 May and four days later hit Japanese installations on Wake.

On 1 April 1944, an aircraft ambush by the Americans, made possible by Ultra radio intelligence, took the life of Admiral Koga, who was replaced as commander of the Combined Fleet by Admiral Soemu Toyoda, a more vigorous figure who decided to lay an elaborate trap to destroy the enemy carriers. To do this, Toyoda intended to lure the 5th Fleet into the waters between Yap and the Palaus where his land-based aircraft might lend support to Japanese carrier operations. In effect, this would place the Americans between fixed and mobile air bases, the very thing that had brought grief to Yamamoto off Midway. After the withdrawal from Rabaul in February, all front-line Japanese land-based aircraft—about 500 planes—had been shifted to four bases in the Marianas, Yap, and Babelthuap in the Palaus and to the rear at Iwo Jima. Toyoda stationed Vice Admiral Jisaburo Ozawa's Mobile Fleet of nine miscellaneous carriers and five battleships at Tawitawi, but this primitive, poorly chosen anchorage lacked the shore installations necessary to prepare the new carrier air groups. Ozawa put to sea to work up his carriers in mid-May and passed through the San Bernardino Strait, but was located off the southern tip of the Sulu Archipelago by American submarines, who put Nimitz on alert that the Japanese were preparing for a major counterattack.[3]

The invasion of the Marianas was an immense undertaking, surpassing by far in scale and complexity any campaign contemplated before the war. The distances to be covered by the invaders were formidable: the Marianas were over 3,500 miles from the Pacific Fleet base at Pearl Harbor, and about 1,000 miles from carrier anchorage and service base at Majuro Atoll in the Marshall Islands. The 5th Fleet under newly promoted Admiral Spruance was divided into Mitscher's Fast Carrier Force—which was composed of fifteen heavy and light carriers embarking 902 aircraft, seven fast battleships, twenty-one cruisers, and sixty-nine destroyers—and Turner's Expeditionary Force. Most of the fighter squadrons flew F6F Hellcats and most of the bombing squadrons flew SB2C Helldivers, although a handful of older SBD Dauntlesses could still be found on the flight decks. The vastly reduced torpedo bombing squadrons flew both TBF and TBM Avenger torpedo planes. There were even three radar-equipped F4U-2 Corsairs operating from the *Enterprise* for night operations. These arms were, in turn, supported by Vice Admiral William C. Calhoun's huge Pacific Fleet Service Force, which was made up of Rear Admiral Augustine Gray's Oiler Force and Rear Admiral Worrell Reed Carter's service bases and ships.

On 6 June 1944—the same day on which the Allies crossed the English Channel and landed in France on the other side of the world—the Fast Carrier Force stood out of Majuro and appeared off the Marianas five days later. Over the next forty-eight hours, they attacked the Japanese land-based air forces at Guam, Rota, Saipan, and Tinian, the southernmost islands in the archipelago—and the only ones of any strategic importance. Although over eighty Japanese land-based aircraft were splashed or damaged on the ground, accurate, heavy enemy antiaircraft batteries exacted an unexpectedly high toll of the attacking American aircraft. "Bombing of runways and AA [antiaircraft] installations is . . . futile," one pilot complained, a position supported by another's observation that "the constant cratering of runways . . . requires great expenditures of bombs and permits the Japanese to display their ability to fill in holes."[4]

On the morning of 13 June, Spruance withdrew Rear Admiral Montgomery's carrier task group—which included the heavy carriers *Bunker Hill* and *Wasp* and the 11,000-ton light carriers *Monterey* and *Cabot*—and deployed it to a station north of Saipan to cover the landings there. Montgomery's ships were soon joined by Rear Admiral John W. Reeves' task group composed of the veteran heavy carrier *Enterprise,* the new heavy carrier *Lexington,* and the light carriers *Princeton* and *San Jacinto.* Spruance, hoping to thwart the Japanese from shuttling planes from the Home Islands via Iwo Jima to the Marianas, ordered Mitscher to send two carrier task groups north to attack airfields in the Bonin Islands. Mitscher led Rear Admiral J. J. Clark to believe that this movement would precipitate the major action of

Marine Corps Major General Harry Schmidt (*left*), Admiral Raymond A. Spruance, Commander, Fifth Fleet (*center*), and Vice Admiral Richmond Kelly "Terrible" Turner, Commander, Fifth Amphibious Force, on Tinian Island, 3 August 1944.

A squadron of Hellcat fighters waiting to take off during the Battle of the Philippine Sea, June 1944.

the battle, so Clark, a volatile, aggressive spirit, was angered when Rear Admiral William K. Harrill, who commanded a task group of one heavy and two light carriers, did not want to detach his carriers and intended, instead, to appeal or ignore Mitscher's order. Clark shamed Harrill into changing his mind, but the episode led Clark to denounce Harrill to Mitscher later, and this cost Harrill his command when the battle was over.[5]

The fleet action began to develop when Clark drove Harrill northward, and at 1330 on 16 June, they launched the first of two days of air strikes against Iwo, Haha, and Chichi Jima, damaging or destroying almost 100 planes and disrupting a vital link in the air shuttle from Japan to the Marianas. At the same time, Spruance had directed Admiral Lee to bombard Saipan with the Screening Force, but Lee refused to send his new battleships closer than 10,000 yards inshore, his spotting plane pilots failed to fix the enemy's positions, and most of the high-explosive shells did little damage. The next day, Rear Admiral Jesse B. Oldendorf's Bombardment Force of old, slow prewar battleships appeared off Saipan. This task group—which included several veterans of Pearl Harbor—was now dedicated to offshore naval gunfire bombardment, and the ships were allowed to move close inshore and inflict serious damage on the Japanese installations.

Meanwhile, the Expeditionary Force, embarking over 127,000 Marines and Army troops, was steaming into the Marianas. Forager, the codename for the invasion of the Marianas, envisioned the capture of Saipan by an amphibious operation and the later seizure of Tinian and Guam by amphibious forces supported by shore-to-shore movements. Staging from Hawaii, Admiral Turner's Northern Attack Force was to take Saipan and Tinian, while the Southern Attack Force under Rear Admiral Richard Conolly, which staged out of the Guadalcanal area, was to capture Guam. At 0542 on 15 June, Turner ordered the invasion of Saipan to begin. With air support from the escort carriers, sixty-four LSTs carried the assault troops to the offshore line of departure where a landing flotilla of over 600 LVT amphibians and supporting gunboats were ready for the run to the beach along channels cleared and marked by underwater demolition teams who had landed earlier that morning. In waves of balletlike complexity, Commodore P. S. Theiss sent ashore over 8,000 Marines within about twenty minutes, and by nightfall that figure had increased to over 20,000. The Japanese, with their fanatical tenacity, skill with mortars and artillery, and ability to exploit the difficult terrain, put up a more successful resistance to the invasion than the Americans expected. The next day, upon learning that the Mobile Fleet had put to sea, Spruance committed his strategic reserve division to Saipan, augmented his Screening Force at the expense of the Bombardment Group that was defending the transports, and ordered Turner to withdraw his transports from Saipan on the evening of 17 June. Although the final outcome of the fighting on the island was never in doubt, a full three weeks passed before the Japanese garrison was finally defeated.

To eject the Americans from the Marianas, the Japanese implemented a strategic plan characterized by great complexity. Fearing in May that the Americans would reenter the central Pacific, Admiral Toyoda had deployed two dozen submarines along a picket line to the east of the Marianas, a movement revealed to Nimitz by Ultra intercepts. "A Japanese submarine commander's operational order was intercepted and partially decrypted" in May, according to Captain Holmes, and "subsequent plotting and additional decryption . . . yielded fairly reliable information on the position of the patrol line." This led Spruance to deploy an antisubmarine carrier and several destroyer escort groups to attack the enemy submarine barrier, a counterstroke that completely disrupted this Japanese operation. Lieutenant Commander W. B. Pendleton in the destroyer escort *England* sank six Japanese submarines during the last twelve days in May. The effect of this successful antisubmarine counterattack was to blind the Japanese to the progression of the 5th Fleet into the Marianas during the second week of June. Nevertheless, when Toyoda learned that American carrier aircraft were attacking the Japanese airfields on Saipan on 11 June, he instantly realized that he had badly misjudged where the weight of the American advance would land.[6]

Recalling his carriers to the Philippines, Toyoda reinforced Admiral Ozawa's Mobile Fleet so that it now numbered 5 battleships, 13 cruisers, and 473 aircraft distributed among 9 heavy and light carriers of various classes. Ozawa knew that the opposing naval air forces were superior in numbers, but he intended to overcome his inferiority by advancing his carriers into the Philippine Sea and taking station outboard of the American carriers, still near enough to the Marianas so that his planes might shuttle between the Mobile Fleet and Rota and Guam. Ozawa also planned to exploit the superior range of his attack aircraft, which, since they carried more gas, no heavy self-sealing fuel tanks, and less armor than the American planes, had a striking radius of more than 300 miles. The striking radius of American aircraft was about 200 miles. His plan concentrated all the Mobile Fleet against a single object, the American carriers, but victory greatly depended upon a level of tactical and strategic coordination that the Japanese fleet had as yet been unable to attain.

To alert the 5th Fleet to a Japanese counterattack, Admiral Lockwood had positioned a large force of picket submarines off the Philippines where they might warn Spruance of enemy ship movements. On the morning of 15 June, the submarine *Flying Fish* reported that Japanese warships had just passed through the San Bernardino Strait. Unable to maintain contact, she withdrew to Brisbane shortly thereafter, but at 1845 Lieutenant Commander Slade D. Cutter in the submarine *Seahorse* saw smoke on the horizon about 200 miles east of Surigao Strait. Although one of his motors went out and he too lost contact, Cutter broadcast a report to Pearl Harbor that was relayed to Spruance in the flagship cruiser *Indianapolis*. These reports not only revealed to Spruance that Ozawa was steaming into the central Pacific but also misled him into believing that Ozawa planned to attack the 5th Fleet from two different directions, a conviction that guided Spruance's entire conduct of the action in the Philippine Sea. Admiral Conolly was scheduled to land on Guam on the 18th, but Spruance now canceled this operation, reinforced his long-range patrol plane reconnaissance, and directed Mitscher to order Clark's and Harrill's task groups to rendezvous with the Fast Carrier Force 160 miles west of Tinian on the afternoon of 18 June. "Our air will first knock out enemy carriers [and] then will attack enemy battleships and cruisers to slow or disable them." He cautioned Mitscher, however, that the Fast Carrier Force also "must cover Saipan."[7]

The stage was set for a fleet action when, on 17 June, Commander Herman J. Kossler in the submarine *Cavalla*, after trailing a pair of Japanese oilers, sighted part of the Mobile Fleet at 2115 and radioed that it was about 800 miles southwest of Saipan. Kossler's message reinforced Spruance's conviction that Ozawa intended to outflank the Americans to the south. Mitscher believed that the *Cavalla*'s contact was the Mobile Fleet's main body and told Spruance that he intended to steam to the southwest, locate the enemy with his search planes, and engage in a surface action that night. Thus, during the 18th, the two fleets steamed toward each other like partly blinded boxers in a very large ring. The Japanese search planes could fly out to 560 miles, so they possessed a significant advantage over the Americans, whose searches were limited to roughly 325 miles. However, at 0800, when the first air contact was reported, the rival carrier forces were only about 350 miles apart, and Ozawa decided to increase this. He reckoned that at this distance his attack aircraft could reach the American carriers but that the enemy planes, limited by their 200-mile striking radius, could not retaliate. Believing that he had opened the distance to about 400 miles at 1540, Ozawa turned to the south and instructed Vice Admiral Takeo Kurita's Van Force of battleships and three light carriers to take station about 100 miles to east of the six-carrier main force. When night fell on 18 June, Ozawa knew the approximate location of the American carriers and was ready to attack them at dawn.

Spruance was not apprised of the enemy fleet's exact location on 18 June, although he understood that Ozawa had entered the Philippine Sea and Mitscher believed that the enemy was approaching the Fast Carrier Force from the southwest. If the Americans continued steaming westward during the day and launched search planes to fix the position of the Japanese carriers, Mitscher reasoned, then Lee's fast battleship Screening Force might meet the enemy at night and defeat him using search radars to dominate the gunnery duel. "Do you desire night engagement?" Mitscher asked Lee. Lee was a blooded veteran of several night actions in the Solomons, so Mitscher was greatly surprised when Lee replied that he did not want to do battle with the Japanese battleships that evening inasmuch as the "advantages of radar [are] more than offset by difficulties of communications and lack of training in fleet tactics at night." Spruance, who evidently thought that a daytime action between battleships was still possible, supported Lee on the basis that the Japanese, with their superior training, might enjoy an advantage at night.[8]

The ranges of the contending aircraft were a major factor in the battle. Mitscher's search planes did not possess the range to locate and monitor the Japanese fleet, whereas the Fast Carrier Force was constantly trailed by the enemy's longer-range scouts. When night fell on the 18th, Spruance told Mitscher that he in-

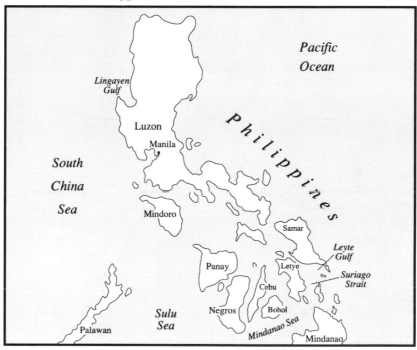

The Philippines

tended to continue to steam westward until 0200 the following morning and send out a night search for the enemy, but that if Ozawa's ships were not found, the Americans would turn back to the east and head toward Saipan. Mitscher protested, but to no avail. Ozawa's mission, Spruance believed, "was to protect Saipan, and this could be most effectively done by destroying the transports and the support forces." His mind did not change even after he received a message from Pearl Harbor that radio intelligence had located Ozawa's flagship about 350 miles to the southwest of the Fast Carrier Force. However, the meaning of this message was obscured by another report that the Japanese were jamming a radio frequency over which the submarine *Stingray*, now about 135 miles south of Ozawa's position, was trying to broadcast. Worried that the *Stingray* meant to report contact with a second enemy task force, Spruance turned aside one more protest by Mitscher, and the Fast Carrier Force steamed away from the enemy in the middle of the night.[9]

At 0530 on 19 June, Admiral Mitscher turned the Fast Carrier Force northeast into the wind and launched the combat air patrol fighters. Within moments one enemy search plane was splashed, but another escaped and broadcast the Americans' exact location to the Mobile Fleet. Mitscher next launched scout planes to locate the enemy carriers, but they had no luck that morning. Mitscher now was told that several Japanese aircraft had taken off from Guam, so he instructed Admiral Clark to dispatch a squadron of F6F Hellcats on a sweep over the island, where they successfully disrupted the enemy attack. Shortly after 0800, Spruance learned from a PBM Mariner contact report—which was already eight hours old—that the Mobile Fleet was 360 miles to the west of the Fast Carrier Force. He now realized that his ships would have to absorb a Japanese blow before they could close, turn once again into the wind, and counterattack.

Despite this unsettling turn of events, the Battle of the Philippine Sea opened with good news for the Fast Carrier Force. A few days earlier, Admiral Lockwood had drawn a great square over a map of the Philippine Sea, divided it into quarters, and deployed several submarines to patrol each quarter. Their work was made difficult, however, by Spruance's decision to impose radio silence on the Fast Carrier Force and by his cautious approach to the enemy fleet. On 18 June, Lockwood had shifted this square to the south, and when dawn broke the next day Lieutenant Commander James W. Blanchard in the submarine *Albacore* found himself right in the middle of the Mobile Fleet. Evading one escort and closing to within 5,300 yards of a larger target, Blanchard fired six bow tubes against Ozawa's flagship *Taiho*, evaded a Japanese depth-charge counterattack, and then heard "a distant and persistent explosion of great force" after one of his torpedoes entered the starboard side of the carrier. Ozawa did not think the damage was serious and assigned an inexperienced junior officer to supervise damage control. Gas filled up the forward elevator pit, and he allowed the fumes to disperse by opening up the entire ventilation system, thus turning the ship into a floating gas bomb. Ozawa, unaware of this danger, had already launched the first of four successive flights of escorts and attackers, a total of 326 aircraft, which headed eastward to strike the Fast Carrier Force.[10]

Mitscher could call upon seven heavy and eight light carriers embarking over 900 aircraft to meet them. He now recalled the

strike against Guam and sent aloft all of his 425 dive bombers
and torpedo planes, thereby clearing the carrier decks for defensive operations. Lee positioned his battleships to the west of the
carriers, where his radars might detect incoming aircraft without
clutter and where he could establish an effective antiaircraft
gunfire barrier. When the Japanese aircraft approached the
American ships, they fell from the sky with such ease and in such
astounding numbers that one Navy pilot compared it to "an old-
time turkey shoot," a phrase aptly describing the thoroughly one-
sided slaughter. Many of the Japanese aircraft were intercepted
as far out as fifty miles from the American formation, and a mere
handful actually penetrated both the lethal combat air patrol
and the antiaircraft screen. Everything worked for the Americans. They overheard the enemy's air controller and translated
his instructions to his aircraft throughout the battle. And atmospheric conditions created incoming vapor trails, which greatly
simplified the problem of vectoring fighters against incoming
bombers. One Japanese dive bomber struck the *South Dakota*, but
this single hit—the only one that day—failed to put the sturdy
battleship out of action. During the Marianas "Turkey Shoot,"
the Americans lost twenty-nine aircraft, although some of their
aircrews were saved, while the Japanese lost 240 planes, the third
and last major gutting of her carrier-based air forces. A handful
of enemy aircraft attackers reached Guam, and to destroy them
Mitscher sent another sweep over that island, which cost the
Japanese at least another fifty planes.[11]

Amidst this catastrophe, the Japanese suffered another demoralizing loss when Commander Kossler in the *Cavalla* reappeared on the scene and pumped three torpedoes into the heavy
carrier *Shokaku*, causing fires that signaled the onset of her
demise. At 1530, the deck of the *Taiho* was cleaved in two by a
tremendous gas explosion, the sides blew off the ship, and she
settled in the water. She was followed about ninety minutes later
by the *Shokaku*, an esteemed veteran of several campaigns. During the night of 19 June, Ozawa, who had transferred his flag to
another ship, steamed to the northwest to lick his wounds and
figure out what to do next.

When a report of the *Shokaku*'s sinking reached Spruance,
he estimated that Mitscher's combat air patrol had eliminated at
least half of Ozawa's planes. He also now knew that part of the
Mobile Fleet was to the west but still suspected that the Japanese

intended to execute an end run. He intended "to attack the enemy tomorrow if we know his position with sufficient accuracy," he told Mitscher, otherwise "we must continue searches tomorrow to ensure adequate protection of Saipan." Supremely confident that he could overwhelm the enemy carriers and their greatly reduced air groups, Mitscher now took note of Rear Admiral Harrill's overly cautious concern about refueling his destroyers and instructed him to detach his task group and take station off Guam. Ozawa had begun to retire at 2000, and two hours later Spruance returned tactical command of the carriers to Mitscher, who sped to the northwest in pursuit of the crippled Mobile Fleet.[12]

Owing to the lack of night search planes, Mitscher waited until dawn on 20 June to launch his patrols, and it was not until 1540 that Lieutenant R. S. Nelson flying a torpedo bomber from the *Enterprise* informed the Fast Carrier Force that the Mobile Fleet was about 275 miles from the American position. Given this distance, and the time of day, Mitscher calculated that a flight of attack aircraft could reach the enemy before twilight, press home an attack for about thirty minutes, and still have enough gas to make it back to their carriers. Finding the Fast Carrier Force at night would be difficult, however; many of the planes would be lost at sea, and a large fraction of the pilots were not qualified to make night landings on the heaving carrier decks. Mitscher was nonetheless anxious to sink the remaining enemy carriers and, within a few minutes, with Spruance's backing, he took a calculated risk. At 1625 the American carriers turned into the wind and launched the first of 215 aircraft, which sped into the Pacific after Ozawa's hapless Mobile Fleet.

Slightly over two hours later, they appeared over the Japanese ships, then facing the late afternoon sun and defended by fewer than seventy-five aircraft of various types. The defending planes were quickly splashed at the cost of only twenty American aircraft. The F6F Hellcats thus cleared the way for the attackers to pummel the Mobile Fleet, but there was so little daylight left that the attack could not be coordinated and each pilot was freed to conduct his own individual assault on one of the vessels below. Owing to the success of the American dive bombers in the action off Midway two years earlier, the Navy's torpedo planes often thereafter went into combat armed with bombs, but now in the Philippine Sea these bombers could not sink any carriers, although they did destroy two oilers and a transport and badly damaged the carriers *Zuikaku* and *Chiyoda*, the fast battleship *Haruna*, and a cruiser. On the other hand, Lieutenant George P. Brown's section of four TBF Avengers, part of the only squadron in the task force still armed with torpedoes, put one or two fish into the side of the carrier *Hiyo*, causing her to erupt into flames that sent her plunging to the bottom two hours later.

The Battle of the Philippine Sea ended around 1900 when night began to fall over the Mobile Fleet and the remaining 190 American aircraft turned back for the long return flight to the Fast Carrier Force. A few crippled planes went down on the way, several pilots got lost and were never recovered, and many ran out of gas before reaching the carriers—which were, according to standard carrier doctrine, lit up with deck and running lights and fully ready for nighttime recovery operations. When large numbers of planes, all low on fuel, arrived over the carriers, chaos ensued. Although the first aircraft to land did so almost without incident, the flight decks were soon cluttered with wrecks. Some scared and weary pilots crashed their planes against the carriers, and a large number simply tried to ditch in the vicinity of a friendly ship. Of 226 aircraft that Mitscher had sent out against the Japanese fleet that day, nearly half—99 planes—were lost. By 2200, when recovery operations ended, the destroyers were already conducting a massive search and rescue operation. They pulled 101 pilots and bombardiers from the ocean on the 21st, and within the next few days another 59 men were rescued. "Planes could be replaced," Admiral King reflected, "but pilots could not," and as a result of the extraordinarily successful rescue effort following the battle, fewer than 50 Navy pilots and crewmen perished in the Philippine Sea. On the other side, including the aircraft destroyed in the Bonins, the Japanese lost over 525 planes and most of their aircrews. According to King, this blow "crippled Japanese naval aviation for the remainder of the war."[13]

This rescue operation marked the end of the Battle of the Philippine Sea, but the engagement brought about an instant controversy among the American admirals. To cover the rescue vessels during 21 June, Mitscher turned the Fast Carrier Force to the east, away from the Mobile Fleet, which was by now escaping to the northwest beyond the range of American search planes. Another air strike was launched that morning, but it failed to locate Ozawa's fleeing ships. After plucking some more pilots out of the water, Spruance sent one carrier task group north for a lightning strike on the Bonins and ordered the rest of the task force to head back toward Saipan that evening. However, Spruance's decision to retire on the 19th was already the source of controversy. "The Japanese . . . had always operated with divided forces, from different directions," Spruance later asserted in his own defense. "At Saipan I had no idea from what direction, or directions, they would attack. Our landings were in an early and critical stage. Our amphibious shipping . . . had to be protected from attack."[14]

Spruance's conduct of the battle was bitterly condemned by Admiral Mitscher and his turbulent chief of staff, Commodore Arleigh Burke, and their complaints were echoed by Admiral Towers in Hawaii. They contended that the root of the problem was that Spruance was a "battleship admiral" whom Nimitz never should have entrusted with command of the Fast Carrier Force. The Marines on Saipan had run into sustained opposition shortly after they landed, but by 18 June, General Smith had overcome this and Turner withdrew most of the transports for two or three days to an anchorage 200 miles to the east of Saipan. Therefore, the critics charged, Spruance might have ordered the transports to keep entirely away from the beaches without at all endangering the Marines. Furthermore, to defend the transports and the beaches, Admiral Turner had at his command Oldendorf's seven old battleships and eleven escort carriers, a slow but powerful force clearly up to the job of repulsing a flanking thrust by some fraction of Ozawa's Mobile Fleet. Also lying in wait for an enemy move in this direction were the five escort carriers attached to Admiral Conolly's Southern Attack Force, which by themselves operated roughly eighty Wildcats and fifty Avengers. "Spruance was still thinking in terms of a surface action," concluded the distinguished veteran aviator Admiral Frederick Sherman, and "did not grasp the tremendous power of our air weapons or their ability to strike in any direction to the limit of their fuel supply." Admiral King, who loudly defended Spruance's conduct of battle, nonetheless had already come up with one way to lessen the tension between the aviators and the surface ship officers. He ordered each of the major battleship admirals to name an aviator as his chief of staff and insisted that each of the carrier task force commanders select a surface officer to be his chief of staff. Thus, Rear Admiral Robert Carney, a battleship sailor, became Halsey's chief of staff, and destroyerman Commodore Burke went to work for Mitscher.[15]

Spruance wanted the strikes against the Palaus to cover the invasion of the southern Marianas, two operations that marked the end of the second stage of the great central Pacific campaign. Although Ozawa's counterattack in the Philippine Sea had been successfully repelled, the battle for Saipan continued to rage ashore until nearly all of the 24,000-man enemy garrison were killed after a last, suicidal charge against the Marines' lines on 7 July. Two days later, the Americans found the body of Vice Admiral Nagumo, the island's commandant, who had committed suicide.

Without the distraction of a naval battle, Spruance next turned on Tinian, only 3.5 miles from Saipan. Tinian's garrison was brought under fire by the heavy American artillery on Saipan, and on 25 July, LVT amphibians landed Marines along two narrow beaches on the island's northwest tip. This choice of a landing site surprised the Japanese, who congregated at Tinian Town on the southwest corner of the island. They were overrun in eight days of bitter fighting. Since Spruance had already committed his reserve division to the battle for Saipan, Admiral Turner and General Smith wanted to wait for another Army division to be shipped from Hawaii to the central Pacific before invading Guam. While these troops were en route, Spruance instructed Rear Admiral Conolly to bombard airfields and fortifications on Guam, an unusually successful thirteen-day operation, which dislodged most of the defenders' heavy artillery. The Marines landed on both sides of Apra Harbor on 21 July, established a long, shallow beachhead, and moved inland over difficult terrain against fierce but disorganized Japanese defenses. By 10 August organized resistance on Guam collapsed after a series of bloody, suicidal "banzai" charges.

With the seizure of the Marianas, Nimitz had gained a position from which the Pacific Fleet might strike at several Japanese strongpoints along an arc stretching from the Home Islands to the critical oil fields of the Dutch East Indies. Naval Construction Battalions, nicknamed Seabees, quickly erected a large base at Guam, which was eventually capable of supporting up to one-third of the Pacific Fleet, while runways were constructed on Saipan and Tinian to handle the long-range B-29 Superfortresses of the new 20th Air Force, a command established by General Arnold to bomb Japan from bases in the Marianas and China. Japan's entire Pacific empire was now exposed to the next American thrust.

Chapter Twelve

The Return
to the Philippines
1944

Admiral King and General Marshall deadlocked over the next Pacific offensive operation in the summer of 1944. The Army chief of staff still supported MacArthur's plan to move his Southwest Pacific forces from New Guinea to the Philippines. King, dedicated to the principle of economy of force, wanted Admiral Halsey's 3rd Fleet to outflank the Philippines and seize Formosa, thus severing Japan's communications with the Philippines, the Dutch East Indies, and Southeast Asia. "A direct attack on Formosa, without reference to the Philippine Islands," he argued, "would dominate the sea lanes by which Japan received essential supplies of oil, rice, and other commodities from her recently conquered empire." The Filipinos might also be spared from the ravages of more war. Although Formosa, long in Japanese hands, was well defended, the Army Air Force wanted its several large airfields for strategic bombing operations against Japan's Home Islands, and Formosa's protected anchorage might be used by the Pacific Fleet to stage a landing either on the China coast or Kyushu under the cover of land-based fighters. King reasoned that a leap from the Marianas to Formosa would demonstrate that an invasion of the Philippines by MacArthur was unnecessary. However, the best strategist in the Pacific theater, Admiral Forrest Sherman, believed that King's Formosa plan was "so ridiculous and so impossible . . . [and] so

obviously bad that they would cancel the idea" for lack of Army
service troops and shipping to support the operation.

On 17 July, King and Nimitz landed on Saipan to meet with
Spruance to discuss Pacific strategy. When King asked him where
the Pacific Fleet should next appear, Spruance recommended
Okinawa, but cautioned King that many problems had to be
overcome. Heavy munitions would have to be transferred at sea
while the ships were under way instead of at anchor alongside the
supply ship in a protected lagoon, and the carriers, having to operate between Okinawa and Japan, might be subjected to continuous attacks by Japan's remaining land-based air forces. Nimitz
turned the munitions problem over to Vice Admiral Calhoun,
the innovative head of the Pacific Service Force.

Marshall was still reluctantly supporting MacArthur's demand that he be allowed to return to the Philippines, the scene
of his humiliating 1942 defeat. It was the "slow way" to approach
Japan, Marshall admitted, and "would take a very much longer
time to make the cut across" from the Marianas to Formosa. In
July 1944, days after King returned to Washington from his visit
to Saipan, the cruiser *Baltimore* brought FDR and Admiral Leahy
to Pearl Harbor, where they met with MacArthur and Nimitz to
discuss Pacific strategy. MacArthur strongly urged Roosevelt to
back the invasion of the Philippines, while Nimitz' explanation
of the Formosa alternative was unconvincing. FDR intended the
meeting to be an election-year showcase of his role as commander in chief, not a working conference where decisions were
made, and he told Nimitz and MacArthur that the JCS would decide the matter. During 1944, with his mental powers clearly on
the decline owing to illness, FDR distanced himself considerably
from the formulation of grand strategy, and he met in Washington with the JCS less than ten times that year. When King and
Marshall took up Pacific strategy again in August, King was confronted with Nimitz' argument that he did not have enough service troops to conduct the Formosa operation. In addition, Admiral Leahy, representing the White House, favored MacArthur's
plan. King assumed that this meant that Roosevelt was eager for
American troops to reenter the Philippines before the November
1944 presidential elections. This consideration was decisive and
led King to agree resignedly that MacArthur might land on Mindanao, the southernmost of the major Philippine Islands. Some

on King's staff reasoned that MacArthur would get "bogged down" on Mindanao and that Nimitz could then get on with the Formosa campaign. Of course the JCS viewed the Philippines as another stepping stone on the road to Japan's Home Islands and never dreamed that MacArthur intended to attempt to subdue all the enemy occupation forces in the islands and then head south to liberate the Dutch East Indies.[1]

When it had appeared in late 1943 that the South Pacific campaign would soon wind down, Roosevelt asked King how he intended to employ Halsey in the future. Before FDR registered this not-too-subtle hint, King had given little thought to the question. Halsey was his most successful and popular fleet commander in the Pacific. Like everyone else in the Navy, King recalled with affection and respect Halsey's gritty victory in the Solomons. He also secretly admired the way that Halsey stood up to MacArthur in various interservice quarrels. On the other hand, King's respect for Spruance's ability was unreserved. Retiring, thoughtful, and meticulous, Spruance had, in King's opinion, won off Midway by showing a willingness to take a calculated risk and in the Philippine Sea by refusing to take an unnecessary gamble. Once Halsey reentered the Pacific theater, however, he would, with his seniority and greater experience, supersede Spruance—an awkward situation King clearly wanted to avoid. King also wanted to reward Admiral Turner with a fleet command.

At the Cairo Conference in November 1943, Admiral Cooke devised a novel way to solve this problem and still satisfy the president. Halsey, Spruance, and Turner and their respective staffs would trade places in command of the same ships during successive operations. While one team conducted an operation, the others would rest from the last one and plan the next one. Nimitz agreed to the scheme with one exception: he disliked Turner and did not want him to have a fleet command. King had already assigned numerical designations to every fleet in the Pacific, Atlantic, and Mediterranean, and thus when Halsey relieved Spruance, the 5th Fleet became the 3rd Fleet, and vice versa. Not only did Cooke's scheme satisfy Roosevelt, who appreciated Halsey's immense popularity at home, but it also provided Nimitz with two veteran fleet commanders each of whom had demonstrated truly extraordinary ability.

Before advancing to Formosa or the Philippines, Nimitz intended to occupy the western Carolines—the Palaus, Yap, and

"Murderers' Row." The carriers *Wasp* (CV-18), *Yorktown* (CV-10), *Hornet* (CV-12), and *Hancock* (CV-19) in Ulithi Atoll on 2 December 1944 during the campaign for the Philippines.

Rear Admiral Arthur D. Struble. Commander, Mindoro Attack Force, December 1944

Ulithi Atoll, all of which lay along a line between Guam and the island of Morotai. At the same time, MacArthur proposed to advance into the Moluccas as a first step toward the reoccupation of the Philippines, but instead of assaulting the large Japanese garrison on Halmahera, he decided on a landing to the north on Morotai. Late in July, Nimitz and MacArthur agreed that the invasions of the Palaus and Morotai would take place on the same day, 15 September 1944, and that Nimitz was to follow up by occupying Yap and Ulithi on 5 October.

The landing conditions at Morotai were some of the worst encountered in the Pacific, but MacArthur's troops met only a small band of dispirited Japanese who put up little resistance. The 40,000 enemy defenders of the Palaus knew that they had been isolated, but they were better led and grimly dedicated. The fast battleship *New Jersey*, flagship of the new 3rd Fleet commander, Halsey, stood out of Pearl Harbor on 24 August and rendezvoused with Mitscher's Fast Carrier Force two weeks later. Before he turned the fleet over to Halsey, Spruance had sent the Fast Carrier Force into the western Pacific in early August to conduct major strikes against the Bonins, the Volcanoes, and the Ryukyus and thus divert Japanese attention from the Palaus landings. Whereas Nimitz and Rear Admiral Robert Carney, Halsey's new chief of staff, were eager to invade the western Carolines, Halsey argued that while "Ulithi had a useful anchorage," he "saw no need for any of the other islands."

On 6 September, three task groups from Mitscher's Fast Carrier Force launched the first of three days of air strikes on the Palaus, while the fourth carrier task group pounded enemy installations on Yap. These targets had just been struck by Southwest Pacific Air Force B-24 land-based bombers. The air strikes were followed up by a three-day prelanding bombardment conducted by Admiral Oldendorf's old battleships, and, apparently as a result, when Admiral Theodore Wilkinson landed Marines and Army troops on Peleliu on 15 September they encountered only weak resistance on the beach. Unbeknownst to the Americans, the Japanese had decided early on not to contest the landing beaches but instead to construct a system of deep defenses in which their troops would remain sheltered in caves until the Americans came ashore. Then they would venture out between the salvoes of the battleships to conduct brief, violent counterattacks.

For three days, Major General Roy Geiger's Marines on Peleliu required continuous close ground support from Rear Admiral Ralph Davison's carrier task group. This work was then taken over by Rear Admiral Ralph Ofstie's escort carriers. While all the Marines' heavy artillery was put ashore within two days of the landing on Peleliu, and Marine F4U Corsairs used 1,000-pound bombs and napalm canisters on enemy positions soon after the landing, the Japanese defense was so stubborn that Geiger did not declare the island secure until 22 September. To his distress, scattered but organized resistance continued for another two months. On the other hand, the small island of Angaur fell within three days, and a regimental combat team easily overcame light opposition and occupied Ulithi Atoll. The cost of these various operations was 9,800 American dead and wounded, a stunning toll. Although the anchorage at Ulithi later proved to be invaluable for the Pacific Fleet, the Palaus' airfields were for a variety of reasons incapable of supporting later operations. This lent support to Halsey's charge that King and Nimitz had insisted on an operation that was both costly and strategically unnecessary.

King was more anxious for Halsey to enter the western Carolines than he was for MacArthur to advance into the Philippines, a campaign that King still believed would divert the thrust of the central Pacific advance away from the Formosa–China Coast–Japan triangle. He reluctantly agreed nonetheless to instruct Halsey's 3rd Fleet to support MacArthur's movement from the Vogelkop Peninsula via Morotai to southern Mindanao. The Mindanao landing was scheduled to take place on 25 October 1944. King also agreed to MacArthur's plan to invade Leyte on 20 December, but he still held out for a descent on Formosa rather than a costly, protracted campaign on Luzon. Even General Marshall now confessed that King was articulating the preferable strategy. "The best operation," he told the JCS on 5 September, "would be to seize Formosa and then move back to the Luzon operation." He did not explain why it would be necessary to land on Luzon at all after taking Formosa.[2]

To reduce Japanese land-based air strength in the Philippines in preparation for the Mindanao landings, Halsey struck northwestward from the Palaus on 10 September, assuming tactical command of the Fast Carrier Force after a series of disputes with Mitscher over the proper conduct of air operations. Two days later, Halsey sent air strikes against enemy bases in the Visayan Islands in the central Philippines. Over the next forty-eight hours, the attack carrier air groups shot down or destroyed over 450 enemy aircraft, sank nearly 50 transports, freighters, and lesser vessels, and pounded ground targets, which had been stripped of their air defenses. The Fast Carrier Force operated without interference from Japanese aircraft throughout September, and the Philippine resistance reported to Halsey that the enemy's aircraft inventory on Mindanao was low. "We had found the central Philippines a hollow shell with weak defenses and skimpy facilities," he recorded, and this prompted him to propose to Nimitz and King that the invasion of Mindanao be scrapped in favor of a movement by MacArthur to Leyte on 20 October.

This error-ridden assessment of enemy air power—attributable largely to Carney's lack of control over Halsey's staff, a situation that Halsey tolerated—compelled the JCS to reexamine the problem of Pacific strategy just at the moment they were settling down for another major Anglo-American summit conference at Quebec. Both Nimitz and MacArthur agreed with Halsey's plan, in part because neither of them now wanted to bypass Luzon. Both surely realized that accelerating the Philippine campaign would greatly undermine King's position on this issue. King, who had consistently urged that the Pacific offensive be speeded up, could scarcely argue against this request. Once he and Marshall had agreed to revise their directive to their Pacific commanders concerning the Leyte operation, King admitted that he could not hold out alone against an invasion of Luzon. On 3 October he reached a compromise with Marshall. MacArthur was to invade Luzon on 20 December and Nimitz was to occupy the Bonins and the Ryukyus early in 1945. Marshall and King clearly believed that MacArthur only intended to liberate key areas of Leyte and Luzon. They never suspected that he planned to attempt to evict the Japanese from every inch of the many hundreds of Philippine Islands before concerning himself with the enemy's Home Islands.

General Marshall, the foremost advocate of the dubious principle of unity of command, was largely responsible for the confusing command relationships that afflicted the American conduct of the Leyte invasion, but King, who knew MacArthur to be unstable, was also to blame. The Pacific and Southwest Pacific theater principals clearly understood the command arrangements for the Leyte invasion, but the JCS's hasty decision to by-pass Mindanao, substitute Leyte, and move up the date of the landing left little time for consultations among the various ground, naval, and air staffs. King's strong distrust of MacArthur denied him overall command, and Marshall's refusal to subordinate MacArthur to Nimitz denied the admiral the theater command he richly deserved. The JCS told Nimitz to assign Halsey to support the landings, which were to be conducted under MacArthur's command by Admiral Kinkaid's 7th Fleet. Because the 7th Fleet contained no carriers to provide an air defense for the beaches or close ground support for the assault troops, Nimitz assigned eighteen 3rd Fleet escort carriers under Rear Admiral Clifton Sprague to Kinkaid for this work. Nimitz also lent Kinkaid Rear Admiral Jesse Oldendorf's old battleship Bombardment Force, which was to provide the landing troops with a preinvasion offshore gunfire bombardment.

In effect, Nimitz had stripped Halsey of most of his fleet, for he now commanded only Mitscher's four fast carrier task groups and Admiral Willis Lee's line of six fast battleships and eight heavy cruisers. On and after 21 October, the Fast Carrier Force was to provide "strategic support" for Admiral Daniel Barbey's Northern Amphibious Landing Force and Wilkinson's Southern Landing Force by destroying Japanese air or naval forces that menaced the beachhead or the 7th Fleet's assault shipping. Halsey was under no obligation to concern himself with the landings, however, and Nimitz issued him orders stating that "in case opportunity for destruction of major portion of enemy fleet is offered or can be created, such destruction becomes the primary task." In short, Nimitz hoped Halsey would not emulate Spruance's tactical conservatism in the Philippine Sea, when the relative strength of the opposing fleets had been somewhat less disproportionate. Navy code breakers had not picked up Japan's plan to defend Leyte, and so Halsey reasoned that he might not encounter a fleet action in the Philippines. However, Rear Admiral Raymond Tarbuck, the Navy's liaison at MacArthur's rear headquarters, was drawing on several intelligence sources and crafting a canny estimate of the enemy's intentions. He predicted that the Japanese fleet would descend on Leyte Gulf, but MacArthur's intelligence chief, Major General Charles Willoughby, ignored Tarbuck's work and refused to forward it to Kinkaid, and Tarbuck did not act on his own.[3]

At dawn on 10 October, Halsey's carriers stood off Okinawa and launched several deck load strikes, which sank 19 small Japanese combatants and destroyed or damaged over 100 aircraft. The next day, he sent a flight of fighters over Luzon, then refueled his carriers and turned to the north to pounce on Formosa, where a formidable air battle took place on 12 October. Although the Japanese were braced for this blow, many of their green pilots had as few as thirty hours in the air, and few were capable of dealing with the overpowering, highly coordinated American air strikes. The Japanese defenders conducted over 600 sorties during the three-day battle, splashing 76 Americans and putting torpedoes in the heavy cruiser *Canberra* and the light cruiser *Houston*. However, these successes were purchased at a terrible price: the sinking of over 100 small ships and landing vessels and the loss of about 520 military aircraft. Such results assured the Americans that they would enjoy unchallenged air superiority over Leyte Gulf. Moreover, Halsey would profit from another, less visible advantage over the enemy—the support he expected to receive from the Pacific Fleet Service Force. Guarded by a force of escort carriers and destroyers, Rear Admiral L. E. Pare's At-Sea-Logistics Service Group included thirty-four fleet oilers and several tugs. For thirteen out of the next sixteen weeks, Pare's ships remained at sea to fuel and replenish the thirsty 3rd Fleet.

The first American landing in the Philippines came on the evening of 17 October when an Army battalion went ashore on some small islands at the entrance to Leyte Gulf to erect navigational lights that were to guide the attack shipping to the beaches. The first shot was fired by the cruiser *Denver* in support of the 6th Army Rangers, who went ashore and secured the first beachhead in the evening. The next morning, Kinkaid directed Oldendorf's old battleships to steam into the Gulf to cover the work of the busy minesweepers and Navy UDT teams, while Halsey's carriers launched sweeps against the enemy's airfields in the northern Philippines. That night, Oldendorf began to shell the beach defenses and, at 0600 on 20 October, air strikes were launched from the escort carriers to cover the landings, which began at 1000. Covered by Rear Admiral G. L. Weyler's Gunfire Support Group, consisting of the Pearl Harbor veterans *Mississippi*, *Maryland*, and *West Virginia*, and a destroyer screen, Barbey's 7th Fleet Northern Attack Force landed assault troops three miles south of the vital Tacloban airstrip. At the same time, Wilkinson's Southern Attack Force, provided by the Pacific Fleet and covered by Oldendorf's old battleships, put ashore an Army corps between the small ports of Dulag and San Jose. The Japanese mistakenly allowed five waves of assault troops to land before opening fire at the landing craft, and the Americans easily overwhelmed this light resistance so that by noon one entire beachhead was secure. In a smartly pressed uniform, MacArthur waded ashore while a host of waiting newsreel cameras recorded the inevitable historic declaration, "I have returned."[4]

MacArthur's dramatics notwithstanding, the amphibious landings at Leyte went quite smoothly, although Rear Admiral Walden Ainsworth nearly lost his flagship, the cruiser *Honolulu*, to a stray Japanese torpedo plane and indiscriminate American antiaircraft fire. By that evening, elements of General Walter Krueger's 6th Army had captured the Tacloban airstrip, at which point the Japanese commander decided to withdraw from the perimeter of the beachhead to prepared defensive positions in the interior. By the evening of 21 October, Kinkaid had put more than 132,000 American troops ashore, Tacloban village and the nearby Dulag airstrip had been overrun, and all but about 50 *Liberty* ships, attack transports, and miscellaneous landing vessels had stood out of the Gulf. So far, there was little evidence that the Japanese intended to deploy their crippled fleet to contest the invasion of the Philippines.

In early October, since naval intelligence had collected some preinvasion clues suggesting that the enemy would seek a fleet action, Admiral Lockwood deployed two separate submarine squadrons to stations between Japan and the Philippines to observe enemy movements. Commander Thomas Wogan in the *Besugo* was watching the Inland Sea when, on the morning of 15 October, he sighted three cruisers and several destroyers about 7,500 yards off his bow. Wogan surfaced and reported to Lockwood that the enemy formation was returning to the Inland Sea. The next night he observed a second group of ships nearby, broadcast a contact report, and then attacked the enemy and blew off the bow of the destroyer *Suzutzuki*, which withdrew to Kōbe. These encounters convinced Wogan that the enemy fleet was retiring to the Inland Sea, and on 18 October Lockwood agreed to Wogan's request to reduce the coverage of those waters and to resume his normal hunting patrol. As a result, four

Japanese carriers under Vice Admiral Jisaburo Ozawa steamed safely through the Palawan Passage two nights later, unnoticed by the remaining American lookouts.

Then, in the early morning of 23 October, Commander David McClintock in the submarine *Darter* surfaced and reported to Halsey that he had sighted an enemy battleship-cruiser force steaming north through the Palawan Passage between the South China Sea and the Palawan Reefs. McClintock submerged, closed on these ships, and at 0630 fired a salvo of torpedoes that struck and sank the heavy cruiser *Atago* and disabled the heavy cruiser *Takao*. Within a short time, Commander Bladen D. Claggett in the submarine *Dace*, which had also broadcast a contact report to Pearl Harbor, approached the nearby *Maya* and drilled the heavy cruiser with torpedoes until she went under. Confounded by this unexpected loss of his flagship, Vice Admiral Takeo Kurita shifted to the superbattleship *Yamato* and continued steaming toward the entrance to the Sibuyan Sea.

The action in the Palawan Passage and intercepts picked up by his shipboard radio intelligence unit alerted Halsey to the imminence of a Japanese counterattack. Once again, however, Admiral Toyoda's strategic plan called for more ships and planes than his fleet possessed and required a level of tactical coordination that his admirals had seldom achieved. Moreover, the Japanese carriers lacked any striking power, having been unable to reconstruct their naval air squadrons destroyed earlier in the Solomons and the Philippine Sea and, more recently, over Formosa. They were desperately short of spares, fuel, engines, and mechanics to maintain their remaining aircraft inventory. The result was that six carriers of various sizes had been left behind in Japanese home waters owing to the lack of planes and trained aircrews. Ozawa commanded a Northern Force composed of three light carriers, two converted battleship-carriers, and the veteran fleet carrier *Zuikaku*. His entire Northern Force embarked only 116 aircraft, and a substantial fraction of these planes were unready for sustained operations. For these reasons, Ozawa's carriers could only serve as decoys. He was to appear off Luzon, lure Halsey's 3rd Fleet away from Leyte Gulf, and so expose the beachhead. Toyoda assigned the striking roles to Admiral Kurita's Central Force, composed of the superbattleships *Yamato* and *Musashi*, three older battleships, and twelve cruisers, and to Vice Admiral Shoji Nishimura's Southern Force comprising the battleships *Fuso* and *Yamashiro*, the heavy cruiser *Mogami*, and four destroyers. At the same time as Ozawa was to appear off Luzon, Kurita was to cross the Sibuyan Sea, steam through the San Bernardino Strait, and enter Leyte Gulf from the north. Nishimura would concurrently sail from Brunei, transit the Surigao Strait, and approach Leyte Gulf from the south.

Halsey concentrated the 3rd Fleet northeast of Samar to provide strategic cover for the beachhead on Leyte Gulf on 23 October and then steamed to the south that night and arrived at a position 125 miles east of central Luzon at dawn on the 24th. He now knew that the Japanese carriers were at sea—but not where they were—and that Luzon-based enemy scout planes had located his ships. Again the Americans would absorb the first blow. Between 0800 and 1200 three waves of attackers hit Admiral Frederick Sherman's task group. Bracing for the attack, he sent all his fighters aloft and hid his ships under cloud cover. During this attack, Commander David McCampbell flying off the *Essex* shot down nine enemy aircraft, the highest number ever by a carrier fighter pilot. Not one enemy aircraft penetrated Sherman's combat air patrol, but at 0915 he turned back toward Leyte Gulf again, and during this movement one Japanese bomber broke through his defenses and hit the 13,000-ton light carrier *Princeton*, causing a fire on the hangar deck that reached the torpedo storage area. Just after the cruiser *Birmingham* came alongside the stricken ship to take her in tow, an explosion blew the carrier's flight deck into the air and heavy debris rained over both vessels. There was no choice but to scuttle the *Princeton*.

While this action was under way, Halsey launched search planes to the west to locate the enemy fleet, and at 0905 Davison's Helldivers found that Nishimura's Southern Force had entered the Surigao Strait. Scouts from Rear Admiral Gerald Bogan's carrier task group discovered Kurita's Central Force east of Mindoro in the Sibuyan Sea at roughly the same time. Halsey had already sent Vice Admiral John McCain's carrier task group to refuel at Ulithi, but he now ordered McCain to return at top speed and rejoin the 3rd Fleet, and Bogan, Sherman, and Davison were told to concentrate their attacks on the larger of the two approaching enemy formations, Kurita's Central Force. They claimed the 72,000-ton superbattleship *Musashi*, holed four destroyers, and forced one cruiser to limp home. At 1400, Kurita decided to retire, and an aircraft flying off the heavy carrier

Intrepid watched his ships turn to the west and head away from the San Bernardino Strait at high speed. When Halsey heard this news he reasoned that the Central Force no longer posed a threat to the Leyte Gulf beachhead. While Sherman's naval bombers attacked Kurita's retiring ships, his fighters were dealing with an assault on his task group by seventy-six Japanese warplanes from Ozawa's carriers to the north, thus alerting Halsey to the general location of the enemy flattops. To the south, guarding the Surigao Strait, stood Kinkaid's 7th Fleet of six old battleships, sixteen escort carriers, and eight cruisers.

The likelihood of a battle in the Surigao Strait emerged at 0900 on the morning of 24 October when scouts from Admiral Davison's carrier task group located the enemy's Southern Force. Seaborne and land-based air attacks inflicted minor damage on this formation, but the Japanese continued to the south, so Kinkaid made ready for a night surface action by stationing PT boats off the coast of Panaon Island at the southern edge of the mouth of the Surigao Strait. To anchor the northern end of this barrier, he positioned two squadrons of destroyers to shield Oldendorf's Bombardment Group. Toyoda followed Japanese fleet doctrine by splitting up his inferior forces and instructing them to converge at the decisive moment. He had even divided the Southern Force into Nishimura's van, comprising the battleships *Fuso* and *Yamashiro*, the heavy cruiser *Mogami*, and four destroyers, and the rear, a cruiser-destroyer force under Vice Admiral Kiyohide Shima. When Nishimura entered the Surigao Strait at 2300 on the 24th, however, forty miles separated these two formations and prevented them from supporting each other.

Kinkaid was alarmed when he received word of Nishimura's appearance at the mouth of the Surigao Strait. American intelligence had predicted that the Japanese fleet would not contest the Leyte landing but would wait for an invasion of Luzon. This would bring the American carriers into the South China Sea, which was ringed by Japanese airfields in the Philippines, Formosa, and Indochina. It was now clear to both Kinkaid and Halsey that something else was afoot. Kinkaid instructed Oldendorf to check Nishimura's progress, and Oldendorf's battleships steamed south to the Surigao Strait to defend the 7th Fleet's southern flank. Between the southernmost tip of Leyte and Hibuson Island to the east, Oldendorf established a fifteen-mile line of six battleships and eight heavy and light cruisers. One destroyer division was to screen the battleships; three others were to attack the enemy. Finally, he instructed Lieutenant Commander R. A. Leeson to station his PT boats up and down the strait to act as radar pickets and to harass the Japanese when they fell into the trap.

At 2236, the *PT-131*'s radar located the Japanese battleships and radioed a contact report to Oldendorf. During the next two hours, the American PT boats launched successive torpedo attacks against their opponents, but the Japanese repelled each thrust and suffered no losses. In the meantime, Captain Jesse G. Coward and his five destroyers braced for combat, and at about 0230 he led his ships south from Hibuson Island in a high speed run toward the enemy. Thirty minutes later, when Coward was within range of the Japanese column, he ordered his captains to fire their torpedoes and turn away. Three Japanese destroyers were sunk, and the battleship *Fuso* was hit and fell out of the formation, leaving a badly decimated force that next had to face Oldendorf's powerful, veteran line. At 0351, Oldendorf's battleships were thirteen miles from the enemy, having effectively crossed Nishimura's "tee," and so achieved the most advantageous tactical disposition possible in a gunnery duel.

Oldendorf now ordered his ships to open fire. Radar-directed salvoes from the American battleships riddled the *Yamashiro*, Nishimura's flagship, and she was sent under by a daring destroyer torpedo attack. Also struck repeatedly, the heavy cruiser *Mogami* turned south to withdraw from the battle. By this time, Shima, having already lost the cruiser *Abukuma* to a torpedo attack by the *PT-137*, was advancing into the midst of the carnage. A few minutes later, he navigated his flagship, the cruiser *Nachi*, into a collision with the burning *Mogami*. Within another hour, three American cruisers had overtaken the crippled *Mogami* and pounded her once more, but found they could not sink that sturdy ship. When dawn broke over the battle, TBF Avengers from Rear Admiral Thomas Sprague's escort carrier task unit appeared over the Surigao Strait and pursued the stricken cruiser into the Mindanao Sea, and she finally went down a few hours later. By now Oldendorf had called off the chase, regrouped his ships, and was heading north. Aside from some damage to the PT boats, the only American casualties were sustained when the destroyer *Alfred W. Grant* got caught between the American and Japanese broadsides. In the Surigao Strait, Oldendorf had won one of the most perfectly conducted battles in naval history.[5]

While the enemy was being ambushed in the Surigao Strait, a battle far to the north off Cape Engaño, Luzon, was taking shape. Throughout the 24th, Halsey had sent out search planes to locate Ozawa's Northern Force, which, ironically, was trying to expose itself so as to lure the Fast Carrier Force away from Leyte Gulf. It was Ozawa's long-range scouts that first fixed the position of the 3rd Fleet, however, and at 1145 he launched the seventy-six-plane strike against Sherman's task group, but this flight was torn apart by the dense American combat air patrols. Then, at 1700, Halsey received a report from Admiral Mitscher that his search planes had found Ozawa's force, which was said to include one or two large carriers escorted by four battleships or heavy cruisers and a powerful light cruiser-destroyer screen. Inasmuch as such search plane reports invariably contained errors, Carney, Halsey's chief of staff, later contended that Halsey still "was not clear" about "the number and types of ships" in Ozawa's force. Nonetheless, Halsey had by now pieced together the general outline of the Japanese strategic counterattack and knew the approximate disposition of the enemy forces. Kinkaid had dispatched Oldendorf's old battleships to meet Nishimura's Southern Force, and Bogan's carrier task group had driven Kurita's Central Force to withdraw to the Sibuyan Sea. That left only Ozawa's carriers and battleships to be dealt with.

Earlier that afternoon, Halsey had decided that once his search planes located the Northern Force carriers, he would take Bogan's and Davison's carrier task groups north, rendezvous with Sherman's carriers off southern Luzon, and pursue and engage Ozawa's ships. The conduct of the upcoming battle was immeasurably confused, however, when Halsey announced to his admirals that he also intended within a short time to establish a fourth formation, Task Force 34, consisting of four fast battleships and five cruisers under Admiral Lee. It appeared that Halsey intended Lee's battleship-cruiser force to stay behind and take station off the San Bernardino Strait between Luzon and the island of Samar in order to protect the remaining amphibious ships anchored in Leyte Gulf. How Halsey intended to handle Ozawa's battleships if he came upon them at night was not explained.

Halsey told Carney at 2000 that the 3rd Fleet was to head north, instructed him to issue the necessary orders, and then retired to his sea cabin after forty-eight hours on the bridge without sleep. Carney broadcast orders in Halsey's name telling Mitscher to head due north at high speed, directing McCain's carrier task group to rejoin the 3rd Fleet, and informing Kinkaid, Nimitz, and King that "strike reports indicate enemy force in Sibuyan Sea heavily damaged. Am proceeding north with three groups to attack enemy carrier force at dawn." Carney's inexplicably imprecise explanation of what Halsey had done left everyone with the impression that the three carrier task groups were steaming northward but that Lee's newly formed battleship task force was being left behind to guard Leyte Gulf.[6]

MacArthur's nearby presence now made itself felt. In accordance with Army doctrine, he had insisted that Kinkaid, his subordinate, not communicate directly with Halsey, who reported to Nimitz. Instead, messages between the 3rd and 7th fleets were relayed to an understaffed, poorly managed Army radio station on Manus Island for decoding and retransmission. Kinkaid did not protest this preposterous arrangement to the JCS or warn King via the Navy's back-channel of what was afoot. Kinkaid's staff arranged to monitor Halsey's broadcasts secretly, but this roundabout means of solving the problem was not wholly successful. Both Halsey and Carney were aware of MacArthur's edict, but neither did anything serious to have it rescinded. Nor did Halsey or Kinkaid take into account that poor communications would inevitably lead to some absence of coordination of their respective movements.

Halsey's message announcing the formation of Lee's task force was overheard by Nimitz at Pearl Harbor and by King in Washington, but it was not addressed directly to Kinkaid, although Kinkaid's communicators picked it up and passed it to him. Misled by Carney's imprecise wording into believing that Lee's battleships were watching the San Bernardino Strait, Kinkaid turned his attention back to Oldendorf's upcoming battle in the Surigao Strait. "We notified Halsey of our expected night engagement with the enemy Southern Force, and that we would be able to take care of them without any assistance from him if he would handle the Jap Center Force," recalled Kinkaid's chief of staff. For the moment, however, none of Kinkaid's 7th Fleet senior staff thought to query Halsey's flagship to confirm the exact whereabouts of the 3rd Fleet. And Kinkaid's communicators unfortunately did not intercept a second message from Halsey to his admirals that clarified the first message with the statement that "if the enemy sorties, TF 34 will be formed when directed by me." Neither King nor Nimitz received this message. As a result of this lapse in fleet communications among the highest levels of the American command, Kinkaid misunderstood Halsey's intentions, and so did King and Nimitz.[7]

At 2022, after assessing the reports on Ozawa's Northern Force, Halsey steamed to the north with Lee's battleships and Bogan's and Davison's task groups. They came upon Sherman's carriers at midnight, and the entire 3rd Fleet sailed north in pursuit of Ozawa on the morning of 25 October. For reasons that are not altogether clear, however, Halsey held to a speed of only 16 knots. After a false alarm at 0220 occasioned by a report from the carrier *Independence*'s night scout planes, Mitscher's search aircraft found the Northern Force at 0710 to the east of Cape Engaño at the northern tip of Luzon, over 300 miles from Leyte Gulf, and Halsey now transferred tactical command of the carriers for the upcoming battle to Mitscher. Unbeknownst to Halsey, or anyone other than Mitscher's staff, Mitscher had suffered a seizure that evening and had taken to bed. He was so ill that Commodore Burke, his chief of staff, was in practical command of the carrier task force, and it was Burke who now issued the order in Mitscher's name that the air attacks be launched at dawn.

The first Helldivers and Avengers appeared over the Northern Force at 0800, opposed by only a handful of Japanese aircraft, which were quickly splashed. The dive bombers sank the carrier *Chitose* and a destroyer, while the torpedo planes put one fish into the side of the veteran carrier *Zuikaku*. During the second strike, the dive bombers crippled the light carrier *Chiyoda*. At noon, Sherman and Davison launched a combined third strike of more than 200 aircraft, which loitered over Ozawa's ships for over an hour, sinking the *Zuikaku* and damaging the light carrier *Zuiho*. She went under when a fourth wave of attackers came on the scene in the afternoon. The fifth and final American strike was unable to sink the rugged converted battleship-carrier *Ise*, which defended herself with formidable antiaircraft gunfire. At 1415, Mitscher detached Rear Admiral Laurence T. Dubose's cruiser group to finish off the abandoned *Chiyoda* and, later that night, the destroyer *Hatsuzuki*. Although Dubose could not overhaul the fleeing battleships *Ise* and *Hyuga* and seven other ships before they came within range of land-based fighters from Formosa, Lockwood had stationed two submarine formations north of Luzon and the *Jallao* sank the already damaged light cruiser *Tama* at the close of the action off Cape Engaño.

By this time, Halsey had long since left the scene owing to the crisis off Samar. During the overnight run to the north, doubts had begun to flower among Halsey's staff over his decision to leave the San Bernardino Strait uncovered. Halsey himself still believed that Kurita's Central Force posed no threat to the 7th Fleet or the Leyte Gulf beachhead. One reason was that after the attack on Kurita's ships in the Sibuyan Sea, Commander Douglas Moulton, Halsey's air operations officer, had impressed him with the extent of the damage that the American air strikes had inflicted on Kurita's ships. As a result, when Halsey received a message shortly after 2000 that a Hellcat night fighter flying off the *Independence* had sighted the Central Force in the Sibuyan Sea and reported that Kurita had turned around and was now steaming eastward toward the San Bernardino Strait, he questioned its accuracy. Halsey was under the impression that Carney on his behalf had informed Kinkaid that the 3rd Fleet was steaming north to attack Ozawa. What Halsey did not know was that Kinkaid was still under the misapprehension that the 3rd Fleet's fast battleships were covering the exit from the San Bernardino Strait. Watching the strait was Kinkaid's job, he believed. Halsey had also been told that Ozawa's Northern Force carriers were being escorted by at least four battleships, including the superbattleship *Yamato*, and if the 3rd Fleet were to meet them in a night action Halsey would need Lee's six fast battleships with his Fast Carrier Force.[8]

Neither Mitscher nor his chief of staff, Burke, figured out until midnight that Lee's battleships had not been left behind. Burke wanted Mitscher to protest Halsey's decision, but Mitscher, now extremely ill, refused. "If he wants my advice he'll ask for it," he told Commander James Flatley. Bogan reiterated to Halsey the importance of the *Independence*'s reports, but the frosty reception to this news from the fleet staff deterred him from continuing to question Halsey's decision. Lee, the object of all this attention, had by midnight deduced the Japanese battle plan and warned Halsey that Ozawa's carriers were mere decoys, but his advice was also gruffly dismissed by chief of staff Carney. As a result, the entire 3rd Fleet, less McCain's carrier task group— which was still to the south of the Philippines—continued to steam to the north and made ready to attack Ozawa at dawn on the 25th.[9]

Halsey's understanding of Kinkaid's obligations was not unreasonable, and only Kinkaid's conviction that the Japanese did not intend to reenter the San Bernardino Strait explained his utter neglect of that possibility. Although both Wilkinson, his amphibious commander, and Captain Powell of the 7th Fleet staff urged Kinkaid to make certain that Clifton Sprague's escort carrier group conducted night searches around Leyte Gulf and that Rear Admiral Felix Stump's escort carrier task unit was ready to launch anti-ship strikes, he rejected the suggestion. It was not until 0430 on 25 October that Kinkaid directed Stump to send a flight of ten bombers and fighters to the north at dawn, but he did this not to check up on Kurita but to pick off any ships from Ozawa's Northern Force that managed to outflank the 3rd Fleet. "I did that mostly out of curiosity," he remembered, "to know what was going on up there." These planes were launched at 0645. Kinkaid had also arranged much earlier for a PBY Catalina to patrol off Samar that night, but its search was uneventful. Kinkaid met his staff at 0400 to review events, but it was only as an afterthought that his chief of staff, Captain Richard Cruzen, pointed out that "we've never asked Halsey directly if Task Force 34 is guarding the San Bernardino Strait." Admitting that this was the case, Kinkaid at last ordered Cruzen to query Halsey to confirm that Lee's battleships were indeed stationed off the San Bernardino Strait. "I thought . . . Lee . . . was up there with Task Force 34," he recalled.[10]

Kinkaid's questioning message was broadcast at 0412, but it was routed to Manus Island where it was deciphered and retransmitted—with the result that Halsey did not receive it for over two and one-half hours, another testament to the sloppy work of Army and Navy communicators that night. Distressed by the message, Halsey warned Kinkaid over a direct circuit that Lee's battleships, Task Force 34, were "with carrier groups now engaging enemy." Kinkaid was stunned. King, who overheard this response, was furious, and Nimitz was thoroughly confused. Nimitz radioed Halsey asking, "Where is, repeat, where is, Task Force 34?" To confound Japanese radio intelligence, padding was added to this message, which made it read: "Where is, repeat, where is Task Force 34? The world wonders." This enraged Halsey, who thought that Nimitz was questioning his judgment in the middle of the battle—something Nimitz might have done much earlier in the day—and Halsey replied briskly that Lee's battleships were still with the Fast Carrier Force. Within a short time, however, Halsey realized that he had made a mistake. He detached Bogan's carrier task group and Lee's fast battleships, and this new formation headed south to join the battle that had unexpectedly developed in Leyte Gulf.[11]

Halsey's change of heart was occasioned by the news that Kurita's Center Force of four battleships and eight cruisers had erupted from San Bernardino Strait at 0100 on 25 October, initiating the action off Samar. Kurita had a tempting target. "Our beaches were full of ammunition, food, everything we needed," Kinkaid said. "Our Army commanders were camped just a few yards from the beach . . . and were wide open. Just two cruisers loose in that gulf could have . . . delayed the operation for many months, maybe stopped it altogether." This apocryphal estimate was somewhat exaggerated, but Kurita's strategy clearly endangered the landing. Steaming south along the coast, the Japanese formation surprised Clifton Sprague's task unit of six escort carriers, three destroyers, and four destroyer escorts at about 0650. It was now evident to Kinkaid that Lee's fast battleships were not guarding the San Bernardino Strait.[12]

Kurita intended to run down and isolate the slow escort carriers and sink them with gunfire. With Kurita's heavy ships in hot pursuit, Sprague steamed to the south into the wind while launching his aircraft and ordering his destroyers to fend off the enemy with a series of desperate torpedo attacks. The first of these attacks forced Kurita's flagship, the superbattleship *Yamato*, and another Japanese battleship to turn northward so as to present a thin profile to the charging American destroyers, but this maneuver left Kurita cut off from the key friction of the engagement. Additional torpedo attacks cost the Japanese three cruisers and a fourth was crippled by a dive bomber, but the Americans lost the destroyers *Hoel* and *Johnson* and the destroyer escort *Samuel B. Roberts*. Kurita's ships were now within gun range of Sprague's escort carriers. They sank the escort carrier *Gambier Bay* and the *St. Lô*, but aircraft from Stump's nearby escort carriers promptly counterattacked. Just at the moment when the enemy cruisers were about to sink more American ships, they received an order from Kurita to retire to the north to protect the *Yamato*. Throughout the war, when faced with the prospect of a decisive battle, Japan's admirals more often than not shrank from pressing a tactical advantage because of their overriding fear of losing ships. And Kurita had been misled by the fury of Sprague's air operations into believing that he was really facing

Halsey's Fast Carrier Force—despite considerable intelligence to the contrary. To the astonishment of the Americans, Kurita's formation now entered the San Bernardino Strait and escaped to the east, thus bringing to a close the amazing action off Samar.

King believed that both Halsey and Kinkaid had committed serious errors in conducting the Battle of Leyte Gulf. Admiral Cooke, who flew out to the Pacific and discussed strategy with all the key commanders in January 1945, reached the same conclusion. For the Navy to admit this openly, however, would strengthen General Marshall's ongoing argument that MacArthur be given overall command of the Pacific campaign, and King was not about to provide the Army with such devastating ammunition. Moreover, Halsey was a national hero of truly outstanding ability for whom both King and Nimitz had genuine respect and affection, and Kinkaid had in many battles proven his mettle as one of the Navy's most gifted combat commanders. And King was not inclined to criticize admirals who fought their ships. By any reckoning, the outcome of the invasion of Leyte Gulf was a great victory for both Halsey and Kinkaid. While the Japanese fleet had not been annihilated, it no longer posed a serious threat to the Pacific offensive.[13]

The Japanese nonetheless attempted to reinforce their isolated garrison on Leyte during late October and November by carrying troops to that island from elsewhere in the Philippines using a variety of makeshift transports. In addition, the enemy ferried aircraft from Japan to Formosa and from Formosa to Luzon, a distance of about 400 miles, and from Luzon to Leyte, another 400 miles. General Kenney, who commanded the Southwest Pacific Army Air Forces, took two weeks to establish a single P-38 fighter group ashore at Tacloban, so Halsey had to hold the Fast Carrier Task Force off Leyte to provide air cover for the Army's lodgment much longer than originally planned. Theretofore, the attack carrier air groups had been thrown against land-based air forces during raids or brief sweeps, but now in the Philippines they faced a high concentration of enemy air forces with over 400 aircraft distributed among 60 airfields on Luzon alone. In addition, the Japanese flung the first kamikaze suicide attack planes at the 3rd Fleet carriers. American losses escalated as a result. On 29 October, Halsey instructed admirals Bogan and Davison to steam north and attack several Japanese airfields around Manila to reduce the pressure on the Army on Leyte, but the kamikazes took a fearful toll. The escort carriers *Intrepid* and *Belleau Wood* were damaged so badly that they had to withdraw to Ulithi for repairs, and one lone kamikaze evaded several layers of defenses and injured the escort carrier *Franklin* at the Ulithi anchorage. At the end of the month, Halsey also retired to Ulithi to regroup his forces, replace a few commanders, and devise tactics to deal with the kamikazes, which now clearly posed an unexpected menace to the 3rd Fleet.[14]

After Halsey withdrew, the Japanese air operations over Leyte intensified, so MacArthur asked for renewed support from the 3rd Fleet. Halsey brought the carriers north again, and on 5 November, he launched additional air strikes against Manila, which destroyed more than 200 enemy aircraft during two days of fighting. The kamikazes counterattacked, however, and one suicide plane evaded the combat air patrol and crashed onto the *Lexington*'s flight deck. Over 180 sailors were killed or wounded, but the carrier nonetheless continued to operate. The strikes against the Manila bases considerably reduced Japanese air strength in the Philippines, but MacArthur once again asked Halsey for another round of carrier air attacks against enemy forces in Luzon to prevent further reinforcements from reaching Leyte. On the whole, neither Halsey's 3rd Fleet nor Kinkaid's 7th Fleet did a good job of interdicting the movements of Japanese troops and supplies from Luzon to Leyte. King was by this point thoroughly alarmed, especially over the increasing loss of Navy fighters and the kamikaze menace. He ordered an increase in the proportion of fighters in each carrier's air group from thirty-six to fifty-four and a corresponding decrease in the number of bombers, and in the fall he expanded the Navy's pilot training program to provide a complete, freshly trained replacement air group for each fast carrier. It was ironic that the carriers' offensive punch had to be reduced just at the moment that the air groups were being called on to provide more air cover and close ground support to troops ashore.

On 13 November, Halsey sent carrier air strikes against Japanese coastal shipping that sank a light cruiser, four destroyers, and seven cargo ships. Nearly two weeks later, a flight of naval bombers from the carrier *Ticonderoga* sank the heavy cruiser *Kumano* off Luzon and disrupted the progression of two large troop convoys. Again, the Japanese threw kamikaze attacks against the American task force, badly damaging the carriers

Essex, Intrepid, and *Cabot.* By this time, the Army Air Force had finally established land-based air superiority over Leyte, and Krueger's troops were about to close the noose around the tenacious Japanese garrison, although MacArthur's hyperbolic declaration on Christmas day that the Leyte campaign was at an end proved to be curiously premature.

The landings on Mindoro, scheduled for 5 December, set the stage for one of the worst crises of the war between MacArthur and the Navy. While it was clear by 16 November that the Army Air Force had not established air superiority over Luzon, MacArthur nevertheless announced that day that he intended to keep to his schedule for the Mindoro and Lingayen Gulf operations. He asked Nimitz to have Halsey's carriers steam back to the Philippines, but Nimitz replied that these ships needed two weeks at Ulithi for rest and replenishment before their scheduled return at the end of the month. When Halsey's 3rd Fleet did reappear off the Philippines on the 25th, it was hit by waves of kamikazes that damaged four of the nine fast carriers, forcing him to cancel strikes planned for the following day and to instruct three of his four task groups to return to Ulithi for repairs. MacArthur stuck to his timetable, matters worsened, and Kinkaid, whose 7th Fleet was responsible for the Mindoro landing, began to stew. On the 21st, General Kenney declared that he could not provide land-based air cover for Rear Admiral Arthur D. Struble's Mindoro Invasion Force, which was scheduled to depart for the beachhead on 2 December. Struble in turn demanded "that Naval Air provide air cover for the convoys and over the beach area if the Army is unable to provide such cover."

Struble was now adamant that the Mindoro landing be canceled altogether, but when Kinkaid brought this word ashore to MacArthur at Tacloban on 30 November he discovered that the general still "insisted upon not delaying the operation and that Jap air was weak." The following evening Kinkaid notified MacArthur that he was willing to risk being relieved by formally appealing MacArthur's decision over his head to King. At this moment Halsey entered the fray, telling MacArthur that his carriers could not return to the Philippines in full strength unless the Mindoro operation were postponed for ten days. With Kinkaid willing to create a true crisis in command over the issue, MacArthur had no choice but to back down, accept Halsey's plan, reschedule the Mindoro landing for 15 December, and put off the Lingayen Gulf landing until 15 January.[15]

Now under the command of Admiral McCain, the Fast Carrier Force departed Ulithi on 10 December and appeared in Philippine waters two days later. McCain was a creative tactician who had not only to shut down the Japanese air pipeline to the Philippines but also to devise ways to deal with the kamikazes. His air operations officer, Commander John Thach, had presented him with a plan to create a continuous "air blanket" over Luzon to obstruct enemy aircraft movements. On the 13th he sent fighter sweeps over the central Philippines and the following day began three days of highly successful air blanket operations using over 200 planes to cover the enemy's airfields from dawn to dusk. To confound kamikaze attacks on the carriers, McCain stationed pairs of picket destroyers at points on an arc about sixty miles from the task force. One destroyer provided the team with fire support while the other, embarking a fighter director, controlled two fighters hovering overhead. Flights of American aircraft returning to the task force were told to circle over the ships to allow the pickets' fighters to pick out and splash intruding kamikazes. Since the pickets were fitted with air search radar, they also provided the carriers with an excellent early warning system. In addition, McCain replaced the usual carrier combat air patrol of three low-flying fighters with a section of five or six fighters that patrolled the airspace between the picket formations and the task force. Twenty-eight fighters were needed to put this plan into effect, however, further reducing the carriers' offensive punch. This soon led King to make two quick decisions. He ordered that the number of fighters in each attack carrier air group be increased from fifty-four to seventy-three, leaving room on the deck for only fifteen bombers, a goal that was reached in mid-March 1945. He also agreed to allow new F6F Hellcat fighters to be altered to carry three 1,000-pound bombs and six new 5-inch rockets, in effect transforming the aircraft into a practical fighter-bomber capable of delivering a payload equal to that of the Navy's SB2C Helldiver.

When Struble's Invasion Force approached Mindoro, the Japanese responded with the first large-scale kamikaze attacks, but McCain's air defense plan was so successful that none of these aircraft reached the fast carriers, although a destroyer was lost on the 14th and the cruiser *Nashville* and a screening destroyer were damaged. A six-escort carrier covering force provided air cover and close ground support the next day when Struble put ashore 27,000 Army troops on Mindoro's southwestern coast.

The weak Japanese beach defenses collapsed within hours, and five days later organized resistance was at an end. Kenney's Southwest Pacific Air Force now operated from bases within range of Leyte and Luzon from which they could support the final movement into the northern Philippines. The 3rd Fleet was badly battered on 18 December when Halsey navigated his formations into the center of a violent typhoon, however, and he was forced to retire again to Ulithi for repairs and preparations for the upcoming landing in the Lingayen Gulf.

Chapter Thirteen

From Yalta to Hiroshima
1945

Before American military leaders could decide how to force Japan to surrender, they had to bring an end to the distraction of General MacArthur's Philippine campaign. Lingayen Gulf was the gateway to Manila, and once General Kenney had established his Army Air Force on Mindoro, MacArthur prepared to invade Luzon. For this operation, Admiral Kinkaid named newly promoted Vice Admiral Oldendorf to command the Bombardment Group of six old battleships and a dozen escort carriers and instructed him to cover the movement of the 7th Fleet Amphibious Force into Lingayen Gulf. Admiral Nimitz had lent Kinkaid Rear Admiral Calvin T. Durgin's eighteen escort carrier task group screened by twenty-seven destroyers, and it was to provide air cover and antisubmarine defenses for the invasion convoys' movement from New Guinea to Lingayen Gulf. Oldendorf's Bombardment Group was in the Sulu Sea headed for the Gulf when, on 4 January, it first attracted kamikaze attacks, which sank the 10,400-ton escort carrier *Ommaney Bay* on 4 January. The escort carrier *Manila Bay*, the flagship cruiser *Louisville*, the Australian cruiser *Australia*, and the destroyer escort *Stafford* were damaged the following day. By this time, Halsey's 3rd Fleet Fast Carrier Force had stood out of Ulithi with orders from Nimitz to establish air control over the northern Philippines by attacking Japanese fields there and on Formosa. Air blanket operations over Luzon and sweeps over Formosa during the first week of

January 1945 stanched the flow of enemy reinforcements to the
Philippines, but storms forced Halsey to shift his attacks back to
Luzon by 7 January, just as the kamikaze blitz against the Invasion Force reached its peak. Oldendorf's old battleships arrived
off Lingayen Gulf late on 6 January, three days ahead of the Amphibious Force.

Oldendorf entered Lingayen Gulf on the morning of the
7th, his ships a magnet for large numbers of kamikazes. The area
was swept for mines, and the Bombardment Group thoroughly
shelled the beachhead. Rear Admiral T. E. Chandler was killed
when an enemy bomber crashed into the battleship *New Mexico*,
the *Louisville* suffered more damage, and the battleship *California*, the cruisers *Columbia* and *Nashville*, and the Australian cruiser *Australia* were also hit. The minesweeping destroyer *Long* was
sunk. The minecraft *Hovey* and *Palmer* fell victim to suicide missions the next day. "Should suicide bombers attack [the] transports," Oldendorf warned Kinkaid, the "results might be disastrous." Informed by the earlier chaos in Leyte Gulf, Kinkaid now
ignored the joint chain of command and asked Halsey directly to
bring the 3rd Fleet fast carriers up to the west of Luzon "to give
direct support [to the] objective area . . . during period loaded
transports in that area."[1]

Although a large number of American ships were damaged,
before the invasion troops landed, Japanese plane losses were too
great to allow them to continue. Kamikaze squadrons were withheld from the Philippines after 8 January, although Japanese
pilots often struck targets of opportunity. Admiral Barbey's 7th
Amphibious Force appeared off the village of San Fabian in the
southwest corner of the Gulf on the morning of the 9th, about
the same time that Admiral Wilkinson's Invasion Group arrived
to the north. Pummeled by the battleships, the defenders were
unable to put up much resistance against the landings. Four
Army divisions stormed ashore, overran light opposition, and advanced four miles inland by the end of the day. Because Halsey
had decided by this time to strike into the South China Sea in
search of the Japanese fleet, however, the 7th Fleet in Lingayen
Gulf did not have enough fighters to put up a combat air patrol
of sufficient density to prevent minor losses from occasional
kamikaze attacks, which sank four Allied ships and badly damaged another forty-two.

Despite early progress, MacArthur's advance on Manila was stalled at San Fernando, so on 29 January, Struble landed another Army corps on nearby beaches, thus outflanking the enemy's main body. Two days later, Rear Admiral William Fechteler's amphibious task group put ashore another Army division at Nasugbu, thus menacing Manila from the southwest. General Tomoyuki Yamashita, who commanded Japanese forces in the Philippines, directed that the capital be evacuated, but Rear Admiral Sanji Iwabuchi, the naval base commander, ignored this order and organized a well-conducted, fanatical defense, which cost the Americans dearly in block-to-block fighting and resulted in the thorough destruction of the beautiful old city. The last Japanese defenders were cleaned out by 4 March, but Yamashita and over 100,000 men continued to resist in northern Luzon and elsewhere in the Philippine Islands. Throughout the spring and summer of 1945, Barbey and Fechteler conducted over a dozen minor, often bloody landings aimed at overrunning and pinning down or isolating these widely scattered forces, but Yamashita and his main army, despite horrific losses, refused to surrender until mid-August. MacArthur was repeatedly urged by the JCS to call off these costly, useless diversions, but to no avail.

Halsey had again shifted command of the Pacific Fleet Amphibious Forces to Kinkaid for the invasion of Luzon, stripping the 3rd Fleet down to the heavy attack carriers and fast battleships. The stage was set for the Battle of the South China Sea. The battle began to take shape in early January 1945 when Halsey received a report from naval intelligence that the Japanese battleships *Ise* and *Hyuga* were berthed in Camranh Bay on the Tonkin Gulf and were preparing to sortie against the American fleet off Luzon. This plan was suicidal. The Japanese Navy no longer had enough spares or oil to conduct fleet operations. On the 9th, the day on which MacArthur waded ashore in Lingayen Gulf, Halsey's 3rd Fleet charged through the Luzon Strait, entered the South China Sea, swung to the southwest, and closed on the Indochina coast. Standing off Camranh Bay three days later, Admiral McCain, commanding the Fast Carrier Force, hurled over 1,200 air sorties over Indochina, sinking fifteen warships, including one light cruiser, twelve tankers, and seventeen freighters, and destroying over 100 aircraft on the ground. This almost shut down Japanese shipping in Indochina waters. Searching for more targets, Halsey now steamed northeast to Formosa, hit the airbase at Takao, and damaged about thirty planes on the ground. He lost twenty-two planes to antiaircraft fire during a desultory raid on Hong Kong, however, and was forced by bad weather to retire through the Luzon Strait back to the Ulithi anchorage.

The September 1944 compromise between Admiral King and General Marshall, which had allowed MacArthur to invade Leyte and Luzon, provided that Nimitz' Pacific Fleet would capture the Bonin Island group around the end of January 1945 and the Ryukyus in March. As this would outflank Japan's Formosa-based air forces, King now abandoned his plan to invade the Formosa stronghold. In spite of this agreed-upon timetable, MacArthur's slow progress in the Philippines forced Nimitz to postpone the Bonins operation for several weeks. Shortly after the action in Leyte Gulf, King toyed with the idea of allowing Halsey to keep command of the Fast Carrier Force while placing Spruance in overall command of the Bonins-Ryukyus campaign, but he dropped this scheme as unworkable and instead directed Spruance to relieve Halsey at Ulithi on 25 January 1945. For the last time in the war, the 3rd Fleet became the 5th Fleet, and Mitscher, who had partly recovered, again relieved McCain, who was also ailing, in command of the Fast Carrier Force.

The invasion of Iwo Jima in the central Bonins was preceded on 16 February by air strikes launched by Mitscher's Fast Carrier Force at airbases around Tokyo; the idea was to divert the Japanese from the upcoming operation and reduce their air operations south of the Home Islands. These fighter sweeps shot down over 300 aircraft at a cost of 60 American planes. Rear Admiral William Blandy's Bombardment Group of eight old battleships and five heavy cruisers appeared off Iwo Jima that same day and subjected the defenders of the small, pear-shaped island to a murderous naval gunfire for three days. The attack carriers returned to the Bonins on the 18th and launched air strikes to supplement the battleship-cruiser bombardment. That afternoon, the Amphibious Force, which staged from Eniwetok, Saipan, and Ulithi, was seen on the horizon.

When Admiral Turner ordered the Landing Force to head for the beaches at 0645 on 19 February, Blandy's Bombardment Group shifted its fires to inland targets. The assault troops met rugged pockets of resistance on the beaches, but it soon became apparent to Turner that the enemy would not contest the landing and had chosen instead to conduct a defense-in-depth. Although nearly 30,000 Marines landed on Iwo Jima before the end of the day, their subsequent advance was slowed down by stubborn Japanese defenders, who had hidden in caves during the preliminary naval bombardment only to emerge when the Americans reached the shore. To overcome the well-camouflaged Japanese artillery, Blandy's Bombardment Group each morning brought under fire preselected targets that were blocking the path of that day's movement on the ground. Spotting planes from Durgin's Escort Carrier Group, which also provided combat air cover for the landing, sought out enemy strongpoints and directed fire from one of a group of destroyers, each of which had been assigned by Turner to support an individual Marine battalion. A handful of enemy I-class submarines carrying human-torpedo suicide squads were easily dealt with, and neither they nor the occasional lone kamikaze raider disrupted the invasion.

After some of the most vicious fighting in the entire war, elements of the 3rd Marine Division scaled the promontory of Mount Suribachi on 23 February, and a few days later the enemy was isolated in a pocket on the northern end of the island. An Army Air Force B-29 Superfortress, low on fuel after a bombing mission over Japan, landed at the recently captured airfield on 4 March, but the defenders did not launch their last "banzai" charge against the invaders until the 26th when they were all killed. Nearly 5,000 Americans, mostly Marines, died during the battle for Iwo Jima. Over 100 long-range Army Air Force P-51 fighters arrived at Iwo Jima in early April and began escorting flights of 20th Air Force bombers from Tinian and Saipan over Japan. Meanwhile, a shortage of Army service troops led Nimitz to cancel the third and last phase of the Bonins campaign, landings on Miyajima and some nearby islands, and to regroup the Pacific Fleet in preparation for the descent on the Ryukyus.

Spruance did not possess good tactical intelligence about Okinawa's defenses. He knew that the enemy would ferociously resist an invasion, however, because the establishment of airbases on Okinawa would give the Americans control of the East China Sea and bring Army Air Force fighters to within 325 miles of southern Kyushu. The Japanese Army on Okinawa was thought to number more than 75,000, so Nimitz organized the 10th Army, consisting of three Marine and four Army infantry divisions, under Lieutenant General Simon Bolivar Buckner. Turner, again commanding the Pacific Fleet Amphibious Force, would have to land and support nearly 290,000 combat and service troops during the course of the campaign, which Nimitz predicted would last about one month. Moreover, the menace of the kamikazes was omnipresent.

On 17 March, Mitscher's Fast Carrier Force of ten heavy and sixteen light carriers, divided into four task groups, appeared off Kyushu and launched air strikes against shipping in the Inland Sea and military targets at Kōbe and Hiroshima. The Japanese responded with kamikaze attacks that damaged the new heavy carriers *Wasp* and *Yorktown* and caused a fire on the carrier *Franklin* that cost over 700 American lives. Captain Leslie H. Gehres and his intrepid crew saved their ship during a heroic damage-control effort that was aided by new firefighting equipment developed by the Bureau of Ships. The heavy cruiser *Pittsburgh* towed the *Franklin* away from danger, and she made her way back home after makeshift repairs. The Japanese paid a heavy price for these attacks, losing over 500 aircraft in the air and on the ground, a crippling blow to the defenders on Okinawa. Nimitz then exercised his rights as theater commander to divert the 20th Air Force B-29 Superfortresses from strategic bombing missions against Japanese cities and on 29 March sent them instead on raids against airfields and harbors in southern Japan. He also instructed the 20th Air Force to conduct an aerial minelaying operation that was so successful that it nearly shut down shipping in the Inland Sea over the next few months.

The Okinawa campaign began on 26 March with two important preliminary landings. To secure a sheltered anchorage that could be transformed into an advance base for the replenishment and repair of his ships, Turner instructed Blandy's Escort Force to cover the landing of an Army division on Kerama Retto, a group of islands about twenty miles from Okinawa. Next, Turner sent troops ashore on Keise Shima, a small island that was so close to Okinawa that an artillery base was established there to provide 155mm fire support for the main landings. In the meantime, Admiral Morton Deyo's Bombardment Group of old battleships and heavy cruisers pounded the defenders on Okinawa during eight days of preliminary naval bombardment. In retrospect, it was clear that this shelling lasted far too long and used up ordnance that might otherwise have been expended later against targets farther inland.

At 0640 on 1 April, Deyo in the battleship *Tennessee* and Rear Admiral Bertram J. Rodgers in the cruiser *Birmingham* closed to within about 1,900 yards of the southern beaches and their heavy batteries opened fire. After an hour, the bombardment was lifted to allow dive bombers from the Escort Force to attack preselected targets. Admiral John Hall's Southern Attack Force moved into position in the meantime, and at 0800 the first of eight waves of landing craft, led by LCI gunboats, ran inshore along swept channels and put the assault troops on the beach. This landing proceeded so smoothly that by noon the Army had overrun its first objective, the Kadena airfield, while the Marines with the Northern Attack Force had seized the airstrip at Yontan. At the end of the first day, around 60,000 Americans had been landed on Okinawa, holding a beachhead about seven miles wide and over two miles deep. "It looks like the Japanese have quit the war," Turner told Nimitz. Meanwhile, a Demonstration Force under Rear Admiral Jerauld Wright feigned preparations for a third landing at the southern tip of the island to confuse and distract the Japanese defenders. Under Major General Geiger, the 3rd Marine Amphibious Corps in the north wheeled left and, supported by offshore gunfire from the *Tennessee*, moved north against light opposition, while Major General John Hodge's Army corps crossed the center of the island and turned to the south where the bulk of the Japanese Army lay in wait.[2]

Before the Americans had landed, the Japanese decided not to contest the beaches, but instead to man a maze of heavily defended artillery, mortar, and machine gun positions concealed in natural and manmade caves on the slope of Kakazu Ridge, one of a series of mountains that ringed the strongpoint of Shuri. Small, specialized shallow-draft Navy mortar craft moved close inshore to provide flanking gunfire support against enemy targets otherwise hidden from the Marines' artillery. After repeated offensives failed to take this position, Hodge proposed that Turner conduct an amphibious landing with his reserves to outflank the Shuri stronghold. The stalemate had resulted not only from the stiff Japanese defenses but also from the lack of land-based close air support for the ground troops. Soon after the amphibious landing, Marine Corsairs began to operate from the two captured airfields, but a Japanese artillery counterattack and a rainstorm put one of these fields out of commission until May. General Geiger's troops took the offshore islet of Ie Shima during his drive to the north, but Army Air Force P-47 Thunderbolts did not arrive there until 13 May. In addition, General Arnold in Washington had instructed the Army Air Force engineers to give priority to constructing airfields on Okinawa for long-range bombers rather than building airstrips for fighters. When Spruance learned about this directive, however, he went ashore and angrily ordered the chief engineer on the scene to reverse his priorities.

In the meantime, the 5th Fleet was being attacked by kamikazes while having to deal with the desperate sortie of the superbattleship *Yamato*. On 5 April, Admiral Toyoda had instructed Vice Admiral Seiichi Ito, who commanded a task force composed of the 72,908-ton *Yamato*, the light cruiser *Yahagi*, and eight destroyers, to steam from the Inland Sea to the southeast and attack American amphibious shipping off Okinawa. Only 2,500 barrels of oil could be found for the ships, not enough for a round trip, so Ito planned a one-way suicide mission. Soon after the *Yamato* task force put to sea it was sighted by Lieutenant Commander John Foote in the *Threadfin*, one of a large number of American submarines that Lockwood had deployed to the area to attack enemy shipping and prevent the 5th Fleet from being surprised. Under orders to report any contacts before attacking, Foote closed to within four miles, surfaced, and radioed Lockwood the composition, course, and speed of the enemy formation. Although he soon resumed the chase, Foote quickly fell behind the Japanese ships, which were steaming to the south at 22 knots. The *Yamato* task force next came upon Lieutenant Frederick Janney in the *Hackleback*, who broadcast a contact report to Lockwood and then tried to close three times but was prevented from attacking the battleship by a strong enemy destroyer screen.

Alerted but not alarmed by these reports, Mitscher positioned three task groups north of Okinawa to interdict Ito's task force. At dawn on 7 April, he launched armed search planes that located the enemy at 0823 heading west through the Van Diemen Strait. Soon a pair of tender-based PBM Mariners from Okinawa appeared overhead to keep track of the Japanese formation and direct the attack aircraft to their targets. At 1232 a flight of TBM Avenger bombers from Admiral J. J. Clark's task group attacked the *Yamato* and put four torpedoes into the ship. Shortly thereafter, another squadron of torpedo bombers from Admiral Radford's task group struck the vessel with six more torpedoes, while at roughly the same time Helldiver dive bombers armed with 1,000-pound bombs wrecked the battleship's topsides. She began to list, and at 1423 the great *Yamato* slid under the water. It took twelve bomb and seven torpedo hits to sink the rugged *Yahagi*. The Americans also sank four Japanese destroyers and inflicted serious damage on the four survivors, which escaped from the battle and retired to the naval base at Sasebo.

After sinking the *Yamato*, the Fast Carrier Force shifted gears once again and resumed combat air patrols and close ground support for General Buckner's troops on Okinawa and girded for another wave of kamikaze attacks. Writing two days before he flew against the American fleet for the last time, kamikaze pilot Yoshi Miyagi compared his suicide plane to "a particle of iron attracted by a magnet—the American aircraft carrier." Turner's Amphibious Force had already established a system to defend against the successive waves of kamikazes. On 26 March, he had stationed sixteen radar picket destroyers at distances from 15 to 100 miles from Okinawa to locate incoming Japanese aircraft and assist fighters from the Escort Force in intercepting them. Near the beaches, cruisers and destroyers provided a second shield of antiaircraft gunfire. And when the Fast Carrier Force finished off the *Yamato*, Mitscher established his own system of distant radar pickets, which reinforced Turner's dispositions. Nevertheless, the suicide planes often penetrated these powerful screens.[3]

On 31 March, a kamikaze crashed into the flagship *Indianapolis*, forcing Spruance to shift his flag to the battleship *New Mexico*. The first large suicide flight to attack the fleet after the landings, consisting of 335 kamikazes and 341 other aircraft from Kyushu, appeared on the scene on 6 April. Four kamikazes crashed into the *Newcomb*, inflicting serious damage not only on this radar picket destroyer but also on the destroyer *Leutze*, which came to her assistance. That afternoon, kamikazes sank the radar picket destroyer *Bush* and the nearby destroyer *Calhoun*, which had been assisting her. Mitscher's experienced combat air patrol prevented the Japanese from finding the Fast Carrier Force that day, but nearly 200 enemy planes hit Turner's Amphibious Force, sinking an LST and the destroyer *Emmons* and damaging two ammunition ships. The next day, a kamikaze evaded the combat air patrol and crashed onto the carrier *Hancock*'s flight deck, causing a fire that forced the ship to withdraw. The Japanese lost hundreds of planes during this initial assault, however, and several days passed before they were able to resume the offensive.

On 12 April, 185 kamikazes and 195 fighters, bombers, and other aircraft attacked the American ships, sinking the radar picket destroyers *Purdy* and *Abele*, the latter being hit by the new rocket-assisted 2,600-pound Baka bomb. The third kamikaze wave struck four days later, sinking the destroyer *Pringle* and damaging the fast carrier *Intrepid*. Although the radar picket *Laffey* was hit by four bombs and six suicide planes, Commander Frederick J. Becton's crew shot down eight kamikazes in eighty minutes and then conducted a damage-control operation that saved the ship. Following a lull in the action pockmarked by sporadic attacks, another large flight of kamikazes headed toward the fleet on 3 May, sinking the destroyers *Ingraham* and *Morrison* and two LSMs. Another big flight of 150 suicide planes struck one week later, putting the fast carriers *Bunker Hill* and *Enterprise* out of action, and 165 kamikazes approached the American ships on 23 May, with the destroyers again taking the worst of it. The destroyers *Bates* and *Berry* went under, as did the *LSM-135* and five other naval vessels. Four days later, the eighth kamikaze wave caused the loss of the radar picket destroyer *Drexler* and badly damaged the pickets *Braine* and *Anthony*.

Despite these heavy losses, the Navy's destroyers were far better prepared to withstand the rigors of the air war now than in 1942, when the prewar *Farragut*, *Benson*, and *Gleaves* classes had borne the brunt of the fighting. With the construction of large numbers of 2,100-ton *Fletcher*-class destroyers, which entered the fleet starting in late 1942, the Navy finally deployed a large, multimission destroyer that could be adapted to the successive wartime adjustments in armaments and control systems needed to meet the Japanese air threat. With the pronounced shift from the surface actions of the South and Southwest Pacific in 1942 and 1943 to the carrier escort role in 1944, destroyers became increasingly specialized, armed either as antisubmarine or antiaircraft escorts or as antiaircraft radar pickets. Fighters accounted for most of the 2,800 kamikaze and supporting enemy aircraft splashed off Okinawa, but the presence of the sturdy mobilization destroyers serving as radar pickets turned the menace of the suicide attacks into a manageable threat. The Navy never did devise a satisfactory strategy or set of tactics to deal with the kamikazes, however, and this menace worried Admiral King whenever he thought of invading Japan.

The protracted fighting on and around Okinawa, originally estimated to last one month, continued until 21 June when the island was declared at last to be secure. The kamikaze attacks cost 15 naval vessels sunk and 200 damaged, many of which were later

U.S. Army Signal Corps

Churchill, Roosevelt, and Stalin met at Yalta on the Crimean Peninsula in January 1945 to arrange for the defeat of Japan and to shape the postwar peace. Roosevelt, now the senior Western partner, effectively agreed that Stalin might establish satel lites in Eastern Europe. Stalin was also offered concessions in the Far East to persuade him to declare war on Japan and remain aloof from the postwar struggle in China. Fleet Admiral King stands behind Churchill, Fleet Admiral Leahy stands behind Roosevelt, and General of the Army Marshall stands behind Leahy.

scrapped, while the fighting at sea and ashore cost 13,000 American lives. Of the 100,000 Japanese and Okinawan defenders, only 11,000 were taken prisoner at the end of the grim battle. The day after the fall of Okinawa, Emperor Hirohito instructed his cabinet to secretly explore a negotiated peace.

On 27 May 1945, Halsey had relieved Spruance, and the 5th Fleet became the 3rd Fleet for the last time in the war. Mitscher, seriously ill, returned to Washington and was again succeeded in command of the Fast Carrier Force by Admiral McCain, who was also not well. Unlike Spruance, Halsey refused to be tied down to the waters around Okinawa and immediately took tactical command of the carriers, sending one task group to Leyte for repairs and steaming north with the rest to attack Japanese airfields on Kyushu for two days starting on 2 June. When he began to withdraw, however, Halsey once again ran the Fast Carrier Force across the path of a typhoon, which cost the heavy cruiser *Pittsburgh* her bow, damaged the carriers *Bennington* and *Hornet*, and destroyed seventy-six planes. Vice Admiral John Hoover headed a court of inquiry that investigated the tragedy and condemned Halsey's "ineptness" in dealing with the typhoon, but Fleet Admiral King quietly laid aside Hoover's outrageous recommendation that Halsey be sent ashore. On 7 June, the Fast Carrier Force had struck Kyushu once again, and a week later it returned to Leyte Gulf, after having spent three months at sea since the start of the Okinawa invasion.

While the battle for Okinawa raged in the Pacific, victory was finally won in Europe. In November 1944, President Roosevelt had easily defeated his Republican challenger, New York Governor Thomas Dewey, and won an unprecedented fourth term in the White House. Two months later, in January 1945, he met Churchill and Stalin at a second Big Three summit at Yalta on the Crimean Peninsula on the Black Sea. Their attention first turned to Germany. Although Eisenhower's offensive had been momentarily halted by a violent German counteroffensive at the Battle of the Bulge the preceding December, the Allied Army resumed its offensive after New Year's Day and was expected to cross the Rhine within a month or two. On the Eastern Front, the Soviets had crossed into Poland and occupied Warsaw and were fast approaching the Vistula River. The Big Three at Yalta divided postwar Germany into three occupation zones—later expanded to four when France returned to the ranks of the major Allied powers. FDR agreed that the Soviets could extract heavy reparations from Germany, but he had begun quite belatedly to be concerned about the fate of eastern Europe and, as an afterthought, persuaded Stalin to sign the Declaration of Liberated Europe. In this document, the Russian dictator promised to tolerate the revival of political freedoms in eastern Europe, freedoms that he had long ago suppressed at home.

"The major business of the Yalta Conference was done at the plenary meetings between the heads of state," King wrote, and neither he nor Marshall attended these sessions. The most pressing issue at the summit concerned Soviet participation in the war against Japan, and this was an issue with which the JCS were deeply involved. Since the 1941 Russo-Japanese Nonaggression Pact, the Soviets had remained neutral in the Asian war, although Stalin told Secretary of State Hull at the October 1943 Moscow Conference that Russia would declare war against Japan soon after Germany surrendered. As usual, the Americans were divided as to how Japan was to be brought to book. Approaching the Home Islands via the cold waters of the North Pacific had already been ruled out. Although the Soviets offered the use of Petropavlovsk on the Kamchatka Peninsula as an advance naval base for the Pacific Fleet, King did not take this proposal seriously. Not only had the Soviets refused to cooperate with the Army Air Force in establishing airbases on Russian territory for shuttle-bombing, but also the primitive naval facility at Petropavlovsk was closed by ice from November to May. Both King and Marshall wanted the Red Army to tie down the large Japanese Army then occupying China, however. Thus, on the eve of the Yalta Conference, they told FDR that they preferred "Russian entry at the earliest possible date . . . and are prepared to offer the maximum support possible without prejudice to our main effort against Japan." MacArthur agreed with this early assessment, telling Navy Secretary James Forrestal in February 1945 that American "strength should be reserved for use in the Japanese mainland, and that this could not be done without the assurance that the Japanese would be heavily engaged by the Russians in Manchuria."[4]

Roosevelt apparently did not believe that Stalin intended to honor his 1943 pledge to declare war against Japan unless there was, to use King's term, some "sweetening" in the form of more Lend Lease aid and political concessions. At Yalta, Stalin made surprisingly few political demands on Far Eastern issues, expanding, instead, on concessions that Roosevelt put on the table. FDR's motives in these negotiations are unclear. He apparently did not believe that Russian troops were needed to defeat the Japanese Army in China but instead saw an agreement with Stalin on this issue as a means to arrange a treaty of friendship between Russia and Nationalist China. To tempt Stalin into declaring war on Japan, he offered the Soviets control of Darien and Port Arthur in Manchuria, exclusive management of the Manchuria Railroad, and Lend Lease supplies to equip thirty more Red Army divisions. Stalin agreed that "China shall retain full sovereignty in Manchuria," but only after the British and

Americans promised that "the preeminent interests of the Soviet Union shall be safeguarded." The outcome of this arrangement would, the president hoped, somehow discourage Stalin from supporting a postwar insurgency by the Chinese Communists against Chiang Kai-shek's battered Nationalist regime. Roosevelt had already been presented with evidence that Stalin intended to enter the Far Eastern war regardless of the outcome of his dealings with the West, however, and King felt that the "price asked [by the Russians] was far too high." Marshall was far more ambivalent. Nonetheless, in a moving address to Congress on 1 March 1945 after he returned from Yalta, FDR asserted that "never before have the major Allies been more closely united— not only in their war aims but in their peace aims."[5]

On 7 March 1945, when victory in Europe was only weeks away, Eisenhower shrewdly employed his Ultra intelligence to seize the Remagen Bridge over the Rhine, then surged his armies into the industrial heart of western Germany. Landing craft and naval boat crews under the command of Admiral Alan Kirk in France and Vice Admiral Robert Ghormley in Germany lifted thousands of American soldiers, tanks, and jeeps across Europe's rivers from the Seine to the Rhine. Once the Anglo-American armies reached the Elbe River, Churchill urged Eisenhower to continue his eastward movement and take Berlin, but the general refused to do this on the grounds that he would eventually have to evacuate his troops from the area since the Allies had already agreed that Berlin would fall within the Russian occupation zone. Before the Red Army overran the German capital, Hitler committed suicide, leaving to Admiral Dönitz the thankless task of surrendering to the Allies on 8 May 1945.

Two months earlier, Roosevelt had reversed his prewar position by announcing that "the defeat of Germany will not mean the end of the war against Japan." Before he could address the strategic problem of how to compel Japan to surrender, however, FDR died suddenly on 12 April 1945. A few days later, Harry S. Truman, the vice president, moved into the White House, and he soon discovered that the JCS were sharply divided over how to defeat Japan. King favored seizing the Chüsan–Ning-po area along the Chinese coast. From there, he intended to tighten the naval blockade around Japan, intensify strategic bombing operations, and prepare for an invasion of the southernmost Japanese island of Kyushu. For at least two years, Admiral Cooke had viewed the establishment of an American base on the China coast as a necessary preliminary to any descent on the Home Islands, and King had told Nimitz as early as December 1942 that "eventually we go up the China coast" to reach Japan.[6]

Throughout the war, the Americans had clung to wildly exaggerated expectations of what the Chinese were willing or able to do to assist in the defeat of Japan. In 1942, King had established Naval Group China, whose commander, Commodore Milton Miles, organized a large Navy liaison mission to assist the Nationalist government in Chungking. Called the Sino-American Cooperative Organization, Miles' command was effectively beyond the control of the Army's theater commander, General Joseph Stilwell, who was furious when Miles somewhat naively fell under the influence of Tai Li, a murderous reactionary who directed the Blue Shirts, Chiang Kai-shek's brutal political secret police. For two years, Stilwell tried to cajole and shame Chiang into taking the offensive against the Japanese, but the generalissimo was convinced that the Nationalists had to husband their resources for the inevitable postwar struggle with the Communists. Stilwell's position was eroded by his notorious lack of diplomatic skills and by a serious misunderstanding of Chinese strategic priorities. Although Japan occupied Manchuria and the entire Chinese coast, Stilwell nonetheless insisted that Chiang allow him to send China's best divisions south to Burma to evict the Japanese from that British colony. Roosevelt was incapable of adhering to a consistent line. He backed Chiang one week, Stilwell the next. A locust swarm of presidential envoys—none equipped with military experience or in any way acquainted with China's unique problems—plagued both Stilwell and Chiang throughout the war.

Commodore Miles disliked Stilwell, wanted to fight the Japanese, distrusted Mao Tse-tung's rival communist regime, and appreciated Chiang's predicament. He did not object to Stilwell's strategic concept, however, nor did King, who generally supported more active operations in the Indian Ocean and Southeast Asia on the grounds that this would divert Japanese resources from the main front in the Pacific. Miles undercut Stilwell's influence with Chiang by convincing the generalissimo that the United States would never abandon its Nationalist allies. Under Miles' energetic leadership, Naval Group China grew into an enormous command that conducted commando operations against Japanese outposts, observed Japanese shipping along the

China coast, and collected important intelligence about Japan's occupation forces in China. After the fall of the Philippines, King wanted the Pacific Fleet to establish a lodgment on the China coast in the vicinity of Chūsan–Ning-po, and he intended Miles' observers and commandos to provide landward support for this amphibious operation. This edifice began to collapse when Stilwell and Chiang's relationship reached the breaking point in late October 1944, just as the JCS began to focus on King's plan. FDR relieved Stilwell at Chiang's request and replaced him with a more able figure, Lieutenant General Albert Wedemeyer, who correctly assessed the Nationalists' conundrum and sympathized with China's cause but still could not persuade Chungking to undertake an offensive against the Japanese. Despite the similarity of their general views, Miles protested Wedemeyer's move to bring his hitherto independent Naval Group China under the Army's theater command. At the bar of the Cathay Hotel in Chungking in June 1945, Miles got drunk and cursed Wedemeyer, only to find himself placed under arrest by the general's chief of staff. Cooke persuaded King to recall Miles quietly to save his career—Miles retired a few years later with the rank of vice admiral. More important, the blazing dispute between Chiang and Stilwell had by the end of 1944 convinced the JCS that they could expect little assistance from China in the final phase of the war against Japan.

The views of the Pacific and Southwest Pacific theater commanders on how to deal the final blow to Japan were difficult to grasp. Meeting at Leyte in November 1944 with Admiral Forrest Sherman, Nimitz' chief planner, MacArthur declared that "his troops were keyed up to take the Philippines but wanted to go home after that," a bizarre reason he used to justify a pronouncement that he was "particularly emphatic against invading Japan." Indeed, MacArthur spent much of the spring of 1945 embroiling himself in Philippine politics and preparing for Operation Oboe, a plan to occupy British Borneo as a stepping stone to the Dutch East Indies. Late that spring he told General Eichelberger that his 8th Army would invade Java in September, although by that time MacArthur was under orders from the JCS to draw up plans to invade Japan in October. Kinkaid was in the Leyte area impatiently awaiting orders while Barbey's 7th Amphibious Force landed in the central and southern Philippines. He flew back to Washington to talk to King in May, visited MacArthur in Manila and Nimitz at Guam, but as of early August Kinkaid had not been asked what role his huge 7th Fleet might play in the Kyushu landings. In short, MacArthur did little or nothing to plan for the Kyushu operation, codenamed Olympic, or the invasion of Honshu, codenamed Coronet. For his part, Nimitz was vacillating between invading Japan and seizing a lodgment on the China coast.[7]

Because the Chūsan–Ning-po plan did not have Nimitz' wholehearted support, King abandoned it and agreed to the Army's strategy of landing on Kyushu, the southernmost of Japan's Home Islands. King did not at the time claim that the combined effects of a naval blockade and strategic bombing would force Japan to surrender, but he did stress in JCS meetings the value of tightening the noose around the Home Islands so as to reduce opposition to the Kyushu landings. Marshall, on the other hand, wanted to devote all American resources in the Pacific first to Olympic and then to Coronet. Washington had an imperfect understanding of Japan's increasingly isolated condition. It was known that in Moscow in April Soviet Foreign Minister Molotov had handed Ambassador Sato formal notice of the abrogation of the 1941 Neutrality Pact, that the Japanese fleet had been virtually destroyed, that Japanese industry had ground to a standstill, and that Japan's air defenses had been badly mauled. Yet after the grim struggle for Okinawa and the fanaticism illustrated by the kamikazes, it seemed unlikely that the Japanese would surrender or succumb to anything less than an invasion and occupation. Navy Secretary James Forrestal, who had succeeded Frank Knox after the latter's death in 1944 and retained his job after Truman shuffled his cabinet in June 1945, explained that "even if we wished to besiege Japan for a year or a year and a half, the capture of Kyushu would be essential." When asked that month by Admiral Cooke if Japan was ready to surrender, Captain William J. Sebald, the Navy's foremost expert on Japanese politics, replied that the enemy would not accept those terms but might be tempted by some "face-saving" device. The Truman administration was now completely adrift, and Forrestal unexpectedly took the lead by arranging for Truman to meet with King and Marshall on the afternoon of 18 June and discuss their plans to invade Japan. At this meeting, a watershed in American history, the president and the JCS for the first time formally examined the strategic possibilities of using an atomic bomb to end the war.[8]

All discussions within the administration on how best to employ the bomb started with the assumption that Japan would not surrender before Kyushu, and perhaps Honshu, were overrun. Admiral Leahy was so alarmed about casualty estimates for these operations that he tried to pin down Marshall and King, but "nobody knew what the opposition might really be so there never was an answer," recalled Commander Robert Dennison, Leahy's aide. After their ships and troops had endured the kamikazes and suicide banzai charges on Okinawa, the JCS were so desperate to "cope with the . . . last ditch defense tactics of the suicidal Japanese" that they even discussed the possibility of using gas warfare. Marshall "sought to avoid the attrition we are now suffering from such fanatical but hopeless defense methods," arguing that "gas . . . was no less humane than phosphorous and flame throwers and need not be used against dense populations of civilians." However, Leahy reminded Marshall and King that Roosevelt had announced in 1943 that the United States would not use gas, pointed out that this position was "beyond the possibility of change," and told them to drop the plan.[9]

A more realistic alternative to gas warfare or an invasion was to use atomic bombs against Japan. Although all the industrial powers except Russia tried to develop war-winning secret weapons—jet planes, rocket-delivered munitions, poisons, and death rays attracted the most serious attention—the Americans narrowed their choices considerably in 1942 with the inauguration of the Manhattan Project. The discovery of the process of nuclear fission in January 1939 had led physicists to conclude that splitting the atom would release unprecedented energy and that this might create a highly destructive explosion. Nobel prize–winning physicist Enrico Fermi discussed the fission process at the Navy Department on 17 March 1939 with Ross Gunn, a brilliant physicist who worked at the Naval Research Laboratory. Armed with the concept that atomic reactions might be used for weapons or to propel vessels, Gunn obtained a small grant from Rear Admiral Harold Bowen, the resourceful chief of the Bureau of Engineering, and set out to prove that the rare uranium-235 isotope could be used to produce fission. At about the same time, Albert Einstein, the father of modern nuclear physics, wrote to President Roosevelt warning that the Germans were probably trying to build an atomic bomb and predicting grave consequences if they succeeded. FDR was irresponsibly slow to react, appointing a series of powerless interim committees to study the question, which evolved at a glacial pace into the civilian Office of Scientific Research and Development under Massachusetts Institute of Technology administrator Vannevar Bush in June 1941.

Bush was determined that scientists play a prominent role in the war effort and that OSRD become his vehicle to influence military and naval policy and strategy. This caused constant friction with the JCS, and especially with King, who believed many of Bush's ideas to be impractical and insisted that the work of Navy civilian scientists be kept in line with operational reality. Vice Admiral Julius A. Furer, who headed the Navy's wartime scientific research, felt that Bush was "very much put out over the fact that he is not called in by King to discuss the grand strategy." Owing to Admiral Bowen's energy and insight, however, the Navy's atomic project was well under way at the start of the war. A brilliant, tempestuous figure whom Admiral Stark sidelined to the Naval Research Laboratory, Bowen arranged for the construction of Ross Gunn's small isotope-separation device, established wide-ranging contacts with civilian universities, and called on the formidable resources of the Navy's rapidly expanding Bureau of Ordnance. Nevertheless, Bush insisted on excluding the Navy from the atomic bomb project and convinced Roosevelt in early 1942 to assign the work to the Army Corps of Engineers. The establishment of an entirely new organization to construct a bomb, a hallmark of FDR's whimsical, haphazard administration of the entire war effort, ensured additional delays, and it was not until September 1942 that General Marshall got around to naming Major General Leslie R. Groves to manage the top-secret Manhattan District atomic bomb project.[10]

These maneuvers led to the exclusion of Ross Gunn and the rest of the Navy from the Manhattan Project, but Gunn's isotope separation work was taken up by Philip H. Abelson, a scientist whom he had brought to the Naval Research Laboratory in 1941. Groves refused to support Abelson's construction of a thermal diffusion plant, but the Navy did, and it was built in early 1944 at the Philadelphia Navy Yard. That summer, Abelson's plant began to produce small quantities of uranium-235, something the vast Army project had as yet been unable to do. Groves now turned to King, who, on 26 June, asked Abelson to assist the Manhattan scientists. Using Abelson's blueprints, Army engineers constructed a thermal diffusion plant as part of the Oak Ridge, Tennessee, facility, which was to produce the uranium-235 and the rest of the first Mark-1 atomic bomb in the spring of 1945. Bush's policy of excluding the Navy from the work of the Manhattan Project eroded once more when Rear Admiral George Hussey of the Bureau of Ordnance assigned Commodore William O. Parsons to work with the top team of War Department scientists at the Los Alamos weapons laboratory. A brilliant line officer, Parsons soon became a leading figure at Los Alamos and a confidant of the project's eccentric scientific director, J. Robert Oppenheimer. Parsons employed the Bureau of Ordnance to manufacture the nonnuclear explosives for the uranium-gun Little Boy bomb and the armored shell for the plutonium-implosion Fat Man weapon. Although they monitored the Manhattan District's work, the JCS dared not risk taking the bomb into account in planning the invasion of Japan. They were uncertain if and when the weapon would be ready, and Admiral King was especially concerned that public support for the war against Japan would flag should the momentum of the campaign not be maintained.

Before they took up the issue following the liberation of the Philippines, King and Marshall negotiated a new directive to sort out their respective commands in the Pacific for the final phase of the war. Marshall demanded that MacArthur be given overall charge of the Pacific theater, while King insisted that Nimitz rightly deserved this honor. MacArthur, a longtime advocate of a unified command, surprised the JCS by declaring, "I do not recommend a single unified command for the Pacific." The old Southwest Pacific and Pacific theater boundaries no longer made any sense, however, so the JCS agreed on 3 April 1945 that Nimitz would gradually relinquish control over all Army forces in the Pacific to MacArthur, who would in turn transfer command of the 7th Fleet and those Marine divisions still in the Southwest Pacific to Nimitz. However, Arnold of the Army Air Force demanded that the B-29 Superfortress bombers be organized into an independent Strategic Air Force command under General Carl Spaatz, who was transferred to the Pacific in 1945 in spite of his uneven record in command of American bombers in Europe.[11]

Soon thereafter, Nimitz moved the rest of his Pacific Fleet headquarters forward from Oahu to Guam to begin planning for the Kyushu operation, while King and Marshall negotiated an interservice treaty to solve the problem of command. King conceded that Marshall could designate MacArthur as the supreme commander for the invasion of Japan, while Marshall agreed that Nimitz, as the naval and amphibious commander, would enjoy the right to appeal MacArthur's decisions to the JCS. In effect, the quarrel-laden but surprisingly successful system of divided command that had driven both men across the Pacific was to be maintained until Japan capitulated. Nimitz ordered Spruance to plan for Operation Olympic, the Kyushu invasion, while Halsey and his 3rd Fleet staff prepared to direct the far larger and more daunting Operation Coronet, the invasion of Honshu.[12]

As late as 17 June 1945, Truman was unaware of this compromise. "I have to decide Japanese strategy," he wrote in his diary that night. "Shall we invade Japan proper or shall we bomb and blockade? That is my hardest decision." The JCS, armed with an agreement on Olympic, if not Coronet, met Truman at the White House the next day. Major General Curtis Lemay's 20th Army Air Force had inflicted stupefying damage to Japan's cities since March, using incendiary bombs to create urban firestorms with which the Japanese firefighting establishment was unprepared to deal, but Lieutenant General Ira Eaker, who represented the Army Air Force at the 18 June White House meeting, admitted that bombing alone would not bring Japan to surrender. Marshall then explained the invasion plans. He was ably supported by King, who told Truman that he "was impressed with the strategic location of Kyushu, which he considered the key to the success of any siege operation" of Honshu. "We should do Kyushu now," he said, "after which there would be time to judge the effect of possible operations by the Russians and the Chinese." Admiral Leahy, not Admiral King, was unhappy with the Kyushu plan. Whereas King wanted to land on Kyushu "at the earliest practicable date," Leahy preferred to bomb Japan into surrendering and now argued that the casualty count for Kyushu would equal that of Okinawa, where over one-third of the American combat troops had been killed or wounded. King shot back that the costly frontal assaults dictated by Okinawa's topography would be unnecessary on Kyushu, where there was "much more room for maneuver." This argument ended when Truman approved both invasion plans. But before the meeting adjourned, he asked what the JCS proposed to do if an atomic bomb, scheduled to be tested in July, became available in August. Secretary of War Stimson had already convened a War Department target-

The *LST-834* on the morning of 1 April 1945 approaches Okinawa with the *LCT-1415* embarked.

On 2 September 1945, Fleet Admiral Chester Nimitz signs the document of surrender on behalf of the United States on board the battleship *Missouri* in Tokyo Bay. Behind Nimitz are General of the Army Douglas MacArthur (left), Fleet Admiral William F. "Bull" Halsey, Commander, Third Fleet (center), and Rear Admiral Forrest Sherman, Nimitz' chief planner.

ing committee, which formally proposed to bomb the cities of Hiroshima, Nagasaki, and Niigata. If the bomb was available, Marshall now said, it should be used. King agreed with Marshall, and when Assistant Secretary of War John J. McCloy suggested that the weapon be demonstrated by bombing an offshore island before attacking a city, King joined Marshall in ridiculing McCloy's unworkable scheme.[13]

Truman and the JCS flew to the Berlin suburb of Potsdam in July for the last of the wartime Big Three summit conferences. There, Stalin reaffirmed his intention to declare war on Japan in August, and Truman agreed to make good on the concessions made by FDR at Yalta. While at Potsdam, Truman received the news from Alamogordo, New Mexico, that the first test of an atomic bomb, codenamed Trinity, had been successful. There were rumors abroad by this time that Japan intended to sue for peace and ask for talks about occupation terms. Truman did not want to dicker with Tokyo, and the Joint Chiefs were concerned that negotiations would undermine public support for continuing the war. Truman learned from deciphered Japanese communications that Tokyo was about to ask Moscow to assist in such a negotiation, a preposterous diplomatic maneuver that stunned the Allies. These intercepts also made it clear that the Japanese would not abandon their emperor system and that they still believed that they could haggle over a number of postwar occupation terms. The upshot was the Potsdam Declaration, in which the United States and Britain called upon Japan to surrender or face "prompt and utter destruction" in the near future. Tokyo's reply was confusing and equivocal, an ill-conceived play for time. The intention was to give the peace faction within the Japanese cabinet more opportunity to convince the fanatics to surrender, but neither the peace faction nor the fanatics were willing for the moment to accept terms that did not include preserving the emperor's position. For all practical purposes, Japan now sought a negotiated settlement "short of unconditional surrender" that Truman was demanding.[14]

While the Potsdam Conference was in session, Captain Charles B. McVay in the recently repaired cruiser *Indianapolis* stood out of San Francisco Bay at 0800 on 16 July 1945 carrying one of only two finished atomic bombs in the American arsenal. Several days later she arrived at Tinian Island in the Marianas, where McVay transferred custody of the bomb to Army Air Force

Colonel Paul Tibbets, the pilot of the *Enola Gay*, a specially configured B-29 Superfortress, and Commodore William Parsons,
the weapons officer for the upcoming mission. McVay then received routing instructions from Captain Oliver Naquin at Guam
to steam unescorted across the Philippine Sea and rendezvous
with a new training group off Leyte Gulf. Although Naquin's office had received a report that Japanese submarines were patrolling the area that the *Indianapolis* was about to enter, he did
not warn McVay of this danger. Just before midnight on 29 July,
the submarine *I-58* fired a salvo of torpedoes that so badly damaged the *Indianapolis* that McVay, who had taken few precautions
against a torpedo attack, was forced to abandon ship without issuing a distress call. Over 800 sailors escaped by jumping into the
water or climbing onto life rafts. When the cruiser failed to arrive
in the Philippines, it went unnoticed because Guam had neglected to inform 7th Fleet headquarters of her movements. A Navy
patrol plane sighted the survivors three days later. Only 316 men,
survivors of a harrowing ordeal in shark-infested waters, were
rescued. Naquin escaped blame, but a court-martial convicted
McVay of being responsible for this unnecessary tragedy.

The JCS intended the atomic bombing to appear to the
Japanese cabinet as a continuation of the current conventional
bombing campaign and to lead them to the erroneous conclusion that the United States possessed a large stockpile of these
fearsome weapons. Truman had already ordered the use of
bombs in June, and nothing that happened at Potsdam changed
his mind. Thus, in July, Arnold directed General Spaatz to drop
both available bombs in quick succession. On the morning of
6 August, the *Enola Gay* appeared over Hiroshima, Parsons
armed and dropped the Little Boy bomb, and it burst in the air
at 0915. Three days later the Fat Man bomb exploded over
Nagasaki. That same day, 9 August, Russia declared war on Japan
and the Red Army invaded Japanese-occupied Manchuria. The
political shock of these events in Tokyo was overpowering—and,
in Washington, altogether unexpected. On 11 August, King
broadcast a historic message to the Pacific Fleet at Pearl Harbor:
"This is a peace warning." Neither Hirohito nor his cabinet was
prepared to surrender unless the Americans agreed to allow him
to keep his throne, however. Truman, confronted with this last
gasp of fanaticism, backed down and instructed Secretary of
State James Byrnes to convey to Tokyo his assurance that

Hirohito would be neither ousted nor tried for his war crimes. Although Toyoda, the resolute Navy minister, and General Yoshijiro Umezu, the fanatical Japanese Army chief of staff, wanted to fight on, once his own safety was assured Emperor Hirohito emerged from his supposed wartime silence and instructed his cabinet to announce Japan's surrender at 1449 on 14 August.[15]

To please President Truman, Secretary of the Navy James Forrestal arranged for the battleship *Missouri* to be the site of the official surrender. The State Department, heedless of the military politics and honor involved, had appointed MacArthur to sign the instrument of surrender. When Admiral Cooke discovered this unwitting slight, he confronted Marshall and arranged a compromise. MacArthur, a superb speaker, conducted the ceremonies for the Allied powers, while Admiral Nimitz, the Nelson of the Pacific, signed the surrender document on behalf of the United States. "Just as the ceremony ended there was a big flyover of U.S. planes," recalled the *Missouri*'s skipper, Captain Stuart A. Murray. "It was really quite a sight." No one disagreed. The avatar of Japan's destruction, Fleet Admiral King, remained in his office in Main Navy in Washington, working as usual. On 2 September 1945 on the *Missouri*'s deck in Tokyo Bay, the Second World War ended.[16]

Chapter Fourteen

The Beginnings of the Cold War
1945–1949

Harry S. Truman, who became president after Roosevelt's death in April 1945, promised to follow Roosevelt's line on foreign policy, although no one quite knew what this was. Other than expecting the United Nations to play a major role in the postwar international system, FDR had always been disarmingly vague about his postwar plans. The JCS had been concerned about the expansion of Soviet influence in Europe since 1942, and Churchill began to harp on this theme two years later. Roosevelt ignored the problem. According to Navy Secretary Forrestal, those who disagreed were "apt to be called a goddamned fascist or imperialist, while if Uncle Joe [Stalin] suggests that he needs the Baltic Provinces, half of Poland, all of Bessarabia, and access to the Mediterranean, all hands agree that he is a fine, frank, candid, and generally delightful fellow." Soon after the Yalta Conference, there were signs of friction over postwar Europe between the West and the Russians, and only days before his death FDR told Churchill that "our Armies will in a very few days be in a position that will permit us to become 'tougher' than has heretofore appeared advantageous to the war effort."[1]

Despite the rosy public glow of Soviet-American relations when Germany surrendered, World War II had upset the classical relationships of international affairs and left the United States and the Soviet Union as the only two great powers on the field. France, occupied for four years by the Germans, was in disarray, and Britain, having fought one or more Axis powers for six years, was bankrupt. Germany and Japan were in ruins. "The whole world structure and order that we had inherited from the nineteenth century was gone," observed Assistant Secretary of State Dean Acheson. In June 1945, Truman had a testy exchange with Soviet Foreign Minister V. Molotov over Soviet policy in eastern Europe on the eve of the UN organizing conference. When, the following month, the president, the new secretary of state, James Byrnes, and the JCS met the Russian and British leaders at the last postwar Big Three summit in the Berlin suburb of Potsdam, these differences came to the fore, although the Allied unity prevailed until Japan formally surrendered in early September. Potsdam demonstrated, however, that great power diplomacy, not the UN, was destined to dominate postwar international politics.[2]

Following Japan's capitulation, Truman's gaze turned to demobilization and domestic policy, although a series of Russian probes on Europe's periphery was already bothering American strategists. The Soviets clearly intended postwar Scandinavia to be within their sphere of influence. In 1944, Molotov had told Norwegian Foreign Minister Tryvge Lie that Stalin wanted Norway to revise the 1920 Spitzbergen Treaty, cede Bear Island to Russia, and allow the Red Army to garrison the Svarland Archipelago. Russian troops took the German surrender in northern Norway in 1945. The Norwegians, who were historically neutral, felt naked, having no security guarantees from either Britain or the United States, so Lie negotiated with Moscow until the Russians withdrew later that year. He then rejected Stalin's territorial demands, broke off the talks, abandoned neutrality, and in desperation turned to Washington for support. Stalin also sought concessions out of the Italian empire in North Africa, which the Allied powers intended to dismember to punish Italy for her role as Germany's major European ally. In 1945, the Kremlin demanded naval bases in the Dodecanese and a role in Libya's occupation, positions Molotov forcefully advanced at the London Conference of Foreign Ministers at the end of the year.

Faced with Russian demands for specific bases outflanking western Europe, the JCS advised Truman to oppose such transfers. "Until the postwar situation and Soviet policy can be seen more clearly, we should . . . resist demands and policies which tend to improve [the] Soviet position in western Europe." Fleet

Admiral Chester Nimitz, the new CNO, and the new Army chief of staff, General of the Army Dwight D. Eisenhower, were becoming alert to a Soviet drive to acquire positions astride the Allied sea lines of communications from the Norwegian Sea to Gibraltar to Suez. Truman backed the Norwegians and arranged for London to take the lead in Libya by rejecting the Russian proposal and establishing instead a joint Italo-British government, which handed power over to a native monarch, King Idris I, in 1952. "The Russians are using their position as a victorious nation to take whatever they can without coming into actual conflict with the West," the director of ONI warned Nimitz in December 1945.[3]

The first postwar crisis over Iran fed the fires of this distrust. Soon after Germany invaded Russia in 1941, Stalin and Churchill had agreed to jointly occupy Iran to prevent a pro-Axis coup in Tehran and protect her oil and the Lend Lease pipeline up the Persian Gulf to Russia. Each power agreed to leave Iran within six months after Germany surrendered. The young shah, Reza Pahlevi, opposed the Anglo-Russian occupation and welcomed the wartime creation of the American Lend Lease commands in the Persian Gulf. He expected to use American influence to force Britain and Russia to leave Iran when the war ended, and to this end he granted American firms important oil concessions in 1945. The British withdrew on schedule later that year, but the Red Army remained behind in northern Iran, created a shabby puppet government in the province of Azerbaijan, and supported a separatist Kurdish republic. At the shah's behest, Truman issued sharp warnings on this issue to Stalin in early 1946. Within weeks the Russians quit Iran and the separatist movements collapsed, leaving Truman to conclude that his threats had produced the Soviet response, although some evidence contradicted this interpretation.

Washington's interest in the Near East and Middle East was further stimulated by the Turkish crisis, which Navy strategists believed to be rooted in the historic Russian drive to acquire a warm-water port on the Mediterranean. In the waning months of World War II, Moscow informed Ankara that the 1921 Russo-Turkish Nonaggression Pact "no longer corresponds to the new situation," and in June 1945 insisted that Turkey cede two of her northern provinces and air and naval bases along the Dardanelles to the Soviet Union. The Turks rejected these demands and anxiously cast about for help from the Western powers, who were, however, still irked by Turkey's evasive wartime neutrality. U.S. Army planners pointed to the British Navy's general postwar drawdown in the Mediterranean, as well as to the postwar proliferation of America's overseas bases, and suggested that Truman agree to the Soviet proposal, but Vice Admiral Russell Willson strongly dissented, arguing instead that Washington back the Turks. The JCS sided with Willson and asked Secretary Byrnes to hold firm against giving "bases or other rights for direct or indirect military control of the Straits" to the Soviets. With American support, the Turks for the moment stood up to Stalin, but Forrestal worried that "Russian pressure was compelling Turkey to maintain an army of six hundred thousand men, which was a great drain upon their resources" and would in the course of a few years lead to "bankruptcy" and eventual Soviet domination. Turkey was the "most important military factor in the Eastern Mediterranean and Middle East," Navy planner Rear Admiral Cato Glover maintained, and the United States had "to oppose the apparent Soviet policy of expansion in the area."[4]

America's first postwar military involvement in the Near East came about under odd circumstances. Turkish Ambassador Mehmed Munir Ertegun had died in Washington in 1944, but his remains could not be returned home until the end of the war. At the end of 1945, when the need to use warships to bring American troops home from Europe was slackening, the State Department requested that the Navy assign a cruiser to this diplomatic duty. Admiral Richmond Kelly Turner, the American representative on the UN Military Committee, proposed to Vice Admiral Forrest Sherman, the Deputy CNO, that the mission be used to transform a routine ship's visit into a special diplomatic signal. "The grandest funeral cortege in the history of our country," he said, would show the Russians that Truman supported Turkey. Forrestal was already considering an instruction to Admiral Marc Mitscher, the new commander in chief of the Atlantic Fleet, to conduct his spring exercises in the Mediterranean, but the White House apparently concluded that this show of force would somehow be overly provocative. Truman was extremely reluctant to break with Stalin and cause the collapse of the wartime Grand Alliance, and in early 1946, he consistently preferred diplomatic persuasion over confrontation in his dealings with the Soviets.[5]

James V. Forrestal. Undersecretary of the Navy, 1941–1944; Secretary of the Navy, 1944–1947; and Secretary of Defense, 1947–1949.

Foreshadowing the articulation of the Truman Doctrine, the post–treaty-class battleship *Missouri* (BB-63) (*center*) anchors off Istanbul in April 1946, a signal of U.S. support of Turkish resistance to Stalin's demands that the Ankara government cede two of its provinces to the Soviet Union and permit the Red Army to occupy the Dardanelles Strait.

Forrestal, who took a less benign view of Stalin's motives, adopted Turner's concept and ordered that a task force built around the battleship *Missouri* carry Ertegun's remains back to Turkey. On 26 February, Byrnes agreed that the battleship should visit the Near East, and also that Forrestal should station a carrier task force in the Mediterranean in the near future. Two days later, he announced that the State Department was taking a "tougher" line with the Soviets. Truman was unwilling to go this far, however, and on 10 March Forrestal confessed to former Prime Minister Winston Churchill, then in the United States on a speaking tour, that "the plans to have" the *Missouri* "accompanied by a task force of substantial proportions had been abandoned." Churchill observed that "a gesture of power not fully implemented was almost less effective than no gesture at all. . . . To make the gesture effective the entire task force should sail into the Sea of Marmara." Truman, not wanting to provoke the Russians, evidently prevented Forrestal from acting on Churchill's advice before the *Missouri* sailed on 22 March.

None of this marred the Turks' affectionate welcome when Admiral H. Kent Hewitt arrived in Istanbul in the *Missouri* on 5 April, an event Ankara interpreted as a sign that the United States would use force to uphold Turkey's position on the straits question. The cruiser *Providence*, the destroyer *Power*, and two Turkish destroyers escorted the battleship to Greek waters, where she was met by two destroyers of the Royal Hellenic Navy. "We are clearly aware of the meaning of this majestic procession," a Greek newspaper reported. "Russia stands threateningly at the land gates of Turkey; America stands likewise at the sea gates of Turkey. . . . It declares: 'Do not be afraid, I am here.'" This dramatic impression was confirmed by Truman, albeit hesitantly, in a Chicago speech nine days later. And when the *Missouri* returned to Algeciras Bay, Hewitt announced a new schedule of port visits in the Mediterranean "on a scale never known before." The first evidence of this more muscular policy emerged in late June when Vice Admiral Bernhard Bieri in the 10,000-ton cruiser *Fargo* visited Trieste on the Adriatic to illustrate America's support for Italy's claims to the surrounding region and to provide a regional counterweight to a nearby troop buildup by communist Yugoslavia.[6]

Hewitt's visit to Athens was also intended as a show of support to the Greek government, now facing an armed communist insurrection. Buoyed, the Greeks soon asked for more help. Forrestal approached Byrnes on 6 June 1946 "about sending casual cruisers unannounced—not as a fleet or a task force, but in small units—into the Mediterranean so that we may establish the custom," and Byrnes approved of the plan. Serious fighting broke out in Greece on 2 August, the same day that Forrestal announced that a task force built around the carrier *Franklin D. Roosevelt* was entering the eastern Mediterranean to visit Piraeus. Coinciding with the opening shots of the Greek civil war, this three-week cruise was designed to suggest to both Athens and Moscow that Washington might use force to ensure Greece's independence. Renewed Soviet pressure on Turkey and the fighting in Greece was the last straw, and Truman, acting on a consensus of his advisers, decided at long last on 15 August to support Greece and Turkey "to the end," accepting the possibility that this might lead to war with the Soviet Union. Forrestal moved rapidly, ordering Admiral Mitscher to announce one month later that the Navy would "maintain an enlarged fleet in the Mediterranean for some time to come." When the carrier *Randolph*, three cruisers, and eight destroyers appeared in Italian waters in late September, Nimitz established the 6th Task Group, and on 30 September 1946 Forrestal declared that an American carrier task force would remain in the Mediterranean on a "permanent" basis.[7]

The impact on Moscow of these ships' visits was hard to measure, but they did underscore the vulnerability of Russia's southern flank. The "Red Army which dominates eastern Europe and could not be removed by a diplomatic frontal attack, can be outflanked in the eastern Mediterranean," declared liberal columnist Walter Lippmann on 2 November. As evidence of American backing for the regimes in Athens and Ankara, the ships' visits were also valuable. In April 1947, the Greek prime minister asked that the 6th Task Group visit Greece more often, and later that month the carrier *Leyte Gulf*, three light cruisers, and five destroyers rendezvoused in Suda Bay in Crete and slowly steamed through the Greek islands and around the peninsula. Gradually, the number of ships in this force increased until, in January 1948, it consisted of two carriers, one cruiser-destroyer division, and amphibious ships carrying a Marine battalion landing team. When Admiral Sherman assumed this command that month, it was redesignated the 6th Task Fleet. Until the Korean War, the

Navy deployed three *Essex-* and three *Midway-*class carriers in the
Atlantic, keeping one or two fast carriers in the Mediterranean at
all times. "Until long-range bombers are developed capable of
spanning our bordering oceans and returning to our North
American bases," Nimitz declared, "naval air power launched
from carriers [in the Mediterranean and Norwegian Sea] may be
the only practical means of bombing enemy vital centers in the
early stages of a war." At the time, however, the 6th Task Fleet was
incapable of delivering nuclear weapons against targets in central Europe or the Soviet Union.[8]

The birth of the 6th Fleet and its deployment in the
Mediterranean coincided with the development of the first
American postwar strategic plans to deal with the Russian military threat there and in western Europe. These plans were necessary for the Navy to defend budget requests to Congress, procure
new ships and weapons, and identify shortcomings in the fleet
and shore establishment. On the whole, the Navy was poorly prepared for Cold War planning in part because Russia, the only
possible opponent, was not a naval power. In March 1946, the
Joint Strategic Plans Group drafted studies of particular problems; they became known collectively as the Pincher plans, a reference to Admiral Sherman's preference for an American strategy that pinched at the flank of Soviet strength in central Europe.
At the end of 1946, the vast area of western Europe from the Elbe
to the Channel was defended only by a shell of the once great
wartime Anglo-American armies. France's small reconstituted
army was the largest force standing between the Elbe and the
Channel. On the eastern side of what Churchill termed the Iron
Curtain, Stalin had at his disposal over 200 divisions and more
than 13,000 military aircraft. The Soviet Navy was thought to be
"of low combat value," according to naval intelligence, but the
Red Army and Air Force were perfectly configured to overrun
West Germany, Belgium, the Netherlands, France, and Italy. That
Stalin would do this if war erupted was the basic assumption
made by Sherman when, on 14 January 1947, he explained the
Pincher plans to Truman. Shortly thereafter, the JCS decided
that "the most vulnerable side of our defensive area will be in the
Atlantic, with the Mid East next and Asia and the Pacific at the
bottom of the list." In short, "Europe first"—the great legacy of
Admiral Stark's 1940 Plan Dog memorandum—was to be the
pillar of America's postwar strategy.[9]

Although Truman claimed to recognize both the political and military threats, he was unwilling to reconcile this analysis with his defense policies. After the Iranian affair in early 1946, he concurred with Sherman's argument that Russian strategy had "begun to look like a giant pincers movement against the oil-rich areas of the Near East and the warm-water ports of the Mediterranean." Instead of reacting to this threat, however, Truman hesitated, unwilling to launch a program of postwar rearmament owing to its costs and to his overconfidence in America's monopoly of atomic weapons. As a result, from 1946 to 1950 military spending and readiness remained low relative to the threat that Truman and the JCS perceived and to the overseas obligations the administration was accumulating.[10]

"We have emerged from this war the most powerful nation in the world—the most powerful nation, perhaps in all history," Truman wrote in 1944, but he relied nonetheless almost exclusively on the atomic monopoly after Hiroshima to bolster his increasingly assertive diplomacy. In 1946, Congress rejected the president's call for a postwar draft embodied in the Universal Military Training bill and thus dealt a body blow to his military policy. Both Truman and General George Marshall, who became secretary of state in January 1947, "placed much more importance on our atomic power than was justified," complained Admiral Arthur Radford, the Deputy CNO for air. This faith, however, was widely shared. Nonetheless, in April 1950, diplomat Charles Bohlen, a Soviet specialist, observed that "it is difficult to deduce any evidence that this monopoly on our part influenced Soviet policy during this period or abated its aggressiveness."[11]

Owing to Truman's reliance on the atomic monopoly, the Navy was eager to develop seaborne forces to deliver these weapons against the Soviet Union. Soon after Japan surrendered, Admiral Randall Jacobs, the wartime chief of naval personnel, warned that "technology had whittled down time and space until we shall have no leeway." The atomic "bomb of today is in the same relative state of development that the airplane was in 1918. What will it be when the next war opens?" The threat that atomic weapons in hostile hands posed to the fleet was demonstrated during the summer of 1946 when Vice Admiral William H. Blandy conducted Operation Crossroads, codename for two major tests designed to determine the impact of atomic bombs on warships at sea. For the Able test, an Army Air Force B-29 dropped one airburst Mk-3 atomic bomb over the old battleship *Nevada*, a Japanese cruiser, the modern submarine *Skate*, and several destroyers that were riding at anchor off Bikini Atoll. Few ships were sunk, but every vessel that remained afloat was badly damaged. The Baker test, an underwater blast, created a turbulence that lifted the 26,000-ton battleship *Arkansas* out of the water and sank eight more ships, including the venerable carrier *Saratoga*. "The shock wave, saturated with steam and vapor, rolled out and over the ships," covering them with tons of radioactive water, marveled Admiral Glover, whose flagship was stationed 10,000 yards from the blast. Hyperbolic newspapermen had led the public to believe that the bombs would disintegrate every ship, and because this did not happen, many observers questioned the lethality of atomic weapons, but this wrongheaded notion had no influence on high-level Navy policy.[12]

Less than three weeks after Japan surrendered, the JCS warned Truman that the United States "cannot afford . . . to permit the first blow to be struck against us" in the next war. "Our government . . . should press the issue to a prompt political decision, while making all preparations to strike the first blow if necessary." Fleet Admiral Leahy, the chairman of the JCS, advised Atomic Energy Commission chairman David Lilienthal on 29 October "that for a war [with the Soviets] a military requirement exists for approximately 400 atomic bombs . . . of destructive power equivalent to the Nagasaki-type bomb." The JCS were told that year that the Soviets might construct an atomic bomb within five years, but that a worldwide shortage of uranium would limit the size of the Soviet stockpile of atomic weapons for another decade. This calculation was upset in 1947 when American intelligence learned that the Soviets were mining uranium at a secret, hitherto unknown site in Russia, probably had access to large quantities of the ore, and were investing heavily in atomic bomb development. The JCS then estimated that by about 1956 the Kremlin would possess an arsenal of such weapons and bombers capable of reaching the United States from bases in northern Russia.[13]

Western Europe's weakness and the hollow shell of the postwar American atomic monopoly truly alarmed Admiral Sherman. Hard upon Japan's surrender, Truman had agreed to Secretary of War Stimson's plan to transfer control over all international atomic energy projects to the UN. Predicting wrongly that the Soviets would agree to this scheme, called the Baruch Plan, Truman did nothing to promote immediate postwar atomic bomb production and sought no advice as to how the JCS intended to fight a war with these weapons. Therefore, America's atomic stockpile remained small, numbering less than a dozen bombs in 1946 and roughly twice that in 1947. None were assembled, and one expert reckoned that only about two-thirds of them would function. In late 1946, there were only twenty-nine finished detonation mechanisms for the Mk-3 Fat Man bomb, and only seven cores in existence. These figures did not substantially increase until 1949.

Forrestal backed the strategic concept of an immediate, retaliatory air-atomic offensive, but he noted that it was an "unresolved question" as to "whether unescorted big bombers can penetrate to targets that have a vigorous fighter defense." Air Force leaders, who believed in the invulnerability of large formations of mutually supporting manned bombers, were in agreement with General Arnold's argument that "the influence of atomic energy on air power" had already made the strategic air forces "all-important." The United States should "concentrate our attention on the role of present-day air power as a means of employing atomic bombs offensively," Arnold asserted. The JCS proposed to use atomic weapons "to destroy the will of the Soviet Union to continue hostilities by a major offensive effort in western Europe and a defensive in East Asia" and pointed to the need for peacetime "forces capable of immediate retaliation for the purpose not only of reducing or limiting the aggressor's capability of continuing the attack, but also as a deterrent to its initiation." The Army, drastically reduced by demobilization, could not prevent the Soviets from overrunning western Europe. Whereas the Army and Navy viewed atomic weapons as one element in an American strategy, the newly independent Air Force regarded them as the only decisive instrument capable of destroying Soviet military capacity and will.[14]

Owing to the "limited supply of atomic bombs" and the lack of ground forces, the Navy favored a flanking strategy in Europe that relied on conventional ordnance during the first phase of a general war. The Mediterranean was the only area "where Allied naval and air superiority could be brought to bear against the Soviet Union without being exposed to the full force of the Red Army." Up to eight carriers might be concentrated in the

Mediterranean to "seize control of the Aegean Sea and the Turk-ish Straits" and attack Russia's Black Sea ports. "The carrier at-tack force is the only [American] weapon . . . which can deliver early and effective attacks against Russian air power and selected shore objectives in the initial stages of a Russo-American con-flict." Sherman even considered sending the large *Midway*-class carriers into the Norwegian Sea to support the West's northern-most position and to bomb Murmansk and other targets on the Russian's northern flank, but the discouraging results of Opera-tion Frostbite in 1946—carriers could operate aircraft in Arctic areas but at a very low tempo—led him to decide not to try to ad-vance into the Norwegian Sea. This meant, of course, abandon-ing Sweden and Norway and retiring to the British Isles, Iceland, Greenland, and the Azores.[15]

This laid the groundwork for the first Swing Strategy, which called for shifting forces from the Pacific to the Atlantic and Mediterranean theaters. One carrier—presumably one undergo-ing repairs when the war broke out—was to be left in the Pacific, and that theater was to be held thereafter only by those Air Force fighters and bombers already stationed in Alaska, the Philip-pines, and Japan. The Pacific Fleet's Trident war plan called ex-plicitly for a Swing Strategy. When the Red Army crossed the Elbe, the Pacific Fleet was to head for the Atlantic, leaving only one carrier at Pearl Harbor, which was to roll up Soviet shipping in the western Pacific and attack Port Arthur and Vladivostok to divert Soviet attention from Europe. The Atlantic Fleet, with two fast carrier task forces and the 8th Fleet as a striking arm, was to defend transatlantic communications to Britain, help the Royal Navy protect the English Channel, hold Norway, and support Western forces in Italy, Greece, and Turkey.

Sherman believed, however, that Stalin might launch a pre-emptive attack on Turkey and Iran in an attempt to cut off Britain from Persian Gulf oil. "Control of the Eastern Mediter-ranean area and Middle East oil resources" would be "the great-est strategic objective . . . for both the Soviets and the United States" during the first stage of the war, he predicted. He often went so far as to depict the area as the primary theater of opera-tions. Admiral Richard L. Conolly, who commanded the Eastern Atlantic and Mediterranean theater, visited Saudi Arabia and Bahrain in May 1947, and the following year Rear Admiral Harold Martin took a carrier task force into the Persian Gulf.

The Middle East Force, usually consisting of a seaplane tender and two destroyers, was established in early 1948, and soon berthing space was leased at Manama in the Bahrain Islands, a British protectorate. Forrestal intended such forward deployed forces—which might deter, police, or fight—to become an "accepted feature" of Cold War American grand strategy.[16]

The JCS were divided, however, over the strategic importance of the Mediterranean, the Near East, and the Persian Gulf. The Army urged in February 1946 that the United States not commit itself to defend the Near East owing to the extended lines of communications to that region, the shortage of forces in the area, and the greater urgency of holding western Europe. Eisenhower wanted to establish a perimeter around Greece and Turkey, whereas Nimitz stressed the importance of Middle East oil to Europe's war effort and pointed to the ease with which the Red Army might occupy Iran, then the region's largest oil producer. After contending with Soviet threats to Iran, Greece, and Turkey, however, Eisenhower's view modified somewhat, and Britain's Field Marshal Bernard Montgomery found in September 1946 that the JCS were alarmed about the Near East and uncommonly united about the area's importance. Two years later, the Navy had developed an emergency war plan that aimed at strengthening the 6th Fleet by sending nine carrier task forces into the area, establishing advance bases in Morocco and Egypt, and recovering Italy from the Red Army, but the means to support this strategy never materialized. The postwar world oil production boom ultimately undercut the economic argument behind Sherman's strategy, and the issue of the defense of the Near and Middle East lay unresolved for many years thereafter.[17]

Because of the haste with which Truman had demobilized America's wartime armed services, the naval forces to meet many of the new challenges of the Cold War no longer existed. Forrestal warned Truman at a cabinet meeting on 26 October 1945 that overly rapid demobilization "threatened to jeopardize our strategic position in the midst of postwar tensions that were building up." The president himself confessed that the armed forces were in danger of "disintegration," but he did nothing to stop it. One source of worry, British planners learned, was that "the Americans . . . are very Pearl Harbor conscious." "In future wars—and eventually the idealists will succeed in babbling us into other wars—we shall never again have the time with which

to build the implements of war, train men, and construct ships,"
said Admiral Thomas Gatch, a veteran of the Pacific, who complained about the pace of premature scrapping and mothballing.

The Navy's failure to articulate and publicize its role in postwar military policy now came home to roost. Postwar planning
within the wartime Navy was overly secretive, in part because Admiral King preferred the Navy to work alone in 1945 and failed
utterly to convey to the White House, Congress, or the Army his
vision of postwar naval policy and strategy. He had drafted a plan
in 1944 for a postwar fleet composed of 12 heavy carriers, 20 escort carriers, and 12 battleships, but before King retired in
December 1945 he revised these figures and urged Congress to
maintain at least 14 heavy carriers, 5,000 aircraft, 5 battleships,
and nearly 30 cruisers. Many aviators agreed with Radford's
claim that "until the world settles down" King's plan was too
"conservative in estimating its needs for air power." Chairman
Carl Vinson of the House Naval Affairs Committee introduced
legislation to enact King's plan, but soon it was clear that Truman was unprepared to back the bill. It was "entirely too ambitious . . . and utterly out of the question," said Harold Smith, Truman's budget director. Nimitz was unwilling to challenge this
assessment, and when Congress late in 1945 asked Vice Admiral
Louis Denfeld, the new Deputy CNO, about the size of the postwar fleet, he declared that the Navy was "unable to make any other representation until we have a more definite national policy
than we have now."[18]

Demobilization inflicted an excessive toll on the fleet and
shore establishment. From 1 October 1945 to 1 May 1946, the
Atlantic and Pacific fleets deployed battleships, carriers, cruisers,
and troop transports to bring home more than 2 million American soldiers and Marines in Operation Magic Carpet. At the
same time, the size of the Navy Department declined dramatically, the number of naval personnel alone dropping from over 3
million to less than 1 million by June 1946. The Bureau of Ships
canceled over $1 billion in wartime shipbuilding contracts, over
7,000 vessels were declared war surplus, and 2,000 more were
mothballed in the 16th and 19th Reserve Fleets. The fleet still
counted fifteen heavy carriers one year after Japan surrendered,
but Nimitz had allowed altogether too many supporting ships to
be mothballed. The Marine Corps fell below 100,000 troops.
There were other costs. The carrier *Philippine Sea*, commissioned

on 11 May 1946, could not get under way for lack of a crew. "We have a very large number of vessels in the active fleet which cannot go to sea because of the lack of competent personnel," Admiral Dewitt Ramsey, the Vice CNO, warned Forrestal on 22 August. Retrenchment affected Army and Air Force strength and readiness as well. Almost every wartime American bomber base in Europe and Britain was shut down, and London warned Washington in 1946 that six weeks would pass after the outbreak of war with Russia before a single British airfield could be readied to handle American bombers. And the JCS estimated that within that span of time the Red Army might cross the Elbe, drive to the Rhine, invest Paris, occupy the Channel coast, strike into Italy, and advance into the Balkans and Middle East. It was in part to counter such an offensive that the 6th Fleet was established, a step that represented a major recasting of the longstanding American naval strategy whose architects had for decades considered the Mediterranean to be the Royal Navy's lake.[19]

Despite a $3.75 billion American loan in July 1946, Britain had sacrificed so much to defeat Germany that her economy was in tatters and the postwar socialist Labour government, committed to dismantling the Empire, was unable and unwilling to continue bearing the burden of world power. In Moscow in October 1944, Churchill had sought a way around the problem of postwar Europe by negotiating an agreement with Stalin, which divided eastern Europe into spheres of influence, but Stalin soon violated this accord. The Moscow arrangement, which put Greece within Britain's orbit, led Churchill to send British troops to Athens later that year, and they helped to oust the Germans, restore the prewar monarchy, and crush a brief, violent communist rebellion in early 1945.

Greek elections in March 1946 brought to power a conservative coalition, but that month the Communists ignited a second uprising against Athens, aided by Marshal Josip Tito, the communist dictator of neighboring Yugoslavia. Soon the Soviets approached the Athens government with an offer to quell the communist uprising in return for a lease to a naval base in the Aegean for Russia's Black Sea Fleet. The Greeks, buoyed by the visit of the *Missouri*, stiffly rejected the menacing Soviet plan. The Americans were fully aware that the Athens regime was corrupt and inept, but when Britain announced in February 1947 that she could no longer afford to support the Greeks, or the Turks,

Washington reacted with alarm. "If Soviet power is to be secure," predicted George Kennan, head of the State Department's planning staff, then the "international authority" of the United States had to be broken. Admiral Glover of the Navy's War Plans Division was pessimistic about the outcome of the Greek civil war but argued that, "if properly equipped and supported," the Turks were "capable of offering material resistance, even to the Soviets."[20]

Prodded by Marshall and Forrestal, the new secretary of defense, who reminded Truman of his August 1946 decision on the importance of the Near East, the president went before Congress on 12 March 1947 and declared that "totalitarian regimes imposed on free peoples, by direct or indirect aggression, undermine the foundations of international peace and hence the security of the United States." Under the rubric of the Truman Doctrine, he proposed to defend Greece and Turkey against Soviet aggression and asked for military aid for both countries without which "confusion and disorder might well spread throughout the entire Middle East." Forrestal held that "Turkey is strategically more important than Greece since . . . it dominates the major air, land, and sea routes from the USSR to the Cairo-Suez area and to the Middle East oil fields," but Greece faced a more immediate peril. Reacting quickly, Congress enacted an aid package of $250 million for Greece and $150 million for Turkey, and soon the carrier *Leyte* led a task force back to Athens to herald the new American commitment. Finally, Truman directed the JCS in November to consider that "the security of the Eastern Mediterranean and of the Middle East is vital to the security of the United States."[21]

Before American arms and advisers reached Greece, however, the Communists had established a rival government and launched an offensive of bombings, ambushes, and kidnappings designed to undermine the royalists. "How large a part of our Mediterranean fleet [could be moved] to Greek ports?" Truman anxiously asked Forrestal when the crisis worsened in July 1947. Emboldened by early success, the Communists chose Christmas Eve to lay siege to Kónitsa in the northern Grammos Mountains in northwestern Greece, which they planned to make their capital. Moscow was already rethinking its support for the uprising, however. According to Yugoslav diplomat Milovan Djilas, the establishment of the 6th Fleet profoundly influenced Stalin's thinking. "Do you think that . . . the United States . . . will permit you to break their sea line of communication in the Mediterranean Sea?" the dictator asked. "Nonsense! And we have no navy. The uprisings in Greece must be stopped and as quickly as possible." American military aid reached Greece in August, and the Greek Army saved Kónitsa and staged a counteroffensive in 1948, overrunning rebel strongholds in the Grammos and Vitsi mountains. At the same time, Stalin's relations with Tito soured, and in June 1948 he expelled Yugoslavia from the Cominform, an important Moscow-based, international communist directorate. Tito was forced to turn to Washington for reconstruction aid, which Truman wisely extended without attaching explicit conditions. Tito reciprocated by closing the frontier between Yugoslavia and Greece in 1949, and in August of that year the Greek Army closed the final chapter on their civil war.[22]

The Greek civil war provided Truman with one model for his new policy of containing Soviet power in Europe. Behind the shield of the 6th Fleet, American aid and advisers had revived the Athens government and provided the means for the Greek Army to take the offensive against the Soviet-backed insurgency. Secretary of State Marshall was one of the architects of this "containment" policy, but this catchword was coined by Kennan, the author of a 4,000-word "long telegram" from the Moscow embassy in 1946 that pointed out the imperialist character of Russia's conquest empire and argued that Moscow's expansionism was not wholly defensive. It was dosed, he claimed, by other factors: Russia's cultural paranoia, Stalin's madness, and communist fanaticism. Forrestal, who saw in Kennan someone to articulate his own concerns, arranged for him to rewrite a paper on Soviet foreign policy, which Kennan published under the pseudonym "Mr. X" in the July 1947 edition of *Foreign Affairs*, an influential quarterly. His earlier analysis of recent Russian history was restated in this piece, which urged that the United States adopt a long-term policy of containment to prevent Moscow from acquiring more satellites and to put enough pressure on the communist system to cause its internal collapse in the long term. Kennan brilliantly codified concepts developed by Forrestal and others, but neither then nor in later years did Kennan understand that only unrelenting American military power would bring about the result he sought.

In early 1947, Marshall had flown to Moscow to repair relations with the Russians, but this conference broke up amidst mutual recriminations and he returned to Washington determined to shore up western Europe and prevent a Soviet takeover there. Although he consistently opposed postwar American rearmament, in June he proposed to extend $17 billion in economic aid to western Europe over the next four years, a proposal that came to be known as the Marshall Plan. When Congress enacted the Marshall Plan, Moscow reacted by forcing Hungary, Romania, Poland, Bulgaria, and Finland to sign mutual assistance treaties with the Soviet Union in February 1948 and by arranging a communist coup that overthrew Czechoslovakia's democratic government that same month. Stalin also levered Finland into signing a one-sided Friendship Treaty in April and menaced Norway and Denmark once again with a ham-fisted diplomacy that caused both countries to abandon their historic neutrality and cast their lot with the West.

Stalin also teamed with the French to thwart Anglo-American steps to reduce the cost and severity of the four-power occupation of Germany by increasing German industrial production. Washington and London responded by imposing currency reforms in their occupation zones to stimulate the German economy, but Stalin reacted on 24 June 1948 by closing off all roads and waterways to the city of Berlin, which was governed by all four Allied powers but was situated within the Soviet occupation zone. American opinion was divided as to how to respond to this provocation. Despite three years of preparations, only one Air Force bombardment group was capable of delivering atomic bombs, and these planes were stationed in New Mexico. Nonetheless, Defense Secretary Forrestal publicly announced that he was deploying two atomic-capable heavy bombardment groups to Britain during the summer. He wanted to use the Berlin Blockade crisis to get Congress to rearm, but Marshall again thwarted this policy on the grounds that it might be rejected and "the reverberations might cause us to lose our support in western Europe." Instead of withdrawing from Berlin, as some advised, or sending an armored column up the Autobahn to break the blockade, as others suggested, Truman chose to sustain the city by a huge airlift, conducted mainly by the Air Force but supported by land-based Navy planes. This lasted until Stalin called off the blockade in the spring of 1949. However, Truman once more rejected Forrestal's rearmament plan.[23]

The Czech coup and the Berlin Blockade led Washington and London to worry that the Soviets were about to invade western Europe. Truman cited the "growing menace" of Soviet policy when he asked Congress to reintroduce the Selective Service draft in March 1948, and on 12 April, the JCS approved the Half-moon Plan, an emergency war plan that embodied the air-atomic offensive as a counter to a Soviet invasion. One month earlier, Canada, Britain, France, Belgium, Luxembourg, and the Netherlands had signed a military alliance, the Brussels Treaty, and shortly thereafter Secretary Marshall agreed to a British proposal that the United States join this alliance. This commitment was supported by Forrestal, but the JCS, suspicious of new calls on their meager forces, warned on 28 April of the treaty's "harmful influence on our global strategy" and the danger that the new allies might engage in "undue interference with our own military requirements" unless Truman rearmed.[24]

Truman ignored these concerns, although he did promise to ask Congress for a small supplemental appropriation to cover any new military assistance costs, but Undersecretary of State Robert Lovett pointed out that the administration was so distrusted on the Hill that the proposed Atlantic alliance would be jeopardized by any association with a new foreign military aid program. In April 1948, their appetites whetted by the hope of more American aid, the British and French rushed a delegation to Washington, where they negotiated most of the details of the new arrangement. Three months later, at the height of the Berlin crisis, Senator Arthur Vandenberg, a Michigan Republican, who chaired the Foreign Relations Committee, persuaded the Senate to pass a resolution favoring an American military commitment to the defense of western Europe. "Its implications are . . . very great, and can extend to United States' involvement in global warfare," the JCS told Forrestal. Passage of the Vandenberg Resolution demonstrated that an alliance with the Brussels Powers would be welcomed by both parties in Congress. Transatlantic talks continued during the summer, and a draft treaty was ready in September. Admiral Louis Denfeld, who had succeeded Nimitz as CNO in late 1947, reasoned that a European alliance would impose immense burdens on the postwar fleet, but during the negotiations the new secretary of state, Dean Acheson, told the JCS that military assistance to rebuild western Europe's armed forces would take precedence over deploying American forces overseas. The JCS assumed that any American forces sent to Europe would be withdrawn once the Allies had improved their own defenses.[25]

After Truman was reelected in November 1948, the North Atlantic Treaty was delivered to the Senate where it was approved by a wide margin on 21 July 1949. Its most important article provided that each signatory power was to consider an attack on any other member of the alliance an attack on its home territory. In short, the United States was committed formally to defend western Europe. Norway withdrew from its weak defense pact with neutral Sweden and entered NATO, although Soviet outrage was so loud that the Norwegians, in an attempt to appease Moscow, announced that no foreign forces would be based permanently in Norway. The Danes followed suit in 1952. One year earlier Greece and Turkey had been invited to join the alliance to strengthen its southern flank. Little attention was thereafter paid to the Navy's flanking strategy, however, inasmuch as the NATO powers concentrated on defending western Europe on the Rhine. "If the Western Powers lose western Europe and they lose the Rhine they lose the war. On the other hand, the loss of the Middle East in the early stages of a global war would not, in itself, be fatal," the JCS concluded. Plans to send forces into the Persian Gulf during a NATO war were soon dropped. In the space of four short years after the collapse of FDR's wartime Grand Alliance at Potsdam, the menace of Stalin's adventurism had forced the United States to abandon its historic independence in foreign policy and commit itself in peacetime to preparing strategies for waging coalition warfare on an unprecedented scale.[26]

The Communist victory in the Chinese civil war also unhinged America's postwar expectations and raised the questions of whether and how to apply the grand strategy of containment to Asia. Since 1926, the United States had recognized Generalissimo Chiang Kai-shek, the head of the Nationalist Party, as China's chief of state, although Chiang's army never completely defeated the rival warlords and lost ground consistently to the Japanese after they invaded China in 1937. Upon being forced to retire up the Yangtze River from his peacetime Nanking capital to the remote, inland Chungking capital in 1939, Chiang rightly concluded that his army alone could not defeat the Japanese and that his best policy would be to stimulate a war between the United States and Japan, wait for the Americans to crush the Japanese, and then reestablish the Nationalists' authority and deal with its communist opponents. During World War II, the Roosevelt administration supplied China with Lend Lease supplies and credits, a large Army Air Force was positioned in India to support another large tactical Army Air Force in China, and the U.S. Navy established a huge military assistance program known as the Sino-American Cooperative Organization in Chungking. None of these expensive efforts nor Chiang's Nationalist Army contributed in any significant way to Japan's defeat.

To the dismay of many of his closest advisers, and of Churchill and Stalin, Roosevelt often treated wartime China as a Great Power and talked of a postwar global order dominated by the "four horsemen," the United States, the British Empire, the Soviet Union, and China. He evidently assumed that China would be the strongest postwar power in the Far East, owing to the imminent collapse of the Japanese Empire and the demise of European colonialism, and that China would be bound to the United States by the ties of history and mutual interest. Chiang was invited to the 1943 Cairo Conference to discuss grand strategy with Roosevelt and Churchill, and two years later, China was accorded one of the five permanent seats on the new UN Security Council. The United States denounced the "unequal" nineteenth century Wanghia and Tientsin treaties and the 1902 Boxer Treaty, which had provided the legal basis for the Navy's prewar Yangtze Patrol, and forced the British to abandon the "treaty port" system, which had involved the U.S. Navy's Asiatic Squadron in Far Eastern affairs for a century. At the January 1945 Yalta Conference, in order to prevent Stalin from reasserting Russia's longstanding interests in the Far East and to align Moscow with the Nationalist regime, President Roosevelt laid the foundations for the 14 August 1945 Sino-Soviet Friendship Treaty. Following the Yalta prescription, this agreement, signed on the eve of the formal Japanese surrender in Tokyo Bay, gave the Soviets the right to occupy the important North China ports of Darien and Port Arthur and to control the Manchurian railroad system. Stalin, who seemed for the moment to prefer a weak China under the Nationalists to the communist insurgents, recognized Chiang Kai-shek's regime and gave the appearance of supporting its return to power, although the reality of Soviet foreign policy was quite different.

World War II only partly suspended the civil war between the Nationalists and Mao Tse-tung's Communist Party. Allied to the Nationalists before 1927 but bitter enemies thereafter, the Communists had established a soviet in rural Kiangsi Province after being driven from the large coastal cities by Chiang's great unifying expeditions of the 1920s. It was during this formative period that Mao became party chairman, developed his doctrine and tactics of peasant revolution, and withstood Nanking's 1933 "bandit campaign" by means of the 3,000-mile Long March, which ended with the reestablishment of another soviet in remote Yenan Province in 1936. By 1945, the Communists controlled territory containing nearly 100 million people and had raised an army of roughly one million effectives supported by a village militia of two million men. The Soviet army's invasion of Manchuria in August 1945 ended with the surrender of over 600,000 Japanese troops, and the Russians armed the Chinese Communists with over 300 Japanese tanks, 4,800 machine guns, 2,300 trucks, 1,200 heavy guns, and over 300,000 captured rifles. In short, the largest stock of Japanese arms outside of the Home Islands was turned over to the Chinese Communists. Thus fitted out with modern weapons, Mao's army was more than ready for the upcoming conflict with Chiang's ill-equipped, poorly trained Nationalist forces, which had lost over 100,000 of its best officers during the eight-year-long struggle with Japan.

When Japan surrendered, Truman had devised no alternative to Roosevelt's China policy. Fleet Admiral Leahy, the chairman of the JCS; Fleet Admiral King, the CNO; and Navy Secretary Forrestal worried that the Soviets would support the Chinese Communists in a renewed civil war, but they, Truman, and Secretary of State James F. Byrnes were transfixed by the problems of Europe and paid little attention to the swirl of events in the Far East until late 1945. Admiral King's proposal at the July 1945 Potsdam Conference to use Admiral Thomas Kinkaid's 7th Fleet to occupy Darien and Port Arthur before the Soviets arrived and to play them as bargaining chips was dismissed without a fair hearing. All Washington was reluctant to become involved in the fighting in China. Organized in 1942, Commodore Milton Miles' Naval Advisory Group had thereafter become entangled with Tai Li's Blue Shirts, the murderous Nationalist secret police, "a political involvement which cannot fully be put on paper," according to the commodore. Lieutenant General Albert C. Wedemeyer, the commander of the Army's China theater, disliked Miles' antics, however, and the Sino-American Cooperative Organization was shut down soon after Japan surrendered.[27]

Japan's capitulation found General Wedemeyer and Admiral
Kinkaid with orders to assist the Nationalist regime—the only officially recognized government—in reasserting its authority by
taking the surrender of Japanese forces in China and by transporting Japanese troops back to their Home Islands. American
warships stood into South China's ports beginning in September,
and Kinkaid went ashore in mid-month to make arrangements
with Wedemeyer to start repatriating the Japanese Army, to occupy South Korea, and to land Marines in North China. In late
September, Vice Admiral Daniel Barbey's 7th Amphibious Force
landed the 25th Army at Pusan and Inchon and these troops advanced on Seoul and took the surrender of the Japanese forces
on the Korean peninsula. Barbey's ships also landed Major General Keller E. Rockey's 1st Marine Division at Taku on the 30th,
and within days, the Marines had occupied nearby Tientsin and
Peiping and key positions in the area. Eventually, the Marines patrolled the main cities of Hopei Province and the Shantung
Peninsula, helped move relief supplies to North China, and rode
coal trains in Hopei, guarding against attacks by bandit gangs or
communist raiding parties. However, there were already signs of
trouble on the horizon.

To assist Chiang in reasserting his authority, the JCS agreed
in mid-September to a Nationalist plan to transport Nanking's
forces to North China and Manchuria. Such a movement had
been envisioned before the Japanese surrender, and the Sino-
Soviet Friendship Treaty specifically provided for the use of Sovi-
et-occupied Darien by the Nationalist Army to this end. In mid-
October, the 14th Army Air Force airlifted 65,000 Nationalist
troops, organized into two armies, to the Peiping-Tientsin area.
Meanwhile, two 7th Fleet transport squadrons, carrying 56,000
Nationalist soldiers and led by the recently commissioned 14,800-
ton fast attack transport *Randall*, were steaming from the South
China port of Kowloon to Darien. Already, Commander Chester
R. Wood with a destroyer squadron had attempted to put into
Darien to look into the fate of 1,500 Allied prisoners of war who
were thought to be there. He found that port occupied by the
Chinese Communists, who refused to permit him to come
ashore. Another communist military commander had refused to
allow Barbey to land the 6th Marine Division at Chefoo, and Admiral Kinkaid had had to divert them to the large port of Tsingtao. Communist authorities in Darien also refused to allow the

Nationalist armies to be put ashore, even after Kinkaid sent a cruiser-destroyer formation to the port to reinforce the point that the Nationalists were acting within their treaty rights. Frustrated, Kinkaid had to divert these troops to the ports of Chinwangtao and Taku. By this time, heavy fighting between the Communists and the Nationalists had broken out in Manchuria, on the Shantung Peninsula, and in other parts of North China.

In late 1945, Truman sent the Marshall mission to China to end the civil war, bring stability to the region, and so limit the American commitment to East Asia at a time of growing tensions in Europe and the Near East. Washington had so far received conflicting advice from its on-scene commanders. By November, Wedemeyer was so frustrated in dealing with the contending factions that he proposed that the United States either openly back the Nationalists or withdraw altogether. Kinkaid agreed. Admiral Barbey, on the other hand, opposed further involvement of the 7th Fleet or General Rockey's Marines in the jockeying for positions and encouraged Washington to arrange a compromise between both factions under which Chiang Kai-shek would share power with Mao Tse-tung and Mao would recognize Chiang's position as chief of state. "This in effect will be a loose federation of states," Barbey supposed, "but will make possible a development of Chinese nationalism which may someday result in the followers of Mao Tse-tung thinking of themselves as Chinese first and Communists second."[28]

Truman agreed with this line of reasoning and named General of the Army George C. Marshall, the widely acclaimed Army chief of staff, as his special ambassador to China. Marshall was about to retire and was therefore available for a diplomatic post. He had served in China in the 1920s, dealt with the Chungking government during World War II, and enjoyed an unusually close relationship with Madame Chiang Kai-shek, the dictator's American-educated wife. The State Department and the War Department wanted to put the 7th Fleet at the disposal of either General Marshall or General MacArthur, the commander of the newly created Tokyo-based Far Eastern theater, but Admiral King objected to this and successfully insisted that the Navy needed its own independent voice in Asian waters. Admiral Charles M. Cooke, King's principal wartime deputy, who was slated to become CNO when Fleet Admiral Nimitz retired in 1947, was chosen to command the 7th Fleet, owing to his vast experience as a strategist and his proven ability to work with Marshall and General Wedemeyer. As for Marshall's goals, he was to offer his services as an honest broker, Truman declared, but was not to assist one side or the other in the civil war. Because the Soviets were clearly now supporting the Communists, complained Leahy and Forrestal, this instruction "practically places us on the side of the Chinese Communists."[29]

General Marshall arrived in China in December 1945, and Admiral Cooke took command of the 7th Fleet—soon renamed U.S. Naval Forces, Western Pacific, to emphasize its independence from General MacArthur's neighboring, Japan-based Far East theater—one month later. Marshall was stunned by the weakness, corruption, and ineptitude of the Nationalist regime and offended by Chiang's blind truculence. Marshall quickly learned, however, that neither side in the civil war was confident of victory, and by 10 January 1946, he had arranged a ceasefire and brought Mao's lieutenant, Chou Enlai, to Nanking for talks on reorganizing the government. Cooke had little hope that the ceasefire would last or that a negotiated settlement would end the decades-long civil war. Should the Communists win, he predicted, they would ally China with their Soviet patrons, a combination that would irremediably complicate the problem of American global postwar strategy. Cooke, who fully understood the many shortcomings of the Nationalist regime but who was overly sympathetic to Chiang and his reactionary clique, concluded that the only correct American policy was to provide limited military support to Chiang Kai-shek's forces and prepare for a protracted, bloody struggle. In December 1945, Admiral Barbey had replaced the Sino-American Cooperative Organization with an aid agreement between the Nanking government and the U.S. Navy, the main features of which were the establishment of a training center for the Chinese Navy at Tsingtao, the finest natural harbor in North China, and the transfer of some LST landing ships and other craft to the Nationalists. Cooke worked feverishly to expand the center, enlarge the Chinese Navy, and improve its training regimen so that it might support the Nationalist Army in the inevitable conflict.

In March 1946, the first ceasefire broke down. Marshall was in Washington at the time lobbying Congress for economic aid for a new coalition government and arranging with the War Department for American forces to be withdrawn from the China theater. That month, acting on an earlier commitment to Chiang made by General Wedemeyer and approved by General Marshall, Admiral Cooke had instructed the 7th Fleet Amphibious Force to transport 200,000 Nationalist troops, divided into five armies, from Kowloon and other South China ports to Manchuria where they were to reestablish Chiang Kai-shek's authority. The 7th Fleet also shipped weapons and munitions of all kinds to the Nationalist forces in Manchuria, and Cooke created a Navy cargo service on the Yangtze to ship food and medicines up to Hunan to combat a famine in the valley. American military commanders in China, including Wedemeyer and Cooke, had warned Chiang not to disperse his armies in the north, but the generalissimo correctly replied that he could not allow the Communists to completely occupy Manchuria, China's industrial heartland. He assumed that the United States would never abandon his cause—a view Cooke constantly reinforced—and so supposed that the 7th Fleet would always be ready to provide his forces in Manchuria with the logistical support necessary to hold the province's larger cities. When the Nationalists reached Manchuria, they discovered not only that the Soviet Army had turned over all of its captured Japanese equipment to the Chinese Communists but also that the Soviets had moved all the railroad rolling stock and heavy factory machines back to Russia and had put the few remaining South Manchurian Railroad locomotives and cars at the disposal of Mao's troops.

By the time George Marshall returned to Nanking, fighting had broken out throughout North China. The Communists had captured Changchun in Manchuria, and the Nationalists had responded with a counteroffensive. Marines holding positions in and around Peiping, Tientsin, and Tsingtao had come under fire. On 21 May, a gunfight erupted between a Marine patrol and a Communist unit south of Tientsin in which one American was killed. Four more Marines died when the Communists ambushed a motor convoy near Tientsin a month later. Then, on 19 June, ships of the newly trained Chinese Navy went on the offensive and shelled the communist-held ports of Chefoo and Weihaiwei on the Gulf of Chili. After difficult negotiations, Marshall arranged a second ceasefire, which included a mutual agreement to disengage. Acting under Marshall's orders, Admiral Cooke directed the 7th Fleet Amphibious Force to rescue 3,000 communist troops who had been isolated north of Chefoo by a superior Nationalist body.

While Marshall was now more eager than ever that American forces be withdrawn from China, Cooke was more firmly convinced that the Marines were providing the only brake on the renewal of hostilities in North China and a convenient shield behind which the Nationalists might consolidate their holdings. Supposing that the ceasefire would not endure unless they did something dramatic, Marshall and Ambassador John Leighton Stuart issued a joint statement on 11 August warning that a renewal of the war would devastate China. On the grounds that Chiang would not abandon his offensive and agree to a third negotiation unless he was convinced that the United States was prepared to abandon his government, Marshall asked Truman for permission to impose an embargo on the transfer or shipment of American arms to the Nationalist armies. He also wanted to withdraw the Marines from North China. Navy Secretary Forrestal, who visited the Far East in July, was opposed to the embargo and the withdrawal of the Marines, as was Admiral Leahy. They also supported Admiral Cooke's contrary proposal to increase American naval forces in China, establish base facilities at Tsingtao and Shanghai, and expand the training program for the small Chinese Navy. "Should [the United States] fail to assist the Central Government in China," Leahy confided to his diary, "we would have no friends in either faction and no friends in China."[30]

Truman was caught in the maw of conflicting advice. The Joint Chiefs supported Cooke and opposed abandoning Chiang, but their concerns centered on Europe and the Near East. Forrestal supported Cooke, but Secretary of War Robert Patterson backed Marshall and urged the White House to withdraw from China. So did Marshall's able deputy, Undersecretary of State Robert Lovett. According to Admiral Radford, the Vice CNO, "President Truman . . . was inclined to lean heavily on a few intimate advisers, and once he had made up his mind he did not change it readily." Of this circle, Marshall was clearly the most important. Truman rarely disagreed with Marshall and almost never overruled his most valued adviser. Moreover, as Radford pointed out, Truman often established policy based on his personal reaction to various figures. "He told me once that he just could not stand President Chiang Kai-shek." Agreeing with all of Marshall's proposals, Truman approved the embargo, instructed the JCS to begin withdrawing the Marines from North China, and issued an unusually blunt warning to Nanking to the effect that the United States would not involve itself further in the civil war.[31]

Marshall all but confessed, in October 1946, that his great mission had been a failure. In spite of the embargo, the Nationalist offensive had gained a deceptive momentum. At the end of the year, the general returned to Washington, and in January 1947, he replaced Byrnes as secretary of state. In the intervening months, the Marines in North China, who had numbered 50,000 at the start of 1946, were reduced to 34,000. Cooke had become so vocal in his opposition to Truman's policy that one of Marshall's first acts when he arrived at the State Department was to issue a directive to the admiral to "withhold . . . military aid to China in any form which would contribute to or encourage civil war." He also demanded that Cooke withdraw the Marines from the area around Peiping and Tientsin. This "failure to support Chiang would result in victory for the Communists," Cooke shot back. To underscore the importance of the issue, Forrestal arranged for the admiral to return to Washington in February to explain his reasoning to the president. At the end of this stormy session at the White House, Truman told Cooke that he had "never heard some of these things [explained] that way before," an artful distortion given the debate raging in Washington over China policy at the time. Cooke's visit coincided with the president's enunciation of the Truman Doctrine and his request to Congress for $400 million in military and economic aid to Greece and Turkey, and Admiral Leahy pointed out that logic demanded that the new strategy of containment of Soviet influence be extended to the Far East. Marshall, who now saw China as nothing more than a bog, resisted every argument and persuaded Truman to adopt a policy of thorough disengagement.[32]

Cooke, realizing that his stand on China had cost him the CNO billet, returned to Tsingtao unhappy with the entire state of affairs. Under orders to withdraw a Marine garrison from a large American ammunition dump at Hsin Ho near Tangku, he dallied and delayed, playing for time. On 5 April 1947, the Communists attacked Hsin Ho, killing five Marines, and within days Cooke received another order from Marshall directing him to abandon the position. He did not do so until the 21st, by which time the Nationalists had organized a force to defend the dump. It was now clear to Washington that Marshall's embargo and Truman's threats had done nothing to bring the warring parties back to the negotiating table and that the Communists were about to thrash Chiang's army in Manchuria. Cooke, arguing that Marshall's policy embodied only "drift" and so relinquished any attempt to control events, helped to reignite the debate in Washington with a mid-summer proposal to transfer 271 smaller American warships and landing craft to the Chinese Navy, provide the Nanking government with substantial economic aid, and end the futile, self-defeating arms embargo. In effect, Cooke was arguing that it was better for American interests in the Far East for the Chinese civil war to continue than for the Communists to emerge victorious.

Forrestal, now secretary of defense, was behind Cooke's plan, while Marshall and the State Department were predictably against it. To avoid making a hard decision, Truman decided to send General Wedemeyer back to China on a fact-finding mission in August. Wedemeyer's carefully crafted report on this mission catalogued the many faults of the Nationalist regime and even suggested for the first time that the end of Chiang's government was near. Many Nationalist officials were "corruptly striving to obtain as much as they can before the collapse," he warned. Despite this dreary portrayal, Wedemeyer concluded that the United States had no realistic option but to end the embargo and support Chiang Kai-shek, the alternative being a Communist government in China and a Sino-Soviet alliance. Marshall wholly disagreed with this reasoning, as did Truman, and the Wedemeyer report was quickly suppressed. In mid-September, Cooke was ordered to begin the final withdrawal of the Marines from the Peiping-Tientsin corridor.[33]

When Vice Admiral Oscar Badger relieved Admiral Cooke on the deck of the flagship *Estes* as commander of the 7th Fleet in February 1948, the Nationalists had long since gone over to the defensive in Manchuria and their position throughout North China was in peril. The 4th Marines, now numbering only 3,600, had been withdrawn to Tsingtao. In April, the Communists overran Weishan, an important railroad junction, thereby severing the rail link between Tsingtao and the rest of North China. Marshall and Lovett wanted Admiral Badger to evacuate that port but he resisted, pointing out that the Nationalist garrison was not strong enough to hold the vital position by itself. After months of discussion, Badger was directed by Undersecretary Lovett in June 1948 to establish his own timetable for the withdrawal but not to collaborate with or assist the Nationalists should the port be attacked.

The drift depicted by Cooke a year earlier was evolving into a thorough disaster for American interests in the Far East.

Chiang Kai-shek temporarily resigned the presidency of China in April and went into a brief retirement, Madame Chiang visited Marshall in Washington, and the Nanking regime sank further under the weight of rampant official corruption, spiraling inflation, food riots in the major cities, and repeated military disasters. Major General David Barr, sent out by the Army to advise the Nanking armies in 1948, often contrasted the overall lack of aggressiveness of Nationalist troops and the incompetence of their officers with the dedication of the Communist armies and the skill and ferocity of their leaders. Republicans back home had come to view Truman's China policy as an election year issue, and they took up the Nationalist cause, a belated, cynical, partisan ploy. In return for their votes for Marshall Plan aid to Europe, Congressional Republicans insisted that Truman sign the China Aid Act of April 1948, which provided an outright, unconditional $125 million grant to Nanking and $338 million in economic assistance. Nanking immediately ordered payment for arms from the $125 million grant, but the State Department delayed the dispersal of these funds. At length, Chiang spent most of the $125 million grant on his useless air force and to enrich his Nationalist cronies.

Admiral Badger took this opportunity to put forth an unusual plan that he thought might result in the Nationalists holding Hopei Province, securing the corridor from Peiping to the sea, and reestablishing themselves on the Shantung Peninsula. Badger recognized General Fu Tso-yi, who commanded the Peiping military region, as one of the few truly able commanders in the Nationalist Army, and the admiral proposed that China Aid Act munitions be shipped directly to Tsingtao and distributed to Fu's loyal divisions. This was one way to bypass Chiang's venal officials in Nanking. Even Truman liked the scheme, but its implementation was delayed by an unusual coalition of anti-Chiang officials at the State Department and the Nanking government, which protested that the Badger plan would violate its sovereignty. In November, however, the Nanking regime agreed to a single shipment of weapons directly to Fu's embattled army. It was too late. On 23 September, soon after the Nationalist garrisons in Changchun and Mukden, Manchuria, surrendered, the Communists had captured Tsinan, an important railroad junction connecting Hopei Province with Nationalist base areas in South China. Two months later, a former U.S. Navy LST at Taku off-

loaded arms and munitions destined for Fu's army. The stocks
were useless. Ammunition clips and tripods for the machine guns
were missing, and the shipment contained no spares. "You will
hear it said that the Nationalists never lost a battle for want of
ammunition," Admiral Badger told Admiral Radford, the new
commander in chief of the Pacific Fleet. "While this may be tech-
nically true, it is also true that there were many battles that they
could not fight because they had no ammunition."[34]

On 4 November 1948, Ambassador Stuart in Nanking officially warned all American nationals to leave China. Over the
next several months, the small Marine garrisons in Nanking and
Shanghai assisted in the evacuation of missionaries from the
Yangtze Valley and thousands of resident American nationals
from the Shanghai area and from various cities along the coast
and the old settlements. Badger instructed Rear Admiral Francis P.
Old to suspend training and shut down the Naval Advisory
Group at Tsingtao. He wanted to hold out there, and Forrestal
supported him, but Truman once again sided with Marshall and
Lovett and Badger was ordered to withdraw. When Captain
Charles W. Moses in the command ship *Eldorado* arrived in Tsingtao to relieve the *Estes* in January, "the Communist lines were
about 25 miles to the west [of the city]. Marine helicopter pilots
made daily reconnaissance flights over the Red positions, and we
were invited to go along on one of the missions. We were not
fired upon as we made our low-level passes. At that stage of the
game it was evident they were not interested in us." A few days later, Badger in the *Eldorado* stood into Shanghai and dropped anchor in the Whangpoo anchorage alongside the British cruiser
Amethyst. For reasons that defy understanding, Chiang had refused to allow his generals to consolidate their forces on the
Yangtze and defend the Nationalist holdings in South China. Instead, he instructed them to abandon Nanking and flee to the
offshore redoubt on Formosa. "A large [communist] force was
encamped along the right bank of the Yangtze, ready to cross
over and seize Shanghai," Moses recalled. The 1,450-ton attack
transport *Diachenko* had been busy evacuating Americans from
various Chinese ports since her arrival for the second time in the
Far East in mid-1948, and she was now ready to steam upriver to
Nanking to rescue a party of Americans there, but Badger decided that the opposing communist artillery on the river banks
made this mission too dangerous and called it off. When the

British sent the cruiser *London* upriver, she was mauled and had to withdraw, while the *Amethyst* was trapped on the Yangtze off Nanking and had to fight her way back to the sea.[35]

In February and March 1949, Badger arranged for American naval activities in Tsingtao, Nanking, Shanghai, and elsewhere in China to be suspended, and all Navy personnel and their dependents were evacuated to the 7th Fleet base at Subic Bay in the Philippines or to Guam. The end of the Chinese civil war was fast approaching. That March, the Nationalist Chinese Navy cruiser *Chungking* and the former Royal Navy cruiser *Aurora*, which had spent a year training in British waters, defected to the Communists. Acting on strict orders from Washington, Badger refused to help Nationalist Air Force planes locate the ship, explaining resignedly that "forces of this command cannot participate in fratricidal war." General Fu, cut off from his base support in South China, withdrew his army to Peiping, which was soon surrounded. He negotiated a bloodless surrender and wangled a place for himself in the upper reaches of the new communist government.[36]

The last stage of the civil war forced Washington to examine the issue of whether the 7th Fleet should defend the Nationalist redoubt on Formosa. One of the first missions of the *Diachenko* when she had arrived on her first tour in Asian waters in November 1945 was to transport the 62nd Nationalist Chinese Army from Haiphong, French Indochina, to the Chinese offshore island of Formosa, now known as Taiwan. The native Taiwanese, oppressed by Japan for forty years, nurtured the hope during World War II that when Japan was defeated they might win their independence from China. The arrival of the Nationalists in late 1945 dashed this hope, however, and within two years Chiang's brutal military governor had killed tens of thousands of Taiwanese and laid the foundation for the exile of the dictator and his circle on the island. Supposing that the United States would, at least, prevent the Communists from overrunning Formosa, Admiral Badger proposed on 5 January 1949 to move the naval training center from Tsingtao to Keelung, the island's major port, but he was overruled by Dean Acheson, who had just replaced Marshall as secretary of state.

Acheson, the legatee of the Truman–Marshall China policy, realized that Chiang's cause was lost and that this would upset the entire postwar structure of Asian politics. He correctly reasoned that the only hope for restoring stability to the Far East was to scrupulously avoid any further American interference in the Chinese civil war and encourage Mao Tse-tung not to ally Communist China with the Soviet Union. As a result, when Acheson learned that Badger in the *Eldorado* had visited the ports of Keelung and Takao in February, the secretary asked the CNO, Admiral Denfeld, to instruct the 7th Fleet commander that his ships were "not to be stationed at or off Formosan ports in support of political . . . measures." What to do about defending Formosa had not been resolved in Washington when Mao Tse-tung, his armies triumphant everywhere, established the Peoples Republic of China in October 1949. And in February 1950, when Mao journeyed to Moscow to sign the Sino-Soviet Alliance, it was clear that Acheson's attempt to divide China and Russia had failed. The Navy's able on-scene commanders, admirals Cooke and Badger, had correctly predicted the likely outcome of the conflict, but little evidence supports their assertion at the time and later that more American aid would have saved Chiang's brutal, inept, and unpopular regime. The end of the Chinese civil war in 1949 closed a long chapter on the U.S. Navy's involvement in the Far East, but the menacing 1950 Sino-Soviet Alliance heralded a new phase of the Cold War in which Navy men would play a major part.[37]

Chapter Fifteen

Defending Containment and Resisting Unification
1948–1949

The Navy viewed the postwar fight over American military strategy and unification as a struggle for its very existence. Wartime interservice disputes—especially the bitter struggles between Nimitz and MacArthur—had received thorough scrutiny in the press. Roosevelt ignored the problem and treated the Army-Navy rivalry as would the benign father of a pair of quarrelsome sons. Nevertheless, throughout the war General Marshall pressed the Army's case for unity of command in the operational theaters, and in 1944 he discreetly urged his many admirers in Congress to amalgamate the military services when the war was over. Admiral King was far less adept in dealing with this volatile issue, and his unbending opposition to any postwar unification plan made him, and fellow Navy men, appear to be self-serving, unregenerate reactionaries.

Public opinion formed up behind unification in late 1945 when a joint congressional committee investigated the Pearl Harbor fiasco and exposed many of the sensational military secrets behind this tragedy. During the highly partisan hearings, minority Republicans tried to prove that Roosevelt and his circle were responsible for the disaster, whereas majority Democrats stoutly defended the administration. Both factions felt free to attack the Navy. The press, however, derived from all this an ill-considered consensus that a collection of backward-looking "battleship admirals" had dominated the prewar Navy, that they had stubbornly ignored the threat from aircraft to the battle line, and that as a result, the Pacific Fleet had been caught napping on 7 December. All sides agreed that the 1941 Hawaiian commanders, Admiral Kimmel and General Short, had committed "errors in judgment" and failed "to discharge their responsibilities" under "the principle of command by mutual cooperation." Still, many found it hard to attribute the disaster at Pearl Harbor merely to good enemy planning or to Kimmel's bungling.

Congress' decision to publish a small fraction of the related intelligence led to charges that Pearl Harbor was the result of a nefarious plot. Republicans wrongly accused Roosevelt, secretaries Stimson and Knox, and General Marshall, by now a partisan figure, and even Admiral Stark, of deliberately withholding Magic intercepts from Kimmel so as to induce Japan to somehow involve the United States in the war. Kimmel, shattered by the disaster to his command and desperate to salvage his blackened reputation, was delighted with this turn of events. These thoroughly unfounded allegations not only tarred Stark, who felt sorry for Kimmel and refused to the end of his days to respond in kind, but also tended to support more temperate observers who argued that the main culprit was a lack of prewar interservice cooperation. When the success in the European theater was compared to the Hawaii debacle, Eisenhower's unified command appeared to be an important ingredient in the campaign. This was an error-filled assessment that the Army nonetheless forcefully advanced.

Soon after Japan surrendered, Truman announced his intention to unify and amalgamate the War and Navy departments. His plan was a byproduct of his interwar indoctrination at Army schools for Missouri National Guard officers and was closely related to his Universal Manpower Training conscription scheme, which entailed drafting 18-year-old male Americans and compelling them to undergo some military training. Roosevelt had rejected several unification plans, but Truman disliked his predecessor's untidy methods and believed that organizational orderliness created good government. Marshall endorsed unification before his retirement in December 1945, and his successor, Eisenhower, immediately took up the cause. Both men also supported an independent Air Force with a status equal to that of the Army and the Navy. Army Air Force leaders wanted independence. They believed that long-range, land-based bombers would dominate warfare in the future, and their attitude toward naval aviation was summed up by Lieutenant General James Doolittle, who told Congress in late 1945 that "the carrier has two attributes. One attribute is that it can move about. The other attribute is that it can be sunk."[1]

The attitude of most Navy leaders did not harden until they returned to Washington after the war and found the Navy under siege over this issue and many others. Nimitz announced in early 1944 that he favored unification, but by the time he became CNO in December 1945 his position was reversed. "Nimitz, Halsey, and other naval commanders had been in thorough agreement on the merger but had been dissuaded from that view by the influence of King," Secretary of War Robert Patterson complained to Navy Secretary Forrestal. Forrestal recognized that Nimitz was too tied to the past to be an effective spokesman for the postwar Navy, but when he tried to prevent Truman from naming him to succeed King, King had intervened and Nimitz became the first postwar CNO. In short order, Nimitz' resistance to unification quickly exhausted his stock of good will with Truman. At the same time, King and other admirals became unhappy with what they considered Nimitz' overly restrained defense of the Navy's position, and King joined a chorus of admirals demanding that Nimitz be retired in the summer of 1946. Truman considered giving Nimitz the sack that July, but in a strange twist of fate, Forrestal sprang to his defense. Nimitz was amiable but politically inept, and this meant that Forrestal had to take the lead on unification. Truman had a "fixation" about unification, he observed, "not so much from the belief that it will provide greater efficiency in . . . operations or procurement, but because of its relation to education and universal military training."[2]

Nimitz realized that Congress would create an independent Air Force—which the Navy had for many years opposed—but he hoped to abort any further encroachment on Navy prerogatives. He correctly insisted that the Army Air Force's doctrine of the "unity of the air" would generate demands for Air Force control or absorption of Navy and Marine Corps land-based aviation. He also held that the establishment of a supreme American military chief of staff—another of the Army's proposals—would not only dilute civilian control over military operations but also blur service interests. Most Navy officers "preferred to see the Army integrate its air component with its ground forces," insisted Vice

Admiral Arthur Radford, the Deputy CNO for air, but this was an impossible proposition that harkened back to the War Department's arrangements after World War I. And the Marine Corps was worried that it was about to be relegated to the status of Britain's Royal Marines, who in peacetime guarded docks and quelled mutinies. The "Army seemed determined," Radford wrote, "to shrink the Marine Corps" to the size of a "naval police or guard force" capable only of conducting small wartime commando raids.[3]

When Congress first grasped this nettle in 1945, the debate took such an ominous course that Forrestal decided that the Navy would have to compromise or face defeat. He was bent on sabotaging Truman's unification policy and did so by adopting the coloring of a compromiser. Forrestal appeared to be compromising when he instructed Nimitz to transfer his headquarters from Main Navy on Constitution Avenue to the Army's new Pentagon Building across the Potomac, a move that King had refused to make. Already, in October 1945, Forrestal had presented Truman with a complex "comprehensive and dynamic" plan drafted by a former business associate, Ferdinand Eberstadt. It retained the separate military departments and stressed the need to improve the coordination of foreign policy and military planning through the vehicle of a national security council composed of the president's most senior lieutenants. Forrestal appointed Radford to assist the Senate Military Affairs Committee in preparing the enabling legislation, but they ran aground over fundamental disagreements about the mission of the Air Force, the establishment of a single, Washington-based supreme chief of staff, and the future of the Navy's land-based aviation and of the Marine Corps.[4]

From his lofty post as chairman of the JCS, Admiral Leahy was perfectly positioned to persuade Truman that creating a single chief of staff was "dangerous to civilian control of the military," and on 15 June 1946 the president announced that he was dropping this demand and would compromise on other issues. He intended to maintain the existing separate military departments, reaffirmed the Marines' independence, and allowed the Navy to keep its land-based patrol planes. Over the next few months, Admiral Forrest Sherman and Army General J. Lawton Collins negotiated a formula for the organization of the military services that, with minor changes, formed the basis of the

National Security Act of 1947. Among other things, this law creat-ed the National Security Council to replace the three-year-old State-War-Navy Coordinating Committee, established a cabinet-level Department of the Air Force, created a National Military Establishment, and authorized the new secretary of defense to oversee the Department of the Air Force, the renamed Depart-ment of the Army, and the Navy Department.[5]

Under the new law, the first secretary of defense, James Forrestal, was empowered only to "coordinate" the military de-partments with the assistance of the JCS. Radford recalled that one of Forrestal's major goals was that any reorganization be un-dertaken "without sacrificing the autonomy of the Navy." Chair-man Vinson of the House Naval Affairs Committee had been "violent" in opposing any step that threatened Admiral Leahy's dual positions as JCS chairman and the president's military chief of staff. Even before the measure was enacted, the JCS had estab-lished in January 1947 a system of unified commands that includ-ed the European, Far East, Pacific, Alaskan, Northeast, Atlantic and Caribbean, and Strategic Air Commands.[6]

Coincident to the passage of the National Security Act, Tru-man directed the JCS in January 1947 to "formulate integrated plans and make coordinated preparations" for war, but this could not be done without a joint statement on the "roles and mis-sions" of the respective forces. Eisenhower and Nimitz were un-able to reach an agreement on these issues that year, so after Admiral Louis Denfeld succeeded Nimitz and General Omar Bradley relieved Eisenhower at the end of 1947, Forrestal de-cided to convene the new chiefs, less Admiral Leahy, at Key West, Florida, where they negotiated the required agreement in March of the following year. In short, the 1948 Key West interservice treaty assigned to the Army the mission of conducting ground operations; to the Marine Corps, amphibious operations; to the Air Force, strategic bombing, developing and firing offensive long-range rockets, defending American airspace, and providing air support of Army ground operations; and to the Navy, con-ducting operations at sea against enemy naval forces and bases. The Army and Air Force were promised that the Navy would "not develop a separate strategic Air Force," but Denfeld reserved "the right to attack inland targets . . . from which enemy aircraft may sortie to attack the fleet." Air Force General Hoyt Vanden-berg acknowledged the "right and need for the Navy to participate in an all-out air campaign" and pledged that the "Navy is not to be denied the use of the atomic bomb." Although admirals Leahy and Mitscher expressed reservations about endowing the fleet with atomic bombs of mass destruction for use against cities and their civilian populations, Rear Admiral Jeraud Wright in 1946 had pointed out that the development of naval aircraft or ship-launched missiles to deliver heavy atomic bombs would strongly reinforce the arguments for laying down a new class of supercarriers. Most Navy men believed that, considering the absence of a Soviet blue-water fleet, the Navy's future was tied to the strategic bombardment mission.[7]

Soon after Forrestal negotiated the Key West agreement, the JCS voted to allow the Navy to "proceed with the development of an 80,000-ton carrier and . . . high altitude aircraft to carry heavy missiles." When Forrestal returned to Washington, he told Truman that the JCS had agreed that the fleet "was not to be denied use of [the] A-bomb," an assertion that varied from the Air Force's revised understanding of the pact. This arrangement was undermined by the rivalry between the Air Force and the Navy over control of the Joint Special Weapons Project, the military agency that stored, assembled, and dispensed nuclear weapons. Denfeld rightly worried that in time of crisis the Air Force would refuse to dispense atomic bombs to the Navy. For its part, the Air Force "actually feared that the Navy might set up a strategic Air Force of its own and threaten their existence," Admiral Sherman admitted. Forrestal tried again to resolve the issue of roles and missions during the Newport Conference at the Naval War College in August 1948, but this failed. Owing to continuing competition over shares of the 1950 defense budget and Denfeld's insistence on laying down the supercarrier *United States*, building the atomic-capable AJ Savage carrier-based jet bomber, and developing second-generation heavy attack aircraft, relations between the Navy and the Air Force worsened.[8]

Navy men fully understood that political necessity meant that maintaining a large postwar fleet hinged on the development of a new generation of heavy carrier-based jet bombers capable of delivering atomic bombs on Soviet territory. One of the first steps was to improve the existing carriers, and this was taken by Nimitz in June 1947 when he approved Project 27A, a conversion program that gave nine *Essex*-class carriers the capacity to operate 40,000-pound jet aircraft. The *Oriskany* entered the yard

One of the three World War II–era 51,000-ton attack *Midway*-class carriers that were not completed until 1945.

An artist's concept of the 65,000-ton flush-deck postwar supercarrier *United States* (CVA-58), a ship designed to operate very heavy naval bombers and so assure that the U.S. Navy might participate in delivering nuclear weapons against the Soviet Union. Secretary of Defense Louis Johnson's cancellation of work on the carrier led directly to the 1949 "Revolt of the Admirals."

that October, and the last 27A conversion was completed six years later. "The next step is the development of a new carrier capable of operating aircraft of a gross take-off weight of 60,000 pounds," observed Captain George B. Chafee of the Bureau of Aeronautics. This was the flush-deck supercarrier *United States*, the centerpiece of Denfeld's building program, a vessel designed to handle naval jet bombers that could deliver the heavy 5-ton airburst Mk-3 Fat Man atomic bomb against Soviet targets. Owing to the scarcity of atomic bombs, Navy leaders argued that these weapons could be delivered more reliably and effectively by carrier-borne bombers—and eventually by ship-based missiles— than by unescorted, long-range, land-based Air Force bombers. With the backing of John Sullivan, who became secretary of the Navy in early 1947, Denfeld persuaded Truman to approve the construction of the supercarrier on 25 July 1948, and he negotiated a compromise with generals Bradley and Spaatz that preserved the ship in the JCS budget for 1949. To keep the supercarrier project alive, Denfeld reduced the fleet from 730 to 690 ships, cut the number of deployed attack carriers from 11 to 8, decommissioned all but one battleship, and slashed the Navy's aircraft inventory from 2,500 to 1,500 planes. Several important projects were canceled, including one aimed at developing a drone version of the AJ Savage bomber and another aimed at constructing a submersible bombardment missile–launching barge. According to Admiral Radford, once the *United States* was commissioned the fleet could "operate heavy land planes of at least B-29 size" and "challenge the Strategic Air Force."[9]

The Air Force had its own plans, however. In late 1948, after Stalin blockaded Berlin, General Spaatz reintroduced an Air Force plan to substantially increase the number of Strategic Air Command air wings by acquiring a very large number of new prop-driven, long-range B-36 bombers. In the past Forrestal had been wary of an overreliance on an air atomic offensive, but he was alarmed about defending the West after an inspection tour of American forces in Europe that November and returned to Washington more willing than ever to back the Air Force's case for more land-based bombers. He did not remain in office long enough to resolve the question, however. Owing to a deep and widening breach over foreign policy with Truman and Marshall, Radford observed, Forrestal "lost his standing with the president." Then a few days before Christmas, Forrestal was overcome by paranoia and abandoned his long and fruitless campaign to persuade the White House and State Department to increase military spending.[10]

Few expected Truman, an unpopular but feisty president, to be reelected in 1948. However, he not only defeated Thomas Dewey, the Republican candidate, but also returned Democratic majorities to both houses of Congress. Forrestal was by now gripped by such bizarre behavior that he was forced to resign from the cabinet. A few months later he committed suicide at the Bethesda Naval Hospital. In January 1949, Truman named to the Defense Department post Louis Johnson, Roosevelt's sometime assistant secretary of war and Truman's chief fund-raiser. He "came into office believing that unification was the cure to all the evils in the armed forces," according to Commander Robert Dennison, Truman's naval aide. From the first day "he was openly prejudiced against the Navy, quite bitter about the Navy." Johnson intended to "crack heads" by slashing the Marine Corps, eliminating the Navy's role in strategic bombardment, and merging naval aviation into the Air Force, then headed by Truman's protégé, Secretary Stuart Symington of Missouri.[11]

Johnson immediately took under review both the B-36 bomber and the supercarrier programs with an eye to reducing the Defense Department budget. On 15 April 1949, he asked General Eisenhower, then serving as the temporary JCS chairman, to reevaluate the Navy's shipbuilding plans. "Our present Navy can scarcely be justified on the basis of the naval strength of any potential enemy," Eisenhower believed, and he told Johnson that the *United States* should be canceled. Denfeld objected heatedly, arguing that constructing the aircraft carrier was "fully warranted as insurance to cover the unpredictable exigencies of the future." At the opposite pole was Vandenberg, the Air Force's new chief of staff, who asserted that the *United States* was "designed for bombardment purposes" and that the "relative value of the large carrier . . . is of a low order."[12]

On 23 April, thunder struck. After secretly obtaining Truman's approval, Johnson publicly announced the cancellation of the *United States*. Admiral Denfeld, who was not informed in advance of this decision, was furious but impotent. Truman had just been reelected, and few Republicans attached any political significance to the issue. Secretary Sullivan, an unpopular figure among Navy men who had refused to allow the Navy's public relations office to respond to the Air Force, had already handed a pro forma resignation to Johnson on 26 March, but he was so upset by the cancellation that he angrily submitted a second letter resigning in protest. Johnson's decision, Sullivan charged on 19 April, would "result in a renewed effort to abolish the Marine Corps and to transfer all Naval and Marine Aviation elsewhere." Sullivan's resignation meant little outside Washington, however, and, as if to mock the Navy, Truman chose as his successor an Omaha banker, Francis Matthews, who added insult to injury by declaring that the only thing he knew about naval affairs was that he had once learned how to row a boat![13]

Up to this point Admiral Denfeld, beset by myriad lesser and greater problems, had taken little part in the propaganda war. Like Nimitz, he wanted to solve the problem within the JCS and disliked squaring off with the Air Force in public. When Johnson canceled the supercarrier and Sullivan resigned, however, Denfeld swung into action. He found the means to counterattack in a thinly disguised Navy propaganda unit first organized in 1946 by Rear Admiral Thomas Cassidy. Urged on by Radford, a violent partisan of Navy air, Cassidy used the Scorer committee to advance the Navy's case by monitoring Air Force propaganda. This was continued after 1948 by his successor, Captain Arleigh Burke, who undermined confidence in the Air Force on the Hill by focusing his criticism on the new B-36 bomber, the ill-fated plane that General Vandenberg had mistakenly chosen to be the mainstay of the new Strategic Air Command. Burke provided reporters with evidence that the prop-driven, four-engine B-36 was underpowered, incapable of attaining high-altitude cruising speeds, and inexplicably vulnerable to a new generation of jet interceptors.

Burke worried that the overheated partisans would embarrass the Navy, however, and he was furious when Cedric R. Worth, a former Hollywood publicist, and Commander Thomas D. Davies, who worked for Navy Undersecretary Dan A. Kimball, stitched together a scathing report on the B-36 issue that Worth secretly circulated to the press. Worth's report exposed Secretary Johnson's unsavory business connections with Consolidated Vultee, the firm that was building the B-36, charged him with a sinister conflict of interest, and asserted that Air Force Secretary Symington was dispensing profitable B-36 contracts to his former employer, Emerson Electric. Worth concluded that the bomber should be canceled. When this sensational indictment was published, Republican Congressman James E. Van Zandt demanded a special investigation, but Democrat Sam Rayburn, the Speaker of the House, instead assigned the question to Vinson's House Armed Services Committee. When Worth surprised everyone by testifying that his charges were based mostly on rumors, the affair backfired on the Navy; it now appeared that the Navy was unjustly blackening Johnson's name merely because he had taken a hard policy decision against the admirals.

Although the quarrel over unification had gone on since 1945, the Navy paid little attention to the specific issues at hand until Worth's paper became public. The results of the first Vinson hearings left Captain John G. Crommelin, a highly decorated naval aviator, believing that Congress had not fully grasped Johnson's alleged scheme to abolish naval aviation and destroy the Marine Corps. There were "endless secret telephone calls . . . [by] Crommelin and others to the press," recalled *New York Times* reporter Hanson Baldwin, a Naval Academy graduate, and "intense rumor-mongering and propagandizing . . . by many in the Navy as well as many in the Air Force." Burke understood that the situation was getting out of control and urged Crommelin to restrain his anger, but to no avail. Crommelin finally called reporters to his home one dark night and told them that the Navy was being "nibbled to death" by Johnson and the Army–Air Force majority on the JCS—an emotional, impolitic, but fairly accurate representation of what Johnson and the generals were trying to accomplish. Against Burke's advice, Crommelin also leaked to the press a letter to Secretary Matthews from Vice Admiral Gerald F. Bogan, a veteran aviator who commanded the 1st Task Fleet. "The morale of the Navy is lower today than at any time since I entered the commissioned ranks," Bogan charged. "This descent . . . stems from complete confusion as to the future role of the Navy." The furor that followed the publication of Bogan's letter moved Chairman Vinson to convene a second set of House Armed Services Committee hearings to investigate the cancellation of the *United States*.[14]

When these hearings opened on 6 October 1949, the first witness, Secretary of the Navy Matthews, was under enormous pressure both to defend the Truman administration and, in the same breath, shield the Navy from Johnson's depredations. Trying to walk this tightrope, he badly miscalculated the depth of resentment among Navy men over Truman's military policy and Louis Johnson's brief stewardship of the Defense Department. Conceding that Crommelin reflected the views of "several naval aviators," he foolishly went on to say that "they do not reflect the views of anything approaching a majority of naval officers." Vice Admiral Radford, fearing that Denfeld would vacillate, had instructed Burke to prepare a number of Navy witnesses to rebut this stance, and there followed an embarrassing parade of admirals who gave the lie to Matthews' claim of harmony. Radford, who orchestrated the Navy's case, testified that he did not believe that the Air Force's "retaliatory atomic blitz . . . theory" was either "an effective deterrent to a war, or that it will win a war." Burke said that carrier task forces could support "our sister services under some circumstances in which they could obtain the help from no other sources, as is now the case in the Mediterranean."

But it was Admiral Denfeld, theretofore condemned by many as a retiring compromiser, who provided the greatest surprise. He brusquely summed up the Navy's testimony by indicting both Johnson and Matthews. "The entire Navy," he said, had "real misgivings over the reductions" to the shipbuilding program, which were "arbitrary" and would "impair, or even eliminate, essential naval functions." Denfeld had been told by Johnson some weeks earlier that he was to be reappointed to a second two-year term as CNO, but when Johnson read Denfeld's testimony he told *Washington Post* gossip columnist Drew Pearson that the CNO would soon be relieved. In another gratuitous slight, the news that Truman would name Admiral Forrest Sherman the next CNO was leaked to the press by the White House before Denfeld was personally informed.[15]

Johnson and generals Vandenberg and Bradley hastened up to the Hill to counteract the admirals' testimony. Vandenberg asserted that there was "no necessity for a ship with those capabilities [of the *United States*] in any strategy plan against the one possible enemy." Bradley, the new JCS chairman, launched into a homey, personal characterization of Denfeld, Radford, Sherman, and the other "fancy Dans who won't hit the line with all they have on every play, unless they can call the signals," accusing them of "open rebellion against . . . civilian control." Reports of this insulting, undeserved outburst gave the entire affair its name, "the revolt of the admirals." With this bit of bombast,

Bradley unwittingly intensified the deeply felt personal animosity that pervaded the entire struggle over unification and confirmed the view of Navy men that unification was in fact little more than a convenient vehicle by which the Army and the Air Force could degrade the Navy's role in the national defense. "The practical outcome of the 'Admirals' Revolt' was the professional death of Louis Denfeld," Bradley wrote. And, "although Matthews had lost all effectiveness as secretary of the Navy," Bradley observed, "Johnson kept him . . . because he had been loyal to him and the administration." Moreover, Johnson's political position was immeasurably strengthened by the Vinson hearings, because Johnson now appeared to be the object of unfair Navy-generated rumors and also seemed to be making hard, money-saving decisions in line with the president's military policy.[16]

Vinson's purpose in exposing these open sores was unclear. He may have wanted to reassert his traditional influence over American naval policy, but he was also capable of indulging in a bit of devious whimsy. Two years earlier, for instance, he had introduced a bill to abolish flight pay, a step that Radford believed the chairman took merely to bring "the Air Force and the Navy [up to Congress] testifying on the same side of the fence." Vinson was truly outraged, however, when Johnson relieved Admiral Denfeld, inasmuch as Johnson had promised Vinson before the hearings that he would not inflict "reprisals" for frank testimony. The step was condemned by a majority of the Armed Services Committee, and a minority even attempted to have the matter referred to the Justice Department—on spurious grounds. Vinson agreed in October 1949 that Johnson had done "the right thing in canceling the carrier," but the committee's March 1950 report condemned the "manner of cancellation." The nub of the dispute was "simply a matter of the proper allocation of war missions between the Navy and Air Force." Truman's paltry defense budgets meant that the country "cannot afford the luxury of two strategic air forces" and "should reserve strategic air warfare to the Air Force." The report also found that "too much joint planning is concentrated on individual service questions of a highly technical nature" and that Johnson had paid insufficient attention to the needs of the specific services. "The whole performance is humiliating," Eisenhower observed bitterly.[17]

Closely related to the acrimonious struggle over unification was the question of what strategy and military policy the United

States should adopt after the Communists had finally won the Chinese civil war in October 1949 and Moscow and Peking had negotiated the Sino-Soviet Alliance of February 1950. This unhappy turn of events, coupled with the vast new American military obligations to the NATO powers, led Secretary of State Dean Acheson to urge Truman to revise his defense policy and approve a major rearmament program. Acheson's reasoning was reinforced by the stunning announcement on 23 September 1949 that the Soviets had exploded an atomic bomb, some five years earlier than most American officials expected. This meant that NATO would have to embrace more than a simple American pledge to wage an air atomic offensive to defend Europe and led the following year to an agreement to create a NATO military organization. In January 1950, Truman reacted to the news of Russia's possession of the atomic bomb by declaring that the United States would develop a more destructive hydrogen bomb, but the response to this decision demonstrated that political support for rearmament was by no means universal. Maryland Senator Millard Tydings, a liberal Democrat, asked Truman on 6 February not to proceed with the hydrogen bomb project, but instead to invite Stalin to join him in convening a world disarmament conference. At the time, Defense Secretary Johnson was slashing the JCS budget for 1951. Irritated by their naive view of Soviet goals, Acheson assigned an assistant, Paul Nitze, to draft a rearmament program that would "bludgeon the mass mind" of Washington into realizing the need to bring defense spending into line with America's new overseas obligations.

The result of Nitze's work, a paper called NSC-68, supposed that in a general war the Red Army would overrun most of western Europe, invade Turkey, Iraq, and Iran, and attempt to occupy the Arabian Peninsula. The Soviets had 175 divisions and 24,000 aircraft in eastern Europe and the Balkans and 400 submarines defending their coastal waters, whereas NATO had barely ten divisions in West Germany, and the United States had fewer than two divisions in Europe, fewer than six at home, and four in Japan. And Field Marshal Montgomery, the NATO ground commander, reported that he could not resist a Red Army drive to the Rhine. With no foothold in Europe, Anglo-American forces would be hard pressed to defend the British Isles while at the same time launching an air atomic offensive against the Soviet Union. An early war plan, Offtackle, using existing forces, accepted a withdrawal from Europe and the need to mobilize new forces before returning to the Continent. Once the United States was committed to NATO, however, this was clearly impossible. Dropshot, the current war plan, called for holding a position of forward defense in Europe and building up for a decisive counterattack against Russia, but it presumed huge increases in American defense spending.

"Acheson believed that American nuclear weapons were unlikely to stop the Russians if they had once embarked upon an invasion of western Europe; in his judgment, even attacks upon the Russian homeland would not stop such an attack," Nitze said. The Soviets now possessed the means to produce atomic bombs and would soon have an inventory of long-range bombers capable of attacking targets in western Europe and, someday, in the United States. "Only if we had overwhelming atomic superiority and obtained command of the air might the U.S.S.R. be deterred from employing its atomic weapons," he wrote. To revise the strategic balance and correct what the Soviets termed the "correlation of forces," Nitze proposed a large-scale rearmament program to widen America's narrowing superiority in atomic weapons and counterbalance the Red Army in Europe. His pathbreaking study underlined the widely accepted assumption of American strategists that the next war would see the United States employing nuclear weapons. Many Navy leaders found flaws in this reasoning, but they failed to convincingly articulate their dissent.[18]

To meet the commitments Truman had accumulated, Nitze proposed to increase the Army to 12 divisions, build up the Air Force to 69 air wings, and reinforce the Navy with new construction until the fleet deployed 9 heavy carriers and roughly 300 greater and lesser combatants. "A substantial and rapid building up of strength . . . to support a firm policy intended to check and roll back the Kremlin's drive for world dominion" was essential, Nitze wrote, a conclusion the JCS heartily endorsed. In 1946, Admiral Nimitz had established a goal of deploying six heavy carriers with the Atlantic Fleet and the same number in the Pacific, and under this plan a four-carrier task force would always be available for emergencies in either theater. Admiral Sherman argued the following year, however, that two four-carrier task forces would be required just to fulfill the fleet's obligations in the eastern Atlantic and the Mediterranean under the hastily crafted, emergency Pincher plans for defending Europe and its flanks. The increasing dedication of American forces to a Europe-first strategy and the reduction of the fleet had forced Denfeld to make further adjustments, and by 1949 only two heavy carriers were on station in the Pacific and Far East theaters. Moreover, Defense Secretary Johnson now intended to reduce the fleet to only six attack carriers, a figure that allowed for only one carrier task force in the Atlantic and another in the Mediterranean, but none in the western Pacific. Finally, the practical outcome of the "revolt of the admirals" was to allow Louis Johnson not only to deprive the Navy of much of its role in an air atomic offensive but also to fold up the 7th Fleet.

The trend toward a Europe-first approach became even more pronounced with the signing of the NATO treaty and the communist victory in China, which, Vice Admiral Oscar Badger, the commander of the 7th Fleet, pointed out in late 1949, would result in a "lessening of naval commitments in Asia." Sherman, the architect of the 6th Fleet's deployment to the Mediterranean, adopted a broader view after he became CNO in December 1949, arguing that one heavy carrier should be attached to the 7th Fleet to create a "stabilizing influence" in the Far East in the wake of postwar turbulence. Owing to his persistence, a skeleton carrier task force was attached to the 7th Fleet in early 1950.[19]

Although Sherman begrudgingly accepted Johnson's decision to cancel the construction of the *United States*, he promptly renewed Denfeld's earlier call for modernizing the *Essex*-class attack carriers so that they might operate long-range jet bombers. In 1949, Johnson agreed, perhaps as a sop to the Navy, to allow the Navy to begin work on the first two of fifteen *Essex*-class carriers to be modernized over the next decade. Their flight decks were strengthened, elevator lift increased, jet fuel capacity enlarged, deck mounts removed, islands streamlined, and hulls widened. This work resulted in a substantial increase in the displacement of the ships. To deliver atomic bombs, the Navy intended to rely at first on the rugged prop-driven Douglas AD-1 Skyraider. This product of wartime carrier bomber experience entered the fleet in December 1946 and quickly became the mainstay of the attack squadrons, replacing the traditional scout, dive, and torpedo bombers. Although famed aeronautical engineer Ed Heinemann of Douglas Aircraft had designed the AD Skyraider as a light attack plane, she was capable of lifting more ordnance than any other contemporary light attack aircraft or fighter-bomber. The Skyraider, which could carry light atomic bombs, remained the most reliable nuclear-capable naval aircraft until 1956, but she was slow and thus vulnerable to Soviet MiG-15 interceptors. At the same time, twelve P2V Neptune land-based patrol bombers were converted to carry heavy atomic bombs.

Captain James Holloway proved that the Neptune might take off from a *Midway*-class carrier, but the plane was simply too large to land on the flight deck. As a result, during long-range nuclear strike missions the Neptune aircrews would have to land at friendly airfields or ditch within the vicinity of American warships. In September 1949, the first AJ Savage auxiliary-jet bomber entered the fleet, and these planes soon began to replace the Neptune patrol bombers as the fleet's primary nuclear strike aircraft. A prop-driven aircraft with a fuselage-mounted Pratt and Whitney jet engine, the Savage could carry one heavy atomic bomb. Soon after the Savage entered the fleet, Admiral Sherman demanded that the JCS assign the heavy attack aircraft carriers as part of the nuclear striking forces, a proposition that Bradley and his fellow West Pointers doggedly resisted. It was ironic that the Savage, designed to carry 10,000-pound Nagasaki-type bombs, became operational just about the time that a new 3,000-pound bomb with greater yield became available in large numbers; with these destined for the 6th Fleet, the Navy could at last claim a share of the strategic nuclear bombardment mission. Riding the trend toward a new policy envisioned in Nitze's NSC-68, Sherman accomplished the extraordinary feat of persuading the JCS in April 1950 to approve the construction of the first *Forrestal*-class heavy attack carrier. The Air Force strongly objected to the renewal of any carrier-building project, however, and Sherman had no assurance that Secretary Johnson's views had changed.

In the spring of 1950, Louis Johnson not only wanted to strip the fleet of its strategic bombing mission but also opposed the larger rearmament plan advanced by Acheson and Nitze in NSC-68. As a result of the bitter divisions within the JCS and Bradley's inability to master the situation, the chiefs played almost no role in formulating this major military policy proposal. Truman also disliked Nitze's plan. Announcing that he needed "further information" about it, he referred the proposal to Budget Director Frank Pace, who had already gone on record against a substantial rearmament program. Then, on 5 May, Truman declared during a press conference that reports of impending increases in defense spending were "incorrect." Thus, on the eve of the Korean War, Truman had revolutionized American foreign policy by negotiating a long-term, overseas military alliance with western Europe, by promising to defend the Philippines and Japan, and by laying down the outline of an overarching global policy of containment of Soviet influence, but he remained stubbornly unwilling to pay the price to honor these new obligations.[20]

Chapter Sixteen

The Korean War
1950–1951

At 0400 on Sunday, 25 June 1950, six divisions of the North Korean Army, spearheaded by 150 Soviet-built T34 tanks, crossed the 38th parallel, invaded South Korea, and advanced on the capital, Seoul. By that evening, the Communists had driven over fifteen miles into South Korea, the South Korean Army was in full retreat, and President Syngman Rhee's government was preparing its escape. Confusion was rife in the Allied camp. A South Korean PT boat reported sighting and taking under fire a Russian cruiser; within moments an American cruiser announced that the Communists were sending their PT boats out on suicide missions and that one had just been sunk by American naval gunfire.[1]

Before the outbreak of hostilities in 1950, Korea's postwar problems had not gripped American attention. On the eve of the Japanese surrender in 1945, the State and War departments had decided, without consulting the Navy, to allow the Red Army to occupy the northern, industrial half of the Korean Peninsula above the 38th parallel, while the Americans occupied the agrarian half to the south. The Red Army imposed a communist regime in North Korea headed by Kim Il Sung, a wily, strong-willed puppet who ruled from his newly established captial, Pyongyang. General John Hodge, the American occupation commander in South Korea, helped to organize a democratic government there, although he crossed swords repeatedly with

Rhee, a volatile conniver, who wanted the United States to help him reunite Korea.

"The Russians have no thought of unifying the Korean nation . . . until Russia is sure that all Korea will be communistic," Hodge told Navy Secretary Forrestal in early 1946, and he saw no evidence that the Americans were prepared to check the "military maneuvering of the Soviets." Hodge's military advisory mission trained and lightly armed some 90,000 fresh South Korean soldiers, but Rhee used his army to provide jobs for his many relatives and partisans and to maintain order at home, and he failed to prepare to defend the 38th parallel. Eisenhower and Nimitz, adhering to a Europe-first strategy, voted to vacate the peninsula in 1947. Two years later, when the last American combat unit left South Korea, the JCS agreed that the country "would be a liability" to the American position in the Far East, which was moored, once the Communists ousted the Nationalists in China, in Japan and the Philippines. Withdrawal of the occupation troops was completed in June 1949, leaving only 500 Americans with the military advisory group in South Korea one year later.[2]

In a major address in February 1950, Secretary of State Dean Acheson reiterated the administration's support for Japan and the Philippines by drawing a defensive "line" in the Far East that inadvertently excluded South Korea and Taiwan. Acheson's speech created confusion and the feeling that "American policy objectives were not clear in the Pacific area," observed Admiral Arthur Radford, who commanded the Pacific theater. Admiral Forrest Sherman, the new CNO, wanted to reaffirm American support for Seoul, and in the spring of 1950 he instructed Radford to schedule frequent visits by American warships to South Korea's ports. The carrier *Boxer* was welcomed when she stood into Inchon on 5 April, her air group staged a flyover of Seoul, and the crew went ashore for liberty. "Come again, come often, and stay longer," Rhee said sadly when the task group departed. Acheson's speech may have encouraged Stalin to approve Kim Il Sung's plan to invade South Korea, but Stalin was also mindful of the weak, unpopular Rhee government, the withdrawal of the U.S. Army, and the absence of any defense treaty between the United States and the South Korean regime.[3]

When Truman learned that the North Koreans had crossed the 38th parallel on 25 June, he quickly agreed to order the 7th Fleet and the Far East Air Force to support the retreating South

Korean Army, but several days passed before he was willing to commit the U.S. Army or Marines to the peninsula. He did not want to declare war on North Korea as he had no idea of Soviet plans, and he decided instead to ask the United Nations to endorse a "police action" to check Pyongyang's aggression. Inasmuch as he did not first turn to Congress for support, however, Truman unwittingly exposed himself to partisan criticism when the tide of war later turned against the Americans. At the time of the North Korean invasion, a special session of the Security Council was meeting at Lake Placid, New York. Fortunately for the administration, the Soviet ambassador was boycotting this session in protest of the United States' refusal to transfer China's seat from Chiang Kai-shek's Taiwan government to the communist regime in Peking. As a result, the Soviets had no means to veto a June 27 UN resolution condemning North Korea for a "breach of the peace" and authorizing "a police action" by member states to defend South Korea. Although this resolution assured Washington of allied diplomatic support, Truman came close to establishing the unhappy precedent of giving an international body direct influence over American military operations.

The JCS believed that Moscow had sponsored North Korea's attack, and the National Security Council worried that it might be "the first phase of a general Soviet plan for global war." Truman wrote on 30 June that "Russia is figuring on an attack in the Black Sea and toward the Persian Gulf." He believed that Stalin's strategy was to use the Korean War to divert American forces to Northeast Asia. Others maintained that the invasion of South Korea was simply a probing maneuver by Stalin to test American will. Almost no one in Washington gave sole credit to Kim Il Sung for the idea. Sherman's counsel during these days was mixed. He understood that there were "hazards involved in fighting Asiatics on the Asian mainland" that "should be avoided if possible," but he reasoned at the same time that the commitment of American soldiers and Marines was probably "unavoidable" to assist the South Koreans in "resisting aggression." To demonstrate to the NATO powers, Japan, and the Philippines that the United States would resist Soviet military expansionism, Truman extended the policy of containment to Asia after the fall of Seoul on 28 June.[4]

General MacArthur, the commander of the Far East theater, had already obtained Truman's permission to provide air and naval support to the South Koreans. This move was fathered by the short-lived hope in Washington that the North Korean invasion might be contained by a combination of American naval air operations, land-based American air power operating from South Korean and nearby Japanese bases, logistic support for the South Korean Army, and sealift provided by the 7th Fleet. Sherman held this view for two or three days, at least until Washington learned that South Korea's army was rapidly disintegrating. Truman, now under tremendous pressure to do something, finally agreed to Sherman's proposal to announce the imposition of an American naval blockade of North Korea on 28 June. What these steps "will do to Mao Tse-tung we don't know," Truman noted, but "we must be careful not to cause a general Asiatic war."[5]

Sherman believed wrongly that Peking had either inspired or knew in advance of North Korea's offensive, and he feared that the Chinese intended somehow to exploit the war to lift an army across the Straits of Formosa, invade Taiwan, and reunite China. Ironically, a few days after the North Korean invasion, Chiang Kai-shek offered to send two Nationalist divisions from Taiwan to South Korea, a proposal that excited Acheson's fear that Chiang himself would use the war as an excuse to reestablish his regime on the mainland. To prevent a resumption of the Chinese civil war, Truman "ordered the 7th Fleet to prevent any attack upon Formosa" and called "upon . . . Formosa to cease all air and sea operations against the mainland. The 7th Fleet will see that this is done." Vice Admiral Arthur Struble, the veteran commander of the 7th Fleet, established a barrier patrol over the Formosa Straits, but during the next several weeks it amounted to little more than a few destroyer patrols and an occasional overflight. Then, in July, he sent the cruiser *Juneau*, two destroyers, and an oiler to Keelung, Taiwan, and the following month the Formosa Patrol was organized by Rear Admiral Thomas Binford. When the CIA reported a buildup of Chinese amphibious shipping and paratroops near the Taiwan Strait, however, Struble cautioned that the 7th Fleet was not strong enough to simultaneously support the South Koreans and turn back an invasion of Taiwan.[6]

These issues diverted Truman's gaze from the central question of whether to use American troops to defend South Korea. On 30 June, after much teeth gnashing, he gave MacArthur command of UN forces in the Far East and instructed him to transport American soldiers and Marines from Japan and Okinawa to the Korean front. MacArthur fed his four understrength divisions onto the Korean battlefield in July, while Lieutenant General George Stratemeyer of the Far East Air Force shifted some land-based fighter squadrons from Japan to South Korea. They easily destroyed most of the Communists' front-line MiG fighters, but the North Korean offensive soon imperiled most of South Korea's military airfields, and in late July, Stratemeyer had to withdraw his fighters back to southern Japan. The Air Force had already converted most of its fighter squadrons to jets, but none of these short-range aircraft could make the long flight from Japan to the battle front carrying a full payload. As a result, the gap in American power created by the flaws in the Air Force's tactical air policy had to be bridged by the Navy's carrier air arm.

When the war erupted, Sherman had nine heavy and light carriers assigned to the Atlantic Fleet, one in the Mediterranean with the 6th Fleet, three on the Pacific coast, and one in Hawaii. Only the carrier *Valley Forge* was attached to Struble's small 7th Fleet. Counting the 7th Fleet's air group and two fleet service squadrons, there were fewer than 100 aircraft under Struble's command, although one squadron was equipped with the Navy's powerful new Grumman F9F Panther jet fighter. Vice Admiral C. Turner Joy's Japan-based Far East Naval Force consisted of only one light cruiser, four destroyers, five amphibious ships, six minesweepers, and two patrol bomber squadrons. His most pressing prewar mission had been to defend Japanese shipping in the Straits of Tsushima against Korean pirates. By the end of June, Sherman had directed Struble to support MacArthur's operations, and decided to strengthen the 7th Fleet with at least three heavy carriers within the next few months. The CNO also instructed Rear Admiral James Doyle to organize a vastly strengthened 7th Fleet Amphibious Force by drawing ships from Radford's huge Pacific Fleet.

Riding at anchor in Hong Kong harbor on 25 June, the *Valley Forge* was replenished at the Navy's new base on Subic Bay in the Philippines before steaming north and launching the first air patrols over the Formosa Strait on 29 June. Following the Lake Placid Resolution, the British placed their Far East Fleet under Struble's command, and on 3 July the British light carrier *Triumph* rendezvoused with the *Valley Forge*; together they launched air strikes composed of older prop-driven F4U Corsair fighter-bombers and new Douglas AD Skyraider attack aircraft against Pyongyang. During this operation, a pair of North Korean Yak-9 fighters were shot down. The following day Struble flung air strikes against a large railroad bridge south of occupied Seoul and allowed his planes to attack targets of opportunity. The Carrier Force soon had to retire to Okinawa's Buckner Bay to replenish, however, leaving the North Koreans free to continue their dogged advance. To strengthen his right flank, MacArthur decided to ship an Army division from Japan to the Korean port of P'ohang-dong, north of Pusan. On 18 July Struble's Carrier Force appeared off P'ohang, Doyle's 7th Amphibious Force entered the harbor, and the troops went ashore during an unopposed debarkation. They could not prevent the North Koreans from advancing on their lines, however, and so Lieutenant General Walton Walker, who commanded the newly established 8th Army, was forced to withdraw to the west and establish a last line of retreat to the south and east of the Naktong River, which surrounded the landward flank of the critical port of Pusan.

Doyle's landing at P'ohang and Walker's establishment of the Pusan perimeter coincided with the beginning of the end for North Korea's offensive. While the Communists spent their forces against the Allied lines, American ships carrying reinforcements, munitions, and other supplies began to arrive in the Far East in large numbers. On 20 July, during the battle for Taejon, the U.S. Army introduced a more powerful Bazooka hand-held rocket launcher, which quickly stopped ten enemy tanks, and that same month the first shipment of 500 American tanks reached Pusan. In addition, Sherman alerted MacArthur that the 1st Marine Division was scheduled to arrive in Japan in August. To reinforce the 7th Fleet, Sherman stripped the escort carrier *Sicily* of her antisubmarine aircraft, assigned her a new fighter-attack air group, and sent her into the western Pacific on 2 August. He also detached the *Princeton* from the Pacific Fleet and sent her to Japan and instructed the heavy carrier *Leyte Gulf* to speed from the Mediterranean through the Indian Ocean and on to the Far East. Despite heavy losses, however, the North Koreans continued to advance throughout July against General Walker's hard-pressed 8th Army. After the Air Force withdrew from South Korea owing to the insecurity of its bases, Walker asked MacArthur to allow Struble to provide direct close air support for the front. On 22 July, the Carrier Force launched the first ground support strikes, rearmed and refueled for the next two days, and then steamed to a station thirty miles south of P'ohang to renew its attacks. These carrier strikes made up for the Army's lack of artillery, and Walker later observed that the carriers made it possible for his infantry to conduct its gallant defense of the Pusan perimeter.

Once Truman had committed the United States to defend South Korea, both the JCS and MacArthur considered ways to conduct a counteroffensive. Flanking amphibious operations were commonplace in the Pacific war, but in the European theater, where General Bradley and General J. Lawton Collins, the new Army chief of staff, had served, the only shore-to-shore landing that outflanked opposing ground and air forces was the 1944 Anzio fiasco. The Army was loathe to repeat that experience, and Bradley had even asserted in 1949 that, with the advent of jet aircraft and nuclear weapons, "large scale amphibious operations . . . will never occur again." Navy and Marine Corps leaders still believed amphibious landings to be feasible, however. It occurred to Sherman, an experienced strategist, to counter North Korea's offensive by landing behind the enemy's lines, but it was MacArthur who first proposed such a step on 2 July. His plan, codenamed Bluehearts, called for a Marine Corps regimental combat team and an Army division to land in late July at Inchon, a port only a few miles from Seoul, advance on the capital, and sever the enemy's western north-south supply lines. This plan distressed Admiral Joy, however, inasmuch as western Korea's coastal waters were characterized by mud banks, high tides, rocks, shoals, and other hazards to navigation and so seemed wholly unsuitable for amphibious landings. And when Sherman heard the news, he reminded MacArthur that the Marines would not arrive in the Far East until August. As the only available Army division was already committed to the Pusan perimeter, Bluehearts was canceled.[7]

Prospects brightened for a flanking counteroffensive when Sherman alerted MacArthur on 10 August that he was shipping another Marine regiment to Korea and that this would bring the 1st Marine Division up to full strength by the end of the month. MacArthur turned again to Bluehearts; gave the slightly revised plan a new codename, Chromite; and committed to it the Marines, the last Army occupation division in Japan, and 9,000

South Koreans from the Pusan perimeter. In spite of MacArthur's hyperbolic optimism, Admiral Sherman was so uneasy about the Inchon landing that he flew to Tokyo to discuss it with the Far East commanders.[8]

Hard upon arriving on 21 August, Admiral Sherman found out that Admiral Doyle, the 7th Fleet amphibious commander, and General O. P. Smith, the highly respected leader of the 1st Marine Division, "did not want to go to Inchon," preferring instead to land about thirty miles to the south at Posung-Myon. "The current intelligence disclosed no enemy there," Marine Colonel Victor Krulak recalled. Unlike Inchon, "we would avoid landing in the heart of a major city, and we would not have to land at a specific time . . . during the only day on which a tide high enough for beaching the LSTs occurred in more than a month." Sherman appeared to agree with Doyle and Smith for the moment and clearly was annoyed when he found out that Doyle "had not been asked . . . my opinion about this landing" by MacArthur. Admiral Radford was "convinced that Inchon was the place to land," however, and, just before the admirals met with MacArthur, Sherman changed his mind and told Struble that he would "back the Inchon operation completely."[9]

When the high-level conference convened, MacArthur outlined the Chromite plan and Sherman explained the Navy and Marine leaders' reservations. MacArthur intended to take Inchon, liberate Seoul, and trap North Korea's army—exhausted by its own recent offensive and short of reserves—in South Korea, crushing it between forces converging from Inchon and Pusan. Doyle argued that MacArthur was violating every known principle of amphibious warfare. MacArthur wanted to send ships up the narrow Flying Fish Channel leading to Inchon, a passage guarded by Wolmi Do Island's heavy guns, and to disembark his assault troops in an area of thirty-foot tidal range onto docks situated in the middle of a city known to contain an enemy garrison. The distance between Inchon and the Pusan perimeter was so great that the two forces would not be mutually supporting. Also, it was unlikely that the Inchon landing would be a surprise inasmuch as MacArthur's security arrangements were exceptionally poor, and the landing was already known in Japan as "operation common knowledge." Troops put ashore at Posung-Myon, on the other hand, might ignore Seoul, wheel to the south, and quickly link up with the 8th Army. MacArthur himself

The Navy's high command in the early phase of the Korean War. Admiral Forrest Sherman (*left*) visits Pusan, South Korea, in August 1950 to discuss strategy with Admiral Arthur W. Radford, CinCPac (*left center*), and Vice Admiral C. Turner Joy, Commander, U.S. Naval Forces Far East (*right center*).

Vice Admiral Arthur D. Struble. Commander, 7th Fleet, 1950–1951.

even admitted that the Inchon landing was a "daring risk," but he depicted this as an advantage.[10]

During the conference when Sherman confronted him, Doyle admitted that "the best I can say is that Inchon is not impossible." He was especially worried about bringing the transports into Flying Fish Channel because the enemy could easily defend the passage with its shore batteries and mines. This attitude smacked of defeatism, Sherman thought. "I wouldn't hesitate to take a ship up there," he remarked acidly. "Spoken like a Farragut," MacArthur exclaimed. "Spoken like John Wayne!" Admiral Doyle snapped. While MacArthur had convinced Sherman not to veto Chromite, the CNO still had his doubts. He privately warned MacArthur "that Inchon was a dangerous enterprise if any resistance developed," and wrung from the general a promise to land there "only if there were none." How much resistance the landing force might face in retaking Seoul was evidently not discussed.[11]

MacArthur had Sherman's backing for Inchon, but Sherman could not persuade MacArthur to give him a complete operational plan for the landing, and when the JCS instructed MacArthur to forward a copy to Washington, he ignored them. "We were," Collins complained, "in the dark." They had no idea of his plan of maneuver once Inchon was secure. The Marines were now united in favor of landing at Kunsan, 40 miles south of Inchon, a site with many of the attributes of Posung-Myon, and the JCS had prepared a plan for a landing there. MacArthur, however, insisted on landing at Inchon, and Sherman was supporting him. While Admiral Sherman wanted MacArthur to bypass Seoul, turn to the south, and crush the North Korean Army against the Pusan perimeter, MacArthur doggedly rejected this advice. Neither Bradley nor Collins shared Sherman's confidence in Chromite, but they both were in awe of MacArthur and fearful of opposing him. They "did not want to approve the Inchon landings," Radford observed, "but did not know how they could turn it down." Lacking full details of what was afoot, the JCS nonetheless grudgingly approved Chromite on 28 August.[12]

Three days later, an American raiding party crept ashore on Wolmi Do Island, reconnoitered the harbor, the adjacent mud flats, and the enemy's defenses, measured the tides, and radioed their findings to Doyle. So ill-prepared was the North Korean garrison that the Americans even erected a small lighthouse on the island to guide up the channel the invasion force of 230 ships, which was just then about to converge off Korea's west coast. In planning the operation, Struble decided to attempt the landing without a preliminary offshore naval bombardment to achieve surprise, but on this point Doyle finally stood his ground, insisting gruffly that the defenders be softened up before he ordered the Marines to go ashore. On 13 September, Struble sent Carrier Force attack aircraft against targets to the north and south of Inchon, and the Navy staged a small diversionary landing at Kunsan. And at dawn that same day, the destroyer *Collett* led Rear Admiral John H. Higgins' Support Force up Flying Fish Channel, four cruisers stood off about 15,000 yards from Inchon and bombarded the defenders, air strikes from the small carrier Escort Force hit Wolmi Do Island, and the Destroyer Force charged up the channel and took station 800 yards from the docks.

Old Russian-built contact mines defended the channel, but the Communists had miscalculated Inchon's tidal range and therefore set their mines for the highest possible water level. The Americans spotted these mines, and Admiral Higgins' ships had no difficulty avoiding them. After shelling the North Koreans for an hour, they retired safely with only minimal damage to the destroyers. The lack of good fire discipline and the exposed gun positions of the North Korean batteries hinted at the true weakness of the entire communist position at Inchon. The Americans discovered, however, that the North Koreans had been quick to exploit Wolmi Do's caves, and not even low-level bombing by the Escort Force's planes dislodged them. The next day, Higgins' ships again shelled Wolmi Do for an hour during high tide, and the cruisers took the communist shore batteries under indirect fire.

On 15 September, Captain Virginius Roane's Transport Force, carrying over 60,000 Americans and 6,000 Koreans of Lieutenant General Edward Almond's X Corps, anchored off Inchon. The 1st and 5th Marines boarded their landing craft and the first wave sped to the landing zone. Charging up the seawall and onto the docks, the Marines overcame light opposition and easily invested three positions to the west and south of the city. Supported by forty-seven old LSTs, the 1st Marine Division and the 7th Infantry soon took the city, then raced overland a few miles and encircled Seoul. Simultaneously, the 8th Army and the South Koreans moved slowly out of the Pusan perimeter in an offensive that began on 16 September. Retreating for the first time, the North Koreans were routed by this unexpected American offensive and hampered by South Korea's mountainous terrain, which limited communist logistics to two lines of communication. One, the Seoul highway, was cut when the Marines took the capital, which was defended by an enemy division that MacArthur's Army intelligence had inexplicably failed to locate. The other, the east coast road, was hit repeatedly by 7th Fleet attack aircraft and by offshore gunfire from a cruiser-destroyer group that Struble had sent into the Sea of Japan. Meanwhile, a South Korean drive northward from the Pusan perimeter to P'ohang was supported by the 16-inch guns of the battleship *Missouri*, which had just arrived in the western Pacific. Finally, on 28 September, advance units from the Pusan area linked arms with American scouts from Seoul.

Routed on both fronts, the North Koreans fled in retreat, pursued by Almond's X Corps along the Seoul-Pyongyang road on the west coast and by Walker's 8th Army up the east coast highway. Despite tremendous losses, however, the North Koreans conducted successful rearguard actions, saved a large fraction of their equipment, and thwarted a lightning advance by the Americans across the 38th parallel. By now unrestrained praise over the Inchon landing was feeding MacArthur's considerable ego. In a fit of hyperbole, Truman declared that, compared to Inchon, "no operations in military history can match." And General George Marshall, who became secretary of defense in August after Truman at long last fired Louis Johnson, told MacArthur on 28 September "to feel unhampered strategically and tactically to proceed north of the 38th parallel," a bold and stunning change in American foreign policy and war aims. Truman was bent on punishing the Communists for committing aggression, and on 2 October he instructed MacArthur to liberate North Korea from communist rule. This was a worthy objective, fully justified on the compassionate grounds of freeing the North Koreans from the brutality of Kim's communist tyranny, but Truman failed utterly to comprehend the likely repercussions of his decision. MacArthur, who directed operations in Korea from a faraway headquarters in downtown Tokyo, now pressed his generals to advance, but for reasons that surpass comprehension, he kept the field force commands divided between Almond's X Corps in the west and Walker's 8th Army in the east.[13]

Over the horizon was disaster, one harbinger of which was the Wŏnsan landing, derisively labeled "Operation Yo-yo" by many participants. To jump across Korea's waist and block the enemy's northward retreat, MacArthur decided on 2 October to land troops at Wŏnsan, a large port situated on the peninsula's northeast coast about 90 miles from Pyongyang and 110 miles from Seoul. To take Wŏnsan, he detached the 1st Marine Division from X Corps, withdrew them from the battle for Pyongyang, and ordered them to board Captain Roane's attack transports at Inchon on the 9th. Roane was to put to sea and rendezvous eight days later with a second transport force carrying an Army division from Pusan, steam into the Sea of Japan, and land at Wŏnsan on 20 October. Admirals Struble, Joy, and Doyle were aghast when they learned of this silly plan. Withdrawing the Marines from X Corps weakened Almond's front, and embarking these troops and reloading their equipment foolishly jammed more shipping into Inchon than that small port could absorb. Desperately needed supplies for the X Corps offensive could not be unloaded. The Wŏnsan operation also lapped up shipping from Japan needed to support the movement to the Yalu River. And, although Wŏnsan was not well defended, naval intelligence was by now aware that its narrow shipping channel leading to the harbor was heavily mined.

MacArthur was fortunate to achieve surprise at Inchon, but he could not reasonably expect to do the same thing twice. Owing to the 7th Fleet's success in sweeping the poorly laid mines at Inchon, he was reluctant to allow even five days for minesweeping operations at Wŏnsan. Inasmuch as supplies were still in short supply, Struble felt that the entire Wŏnsan operation was a dreadful waste. By now the North Korean Army had regrouped in the hills south of Wŏnsan but had given up on defending the coastal road owing to its great fear of American offshore naval gunfire. The result was that the advancing South Koreans moved north without check up the highway, crossing the 38th parallel on 1 October and closing on the outskirts of Wŏnsan within a week. Joy, openly more concerned about the minesweeping problem than about anything else, predicted that the South Koreans would enter the city before the landing force was put ashore. MacArthur suggested shifting the landing site to Hŭngnam, but Joy pointed out that there was little intelligence on Hŭngnam and not enough amphibious shipping to move that far north.

On the night of 6 October, Doyle sent raiders ashore near Wŏnsan to reconnoiter the beaches, and two days later Navy PBM Mariner patrol planes appeared overhead to begin minesearching operations in the channel leading to the port. With four *Essex*-class carriers, one battleship, and several cruiser-destroyer groups composing his Covering Force, Struble arrived off Wŏnsan in the battleship *Missouri* a few days later. He was alarmed by news that five vessels had been sunk in Korean waters by enemy mines over the past two weeks. He was now all too aware that the postwar Navy had lost interest in minesweeping and had demobilized most of its minesweeping vessels to keep pace with Truman's niggardly defense budgets. The Bureau of Ordnance had wanted to retain some minesweeping capability for the postwar fleet, but the most talented officers left the field and the "whole program sort of remained in the doldrums," according to Commander Kenneth Veth, a mine warfare expert.[14]

In August Admiral Radford had dispatched several minesweepers from the Pacific coast and Hawaii to the Far East, and Admiral Joy had commandeered eight Japanese Navy sweepers for the 7th Fleet, but Captain Richard T. Spofford's Protective Group, which started to clear the waters near Yo Do Island in the Wŏnsan channel on 10 October, was still seriously understrength. Moreover, Spofford misunderstood the Navy's minesweeping doctrine and decided to search and sweep at the same time. After destroying eighteen mines and clearing a ten-mile-long segment that afternoon, the formation retired, returning the next day to within four miles of the shoreline. On 12 October, Spofford again assigned the minesweepers *Pledge, Pirate,* and *Incredible* to lead the formation into the minefield. They had no paravanes to stream ahead of the vessels, and Spofford failed to send out small boats to explore the area before sweeping it. To make matters worse, Rear Admiral Higgins in the nearby cruiser *Rochester* had failed to provide a direct communications link between the cruiser's supporting helicopter and Spofford's minesweepers below, and when the helicopter pilot located an uncharted minefield, Spofford was confused by the information and failed to alert his minesweepers. Suddenly, at 1209, the *Pirate* collided with a mine, blew up, and went under in four minutes.

Stunned, the *Pledge* came to a full stop, cut her sweeping gear, and started to rescue the *Pirate*'s survivors. This commotion attracted the attention of North Korean gunners in concealed positions on nearby Sin Do Island, and they promptly took the American ships under fire. Bracketed by shells, Lieutenant Richard Young in the *Pledge* was instructed by Higgins to retire,

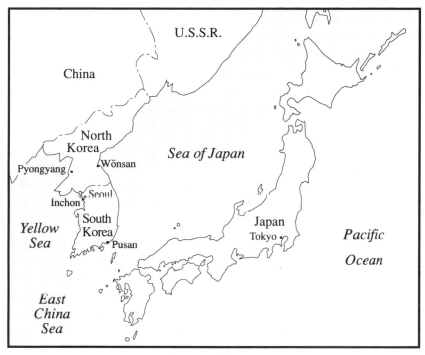

China

U.S.S.R.

North
Korea
Pyongyang. Wŏnsan

Sea of Japan

Seoul
Inchon
South
Yellow Korea
Sea Pusan

Japan
Tokyo

Pacific

Ocean

East
China
Sea

Korea and Japan

but unfortunately Young's maneuvering led his small vessel into another undiscovered minefield and at 1220 she struck a mine. The explosion split the *Pledge* apart from the keel to the open bridge and she, too, went under. Although air strikes from the carriers eventually silenced the Sin Do batteries, Struble had little choice but to postpone the Wŏnsan landings until sweeping operations were safely concluded. Captain Roane's Transport Group arrived in the Korean Gulf on 19 October, but the Marines had to wait in their ships at anchor for another week before Struble was willing to allow them to land. When they finally marched into Wŏnsan, they found that the city had been in the hands of the South Koreans for several days, that the 1st Marine Air Wing command was already operating, and that a USO show featuring comedian Bob Hope was in progress.[15]

After Walker's 8th Army crossed the 38th parallel on 9 October, Truman decided for partisan political reasons to bask in MacArthur's reflected glory, and six days later, with a large entourage, he flew out to the Pacific to meet the general at Wake

Island. Always willing to provide an easy answer to any hard question, the incurably long-winded MacArthur told Truman that the American troops would be "home by Christmas" and that he saw no signs that China intended to enter the war. This assessment was, of course, based on the same CIA intelligence to which the president and the JCS were privy. MacArthur's assertion that China would not intervene was supported by a staff evaluation of the impact of carrier- and land-based tactical air power on the fighting so far in Korea, a report that concluded that the air forces had contributed significantly to the destruction of the North Korean Army. As North Korea's army was known to be far better equipped, if much smaller, than China's, MacArthur reasoned that his air and naval forces constituted a powerful deterrent to Chinese intervention. Truman later claimed that he went to Wake Island to review Asian policy and improve his poor relations with MacArthur, but his failure to properly staff the meeting, the absence of an agenda, and the frivolity of the talks gave the lie to this distortion. In fact, by October 1950, Truman feared MacArthur's political allies, understood that the general still nursed presidential ambitions, and knew full well that he had a habit of ignoring unwelcome orders.[16]

The possibility of China's intervention in the Korean War first became an important issue for American strategists in September 1950 when Truman asked the UN to approve MacArthur's operations north of the 38th parallel. Opposing this resolution, India's delegate cautioned that the U.S. Army's presence on the Manchurian border would provoke a reaction from Peking, but because most communist capitals were issuing daily propaganda threats of all manner of dire consequences, no American leader paid heed to the Indian claim. MacArthur knew on 14 October that there were thirty-eight Chinese divisions in Manchuria, but neither the Far East command nor the JCS predicted that they would soon be sent into combat. Five days later, the North Koreans were driven from Pyongyang, their capital, and on 26 October American and South Korean advance units reached positions on the Yalu River. Unbeknownst to Washington, three weeks earlier the Chinese Communist Party's Central Committee had assembled in Peking to discuss the American presence on the Korean peninsula and, after a debate lasting two days, Chairman Mao Tse-tung announced secretly that China would enter the war on the grounds that once American troops reached the Yalu they might be tempted to cross over into Manchuria. General Peng Dehuai moved the first Chinese troops across the Yalu on the night of 13 October. Under the cover of darkness, on side roads and through treacherous mountains, roughly 200,000 more men followed him into northwestern Korea later that month and in early November.

Peng jolted MacArthur's forces with slashing attacks on 25 October, mauling a South Korean corps on the flank of the 8th Army. "An entirely new war against an entirely new power of great military strength" now faced his forces, MacArthur told the JCS. He ordered Admiral Struble and General Stratemeyer to bomb a long list of targets between the front and the border, as well as the Sinŭiju bridges, which carried most communist military traffic across the Yalu River from China to North Korea. Soon after the JCS reviewed the directive, MacArthur was hastily instructed not to strike Chinese territory as this might cause the Soviets to intervene under the secret terms of the February 1950 Sino-Soviet alliance. MacArthur appealed this order to Truman, and he overruled Bradley and Sherman against the advice of Secretary of State Acheson and Defense Secretary Marshall. Meanwhile, a new threat to the American air forces appeared on the scene on 1 November when a flight of six Soviet-built MiG-15 jet fighters crossed the Yalu and attacked a section of Air Force prop-driven fighter-bombers. Not only did the MiGs' appearance menace American bombing operations, the planes also seemed to outperform the Navy's F9F Panther fighters and the Air Force's F-80 Shooting Star interceptors. Stratemeyer called on Struble to conduct a joint air campaign against the Sinŭiju bridges, but Struble demurred, pointing out that the 7th Fleet was already fully occupied with close ground support operations. Stratemeyer then appealed to Joy, who overruled Struble and instructed him to participate in the bridge-busting operations, which the Air Force inaugurated on 8 November.[17]

Next day the carriers *Philippine Sea* and *Valley Forge* sent air strikes composed of AD Skyraider bombers escorted by F9F Panthers and F4U Corsairs from the carrier station in the Sea of Japan 225 miles across the length of northeastern North Korea to the Yalu bridges, which were defended by thick antiaircraft fire from both banks of the river and by MiG fighters. During this action, Lieutenant Commander William T. Allen became the first naval aviator to shoot down a hostile jet when he splashed a

MiG-15 on 9 November, the first of three losses by the Communists that day. The American bombing campaign dropped three highway bridges at Sinŭiju and two more bridges at Hyesanjin, but the Sinŭiju railway bridge seemed immune to attack and remained standing when the operation ended on 21 November. Despite the ability of the F9F Panther to overwhelm the poorly handled MiG fighter, the captain of the *Valley Forge* reported that "if they had been manned by pilots as aggressive and well-trained as ours . . . plane losses would have been great." The appearance of the MiGs moved the Bureau of Aeronautics to ask Grumman to convert the Panther into the F9F-8 Cougar and to hasten the development of the new F3H Demon fighter; however, these planes did not enter the fleet in any numbers until 1953, leaving the F9F Panther as the workhorse of the fighter squadrons. The disappointing results of the Sinŭiju bridge campaign also exposed the intractable tactical frustration the 7th Fleet and the Far East Air Force would encounter when they were diverted from ground support operations to an interdiction effort against fixed enemy means of communications. While four of twelve bridges across the Yalu had been badly damaged or destroyed, Peng's Chinese Army had already crossed into North Korea and the Yalu River was on the verge of freezing over.[18]

The Chinese attacks against the Allies stopped unexpectedly on 10 November. Despite evidence to the contrary, MacArthur now insisted that only a few Chinese troops had crossed the Yalu. He refused to give command of the entire front to either General Walker or General Almond, announced that the war would be over by Christmas, and badgered Almond to continue his advance north of Pyongyang. The JCS met with Acheson and Marshall on 21 November to discuss the meaning of Chinese military behavior, but adhered "to the custom of yielding to the man on the scene." On the night of the 25th, Peng attacked again, this time hitting the right flank of the 8th Army, eviscerating one South Korean corps, and nearly cutting off the main Allied line of retreat. Two days later, an entire Chinese Army group fell on the 1st Marine Division west of the Chosin Reservoir, then mauled the 7th Infantry Division to the east. Part of X Corps retired back to Seoul, while the Marines fought their way through seven Chinese divisions to get past the Chosin Reservoir and onto the road to the east coast port of Hŭngnam. By 1 December, their situation was desperate. Struble sent a pair of PBM Mariner patrol bombers into the Chosin area to shuttle out the Marines, but the reservoir was frozen solid and the planes were unable to land on the ice. Sherman had sent the attack carrier *Leyte Gulf* to join the *Philippine Sea, Princeton,* and *Valley Forge* of the 7th Fleet Carrier Force, and Struble moved these ships into the northern Sea of Japan to support the Marines along the Chosin-Hŭngnam line.

The Navy now began to organize the remarkable evacuation of Hŭngnam. Joy assembled all available transport shipping in the region. An Escort Force of three light carriers steamed north to give close ground support to the withdrawal to Hŭngnam, and General Smith's Marines finally reached the port on 10 December. To defend the city, Struble then brought up the battleship *Missouri* and a Gunfire Support Group of two heavy cruisers and eight destroyers. When the Chinese offensive reached the Hŭngnam pocket, MacArthur and Struble considered a plan to hold Hŭngnam, but the weight of the attack was so great that they had no choice but to evacuate the Marines. Doyle's Amphibious Force lifted the Army's 3rd Division out of Wŏnsan, then steamed into Hŭngnam on 10 December with seventy-six transports and cargo ships. The entrance was well mined, so a narrow channel was swept and minesweepers escorted the transports and freighters into the harbor. Nearly 100,000 troops and just as many Korean refugees were crowding into the city, and Doyle was determined to save them all. Air operations were hampered by freezing weather, so the Gunfire Support Group closed to support the withdrawal. To stun the Chinese, who had massed their forces on the reverse slopes of the surrounding mountains, Doyle also employed three rocket ships. The cruisers took station ten miles out to sea to provide additional gunfire support, while the destroyers steamed into the swept channel leading to the harbor and covered the embarkation.

The defenders of Hŭngnam withstood two major Chinese assaults while all the troops and refugees boarded the ships, taking with them most of their arms and vehicles. On 23 December, while the destroyers' 5-inch guns covered the last large troop movement to the ships, the battleship *Missouri*'s main battery was brought to bear on the Ori-ri-Hŭngnam Road to prevent a final communist lunge at the city. Admiral Roscoe Hillenkoetter's Gunfire Support Group then established a ring of fire around the harbor, a barrage laid down on a belt 2,500 yards long and

3,000 yards deep, and this prevented the attackers from harassing the final, tragic, but successful embarkation. "As we pulled out [in the flagship *Mount McKinley*]," Doyle recalled, "Almond and I saw . . . Chinese Communist troops coming over the ridge behind Hŭngnam, only three or four miles away." After directing some desultory fire in that direction, Hillenkoetter turned his guns on the harbor and railroad yard, blasting freight cars and locomotives, deserted buildings, and track. On Christmas Eve, a Navy UDT team blew up the warehouses and docks just before Doyle cleared the channel and entered the Sea of Japan. The desperate battle for Hŭngnam was over.

Unnerved by these setbacks, MacArthur began to panic. Half of the troops from Hŭngnam were landed at P'ohang and had to march back north to reinforce the 8th Army, while the rest sailed south to Pusan to refit before heading up the peninsula once again to fight on the Allied lines south of Seoul. On 1 December, Sherman, informed by Joy's private reports about affairs at the Far East theater headquarters, first expressed skepticism about MacArthur's state of mind and his reliability. Although the front was stabilized by New Year's Day, MacArthur claimed on 9 January 1951 that he had "insufficient strength to hold a position in Korea," an assessment not shared by many of his field commanders. Sherman was by now having a "difficult time" adjusting to MacArthur's "mercurial shifts." MacArthur asserted that he would have to abandon the peninsula within a few weeks and told Washington his troops were distressed, but when Radford visited South Korea on 20 January to "assess morale" he reported back to the CNO that there was "no pessimism in the Navy's high command."[19]

In December 1950, MacArthur began to reiterate two prescriptions to alleviate his situation, remedies that appeared to be bold but that the JCS had already studied and rejected. He urged Truman to accept Chiang's offer to send Taiwan divisions to fight in Korea, an idea the JCS considered foolhardy inasmuch as Chiang could not even defend Taiwan against a communist invasion. Moreover, South Korean President Rhee was violently opposed to introducing more Chinese troops into his country. MacArthur also wanted to impose a naval blockade on China, but Sherman rejected this on the grounds that it might engage the United States in a direct war with Peking. A blockade would do little to reduce the flow of supplies from Vladivostok and Soviet-controlled Port Arthur to North Korea. So uneasy was the State Department about confronting Peking that policy planner Paul Nitze declared that a planned 7th Fleet sweep along China's coast was overly provocative. Moreover, the Navy was already straining to meet its many other obligations. When the war began, the fleet included only about 280 warships, and Sherman understood that he did not have enough ships to blockade China's coast and concurrently meet other commitments. By redeployments and recommissioning, he had created a major fleet off Korea almost from scratch, and by the end of 1950 there were more naval aircraft in the Far East than the carriers could operate. The price of this policy was the shrinking of the Atlantic Fleet and the 6th Fleet, a force in which Sherman justifiably took much personal pride. Nonetheless, by the end of the year he had decided to rotate the large nuclear strike *Midway*-class carriers into the Mediterranean and had sadly warned admirals Struble and Radford that they could expect no additional platforms in the Pacific theater for another two years.

China's intervention in Korea moved Truman in December 1950 to declare a national emergency, quadruple annual military spending to about $50 billion, and approve in the process Sherman's substantial shipbuilding program. Truman mentioned in public that he was thinking of using nuclear weapons in Korea, but Sherman told the JCS that it would be wise to "delay a general war with Russia until we have achieved the necessary degree of military and industrial mobilization." Despite the completion of the carrier *Oriskany* in September, the fleet was still short of carriers, so the CNO issued orders to recommission the *Bonhomme Richard*, *Essex*, *Antietam*, *Kearsarge*, and *Lake Champlain*. Truman's emergency message asked Congress to increase the Army to eighteen divisions because of the war in Korea, but overshadowing the war was the American naval and military commitment to NATO, and so at the same time Truman named General Eisenhower to be the first NATO supreme commander and promised to send four divisions to Europe within the next two years. Likewise, General Vandenberg advised the JCS that the number of Air Force bombers and attack aircraft assigned to the Far East was hardly enough to execute the vast bombing campaign for which MacArthur was pleading and that new bombers were already committed to NATO. There was more than a bit of dissention over these decisions, Radford complaining that the "Joint Chiefs should not have divided their efforts between the Far East and Europe in trying so desperately to build up."[20]

Radford was also more enthusiastic about a bombing campaign against China than was Sherman, who feared that attacks against the communist sanctuary in China would provoke Chinese strikes against the equivalent "sanctuaries" Americans found on their carriers or at air bases in Japan. Although the possibility that the Communists might violate this tacit accord meant that the defense of the fleet and the air bases had to remain alert, as the war droned on such an escalation of hostilities became less probable, and the American air commanders were able to shift more fighters from defensive to offensive operations.

Under the press of the Chinese offensive and the lack of an easy alternative to defending the front lines on the peninsula, the European allies' enthusiasm for the Korean War waned, and they failed to honor their earlier troop commitments. At the same time, General Collins was bluntly telling MacArthur that, because of the need to build up the NATO army in Europe, no more American divisions would be spent defending Korea. "Korea is not the place to fight a major war," the JCS told MacArthur on 29 December 1950.[21]

Ironically, the momentum in Korea shifted rapidly during the next few weeks. In December, an accident claimed General Walker's life, and Collins used the opportunity to name his replacement to consolidate the command of ground forces in Korea under General Matthew Ridgway, an officer in whom MacArthur unexpectedly reposed complete authority. Ridgway's initial survey of the front conflicted with MacArthur's gloomy assessment, and within a few weeks Struble confided to Sherman that Ridgway was planning a major counteroffensive. In Operation Roundup, which began on 5 February, Almond's X Corps in the east advanced into the teeth of an attack by a full Chinese Army group, then fell back to prepared artillery positions and called in massive air strikes from the Air Force and the 7th Fleet Carrier Force. Within a week, the Chinese and North Koreans had lost so many men that they quit the battlefield and withdrew in panic.

Ridgway launched Operation Thunderbolt in the west on 25 January, an advance that culminated in the contest for Suwŏn on

9 February and that cost the Communists 4,000 soldiers in four hours of fighting. Operations Killer in February and Ripper in March were slugfests between American artillery and air power and communist infantry, with offshore naval gunfire support being provided by the West Coast Blockade Force led by a small formation of British destroyers. Heavy losses caused the Chinese to abandon Seoul without a fight on 15 February. Over the next six weeks, Ridgway kept up the tempo of operations while preparing to confront the Communists along the southern edge of the "iron triangle" defensive positions in central Korea. The fury of the air campaign in the north also intensified, and on 2 April a section of Phantoms, the first naval jet bombers, flew off the *Princeton* and struck railroad bridges near Songjin. One month later, Douglas AD Skyraiders armed with Mark XIII aerial torpedoes destroyed the gates to the Hwachon Dam, releasing thousands of tons of water in the reservoir and flooding the Han and Pukhan river valleys. This temporarily shut off logistics support to the Chinese armies at the very moment that they were trying to erect defensible lines to slow down the American onslaught in the south.

Ridgway's victories raised morale in Washington, but China's intervention had sapped Truman's will to win the war. After Ridgway retook Seoul, the JCS told MacArthur once again that no additional American troops would be sent to Korea and prodded him to accept the reality that the tactical stalemate had produced a strategic victory of sorts. On 20 March, the JCS sent MacArthur a draft of an announcement prepared for Truman stating that "before any advance with major forces north of the thirty-eighth parallel," the United States intended to seek a ceasefire and a negotiated settlement. Three days later, MacArthur countered with a public threat against China. The UN, he blustered, might "depart from its tolerant effort to contain the war to the area of Korea, through an expansion of our military operations to its coastal and interior bases," and he called on Peking to surrender.[22]

Truman, insecure and hypersensitive, was furious at MacArthur's apparent challenge to his authority, but the JCS for the moment sided with the general. They urged the 7th Fleet to prepare for attacks against targets in China and cautioned Truman not to negotiate a ceasefire that would tie down American troops in Korea. Owing to his low standing with the public,

Truman dared not act unless the JCS agreed with him, so he cunningly obscured his differences with MacArthur's ultimatum. Though still in awe of MacArthur, the JCS were nonetheless agitated by his recklessness. They were very secretly considering using atomic bombs to end the war, and Truman had ordered that nine bombs be transferred by the AEC to the Air Force and be sent to Guam, but neither he nor the JCS intended to place these weapons in MacArthur's unsteady hands. As a result, the JCS began to discuss relieving their Far Eastern general.

Within a week, Congressman Joseph Martin, the Republican House Minority Leader, published an open letter from MacArthur that urged the "utilization" of Chiang's divisions in Korea. "If we lose this war to Communism in Asia the fall of Europe is inevitable," he wrote. "Win it and Europe most probably would avoid war and yet preserve freedom." This bizarre concept directly contradicted the NATO-based, Europe-first strategy the JCS had adopted to fight the Cold War. Although this letter was an unexceptional example of MacArthur's penchant for bluster, Truman contended ingenuously that it constituted unbridled insubordination. He wanted to relieve MacArthur instantly, but Defense Secretary Marshall warned him that the political costs of this step would be alarmingly high for an unpopular administration. Marshall and Bradley drafted a reprimand for Truman to send to MacArthur, but Truman rejected it. They then proposed that MacArthur be brought home to receive it, but Acheson, who despised MacArthur, scotched this idea. Before Truman could order that MacArthur be relieved, he needed the "unanimous" consent of the JCS. After two days of discussion they agreed without dissent and with surprisingly little reluctance.

On 11 April, Truman ordered Ridgway to relieve MacArthur in the Far East command. Truman, never a popular figure, was excoriated by most politicians and vilified by public opinion. He became an easy target of scorn and derision. While the political storm swirled, Congress held hearings on MacArthur's relief and he became the star witness. He was allowed to drone on for a week, lost the attention of a fickle public, and made a dramatic error by testifying that he and the JCS held views that "were practically identical." This contrived fib gave committee Democrats the opportunity they were seeking, and Truman dispatched generals Marshall, Bradley, and Collins and Admiral Sherman up to the Hill to put the lie to MacArthur's claim that the JCS supported his actions. The Republicans, who used the occasion to thrash Truman, were reluctant to lionize MacArthur and so hand him their 1952 presidential nomination, while many Democrats, aware of Truman's interest in using nuclear weapons to restrain China, worked to obscure the fact that Truman's and Mac-Arthur's views on how to conduct the war were in truth not that far apart. Interest in MacArthur's relief soon abated, and when he ran for the Republican nomination in 1952, he lost badly.[23]

Ridgway's grinding offensives continued during May. The fear of a renewed Chinese drive moved Truman to transfer atomic-capable B-29 bombers to Japan and permit Ridgway to bomb China, should Chinese aircraft strike American bases in Japan. But Truman had no stomach to press his atomic advantage and he refused to publicize the movements of the B-29s, although his diplomats issued broad threats about using atomic bombs if China refused to negotiate. Mao thought the West toothless, but Stalin apparently took note of the danger. On 23 June, just before Sherman left Washington for Tokyo, Jacob Malik, the Soviet ambassador to the UN, proposed a ceasefire along the 38th parallel, and while Sherman was in the Far East, the Chinese and North Koreans accepted a proposal to meet Ridgway's representative for armistice talks. There was no doubt that the timing of the Soviet proposal was meant to coincide with another American offensive against the "iron triangle" during which Ridgway intended to annihilate the communist armies on the peninsula. On 9 June, Bradley ordered Ridgway to curtail his offensive, and on 5 July truce talks began at the village of Kaesong, with Admiral Joy representing the UN command. A return to the antebellum status quo along the 38th parallel was not an unworthy war aim, but Truman's decision to freeze American offensive operations and create a stalemate before serious talks even began effectively left the decision to end the war in China's hands.

Chapter Seventeen

Stalemate in Korea
1951–1953

After the crises of spring 1951, Truman's policy in the Korean War returned the military initiative to the Chinese for nearly two years. Soon after the Kaesong truce talks began in July 1951, the Chinese and North Koreans demanded that all foreign troops leave the Korean peninsula as the first condition of any ceasefire. This was promptly rejected by Truman. Admiral C. Turner Joy, the chief UN negotiator, reluctantly concluded that the enemy was negotiating merely to prevent the Americans from advancing again into North Korea. General Ridgway's counter-offensive had ended in June 1951 with local victories along the entire front, and Ridgway was preparing to reenter North Korea when Truman ordered him not to do so. Thereafter, Truman refused to consider any war aim other than a ceasefire that would leave both North and South Korea intact. The war was "never stalemated," complained General James Van Fleet, the new 8th Army commander. "It was a sit-down on our part."[1]

The Communists were alert to the immunity conferred upon them by Truman's war policy, and for this reason among others, they refused to abandon their goal of unifying Korea. The weight of American carrier- and land-based air strikes prevented them from mounting another general offensive for the rest of the war, however, so they turned to short, local advances, violent outbursts followed by lengthy periods of inactivity. Truman's decision not to invade North Korea again diminished the need for strategic flexibility and left Van Fleet unable to find any use for the amphibious skills of the 1st Marine Division, so he assigned them to hold a sector on the eastern flank of the UN line. To provide logistics support for the troops on the peninsula, the once powerful 7th Fleet Amphibious Force lost a number of transports, supply ships, and large landing vessels.

The 7th Fleet Gunfire Support Groups were constantly active, but their work was hampered by the lack of shore control parties and trained gunfire control officers, as well as by poor communications and old charts and maps. Spotting for fires was not good. There were few helicopters for spotting, and these machines could only fly over areas where there were no enemy anti-aircraft batteries. Otherwise, the Gunfire Support Groups depended on naval aviators from the Carrier Force who had little or no training in spotting and not much interest in the duty, and neither Vice Admiral Harold Martin, who relieved Struble in command of the 7th Fleet in mid-1951, nor Vice Admiral J. J. Clark, who commanded the 7th Fleet during the last years of the war, was willing to create a specialized unit dedicated to this work. Air photo reconnaissance was seldom employed to support the naval gunfire mission. Instead, most reconnaissance sorties were flown over interdiction targets such as bridges, railroads, tunnels, and roadways.

The failure of another Chinese offensive in November 1951 convinced Peking to adjust its negotiating position, first asking that the truce talks be moved to the village of Panmunjom and then announcing that they would agree to a ceasefire in place. Although Truman wanted an armistice on almost any terms, progress was now checkmated by Ridgway, who resurrected an earlier proposal that the Communists return the ancient capital of Kaesong to the South Koreans. Control of this city had been disputed ever since the truce talks began. On 24 July, Joy had instructed the West Coast Bombardment Force to conduct a sustained shelling of the communist batteries on the northern bank of the Han River estuary so as to move them away from the Kaesong area. When Rear Admiral George C. Dyer assumed command of the West Coast Bombardment Force in September 1951, he pressed his destroyers upriver, slowly forcing the Communists to retire to new defensive works to the northeast. The pressure had escalated around Kaesong on 3 October when the escort carrier *Rendova* was assigned to provide combat air cover for the bombardment destroyers with its F4U Corsairs and to hit opposing Chinese artillery. Later that month, however, the JCS told Ridgway that Truman did not support his position on Kaesong, and in the meantime Joy had persuaded the Communists to incorporate in the armistice a demilitarized zone four miles wide along the front line. The negotiators also agreed on a map that fixed the location of their respective forces in the Han River area, and with this settled, Dyer was instructed to end the bombardment on 27 November.

Still there remained several obstacles to a truce, the major ones being the likeminded unwillingness of the Seoul and Pyong-yang regimes to abandon their plans to unify Korea and the repatriation of North Korean prisoners of war held in South Korea. The communist powers wanted the allies to return all of their POWs, but both Washington and Seoul refused to forcibly repatriate those—roughly half— who did not want to return to communist rule. The inability to arrive at a compromise on the POW question "cost us over a year of war," according to Joy. Other issues arising from the fighting front intruded into the truce tent, one being ultimate possession of several offshore islands. The Navy's ongoing siege of Wŏnsan had coincided with Ridgway's first offensive, Operation Killer, a movement begun in February 1951 that forced the Chinese to withdraw north of the 38th parallel. To divert the enemy, Rear Admiral A. E. Smith decided to establish a staging point on North Korea's coast in case the allies made another amphibious flanking maneuver and at the same time to reduce communist coastal mining operations and junk traffic. He had minesweepers sent in to clear Wŏnsan Channel on 12 February, and four days later a pair of destroyers bombarded Wŏnsan. After an air strike from the Carrier Force against a communist battery on Sin Do Island, a landing party of South Korean Marines went ashore on 19 February without opposition. Nearby Yo Do and Ung Do islands were seized later in the year. Wŏnsan and the communist artillery in the surrounding hills were attacked repeatedly during the long siege.

Truman's decision in June 1951 not to allow Ridgway to cross into North Korea raised the question of what to do about these offshore islands, and Joy directed that they be held as useful pawns during the negotiations. His purpose was to keep these positions as part of a ceasefire in place, so the 7th Fleet continued to harass Wŏnsan with grim regularity. On 16 July, the 16-inch guns of the recommissioned battleship *New Jersey* were brought to bear on the enemy positions, air strikes from the Carrier Force were launched on 18 September as part of the interdiction campaign, and at the end of the year the battleship *Wisconsin* brought communist positions around Wŏnsan under fire. Once the negotiators at Panmunjom had agreed that the basis of any truce would be a mutual withdrawal from isolated positions above and below the ceasefire line, however, all talk of holding the Wŏnsan islands ended. Still, in 1952, Admiral Clark continued harassing operations against the city and the coastal defense artillery to supplement the interdiction effort and to shut down communist maritime activity along the North Korean coast.

Following Ridgway's spring 1951 counteroffensive, the Communists had few tanks left, and they seldom thereafter concentrated their armor into offensive formations, thus depriving the Gunfire Support Group's battleships and cruisers of their favorite targets. Conditions along Korea's east coast were far more suitable for close-in bombardment operations than on the west coast, and offshore gunfire became a practical necessity inasmuch as the South Korean corps defending this flank had no organic artillery. The battleships fired at average ranges of 30,000 yards, the heavy cruisers' 8-inch guns from 20,000 yards. The American batteries were especially effective against communist truck convoys and depots, supply dumps, and field artillery, at least on those occasions when they were brought out into the open. The Chinese specialized in the art of concealment, however, and they educated their North Korean allies in the burrowing tactics adapted from those used by the Japanese during the Pacific war. On reverse slopes and in the folds of the hills, the Communists dug intricate, dense networks of bunkers and tunnels that they covered with logs, earth, rocks, and sand; key Chinese and North Korean command posts and artillery batteries were covered by reinforced concrete. These defenses immeasurably complicated the Gunfire Support Groups' task.

Hampered by poor spotting and imperfect aerial reconnaissance, Navy gunfire against these targets was often ineffective. One intelligence assessment issued on 1 July 1952 by Vice Admiral Robert P. Briscoe claimed that communist coastal defense artillery was "organized and equipped" so that they could "be employed on the main battle line if required." The Communists' "main coastal defenses . . . are standard artillery pieces, rather than immobile or semi-mobile guns." Movement and rotation of these guns made it "very difficult" for the ships "to produce any acceptable estimate of the number of artillery pieces in a specific area at a given time." The Communists used the same tactics to strengthen their coastal defense artillery, which was highly mobile and cleverly concealed. The hydrography of the west coast favored the Communists, and only along one stretch north of Seoul might British and American destroyers get close enough to deliver effective fires. Although the overall volume of allied counterbattery fire increased significantly in 1952, especially during the latter half of the year, early the following year the West Coast Blockade Force commander pointed out in despair that the Communists had erected a network of "practically invulnerable emplacements."[2]

The land- and carrier-based air forces were critical to slowing down the Chinese offensive in the winter of 1951. For guidance on how to do this, Air Force leaders relied on their experience in World War II, when, occasionally, bombing had isolated an enemy front line from its logistic support. Admiral Struble, who commanded the 7th Fleet until spring 1951, did not share the Air Force's enthusiasm for an air interdiction strategy in North Korea, however, and resisted General George Stratemeyer's plan to dedicate the Carrier Force to this campaign. The static front on the peninsula meant that the Communists did not need to rapidly move large bodies of troops or supplies, he argued. It reduced their need for predictable logistics and allowed them to exploit bad weather, camouflage, concealment, darkness, and dispersal to frustrate interdiction operations. Navy involvement in Operation Strangle, the poorly conceived air interdiction campaign, evolved from MacArthur's call to the carriers to support the troops in northeast Korea during the retreat from the Yalu river. To meet this emergency, he also asked Struble to sever communist communications between the Yalu and the front. Maintaining that "the results to be obtained from such operations are only partial," Struble replied that using the carriers for "strong close air support . . . will do more to hurt the enemy potential than any other type of operation in which we can participate."[3]

Admiral Joy sided with Stratemeyer, however, overruled Struble's objections, and ordered him to mount "deliberate, methodical total destruction of all piers, spans, approaches, and embarkments of each vital bridge" in northeastern Korea. Pointing to the Wŏnsan-Ch'ŏngjin Railroad, which consisted of 1,140 miles of track and 956 bridges, Joy insisted that bombing these targets would leave the line "seriously impaired" since the Chinese "cannot accomplish makeshift repairs when nothing remains upon which to make them." While the front was fluid, 7th Fleet and Air Force interdiction strikes clearly retarded the communist advance, but with the onset of the summer stalemate the entire American air war was reorganized, and Ridgway, the new theater commander, adopted a different strategy.[4]

Stratemeyer, a disciple of the Air Force doctrine of the unity of air power, insisted that his Tokyo headquarters direct all air operations over Korea. His demand was backed first by MacArthur, and later by Ridgway, both of whom dismissed the Navy's objections to this arrangement. Unfortunately, Stratemeyer's highly centralized methods of command quickly swamped the fragile Air Force communications network, a primitive system that was one of the legacies of the lack of postwar Air Force interest in tactical operations. Stratemeyer ignored this problem and convinced Ridgway to apply the Air Force system to ground support operations, but the results were so poor that General Collins, the Army's chief of staff, spread rumors that he intended to develop the Army's own tactical air force. Joy's support of Operation Strangle was not wholly ill advised. Japan's long occupation had left Korea with an impressive network of railroad tunnels and bridges, a transportation system that at first appeared to be an ideal target for the American air forces even before Truman's stalemate policy gripped military strategy in Korea. North Korea's railroad bridges seemed to be particularly well suited to the capabilities of the Navy's AD-1 Skyraider bombers, which could deliver large payloads with unprecedented accuracy, and this in part had caused MacArthur in January 1951 to instruct Struble to fling the heavy carrier air groups against North Korea's bridges and tunnels.

As a first step, Rear Admiral Ralph A. Ofstie of the 7th Fleet Carrier Force sent reconnaissance flights over the length and width of North Korea to photograph the entire railroad bridge system; occasional attacks on these spans followed. On the morning of 2 March, Lieutenant Commander Clement E. Craig, flying off the *Princeton*, discovered that a single bridge, just south of Kilchu, was situated near a junction of three railroads along which moved southbound trains laden with communist supplies from Manchuria. That afternoon, Ofstie sent one air strike against the Kilchu bridge, and the next day a second flight hit some nearby spans. There were additional strikes throughout the month, and by 27 March all six spans of the bridge had apparently been knocked out. Ofstie had to suspend this series of attacks unexpectedly in April in order to deploy the fast carriers south to patrol the Taiwan Straits following a rumor that the Chinese were about to invade Taiwan. When this alarm proved to be false later that month, he was told to divert his aircraft once again to close ground support operations to check China's spring offensive. By the time that Rear Admiral G. R. Henderson relieved Ofstie on 7 May, large communist work crews had repaired a great deal of the damage to the Kilchu and other damaged bridges upon which North Korea's railroads depended.

Carrier air attacks against the bridges continued on a sporadic basis during May, but this campaign's impact on the battlefield was doubtful. Henderson asserted in June that the bridge interdiction campaign was failing, pointing out that it had not prevented the enemy from mounting two spring offensives. While they repaired damage to the east coast railroad, the Communists had shifted most of their freight to the west coast lines; at the same time, they began to move a large fraction of their supplies in nighttime truck convoys. On the average, it was taking a dozen or more Skyraider strikes to destroy a single bridge. Most of these bridges merely forded shallow creeks and rivers, and the Communists soon discovered that by using their surplus manpower they could effect repairs quickly or erect a substitute span with relative ease. Moreover, Henderson admitted that he did not have enough naval bombers both to attack North Korea's highways at night and to continue the concurrent daytime railroad-bridge campaign.

To solve this problem, Ridgway drew a 100-mile-wide belt across southcentral North Korea. Within this belt, the Air Force was to hit the enemy's transport system in the western sector, the 7th Fleet Carrier Force would hit the center, and the land-based 1st Marine Air Wing, the east. This shift in air strategy came in July, just before the task force's offensive punch was strengthened by the arrival in the Far East of the fast carrier *Essex*. This ship had been modernized recently to handle the first squadron of McDonnell F2H Banshees, a heavy twin-jet fighter that was nonetheless inferior in maneuverability and speed to the communist MiG interceptor. Unprecedented American coordination in air operations marked the new concentration against the transportation system in the North Korean belt, but within two weeks there was irrefutable evidence that Operation Strangle had not reduced the number of communist trucks running between the Yalu and the battlefront. In large measure, this was because a bomb crater in a road did not guarantee that the road was closed thereafter to traffic. The futile highway bombing continued throughout August nonetheless, when Admiral Martin finally persuaded Ridgway to abandon it.

Martin urged Ridgway once more in September 1951 to assign the 7th Fleet carriers to close ground support, but Ridgway and Stratemeyer again rejected the Navy's proposal. Instead, on 20 September, Ridgway told Martin to withdraw the carriers from ground support operations, which were taken over by the Air Force and Marine Corps aircraft. Under the new arrangement, Martin was to concentrate his carrier air attacks against North Korea's railroad tracks, a costly and wrongheaded decision that forced the task force to rethink its attack doctrine. To compel the Communists to disperse their repair crews, Rear Admiral W. G. Tomlinson of the 7th Fleet Carrier Force dictated that targets be spread out over a wide area and that individual targets be separated by at least one mile. Tomlinson's tactics had the advantage of reducing the menace to Navy aircraft from communist antiaircraft batteries that had already taken a heavy toll in attack aircraft. It appeared at first that the attacks on the railroad tracks were affecting communist logistics, and during October, the lines were broken at over 1,000 locations. This was duplicated in November and again in December, months when the flying weather was especially poor. "An almost complete interruption of eastern rail line movement was accomplished by this effort," reported Rear Admiral John Perry in January 1952.[5]

Before Christmas 1951, however, there was ample evidence that Perry's self-congratulatory estimate was far wide of the mark. About 500 heavy antiaircraft guns and nearly 2,000 automatic weapons in North Korea were taking a fearful toll of American aircraft, and the number of artillery pieces along the coast had increased so greatly that Gunfire Support Group ships could no longer remain close inshore during bombardment operations. And, on 27 November 1951, south of Pyongyang, communist

MiGs had attacked a flight of bombers from the carrier *Bonhomme Richard*, a signal of a new threat to the Navy pilots and of China's intent to contest the airspace over Korea's waist. Coupled with this more active defense of North Korean territory was the appearance of a sophisticated communist labor organization dedicated to the swift repair of damaged railroad tracks, bridges, and tunnels. "It was really astounding," Admiral Andrew Jackson recalled. "We would bomb a section of the railroad and take photographs before the end of the day, and the railroad would be cut in eight or ten or fifteen or twenty places. They would keep rails alongside, and then they had all this manpower, and they would come in at night and repair it overnight."[6]

The naval air effort in the Korean War was prodigious, with eighteen fleet carrier deployments to Korean waters and naval bombers dropping over 272,000 tons of bombs during 177,000 sorties, only 7,000 less than the fleet had dropped in World War II. The total ordnance expended in Korea exceeded the total for the earlier conflict by 74,000 tons, and the 272,000 tons of rockets fired exceeded the World War II total by 60,000 tons. The reasons for this were many. The more modern planes carried heavier bombloads, the average attack aircraft spent more time over its target, several strikes were launched daily, and the targets were close to the task force. Two related, persistent problems hindered Navy air operations in Korea, however. The first was the dreadful weather, and the second was the differing speeds of the Navy's attack planes and fighter planes. This greatly complicated the coordination of strike missions and probably accounted for a large fraction of the heavy losses of attack aircraft.

The Communists' agility in adjusting to the interdiction campaign discouraged the American high command. "To continue the rail attacks would be . . . to pit skilled pilots [and expensive aircraft] against . . . coolie laborers armed with pick and shovel," concluded an Air Force observer in early 1952. That January, Admiral Clark of the Carrier Force devised an alternative, Operation Package. To shut down the east coast railroad net, he selected five targets along the northeast coast against which he alternately hurled naval air attacks and naval gunfire bombardment by the battleships, cruisers, and destroyers of the East Coast Bombardment Force. In February, Clark concentrated on a railroad junction at Kowon, twenty-two miles northwest of Wŏnsan, a successful operation that disabled this vital facility for over a month. Each carrier in the 7th Fleet Carrier Force had to be replenished every three days, however, and bad weather over the Sea of Japan often impeded air operations. So, when attack aircraft were unavailable, patrol destroyers guided by radar buoys planted offshore took the communist repair gangs under fire.[7]

Also in January 1952, Clark launched Operation Derail against eleven rail targets, which were assigned to the battleships and heavy cruisers, although the extent of North Korean mining now forced the ships of East Coast Bombardment Force to keep well out to sea during bombardment operations. Operations Package and Derail cost the Communists dearly, but Clark soon discovered that the only way to completely disrupt a railroad was to attack it continuously, and he did not have enough ships or aircraft to do this on a large scale. The results of Air Force operations on the west coast were the source of just as much despair. The railroad track campaign had been no more effective than the earlier air strategies in isolating the Chinese armies on the front line from their logistic support. "The interdiction program was a failure," Clark reported. "It did not interdict. The Communists got the supplies through. . . . They had enough supplies to spare so that by the end of the war they could even launch an offensive."[8]

The JCS again completely reshuffled the Far Eastern command in May 1952, but the new leaders were soon overcome by the same sense of angry frustration that their predecessors had lived with for nearly a year. When General Eisenhower resigned his NATO command to run for the presidency, the JCS made the unfortunate mistake of sending Ridgway to Europe and replacing him in the Far East with General Mark Clark. Claiming that "there is nothing left to negotiate," Turner Joy retired from the Panmunjom truce talks. Vice Admiral Briscoe took command of the Far Eastern Naval Forces, and Vice Admiral J. J. Clark relieved Martin in command of the 7th Fleet.[9]

Ridgway had been committed to the interdiction campaign, but General Clark was less certain that this strategy was the best way for the mobile Carrier Force to support the front lines. An alternative to attacking North Korea's railroads was striking her industrial targets. Although there were few manufacturing centers in North Korea, the country did depend upon hydroelectric power produced by a complex of dams and generating plants that fed electricity not only to North Korea but also to China. MacArthur had wanted to attack the Yalu dams when the Chi-

Grumman F9F-2 Panther fighter after flying off the attack carrier *Philippine Sea* (CVA-47) and dropping a pair of 250-pound bombs on a target over North Korea. The Panther was the first Navy carrier-based jet fighter-bomber flown in combat during the Korean War.

nese crossed the river in November 1950, but the JCS suspected that this was a ploy to widen the war, and they banned bombing that violated Chinese airspace. This restriction was reiterated when the Kaesong truce talks started in July 1951, and Ridgway consistently opposed Martin's and Ofstie's plans to attack the Yalu installations. Confronted by a diplomatic and military stalemate upon his arrival in the theater in May 1952, General Clark found that a number of targets south of the Yalu were not restricted by the earlier directive, and he urged Washington to approve these attacks. With Truman's consent, the JCS agreed, while cautioning General Clark not to conduct air operations within twelve miles of the Soviet border or within Manchurian airspace.

Admiral Clark moved promptly to test the new strategy of bombing North Korea's industrial targets. In the first joint air operation of the Korean War, on 23 June 1952, the 7th Fleet

Carrier Force and the Air Force mounted a coordinated attack on the Suiho hydroelectric complex. Thirty-five AD Skyraiders and thirty F9F Panthers from the carriers *Princeton, Boxer,* and *Philippine Sea* bombed the Suiho plant, while Air Force F-86 Saberjets provided combat air cover for the attack aircraft. The Skyraiders dropped their bombs on the target while the Panthers suppressed the North Korean antiaircraft batteries; then the Saberjets came in and dropped their ordnance. None of the 200 Communist fighters based across the Yalu made any attempt to contest the airspace or to repulse the attack. During the next three days, Admiral Clark launched over 500 sorties against the Suiho system, while 700 Air Force sorties were recorded against this and twelve other installations. North Korea was held in the grip of a complete power blackout for two weeks, and the disruption was not totally relieved for another several months.

Less politically sensitive than hitting the Yalu dams was the question of bombing Pyongyang, which both Air Force General Weyland and Admiral Clark had proposed in May. Mark Clark approved the operation only with great reluctance, however, as a large POW camp was located on the outskirts of the North Korean capital. On 11 July, 1,254 sorties were flown against the city, and when darkness fell, Air Force B-29 bombers struck the remaining targets. After two more attacks in August, the UN commanders agreed that there were not enough targets left in or around Pyongyang to justify further operations.

The air campaign found lucrative industrial targets elsewhere. On 27 July 1952, naval aircraft from the carrier *Bonhomme Richard* hit a mine and mill at Sinbdok, and fighter-bombers from the *Princeton* struck a magnesite plant at Kilchu the next day. On 28 August, a special guided missile unit launched six F6F Hellcat drones from the carrier *Boxer,* followed by a section of AD Skyraiders. Using radio controls, the Skyraiders directed the Hellcat drones to a North Korean railroad bridge, and two of the drones were crashed into one of the spans and a nearby power plant. The first use of seaborne guided missiles in war, this operation illustrated another means by which ships might attack targets inshore. On 1 September, planes from the carriers *Boxer, Essex,* and *Princeton* hit the Aoji-dong oil refinery only eight miles from the Russian border. Despite the grim ferocity of these attacks, the new industrial campaign was no more effective than the earlier railroad offensive in convincing Moscow and Peking to agree to an armistice under Allied terms. The Communists were "unde-moralized," and they were continuing "to provide themselves with sufficient logistical support," at least enough to continue to mount local operations, General Clark reported on 29 September.[10]

After nearly two years of fighting, the war in Korea had come to a complete stalemate. The absolute superiority of American naval and land-based air forces was balanced by the marginal numerical inferiority of the UN ground forces and the proximity of secure Chinese and Russian bases to the central Korean battlefield. Along a front line that stretched from just south of Kosong on the Sea of Japan in the west to the valley of the "iron triangle" in the center of the peninsula and then south-east to the village of Panmunjom near the Yellow Sea, roughly 247,000 American, South Korean, and British Commonwealth troops faced a communist force of about 200,000 Chinese and 83,000 North Koreans. In reserve and supporting units, the Communists also held an edge in manpower. About 620,000 ene-my troops were behind the front lines, but the allies counted fewer than 450,000 men in reserve. Beyond the Korean peninsu-la, the Chinese and Americans paid reciprocal respect to one another's sanctuaries. The Americans did not enter Manchurian airspace, and the Communists did not attack the 7th Fleet Carri-er Force, which operated off Korea, or U.S. Air Force or Navy bases in Japan.

"The enemy had sufficient manpower . . . to block our offen-sives," General Clark now concluded, and any renewed drive into North Korea by the allies would require not only "lifting our self-imposed ban on attacks on the enemy sanctuary north of the Yalu" but also "more trained divisions and more supporting air and naval forces." Despite a herculean effort by the new CNO, Admiral William Fechteler, to send ships to the western Pacific, the need to support the new naval commitment to NATO had stretched thin fleet resources, still burdened by Truman's nig-gardly postwar defense policy. Throughout the summer, without any prospect of major reinforcements, both sides in Korea hard-ened their defenses while conducting small probing operations on the ground.[11]

Convinced that "military victory . . . is not feasible," Mark Clark nonetheless ordered Briscoe to stage a demonstration to "alarm" the enemy by landing an Army regimental combat team at Kojo on North Korea's east coast. A new joint amphibious task force was established under Admiral Clark, and an airborne regiment was withdrawn from the lines and prepared for an airdrop. On 12 October, the battleship *Iowa* led a Gunfire Support Group that shelled the Kojo beaches, while planes from 7th Fleet Carrier Force bombed and strafed nearby communist defenses. Three days later, the amphibious ships closed on the beaches, and assault troops boarded their landing craft and sped toward the landing zone. Suddenly they were ordered back. Many felt betrayed, and Briscoe later claimed that General Clark had "not decided until the troops were loaded that it would be a feint." The final, tragic hours off Kojo were marred by unexpectedly high winds and nasty seas that made it difficult to recover the landing craft, and several men lost their lives. The Kojo feint accomplished nothing. The enemy transferred a few troops to Kojo after the naval bombardment, but when the landing forces moved toward the beach, they were met by only desultory counterbattery fire. Reflecting on this lost opportunity, Briscoe maintained that the Kojo operation "would have broken the back of the Chinese Communists" because of the "concentration of communist forces near the battleline." Kojo symbolized the foolishness of Truman's stalemate strategy and the frustrations of fighting a bitter "no win war."[12]

The Communists adjourned the Panmunjom talks in October 1952 and mounted an offensive against the 1st Marine Division, then holding a defensive salient known as the Hook, which guarded the approach to Seoul. Admiral Clark assigned to the fast carriers close air support of the front lines, while the bombardment ships took up the slack by concentrating their fires against targets along North Korea's coast. In some of the bitterest fighting of the war, the Marines withstood these attacks, and by the end of the month the offensive had been repulsed. General Clark's frustration was vented in a 16 October report to the JCS proposing that they ask Truman to approve another amphibious landing in North Korea and to accept the need to widen the war by imposing a blockade of China. Not only did he want to bomb Manchuria, he also proposed to use atomic bombs against both China and North Korea. Clark's plan was treated with reserve in Washington. Truman had dropped out of the Democratic presidential primaries earlier in the year upon Eisenhower's announcement that he was a candidate, and when Clark's strategy reached the capital the elections were only two weeks away. The JCS expected the next president to adopt a new strategy in the Korean War; therefore, they tabled General Clark's proposals.

Truman's inconsistent handling of foreign affairs and military policy placed him so low in public esteem by 1952 that even those decisions that showed his spine somehow backfired. When General Clark authorized Admiral Clark to instruct the 7th Fleet to bomb the Suiho hydroelectric complex in June 1952, congressional Republicans embarrassed Secretary of Defense Robert Lovett by asking why Truman had not approved the attacks earlier in the war. Aware that he could not be reelected, Truman announced that he was retiring, and after a wild scramble for the nomination, the Democrats selected Illinois Governor Adlai Stevenson, a former Navy Department official, as their candidate. Stevenson could not decide during his campaign whether to defend Truman or distance himself from the administration. The Republicans chose General Eisenhower, who promised to "go to Korea" and seek a solution to the stalemated war, which was, by now, a divisive partisan issue. To influence the election, the Communists announced at Panmunjom on 8 October 1952 an "indefinite adjournment" of the truce talks and threatened to resume offensive operations. In the election, Eisenhower crushed Stevenson and carried Republican majorities into both houses of Congress in 1953.

Despite his campaign promise to end the war, Eisenhower took a full three months to decide that the only way to do this was to threaten to use nuclear weapons against North Korea and China. When Eisenhower visited Korea in late 1952, he pointedly ignored Syngman Rhee and spent his time with the battlefield commanders. "I stayed up all night arguing with him that in our first test of arms with communism we should win," General Clark recalled. "I proposed to do so by the use of my air and naval power, by hitting targets in Manchuria, North China, and knocking out the bridges over the Yalu." However, Eisenhower's first meeting with his National Security Council in January 1953 found him declaring that the United States "could not go on [fighting] the way we were indefinitely" in Korea and "should consider the use of tactical atomic weapons" to bring about an armistice. The idea of using nuclear weapons in Korea was not new, having been advocated by many Republicans since 1950, and MacArthur told Eisenhower soon after the elections that he too favored this step. To this groaning voice of Armageddon was added Admiral Radford's urging that the president begin "to think" about using nuclear weapons.[13]

The JCS had studied the use of nuclear weapons against China on several previous occasions and had always reached the conclusion that it would risk Russian intervention and a full-scale nuclear war. Truman's circle consistently refused to make this move. General Bradley, for example, pointed out that the NATO allies would balk, and General Collins argued that the Communists were so well entrenched in North Korea that they would probably "not be hurt" too badly by nearby nuclear explosions. There "were no good strategic targets within the confines of Korea," claimed General John Hull, an Army planner. Eisenhower, while admitting that the use of atomic bombs to end the Korean War might temporarily disrupt NATO and might provoke a violent Chinese reaction, nevertheless told his advisers that his "only real worry . . . was over the possibility of intervention by the Soviets."[14]

In spite of this strong talk, the Chinese apparently believed that Eisenhower's failure to launch an immediate offensive into North Korea indicated his determination to continue Truman's stalemate strategy and seek a negotiated truce. With this in mind, they launched their own offensive in the spring of 1953 to gain as much territory as possible before the war ended. The Soviets had provided their allies with hundreds of MiG fighters, and in March, General Clark was alerted to the upcoming offensive by their renewed activity over North Korea. The Communists also strengthened their defenses on North Korea's east coast, installing fire control radars and anchored ranging buoys to improve their coastal defense gunfire. Fearing that the enemy was about to attack the islands off Wŏnsan, Admiral Clark reinforced the blockade force and flung air strikes against communist concentrations on the peninsula. On 5 May 1953, the battleship *New Jersey* fired 115 rounds into the Hodo Pando complex, silencing these guns until the end of the month. After renewed enemy activity, the area was saturated on 17 June by the destroyers *Irwin*, *Rowan*, and *Henderson*, but the opposing batteries continued to return fire. A gunfire group consisting of the *New Jersey* and the cruisers *Bremerton* and *Manchester* returned to the waters off Hodo Pando on 11 July, fired 164 rounds over forty-eight hours, and finally silenced their opponents for the rest of the war. The East Coast Bombardment Force also increased its shelling of inshore targets, while continuing the frustrating campaign against the coastal railroads. For the 7th Fleet Carrier Force, attention turned in March back to the bombline and close ground sup-

port, although Admiral Clark's Cherokee strikes against preselected targets continued into the summer. And the West Coast
Bombardment Force, where British cruisers and destroyers operated, shelled enemy positions at Wolsa-ri, Sok To, and Ch'o-do.
All the while the UN commanders braced for the expected communist offensive.

After considerable gnashing of teeth, Eisenhower decided
on 20 May 1953 that atomic blackmail was the only way to end
the Korean War. That same day the reconstituted JCS, now led by
the new chairman, Admiral Radford, proposed "air and naval operations directly against China and Manchuria" and "a coordinated offensive to seize a position generally at the waist of Korea."
Secretary of State John Foster Dulles was at the time traveling in
India, and the next day he conveyed a veiled threat along this
line to Prime Minister Jawaharlal Nehru, who apparently relayed
it to Peking. Analogous warnings were privately passed along to
the communist delegation at the Panmunjom truce talks. The
Chinese may have been preparing for this moment, for at the
end of March Foreign Minister Chou En-lai had agreed to an unprecedented exchange of those sick and wounded POWs who
wanted to be repatriated. Two weeks after Eisenhower issued his
dire warning, the Communists accepted a compromise on the
entire POW issue, which they had previously rejected.

The communist powers agreed to a ceasefire on the condition that all their POWs be returned, but South Korea's Rhee rejected "any ceasefire which leaves our country divided. No matter
what arguments others may make, we are determined to unify our
fatherland with our own hands." To disrupt the talks he refused to
force North Korean POWs to return to Pyongyang's custody, and
in June he defied his American patrons by allowing 27,000 communist POWs to escape en masse from his camps. If the truce
talks collapsed now, warned the JCS, then Eisenhower should consent to the "extensive strategical and tactical use of atomic
bombs" against targets in China. Although both Peking and
Pyongyang were furious at Rhee's egregious violation of earlier
agreements, they were in no position to continue fighting. Their
economies had been shattered by the war, their ablest strategists
were wounded or dead, and they needed to consolidate their unpopular regimes. It was ironic that the sturdiest roadblock to a
truce at the last moment was not the communist alliance but
Rhee's government in Seoul. Eisenhower did not concern himself

with appeasing Seoul, however, and instructed his negotiator at Panmunjom to refer the POW issue to a powerless neutral commission. This face-saving compromise was accepted by the Chinese and North Koreans, who really had no alternative.

Eisenhower's nuclear diplomacy led to an armistice signed at Panmunjom on 27 July 1953. Korea was divided and scarred, but Seoul's elected, pro-American government had been saved. Americans were for good reasons greatly excited in 1953 that the Korean War was over, but their sense of relief was alloyed with anxiety. For reasons that were hard to grasp, the foreign policy of containment did not seem to be working. "Korea offers little evidence," observed Commander Samuel Stratton, that "stopping communism's expansive drive will in itself be enough to start the gradual break-up of Soviet power."[15]

Chapter Eighteen

The New Look and Massive Retaliation
1953–1957

President Eisenhower's military policy, which he called the New Look, rested on the assumption that the United States had to "achieve both security and solvency." Holding that "the foundation of military strength is economic strength," he asserted that "savings must be made without reductions of power." He was acutely aware of the short-term costs of sustaining a long-term foreign policy of containment, which was intended to wear down the Soviet Union and ultimately win the Cold War, although he agreed with the essential premises of Truman's foreign policy, accepted the objectives of containment, and supported the primacy of a Europe-first strategy implicit in the NATO alliance. However, he rebelled against waging limited wars, like Korea, on the Eurasian periphery against Soviet clients and proxies, and he considered the force levels fixed by NSC-68, Truman's 1950 rearmament program, and NATO's huge 1952 Lisbon Conference arms plan to be too costly. From $13 billion in 1950, on the eve of the Korean War, annual defense spending had grown to over $50 billion when Eisenhower took office. Partial demobilization in 1953 met some of his cost-cutting goals, but he still saw the Defense Department as the place in the federal budget "where the largest savings can be made." To flesh out the New Look, he directed the JCS in early 1953 to develop a military policy and grand strategy that avoided "the serious weakening of the economy . . . that may result from the cost of opposing the Soviet threat over a sustained period."

The JCS, not surprisingly, found their past "military plans and their implementation since 1950" to be "sound and adequate," cautioned against any reduction in post-Korea forces, and pointed out projected gaps in the current defense posture. "We continue to place our emphasis . . . on peripheral deployments overseas," the Army and Air Force complained, with the result that "our freedom of action is seriously curtailed." Realizing that this line would hardly satisfy Eisenhower, the JCS Chairman, Admiral Arthur Radford, devised a way around the impasse by proposing that Secretary of Defense Charles Wilson direct the chiefs to craft a strategy based on the assumption that "atomic weapons . . . will be used in military operations by U.S. forces engaged whenever it is of military advantage to do so." American defense policy "is based on the use of atomic weapons in a major war and is based on the use of such atomic weapons as would be militarily feasible and useful in a smaller war, if such a war should be forced upon us," he told Congress. "In other words, the smaller atomic weapons, the tactical weapons, have now become the conventional weapons."[1]

Radford believed that Truman's containment policy—coupled with Truman's unwillingness to use nuclear weapons in Korea—had resulted in the overcommitment of America's conventional forces. He was repulsed by the destructiveness of these weapons but felt that the Cold War had "entered a state where atomic weapons are now conventional." Moreover, Radford rejected the wholly Europe-first approach taken by Truman and drew no sharp distinction between the Soviet challenges in Europe and the Far East. "The Asian problems were basically caused by the same communists who were causing us difficulties in Europe," he insisted. He therefore welcomed a grand strategy of Massive Retaliation with nuclear weapons should the Soviets persist in trying to expand along the Eurasian periphery, but the practical result of this thinking was that, as Radford confessed, "after the [nuclear] deterrent forces were decided upon, almost every other activity had to give."[2]

The JCS were fully aware that the "increasing Soviet atomic capability will tend to diminish the deterrent effect of United States atomic power against peripheral aggression." Should the Soviets develop a credible arsenal of atomic or thermonuclear bombs, this "could create a condition of mutual deterrence in which both sides would be inhibited from initiating general war," a state of affairs allowing the Soviets to "pursue their ultimate objective of world domination through a succession of local aggressions." Inasmuch as no effective defense against incoming nuclear weapons was likely to be perfected, Eisenhower concluded tentatively that the only real chance to survive a nuclear exchange was to strike first. Massive Retaliation was not a recipe for a preventive first strike, but it provided for a preemptive attack. Nonetheless, the JCS gave Eisenhower little help as to how to identify an aggressive act of such magnitude that it warranted nuclear retaliation.[3]

Admiral Robert Carney, the new CNO, disagreed with Radford's extreme confidence in Massive Retaliation as a deterrent to Soviet aggression-by-proxy outside of Europe and remained convinced that powerful, forward-deployed air, sea, and ground forces would be necessary to parry Soviet thrusts in Asia or the Middle East. He even questioned whether nuclear weapons would be used to defend NATO unless all Europe was overrun. To Carney, it appeared unlikely that any president would order Massive Retaliation to respond to an ambiguous case of Soviet-backed aggression not directly tied to NATO, Japan, or the United States. Indeed, at the time and for decades thereafter, the NATO powers were not wholly convinced that the Americans really intended to use nuclear weapons to defend Europe. Reacting to Russia's new arsenal of atomic bombs, the NATO powers met at Lisbon in 1952 and agreed to establish a front-line army of nearly fifty divisions, and the Americans promised to maintain one or two carriers in the Mediterranean. Eisenhower, who negotiated this Lisbon Plan, understood that its ground force goals could not be met and so decided to depend "primarily upon a great capacity to retaliate, instantly, by means and at places of our choosing," instead of trying to match Soviet troop and air strength in central Europe.[4]

Carney's reservations about the New Look, which shifted a large fraction of the defense budget from the Navy and the Army to the Air Force, did not lead him to completely oppose Massive Retaliation, however. American forces should not "rush around plugging the dike" in regional conflicts like Korea, the Taiwan Straits, or Indochina, he declared, but instead should "take the rougher road." Many even understood this to "be suggesting a preventive war" using nuclear weapons against the Soviet Union. In spite of his reservations about the New Look, Carney foolishly passed up the chance to align himself with General Matthew Ridgway, the new Army chief of staff, who was vainly protesting manpower cuts imposed by the New Look. "Admiral Carney and General Ridgway were about to kick over the traces" just before the New Look was promulgated, Radford recorded, "but they did not." In sum, both Carney and Ridgway took equally parochial positions. Whereas Ridgway advanced the view that limited wars—conflicts in which the Army would take the lead—were the most likely future threat to American security, Carney saw in Massive Retaliation a means to justify Navy investments in heavy naval bombers, large carriers, and nuclear-tipped bombardment cruise and ballistic missiles, even though he disliked the New Look emphasis on the Air Force. The Navy simply wanted "a little bit of everything" with no "positive prescription for fighting any particular kind of war," claimed Air Force General Thomas White. For its part, the Air Force believed that the antidote was a preventive or preemptive first strike and argued that only by this means might the United States survive a nuclear war with the Soviets.[5]

Eisenhower's adoption of Massive Retaliation reinforced the thinking behind Admiral Sherman's earlier policy of developing the postwar Navy around large carrier task forces embarking heavy nuclear-capable aircraft. In line with the Europe-first orientation of Truman's early containment policy, Sherman had implemented a strategy that gave top priority to the Atlantic and Mediterranean theaters. Not even the 7th Fleet's demand for carriers during the Korean War had altered this approach. During the first year of that war, while eight out of fourteen heavy carriers were assigned to the Pacific Fleet, only about one-third of the total Navy was deployed in the entire Pacific theater. Sherman held the *Midway*-class heavy carriers in the Atlantic and Mediterranean and dedicated them to nuclear and conventional strike missions against the Soviet Union. Admiral William Fechteler had continued this strategy when he became CNO in 1952, advising the NATO powers that if war with the Soviet Union erupted, then the United States planned to shift at least three or four carriers and twenty-five other major warships from the Pacific to the Atlantic. It was on this understanding that the JCS included the carriers as part of the Strategic Striking Forces.

Fechteler's 1952 plan was to keep two carriers in the 7th Fleet and two forward-deployed with the 6th Fleet in the Mediterranean after the Korean War. The following year, however, Admiral Carney expressed concern that the withdrawal of so many carriers from the western Pacific would be "interpreted as a diminution of U.S. interests in defense of those areas." As a result, Carney decided in 1953 to leave three carriers in the 7th Fleet. Using a deployment-to-overhaul ratio of about 3 to 1, he persuaded Eisenhower to allow the Navy to maintain a total of fourteen or fifteen heavy carriers. In 1955, he justified his decision to station nine of fifteen carriers on the West Coast or in the Pacific theater on the grounds of a Swing Strategy. Under this formula, the Pacific Fleet carriers might be employed for limited war or presence to reassure allies in peacetime, but during a general war in Europe most of them would steam into the Atlantic to support NATO's retaliatory forces. A corollary of the Swing Strategy was that the Navy had to be ready to fight in either a conventional or nuclear environment. The Navy's Strategic War Plans Division, however, worried that the decision to station three carriers in the western Pacific "resulted in a poor disposition of the fleet to meet . . . commitments of a general war" in Europe. These continuing discussions led finally to a fairly settled strategy for the aircraft carriers. The 2nd Fleet at Norfolk and 6th Fleet in the Mediterranean would each include a heavy carrier strike force composed of two or three Forrestal-class or modernized Midway-class carriers. In the Pacific, only the 7th Fleet included an equivalent carrier air group of the same composition.[6]

Eisenhower's dedication to Massive Retaliation proved to be far less rigid than his doggedly noninterventionist foreign policy and his adherence to the principles of national solvency embodied in the New Look. The practical result of the New Look was to allot about 47 percent of the post–Korean War defense budget to the Air Force, about 29 percent to the Navy and Marines, and 22 percent to the Army. Unwilling to become involved in ground wars outside of Europe, Eisenhower felt uneasy with Massive Retaliation nevertheless, and had no serious plans to employ nuclear weapons in limited wars. He sought some sort of rapprochement with the Soviet Union through the vehicle of arms control. Moreover, in 1955 General Maxwell Taylor, who had just succeeded Ridgway as Army chief of staff, inaugurated a thinly veiled public assault on Massive Retaliation and the cutbacks in conventional forces dictated by the New Look. Because their B-52 bomber and intercontinental ballistic missile programs profited most from the New Look, however, Air Force generals strongly supported the continuance of this approach. Admiral Arleigh Burke, who relieved Carney as CNO in 1955, was an early supporter of Massive Retaliation, but he soon began to take a less rigid posture. Before this, however, he sought to enhance the Navy's role in delivering nuclear weapons by implementing a new carrier strategy and constructing a sea-launched ballistic missile force. His objective was to support the president's goal of erecting American forces able to hit Russia "from any point on the compass" with nuclear weapons.[7]

With the introduction of the B-52 bomber into the Strategic Air Command in 1955, Burke kicked off a campaign to eliminate the Swing Strategy and establish instead a strategic naval nuclear strike force in the Pacific. On 1 May 1956, he pointed out to the State Department "that Naval Forces . . . will be the primary source of U.S. strength in the Western Pacific, whereas in the European Theater, other elements of this and other nations' armed forces would most surely dominate." In the wake of the blow to Britain and France over Suez that year, however, the State Department resisted Burke's plan to withdraw one of the heavy carriers from the Atlantic and restore the 7th Fleet to three deployed carriers. Burke insisted that he needed one carrier in the western Pacific to defend South Korea and Japan and at least two carriers ready to conduct the general war operations of attacking Soviet ports, military installations, and naval bases in the Far East. Admiral Harry D. Felt, the commander in chief of the Pacific theater, was told in 1958 to incorporate into his war plans the assumption that the Pacific Fleet would possess all those ships not already dedicated to NATO during a general war. Burke then exploited the eruption of the second Taiwan Straits crisis in 1960 to persuade Eisenhower to authorize the stationing of a third heavy carrier with the 7th Fleet and assign it a nuclear strike mission. This, in effect, constituted a further erosion of the Europe-first strategy envisioned by Navy leaders at the onset of the Cold War.[8]

During the Korean War, the Navy had commissioned or recommissioned twenty-four aircraft carriers of all types, raising the number of flight decks in the fleet to thirty-nine. Admiral Sherman had reactivated nearly 300 other warships and auxiliaries to support the 7th Fleet in the Far East and to back up the new American commitment to NATO in the Mediterranean and North Atlantic. Ten of the reactivated *Essex*-class carriers were vet-

erans of World War II, but these ships were too small to handle a
large number of jet strike aircraft in peacetime. Following the
Korean War, many of the smaller carriers again went into mothballs because Admiral Sherman wanted a much larger carrier for
nuclear strike and conventional attack missions, and the *Essex*-
class carriers were to be dedicated to antisubmarine warfare. The
Essex was tested at sea in this role the following year, and shortly
thereafter she was redesignated as an antisubmarine warfare carrier, and during the decade, fifteen vessels of her class were converted to antisubmarine carriers. While understanding that, for
the present, Soviet submarines were dedicated to the coastal defense of Russian home territory, Sherman reckoned that one day
they would venture out into the Atlantic and Pacific and he wanted the Navy to be prepared for this. Believing that "the worst
place to protect a convoy is at the convoy," the CNO intended to
develop offensive, hunter-killer carrier task forces to obstruct the
Soviets from entering the larger oceans.

The capstone of Sherman's shipbuilding program was the
heavy, angled deck *Forrestal*-class carrier, and in 1952 the Navy
had persuaded Congress to agree to a plan to lay down one of
these ships every year for the next ten years. Sherman's shipbuilding plan was animated by the introduction of jet aircraft
into the Navy during the Korean War, when over 1,500 jets were
added to the Navy Department's inventory. These new aircraft
endowed the fleet with strengthened combat air patrols and offensive strike punch, but they also posed serious operational
problems. For one thing, to carry nuclear weapons, early jet attack aircraft had to be large and heavy, necessitating the installation of more powerful and rugged catapults, heavier arresting
gear on the flight decks, and more lift and capacity for the ships'
elevators. In addition, there was a new premium on safety. Propeller-driven aircraft landed on a carrier deck at about 75 miles
per hour, and commonplace barrier crashes on axial decks at this
speed were usually minor, seldom fatal. A jet aircraft approached
the carrier at 125 miles per hour, however, and when its tailhook
missed the deck arresting wires, the plane almost invariably penetrated the barriers, destroying aircraft and injuring or killing pilots and deckhands. In May 1951, at the suggestion of the British
Admiralty, an angled landing strip was painted on the flight deck
of the heavy carrier *Midway*. Tests showed that this scheme improved the arrangement of the aircraft on the deck and allowed

concurrent launching and recovering operations. In 1952, Admiral Fechteler sent the *Antietam* into a shipyard to be fitted with a real angled deck. By merely building the landing deck at a 10.5-degree angle with respect to the keel of the ship, safety was greatly increased for everyone involved in flight operations. Another British innovation, the mirror landing system, also improved the safety record of the air groups in the fleet.

The first class of carriers embodying these improvements were the *Forrestals*, the lead ship in the class having been approved by Defense Secretary Johnson a bare two weeks after the June 1950 outbreak of the Korean War. A scaled-down version of the canceled supercarrier *United States*, the 56,000-ton *Forrestal* was designed to handle the A3D Skywarrior heavy naval bomber. She was the first carrier with the space and facilities to store, maintain, and operate up to 100 jet aircraft. When she was ten months into construction, an angled deck was added, and steam catapults, another British innovation, were installed. She entered the fleet in October 1955. The *Forrestal*-class carriers were equipped with four steam catapults, as opposed to two on the *Essex*-class and three on the *Midway*-classes, allowing up to eight aircraft to be launched every sixty seconds. The *Forrestal* was the first of the twelve large postwar carriers to be commissioned, and the first to be designed from the keel up to launch, store, recover, and maintain jet aircraft. When she was commissioned, the carriers *Saratoga*, *Ranger*, and *Independence* were already under construction. Furthermore, Burke was pushing for eight more carriers to bring Navy levels to twelve *Forrestal*-class and three modernized *Midway*-class carriers, and he persuaded Congress to authorize the construction of the *Kitty Hawk* and, the following year, the *Constellation*.

The most important mission of the Navy's carriers in the 1950s was to deliver nuclear weapons against Soviet targets. During the Korean War, Sherman had deployed his *Essex*-class carriers to Asia and had rotated the larger *Midway*-class carriers into the Mediterranean. In an exercise in February 1951, the *Coral Sea* steamed into the Mediterranean carrying nonnuclear components for an atomic bomb. Soon, a flight of six twin-engine A-J Savages, the first naval jet bomber, and three P2V Neptunes flew from Bermuda to Port Lyautey, French Morocco, where they joined the carrier *Franklin D. Roosevelt*, which steamed to a launching station south of Greece. In February 1952, the first of the A-J Savage squadrons was assigned to the *Midway*-class carriers. The fear of storing nuclear weapons on board American warships was still profound. Therefore, if war erupted between Russia and the United States, it was Sherman's plan to ship the 5-ton Mk-3 airburst implosion bombs to Morocco in Navy transport aircraft. There they would be transferred to one of the 7th Fleet's heavy *Midway*-class carriers, which was to steam into the eastern Mediterranean and begin bombing operations against targets in southern Russia. Although the A-J Savage could lift the heaviest Mk-4 airburst atomic bombs, her top airspeed was only 385 knots, and this made her vulnerable to MiG interception. An alternative appeared during the Korean War with the arrival in the fleet of

The submarine *Grayback* (SSG-574) is about to launch a Regulus II cruise missile off the California coast in September 1958. Sea-launched cruise missiles of the 1950s were capable of delivering nuclear weapons against some larger coastal Soviet targets, but continuous mid-course corrections were necessary and the vehicle suffered from poor terminal guidance. The Navy installed deck rails on one nuclear- and four diesel-powered submarines so that they could launch the more primitive Regulus I bombardment cruise missile, which entered service in 1953, but Admiral Burke cancelled the Regulus II program five years later to pay for the costly Polaris ballistic missile program.

McDonell's F2H Banshee heavy fighter-bomber, but it soon was understood that the Banshee was inferior to the new Soviet MiG-15 fighters, so after tests with the Atlantic Fleet, the Banshee squadrons were transferred to the Pacific. The Banshee was never pitted against MiGs as a fighter, but the plane was successfully employed in Korea to conduct air strikes and to fly photo reconnaissance missions. She lacked flexibility as a strategic bomber, however, because she could only deliver the 1.5-ton Mk-8 atomic bomb, an inefficient impact device useful against only high-value hard military targets.

Hard upon Truman's rejection of the Navy's nuclear strategy, advances in atomic bomb designs undermined the Air Force's monopoly of these weapons. In 1948, the Bureau of Ordnance had helped design the Mk-8 bomb, which was armed with a time-delay fuse to allow a slow, propeller-driven aircraft to deliver it safely, and two years later the Navy supported an Army plan to develop a nuclear artillery shell from the Mk-8 design. This led to the 1956 AEC announcement that the Los Alamos Weapons Laboratory had perfected a 1.5-ton thermonuclear implosion bomb and proposed to build an even smaller device, the Mk-7. Armed with these small weapons, nuclear-capable naval bombers might one day operate not only from the large *Midway*-class carriers but also from the more numerous *Essex*-class decks. In the meantime, improved manufacturing methods led to the serial production of nuclear weapons starting in 1949 and a vastly increased stockpile, with the result that scarcity of nuclear weapons as a determinant of strategy soon vanished.

The Navy's basic strategic concept in the 1950s was to use its hunter-killer submarines and *Essex*-class antisubmarine carrier task forces, aided by the new SOSUS ocean-floor underwater hydrophone system, to advance ahead of the attack carriers into the eastern Mediterranean and up the Norwegian Sea. From stations off the Kola Peninsula and Greece, the *Forrestal*- and *Midway*-class carriers would launch heavy naval bombers carrying nuclear weapons against Soviet naval forces, bases, and associated maritime industries. The Navy had invested tremendous effort and expense after 1945 in heavy attack aircraft, but by the end of the Korean War none of these planes could conduct long-range, high-speed deliveries of the most lethal high-yield nuclear weapons. While the A-J Savage endowed the Navy with the semblance of a nuclear delivery capability, it was slow, too bulky for efficient deck handling, and so unreliable that it had to be grounded from June to October 1951 for "extensive safety modifications." The need for a naval jet bomber that might strike targets 1,500 miles from a carrier, thereby providing the fleet with the ability to reach almost every target in the Soviet Union, had moved aircraft designer Ed Heinemann of Douglas Aircraft to develop the 70,000-pound very heavy attack A3D Skywarrior. The first pure jet naval bomber, the Skywarrior could operate from either a *Midway*-class or a converted *Essex*-class carrier. She had her maiden flight in October 1952 and entered the fleet in large numbers four years later.[9]

In 1954, Rockwell offered an unsolicited proposal to the Navy Department to build the level-flight supersonic A-5 Vigilante, an all-weather, seaborne strategic bomber, which operated an inertial navigation system and a low-altitude bombing system that used a "loft" technique for delivering nuclear munitions. The Vigilante could make a supersonic treetop run at a target, pull into a loop, release an atomic bomb on target, and return to her carrier. In 1955, Admiral Burke asked Congress for funds for the Vigilante program, and these planes started to enter the fleet five years later.

The development of smaller atomic bombs and the successful hydrogen bomb program created a family of lightweight nuclear weapons suitable for both strategic and tactical applications. This lessened the Navy's need to continue building large numbers of heavy attack bombers late in the decade. At the same time, the failure of the interdiction campaign during the Korean War highlighted the need for a new generation of all-weather medium bombers equipped with superior radars to carry small nuclear weapons or deliver conventional ordnance with pinpoint accuracy. The Bureau of Aeronautics asked for proposals for such an aircraft in 1956, and Grumman responded with a design for the A-6 Intruder. Lack of funds—owing to the Polaris and antisubmarine warfare programs—hampered the development of this plane until 1960, when the first Intruders arrived at Oceana Naval Air Station.

The lethality of the Soviet-built MiGs in the Korean War and the vulnerability of the carriers to nuclear weapons drove the Navy to strengthen fleet air defenses in the 1950s. Admiral Sherman and his successors chose two avenues of approach to this problem: improved jet fighter interceptors and missile-armed surface escorts. Grumman converted the successful F9F Panther into the Navy's first supersonic jet fighter, the F9F-6 Cougar, which entered the fleet in November 1952. She was followed by the trouble-plagued F3H Demon, an unpopular plane that was first deployed in 1956. The Demon was intended to provide defense against a new generation of high-speed, high-altitude, nuclear-capable Soviet coastal bombers equipped with radar and armed with air-launched anti-ship missiles. As a countermeasure, the Navy's early jets were armed with unguided air-to-air rockets until the Sidewinder self-guided heat-seekers entered the fleet. Cougars flying off the *Randolph* in the Mediterranean were armed with the first operational Sidewinders in July 1956. The Demons were similarly armed shortly thereafter, and they also carried the longer range Sparrow air-to-air missile, a weapon that greatly increased the distance between the air battle and the carrier task force. However, the Navy's finest early jet fighter was the high powered F8U Crusader, a plane that first took off on 25 March 1955. A supersonic fighter equipped with guns and missiles, she was a radical change from the slower and more cumbersome aircraft that fought the Korean War. A contract was quickly let and deliveries to the Navy began in 1957, but by this time Admiral Burke was pressing for yet another fighter.

In cooperation with McDonnell Aircraft, in 1953, the Bureau of Aeronautics began to develop the F4H Phantom, the first fighter to be armed only with missiles, and her maiden flight took place on 27 March 1958. Capable of Mach 2.2 speed, the Phantom represented a decision by the bureau to revert to the prewar practice of flying two-man fighters with a pilot and a radio intercept officer. Although the Crusader had better handling characteristics than the Phantom, the new Deputy CNO for air, Vice Admiral Robert Pirie, believed in "twin-engine aircraft on our carriers because of the likelihood that in case of trouble the pilot might bring a twin-engine aircraft home, while a single-engine aircraft pilot would probably have to eject and lose an aircraft." The sleek Phantom was so promising that Burke agreed to serial production. Deliveries started to arrive three years later, and she became the Navy's workhorse in the 1960s, although the early versions had their share of problems. The Phantom was supposed to loiter at low speed over the task force, but she used so much fuel to climb at high speed that she barely had enough left to descend and refuel. Therefore, in 1957, the Navy turned the slow, long-range S-2 Tracker into a combat air patrol fighter, thus freeing the Phantom for purely offensive operations. Thus arose the need for the even heavier fleet air defense Douglas F6D Missileer, a slow, sluggish plane designed to carry the long-range Eagle standoff air-to-air missile. The concept of a slow fighter was unpopular, however, and traditionalists prevailed on Secretary of Defense Thomas Gates to cancel the airframe part of the Missileer contract in December 1960.[10]

The second major postwar fleet air defense countermeasure had originated with Project Bumblebee late in World War II and evolved into the very costly, mostly unsuccessful first generation missile-armed surface escort program. The missile-bearing escort ship was to be charged with providing close-in, second-line protection for the nuclear attack carrier task force. The invention of the transistor shortly after the war allowed electrical engineers to reduce considerably the relative size of air search radars and associated computer equipment, thus allowing the Navy to install systems of unprecedented, but still primitive, processing capability in surface escorts. Because these new cruiser and destroyer radars might also be used to direct fighters toward approaching enemy aircraft, the need for outlying radar picket destroyers diminished, and they were phased out of the task force formations after 1960. The new radars' second function was to support a family of missiles designed to enhance the defense of the heavy carrier. The small, rocket-powered, supersonic Terrier surface-to-air missile, which had a range of about twenty miles, later extended to forty, was developed for destroyers. The converted cruiser *Boston* carrying a Terrier battery was recommissioned in November 1955 and the cruiser *Canberra* followed the next year. Burke also arranged for six older 11,000-ton *Cleveland*-class cruisers to be recommissioned as austere missile escorts armed with Terrier and Talos launchers. Capable of delivering either a small nuclear device or conventional explosives, the Terrier entered the fleet in large numbers by 1960, and the larger ramjet, supersonic Talos surface-to-air missile was introduced that year as well. Armed with either nuclear or conventional ordnance, the Talos had a range of 50 to 100 miles and was installed only in cruisers or frigates. Ships as small as destroyer escorts, however, could launch the rocket-powered, supersonic Tartar, a surface-to-air missile with a range of about ten to twenty miles.

To defend the *Forrestal*-class carriers against air-launched missiles, Burke persuaded Congress to authorize the construction of nine 7,800-ton *Leahy*-class guided missile destroyers and to arm them with the Terrier missile. The lead ship in this class, wholly devoted to fleet air defense, entered the fleet in 1962, but these heavy escorts paid a price in their gunnery, and future cruisers, it seemed, would be incapable of independent action inasmuch as they were being designed solely to protect the carriers. Despite immense expenditures, however, various defects so hounded these surface-to-air missiles that as late as 1965 none of them were truly adequate for fleet air defense.

The competing needs of building missile-bearing and antisubmarine escorts profoundly influenced the development of postwar destroyers. Before the Korean War, Congress had authorized the construction of four large 4,855-ton *Mitscher*-class destroyers, the only all-gun, frigate-type escort the Navy ever built. Originally intended as high-speed escorts with strong antiaircraft defenses, these ships were also armed with guided torpedoes, the Alpha automatic rocket launcher, and depth-charge racks, and were dedicated in the 1950s to antisubmarine operations in the North Atlantic as part of a hunter-killer antisubmarine task force built around an *Essex*-class carrier. They were also capable of providing offshore gunfire support for amphibious operations. At the same time, the Navy converted twenty-four *Gearing*-class destroyers into radar pickets by removing their torpedo tubes and installing an air search radar. Concern about the menace of Soviet air-launched nuclear-tipped missiles after the Korean War led to the development of a new task force formation that provided for greater ship separation but still required a large number of antisubmarine escorts, and to fill this need between 1954 and 1957 thirteen small, austere 1,914-ton *Dealey*-class destroyers entered the fleet to be used exclusively for antisubmarine operations.

The *Forrest Sherman*-class destroyers, laid down from 1953 to 1957, evolved from the earlier experimental *Mitscher*-class. Owing to the need for fleet air defense, these general-purpose destroyers were armed with 5-inch and 3-inch guns and provided excellent close-in conventional antiaircraft defenses. In 1954, however, Admiral Carney approved a Long-Range Shipbuilding Plan encompassing the idea that the Navy abandon its traditional multipurpose destroyer and build instead three specialized types: an antiair missile–bearing destroyer, an antisubmarine destroyer, and an austere ocean escort. The outcome was a large escort program begun in 1956 with congressional approval to lay down nineteen cruiser and destroyer missile escorts within two years. The *Forrest Sherman*-class was succeeded after 1957 by the construction of the first of eighteen missile-armed *Charles F. Adams*-class destroyers, vessels that entered the fleet from 1960 to 1964. Designed in 1956, the first of ten gun and Terrier missile-bearing *Coontz*-class 5,800-ton frigates was laid down the following year. At the same time, Burke did not neglect the antisubmarine forces, and he had two 2,650-ton *Bronstein*-class destroyers converted to carry DASH drone antisubmarine helicopters, improved sonar systems, and ASROC antisubmarine missile launchers. The *Bronsteins* were clearly a transitional measure that masked the growing differences between air defense and antisubmarine escorts.

The need for missile-bearing screening ships for the heavy attack carriers conflicted with demands for effective antisubmarine escorts to defend troop transports and cargo convoys. Although the Soviets maintained a very large fleet of submarines after World War II—including a number of captured German Type XXI submarines—most of these were old, slow boats dedicated to coastal defense. Moreover, the carrier task forces enjoyed such a significant advantage in speed that the Russian diesel submarine appeared to pose little threat to the American formations. On the other hand, coastal submarines deployed to protect Russia's "blue belts" were intended to interfere with carrier movements within range of her ports. Also, the U.S. Navy knew that the advent of nuclear-powered submarines would change this equation, and the CIA estimated in 1955 that the Soviets intended to build more than 100 attack submarines over the next few years and planned to send them against NATO's sea lines of communication.

Here again, tension arose between the advocates of offensive, hunter-killer antisubmarine operations and those who propounded the virtues of defensive convoy escorts. Unwilling to expect that code breaking would provide a decisive edge, as many imagined it had in World War II, the Navy was left with no other means of detecting a hostile submarine at long range, so Admiral Sherman ordered the development of a large system of passive ocean-floor hydrophones, SOSUS, which was designed to locate submarines at a distance—in its early version within a radius of about fifty miles or less—that varied proportionate to the noise they produced, local oceanographic conditions, and the speed and memory of the associated signal processing computers. Under a project codenamed Caesar, the Navy began to install hydrophones on the continental shelf off the East Coast in 1950, work that was completed four years later. SOSUS cables and hydrophones, separated by intervals of five to fifteen miles, were also laid off Denmark, Iceland, Norway, the North Cape, Italy, Spain, Turkey, and around the British Isles by the end of the decade. SOSUS acoustic networks were established on selected segments of the continental shelf on the Pacific Coast, Hawaii, the Aleutians, Korea, Japan, and the Philippine Islands in the 1960s. Soon after the Soviets had sent their attack submarines to Cuba during the 1962 missile crisis, the Navy placed a SOSUS array between Bear Island and Norway at the edge of the Barents Sea and another parallel to the Kamchatka Peninsula.

Navy planners in the 1950s had identified SOSUS as the third line of defense against Soviet submarines, the first being attack submarine and hunter-killer carrier sweeps into the Norwegian Sea and against the Kola Peninsula and into the eastern Mediterranean, the second being followup antisubmarine task force sweeps against enemy submarines that escaped. The weakness of the SOSUS system was, however, that considerable time elapsed between the moment it acquired an ocean sound signal and the moment the computers processed it and fixed the position of the opposing submarine. Prosecuting contacts originated by the SOSUS hydrophones required a large number of land-based WV-2 Warning Stars and P-2 Neptune patrol planes operating long-range radars on barrier patrols and, eventually, a complex supporting air-dropped sonobuoy system. The SOSUS network was designed to provide sufficient warning of Soviet submarine movements such that American antisubmarine forces might be deployed to intercept and attack them. One product of this enormous investment was Admiral Burke's 1955 decision to concentrate on the development of offensive antisubmarine weapons, ships, and locating systems and to abandon for the most part the older convoy and escort strategy. An existing shortage of P-2 Neptunes had created a gap in the air coverage of the North Atlantic, however, and Burke found that he could fill this only by assigning it to the antisubmarine hunter-killer *Essex*-class carriers and so reduce their availability for offensive tasks. The appearance in the fleet of large numbers of Lockheed P-3 Orion long-range patrol planes eventually closed this mid-Atlantic air gap and permitted Burke a few years later to reassign these carriers to offensive antisubmarine operations and screening duty with the heavy attack carriers.

Sustaining these carrier-based programs was not an easy task for either Admiral Carney or Admiral Burke, both of whom confronted persistent opposition to Navy shipbuilding plans from the Army and Air Force. General Taylor admitted that the carrier task force had proven useful during the Lebanon crisis of 1958 and that the defense of Taiwan was "largely an air and naval operation," but the Army's chief of staff asserted that larger limited wars "related to sustained combat on the ground, which is an Army task," for which the Army was unprepared. "We have an ample number of carriers," Taylor told Congress. The Navy also had to contend with sophists like Dr. Herbert York, the Pentagon's eccentric research director, who argued that in a war with "a highly sophisticated enemy like Russia, they [the carriers] are going to be blown up." In the end, Secretary of Defense Neil McElroy supported the Navy's assessment and announced in 1959 that the carrier task forces provided "a very effective limited warfare capability in places where overflight rights for aircraft are often unattainable and in places where landing fields often do not exist."[11]

In spite of this new construction, the overall size of the postwar Navy diminished after the Korean armistice owing to the cutback in conventional forces dictated by the New Look, the escalating cost of new aircraft, radars, and missiles, and the burgeoning expense of the nuclear submarine programs. From slightly over 1,000 warships of all types in 1953, the fleet shrank to 967 vessels four years later, and to just over 800 by the end of the decade. To slow this trend, Burke introduced the imaginative FRAM warship modernization program, which extended the shiplife of over 250 World War II–vintage ships by about five to eight years each. Perversely, the cost of the FRAM program forced Burke to divert even more funds away from new cruiser, destroyer, and auxiliary shipbuilding accounts. In 1957, the Navy's Long-Range Objective Group warned Burke that the root of the problem lay with the acceptance of a grand strategy of Massive Retaliation, an argument that moved the admiral to renew his search for an alternative strategy to meet the challenge of a fast-approaching era of mutual nuclear deterrence.

Chapter Nineteen
Enforcing Containment in Asia
1953–1956

Truman's decision to defend South Korea and Taiwan in 1950 extended the containment policy to the Far East, but it fell to Eisenhower to decide how to prevent Moscow from advancing elsewhere in Asia. FDR had probably intended to prevent the French from returning to Indochina after World War II, but Truman revised this hopeless policy and only a few months after the Japanese surrendered in September 1945, the French Army marched back into Hanoi. There they found that Ho Chi Minh, the founder of the Vietnamese Communist Party, had already proclaimed the establishment of an independent Vietnam. Ho quarreled with the French, withdrew to the countryside, and launched a guerrilla campaign with his Vietminh Army. Supported by Russia and China, the Vietminh offensive escalated in ferocity to a pitch that moved John K. Melby of the State Department to warn in 1950 that the French were "moving into a debacle which neither" France nor the United States "can afford." Truman agreed that year to support the French anti-Vietminh campaign in Indochina as part of a broader effort to contain communist expansion in the Far East, and the French military position soon improved under the inspiring leadership of General de Lattre de Tassigny.

The harsh but successful de Lattre offensive caused Army Lieutenant General John O'Daniel, who visited Vietnam in October 1953, to report "clear indications of real military progress by

French Union Forces" within the past six months. Admiral Felix Stump, the commander in chief of the Pacific Fleet, was less certain. Pointing to the lack of Vietnamese support for the French, he predicted that the French would lose unless they captured the psychological initiative from the Vietminh. The Vietminh had crossed into northern Laos to link arms with the small communist Pathet Lao Army earlier in the year, so General Henri Navarre, France's new commanding general, placed paratroopers in the valley of Dien Bien Phu in northwest Tonkin in November to obstruct the Communists' supply lines. He intended to support Dien Bien Phu by means of an airlift, but the valley contained only one airstrip and the Vietminh moved artillery into the surrounding hills and brought it under fire. By March 1954, roughly one French division was surrounded by a Vietminh army four times its size.[1]

The first call for American intervention in Indochina came from General Paul Ely, the French chief of staff, who arrived in Washington in late March 1954 to ask that planes be transferred to the French air forces in Indochina. He found both Eisenhower and Secretary of State Dulles worried not only about a French defeat at Dien Bien Phu, but also about Chinese intervention in Vietnam. At the time, Admiral Radford, the JCS chairman, had in hand a plan devised by a joint military committee in Saigon for the 7th Fleet Carrier Force and B-29 bombers from Clark Air Base in the Philippines to bomb the Vietminh emplacements around Dien Bien Phu. This plan included the possible use of nuclear weapons in a tactical role, something for which they had been neither designed nor tested. Radford, who was vigorously advocating intervention, believed that the "Chinese Communists engaging the French in Indochina have been using similar tactics" to those employed in Korea, an analogy that eluded others. The JCS were sharply divided over the merits of his plan, however. Air Force General Nathan Twining agreed to it as a last resort, but the Army's General Ridgway, who distrusted the French, cited the poor record of the American tactical air forces in Korea as evidence that Radford's strategy would fail. He stood ruggedly opposed to intervention. Admiral Carney, the CNO, agreed with most of Ridgway's assessment.[2]

The issue came to a head on 4 April, when French Premier Joseph Laniel formally asked Eisenhower to permit "immediate armed intervention by US carrier aircraft at Dien Bien Phu . . . to save the situation." Although he was prepared to act, Carney opposed direct American intervention unless the Chinese entered the Indochina War, and he had already armed himself with a detailed estimate of the futility of the French military position. Over the past several months, Carney had rotated several carriers in and out of the Tonkin Gulf, and on his orders they conducted reconnaissance flights over Dien Bien Phu to identify Vietminh artillery positions and lines of supply. By this time, the Navy was already providing the French with substantial assistance. Ninety-five amphibious landing craft had been transferred to the French Navy, and a large number of armored river craft had been provided under the Mutual Defense Assistance Act. In addition, the carrier *Belleau Wood* had been lent to the French fleet in 1951; recommissioned the *Bois Belleau*, she reached Saigon on 30 April 1954.[3]

Although Carney opposed intervention, he instructed Vice Admiral William Philipps in January 1954 to establish the Fair Weather Task Force built around the carrier *Wasp* and told him to prepare to enter the Tonkin Gulf on short notice. On 19 March, Carney directed Philipps to steam into the Gulf, put his task force on a twelve-hour alert, and ready his air groups to launch strikes against the Vietminh's positions around Dien Bien Phu. Despite these precautions, Carney knew that a few bombing runs on well-entrenched troops would not silence the Vietminh, and he steadfastly resisted the use of nuclear weapons to salvage the French colonial empire in Southeast Asia. Vice Admiral Arthur C. Davis, who was in charge of aid to the French, put the case in stronger terms, insinuating that the JCS were in danger of being "self-duped" by Radford "into believing the possibility of partial involvement" in the Indochina War. Asserting that "one cannot go over Niagara Falls in a barrel only slightly," he agreed with Carney's discouraging assessment that "naval and air units only" would not defeat the Vietminh at Dien Bien Phu. "Involvement of United States forces in the Indochina War should be avoided at all costs," Davis concluded.[4]

Eisenhower was shrewdly ambiguous about his plans. At a 7 April press conference, he explained his faith in the domino theory, a concept that held that if Vietnam came under communist rule, then so too would the rest of Indochina, thereby increasing the threat to neighboring Thailand, Burma, Malaysia, Indonesia, and the Philippines. Later portrayed as a fanciful anticommunist bogey, the domino theory in fact rested upon a realistic appraisal of Vietnamese imperialism that had shaped the early modern history of Southeast Asia. Mindful of this long-term peril, Eisenhower was also aware that he could not appear to abandon France in her hour of need. Sherman Adams, the White House chief of staff, observed that the president wanted to help the French at Dien Bien Phu in large part "because he and Dulles were anxious to win the French over to the proposed European Defense Community treaty" under which West Germany was to enter NATO and be rearmed.[5]

Washington was in the grip of a crisis over Dien Bien Phu when Eisenhower directed Dulles to convene a meeting between Radford and congressional leaders at the State Department on 3 April to go over the joint military committee's plan. Senate Majority Leader Lyndon Johnson resisted Dulles' request for advance approval from Congress authorizing the president to order naval and air forces in Indochina to attack the Communists at Dien Bien Phu. Johnson demanded that, as a condition of American assistance, the French first had to agree to shut down their colonial empire and the British had to obligate themselves to fight alongside the Americans in Southeast Asia. When Dulles flew to London to sound out the British, he was amazed that neither Prime Minister Churchill nor Foreign Secretary Anthony Eden was behind intervention. Even Eisenhower quietly agonized over Eden's "woeful unawareness" of the situation at Dien Bien Phu. On the 26th, however, he admitted at long last to congressional leaders that intervening unilaterally to save France in Indochina would be a "tragic error." A few days earlier, the defenders of Dien Bien Phu were blanketed by a monsoon and trapped in a sea of mud, and on 1 May, the Vietminh launched its final, violent offensive. The French surrendered six days later.[6]

As an alternative to Western intervention, Eden had already persuaded the Russians to help organize and co-chair a conference of all parties to the Indochina War. This conference had convened in Geneva earlier in the year. After the French Army was crushed at Dien Bien Phu, Eisenhower insisted that Paris negotiate an armistice with the Vietminh at Geneva. To keep the Communists uncertain about his plans, however, he ordered Carney to convene a meeting in June with French, British, and Australian military representatives at the Pentagon, where the use of American forces to resurrect the French position in Indochina was discussed. This course of action ran directly counter to the trend of public opinion in the United States and France, and the utter futility of the Pentagon talks became evident on 30 June when a new French premier, Pierre Mendès-France, took office and promised to end the war within a month. When Mendès-France agreed to arrange for the defeat of the European Defense Community Treaty in the French Chamber of Deputies, the Russians reciprocated by levering the Vietnamese Communists into accepting a compromise to settle the Indochina War. Signed on 20 July 1954, the Geneva Accords signaled the end of the French colonial empire in Southeast Asia by dividing Indochina into the independent nations of Cambodia, Laos, and Vietnam. In Vietnam, a thin demilitarized zone was established along the 17th parallel. The Vietminh promised to withdraw north of this line, while the French and their Vietnamese clients were obliged to retire to the south of it. Although the Geneva Accords called for the reunification of Vietnam on the basis of free nationwide elections in 1956, none of the participants intended to honor this impractical provision and all effectively agreed to the partition of the country.

Once the ink was dry on the Geneva Accords, Eisenhower set out to establish a stable anticommunist government in South Vietnam under Emperor Bao Dai, a sometime French puppet. General J. Lawton Collins, the former Army chief of staff, flew to Saigon to implement a large-scale military assistance program, and Dulles asked Congress to aid Bao Dai's regime. While the armies marched north and south across the demilitarized zone, tens of thousands of Vietnamese who had associated themselves and their futures with France's cause were stranded in North Vietnam. To transport these mostly Roman Catholic families to the south, Carney sent Rear Admiral Lorenzo Sabin's 7th Fleet Amphibious Force into the Gulf of Tonkin, and this assemblage of landing ships, transports, and other vessels shuttled nearly 300,000 refugees from Haiphong to Saigon. Operation Passage to Freedom also liberated a huge quantity of guns, vehicles, and other military stores from French depots in Hanoi, cargo that was shipped to Saigon and used to equip the new South Vietnamese Army. By the time this operation ended in May 1955, Ngo Dinh Diem, a young, wily nationalist, had overthrown

Emperor Bao Dai and had become South Vietnam's new president. Later that year, during a visit to Washington, he signed a mutual security pact with the United States.

On 12 January 1954, before Dien Bien Phu fell, Dulles had worried aloud that a Western collapse in Southeast Asia would have "grave consequences which might not be confined to Indochina." The Indochina War also demonstrated that Eisenhower's views on American strategy in Asia were not settled. In a televised speech on 2 February 1953, he had declared that he would not accept "a posture of paralyzed tension" in the Far East, but at the same time he admitted privately that dislodging the Chinese communist regime in Peking was not possible. As part of his multifaceted attempt to coerce the Chinese to agree to end the Korean War, Eisenhower had increased military aid to the government of Chiang Kai-shek in Taipei in 1953 and publicly instructed the 7th Fleet not to "prevent" an invasion of the mainland by the Nationalist armies on Taiwan—an improbable move, given the frailty of Chiang's regime. As an added step, Eisenhower persuaded the aging Chinese tyrant to deploy one of his few fighting divisions to the Tachens, offshore islands about 200 miles above Taiwan's northern tip that the Nationalists still controlled. The Nationalists also established garrisons on Matsu and Quemoy islands situated in the Taiwan Strait separating Taiwan and mainland China.[7]

The Nationalist army division was still in the Tachens when, in August 1954, Dulles flew to Manila to announce with some reluctance the formation of the Southeast Asia Treaty Organization. SEATO was designed to check the spread of Soviet and Chinese influence in the region, and Peking responded that month by declaring its intention to invade the Tachen Islands. This thoroughly alarmed Admiral Carney, who sent a 7th Fleet task force to visit the Tachens on 19 August, but the gesture was ineffective. One week later, Chinese commandoes raided Quemoy. Air attacks and bombardment by the mainland batteries against the offshore islands started on 3 September, and Peking announced that this was a prelude to an invasion of the Tachens. Carney now dispatched another task force into the Taiwan Straits, but Eisenhower ordered that these ships not take the Chinese batteries under fire. Uniquely inept, the Taiwan Navy shortly thereafter lost the destroyer *Tai Ping* to a brilliant sortie by a Chinese motor torpedo boat squadron.

The Navy's first nuclear-powered escort, the destroyer *Bainbridge.*

Between August 1954 and May 1955, ships of the U.S. Navy's Operation Passage to Freedom transported over 300,000 Vietnamese civilians and soldiers, munitions, and military supplies from the port of Haiphong in North Vietnam to South Vietnam under the terms of the Geneva Accords on Indochina.

Grasping at a fading hope, Chiang begged Eisenhower to allow the 7th Fleet to shell the mainland, and Admiral Felix Stump, the commander in chief of the Pacific Fleet, endorsed this plan. Restrained as usual, Eisenhower scoffed at Chinese Premier Chou En-lai's contention that China would soon liberate Taiwan, but at the same time he ignored Carney's proposal that Chiang be "unleashed" and permitted to attack the mainland, and the White House sent word to Chiang that Eisenhower wanted all Nationalist raids on the mainland to be "suspended." He also vetoed Stump's plan to send American naval attack aircraft against the onshore batteries. He did, however, agree to Radford's proposal to keep two carrier task forces in the area and on alert, and the White House issued a public warning to Peking that an attack on Taiwan "would have to run over the 7th Fleet."[8]

To wriggle out of the crisis, Eisenhower instructed Chiang to back down and withdraw his troops from the Tachens, and in return he promised that the 7th Fleet would defend Quemoy and Matsu. To legitimize American deterrence of a Chinese offensive, Dulles hastened negotiations on a mutual defense treaty with Taipei, which was signed on 2 December, and early the following year Congress passed the Formosa Resolution, which authorized the president to defend Chiang's regime but did not address Taiwan's claim to the offshore islands. The Chinese response was to resume bombarding the Tachens on 10 January 1955. Eight days later they occupied Yikiang, a small island in the Tachens within gun range of China's mainland, and boldly announced that this was the first step in the campaign to recover Taiwan. Yikiang was "of little or no military value," Eisenhower said, and he calmly ignored its loss. Reassured by the American guarantee of Taiwan, Chiang now agreed to withdraw his forces from the exposed islands, and Eisenhower told Carney to have Vice Admiral Alfred Pride's 7th Fleet evacuate Chiang's defenders from the Tachens. Beginning on 6 February, Pride personally supervised a four-day evacuation of 27,000 troops and over 8,500 tons of equipment from the Tachens, an operation that was covered by 7th Fleet aircraft. Just after this withdrawal, however, Peking broadcast more threats, making it appear as though Eisenhower's attempt to reach an accommodation over the offshore islands had failed and moving him to speculate offhandedly during a March press conference that war with China might be "only weeks away."[9]

Carney, traveling in the Far East when this statement was published, failed entirely to discern the difference between Eisenhower's belligerent public posturing and his private resolution not to allow a minor issue to lead to war with China. The basic question, according to Sherman Adams, was "whether the United States should defend the islands of Quemoy and Matsu from a threatened invasion," and he understood that "Eisenhower had no desire to provoke a war with China unless Formosa itself was in jeopardy." Carney, insensitive to this distinction, met with a few reporters on 24 March for a confidential briefing, during which he predicted that should the attacks persist, the JCS would propose to use nuclear weapons against China. One journalist published these comments, which provoked the president to write in his diary that "hostilities are not so imminent" as Carney believed. Eisenhower reacted to Carney's remarks "with irritation bordering on despair," Adams recorded. "I have become accustomed to the fact that most of the calamities that we anticipate never really occur," the president observed.

When Dulles reported from Taipei that there was "an even chance" that American forces would have to fight, and Radford advocated air strikes against Chinese airfields and a warning to Peking and Moscow that the United States would use nuclear weapons to defend Quemoy and Matsu, Eisenhower swung into action. He rejected the air strikes, but at a press conference declared that nuclear weapons "can be used on strictly military targets . . . just exactly as you would use a bullet." At long last Peking read the signal, soon ended the bombardment of Quemoy and Matsu, and appealed to Washington for reduced tension in the area. At the Bandung Conference of neutral, nonaligned Asian and African states, Chou En-lai suggested talks in Geneva between China and the United States to wind down the Tachens affair. These meetings produced no overall settlement to the problem of Taiwan but did allow both sides to back down and save face at the same time.[10]

Eisenhower crafted an equally artful policy to deal with two willful NATO allies during the 1956 Suez crisis. Humiliated by Israel during her war for independence in 1948 and 1949, the Egyptian Army overthrew King Farouk three years later and brought to power Colonel Gamal Abdel Nasser, a spellbinding spokesman for anti-imperialism and Arab nationalism who dedicated his regime to the conquest of Israel and tried to exploit the Cold War to this end. This effectively ended Britain's long-time dominance of Egypt and put at risk her long-standing influence in the Middle East and Africa. Dulles wanted to organize an anti-Soviet coalition of Arab states to prevent Moscow from capitalizing on the decline of Anglo-French influence in the Middle East, but he found in 1953 that "many of the Arab League countries are so engrossed in their [regional] quarrels . . . that they pay little heed to the menace of Soviet communism." There was a "vague desire to have a collective security system" in the area, but "no such system can be imposed from without." Nasser wanted the United States and Britain to finance his major economic development project, the Aswan Dam, and to agree to Egypt's domination of neighboring Sudan, but in September 1955 both Washington and London withdrew their support for the dam and refused to sell arms to Egypt, so he turned to the Soviets for assistance. Khrushchev promised to construct the dam and also backed Nasser's call for pan-Arab unity against Israel, supplying Czech weapons and Soviet advisers to the Egyptian Army.[11]

Anthony Eden, who succeeded Churchill as Britain's prime minister in 1955, was embroiled with Egypt in disputes over control of the Suez Canal and the status of the Sudan. Finally in June 1956, he agreed to withdraw the British Army from Egyptian territory, but Nasser shocked London only six weeks later with the announcement that Egypt was nationalizing the canal. Without Suez, Eden reckoned, Britain would no longer rank among the great powers. At the same time, Nasser's call for Arab nationalism frightened the French, who faced an Egyptian-supported insurgency in Algeria. For their part, the Israelis were now concerned that Soviet military assistance might provide Egypt with the means to overrun their small country. Dulles was in London on 2 August when he warned Eisenhower that Eden seemed likely to order the Anglo-French expeditionary force then assembling in the Mediterranean to "move into the Canal area with force," and the next day British, French, and Israeli envoys met secretly in Paris and signed a military alliance, unbeknownst to the Americans. Their plan was for the Israelis to attack Egypt, cross onto the Sinai, and advance toward Suez. At this point an Anglo-French expeditionary force was to land under the pretext of protecting the canal. Eden supposed that the affair would end in the overthrow of Nasser's regime.[12]

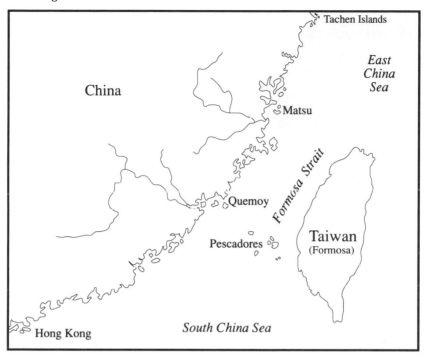

China's Offshore Islands

Eisenhower, who followed a policy of evenhanded neutrality between the Arabs and the Jews in the Middle East, disliked Nasser's aggressive nationalism and needlessly feared that Nasser would allow Egypt to become a Soviet puppet. "The British have never had any sense in the Middle East," he observed, recognizing that should Britain try to recover the canal by force, the Arab world would be roused against the West. When the Suez crisis first erupted in June, the Saudis and the Persian Gulf sheiks were so alarmed by Egypt's posturing that the JCS agreed with Admiral Burke, the CNO, who proposed to send a pair of destroyers from the 6th Fleet to the Persian Gulf to strengthen the Middle East Force and reassure these American friends. Nasser responded to this well-publicized movement by delaying the passage of the destroyers from the Mediterranean through the Suez Canal, a step that alarmed Burke, who told Vice Admiral Charles Brown to place the 6th Fleet on alert for four days. Only after Eisenhower announced that he favored a peaceful resolution of the

Anglo-Egyptian crisis did Nasser allow the American warships to proceed to the North Arabian Sea.[13]

In the meantime, British General Sir Charles Kneightly, the Anglo-French expeditionary commander, had encountered repeated delays in assembling the forces necessary to occupy the canal. Malta, the Royal Navy base with a deepwater port nearest to the scene of the crisis, was over 1,000 miles from Egypt. Ships, troops, and equipment had to be sent into the Mediterranean in the fall during a buildup hampered by confusion and poor timing, which the allies could not conceal from Brown, who exercised the 6th Fleet in the Ionian Sea in October. Eisenhower repeatedly told Eden not to act until Dulles tried to negotiate a settlement. Eisenhower erred, however, by allowing London to believe that he was willing to back the use of force against Nasser as a last resort. While the Anglo-French fleet, which was composed of seven aircraft carriers, a flotilla of landing craft, 130 warships, and several divisions of specialized troops, assembled south of Cyprus, Eden was busy trying to convince Eisenhower and Dulles that he intended these preparations merely to bluff Nasser into backing down and returning the canal to international supervision. Nasser refused to play, however, and became more truculent and abusive than ever.

After being alerted by the CIA that the Israelis intended to attack Egypt, Eisenhower warned Israel's prime minister, David Ben-Gurion, that the United States stood firmly against such outright aggression. Israel was already committed to the Anglo-French scheme, however. Jumping off on the evening of 29 October, the Israeli Army slammed onto the Sinai Peninsula, crushed Egyptian resistance, and reached the Suez Canal within the week. Eisenhower, furious with Tel Aviv, announced that the United States would "redeem our word about supporting any victim of aggression," in part on principle, in part because a failure to do so would allow the Soviets "to enter the situation in the Middle East." The next day, Washington asked the UN to arrange a ceasefire, only to be stunned by the issuance of an Anglo-French ultimatum to both parties to withdraw from the Suez Canal area. Because the Israeli Army had yet to complete its fight across the Sinai, the threat applied only to the Egyptians, and its timing clearly exposed the prewar conspiracy among the British, French, and Israeli governments.[14]

Eisenhower's policy confused not only the British but also the JCS and the responsible American commanders in the Mediterranean. Glad that the Europeans were "punishing" Egypt, Admiral Cato Glover, the commander in chief of NATO South, "felt certain" that Eisenhower would "cast our political lot" with Britain and France. Indeed, when Burke directed Brown to "prepare for imminent hostilities" in the area, the 6th Fleet commander responded, only half in jest, "Which side are we on?" On 3 November, the Russians supported an American motion before the UN Security Council calling for a ceasefire. Ben-Gurion, unwilling to alienate the Americans, publicly accepted this resolution, only to reverse his stance the next day under pressure from Britain and France. Israel's ruthless rejection of the first UN ceasefire plan provided Eden with a public excuse to give the order to Kneightly to invade Egypt.[15]

At 0800 on 5 November, British helicopters landed airborne troops around Port Said and Port Fuad, and the next day British units laid siege to Port Said. The European forces humiliated the Egyptian Army, but the Suez operation proved to be an embarrassing fiasco for the West. Blockships were sunk in the Suez Canal on Nasser's orders, effectively closing the waterway and thwarting Eden's professed goal of keeping it open to international shipping. Furthermore, Nasser's government withstood the loss of Port Said and the defeat at the hands of the Israelis on the Sinai, and with his emotional but accurate portrayal of Egypt as the victim of an imperialist-Zionist conspiracy, his popularity in the Arab world soared. Eisenhower now took steps to threaten the British pound sterling and so to force Eden to concede defeat and accept the ceasefire. The invasion had failed either to keep open the canal or to topple Nasser, and London and Paris had no choice but to withdraw their forces once a 6,000-man UN peacekeeping contingent arrived on the scene. Eden resigned in disgrace, Britain's historic influence in the Middle East plummeted, and Eisenhower was left to figure out how the United States might deal with this newly created vacuum of power.

Chapter Twenty

The Advent of Polaris
1957–1960

America's nuclear-powered fleet resulted from the concurrent development of atomic fission reactors and the Navy's dogged determination to break the Air Force's early postwar near monopoly of delivering nuclear weapons. Soon after World War II ended, Vice Admiral Earle W. Mills, the able chief of the Bureau of Ships, set about to develop nuclear propulsion plants for ships and submarines. Mills was concerned that the Soviets had captured a large number of advanced German submarines and that they intended to build their own large submarine fleet, a danger frequently cited by Navy propagandists during the unification struggle. "They now have over five times the number of undersea craft that Germany had at the outbreak of World War II," asserted Captain Arleigh Burke in 1948. Some held that within a decade Soviet submarines might challenge the U.S. Navy for control of the Atlantic. As a first step, Mills assembled a small engineering team under Captain Hyman Rickover, who was directed in 1947 to provide liaison between the Navy and the newly established Atomic Energy Commission.[1]

Navy submariners claimed that the best antisubmarine weapon was an attacking submarine. In a 1949 exercise, four modernized fleet-type submarines conducted successful offensive antisubmarine sweeps ahead of a carrier task force in the Barents Sea. Speed and stealth were the greatest tactical problems of antisubmarine warfare. Destroyers were fast, but noisy.

Diesel submarines were quiet, but their electric drives were slow and they needed to surface frequently to recharge their storage batteries. If the submarine could be unchained from its battery, greater undersea speed might be achieved. Mills told Rickover to get the AEC to assist the bureau in building a small prototype reactor to install in a submarine hull. Rickover convinced the AEC to name him to head its Naval Reactors Section, and he then told Mills that the Navy's relations with the AEC hinged on his, Rickover's, acceptance of the appointment. The AEC valued the Navy as a customer; at the same time, the Bureau of Ships was led to believe that only Rickover could ensure that the AEC would assist the Navy's nuclear program. Rickover was thus, for no good reason, given a warrant to grasp the chokepoint between the provider of nuclear services, the AEC, and one of its important clients, the Navy.

At the moment, the AEC was embarking on an ambitious program to build civilian reactors, and erecting a small naval prototype advanced its plan to widen its constituency. In April 1950, after tests proved that a shipboard reactor was feasible, Mills persuaded the Navy's General Board—in one of its last acts before being disestablished—to agree to the construction of a submarine propelled by an atomic power plant. Later that year Admiral Sherman, the CNO, got Congress to approve building two experimental submarines, one with a "closed" diesel system, which was never completed, the other with a nuclear power plant. On 13 July 1951, Navy Secretary Dan A. Kimball let the contract for the *Nautilus* to the Electric Boat Company of Groton, Connecticut. Rickover was placed in charge of the *Nautilus'* reactor.

The Navy pursued a policy of concurrently developing reactors and hulls for the new submarines. Shortly after World War II, fifty-two fleet submarines were modernized and converted under the Guppy program. The hulls were streamlined and snorkel breathers and high-capacity storage batteries were installed—measures that doubled their underwater speed. Another ten fleet submarines were converted into radar pickets by streamlining the conning tower and adding a snorkel system. The shortened, streamlined hull of the *Tang*-class, the first postwar submarine, which entered the fleet starting in 1951, afforded greater submerged maneuverability and increased diving depth. Higher speed meant that the submarine's hull had to be completely reshaped, however. Several years earlier, Mills and his Bureau of

Ships designers had fashioned a teardrop hull for the experimental submarine *Albacore*. Whereas all previous submarine hulls were designed with a sharp bow to slice the ocean's waves, the teardrop hull was smooth and slim, its bow tapered and rounded like a porpoise's snout. The *Albacore* was fitted with a large, single propeller, reversing a long Navy tradition of providing submarines with two propellers as a safety precaution. Designers also relocated her rudder and stern plates forward of the propeller and eliminated the conning tower. Launched in 1952, the *Albacore* made 29 knots during sea trials off Portsmouth, and one study suggested that she might be capable of making 50 knots underwater. With the advent of the teardrop hull and the small nuclear reactor, a new generation of submarines was born.

Admiral Carney, who became CNO in 1953, adopted a balanced fleet policy that year, refused to accelerate the nuclear propulsion program, and asked Congress one year later for funds to build only three submarines, two with diesel engines and one with a nuclear reactor. Nonetheless, he was excited about the prospect of nuclear-powered attack submarines. Although the *Nautilus* fell short of her design goals, Commander Eugene Wilkinson put to sea on 17 January 1955 and broadcast the historic message, "Underway on nuclear power." The *Nautilus* provided submerged endurance limited only by the needs of the crew, and was advertised as a great success.

The success of the *Nautilus'* sea trials persuaded Carney to ask Congress to authorize the five-vessel *Skate*-class nuclear attack submarines, but they did not benefit from the results of the *Albacore* trials and were really scaled-down versions of the *Nautilus*. Later in 1955, when Admiral Burke became CNO, he decided to install the SW2 reactor in a submarine that incorporated the teardrop hull, and in January of the following year he asked Congress for funds to lay down six *Skipjack*-class attack submarines, vessels that did benefit from the *Albacore* trials and married the *Nautilus'* SW2 reactor, the teardrop hull, and the single screw. This produced a 50 percent increase in speed for the same horsepower and displacement, tremendous maneuverability, and unprecedented endurance. And, in a dramatic gesture, Burke announced that all future submarines would be nuclear powered.

Carney was intent that the Navy participate in strategic nuclear warfare by having vessels capable of delivering sea-based nuclear weapons against the Soviet Union. Until the Korean War,

The 4,092-ton experimental attack submarine *Nautilus* (SS-571), the Navy's first nuclear-powered vessel, was put to sea on 17 January 1955.

Vice Admiral William F. Raborn. Director, Special Projects Office (Polaris system), 1955–1962; Director, Central Intelligence Agency, 1965–1966.

The 5,600-ton nuclear-powered *George Washington* (SSBN-598), the first fleet ballistic missile submarine, was commissioned on 30 December 1959. On 20 July 1960, she fired the first sea-launched Polaris ballistic nuclear-tipped missile.

the most promising means of doing this was by using carrier-borne naval bombers, but improvements in bombardment and ballistic missiles seemed the wave of the future after 1953. For rockets, the Navy adopted two postwar models, the Germans' V-1 and V-2, and in 1946 Admiral Nimitz divided the naval rocketry effort into two parts. The rocket program aimed at exploiting V-1 technology. The Navy's KUW-1, a copy of the V-1, was launched in January 1946, and a year later a Loon missile was fired from the deck of the submarine *Cusk*. In January 1949 another Loon was launched from the deck of the recently commissioned experimental missile ship *Norton Sound*. The pilotless aircraft program was intended to duplicate the kamikaze but without the unacceptable loss of the pilot. The first version of the air-breathing, turbojet Regulus I was ready to fire before the Korean War. A surface-to-surface missile designed to carry a Mk-5 atomic bomb, the Regulus I had an airspeed of 600 miles per hour, a range of 500 miles, and a radio system that guided it to fixed targets. It was inaccurate and could not hit moving targets, however, and so was inferior to the contemporary generation of heavy naval bombers, although it was cheaper to build and deploy and did not put pilots at risk. And its entry into the fleet added a potent nuclear bombardment threat to some Soviet ports and exposed coastal installations.

Secretary of Defense Louis Johnson slashed funds for Navy missiles in 1949, but two years later, after he was fired, Admiral Sherman restored several programs and persuaded Congress to authorize the conversion of the submarine *Tunny* so that she might fire the Regulus missile. The Navy's first postwar missile, the ill-designed ramjet Rigel, was canceled in 1953, but in July of that year another Regulus I was successfully fired from rails on the *Tunny*'s deck. The Regulus I became operational in 1956, but as a delivery vehicle for nuclear weapons it was vulnerable to enemy jet interceptors and had limited striking range.

By this time, the enthusiastic chaos of interservice competition had invested American missilery. The Navy was developing the Regulus and the expensive Vanguard carrier-launched aerodynamic rocket, but because the 1948 JCS Key West agreement assigned long-range strategic missiles to the Air Force, the Navy was not formally associated with any ballistic missile program. Moreover, Navy men had little faith in sending large, liquid-fueled ballistic missiles to sea. The Army was developing the

Matador and the Mace, land-based versions of the Regulus, the tactical Redstone rocket, and the medium-range Jupiter ballistic missile. The Air Force was building the Snark intercontinental aerodynamic missile, the supersonic Navaho system, and the medium-range Thor and the intercontinental Atlas and Titan ICBM ballistic rockets.

In 1955, under congressional pressure, Eisenhower reluctantly imposed a template of greater order over these diverse projects. He commissioned a study by MIT official James Killian, Jr., who recommended that the Air Force develop an intercontinental ballistic missile; the Army, a tactical rocket; and the Navy, a ship- or submarine-launched, intermediate- or long-range ballistic missile. The fate of the air-breathing cruise missile was left in limbo. The Killian Report thus brought the Navy into the strategic ballistic missile field and resulted in the suspension of most primitive aerodynamic systems and a new focus on intercontinental ballistic missiles. On 15 September 1955, Eisenhower fixed a requirement of a minimum range of 1,500 miles for both sea- and land-based ballistic missiles, and Defense Secretary Wilson announced that the Navy would participate in the Army's Jupiter missile program. However, Burke regarded the liquid-fuel missiles as too volatile for shipboard launchers, and the six-story Jupiter too long to be sea-launched. Rear Admiral John A. Sides, the Assistant CNO for guided missiles, wanted the Navy to abandon the ballistic missile to the Air Force and concentrate instead on perfecting nuclear weapons–bearing cruise bombardment missiles. Burke disliked the Jupiter program but rejected Sides' assessment, and in September 1955, he selected Sides' former chief of staff, Rear Admiral William Raborn, to superintend the Navy's part of the Jupiter program.

In March 1956, Raborn and his technical director, Captain Levering Smith, abandoned the liquid-fuel propellant in favor of a new, safer, equally efficient solid-fuel rocket. Another milestone was reached that September when the country's leading nuclear physicist, Edward Teller, announced that within a few years the AEC would produce a warhead considerably lighter and smaller than the one the Jupiter was designed to deliver. This led Raborn to propose that the Navy divorce itself from the Jupiter project and instead build its own sea-launched ballistic missile, the intermediate-range Polaris. "The attractive feature was that Polaris would be a purely Navy system, without the . . . complications of

Army collaboration," recalled William A. Whitmore, the project's chief scientist. Inasmuch as the "Polaris would not be capable of precise attacks on hard targets" and so would hit "soft target areas such as urban industrial complexes . . . competition with nuclear delivery by [Air Force] manned aircraft" was reduced. Burke's Project Nobska, which studied means to defeat the Red Navy's growing submarine force, advocated building a force of American ballistic missile–bearing nuclear submarines so that the Soviets would have no choice but to commit their own attack submarines to strategic antisubmarine warfare.[2]

The shock of Russia's successful Sputnik satellite coincided with these developments. On 3 August 1957, a Soviet SS-6 ballistic missile rocketed from its launch pad into space and impacted deep in Siberia. Five weeks later, Sputnik, the first artificial space satellite, shot into earth orbit. This did not change the balance of power, but it altered the world's perception of Russia's relative strength, and Khrushchev's plan to build a large arsenal of cheap ICBMs irremediably complicated America's strategic problems. Senate Majority Leader Lyndon Johnson assailed Eisenhower for losing the lead in space and demanded an expensive program to build ballistic missiles for space exploration and defense. Eisenhower was unmoved. He tried to deflect the criticism by appointing a commission chaired by auto executive H. Watson Gaither and charging it with studying the issue. To his surprise, the Gaither Report, issued on 7 November, argued that the Soviet Union was devoting a larger fraction of its economy to defense than the United States, and claimed that Sputnik posed a challenge to American technological superiority in the strategic arms competition. This was a charge that Eisenhower could not ignore.

The Gaither Report not only supported accelerating work on the Air Force's solid-fuel Minuteman ICBM project, but also strengthened the Navy's case for building a submarine-launched ballistic missile. Indeed, Gaither specifically proposed that the Navy build and deploy eight nuclear-powered ballistic missile submarines. As a result, Eisenhower made an "open-ended" commitment to construct the Polaris system. On 14 November, Navy Secretary Thomas Gates accelerated the construction of the Polaris missile and asked Congress to increase the authorization for ballistic missile submarines from one to three by 1960. Despite Air Force opposition, Eisenhower agreed to this schedule.

In the summer of 1958, this number was increased by Congress and funds were voted to build six fleet ballistic missile submarines of the *George Washington* class.

The enormous costs of the Polaris program had created a crisis in the entire shipbuilding program by May 1958, however. Owing to lack of funds, Burke mistakenly canceled the promising Regulus II cruise missile program and ordered that no more diesel submarines be converted to carry guided missiles. He also canceled the Triton missile program. However, five diesel submarines armed with Regulus I cruise missiles were deployed in the Pacific until the Polaris ballistic missile boats entered that theater in 1964. Nevertheless, Eisenhower was reluctant to release the funds for the ballistic missile submarine program unless Burke could assure him that the Polaris' warheads were large enough to destroy their targets and until the technique for a submerged launching was proven. In addition, the president was concerned about command and control of the Polaris-bearing submarine force.

When Burke had become CNO in 1955, he discovered that there was little agreement within the Navy that the submarine-launched ballistic missile was desirable, feasible, or necessary. Many Navy leaders believed that perfecting a long-range, under-sea-launched ballistic missile was overly expensive or improbable, and naval aviators worried that it would deprive the carriers of any role in a nuclear war. The ballistic missile submarine had no patrons outside the Navy other than a handful of self-interested contractors. Burke's wise decision to turn the program over to Raborn, who was respected, rather than Rickover, who was not, ensured that those foes of the program rarely emerged. Owing to Raborn's skill, within a few years there were no doubters left. At the Electric Boat Company, the diesel submarine *Scorpion* was bisected to allow for the installation of a 110-foot missile tube compartment. In early 1958, two pressure-resistant cylinders to carry the Regulus II missile were installed into the forward part of the pressure hull of a converted *Grayback*-class submarine, and the following year the first nuclear-tipped Regulus missile was deployed. An additional diesel submarine was to be converted to fire the Regulus, and in 1958, orders were placed for four more nuclear-powered submarines to carry this missile. Raborn had decided in the meantime on the characteristics of the new fleet ballistic missile submarine. She would have a porpoise-shaped hull like the *Albacore*, a nuclear propulsion plant, and a battery of sixteen tubes to launch the solid-fuel Polaris A-1 ballistic missile. That this figure was chosen by lot demonstrated Burke's eagerness to build the platform and the lack of strategic thought behind it. Whether it was best to establish a small force, with each submarine bearing a large number of missiles, or a large force, with each boat bearing a small number of missiles, did not figure in this decision. Solid-fuel missiles had less thrust than comparable liquid-fuel vehicles, however, thus creating a need greater than ever for nuclear warheads smaller than the 1,600-pound device built for the Jupiter rocket.

Burke ended Navy participation in the Jupiter program in August 1956. Earlier that year the AEC had reported that a 600-pound missile-borne warhead would not be available until 1965. Therefore, to meet Eisenhower's deadline, Burke and Raborn were forced to accept a limit to the range of the Polaris A-1 missile of 1,200 miles, a hitherto unacceptable figure. "Most targets of naval interest are more suitably attacked by aircraft, or air breathing missiles," Burke said, but he was desperate to keep a strategic role for the Navy and reasoned that the sea-based ballistic missile would need to attack not only naval targets but also "very highly defended population or industrial targets." Burke canceled the Regulus program to pay for the Polaris missile, but the Air Force worked to prevent the Navy from deploying ballistic systems nevertheless. A Navy plan to arm six guided missile cruisers with eight Polaris missiles launchers each—an interim measure until the fleet ballistic missile submarines put to sea— was defeated in June 1959 within the JCS by General Thomas White and the Air Force.[3]

To answer his partisan critics, Eisenhower called for several stage-managed spectaculars that might capture the public's imagination. The most wasteful result was NASA's decision to conduct the utterly useless manned Mercury and Apollo space shots. The Navy also supported this public relations extravaganza. In October 1958, the nuclear-powered *Seawolf* completed a 60-day, continuously-submerged cruise covering a distance of over 13,000 miles, thus demonstrating the practicality of long-term underwater deterrent patrols. Burke also sent the *Nautilus* on an August 1958 cruise under the North Pole, and in May 1959, the nuclear submarine *Skate* actually punched a hole in the ice pack near the North Pole, thus publicly exposing the vulnerability of Russia's northern polar flank. The final extravaganza occurred on 20 July 1959, when the submarine *George Washington* conducted the first successful underwater launch of an A-1 Polaris missile. At last, on 15 November 1960, she stood out of Charleston en route to her first deterrent patrol in the Norwegian Sea. The *George Washington* was built by cutting in two an attack submarine hull and inserting the missile battery section. Within two months of her maiden voyage, however, the keel was laid for the first of an entirely new class of ballistic missile submarines, the *Ethan Allen*s, which entered the fleet beginning in May 1962. While the primary mission of these ballistic missile-bearing submarines, and their successors, was to deliver nuclear weapons against Soviet territory, Admiral Burke made certain that they carried antisubmarine weapons and expected that once they had launched their Polaris missiles they would function as attack submarines.

Burke's advocacy of the Polaris program signaled that he was no early critic of Massive Retaliation. Indeed, he had lined up behind Admiral Radford in a showdown over Massive Retaliation in 1955 with the Army's chief of staff, General Maxwell Taylor, but after the shock of Sputnik, Burke moved closer to Taylor's position. The new look placed "undue reliance upon nuclear weapons," Taylor wrote, "to the impairment of the conventional capabilities of all services." Burke reckoned that the United States would not initiate a nuclear war once the Soviets acquired their own nuclear stockpile and delivery systems, and he felt that Massive Retaliation would not deter local aggression, often quite ambiguous in origin, even if it were backed by the Soviets or their clients or proxies. Even Secretary Dulles, an early apostle of Massive Retaliation, was asking the JCS to devise a more supple strategy that would "convince U.S. allies that local attacks can be countered without necessarily inviting all-out nuclear war" and "decrease the danger of local conflicts, which might escalate into general war."[4]

Massive Retaliation exerted a pernicious hold over the Eisenhower administration, nonetheless. Secretary of Defense Neil McElroy declared as late as 1958 that Washington "must . . . make it obvious to any potential enemy that we have available and are prepared to use weapons of retaliation so devastating that the cost to an aggressor of an attack on us would be unbearable." Three months later he added that "we better never let anyone get the mistaken idea that we are not going to use our big weapons if they are needed."[5]

The long-awaited Soviet counterpoint arrived the following year when Khrushchev boasted somewhat prematurely that the Soviets "had now stockpiled so many missiles and so many atomic and hydrogen devices that, if we were attacked, we could wipe all our probable enemies off the face of the earth." Burke wanted to disregard the premier's hyperbole and address the underlying reality that Soviet possession of a credible retaliatory nuclear force negated the political utility of Massive Retaliation.[6]

In 1959, Burke put forth the concept of "finite deterrence" as an alternative to Massive Retaliation. Burke broadcast his views by arranging for Commander Paul H. Backus, a member of the secretary of the Navy's ballistic missile committee, to publish a major article on the subject in the Naval Institute *Proceedings*. As Backus outlined the new strategy, once the Soviets had deployed ICBMs, Massive Retaliation would be irreparably harmed because an American decision to launch a countervalue attack against Soviet cities might provoke a retaliatory blow against America's urban centers. An attempt to hold on to Massive Retaliation by hardening ICBM silos to "blunt" a Soviet counterforce first strike would guarantee a new and futile arms race. Thus, Backus reasoned, the United States should abandon Massive Retaliation and adopt finite deterrence. This strategy assumed that the constant menace of an effective American countervalue stroke would deter a thermonuclear exchange.[7]

The strategic force necessary to effect such a retaliatory attack was fairly easy to estimate, Burke claimed in March 1958. "You can take from the number of Russian cities the number of megatons it takes to destroy a Russian city, the reliability of the missile, the accuracy of the missile, and you can compute it pretty accurately yourself. And then you double it just to make sure." He told Congress in 1960 that "no matter what Russia does [in a nuclear war] there is no possibility she can avoid destruction." Increases in Soviet strategic nuclear forces would simply "not affect our deterrent capability." Vice Admiral Chick Hayward, in arguing for the abandonment of the Air Force ICBM program, contended that about forty-five Polaris submarines would "come close" to displaying at sea nearly all the strategic nuclear forces needed to deter the Soviets from attacking either western Europe or North America.[8]

With between 100 and 200 major Russian cities as targets, finite deterrence would clearly require no more than 200 to 400

missiles and far fewer launchers, a number that, not coinciden-
tally, closely approximated the total number of missile tubes
available in a Polaris submarine fleet of 30 to 40 vessels. The
Polaris submarines would be "relatively invulnerable," Commander Backus supposed, so "no matter what the Russians tried to
do, we might in fact truly put behind us the frightening possibilities of general nuclear war." General White of the Air Force
countered that "finite deterrence is purely a bluff strategy and
does not include the capability for military victory." Burke's
claim that the second-strike fleet ballistic missile submarines constituted an "alternative undertaking" to the Air Force's planned
preventive nuclear strike particularly enraged White and his subordinates. Partly as a result of Burke's efforts, however, countervalue later emerged as an alternative to the counterforce aspect
of mutual deterrence.[9]

Taylor supported this line, testifying on 29 January 1959 that
the United States already possessed ten times as many vehicles as
needed to deliver nuclear warheads against Soviet targets. Instead
of increasing the weapons stockpile, building more manned
bombers and ICBMs and laying down additional Polaris submarines, he wanted to abandon the strategy of Massive Retaliation
altogether and increase America's conventional arms. "There is,"
he concluded, "a fundamental need to determine standards of
sufficiency in the various categories of military forces which we
maintain." Leaping to the defense of Massive Retaliation, General
Curtis LeMay, who headed the Strategic Air Command, asserted
that "protracted war passed with the advent of the nuclear age."
The Americans already had a retaliatory "overkill" capacity, Burke
responded in February 1959, and needed to pay more attention
to their conventional forces. "I think there is nothing Russia can
do to prevent her from being destroyed . . . We would break her
back." Vice Admiral Charles E. Brown, who commanded the 6th
Fleet, went one step further, insisting that he "would not recommend the use of any atomic weapons no matter how small, when
both sides have the power to destroy the world. . . . I have no faith
in the so-called controlled use of atomic weapons."[10]

The crisp debate provoked by Burke's advocacy of finite deterrence exposed the differences between the Air Force and the
Navy over Massive Retaliation, but Eisenhower was unwilling to
choose between the two options, as was his new defense secretary, Thomas Gates, although he refused to ask Congress to pay

for the large number of land-based ICBMs necessary for a preventive or preemptive first-strike, counterforce capability. Gates backed the Polaris system and augmented forces useful only in conventional wars, however, and he accepted a preemptive, retaliatory strategy, not the preventive, first-strike strategy the Air Force espoused. Even this left many Navy leaders uneasy. Upon examining the first Strategic Integrated Operating Plan, Admiral Harry Felt, who took command of the Pacific theater in 1958, found that the Air Force's overly redundant target list left him "more concerned about residual radiation damage resulting from our own weapons than those of the enemy." Eisenhower was also concerned that LeMay's plans included "unnecessary and undesirable overkill," but he left the choice between prevention, preemption, or deterrence to be resolved by his successors. In effect, his decision not to choose killed any strategy of limited retaliation.[11]

Although Eisenhower rejected the implications of finite deterrence, Burke had irreparably discredited Massive Retaliation by suggesting that the establishment of an invulnerable second-strike Polaris missile fleet might permit the United States to control the escalation of a nuclear war. Eisenhower's response was to question how effectively the Navy could broadcast its launch messages to Polaris-bearing boats at sea, a technical issue of command and control that dogged American strategists for the next several decades. The longer a submarine remained deeply submerged, the safer she was. However, very low frequency radio transmissions used for fleet communications could penetrate only a few feet underwater. Very slow ELF transmissions penetrated several hundred feet underwater, and an experimental transmitter on the North Carolina coast broadcast an ELF signal that was successfully received by the nearby submerged submarine *Seawolf*. The ELF system eventually solved the command and control problem, but the early Polaris missile boats relied on a primitive communications system, a fragile link in the chain of logic about developing a truly flexible nuclear deterrent. One result of the tenuous communications, however, was the decision to endow each submarine's skipper and his launch officer with the ability to launch his missiles.

In April 1959, the JCS first considered who would command the Polaris missile–bearing submarine fleet. Prior to the passage of the 1958 Defense Department Reorganization Act, the CNO in effect exercised direct command over all the numbered fleets and loaned ships to the unified theater commanders only for joint exercises and emergencies. After 1958, the unified commanders assumed command of the numbered fleets, but this simply transferred the Atlantic and Pacific fleets to admirals headquartered in Norfolk and Hawaii respectively. Rather than assigning the Polaris submarines to these unified commanders, Air Force General Thomas White wanted to merge them with the B-52 bombers and ICBMs into a single unified strategic command. Apoplectic that an Omaha-based Air Force general was to direct the movements of submarines at sea, Burke condemned White's scheme as "unsound and impractical." Before and after the submarine fired her missiles, he pointed out, she had to conform to the movement of other vessels in her operating area. "To depart from the principle of the integrated, balanced fleet . . . by assigning Polaris submarines to a command charged with operating land-based strategic bombers and missiles would decrease our Nation's ability to strike back."[12]

Burke wanted to establish an operational submarine command for the Atlantic that would conduct deterrent patrols under the supervision of the Atlantic Fleet theater commander. Inasmuch as after 1958, the latter reported not to the CNO but to the chairman of the JCS, it went halfway to meeting the Air Force's position. Gates agreed, and in 1960 vested operational control of the Polaris submarines in the commanders of the numbered fleets, but also, over Burke's objections, he established the Joint Strategic Target Planning Committee in Omaha under an Air Force general whose deputy was always to be a Navy vice admiral. The committee was to compose a Strategic Integrated Operating Plan, or SIOP, designed to efficiently employ America's limited nuclear arsenal.

Speed, endurance, and long cruising radius—the characteristics of the ballistic missile submarine—were also important to the development of nuclear-powered attack submarines. The Navy entered the Cold War with a large inventory of wartime anti-ship fleet submarines, only to learn in 1945 that they were inferior to the most recent captured German Type XXI designs. Traditionalists favored continuing to build general-purpose submarines, a type that evolved into the new *Tang*-class, but concern about Soviet submarines after the Korean War prompted the Navy to lay down the experimental *Barracuda*-class boats and to convert several fleet submarines for antisubmarine work. In the meantime, the nearly simultaneous appearance of the teardrop hull and the shipboard reactor offered a solution to the problem of a lack of sustained high submerged speeds, which had dogged submarines since World War I. As a result, the first American nuclear-powered submarines were to be attack types.

By 1957, Burke was convinced that the antisubmarine warfare mission constituted the major argument in favor of attack submarines. The product of this conviction, the *Skipjack* class, combined high speed, deep diving, and tubes for the SUBROC, a ballistic rocket carrying a nuclear warhead that was designed to strike targets forty miles away. In 1954, Carney had identified offensive antisubmarine warfare as the primary mission of the nuclear-powered *Nautilus* and her successors, but one year later Rear Admiral Frank Watkins, who commanded the Atlantic Fleet submarines, conducted an exercise during which the *Nautilus* stalked an antisubmarine hunter-killer carrier task force. Owing to her great speed, invisibility, and immunity from air attack, the *Nautilus* overtook the task force, penetrated the screen, and launched simulated torpedo attacks against the carrier at will. This convinced Burke to establish a second program—parallel to the Polaris effort—to develop the *Skipjack* class of fast attack nuclear-powered submarines. By the time the first of the *Skipjack*-class nuclear attack submarines entered the fleet in April 1959, the hull of the lead boat in the next class, the *Thresher*, was already laid down. Rickover chose to use the *Nautilus*-type reactor in the heavier *Thresher*s, however, thus considerably reducing the vessel's speed, for the hull had to be enlarged to install a new, large active-passive sonar system.

The early nuclear-powered aircraft carrier program was far less successful. In August 1950, Admiral Sherman had asked Admiral Mills of the Bureau of Ships to design "a large carrier with an atomic power plant." Three months later, Sherman persuaded the JCS to agree to this project on the grounds that such a carrier would be "capable of operation without refueling for very long periods of time." Unlike the small power plant required to move a submarine, however, a large reactor capable of turning up to eight shafts would be needed for an aircraft carrier. The enormous costs alarmed even the AEC and Admiral Fechteler, the CNO, who in May 1953 came out against the project. Captain Rickover had tried to cultivate support among the commission members for the carrier reactor, but this failed when Secretary Wilson made the stunning public announcement that Rickover's advocacy conflicted with Defense Department policy.[13]

Carney asked for no funds for a nuclear-powered carrier in 1954. He wanted to build the vessel, but the Navy's shipbuilding account had already been reduced to support Air Force expansion dictated by the New Look. Rickover continued to lobby on the Hill to develop multiple large-ship reactors to power one of the new *Forrestal*-class carriers, however, and soon after Admiral Burke succeeded Carney as CNO in the summer of 1955, he decided to appease Rickover and the Navy's aviators with one stroke. He asked the Bureau of Ships to draw up the requirements for a nuclear-powered attack carrier that September, and the following year persuaded Congress to authorize the construction of the *Enterprise*, the first nuclear-powered carrier. Inasmuch as Congress was unwilling to authorize more carriers either in 1957 or 1958, Burke suspended the program and asked Congress for another vessel in 1959. Burke's and Rickover's energetic lobbying produced a favorable House vote for a reactor-driven carrier, but senators Symington and Jackson, the champions of the Air Force's new Minuteman ICBM program, killed the measure in the Senate. Although funds for long–lead-time items for a second *Enterprise*-class carrier appeared in the resulting compromise legislation, Eisenhower impounded these appropriations. For the moment, nuclear-powered carrier construction was suspended.

The high cost of large reactors also led to the suspension of the Navy's nuclear-powered cruiser and destroyer programs during Eisenhower's presidency. This outcome was tinged with irony because the first concrete proposal to install a nuclear propulsion plant in a warship emerged in 1946 when General Electric engineers suggested using an atomic reactor to drive a destroyer. Within a few years, however, Rickover decided to construct successively larger submarine reactors before designing a reactor for ships. Although Carney was unenthusiastic about building nuclear-powered cruisers or destroyers, Burke reversed this policy in September 1955 and approved plans to lay down the nuclear-powered cruiser *Long Beach*. Originally designed to displace 7,800 tons and cost $142 million, when the *Long Beach* entered the fleet in 1961 she displaced over 14,000 tons, cost $320 million, and had space amidships for radars and launchers for Regulus II bombardment missiles.

In the meantime, Rear Admiral Joseph Daniel, who commanded the Atlantic Fleet's destroyers, overcame formidable opposition and persuaded Burke in 1955 to lay down an experimental nuclear-powered destroyer on the grounds that a reactor plant would release the destroyer from the traditional need to refuel at sea every two or three days during fleet operations. By the time Congress authorized the ship, however, Rickover claimed that he did not have a reactor small enough for a destroyer. As a result, the vessel's hull size was increased, and when the large nuclear-powered destroyer *Bainbridge* entered the fleet, she displaced over 8,500 tons and cost $108 million, over twice the figure for an oil-fired escort frigate. Rear Admiral Ralph K. James sounded the death knell for a nuclear surface fleet when he told Congress a few years later that "two nuclear surface ships just cannot do the work of three others." The real price of these costly experiments with shipboard reactors was the continued overall decline in the size of the fleet, which fell below 800 ships before Admiral Burke retired in 1961.[14]

Chapter Twenty-one

Policing the Eisenhower Doctrine
1957–1958

Fear of Soviet penetration in the wake of Europe's decline moved Secretary Dulles to impose some measure of mutual security over the Middle East. He helped the British organize the 1955 Baghdad Pact, which created METO, the Middle East Treaty Organization, whose members—Britain, Turkey, Iraq, Iran, and Pakistan—promised to defend one another against a Soviet invasion. Egypt refused to be drawn into METO, however, and, following the Suez crisis, Nasser and Khrushchev signed the 1957 Russo-Egyptian Friendship Treaty. Moscow also established closer ties with Syria. Eisenhower, determined to obstruct Soviet policy in the Middle East, told Congress on 5 February 1957 that the "independence" of those nations was "vital to the national interest of the United States" and asked for a resolution committing American "armed forces to assist any nation" that was resisting an "armed attack from any country controlled by international communism." Congress passed the resolution by large majorities and appropriated $200 million to aid the Baghdad powers, and on 9 March the president signed the bill that became known as the Eisenhower Doctrine. The United States formally joined METO's military organization in June. Khrushchev denounced the Eisenhower Doctrine as "gross interference" and Nasser labeled the Baghdad Pact an "imperialist plot."[1]

An aborted coup in Jordan first brought the 6th Fleet into play to support the Eisenhower Doctrine. Jordan's King Hussein had thwarted one attempt on his throne by pro-Egyptian rebels in April 1957 but feared that others would follow and begged Washington for assistance. Eisenhower invoked his doctrine, dispensed some aid, and declared that he was committed to Hussein's autocratic regime. This greatly pleased Admiral Arleigh Burke, the CNO, and on 20 April he instructed the commander of the Eastern Atlantic and Mediterranean theater, Vice Admiral James L. Holloway, to send the 6th Fleet into the eastern Mediterranean. Under Vice Admiral Charles R. Brown, the light carrier *Lake Champlain*, the battleship *Wisconsin*, two cruisers, and twenty-four destroyers took station off Crete, while Brown sent the new heavy carrier *Forrestal* and an amphibious task group carrying 1,800 Marines to the waters off Lebanon. Brown sent some of the Marines into Beirut on liberty to suggest that the United States had no fear of putting troops ashore. By that time, Hussein had thwarted another coup and salvaged his regime. This affair and the move by Syria into Russia's orbit led to another crisis between Syria and Turkey in August 1957, during which Eisenhower invoked the NATO treaty and promised to defend the Ankara government against Syrian or Soviet aggression or subversion.

Until 1958, neutral Lebanon seemed to be immune to Arab radicalism, Soviet provocation, and the ongoing Arab-Israeli struggle. A former French colony, Lebanon had won its independence in 1943 while Germany occupied France and French forces overseas were in disarray. To maintain domestic peace, the Lebanese carefully crafted a constitution under which the Christians, a slight minority, held the presidency, while a Muslim, representing the religious majority, served as prime minister. In May 1958, however, President Camille Chamoun undermined Muslim confidence in the national government by amending the constitution so that he might succeed himself. Chamoun's arch rival, former Prime Minister Saeb Salem, assembled a Muslim force of 10,000 men, which was armed by the Syrians, and challenged the central government. On 8 May, riots in Tripoli spread to the Muslim quarter of the capital, and Muslim militiamen took control of the Bekaa Valley along the border with Syria. Civil war on a small scale erupted, but General Fouad Chehab, the head of the Lebanese Army, was afraid to order his troops into the breach for fear that some Muslims in his ranks would desert.

Eisenhower received conflicting advice. Noting that the basic cause of the Muslim uprising was Chamoun's drive to upset

Lebanon's constitutional balance, some warned the president that intervention would only reinforce Nasser's charges of American imperialism and alienate Muslim opinion. Led by Burke, the interventionists cited the danger of a Syrian invasion of Lebanon and pointed to the need for a symbolic act of American muscularity in the Middle East. In effect, American military success in Lebanon seemed to be virtually assured owing to the small number of rebels, their widely dispersed positions, the weakness of the Syrian army, and the support of the Turks, Israelis, and Jordanians for American intervention.

Later that May, Burke ordered Admiral Holloway to send Vice Admiral Brown's 6th Fleet back into the eastern Mediterranean. He also named Rear Admiral Howard Yeager to take

Admiral Arleigh Burke. Chief of Naval Operations, 1955–1961.

U.S. Navy Department

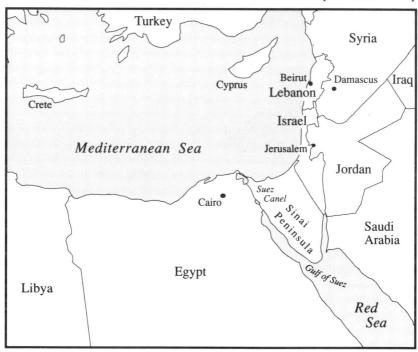

Eastern Mediterranean

command of the 6th Fleet Amphibious Force, which would be responsible for any landing operations in Lebanon. Two Marine battalions under Brigadier General S. S. Wade boarded the command ship *Mount McKinley*, which steamed from Italy to the familiar anchorage off the coast of Cyprus. Brown arrived there within days with the heavy carrier *Saratoga*, the attack carriers *Essex* and *Wasp*, two cruisers, several divisions of destroyers, and other supporting vessels. Brown had already approved Operation Bluebat, a plan for the Marines to take control of Beirut before the Muslim rebels could occupy the entire city or get any direct support from the Syrian 1st Army, which had just recently massed on the Lebanese frontier. Burke wanted a landing to appear to be easy and attractive to the president, but Saeb Salem boasted that if "one Marine sets foot on the soil of my country," he would "commit my forces against them." Eisenhower wearily agreed to Burke's contingency planning, but he would not commit himself to intervention, although the new British prime minister, Harold Macmillan, was persuaded by Holloway on 22 May to send British forces to Jordan if the Americans landed in Lebanon.[2]

Eisenhower's restraint evaporated when he learned of the Iraqi coup of 14 July 1958. Led by Brigadier General Abdul Karim Kassem, Muslim radicals took control of Baghdad, executed the corrupt monarch, King Feisal II, and most of the royal family, and established a new pro-Soviet regime. Chamoun was afraid that he would be next, and he begged Eisenhower to intervene in the Lebanese civil war by sending in the Marines, and Jordan asked again for British help. "The Central Intelligence Agency and the military intelligence sources had given the President no forewarning of the sudden revolt in Iraq," complained White House chief of staff Sherman Adams. Thus, when Kassem announced his support of Nasser and Arab nationalism, Eisenhower felt that he had no alternative but to intervene in Lebanon. He phoned Burke at 1800 and directed him to order Brown to land the Marines and have them occupy Beirut the next morning. Yeager's Amphibious Force was only 120 miles off the Lebanese coast when Burke relayed Eisenhower's instructions to the 6th Fleet. From Crete, 350 miles from Lebanon, Brown launched aircraft from the *Essex*, which refueled at British air bases on Cyprus, then flew south to cover the prearranged landing zones on the outskirts of Beirut.

In Beirut, only ninety minutes before the Marines were to land, however, Ambassador Robert McClintock belatedly concluded that Operation Bluebat was altogether unnecessary. Not keen about intervening in the civil war, he arranged a hasty midnight conference with Chamoun to discuss the landing. Chamoun, facing the opposition of his own supporters and General Chehab to American intervention, got cold feet at the last moment, and begged McClintock to instruct Admiral Holloway to have the Amphibious Force steam into Beirut harbor but not allow the Marines to come ashore. It was now clear to McClintock that "many elements in the Lebanese Army were at that moment preparing to resist the American landing by force."

With no time to waste, he tried to contact the landing forces but could not establish communications, so he sent an envoy to stop the Marines on the beach. At 1504, Yeager's LVTP beaching craft disembarked four companies of Marines. They were met on the pleasant, sandy beach by bikini-clad sunbathers, a swarm of soda vendors, and gangs of small boys who tried to help the Americans get their heavy equipment ashore. Lieutenant Colonel Harry Hadd established a defensive perimeter around the area, chased the bathers away, secured the nearby roads, and cut off all traffic to the beach. Commander John Baker, McClintock's emissary, now arrived on the scene. Admiral Brown's ill-informed 6th Fleet planners had assumed that the Lebanese Army would welcome the landing, but Baker warned Hadd that this was not now the case and that General Chehab was now demanding that the Marines return to their ships before they were attacked by the Lebanese Army. Hadd, a narrow-minded figure who had no understanding of the stakes involved, refused to budge. The Marines had landed, and Hadd intended to stay. McClintock was furious. Hadd's position "was in no way responsive to the critical need of the situation, which called for a flexible approach," he observed bitterly.

Compounding this debacle, poor logistics planning embarrassed the Marine landings, which had been plagued from the start by dreadful tactical intelligence despite the easy availability of information about the beaches. The Marines found that they could not drive their vehicles around in the soft sand and that a sandbar prevented the large LST landing ships from beaching, thus forcing the troops to carry their supplies ashore by hand. Not until 2000 did the *Fort Snelling* arrive, carrying special pontoons, which Hadd used to erect a causeway between the LST *Traverse Country* and the beachhead. Next, a landing craft from the *Traverse County* ran aground on the sandbar and failed to reach the beach until the following morning. Only then was Colonel Hadd able, for the first time, to start bringing ashore his heavy equipment from the large landing craft. It was fortunate that neither the Lebanese Army nor the rebels decided to oppose this poorly conducted landing.

While the Marines were struggling onto the beach, Holloway was flying from London to Beirut Airport, where his plane touched down at 0400 on the morning of 16 July. After shifting his flag to the command ship *Taconic*, then riding at anchor in Beirut harbor, he met with McClintock, who warned that General Chehab had lost control of several units of the Lebanese Army that were opposed to the landing. Chehab arrived and told Holloway that two Lebanese tank formations were blocking the highway between the beachhead and the city. Holloway, who at long last realized that Lebanon's politics were irremediably complicated, was not itching for action. He told Colonel Hadd not to drive up the road to the capital, then convinced Chehab to agree to walk ahead of the American columns and try to persuade his men to accept the temporary American presence. With McClintock and Holloway arm in arm, Chehab escorted the Marines into Beirut, where they bivouacked around the docks and the northern bridges. So far, not a shot had been fired.

During the night of 16 July, however, the Muslim rebels sniped at a few American outposts and began to harass the Marines' positions. Holloway had positioned them between the opposing Christian and Muslim militias, and McClintock recalled that they were "maintaining an uneasy stalemate between the two" armed bands. General Wade had come ashore by this time to take command of the Marines, and he quickly realized that his men had lumbered into the middle of a civil war of Byzantine complexity and that none of the American diplomats wanted him there. Despite more shooting, local agreements between Chehab's troops and Wade's Marines solved most of the problems. On the 17th, the carrier *Saratoga* anchored off Beirut, and Holloway decided to stage a demonstration to impress the Lebanese Army, the rebels, and their Syrian patrons. Fifty-three A-3D Skywarriors, F-86 Crusaders, and A-4D Skyhawks streaked over Lebanon, violated Syrian airspace, and continued on toward the west bank of the Jordan River. A few of the planes were hit by small-arms fire from Muslim villages, and the American pilots could see small Arab children throwing rocks into the sky.[3]

When Burke had first raised the issue of intervention in May, Army Chief of Staff General Maxwell Taylor demanded that his troops be deployed to Lebanon alongside the Marines. Thus, on 19 July, the 24th Airborne Brigade, which was airlifted from Europe to Turkey, began to arrive at Beirut Airport.

Eisenhower was by now disillusioned with the entire Lebanese adventure. He claimed on 17 July that the Marines were not there to intervene in Lebanon's politics, which was, after all, the reason Chamoun wanted the Marines to land in the first place. Instead, they were in Lebanon "to protect American lives . . . [and] by their presence to assist the government of Lebanon to preserve its territorial integrity and political independence." Annoyed by the confusion on the scene, he had already sent a veteran diplomat, Deputy Secretary of State Robert Murphy, to Beirut with orders to relieve Holloway of the responsibility for the political situation. Murphy reached Beirut on the 17th and found "about seventy or seventy-five warships of the Sixth Fleet . . . near Beirut harbor, providing quite a spectacle for the fashionable diners on the terrace of the Pigeon Rock Restaurant. Marine columns were marching past the luxurious St. George's Hotel, where girls were sunning themselves on yachts in the hotel's private basin while Navy jets from the carriers *Saratoga* and *Essex* were shrieking over the city." After meeting with Chamoun, Murphy concluded that he "was a victim of his own political excesses" and had "overreached himself in the brambles of Lebanese politics." There was no evidence that Soviet agents or Lebanese Communists had played a "direct or substantial part in the insurrection."[4]

Murphy next arranged a secret meeting with Saeb Salem, the Muslim leader, who explained that his uprising was aimed at getting Chamoun to obey the constitution and leave office when his term expired. This seemed reasonable to Murphy, and he persuaded Salem to accept a scheme under which Chamoun would retire and special elections, rigged to assure the necessary result, would bring General Chehab into the presidential palace. The elections were held on 31 July, the day on which Eisenhower—thoroughly unhappy with the whole incident—instructed Secretary Dulles to announce that all American forces would leave Lebanon after Chehab took office in late September. The British, who at the same time had landed paratroopers in Amman, Jordan, to support Hussein, asked the UN to consider the entire matter, and the General Assembly issued a meaningless resolution that fall. According to Adams, Eisenhower and Dulles "were under no illusions that they had solved any problems in sending the Marines to Lebanon," and Dulles confessed that it was just a matter of "using military force only to prevent the dangerous situation from getting any worse."[5]

The Kremlin was dyspeptic, but Khrushchev would do nothing to intervene in Lebanon without a Mediterranean fleet, and Sherman Adams recalled "a change in the tone of Khrushchev's letters to the President in subsequent months, a more conciliatory note." The Soviets were not inactive, however. Admiral Sergei Gorshkov, the new commander of the Soviet Navy, deployed eight diesel submarines and a tender to the Albanian port of Vlorë during 1958, but this feeble effort did not overly concern Holloway. Moscow increased its military aid to Egypt and Syria soon after the crisis, pleased its Arab partners by denouncing Israel, and capped Russian achievements in the Middle East by signing a new military alliance with Iraq. A few days after President Chehab took office in Beirut, Admiral Brown withdrew the Marines, and the Air Force transported the Army brigade back to Europe. The Lebanese fiasco ended on 25 October 1958 when the last troops flew out of Beirut, leaving behind a legacy of bitterness among the Muslims and a shaky sectarian coalition government propped up by the fear of a renewed civil war and the threat that the 6th Fleet might return. "Sending the Marines to Lebanon . . . was a frustrating and unhappy experience for Eisenhower," Adams wrote. The president had "overestimated the gravity of the Lebanon situation and the effects of his intervention in that Middle East brushfire."[6]

The landing in Lebanon refreshed the charge of Western imperialism in the Middle East, and anti-American radicalism captured the Arab mood of the moment. Although Lebanon was intact, the Eisenhower Doctrine was in shreds, as evidenced by the deterioration of the Baghdad Pact. When Iraq came under the sway of militant Arab socialists, Secretary of State Christian Herter, who replaced Dulles in 1959, arranged for METO headquarters to move to Ankara and for the name of the shaky alliance to be changed to the Central Treaty Organization. CENTO, however, was a mere shadow of Dulles' dreams for METO, and to ensure an American military influence along the northern tier, Washington had to negotiate new and expensive bilateral military arrangements with Pakistan, Turkey, and Iran.

A sidebar to the Lebanese affair was an attempt by Burke to engage the Eisenhower administration in a new commitment to defend the Persian Gulf's oil sheiks under the guise of supporting the Christian government in Beirut. First, the pair of destroyers assigned to the Middle East Force was reinforced by the arrival of a third ship and some additional auxiliaries in the Gulf. On 16 July 1958, the same day that Burke directed Admiral Brown to land the Marines in Lebanon, he instructed Admiral Harry D. Felt, the commander in chief of the Pacific theater, to ship a Marine battalion landing team in three transports from Okinawa via the Indian Ocean to the Middle East Force's Bahrain anchorage. Their presence offshore would signal American support for Saudi Arabia, Iran, and the Persian Gulf sheiks, he asserted. London objected to any American interest in this traditionally British sphere of influence, however; Dulles was aghast at the prospect of new complications; and the oil sheiks uniformly opposed an increased American presence in their backyard. Burke was abruptly told by Eisenhower to send the Marines back to Okinawa, the president's taste for Middle East interventionism having already gone sour.

Within weeks of the July 1958 Lebanon affair, Eisenhower turned to deal with another crisis between China and Taiwan over the offshore islands of Quemoy and Matsu. The region was, by this time, more than ever one of Navy concern since the disestablishment of the Army's Far Eastern unified command in July 1957 and its incorporation within the unified Pacific theater, then commanded by Admiral Felix Stump. At the same time, the Army and the Air Force pressured Burke to accept a truly unified command in Hawaii by divorcing direct control of the Pacific Fleet from the more prestigious theater billet, a step the CNO took with great reluctance in January 1958.

These arrangements were in place only a few months before the second Taiwan Straits crisis erupted. Following the confrontation between China and the United States in 1954, Eisenhower had instructed his ambassador to Poland to arrange for regular talks with his Chinese counterpart in Warsaw. Objecting bitterly to any rapprochement, Chiang threatened to invade the mainland in 1957 and posted one-third of the Nationalist Army, about 100,000 men, on Quemoy and Matsu. Mao responded by threatening again to overrun Taiwan, and in July 1958 the Communists reactivated two airbases in Fukien Province across the straits from Taiwan to deal with Taiwan Air Force overflights. From these bases later that month the Chinese Air Force started its own overflights over Quemoy and Matsu. This coincided with Khrushchev's four-day visit to Peking, a vain attempt to repair growing strains in the Sino-Soviet Alliance. Before departing, he and Premier Chou En-lai issued a joint communiqué reaffirming their support for the reunification of China and Taiwan under Mao's rule.

On 9 August, the day on which the Nationalist garrisons on Quemoy and Matsu were to be inspected by Taiwan's war minister, the mainland batteries bombarded the islands. Chiang doggedly refused to retire from these exposed positions. "Withdrawal from Matsu and Quemoy weakens our material strength and undermines our moral position," Taiwan's ambassador to the UN explained. After the 1954 Taiwan Straits crisis, Dulles had assured Chiang that he would not "stand alone" against an invasion by Mao's army. Burke suspected that the shelling might be the prelude to an invasion, an interpretation supported by a 27 August Peking broadcast declaring that the Communists intended to "liberate" Taiwan and a proclamation issued two days later announcing that a "landing is imminent."[7]

The Formosa Resolution passed by Congress in 1955 empowered the president to take military action to defend Taiwan, the Pescadores, and "such related positions and territories of that area now in friendly hands" as he deemed necessary to protect the Nationalist stronghold. Admiral Felt put his forces on alert on 6 August and then reviewed his plans to defend Taiwan. Eisenhower had always been purposefully vague about committing the United States to the defense of Quemoy and Matsu, however, so the JCS in the summer of 1958 were uncertain what course to follow. After the heavy communist bombardment on 9 August, Burke instructed Felt to deploy the *Hancock* and *Lexington* to stations east of Taiwan, and these carriers were joined by most of the rest of the 7th Fleet soon after. Burke also sent the carrier *Midway*, which was armed with nuclear weapons, from Pearl Harbor to the Far East, and he shifted the antisubmarine carrier *Essex* from the Mediterranean into the western Pacific. Then, on 25 August, the JCS approved Felt's decisions to move a Marine air group from Japan to Taiwan where it could conduct fighter sweeps of the Taiwan Straits, and to rush an amphibious task force with a Marine battalion landing team into the area. Anxious to defend Chiang's position, Burke also increased the tempo of the long-standing American destroyer patrols in the Taiwan Straits. Air Force transports lifted advisers, equipment, and arms to Taiwan, including the Navy's new Sidewinder heat-seeking, rocket-powered, air-to-air missile. On 25 September, four Taiwan Air Force F-86Fs armed with Sidewinders shot down four communist Chinese MiG-17s over the straits, the first combat kills for any air-launched missile.[8]

The Quemoy and Matsu shelling raised anew the wisdom of applying Massive Retaliation to a regional crisis in which the Soviets were only indirectly involved. The issue was first raised by Felt, whose stocks of conventional ordnance were low because of budget cuts imposed by the New Look. If war erupted between China and the United States, he warned, Eisenhower might soon have to quit the region or escalate to the use of tactical nuclear weapons. Felt did not believe that the use of tactical nuclear weapons by the United States against China would necessarily lead to a general nuclear war with the Soviet Union. Burke also urged a bold line, insisting that the Americans had to challenge the Russian policy of "creeping aggression" by proxy, but understood that Massive Retaliation was not serving American ends in Asia. Even Dulles agreed with the JCS that nuclear weapons would have to be employed if the communist Chinese invaded Quemoy and Matsu. "There is no use of having the stuff and never being able to use it," he noted in frustration.[9]

Eisenhower was uneasy about another Asian imbroglio, but because the Nationalist airlift to Quemoy and Matsu could not sustain the troops stationed there, he reluctantly approved Burke's plan to have a 7th Fleet task group escort a convoy of Chiang's LSTs to within three miles of the islands on 7 September. For this scheme to work, however, American advisers had to be put ashore on Quemoy and Matsu, and Dulles resisted this because their presence might provoke Peking. Burke countered that defending the islands was more important than appeasing the Communists and claimed that having advisers ashore was necessary to implement the 7th Fleet convoy plan. Eisenhower relented, while assuring Dulles that he intended to minimize the number of advisers allowed to work on the islands. Later that same day, he received a threatening message from Khrushchev, who raised the stakes a bit by declaring that "an attack upon the Chinese People's Republic . . . is an attack upon the Soviet Union." Eisenhower dismissed this bellicosity as a "bluff," but at the same time turned aside Burke's alarming proposal to send carrier air strikes against the mainland artillery batteries.[10]

By this time, both Eisenhower and Mao had simultaneously reached the conclusion that the trivial affair had taken on an unwarranted dimension. Before the first American escort force put to sea, the Chinese lifted their bombardment of Quemoy and Matsu, although they resumed shelling the islands on a sporadic basis during the next four weeks. By the end of the month, however, the 7th Fleet Escort Force had developed a routine in which large American LSD landing ship docks would take station off the islands beyond the range of the communist guns. Small Nationalist amphibious craft would then run up onto the beaches to offload enough supplies to support the huge garrisons. During the intervening bombardments, however, two American advisers with the Nationalist forces on Quemoy were killed.[11]

President Eisenhower explained to the Chinese that he could not allow the Nationalists to be dislodged from the offshore islands but that he did not intend to precipitate a war over the issue and would restrain Chiang from any more provocative adventures. Both sides had made their points, and they arrived at a quick, face-saving resolution of the problem. On 6 October 1958, the Communists announced a unilateral ceasefire that was to last one week; in response, Eisenhower dispatched Dulles to Taipei where he browbeat Chiang into agreeing publicly to foreswear the use of force to "free" the mainland from the grip of the Communists without "advance consultation" with Washington. Although the Chinese resumed their shelling of Quemoy and Matsu in mid-October, they did so on alternate days, thus making Nationalist resupply of the islands a regular, benign operation that lasted, surprisingly, for nearly another decade. Referring to Eisenhower's ability to employ a powerful, measured response via the 7th Fleet to support his diplomacy during the Quemoy and Matsu crisis, Mao wondered, somewhat whimsically, "Who would have thought . . . a few shots . . . would stir up such an earth-shattering storm?"[12]

The two Taiwan Straits crises underscored fundamental differences between Eisenhower and the JCS, a schism that first arose during the development of the New Look in 1953. Eisenhower was a long-time advocate of military unification, and soon after entering office he appointed a panel headed by former Assistant Secretary of State Nelson Rockefeller and ordered it to reorganize the Defense Department. Rockefeller's group proposed Reorganization Plan Number Six, which placed the secretary of defense in the military chain of command, relieved the individual service chiefs of their executive authority over the various unified commands, and transformed the civilian service secretaries into the "operating heads" of the military departments. War plans were now to be drawn up, not by the individual services, but by the JCS, the unified theater commanders in the Atlantic, Pacific, Europe, and the Far East, and the Air Force's Strategic Air Command. Despite the Navy's objections, the Rockefeller Plan was enacted by Congress on 30 June 1953. Because it permitted the secretary of the Navy to designate the CNO to act on his behalf on "military" matters, it did little to diminish the CNO's authority over the fleet. However, the law named the

CNO as the president's principal "naval advisor," and Carney interpreted this to mean that he was to have direct access to the president, a position vigorously opposed by Defense Secretary Wilson. Moreover, Carney refused to allow Navy Secretary Charles Thomas to read the "blue flag" radio message traffic among the admirals. In December 1954, when Carney brought the issue to a head, Eisenhower agreed with him and overruled Wilson, but this Pyrrhic victory was short-lived. A few weeks later, Wilson and Thomas agreed not to reappoint Carney to a second two-year term as CNO.

In 1957, two years after Burke—whose promise to share the "blue flag" traffic with Thomas helped to win him the job—succeeded Carney, Defense Department organization reemerged as an issue, owing to shock in Washington over the Sputnik space shot. Senate Democrats alleged that interservice rivalries were retarding the growth of American rocket, missile, and space technology. "Waste in the allocation to the three services of responsibility in the missile field," Senator Stuart Symington charged, had "delayed in giving overriding priority to the ballistic missile program." This was underscored by the seminal 1957 Gaither Report on national defense, which recommended that war planning and operational control of the fighting forces be centralized under the secretary of defense, leaving the three military departments to train, assemble, and administer their forces and develop, procure, and maintain new weapons. Long an advocate of amalgamation, Eisenhower concurred and announced on 7 November 1957 that he would not allow "such things as alleged inter-service competition . . . to create even the suspicion of harm to our scientific and development program." He turned space exploration over to NASA and decided once again to reorganize the Department of Defense.[13]

In his January 1958 State of the Union Address, Eisenhower promised to send to Congress a plan to "achieve real unity" among the military forces, which would "end inter-service disputes." Distressed by the postwar unification fiasco, he had named a new set of Joint Chiefs in 1953 and, in effect, instructed them not to bicker, but the bickering continued nonetheless. Four years later a second set of personalities populated the JCS, but they also bickered. Eisenhower now intended to punish the chiefs by depriving them of some of their powers. Air Force General Nathan Twining, who succeeded Admiral Radford as

JCS chairman in 1957, claimed that the Army, Navy, and Air Force departments each sought "service self-sufficiency" and urged that the powers of the secretary of defense be expanded and that several more four-star unified and specified commands be established. "We are going to have to go to something that is tantamount to a single service," insisted General Thomas White, the Air Force chief of staff. On the other hand, former Secretary Wilson pointed out that he had encouraged competition among the services in order to develop new weapons that, once constructed, would "fit into the previously agreed division of [operational] responsibility."[14]

Admirals Radford and Burke stiffly opposed Eisenhower's plan. When General Carl Spaatz, a retired Air Force chief of staff, proposed the creation of "a single military chief of staff under the secretary of defense plus a general staff," or a combination within one service of all military forces, Radford replied that "we would still have competition within this single uniform." Reflecting traditional Navy attitudes, Burke claimed "that the three services watching each other is a pretty healthy thing, because no one can get really off the beam." Nonetheless, in April 1958, Eisenhower sent to Congress a set of proposals to reorganize the Defense Department. These proposals had been prepared by a committee of military elders selected by Neil McElroy, the new secretary of defense. "Separate ground, sea, and air warfare is gone forever," the president maintained. "If ever again we should be involved in war, we will fight it in all elements, with all services, as one single concentrated effort." Prior to 1958, the CNO effectively controlled the movements of the numbered fleets, assigning ships and aircraft to the unified theater commands only for joint exercises or during emergencies. Among other things, Eisenhower wanted to repeal the authority of the CNO to direct fleet operations and transfer this responsibility to the secretary of defense, the JCS, and the unified commanders, thus turning "all of our operational forces . . . into truly unified commands."

Despite Burke's opposition, Congress passed a Defense Reorganization Act in August 1958 that embodied nearly all of Eisenhower's proposals, although the new law neither established a single military chief of staff nor emasculated the individual military departments. Earlier Defense Department legislation had described "three military departments separately administered," and on this occasion the Navy's patron on the Hill, Con-

gressman Carl Vinson, the aging, tyrannical chairman of the
House Armed Services Committee, insisted that the law stipulate
that the Army, Navy, and Air Force departments be "separately
organized" under the Department of Defense. Vinson also appended a provision to the act requiring that any service secretary
or service chief might present Congress with recommendations
that differed from administration policy, an injunction characterized by Eisenhower as allowing "legalized insubordination."

Eisenhower complained that his "efforts to modernize the
armed forces seemed to be futile." He may have been alluding to
just this sort of resistance to political control in his famous 1960
"farewell address," in which he warned the nation against the
growing "military-industrial complex," an elite of military officers, scientists, engineers, defense contractors, and Pentagon bureaucrats whose arcane, technological product was beyond the
ken or control of the public and politicians alike. This important
address might be taken either as a warning or as a confession that
Eisenhower himself had failed to impose his tremendous grip on
the daunting problem of military policy and nuclear strategy in
the Cold War.[15]

Chapter Twenty-two

The Navy on the New Frontier
1961–1963

In the presidential election of 1960, the Republicans turned to Vice President Richard M. Nixon, who defended Eisenhower's record of containment. The Democratic nominee, Massachusetts Senator John F. Kennedy, accused Eisenhower of allowing a "missile gap" to develop between Soviet and American strategic forces that "invalidated the original strategic concept of NATO, by outflanking its key [nuclear] element." In a bitterly fought campaign, Kennedy was elected by a narrow margin.[1]

Kennedy and his Defense Secretary, Robert McNamara, abandoned Massive Retaliation and crafted in its stead a grand strategy they called "flexible response." It had two components: the Grand Design for Europe, and counterinsurgency in Asia, Africa, and Latin America. The Grand Design, Kennedy's answer to the proliferation of nuclear weapons among the NATO powers, began to take shape when McNamara denounced the British and French nuclear forces as "dangerous, expensive, . . . and lacking in credibility." Then, in August 1961, at the height of the Berlin crisis, Europe was thrown into turmoil when Soviet Premier Nikita Khrushchev erected a wall to divide the occupied German capital. "If other nations—particularly the French—make their own H-bomb, Germany may well be sucked in, too," announced West German Defense Minister Franz Josef Strauss.[2]

Kennedy's Grand Design was intended to vaccinate against this nuclear fever. Eisenhower's last secretary of state, Christian

Herter, concerned about controlling land-based medium-range ballistic missiles in Europe, had concocted a plan to establish a sea-based, nuclear-armed Multilateral Nuclear Naval Force of ships manned by mixed crews from various allied navies. He presented this plan to a December 1960 NATO meeting, but to Herter's dismay only Germany and Italy expressed any interest in the concept. Kennedy was uneasy about creating another nuclear-armed command, but he nonetheless adopted Herter's plan and at a 1961 NATO summit in Ottawa offered to "commit to NATO . . . five—and subsequently more—Polaris submarines subject to any agreed NATO guidelines on their control and use" and to establish "a NATO sea-borne force which would be truly multilateral in ownership and control." The MLF was to consist of twenty-five missile-bearing cruisers, submarines, and escorts, each manned by a mixed crew and armed with eight Polaris ballistic missiles. In effect, the MLF offered a depot for British and French nuclear weapons and forces, "an opportunity" for the Germans "to participate" in nuclear strategy, and a means for the United States to control their use.[3]

The Army and Air Force opposed the plan, and Admiral Rickover told Kennedy that he was against sharing reactor secrets with the Europeans, but in the summer of 1962 Admiral Claude V. Ricketts, the Vice CNO, issued a report that graced the MLF with the Navy's blessing. That October, Vice Admiral John M. Lee accompanied diplomat Gerard Smith to Europe where they explained to NATO's defense ministers how the MLF would function. Germans, Belgians, and Italians were keen for the concept, the Lee-Smith mission found, but the British and French opposed it. Taking the first step, McNamara ordered the new CNO, Admiral George Anderson, to arrange for trials with a multinational crew manning the newly commissioned guided missile destroyer *Claude V. Ricketts*—named for the widely admired officer who had died suddenly—and to persuade the Italian Navy to install launching tubes for Polaris missiles in the cruiser *Garibaldi*, then being overhauled. Privately, Kennedy "really considered . . . the MLF" to be "something of a fake" inasmuch as he "could not see why Europeans would be interested in making enormous contributions over which they had no real control."[4]

Britain's Prime Minister Harold Macmillan and France's President Charles de Gaulle, acting separately, thwarted Kennedy's Grand Design. To get the British to allow the U.S.

Navy to base Polaris-bearing submarines in Holy Loch, Scotland, Eisenhower had arranged for them to buy the new, trouble-plagued Air Force Skybolt ICBM, but when five successive Skybolt test launches failed, McNamara decided to abandon the program. Learning of this from Kennedy on 18 December 1962 at a summit conference in Nassau, Macmillan not only demanded that Polaris missiles be transferred to Britain in place of the Skybolts but also insisted on the right to retract Royal Navy ballistic missile submarines from NATO should they be needed on behalf of Britain's "supreme national interest." Holy Loch was needed to support deterrent patrols in the Norwegian Sea, and with this at stake Kennedy had to agree to Macmillan's plan. Admiral Anderson, the CNO, warned that substituting the Polaris for the Skybolt missile would doom the MLF plan. He argued, according to Admiral I. J. Galantin, that "whatever progress had been made toward acceptance of an MLF NATO nuclear forces as a substitute for individual national forces could be all but wiped out by the bilateral US-UK program."[5]

In 1963, the Royal Navy laid down four nuclear-powered, Polaris-bearing *Resolution*-class submarines, evidence of an Anglo-American special relationship, which angered de Gaulle, who believed that France was destined to lead NATO in Europe, that the Americans were untrustworthy, and that the French needed a means of defending France without American assistance. Kennedy had offered to sell *Lafayette*-class fleet ballistic missile submarines to France in the fall of 1962, and at Nassau, Kennedy and Macmillan jointly invited de Gaulle to join the MLF, but he was infuriated by what he perceived to be condescension. To punish Macmillan, de Gaulle vetoed Britain's membership in the European Common Market and accelerated the construction of France's nuclear *Force de Frappe* without consulting Washington. He also announced that if the West Germans were given access to nuclear weapons, even under the umbrella of the MLF, then France would withdraw her support for the Holstein Doctrine and German reunification. While Macmillan supported Kennedy's claim that nonnuclear NATO allies would be less likely to want their own nuclear arsenals once they were allowed a share, albeit contrived, in their own strategic defenses, the British did, from the start, question the practicality of operating a large multinational fleet of twenty-five ballistic missile–bearing ships. Related tensions within NATO gnawed away at the MLF plan until 1964, when the Turks withdrew their support to show dissatisfaction with Washington's failure to back them against the Greeks in a quarrel over newly independent Cyprus. Under French pressure, the Belgians also soon refused to participate. The scheme had a momentum of its own nonetheless, and in the spring of 1965 a mixed crew from six NATO navies manned the *Ricketts* during a demonstration deployment in the Caribbean Sea and European waters.[6]

Unhappy with the imminent demise of the MLF, Prime Minister Harold Wilson's new Labour government put forth an alternative in late 1964, the Atlantic Nuclear Force. Under Wilson's plan, the British would place their Polaris submarines and long-range V-bombers under multilateral control if the French would do the same, but de Gaulle arrogantly refused. The French Navy had already laid the keel for the *Le Redoubtable* in 1963, the lead vessel in a new class of French nuclear-powered fleet ballistic missile submarines, and France also began to build medium-range ballistic missiles and a wing of twenty-four Mirage IV nuclear weapon–bearing fighter-bombers. In March 1965, Paris announced the deployment of the jet bombers and unilaterally adopted a strategy of Instant Response to a Soviet invasion, the very opposite of McNamara's graduated response. De Gaulle also withdrew all French military forces from the NATO military command that year, and the first British and French ballistic missile–bearing submarines both put to sea in 1969. Although McNamara was still arguing in January 1964 that the MLF "would have a clear military utility," he admitted now that "its purpose would be primarily . . . to increase the political unity among the members of NATO." The NATO powers, who moved the alliance's headquarters from Paris to Brussels in 1967, adopted that same year a grand strategy of flexible response coupled with a forward defense of West Germany. Under this formula, the allied armies and air forces would hold the Elbe River as long as possible so as to give time for a political settlement, allow allied leaders to react with nuclear weapons, and prevent the French from implementing their Instant Response strategy. In short, McNamara's demand for a centralized American monopoly over the direction of a nuclear war was in shambles and with it went the MLF plan and Kennedy's Grand Design.[7]

Kennedy's flexible response strategy also called for a regional strategy of counterinsurgency to thwart Soviet-backed insurrections in Asia, Africa, and Latin America. Kennedy's Latin American policy was shaped by the conflicting heritage of pre–World War I interventionism, sanctioned by the Monroe Doctrine and the Roosevelt Corollary, and the Good Neighbor Policy and the noninterventionist liturgy embodied in the 1947 Rio Treaty. As an alternative to intervention, Truman and Eisenhower accepted costly aid programs, and Kennedy increased aid under the Alliance for Progress. The Good Neighbor Policy was poorly suited to the Cold War, however, especially when the Soviets violated the Monroe Doctrine and Cuba's Fidel Castro tested Kennedy's grit.

Castro had ignited a brief uprising in 1953 against the Cuban dictator Fulgencio Batista, the leading figure in Cuban politics for two decades. Batista crushed Castro's first insurrection, but Castro landed in Cuba again three years later, took to the mountains, and launched a successful guerrilla insurrection. Eisenhower adopted a policy of strict neutrality and slapped an arms embargo on the shipment of weapons to Cuba. Admiral Burke, then CNO, regarded Castro with distrust from the start and in vain urged the administration to prevent Batista's defeat. At the height of Castro's summer offensive in June 1958, a guerrilla band stopped a bus returning to the Guantánamo Naval Base, kidnapped thirty-one Marines, and imprisoned them in the mountains. The mastermind of this outrage was Raul Castro, Fidel's brother, who apparently believed that Eisenhower would ransom the hostages with arms for the rebels. When Burke heard this news, he was furious. "The Navy recommended an immediate intervention in Cuba in divisional size, with whatever naval support would be required to rescue the thirty-one Marines," according to Undersecretary of State Robert Murphy. However, Eisenhower rejected an invasion or armed intervention on the grounds that "getting into the island would not be difficult but that getting out would be interminable." Instead, after waiting for three weeks, he threatened to resume arms shipments to Batista, with the result that Fidel released the Marines to the American consul in Santiago.

Lack of popular support and Eisenhower's arms embargo now virtually ensured Batista's defeat, and Castro entered Havana in triumph on New Year's Day 1959. At first this did not worry Washington. Allen Dulles, the CIA director, assured Congress on 26 January that Castro was "not working for the communists" and had not exhibited "any communist sympathies." Eisenhower was therefore genuinely surprised when Castro murdered or imprisoned his democratic opponents and turned to Moscow in 1960 for political support and economic and military aid. Khrushchev and Castro signed a military assistance treaty that year that heralded Cuba's entry into the Soviet orbit, although the Russians brushed aside Havana's request to join the Warsaw Pact. Washington reacted to this violation of the Monroe Doctrine by embargoing Cuban sugar, welcoming the flight of the Cuban middle class to Miami, and devising plans to overthrow the Castro regime.[8]

Soon after, Khrushchev declared that the Kremlin supported "wars of liberation" in the Third World, and so opened the door to a new phase of the Cold War. Castro needed no prompt-

Admiral Robert L. Dennison. Commander in Chief, Atlantic, 1960–1966.

U.S. Naval Institute

ing to subvert other Latin American regimes, a policy for which Cuba was condemned by the Organization of American States. As early as April 1959, Castro had sent commandos to Panama with orders to conduct guerrilla operations against the pro-American regime in Panama City. To counter this threat to the Canal Zone, Eisenhower agreed to Admiral Burke's plan to dispatch a small task force to the waters off Panama, where these ships joined the Colombian Navy for maneuvers. These patrols prevented additional Cuban landings and demonstrated American support for the dissolute regime in Panama City, but the display of force was largely superfluous. The ragtag Cuban guerrillas were quickly captured by the Panamanian National Guard, and they were soon disavowed by Castro.[9]

Despite this setback, Radio Havana issued a call to leftists throughout the hemisphere to take up arms against their governments. In November 1960, communist-sponsored armed uprisings in Guatemala and Nicaragua created a minor panic in Washington that led to the deployment of the Caribbean Task Force. This command, composed of the carrier *Shangri-La* and several destroyers, patrolled the western Caribbean into December "to prevent intervention" by Cuba "through the landing of armed forces or of supplies from abroad." Although the pro-American military regimes in Guatemala City and Managua quashed these hapless left-wing insurrections, the sum of Cuban-inspired political and military subversion in Latin America was impressive, and Washington now decided the need to overthrow Castro was acute.[10]

The Democrats were in high dudgeon over this state of affairs. In his 1960 campaign, Kennedy had denounced Eisenhower for not acting against Cuba and called for a "serious offensive" against Castro. Once in office, he decided to do something stiff. CIA Director Dulles offered up Operation Zapata, a plan to transport a brigade of CIA-trained Cuban renegades from Nicaragua to Cuba, where they might establish a mountain redoubt and organize an insurrection aimed at toppling Castro's regime. On 28 January 1961, Kennedy turned to the JCS for their advice on Operation Zapata, but he prohibited them from reviewing it with their staffs and announced prematurely that the landings would be directed by Richard Bissell, the CIA's deputy director. Burke believed that the political objective of overthrowing Castro was correct, but he argued that the renegade landing force would not succeed without adequate air cover, communications, and logistical support. Aware that Operation Zapata's security was poor, Burke failed in his duty as the president's "principal naval adviser" to warn Kennedy of the exact flaws he found in the landing plan. The JCS was wary of the plan to land at the remote swamp known as the Bay of Pigs, and preferred to land the renegades at Trinidad, about thirty-five miles away, but Kennedy had personally selected the Zapata Swamp. Burke was successful in opposing Secretary of State Rusk's bizarre scheme to have the renegades launch their offensive from the Guantánamo Naval Base. Burke wanted so badly to believe that Castro could be removed, however, that he signed a final 7 February JCS assessment stating that Operation Zapata enjoyed "fair prospects." Subsequent quibbling over precisely what this term meant served only to exaggerate the failure of Burke and the rest of the JCS to give Kennedy straightforward advice.[11]

In March, Admiral Robert Dennison, the commander in chief of the Atlantic theater, ordered Rear Admiral John A. Clark to put to sea in command of a Caribbean Task Force composed of the antisubmarine carrier *Essex* and five destroyers, rendezvous with five transports carrying the Cuban renegades from Nicaragua, and escort them into the Bay of Pigs. Hoping to avoid charges that American forces were invading Cuba and thereby violating the Rio Treaty, Kennedy directed Clark to send his destroyers no closer than five miles offshore and not to provide the landings with gunfire support. Defense Secretary McNamara's orders to Dennison rigidly stipulated that Clark not open fire on Castro's forces except to defend his ships. "You mean I'm to go down there armed to the teeth but I'm not supposed to do anything?" Clark growled. "Yes, my darling daughter," Dennison snorted, "don't go near the water!" Neither Dennison nor Clark was deluded by Bissell's argument that the Cuban people would rise up against Castro and that the Cuban Army would "jump aboard" the renegades' bandwagon. At the last moment, General Lyman Lemnitzer, the JCS chairman, appealed to JFK to allow the Caribbean Task Force to provide the Zapata Brigade with air cover, but Kennedy would only permit Clark to provide the assault troops with early warnings of incoming communist aircraft.[12]

Mishaps and blunders characterized the operation from start to finish. On the night of 16 April, Commander Peter Perkins in the destroyer *Eaton* led the brigade's ships into the Bay of Pigs. The destroyer *Murray* remained behind to cover the rear, and the exile brigade landed in the remote, sparsely populated Zapata area. The carrier *Essex* stood off the coast, fully prepared to launch air strikes to prevent Castro from containing or bombarding the beachhead, but Kennedy would not change his mind. Communications linking the landing force and its support ships were poor, and the cargo ships were incorrectly loaded for a forced landing. While these problems were being sorted out, Castro surged troops, artillery, vehicles, and aircraft to the Zapata Swamp, isolated the lodgment, and reduced the trapped renegade brigade. The CIA intended to stage a diversion on the other side of the island, but their agents failed to bring it off. And there was no uprising. Castro was genuinely popular, and the Cuban people now believed that the Zapata landings heralded the return of Batista's hated clique.

Burke pleaded with Kennedy for two days to order the *Essex*'s air group to defend the beachhead, but the president turned this down on the grounds that he wanted no direct American involvement with the operation. To Burke, this made no sense. American sponsorship of Operation Zapata was evident. Though Kennedy allowed the CIA to launch a flight of old B-26 bombers from Nicaragua, they were shot down by Cuban Sea Fury fighters and T-33 trainers before they reached the beachhead. At last, on 19 April, with the landing in jeopardy, the president relented a bit, permitting Burke to order unmarked fighters from the *Essex* to escort another inbound flight from the rebel staging area in Nicaragua, but the two friendly air formations never made contact with one another. With defeat imminent, Burke finally obtained Kennedy's permission for Clark to send Captain Robert R. Crutchfield's destroyers into the Bay of Pigs at night under the guise of a humanitarian mission to rescue the Zapata Brigade. However, they picked up only a handful of rebels who had been isolated from the main body and were stranded on outlying keys. On the 20th, when the battle was almost over, Ambassador Charles Bohlen, the State Department's foremost Soviet expert, urged JFK to allow the Caribbean Task Force to land Marines to support the invasion, but this last-minute plea was rejected. Within hours, Castro's army captured most of the renegades. They were ransomed later that year for American trucks.

Kennedy publicly took responsibility for the Bay of Pigs tragedy but privately sought revenge. General Maxwell Taylor, the former Army chief of staff and intimate of Attorney General Robert Kennedy, the president's brother, was brought out of retirement and into the White House as a special military adviser. Within a year, he relieved Lemnitzer as JCS chairman. JFK sacked CIA director Dulles and replaced him with California business tycoon John McCone. He told Taylor and Burke to prepare a critique of Operation Zapata, but their findings dwelt only on the military aspects of the plan and carped about the president's failure to entrust its execution to the JCS. Burke had not made himself a favorite at the White House during the Bay of Pigs crisis; one of Kennedy's liberal aides complained that the CNO was an inveterate interventionist and the "chief voice of the counterrevolutionary line." Burke himself reckoned that "there was nothing I could accomplish" with McNamara as secretary of defense, so he retired at long last, and on 1 August 1961, Navy Secretary John Connally personally selected his relief, Admiral George Anderson, a distinguished naval aviator. Trouble inhered in the distrustful relations between the president and the JCS. Kennedy boasted that he "could have managed the military responsibilities of the Bay of Pigs better than the military experts," and Theodore Sorensen, his speechwriter, observed that JFK had "little confidence" in the chiefs after the awful spring of 1961.[13]

Kennedy tried to improve relations with Khrushchev when they met 3 June 1961 in Vienna. He told the premier that "there could be no agreement between us so long as he supported Communist subversion all over the world, but he never gave way, never gave an inch." Kennedy, now more than ever determined to overthrow Castro, ordered the Defense Department and the CIA to implement a somewhat fanciful covert action plan codenamed Mongoose. Its creators hoped to improve intelligence about Cuba by more carefully interrogating refugees and by infiltrating eleven teams of CIA agents into Cuba to work with over 200 subagents and informers to subvert and sabotage the Cuban economy, all of this with the aim of "overthrow[ing] the Communist regime" by late 1962. The resulting activity worried Castro and the Russians and may have led Moscow to think that it foreshadowed an American invasion of Cuba, although Kennedy did not plan such a step and did nothing whatever to prepare for it. The Russians still refused to admit Cuba to the Warsaw Pact, but because of an ongoing rift with China over Moscow's leadership of the communist bloc, they could ill afford to lose their new satellite.[14]

The 1962 Cuban Missile Crisis was thus rooted in the affront Castro posed to the Monroe Doctrine and to the Kennedy brothers personally, as well as in the Soviet commitment to defend Cuba from an imaginary American invasion and in Khrushchev's assessment of Kennedy at the Vienna summit, where he had taken the young president's measure and somehow found it wanting. The Americans had their own reasons to worry. There was a prodigious buildup of Soviet military power in late 1961 and 1962 in Cuba, including over forty Russian-operated MiG fighters, forty-two Il-28 light bombers, 42,000 Red Army combat troops and assorted technicians, *Komar*-class missile–bearing patrol boats, and short-range, AS-1 Kennel shore-to-ship cruise missiles.

What turned this regional quarrel into a genuine superpower crisis, however, was Khrushchev's use of the movement of defensive arms to Cuba to mask the installation of forty-eight SS-4 Sandal medium-range and thirty-two SS-5 Skean intermediate-range ballistic missiles at remote sites in Cuba. This upset the existing strategic nuclear balance of power. After the April 1962 discussions with Soviet Defense Minister Rodion Malinovsky highlighted the problems that the upcoming placement of American Jupiter medium-range ballistic missiles in Turkey posed for Soviet military strategists, Khrushchev devised a plan to position Russian "missiles with nuclear warheads in Cuba without letting the United States find out they were there until it was too late to do anything about it." The MRBMs and IRBMs would be useful in "protecting Cuba," he boasted to the Politburo, and "our missiles would have equalized what the West likes to call 'the balance of power.' "

One reason for his concern about the strategic nuclear balance was that Kennedy's policy of accelerating the construction of Eisenhower's missile-bomber-submarine strategic triad was bearing fruit. At the time, the U.S. Air Force deployed over 200 Atlas and Titan ICBMs, nearly 200 Thor and Jupiter IRBMs in Britain, Italy, and Turkey, and 600 long-range B-52 and 1,100 medium-range B-47 manned bombers; and the Navy operated 8 *Ethan Allen*-class submarines armed with 128 tubes capable of launching Polaris A-1 or A-2 medium-range ballistic missiles. The Russians, on the other hand, had only 14 SS-6 Sapwood liquid-fuel ICBMs, 50 SS-7 Sadler and SS-8 Sassin solid-fuel ICBMs, 140 Bear and Bison long- and medium-range bombers, and 25 submarines capable of firing and refiring about 60 SS-N-4 Sarks, a highly unreliable sea-launched, medium-range ballistic missile. This meant that in a full-throttle exchange, the United States might attack the Soviet Union with roughly 4,000 nuclear weapons, whereas the Soviets had only about 500 to use against America and her NATO allies. Informed by the radio-transmitting Samos II reconnaissance satellites and other sources of this growing disparity in the rival strategic nuclear forces, McNamara had gone so far as to announce confidently in May 1961 that he was implementing a "no cities" counterforce strategy, which would wipe out in a single strike the entire Soviet bomber and missile inventory. Positioning the Sandals and Skeans in Cuba was intended therefore to right this imbalance and greatly complicate McNamara's counterforce strategy by doubling the number of quick-draw Soviet ballistic missiles within easy range of American targets.

Marshal Sergei Biryuzov, heading a secret mission to Cuba in May, reported that Castro, fearing an invasion, had approved of Khrushchev's plan. Biryuzov told Khrushchev that his team had identified four likely Sandal sites in San Cristóbal and two in Sagua la Grande and two Skean sites in the vicinity of Remedios in Las Villas Province and Guanajay in Pinar del Río Province, and that the missiles could be deployed and made operational before American intelligence got wind of what was afoot. The deal was consummated in early July during a two-week trip to Moscow by Raul Castro, who negotiated a secret five-year treaty that provided for the stationing in Cuba of the ballistic missiles and accompanying Soviet ground and air forces and surface-to-air missile batteries that were to act as a "trip wire" in the event of an American air attack on the missile sites or an invasion. Soviet communications security for these talks was tight because, as Foreign Minister Andrei Gromyko had warned, revealing the plan before the midterm November 1962 elections in the United States was sure to trigger a political "explosion" that Kennedy could not ignore.

Soviet security notwithstanding, "the president became aware of the planned introduction of Russian missiles into Cuba sometime in early July," according to a diary kept by Commander Gerry McCabe, Kennedy's assistant naval aide. The exact source of Kennedy's carefully guarded, codename intelligence is unclear, but he had many means of learning what Khrushchev was up to. While the Russians hand-carried all sensitive diplomatic traffic, assembling and transporting the ballistic missiles, specially built trucks, and oddly configured fuel containers within the Soviet Union was a huge logistical task involving hundreds of routine movement orders inviting American interest. Moreover, there were several Western spies in the upper reaches of the Soviet government. Orbiting high above the Soviet Union, the Corona and Samos II, recently launched American satellites, provided nearly complete photographic coverage of the key ports of Odessa and Leningrad, where the ships, missiles, and support equipment destined for Cuba were assembled. And while Raul Castro was still in Moscow, Commander Thomas Cosgrove, the skipper of the 11,000-ton *Oxford,* an ex-*Liberty*-class cargo ship converted into a sophisticated signals collecting vessel for the National Security Agency in 1961, was handed urgent orders to stand out of Norfolk and position his vessel twelve miles off Havana. She arrived on station on 23 July. With her large antennae and other emissions-collecting gear, the *Oxford* intercepted and deciphered Cuban and Soviet communications to and from Havana and tracked Soviet vessels appearing in Cuban waters for the next several months. Because the Cubans, then relying on an ITT telephone system whose layout was known to the CIA, were less cautious than the Soviets, the *Oxford*'s deployment provided Washington with an intelligence cornucopia from late July onward.

Forward deployed U.S. Navy forces first detected the Soviet sealift. Operating from bases in Greece, Sicily, and Spain, patrol squadrons of the 6th Fleet watched the increasing flow of outbound Soviet merchantmen, as did their counterparts based in Scotland, Iceland, Nova Scotia, the Azores, and Bermuda. Long-range patrol planes tracked the arms-laden freighters through the Mediterranean and Baltic seas strategic chokepoints and across the Atlantic. "It wasn't limited to sightings at sea," recalled Admiral Dennison, commander in chief of the Atlantic Fleet. "We had intelligence sources in various parts of Europe and naval attachés all over the place" who reported the suspicious Soviet merchantmen. The "ships that were coming through the Dardanelles and the Bosporus and through Gibraltar or through the Channel, and those that came down past Iceland and off our own coast were . . . photographed." Operating closer to Cuba, P-2V Neptune maritime patrol aircraft flying out of Norfolk, Jacksonville, Key West, Puerto Rico, and Guantánamo shadowed the freighters into Cuban ports and "observed every Red Bloc merchant ship that came into our waters," according to Rear Admiral Edward O'Donnell, the commandant of the Guantánamo Naval Base. "When the whole thing was over we were able to fix that we really hadn't missed any." Suspicious of the early buildup, O'Donnell positioned a ship in the Windward Passage to report "any spot on their radar" that failed to identify herself and vector a nearby patrol plane to intercept the vessel. "We picked up quite a bit of information from that small ship sailing around slowly in the Windward Passage," he observed. In July alone, Navy surveillance detected thirty Soviet merchantmen arriving in Cuba, a 50 percent increase over the month of June. Six to ten times in July alone, Navy and Air Force F3D-2Q Skynight, AD-5Q Skyraider, WV-2Q Constellation, and A3D-2P Skywarrior electronic warfare aircraft flew around the island, skirting Cuban airspace, to monitor and intercept communications and electronic emissions. One of the surveillance operations, codenamed Quick Fox, used two Air Force C-130 cargo transports to eavesdrop on Russian and Cuban military message radio communications throughout the island after 1 August.

For reasons that defy comprehension, Kennedy did nothing to prevent the missile shipments from arriving in Cuba. Instead, he restricted the dissemination of information about them within the American intelligence community. Nonetheless, CIA director McCone apparently pieced together Khrushchev's plan in mid-August and raised the alarm, but McNamara, Secretary of State Rusk, and Attorney General Robert Kennedy insisted that the Soviet buildup in Cuba was entirely defensive. Navy leaders were not so easily misled. The Navy representative on the Joint Strategic Survey Committee warned the JCS in mid-August that ballistic missiles were about to arrive in Cuba, but General Maxwell Taylor, the JCS chairman, turned down a plea that the assessment be sent up to the White House. Robert Kennedy did ask Assistant Attorney General Nobert Schlei on 22 August to study ways by which the missiles might be removed from Cuba, and Schlei recommended the establishment of a "visit and search" naval blockade. The following day the president ordered the JCS to study "military alternatives . . . to eliminate any installations in Cuba" including "pinpoint attack [surgical strike], general counter-force attack [with nuclear weapons against the Soviet Union], and outright invasion." On 29 August, however, when two Navy P-2V Neptune patrol planes monitoring shipping off Cuba were fired upon by Cuban patrol boats, the president had future flights restricted rather than intensified. And he still took no action to stop ships carrying the missiles and warheads from reaching Cuba.

Kennedy's hand was first called on 31 August, when Senator Kenneth Keating, a New York Republican, delivered an electrifying speech on the Senate floor in which he denounced the White House for allowing Cuba to be transformed into a Soviet bastion, speculated that the Soviets were installing missiles in Cuba, and implored Kennedy to take action. The White House responded to Keating's sensational charge by announcing on 4 September that "offensive ground-to-ground missiles . . . either in Cuban hands or under Soviet direction" would cause "the gravest issues to arise." Khrushchev replied on the 11th, claiming that the weapons he was shipping to Cuba were "exclusively for defensive purposes" and declaring that "an attack on Cuba" or "on Soviet ships" would start a general war. It would be "impossible for an aggressor to attack Cuba and count on the attack going unpunished," the Kremlin warned, a major change in Soviet policy. Two days later Kennedy scoffed in public at Keating's claims about the missiles and agreed with Khrushchev's contention that they did "not constitute a threat to any other part of this hemisphere."

The second phase of Khrushchev's plan was almost complete by this time. Guantánamo-based Navy patrol planes were shadowing the Vladivostok lumber carrier *Omsk* when, on 11 September, she stood into the port of Casilda on Cuba's southern coast. Soviet military personnel offloaded her cargo of Sandals and trucked them up to the Sagua la Grande site. The lumber carrier *Poltava* docked at Mariel four days later, and her missile cargo was offloaded and transported by a heavily guarded convoy down to San Cristóbal on the night of the 17th. "The ports into which the ships sailed," according to Admiral O'Donnell, "really helped to localize the probable sites of the missiles." About the same time, a recently arrived Cuban refugee provided a CIA Mongoose team with a description of a truck convoy he had seen and a remarkably accurate sketch of the rear section of one of the Sandal missiles. And on the 16th, Atlantic Fleet P-2V Neptunes photographed large crates strapped to the deck of the Soviet freighter *Kasimov* and Defense Intelligence Agency photo interpreters discovered that they contained the dismantled components of Il-28 Beagle bombers. Again the Navy representative on the Joint Strategic Survey Committee begged General Taylor to raise the alarm at the White House, but for a second time Taylor heaped scorn on the admiral's assessment. "The fact of the missiles was known a long time before [the October crisis] from many sources," noted Rear Admiral Chick Hayward, who commanded the 2nd Fleet's carriers. "We certainly . . . did not need to let it progress to the so-called 'eye ball' confrontation that happened." At roughly the same time, in mid-September, the Navy received more alarming news. An Atlantic Fleet maritime patrol plane had sighted a Soviet *Zulu*-class diesel submarine armed with nuclear-tipped, 75-mile-range bombardment cruise missiles. "She'd been on a covert patrol . . . near the East Coast of the United States," recalled Admiral Dennison.

By mid-month it was evident that Kennedy's warnings were having no effect on Khrushchev, who forged ahead with the deployment in the absence of any stiff action by the United States to stop it. Khrushchev now suspected that Kennedy was aware of what the Soviets were up to and knew that he had as yet failed to react. "The Americans became frightened," he wrote, "and we stepped up our shipments." U-2 overflights in late September and early October provided photography that documented the deployment, and Kennedy could not prevent this news from reaching Republican hands. He was stunned by Keating's 10 October speech to the Senate in which he declared that "construction had begun on at least a half a dozen launching sites for intermediate-range tactical missiles" in Cuba and demanded that Kennedy "let us have all the facts, and have them now." The next day Kennedy further tightened access to intelligence about the missiles, but it was too late. Within a week he was at long last forced to act.

Pictures of the San Cristóbal site were taken by two U-2s on the 14 October and delivered to the White House the next day. Navy leaders were not surprised. "We knew three weeks before . . . that there were missile sites," noted Vice Admiral Herbert D. Riley, the director of the Joint Staff. "The military got the information and passed it on to the Chiefs and to the White House, and they sat on it for a while hoping it would go away. . . . But we had beautiful pictures of those sites and the stuff going in." The U-2 photography "was not particularly a surprise to me," recalled Admiral Anderson. "We sort of expected it." Kennedy, worried that these photographs would soon fall into Republican hands, let down his guard for a moment when he told an aide that "Keating will probably be the next president of the United States."

White House assistant Richard Neustadt, a sometime Harvard political science professor, had just finished gutting Eisenhower's well-functioning NSC staff system, so Kennedy was now forced to turn to an ad hoc "war cabinet" called the ExComm, a mixed group of old cronies and partisan cabinet officials "many of whom had little knowledge in either the military or diplomatic field," noted former Secretary of State Dean Acheson. Kennedy did not disclose to the ExComm the intelligence he had received in July, and those who briefed the group during the October crisis apparently ignored or glossed over other important information. Acheson, who attended these early meetings, was so disgusted by Kennedy's amateurism and the "repetitive, leaderless" ExComm sessions, which he considered to be a "waste of time," that he stormed out of the White House in a rage four days later. During meetings on 16 October, Kennedy's advisers were divided on the importance of the missiles in Cuba. "I don't think there is a military problem here," Secretary McNamara insisted. "This is a domestic political problem." Taylor strongly disagreed, pointing out that the Sandals and Skeans served as "important adjunct and reinforcement to the . . . strike capability of the Soviet Union" and alluding to early warning problems raised by the Joint Strategic Survey Committee a month earlier. Whether the problem was political or military, the ExComm decided that Kennedy had to do something to force the Soviets to withdraw the missiles from Cuba. Inasmuch as selective air strikes against the missile sites could not guarantee their destruction, the issue resolved itself into a question of a thorough air offensive against the enemy's air forces, ground-based air defenses, and the missile sites; an invasion; or Schlei's "visit and search" blockade.

The JCS had devised several contingency plans to deal with Cuba since Castro took power in 1959, and in mid-1961 turned over this task to Admiral Dennison's Atlantic command. He appointed the commander of the 2nd Fleet to lead any operations against Cuba, and his staff drew up one plan for air strikes, OpPlan 312, and two plans for an invasion, OpPlans 314 and 316, and continually updated them as the crisis worsened in 1962. Operation Rockpile, a September version of OpPlan 312, provided for attacks by Florida-based Air Force bombers and fighter-bombers and planes from Rear Admiral Hayward's two-carrier 2nd Fleet Covering Force against the Cuban-based MiG fighters, their bases, and the Soviet SA-2 Guideline surface-to-air missiles defending the Sandal and Skean sites. OpPlan 316, the preferred scheme for an invasion, provided for a parachute assault south of Mariel by two Army airborne divisions and a concurrent amphibious landing at Tarata, west of Mariel, by the 2nd Marine Division supported by elements of the Army's 1st Armored Division. Once a beachhead was established, Vice Admiral Horacio Rivero's Atlantic Amphibious Force was to transport the Army's 1st and 2nd Infantry Divisions from Florida to the lodgment. Over 100,000 troops and Marines would be needed for the invasion.

By the time the ExComm convened in the White House in mid-October, the Navy had already swung into action. Rivero's Amphibious Force was off Puerto Rico participating in an annual amphibious exercise, and on the 16th other warships began to put out of Norfolk to strengthen his command. The attack carrier *Independence* and her destroyer screen steamed out of Norfolk that same day and headed south for a position from which her air group might attack the missile bases once the order came. Three days later, Hayward in the *Enterprise*, her air group strengthened by the addition of Marine A4D Skyhawk light bombers, followed the *Independence* southward. "My . . . attack force . . . had as its primary mission to destroy the missile sites located in Cuba," Hayward recalled. "After we had done the first task, the second was to provide the air support for the proposed landing west of Mariel."

The JCS also met on the 16th to consider the military options for removing the ballistic missiles. They concluded that the plan for selective strikes against only the MRBM bases was militarily unsound and told McNamara that any air strike had to encompass "all missile sites, all combat aircraft and nuclear storage, combat ships, tanks, and other appropriate military targets in Cuba, in conjunction with a complete blockade." Only an attack on this comprehensive list of targets would ensure the safety of the air strike force and destroy the missile sites. At the same time, only a complete blockade of shipping to Cuba would prevent Soviet reinforcements from reaching the island. The air strike could be launched within twenty-four hours after authorization, and the 2nd Fleet was moving into a position from which to impose the blockade. To ensure that no missiles or warheads remained in Cuban or Russian hands, Rivero's Amphibious Force was poised to invade Cuba. Likewise, the chiefs added, should Kennedy decide on the "elimination of the Castro regime," American troops would have to invade Cuba.

Kennedy was apparently reluctant to meet with the JCS, but on the 19th they had their only chance to present their "individual and corporate views" to him at the White House. They again recommended a surprise attack on the bases and any other target capable of a retaliatory response and a complete naval blockade of the island. The air strike, they admitted, was unlikely to destroy all of the missile launchers and might give the Soviets the opportunity to disperse any undamaged launchers into the Cuban jungle, and therefore additional air strikes and an invasion would ultimately be necessary. The chiefs predicted that the Soviets would not retaliate against the United States for an air strike or an invasion of Cuba, or at least that they would not initiate a nuclear exchange that would lead to World War III. Khrushchev's most likely countermove would be to blockade West Berlin. Kennedy was unconvinced. He continued to fear a stronger Soviet reprisal if an American air strike or invasion killed Russian troops. The meeting, Taylor recalled, "may not have been particularly helpful to the president, but it certainly made the Chiefs feel better." Ever since the Bay of Pigs fiasco, Kennedy had looked upon the JCS with a wary eye, and the meeting on the 19th probably reinforced his conviction that the chiefs were unsophisticated bumblers whom he ought not to trust. "These brass hats have one great advantage in their favor," he scoffed. "If we . . . do what they want us to do, none of us will be alive later to tell them they are wrong." However, Kennedy had no one but himself to blame for allowing the missiles to reach Cuba in the first place.

Unbeknownst to Kennedy or his circle, considerable disagreement over invading Cuba existed within the JCS and its subordinate commands. "As a body [the JCS] never recommended the invasion of Cuba," according to Taylor, but did call for "merely the preparations for an invasion that would reinforce the President's hand" in dealing with Khrushchev. This was an inaccurate rendering of what really transpired. Admiral Anderson and Generals Wheeler and LeMay all favored an invasion. Only

Taylor abstained. "Once you invade Cuba," he argued, "what are you going to do with it? Sit on it for eternity?" Any invasion would plant "the seed of guerrilla warfare against our occupying forces, and again tie down a large part of our conventional strength." The air strike, Taylor believed, would provoke Khrushchev to voluntarily withdraw any remaining missiles.

Anderson was the strongest advocate of invading Cuba and of challenging Castro, not Khrushchev. He favored "going from one end of the island to the other" in a "massive invasion . . . coupled with a massive propaganda campaign of all sorts, leaflets, and radio broadcasts to get the support of the Cuban people." Members of the CNO's staff, however, felt that an invasion would be far too costly in ships and men. Captain Turner F. Caldwell's "Cuba Watch" committee had reported to Anderson and the JCS in early October on a study that examined the forces required for an invasion of Cuba. "The study," Caldwell observed, "asserted that an invasion would need 500,000 men, take six months to mount, and require the mobilization of twenty or so large civilian ships." OpPlan 316, however, called for only 109,000 troops. The JCS "did not comment on this latter requirement," he noted, "nor start any action to implement the recommendations of the study." And Admiral Dennison in Norfolk opposed invading Cuba.

Navy men were concerned about invading Cuba owing to the shortage of amphibious shipping available for the three Army divisions. Admiral Rivero's Amphibious Force embarked the 2nd Marine Division's assault troops, but he had only eight LSTs to handle the 1st Armored Division's landing force and they could not carry all of its heavy vehicles. Moreover, he needed even more cargo shipping and landing ships to land the rest of the division after the initial assault. Admiral Anderson ordered that eleven LSTs be activated from the Atlantic Reserve Fleet and that an additional twenty commercial cargo ships be chartered, but this was not done until 26 October, and the Reserve Fleet's World War II–vintage LSTs needed refitting and the commercial ships still had to be assembled at the embarkation ports before any invasion could be mounted. The ships carrying a 10,000-man Marine expeditionary brigade from California were not scheduled to enter the Panama Canal until 8 November, and until they joined his command, Rivero did not have enough assault troops to conduct a landing. Owing in part to the shipping problems, "even though our plans did provide for it," said Dennison, "no-body . . . that I know of felt that invading Cuba was the right thing to do."

After considerable teeth gnashing, on 21 October the president at last sided with McNamara and Robert Kennedy, who favored imposing a blockade and seeking diplomatic support from the OAS before taking any stiff action. As Acheson had pointed out, however, a blockade would do nothing to force the Soviets to withdraw the missiles already in place, missiles that were in all likelihood now ready to be fired. Kennedy had not acted earlier to halt the deployment of the missiles, and he now chose the path of least resistance in seeking their removal. He explained his decision to Admiral Anderson, and the CNO in turn described how Vice Admiral Alfred Ward's 2nd Fleet would locate, shadow, stop, and search vessels crossing the blockade line that Anderson had located 500 miles off Cuba. Anderson, Dennison, and Ward understood that "intercept" did not mean "stop and board" and that the president would decide which ships the Blockade Force would stop and board regardless of whether they were within the blockade zone. "In other words," recalled Dennison, "the line wasn't necessarily static. We just didn't sit there. We knew where these ships were and went out to intercept them." Should a Cuba-bound freighter refuse to stop after being challenged, Anderson told Kennedy, a Blockade Force ship was to fire a shot over her bow and follow this with a shot at the rudder or other nonvital part. Unbeknownst to Anderson, however, Ward did not intend to fire on any cargo ship that ignored his orders; he planned instead to have one of his heavy cruisers "ram it," put a prize crew on board, and haul it into a Florida port.

The JCS now told its unified theater commanders and all strategic forces to assume a Defense Condition Three alert at 1900 on 22 October, the very moment that Kennedy was scheduled to appear on nationwide television and announce the blockade. In Norfolk, the remaining ships of the Blockade Force prepared to put out to sea. At an early-morning presail conference with the ships' commanding officers that day, Admiral Ward explained the upcoming operation. "They were all highly enthusiastic," he said. "The consensus was that such action was long overdue." At 2100 that evening, Ward boarded his flagship, the cruiser *Newport News*, and she stood out to sea to rendezvous with the rest of the blockade vessels, which were already moving into position. The JCS had named Admiral Anderson to handle blockade operations, but Kennedy made it known that he alone would decide which vessels the Blockade Force was to stop and board. His orders were issued to McNamara or General Taylor, who in turn informed Admiral Anderson in the Navy's Flag Plot in the Pentagon. Anderson relayed these orders to Dennison at Atlantic Fleet headquarters in Norfolk or, on occasion, communicated instructions directly to Ward in the *Newport News*. Contrary to some ill-researched accounts, the White House never communicated orders directly with the ships at sea. "I know of no incident when civilian authorities gave orders directly to afloat forces," recalled Captain Carmichael.

At 1900 on the 22nd, Kennedy addressed the nation from the Oval Office. In a seventeen-minute statement, he claimed that he had only recently learned about Khrushchev's plan to turn Cuba into a strategic missile base. "To halt this offensive buildup, a strict quarantine on all offensive military equipment under shipment to Cuba is being initiated." He demanded that Khrushchev "halt and eliminate this clandestine, reckless, and provocative threat" and declared he would regard an attack on the United States by the ballistic missiles in Cuba "as an attack by the Soviet Union." By this time, several of the Soviet ballistic missile batteries were already operational. The CIA reported that two of the San Cristóbal sites, a total of eight launchers, were ready to fire. "We understood operational to mean that everything was there that was needed to fire the missiles," recalled State Department functionary Raymond Garthoff. The DIA estimated that the entire launch sequence—fueling, warhead mating, targeting, and counting down—would take about eight hours to complete. The two bases at Sagua la Grande were also capable of launching their ballistic missiles, while the Guanajay and Remedios sites were still being constructed and would not be operational until December.

Soon after Kennedy's address, the JCS issued the rules of engagement for the Blockade Force. Drawn up by Captain Caldwell, approved by McNamara on the evening of the 21st, and sent out to the Atlantic Fleet two days later, these orders merely reiterated long-established Navy procedures for searching and boarding ships. Any "ship, including surface warships, armed merchant ships or submarines, or any aircraft which take actions which can reasonably be considered as threatening a U.S. ship

. . . may be subjected to attack to the extent required to terminate the threat." In short, this authorized Blockade Force ships, if sufficiently threatened, to fire before being fired upon, although they already had this authority under existing peacetime rules of engagement.

The fear that Russian submarines might escort merchantmen into the blockade zone, carry nuclear warheads to Cuba, or attack the invasion transports required that they be included in the blockade order, and the CNO had discussed this with the president on the 20th. Kennedy's quarantine proclamation did not specifically mention hostile submarines, but it did announce that "any vessel or craft which may be proceeding toward Cuba may be intercepted," and Admiral Dennison's order, issued to the Blockade Force on the 23rd, directed that "all ships, including combatant, surface and sub-surface, . . . designated by Cin-CLantFlt . . . will be intercepted by this force."

Reports of Soviet submarines operating from Cuba had been received in Washington for some time. "We'd had low-level reports . . . that Soviet submarines would be based in Cuba, and the buildup of weapons in Cuba made these reports somewhat significant," Dennison noted. The first news that the Russian boats were operating near the quarantine area came on 22 October, when Navy patrol aircraft photographed the Soviet replenishment ship *Terek* in the vicinity of the Azores. Alongside the *Terek* was the cruise missile–bearing Zulu-class submarine, which showed signs of her lengthy western Atlantic deployment. "We had known that Soviet submarines were operating south of Iceland," Ward recalled, "but this was the first time we had found any as far south as Cuba." The Navy's SOSUS underwater listening arrays also picked up contacts. "We had rather good information ever since we had SOSUS installed," observed Vice Admiral Charles D. Griffin. Kennedy was told on the evening of the 23rd that three Soviet submarines were heading for the Caribbean. According to his brother, Robert, the president instructed McNamara "to give highest priority to tracking the submarines and to put into effect the greatest possible safety measure to protect our own aircraft carriers and other vessels."

Armed with the blockade order and the revised rules of engagement, Admiral Ward's 2nd Fleet now made ready for action. He would directly command the Blockade Force and be responsible for tracking, intercepting, and boarding all suspicious ships bound for Cuba. Rear Admiral John W. Ailes in the cruiser *Canberra*, who commanded a 2nd Fleet cruiser-destroyer task group, was to establish and maintain the destroyer blockade stations. Vice Admiral Edmund B. Taylor's Norfolk-based Atlantic Fleet Antisubmarine Force, which included a hunter-killer task group built around the antisubmarine carrier *Essex*, was to provide air support and surveillance for the Blockade Force. Four more hunter-killer groups were steaming in and around the blockade zone, and maritime patrol planes operated continuously off the East Coast and from naval stations throughout the Atlantic theater. Admiral Hayward's Covering Force, consisting of the attack carriers *Enterprise* and *Independence* and their screens, were on the prowl northwest of the Bahamas on the 20th, but Hayward shifted his ships to a position between Cuba and Jamaica on the 23rd to be ready to support the Guantánamo base should Castro decide to attack it. By this time, at total of 183 ships representing the might of the Atlantic Fleet were patrolling the waters around Cuba. "Whatever we did," recalled Captain Isaac Kidd, the CNO's executive assistant, "it had to be credible to the Soviets . . . so there could be no question that we came with enough power to the ball game to win."

The blockade proclamation—which Kennedy and his circle euphemistically called a "quarantine"—took effect at 1000 on the 24th. Before dawn that morning, according to the Navy's shipping intelligence, seventeen Soviet dry cargo ships and five tankers in the Atlantic were en route to Cuba. This included four vessels that were suspected of transporting ballistic missiles, the lumber carriers *Poltava*, *Kimovsk*, *Okhotsk*, and *Orenburg*. At this time, however, explained Commander McCabe, the Navy "knew the ships had left, we knew that the missiles were in the ships, but we had no idea where in the hell those ships were." Because Admiral Taylor's P-2V Neptunes were busy at the moment with an oceanwide submarine hunt, General LeMay offered to have his B-52 bombers "locate all ships in the Atlantic within four hours," and he kept his promise. "Not only did he fly every single plane the Air Force had out over the Atlantic," recalled McCabe, "but they sent in every single contact report, from a fishing smack, to the biggest vessel they could find floating on the Atlantic and they swamped the White House Situation Room." The Air Force "just wanted to rub the Navy's nose in it, and they did," with the result that when the blockade went into effect the first Soviet ships to approach the blockade line were already under surveillance.

Dennison in Norfolk now decided that the freighters *Kimovsk* and *Poltava*, which he believed might be carrying missiles, should be the first vessels to be intercepted. Both were well beyond the 500-mile arc, but Ward ordered the destroyer *Lawrence* to shadow the *Poltava*, although she would not enter the blockade zone for another day. The *Kimovsk* was expected to cross into the zone on the evening of the 24th, and Ward directed the *Essex* hunter-killer group to intercept her inasmuch as there had been three recent submarine contacts in her vicinity. The Red Navy did not use its submarines to escort the lumber transports, however, and the suspicious Soviet ships, scattered across the Atlantic, gradually slowed down and reversed course to avoid the American blockade. "The [missile carrying] ships never got much beyond the Azores," recalled Anderson. Shortly thereafter, Ward received "information from the highest authority [that] prescribed: Do not stop and board. Keep under surveillance. Make continuous reports."

The elation over the apparent success of the blockade was short-lived, however, for that evening Kennedy received a message from Khrushchev warning that the "Soviet government cannot give instructions to the captains of Soviet vessels bound for Cuba to observe the instructions of American naval forces blockading the island." The president also soon learned that only fourteen of the twenty-two Soviet ships bound for Cuba had reversed course. Of the remaining eight, five were tankers and three were freighters. Secretary of State Rusk claimed that the Soviets had "blinked." In fact, they had yet to flinch. Kennedy now ordered that American strategic nuclear forces be put on a Defense Condition Two alert—meaning that they were to be deployed for combat—and Admiral Anderson ordered two Polaris-bearing ballistic missile submarines to steam to their assigned patrol areas in the Norwegian and North Seas. The new submarine *Abraham Lincoln* stood out of Holy Loch, Scotland, within fifteen hours, but her sister boat, the *Thomas A. Edison*, was not on station until early November. Six Polaris-bearing submarines, out of an eight-boat force, were already on their assigned launching stations.

As the deterrent force was made ready, the first positive contact with a Soviet submarine occurred on the afternoon of the 24th in the Atlantic, marking the opening round of what Vice

Admiral Griffin termed "an absolutely magnificent antisubmarine workout." Over the next two days, the antisubmarine forces located five *Foxtrot*-class diesel-electric Soviet attack submarines. "It was some surprise to me when we found they were operating so close [to Cuba]," recalled Ward. One of the submarines was prowling the waters near the Windward Passage and attempting to close on Hayward's two-carrier Covering Force. This surprisingly aggressive tactic forced Hayward to move his formation off station and shift to a new operating area south of Jamaica, where shoal waters made submarine operations difficult, and the carriers adopted "evasive steering [and] zig-zagging" maneuvers to confuse their Soviet opponent. The *Foxtrot*-class submarine was eventually discouraged by American destroyers, who sat on top of her and pinged her mercilessly with active sonar. The antisubmarine forces also dropped harmless PDC depth charges on submarine contacts. This notified the prey that she had been located, the Navy's long-time standard operating procedure for dealing with Soviet boats, which were quite familiar with the rules of chase. Taylor's antisubmarine forces also found four other Soviet boats in the North Atlantic. Wary of other Soviet submarines making their way south into the blockade zone, he ordered seventeen Neptune patrol planes and ten American attack submarines to establish an "Argentia Sub-Air Barrier" from 27 October to 13 November, but during this time no new contacts were made.

On the second morning of the blockade, Soviet-flagged ships crossed into the quarantine zone for the first time. Intercepted by the *Essex* and the destroyer *Gearing*, the Soviet-flagged tanker *Bucharest* was hailed by a flashing light signal, but after the usual dipping of colors, she was allowed to proceed unchallenged while Kennedy and the ExComm debated whether to stop her. "*Bucharest* was tracked on and off for the next few days," Ward observed, "with orders coming from Washington to track her, then to trail her out of sight within radar range, then to discontinue trailing, then to resume contact and resume trailing." The indecision ended that evening, when Kennedy finally chose to allow the tanker to continue on her way without being boarded.

Kennedy's blockade, twenty-four hours old on the 25th, stopped only one ship and proved to be little more than a traffic nuisance for Cuba-bound merchantmen. Overly anxious to avoid confronting the Soviets, Kennedy now ordered Ward's Blockade Force to stop and search the hapless Lebanese freighter *Marucla*, which was sailing under Soviet charter. The destroyer *Pierce* had sighted the *Marucla* that morning, and Ward received the order to intercept her before nightfall, but the *Pierce* had already stopped tailing her and Ward had to use aircraft flying off the antisubmarine carrier *Randolph* to locate the phantom freighter that afternoon. Once she was found, the *Pierce* began closing on her position, as did the nearby destroyer *Joseph Kennedy*. Vice Admiral "Beakley [the deputy commander in chief of the Atlantic Fleet] had suggested that it would be nice if [the] *Kennedy* was one of the first ships to board a ship suspected of carrying forbidden cargoes," recalled Admiral Ward, who arranged that the *Marucla* be stopped and searched at first light on the 26th.

At 0600 the following morning, the *Pierce* closed on the *Marucla* and ordered her to heave to and prepare to be boarded. The Greek captain happily obliged the two American destroyers and responded promptly to the *Pierce*'s signals. Led by the executive officers of both destroyers, Lieutenant Commander D. G. Osborne and Lieutenant Commander K. C. Reynolds, an unarmed boarding party in service dress white uniforms took a whaleboat over to the Soviet-flagged vessel. A two-hour search of the ship revealed that "no prohibited materials were on board," Reynolds reported, "so I therefore recommended that the SS *Marucla* be cleared to proceed," and Admiral Ward agreed. Kennedy's decision to stop the *Marucla* was at once a signal to Moscow that he intended to enforce the blockade and a confession that he hoped to avoid a more direct confrontation by stopping Soviet-owned shipping in international waters.

In spite of the Navy's enormous effort to establish and enforce the blockade, during the entire Cuban Missile Crisis Ward's 2nd Fleet stopped and inspected only one ship at sea, the benign *Marucla*. "It was little more than a stunt," said Dennison, "a demonstration that we were effective." Ward was directed to allow other suspicious vessels, including several Soviet ships, to proceed on to Cuba without interruption. The master of the Swedish ship *Collangatta*, chartered by the Soviet Union and carrying a load of potatoes, reportedly ignored attempts by an American destroyer to hail her on 26 October, broadcast a message to the Americans to "go to hell," and steamed through the blockade zone. Two Soviet ships were within the quarantine zone when the blockade took effect—the freighter *Leninsky Komsomol*, which carried a load of crated Il-28 bombers, and the tanker *Vinnitsa*—but Kennedy allowed both to proceed into Cuban ports. Still another ship that was not stopped was the East German passenger liner *Voiderfreund*, although Commander Foust, after intercepting her and examining her topside, sent several messages to Ward advising that she should be searched. He was frustrated when Ward told him to allow her to proceed. "They didn't stop the one we said they should [the *Voiderfreund*] and they had us stop the one we said they shouldn't [the *Marucla*]."

On the evening of the 26th, following this token search, the stage shifted rapidly from the Caribbean to Washington. The White House received a rambling letter from Moscow, which Khrushchev wrote himself, offering to pull the Sandals out if Kennedy agreed to "declare that the United States will not invade Cuba with its troops and will not support any other forces which might intend to invade Cuba." Hopes for a quick settlement were soon shattered, however. The next morning brought another message from Moscow, this one adding the removal of the Jupiters in Turkey to the earlier proposal. A CIA update on the 27th listed three of the four missile sites at San Cristóbal and two sites at Sagua la Grande as operational. And the latest message from Moscow, by mentioning the Jupiters, had placed Kennedy in an awful position. The fifteen Jupiters, first-generation, solid-fuel ballistic missiles, defended from a landward attack by the large Turkish Army, had been installed earlier that year and Kennedy had signed the order making them operational in July. They were a valuable adjunct to NATO's nuclear strategy.

Kennedy understood that an explicit, publicized swap of the removal of the Sandals for the withdrawal of the Jupiters would result in domestic political disaster for the Democrats. He was willing to make the trade, but he could not allow it to appear as though he had succumbed to Khrushchev's blackmail. Therefore, he momentarily ignored the issue of the Jupiters mentioned in Khrushchev's second letter and replied instead to the first letter, which had not referred to them. He agreed not to invade Cuba if Khrushchev withdrew his missiles from the island. A letter accepting this arrangement was drafted and quickly sent on its way to the Kremlin. Concurrently, Robert Kennedy assured the Soviet ambassador in Washington in private that the Jupiters would be removed from Turkey once the crisis over Cuba was at an end. Determined not to allow the issue of the Jupiters to obstruct a settlement of the Cuban crisis, the president devised a contingency plan. He instructed Secretary of State Rusk to prepare a statement to be made by U Thant, the UN Secretary General, "proposing the removal of both the Jupiters and the missiles in Cuba." It was a last, desperate card that was not played.

Krushchev retreated the next morning and accepted Kennedy's terms. The United States promised not to invade Cuba and the Soviets announced that they would withdraw the Sandal and Skean ballistic missiles and Il-28 Beagle bombers. The crisis then began to draw down. Ward's Blockade Force remained in position surrounding Cuba, however, and preparations for an invasion continued. On the 30th, the destroyer *Cecil* reported that her quarry, a Soviet *Foxtrot*-class submarine, had surfaced after a chase lasting thirty-five hours. "When the submarine surfaced, it was on course 090 as prescribed by our instruction to Moscow of October 24," wrote McNamara's assistant, Adam Yarmolinsky, weeks later, perhaps indicating that Moscow had informed her submarine skippers of the American fleet instructions or had ordered them home shortly before the quarantine took effect. That same day, Kennedy suspended the blockade while U Thant flew to Havana to try to convince Castro to allow neutral inspection teams to observe the dismantling of the missile sites. Castro angrily turned down this plan, but American photo reconnaissance revealed that the Soviet sites were being dismantled anyway, so Kennedy did not object. After U Thant left Havana, however, Kennedy reimposed the blockade with great bravado on 2 November, only days before the critical midterm congressional elections.

Ward's next job was to see that the Sandals were removed from Cuba under the terms of an agreement with the Soviets, which allowed the Blockade Force to inspect the outgoing Soviet freighters. On 7 November, the Soviet UN delegation gave Adlai Stevenson, the American ambassador to the UN, the names of nine Soviet ships scheduled to transport the missiles back to Russia, their dates of departure, and the number of missiles each vessel would be carrying. This document did not provide any information as to their courses, and, in any event, the Soviet ships did not pass through the designated rendezvous points. "Don't wait," Dennison told Ward. "Find them!" Four days later, the nine Soviet lumber carriers had been located and visually inspected by the

Blockade Force to ensure that all forty-two of the Sandals had been removed. Kennedy ordered the quarantine to remain in effect until the Il-28 bombers were withdrawn as well.

Kennedy still had to approach Ankara and NATO headquarters and explain why he was withdrawing the Jupiters from Turkey. The Turks extracted concessions in the form of more foreign aid and Kennedy's agreement to station one of the Navy's nine available Polaris-bearing ballistic missile submarines in the eastern Mediterranean as a substitute for the Jupiters. The Navy was already studying a plan to send missile submarines into the Mediterranean and the Indian Ocean once they became available, to "stress" the Soviets and force them to invest in air defense radars to monitor the southern hemisphere missile approaches to their home territory. Although Polaris boats usually attempted to blend into the ocean during their seventy-day deterrent patrols, on this occasion Kennedy ordered the fleet submarine *Sam Houston* to visit Izmir, Turkey, in April 1963 and to make herself visible, albeit briefly. Shortly afterward, on the 25th of that month, McNamara reported to the White House that "the last Jupiter missile [in Turkey] came down yesterday [and that the] last Jupiter warhead will be flown out at the end of the week."

While Kennedy's handling of the crisis drew high marks from many, the Navy's reaction was mixed. "It was a defeat," said Vice Admiral Hayward, "and a cheap success for the Soviets." The CNO, Admiral Anderson, agreed. He believed that Kennedy might have pressed Moscow to retreat even further and erred by handing Khrushchev "the concession that we would pull our missiles out of Turkey." Dennison, on the other hand, reasoned that Kennedy "made a very wise decision in using naval power" and in not ordering the invasion, and admirals Ward, Rivero, and Kidd agreed. "It would have been wrong for us to invade that little country," Rivero concluded. Former Secretary of State Acheson, who was thoroughly disgusted with the Kennedy brothers' lack of grit, attributed Kennedy's apparent success in the Cuban Missile Crisis to "plain dumb luck."

Kennedy moved swiftly from confrontation to appeasement, reviving Eisenhower's dormant arms control policy and persuading the Soviets to sign a treaty prohibiting tests of nuclear weapons in the atmosphere. In the 1950s, while the Soviets believed their nuclear arsenal was inferior, this diplomacy had failed. After they had reviewed the successful test results of a

September 1961 50-megaton above-ground blast and had recovered from the shock of the Cuban Missile Crisis, however, the Soviets were ready to deal. Khrushchev agreed to a compromise stitched together by the British, and in 1963 Britain, Russia, and the United States signed the atmospheric Nuclear Test Ban Treaty. In doing so, however, Kennedy established an important political precedent by failing to link major American concessions on arms control to a modification of Soviet foreign policy.

Cuba was not the only Latin American country to which Kennedy tried to apply counterinsurgency and gradual escalation. Since FDR had replaced the Roosevelt Corollary to the Monroe Doctrine with his Good Neighbor Policy, the United States' relations with Latin America had taken a back seat to the problems of Europe and Asia. The 1947 Rio Treaty and the establishment of the OAS were intended to provide a diplomatic framework for hemispheric security against Soviet aggression and to foreclose the need for unilateral American intervention. Latin America's governments paid less heed to Kremlin-sponsored communist subversion than to signs of American domination, however, and Washington, while aware of this sensitivity, nonetheless reacted with alarm to the most fleeting evidence of Soviet penetration. Eisenhower had used the CIA to support a 1954 coup in Guatemala that overthrew Jacobo Arbenz Guzmán, the left-leaning president, but he had refused to intervene in Cuba, leaving to John Kennedy the problem of how to deal with an established Soviet client on the other side of the Florida Straits. Kennedy promised in 1961 to uphold the Good Neighbor Policy but found this pledge hard to keep. Early on he used diplomacy and economic aid to prevent coups in Latin America, but when this policy failed he reverted to a more pragmatic approach. His successor, Lyndon Johnson, took the same line in 1964 when an elected left-wing president was ousted by the Brazilian Army. Moreover, one outcome of the Bay of Pigs fiasco and the Cuban Missile Crisis was a firm resolve in Washington not to allow Castro to export his revolution through subversion or aggression. President Johnson was the legatee of this policy.

The CIA-assisted assassination of the Dominican Republic's dictator Rafael Trujillo Molina highlighted the impracticality of Kennedy's early policy of seeking concurrent economic growth and political democracy in the hemisphere. In power since 1930, Trujillo had always been careful to maintain close ties with Washington. "He may be an S.O.B.," FDR once remarked, "but he is our S.O.B." When Trujillo was gunned down on 30 May 1961, his playboy son succeeded to the presidency, and Kennedy worked relentlessly during the summer and fall to orchestrate his downfall. The Dominican Republic, he predicted, might have "a decent democratic regime, a continuation of the Trujillo regime, or a Castro regime. We ought to aim at the first, but we really can't renounce the second until we are sure that we can avoid the third." The pressure escalated until November when Admiral Dennison organized a Caribbean Task Force consisting of the carriers *Franklin D. Roosevelt* and *Valley Forge* and a six-ship amphibious group embarking 1,800 Marines. On 19 November, Kennedy positioned these ships off Santo Domingo as a show of force.[15]

The threat of American intervention forced the Trujillo family into exile, and an army junta scheduled free elections in 1962. Juan Bosch, an eccentric Marxist, prevailed at the polls, but his socialist policies and support for Castro soon alienated conservatives. Nine months later, on 26 September 1963, General Wessin y Wessin, the commanding general, overthrew Bosch, who escaped with his life only because of the intervention of Marine Colonel David Wolfe, the intrepid American defense attaché in Santo Domingo. Bosch's successor was Donald Reid Cabral, a progressive oligarch, but Reid's inept reforms angered both left and right, while Bosch, now in exile in Puerto Rico, and some younger army officers plotted his return to power. On 24 April 1965, members of this clique stormed the presidential palace, ousted Reid, and invited Bosch to return to head a new government. When Wessin learned what was afoot, he put a gun to the head of the air force's commanding general and made him order his planes to strafe the presidential compound. Rebel forces congregated in Santo Domingo, and a small band of communist agitators assembled a mob, took to the streets, and assaulted their democratic opponents. Hundreds were killed in these riots. Armed bands of no particular political persuasion soon ruled the capital.

Admiral Dennison had already put Vice Admiral Kleber Masterson's 2nd Fleet on alert, and on 24 April the JCS instructed Dennison to draw up plans to evacuate over 1,200 Americans from the Dominican Republic. Captain James A. Dare's Amphibious Ready Group was riding at anchor off Puerto Rico at 1100 that day when Dare received word that his command had been assigned this mission. Steaming toward the war-torn island, Dare planned to use the LSD *Fort Snelling* to evacuate the island's southeastern ports, to employ the assault ship *Rankin*'s landing craft to rescue Americans from the northern ports, and to concentrate the rest of his ships off Santo Domingo. Arriving off the capital on the morning of the 26th, Dare kept his formation out of sight of land for the rest of the day.

Masterson told Dare to move inshore that night, and on the morning of 27 April two Marine HU-1E helicopters landed at the Punta Accedo Airport, picked up American Ambassador W. Tapley Bennett, and returned him to the helicopter carrier *Boxer*, where he approved Captain Dare's evacuation plan. Dare now learned that the rebels, upon discovering that over 1,000 Americans were assembled at the Embajador Hotel, had broken in and terrorized them with automatic weapons fire. "This fixed attention on [nearby] Port Jaina as the only safe evacuation site," he recalled. At 1300 the amphibious ship *Ruchamkin* and the LST *Wood County* pulled into Port Jaina, slightly to the west of Santo Domingo. With her high speed, easy maneuverability, and shallow draft, the *Ruchamkin* easily shuttled between piers and picked up scattered groups of refugees. To provide an additional show of strength, Ambassador Bennett asked Dare to move the *Boxer* and the LPD *Raleigh* into the harbor where they would be within sight of the rebel forces downtown. Over 1,000 Americans had been bussed to Jaina; about half were taken by helicopter to the *Boxer* and the *Raleigh* and the rest boarded the landing ships.

As the fighting between the loyalists and the rebels intensified in Santo Domingo during the day, more American evacuees arrived at the hotel. To rescue them, over 500 heavily armed Marines were airlifted from the *Boxer* to the embassy area on the night of the 27th, and nearly 700 American civilians were flown back to the carrier. "Those in the embassy were pinned down for about 15 minutes by [rebel] snipers in the vicinity," Dare reported, and "the Marines on the ground returned fire."[16]

In the midst of the evacuation, at 1700 on the 27th, Molina Urena, who had replaced Reid as the head of a provisional junta, met with the rebel leader, Colonel Caamano, at the American embassy. Both men asked Bennett to mediate between the rebels and Wessin. When Bennett refused to intervene, Urena resigned, but Caamano vowed to fight on. Nonetheless, reports of Dare's successful evacuation and the collapse of the Urena junta led President Johnson to conclude that night that the crisis was over and that no further intervention by American forces would be necessary.

This picture changed by the morning of 28 April. Caamano had regrouped his rebels, established a stronghold in the capital's business district, and held off the loyalists at the Duarte Bridge. To reestablish control outside of Santo Domingo, Wessin now agreed to the formation of a new anti-Bosch junta led by Air Force Colonel Pedro Benoit. Ambassador Bennett welcomed this step, but he now believed that the rebels were under communist control, that the loyalists could not restore order, and that the civil war was "between Castro-type elements and their opponents." At 1500, Benoit asked that the United States interpose its forces between the warring factions. "The time has come to land the Marines" and thwart the rebel attempt to "convert the country into another Cuba," Bennett told Washington an hour later. When this cable reached the White House "we had no option," recalled Undersecretary of State George Ball, and Johnson ordered Admiral Masterson to land the Marines.[17]

Captain Dare had already devised a plan, codenamed Barrel Bottom, to lift more Marines to the embassy area and to land Marine tanks on a beach just outside Port Jaina. On 28 April, after Washington approved Barrel Bottom, Admiral Masterson arrived on the *Boxer* and took command of the growing joint task force and the intervention. At 1730 the first wave of LVTs drove onto the beach and landed tanks, which formed up into a column and headed down the main highway to the embassy. There they met up with the rest of the battalion, which had already arrived by helicopter and had established a security zone in the area. It soon became clear to Dare that "the rebel forces were expanding their operations while the [loyalist] junta forces were stalled" on the Duarte Bridge. LBJ now hesitated, however, telling Bennett to have Dare restrict the Marines to patrols around the embassy area.

A few minutes later, Johnson polled his advisers during a conference call between the White House and Santo Domingo. At the end of the call he revised his policy and directed that the entire 82nd Airborne Division be airlifted to the Dominican Republic to prevent a communist takeover. "What can we do in Vietnam if we can't clean up the Dominican Republic?" Johnson was heard to ask. A few hours after the Marines went ashore, he announced his decision on national television, and the State Department asked the OAS to mediate the dispute. On 29 April, 2,000 Army paratroops arrived at the San Isidro Air Base, where Wessin and the new junta had made their headquarters, thus creating the incorrect but sinister impression that the United States was siding with Wessin's right-wing loyalists. The Army and Marines linked up within days, dividing in half the area of the city still held by the rebels. Eventually, over 23,000 American troops were landed in and around Santo Domingo. The OAS asked the junta and the rebels for a ceasefire, established an international security zone, and assembled a multinational peacekeeping force to join the American troops and Marines in Santo Domingo. "Many OAS states were ambivalent," recalled Army General Bruce Palmer, who relieved Admiral Masterson as joint expeditionary commander on 1 May. They were "publicly denouncing the U.S. unilateral intervention" while "showing their own shared concern about communism in the region by private, discreet expressions of support."

The American left, Johnson's natural allies, reacted with alarm. The *New York Times* and the *Washington Post* castigated LBJ's abandonment of the Good Neighbor Policy. Johnson reacted, according to Ball, by directing "day-to-day policy and became, in effect, the Dominican desk officer." He accredited personal envoys to both factions in Santo Domingo, sent a special commission to the scene, and completely undermined the authority of both Ambassador Bennett and General Palmer. It was soon evident that neither the Cubans nor the Soviets had played any role in the uprising—other than welcoming it. Nevertheless, the intervention led to an end to the civil war. The landing had so stunned the rebels that they agreed to a settlement negotiated by the OAS on 9 May. Less than three weeks later, the Marines and other American troops began to withdraw from Santo Domingo and a new junta took power. Free elections in 1966 resulted in Bosch's defeat and the election of Joaquín Balaguer, an able pro-American moderate, but the respective factions jousted for control of the country for the next two decades.

LBJ used the Dominican Republic intervention as the occasion to enunciate a new Johnson Doctrine, under which the United States was obligated to intervene unilaterally to prevent the establishment of a second communist government in Latin

America. For several years, the example of the Dominican Republic vaccinated the virus of Latin American radical nationalism. However, Johnson's willingness to intervene in foreign politics, his hand-wringing indecisiveness, and his habit of personally managing overseas operations were harbingers of his troubles in Vietnam.[18]

Chapter Twenty-three
Flexible Response
1961–1963

The Kennedy administration came to Washington intending to completely revise American military policy and strategy. Kennedy believed that Eisenhower's grand strategy of Massive Retaliation had led the JCS in the 1950s to prepare "to fight the one kind of war we least want to fight and are least likely to fight." The result was to drive American strategists "into a corner where the only choice is . . . world devastation or submission—a choice that necessarily causes us to hesitate on the brink and leaves the initiative in the hands of our enemies." Kennedy's alternative to this strategy was termed Flexible Response. McNamara's first step in implementing the new approach was a wholesale shakeup of the Defense Department, with the aim of greatly strengthening the powers of the secretary of defense. According to McNamara, Eisenhower had fixed a budget ceiling, "the three military departments" established "their requirements largely independent of each other," and the JCS and the secretary umpired disputes.[1]

The JCS could not solve conflicts between strategy and service demands on their own inasmuch as they were "regularly subjected to massive institutional pressures for setting even higher requirements," according to Alain Enthoven, who headed McNamara's new Systems Analysis Office. The Army was stockpiling enough munitions for a European war lasting two years, but the Air Force refused to buy transport planes on the grounds that Massive Retaliation would obliterate the Soviet Union within

a few days. McNamara charged that the Navy was the most wasteful and ill organized of the services, wanting enough ships and
planes to participate in either of these war plans; conduct another, simultaneous limited war on the Eurasian periphery; and be
ready to intervene in the Third World. McNamara's convictions
and his arrogance led him to treat the views of the JCS with cava-
lier indifference. They had "nothing to lose from calling for
more forces and much to lose from accepting less," Enthoven
observed. This unhelpful attitude engendered considerable hostility to McNamara within the services and generated resistance
to the changes that he was determined to impose. The hubris of
McNamara's circle exacerbated the problem. Vice Admiral
Robert Pirie, the Deputy CNO for air, was deeply offended by
McNamara's aides, "a group of amateurs teaching professionals
how to run their business" that included "foreigners who had
questionable security clearances." The result was "a fantastic
amount of antagonism" between McNamara and the uniformed
military, according to Deputy Assistant Secretary of Defense
Henry Bowen. "The military had a sense that important variables
were being left out [of McNamara's systems analysis]—such as a
feeling for the enemy, his intentions, and other intangibles."[2]

To impose his will, McNamara enlisted a crew of young assistants, who were quickly but inappropriately labeled "whiz kids"
by reporters. Harold Brown, Paul Nitze, Cyrus Vance, Roswell
Gilpatrick, and systems analyst Enthoven were installed in a vastly
expanded Office of the Secretary of Defense. Each new assistant
secretary was authorized to oversee a different functional area of
military activity. Vice President Lyndon Johnson's cronies ran the
Navy Department. John Connally, Kennedy's first secretary of the
Navy, spent his time in Washington running for governor of
Texas. He resigned in December 1961 and was replaced by another Texan, Fred Korth. Both men closely allied themselves with
McNamara. McNamara created a five-year Defense Department
plan that reflected his quantitative approach to military policy
and strategy. Under this plan, missions were defined not by service but by function, an attempt to avoid duplication and the allegedly wasteful tensions of interservice rivalry. Ships, tanks, rifles, manpower, and aircraft were assigned measures of utility not
by sources or users, but by functions and cost. To endow grand
strategy with the same rationality he believed he was bringing to
Defense Department management, McNamara accelerated for-

mer Defense Secretary Gates' work on the Single Integrated Operating Plan, a plan for fighting nuclear wars that for the first time coordinated the delivery of all nuclear weapons against the Soviet Union, its Warsaw Pact allies, and China.

McNamara also completely reorganized the Navy in 1963, claiming all along that he did not intend to "affect the traditional bilinear organization of the Department." The new Bureau of Naval Weapons incorporated, but did not abolish, the old Bureau of Ships, the Bureau of Yards and Docks, and the Bureau of Supplies and Accounts. To supervise the material bureaus, McNamara created a chief of naval material, who was to report to the secretary of the Navy. Navy Secretary Paul Nitze, who replaced Korth in 1963, disliked this arrangement, arguing that it was a legatee of the "Navy's antiquated bilineal organizational structure which had part of the service reporting to the secretary of the Navy and the other part reporting to the CNO." In 1966, he persuaded McNamara to abolish all the bureaus except Personnel and Medicine and Surgery and create six functional commands in their place. The Air, Ship, Ordnance, Electronic, Supply, and Facilities Engineering Commands now fell within the new Naval Material Command, thus establishing a "true Material Command that would report to me through the CNO," Nitze recalled. From 1958 to 1966 the main job of the CNO was almost wholly transformed. Instead of directing global fleet operations, he now became in effect manager of the Navy's shore establishment.[3]

McNamara also moved to implement the strategy of Flexible Response, quickly dismissing the Democrats' 1960 election charge that a "missile gap" existed between the superpowers. "Although there might have been a missile gap, there certainly was no deterrent gap, and . . . in any event there almost certainly would not be a missile gap at any time in the near future," he declared in mid-1961. Flexible Response was intended to provide the president with a menu of nuclear and conventional retaliatory forces to fit each general war strategic situation. This approach justified rather than rationalized the existing, haphazard triad of B-52 bombers, ICBMs, and fleet ballistic missile submarines that had been born out of the feverish interservice arms race of the 1950s. During a crisis, American bombers might fly to the edge of Soviet airspace to signal determination, the ICBMs might be fired to respond to a Soviet first strike, and the submarine-launched Polaris missiles might be kept in reserve to men-

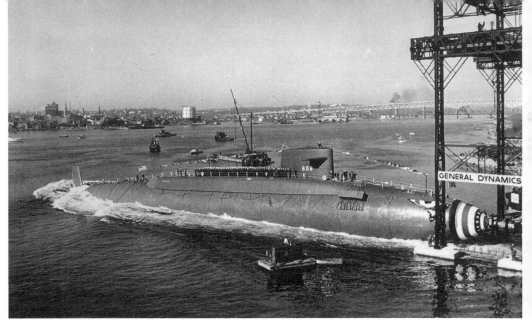

The Polaris missile–bearing, nuclear-powered submarine *Ethan Allen* (SSBN-608) down the ways at Electric Boat shipyard in Groton, Connecticut, 22 November 1960.

ace the enemy with a second-strike retaliatory blow. Although he accelerated construction of the *Ethan Allen*-class Polaris-bearing submarines, their closely related successors, the *Lafayettes*, and the Air Force's Minuteman ICBMs, McNamara had no faith in nuclear war fighting and discouraged continued Air Force attempts to craft a first-strike preventive or preemptive counter-force strategy or to develop other weapons to attack the growing Soviet strategic rocket forces. While he at first favored a retaliatory counterforce strategy, he soon turned toward a more limited "cities only" countervalue approach. "We must have sufficient strategic forces to absorb a full Soviet strike, and survive with sufficient strength to absolutely destroy the Soviet Union," he declared, but he intended to build up no further.[4]

As part of his early improvement of America's strategic forces, Kennedy asked Congress for five more Polaris submarines in early 1961, and for five more that summer, bringing the total to be constructed to twenty-nine boats. Six fleet ballistic missile submarines were ordered in each of the following two years, for a total of forty-one. To pay for accelerating this program, however, McNamara canceled Burke's plan to prepare the nuclear-powered cruiser *Long Beach* to fire Polaris missiles. He was encouraged to do this by the development of the new *Lafayette*-class submarine, a vessel that dove deeper and displaced more than the *Ethan Allen,* and by the introduction in 1962 of the 1,500-mile-range Polaris A-2 submarine-launched ballistic missile. It was replaced after 1964 by the Polaris A-4, a vehicle armed with multiple warheads that were intended to compensate for the submarine launch's inaccuracy by hitting each target with three small-yield nuclear weapons. To pay for this, McNamara canceled the Air Force's cruise missile program, refused to lay down another nuclear-powered carrier in 1963, and reduced the Navy's other shipbuilding accounts.

McNamara's declaration that the bomber-missile-submarine triad would meet the needs of Flexible Response left the mission of the Navy's *Midway*-class and *Forrestal*-class heavy attack carriers in doubt. Admiral Burke, the CNO, persuaded him to dedicate the carriers to the nuclear delivery mission when the SIOP was first revised in 1961, but in February 1962, soon after Burke retired, McNamara announced that "our [missile and bomber] forces would destroy virtually all Soviet targets without any help from deployed tactical air units or carrier task forces which . . . have the capability of attacking these targets with nuclear weapons." He pointed out that some carrier aircraft could not attack land targets in bad weather, some could not operate at night, all had a limited operating radius, and none could reach targets in the Soviet Union before their carriers steamed to their preassigned launching positions. The establishment of the Polaris and Minutemen strategic missile forces meant that "the need for the attack carrier in the general war role will diminish." Putting the best face he could muster on this defeat, Admiral Anderson, now CNO, got McNamara to admit that the carriers still retained a "significant nuclear strike capability," and the JCS crafted a face-saving compromise that identified them as "strategic reserves." Admiral Horacio Rivero, the Vice CNO, maintained that McNamara's decision at least had the virtue of removing "a restraint" on carrier operations and "restored flexibility" to their movements.[5]

Admiral David McDonald, who became CNO in 1963, agreed to McNamara's decision to drop the carriers from the nuclear strike forces but bitterly resisted his plan to reduce carrier-based naval aviation from fifteen to twelve air wings, as this would make it impossible to continue to operate fifteen attack carriers or to forward deploy five or six attack carriers with the numbered fleets. Kennedy and McNamara "were going to reduce the number of carriers, if they never did anything else," according to McDonald. McNamara relieved American carrier task forces of their strategic mission in 1963 and dedicated them to interdicting enemy forces and to close support of ground operations. He also announced in January 1964 a radical reduction in plans to procure new naval aircraft, justifying this on the grounds that new Soviet land-based attack aircraft had longer ranges and could operate from relatively primitive airstrips, thus lessening the carrier's ability to survive an attack from the air. McNamara also told the Navy to cancel the A-5 Vigilante, a supersonic naval bomber, and directed that those Vigilantes already flying be converted to reconnaissance aircraft. Instead of buying additional heavy attack planes, he procured more older A-4 Skyhawks, new A-6 Intruder bombers, and A-7 Corsair II bombers. McDonald sternly resisted any overall reduction in the number of carriers or air wings, however. This "might be the Secretary of Defense's plan," the CNO told Congress bluntly, but it was "not the Navy plan today."[6]

During the 1961 Berlin crisis, McNamara had agreed to expand the carrier fleet to sixteen attack carriers and ten antisubmarine carriers, but after he removed the carriers from the SIOP, the JCS turned aside the Navy's protests and agreed only to support a fleet composed of fifteen attack carriers and nine antisubmarine warfare carriers. Air Force and Army members of the JCS also opposed constructing the next ship in the *Forrestal*-class carrier program, but the chairman, General Lemnitzer, supported Admiral Anderson on this issue. McNamara held that the carrier's role in general and limited wars was declining as a result of the threat from air- or surface-launched anti-ship missiles; however, he admitted that there were "many potential trouble spots in the world where the attack carrier is and will continue to be the only practical means of bringing our air striking power to bear" but predicted that the importance of the carrier—even in limited wars—would decline with the advent of more sophisticated missiles.[7]

Kennedy's grand strategy of Flexible Response and its corollary, counterinsurgency, led McNamara to reason that the United States needed forces capable of fighting "two and one-half wars" simultaneously. "This meant meeting, simultaneously, a Warsaw Pact attack in Europe and a Chinese attack in Asia, while maintaining the ability to meet a minor contingency in the

Western Hemisphere or elsewhere," Enthoven recorded. Considering his emphasis on building up America's conventional forces, McNamara paid surprisingly little heed to the reductions in fleet strength that had begun to occur as a result of the "bloc obsolescence" of entire classes of World War II–era ships. He refused to replace the *Essex*-class antisubmarine carriers, deciding instead that antisubmarine operations would eventually be transferred to the attack carriers. This forced the Navy's fifteen heavy-carrier fleet to absorb the antisubmarine obligations of the nine old *Essex*-class small carriers as they were decommissioned in the 1960s and early 1970s. Moreover, he abandoned Eisenhower's one-carrier-each-year policy and replaced it initially with a plan to build one carrier every other year.[8]

After approving the construction of the carrier *America* in 1959, Congress, successive administrations, and the Navy were paralyzed over whether the next carrier should be oil fired or nuclear powered. When the nuclear-powered carrier *Enterprise* was commissioned on 25 November 1961, her cost was nearly $450 million. Costing less than half that figure each, the oil-fired carriers *Constellation* and *Kitty Hawk* entered the fleet that same year. Admiral Anderson preferred that the next carrier be nuclear powered, but in the spring of 1962 McNamara, supported by Navy Secretary Korth, announced that she would be oil fired. "I am absolutely certain of one thing," McNamara told Korth, "that six conventional task forces are superior to five nuclear task forces." On 8 October 1963 he instructed the Navy to install an oil-fired plant in the new carrier, which was soon named the *John F. Kennedy*. Apoplexy gripped the air admirals. "It was still another stupid and shortsighted decision," fumed Admiral Pirie.

McNamara refused to build another carrier for the next several years, but the inauguration of Rolling Thunder air operations in Vietnam once again proved the usefulness of carriers in limited wars. In addition, Admiral Rickover had developed a large, powerful carrier reactor to replace the *Enterprise*'s eight small reactors, and he saw to it that Congress would not approve another oil-fired carrier. Years later, Navy Secretary Paul Nitze wrote of "the ever-present difficulty of dealing with Vice Admiral Hyman Rickover and his numerous friends in Congress. Any decision that went against their wish for an all-nuclear Navy inevitably became a hotly-contested, time-consuming battle." To replace the retiring *Essex*-class antisubmarine carriers, McDonald proposed in 1966 to lay down a new class of 74,000-ton nuclear-powered *Nimitz*-class multipurpose carriers that would embark a squadron of S-2 Tracker antisubmarine aircraft in addition to the usual mix of fighters and attack bombers.[9]

McDonald was successful in advancing the case for maintaining a fifteen-carrier fleet because of the increasing difficulty in the 1960s of obtaining basing and overflight rights for land-based Air Force aircraft in the Mediterranean and Middle East. Congress reluctantly agreed to a compromise plan to build three *Nimitz*-class carriers over a period of three years under a single contract, but the costs of the Vietnam War forced the Navy to abandon this scheme. The *Nimitz*, laid down in 1968, was not completed until 1975; the keel of the *Eisenhower* was not laid until 1970 and she did not enter the fleet for another seven years. As a result of continued economies by the Nixon administration, construction of the third ship in this class, the carrier *Carl Vinson*, did not even begin until 1975. McNamara's general opposition to carrier construction also manifested itself when it came to building helicopter carriers to support Marine Corps operations ashore. Construction of the seven-ship *Iwo Jima*-class helicopter carriers was stretched out into the next decade, and Admiral Anderson had to fill the gap by scheduling the conversion of three *Essex*-class carriers into amphibious carriers. Even this scheme received low priority from the secretary of defense.

The need for missile escorts for the carriers was reinforced by a 1960 Navy study that pointed to the upcoming danger to the task forces from land-based Soviet aircraft bearing air-to-surface missiles. One response to this threat was the nine 6,570-ton *Belknap*-class guided missile frigates, which entered the fleet between 1964 and 1967. Operating a drone antisubmarine helicopter and armed with Terrier missiles and launchers capable of firing the ASROC antisubmarine missile, they served both as antiaircraft and antisubmarine escorts. The *Belknap*-class cruisers were too few in number and too expensive to use for convoy escorts, however. Once the nuclear-powered cruiser *Long Beach* entered the fleet in 1961, Rickover agitated for another nuclear-powered cruiser, but Admiral Burke and his successors opposed building more nuclear-powered ships, other than carriers, owing to the high costs. "If we had to make a choice between seven conventional frigates and four frigates of the nuclear type," Burke told Congress in 1961, then "we would have to take the seven frigates because we need the ships so badly." Congress nonetheless rewarded Rickover for his persistence that year by authorizing the 9,200-ton nuclear frigate *Truxtun*, which entered the fleet in 1967. Nearly the size of a cruiser, she cost almost as much as an oil-fired carrier, clearly far too expensive for a missile or antisubmarine escort. The *Truxtun* was only one of seven missile frigates authorized by Congress in 1961, vessels that were to carry the Typhoon surface-to-air missile, but problems in developing this ill-designed weapon resulted not only in its cancellation but also in the suspension of the heavy frigate program.[10]

This coincided with McNamara's renewed concern about the lack of antisubmarine escorts, and by 1963, having turned against building larger cruisers and frigates, he announced instead a preference for a new class of small, austere oil-fired escorts. Despite Navy opposition, he would thereafter support only continued construction of the 2,440-ton *Garcia-* and *Brooke-*class destroyer escorts and the 3,040-ton *Knox-*class destroyer escorts. Rickover lobbied for funds to construct at least twenty-five 10,000-ton nuclear-powered guided-missile destroyers, but in 1966 McNamara would agree to lay down only one of these new vessels—and that was forced on the administration by Congress. And, the following year, he decided that the *Nimitz-*class nuclear carriers would have to be defended by oil-fired escorts. As a result, in June 1970, the Navy awarded a contract to Litton to build thirty 7,180-ton *Spruance-*class destroyers, which operated a LAMPS helicopter and were armed with the Sea Sparrow and Standard missiles, an ASROC antisubmarine rocket launcher, and two 5-inch guns.

The 1959–61 Berlin Crisis and the development of long-range Soviet attack submarines renewed concern within the Navy over the fleet's escort and antisubmarine capabilities. Soviet Navy submarine operations during the Cuban Missile Crisis in 1962 reinforced this view. When President Kennedy entered office, Vice Admiral Hyman Rickover had already become an extraordinary national figure whose reputation exceeded his actual role in the determination of shipbuilding policy. On the other hand, Rickover did exercise an iron grip over the design, construction, and daily operation of all nuclear submarines. While viewed by the public as a maverick, in practice Rickover was quite conservative. For many years he resisted the installation of transistorized electronic equipment and continued to rely on vacuum tubes for some systems long after they were obsolete. The goals of his program were almost unrelated to strategic, tactical, or political issues, centering singlemindedly on the development of an all-nuclear fleet. While the public at this time perceived nuclear reactors to be clean, efficient, and safe, Rickover evidently reckoned that one horrendous accident might easily undermine this confidence and destroy the Navy's entire nuclear propulsion program. He recognized earlier than most that safety stemmed from reliability as well as from constant training, carefully regulated procedures, and relentless attention to detail.

High costs attended this conservative approach. Rickover refused, for instance, to install superpressured steam mechanisms in his reactors. He also sturdily rejected alternatives to the old water-cooled reactor to which so much of his technical expertise had been devoted. By 1960 theoretical studies had demonstrated the potential of liquid metal or gas as a substitute for water to transfer heat from the reactor core to the boiler, but Rickover punished advocates of this technology within the Navy's Nuclear Reactors Branch and hounded private firms interested in this approach. He also tended to be oblivious to the tactical restrictions his conservatism imposed on American submarines. The record-breaking 30-knot flank speed of the original *Skipjack* class was produced by an S5W reactor working against only 3,500 tons of submarine. Rickover installed the same S5W reactor in the succeeding 4,500-ton *Thresher*-class boats, laid down in May 1958, and in the third class of nuclear-powered attack submarines, the 4,650-ton *Sturgeon*s, laid down in 1963. As a result, the latter two classes were each a few knots slower than the *Skipjack*s. Because attack submarines clearly added to the Flexible Response strategy, McNamara supported an expanded building program and persuaded Congress to lay down eight attack submarines in 1962 and six each year for several years thereafter.

The *Thresher*, lead ship in the class that followed the *Skipjack*s, was slower than her predecessors, but she was quieter and had more sophisticated passive sonars and greater safe diving depths. Before she went out on her sea trials in 1961, she was virtually transformed into a floating sound laboratory. Whereas the *Skipjack*'s turbines had been bolted to the hull, the *Thresher*'s machinery was suspended on special decks and encased by rubber, and her propeller shaft was fitted with devices that deadened sound in the water. The *Thresher*'s initial sea trials proceeded without incident, although the full schedule of deep-diving and full-power tests was never conducted. Her storage pressure in the ballast tanks had been increased by 50 percent, and the components were tested individually, but testing the entire system at sea was inexplicably postponed. Nonetheless, she completed a successful shakedown cruise during which she operated at test depth on over forty occasions. Then, tragedy struck. On 10 April 1963, while conducting additional sea trials east of Boston, the *Thresher* decelerated to the very slow underwater speed required for a rapid descent. Suddenly, flooding was reported to the bridge. The captain gave orders that full power, full rise be applied to the control planes, and that the main ballast tanks be blown. The vessel accelerated and ascended, but within a few moments the main propulsion plant failed. The high-pressure air-blowing system could not overcome the negative buoyancy caused by the flooding, and the *Thresher* plunged to the bottom of the ocean floor—over 8,500 feet—killing all 129 naval and civilian personnel on board.

The *Thresher*'s loss threw Rickover into a panic. Upon learning of the tragedy, he telephoned his old adversary, Rear Admiral Ralph K. James, the chief of the Bureau of Ships, in an effort to dissociate himself from the disaster. He asserted that he "was not the submarine builder," James recalled, "simply the nuclear plant producer," a position that James considered "thoroughly dishonest." To distance himself from the accident, Rickover insisted from start to finish, from the Navy's court of inquiry through special hearings by Joint Atomic Energy Committee on the Hill, that "the nuclear power plant did not contribute to this casualty" and that he was not responsible for any other feature of the vessel. He blamed instead mismanagement by Admiral James' Bureau of Ships, shoddy shipyard welding techniques on the submarine hull, and the frequent rotation of shipyard officers—not the nuclear-trained submariners whom he controlled. Rickover took several steps to avert another disaster, however, including reducing the maximum allowable time between a reactor scram and a restoration of full power.

The Navy's inquiry into the tragedy concluded that a pipe had failed in one of the seawater systems, and that this had caused an electrical short circuit, which led to the fatal loss of power. Although he could not prove it, Admiral James believed that "a discharge of a stream of water on the nuclear control board . . . scrammed the power plant." Another theory held that the control valves, which led to the ballast tanks, had acted like expansion valves when air expanded into the tanks at very high pressure, causing moisture in the high-pressure air to freeze and block further inflow. The Navy's official announcement ambiguously stated that "a piping system failure had occurred in one of the *Thresher*'s salt water systems, probably in the engine room." This announcement meant that Rickover had effectively won the day. The unfortunate practical outcome of the *Thresher* tragedy was to increase rather than diminish Rickover's already immense, autocratic authority over nuclear submarine policy.[11]

While Navy men were sharply divided over Rickover and his nuclear power program, they closed ranks in the dispute with Secretary McNamara and the Air Force over the TFX fighter-bomber. Although professing to do otherwise, from almost the moment McNamara took office, he wittingly encouraged a renewal of the traditional rancor between the Navy and the Air Force, which reached its zenith over the TFX. In February 1961, McNamara directed Admiral Burke and General LeMay to prepare a design for a new fighter-bomber for both services, work that was to be guided by the principle of interservice commonality. The basis for this new plane was to be the TFX, an aircraft conceived by the Tactical Air Force Command to replace its aging F-105 fighter. The Air Force wanted a plane that could take off from sodded fields, fly nonstop at 700 miles per hour across the Atlantic, carry a huge payload, and operate efficiently at high and low airspeeds. The Navy, by contrast, needed a somewhat lighter, highly maneuverable tactical fighter with a very complex missile system, or a plane akin to Douglas' heavy missile–bearing F6D Missileer air defense fighter, which was still on the drawing board. Of particular importance was that the new aircraft have a short, fat fuselage, so that it would fit on flight deck elevators, and a 4-foot-diameter radar dish. Because McNamara had decreed that "changes to the Air Force tactical version to achieve the Navy mission shall be held to a minimum," he ruled that the plane would be long and slender and have the 3-foot radar dish proposed by the Air Force. This latter decision meant that the TFX's radar would be no better than that used by the Navy's older F-4 Phantom.[12]

There were other problems. The Air Force wanted the plane to be fitted with large, single wheels to roll over grassy, unpaved runways; the Navy wanted small wheels set in pairs, to keep the plane on a good center of gravity during carrier recoveries and to prevent a crash if one tire blew out. To save money, McNamara and his director of research, "whiz kid" physicist Harold Brown, ruled that both the Air Force and Navy versions of the plane would have single wheels. Rear Admiral Frederick L. Ashworth, the Navy's sole representative on the Defense Department's Source Selection Board, wanted to scrap the TFX entirely, but when McNamara canceled the F6D Missileer fighter in June 1961, the Navy had no choice other than the TFX for a modern fighter-bomber. By this time both Boeing and General Dynamics had submitted proposals to build the plane. Navy Secretary Fred Korth, a Texas banker with ties to General Dynamics, favored that firm, and for reasons that are not altogether clear, Admiral Anderson in October 1962 announced that the Navy would accept either proposal. One month later, the Boeing design was accepted by a unanimous vote of the Source Selection Board.

Only days later, on 13 November 1962, McNamara stunned everyone by awarding the TFX contract to General Dynamics, based in Texas. The Navy's version was awarded to a subcontractor, Grumman Aircraft of New York. Partisan politics obviously figured in the decision. Texas and New York, swing states, were far more important to Kennedy's 1964 reelection campaign than Washington State, where Boeing was located. Trying to muffle the ensuing uproar, McNamara disingenuously denied his partisan motives and challenged the Source Selection Board's technical recommendations during acrimonious Senate hearings, which kicked off in February 1963. Anderson and LeMay were equally apoplectic over the decision, as was Washington's Senator Henry Jackson, a Kennedy loyalist. From the Navy's standpoint, however, the Senate's challenge to McNamara was inadequate because its criticism was aimed at his decision to award the contract to General Dynamics, not at the concept of commonality. McNamara and Anderson already disliked each other, and when the CNO testified that he and the rest of the uniformed Navy opposed the TFX decision, McNamara and Kennedy exiled the admiral to the American embassy in Portugal. Admiral David McDonald, their choice to succeed Anderson, did not want the job initially, but he was persuaded to accept it, and on 21 May 1963 the White House announced the change of command.

Once McDonald took office as CNO, recalled Rear Admiral Gerald E. Miller, the team responsible for the Navy's TFX project "avoided any discussions with the CNO in order to protect him from higher authority." This did not mean that the Navy's opposition to the TFX, now designated the F-111B Aardvark, was any less than relentless or uniform. "Many of its aspects were impressive," he observed, "but the bird was not a fighter; it had no place in the Navy's inventory; and we needed a fighter." Miller "knew we should kill the plane . . . and we proceeded." At the same time, the rippling effects of the F-111 scandal started to spread within the Kennedy administration. Secretary Korth, who supported McNamara's decision, was attacked by Congress for his financial ties with General Dynamics, and when he was accused in Texas of the additional charge of stock fraud he resigned in disgrace. Korth was replaced in early November 1963 by Paul Nitze, McNamara's most durable assistant. Soon after, President Kennedy decided to collect interest on the partisan capital he had earned by delivering the F-111 aircraft contract to General Dynamics. Late in the month he flew south for a round of speeches in Texas, appearing in Fort Worth on 22 November 1963 and praising the F-111 as "the best fighter system in the world." Later that day, Kennedy flew on to Dallas, where he was shot and killed by an assassin.[13]

Although Admiral Anderson was dismissed in June 1963, he had by that time already laid the groundwork for one alternative to the TFX by commissioning a study on naval attack aircraft that was completed one month before he left office. Most existing Navy attack aircraft were designed shortly after World War II to penetrate primitive Soviet air defenses and deliver a single atomic bomb against a Russian or Warsaw Pact military target, but many of these planes were very old, and most were ill suited to conventional warfare. Admiral McDonald proposed to develop a new subsonic all-weather, night-fighting attack aircraft that could carry a large load of conventional iron bombs, fly long-range missions, and loiter over targets. Since McDonald believed that the fighters from a carrier task force would be assigned to achieve air superiority over an enemy target, he was not troubled by the inability of the new A-7A Corsair II to penetrate stiff opposing air defenses. The Air Force was, predictably, opposed to the production of this aircraft, but McDonald cleverly avoided a protracted dispute on the issue by bypassing the JCS and securing McNamara's approval for the plane, using the argument that its acquisition would permit the fleet to adapt to its new role as a purely conventional warfare arm.

This accomplishment notwithstanding, McDonald failed to persuade McNamara to drop the TFX. McNamara, incensed at the way his pet project was being abused by the Navy, dug in his heels, demanded that more planes be produced, and ignored Vice Admiral Tom Connally's plan to begin anew the search for a replacement for the aging F-4 Phantoms. McNamara repeatedly asserted that allowing the Navy to design its own fighter would violate the principle of commonality. One of McNamara's more pliable disciples, Assistant Secretary of the Navy Robert A. Frosch, insisted as late as 1967 that the F-111B "meets our fleet air defense requirements," even though only one-third of the parts in Grumman's Navy F-111B were common to the Air Force's F-111A produced by General Dynamics. Nevertheless, on the eve of McNamara's ouster from the Defense Department, Admiral McDonald was forced by the new Deputy Secretary of Defense, Paul Nitze, to purchase five F-111Bs for research and to sign a contract for serial production.[14]

Grumman was not blind to the reality that its association with the F-111B would cost it dearly over the long term in the coin of ill will among naval aviators; furthermore, Grumman engineers recognized the truth in many of Admiral Connally's pestering complaints. One of the major original problems with the F-111B was a weak swing box for the swept wings, but by the time that Grumman had devised a more durable device, a far lighter and more agile aircraft design was within reach. Without any formal Navy assistance, Grumman proposed in October 1967 that the Navy consider the variable geometry F-14 Tomcat fighter as an alternative to the F-111B. The plane combined a lightweight airframe with the powerful TF-30 engine, carried the AWG-9 weapons guidance system, was armed with one gun, and could fire Sidewinder, Sparrow, and Phoenix missiles. The new CNO, Admiral Thomas Moorer, understood that Congress would not pay for two different Navy fighters, so he dispatched Admiral Connally to shoot down the F-111B before the Senate Armed Services Committee in 1967. At the end of a long day of testimony, Admiral Miller arranged for the chairman, Senator John Stennis, to ask Connally what he personally thought of the plane, and Connally replied, "There is not enough thrust in all of Christendom to fix that aircraft!" Congress cut off funds for the F-111B, and Defense Secretary Clark Clifford canceled the program in July 1968. The bitter, seven-year struggle between McNamara and the Navy over the TFX was the second act in a drama that climaxed during the Vietnam War.[15]

Chapter Twenty-four

To the Tonkin Gulf Incident
1961–1964

Kennedy's application of Flexible Response to Asia to check Soviet support for Third World wars of national liberation inspired the strategy of counterinsurgency. This approach was first tested in Laos, a nation carved out of French Indochina by the 1954 Geneva Accords and governed by a quarrelsome oligarchy headed by Prince Souvanna Phouma. North Vietnam organized a band of disaffected Laotians into the Pathet Lao army, which launched a small-scale campaign of subversion against Souvanna Phouma's regime in 1957. Souvanna Phouma's inability to deal with this threat in part accounted for Eisenhower's decision to lend American backing to his rival, General Phoumi Nosavan, who seized power a year later. As a result, when Souvanna Phouma returned to office in August 1961, he sought assistance from Moscow, only to be ousted once again by the army. These upheavals within the faction-ridden elite only benefitted the Pathet Lao, and a renewal of its insurrection led Phoumi to appeal to Washington for support. Eisenhower understood Laos to be the strategic "key to the entire area" of Southeast Asia and told Kennedy in late 1960 that the United States might have to intervene to save Phnom Penh's pro-American government.[1]

JFK at first agreed with the assessment of his favorite general, Maxwell Taylor, who regarded control of Laos as the solution to the Indochina riddle and South Vietnam as "only a secondary theater." The JCS, alarmed by North Vietnam's attempt to overrun Laos and intimidate neighboring Prince Sihanouk of Cambodia, urged the president to save Phoumi's government. On 28 March 1961, Kennedy brashly promised to defend the status quo. Admiral Harry D. Felt, the commander in chief of the Pacific theater, had already positioned one carrier task force in the Tonkin Gulf and now sent the carrier *Coral Sea* and an amphibious task group carrying a Marine battalion into the Gulf of Thailand. They remained on station there for the next five weeks. When the tide of battle in northeast Laos turned against the Royal Laotian Army, General Lyman Lemnitzer, the JCS chairman, told Kennedy that if the chiefs "are given the right to use nuclear weapons," then "we can guarantee victory." Such alarmist pronouncements and the difficulty of intervening in land-locked Laos moved Kennedy to approve a compromise arranged by Assistant Secretary of State Averell Harriman in Geneva. Under this agreement, Souvanna Phouma returned to power as the head of a neutralist coalition and the Pathet Lao was allowed to retain control of Laos' two northern provinces, the site of the northernmost segment of the Ho Chi Minh Trail. Admiral Burke, a bitter, isolated opponent of the ceasefire that went into effect on 3 May 1961, asked in vain, "Where do we draw the line?"[2]

Burke correctly predicted that this settlement would not last long. Neither Phoumi nor the Pathet Lao would cooperate with Souvanna Phouma's coalition, and he was increasingly offended by Hanoi's presumption that the Vietnamese should dominate the other peoples of Indochina. The ceasefire evaporated in early 1962, and later that spring the Pathet Lao thrashed Phoumi's army in northwest Laos. Deeply disturbed that Harriman's arrangement was being sabotaged, Kennedy decided to show his support for Laotian independence and shore up the friendly regimes in nearby Thailand and South Vietnam. Admiral Felt, anticipating this sorry turn of events, had once more sent the 7th Fleet carriers *Hancock* and *Bennington* and a 1,500-man Marine battalion landing team to the familiar station in the Gulf of Thailand. On the morning of 17 May 1962, the carrier air groups covered the unopposed landing of the Marines, who were trucked north to an American base at Udorn, Thailand, on the Laotian border. Kennedy intended by this show of force to signal Hanoi that he would not allow the Communists to defeat the Royal Laotian Army. Secretary Rusk dispassionately referred to this as one of a number of "precautionary moves," and Admiral Anderson proposed next that the carriers attack the Ho Chi Minh Trail in Laos. "It is essential that we convince the North Vietnamese government that we will not tolerate further incursions by them into other Southeast Asian countries," he warned, predicting that unless Hanoi's aggression were checked, "military measures may eventually be required in North Vietnam or even in Communist China." There was little support within the Kennedy administration for intervention in Laos, however, and even Anderson confessed that "it was difficult to determine just who were our friends."[3]

The second Laotian crisis ended as suddenly as it had erupted. Unwilling to draw too much American attention to Indochina, Hanoi instructed the Pathet Lao to agree to another ceasefire, and a second coalition was organized under Souvanna Phouma. The Marines in Thailand returned to their ships, and a small American military advisory group withdrew from Laos. This arrangement was given the support of the great powers, who reconvened the Geneva Conference and agreed on the future neutrality of Laos in a protocol issued on 23 July 1962. Like the earlier agreement, it ignored the root cause of the fighting, which was a brew of Soviet-inspired expansionism and classical Vietnamese imperialism. Although the Americans scrupulously complied with this agreement, the North Vietnamese remained in Laos and in possession of the Ho Chi Minh Trail. Kennedy's failure to demand that the Communists back down—a habit illustrated during the Cuban Missile Crisis—augured ill for the independence of the nations of the region. Within a year the arrangement had collapsed again, and Kennedy was forced to resume military assistance to Souvanna Phouma's frail regime and the inert Royal Laotian Army. The fiction that the Harriman arrangement had neutralized Laos remained, however.

The skirmish in Laos presaged the tragedy of Vietnam, the former French colony that had been divided into two states by the 1954 Geneva Accords. In newly established South Vietnam, President Ngo Dinh Diem, a truculent, scheming American client, held sway over a corrupt, repressive regime that represented the interests of Roman Catholic refugees from North Vietnam and their political allies, the absentee South Vietnamese landlord aristocracy. In North Vietnam, after partition, President Ho Chi Minh established a vicious police state, destroyed the middle class, instituted a brutal land redistribution program, and followed the lead of Moscow and Peking in foreign policy. Ho was dedicated to the reunification of Vietnam and to Vietnamese domination of Indochina. Over 10,000 communist Vietminh agents remained behind in South Vietnam after 1954, and when Diem launched an unsuccessful campaign to wipe them out three years later, Ho countered by organizing the Vietcong army and establishing the National Liberation Front, the political arm of North Vietnam's communist-led coalition. Small-scale guerrilla operations directed by the North Vietnamese government in Hanoi against the South Vietnamese regime in Saigon began in 1960. To supply the Vietcong, the North Vietnamese built the Ho Chi Minh Trail, a complex of roads, paths, small bridges, waterways, and depots leading from North Vietnam through eastern Laos and Cambodia into South Vietnam. Alert to the danger of American intervention, the Communists decided when building the Ho Chi Minh Trail to avoid as much as possible creating chokepoints in their logistics system. As the insurgency gathered steam, Saigon's inert army was able neither to contain the Vietcong, which was responsible by 1963 for the loss of about one battalion of South Vietnamese troops each week, nor to overcome the increasingly violent opposition to Diem's Saigon government from several domestic fronts—South Vietnam's Buddhists, a small faction of Western-educated democrats, and the corruption-ridden armed forces.

American concern for Diem's long-term stability first arose in 1959, but it was not until May 1961 that Kennedy announced huge increases in military and economic aid to Saigon. He established three objectives for this effort: to sever the logistical support from North Vietnam to the Vietcong, restore Saigon's prestige, and thereby eventually defeat the Communists' attempt to unite the country. Because Hanoi was shipping large quantities of munitions from North Vietnam to South Vietnam, the Kennedy program included funds and equipment to enlarge the South Vietnamese Navy's paramilitary coastal Junk Force, which was manned by civilian irregulars and supervised by regular naval officers. In December 1961, Admiral Felt deployed American oceangoing minesweepers to the Gulf of Tonkin, where they joined South Vietnamese Navy units in conducting barrier patrol operations near the 17th parallel. The Americans used radar to direct the South Vietnamese vessels in intercepting and searching suspicious craft, but this operation was notably unsuccessful.

In November 1961, Kennedy sent General Taylor and State Department official Walt W. Rostow to South Vietnam, but upon their return they reported that there was no way to "limit . . . our possible commitment [to Saigon] unless we attack the source in Hanoi." Like his successors, Kennedy refused to confront the fact that North Vietnamese policy was the source of most of South Vietnam's woes and instead adopted half measures that were palliative rather than therapeutic. Taylor urged Kennedy to send 8,000 American combat troops to South Vietnam for base defense, but this was strongly challenged by Admiral Felt, who wanted Washington to take even more vigorous steps. Admiral Anderson and the rest of the JCS worried that the United States would "get increasingly mired down in an inconclusive struggle" and unsuccessfully sought a firm, long-term commitment from Kennedy to the unstable Saigon regime before more Americans were shipped to South Vietnam. Kennedy opted instead for gradual escalation, dispatching more than 16,000 American advisers to South Vietnam in driblets over the next two years. In late February 1962, American destroyers were again deployed to the Gulf of Thailand to conduct combined barrier patrols with the South Vietnamese Navy between the Ca Mau Peninsula and Phu Quoc Island near the Cambodian border. These operations suggested that there was "no large-scale communist infiltration from [the] sea," and the occasional deployments evidenced no long-term Kennedy commitment to the naval defense of South Vietnam.[4]

These half-hearted measures hardly prevented the Vietcong from gathering momentum and undermining Washington's faith in Saigon's will and capacity to resist. The inability of the Americans to induce Diem to reform his government and move vigorously against the Communists perplexed Kennedy, who articulated every danger of direct American involvement in the Vietnam War but steadily increased the commitment to Saigon nonetheless. In October 1962, Taylor, now the chairman of the JCS, visited South Vietnam to report again on progress in the war. The result of Taylor's second mission was Project Beef Up, more military advisers and aid and the assignment of a handful of American advisers to combat billets. A small fraction of this new program was invested in the South Vietnamese Navy, which by the end of 1963 included 50 patrol ships and mine vessels and an assortment of about 200 various riverine warfare craft.

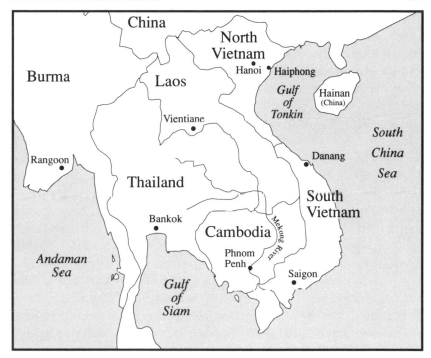

Vietnam

Kennedy also established a special office for counterinsurgency in the Defense Department in 1962 under Marine Major General Victor Krulak, but JFK's skepticism about the situation in South Vietnam was unrelenting. When Krulak and diplomat Joseph Mendenhall came back with opposing findings after a September 1963 inspection trip to Saigon, Kennedy asked in exasperation, "You two did visit the same country, didn't you?"[5]

None of Kennedy's half measures seemed to help South Vietnam. The military situation deteriorated in 1963, owing to increased communist infiltration and bolder ambushes against government forces and bases and to the collapse of the Strategic Hamlet Program. This program, vigorously backed by General Paul Harkins, the chief American adviser in Saigon, was a scheme to resettle hostile peasants. Both the Strategic Hamlet Program and Harkins, who had staked his reputation on the plan, were thoroughly discredited by the end of the year. Kennedy's limited advisory effort had failed to stem the tide of the Vietcong in

South Vietnam, while Saigon's politics were turning against Diem. Admiral Felt in Hawaii dejectedly complained to his special adviser on Indochina, Captain Philip Bucklew, that "all I get from Vietnam are glowing reports [from Harkins] of our accomplishments and meanwhile we are getting the hell kicked out of us."[6]

In the fall, South Vietnam's generals concluded that Diem had to be overthrown if Saigon was to survive. Kennedy concurred. The White House instructed Ambassador Henry Cabot Lodge to give the green light in October 1963 to General Dong Van Minh, who led a successful coup against the palace during which Diem and his brother, the secret police chief, were assassinated. But the Diem coup resolved nothing and led immediately to a struggle for power among South Vietnam's generals that drained Kennedy's enthusiasm for the war. The Diem coup and Kennedy's assassination a few weeks later also forced North Vietnam to decide what to do next, a question the Hanoi Politburo debated in a stormy session in December. Ho persuaded his colleagues that South Vietnam was mortally weakened and that they should exploit this opportunity—and their possession of the Ho Chi Minh Trail, now sanctified by the 1962 Harriman regulations—by increasing infiltration into South Vietnam. This decision set the stage for the Vietcong's 1965 offensive.

On 22 November 1963, Lyndon Baines Johnson took the oath of office aboard *Air Force One* en route from Dallas to Washington only hours after Kennedy's assassination. A legislator by trade and instinct, LBJ moved rapidly to enact a legislative program of welfare measures and civil rights acts under the banner of the Great Society. In 1964, the Republicans reacted to this liberal policy by nominating for president Senator Barry Goldwater of Arizona, a distinguished conservative who opposed the 1963 Civil Rights Act and Kennedy's Atmospheric Test Ban Treaty. During the presidential campaign, LBJ and the Democrats portrayed Goldwater as a crazed warmonger who was overly eager to involve the United States in the Vietnam War. The Tonkin Gulf incident, however, nearly forced Johnson to show his own carefully concealed hand on Southeast Asia.

The South Vietnamese had been staging small raids against North Vietnam's southern ports since 1961 to retaliate for Vietcong atrocities and to gather intelligence. Also in 1961, the 7th Fleet had begun to conduct Desoto Patrols, missions that brought American warships near the coasts of a number of communist countries in Asia to gather intelligence by intercepting communications and by observing movements ashore. Two years later, Desoto Patrols were a regular feature of the American presence in Southeast Asia. In addition, by 1964 unarmed RA-8 Crusader and escort fighters from the 7th Fleet Carrier Force flew increasingly frequent reconnaissance missions over South Vietnam, Cambodia, and Laos to gather intelligence about infiltration along the Ho Chi Minh Trail. Flying one of these missions off the carrier *Kitty Hawk* in May 1964, Lieutenant Charles F. Klusman was shot down over Laos, but he soon escaped from his communist captors. To punish the Communists for firing on American reconnaissance flights, heavy, prop-driven AD Skyraider bombers occasionally flew retaliatory strikes against hostile positions in both Laos and South Vietnam. Earlier that year, on 17 March 1964, Johnson had approved Operation 34A, an elaborate plan for a higher tempo of secret military operations against North Vietnam, intended to force Hanoi to withdraw from South Vietnam by "progressively escalating pressure" on a small scale. These pinprick raids featured air strikes by T-28 trainers flown by Thai pilots against North Vietnamese ports and villages and coincided with the American reconnaissance flights over the Ho Chi Minh Trail. By early June 1964, two American pilots had already been lost on these missions.[7]

One phase of Operation 34A included raids by South Vietnamese Navy patrol boats against North Vietnamese coastal installations. General William Westmoreland, who had just taken command of the American military advisory group in Saigon, wanted one of these operations to occur on the night of 30 July. To evaluate the success of these raids and acquire radio and other emissions intelligence during a period of intense electronic activity, Admiral U. S. Grant Sharp, the new commander in chief of the Pacific theater, ordered that more Desoto Patrols be sent into the Tonkin Gulf. Sharp directed Captain James Herrick in the destroyer *Maddox* to steam into the Gulf to monitor South Vietnamese attacks against Hon Me and Hon Ngu, North Vietnamese islands situated a few miles off the coast. Herrick entered the Gulf on the afternoon of 31 July with orders to stay at least eight miles away from the mainland because North Vietnam claimed a five-mile territorial limit, but the commodore soon passed within five miles of the islands of Hon Me and Hon Ngu.

On 2 August, the *Maddox* was about thirty miles off North Vietnam's coast observing thick coastal junk traffic in the Gulf. Herrick was aware of the South Vietnamese raids against the off-shore islands and the port of Vinh Son. At about noon, the destroyer's radar picked up three North Vietnamese P-4 motor torpedo boats speeding along a parallel course but still far out of torpedo range. Within an hour, however, these obviously hostile vessels began to close on the *Maddox* at 40 knots. Herrick turned to the south and increased his speed, and at 1440 he radioed for assistance from the carrier *Ticonderoga*, then stationed at the edge of the Gulf. The engagement began at 1508 when the *Maddox* fired three warning shots from her 5-inch battery at the approaching boats. Meanwhile, in Washington, Secretary McNamara was attempting in vain to establish radio communications with the destroyer in the Tonkin Gulf so that he might direct the battle from his Pentagon office.

Earlier that afternoon, Commander R. F. Mohrhardt, with a section of three F-8 Crusader fighters, lifted off the carrier *Ticonderoga* on a routine training mission, unaware that the *Maddox* was under attack by the North Vietnamese. Forty-five minutes later, Mohrhardt was sent 300 miles to the north to help the American destroyer. In about thirty minutes his planes arrived over the battle. Because it was still daylight, he easily surveyed the scene. The *Maddox* was steaming to the south at flank speed, but she was being overtaken by the North Vietnamese formation. Taking command of the battle, Herrick ordered Mohrhardt to attack the enemy. One section of American naval aircraft hit the trailing vessel with 20mm cannon fire and 5-inch Zuni rockets, and Mohrhardt saw the "boat burning and smoking heavily in the stern and the crew throwing gear and smoke lights over the side." Within a few moments, she sank. The next boat was shot up just after she fired a torpedo, which missed the *Maddox* by a few hundred feet. The third attacker closed to within 1,700 yards of the *Maddox*, opened up with her machine guns before being hit by the destroyer's 5-inch guns, and passed by her stern in a frantic attempt to withdraw. Badly damaged, the two communist vessels retired to the north.[8]

When Admiral Sharp relayed word of the first Gulf of Tonkin incident to Washington, Secretary Rusk's immediate reaction was to send an angry but useless protest to Hanoi. At the same time, Sharp asked the JCS for permission to reinforce the

Maddox and send her back into the Gulf. "We cannot sit still as a nation and let them attack us on the high seas and get away with it," McNamara confessed, but he encouraged President Johnson to treat this first attack in the Gulf of Tonkin as an honest "mistake." Rusk felt that the "OpPlan 34A activities are beginning to rattle Hanoi, and the *Maddox* incident is directly related to their effort to resist." Despite this contradictory interpretation of the episode, Rusk agreed with McNamara on one point. "We have no intention [of] yielding to pressure." Undersecretary of State Ball objected to reinforcing the *Maddox*, however, and dismissed as "a hollow bravado" the decision to send the Desoto Patrol back into the Tonkin Gulf. Captain Herrick was also uneasy about reentering the Gulf, complaining that the Desoto Patrol destroyers did not carry enough fuel "for long patrol where high speeds are required" and that his "gunnery . . . [was] not well fitted for anti-PT [operations] even in daylight."[9]

On a Desoto Patrol in the northern Tonkin Gulf, the destroyer *Maddox* (DD-731) was attacked in daylight on 2 August 1964 by North Vietnamese fast patrol vessels. In company with the destroyer *C. Turner Joy*, she reentered the Tonkin Gulf and reported another attack on the night of the 4th, an action that the Johnson Administration used to convince Congress to pass the controversial Gulf of Tonkin Resolution.

The attack carrier *Constellation* and the destroyer *C. Turner Joy* were riding at anchor in Hong Kong when the North Vietnamese attacked the *Maddox* on 2 August. After the White House approved another Desoto Patrol, Vice Admiral Ray Johnson, who commanded the 7th Fleet, ordered Commander Robert C. Barnhart in the *C. Turner Joy* to rendezvous with the *Maddox* and reinforced the Tonkin Gulf Task Force by directing the *Constellation* and the antisubmarine carrier *Kearsarge* to join the *Ticonderoga* at the southern edge of the Gulf. The ships might fire on the North Vietnamese, McNamara decided, but only after they had first been attacked. Herrick's patrol on 3 August was uneventful. The two-ship Desoto Patrol sailed north, staying about sixteen miles off North Vietnam's coastline, but that evening the formation changed course and started to retire to a position roughly 100 miles to the southeast. The day before, an NSA listening station in Thailand had intercepted a message from Vinh to Hanoi mentioning North Vietnamese naval operations in the near future. For the night of 3 August, Westmoreland had ordered another 34A operation by fast South Vietnamese patrol boats, which were to attack communist targets in the Rhon River estuary and a radar installation at Vinh Son. In response to these attacks, a small squadron of North Vietnamese junks and P-4 motor torpedo boats stood out to sea on 4 August.

On the morning of 4 August, the Desoto Patrol again steamed northward into the Gulf, and at 1435 the ships turned to the southwest, movements covered by nearby combat air patrol aircraft from the carrier *Ticonderoga*. Three hours later, Herrick changed course again and headed eastward. For several hours that day, a North Vietnamese motor gunboat shadowed the American ships at a distance of about fifteen miles. Alerted to the danger by the earlier attack, new radio intelligence, and North Vietnamese movements, Admiral Johnson had explicitly instructed Herrick not to shrink from a surface action. Were the destroyers to be "confronted with attack" by the North Vietnamese, Herrick was to "use all means available to destroy [the] enemy including aggressive pursuit."[10]

At 2041 Commander Herbert Ogier, the captain of the *Maddox*, reported to Herrick that the ship's long-range, surface search radar had acquired a contact to the northeast. Within the next hour, two more enemy P-4 motor patrol boats were identified heading toward the Americans at high speed on an intercepting course. Upon hearing this news, Herrick made the surprising decision to retire, and the Desoto Patrol turned to the southwest at a speed of 30 knots. This change of plans angered Admiral Johnson, who tried in vain to get Herrick to stand and fight. The opposing forces appeared to be converging, and at 2239, with only 7,800 yards separating them, the *C. Turner Joy* opened fire, followed within moments by the *Maddox*. Within seconds, the North Vietnamese launched a torpedo that Ogier in the *Maddox* had to swerve hard to avoid. After falling back for a moment, the enemy renewed the chase, and a few minutes later the North Vietnamese boats were thought to be close enough to be taken under fire again by Barnhart in the *C. Turner Joy*.

Herrick by now had asked Rear Admiral Robert B. Moore with the *Ticonderoga* task force for air support, and within twenty minutes a pair of A-4 Skyhawks arrived over the battle and were joined shortly by a pair of AD Skyraiders and a lone F-4 Phantom fighter. Herrick could not figure out what was happening. The crew of the *C. Turner Joy* reported that a large cloud of black smoke erupted from one of the targets, but when Commander James Stockdale dipped down a bit to locate the North Vietnamese in a fast flying pass, he saw no phosphorescent waves other than those made by the destroyers and was unable to locate and attack the enemy boats. Many years later Stockdale asserted that because he did not see the enemy on the night of 4 August, no attack had taken place. Several miles away, however, Commander George H. Edmondson was flying his slow, prop-driven AD Skyraider at 700 feet, below the clouds, when he sighted gun flashes and antiaircraft bursts, and in one pass over the destroyers he clearly saw and reported a "snakey" wake 1.5 miles ahead of the *Maddox*, the lead destroyer.[11]

Following the *C. Turner Joy*'s first radar contact, Herrick reported to Sharp that he was engaging three North Vietnamese torpedo boats, a description of the battle later suggested by radio intelligence. Confusion reigned on board the *Maddox*, and Herrick was worried about the conflicting radar and sonar reports and the lack of confirmation from Stockdale's aircraft. Anxious to leave the Gulf in spite of Admiral Johnson's orders that he remain on station, Herrick now warned his superiors that he could not be certain about some aspects of the attack until an air search was conducted at dawn. The "entire action leaves many doubts," he declared. Sharp told McNamara, "Reports from the ships were not conclusive [but] the weight of evidence [including some radio intercept intelligence] supported" the conclusion "that an attack, in fact, occurred." Eighty minutes later, after checking with Ogier, Herrick informed Sharp that the destroyers had indeed been attacked. Admiral Johnson was "convinced beyond any doubt" that the destroyers had been "subjected to an unprovoked surface torpedo attack on the night of 4 August." Admirals Sharp, Moorer, and Johnson, certain that the attack had taken place but furious with Herrick for disobeying orders, apparently ignored the confusion in Washington generated by Herrick's single, ambivalent message about the radar contacts. "The second attack was always questioned," Admiral McDonald, the CNO, recalled. President Johnson, surprisingly unconcerned about specifics, told Undersecretary Ball just two or three days after the incident that "those dumb, stupid sailors were just shooting at flying fish."[12]

At a soft point in his reelection campaign, LBJ was being pressured by southern Democrats and conservative Republicans not to allow the Communists to overrun South Vietnam. To avoid further commitment to the ground war in South Vietnam, the president decided to retaliate against North Vietnam, and at 2340 on 4 August in Washington, the White House announced that "our response for the present will be limited and fitting" retaliatory air attacks by the 7th Fleet. This midnight broadcast not only alerted the Communists to what was afoot but also exposed the fundamental weakness that would infect Lyndon Johnson's entire war policy. He wanted the North Vietnamese to quit supporting the Vietcong but was unwilling to do anything truly stiff to achieve that end. That night he worried in public about "the risk of spreading the conflict," and soothed Ho Chi Minh in Hanoi with the promise that "we seek no wider war." This squeamishness was no vaccine for the pox of Vietnamese imperialism.[13]

To punish Hanoi, Johnson approved the first Pierce Arrow retaliatory air raid against a handful of military targets in North Vietnam. McNamara prepared a detailed plan for these strikes, and General Earle Wheeler, the new chairman of the JCS, was told to transmit it to Admiral Sharp. At 1230 on 5 August, Admiral Moore launched sixty-four aircraft against four targets in North Vietnam. Half of the *Ticonderoga*'s A-4 Skyhawks were still at Cubi Point in the Philippines, however, so these aircraft had to fly out to the carrier, get armed, and join in the attack. Led by Commander Wesley L. McDonald, twenty-six aircraft from the *Ticonderoga* struck ten oil dumps at Vinh, while F-8 Crusaders hit a flotilla of North Vietnamese patrol torpedo boats at Quang Khe, fifty miles north of the demilitarized zone. The Crusaders failed to arrive on time to support the Skyhawk attack on Vinh, however, with the result that the attack "was all improvisation," observed Captain R. N. Livingston. Another communist PT boat base to the south at Loc Chao was attacked by a mixed flight of fighter and attack aircraft from the *Constellation,* and planes from this carrier also hit the enemy's northernmost patrol boat base at Hon Gai on the outskirts of the port of Haiphong. There, North Vietnam's antiaircraft defenses were strong enough to shoot down an A-4 Skyhawk piloted by Lieutenant Everett Alvarez, who became one of North Vietnam's first American prisoners of war. And it was the first and last time that the old, vulnerable A-1 Spads dropped bombs on North Vietnam. "We knew we were seeing a war start," Commander Stockdale recalled.[14]

LBJ now chose to exploit the Gulf of Tonkin incident to get congressional backing for his new strategy, one that coupled a more vigorous counterinsurgency in South Vietnam with spasmodic, punitive Pierce Arrow air strikes against North Vietnam. On 5 August he asked Senator J. William Fulbright, the chairman of the Foreign Relations Committee, to arrange for the expedited passage of a congressional resolution expressing approval for his policy. Johnson foolishly failed, however, to explain fully the events surrounding the attack on the Desoto Patrol to his fellow Democrats on Capitol Hill. The Gulf of Tonkin Resolution, passed almost without dissent, authorized the president to "take all necessary measures to repel armed aggression" in Indochina and affirmed congressional support of the president's military policy "until the peace and security of the area is reasonably assured." Soon afterward, Admiral Sharp shifted the carrier *Ranger* and her escorts from San Diego to the western Pacific, and more than fifty Air Force F-102 fighters and B-57 Canberra bombers flew from the Philippines to South Vietnamese airfields at Danang, Bien Hoa, and Tan Son Nhut near Saigon.[15]

Johnson refused to do anything truly stiff, however. His first object was to win reelection, and his most successful campaign tactic was to attack Senator Goldwater as a trigger-happy warmonger. Thus, 34A operations against North Vietnam's coast were suspended until October, and then only occasional forays were permitted for the rest of the year. Admiral Sharp pressed Washington to continue the Desoto Patrols, but McNamara instructed him to suspend these operations also, and more than a month passed before American warships reentered the northern Tonkin Gulf. Claiming that this would signal Hanoi that Washington was willing to allow the 7th Fleet to be driven out of international waters, the JCS finally persuaded McNamara to agree to another Desoto Patrol the following month, although he insisted that the ships steam no closer than twenty miles from North Vietnam's mainland.

The destroyers *Morton* and *Richard E. Edwards* sailed into the northern Tonkin Gulf on 17 September, but the North Vietnamese did not react until the following evening, when a formation of high-speed patrol boats stood out to sea and began to run down the American ships. The Communists opened the engagement with a long-range torpedo attack, but the *Edwards* maneuvered violently to evade these weapons, while both American ships brought the enemy under such a withering fire that he was forced to retire. Sharp wanted to retaliate, but the president not only turned down this proposal but also ended the Desoto Patrols for good. Next, on 1 November, only days before the American elections, the Vietcong launched a vicious mortar attack against the Bien Hoa Air Base on the outskirts of Saigon. Johnson and McNamara, fearful of calling attention to the dilemma of Southeast Asia, abruptly rejected Admiral Sharp's plea for another Pierce Arrow strike against North Vietnam.[16]

Kennedy's legacy, Goldwater's gritty, unpopular conservatism, and Johnson's manipulation of the news led to a Democratic landslide on 4 November. Within a few days, however, the president was confronted by more Vietcong attacks on American advisers in South Vietnam. He finally agreed to Admiral Sharp's plan to initiate Operation Barrel Roll, a series of armed reconnaissance flights conducted jointly by the Air Force and the Tonkin Gulf Carrier Task Force against the Ho Chi Minh Trail in Laos. By early January 1965, these daytime strikes had damaged the main road from North Vietnam to the Plain of Jars in Laos, forcing the Communists to reduce the size of their truck convoys and to begin moving them by night. Unfortunately, an attempt to counter this step with nighttime AD Skyraider strikes resulted in a tragedy when the Americans mistakenly bombed a village garrisoned by the Royal Laotian Army and provoked a bitter protest from Phnom Penh to Washington. On Christmas Eve, Vietcong sappers bombed the Brink Bachelors Officers' Quarters in Saigon, but this time the White House brushed aside the pleas of the JCS for another violent American reaction. Unsteady and uncertain, President Johnson twisted and turned, confusing his military advisers and leaving the American people with no firm direction as to the course he planned to take in the Vietnam War.

Chapter Twenty-five

Gradual Escalation in the Vietnam War

1965

On 7 February 1965, the Vietcong staged a heavy mortar attack on Camp Holloway at Pleiku in South Vietnam's Central Highlands, a milestone that winter of escalating communist violence that General Westmoreland estimated was costing the South Vietnamese Army "about a battalion a week." According to the CNO, Admiral McDonald, "the Joint Chiefs felt that if we didn't intervene militarily, South Vietnam would fall," but they hoped that American forces could "win it quickly" and turn internal security back to the quarrelsome South Vietnamese. President Johnson and Defense Secretary McNamara were still clinging to the cautious strategy of "sustained reprisal," which embodied discrete reactions to each communist provocation with minor air raids against North Vietnam.[1]

To retaliate for the attack on Pleiku, McNamara ordered Rear Admiral H. L. Miller, who commanded the Tonkin Gulf Task Force, to launch Operation Flaming Dart I. Miller recalled the carriers *Coral Sea* and *Hancock*, then en route to Subic Bay in the Philippines, and they joined the *Ranger* in the Gulf of Tonkin shortly after noon on the 27th. Later that day, forty-nine attackers from the *Coral Sea* and the *Hancock* hit an enemy army barracks and port facilities at Dong Hoi, just north of the demilitarized zone. As the target for a flight from the *Ranger*, McNamara personally selected another North Vietnamese barracks at Vit Thu Lu, fifteen miles inland and only five miles from the DMZ.

The northeast monsoon engulfed the area, but McNamara refused to allow the American naval aviators to attack targets of opportunity, and Air Force attacks on other installations were also turned back because of low visibility. "If that target was closed," Miller complained, "there was no recourse but to drop the ordnance in the water."[2]

Beyond some minor damage to a few buildings and one staging area, the first Flaming Dart strikes achieved none of their objectives. Ho Chi Minh issued an icy denunciation of the United States and, on 10 February, the Vietcong blew up the American enlisted barracks at Qui Nhon. Under pressure from the JCS and Admiral Sharp, McNamara agreed to more "sustained retaliation." The next day, Admiral Miller launched Flaming Dart II, which called for ninety-nine carrier-based aircraft to hit an enemy army barracks at Chanh Hoa. This time, McNamara not only selected the targets but also specified the aircraft to be flown, the ordnance each would deliver, and the fusing of the bombs. He dictated the timing of the attack, set for 0900 to coincide with Johnson's announcement in Washington of the strikes. McNamara's choice of the early morning hour was poor, for the fog, drizzling rain, and clouds down to 500 feet limited visibility to less than one mile, even at very low altitudes. Instead of the punishing blow Sharp intended to deliver, McNamara settled for "a small strike against rather insignificant targets in the southern part of North Vietnam." This was "generally ineffective as a reprisal action." In addition, Chanh Hoa's antiaircraft defenses were ready, and they shot down three American aircraft from the *Coral Sea*. The Flaming Dart II strike achieved no more than the first. Over 480 bombs were dropped and three American aircraft were lost to flak, but only twenty-three of seventy-six targeted buildings were damaged. Clearly, American attack aircraft were at a tremendous disadvantage against well-defended, fixed targets in North Vietnam, a disadvantage that would not be fully overcome until the introduction of laser-guided munitions seven years later. By design or happenstance, moreover, Vietcong operations in South Vietnam intensified after Flaming Dart II.[3]

Washington now feared that South Vietnam was about to collapse. After the November 1963 coup had toppled Diem, General Minh took power, but neither Minh nor his many successors had the will or means to reform Saigon's government or to take the offensive against the Vietcong. "The best thing about [General Nguyen] Khanh's government," reported Ambassador Taylor at Christmas, 1964, "is that it has lasted six months and has about a 50-50 chance of lasting out the year." Reforms, McNamara believed, would not reverse the course of the war. Khanh was ousted in 1965 and a short-lived civilian government took power. In May a new junta took over, this one headed by Air Marshal Nguyen Cao Ky as prime minister and General Nguyen Van Thieu as head of South Vietnam's armed forces. The South Vietnamese Navy was a pawn in each upheaval. "You are up to your neck in politics," Taylor angrily told Ky and the Navy's Admiral Cang. The Thieu-Ky clique ruled Saigon until the end of the war. "South Vietnam is a country with an army and no government," observed Undersecretary of State George Ball resignedly.[4]

The South Vietnamese Navy was peculiarly luckless. Captain Philip Bucklew alerted Admiral McDonald to the extent of the problem in January 1964. Bucklew, who headed a U.S. Navy team studying the problem of infiltration, regarded seaborne infiltration as the most economical way for North Vietnam to provide the Vietcong with standardized ammunition and arms. Apprised of the South Vietnamese Navy's corruption and ineptitude, he urged that the entire American naval effort in Indochina be reorganized. Coastal patrols were futile without aggressive inland riverine operations in the Mekong Delta. The charter of Captain William Hardcastle's Naval Advisory Group in Saigon was broadened by Sharp in May 1964, tests were rushed to completion on the 36-foot PFC Swift patrol craft, and a huge construction project was begun to enlarge the South Vietnamese Navy's bases at Danang and Camranh Bay. However, McNamara refused to allow the Navy to act on many of Bucklew's proposals—such as interdicting communist shipping to Cambodia's port of Sihanoukville—until one year later, when the Vung Ro Bay incident led to a change in policy.[5]

The Vung Ro Bay affair began to evolve at 1030 on 16 February 1965 when a U.S. Army UH-1B Iroquois helicopter spotted a camouflaged 180-ton ship lying in the bay on South Vietnam's south-central coast. Lieutenant Commander Harvey P. Rodgers, the naval coastal zone adviser, called for an aerial reconnaissance patrol that confirmed the vessel's location. He then asked for air strikes to hit the ship. Four separate attacks crumpled her onto her port side in shallow water, and the planes strafed nearby beaches where dozens of large crates containing arms had been offloaded. Lieutenant Commander Thoai of the South Vietnamese Navy, who commanded the second coastal zone, was trying to arrange for South Vietnamese Army troops from nearby Tuy Hoa to be transported to Vung Ro Bay on board the *LSM-405* and for support by a South Vietnamese coastal group and a SEAL team, which was to be assigned to conduct salvage operations. The *LSM-405* reached Tuy Hoa early on the 17th, but the local South Vietnamese province chief refused to provide any troops for the mission on the grounds that it was too dangerous, Vung Ro Bay being known as a Vietcong stronghold. Therefore, when the landing craft anchored off Vung Ro Bay at 1430 that afternoon, there were no troops to go ashore. Commanders Rodgers and Thoai both anxiously called for more air strikes, but no planes appeared over Vung Ro Bay, and when Thoai twice attempted to enter the bay he was driven off by small arms fire.

Word of the Vung Ro Bay incident had by now reached Brigadier General William E. DePuy, and he convened a conference at Nha Trang to pressure the South Vietnamese Army to do something about the ship and the nearby arms cache. By this time, Thoai in the patrol escort *PCE-08* had reappeared off Vung Ro and instructed the LSM's captain to accompany him into the bay. After shooting up the area, they retired to Dai Lanh to embark South Vietnamese Special Forces for another attempt to enter the bay. At 0550 on 19 February, Lieutenant Franklin W. Anderson in the *PC-04* rendezvoused with the South Vietnamese Navy formation at the mouth of Vung Ro. At 0800, all three vessels entered the bay, and, after three attempts to land, South Vietnamese troops finally got ashore.

They discovered crates of machine guns, ammunition, medical supplies, and 4,000 small arms on the beach. Some of the guns and munitions were loaded on board the South Vietnamese vessels, but the troops started to loot the crates in search of drugs and their officers refused to stop them. Thoai did not believe that he could hold the beach overnight, so, overruling Lieutenant Anderson's violent objections, he reembarked the South Vietnamese troops, stood out to sea, and refused to approach Vung Ro before dawn the next day. The Saigon regime was now under the bright glare of intense American scrutiny. At 0600 on 20 February, South Vietnamese Navy headquarters instructed Thoai to land again, but when the troops got ashore the South Vietnamese Special Forces commander refused to direct his men to load the crates onto the LSM, instead allowing them to loot the medical supplies once again. Anderson and a few other American advisers located several more communist caches around the beach, and the South Vietnamese continued their looting spree for several days.[6]

The Vung Ro Bay incident illustrated the unfortunate subordination of South Vietnam's navy to the army. The four naval zones of South Vietnam were divided in rough conformity to the army's corps organization, the commander of each zone assuming responsibility for coastal security and inland riverine operations under the local army general. A dense mangrove swamp bisected III Corps and IV Corps, and in 1964 the South Vietnamese Joint General Staff in Saigon termed this area the Rung Sat Special Zone and set it aside as its navy's only territorial command. In effect, this gesture signaled that the Saigon army had abandoned any attempt to wrest the Rung Sat from the Vietcong. If the South Vietnamese Navy ventured into other areas, its vessels fell under the operational command of the local civilian province chiefs or the army's corps commanders.

Progeny of the French, the South Vietnamese Navy had operated exclusively as an inland riverine force during the Indochina War. With the help of American naval advisers during the Diem dictatorship, it had developed a small, ineffective Sea Force that operated a few ships transferred from the French and American fleets. By 1965, the Sea Force was composed of 16 ships and 2,000 men, few of whom ever put to sea. The paramilitary Junk Force counted up to 600 vessels on coastal patrol, and another 190 inshore, but at least half of this number were unable to operate for want of equipment or maintenance. American naval advisers with both forces were constantly frustrated by the Vietnamese sailors' lack of training, the officers' lack of enthusiasm for the war, and the disinterest in the naval effort that Saigon's corrupt junta demonstrated daily. The clique that ran the South Vietnamese Navy was so corrupt that between April 1965, when its chief of staff was assassinated, and 1967, it had four different commanders, including one army general. However, Saigon's generals valued the navy, for its vessels were useful in ferrying troops to the capital during coups. As a result, observed Rear Admiral Robert Salzer, South Vietnam's navy was "pre-occupied with staying out of trouble with the all-powerful army."

For the most part, however, the Saigon juntas paid little attention to South Vietnam's navy, and its officers and sailors enjoyed precious little prestige in the larger society. They were "held in very low esteem within the South Vietnamese military," remarked Rear Admiral Arthur Price, Jr. Another problem was that the South Vietnamese Navy "did not have a good rapport with the people" it was supposed to defend. American advisers had worked hard to improve the South Vietnamese Navy's morale and performance for a decade but accomplished little. In September 1965, one adviser on board a South Vietnamese Sea Force patrol vessel watched in silent frustration while the ship searched 169 junks, steamed about without radar because the captain had given the repairmen leave, and stayed at sea rather than venture inshore where traffic was heavy. That same month, the U.S. Coast Guard cutter *Point Glover* sank a 42-foot motorized junk carrying weapons, and the Coast Guard water patrol boat *Point Marone* destroyed an armed Vietcong junk off Ha Tien near the Cambodian frontier. Most U.S. Navy observers agreed with General Westmoreland's observation that saving South Vietnam in 1965 "could not depend on the Vietnamese."[7]

On the eve of the Pleiku and Vung Ro Bay incidents, McGeorge Bundy, the president's national security adviser, had warned LBJ from Saigon that "without new U.S. action, defeat appears inevitable." Bundy urged the adoption of a "policy of graduated response" to effect what he would later term a "denial of victory" strategy. At the same time, Westmoreland formally asked McNamara to send American combat ground, naval, and air forces to South Vietnam to engage the Vietcong and the North Vietnamese. Sharp, Westmoreland's nominal superior, backed the general's plan, and he appended to the proposal a plan of his own, which he had worked on since August 1964, to mount Rolling Thunder One, a sustained strategic bombing campaign against North Vietnam. These plans were approved by the JCS, who added some measures of their own and sent them up to McNamara and Johnson. To defeat the Communists, insisted General Earle Wheeler, American forces in South Vietnam "must take the fight to the enemy."[8]

In March 1965, McNamara announced dramatically that he would do "anything that will strengthen" South Vietnam, but within days he privately reversed course, rejecting steps proposed by the JCS to call up the reserves, lengthen the draft, lift service manpower ceilings, and ask Congress for supplemental appropriations to increase military assistance to Saigon's army and navy. General Taylor, the new ambassador in Saigon, also wavered. He warned that the introduction of Americans into combat in South Vietnam would lessen the independence of the regime in Saigon, which Washington wanted to help. Comparing Vietnam to Korea, Taylor wondered aloud if Johnson and McNamara possessed the will to stay the course in another land war in Asia. Undersecretary of State Ball adopted a more defeatist line. Castigating the "air power zealots," whom he claimed now "realized that bombing alone would not critically reduce the enemy's fighting capacity," Ball proposed a "general amnesty" for the Vietcong and the "creation of a coalition government" under international supervision. Then, he told Johnson, "the United States would withdraw."[9]

Secretary of State Rusk rejected a policy designed to facilitate withdrawal, arguing that this would destroy American influence in Asia and undermine Washington's guarantees to South Korea, Japan, and the Philippine Islands. McNamara agreed with this analysis, although he persuaded the president to steer a "middle course" between the muscular strategy proposed by the JCS and Admiral Sharp and the policy of appeasement and retreat advocated by Undersecretary Ball. Johnson agreed in June to commit American troops and Marines to ground combat in South Vietnam and directed McNamara to deploy American naval forces to support the Army within South Vietnam. Finally, he agreed to meet the JCS demand that McNamara's air policy of "sustained reprisal" be abandoned in favor of a strategy dedicated to interdicting the communist logistics system in North Vietnam, but he turned down a JCS plan to use mass and shock in an air blitz to crush North Vietnam's weak, poorly arranged air defenses. General John McConnell, the Air Force chief of staff, warned McNamara that graduated air strikes would fail, but McNamara nonetheless assured Johnson that a policy of "gradual escalation" would inflict sufficient pain on North Vietnam to induce Ho Chi Minh to send negotiators to the bargaining table. On 7 April, the president had announced that the Americans "would not grow tired" or "withdraw under the cloak of a meaningless agreement," but he reduced the ferocity of this threat by marrying it with a promise that Washington stood "ready . . . for unconditional discussions."

The first American combat troops in Vietnam were Marines. At 0300 on 7 March, the 9th Marine Expeditionary Brigade under Brigadier General Frederick Karch sped upriver in boats, which landed them on a sand ramp in downtown Danang six hours later. They marched up to a nearby Air Force base used to fly strikes into North Vietnam and dug foxholes. The Vietcong's violent reaction to their presence underscored the need for more combat troops for active base defense. McNamara instructed Karch that the president did not want the Marines to undertake extensive patrols that would result in combat casualties. However, the ferocity of the Vietcong reaction was such that LBJ agreed on 6 April to send two more Marine battalions to Danang and Phu Bai and approved a "change of mission . . . to more active use" of these troops. Conditions worsened. Westmoreland reported on 7 June that the South Vietnamese Army was near collapse. There was "no course of action open to us except to reinforce" the American advisory group with thirty-five Army maneuver battalions and to take over the war from the South Vietnamese. Later that month, Johnson decided to commit American forces to ground combat in South Vietnam, and within two months the number of men of all three services under General Westmoreland's command had jumped to 125,000, later raised to 219,000. Lieutenant General Lewis Walt, who now took command of the Marines in I Corps, laid out a plan for what he called an Inkblot strategy of slowly establishing very secure rear bases, developing local self-defense forces, and expanding the perimeter of these pacified areas to nearby villages.

Westmoreland disagreed with Walt's Inkblot strategy, however, holding that it would expose South Vietnam's major cities to continuous enemy attacks. Ordered by LBJ to keep South Vietnam's civilian casualties low, respect Cambodian and Laotian neutrality, and not invade North Vietnam, Westmoreland decided to rely on heavy firepower, helicopter mobility, and American air power to search out, trap, and defeat the Vietcong in pitched battles. He was left with little choice about conducting simple heavy firepower operations—his Army maneuver battalions, composed mostly of short-term enlistees or short-term conscripts, were incapable of executing more complex maneuvers. Therefore, he quickly set about constructing a string of heavily fortified firebases around which he would conduct aggressive search and destroy operations intended to flush out the Vietcong and bring him to book. "Now we were committed to major combat in Vietnam," LBJ observed.[10]

For his part, Sharp, who remained in Hawaii, was not equipped with the temperament or the ability to plant his own imprint on grand strategy in Southeast Asia, let alone on ground strategy in South Vietnam. Whereas Hanoi treated Indochina as a single theater, Johnson and McNamara dealt with South Vietnam, North Vietnam, Laos, Cambodia, and the neutral powers as separate problems. Sharp strongly disagreed with this approach, but he was unable to persuade LBJ to upset it. Nor was Sharp capable of imposing a single ground strategy on his Army and Marine Corps subordinates in South Vietnam. In March, he agreed with Westmoreland's plan to establish firebase enclaves from which to conduct search and destroy patrols, but later in the year he seemed to back Walt's Inkblot approach. On the whole Sharp was overly reluctant to impose his will on either Westmoreland or Walt and so failed as a unified commander to bring order and coherence to American strategy in South Vietnam.

One reason for this was that Westmoreland quickly established a back channel to General Wheeler of the JCS, and LBJ quite often bypassed the JCS and Sharp to deal directly with Westmoreland. In refusing to take a strong stand against these practices, Sharp undermined his own position on other issues. Westmoreland "generally makes the decisions with regard to the ground war," Sharp told Congress in 1967, an oblique explanation of his refusal to make a firm choice between the opposing Army and Marine Corps ground strategies. When Westmoreland made a bid to take over both Air Force and Navy air operations over the southern half of North Vietnam in early 1965, however, Sharp resisted the encroachment and effectively slapped the general's wrist. Nevertheless, he was overruled by the White House on most of the larger issues of the war and failed utterly to convince Johnson or McNamara to agree to a plan developed by General Krulak, who commanded the Pacific Fleet Marine Force, and Westmoreland to establish an American ground force in Laos to shut down the Ho Chi Minh Trail. For reasons that defy understanding, LBJ was committed to upholding Harriman's 1962 Geneva Protocol on Laos, although he knew full well that for years North Vietnam had made a mockery of Laotian neutrality. Possession of the Ho Chi Minh Trail gave North Vietnam the whiphand throughout the war.

The start of Westmoreland's search and destroy operations in 1965 created the need for more close ground support for the Army and the Marines than the Air Force could then provide, as the number of secure airbases in South Vietnam from which American jets could safely operate was limited. However, the carriers were now on call. In April, naval aircraft from the *Coral Sea* and *Midway* and Marine F-8 Crusaders from the *Oriskany* supported the Marines and the Army by hitting several minor communist targets in northern South Vietnam. These strikes so impressed Westmoreland that he asked Sharp to establish Dixie Station, about 100 miles southeast of Cam ranh Bay, on 16 May. About the same time, Rolling Thunder bombing against North Vietnam was getting under way. With four carriers in the 7th Fleet, Vice Admiral Roy Johnson positioned one on Dixie Station and two on Yankee Station south of Hainan Island in the northeast Tonkin Gulf. Aviators, aircraft, and carriers that arrived in Southeast Asia over the next year were first assigned to Dixie Station, operating against the Vietcong in South Vietnam before moving north to Yankee Station to participate in Rolling Thunder operations over North Vietnam. Indeed, until 1967 over one-third of all air strikes against targets in South Vietnam were flown by the Tonkin Gulf Task Force.

Coupled with the commitment of American forces to combat was the transformation of the U.S. Navy's small Saigon advisory group into a major command. In May 1965, Sharp established the Naval Forces Vietnam command, a billet first held by Rear Admiral Norvell G. Ward, an outstanding organizer. Naval Forces Vietnam fell under Westmoreland's organization, but Westmoreland had little time for the Navy and so left Ward to operate what became almost an independent command. Ward divided his command into two elements: an enlarged advisory group, which continued to support the training of the South Vietnamese Navy, and three operational task forces—Market Time, Game Warden, and the Mobile Riverine Force. Vietcong sapper attacks in early 1965 showed that sabotage was a deadly menace to the security of American forces in South Vietnam, and a closely aligned problem was harbor security, an especially important Navy mission once American combat troops started to arrive in South Vietnam in large numbers. In 1964, a Vietcong mine sank an American aircraft transport at her berth in Saigon, and the problem threatened to grow worse with the influx of American forces and supplies into the country. To meet this challenge, Ward created the Coastal Surveillance Force and charged it with executing Operation Stable Door. Five Harbor Entrance Control Posts were established to provide day and night radar and patrol boat surveillance over anchorages and approaches. Stable Door was so successful that at no time during the conflict were these sophisticated defenses penetrated from the sea, although local Vietcong sabotage mounted from the landward approaches to the harbors persisted on a small scale.

The decision to initiate the Market Time coastal surveillance campaign stemmed directly from the Vung Ro Bay incident, an event that ended any doubts about the South Vietnamese Navy's inefficiency. "Most of their supplies were coming down by sea," Westmoreland recalled. "It became pretty obvious that we had to close the sea route." This did not solve the riddle as to what extent the Americans should participate in coastal surveillance operations, although there was an unhappy, self-defeating tendency to shove aside the South Vietnamese as much as possible. The Communists used two types of vessels for infiltration operations, steel-hulled trawlers and motorized coastal junks. Captain Hardcastle believed that the South Vietnamese Navy could handle the junks and sampans in shallow waters, but that the 7th Fleet should establish a separate task force to interdict the larger North Vietnamese vessels. Although this arrangement was unwieldy, Sharp had been enjoined by the Vice CNO, Admiral Horacio Rivero, not to allow any 7th Fleet ships assigned to Market Time to fall under Westmoreland's Army headquarters. Sharp therefore initially assigned the Market Time Force to the 7th Fleet.[11]

Since the 1950s North Vietnamese 275-foot diesel trawlers had made their way from Haiphong into the South China Sea and then north toward South Vietnam's coastline. They dashed ashore at night, favoring anchorages at the mouth of the Bo De River or the U Minh Forest in the Delta, off the Hon Heo Peninsula at the mouth of the Sa Ky River, or off the Lo Dieu beach on the Annam coast. Staunching this means of infiltration was the job of the Market Time campaign, which began on 16 March 1965. The complexities of the mission were prodigious, for at least 50,000 civilian vessels plied the coastal waters of South Vietnam each year, and the Communists mixed in easily with innocent Vietnamese fishermen and water tradesmen. The fraction that carried supplies to the Vietcong would never be known, but Hardcastle estimated that the Vietcong received about three-quarters of his arms, ammunition, equipment, and medicines by sea. Vice Admiral Paul P. Blackburn of the 7th Fleet initially assigned two destroyers to the Market Time Force. The first was stationed off the DMZ, the second near the southwest frontier of South Vietnam in the Gulf of Thailand.

These areas of operation were the scenes of the most intense communist shipping effort, and it soon became clear that the Market Time Force did not possess enough vessels to cover the lengthy, twisting coastline. Blackburn increased the total number of Market Time destroyers to ten, then in the summer gradually replaced them with smaller radar-equipped destroyer escorts and minesweepers. And on 20 July 1965, eight 64-ton Coast Guard WPB cutters reached Danang, and another eighteen of these highly capable ships were deployed to Southeast Asia later in the war. Nonetheless, the appearance of these vessels in South Vietnam did not entirely solve the problem. Coast Guard cutters operated only from An Thoi and Danang, and 1,000 miles of South Vietnamese coastline separated these two bases, leaving, in 1965, a vast area covered only by two destroyers and a pair of oceangoing minesweepers.

To extend the reach of the destroyers, Blackburn assigned a pair of shore-based P-2 Neptune patrol planes to the Market Time campaign. They operated out of the American air base at Tan Son Nhut near Saigon. Additional patrols were undertaken by P-3 Orion patrol planes and P-5 Marlin seaplanes, the Navy's last flying boat, which flew out of Langley Point in the Philippines. This skeletal force was enlarged to twenty-eight aircraft by the end of April, with more to come. The following month, President Johnson authorized the Market Time Force to search suspicious vessels beyond the territorial waters of South Vietnam. The value of this operation was almost immediately evident: on 10 May 1965, a 100-ton North Vietnamese steel ship was sunk by a Market Time patrol, and on 20 June another small North Vietnamese cargo ship was sunk by the force. From its inception, however, Market Time was controversial. "McNamara and his boys [Navy Secretary Paul Nitze and systems analyst Alain Enthoven] put intense heat on" Blackburn to organize the campaign, the admiral recalled, and "like so many of their strongly held ideas, this one wasn't very bright."[12]

Command of Market Time passed from the 7th Fleet to Ward's Naval Forces Vietnam organization on 1 August. By this time he had divided South Vietnam's coastal waters into a belt with nine patrol zones, each about 40 miles deep and 100 miles long. Within each zone Market Time operations were divided into three rings. Patrols in the inner ring were left to the South Vietnamese Navy's Coastal Force; the South Vietnamese Sea Force, which had been merged with the old Junk Force, was responsible for coverage throughout the middle ring. Reluctant to initiate combat, the South Vietnamese Navy boarded very few suspicious craft. They were also hampered by their atrociously poor shiphandling, constantly having trouble bringing their vessels alongside junks and sampans.

Operating in the outer ring about forty miles offshore, the U.S. Navy's Coastal Surveillance Force was assigned to implement Market Time by shutting down the communist supply lines, and Ward stationed one destroyer or oceangoing minesweeper in each of the patrol zones. By the end of the year, most of the early destroyers had been replaced by destroyer escorts, which had better fuel efficiency and were equipped with superior radars and electronic equipment. Ward also erected five coastal surveillance centers at Danang in the north and at Qui Nhon, Nha Trang, Vung Trang, and An Thoi on Phu Quoc Island in the Gulf of Thailand near the Cambodian border. Although Market Time evolved into a joint air-surface search operation, most of the searching was conducted by coastal surveillance vessels.

By the end of July, the forces operating with the Market Time Force had grown to include seven radar picket ships, two oceangoing minesweepers, three converted LSTs providing radar cover of the mouths of major rivers, and seventeen Coast Guard cutters. And, to strengthen the Market Time Force, McDonald, the CNO, ordered the Navy that month to acquire another fifty-four PCF Swift boats that would be added to the Market Time Force for inshore patrols. By late 1967, Market Time craft were visually inspecting about 1,500 coastal junks every day, and Navy strategists believed that the campaign was putting a dent into communist logistics. One frequently cited 1964 Navy survey estimated that 75 percent of the enemy's supplies were being shipped into South Vietnam, but two years later a follow-up report put that figure at only 10 percent.[13]

The North Vietnamese were unwilling to challenge Market Time forces during the rest of 1965, although they resumed their shipping effort during the first six months of the following year when the Coastal Surveillance Force captured about six large communist junks each week. Smaller, motorized junks and sampans were harder to identify, as they were nearly indistinguishable from innocent waterborne traffic. By mid-1966, the number of larger junks intercepted diminished considerably, and Market Time appeared to deter the North Vietnamese from resuming this means of infiltration for another two years, although the campaign did not by any reckoning succeed in preventing enemy movements along South Vietnam's coast. Captain Robert Kallen, Secretary Nitze's talented assistant, urged that the South Vietnamese Navy be equipped and trained to handle all of the off-shore patrols, but training and equipping the South Vietnamese was not a high priority in the early years of the war. Later assessments of Market Time were quite critical. It was an "over reaction" to a minor problem, concluded Admiral Blackburn, an early critic, while Rear Admiral H. S. Ainsworth, who commanded the 7th Fleet's Patrol Wing, reasoned that the "forces employed . . . were extravagant in relation to the threat and the value of the cargo delivered by the [North Vietnamese] trawlers."[14]

On the other hand, the role of the major communist powers in supporting North Vietnam's war effort was unquestioned. Early Market Time patrols, special radio intelligence, and photo reconnaissance of North Vietnam informed Admiral Ward that Russia and China were providing the bulk of the war materiel for the infiltration campaign, and this and other evidence reinforced Lyndon Johnson's strong conviction that Moscow and Peking were working in close concert to expand communist influence in Southeast Asia. The foremost advocate of this partly wrongheaded concept was Secretary of State Rusk, a veteran of the bitter Korean conflict, who steadfastly refused to accept abundant proof that the Sino-Soviet Alliance was in shambles and that the Chinese were pursuing an independent line aimed at reducing Russian influence in Asia, the Middle East, and Africa. China's interests in the Vietnam War were more ambiguous than in the Korean conflict, and Peking's capacity to support an army in North Vietnam clearly was limited. Nonetheless, LBJ decided that the best way to prevent being bogged down in

Southeast Asia was to avoid goading China to intervene in Vietnam—as it had in Korea. Peking "had to understand that the retaliation was aimed only at North Vietnam, not Red China, and that the objective was limited," he had told congressional leaders during the 1964 Tonkin Gulf crisis. He was sure that bombing Hanoi or Haiphong or invading North Vietnam would bring China's army rushing south to support Ho Chi Minh's regime. Whenever he wavered from this unsound conclusion, McNamara or Rusk was ready to shore it up. If Rolling Thunder were to be loosed against Hanoi or Haiphong, McNamara's systems analysts argued, "the chances of a direct confrontation between China and the United States appeared high."[15]

Not only was Rolling Thunder One crippled from the start by the unilateral establishment of sanctuaries where the 7th Fleet and the Air Force were not allowed to attack, but in the spring of 1965 the North Vietnamese quickly stiffened their defenses and braced for the onslaught from the air. On 3 April, an Air Force Crusader was attacked by three MiG-15s near Thanh Hoa, and the first dogfight of the war ensued. The following day, MiG-17s shot down two Air Force fighters. Nevertheless, LBJ imposed his first bombing pause on 11 May in an attempt to persuade North Vietnam to negotiate, but stony silence met his diplomacy. One week later, Rolling Thunder Two began, and with it came approval to hit new targets in North Vietnam—the bridges between Hanoi and the Chinese border, army barracks, lines of communications, and then in December, the Hanoi thermal power plant. No MiGs rose to challenge Navy aircraft until 17 June 1965 when Commander Louis C. Page's section of Phantoms was attacked by four MiG-17s south of Hanoi. During this air battle, the Americans shot down a pair of North Vietnamese planes with air-to-air Sparrow missiles. By this time, American naval intelligence had already counted over seventy MiGs in operation over the skies of North Vietnam, but McNamara stubbornly refused to allow Rear Admiral Edward C. Outlaw, the Tonkin Gulf Task Force commander, to strike any of the MiG airbases for fear of killing Russian technicians.

Outlaw was furious with this edict, and when Navy Secretary Nitze visited the *Midway* on Yankee Station in the Tonkin Gulf on 20 June, the admiral tried a ruse. He believed that, if tempted enough, the MiGs would attack a section of four slow, prop-driven AD Skyraiders, which he sent on a flight over a North Vietnamese airbase under the pretense that the planes were to fly cover for a rescue mission. While Nitze listened to the action over the radio on the carrier's flag bridge, a pair of MiG-17s jumped the Skyraiders. The Americans dove down to 500 feet, scissored, and Lieutenant Clinton B. Johnson and Lieutenant (j.g.) Charles W. Hartman achieved a tail-on position from which they shot down one MiG with 20mm gunfire. Although Nitze was impressed with the danger to the American aviators from the MiGs, he nevertheless refused to ask McNamara to lift the iron curtain of restrictions that had so far immunized the communist sanctuaries in North Vietnam.

While Johnson and McNamara dithered, the North Vietnamese strengthened their air defenses. On 5 April 1965, an RF-8 Crusader photo reconnaissance flight returned to the *Coral Sea* with pictures of an SA-2 Guideline SAM site that had been erected by Russian technicians fifteen miles south of Hanoi. Outlaw flew to Saigon where he met with the Air Force commander, and they agreed to a joint strike against the SAM site. They quickly discovered, however, that McNamara was worried that American ordnance might kill or injure the Soviet ground personnel. "After what seemed an inordinate delay," Outlaw recalled, the proposal to attack the missile site was "disapproved," and the missions against the Guideline battery were canceled. McNamara's logic was "beyond comprehension. It was feasible to have destroyed this site and all others still under construction which were ultimately completed."

Two months later, on 24 July, another North Vietnamese SA-2 Guideline shot down an Air Force Phantom jet. McNamara, under intense pressure from the JCS, at long last retreated from his earlier stand and authorized attacks on the SAM sites. On 12 August, Outlaw established Operation Iron Hand, the opening stroke in a long campaign to achieve air control over bombing targets in the skies of North Vietnam. That night, a pair of A-4 Skyhawks lifted off the *Midway* about sixty miles south of Hanoi. Closing on their targets, Lieutenant Donald Brown and Lieutenant Commander Donald Roberge saw two fires glowing beneath the clouds about fifteen miles away, but neither pilot recognized the danger until the Guideline missiles were too close. Too late, they both swerved just as the Guidelines exploded. Brown's plane went up in a fireball, but Roberge, his plane ablaze, limped out to sea and landed on the deck of his carrier.

The menace of the Guideline missiles, nicknamed "flying tele-phone poles" by the pilots, was enhanced by the mobility of the launchers, which could be moved from one site to another with-in three hours.

Outlaw tried new tactics to outwit the North Vietnamese mis-sile batteries. To avoid the Guidelines, American aviators had to release their bombs at about 5,000 to 6,000 feet, too high to as-sure any precision, or to fly in very low, thus exposing themselves to distracting small arms fire and their planes to very accurate North Vietnamese antiaircraft batteries. At first, they tried to roll their planes and pull hard down into a missile to cause it to over-shoot, but the North Vietnamese gunners responded by firing pairs of Guidelines in sequence, the first high as a decoy, the sec-ond, low to catch the attacker when he was descending to escape the initial shot. To overcome these missile tactics, McDonald de-ployed the new air-to-ground Shrike missile with the 7th Fleet. The Shrike was designed to reduce or eliminate North Viet-namese radar operations and when fired, it homed in on the radar dishes that sat atop mobile vans. Because this successful tac-tic forced the missile battalion crews to shut off their radars until the last moment before an American attack, the Shrike decreased the overall effectiveness of the entire missile battery. In response, the North Vietnamese fitted optical sights to their communica-tions vans to visually locate enemy aircraft and adjust the position of their radar antennas before they were energized. This step was not entirely successful. Begun in late 1965, this contest in elec-tronic tactics continued without abatement for nearly three years.

During 1965 and early 1966, air operations progressed north, but McNamara continued to turn his back on Sharp's nag-ging requests to strike Hanoi and Haiphong. He forbade Ameri-can warplanes to fly within thirty miles of Hanoi, ten miles of Haiphong, or ten miles of the Chinese border. There were other problems. The Air Force could not deploy enough fighters to Southeast Asia to support the tempo of low-level, precision bombing attacks with the conventional munitions called for in Rolling Thunder. "For a long time [after the Korean War] the na-tional policy was that we were not going to fight anything except a nuclear war at places and with weapons of our own choosing. We did not even start doing anything about tactical fighter avia-tion until about 1961 or 1962," General John P. McConnell, the Air Force chief of staff, told Congress.

U.S. Navy Department

Four F-4H Phantom fighters in formation over the attack carrier *Forrestal* in the Mediterranean in December 1964.

Furthermore, Navy and Air Force tactical attack doctrines were alien to one another, developed by each service, at least in part, to stress to the outer world the differences between land-based and seaborne aviation. To divide up the air war over North Vietnam, Sharp in early 1965 ordered his two air forces to alternate in attacking North Vietnamese targets every other three hours. In turn, Vice Admiral John Hyland, who commanded the 7th Fleet, assigned one carrier to strike operations before 1200, while a second carrier was responsible for these missions for the rest of the day. By November 1965, however, it was evident to Sharp and Hyland that the entire system was overly complicated, and Sharp abandoned the rotation scheme. To replace it, he divided the map of North Vietnam into six geographical route packages; attacks on each of these areas were rotated back and forth on a weekly basis between the land-based and carrier air forces.

Meanwhile, the Tonkin Gulf Task Force was strengthened by an increase in the number of carriers on Yankee Station and the arrival of more fighter squadrons flying the McDonnell F-4 Phantom fighter-bomber. This versatile aircraft had begun to enter the fleet in 1961, and over the next fifteen years she gradually replaced the older, slower F3H Demon and the slightly younger Crusader. At the time of the Gulf of Tonkin incident, for example, just over half of the Navy's thirty-one fighter squadrons were flying Phantoms. Although a perfected radar coupled with the long-range Sparrow air-to-air missile allowed the Phantom's pilots to engage an enemy beyond visual range, McNamara was so afraid of downing Soviet or Chinese aircraft over North Vietnam that he issued instructions that American fighters were not to fire their missiles until they saw their opponent. These and other overly restrictive rules of engagement partly explained the preference of Navy aviators for the close-in Sidewinder missile during aerial combat.

The Tonkin Gulf Task Force adjusted to the heavy tempo of daily air operations by trying to integrate new weapons, planes, and equipment into the air war. On 27 June 1965, the carrier *Independence* arrived on Yankee Station with a squadron of Grumman A-6 Intruders on board, a milestone in the history of Navy air. This expensive, rugged, subsonic, all-weather, all-purpose naval bomber was being deployed to Southeast Asia two years after it had entered the fleet. Although the Intruders had greater endurance than their Phantom escorts, early Intruder operations were plagued by problems. The plane incorporated a fragile link between the bomb-rack ejection switch and an electronic device that simultaneously fused the bomb. Three Intruders were blown up when the fusing system functioned even after the ejection rack had jammed. The electronic system was replaced with mechanical fuses, but the malfunctioning bomb racks continued to plague the plane for some time thereafter. The plane's payload and accuracy were so impressive that carrier skippers often used them for daylight strikes, although the Intruder's great advantage was its ability to fly in bad weather and deliver an attack at night. Many early Intruder strikes were quite successful, but in September, enemy 37mm antiaircraft gunfire shot down an A-6 during a night attack on a North Vietnamese torpedo patrol boat in the Tonkin Gulf. And, during early 1966, six Intruders from the carrier *Kitty Hawk* were downed in quick succession over North Vietnam. Soon after, the Navy ruled that the Intruder could not descend below 2,500 feet to deliver its payload. Intruder losses to conventional antiaircraft gunfire highlighted the lethality of many of North Vietnam's primitive weapons. They also compelled the Navy to dedicate its lighter attack aircraft to low-value targets and to restrict the expensive Intruders to targets where the danger from indiscriminate rifle or antiaircraft gunfire was not so great.

Another milestone in naval aviation was reached in 1965 with the arrival of the *Kitty Hawk* in the Tonkin Gulf in November, bringing into battle for the first time the Navy's turboprop E-2 Hawkeye airborne early warning aircraft, which easily detected hostile aircraft and directed American fighters or attack air-

A wooden-hulled, shallow-draft, 57-foot minesweeping boat (MSB-52) steams down the vital Long Tau River in order to keep the channel from the Tonkin Gulf to Saigon open to shipping.

The heavy cruiser *St. Paul* (CA-73) exchanges fire with a North Vietnamese coastal artillery battery on 4 August 1967 during Operation Sea Dragon. The cruiser was bombarding the Cong Phu railway yard 25 miles south of Thanh Hoa.

craft to their targets. The *Kitty Hawk* also was equipped with the
new Naval Tactical Data System, which enhanced surveillance,
tracking, and intercept operations. A further milestone was
passed on 2 December when Captain James L. Holloway III in
the nuclear-powered carrier *Enterprise* joined the antisubmarine
carrier *Intrepid* on Dixie Station. The *Enterprise* embarked a number of RA-5 Vigilantes, which had been developed as heavy attack
bombers but were successfully converted to electronic and photo
reconnaissance aircraft. The Vigilante served the carrier's newly
devised, computerized Integrated Operational Intelligence Center, which was used to compose an electronic portrait of air operations from a variety of visual, radar, and electronic sources.

After working on Dixie Station, Holloway steamed north
to Yankee Station off North Vietnam where the *Enterprise* joined
in Rolling Thunder Two operations beginning on 17 December,
and within a week the carrier's air wing had established a
new record by flying 165 combat sorties on one day. Admiral
McDonald was at the time pleading with McNamara to allow
Sharp to hit several important industrial targets within the
restricted Hanoi-Haiphong zone that the defense secretary had
established on 13 October. Johnson and McNamara relented
a bit, and on 22 December the Tonkin Gulf Task Force carriers
launched the biggest naval air strike thrown against North Vietnam to date. From the south aircraft from the carriers *Ticonderoga* and *Kitty Hawk* approached the giant Uong Bi thermal power
plant fifteen miles south of Haiphong, while planes from the
Enterprise screamed in from the north. Every complex in the facility was billowing flames when the last wave of American attackers
left the target at 1600.[16]

McNamara's approval of the Uong Bi strike—the first industrial target in North Vietnam to be hit—led Admiral Sharp to believe for the moment that Johnson's air strategy was about to
change, and he expected the operation to convince Hanoi that
its entire economy would soon be ravaged by bombing. Before
the North Vietnamese could absorb this message, however,
McNamara convinced LBJ to initiate a "peace offensive" on 24
December 1965 aimed at bringing Hanoi to the bargaining table.
Assistant Secretary of State Averell Harriman, who had negotiated the discredited 1962 Laotian arrangement, was sent to
Europe, where he visited over a dozen communist capitals in a
particularly humiliating and wholly fruitless quest for "peace feel-

ers" from Hanoi. Johnson declared another "bombing pause," and McNamara ordered Sharp to suspend Rolling Thunder operations over North Vietnam. Johnson claimed that his war policy was grounded on the principle of the sovereignty of small states and the inviolability of established international frontiers, but his diplomacy suggested that he neither believed in the soundness of those principles nor fully understood North Vietnam's grim dedication to violating them. From Sharp's vantage point, about the only virtue of the 1965 Christmas bombing pause was that it coincided with the height of the northeast monsoon, which brought to the skies over North Vietnam heavy cloud cover, dense fog, and daily thundershowers between November and March. Unbeknownst to Navy men, the wild oscillations in Johnson's foreign policy and military strategy in Southeast Asia had only begun.

Chapter Twenty-six

The Navy's Air War in Vietnam
1966–1968

Lyndon Johnson's 1965 "peace offensive" entailed a thirty-seven-day suspension of Rolling Thunder over the Christmas and New Year's holidays and a renewed diplomatic effort to persuade the North Vietnamese to negotiate an end to the war. Johnson outlined a fourteen-point peace formula and proposed talks on the basis of the Geneva Accords, but in the same breath he refused to recognize the legitimacy of the communist National Liberation Front. This was Hanoi's minimum stated demand. In January 1966, pressure from the JCS and Congress to resume Rolling Thunder was starting to weigh heavily on the White House. "A properly oriented bombing effort could either bring the enemy to the conference table or cause the insurgency to wither from lack of support," claimed Admiral Sharp. While McNamara was inclined to suspend Rolling Thunder altogether before Hanoi made reciprocal concessions, Johnson refused to do so without advance word from the North Vietnamese, a step that Ho Chi Minh was obviously unwilling to take.[1]

Not only did Hanoi reject every American overture, but also the Communists used the breather of the bombing pause to deploy new heavy artillery to the DMZ, establish 400 new antiaircraft sites in North Vietnam, and erect 20 early warning and fire-control radars. They dug underground fuel farms, camouflaged numerous military installations, and ran hundreds of truck convoys into the DMZ. By 31 January 1966, when Johnson confessed that his diplomacy had collapsed, North Vietnam had mostly rebounded from the minimal losses sustained during the Rolling Thunder Two strikes of the previous year. Even the Uong Bi plant had been partially rebuilt and was again supplying all the electricity to Haiphong and about one-third of the electrical power needs of Hanoi. Ho Chi Minh had also prepared his people to absorb more punishment during the coming spring and summer. Indeed, the JCS soon thereafter warned McNamara that "the heavily restricted air campaign had undoubtedly contributed to Hanoi's belief in ultimate victory."[2]

Nonetheless, Johnson refused to change his air strategy in Indochina. During the bombing pause, Vice Admiral John Hyland, the commander of the 7th Fleet, had not been inactive; aircraft from the Tonkin Gulf Task Force hit targets along the Ho Chi Minh Trail in Laos and flew close ground support missions for American troops in South Vietnam. When LBJ ended the bombing pause and approved Rolling Thunder Three, McNamara convinced the president to saddle the renewed bombing with more restrictions by revisiting the president's fear of Chinese intervention. "I am not going to spit in China's face," Johnson coarsely announced.[3]

Rolling Thunder Three, which began at the end of January 1966, was largely restricted to the southern part of North Vietnam; Hanoi and Haiphong were put "off limits." McNamara set strict target guidelines, limited the number of sorties per day, and ordered Sharp not to attack communist shipping in North Vietnamese waters, despite the fact that American reconnaissance aircraft had photographed Soviet ships entering Haiphong harbor carrying hundreds of Guideline SAMs. The commander of the Pacific Fleet, Admiral Thomas Moorer, recalled that Assistant Defense Secretary John T. McNaughton insisted that the North Vietnamese "are not going to shoot at you. . . . They're just putting those there as a deterrent," and he persuaded McNamara to order that the SAMs not be disturbed. "By the time they shot at us they had put in several installations. We could have made certain they never had one; we could have knocked them out just as fast as they built them," had it not been for McNamara's restrictions. Likewise protected by this apparent immunity, communist shipping into Haiphong began to increase dramatically in February 1966. McNamara also instructed Sharp not to attack North Vietnamese airfields from which Soviet-built

Admiral U. S. Grant Sharp. Commander in Chief, Pacific, 1964–1968.

An F-8 Crusader fighter flies off the carrier *Midway* (CVA-41) on Dixie Station in the Tonkin Gulf and fires an unguided Zuni rocket at a Vietcong target in South Vietnam on 22 November 1965.

AD-1 Skyraiders, the two leading aircraft in each echelon, followed by F-4U Corsairs return to the carrier *Boxer* (CV-21) from an early morning strike.

MiG fighters had begun to operate, and when at long last he approved American strikes against these MiG bases, he strictly limited their frequency and intensity. Admiral McDonald and the rest of the JCS obediently relayed these orders to Admiral Sharp in Hawaii. In the spring of 1967, for instance, General Wheeler warned the Pacific commander that the chiefs "were worried that our air attacks on Hoa Lac and Kep airfields were heavier than needed just to harass and attrite aircraft." As a result, Sharp had to tell his Air Force and 7th Fleet commanders "not to overdo these harassing attacks."[4]

The February 1966 resumption of Rolling Thunder saw no relaxation of the ongoing struggle over strategy in the Vietnam War between Johnson and McNamara on one side and the JCS and Admiral Sharp on the other. In April 1966, the chiefs, trying to force Johnson to reverse course, proposed to cut the southern segment of the Ho Chi Minh Trail by invading Cambodia, sending American troops into southeastern Laos, and menacing the panhandle of North Vietnam. This major proposal was rebuffed by McNamara and Assistant Secretary of State William Bundy, who insisted that any threat to invade North Vietnam would provoke direct military intervention in the Indochina War by the Chinese Army. "They didn't want us in that area because of the . . . international situation," Sharp told Congress in 1967. However, after another of Dean Rusk's diplomatic offensives collapsed, McNamara reluctantly agreed to Rolling Thunder Four, shifting from attacks on primitive military bases and supply dumps to interdiction and economic targets, lifting many of the restrictions on Alpha bombing strikes, and initiating the POL—petroleum, oil, and lubricants—campaign aimed at slowing down North Vietnam's economy. McNamara still refused to endorse an industrial bombing strategy, continued to put Hanoi and Haiphong off limits, and turned down a plan to destroy the Red River dam system, the single most important landmark of North Vietnam's agricultural economy.

Hampered by McNamara's refusal to hit Hanoi and Haiphong, Sharp resorted to an interdiction strategy in Rolling Thunder Four, following a detailed study of North Vietnam's transportation system, which, although primitive, did not want for internal lines of communication. Four highways and two railroads linked North Vietnam with China, and another railroad and major highway connected Hanoi to the nearby port of

Haiphong. Goods also moved along the many waterways of the Red River and San Thai Binh River deltas. Shallow-draft junks served Hanoi and Nam Dinh, even at low water, and the North Vietnamese also used shallow-draft steamers, barges, tugs, and hundreds of sampans to transport supplies from the coast to inland railheads and highway depots. However, all movements into the interior from China or from North Vietnam's ports had to be funneled through Hanoi or Nam Dinh, junctions served by only a single southbound railroad and one highway. To the south, below Than Hoa, there was just one road to move goods to the DMZ. And, south of Ninh Binh, there were only four major ports and almost no inland waterways. This geography caused Sharp to concentrate his naval air strikes south of Hanoi, where the rail and road network diminished considerably, and where the flow of arms and equipment to South Vietnam was not supported by rivers, canals, or streams. The Air Force was to attack targets to the north of and around Hanoi, and in the northeastern portion of the country.

The Rolling Thunder Four interdiction campaign against bridges, railroads, rolling stock, and truck depots south of Hanoi began in April 1966, when the monsoon let up and normal flight operations resumed, but it was hamstrung from the start by McNamara's restrictions. American bombers "couldn't come within thirty miles of China, and we couldn't come within ten miles of Hanoi," Admiral Moorer recalled bitterly. The enemy arranged his defenses in accordance with McNamara's restrictions as much as the Americans did their attacks. Inasmuch as Hanoi was only seventy-five miles from the Chinese border, "you had only thirty miles to attack them. They only ran the trains at night, and they'd hide in the tunnels in the daytime and dash across that thirty-mile thing." There was a concurrent effort to increase the tempo of Skyhawk attacks against communist truck convoys along the Ho Chi Minh Trail. The North Vietnamese accordingly reduced their dependency on daytime truck movements, established a string of well-camouflaged way stations, and adopted a complex system of nighttime truck convoys. To disrupt this system, Skyhawks began to operate over the trail in pairs, one aircraft carrying flares, which were dropped to illuminate targets, the other delivering 500-pound bombs. Sending these costly aircraft against trucks, however, was an unacceptably expensive way of conducting interdiction operations.[5]

Rolling Thunder Four allowed Sharp to inaugurate bombing attacks against four key bridges and the major railroad line in the northeastern quadrant of North Vietnam. The defense secretary also agreed to stepped-up attacks on the vital Vinh-Ben Thuy industrial complex. The Uong Bi power plant was hit for a second time on 18 April by Commander Ronald J. Hayes, who led a section of A-6 Intruders in a strike so perfectly executed that the American pilots, who approached the target at low level from opposite directions, dropped their bombs and escaped before the defending antiaircraft batteries could even open fire. Although the Air Force bore the greatest burden in the interdiction campaign, attack aircraft from the Tonkin Gulf Task Force frequently brought bridge, rail, and truck targets in the vicinity of Haiphong and along the coast under attack. By this time, however, the North Vietnamese had positioned formidable antiaircraft batteries to defend the key spans, increasing the cost to the Americans of these operations. Repeated attacks were necessary to disable a bridge for more than a few days, and dropping an entire span became progressively more dangerous. Nevertheless, in a daring surprise nighttime attack on 12 August 1966, an Intruder dropped five 2,000-pound bombs directly onto the large Hai Duong bridge that linked Hanoi and Haiphong, inflicting major damage to the target and escaping without a scratch.

The cost of the air war had become formidable. During April 1966 alone the Tonkin Gulf Task Force flew over 6,500 sorties, mostly in poor weather against the Vinh-Ben Thuy complex, and lost twenty-one aircraft and fifteen air crewmen. Until that month, the Tonkin Gulf Task Force and the Air Force had alternated bombing fixed targets in the six geographical route packages each week, but this system worked poorly because the Navy and the Air Force used different systems and the Navy did not want to operate under the thumb of overburdened Air Force air controllers. Moreover, the Air Force still lacked enough secure air bases within South Vietnam from which to operate in support of Westmoreland's troops. Admiral Sharp decided to assign targets along the coast and around Haiphong to the Tonkin Gulf Task Force and to allow the Air Force to concentrate on the rest of North Vietnam—except for the area just north of the DMZ, which was the responsibility of the Marine air wing and Air Force aircraft based in South Vietnam. As a result, American pilots soon became familiar with the terrain, defenses, and targets within their respective route packages, and this heightened sensitivity to the combat environment led to more effective bombing strikes and reduced aircraft losses. Nevertheless, although the Air Force wanted to consolidate all air operations over Indochina under its control, the Navy, alert to the difficulty of coordinating carrier- and land-based air operations, resolutely resisted. According to Air Force General William Momoyer, "the route package system was . . . an approach which, however understandable, inevitably prevented a unified, concentrated air effort."[6]

These refinements led to an increase in the tempo of the air war during Rolling Thunder Four. In the summer, a southwest monsoon covered the Gulf of Tonkin and North Vietnam. Even when the skies were clear and the drizzle and fog of winter had drifted away, tropical storms, typhoons, and high humidity complicated air operations, rusted planes, sickened pilots, and occasionally drew odd shapes on radar screens. In July, Admiral Hyland established a radar picket destroyer station in the Gulf to identify and track all aircraft over the eastern region of North Vietnam as well as those flying over the northern half of the Gulf. The destroyers deployed to PIRAZ picket radar stations vectored American naval aircraft to their targets beyond the coastline and warned pilots and the Tonkin Gulf Task Force of approaching MiGs. In addition, Hyland established one northern and one southern search and rescue station in the Gulf of Tonkin, each comprising a single destroyer. Between 1964 and 1968, American SAR operations saved 912 naval aviators.

By August 1966, Sharp had assigned four carriers to the 7th Fleet, and Admiral Hyland had moved all of his seaborne air power onto Yankee Station off the coast of North Vietnam. Carriers with large decks, like the *Forrestal* and *Enterprise*, had air wings consisting of nearly 100 planes, while smaller carriers like the *Hancock*, which displaced only 33,000 tons, deployed fewer than 70. The demand for bombers forced Admiral McDonald to change the configuration of the air wings deployed with the Tonkin Gulf Task Force, and by late 1966 most of the carriers in Southeast Asian waters operated only two fighter squadrons and two or three attack squadrons.

Sharp still viewed the interdiction campaign as an unsatisfactory alternative to the shipping and industrial bombing strategy that McNamara stubbornly refused to adopt. In April 1966, McNamara somewhat disingenuously told the JCS that he agreed with a proposal by Sharp to undertake the POL campaign to deprive North Vietnam of gasoline, fuel oils, and lubricants, but that the president had rejected the plan. According to Sharp, the POL plan was soon endowed with "the proportions of a major strategic issue." Although "official intelligence estimates . . . said that, on balance, Chinese or Soviet intervention in the war was unlikely," McNamara's civilian assistants and Rusk's State Department united against the plan. "Some were more concerned over the risk of incurring severe domestic political repercussions" owing to the stirrings of an antiwar movement within the Democratic Party, Sharp noted.

Frustrated at Hanoi's resistance to his diplomatic efforts, LBJ finally agreed to the POL campaign on 23 June 1966, but opposition to the bombing from his sometime supporters in the liberal American press disconcerted him. Sharp was furious that newsmen would openly discuss American strategy and complained that the secretary of defense had "publicly forewarned" the North Vietnamese about American war plans. Two days after he approved the new offensive, Johnson abruptly suspended all POL operations. "In the meantime," Sharp wrote, "there had been enough publicity in the press about hitting POL facilities that the Communists were sparing no effort to disperse their fuel supplies."

After bitter protests from the JCS and Admiral Sharp, Johnson relented and approved a resumption of air operations beginning on 29 June. McNamara warned Sharp, however, that he was to instruct American pilots to take extraordinary measures to keep the level of casualties low in North Vietnam. From 29 June until 15 July, naval aircraft from the carriers *Ranger, Hancock,* and *Constellation* attacked North Vietnamese oil supplies. The *Ranger*'s Skyhawks dropped nineteen tons of bombs on the Haiphong fuel complex and struck the surrounding buildings with Zuni rockets, and the pilots could see only billows of black smoke as they flew away from their targets. Two other major fuel farms, one near Hanoi, the other at Bac Giang, were also struck by the Navy, and the Air Force accounted for additional targets. Photo reconnaissance estimated that at least half of North Vietnam's fuel and lubricants had been destroyed during Rolling Thunder Four, forcing the Communists to disperse existing stocks as well as new shipments, which arrived every day in tankers that were unmolested while they unloaded their cargos at Haiphong.

The cost of these operations to North Vietnam was demonstrated on 1 July 1966, when a Phantom pilot, flying combat air patrol, spotted three motor torpedo boats closing fast on the destroyers *Coontz* and *Rogers*, on station in the northern Gulf of Tonkin. As the ships steamed to the north, the enemy began to charge. Alerted, Admiral Hyland dispatched from the *Constellation* a section of Phantoms that appeared over the battle within minutes and launched rockets and bombs at the torpedo boats and strafed their decks with gunfire. Still ten miles away from the American destroyers, the North Vietnamese fired their torpedoes and turned sharply to escape. At this moment, the *Hancock*'s Phantoms joined the engagement, and all three communist vessels were sunk. From July to December 1966, the Tonkin Gulf Task Force continued the POL campaign against North Vietnam. American naval aircraft attacked small depots, railroad cars, barges, convoys, and even individual trucks, trying vainly to interrupt the smallest mechanisms of communist military activity. In addition, Hyland organized multicarrier strikes against rail junctions at Thanh Hoa, Phy Ly, Ninh Binh, and Vinh.

The North Vietnamese countered the POL campaign mainly by dispersing all of their petroleum supplies and by digging new underground shelters for fuel depots. Despite the fact that the POL campaign compelled the Communists to divert manpower and other resources away from infiltration into South Vietnam, Sharp knew that this would not seriously interrupt enemy activity in the south or force North Vietnam to surrender. "By now the North Vietnamese were storing fuel in barrels in caves, and along the streets of villages in order to make such supplies immune from air attack," Sharp recorded, "since they knew we would not strike a populated area." Because the Russians and Chinese were committed to providing North Vietnam with adequate fuel imports to sustain the communist campaign in South Vietnam, McNamara's restrictions on American air attacks against shipping in Haiphong harbor provided the Communists with the highest trump.

The utility of the highly restricted Rolling Thunder operations was always in doubt. Despite the limits imposed by McNamara, Admiral Sharp believed that the air campaign imposed an enormous penalty on the North Vietnamese and fenced in their strategic options in South Vietnam. McNamara questioned this assertion and controlled the terms of the debate. During the

POL campaign, for instance, Sharp was inclined to accept the view of his operational commanders that their strikes were crippling North Vietnamese truck transportation along the Ho Chi Minh Trail. At the Pentagon in Washington, however, McNamara's systems analysts claimed that the kill ratio for trucks during attacks on the trail was really only about one to ten. To Walt Rostow, the president's national security adviser, this was irrelevant. The function of Rolling Thunder was merely to "impose an awkward inconvenience" on Hanoi, he asserted, thereby forcing North Vietnam to "run its economy and logistical system at a lower throttle." Although Rolling Thunder was failing to cut off infiltration—according to American intelligence, communist troop movements into South Vietnam increased from 35,000 men in 1965 to nearly 100,000 in 1967—some evidence supported the view that the bombing was weakening North Vietnam. Several smaller North Vietnamese cities were almost destroyed, and a British observer reported severe malnutrition among the population of other urban areas. In an unusual fit of hyperbole, Sharp estimated that "North Vietnam was now at least unable to mount a major offensive [in South Vietnam] and had to rely primarily upon increased guerrilla activity and small-scale actions."[7]

The high tempo of air operations over North Vietnam took a steep toll on the Navy's crews, carriers, and planes. For one thing, carrier operations were under way throughout the daylight hours and often into the night, a constant strain on both men and machinery. For another, economy and efficiency dictated that carrier operations be run by the clock. One result of the careful scheduling was that an inevitable element of predictability crept into the strikes, from which the North Vietnamese learned, for instance, that the new, expensive, night-fighting Intruders were not permitted to fly below 2,500 feet and that they were not allowed to make a second run on a target. And weather of all kinds—monsoons, rain, fog, and sudden storms—predictably influenced the timing of air operations. Accumulating all this intelligence, the Communists could often estimate quite accurately when the American bombers would arrive over their targets, and North Vietnam's defenders became quite skilled in exploiting this advantage.

The task force's grueling schedules often led to minor mishaps on the carrier decks, and the grinding wear and tear on the ships was visible when they returned to Pearl Harbor. Combat invoked relaxed standards for most shipboard behavior, including adherence to safety precautions. At no time was the danger of this more evident than when a fire erupted on the *Oriskany* on 26 October 1966. Two sailors were carelessly stowing flares in a locker when one exploded; the flames spread to the nearby ordnance area, then to the hangar deck below and some nearby living spaces. Brave damage-control parties contained the blaze, but not until several bombs had exploded and the resulting fire spilled over the fantail. The loss of life was bad enough, but the carrier and her air group were so seriously damaged that Admiral Hyland had to return the *Oriskany* to the United States for major repairs.

Anticipating that Johnson would order another suspension of Rolling Thunder over the 1966 Christmas and New Year's holidays, the JCS recorded their opposition in advance in late November. Facing a round of criticism in the press owing to the restrictions on the air campaign, LBJ backed off, but McNamara urged him to put a truce into effect during Vietnam's Tet holidays in February 1967. Both Admiral Sharp and General Westmoreland registered their predictable opposition to yet another bombing pause. "It seemed senseless to allow the enemy the luxury of such respites, which, in the end, would only translate to higher casualties on our side," Sharp complained. Secretaries McNamara and Rusk, on the other hand, supported a renewed diplomatic initiative, and British Prime Minister Harold Wilson, Johnson's only backer in Europe, told LBJ that he and Soviet Premier Aleksei Kosygin, then visiting London, were about to negotiate a ceasefire. Johnson, eager for peace talks, ordered another suspension of hostilities in February 1967 and launched a renewed diplomatic offensive, but Wilson's scheme collapsed within days. Ho Chi Minh clearly was not ready for a truce. This was clear evidence that Rolling Thunder had yet to punish North Vietnam enough to force the Communists to reconsider their ultimate war aims.[8]

Not only did the JCS press McNamara to increase Rolling Thunder's target list, but they also repeatedly advocated imposing a naval blockade on North Vietnam. McNamara invariably rebuffed these plans with the argument that the war could be won in South Vietnam without provoking the Chinese—although China by this time was in the maw of the Great Cultural Revolution, a virtual civil war pitting factions of the Communist

Party against one another, and was clearly no longer capable of intervening in Southeast Asia. Playing on the secretary's willingness to support the interdiction campaign, which was merely intended to weaken the Vietcong, Sharp conveyed to Washington a plan to form the Sea Dragon Force composed of one cruiser and one or two destroyers that would operate off the coast of North Vietnam just above the DMZ. In October 1966, McNamara finally approved the inauguration of Sea Dragon operations, although he at first restricted the movement of the task unit to the waters south of the 17th parallel. Once on station, these cruisers and destroyers bombarded coastal highways and communications, shelled coastal batteries and radar sites, and attacked communist supply craft that moved along the shoreline. The American ships worked with Skyraiders and S-2 Trackers from the Tonkin Gulf Task Force to locate and shell targets inshore and attack North Vietnamese craft carrying supplies to South Vietnam. The results were so encouraging that Admiral McDonald and Admiral Sharp begged McNamara to allow them to press the attacks farther north, and in February 1967, McNamara agreed to allow the Sea Dragon Force to operate off North Vietnam's coast up to the 20th parallel.

On 14 February 1967, in the wake of Britain's failure to arrange a ceasefire, LBJ agreed to Rolling Thunder Five, complete with a new target list. The air forces were to concentrate on shipyards, harbor dredges, industrial plants outside Hanoi and Haiphong, and the highway and railroad linking those cities. This phase of the air war also saw the introduction of the Walleye guided bomb, which immeasurably improved bombing accuracy. In addition, the Tonkin Gulf Task Force was allowed for the first time to lay mines at the mouths of North Vietnam's larger rivers, and later in the year mines were dropped along inland waterways and on roads leading to major bridges and military centers. The net result of these measures was to reduce the level of infiltration into South Vietnam, but a successful interdiction campaign was going to demand American patience, a quality that Johnson, McNamara, and their liberal supporters did not possess.

Chapter Twenty-seven

The Naval War in South Vietnam
1965–1967

The February 1967 Tet truce capped a year of frustration and accomplishment for American arms in the Vietnam War. Neither the interdiction phase of Rolling Thunder nor the POL campaign showed any evidence of changing North Vietnam's war policy. Vietcong operations in South Vietnam had continued apace during 1966, and while the Marines in I Corps executed a thinly disguised version of General Walt's Inkblot strategy, General Westmoreland's two Army field forces intensified their search and destroy operations in the central highlands and around Saigon. South Vietnam's larger cities were no longer under attack. By this time, Admiral Ward's Stable Door Force had secured South Vietnam's harbors and his Market Time Force seemed to have succeeded in reducing communist infiltration by sea. In May 1966 the Market Time Force located and sank a 100-ton North Vietnamese cargo ship, and another went down in June.

The success of Market Time operations was difficult to gauge, however. There were not enough American or South Vietnamese ships to search more than a fraction of the junks and trawlers plying South Vietnam's coastal waters, and Coast Guard Captain James A. Hodgman pointed out that "in the Gulf of Thailand all we could do to survey large cargo junks . . . was to check their manifests for form and substance, spot-check their cargoes, and ensure that they were on the trade route between the ports listed on the manifests." Nonetheless, when Rear Admiral Kenneth Veth assumed command of American naval forces in South Vietnam in 1967 he reckoned that the Market Time Force had erected "a pretty tight . . . fence around the coast of South Vietnam" and that "few, if any, enemy trawlers got in with supplies." The Vietcong received about three-fourths of its supplies from coastal shipping in 1965, but this figure may have dropped by 90 percent a year later, and Market Time clearly played a part in forcing the Vietcong some time in 1966 to turn to the newly constructed Sihanouk Trail in Cambodia to support operations in the Mekong Delta.[1]

Admiral Ward's original strategy called for the Coastal Surveillance Force to deploy PCF Swift boats on one-week-long Market Time patrols. Because of a persistent lack of spare parts, unforeseen maintenance problems, and the size of the boats—which were not large enough for extended patrols in deep waters—he had to abandon this plan. Moreover, the crews could tolerate patrols of only two or three days at the most. As a result, each section's time on station was considerably reduced from original estimates, and the intensity of the entire campaign was thereby significantly lowered. Nevertheless, Market Time operations caused Hanoi to adjust the flow of its logistics support to the Vietcong. Instead of shipping munitions into the Gulf of Thailand from Haiphong or Sihanoukville, the North Vietnamese established the Sihanouk Trail, which led north from Sihanoukville to the South Vietnamese border. Within South Vietnam, Game Warden operations, which were designed to interdict the movement of communist supplies on the Delta's many waterways, moved the Vietcong to shift their operations from the larger rivers onto the hundreds of slightly smaller canals and waterways. Unfortunately, the Game Warden patrols did not follow, both because of Admiral Ward's conservative battle doctrine and because of a lack of vessels and crews. While the communist decision to abandon the wider waterways increased the scale of effort required to coordinate logistics with ambushes and other operations, it also spread the Vietcong more thinly over the countryside at a time when communist defensive considerations seemed paramount.

At this time, Ward's attention turned to the increasing Vietcong threat to shipping in the Long Tau channel, a waterway that bisected the Rung Sat Special Zone, an ancient pirate haven known for decades as the Forest of the Assassins. There was little good land in the area, but it was important, owing to its proximity to the channel, which carried almost all shipping up to Saigon. In 1965, Vietcong mines sank the freighter *Eastern Mariner*, and Ward responded on 22 March 1966 by organizing Jackstay, a twelve-day joint operation that aimed at Vietcong bases in the Rung Sat. Army, Marine Corps, Navy SEAL teams in PBRs, and helicopters participated in Jackstay, but the operation was a frustrating failure and only sixty-nine Vietcong dead were found. In August of that year, Vietcong mines damaged the freighter *Baton Rouge Victory* and a South Vietnamese Navy motor launch minesweeper, and the *MSB-54* struck an enemy mine and sank in November. One month later a Russian-made contact mine was found in the shipping channel leading to Saigon.

During the next two years, aggressive minesweeping, drastic chemical defoliation—later found to be deadly to all involved—and occasional riverine patrols reduced the danger from Vietcong mining operations on the Long Tau channel. Vietcong mining operations were conducted by frogmen who attached limpet mines to hulls or by sappers who laid mines in a channel and connected them to detonators ashore. The Vietcong "might have one in one part of the river and another in another part of the river, but that particular mine was monitored by an individual Vietcong," explained Admiral Veth. "He would lie on the river bank and fire. He just touched the wires together and fired the mine when a ship got close." Minesweeping reduced the latter threat, and chemical defoliation along the waterways increased the hazard to the Vietcong of approaching the riverbanks during the daytime. The Vietcong "could not afford . . . to lay a dozen mines in the river," Veth said. "What they had to do was to put down one mine and have control wires leading from that mine to the shoreline." Ward extended his minesweeping operations to other waters, establishing another mine squadron at Nha Be on 22 May 1966. Each of these squadrons operated thirteen 57-foot fiberglass-hulled minesweepers armed with surface search radar, minesweeping gear, machine guns, and grenade launchers. Other minesweeping units were established later in the war at Danang and Camranh Bay to support the Stable Door Force.[2]

Naval Forces Vietnam was not only responsible for the security of South Vietnam's main shipping channels but also for driving the Vietcong from the waterways of the great Mekong Delta. From its origins in the snows of the Himalayas, the

Mekong River grows in size as it winds through Burma, Thailand, Laos, and Cambodia, finally emptying out into the Gulf of Tonkin from the low, flat, muddy Delta of South Vietnam. In 1965, the number of peasant watercraft in the Delta nearly equaled the number of miles in the great labyrinth of watery highways that support South Vietnam's rice culture and commerce. "A sampan there is as essential as an automobile is around Los Angeles," Veth observed. The South Vietnamese Navy had operated its own River Patrol Force in the Delta for many years, but the American Naval Advisory Group reported in 1965 that it was hopelessly inept, starved for resources, and manned by crews who were preoccupied with extortion, smuggling, and piracy. That September, Ward decided to organize the Game Warden Force, and just before Christmas, he established the River Patrol Force under Captain W. C. Witham, a resourceful figure who established his headquarters at Binh Thuy.[3]

The Navy was slow to realize the means necessary to conduct successful riverine warfare. Not until October 1965 did Ward establish a requirement for patrol craft or submit the necessary operational characteristics to the Bureau of Ships. His first plan called for converting small LCPL fast landing craft into patrol vessels for the River Patrol Force, but Admiral McDonald abandoned this scheme when these vessels were found to be too slow. As an alternative, Willis Shane of the Hatteras Yacht Company of North Carolina proposed to install a 220-horsepower General Motors truck engine linked to a set of Jacuzzi waterjet pumps in an existing design for a 31-foot fiberglass pleasure boat hull. By substituting Jacuzzi pumps for the propellers and shaft, the 2-ton PBR river patrol boat could operate safely in the shallow waters of the Mekong Delta and the Rung Sat. Ironically, Shane's firm lost the contract to build the first 120 PBRs, which went instead on 1 November 1965 to United Boatbuilders of Bellingham, Washington. The 28-knot PBR, weighed down by an armored superstructure added to her hull, was heavily armed. These boats stood up well to machine gun fire but could not take a direct hit by a Vietcong rocket, and the PBR's fragile fiberglass hull was always in danger if it collided with an enemy mine. The Vietcong learned to float plastic bags filled with rocks and water down rivers to clog the PBRs' Jacuzzi intakes. The vessel was originally designed as a pleasure craft to operate in clean, tranquil waters, but Vietnam's waters were dirty and corrosive and the average PBR was in commission for only six months. The PBR teams carried a great deal of firepower, but they were also quite noisy, and the boats' GM truck engines could be heard two miles away, often announcing the arrival of a River Patrol section. This led to the development of drift-and-ambush tactics, which allowed a river's current to deliver the PBRs to a predetermined station where they waited for the Vietcong, unaware of the danger lurking nearby, to emerge.

The delivery of the first PBRs in South Vietnam in March 1966 allowed Admiral Ward to divide his River Patrol Force into five River Patrol squadrons and to intensify Game Warden operations. Captain Witham assigned the first PBRs to bases at Nha Be on the Saigon River and Cat Lo on the Vung Tau Peninsula. In April, he began patrols in the Rung Sat Special Zone by sending the LSD *Tortuga* to anchor off the mouths of the Co Chien and Bassac rivers and assigned ten PBRs and a pair of PACV air cushioned vessels to operate upriver from this position. Ten patrol stations, which formed the base for the expanding Game Warden network in the zone, were established, but these early operations resulted in many disappointments. The monsoons were worse than usual that season, and the winds crossing the shallow waters created a heavy chop. On 15 July, for example, one River Patrol squadron reported that half the time the weather was so bad its patrol craft could not operate.

The River Patrol Force began Game Warden operations in the Mekong Delta on 8 May 1966 when Ward ordered the Can Tho River section to start patrolling the Bassac River. Other Game Warden sections started to operate soon afterward from bases on the upper Mekong and on the My Tho, Ham Luong, and Co Chien rivers. They conducted mostly two boat inspection patrols, seldom moving more than thirty-five miles from their bases. Ward's original Game Warden plan assumed that three floating bases and eight facilities ashore would be built to assure that the PBRs would never have to operate more than thirty-five miles from their patrol base in the lower Delta, but bad weather, particularly during the monsoon season, forced Ward to tentatively abandon the offshore bases and turn to the use of support bases on the rivers themselves. However, the Naval Construction Battalions had not completed building three of the bases when the first boats arrived, and Ward learned that Westmoreland had assigned base security to the untrained rabble that made up the South Vietnamese Local Self-Defense Forces.

To counter the Game Warden campaign, the Vietcong avoided concentrating troops at chokepoints or committing major forces to the defense of any particular waterway; alternative lines of communication were abundant. Much too late, Ward abandoned the concept of total offshore support altogether and switched to bases upriver and shore support bases along the rivers' banks, a move that led him to deploy upriver three LSTs from the 7th Fleet. In September 1966, the first specially configured LST floating base arrived on station, but bad weather offshore continued to hamper Game Warden operations. Some shore bases functioned throughout the war, but the diversion of Navy personnel for base security and the vulnerability of the bases to landward attacks by the Vietcong decreased their usefulness. By contrast, the LSTs offered mobility and provided a degree of self-defense, and the PBRs could be brought on board the much larger vessels for repairs. There never were enough bases or craft for Operation Game Warden to be effective, however.

In devising his tactics for Game Warden, Admiral Ward divided River Patrol Force operations into daytime and nighttime segments. After a short time it became apparent that the PBRs would have to patrol in pairs, one advancing in midstream and the second within radar range on one side of the river. In one stroke, however, this reduced by one half the number of patrols that the River Patrol Force could conduct. Because of the density of the daytime maritime traffic, only random checking of suspicious vessels was possible. Upon sighting a suspicious junk or sampan, one PBR would close at an angle intended to bring most of its weapons to bear on the other vessel while the second PBR remained in midstream where she had a clear field of fire against both riverbanks. A party would board the suspect vessel, inspect the cargo, and examine the crew's papers. The danger to the Game Warden sailors from grenade attacks, booby traps, or mines from a Vietcong vessel, and from enemy gun, mortar, or rocket attacks from the riverbanks was omnipresent. Using leaflet drops and loudspeakers, the Game Warden Force tried to warn the peasants of a nighttime curfew, but they were not always successful. After nightfall, however, the Americans had to assume that any craft appearing on the rivers or waterways was hostile.

A River Patrol section of eight boats usually sent out two boats during the day while the remaining six conducted nighttime patrols. The only prudent way to approach a contact at night was to close the other vessel at high speed with lights off, illuminating the suspect vessel only at the last moment and firing on her at the slightest evidence of hostile intent. As the war progressed, American sailors, unable to discriminate easily between friend and foe, became increasingly distrustful of any South Vietnamese, and the peasants, whose vessels, oxen, villages, and families were being destroyed by the war, often reciprocated this hostility. "You give a kid an order to go out on the river and anything that moves on that river is presumed to be the enemy, and all of a sudden he sees something moving and it's nothing more than a family, but his orders are to shoot anything that moves on the river, and he knows that's not the enemy," recalled Captain Howard Kerr. "I don't think we ever resolved that kind of thing." Another irritant was the temporary salt erosion dams constructed by peasants on the Delta's narrower waterways to improve irrigation. These obstructions impeded the movement of the PBR patrols and the Navy repeatedly called upon the Army to bomb and destroy them. Improving the lot of the South Vietnamese peasantry—a strategy graced by the euphemism "pacification"— often conflicted with the need to conduct active operations to evict the Vietcong.[4]

Ward's initial Game Warden battle doctrine called for the PBRs to approach suspicious vessels carefully, withdraw if ambushed, call for reinforcements, and reappear with superior firepower as soon as possible; but this simply provided the Vietcong with a predictable lapse of time to escape and so avoid casualties or pursuit. Ward was an agile tactician, however, and in 1966, when he became convinced that his doctrine was not working, he revised his orders, now telling his River Patrol sections that if they encountered an ambush they should hold their positions, suppress the enemy's fire, and maintain contact until reinforcements arrived. While this was a superior approach, Ward simply did not have enough forces to transform ambushes into battles of pursuit and annihilation. The Game Warden Force was equipped to harass the Vietcong and disrupt its logistics in the Delta, but it could never bring the enemy to book.

Ward was an early advocate of marrying helicopters to the River Patrol sections, but he learned in 1965 that a persistent stateside shortage of Navy and Marine Corps helicopters meant that his needs would not be met soon. This led him to turn for help to General Westmoreland, who provided the River Patrol Force with several Army UH-1B Iroquois helicopters and Army crews to operate with the Navy's new River Patrol squadrons. Each river division of ten PBRs was paired with two helicopters and was supported by an autonomous SEAL team. In August 1966, Ward was able to replace the Army crews with Navy personnel and to assemble the first Helicopter Support Squadron, and on 1 April 1967, Admiral Veth activated the first Navy Seawolf Helicopter Attack Squadron when it arrived at Vung Tau. These armed helicopter units had two missions: to reconnoiter for the enemy and to provide gunfire support for other Game Warden forces. As the eyes of the River Patrol Force, they gathered intelligence on suspicious sampans and attempted to monitor the movements of Vietcong troops and supplies. The Helicopter Attack Squadrons also provided fire support during PBR attacks on communist forces, disrupted riverbank ambushes, and provided airborne medical evacuation for American or South Vietnamese military or civilian casualties. To do any of these things well, however, the helicopters had to arrive on the scene quickly, and during the long winter monsoon lasting from October to April, that seldom happened. The dense fogs either shut down flight operations or forced the pilots to fly by instruments. The summer monsoon from May to September, with its high humidity and constant rain, did not hamper flight operations, but most helicopters in Vietnam had to fly at low levels to avoid detection and hostile ground fire. Under these conditions, cooperating with the PBRs and finding targets were extremely difficult, and there were never enough Navy helicopters in Vietnam to fully implement Ward's operational plan.

After Admiral Veth succeeded Ward in late April 1967, he acquired sixteen OV-10 Bronco reconnaissance aircraft—light two-seaters armed with machine guns, Zuni rockets, bombs, and small missiles. Though more heavily armed and better armored than the helicopters, the OV-10 Bronco lacked the Huey's flexibility and ability to loiter over the battlefield and search for targets. Eight Broncos operated from Vung Tau, and another eight were divided between Binh Thuy in the Delta and the Rung Sat. As in the case of riverine craft, however, the CNO, Admiral McDonald, was unable or unwilling to provide the Game Warden Force with enough helicopters, Broncos, or aircrews, and this partly accounted for its failure to accomplish its mission. In early 1968, only twenty-two Hueys were to be found in the entire Helicopter Attack Force, the Army still provided all the machines, and Veth could not persuade the Navy Department to send him any more. Because it had only a handful of helicopters and aircraft, the Game Warden Force could seldom follow up contacts or turn ambushes into battles of pursuit, although the small, overburdened, noisy naval air force clearly frightened the Vietcong and forced them to consider American air power when they established depots or concentrations. "They'd usually be in an area where they couldn't be spotted from the air," Veth recalled.[5]

The mission of the Game Warden Force was arguably the most important task undertaken by any American combat arm in South Vietnam during the entire war. Laced with rivers and waterways and with a large percentage of the lowlands flooded from June to November, the Delta provided an ideal environment for testing Game Warden's strategy and doctrine, but the overall results at the end of 1967 pointed to failure. Had Ward's plan succeeded, it would have ousted the Vietcong from the Delta and restored the area to Saigon's control. In 1963, the nation was the world's third largest rice producer, but two years later, when Ward inaugurated the Game Warden campaign, roughly three-fourths of the Delta's population and at least two-thirds of South Vietnam's rice production were under Vietcong control. Between 1965 and the end of 1967, Game Warden river patrols registered 400,000 boardings, attacked 2,000 Vietcong watercraft, and killed over 1,400 communist soldiers. From May 1966 to May 1969, some 63,000 patrols detained 482 suspicious craft and more than 18,000 Vietnamese of one political persuasion or another. And the Seawolf helicopters recorded 30,000 flying hours. Nonetheless, in 1969, South Vietnam was reduced to importing rice, one million tons of it, simply to feed its own people. And not once had the Game Warden Force seized an important shipment of Vietcong munitions or supplies, although such shipments were necessary for the enemy to keep active in the Delta.

In part the failure of Game Warden was attributable to the neglect of the campaign by the Navy's higher command, especially by two successive CNOs, Admiral McDonald and Admiral Moorer, who did not invest these naval operations in South Vietnam with much prestige or urgency. Admiral Sharp in Hawaii spent his time on the air war, and by 1966, he had virtually abdicated his authority as a unified theater commander over what went on in South Vietnam to General Westmoreland. Moreover,

Navy men found that "there weren't any incentives to go to South Vietnam," according to Captain Kerr. The Bureau of Naval Personnel in Washington "was simply not supporting that up until" Admiral Zumwalt relieved Veth in September 1968. Moorer, who replaced McDonald as CNO in 1967, "paid little attention to

A Swift PCF fast patrol craft on duty in the Delta during the Vietnam War.

The 8-knot Mobile Riverine Force monitor (LCM-6) was a converted mechanized landing craft, protected against enemy gunfire and rockets by ten tons of plate and bar armor. She usually carried a 40mm automatic cannon in a forward turret, two .50 cal. machine guns and a 20mm cannon atop the wheelhouse, and two rapid-fire grenade launchers.

General Cao Van Vien, the archtypical South Vietnamese military politician, presents an award to Rear Admiral Kenneth L. Veth, Commander, U.S. Naval Forces, Vietnam, 1967–1968.

what was going on in country," viewing the riverine campaign in South Vietnam as "an adjunct to what the major war was," according to Kerr and others.

Another factor was that the shortages of sailors, water craft, and helicopters fueled Admiral Veth's natural tendency to adopt an overly conservative strategy. Because the PBRs were relatively costly vessels, Veth held them on the major waterways and seldom allowed the River Patrol Force to work its way up the thousands of narrow, shallow streams and canals, which the Vietcong were able to use until late 1968 with only occasional harassment. By 1967, the number of PBRs in South Vietnam had risen to 155, the number of supporting naval helicopter squadrons to 7, the number of Game Warden LSTs to 4, and the number of specially trained SEAL reconnaissance commando platoons to 6. These figures testified to Ward's and Veth's unstinting efforts to strengthen the River Patrol Force, but the numbers were grossly inadequate to achieve the goals established for Game Warden in 1965. Neither McDonald nor Moorer treated the PBR boatbuilding program with sufficient urgency, so the River Patrol Force grew to only 230 boats in December 1968, and did not reach an inventory of 250 boats until 1969—although in February 1967, McDonald had fixed this number as a minimum needed for the Game Warden Force to accomplish its mission.[6]

To more directly support what appeared to be Westmoreland's search and destroy strategy, Ward in late 1965 approved a plan devised by Captain David F. Welch to assemble the heavily armed Mobile Riverine Force, a naval command that was to carry specially trained troops deep into the Delta, attack communist strongpoints, and bring the Vietcong to book. Early planning for the Mobile Riverine Force concentrated on organizing units along the lines of the old heavy French naval division, which had operated in the Delta during the 1946–1954 Indochina War, but the impracticality of this scheme soon became clear to Admiral Ward. He decided instead that each river assault squadron would consist of about fifty LCMs serving as armored troop carriers, ten LCMs serving as gunfire monitors and minesweepers, and thirty-two assault support boats. He also arranged to construct a floating base so as to provide full barracks support for an entire Marine brigade, but the problem with this was that the Marines, who were accustomed to cooperating with the Navy and were trained for amphibious warfare, were already committed to I Corps. And Westmoreland's view was that "the Marines had no more experience in that type of operation than the Army." Ward needed troops, and he especially needed helicopters and fire support, and Westmoreland agreed in late 1966 to assign to the Mobile Riverine Force Colonel William B. Fulton's 2nd Brigade, 9th Infantry Division, supported by an artillery battalion, which became the Mobile Riverine Force Afloat.[7]

On 7 January 1967, the first river assault squadron arrived at the Navy's newly constructed base at Vung Tau, the only shore facility of Captain Wade C. Wells' Mobile Riverine Force. Joined by several more squadrons over the next two years, the Mobile Riverine Force carried Army troops up and down the rivers of the Delta in search of the elusive Vietcong. From the start, the flaws in this plan became evident. For one thing, the force was too small to accomplish its mission. For another, Wells and Fulton differed sharply over who should be in command. The Army intended the Mobile Riverine Force to act as an arm of the 9th Division, whereas Wells insisted that it "should act as a separate force, divorced from 9th Division operations, with deployments deep into the Delta" where the Army otherwise would not go.

"Intensive discussions" over command of the river assault squadrons led to an interservice treaty or agreement to conduct operations "at all levels through liaison, cooperation, coordination, and good judgment." In reality, it was "just a nightmare to try to get anything done" with the American or South Vietnamese Army leadership, Captain Arthur Price complained, because Westmoreland, the 2nd Brigade's Colonel Fulton, and the Army's generals "felt that the Navy was there to be a logistics group and move them around as needed." This wrongheaded approach to combined arms operations hampered the effectiveness of the Mobile Riverine Force from its inception.[8]

Veth's strategy was to reduce Vietcong activity north of the Mekong to the Plain of Reeds, shift the Mobile Riverine Force south to the Mekong and Bassac provinces, and then to the area south of the Bassac River. Soon after the first river assault group was assembled, he launched a series of six search and destroy operations against Vietcong concentrations in Long An and Dinh Tuong provinces. Highway 4, the only paved road through the Delta, had been closed to traffic by the Vietcong in 1965, but it was now opened up by the Mobil Riverine Force, allowing the peasants to bring their produce to market. In May 1967, in Silver Raider I, the Mobile Riverine Force attacked the Vietcong in the Rung Sat, a series of large raids on remote enemy bases, which had not been disturbed for many years. On 11 June, Wells' vessels steamed sixty miles from the Dong Tam anchorage on the My Tho River to Nha Be, where Fulton's troops were embarked. One river flotilla then ran down the My Tho to the South China Sea, fighting its way through a series of violent ambushes by three Vietcong companies along the riverbanks and leaving 225 enemy dead at the cost of 60 Americans. By mid-month, the Mobile Riverine Force had sixty-eight LCMs and was fully operational. There was a floating artillery barge with 105mm howitzers linked to the base, and a few Army helicopters were available to support landing operations. On 19 June, the Mobile Riverine Force stood out of Dong Tam and over the next seventy-two hours trapped three Vietcong companies fifteen miles from Saigon, inflicting stinging casualties in a series of bitter firefights. And, in July, the Mobile Riverine Base ships steamed sixty-five miles upriver with troops from the 2nd Brigade, its artillery in tow, joined South Vietnamese Marine and Army units, and thwarted an assault on Dong Tam by two well-armed Vietcong battalions. The Navy in the Delta now possessed some of the means to take the offensive, but the campaign would succeed only if pursuit and annihilation rather than attrition were its goal.

Poor intelligence meant that the Mobile Riverine Force was not often able to exploit the element of surprise, however. The Vietcong enjoyed superb tactical intelligence derived from a thorough knowledge of the Delta's terrain and from networks of sympathizers living on the rivers and canals. And "information provided by the [South] Vietnam Army . . . seldom arrived on time to serve as the basis for an attack," Fulton observed. To overcome these disadvantages, the Americans needed very large numbers of troops and equipment to conduct riverine search and destroy operations, but this reduced their quickness and stealth. Captain Wells also noticed that an alarming trend was emerging. Having planned for each raid to be a three- or four-day event, he found that, owing to poor intelligence, the extremely wet environment that led to a large number of foot problems and equipment breakdowns, and problems with command and control, full-scale Mobile Riverine Force raids were limited to about twenty-four hours each, and at most, eight such raids might be conducted monthly. Ambushing and trapping the enemy were also difficult, as Vietcong battle doctrine emphasized mobility and holding open a line of retreat, and the Communists were usually able to escape from the most threatening positions.

These problems notwithstanding, the Americans still won some notable victories against an elusive, battle-hardened foe. The River Patrol Force established a 30-boat patrol on the My Tho River between the towns of My Tho and Sa Dec on 27 July 1967, while the Mobile Riverine Force embarked nearly 4,000 troops in preparation for the largest combined waterborne operation of the war up to that time. During the fighting that ensued, Wells and Fulton trapped the 263rd Vietcong Main Force Battalion between the anvil of the Mobile Riverine Force on the river and converging elements of the American 47th Infantry, a unit of the South Vietnamese Marines, and the South Vietnamese 7th Division. During this battle, the Vietcong lost over 300 men. Although the enemy withdrew without being shattered, for the moment at least the region around My Tho and Dong Tam was no longer menaced.[9]

The Vietcong soon adjusted to the new threat from the waterways and began to stage ambushes against the Mobile Riverine Forces. "Ambushes of riverine assault craft were all too frequent," observed Captain Joe P. Rizza, Veth's overworked chief of staff. On 12 September, for example, a river assault convoy was attacked by two communist battalions along a two-mile stretch of the Ba Ria, a narrow river flowing north from the Mekong into the Cam Son Special Zone fifteen miles southwest of Saigon. During this firefight, which lasted over four hours, half of the American vessels were shot up, three Americans died, and in the end the Vietcong slipped away. These same units, the 263rd Main Force Battalion and the 514th Local Force Battalion, were found two days later occupying a salient on the Ba Ria to the south. Captain Wells and Colonel Bert David of the 2nd Brigade approved a plan to have a Mobile Riverine Force convoy carry the Northern Blockade Force around the hairpin turn in the river and put the troops ashore at White Beach, thus establishing a position on the enemy's northern flank. A second convoy was then to land the Southern Blockade Force on Red Beach to the south of the Vietcong position. The coup de grace would then be administered by an Army battalion that, acting as a hammer, was moving from the east overland against the Vietcong while the Mobile Riverine Force was providing the anvil that prevented the enemy from retiring across the river.[10]

Lieutenant Commander Francis E. Rhodes in the command boat entered the misty Ba Ria at 0700 on 15 September, making about 8 knots. In single file, his vessels about fifty feet apart, Rhodes' van consisted of two minesweeping ATCs, while the convoy was composed of three sections of ATCs carrying troops, each section guarded by one monitor. Suddenly, at 0730, small arms fire from the jungle near Red Beach spat across the river. Next, two rounds from an RPG-2 antitank rocket struck the bow of the minesweeper *T-91-4* with an impact so great that the crew at first believed that the vessel had hit a mine. After this minesweeper had taken three more rocket hits, Rhodes ordered her to retire, but instead the crew stayed to fight. Within another minute, the convoy was brought under a crossfire by Vietcong machine guns and rockets on the western bank. Rhodes closed up his formation while his sailors began to answer the enemy with 20mm and 40mm machine guns and 81mm mortars, which they aimed at point-blank range into the smoky fog ashore.

Neither side gave way. When the Navy gun crews began to take heavy losses, the soldiers in the ATCs took over and brought their own weapons to bear on the Vietcong. In rapid succession, three enemy antitank mortars hit the command boat. One knocked Rhodes unconscious, but within a few seconds he was back on his feet and resumed direction of the battle. By this time the Vietcong were so close to the bank that many of the boat guns could not be depressed low enough to fire at them. More often than not, only when the Communists emerged from behind trees or popped up from their trenches or earthworks could the sailors hit them, and only a direct hit from a 40mm machine gun or an 81mm mortar through the slit of a Vietcong bunker could knock it out. Artillery rounds began to rain on the enemy from a nearby American firebase at 0740, but the Vietcong were spread out and dug in along a 1,500-meter front, and while 105mm artillery shells might deal with the enemy's shallow holes and open trenches, direct hits from a 155mm gun were needed to silence the bunkers.

Rhodes took stock of his situation five minutes later. The monitor *111-1* had taken two RPG-2 rounds through her armor, several ATCs were shot up, and both minesweepers were disabled. The ATC *111-6* had fought through the ambush and landed a company on White Beach, but Rhodes did not know this, and in any case he had no monitors available to provide them with fire support. Once the Vietcong counterattacked, the troops on White Beach were forced to withdraw. Sensitive to the danger of Vietcong mines, Admiral Veth had dictated that minesweepers proceed in the van of every Mobile Riverine Force convoy, and he often urged his tactical commanders not to risk troop movements without minesweepers in the lead. Although his Army counterpart wanted to fight on, Rhodes now decided to retire and ordered all the boats to retreat south to a position off Red Beach. Dashing through a hail of rocket and machine gun fire, the convoy started to reassemble under the cover of air strikes with napalm and rockets dropped by four A-37s. At 0830, the entire formation arrived off Red Beach, regrouped, and withdrew farther to the south, by which time helicopters were working overtime to take out the casualties.

Rhodes refused to give up, even though every minesweeper and monitor was hit, casualties were high, and three vessels were badly damaged. He quickly planned to renew the attack. Two replacement minesweepers and another monitor arrived at 0900, as well as new crews to replace the dead and wounded, and the river assault squadron was soon back up to full strength. Three

Phantoms appeared overhead and dropped more napalm and bombs on the enemy positions 100 meters from the east bank of the turn in the river. Then Colonel David's artillery opened up, and when Rhodes' watercraft again neared the ambush zone, the big guns walked up the riverbanks just ahead of the boats.

At 1000 Rhodes proceeded north in the second attempt to reach White Beach. This time the Vietcong would not have the element of surprise. Firepower, good tactics, and superb leadership decided the day. In the face of overwhelming American superiority the Vietcong chose to hold its positions, and when Rhodes' formation reached the river bend, a terrifying rocket fire from nearby earthen bunkers roared and struck both of the leading minesweepers. One rocket hit the ATC *111-10*'s starboard canopy, spreading fragments that decimated an entire American platoon and wounded several sailors. Nonetheless, Rhodes pressed on around the bend, his first boats finally reaching White Beach and landing their troops into the face of a furious communist opposition. At this moment, two sections of F-100s began to bomb and strafe the Vietcong defenders near White Beach, and all the while, artillery rounds were landing on the communist positions. Once the troops began to move inland, however, it was too dangerous for the monitors to fire because the sailors could not see the soldiers through the dense jungle.[11]

Rhodes next turned south and landed the Southern Blocking Force onto Red Beach. At the same time, the Vietcong counterattacked White Beach to prevent their bunkers from being overrun. By now David had ordered his hammer force into the jungle to press the Vietcong westward against the riverbank. At noon, the noose around the enemy was tightening. All the American troops were ashore, and they were chasing small elements of Vietcong infantry away from the river, into the jungle, and then over open rice paddies to the north, where communist machine gunners tried to slow down the remorseless American advance. By 1700 on White Beach, however, the troops had advanced only 500 meters beyond the landing zone and still faced stubborn Vietcong resistance. Unwilling to risk a nighttime battle in the jungle, David ordered his men to break contact, establish a perimeter around White Beach, and rest overnight.

The next day, 16 September, most of the 263rd Vietcong Main Force Battalion had vanished from the jungle, slipping silently through the converging American patrols. "Resistance was light" that day, according to Fulton. "Most of the enemy force encountered on 15 September had been killed or had slipped away during the night." In the jungle, the troops found 79 Vietcong bodies and destroyed over 250 bunkers, at a cost of 7 Americans dead and 123 wounded. Following its defeat at the Ba Ria, the Vietcong avoided contact there with the Mobile Riverine Force for several months.

Led by many brave, resourceful tacticians like Rhodes, the Mobile Riverine Force repeatedly cornered the Vietcong and created considerable friction, but it seldom transformed an ambush into an annihilation. The Mobile Riverine Force came into being too late in the war, took too long to assemble and train, and never developed a tactical doctrine that stressed hot pursuit and ruthless annihilation. The South Vietnamese would not participate in Mobile Riverine Force operations, and the force was not scheduled to reach full strength until the fall of 1968, by which time it consisted of only 4 river assault groups operating 184 assault craft, 4 barracks ships, and various support ships, barges, and small craft. Soon after, it was disbanded. Performing creditably for a short time, the Mobile Riverine Force operated far too few vessels carrying far too few troops and far too frequently merely chased the Vietcong around the Delta.[12]

Navy critics of these operations were plentiful. Rear Admiral Charles Rauch charged that, from 1965 to 1968, the Navy was "pretty much a police force that was just simply stopping the sampans and out on the open ocean the trawlers." Admiral Veth was responsible for much of this dismal record, refusing, for example, to mount operations against the easternmost rivers. One of his excuses was that the South Vietnamese Navy would not participate in such costly and dangerous operations. "Veth's idea was to try to get the Vietnamese Navy to do more but I don't think he was interested in opening up new avenues" in strategy against the Vietcong, Admiral Arthur Price charged. Veth was unenthusiastic about "operations way down in the tip of the Mekong Delta" because, he said, "it just didn't seem to be worth the risk for them to go down there." Westmoreland, the South Vietnamese Joint General Staff, and the leadership of the South Vietnamese Navy all opposed aggressive patrols against the eastern waterways. Furthermore, both McDonald and Moorer pressured Veth not to take too many casualties, with the result that Veth "didn't want to see us get involved in any new pieces of real estate and lose lives and boats," Price observed. Veth's "theory was don't go out there and get yourself all shot up, you might accomplish nothing."[13]

Veth was content with the tempo of his ongoing Game Warden and Market Time campaigns and unwilling to transfer vessels and crews from those operations to provide logistical support for mobile inland patrols to challenge the Vietcong supply arteries near Cambodia. "On the rivers . . . there was some agitation to go up a lot of the canals with our riverine boats, and . . . harass the countryside, but for the most part we avoided that . . . because the chance of being ambushed by the enemy was so great and there wasn't that much to be accomplished," Veth claimed. "To have a boat go up a side river and come back down again, if the enemy wanted to ambush it they could do so, if they didn't, all they had to do was hide and you'd never see them. There just wasn't that much to be gained by going up a lot of little canals and streams that ran into the major rivers. So, in general, we discouraged that sort of thing."

The result, according to Lieutenant Fritz Steiner, was that the Mobile Riverine Force became an "elephantine armada of slow-moving modified mechanized landing craft that was mobile in the sense a sloth is agile." Mated with the heavy 9th Infantry Division whose soldiers "were prepared for rice paddy warfare in the wheat fields of Kansas," it was a "lumbering, awkward conglomeration" that "had no chance of catching, let alone beating, the elusive Vietcong and paid a heavy price whenever the Vietcong decided to fight." Although he was not a disinterested party to the controversy, Admiral Zumwalt asserted some years later that when he arrived on the scene in the fall of 1968, there was "a lack of good strategic and tactical planning at all levels" and no sense of mission. And in Washington "the Navy's attitude was that the war was the Army's job."[14]

The failure of what passed for a U.S. Army search and destroy strategy to staunch Vietcong activity in South Vietnam was matched by Rolling Thunder's inability to shut down infiltration or to force Hanoi to the peace table. Hours before beginning the bombing on 2 March 1965, Johnson had announced to his secret White House Tuesday lunch group, "I don't wanna run out of targets and I don't wanna go to Hanoi." After nearly two years of limited bombing, however, a secret January 1967 CIA report argued that the campaign had failed to impair North Vietnam's economy, cripple the Vietcong, or significantly reduce infiltration. Thousands of trucks, railroad cars, and barges had been destroyed, but "the evidence available does not suggest that Rolling Thunder to date has contributed materially . . . to the reduction of the flow of supplies . . . or weakening the will of North Vietnam to continue the insurgency."[15]

Admiral Sharp regarded this as merely more evidence that McNamara should allow unrestricted bombing. "We are just starting to put some real pressure on Hanoi," but complaints from the antiwar lobby about bombing close to Hanoi led to McNamara's 23 December 1966 directive to "stop our pilots from striking within 10 miles of Hanoi" and "avoid even the transit of this area by strike aircraft." Only Johnson or McNamara might approve flights over the prohibited circles around Hanoi and Haiphong. "We had better . . . bring this war to a successful conclusion as rapidly as possible," Sharp replied, otherwise "the American people can become aroused either for or against this war. At the moment, with no end in sight, they are more apt to become aroused against it." The administration wanted to avoid either outcome, however, and actively sought to discourage passion over the war. "We never made any effort to create a war psychology in the United States," Secretary Rusk later confessed. "We tried to do in cold blood perhaps what can only be done in hot blood." The result was that the American soldiers, Marines, and sailors who fought the Vietnam War often had little understanding of the stakes at risk. "Of the thousands of men [I spoke to] I never encountered one who felt he was fighting to defend his homeland or to preserve America's freedoms," recalled Rear Admiral Sayre A. Swartztrauber. "It was simply kill or be killed, do your duty the best you can and count the days until" the time to return home.[16]

This eccentric, passionless attitude toward waging war led President Johnson to insist on bombing pauses for Christmas and New Year's Day 1967, and against the advice of General Westmoreland, he also decided on another truce from 8 to 12 February, when Vietnamese Buddhists celebrate Tet, their most important religious holiday. During the 1967 Tet truce, the North Vietnamese moved over 25,000 tons of material into the DMZ, and when the fighting resumed, allied forces in that area for the first time had to face heavy enemy mortar and rocket fires.

Johnson took the occasion to offer new concessions to North Vietnam, but on 15 February Ho Chi Minh cut short this diplomacy by demanding an unconditional halt to Rolling

Thunder before Hanoi would even discuss negotiations. This bombing pause again permitted an "unprecedented resupply activity" along the Ho Chi Minh Trail, a lack of reciprocity so flagrant that it angered even Johnson. "It seemed pointless," Sharp reflected, "to allow the enemy the luxury of such respites, which, in the end, would only translate to higher casualties on our side." When the unilateral truce collapsed, he proposed to mine Haiphong harbor since "85 percent of the imports [into North Vietnam] come through Haiphong and there is no satisfactory alternate port," but McNamara, strongly supported by Deputy Secretary of Defense Cyrus Vance, discouraged Johnson from taking any stiff measures. He tried to appease the JCS and Sharp by agreeing to an aerial mining campaign on the inland waters of North Vietnam's panhandle and a few new targets for Rolling Thunder, but Sharp realized that Johnson was "obviously choosing the ones that offered the least risk of counter-escalation" by the Communists.[17]

On 20 April 1967, the JCS proposed major changes in American military strategy in the Vietnam War. First, they planned to launch an amphibious "hook" into North Vietnam and establish a lodgment just above the DMZ. Second, they planned to mine Haiphong harbor. Third, they proposed to bomb Hanoi, noting that attacks on most targets other than Hanoi and Haiphong had reached a point of "saturation." Finally, they urged Johnson to agree to Westmoreland's request for another 200,000 troops. Each point was rigidly opposed by McNamara, who convinced Johnson to veto the entire package, allowing only another 50,000 men to be deployed to South Vietnam over the next year. "As time went on," Admiral McDonald lamented, "it didn't make much difference what we recommended."[18]

To keep a tight grip on the conduct of the war, McNamara resourcefully interposed himself between the JCS and the president. Johnson and McNamara selected targets for Rolling Thunder during regular weekly Tuesday lunches at the White House, but General Earle Wheeler, the JCS chairman, was not allowed to attend these crucial meetings until 1967. Following the Gulf of Tonkin incident in 1964, moreover, McNamara worked to limit the number of private discussions between the service chiefs and the president. During the twelve months following June 1965, Johnson saw the commandant of the Marine Corps only four times and the Army chief of staff only twice. Out in the fleet, the complaint was the same. Veth was discouraged that "too much detailed instruction came over from Washington. McNamara was at the bottom of a lot of it," he charged, "and Johnson was at the bottom of a lot of it." McNamara created a system for conducting air operations that was immeasurably complex, both for the Navy and Air Force pilots and their commanders. He effectively selected most of the targets for Rolling Thunder and had Wheeler convey his instructions to Sharp in Hawaii. This system was also applied to bombing operations against the Ho Chi Minh Trail in Laos, and later in Cambodia, although the American ambassadors in Vientiane and Phnom Penh could adjust or cancel missions over these countries at will. Preplanned strikes within South Vietnam, on the other hand, frequently originated in the Pentagon and were conveyed directly from Washington to Westmoreland's headquarters near Saigon, and he would call on the Tonkin Gulf Task Force or the Air Force to carry them out.[19]

On 23 February 1967, McNamara finally agreed to parts of Sharp's plan to mine the waterways of North Vietnam. Fifty percent of North Vietnam's cargo moved on these inland waterways, and during the interdiction campaign in 1966 the Communists had increased their use of barges and sampans to move war materiel from Haiphong east to Laos and down the Ho Chi Minh Trail. Nonetheless, Sharp was unsatisfied with McNamara's decision because the defense secretary still refused to allow the 7th Fleet to attack a large reserved sanctuary in North Vietnam. On the 26th, Commander A. H. Birie's seven A-6 Intruders from the carrier *Enterprise* planted one minefield at the mouth of the Ca River and another at the mouth of the South Giant River. Birie's pilots dropped their mines from low altitudes during dangerous maneuvers, and the success of the operation depended upon great flying skill and precision. In May, another section of A-6 Intruders from the carrier *Kitty Hawk* used radar at night to drop mines at the mouths of the Ma, Tien Giang, and Cua Sot rivers. The Communists reacted quickly, deploying squadrons of small wooden boats to sweep and clear channels in the minefields; three of these vessels were sunk by an American naval aircraft during an attack in May. Despite the success of these missions, Defense Secretary McNamara again rebuffed Sharp's proposal to mine North Vietnam's three deepwater ports—Haiphong, Hon Gai, and Cam Pha.

On the other hand, McNamara did agree in February 1967 to allow Sharp to attack targets from "six systems": electricity, maritime ports, airfields, transport, military complexes, and industries. The interdiction campaign against North Vietnam's bridges was given an immeasurable lift by the introduction of the television-guided, air-to-surface Walleye glide bomb, a weapon first used on 11 March to make three hits on the rugged Thanh Hoa Bridge, which spanned the Ma River about eighty miles south of Hanoi. However, until April the weather was unusually poor over North Vietnam, and American air activity had to be sharply curtailed. Soon after the weather cleared, on 19 and 20 May, American aircraft struck the Hanoi thermal power plant, located near the center of the capital. Ho Chi Minh wrongly assumed that Lyndon Johnson had lifted the restraints from the American bombing arms and apparently feared that the destruction of Hanoi would end the war. A large fraction of North Vietnam's MiG fighters went aloft to challenge the Americans. The Russians complained loudly, the North Vietnamese denounced the United States in bitter terms, and Hanoi's network of propagandists and sympathizers in western Europe took to the streets in a wave of large anti-American demonstrations.

The antiwar movement at home was supported by a growing faction of American liberals who harbored a longstanding, deeply rooted philosophical dislike of bombing cities. The American left also unwittingly romanticized the hard-bitten despots of the Hanoi Politburo and eagerly mouthed the slogans of class warfare and racial hatred contrived by North Vietnam's skillful propaganda. Ever sensitive to the administration's important liberal Democratic constituency, McNamara reimposed a restricted zone ten miles around the city of Hanoi, but American land-based and naval air operations had nonetheless begun to tear away at the North Vietnamese air defenses. "The restrictions should be removed," Sharp pleaded with Washington, "and then when Hanoi screams in anguish we should hit them again." There were few challenges to American aircraft from the enemy MiG fighters after 23 May 1967, and the effectiveness of North Vietnamese anti-aircraft fire diminished. Owing to McNamara's restrictions, however, the "six systems" campaign was no more successful in ending the war than any other Rolling Thunder strike series.[20]

In spite of McNamara's policy, American military operations in South Vietnam during 1967 resulted in unquestioned success. Even the defense secretary admitted on 12 July that "there is no military stalemate" in the Vietnam War. With a strength of 463,000 men, the Americans had fostered the growth of the South Vietnamese Army, Navy, and Marine Corps, whose manpower on paper numbered nearly 600,000 effectives. Although few Americans were comfortable with the performance of any South Vietnamese units, they had suffered almost 48,000 casualties over the past year while the allies had inflicted about 75,000 casualties on the body of 300,000 men fighting for the communist cause. Taking a cue from their mentors, the South Vietnamese Marines often exhibited exceptional bravery. Despite the obviously fraudulent character of the political system in Saigon, a superficial stability grew over South Vietnam in early 1967, a freely elected constituent assembly ratified a new constitution, and in September fairly honest elections brought a surprisingly narrow victory for President Nguyen Van Thieu and Vice President Nguyen Cao Ky. Thieu's regime was, however, corrupt and unpopular, and most American leaders now realized that Ambassador Henry Cabot Lodge was correct when he argued that establishing democratic institutions in South Vietnam during the war was "clearly an impossible task."[21]

In November 1967, President Johnson ordered General Westmoreland back to Washington, where he delivered a triumphal address before a special joint session of Congress, a tasteless ploy that the general recognized was "in reality for public relations purposes." He nevertheless willingly announced that "we are winning" in South Vietnam. Despite repeated warnings from Sharp that much of the military success was transitory, and that the "artificial" limitations on the air war had minimized the effectiveness of Rolling Thunder, Lyndon Johnson refused to veer from his "middle course." The president acknowledged that public opinion in the United States was unhappy with his war leadership. "Americans like . . . it decided quickly," he admitted, but he continued to shrink from doing what was required to achieve that end. The following month, Johnson visited South Vietnam, greeting troops and sailors at the naval base at Camranh Bay, bestowing medals on all in sight, and agreeing in principle to Sharp's strident demand that Washington honor General Westmoreland's request for more ground troops. This concession notwithstanding, by the end of the third year of the Vietnam War, Johnson had rejected almost all of the important advice he had received from the JCS and his theater commander on how to conduct the war.[22]

By now, even Lyndon Johnson was disenchanted with the work of Robert McNamara, who had, ironically, months earlier concluded that the Vietnam War could not be won. On 18 May 1967, McNamara had first proposed to instruct General Westmoreland to shift his strategy from search and destroy operations to an enclave strategy, which consisted of securing South Vietnam's major population centers. At the same time, McNamara became a disciple of an "unconditional bombing halt" as a means to lure the North Vietnamese into negotiations that would permit the United States to withdraw its forces from Indochina. This was a popular feature of the liberal antiwar litany. If such talks could be arranged, McNamara argued, then Johnson should not tie the American negotiating position to the principle of South Vietnamese sovereignty. In short, he wanted the United States to abandon its long-standing support for the integrity of small nations. In public, however, McNamara persisted in his vigorous defense of his air strategy.

When Senator John C. Stennis, a conservative Democrat, got wind of McNamara's vacillation, he convened hearings of a subcommittee of the Senate Armed Services Committee to investigate "the overall policy and philosophy governing" the air war against North Vietnam. Admiral Moorer, the new CNO, hoped that the Stennis hearings would prove to be the catalyst to reversing the administration's policy on the air war. Sharp, who flew from Hawaii to Washington to be Stennis' first witness, offered up a damning indictment of McNamara's strategy when the hearings opened on 9 August 1967. Stennis carefully built up the case against the administration until, on the 25th, McNamara appeared before the committee to defend his policy. He claimed that he had allowed the air forces to strike about 85 percent of the targets recommended by Sharp, asserted that the remainder were not worth the risk of hitting, and concluded that the war could be won with his strategy of restricted bombing in the north and attrition in the south. When asked about the conflicting assessments of Sharp and the JCS, McNamara replied, "I don't believe that there is a gulf between the military leaders and the civilian leaders" over air strategy. General Wheeler, the JCS chairman, believed by many to be all too ready to toady to McNamara, was so outraged at this preposterous testimony that he proposed that afternoon that he and the service chiefs resign en masse the next morning at a news conference. Before the JCS reached any decision, however, Wheeler did a predictable overnight about-face and the next day begged his colleagues to stay on.[23]

To relieve some of this pressure from the JCS, Stennis, and other Senate conservatives—all strong advocates of strategic air power—Johnson rejected McNamara's line on negotiations and decided instead to allow Sharp to attack a few more targets near Hanoi and in the vicinity of the Chinese border. Johnson was angry at McNamara for proposing to abandon the bombing campaign altogether, but the president still refused to accept the stiff, bloody measures espoused by Sharp and the JCS. In a complicated maneuver, Johnson levered McNamara into resigning from the Defense Department in early 1968 with the offer of a sinecure at the World Bank, and the president named as McNamara's replacement the wily Washington attorney Clark Clifford, whom Johnson counted on to revive the pace of the military effort in Vietnam.

The contradictions of Johnson's war policy were most fully exposed when he announced in Texas in September 1967 what soon became known as the San Antonio Formula. He offered to halt Rolling Thunder if North Vietnam would simultaneously agree not to "take advantage" of the opportunity by increasing infiltration into South Vietnam and also promise to join in "productive discussions" during which the United States would negotiate not only with the Hanoi regime but also with the Vietcong. Maddened by antiwar demonstrations led by liberal Democrats who were undermining the constituency behind his Great Society, Johnson in effect declared his willingness to cast South Vietnam adrift in a bid to regroup the Democratic Party at home in support of his presidency. This failed, the antiwar demonstrations grew in size and virulence after Johnson issued the San Antonio Formula, and the White House received only a cold, hostile rebuff from Hanoi. Johnson offered up another bombing pause and peace offensive at Christmastime, but the answer was the same, and so he was forced to agree to another round of bombing, Rolling Thunder Six, which kicked off on 3 January 1968. The policy of bombing and pausing was in disarray, Johnson was thoroughly discredited, and the Vietnam War was heading toward an ironic, violent climax.[24]

Chapter Twenty-eight

The Tide Turns
in the Vietnam War
1967–1968

Throughout the Vietnam War, LBJ worried that the communist bloc would take advantage of the heavy commitment of American forces to Indochina and move aggressively elsewhere in Asia, perhaps on the Korean peninsula. For this reason, monitoring North Korea's military activity assumed considerable importance—it was essential for Washington to have advance warning of trouble. For nearly two decades, the Navy had conducted intelligence-collecting patrols off hostile shores using auxiliary ships that carried signal-intercepting equipment controlled by the National Security Agency. Seven *Liberty*-class and *Victory*-class cargo ships had been converted into technical research ships for these intelligence missions, codenamed Desoto Patrols, many of which had been quite useful.

The presence of these signal-collecting vessels off the coasts of various communist powers caused continuous friction between the Navy on one side and the State Department and NSA on the other. In short, Navy leaders wanted all warships to be armed to defend themselves, the intelligence agencies preferred them to be inconspicuous, and the diplomats asked that their movements not be provocative. Although the *Liberty*-class vessels performed their intelligence gathering admirably, they were quite decrepit, and to replace them in 1964, the Navy selected a number of old attack cargo ships for conversion, one of which entered the fleet as the auxiliary research ship *Banner*. Her sister ship, the ocean research auxiliary *Pueblo*, was recommissioned by Lieutenant Commander Lloyd Bucher in 1966. The State Department initially vetoed the installation of any guns on the ship, but following the 1967 Israeli attack on the *Liberty* a single 3-inch cannon was installed and ten Thompson submachine guns and seven pistols were brought on board. As the ship would be carrying highly secret NSA communications equipment and documents, Bucher asked that he be provided with emergency destruction devices, but someone on the Joint Staff turned down this request on the grounds that during her deployment in the Far East the *Pueblo* would be undertaking a "minimal risk mission." Lieutenant Richard MacKinnon, who handled intelligence on Korea for the Pacific Fleet, disputed this, opposed the mission, and argued his way up to Admiral John Hyland, the commander of the Pacific Fleet, but was eventually overruled.[1]

Standing into the Pacific in October 1965, the *Banner* operated off the coast of North Korea during the latter months of the following year, provoking the North Koreans to deploy several gunboats and patrol craft, which harassed her at close quarters in international waters, and to protest the presence of an "armed spy ship" in November 1967 at the continuing Panmunjom armistice talks. In 1967, tension in Northeast Asia heightened after several small communist raids across the DMZ into South Korea, which cost over 400 American and South Korean casualties, and the unprovoked sinking by North Korean forces of an unarmed South Korean fishing boat in international waters later that year. On 21 January 1968, North Korea's dictator, Kim Il Sung, sent thirty infiltrators into South Korea to storm the Blue House in Seoul and assassinate President Park Chung Hee, but the plot failed and the assassins were all killed or captured. Two weeks earlier, Pyongyang had reiterated its warning about the American "spy ships" and announced that North Korea intended to effect more direct reprisals, causing NSA to issue a special alert to the Joint Reconnaissance Center, which supervised all American military imaging- and emissions-collection activities for the JCS.

These broadcasts and the special alert caused Rear Admiral Frank L. Johnson, the commander of U.S. Naval Forces in Japan, to instruct Commander Bucher "not to appear provocative" during the *Pueblo*'s upcoming deployment off the North Korean coast, but neither Johnson nor Bucher made any special provisions to defend the ship in the event that the North Koreans carried out their threats. Pyongyang issued another blast on 11 January, the day that the *Pueblo* stood out of Sasebo, Japan, passed through the Tsushima Strait, and swung north into the Sea of Japan to take station off North Korea's coast. Eight days later, Pyongyang again specifically warned that the presence of the *Pueblo* constituted a "provocation," but this was taken in Washington as merely another dose of the bluff and bluster that constituted North Korean foreign policy and it was blithely ignored. Soon afterward, Bucher took station fifteen miles off Yodo Island at the entrance to Wŏnsan harbor, which had been transformed only recently into a major Soviet submarine base. On 21 January, the North Koreans sent out a P-4 patrol boat that passed close by the *Pueblo*, and at noon the following day two more North Korean patrol boats approached the *Pueblo*, circled her, took photographs, and observed that Bucher was obeying Admiral Johnson's orders not to uncover his gun. Bucher broke radio silence to report this incident to Johnson's headquarters at Sasebo, but nearly fourteen hours elapsed before communications were established. Sasebo received only two messages that day from Bucher, neither of which suggested that the North Koreans were up to anything other than commonplace harassment. Nevertheless, the *Pueblo* was clearly attracting their attention.[2]

It was breezy and overcast at noon on 23 January when word came down to Bucher from the *Pueblo*'s pilothouse that a vessel had been spotted approaching from the direction of Wŏnsan. She was three miles away, but closing fast. Within minutes, a North Korean subchaser and three P-4 patrol torpedo boats reached the American ship and circled around her for about five minutes. Two of the hostile boats then took station close astern of the *Pueblo*, while the other pair began to zigzag off her bow. Next, a pair of North Korean MiG fighters suddenly appeared overhead. Remembering Admiral Johnson's injunction, Bucher refused to panic or even uncover his single gun. The North Koreans challenged the American vessel, and when Bucher correctly responded, they radioed Wŏnsan for instructions. Finally, at 1252, the captain of the North Korean subchaser issued a warning: "Heave to or I will open fire."

"The harassment now seemed in earnest," Bucher recalled, "but I still thought it was a bluff." He had already decided not to fight his ship inasmuch as she was, in any case, unprepared for such a contingency. Not only was the *Pueblo* weakly armed, but Bucher had conducted few gunnery drills in the past year that she had been at sea, and one gun captain did not even know how to open his ammunition locker. Bucher also decided against scuttling the ship as the water was "too cold for the crew to survive." Keeping Johnson at Sasebo informed of each step, he turned his attention to his secret documents. Reasoning that North Korean divers might recover the papers despite the near freezing temperature of the water, he rejected a suggestion that they be thrown overboard and ordered that they be burned. This unwittingly convinced the North Koreans that the *Pueblo* would not resist a takeover. At 1306, the North Korean commander, without requesting permission from Wŏnsan to fire, advised his base that he intended to "board [the *Pueblo*] and tow to Wŏnsan." The first attempt to board the ship was unsuccessful, however, so the North Koreans opened fire, knocking out some of the radio antennas and wounding Bucher and two sailors who were standing with him on the bridge. "The complete uselessness of further resistance flooded my brain," Bucher recalled.

"We are being boarded," Bucher radioed Johnson. "We need help. Please send assistance." At 1432, the North Koreans took over the *Pueblo* and seized the listening equipment and the secret documents, most of which were still intact. Two hours later, the captured ship passed Ung Do Island, ten miles from Wŏnsan. At 2030, seven hours after the first warning had reached Admiral Johnson, the *Pueblo* was moored at a pier in Wŏnsan harbor. It was still light. The North Koreans put Bucher and his crew in chains and paraded them through a jeering, spitting mob before throwing them into the filthy local prison.[3]

From Bucher's first warning of trouble until *Pueblo*'s arrival off Wŏnsan, Admiral Sharp's entire Pacific theater command reacted slowly. The *Pueblo* and other intelligence-collecting ships were about the only Navy vessels in the western Pacific not under Admiral William Bringle's 7th Fleet command, so he was at first naturally confused about her whereabouts and mission. According to Rear Admiral Horace W. Epes, the *Enterprise* task force, then about 500 miles from Wŏnsan, "had ready-alert fighters, armed for air-to-air combat, but other aircraft would have required arming and readying for any contemplated strike—approximately one-and-a-half hours. We had not briefing materials for pilots on the Wŏnsan area, no rules of engagement, and no definitive mission." Thus, Epes "elected to maintain status quo and await developments," and a full hour elapsed before Admiral Bringle ordered him to "proceed north at best speed" but to "take no action" such as launching fighters to support the *Pueblo* without further orders. Sharp, in Saigon when Bucher first sounded the alarm, did not receive the news until 1700 when he returned to the carrier *Kitty Hawk* on Yankee Station in the Tonkin Gulf. Although enough daylight remained for Japan-based Air Force aircraft or the *Enterprise*'s fighters to reach the

A fast patrol craft (PCF-71), known as a Swift boat, proceeds up one of the many narrow waterways lacing South Vietnam's delta during Operation Giant Slingshot in February 1969. Early in the war the 23-knot, 50-foot Swift boats were dedicated to Market Time coastal surveillance operations, but they were too light to conduct extended high seas patrols.

U.S. Navy Department

U.S. Navy Department

Commander Lloyd M. Bucher (*left*), who had allowed North Koreans to take over his ship, the intelligence collector *Pueblo* (AGER-2), on 22 January 1968, returns from captivity on 23 December 1968. Secretary of the Navy John Chafee prevented the Navy's high command from putting Bucher before a court martial for refusing to fight his ship.

scene or hit Wŏnsan, Defense Secretary Clark Clifford decided against any response and ordered Bringle to have the *Enterprise* stand down. Sharp agreed with this decision. "Once the *Pueblo* entered Wŏnsan harbor, any major U.S. countermeasures would then be of a retaliatory nature . . . [and] could result in a second Korean War."[4]

Already facing a crisis in Vietnam, Lyndon Johnson refused to allow American forces and prestige to be drawn into another conflict on the Asian mainland. Moreover, the JCS warned him that there simply were not enough American forces in the Pacific at the time to make a credible threat of war against Pyongyang.

After flying a Rolling Thunder mission over North Vietnam, a rugged, versatile F-4 Phantom fighter-bomber is towed across the flight deck of the attack carrier *Ranger* on the eve of the 1968 Tet Offensive.

Thus, he had no choice but to allow Bucher and his crew to remain in the hands of the North Koreans, who imprisoned, tortured, and abused them without mercy. One of the wounded sailors died in captivity, but Bucher, two other injured men, and the rest of the crew survived the ordeal. President Johnson quietly named an ad hoc committee, which included the former CNO, retired Admiral George Anderson, to investigate the incident. According to Undersecretary of State George Ball, the group "unanimously agreed on a draft [report] that raised serious doubts as to the exact position of the *Pueblo*" and "was severely critical of the . . . director of the whole enterprise." After eleven months of difficult negotiations, on 22 December 1968, the American representative at Panmunjom signed a statement admitting that the *Pueblo* had "illegally intruded into the territorial waters of North Korea" and offering an official apology, but the State Department disavowed this statement within minutes by issuing a bizarre prearranged announcement that denied the earlier admission.[5]

The North Koreans fulfilled their part of this surreal bargain by releasing Bucher and his crew at Panmunjom that same day. The *Pueblo*'s embittered executive officer, Lieutenant Edward R. Murphy, blamed Bucher for allowing the ship to be taken, and a Navy court of inquiry recommended that Bucher be court martialed for "permitting his ship to be searched while he had the power to resist" and accused Rear Admiral Johnson of being "derelict" in his duty for failing to plan to support the *Pueblo* in an emergency. The threat of an official letter of reprimand ruined Johnson's career. On 6 May 1969, Secretary of the Navy John Chafee announced that Bucher and his men had "suffered enough and further punishment would not be justified." Referring to the accusations against Admiral Johnson, Chafee reasoned that the charge of dereliction might "be leveled in various degrees" against the Navy's entire higher command, including admirals Moorer, Sharp, and Hyland.[6]

While President Johnson's gaze was diverted in late January 1968 by the *Pueblo* incident, the Vietcong launched the violent Tet Offensive, aimed at upsetting completely the politics of the Vietnam War. The North Vietnamese had decided on this move in late 1967, when General Giap had flung several diversionary attacks at South Vietnamese forts along the Cambodian border and laid siege to a Marine firebase at Khe Sanh just south of the

DMZ. Most supplies that entered the country at Danang and that were bound for allied forces in the two northernmost provinces of South Vietnam were transported up the coast and then carried inland up the Cua Viet River into Quang Tri and along the Perfume River into Thua Thien. Mindful of the importance of these lines of communication, the Vietcong often ambushed vessels along the narrow banks of these rivers and frequently targeted them for mining operations. In early 1967, Marine General Walt had asked Westmoreland to deploy Navy patrol craft to fend off these attacks, but Admiral Veth had refused to withdraw vessels from either the Game Warden or Market Time forces at the time.

When the communist offensive in I Corps gained momentum later that year, Westmoreland sent his most trusted deputy, General Creighton Abrams, to establish a northern headquarters at Phu Bai near Hue where Abrams could superintend the defense of the region. Alarmed by the threat to Khe Sanh and Quang Tri Province, Abrams insisted that Veth organize naval escorts to guard allied shipping along the Cua Viet River. Veth was by now convinced of the urgency of the situation in the north, and he directed Captain Gerald W. Smith to establish Task Force Clearwater, another independent naval command, which was to include ATCs, monitors, and a construction battalion detached from one of the Mobile Riverine Force river assault groups. Dividing his task force into two elements, Smith assigned the Dong Ha Security Group the mission of defending the Cua Viet from its mouth to the vital base at Dong Ho, where supplies were offloaded for the airlift into Khe Sanh. The Hue River Security Group was to secure the Perfume River and the nearby waterways from its mouth up to the provincial capital of Hue. By this time, however, the siege of Khe Sanh had been overshadowed by the enveloping fury of the Tet Offensive.

In December 1967, Lyndon Johnson announced another unilateral Christmas truce; the Communists attached no spiritual significance to the event and ignored the ceasefire. This unilateral standdown was followed by the president's proclamation of another brief ceasefire during Tet, when Vietnamese Buddhists celebrated the arrival of the lunar new year. General Westmoreland had drawn the conclusion by this time that the Communists intended to mount a major operation after the new year. Reconnaissance flights from the Tonkin Gulf Task Force during the

Christmas truce provided conclusive evidence that the North Vietnamese had remorselessly built up impressive stocks along the Ho Chi Minh Trail in Laos and Cambodia at supply dumps that were uncommonly close to South Vietnam's border. In early January 1968, a press release from Westmoreland's Saigon headquarters disclosed that captured documents indicated that the Vietcong were planning a large-scale offensive, and twelve days later American troops found a Vietcong general order calling for "strong military attacks in coordination with the uprisings of the local population to take over towns and cities." Westmoreland distrusted this intelligence, however, and focused his attention instead on Khe Sanh, reckoning that the Communists were planning to overrun the northernmost Quang Tri and Thua Thien provinces.[7]

At 0135 on 30 January the Tet Offensive exploded with a violent Vietcong attack on Ban Me Thuot, followed later that morning by assaults on Danang, Qui Nhon, Pleiku, and several coastal cities defended by the South Vietnamese troops, half of whom were on leave for the holiday. Since the Vietcong drew most of its local support from the peasantry and was mostly opposed by city dwellers, this poorly chosen tactic of attacking larger cities did not succeed. In the Delta alone, twenty smaller cities were subjected to furious Vietcong attacks and several were overrun. To the north, Hue fell, but most of South Vietnam stood firm, and the Vietcong bungled its attack on Saigon. Although an isolated group of sappers breached the perimeter of the American embassy compound, the Marine guards killed them before they did any damage, and the capital itself was never seriously imperiled. Another Vietcong sapper unit attacked the South Vietnamese Navy's headquarters in a confused operation in which the communist shock troops clearly expected support from a second party that never appeared. At the end of this small firefight, Admiral Veth inspected the area and discovered the bodies of the Vietcong sappers "lying just like cordwood right outside the gate of the Vietnamese naval headquarters."[8]

In the Mekong Delta, the Mobile Riverine Force was the only allied unit prepared for rapid counteroffensive operations, and Westmoreland put it under Army command and ordered it to recover the ground lost to the Communists. Veth had resisted this command arrangement for some time, but his objections were now overridden by the Army's high command in Saigon.

A 40-knot SEAL team assault boat speeds up the Mekong River near the Cambodian border during a SeaLords operation on 6 June 1970. Navy SEAL commandos conducted special operations against the Vietcong and provided tactical intelligence to the Game Warden and Mobile Riverine forces during the Vietnam War.

The Vietcong had taken My Tho from the South Vietnamese, but the Mobile Riverine Force landed two Army battalions nearby, and they recaptured the city after bitter street fighting. The Mobile Riverine Force was then shifted to the battle for Vinh Long Province, where a joint American task force overcame three Vietcong battalions during a protracted campaign for control of Can Tho, the major city in the Delta. The Vietcong had neglected to position defensive forces on the canals or waterways near Can Tho, so the river assault squadrons were able to move about quite freely. On 8 February, the Mobile Riverine Force was pulled back to the Saigon area, where it remained until Vietcong operations in the vicinity of the capital were suppressed.

The river assault groups were then divided up for the rest of the month and roamed over the Delta in support of the recovery of a number of minor South Vietnamese outposts. Many of these lesser battles were quite costly, as the Army did not have enough helicopters to support Mobile Riverine Force operations. Westmoreland's claim that the Mobile Riverine Force had "saved the Delta" was somewhat exaggerated, but its operations were clearly essential to the ferocious, successful Allied counterattack. A second, less intense wave of communist attacks fell on the Allies later in the spring, and to respond, Veth dispatched the Mobile

Riverine Force to confront the Vietcong in the battle for Cai Lay, where the Americans inflicted 700 casualties on a single enemy battalion. Off the coast, meanwhile, the North Vietnamese mounted a major shipping effort to support the Vietcong's Tet Offensive. The Market Time Force ran one steel-hulled, cargo-laden communist trawler aground near Danang and another aground northeast of Nha Trang. One was intercepted and shot up off the Ca Mau Peninsula, while two more were turned back at sea. Tet was the first unquestioned success for the Market Time campaign.[9]

The Vietcong's major military victory during the Tet Offensive was the seizure of Hue. To recapture the ancient capital, allied forces needed to secure a line of communications from the Gulf of Tonkin up the Perfume River to the city. Admiral Veth instructed Commodore Smith of Task Force Clearwater to support the Marines around Danang and assist in the counteroffensive. Already Smith had established his headquarters and main operational base at Tan My at the mouth of the Perfume River near Hue, about fifty miles south of the Cua Viet River, and he now ordered the Hue River Security Group to support the counteroffensive by escorting the movement of LSMs and LCUs carrying troops up to Hue. Then in late March, Smith moved Task Force Clearwater's headquarters to the Cua Viet River, owing to the importance of repulsing the siege of the Marine firebase at Khe Sanh. Operations along the Cua Viet were especially dangerous, and providing gunfire support for the movement of the Marines upriver was complicated by the treacherous shoal waters and a spell of the worst weather in several months in all of Southeast Asia. In spite of these obstacles, by June the Americans had evicted the Vietcong from Hue and temporarily pacified the banks of the Perfume and Cua Viet rivers.

Many months earlier it was evident that the outcome of the Tet Offensive was a stunning blow to the Vietcong, which lost at least a third of its front-line strength of 80,000 troops in the savage uprising. Tet "was a terribly disorganized effort," Admiral Veth reported, and it "turned out to be a disaster for the enemy." On the other hand, the number of American combat casualties was rising to over 500 each week, a figure that increased during the battle for Hue and the grisly siege of Khe Sanh. The shock to American politics of the Tet Offensive drove Lyndon Johnson from the White House, and inaugurated a new American strategy in the Vietnam War. This resulted in large measure because American newsmen prematurely and incorrectly reported that the Tet Offensive constituted a communist victory. At the height of the American counterattack, the JCS pointed out that in reality the Vietcong had suffered a tremendous defeat, which created a "great opportunity" for General Westmoreland's forces to take the initiative. The JCS urged the president to approve intensified bombing of the Ho Chi Minh Trail in Laos and Cambodia, remove the restrictions from Rolling Thunder that protected Hanoi and Haiphong, and allow the 7th Fleet to execute an "amphibious hook" to establish a lodgment in North Vietnam just above the DMZ.[10]

In December 1967 Johnson had visited the American naval base at Camranh Bay, where he promised to dispatch more soldiers and Marines to South Vietnam if Westmoreland needed them—but only to defend South Vietnam, not to invade the communist sanctuary to the north. When Westmoreland did ask for 206,000 additional men in February 1968, however, LBJ went back on his word and referred the request to Clark Clifford, the new secretary of defense. Clifford not only opposed calling up the reserves so that the Army could meet Westmoreland's requirements but also began to argue that the Vietnam War could not be won. He "suddenly flipped from being an extreme hawk to being an absolute incontinent cut-and-runner," observed his erstwhile friend, Undersecretary of Defense Paul Nitze. Instead of resuming the campaign of attrition, Clifford now proposed that Johnson instruct Westmoreland to end offensive search and destroy operations and redeploy American forces to defend enclaves around South Vietnam's major cities. This plan was approved by Johnson's inner circle—all civilians—a stunning blow to the president's war policy and to Johnson's highly personal stake in the conduct of the war.[11]

At this crisis in his presidency, Johnson was under siege abroad and at home within his own party. France's President de Gaulle repeatedly denounced the United States over the Vietnam War, withdrew France from SEATO in 1966, and evicted NATO headquarters from Paris the following year, although France did not withdraw from NATO's political alliance. West German Chancellor Willy Brandt, a socialist, exploited anti-American mood swings in Europe, abandoned the Federal Republic's longstanding anticommunist Holstein Doctrine, and adopted a policy of *Ostpolitik* designed to improve Bonn's relations with communist East Germany and the Soviet Union. Although Labour Prime Minister Harold Wilson publicly supported the American position in Vietnam, his extreme reluctance in doing so was evidenced by Britain's withdrawal from SEATO in 1967. The left throughout Europe staged a series of huge anti-American demonstrations that year that were surpassed only by the antiwar movement in the United States. And an obscure Minnesota senator, Eugene McCarthy, organized a campaign to deny Johnson renomination by the Democrats and, backed by antiwar protestors, nearly defeated the president in the critical New Hampshire primary in February 1968. The final blow to Johnson's political fortunes came a few days later, when Senator Robert Kennedy, whom Johnson thoroughly despised, declared that he too was a candidate.

Facing near certain political defeat in the upcoming elections, Johnson nonetheless shocked the nation by announcing on 30 March 1968 that he would not seek another term in the White House. He also disclosed that North Vietnam and the Vietcong had agreed to meet with envoys from South Vietnam and the United States in Paris on 3 May to begin peace talks and that he had agreed in return to end Rolling Thunder operations above the 20th parallel, although not between the parallel and the DMZ. In vain Admiral Sharp protested that he could see "no advantage, and on the contrary, the greatest disadvantage from a cessation of our bombing of North Vietnam." He felt that "time is on our side; we can win the war if we continue our present strategy." Sharp's protest of Johnson's decision was to no avail. Johnson also imposed other restrictions on American forces in Southeast Asia, although they were not highly publicized at the time. For example, Vice Admiral William Bringle, the commander of the 7th Fleet, was told to end Sea Dragon bombardment patrols off the North Vietnamese coast north of the 19th parallel. For their part, the North Vietnamese had expressed a willingness to negotiate in Paris in 1968 in order to free their war effort from the shackles of the American bombing campaign and also to gain some time to reorganize and rearm their forces in South Vietnam, forces that had been crushed by Westmoreland's successful response to the Tet offensive.[12]

Johnson also agreed to a new strategy in South Vietnam. "Our orientation seems to have been more on operations than on assisting the South Vietnamese to acquire the means to defend themselves," Defense Secretary Clifford told the Senate. He announced within a few weeks a new strategy aimed at "improving Vietnamese capabilities in order that the U.S. Forces could . . . be withdrawn in significant numbers" from South Vietnam. This step could not be taken without removing Westmoreland, who personified the search and destroy attrition strategy, and so in June 1968, he was returned to Washington and made Army chief of staff, while General Creighton Abrams relieved him in command of American forces in South Vietnam. Abrams was directed by the JCS to secure South Vietnam's borders, eject the North Vietnamese Army, and extend Saigon's control over its own territory, but the JCS no longer expected American forces in South Vietnam to run down and defeat the Vietcong. When Rolling Thunder was scaled back on 31 March, Vice Admiral Bringle assigned the Tonkin Gulf Task Force to conduct interdiction operations between the 20th parallel and the DMZ, and by August the flow of traffic through this vital corridor had been reduced to a trickle. Clifford permitted only an occasional RF-8 Crusader or RA-5 Vigilante reconnaissance flight over Hanoi or Haiphong, however, although he did agree to Admiral Sharp's plea for intensified Barrel Roll strikes against the Ho Chi Minh Trail in Laos.[13]

The end to Rolling Thunder came about as a result of presidential politics in 1968. At a raucous convention, the bitterly divided Democrats selected Vice President Hubert Humphrey as their candidate, but he was unable to unify his party during the subsequent campaign. The Republicans turned to former Vice President Richard Nixon, who promised to end the Vietnam War but refused to discuss in detail how he intended to do this. Instead, Nixon leveled his strongest attacks on LBJ's Great Society domestic policy and the loss of America's international prestige during his presidency, citing the *Pueblo* incident as evidence of this erosion of America's global position. Both the North and South Vietnamese played major roles in the American election by refusing for seven months to agree to the shape of the negotiating table at the Paris peace talks, a deadlock that was used against the Johnson administration by disaffected Democrats on the left and by Nixon's Republicans on the right. Then, on 28 October 1968, only days before the presidential election, LBJ announced that he was ending all bombing of North Vietnam below the 20th parallel because the Communists had finally agreed to sit at a round table and negotiate seriously in Paris. All Rolling Thunder bombing operations over North Vietnam's panhandle, between the DMZ and the 20th parallel, were ended, and Admiral Bringle was told to withdraw the Sea Dragon Bombardment Force from its station above the DMZ. On the morning of 1 November, the last Rolling Thunder mission over North Vietnam was flown off the deck of the carrier *Constellation*. Most Americans viewed Johnson's announcement as a last-ditch, duplicitous maneuver to manipulate the elections, and it backfired when Nixon defeated Humphrey by a slim margin.

Rolling Thunder did not achieve its many objectives by any yardstick. The bombing did not inflict enough distress on North Vietnam to compel Hanoi to renounce or even modify its goals of reunifying Vietnam and gaining military hegemony over Indochina. But Johnson and McNamara ignored the political value of bombing, refusing to hit targets that might cause a large number of civilian casualties or to escalate the war. The result was that most important North Vietnamese political and military targets were never touched, and North Vietnam's population was largely immune from punishment—unlike the long-suffering people of South Vietnam. North Vietnam's Politburo repeatedly demonstrated its willingness to pay an awful price in the blood and sacrifice of its own people to reach its ends. Bombing, by itself, did not lead to Hanoi's decision to join the 1968 Paris peace talks, but it clearly was a major consideration. Nor did bombing shut down the Ho Chi Minh Trail, but it made infiltration very costly. The Vietcong depended on North Vietnam for weapons, munitions, and leadership, but the vehicle of taxes-in-kind in communist-controlled areas of South Vietnam permitted the insurgents to tolerate a considerable disruption to their supple logistics system and still survive, conduct occasional ambushes, menace South Vietnam's Army, embarrass the Americans, and undermine Saigon's authority. In the end, however, the Vietcong was Hanoi's cat's-paw, and the insurgents posed no real threat to South Vietnam's sovereignty without active support from the North. Johnson rejected the one step certain to reach the goals he and Kennedy had set out for American policy in Indochina. An unleashed armada of B-52s, armed with conventional bomb-loads, surely could have laid waste to Hanoi and Haiphong within weeks, destroyed the Red River dams, and so brought

Armageddon to North Vietnam's political and economic fabric—and saved tens of thousands of American lives in the process. But neither Lyndon Johnson nor Robert McNamara possessed the will or stomach to take this single, bloody, apocalyptic, war-winning step.

In short, Johnson and his circle were content with half measures that condemned the Navy and Air Force men who waged the air war over North Vietnam to cycles of suffering, frustration, and resentment over their inevitable failures. "At times it seemed as if we were trying to see how much ordnance we could drop in North Vietnam without disturbing the country's way of life," recalled Commander John Nichols. All six Rolling Thunder campaigns were severely restricted—first by McNamara, and then by his like-minded successor, Clifford, whose first concern was always domestic politics. McNamara's policy of graduated response allowed the North Vietnamese to learn to absorb one easily defined level of punishment, prepare for the next, stiffen their air defenses, and thereby increase the cost of the bombing campaign to the Americans.[14]

From only a few SAM sites in April 1965, the North Vietnamese erected over 600 radar-guided missile sites within the next three years to protect key population centers, military bases, and lines of communication leading to Laos, Cambodia, and South Vietnam. More deadly than the missiles were the enemy antiaircraft batteries, whose able gun crews proved especially effective against American fighter-bombers or flak suppression aircraft, which regularly attacked predictable targets. The Russians also helped North Vietnam construct a sophisticated early warning radar network that alerted the communist missile and antiaircraft batteries to impending American air attacks and brought greatly increased coordination to that country's defenses. Until it was too late, McNamara refused to allow the Navy or Air Force to molest these installations. At the same time, in his search for a negotiated settlement, Johnson rewarded the Communists with the luxury of repeated bombing pauses, during which they repaired the damage from the last round of Rolling Thunder strikes and prepared for the next. With LBJ's March 1968 peace plan and Nixon's election victory in November, this phase of the Vietnam War came to a close, and Americans thereafter sought a formula by which they could safely disengage from Southeast Asian politics.

Chapter Twenty-nine

Defending the Nixon Doctrine

1969–1971

Richard Nixon entered the White House in January 1969 determined to dramatically change American foreign policy and military strategy. Believing that liberal Democrats had invested the State Department, he decided that his National Security Adviser, former Harvard political science professor Henry Kissinger, would formulate foreign policy and conduct the administration's most important diplomacy. Nixon and Kissinger shared an interest in the play of Great Power politics and so viewed the Vietnam War, a faraway conflict in an area of no strategic importance, as an obstacle to establishing a new triangular diplomacy among America, Russia, and China. They intended to reduce tensions in Asia, not pose a new challenge to the Chinese regime. When North Korean MiGs shot down a Navy EC-121 reconnaissance plane in international airspace over the Sea of Japan on 14 April 1969, Nixon was faced with his first test. He had criticized LBJ's handling of the *Pueblo* affair, and Kissinger was now "in favor of going in and taking out a Korean airfield," but Nixon already had one Asian war on his hands. Though he agreed at first with Kissinger's plan, "virtually everybody else in the administration opposed us, because it would cause [antiwar] demonstrations," Nixon recalled, so "I decided against taking any military action."[1]

Nixon also shared his predecessor's lack of faith in the JCS, and he mostly ignored their advice on military strategy in Vietnam. Ironically, his stated aims in Indochina were much the same as those enunciated by Lyndon Johnson. "The true objective of this war is peace," he told the *New York Times,* a preposterous formulation. While the publicly conducted Paris Peace Conference droned on without result, Kissinger flew to the French capital on 4 August 1969 to inaugurate a series of highly secret parallel meetings with Le Duc Tho, North Vietnam's envoy. On that occasion, Kissinger conveyed a bold threat from Nixon: The United States would deliver "savage, punishing blows" against North Vietnam unless Ho Chi Minh promptly withdrew the North Vietnamese Army from South Vietnam and ended his support of the Vietcong insurgency. "We have the enemy licked now. He is beaten. We have the initiative in all areas," announced Admiral John S. McCain, the new commander in chief of the Pacific theater, in January 1969. "The enemy . . . cannot even mount another major offensive."[2]

The Communists had been crushed to their knees by the disaster of Tet, but LBJ's fall and the growing strength of the American antiwar movement heartened Hanoi. Since 1964 Ho Chi Minh had been the object of repeated, mostly hollow American threats, so after Nixon took office, Ho decided to test the new president's mettle. Just before he died in September 1969, Ho responded to Nixon's threat with a message containing what Nixon later described as a "cold rebuff." It was an impasse. In an attempt to exploit Nixon's frustration, Admiral Moorer, the CNO, proposed to carry out the threat by resuming the bombing of North Vietnam, mining Haiphong harbor, and blockading North Vietnam's ports. Kissinger and Secretary of Defense Melvin Laird were alarmed by this proposal; they believed that such strong steps would stimulate more support among Democrats in Congress for the antiwar movement. Together they persuaded Nixon that Moorer's plan would not force Hanoi to withdraw from South Vietnam. In short, Nixon recalled, "we were stuck with the bombing halt that we inherited from the Johnson administration." Nixon was now in a bind. He was interested in the global balance of power, not the fate of Indochina, and he cared not a fig for General Nguyen Van Thieu's inept, venal Saigon regime. After Nixon retreated from his threat to resume the air war, North Vietnam's new leadership saw no reason to negotiate seriously in Paris, thereby forcing Nixon to devise a new strategy to facilitate an American withdrawal.[3]

On 3 November 1969, Nixon laid out his new policy of "Vietnamization," a term he had coined one year earlier. He intended to rebuild Saigon's armed forces and bolster South Vietnam's economy with American aid, while gradually withdrawing American troops and turning over offensive military operations against the Vietcong to the South Vietnamese. A few months earlier, on 25 July, during a stopover at Guam, he had enunciated the Nixon Doctrine, explaining that after pulling out of Vietnam the United States would be generous in providing military and economic assistance to its non-European clients but would expect them in return to defend themselves against communist aggression or subversion. The Nixon Doctrine, Assistant Secretary of State Joseph Sisco explained to Congress in 1972, was "basically a doctrine of disengagement and engagement on a selective basis." One result of this declaration was the little-noticed withdrawal of about 20,000 troops from South Korea, leaving 38,000 American soldiers there to support the South Korean Army in defending the armistice along the 38th parallel. To compensate Seoul, Nixon promised a substantial modernization program for South Korea's armed forces and the continued deployment of a 7th Fleet carrier task force in the region.[4]

The Nixon Doctrine notwithstanding, Admiral Elmo Zumwalt, who became CNO in 1970, pointed out that for the fleet "the western Pacific commitment was irreducible for at least as long as the war continued in Southeast Asia, and probably longer in view of the shaky situation in Korea and the need to keep Japan covered." Moorer and Zumwalt casually read into the president's new formulation a justification for continuing the forward deployment of American naval power. "The credibility of the Nixon Doctrine," Zumwalt wrote somewhat halfheartedly, "clearly depended on U.S. control of the seas." A great deal was made of the Nixon Doctrine, but the official most directly responsible for its implementation, Admiral McCain, later dismissed it, admitting that "no one ever told [me] what the Nixon Doctrine actually meant." Indeed, Zumwalt even concluded "that the Nixon Doctrine was not very convincing even to its author."[5]

The Nixon Doctrine—at least as it applied to Southeast Asia —was intended to divert attention from the Vietnam War and thus allow Vietnamization to take hold. Nixon took some of the wind out of the sails of the antiwar movement by ending the Selective Service draft and instituting an all-volunteer force in

1972 and by publicizing North Vietnam's brutal treatment of her American prisoners of war. In 1969, the Democrats, just repudiated in the presidential elections, started to undercut Nixon's war policy by seeking to have Congress impose legal restrictions on the continuance of American military operations in Southeast Asia. In reply, Nixon turned to the 1964 Tonkin Gulf Resolution, in which Congress had given the president the authority to take steps to protect American forces stationed in Southeast Asia. He needed time for Vietnamization to work, and so he announced that American forces would not leave Indochina until North Vietnam released the American POWs, almost all of whom were Navy or Air Force aviators. When the Democrats argued with this reasoning, the White House denounced them for wanting to abandon the POWs.

Since Nixon had accepted Johnson's decision to trade Rolling Thunder for the Paris peace talks, McCain in November 1968 was forced to revise the strategy for the air war in Indochina. Until Johnson ended air operations over North Vietnam entirely, the Air Force bombed Barrel Roll targets in the panhandle above the DMZ. Nixon then restricted McCain to occasional Blue Tree photo reconnaissance flights over North Vietnam by RF-8 Crusaders and RA-5 Vigilantes; to deal with North Vietnam's dangerous air defenses, the flights were escorted by Iron Hand Skyhawks. Under rules of engagement dictated by Kissinger and Laird, American pilots flying these missions were required to allow the enemy to wait for the most advantageous moment to attack the unarmed aircraft before the victims were permitted to respond with a "protective reaction" strike. Nevertheless, the North Vietnamese response to these escorted reconnaissance flights was so violent that over sixty such American retaliating strikes were flown in 1970, and twice that many the following year.

For the most part, the Communists withheld their fighters from the air war after 1968, but in March 1970 a MiG-21 was shot down by Lieutenant Jerome E. Beaulier and his bombardier, Lieutenant Steven J. Barkley, flying an F-4 Phantom off the *Constellation*. After that incident, however, Navy aircraft were not challenged by the North Vietnamese Air Force until the Easter offensive of 1972. Meanwhile, McCain had reinforced the air campaign against trucking on the Ho Chi Minh Trail with assets freed up in November 1968 by the end of Rolling Thunder. He increased the number of Steel Tiger strikes against northern Laos and initiated joint Navy–Air Force Commando Hunt operations in the Laotian panhandle to destroy North Vietnam's supplies and tie down her manpower. Against the Laotian side of the important, well-defended Ban Karai, Mu Gia, and Ban Raving passes, the Tonkin Gulf Task Force launched Commando Bolt strikes flown by sections of A-6 Intruders assisted by EA-6B Prowler electronic countermeasures aircraft. Along the Ho Chi Minh Trail in Laos, daytime communist truck traffic disappeared, and nighttime convoys seemed to decline to a trickle.

McCain also renewed the use of Tonkin Gulf Task Force carriers for close ground support and interdiction operations in South Vietnam, but this was only a fraction of the overall naval air effort in Indochina. Unfortunately, the anti-truck campaign on the Ho Chi Minh Trail, like the broader interdiction strategy, was a notable failure. McCain was unhappy with these peripheral operations, and during every logjam in the Paris peace talks he pressed Defense Secretary Laird for permission to resume Rolling Thunder. Under Nixon's Vietnamization policy, however, naval air operations were instead sharply curtailed. For example, the three carriers on Yankee Station averaged a total of between 5,000 and 6,000 attack sorties each month against targets in Indochina during 1968; by mid-1970, only 3,000 sorties from a pair of carriers were launched over Laos and South Vietnam. McCain's messages complaining about this state of affairs became "so consistent and so predictable," according to Captain Andrew Kerr, that Laird's staff simply prepared "boiler-plate texts ready for every occasion and merely had to insert the date of the rejection."

Just when the end of Rolling Thunder allowed North Vietnam to begin to recover from the defeat of the Tet Offensive, American forces fighting in South Vietnam were blessed by the arrival in 1968 of two new dynamic commanders: General Creighton Abrams and Vice Admiral Zumwalt. Abrams was the beneficiary of three years of Westmoreland's attrition campaigns, and when he took command in the summer of 1968 he tried to exploit this advantage by assigning American forces to secure key geographical strongpoints, the most vital lines of communications, and major population centers. He was anxious to launch new attacks against Vietcong depots, to retrain and reequip the South Vietnamese Army, and to get these troops out into the field to confront the Vietcong. Although he intended that American forces pursue the Vietcong energetically, he was equally eager to turn over ground and naval operations to the South Vietnamese. Neither Abrams nor Zumwalt welcomed Vietnamization, but they understood that they had no alternative but to carry it out.

Zumwalt, who relieved Admiral Veth in command of Naval Forces Vietnam in September 1968, labored under several burdens, one of which was the widely held view that South Vietnam's navy was not aggressive and was victimized by indifferent leadership. Abrams was "obviously unhappy with Admiral Veth" because he had been "unable to supply . . . leadership and innovation" to the naval campaign, observed Captain Howard Kerr. He blamed this in part on Veth's staff, a "sleepy, large, moribund" group who read their daily message traffic and proceeded to Saigon's fashionable Circle Sportif bar for lunch and tennis. "I found things far worse than I had imagined," Zumwalt recalled. "At command headquarters in Saigon I perceived what can only be described as a country club atmosphere." Passed over for a vice admiral's third star, Veth boycotted a farewell party that Abrams held for him when he left South Vietnam. Zumwalt, his relief, was "more daring" than Veth, according to Rear Admiral Arthur Price, and he brought to his new command an excitement for action that was tempered with the understanding that "domestic politics would drive the situation in Vietnam as much as anything." Indeed, Abrams and Zumwalt agreed even before the 1968 presidential elections that both Humphrey and Nixon intended to withdraw American forces from Indochina, although, as Kerr concluded, Nixon's victory in November "had bought time [for the American withdrawal] that Johnson didn't have and Humphrey wouldn't have had."[6]

Zumwalt found that Operation Stable Door, the continuing effort to secure South Vietnam's ports and harbors, had been the most successful of all the Navy operations. On the other hand, the record of the Market Time campaign in reducing communist shipping from North Vietnam to the Vietcong in South Vietnam was decidedly mixed. If the Tet Offensive proved nothing else, it demonstrated that Market Time had failed theretofore to prevent supplies from reaching the Vietcong in the Delta. In one busy month, September 1968, Market Time vessels inspected over 35,000 watercraft and boarded over 16,000 of them. They also inspected 728 steel-hulled ships, boarded 52, and supported 40 armed guard operations.

Market Time operations were dangerous. On nearly 800 occasions Market Time forces chased evading sampans or exchanged fire with communist gunners. From the Tet Offensive to August 1969, no North Vietnamese trawlers tried to enter South Vietnamese waters, although this trend was reversed after the Communists lost the use of the Cambodian port of Sihanoukville in 1970. Over the next fifteen months, at least one North Vietnamese trawler attempted to reach the Mekong Delta each month. One ship evaded capture and completed its mission; the Market Time Force sank another, which was loaded with sixty tons of munitions, but the rest fled back into international waters when they were discovered. How many vessels completed their missions without being detected was a mystery. The Market Time Force had won a "foothold, no more than that" on the Gulf of Siam coast, according to Captain Robert S. Salzer. The northern extremity "was a smugglers' haven, however, and down the coast it became all Vietcong country, halfway up the neck of the Ca Mau Peninsula."[7]

Despite Veth's conservative tactical doctrine, Zumwalt concluded that the Game Warden Force had been remarkably successful in driving the Vietcong off the Delta's major rivers and canals. Veth had been unwilling to send either the Game Warden or the Mobile Riverine Forces up the more dangerous lesser canals and waterways, however, partly because Ambassador Henry Cabot Lodge and his State Department advisers were reluctant to introduce American forces with heavy firepower into these densely populated areas. It was Captain Salzer's view that Veth compounded this problem by dedicating the Mobile Riverine Force to the support of Westmoreland's search and destroy operations, a role in which it was sadly underused. In short, the Mobile Riverine Force often chased the Vietcong but seldom brought him to book. Zumwalt, who believed the Navy's operations in the Delta were too limited in scope, was also disturbed that in many parts of the Delta there was no allied presence whatsoever. Good intelligence was also at a premium. Although a number of specially trained Navy SEAL teams had arrived in South Vietnam as early as 1965 to conduct intelligence and reconnaissance missions, security for these and other operations posed a major problem. One of the reasons "we had trouble finding the enemy was that if we received intelligence" from SEAL platoons "that they were going to make a crossing . . . in order for us to set up a blockade, it was necessary to get the permission of the government agencies that controlled that river, whether it was a province chief, an army division commander, or whatever," reported Captain Arthur Price. American plans were often "leaked" to the Vietcong by spies and "by the time we got there they were gone."[8]

Zumwalt also inherited the problem of neutral Cambodia, for years a Vietcong sanctuary. In 1967, Prince Sihanouk negotiated a secret agreement with Hanoi under which Cambodian authorities allowed communist ships to enter the ports of Sihanoukville, Kep, and Kampot and to be unloaded there. Stores for the Vietcong were then transported overland along the Sihanouk Trail into South Vietnam, or were shipped in small vessels that hugged the coast and offloaded at depots between Ha Tien on the Gulf of Thailand and Chau Phu on the Bassac River. The Sihanouk Trail entered South Vietnam west of Chau Phu, where the Bassac crossed into South Vietnam from Cambodia, and crossed the Plain of Reeds into the Parrot's Beak, that part of Cambodia that intruded into South Vietnam like a salient. "The Vietcong brought in a lot of supplies through these routes. The CIA misjudged the situation," Westmoreland observed. "Its intelligence didn't confirm it." Veth also understood that "a lot of supplies were being brought in by ship to Sihanoukville. . . . Then these supplies would just move through this ten-mile corridor, all the way down and across to the northern part of the Delta, so the Vietcong had supplies stashed away all along there." Because LBJ demanded that American forces in Indochina respect Cambodia's nominal neutrality, Veth reasoned that he could do nothing to upset the Vietcong's logistics on the Cambodian frontier. Shortly after Zumwalt took command in South Vietnam, his intelligence chief, Captain Rex Rectanus, developed the surprising thesis that not some but most supplies destined for the Vietcong in the southern half of South Vietnam were now being shipped through Sihanoukville. Salzer insisted that "supplies were coming into . . . Sihanoukville and coming down the Gulf of Siam coast about 10–20 miles inland through a canal network. We had a foothold in the town of Rach Gia and no control above that at all."[9]

Zumwalt crafted a new campaign called Sealords, which was intended to attack the most vulnerable links of the Vietcong line of communications. He wanted to shut down infiltration in the Delta, wrest the initiative from the enemy in the Rung Sat Special Zone and secure the Long Tau shipping channel, and start turning some operations over to South Vietnam's navy. The Sealords Plan was fleshed out by Captain Salzer, who was shortly thereafter named to command the new Sealords Force, which would draw its combat units from the Game Warden, Market Time, and Mobile Riverine Forces. Zumwalt decided to reduce Market Time coastal patrols, in part by turning some missions over to the South Vietnamese Navy. This released some Swift PCFs, and Zumwalt used them to replace the PBRs on the larger rivers. The PBRs in turn could be sent upriver to challenge the Vietcong. Salzer planned to "strike down the canal network" and "establish a series of outposts along that river-canal network first, then spread it up to the north."[10]

The broad goals of the Sealords campaign were to seal off the Cambodian border, starve the Vietcong in the Delta, and throw the Communists "off balance." Zumwalt also intended to create some front lines in the war in the Delta for the first time by setting up interdiction barriers along South Vietnam's major waterways. The goal of pacification was to establish physical control over the Vietnamese who lived along the riverbanks, end Vietcong taxation and extortion of the rice growers and fishermen, deny the use of the waterways to the Vietcong, and restore the safe use of those economic arteries to agents of the Saigon regime and the local South Vietnamese. On 5 November 1968, Abrams agreed to support the Sealords strategy. For the first time in the Vietnam War, Captain Kerr recalled, Navy personnel involved in the riverine campaign were "excited" at the prospect of achieving a strategic victory.[11]

The Sealords campaign got off to a quick start on 2 November 1968 with Operation Search Turn. Its objective was to establish an interdiction barrier on the Rach Gia Xuyen and Can Son canals in the Upper Mekong Delta about forty miles from the Cambodian frontier. Captain Ray Hohlman, a vigorous combat commander, stationed his PCFs in the Gulf while a formation of PBRs entered the canal, followed by the Mobile Riverine Force. For five days, Hohlman's vessels fought their way toward the Cambodian border, supported by troops who moved in a parallel line along the banks of the waterway. Fourteen tons of arms were captured and over 200 Vietcong were killed. Search Turn vividly demonstrated the need to push the barrier patrols closer to the border of Cambodia.

Operation Foul Deck was precipitated by an incident at Rach Giang Thanh. On 14 October 1968, Lieutenant (j.g.) Michael Bernique, who was operating at Ha Tien on the Gulf near the Cambodian border, learned that the Vietcong had established a tax-collecting station at Rach Giang Thanh, a small river earlier ruled off limits to American naval operations because of its close proximity to the Cambodian border. Bernique nevertheless drove up to Ha Tien and disrupted this post, provoking the kind of violent reaction from the Communists in the vicinity that Zumwalt had hoped to inspire. In response, on 16 November, Zumwalt ignited Operation Foul Deck, in which Navy patrols were extended on the Rach Giang Thanh–Vinh Te Canal, which paralleled the Cambodian border from the Gulf to Chau Doc on the Bassac River. Three tons of arms were taken and 470 Vietcong died during this operation. Yet another violent, successful barrier operation was Giant Slingshot, which kicked off 6 December 1968. It was formed on the Vam Co Tay and the Vam Co Dong, two rivers that ran down the sides of the Parrot's Beak and converged fifteen miles south of Saigon. This costly operation killed over 1,000 Vietcong, captured over 250 tons of war goods, and opened up the canal from Can Tho toward Saigon, the main trans-Delta route for Vietnamese rice convoys.

American casualties during these operations were high— and often unnecessary. On one occasion, during the Giant Slingshot movement, two PBRs were lost when they were airlifted to a station on a long canal that was so narrow the vessels were unable to turn around when they were ambushed by the Vietcong. The water level was so low that the trapped PBRs were unable to elevate their guns enough to return the enemy's machine gun and rocket fire. To reduce the huge casualties suffered during the first week of Sealords, Lieutenant George Stefencavage proposed that the Americans initiate a series of waterborne ambushes. PBRs had conducted nighttime patrols for several years, but these vessels made too much noise while they were under way to achieve tactical surprise. Instead, Stefencavage wanted to have six PBRs move onto preselected river stations at sunset, steam upriver in the darkness, cut engines, drift over to a bank where they

Captain Roy F. Hoffmann (*left*), **Commander, TF-115 (Game Warden Force), and Vice Admiral Elmo Zumwalt** (*right*) **board the patrol gunboat** *Crockett* **(PG-88) at Camranh Bay, South Vietnam, 7 October 1968.**

would wait until the Vietcong came along, and then ambush them. Zumwalt approved Stefencavage's plan, and within a week it was operational doctrine in the Delta.

Operation Barrier Reef joined Giant Slingshot in the east to form a two-tiered western barrier, thus tightening the noose around communist infiltration routes from the north. This major naval campaign extended the barrier patrols to the Vam Co Dong River, north of the Parrot's Beak, and the Vam Co Tay River to the east. On 2 January 1969, a Barrier Reef Force was established on the La Grange–Ong Lon Canal. Despite the early success of these barrier operations, neither the U.S. Army nor the South Vietnamese were willing to provide the Sealord Force with enough troops to allow Zumwalt to mount vigorous patrols along the riverbanks and thereby create more friction, or to pursue and annihilate the enemy. Nonetheless, the forces involved accounted for nearly 200 dead Vietcong. Vietnamization was starting to take its toll, and in June 1969, the Army decided to withdraw the 2nd Brigade, 9th Infantry, the assault troops assigned to the Mobile Riverine Force since 1967, from South Vietnam. As his operations became more aggressive, Zumwalt hoped that Sealords would so stir up the Communists that they would mount a major counteroffensive and thus force General Abrams or the South Vietnamese to provide him with more troops, but this did not happen.

The saga of Nam Can illustrated the conundrum Zumwalt faced. When he arrived in Vietnam, communist rule in the Nam Can district of An Xuyen Province at the southernmost tip of

Rear Admiral Tran Van Chon (*left*), Chief of Naval Operations of South Vietnam's Navy; Admiral Elmo Zumwalt (*center*), Commander, U.S. Naval Forces, Vietnam, 1968–1970, and Chief of Naval Operations, 1970–1974; and Rear Admiral Frank W. Vanmoy, Assistant Chief of Naval Operations for Plans and Policy, at An Thoi Naval Base, South Vietnam, May 1971.

the Ca Mau Peninsula was unchallenged. Only a small South
Vietnamese garrison held the small city of Nam Can, the capital
of an area thick with mangrove swamps, dense with forests, lacer-
ated by canals and waterways and rivers, and poor beyond description. Nam Can had served before 1966 as an entrepôt for
communist trawlers that slithered down the coast into the
mouths of the rivers of the Ca Mau Peninsula. Supplies were offloaded at Nam Can, then dispersed to Vietcong units in the Delta
or north into III Corps. Market Time operations severed this
communist sea link and forced the Vietcong in some measure to
reverse the flow of their logistics. They established several small
factories on the Ca Mau to manufacture munitions from scrap
metal and duds and increased taxes-in-kind on the peasantry collected by armed sampans at stations along the major waterways.
The South Vietnamese Army at Nam Can city did not try to disrupt this arrangement, and during the Tet Offensive, the Vietcong even seized that outpost and held it in the face of a dispirited counterattack by Saigon troops. The South Vietnamese then
moved the local peasants ten miles north to New Nam Can city,
after which Saigon declared Old Nam Can to be a "free fire
zone." It was soon turned into a rubble heap, a convenient
dumping ground for American pilots who had unused bombs
left over after missions over the Delta.

This stasis was disturbed by Zumwalt's arrival in South Vietnam, for in Nam Can he found a place to test his aggressive
tactics and his pacification scheme. Captain Roy Hoffman sent
three PCFs seven miles up the Ong Doc River on the Ca Mau
Peninsula and four miles along an adjacent canal, destroying
over 100 communist buildings, tents, and dozens of sampans.
Next, in October 1968, Zumwalt dispatched Market Time raiders
along the Cua Lon and Bo De rivers on the Ca Mau while Swift
boats shot up the rivers of the Nam Can district. Zumwalt wanted
to dispute Vietcong control of the region, force the enemy to defend his positions, and call attention to the Communists' presence in the area. Just as he had expected, the Vietcong launched
a furious counteroffensive. Forts were erected along the riverbanks and barriers were hurled across most of the principal waterways to impede the movement of the Market Time craft. As his
next step, Zumwalt assigned a meticulous planner, Captain J. G.
Now, to the command of a Mobile Riverine Force assault group
for Operation Silver Mace I. This force included the APB *Mercer,*

the ARL *Satyr*, three ATCs, monitors, and ASPBs. In December, Now's vessels steamed along the coast from Rach Gia to Son Cua Lon in the first open sea transit of heavy riverine assault craft, and on the 19th his men fell on the barriers. In three days they were all cut and removed.

Zumwalt wanted to keep up the pressure against Nam Can during the winter monsoon, but this proved to be too difficult. Neither the U.S. Army nor the South Vietnamese would support these costly operations. "They were enthusiastic about it until it required soldiers," Salzer reported. And in the fall of 1968, the Army withdrew its helicopter support for Mobile Riverine Force operations at the very moment that Vietcong ambush operations in the Delta began to increase. The following spring, Zumwalt planned another operation, which was to be both joint and combined, but for Silver Mace II he could get only the ragtag elements of South Vietnam's ill-trained reserve Regional and Popular Forces, some Coastal Force junks, a handful of Air Force planes, and his own Market Time units. Nonetheless, in April 1969, LSTs and ARLs anchored five miles off the coast of the Ca Mau Peninsula while the Mobile Riverine Force moved up the rivers, but the Americans killed fewer than twoscore Vietcong and recovered fewer than 400 weapons. Security in any combined operation with the South Vietnamese was almost uniformly poor, and Silver Mace II brought this reality to Zumwalt's doorstep. "Any time you are working with the Vietnamese there are bound to be frustrations," Salzer mused. "With some of them, it was simply [that] the astrologer told them it was a bad day." Not only was security poor, but the stationing of the support ships off the coast limited the extent of American penetration. In addition, intelligence on Vietcong plans and movements was so poor that Salzer claimed that neither Zumwalt nor he had "much faith in it at all."[12]

To keep up the pressure on Old Nam Can, Zumwalt now decided to locate a base on the Cua Lon or Bo De rivers that could support junks, river assault craft, and waterborne patrol forces. By inviting the South Vietnamese Navy to participate in this operation, he intended to help Saigon reestablish its sovereignty over the Ca Mau. The generals of the South Vietnamese Joint General Staff, who had long since given up any hope of wresting control of the peninsula from the Vietcong, offered little backing for the project. And on the whole, General

Abrams' staff agreed, arguing that a base ashore was almost inde-
fensible from a communist attack from the north by land.
Zumwalt revised his plan. Instead of erecting the base ashore, he
decided on 15 May 1969 to build a floating base out of thirteen
Ammi pontoon barges and moor the contraption with 9,000-
pound cement anchors in the middle of the Cua Lon. The
Ammis were fitted out at Nha Be, then carried to the mouth of
the Cua Lon by LSDs from the 7th Fleet.

On 25 June, YFU tugs towed the new Sea Float upriver and
she moored at a midstream station not far from Old Nam Can.
The base was imminently defensible. Vietcong frogmen could
not mine the barges owing to the strong tidal current, and within
a few days the Americans began to plant effective electronic sensors along the riverbanks to prevent the enemy from mounting
rocket or mortar attacks against the Sea Float base. Various medical and economic services were offered to the harried local peasants, both to improve their lives and to counter Vietcong propaganda, although no evidence exists that the peasants responded
by providing the Americans with better intelligence about enemy
movements. Numbed by the fighting, terrorized by the Vietcong,
and oppressed by Saigon's tax farmers, the suspicious, unlettered
South Vietnamese peasantry was too stunned, war-weary, hungry,
and weak to decide the outcome of the war.

Zumwalt established a supporting Sea Float Annex on 24
July 1969 at the junction of the Cua Lon River and the Cai Nhap
Canal about six miles from the main Sea Float base. The craft assigned to the annex sheltered at Sea Float at night and patrolled
during the day. They inspected river traffic, provided medical
assistance, and tried gamely to establish a new hamlet nearby.
The entire effort recorded some modest success, at least on paper. Vietcong tax collections declined, the number of sampans
on the Cua Lon went up, and some Vietnamese moved back to
New Nam Can. With the onset of Nixon's program of Vietnamization, however, hopes began to sour. On 24 October, the
South Vietnamese Navy Coastal Force established a base at Old
Nam Can, and over the next year the U.S. Navy turned over a
huge amount of equipment and a large number of craft to the
South Vietnamese. Meanwhile, the Vietcong slowly reestablished
themselves near Nam Can.

In 1969, Zumwalt also turned his eye to a renewed Vietcong
offensive in the swampy Rung Sat Special Zone. After the Ameri-

cans had taken over fighting the Vietnam War in 1965, their principal concern in this area was to secure the Long Tau shipping channel to Saigon. Beginning in 1967, the extensive use of Agent Orange and other defoliants sprayed from the air had erased vegetation in broad strips along the banks of the channel, thus exposing enemy movements and concentrations to American counterattacks. Despite the heightened tempo of communist operations during the Tet Offensive, the Vietcong had launched only forty-four attacks on shipping in the channel during all of 1968. Between January and June 1969, however, fifty-one separate communist operations were mounted by Doan-10, a Vietcong unit based just north of the Rung Sat in the Nhon Trach district of Bien Hoa Province, about fifteen miles from Saigon. Doan-10's attacks alarmed Veth, but he did little to counter them. He faced indifference at General Abrams' headquarters and opposition from South Vietnam's generals. South Vietnam's command structure, which tied commanders to geographical areas, allowed the generals and provincial officials in Bien Hoa to ignore Vietcong forces, which, although based in that province, only operated in the neighboring Rung Sat—the South Vietnamese Navy's exclusive responsibility.

Zumwalt's attention turned to the Rung Sat during Operation Ready Deck, which began in May 1969 when an Army Skytrain plane was used to lift six PBRs from Vam Co Dong River to the upper Saigon River, blocked to traffic by a bridge that the Vietcong had blown up some months earlier. Then, during June 1969 alone, there were nineteen separate sapper or mine attacks on American or South Vietnamese shipping along the Long Tau channel, causing Zumwalt to reexamine the whole problem of the Rung Sat. By midmonth Zumwalt decided that the only way to secure the channel was to strike at the Vietcong's base at Nhon Trach. General Abrams agreed, but he would not or could not provide American troops for the operation. Neither would the South Vietnamese Army or Marines, so Zumwalt scraped together an international force of Royal Thai Volunteers, First Australian Force troops, and some American sailors. This composite group attacked Nhon Trach on 22 June, overran the base, and provoked a series of firefights with Doan-10. Although the allied troops withdrew from Nhon Trach, they had crippled the Vietcong—there were only two feeble attacks against the Long Tau channel that July. Zumwalt wanted to keep up the pressure, and indeed, the success of the first raid now encouraged the South Vietnamese to participate in another offensive. In August, he organized Operation Friendship and Operation Platypus, combined attacks on the Vietcong's Nhon Trach base by American and South Vietnamese Navy units. Subsequent operations during the rest of the year were codenamed Wolf Pack, and Zumwalt wangled increased, if reluctant, participation in these attacks by the South Vietnamese.

Zumwalt's Sealords campaign forced the Vietcong to relocate virtually all of their munition dumps, training sites, and hospitals in the Rung Sat to other areas and thoroughly disrupted Vietcong movements in the rest of the Delta. The quickened pace of these operations strained all of Zumwalt's subordinates, and Salzer reported that the "fatigue factor was so great" that even "the best river squadron commanders had to be rotated to my staff after six months in combat." Salzer was "less enthusiastic about" using Market Time Force small Swift PCF boats on "hit and run raids" in deep base areas. Nonetheless, between the defeat of the Tet Offensive and the Sealords operations, the Vietcong had suffered what he called a "horrendous blow" from which they "never recovered in the Delta."[13]

The new zest to Navy operations in Vietnam spread to the Tonkin Gulf Task Force. On 9 January 1969, Vice Admiral William F. Bringle, the commander of the 7th Fleet, launched Bold Mariner, the largest amphibious operation of the Vietnam War. Supported by naval gunfire support ships, Market Time craft put two Marine amphibious reconnaissance groups and Army troops ashore to seal off the Batangan Peninsula. In an immensely ponderous and costly operation, over 12,000 Vietnamese were screened, with the result that a lone Vietcong sapper company was discovered and destroyed. Further operations over the next two months failed to dislocate any large enemy formations, but a landing on Barrier Island south of Hoi An in May resulted in 178 Vietcong killed or captured. Bringle continued the campaign throughout the summer, although early operations against islands off the coast by I Corps probably cost the Marines more casualties than they inflicted, owing to the Vietcong's superb land-mining and booby-trap tactics. They were brought to book soon after, however, when Bringle mounted a second descent on Barrier Island by American and South Vietnamese Marines. Nearly 300 Vietcong were killed in heavy fighting.

The Communists had gone on the defensive elsewhere in South Vietnam. The Vietcong was shattered by Tet, and its cadres were decimated by the CIA's successful Phoenix program. Begun much too late in the war, this campaign of arrests and assassinations failed to discriminate carefully between the Vietcong and Saigon's loyal opponents, but thousands of Communists were killed and the insurgency was dealt a last, lethal blow. Abrams could, therefore, deliver his hammer blows at North Vietnam's divisions in South Vietnam.

Time was running out for South Vietnam, however, as Nixon hastened withdrawals of American troops to keep abreast of congressional demands to end the war. In March 1969, Secretary Laird flew to Saigon to meet Abrams and Zumwalt and outlined Nixon's plan for Vietnamization. Zumwalt soon drafted his own plan, entitled Accelerated Turnover, to transfer all operational naval activities to the South Vietnamese Navy by June 1970 and all support functions two years later. He desperately wanted to win, but Vietnamization meant that winning was impossible. He had only his own resources to support his offensives, and those resources were diminishing daily. The upshot was that almost none of the offensives could be sustained under the timetables set down by Nixon and Laird for withdrawal. Moreover, the South Vietnamese were unprepared for Vietnamization. Little had been done to improve South Vietnam's armed forces before 1968, the result of McNamara's presumption that the conflict would be brief and that American intervention would remove the danger to Saigon. Like many Americans, McNamara did not believe that the South Vietnamese could or would fight to defend their own country. When, in August 1968, Abrams asked Veth what naval functions could be assumed by the South Vietnamese Navy, the admiral proposed only to turn over two river assault squadrons to them within the next sixteen months.

The Vietnamization program exposed several accumulated problems. Admiral Salzer wanted the South Vietnamese Navy to operate on the rivers from mobile bases, but the South Vietnamese wanted to be near their families and thus insisted on establishing shore bases. This limited their mobility and effectiveness. In March 1970, Foul Deck operations along the Cambodian boarder were turned over to the South Vietnamese and responsibility for the Giant Slingshot barrier was transferred in May. One year later, in April 1971, the original Sea Float, codenamed Solid

Anchor, the basis of the pacification program on the Ca Mau
Peninsula, fell under the authority of Rear Admiral Chon's naval
headquarters. The Market Time transfers were phased. The inner barrier operations conducted by the WPBs and the PCFs
were finally surrendered to the South Vietnamese Navy in
September 1971. During that year, the South Vietnamese Navy
also received command of the WHEC-class Coast Guard cutters
and an American radar picket ship. By February 1970, shortly before Zumwalt left Indochina, the South Vietnamese Navy was operating more than 50 percent of the boats in the Rung Sat Special Zone.

Zumwalt was allowed to press his Sealords campaign up
close to Cambodia's border when Washington's attitude toward
Prince Norodom Sihanouk's nominal neutrality began to
change. Cambodia's king since 1941 and chief of state since
1960, Sihanouk found himself caught in a cruel conundrum
created by the Vietnam War. He had allowed Hanoi to build the
Ho Chi Minh Trail along Cambodia's eastern border with
South Vietnam because he could not prevent it. "Sihanouk had
made a deal with the North Vietnamese and the Vietcong to
let them occupy ten kilometers of space between Cambodia
and South Vietnam," Admiral Veth had learned from an agent
in the Cambodian cabinet. Under the terms of this accord,
Sihanouk "agreed to let the Vietcong establish camps, supply
dumps, and everything inside the Cambodian border." In return, the North Vietnamese restrained Cambodia's communist
Khmer Rouge insurgency. Veth, aware that possession of the Ho
Chi Minh Trail was one of North Vietnam's major assets, wanted to cross into Cambodia and attack North Vietnam's bases
there, but McNamara told all American commanders in Southeast Asia to "avoid doing anything that might possibly offend
Sihanouk." Both Veth and Westmoreland were frustrated by
McNamara's decision to allow the enemy to hold a sanctuary
"across a border that we wouldn't cross so we couldn't touch
them." During Johnson's presidency, the JCS repeatedly asked
McNamara for permission to bomb the Ho Chi Minh Trail in
Cambodia and Laos, and both Sharp and Westmoreland
begged McNamara for permission to send American forces into
Cambodia. "I did try and try again to cross into Cambodia and
Laos with my own troops," Westmoreland remembered, but
"that was not approved because of the . . . fear it might bring

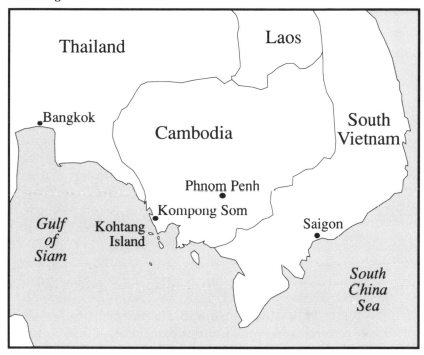

Cambodian Coast

the Chinese to the battlefield." Johnson and McNamara also worried about forcing Sihanouk to abandon his ostensible neutrality and formally ally himself with Hanoi.[14]

The North Vietnamese 1969 Tet Offensive against South Vietnam's cities was a clear violation of LBJ's 1968 understandings with Hanoi, and it led Nixon to approve the Freedom Deal plan for using B-52s to bomb the Ho Chi Minh Trail in Cambodia. Sihanouk secretly agreed to these operations, but at the same time he urged Washington to leave South Vietnam, holding that the Americans lacked the staying power of the brutal men in Hanoi. He flew to Moscow in January 1970 for an extended visit, entrusting his government to General Lon Nol, his prime minister. In mid-March mobs of anti-Vietnamese students sacked North Vietnam's embassy in Phnom Penh, and the next day Lon Nol ordered Hanoi's ambassador to remove North Vietnamese forces from Cambodian soil and demanded that North Vietnamese ships leave the port of Sihanoukville. These demands were rejected in an especially insulting reply. On the 18th, Lon Nol's faction in the Cambodian parliament denounced the old policy of appeasement and deposed Sihanouk in a coup d'état that was welcomed by the Americans. That afternoon, Lon Nol invited the Saigon government to send troops across the border to help the Cambodians defend their sovereignty. Following tentative air and ground probes, two South Vietnamese battalions were sent into Cambodia on 2 April. Meanwhile, Lon Nol ordered the Cambodian Army to move eastward in a vain attempt to trap the North Vietnamese between the two converging forces.

The Lon Nol coup, which transformed Cambodia from a neutral into an ally, caused Nixon to agree to Admiral Moorer's plan to send American and South Vietnamese forces into Cambodia. In a televised speech on 30 April 1970, Nixon announced that he had approved the "incursion" into Cambodia of 32,000 American troops, who attacked the North Vietnamese base in the Fishhook, a sanctuary only fifty miles northwest of Saigon. The South Vietnamese simultaneously entered the Parrot's Beak, another communist enclave in Cambodian territory within thirty miles of Saigon. Vice Admiral Jerome King, who had just succeeded Zumwalt in command of Naval Forces Vietnam, dispatched a large combined American–South Vietnamese naval task force led by Navy river assault craft carrying South Vietnamese Marines up the Mekong River. Its objective was to open the way to Phnom Penh. To support these movements, Admiral McCain initiated Freedom Deal bombing operations against Khmer Rouge concentrations in eastern Cambodia, then expanded the bombing to the southern and western areas of the country—secret bombing that continued to August 1973. He relieved the Air Force B-52s of all responsibilities for Steel Tiger bombing of the southcentral Laotian panhandle, the site of the Ho Chi Minh Trail, and shifted this burden to the 7th Fleet. Vice Admiral William Mack concentrated three carriers on Dixie Station to conduct operations over Laos and to fly ground support missions within South Vietnam.

Nixon bragged that the Cambodian incursion illustrated his eagerness to "go for all the marbles," but he was unwilling nonetheless to widen the war and deny the North Vietnamese the use of the Ho Chi Minh Trail. Instead, American troops and naval units were instructed not to venture more than about twenty miles into Cambodia, a restriction that satisfied neither

The *Truett* (FFG-1095), a *Knox*-class frigate.

the antiwar Democrats at home nor the commanders in Vietnam. When the combined naval task force reached Neak Luong, about halfway to Phnom Penh, the Americans mounted a combined arms attack against the communist ferry-crossing base there. Neither the Army's helicopter gunships from South Vietnam nor the Air Force's Thai-based aircraft could defend the convoys sailing up the Mekong, so the Tonkin Gulf Task Force was called upon to provide air escorts for these movements, which advanced against furious communist resistance. The Americans stopped at Neak Luong, but the South Vietnamese vessels proceeded thirty miles upriver to Phnom Penh, reaching the capital that night. They delivered food, clothes, and medical supplies to a swarm of Vietnamese refugees who had congregated there, and more than 82,000 native Vietnamese were transported from Phnom Penh back to swollen relocation camps in South Vietnam, adding to Saigon's overburdened refugee system. The allies held Neak Luong through June, but then this vital position was abandoned to the Communists when Nixon, bowing to antiwar Democrats, ordered McCain and Abrams to withdraw from Cambodia.

Democrats in the Senate reacted to the Cambodian incursion by passing a measure written by two liberals, Senator Frank Church and Senator John S. Cooper, which cut off funds for this operation. The House rejected the Cooper-Church Amendment, but this attempt to usurp the president's wartime authority as commander in chief disclosed an unexpected depth to antiwar feelings on the Hill, shook the administration, and shattered Nixon's resolve. He announced a premature end to the Cambodian incursion, accelerated troop withdrawals from South Vietnam, and instructed Kissinger to prepare new concessions for North Vietnam's envoy in Paris. Air Force B-52 high-level bombing was allowed to continue against the Ho Chi Minh Trail in Cambodia, but air power alone was inadequate to the task of supporting Lon Nol's fragile coalition, which now faced the fury of North Vietnam and its rearmed Khmer Rouge allies.

Anticipating the upcoming midterm elections, Nixon broadcast his new peace terms in mid-October and promised to increase the pace of American military withdrawal from South Vietnam over the next year, but the North Vietnamese angrily turned down his offer of a ceasefire in place and demanded instead that the Americans overthrow Thieu and replace his Saigon clique with a government controlled by the Vietcong. Hanoi did not intend to tie down its troops to areas of South Vietnam it already controlled when it was planning another offensive. This operation, directed toward South Vietnam's northernmost provinces, was revealed to American intelligence when the Communists began to assemble their assault forces in southeast Laos and northeast Cambodia in late 1970. To thwart this move, Moorer obtained Nixon's permission to employ the American air forces to support Lam Son 719, an invasion of southeastern Laos by the South Vietnamese Army.

On 8 February 1971 two South Vietnamese divisions in

Quang Tri Province crossed over the border a few miles into Laos and occupied the city of Tchepone. This stroke threatened a major artery of the Ho Chi Minh Trail, and the North Vietnamese counterattacked around Tchepone with great ferocity, unexpectedly hurling Russian-built tanks against the poorly led South Vietnamese infantry. To blunt this counterattack, Admiral Mack sent flights of older Skyhawks against the Ho Chi Minh Trail in the Laotian panhandle. Thousands of North Vietnamese vehicles were destroyed by these attacks, but the antitruck campaign failed to prevent the defeat in Laos of the South Vietnamese Army, which retreated in shambles back across the border. Air operations connected to Lam Son 719 interrupted communist logistics but hardly represented a permanent setback to North Vietnam's war effort, and Lam Son 719 clearly proved that South Vietnam's infantry, without American air, artillery, and logistics support, was no match for North Vietnam's armor. Nixon reacted to the shrill but predictable opposition at home to the Laotian incursion—symbolized by the Cooper-Church Amendment—by again slashing American forces in South Vietnam, and by hastening the pace of the Vietnamization turnover program. At the end of 1971, few American combat forces remained in South Vietnam. The Vietcong was destroyed, but Hanoi held the Ho Chi Minh Trail and the North Vietnamese Army in South Vietnam was intact, while the Americans left the battlefield before they had won or lost the Vietnam War.

Chapter Thirty

The Navy and Détente
1969–1973

Richard Nixon presided over a dramatic decline in American military power, an outcome not only of post-Vietnam War demobilization and antimilitary politics in Congress but also of his new foreign policy of détente with the Soviet Union. The centerpiece of détente was the Strategic Arms Limitations Talks, or SALT. Johnson had laid the groundwork for détente during a 1967 meeting with Soviet Premier Aleksei Kosygin at New Jersey's Glassboro State College, but the only outcome of those conversations was the ineffectual Nuclear Nonproliferation Treaty, signed by over 100 nations but rejected by France and China. The Soviets' August 1968 invasion of Czechoslovakia and the Kremlin's enunciation of the Brezhnev Doctrine—reasserting Moscow's supremacy over the Warsaw Pact satellites—undermined LBJ's plan for another arms control summit before the November presidential elections and left relations with Russia chilly when Nixon entered the White House. Both Nixon and Kissinger were convinced that "the simplicities of the Cold War began to evaporate" when the Soviets acquired a large ballistic missile force, however, and they set about to "redesign" American foreign policy.[1]

The first major step in this diplomacy was the unheralded but public acceptance of parity in strategic nuclear weapons between the two great powers. Following the completion of the Minuteman ICBM land-based intercontinental ballistic missile and Polaris SLBM submarine-launched ballistic missile programs in 1967, McNamara resisted adding to the strategic forces on the grounds that both sides possessed enough weapons to ensure Mutual Assured Destruction. Although in early 1963 McNamara had characterized as "irrational" charges that his strategy of "mutual deterrence" would replace American superiority with a "nuclear stalemate," soon after that he confessed that a "full first strike" strategy was "simply unattainable," whereas a counter-value, or "cities only" strategy, was "dangerously inadequate." His approach to the strategic dilemma of the Cold War increasingly assumed that either side might inflict so much damage on the other's cities that neither would initiate a global thermonuclear exchange. McNamara was never certain where this level of destruction should be fixed; he set it at 30 percent in 1965 and lowered it to 20 percent two years later. This thesis hinged on the ability of the American bomber-silo-submarine strategic triad to absorb a first strike and still retaliate with a thorough second strike. Meanwhile, the immense growth of the Soviets' ballistic missile submarine fleet and strategic rocket forces following the Cuban Missile Crisis altered the major index of international military power.[2]

Mutual Assured Destruction was, however, a declaratory policy that set a limit on forces, not a strategic prescription defined by missions and deployments. McNamara did not demand any major changes in targeting plans for the strategic nuclear triad—for which Soviet military forces and bases remained the highest priority. Of course Navy men disliked the policy of Mutual Assured Destruction, as it embodied little consideration for nuclear war fighting in general or for attacks against Soviet ballistic missile submarines in particular. Instead of writing new strategic war plans, McNamara merely conjured up a rationale for holding down spending for new American ballistic missile submarines, third-generation ICBMs, and long-range manned bombers. It was therefore ironic that, by the time he had fleshed out his thesis, the utility of Mutual Assured Destruction was already under attack by two developments. The first was the creation of the Safeguard antiballistic missile system.

In July 1962, a Zeus rocket fired from the secret Kwajalein Missile Range in the Marshall Islands came within lethal distance in mid-air of a Minuteman ICBM that had been launched 4,300 miles away at Vandenberg Air Force Base in California, about the same distance as that between the Soviet missile bases in Siberia and the major cities of the United States. Aware that a functional defense against incoming ballistic missiles would make his nuclear strategy untenable, McNamara tried to starve the Safeguard antiballistic missile system, only to see it repeatedly rescued by Congress. According to his assistant Alain Enthoven, McNamara believed that an ABM system "could not significantly reduce the number of American dead in an all-out nuclear exchange so long as the Soviets were determined to maintain their deterrent." Adding to the controversy over Safeguard were its use of a nuclear explosion to destroy an incoming warhead and the ease with which its radars could be outwitted. However, McNamara caved in to pressure from the JCS and Congress, and agreed in September 1967 to construct a small Safeguard system to defend against missiles launched by accident or by the Chinese or another second-rank power. This compromise pleased no one.[3]

The second development to undermine Mutual Assured Destruction was the invention of the Multiple Independently Targetable Reentry Vehicle, or MIRV. Several of these vehicles could be carried by a single land-launched or sea-based intercontinental ballistic missile. In effect, MIRV promised a tremendous growth in the number of inexpensive nuclear warheads without a corresponding increase in the number of costly land- or sea-based launchers. Coupled with advances in missile guidance systems that improved the accuracy of the individual delivery vehicle, the development of the MIRV imperiled all existing land-based ICBMs and undermined the assumption that either power might absorb a first strike and still be left with a sufficient nuclear arsenal to retaliate with an effective second strike. Inasmuch as the Americans enjoyed a significant lead over the Soviets in MIRV technology, it was in the Kremlin's interest to limit the growth of American strategic nuclear forces while trying to close the gap that still remained before they reached true parity. The Americans, on the other hand, wanted to retard the overall growth of Soviet rocket forces, which Nixon believed Congress was unwilling to match.

After protracted negotiations over these issues, Nixon flew to Moscow, where on 29 May 1972 he and Brezhnev signed two SALT I agreements. Since the Safeguard system was imperfect, Nixon had few qualms about scrapping most of it under the Anti-Ballistic Missile Treaty, which obligated the Russians to desist from erecting an analogous defense. A separate Interim Agreement fixed the Soviets' strategic systems at 1,618 ICBMs, 950 SLBMs, and 62 ballistic missile submarines, whereas the Americans were limited to 1,054 ICBMs, 710 SLBMs, and 41 ballistic missile–bearing submarines. McNamara had curtailed the construction of these vessels when there were forty-one *Ethan Allens* and *Lafayettes* in service, so the SALT I agreement merely recognized a limit that was preexisting and self-imposed. Although the Soviets enjoyed greater numbers of launchers and much greater throwweight under this formula, Nixon defended the inferior limits for the United States on the grounds that American systems were more reliable and accurate. The Interim Agreement allowed either side to vary the mix of its delivery systems, but only the number of sea-based launchers might be increased. Because ballistic missile–bearing submarines were considered second-strike systems, both sides believed that this would contribute to a more stable balance of power. The Soviets regarded the U.S. Navy's antisubmarine forces with alarm, however, and thereafter resisted redistributing their strategic missiles from silo- to sea-based launchers. In a fit of bipartisan euphoria undisturbed by a muffled conservative dissent, the Senate approved the ABM Treaty and passed a resolution in support of the Interim Agreement. Achieving these ends carried a price—the exclusion of the JCS, who opposed the policy, from the negotiations, a practice that even Kissinger, its architect, later confessed was "tactless and unwise."[4]

Nixon inherited not only an arms control policy from Lyndon Johnson but also the seeds of a precipitous decline in the strength of America's conventional military forces. Nixon's decision to reopen relations with China relaxed tensions in East Asia and allowed Kissinger to announce that the administration was devising a one-and-a-half war strategy. The United States "would no longer treat a conflict with the Soviet Union as automatically involving . . . China." Liberal Democrats in Congress, believing the Vietnam War to be a byproduct of rabid militarism, wittingly aided in this decline. They were eager to accelerate withdrawal from Southeast Asia; to reach this end, they cut defense appropriations throughout Nixon's presidency. And a neoisolationist clique in the Senate, led by Majority Leader Mike Mansfield, a Montana Democrat, proposed to withdraw 100,000 American troops from NATO—despite the menace of the Brezhnev Doctrine and an alarming buildup of Soviet ground and air forces in eastern Europe. Nixon was firmly against reducing American forces dedicated to the defense of western Europe, but his protests over other defense cuts were somewhat insincere and mostly ineffective. This set in train a process leading to reductions in naval, ground, and tactical air forces of such proportions that Kissinger worried that the administration was "sliding into a period of relying on Massive Retaliation even though this is absurd." Moreover, the end of the draft and the inauguration of the all-volunteer force increased the percentage of the Defense Department budget spent on personnel, a shift that came at the expense of new equipment, planes, guns, missiles, ships, and operating and maintenance accounts. Contributing to the overall decline was inflation, the product of Lyndon Johnson's refusal to increase taxes to pay for either the Great Society or the Vietnam War.[5]

It fell to Admiral Elmo Zumwalt, who became CNO in May 1970, to devise the Navy's response to these alarming trends. In the 1960s, the JCS had established a "two-war" requirement to meet the goals of Kennedy's "flexible response" strategy, but the enunciation of the Nixon Doctrine, the adoption of détente and SALT I, and the collapse of the partisan political consensus behind containment meant that some reduction was in order. The result was a one-and-a-half war strategy, under which, the Navy told Congress in 1970, "the U.S. will maintain, in peacetime, general purpose forces adequate for simultaneously meeting a major communist attack in either Europe or Asia, assisting allies against non-Chinese threats in Asia, and contending with a contingency elsewhere." Zumwalt supported withdrawal from Vietnam, not only as a political necessity but also because the end of that distraction might lead to a renewed public awareness of the persistence of the Soviet threat. When Nixon signed the SALT I treaties, the CNO was disconcerted by the president's determination "to cede the Soviets' superiority in numbers and throwweight of offensive missiles." For this reason, the admiral aggressively pushed Congress to approve the new Trident ballistic missile submarine program, asserting it was "of extreme importance for us to keep well ahead of them technologically." This view was advanced in tandem with the reassuring thesis that Nixon "saw the Navy as the alternative to Massive Retaliation," a formulation that found little support in the available evidence.[6]

The offsetting edge to SALT I was strategic modernization, and the Navy's principal contribution to this was the Trident ballistic missile system. This concept of the Trident-bearing submarine was the work of Rear Admiral Levering Smith and Rear Admiral George H. Miller, who represented the Navy in 1966 when McNamara assembled the Strat-X panel under the direction of General Maxwell Taylor to study future strategic systems. McNamara's agents on the panel wanted to design a ballistic missile–bearing submarine called the "crawler," which was cheap, slow, and underpowered, but Smith and Miller selected another alternative, which Miller later described as a "rather austere" boat capable of carrying roughly twice the number of missile tubes as the Polaris-Poseidon submarines. Miller and Smith saw no particular need for deep diving capability or even great speed, arguing instead for greater silence, very long range missiles, and greater cruising radius than the Polaris-bearing submarines. They proposed to build an 8,000-ton submarine armed with sixteen launching tubes that could fire her missiles from a station about 4,000 miles from their targets. Smith and Miller argued that a new fleet ballistic missile submarine was needed within the next decade to counter improvements in Soviet antisubmarine tactics and to guarantee that the United States might retaliate against a first strike by the Russians. Admiral Harry Train recalled that he "sold the Trident" within the Pentagon and to Congress on the grounds that "the United States needed a hedge against an antisubmarine warfare breakthrough, the nature of which we could only guess."[7]

The displacement of the hull of the new Trident missile–bearing submarine grew from this early conception, owing to a number of factors. Admiral Moorer, the CNO, wanted to increase the hull size to provide spaces for more computers, a very large fire-control system, and more berthing, which would allow for longer deterrent patrols. And, when Admiral Rickover was asked to provide propulsion for the submarine, he selected the S8G reactor, a plant so large that the displacement of the hull had to be doubled to 18,700 tons. "If Rickover experienced a conflict between the needs of the ship and the needs of the reactor," observed Harold C. Hemmond, an engineer with the Electric Boat division of General Dynamics, "the reactor always won." Although the Trident submarine was now twice as large as a Polaris boat, she nonetheless sported only twenty-four missile tubes, an improvement of merely 50 percent over her predecessor in spite of an enormous increase in cost. This guaranteed that the number of ballistic missile–launching submarines would decline as the Polaris- and Poseidon-bearing boats retired and the Trident-bearing vessels entered the fleet. Although Henry Kissinger reluctantly supported the Trident program, he confessed that he "did not think much of the concept" because "each Trident risked a larger percentage of our sea-launched missile force than did its predecessors."[8]

Zumwalt's dismay at the evolution of the Trident submarine program was complete in 1970. The new CNO was under pressure from Undersecretary of Defense David Packard to reduce the hull size, but the only way to do this, as Admiral Smith pointed out, was to reduce the range of the Trident C-4 missile, an unacceptable option. Confusion and error had even victimized the issue of the number of missile tubes. Zumwalt settled on twenty tubes in an effort to limit the size of the boat, but Defense Secretary Laird mistakenly advised Nixon that twenty-four were needed, an error that neither Laird nor anyone else was willing to correct. The Trident missile promised a significant improvement over the Polaris-Poseidon–bearing submarines, however. The Poseidon C-3 missile carried ten to fourteen 50-kiloton reentry vehicles, whereas the Trident C-4 missile carried eight buses, each containing a larger number of 100-kiloton warheads or dummys. As a result, the *Ohio*-class ballistic missile–bearing submarines would possess far greater throwweight than her Poseidon-bearing predecessors. Zumwalt, aware of Rickover's eagerness to lay down the *Ohio*s, offered to support the program if Rickover would not undermine Zumwalt's high-low shipbuilding program on the Hill. Zumwalt contended that Rickover, the turgid cleric of nuclear reactions, had agreed to this arrangement but later went back on his word. Although the Navy united behind the Trident program in May 1972, Defense Secretary Laird judged it unseemly to ask Congress to authorize the lead submarine *Ohio* on the eve of Nixon's visit to Moscow, where he intended to conclude negotiations on the SALT I Treaty. However, the conservative opposition on the Hill to the administration's arms control arrangements caused Laird within a few weeks to offer up the Trident program to Congress as a vehicle by which the United States might maintain some strategic edge over the Soviets in the wake of SALT I. Zumwalt would sell "a skeptical Congress the proposition that the May 1972 strategic arms limitations agreements made a new class of missile submarines, the Trident, necessary."[9]

The two-year campaign to persuade Congress to build the *Ohio*-class Trident submarines found Admiral Zumwalt and Navy Secretary John Warner, who greatly disliked one another, energetically lobbying on Capitol Hill just when the Cold War political consensus supporting containment was about to collapse and antimilitary sentiment was at its peak. Zumwalt had, however, developed a new concept that reinforced his strategic arguments in favor of building the submarines. The Navy would, he announced, base a flotilla of the new *Ohio*-class submarines at Bangor, Washington. "The West Coast was harder for Soviet ships or planes to reach than the East Coast," he pointed out, and the great depth of Puget Sound "would make it possible for the boats to put to sea submerged and therefore unobserved." Not only would the Pacific Coast homeporting plan give the *Ohio*-class submarines more defensive sea room, but also it would increase the number of deterrent patrols in the Pacific Ocean, where Soviet antisubmarine defenses were weaker than in the Atlantic or the Mediterranean.[10]

The Pacific Coast homeporting plan had the vigorous backing of Senator Henry Jackson of Washington, a powerful moderate Democrat whose budding opposition to the SALT I treaties had begun to bloom. Because support for the Trident program was firm in the House, it was in the Senate that the liberal Democrats made their stand against it, seeking votes from Easterners on the grounds that Zumwalt's homeporting plan made the matter a regional issue. The final test came on 25 September 1973, when on a vote of forty-nine to forty-seven, the members defeated a motion by Senator Thomas McIntyre of New Hampshire to abandon the Trident program. At a "target cost" of $253 million, plus all but 5 percent of all cost overruns, General Dynamics was awarded the contract to build the first *Ohio*. "The terms of the contract were like putting an alcoholic in charge of the liquor store," claimed one former company official. Saddened by this outcome, Admiral Miller wrote that the resulting *Ohio*-class Trident-bearing submarines were "too big, and the missile was too large, and the whole program was too late."[11]

Zumwalt was the first CNO to forthrightly confront the challenge of Admiral Sergei Gorshkov's new missile-bearing Red Navy, which in 1970 regularly deployed out of home waters and had become a formidable blue-water fleet. Although the Soviet Navy was growing rapidly, especially in the number of missile-bearing ships and nuclear-powered attack submarines, Soviet ships had poor reload capacity, their logistics support was lamentable, and it was doubtful that they could sustain protracted combat operations. These factors led Zumwalt to worry that Gorshkov would adopt a surprise "shootout" strategy by surging his ships to forward stations on the eve of a conflict and then having them fire all their missiles concurrent with the outbreak of war, the aim being to instantly attrite the forward-deployed American carrier task forces. Concern about this Soviet "shootout" strategy largely animated Zumwalt's naval policy.

At the end of Moorer's term as CNO in 1970, the Navy included over 1,000 ships and 22 carriers, but these numbers would soon fall sharply, the result of the end of the Vietnam War and the effects of the bloc obsolescence of large numbers of World War II– and Korean War–era vessels. Clearly, more ships were needed simply to meet existing treaty obligations. In addition to the submarines, Zumwalt inherited another high-end program, the nuclear-powered *Nimitz*-class carrier, which was being attacked by antiwar liberal Democrats on the Hill. Congress had forced McNamara in 1966 to ask for funds for the *Nimitz*, and in the wake of the *Pueblo* crisis two years later the Navy persuaded Congress to approve construction of a sister ship, the *Eisenhower*. By 1970, however, liberal Democrats had come to view heavy attack carriers as symbols of the overly muscular interventionist policy of global containment, which they charged had led to America's disastrous involvement in the Vietnam War. "There are times when I think they [the carriers] might get us in trouble" by providing the president the means to intervene in foreign disputes, asserted Senator Walter Mondale, a neoisolationist liberal. Other forces were also at work. The Air Force, traditionally opposed to building more attack carriers, was pressing Congress for research and development funds for its B-1 manned bomber and for a third generation of highly accurate, silo-based intercontinental ballistic missiles. Thus, an unlikely coalition of antiwar Democrats and Air Force enthusiasts lined up against Admiral Moorer's request for authority to lay down the third *Nimitz*-class carrier in 1970.[12]

A bullish, drawling veteran of earlier carrier battles, Moorer seemed almost to relish the ensuing congressional hearings and another round of this old war. "The Navy is obligated to respond to comparisons which have been initiated by critics of the Navy and the opponents of the carrier," he announced triumphantly. He pointed out that the *Essex*-class antisubmarine carriers would soon all be retired and that the nuclear-powered *Enterprise* and *Nimitz*-class carriers and the oil-fired *Midway*s and *Forrestal*s would have to assume some antisubmarine missions. Because the Nixon Doctrine signaled a retrenching policy under which American troops were not to be committed to regional conflicts outside of Europe, only the heavy carriers could provide readily deployable air forces, unencumbered by foreign-controlled basing or over-flight rights that would be needed to support pro-American clients facing the aggression of Soviet proxies. Even Defense Secretary Laird, one year later, insisted that "U.S. ships and war-planes will remain on duty in Southeast Asia after the last American soldier leaves Vietnam. [They will constitute] the realistic deterrent which we will maintain in Asia."[13]

Army General Earle Wheeler, whom Moorer was about to succeed as chairman of the JCS, obliquely disagreed with the admirals' testimony, but the Navy's case carried the day, the liberals lost, and Congress approved construction of the third ship in the *Nimitz*-class, the *Carl Vinson*, later that year. Zumwalt was not entirely pleased with this outcome. Years later he confessed that he felt that so much of the Navy's strength had been invested in heavy attack carriers that "in a limited war fought in a few weeks over a limited objective, the Soviets could prevail by neutralizing most of our aircraft carriers." Nor was Laird, ever sensitive to mood swings on the Hill, anxious for another bout with the Democrats over the issue. With both the *Nimitz* and *Eisenhower* behind schedule, he waited for two years before asking for full funding of $1 billion for the *Carl Vinson* in 1972. The *Nimitz* did not enter the fleet until 1975, the *Eisenhower* not until 1977, and the *Carl Vinson* not until 1979. Owing to the cost overruns, inflation, and Zumwalt's other priorities, a decision on continuing to build the *Nimitz*s would have to await a new administration.[14]

Another vessel at the upper end of the high-low shipbuilding mix was the *Los Angeles*-class attack submarine, which Zumwalt believed to be necessary to prevent the growing fleet of nuclear-powered Soviet attack submarines from assaulting the Atlantic sea lines of communications. Okean-75, a major Soviet naval exercise, suggested that the Red Navy was developing tactics to interdict NATO-bound resupply shipping. Owing to advances in sonar technology, the completion of the second phase of the SOSUS underwater hydrophone network, and the development of effective air-dropped homing torpedoes, the U.S. Navy had withdrawn its attack submarines from their early Cold War stations off Soviet coastal waters and adopted instead a barrier strategy in the Norwegian Sea, along the Greenland–Iceland–United Kingdom line, and at chokepoints in the North Pacific. The object was to thwart the movement of Soviet attack submarines beyond the barriers and thereby prevent them from interdicting NATO-bound convoys or defending their forward-deployed ballistic missile submarines.

In devising this strategy, Zumwalt sought to apply the Nixon Doctrine to Europe, maintaining that it "called for making the naval capability of the NATO allies as large as possible in order that the United States could devote its full attention to its sea control [escort] mission." The effect of this was to abandon any thought of attacking Soviet ballistic missile–bearing submarines, a natural target for American naval forces, in or near their home waters. During the 1970s, the Soviets deployed about ten ballistic missile submarines at any time, but when the new *Delta*s, which carried longer-range missiles, entered the Soviet fleet, they preferred to operate them in the relatively safe waters of the Barents Sea and the Sea of Okhotsk. Fewer and fewer crossed the barriers and operated in the deep ocean basins within range of the U.S. Navy's lethal antisubmarine forces. By adopting a sea control and barrier strategy and conducting antisubmarine exercises in mid-ocean, Zumwalt consciously chose to avoid offensive operations in strategically sensitive regions where the enemy ballistic missile submarines were on patrol. On one occasion, the State Department even announced that this was declared U.S. strategy.

The early *Sturgeon*-class attack submarines, deployed in the 1960s and armed with long-range sonars and the SUBROC antisubmarine nuclear-tipped missile, were designed to execute a barrier and ambush strategy and to provide antisubmarine escorts for the heavy carrier task forces. A few years after the construction of the *Sturgeon*s got under way, however, McNamara withdrew the carriers from the strategic striking forces, arguing that they were hopelessly vulnerable to Soviet attack submarines and that constructing more expensive escorts would not alter this equation. In addition, by 1966 the costs of the Vietnam War had begun to escalate and LBJ refused to ask Congress for new taxes, thereby forcing McNamara to stretch out or cancel a number of current weapons projects. By this time, Admiral McDonald, the CNO, had begun to press the case for an entirely new class of attack submarine to meet the new threat of the second generation of Soviet nuclear-powered attack submarines.[15]

In selecting a new attack submarine, the Navy again faced the seemingly ageless choice between speed and stealth. The experimental submarine *Glenard Lipscomb*, which Rickover persuaded Congress to build in 1967, made only 28 knots, but the installation of a quiet electric drive instead of noisy geared turbines meant that she was a very stealthy boat. Another design, which evolved into the *Los Angeles*-class submarine, was to be powered by the new S6G reactor, which produced twice the power of the older S5W plant. When Rickover first began work on this submarine design, he promised a return to sustained speeds above 30 knots, but there was never much doubt that she would be far noisier than the older *Sturgeon*s, and the compensating speed advantage was lost when Rickover's team gave birth to a 6,900-ton monster—nearly 70 feet longer than her predecessor—equipped with similar weapons and sonars. This caused McNamara to decide to build no more nuclear attack submarines in 1967, and he refused to ask Congress for funds for the program.

Vice Admiral Philip A. Beshany, who directed the development of the *Los Angeles*-class nuclear attack submarine, found it "very difficult to persuade the internal Navy we needed speed . . . to gain an attack position against an opponent who has high speed." He recalled that "some believed we should build more *Sturgeon*-class submarines, or not build at all." Beshany was, however, supported by the CNO, Admiral Moorer, who named him to chair a board that convened to study the problem in 1968 just after McNamara left the Pentagon. Moorer "insisted that the study would be strictly operationally driven and he would not permit technical people to be involved in the decision-making process." This "annoyed" Rickover "considerably," and he sent "an observer [who] . . . monitored the board's final recommendations." Rickover's "approach was at odds with [Defense Department Research Director] Dr. Foster's. The admiral was concerned with the propulsion system, which would provide twice as much power . . . and thought that we should settle for a restructured 637-class submarine," according to Beshany. "Foster said, 'Admiral Rickover just wants to trot out another reactor, and we can't afford that.'" Foster would allow Rickover to have the development

Secretary of the Navy John W. Warner (*left*) and President Richard M. Nixon (*right*) congratulate Admiral Hyman G. Rickover on his promotion to four-star admiral in 1972.

money, but Foster was "not going to build a class of ships—bigger submarines—with no more capability than the 637." Deputy Secretary of Defense Paul Nitze had "developed his own design for a small submarine, predicated on the *Narwhal* reactor," which was a "very quiet submarine." Rickover opposed Nitze's plan, and Moorer "decided [that] he wanted his [own] program to move ahead and would not permit interferences."[16]

While these forces were deadlocked in Washington, Captain Kent Lee guided the nuclear carrier *Enterprise* through the narrow shipping channel in San Francisco Bay out into the eastern Pacific on 5 January 1968 en route to join the Tonkin Gulf Task Force on Yankee Station. During his first day at sea, Lee received a highly secret warning from the Navy Department that SOSUS passive ocean-floor hydrophones had located a Russian *November*-class nuclear attack submarine and that she was closing on the *Enterprise*'s position several hundred miles to the north. Neither naval intelligence nor the CIA had been able to pinpoint the speed of this class of Soviet submarines, but they guessed it to be about 25 knots. Admiral Moorer decided that the *November*'s plan to shadow the *Enterprise* provided him with an ideal opportunity to induce the Soviet captain to show his flank speed, and Moorer instructed Lee to power up his eight reactors slowly to over 35

The 3,600-ton guided missile frigates *Wadsworth* (FFG-9) and *George Philip* (FFG-12). An *Oliver Hazard Perry*-class frigate, the *Wadsworth* was laid down in July 1977 and commissioned on 2 April 1980. Armed with a launcher for Harpoon anti-ship and Standard air-to-air missiles, she is fitted with a pad to operate a LAMPS anti-submarine helicopter.

The *Los Angeles*-class nuclear-powered attack submarine *Minneapolis-St. Paul* (SSN-708).

knots. To the surprise of both men, however, the *November* easily matched the carrier's speed, closed the distance between the two vessels, and trailed the American ship to Pearl Harbor with power to spare.

The incident between the *Enterprise* and the *November* made urgent the business of building a new class of attack submarines to replace the *Sturgeons*, as the attack boats were now assigned to defend the carrier task forces against the faster Soviet nuclear attack boats. This problem was acute owing to the fact that fewer than half of the American attack submarines in commission in 1968 were powered by nuclear plants. Admiral Moorer had two options. Rear Admiral Jamie Adair and Captain Donald H. Kern favored the Conform, a design incorporating a new General Electric natural-circulation reactor and a radical hull shape capable of sustained speeds in excess of 45 knots. An early version of this small reactor had been installed in the submarine *Narwhal*, but Admiral Rickover, whose mean-spirited control of the nuclear submarine program was at its zenith, disliked the concept and ruggedly opposed the Conform project. His alternative was the *Los Angeles*-class submarine, but there was considerable opposition within the Navy to building this vessel. Research chief Foster favored building a quiet, slow, and costly electric drive system much like the one installed in the experimental submarine *Lipscomb* in 1966. He particularly disliked the *Los Angeles*-class design and tried in 1967 to terminate the program. Although in theory Rickover's writ covered only nuclear reactors and, as Foster told Congress, Rickover "claimed no expertise in other aspects of the boat," in practice Rickover had for many years tried to dictate every aspect of the design of all nuclear submarines.

When Foster attempted to kill the program by delays, Rickover sought aid from his allies in Congress. Representative Chet Holifield knew little about naval affairs, but Rickover used shameless flattery to transform Holifield into his mouthpiece on Capitol Hill. Also in Rickover's corner was Senator Stuart Symington, a former secretary of the Air Force, who disliked the Navy with an intensity he could barely articulate and so consistently supported Rickover in an effort to rub salt into the Navy's wound. Senator John Stennis, the chairman of the Armed Services Committee, held hearings on the attack submarine question in the spring of 1968. He was uninterested in the details, but he wanted the Navy to build a new fast attack submarine to counter the growing Soviet naval menace. Inspired by Rickover, Symington mauled Foster during these hearings until Admiral Moorer came up with a compromise: he and Rickover agreed to name a special board, headed by Captain Joe Williams, a highly respected submariner, that would select the design for the new boat. The Williams Board, instructed by Moorer to pick the fastest submarine, soon discovered that Captain Kern's design for the Conform was in many respects superior to that of the much slower *Los Angeles*-class, but the board finally chose the latter design on the basis of overall characteristics.[17]

Meanwhile, Rear Admiral Zumwalt, then working on the problem in the Pentagon, had persuaded his confidant, Deputy Secretary Nitze, to oppose building the *Los Angeles*-class submarines, but Nitze refused to challenge Rickover in front of Congress without Foster's support, and the Williams Board's findings persuaded him to drop the matter. For all practical purposes, Rickover had convinced Senator Stennis to give the fleet a new attack submarine whether the Navy Department wanted it or not. Admiral Moorer, who distrusted Foster and truly reviled McNamara, derived an almost feline pleasure from the simple accomplishment of getting Congress to approve a shipbuilding project that the former secretary of defense stridently opposed. With backing from Stennis and Congressman Holifield, Moorer persuaded the administration and Congress in 1968 to authorize the construction of the lead boat in the class. Rickover rewarded Holifield for his support by naming this lead submarine the *Los Angeles*, the city containing Holifield's district. Zumwalt, who succeeded Moorer as CNO in 1970, believed the *Los Angeles*-class submarines to be too slow, vulnerable, and costly, but he inherited a program he could do little to derail. To get support from Rickover in return for his backing for the *Los Angeles*-class program, Zumwalt negotiated an arrangement under which Rickover promised not to lobby against Zumwalt's high-low mix on Capitol Hill and Zumwalt agreed to support the attack submarine construction before Congress. "All I wanted Admiral Rickover to do was to go along with, at least tolerate quietly, my new [shipbuilding] programs. On 2 June 1970 he agreed to do so." This arrangement, of course, did not last.[18]

Chapter Thirty-one

The End of the Vietnam War
1969–1973

Richard Nixon's decision in 1969 to continue the fruitless public Paris peace talks freed North Vietnam from the burden of defending itself against American airpower for three years. Then the 1972 Easter Offensive erupted. What made this campaign possible was the Soviet conviction that the Sino-Soviet split was irreparable and that China's newly acquired nuclear-tipped ballistic missiles endangered Russia's maritime provinces. The triumph of Mao Tse-tung's anti-Soviet faction in China's great Cultural Revolution and Nixon's shrewd triangular diplomacy meant that a rapprochement between the communist powers was unlikely. Rumors were abroad in 1970 and 1971 that the Soviets intended to launch a preemptive first strike to destroy China's nuclear arsenal, but Nixon and Kissinger sternly warned Moscow against such a dangerous step. The result was that the Brezhnev regime devised a countervailing strategy to which Southeast Asia was one key.

Since 1964, the Soviets had shipped arms to North Vietnam to provide for the air defense of her home territory and to support the Vietcong in South Vietnam. This activity embarrassed the United States, while not creating enough friction to cause a clash between the superpowers. Indeed, it led many American diplomats to want to appease Moscow so that she would reduce her support for Hanoi. Nixon's retrenching policy lessened the likelihood of a superpower confrontation in Southeast Asia, and the Sino-Soviet split provided a new motive behind the Kremlin's strategy in the war. Brezhnev decided in 1971 that a North Vietnamese victory over South Vietnam, Cambodia, and Laos would create a durable Soviet client on China's southern flank. This explained Warsaw Pact shipments to North Vietnam that year that featured a new mix of tanks, self-propelled guns, and heavy vehicles, arms that Hanoi needed to mount its full-scale invasion of South Vietnam in the spring of 1972.[1]

The Americans first noticed these preparations late in 1971, when the pilot of a Navy aircraft flying a photo-reconnaissance mission over the Laotian border saw a North Vietnamese ground crew pushing a new Soviet-built MiG-21 fighter into a cave at the Quang Lang airbase. Vice Admiral William P. Mack, who commanded the 7th Fleet, wanted to test the mettle of the new enemy fighter and so he devised a special Blue Tree operation to provoke the North Vietnamese into sending up the MiG-21s. Under Nixon's rules of engagement, American fighters might challenge these communist aircraft only during protective-reaction missions. Flying off the *Constellation* on 19 January 1972, a section of RA-5B Vigilantes photo-reconnaissance planes crossed into Laotian airspace and flew over Quang Lang, drawing intense fire from the ground—the precondition for launching a protective-reaction strike. These planes were followed closely by escorting A-6 Intruders and A-7 Corsairs, which bombed and strafed the communist airfield. To pounce on any MiGs that arose to defend Quang Lang was a section of F-4 Phantoms loitering on station five miles to the north. Unfortunately, the combat intelligence for this operation was poor, and the Phantoms found themselves positioned directly above a pair of deadly surface-to-air missile sites, whose operators quickly fired a barrage at a Phantom flown by Lieutenant Randy Cunningham and his bombardier, Lieutenant Willie Driscoll. Maneuvering to avoid the missiles, Driscoll caught sight of two MiG-21s escaping from Quang Lang, and Cunningham dipped down to pursue them. In a running air battle at speeds of up to 690 miles per hour often as low as 500 feet above the tree line, Cunningham lost one of the North Vietnamese aircraft but caught up with her partner and shot her down with a close-range Sidewinder missile.

The air battle over Quang Lang preceded the North Vietnamese Easter Offensive, which began on 31 March 1972. When Admiral Zumwalt, as CNO, visited South Vietnam in February, he was warned that the renewed aggressiveness of the North Vietnamese Air Force coupled with the movement of the communist armies into Laos, Cambodia, and north of the DMZ were signals of an impending major operation. The commander of the residue of American forces in South Vietnam, General Creighton Abrams, knew that the Communists were massing troops north of the frontier, but the attack across the DMZ nonetheless caught both Americans and South Vietnamese unprepared. Crushed by the Communists' armor, Saigon's troops disintegrated. Owing to Nixon's policy of Vietnamization of the battlefront, only a handful of American Marine advisers were available around Danang and elsewhere to support the defenders in I Corps. For example, from nearly 40,000 men in 1969, Rear Admiral Robert Salzer's naval command in South Vietnam was reduced to only 10,000 sailors three years later.[2]

Nixon told Admiral Moorer, the JCS chairman, that he wanted "to give the North Vietnamese a bloody nose," but he reacted slowly to the Easter Offensive. Defense Secretary Laird believed that the American public was so weary of the war and so disenchanted with Thieu's dictatorship that Washington should stand aside and let Saigon defend its own interests. Moorer, on the other hand, backed a plan drafted by Admiral McCain, the commander in chief of the Pacific theater, to bomb Hanoi and Haiphong, mine Haiphong harbor, and blockade North Vietnam. Nixon rejected these steps until 15 April, when communist artillery reached Danang's outskirts and shelled the city. In a replay of LBJ's 1964 sustained reprisal policy, Nixon then ordered a single retaliatory attack, codenamed Freedom Train, by Air Force B-52 bombers against the Hanoi-Haiphong oil complex. This had no effect. On May Day the North Vietnamese captured Quang Tri City and advanced on Hue, throwing the city's defenders into panic and creating a riot among the refugees there. Admiral Salzer in Saigon agreed with General Abrams' assessment that the battle would soon turn into a "rout."[3]

Admiral Moorer ordered Zumwalt on 4 May to prepare a plan to retaliate against North Vietnam and not to inform Laird or the other chiefs of his work. Aware that Laird opposed a renewal of the bombing, Moorer and Nixon evidently feared that if he learned of the plan, he would try to undermine it by leaking details to liberals in Congress. Zumwalt preferred mining over a blockade inasmuch as mine warfare was "cheap and relatively

safe and extremely threatening," but by this time both Nixon and
Moorer wanted to use more force. The president appeared on
television four days later to announce that Navy and Marine aircraft from the carrier *Coral Sea* were sowing mines in Haiphong
harbor that would be activated in three days. This operation,
codenamed Pocket Money, was so effective that no vessels entered the harbor for over 300 days. Nixon also announced the
start of Linebacker I air operations against targets in North Vietnam and publicly authorized the "hot pursuit" of communist aircraft into Chinese airspace, although this permission was soon secretly rescinded. For the first time in the war, however, targeting
became a responsibility of the local air commanders, who could
finally strike and restrike targets in North Vietnam at will.
Nonetheless, at the last minute before Nixon's announcement,
Laird convinced the president not to allow American bombers to
attack and lay waste to the population centers of Hanoi or
Haiphong.[4]

Linebacker I began on the night of 9 May. Targets including
rails and roads to China, munitions depots, and fuel farms were
attacked, as were the Thanh Hoa and Paul Doumer bridges, two
spans that had resisted American bombing during the Rolling
Thunder campaign. Naval aircraft also struck the Hanoi Power
Plant in the center of the North Vietnamese capital, as well as
other military targets in the suburbs of Hanoi and Haiphong.
Walleye bombs and bombs guided to their targets by lasers and
wires increased bombing accuracy and, for the first time since
the Flaming Dart operations of 1965, gave the American aircraft
an edge over North Vietnam's fixed defenses. Under presidential
orders that "all entrances to North Vietnamese ports will be
mined," A-6 Intruders and A-7 Corsairs from the carriers *Coral
Sea*, *Midway*, and *Constellation* planted aerial mines in the harbors
of Haiphong, Hon Gai, Cam Pha, and Thanh Hoa in the northern sector and at Vinh, Quang Khe, and Dong Hoi in the panhandle. The North Vietnamese ferociously defended their home
territory, firing salvos of surface-to-air missiles at the rate of
about 500 each month, and her MiG fighters began to stir. During the night of the 9th, the cruiser *Chicago* fired a Talos missile
that splashed one MiG over Haiphong harbor. The following day,
forty-one North Vietnamese Air Force fighters went aloft to challenge the Americans for air superiority. Nixon had belatedly lifted all restrictions on air attacks against most areas of Haiphong

and several other targets in North Vietnam, and Admiral Mack began to launch three strikes daily against different locations in an effort to confuse the defenders.[5]

The first strike on 10 May was a joint Navy–Air Force Alpha mission that included planes from the *Constellation* and hit oil storage depots north of Haiphong. The second attack pounded railroad yards at Hai Duong between the port and the capital. Four F-4 Phantoms flew ahead of the formation to suppress flak, while on their flanks pairs of A-7 Corsairs launched Shrike missiles against defending missile radars. Next came more Phantoms. They conducted bombing runs and rocket attacks, then pulled ahead and above the formation to defend against attacking MiGs while an American destroyer near Yankee Station in the Gulf watched the air battle on radar. While Lieutenant Randy Cunningham became the Navy's only wartime "ace" that day by adding three MiGs to the two he had already splashed, the North Vietnamese claimed six American aircraft at the cost of eleven of their own planes. Over Hai Duong, North Vietnamese MiGs overwhelmed the attackers and forced them to retreat temporarily to the safety of the task force. Air Force fighter-bombers finally destroyed a large span of the well-defended Dragon's Jaw Bridge near Thanh Hoa, and Navy and Air Force restrikes kept it shut down for the rest of the year. Subsequent Linebacker I operations so crippled the enemy's transportation system that most of the major bridges between the Chinese frontier and the Red River Delta and south into the panhandle were rendered useless and the railroad system was left in shreds. North Vietnam turned increasingly to truck transport, but the mining of Haiphong and the destruction of several oil pipelines by American air forces limited the movement of enemy vehicles. As a result, Hanoi could not support its armored and mechanized divisions in South Vietnam, the spearhead in the Easter Offensive.

The renewal of the air war over North Vietnam demonstrated the vast improvements in American naval aviation since the beginning of Rolling Thunder in 1965. From 1963 to 1973, about 3,700 Air Force, Navy, and Marine aircraft were lost in combat in Indochina. Enemy antiaircraft batteries—many defending fixed targets—accounted for roughly 85 percent of this figure. Nearly 1,000 planes were lost over North Vietnam, and about 700 airmen died during various bombing campaigns, and American losses in aerial combat were also high. More disturbing, however,

U.S. Naval Institute

Admiral Thomas H. Moorer. Chief of Naval Operations, 1967–1970; Chairman, Joint Chiefs of Staff, 1970 1974.

was the fact that from 1965 to 1969 only two enemy fighters were splashed for each American plane that went down, a two-to-one exchange rate that compared unfavorably with a ten-to-one exchange rate during the Korean War. This was especially troubling for naval aviators because North Vietnam saved its new MiG-21 fighters for the Air Force's Thunderchiefs and Phantoms and threw its older, slower MiG-17s against the Navy's Crusaders and Phantoms. Most Navy losses resulted from unseen MiGs that crept up behind the wingline and were identified only when they were already sliding in for a missile shot. To reverse this unsettling trend, the Navy's Top Gun School was established in 1967 at Miramar Naval Air Station so that naval fighter pilots might hone their skills in air-to-air combat before deploying to the numbered fleets. From 1969 to 1973, the exchange rate for Navy aircraft improved to about twelve-to-one, and during Linebacker operations in 1972 naval aviators were once again able to aggressively go after North Vietnamese MiGs. From 1965 to 1971, naval aviators shot down twenty-nine MiGs, all with Sidewinders, but during 1972 alone, at least twenty-four MiGs were splashed, again mostly with Sidewinder missiles.

To intensify air operations against North Vietnam, Admiral Moorer surged aircraft carriers into the Gulf of Tonkin, and by July 1972, six were operating with the Tonkin Gulf Task Force. Once again they engaged the enemy in both North and South Vietnam on a daily basis. Moorer even persuaded Nixon to authorize strikes against North Vietnamese railroads near the Chinese border, which the American land-based and carrier bombers soon left in wreckage. From May to September 1972, naval aircraft flew an average of 4,000 day and night sorties each month and accounted for 60 percent of the combat sorties launched in support of South Vietnamese ground operations. The combination of Linebacker I bombing of North Vietnam, the mining of Haiphong harbor, and the close ground support provided to the South Vietnamese Army finally blunted the Easter Offensive, but when it ended in June the Communists still occupied most of Quang Tri Province.

North Vietnam's success in the Easter Offensive led directly to the Paris Peace Accords of January 1973. During the battle for Quang Tri Province, Hanoi learned that the South Vietnamese Army would break without American air, artillery, and naval support. On the other hand, American mining and air operations against Haiphong harbor had soon shut down the communist offensive in the south. In short, getting American air and naval forces out of Indochina became North Vietnam's foremost diplomatic objective. Before 1972, Hanoi ambassador Le Duc Tho had demanded in secret negotiations in Paris that Henry Kissinger agree to a coalition government in Saigon prior to an armistice, but Kissinger had refused to dismantle Thieu's regime for Hanoi and required instead a ceasefire before a new coalition government took power in South Vietnam. Neither Kissinger nor Le Duc Tho believed that Thieu could survive once North Vietnam resumed offensive operations.

North Vietnam occupied so much South Vietnamese territory after the Easter Offensive that Le Duc Tho was now willing to agree to a ceasefire in place and allow Thieu to remain in Saigon if the Americans promised to withdraw all their forces. For his part, Kissinger believed that American public opinion had turned so strongly against the war that he had no choice but to accept this hitherto unsatisfactory arrangement. Indeed, Nixon barely mentioned the Saigon regime in May and June and shrewdly portrayed the summer air offensive and the closing of North Vietnam's ports as a means of hastening the withdrawal of American forces from Southeast Asia. Although both Admiral Moorer and Admiral Noel Gayler, the new commander in chief of the Pacific theater, bitterly opposed the terms of the agreement on the grounds that Kissinger had not provided for the long-term security of the Saigon government, the political force at home behind withdrawal was irresistible. From the Paris talks Kissinger returned to Washington in triumph in October 1972 and announced that "peace is at hand."[6]

The end of the Vietnam War was linked to the 1972 presidential elections. The Republicans renominated Nixon; the Democrats turned to the left and chose South Dakota Senator George McGovern, who promised to end the war forthwith, reduce defense spending by half, and eliminate many of America's global military obligations. Nixon crushed McGovern in a landslide in early November, but liberal Democrats nonetheless strengthened their hold on Congress and they were now more determined than ever to end the war by legislation when they reconvened in January 1973. The North Vietnamese, supposing that they would get better armistice terms out of Nixon after Congress reconvened in January 1973, demanded in late November that several major provisions in the treaty be changed. This bold step led to the breakdown of the Paris talks.

Nixon, who had to do something to save the Paris arrangement before Congress came back to Washington, turned to Admiral Moorer, instructing him on 18 December 1972 to bring North Vietnam to her knees. "This is your chance to use military power to win this war," Nixon told Moorer. For the first time in the war, American airpower was applied against the vitals of the enemy. On 18 December 1972, Operation Linebacker II began when Admiral Gayler dispatched Air Force B-52 bombers from Guam and F-111 fighter-bombers against Hanoi. A-6 Intruders and EA-6 Intruders from the Tonkin Gulf Task Force supported the heavy bombers in special missions, but the aging B-52s bore the brunt of the offensive and withstood the enemy's furious missile defenses, which vainly tried to protect the communist capital. Protests by Democrats, liberal Republicans, and North Vietnamese sympathizers in the United States escalated into a crescendo of pressure on the Nixon White House, and Kissinger even abandoned Nixon by allowing the press to report without contradiction that he opposed the president's decision to conduct Linebacker II. During late December, something of a race ensued between the extent of damage the bombing inflicted on North Vietnam and the amount of political opposition Nixon was willing to tolerate in Washington. This contest lasted until 29 December, when Le Duc Tho, the North Vietnamese envoy, stunned by the damage to Hanoi and Haiphong, conveyed a message to Kissinger that he was ready to resume the talks. The Christmas bombing, lasting only eleven days, devastated large sections of the North Vietnamese capital, while killing only about 1,100 civilians, and forced the Communists to return to the bargaining table, where they agreed to the Paris Peace Accords of January 1973.[7]

The agreement referred to Vietnam as one nation, which Hanoi wanted, but mentioned nothing about South Vietnam's sovereignty, which Kissinger had already bargained away. The North Vietnamese dropped their demand that General Thieu be ousted and were rewarded with a tripartite electoral commission composed of representatives of the Vietcong, the Saigon government, and South Vietnamese neutralists, which was to supervise the ceasefire. Thus, the accords explicitly admitted the illegitimacy of South Vietnam's government. In exchange for releasing all American prisoners of war, the North Vietnamese received a promise that all American forces would withdraw from South Vietnam within sixty days, leaving only a small military aid mission in Saigon. On the other hand, Kissinger agreed to allow the North Vietnamese Army and the Vietcong to remain in place in northern South Vietnam, thus conceding to them the territory that they had conquered during the Easter Offensive. Thieu was apoplectic over these conditions and threatened to disrupt the ceasefire; he had no intention of sharing power and rightly felt that the Americans were deserting his cause.

Nixon warned that, regardless of Thieu's position, he intended to sign the treaty with North Vietnam and withdraw all American forces from South Vietnam. If Thieu agreed to ratify the treaty, Nixon said, then the United States promised to continue aid to Saigon and "respond with full force" should the Communists violate the ceasefire. Thieu had no choice but to sign the accords, although in doing so he accepted the coin of American aid and promises, the political value of which the upcoming Watergate scandal would soon debase. The Christmas bombing and the Paris Peace Accords were a fitting end to the frustrating air war, a poignant illustration of the political utility of strategic airpower against North Vietnam, and a baleful demonstration of the wrongfulness of McNamara's earlier gradual escalation of Operation Rolling Thunder. The Paris Peace Accords, Admiral Kenneth Veth recorded bitterly, were little more than "an invitation for the war to continue at some later date."[8]

The last allied combat operation of the Vietnam War began on the evening of 26 January, when the South Vietnamese Marines mounted an amphibious assault with sixteen tanks and supporting artillery against an enemy position on a small sandspit on the northern edge of the Cua Viet River. To force the North Vietnamese to the other side of the river, the South Vietnamese landed, secured a bridgehead about one-half mile deep, and pushed the enemy into the water with the support of American air strikes. In the midst of the battle, at 0600 on 27 January 1973, the ceasefire took effect and American air support for the South Vietnamese Marines holding the sandspit ended. An American adviser wrote that "the North Vietnamese didn't obey the cease-fire. They opened up with everything from the other side of the river. We couldn't do anything because the air support was turned off." By the end of March, all American forces had left South Vietnam.[9]

On 3 March, Rear Admiral William Lawrence was released by the North Vietnamese after being imprisoned since 1967, and with him came the rest of the 651 American prisoners of war taken by the Communists during the Vietnam War. Malnourished, mistreated, and frequently tortured, they served as pawns for Hanoi and Washington but received the only heroes' welcome of the war when they returned home. A few had aided the enemy, but most stolidly upheld the Code of Conduct in the face of tremendous adversity. Most American prisoners were pilots and career officers, and a large number of these men lost years of professional training during their captivity. Many returned to broken marriages and fractured careers. A few, including Vice Admirals Lawrence and James Stockdale, made major contributions to naval education by infusing the Naval Academy and the Naval War College with the intellectual toughness they had sharpened during their imprisonment. Others, including Rear Admiral Jeremiah Denton and Captain John S. McCain III, remained on active duty for a few years, then translated their skills into electoral politics. A few went berserk. Most melded back into the normal pursuits of American life.

On 6 February 1973, the 7th Fleet's Mine Countermeasure Force began Operation Endsweep to clear all American mines from North Vietnam's coastal waters and remove the Mark 36 destructors from North Vietnam's inland waterways. During the first two weeks of this effort, a pair of destroyers escorted four oceangoing minesweepers, which cleared anchorages off the coast around Haiphong. On 27 February, they were joined by five amphibious ships carrying thirty-one Navy and Marine CH-53 Sea Stallion helicopters, which were invaluable during sweeping operations along the inland waterways. Also cleared were the ports of Hon Gai and Cam Pha as well as the coastal waters off Vinh. After a six-month effort, which involved forty-seven American ships and tugs, Endsweep was complete. The 7th Fleet left North Vietnamese waters for the last time in the Vietnam War.

Chapter Thirty-two

The Interregnum
1974–1976

Free of the Vietnam War after 1973, American strategists turned their attention to the Middle East, where the long-awaited decline of Europe's imperial power was creating a vacuum that endangered Western interests. American commercial relations with Iran went back to World War I, but the tie became a political concern during World War II owing to the strategic importance of Iran's oil and the wartime Anglo-Soviet occupation. In 1946, Truman reinforced Tehran's demand that the Red Army leave northern Iran, and the JCS highlighted the continuing importance of Iranian oil exports for the revival of the economies and military arms of western Europe. Iran's link with the West was threatened again in 1951 by the ascension of Premier Mohammed Mossadegh, a cagy radical who drove Shah Reza Pahlavi into exile and adopted a uniformly hostile attitude toward the West. Two years later, Eisenhower employed the CIA to turn out Mossadegh and restore the shah, who, while recognized as a weak reed, was nonetheless valued for his anti-Soviet posturing.

Following the 1958 Lebanon adventure, Eisenhower signed a bilateral defense treaty with Iran guaranteeing her "independence and territorial integrity." To support this commitment, the Navy had already sent the three-ship Middle East Force into the Persian Gulf, and Admiral Arleigh Burke, the CNO, established a separate Indian Ocean Naval Area as part of the domain of the commander in chief of the Eastern Atlantic and Mediterranean theater. In 1960, Rear Admiral John M. Lee persuaded Admiral Burke and Assistant Secretary of Defense Paul Nitze to propose that a Navy facility be established in the Indian Ocean on Diego Garcia, an eleven-square-mile horseshoe-shaped atoll of low-lying coral and sand, the largest of the five islands constituting the Chagos Archipelago. About 1,200 miles from the southernmost tip of India, Diego Garcia long had been governed by the British as part of the Mauritius Territory. Lee's concept was to use Diego Garcia to support the movement of a carrier task force into the Indian Ocean and to follow this up by sending Polaris-bearing submarines on war patrols in those waters to carry out the Navy's "stressing" strategy. Prime Minister Harold Macmillan considered the Indian Ocean an area of exclusive British naval hegemony, however, so it was not until Labour's Harold Wilson ousted the Tories in 1964 and hastened the process of imperial withdrawal that the issue surfaced again in Washington.[1]

Britain's decline, the United States' ties with Pakistan and Iran, and Soviet attempts to forge an alliance with India drew the Navy inexorably into the Indian Ocean. Successive presidents backed the shah, but his truculence and autocratic ways often strained relations between Tehran and Washington. These tensions were exacerbated when, in 1961, Kennedy tied American foreign aid to Iran to a reduction in the size of Iran's army and a modest program of land reform. Upon hearing this news, the shah's opponents organized riots that rocked Tehran until his army and police put the uprising down without mercy. The episode reinforced the shah's view that democracy was an inappropriate vehicle for his plan to modernize Iranian politics and industrialize her economy.

Iran's instability, a drawdown of British forces in the region, and the absence of Soviet antisubmarine forces in the Indian Ocean led Admiral George Anderson in 1963 to propose that the United States lease Diego Garcia from the British and that the Navy dredge a forty-foot channel in the lagoon for a carrier anchorage. This project was suspended owing to Secretary McNamara's rejection of additional overseas bases and commitments and his general opposition to any policy that increased the need for forward-deployed carriers. In 1964, Lyndon Johnson reversed Kennedy's foreign aid policy by giving Iran $100 million and by lifting Kennedy's restrictions on Iran's purchase of American arms. He also improved ties with Pakistan and agreed to the initiation of the Polaris-bearing deterrent patrols in the Indian Ocean. McNamara resisted extending American military obligations, however, and he vetoed Admiral David McDonald's 1965 plan to support these deterrent patrols by establishing an Indian Ocean station for an antisubmarine task force.

The CNO persisted and, in 1966, convinced McNamara to get Secretary Rusk to negotiate with the British on 30 December a fifty-year executive agreement that permitted the use of Diego Garcia for a fleet radio center, which was intended to supplement the older Asmara, Ethiopia, station. Nevertheless, both McNamara and Rusk stiffly opposed extending the Navy's presence into the Indian Ocean, the Arabian Sea, or the Persian Gulf, thus reinforcing the shah's low level of confidence in American guarantees. This was also shaken by Johnson's refusal to support Muslim Pakistan in her unsuccessful 1965 war against Hindu India. To the Johnson administration, facing the ongoing escalation of the Vietnam War, new commitments in this region were unwise, and the costs of Indochina operations increased so quickly that neither McDonald nor his successor, Admiral Thomas Moorer, were able to exploit the Diego Garcia agreement. The strategic calculus of Southwest Asia changed abruptly in January 1968, when Prime Minster Harold Wilson announced that he would withdraw all British forces "east of Suez" by 1971, thus conceding Britain's unwillingness and inability to sustain its historic commitments beyond western Europe.

At the same time, relations between India and Russia warmed, and in March of that year the Soviets established their first naval presence in the Indian Ocean when Admiral Gorshkov sent a task force comprising a *Sverdlovsk*-class cruiser, a *Kashin*-class destroyer, and a *Kruppy*-class guided missile destroyer to visit Indian ports for four months before returning to the Red Navy's Pacific Fleet base at Vladivostok. More Soviet warships entered the Indian Ocean later in the year, and in December Gorshkov established a fleet anchorage on the Fortune Bank off the Seychelles. Under the terms of a friendship treaty signed in New Delhi on the eve of the Bangladesh War, the Indians allowed the Soviets to erect a naval supply depot and training base at Vishakhapatnam, a port on India's east coast. Far to the west, the Soviets could count on backing from Tanzania's socialist regime, which offered the Russians the use of the port of Dar es Salaam and allowed them to establish an uncommonly large military mission on the offshore island of Zanzibar. The Soviet presence also increased in the Arabian Sea. In the early 1970s, the Soviets established an anchorage off Socotra Island at the eastern end of the Gulf of Aden and, by 1972, had obtained basing rights for their land-based naval aircraft to operate from Aden, Conakry, and Luanda. They also improved their ties with the Iraqis, who attacked Kuwait in 1973 and occupied a strip of Kuwaiti territory in an effort to acquire all the land approaches to the Iraqi naval base at Umm Qasr. The Soviets were not eager to support their clients' adventurism, however, and often imposed a restraining hand. Admiral Gorshkov sent a task force to visit Umm Qasr and personally flew to Baghdad for talks, and the Iraqis withdrew from Kuwait twenty-fours later.

This feverish Russian naval activity in the region unnerved the shah, who was facing a constant threat from enemies on his own frontier. In 1967, Communists armed by Moscow took over South Yemen, and a year later Iraq's new Baath Party regime cemented more intimate military ties with the Soviet Union. Shortly thereafter, the Iraqis began backing insurgencies in the Iranian provinces of Baluchistan and Kurdistan and loudly announced their claim to Iranian territory in the Shatt-al-Arab region and Khuzistan. Mired in the Vietnam War, the United States did nothing to support the shah's friends. Although Nixon "tilted" in favor of Iran's ally, Pakistan, during the Bangladesh War, sending a task force built around the carrier *Independence* into the Indian Ocean, he refused to do more and stood by, to the shah's dismay, while the Indian Army invaded and dismembered Pakistan.[2]

Admiral Zumwalt, the CNO, was chagrined by the difficulty of maintaining the *Independence* task force in the Indian Ocean during the Bangladesh War. The lack of facilities in that area was compounded by the loss of the use of the fine South African naval base at Simonstown. This was a result of pressure from black and liberal Democrats in Congress who wanted to disassociate the United States from the white government in Pretoria. Since assuming command of the Pacific theater in 1968, Admiral John S. McCain had urged the JCS to establish a new 5th Fleet, to station it in the Indian Ocean, and to develop Diego Garcia as a counter to the surge of Soviet forces into that area. An austere communications facility was established on the island two years later, and soon after, Nixon, alarmed by the Russo-Indian coalition, agreed to McCain's plan. On 24 October 1972, Washington and London exchanged notes that expanded the 1966 executive agreement on Diego Garcia to allow the United States to improve the lagoon anchorage, extend the 8,000-foot runway, and improve the fuel storage facilities. Zumwalt then persuaded the State Department to negotiate a simple fifty-year lease of Diego Garcia from the British, and on 20 March 1973 an American naval station was established on the island. The urgency of developing Diego Garcia increased when the Bahrainis threatened to expel the three-ship Middle East Force from its anchorage in the Persian Gulf in the aftermath of the Yom Kippur War, although Kissinger's rapprochement with the moderate Arab regimes led the Bahrainis to allow their eviction deadline to pass by without notice. However, this unsettling episode illuminated the fragility of the American position in the Middle East and Southwest Asia.

As a result, in 1974, Zumwalt persuaded Defense Secretary James Schlesinger to agree to a permanent naval base to support a carrier task force in the Indian Ocean, a decision that was also influenced by increasing Soviet naval activity in nearby Somalia, South Yemen, and Iraq. The JCS had sent a task force built around the carrier *Hancock* into the Arabian Sea for several months in 1973, and the following year Schlesinger and Zumwalt agreed "to keep a carrier . . . [in the Indian Ocean] permanently." Zumwalt asked Congress to authorize the construction of an 8,000-foot runway and an enlarged anchorage at Diego Garcia, but this measure was nearly defeated by liberal Democrats. It was, he observed, "a poor man's counter to the facilities in the Indian Ocean with which the Soviet Navy is now richly endowed." In 1974, Zumwalt got more funds to enlarge the anchorage and extend the runway. In the Senate, however, where anger with the Nixon administration was reaching its zenith, Zumwalt found "much fear" that these measures "implied an under-the-table commitment to some nation or nations in the area."[3]

Senate Democratic Majority Leader Mike Mansfield, a neo-isolationist who wanted to return Okinawa to Japan and withdraw American troops from NATO and the Far East, charged that President Ford, who succeeded Nixon in August 1974, was unnecessarily extending the Cold War into the Indian Ocean. On 19 May 1975, Mansfield introduced a resolution to cut funds for Diego Garcia from the annual Defense Department appropriations bill. Iowa's Senator John Culver, a liberal Democrat, de-

clared that "if we proceed with this expansion in the Indian
Ocean . . . then we will indeed be simply replaying the first act of
a scenario identical with that which took us into the quagmire of
Vietnam." Instead of "automatic military escalation and gunboat
diplomacy," Culver suggested adopting "peaceful, less costly, no-
risk alternatives" such as Indian Prime Minister Indira Gandhi's
scheme to create an Indian Ocean Zone of Peace excluding the
fleets of both great powers. However, Schlesinger exploited the
discovery of a large Soviet missile-handling base at the Somali
port of Berbera in 1975 to persuade Congress to agree to major
improvements to Diego Garcia that year.

Over the next few years, Diego Garcia's lagoon was deep-
ened to accommodate a *Nimitz*-class carrier and a dozen ships of
her battle group—a new term devised by Admiral James Holloway, who became CNO in 1974, to describe a carrier or battleship task force—and a 12,000-foot runway was paved to allow the
air station to handle P-3 Orion maritime patrol aircraft from the
Philippines and, after 1985, Air Force B-52 bomber flights from
Guam. Diego Garcia was really not suitable for a major American
naval base, however. While a Marine battalion landing team
might reach Diego Garcia from Okinawa within two days, its
heavy combat equipment would not arrive by sealift for another
five weeks, the result being that the island was virtually undefended. Nonetheless, an increasing American naval presence in the
Indian Ocean region was the only way, according to Admiral Holloway of "demonstrating our capability to protect the oil lines of
communication" and "providing a military presence to reassure
our friends in the Middle East."

Despite the Navy's new presence in nearby waters, the shah
was dumbfounded by American neutrality during the
Bangladesh War and by Nixon's withdrawal from South Vietnam,
events that led him to regard his many American guarantees as
worthless. This view was underscored by Nixon's refusal to sign
another bilateral defense treaty to replace the old CENTO pact,
which the shah believed had "never been really serious." The
Nixon Doctrine seemed to offer a partial solution to this problem, intended as it was to rescind American overseas commitments by emphasizing "burden sharing" between the United
States and its non-NATO allies. Details of how the Nixon Doctrine was to be applied to the Persian Gulf had been supplied in
November 1970, when Kissinger announced the Twin Pillars Pol-

icy, an attempt to shift the burden of regional defense to Iran and Saudi Arabia by recognizing Iran's regional military hegemony and Saudi Arabia's economic and strategic importance to the West. Under this policy, Washington and London underwrote a new $1 billion Iranian defense buildup that unfolded once the Royal Navy withdrew from the Gulf. On the other hand, Red Navy deployments in the Mediterranean, Arabian Sea, and Indian Ocean, and increased Soviet political interest in Syria and Iraq, discouraged Nixon from thinking that he might shift much more responsibility for policing the Persian Gulf to Iran.[4]

The Twin Pillars Policy was translated into action in May 1972 when Nixon issued a virtual carte blanche to the shah to acquire American planes, ships, and weapons to prepare Iran's armed forces to defend her border with Russia and to police the Gulf. In return, the shah quietly allowed American aircraft to overfly Iran during the Yom Kippur War of 1973, the only leader in the region to do so. He also refused to join in the Arab oil embargo that followed that war, although he played a major role in the OPEC cartel's move to raise oil prices in 1974. Western vulnerability to the embargo and OPEC pricing reinforced the shah's notions of his worth. His muscular pretensions were already evident to his neighbors. After the withdrawal of the Royal Navy from the region in 1971, Zumwalt concluded that neither the Iranians nor the Saudis "believe they need, nor do they enjoy, the permanent showing of the U.S. flag in the gulf." Armed with Nixon's promise to sell Iran four *Spruance*-class destroyers, three diesel submarines, and several squadrons of Navy F-14 Tomcat and Air Force F-15 Eagle fighters, the shah exerted his new authority by occupying Abu Musa and the small Tunb islands, measures that received American approval. After 1973, he helped the Sultan of Oman suppress the communist Dhofar Rebellion from South Yemen, sent troops to Oman, and supported the Omanis with joint naval maneuvers in the Strait of Hormuz. When Iranian forces pulled out of Oman in 1977, it seemed to Washington to be a successful application of the Nixon Doctrine and the Twin Pillars Policy.[5]

In the meantime, the 1971 Bangladesh War between India and Iran's ally, Pakistan, had spurred the Americans to establish a permanent naval presence in the Indian Ocean, a long-term strategy designed to fill the vacuum of power created by the British withdrawal and to thwart the expansion of Soviet influ-

ence in the region. Under Jawaharlal Nehru, India had achieved
her independence from Britain in 1947 with American blessings.
Despite Nehru's lofty policy of nonalignment and his leadership
among the newly independent nations of the Third World, President Eisenhower and his two successors provided generously for
India in their annual foreign aid programs without expecting or
receiving in return much international support from New Delhi.
Although India was a democracy, Indian leaders seemed immune
to understanding that it was American military power that made
their freedom possible. Moreover, Indian leaders usually enunciated their foreign policy in highly offensive terms. Henry
Kissinger observed that, although "Nixon made few changes in
the policies he inherited on the subcontinent," Prime Minister
Indira Gandhi's "assumption of almost hereditary moral superiority and her moody silences brought out all of Nixon's latent in-
securities."

By contrast, American relations with Muslim Pakistan, an
early ally in the Cold War, had always been cordial, and Nixon
even lifted slightly an arms embargo on South Asia imposed
some years before to prevent a repetition of three earlier wars between Pakistan and India. The purpose, according to Kissinger,
was to grace relations with Islamabad with a "somewhat warmer
tone." The Nixon administration was sharply divided over American policy in the region, however. Secretary of State Rogers "felt
that the United States had no vital interests in the Indian Ocean
that the Russians were likely to threaten," whereas the JCS
backed Zumwalt's view that Moscow intended "to complete the
encirclement of China from the south . . . , radicalize as many
Middle Eastern regimes as possible" and "develop a military capability . . . to interfere with oil deliveries to Japan and Europe if
an occasion ever arose to do so."[6]

A terrible famine broke out in East Pakistan in 1971, and
this led directly to the war. The Islamabad regime's inability to
deal with the tragedy gave life to a movement among East Pakistan's Bengalis for independence. India's Gandhi, hoping to dismember and weaken Pakistan, supported this uprising. Dispatched to restore order in the eastern half of the country, the
Pakistani Army created even more disruption by its brutality and
forced thousands of Bengalis to flee across the Indian frontier.
Gandhi turned to the Soviets, and in August she signed a major
military treaty with Russia that was intended to prevent either the

United States or China from intervening to save Pakistan once the Indian Army was ready to invade East Pakistan. This treaty contained a "secret protocol giving the Soviet Navy base rights at Vishakhapatnam," according to Zumwalt, which made India "for some purposes a Soviet client."[7]

The Indian Army invaded East Pakistan on 3 December 1971. On the eve of the war, both the Soviets and the Americans had nominal forces in the Indian Ocean. However, a *Kynda*-class cruiser and a diesel submarine stood out of Vladivostok on 6 December and shaped a course for the Indian Ocean. To show support for Pakistan, Nixon and Kissinger decided four days later to order Admiral McCain to organize an Indian Ocean Task Force comprising the nuclear carrier *Enterprise*, the amphibious assault ship *Tripoli*, three guided missile cruisers, four destroyers, and one attack submarine and to position this formation off the East Bengal coast. Zumwalt opposed this on the grounds that "it was taking an unnecessary risk to put a task group without a stated mission in precisely the place where harm was likely to befall it." He convinced Admiral Moorer, the chairman of the JCS, to rewrite McCain's directive, deploying the *Enterprise* task group instead to a position south of Ceylon, where it would be free from accidental involvement in the Bangladesh War. In Washington, the Navy Department announced that the *Enterprise* task force was being sent into the Indian Ocean to evacuate American residents from East Pakistan, despite the fact that all foreign nationals wanting to leave Dhaka had already done so. The real function of the force was to deter India from further dismembering Pakistan and to persuade Chinese Premier Chou En-lai that the new tie between Peking and Washington would prove useful in balancing the Russo-Indian combination. It was a mere "token of our concern," Zumwalt concluded, inasmuch as nothing Nixon might do could in any way prevent India from evicting the Pakistanis from East Pakistan, which the Bengalis now called Bangladesh. The Indian offensive swiftly overran East Pakistan, which surrendered on 16 December, and the next day a ceasefire went into effect on the western front.[8]

The Soviets responded to the Bangladesh War by detaching a *Kresta*-class cruiser, a *Kashin*-class destroyer, and two submarines from their Pacific Fleet and sending them into the Indian Ocean to visit Bombay and the Indian naval base at Vishakhapatnam, to show support for India, and to thwart any American intervention to save Pakistan from defeat and partition. Owing to the steaming time from Vladivostok to the Indian Ocean, however, this Russian task force did not arrive on the scene until after the war was over. Although the deployment of the *Enterprise* task force into the Indian Ocean had no effect on the war's outcome, the Soviets were clearly stunned by Nixon's bold step. Brezhnev shortly thereafter restated Soviet backing for India's Zone of Peace scheme, claiming that "we have never considered it an ideal situation to have the fleets of the great powers plying the seas for long periods at great distances from their own shores."[9]

The increasing level of American naval activity in the Indian Ocean and the continuing demands for extended deployments in the eastern Mediterranean came at a time when the size of the American fleet was dramatically decreasing. The most visible evidence of this was the retirement of the *Essex*-class antisubmarine carriers. Their functions were to be taken over in some measure by the heavy attack carriers. In the aftermath of the Vietnam War, neither Congress nor the administration was willing to rebuild the carrier force to prewar levels, however. As an alternative, one which he believed was consistent with the Nixon Doctrine, Zumwalt developed the policy of overseas homeporting—permanently basing a carrier in a foreign port—to support the continuance of traditional deployment patterns. "Maintaining five carriers overseas without homeporting required a force of fifteen carriers, nine based on the west coast and six on the east coast," he explained. However, a fleet composed of "twelve carriers can deploy five overseas continuously only by either extending the length of deployments beyond six months, which would damage morale and discourage reenlistments, or basing two or three on overseas ports." Fifteen carriers provided for the Navy's traditional strategic long-term peacetime deployment: two in the Mediterranean, three in the western Pacific, but none for remaining contingencies—and none for the Indian Ocean Fleet.

Zumwalt hoped eventually to reduce to one the number of carriers assigned to the 6th Fleet, a move that would leave the Atlantic Fleet with only five carriers deployed, undergoing overhaul, or working up. By homeporting one carrier in Japan, he might increase the Pacific Fleet to a grand total of seven carriers, of which three would be forward-deployed. Kissinger objected to this, however, citing the traditional commitment of two carrier task forces to defend NATO's southern flank and to replace the

Royal Navy's Mediterranean Fleet. This latter problem became acute in 1975 when Prime Minister Harold Wilson announced that London could not "in the future commit British maritime forces to the Mediterranean in support of NATO." The Royal Navy's attack submarine flotilla had already been withdrawn to Britain's home waters, and her ships and land-based patrol planes retired from the Mediterranean three years later. As a result, Kissinger's argument won the day. Zumwalt was, however, successful in putting across his 1972 plan to homeport the carrier *Midway* at Yokosuka, Japan, largely because Congress refused to allow the Navy to lay down more carriers. Indeed, no carriers were laid down from the *Carl Vinson* to the *Theodore Roosevelt* in 1979.[10]

Overseas homeporting appeared to solve other problems as well, but it was a controversial step. The end of the draft, the unpopularity of military service among American teenagers, and low domestic unemployment conspired to reduce Navy enlistments and reenlistments during the early years of the decade. Zumwalt concluded that one of the major causes of low retention rates was family separations during long overseas deployments and that overseas homeporting would relieve this burden. There was significant opposition to overseas homeporting on Capitol Hill, however. Not only did Zumwalt want to station a task force in Japan, but he also intended to base a 6th Fleet task force in the Aegean Sea. Greece, which had announced that it would welcome American warships, was at the time governed by a brutal military regime, which even Zumwalt said was "an embarrassment to the United States." And, as retired Admiral George Anderson pointed out, in the event of a crisis there, American dependents might be taken hostage.[11]

The State Department was uneasy about Zumwalt's homeporting policy on the grounds that it appeared to tie the United States too closely to the Greek dictatorship. Diplomat Lee Dinsmore naively told Congress in 1972 that "there is a better way for the United States to demonstrate its naval power . . . by a system of roving fleet units. . . . These would be fleet units that are not dependent on homeporting at any one place or on having a base abroad." This eccentric view notwithstanding, Zumwalt went ahead with his plan. In December 1972, a destroyer squadron steamed to Greece and another squadron sailed for Yokosuka, Japan; in 1973, the carrier *Independence* visited Athens; and the

Midway put into her new home port in Japan in September of the following year. Although the plan to homeport a carrier in Greece had to be abandoned when a coup in Athens overthrew the military dictatorship and brought an anti-American socialist to power, Zumwalt's decision to station the carrier *Midway* at Yokosuka proved so beneficial that, in spite of extended deployments into the Indian Ocean during the next decade, retention of sailors in ships based in Japan improved considerably.[12]

Retiring the *Essex*-class antisubmarine carriers created a gaping hole in the Navy's escort and antisubmarine forces, which Zumwalt tried diligently to fill. He assigned some scout planes and antisubmarine helicopters to the attack carriers to convert them into multi-mission vessels, but this failed to solve even part of the problem because these aircraft were frequently diverted to logistics tasks or duty as plane guards. This and other factors caused Zumwalt to adopt a policy that reduced the fleet's traditional reliance on the attack carrier task forces and strike aircraft and shifted some of the burden for escort and antisubmarine operations to other surface ships. The arrival in the fleet of the LAMPS helicopter, for example, extended the range of the destroyers by endowing their radars and missiles with a short-range over-the-horizon reach and led ultimately to the consolidation of surface antisubmarine operations in the destroyer forces.

Zumwalt also moved to reorient the Navy's strategy away from the heavy air strike and close ground support missions that had occupied the Navy during the Korean and Vietnam wars and toward a posture from which the fleet might confront the rapidly growing Soviet missile-bearing surface fleet. At the time, it appeared that "no matter what the length of a conflict [with the Soviets], we would quickly lose the use of our deployed carriers," he later explained. Zumwalt was convinced that heavy carriers might be used to attack enemy naval forces, but only in uncontested waters. After 1962, Admiral George Anderson had toyed for two years with a plan to build a large number of 40-knot destroyer escorts—the oil-fired 5,600-ton Seahawk—but the Atlantic Fleet's submarine warfare commander successfully objected to the program on the grounds that "the first priority should be increasing the number of surface escorts . . . rather than [building] a lesser number of highly sophisticated escorts."[13]

Soon after the Cuban Missile Crisis, McNamara persuaded Congress to authorize the construction of forty-six 4,100-ton

Knox-class antisubmarine destroyer escorts, which operated DASH antisubmarine helicopters and were armed with ASROC antisubmarine rocket launchers and anti-ship and antisubmarine torpedoes. Successors to the 3,400-ton *Garcia*-class and *Brooke*-class destroyer escorts—which bore much of the burden of the Vietnam War—almost all of the *Knox*-class ships entered the fleet during Nixon's first term. To hide the price of fighting the Vietnam War, however, McNamara had dictated in 1965 that the Navy deduct many of the war's expenses from its shipbuilding accounts. As a result, new destroyer construction was abandoned until the Johnson administration was about to leave office three years later. The need for a more powerful antisubmarine escort led Navy Secretary Paul Nitze in 1966 to commission Rear Admiral Zumwalt to conduct a Major Fleet Escort study. In this study, Zumwalt warned of the coming reduction in the size of the fleet owing to bloc obsolescence of World War II–era ships and the end of Admiral Burke's FRAM ship repair and modernization program. "The study did not deal directly with propulsion systems," according to Zumwalt, "but since it recommended a very large building program that ultimately would bring the Navy's

The guided missile destroyer *Henry B. Wilson* fires on Khmer Rouge troops on Koh Tang Island off Cambodia in support of Marines who had landed on 15 May 1973 to rescue the hostage crew of the American container ship *Mayaguez.*

total number of escorts to a minimum of 242 . . . the study did come down by implication on the side of conventional [oil-fired] propulsion for almost all escorts."[14]

Zumwalt proposed to create a new mixed carrier screen composed of six antiaircraft and antimissile escorts and three escorts wholly dedicated to antisubmarine operations. To screen the four nuclear-powered *Nimitz*-class carriers that the Navy hoped to build before 1980, sixteen nuclear-powered antiaircraft escorts would be needed. The remaining eleven oil-fired attack carriers required modernized screens composed of forty-four antiaircraft escorts and twenty-two new, fast antisubmarine escorts. Although the fleet escort study recommended constructing a new class of austere patrol frigates, this plan ultimately led to Admiral Moorer's successful request to Congress in 1968 for funds for the high-speed 7,100-ton *Spruance*-class antisubmarine destroyers. Operating two LAMPs helicopters, the *Spruance*-class destroyer was armed with only two lightweight 5-inch guns, but sported a combined launcher for ASROCs and close-in Standard antiaircraft missiles, bow-mounted sonars, and antisubmarine torpedo tubes. The *Spruances* were not armed with mid- or long-range surface-to-air missiles, although the sister *Kidd*-class destroyers—originally built for sale to the Iranian Navy—were converted later in the 1970s into antiaircraft missile ships. Zumwalt arranged for all the *Spruance*-class destroyers to be built at Litton's newly constructed Pascagoula, Mississippi, shipyard using the most advanced shipbuilding methods. However, corporate mismanagement, Navy-originated design changes, and inflation drove up the cost of each ship from $30 million in 1969 to over $100 million three years later. The escalating cost of the *Spruance*-class destroyers precluded building enough of them to meet the fleet's escort requirements.

The escalating costs of these and other ships and submarines led Admiral Zumwalt, when he became CNO in 1970, to announce a new shipbuilding policy consisting of a what he called a High-Low Mix. He intended to bring the fleet "into balance by supplementing the high-performance [mostly nuclear-powered] ships it was building in small numbers, because they were so expensive that small numbers were all [the Navy] could afford, with new types of ships that had adequate capability for many missions and . . . were inexpensive enough to build in the larger numbers required." Zumwalt proposed, for instance, to supplement the *Knox*-class destroyer escorts with the *Oliver Hazard Perry*-class of slow, low-cost patrol frigates that were armed only with 76mm guns and an austere fire-control system. Designed to tow a modernized array of sonar hydrophones, the *Perry*-class frigate also operated a LAMPs III antisubmarine helicopter. The *Perry*'s antiaircraft system could engage only two targets simultaneously, however, and this was their weakest feature. Single-purpose ships, they were intended to escort resupply convoys to Europe to support NATO in a war against the Warsaw Pact, but not much else.[15]

Zumwalt was determined that the *Perry*-class frigate program succeed, so he named a hard-driving, resolute figure, Vice Admiral Frank H. Price, to superintend it. The rest of Zumwalt's shipbuilding program was not so successful, as he allowed it to fall into the hands of less powerful, lower-level bureaucrats. Because of Price's dynamism and bureaucratic skills, the lead ship in the *Perry* class entered the fleet in 1977, two years ahead of the second ship—a unique schedule wisely arranged so that design defects could be corrected before large numbers of the vessels were constructed. Nevertheless, the aging fleet, bloc obsolescence of World War II– and Korean War–vintage vessels, and escalating construction, maintenance, and repair costs forced Zumwalt to adopt an accelerated scrapping policy to free up monies for new shipbuilding. The result was to reduce considerably the size of the fleet. From a total of 240 cruisers and destroyers in 1964, the fleet was left with only 96 of these types twelve years later. Thus, when Zumwalt recommended that Admiral James Holloway III be his successor in 1974, the new CNO found that the fleet now consisted of only 490 ships, and, as he pointed out, owing to "the reduction of carrier force levels, the surface combatants will [have to] carry a larger share of the sea control [escort] mission."[16]

Zumwalt's High-Low Mix shipbuilding policy reflected in part his conviction that the Navy could no longer afford merely to concentrate on perfecting carrier air strikes but had to deal with the large numbers of missile-bearing cruisers and destroyers entering the Soviet fleets. To confront this emerging threat, Zumwalt accelerated the development of the Harpoon anti-ship missile. During the 1960s, the Navy had borrowed the Army's Lance missile and tried without success to convert it into the Sea Lance bombardment missile, but the project ended in a costly, embarrassing failure. As a result, the Navy possessed no equivalent to the lethal Soviet-built Styx surface-to-surface missile—four of which were used by the Egyptians in 1967 to sink the Israeli destroyer *Eilat*—or the 150-mile-range Strella missile or the 400-mile-range remote-controlled, air-breathing Shaddock missile. "All of our long-range offensive capability was crowded onto the decks of a few carriers," complained Zumwalt, who reasoned that his "most urgent task by far was to develop and deploy a proper cruise missile . . . in surface vessels, particularly escorts, first, then . . . in planes and submarines." The Navy's hugely successful Harpoon missile program promised to reverse this imbalance.[17]

Opposition within the Navy to Zumwalt's High-Low Mix policy was considerable. Many did not favor building single-mission ships inasmuch as these vessels lacked flexibility. The aviators especially feared that long-range cruise missiles would put their carriers out of business. And Admiral Rickover, the aging, sharp-tongued cardinal of nuclear propulsion, still envisioned the day when reactors would drive every ship and submarine in the fleet. Zumwalt later claimed that he and Rickover made a deal under which Zumwalt was to back the construction of more nuclear-powered submarines and the fourth *Nimitz*-class carrier while Rickover was not to oppose building more oil-fired cruisers, destroyers, and escorts. However, Rickover's witting violations of this agreement escalated, and he convinced Congress in 1974 to attach an amendment to that year's Defense Department authorization act requiring that all Navy ships be nuclear powered unless the president certified that this was unnecessary. J. William Middendorf, a decorative Maryland millionaire who served as Nixon's third secretary of the navy, mused that the United States "should have an all-nuclear Navy, but I suspect it would be a pretty small Navy."[18]

Rickover's intrusive, contentious mismanagement of several programs, economywide inflation, shipyard corruption, and general blundering, all conspired to sabotage Rickover's grand plan. By the middle of the decade every nuclear-powered ship and submarine building program was swamped by a vast sea of seemingly unstoppable cost overruns. On 16 February 1974, the nuclear cruiser *California* was commissioned at Newport News Shipbuilding and Drydock Company. Her keel had been laid down seven years earlier, but construction was at least eighteen months behind schedule and the cost of the ship had more than doubled from the original estimate. She was followed a year later by her sister ship, the *South Carolina*, whose history was similar. Cost over-runs caused by design changes, waste, and poor management of the shipyard were at the core of a $900 million claim by Newport News against the Navy Department. Not only did this and other cost overrun disputes with shipbuilders embarrass the Navy, but they also led to an overall reduction in the size of the fleet.

Zumwalt intended to build four 12,000-ton nuclear-powered light strike cruisers, armed with long-range Tomahawk cruise missiles and Harpoon anti-ship missiles and defended by the new Aegis phased-array antimissile, antiaircraft radar system. His successor, Admiral Holloway, who paid lip service to a "careful balance between high-performance, expensive ships and the less expensive ones we can procure in great numbers," supported construction of the nuclear-powered strike cruiser, but President Ford, under pressure from Congress to reduce military spending, canceled the project in 1976. This led Holloway to turn his attention the following year to the oil-fired *Ticonderoga*-class cruisers as a platform for the Aegis air-defense system. During this same round of defense cutbacks, the nuclear-powered destroyer leader program—which had produced six guided-missile–bearing ships between 1967 and 1975—was also canceled by the liberal Democrats who dominated Congress. "In 1976, the Navy will have 490 ships," Holloway worried, "the lowest total in the active fleet since 1939." Although the "newer ships are more powerful and capable than those they replace," the fleet "must still cover the same broad areas." This meant that the Navy had to start to "be concerned with numbers as well as capabilities."[19]

Zumwalt believed that one of the ways he might compensate for the retirement of so many World War II–vintage ships was to improve the Navy's intelligence, communications, and navigational aids. "In order to fight a modern battle successfully it is necessary to transmit and receive rapidly and securely—in other words without deciphering or jamming by the enemy—a staggeringly large volume of data about the rapidly changing speeds, courses, and ranges of hundreds of ships, planes, and missiles, and about changes in the intentions of our own forces and in the estimated intentions of the enemy." In 1964, the first of three Transit launches was completed, giving the fleet its first Navy Navigation Satellite System. Two years later, NASA launched the first of six satellites to be sent into orbit to support the Initial Defense Satellite System, a spartan communications link between

Washington and the major operating forces. Owing to Zumwalt's attention, the vital Fleet Satellite Communications System became operational in 1977, providing enhanced communications to the fleet and the first ship-to-shore, computer-to-computer data links. And one year earlier another team put into orbit the first White Cloud passive electronic ocean reconnaissance satellite, while subsequent launches placed in space the Clipper Bow high-resolution radar satellite and a number of Teal Ruby satellites, which were intended to detect infrared sensor patterns on the oceans.

Although Zumwalt claimed to be pessimistic about the fleet's ability to survive a purely naval war with the Soviet Navy, the American edge in advanced technology—in computers, satellites, and radars, for example, and in aircraft carriers and intelligence gathering—sustained a safe margin of superiority throughout the decade and imposed immense pressure on the Soviets to try in vain to keep pace. By the time President Ford left office in January 1977, however, the trends of the great powers' shipbuilding programs clearly favored the Soviets and there existed a desperate need for what Admiral Holloway termed a "stable, long-term shipbuilding program."[20]

Chapter Thirty-three

The New Isolationism
1975–1977

Nixon wanted to apply his doctrine of retrenchment to the Arab-Israeli dispute and to modify Soviet behavior in the Middle East by linking it to progress on détente. This design was thwarted by the legacy of Lyndon Johnson's policy of providing Israel unlimited arms and by Russia's rugged support of Egypt, Syria, and Iraq—a policy that Leonid Brezhnev reaffirmed in 1964 soon after he ousted Khrushchev from the Politburo. That year, as well, the Arab powers agreed to finance commando operations against Israel by Yasir Arafat's Palestine Liberation Organization. The Israelis used American arms and aircraft to retaliate against PLO bases in Jordan and Syria and for the April 1967 bombing of Syrian military installations only sixty miles from Damascus. The Soviets responded by supporting the Syrians' demand that Egypt's President Nasser provide them with more than mere diplomatic encouragement.

On 16 May 1967, the Egyptians persuaded United Nations Secretary General U Thant to withdraw the 3,400-man UN peacekeeping force, which had patrolled the frontier on the Sinai Peninsula since the end of the 1956 Suez War. Six days later, Nasser announced the closure of the Strait of Tiran at Sharm al-Sheikh, thus cutting off the vital Israeli port of Eilat from the Red Sea. Washington was alarmed, and Defense Secretary McNamara ordered Vice Admiral William Martin, the 6th Fleet commander, to position the carriers *America* and *Saratoga* south of Crete and send the carrier *Intrepid*, which had just entered the Mediterranean en route to the Gulf of Tonkin, to a station off the coast of friendly Libya to await developments. President Johnson announced that the United States would not recognize the closing of the Strait of Tiran, but he was prevented from doing anything stiff by conservatives on the Hill who warned that Congress was ready to oppose any unilateral American action to lift the blockade. Instead, he asked British Prime Minister Harold Wilson to suggest forming a multinational Western naval force to reopen the waterway, but France and other NATO powers rejected this scheme, in part because they opposed Israel's policy and in part because they did not want to involve NATO outside of Europe. As a result, Johnson was unable to round up any international naval support for reopening the Strait of Tiran.

The Israelis had decided by now to conduct a preemptive war, with the objectives of seizing the West Bank of the Jordan River from Jordan, the Golan Heights from Syria, and the Gaza Strip from Egypt. In the early morning of 5 June 1967, Israeli fighter-bombers flew west into the Mediterranean, dropped down so low that they disappeared from ground radars, turned south, entered Egyptian airspace, and within five minutes destroyed or damaged every enemy front-line aircraft. Simultaneously, the Israelis crushed the smaller Syrian and Jordanian air forces during another series of preemptive air strikes. The next day, Israeli armor slashed onto the Sinai, reaching the Suez Canal on 8 June, while another army overran Sharm al-Sheikh on the Egyptian side of the Strait of Tiran on the 7th. Syria refused to declare war on Israel and, indeed, supported a UN ceasefire resolution backed by the Johnson administration. The Israelis, however, intended to occupy Syria's Golan Heights and thereby put an end to the sporadic shelling of Israel's northernmost settlements. The Israeli Army was ordered to be ready to invade Syria on 9 June. The Israelis had masked preparations for this operation because they feared an abrupt shift in American policy once it became evident that Tel Aviv was engaged in a war of expansionist conquest.

The speed of Israel's offensive stunned American intelligence and left LBJ eager to learn the details of Tel Aviv's strategic plans and the Arab response. One ship that the JCS had already shifted to the eastern Mediterranean was the technical research vessel *Liberty*, a converted *Victory*-class cargo ship, which some years earlier had been withdrawn from mothballs and converted into a signal intelligence collector. She carried special communications intercepting equipment, the most distinctive feature of which was a 32-foot antenna aft from which messages could be transmitted directly to the National Security Agency at Fort Meade using the moon as a relay satellite.

Commander William L. McGonagle in the *Liberty* had received orders on 23 May to steam from Rota, Spain, into the eastern Mediterranean. He was to take station off Egypt and intercept, process, and relay the most sensitive Egyptian and Israeli military message traffic back to Washington. Owing to the tension between Israel and Egypt, McGonagle asked that a destroyer accompany his ship into the eastern Mediterranean; this request was denied, although McGonagle was assured that American aircraft would be only ten minutes from his station. The *Liberty* arrived off the Gaza Strip on the evening of 7 June—her electronic interception equipment abuzz—and steamed along a dogleg track from a point off Al-'Arish to a point off Port Said, which kept her about fifty miles from the territorial waters of both belligerents. When Israel invaded Egypt on 7 June, the JCS instructed Admiral John S. McCain, the new London-based commander of American naval forces in European waters, to move the *Liberty* to a position 100 miles off the coast. However, the communications circuits in the region were clogged by message traffic—generated by the commanding general of the Army's Florida-based Strike Command, who picked this moment to convey volumes of war plans to his local commanders—and at least five messages conveying the JCS order to the *Liberty* did not reach her until it was too late.

At 0600 on 8 June, an Israeli reconnaissance transport appeared over the *Liberty*, circled, and then flew away. More than a dozen Israeli aircraft reconnoitered the ship that morning, the last flying over at about 1145. Neither McGonagle nor his crew was concerned. The weather was clear, the *Liberty* was well identified as an American warship by a five-by-eight-foot ensign, and the crew assumed that the Israelis, who were receiving American arms, meant no harm to their vessel. McGonagle alerted the 6th Fleet to the overflights, but hours passed before McCain's order giving Admiral Martin authority to direct the movements of the *Liberty* reached the Mediterranean. The Israelis had delivered an informal request to the State Department that American warships be kept away from the Egyptian coast, but this was not interpreted as a threat to their safety. Next, a CIA agent in Israeli's Tel Aviv military headquarters warned Washington that the Israelis intended to attack the *Liberty* if she came near enough to the war zone to eavesdrop on Israel's military communications. Although none of this reached McCain's headquarters, his able acting chief of staff, Captain Michael Hanley, had already ordered the *Liberty* to withdraw to a position 100 miles off Israel's coast, but this message also failed to reach the ship.

At 1400 two Israeli Mirage III jet fighter-bombers appeared over the *Liberty*, strafed the vessel with cannon fire, and launched a rocket attack that quickly disabled every antenna on the ship. McGonagle returned fire with his four 50-caliber machine guns but was unable to disrupt the Israeli attack. Within minutes, a second section of Israeli Mystère fighters hit the *Liberty* with more cannon fire, rockets, and napalm. At 1453, three torpedo boats from the nearby Israeli naval base at Ashdod arrived on the scene, circled the helpless ship, raked the vessel and American sailors in life rafts in the water with machine guns, and fired at least five torpedoes. McGonagle evaded the first torpedo, but the second detonated against the *Liberty*'s starboard side, tearing a forty-foot hole in her hull. He now ordered his crew to "stand by to repel boarders," but the Israeli boats retired after the torpedo explosion. At 1515 the Israeli attackers broke off, leaving behind 34 American sailors dead and 171 wounded.[1]

The Israelis had successfully silenced the *Liberty*'s listening equipment. McGonagle tried to alert Admiral Martin during the attack, but an Israeli shore communications station jammed five of the six radio circuits available to him; the Israeli jammers were searching for the last one when the Israeli torpedo boats finally withdrew. Less than one hour after the attack on the *Liberty* was over, the Israelis moved to repair the political damage that the operation was likely to cause and to advance against Syria. At 1614, the American defense attaché in Tel Aviv relayed to Washington a message containing an Israeli apology. The Israelis would later make the preposterous claim that their planes and torpedo boats had mistaken the *Liberty* for the smaller Egyptian horse transport *El-Quseir*, although both Tel Aviv and Washington knew that this vessel was anchored in Alexandria. Israeli motor torpedo boats returned to the scene at 1632, and Israeli helicopters appeared overhead soon after and asked McGonagle if they might render assistance. Angry and bitter, he rejected this hypocritical offer.

When news of the attack finally reached Martin, he ordered Rear Admiral Lawrence R. Geis, the 6th Fleet carrier task force commander, to launch an air strike of four fighter-bombers to protect the *Liberty*. Learning that American aircraft were aloft and might be heading to attack the Israeli base at Ashdod, Secretary of the Navy Paul Nitze phoned McCain in London and tried to persuade him to order Martin to recall the strike. Captain Ernest Juehnke, the naval attaché in Tel Aviv, was telling Washington that the attack was inadvertent. Moments later Defense Secretary McNamara contacted Martin directly and ordered him to recall the aircraft. Eight more aircraft were launched after the attack on the *Liberty* ended, but Martin was again instructed to recall these planes. The Johnson administration viewed Israel as a valuable client, and American Jews, who uniformly supported Israeli policy, formed the core of LBJ's Democratic coalition. He could ill-afford to offend them. Under the circumstances, an attack on Ashdod would have been disastrous. On the other hand, McNamara's second order—not to send aircraft to overfly the *Liberty*—was inexplicable. Martin directed the destroyers *Davis* and *Massey* to steam to the rescue of the stricken ship, but she was left without support until the following day.

Once the Israeli attack was over, Commander McGonagle made emergency repairs to his ship, rendezvoused with the destroyers early on 9 June, and evacuated the wounded. The heavy carrier *America* soon arrived on the scene and the task force escorted the *Liberty* back to Malta. There, Rear Admiral Isaac Kidd convened a court of inquiry to investigate the attack. Within hours, Kidd received orders from McNamara not to release any statements critical of the Tel Aviv government. Kidd's final report courageously declared, however, that "the attack of the Israeli aircraft and motor torpedo boats was entirely unprovoked and unexpected." Kidd privately told Admiral McCain that, while McGonagle had failed to prepare his ship for combat, he and his crew had performed heroically during and after the wanton attack. In a politic gesture, McCain accepted full blame for the lack of preparedness and recommended that McGonagle receive the Congressional Medal of Honor. McCain was rewarded in 1968 by Admiral Moorer, the CNO, with a promotion to the Navy's more prestigious Pacific theater unified command. President Johnson had long since adopted a self-conscious policy of ignoring Israeli duplicity and callousness in the *Liberty* incident, so McNamara arranged for McGonagle's Medal of Honor to be awarded quietly at the Washington Navy Yard rather than at the White House, where LBJ usually conducted these ceremonies. A subsequent congressional investigation scored the Defense Department, but the Democrats who controlled the Hill refused to criticize Johnson or his pro-Israel foreign policy.[2]

The disabling of the *Liberty* blinded American intelligence to the movements of Israel's army on 8 June, and the day following the vessel's withdrawal, Israeli troops invaded Syria and overran the Golan Heights. Other Israeli forces evicted the Jordanians from the Arab half of Jerusalem, crossed into Jordan, and occupied the West Bank. Her war aims in hand, Israel accepted the UN ceasefire on the 11th. The Six-Day War emboldened the Israelis, who annexed Jerusalem and the Golan Heights and began to settle the West Bank, and also drew Washington closer to Tel Aviv after France's de Gaulle imposed an embargo on arms shipments to the Israelis. Thereafter, Israel looked to the United States for arms and economic aid. Humiliated by defeat, Egypt and Syria were thrown back on their alliances with the Soviet Union. In return for a Soviet pledge to rebuild the Egyptian Army and Air Force, Nasser granted the Red Navy's Mediterranean Fleet access to Alexandria and other Egyptian naval bases and invited the Soviet land-based naval air force to make use of Egypt's military airfields. Soviet influence in the region increased substantially over the next six years until the outbreak of the Yom Kippur War again upset the regional balance of power.

When Nasser died in 1970, he was succeeded by his protégé, General Anwar Sadat, who one year later renewed the Russo-Egyptian Friendship Treaty under which over 20,000 Soviet military advisers and technicians were stationed in Egypt. Brezhnev negotiated a more generous military assistance pact with Syria two years later, and Soviet influence in the Middle East peaked in late 1972 when a Russian task force entered the Persian Gulf and visited the Iraqi port of Umm Qasr. However, Sadat was unhappy with Russia's inability to lever Israel into withdrawing from the Sinai, the Gaza Strip, and the West Bank, so he secretly decided to cut his ties with Moscow and turn to the West. He ousted most Soviet advisers from Egypt that year and curtailed access rights for Soviet Air Force aircraft to Egyptian military airfields, but he reckoned that before he made his major diplomatic move he needed to win a military victory, so he negotiated an agreement with President Hafez Assad of Syria to coordinate an attack on Israel the following year.

In early October 1973, Sadat, with the support of South Yemen and Ethiopia, blockaded the Bab el Mandeb Straits at the southern end of the Red Sea, about 1,200 miles from the Strait of Tiran, thus isolating the Israeli port of Eilat at the north end of the Gulf of Aqaba. Then, on 6 October, the Egyptian Army crossed the Suez Canal, breached Israel's static Bar Lev defensive line on the east bank, and established a bridgehead on the Sinai. The Syrians simultaneously overran Mount Hebron in the Golan Heights and advanced to a line that menaced Israel's entire northern flank. Sadat's decision to attack on Yom Kippur, a Jewish religious holiday, caught the Israelis completely off guard. They reacted by flinging air strikes at Syria's ports and military bases and by mounting a ferocious armored counterattack on the 10th that thrashed the Syrians, brushed aside a supporting Iraqi division, and within forty-eight hours was within artillery range of Damascus. However, these operations were costly, the Sinai front was unstable, and Prime Minister Golda Meir was so needful of American support that she even suggested to Secretary of State Kissinger at one point that she would fly to the United States on a secret mission "to plead with President Nixon for urgent arms aid."[3]

For his part, Nixon was worried that when the Israelis "finish clobbering the Egyptians and Syrians," they "would be even more impossible to deal with than before." American military and economic assistance to Israel had been significant but relatively small prior to the 1967 Six-Day War, but thereafter the sums appropriated for Israel by the Democratic Congresses climbed, until the total neared $1 billion six years later. On 8 October 1973, even before the issue of immediate military assistance came to a head, the Israelis had begun their own airlift of Sidewinder missiles, spare parts, and electronic equipment, using El Al Airline commercial aircraft, which flew out of Oceana Naval Air Station in Virginia. The following day, the Soviets responded to Arab requests for support with a massive long-range airlift of their own, staged out of Hungary and Yugoslavia. At first, Kissinger was skeptical about Israel's requests for aid, as was Defense Secretary Schlesinger, who wisely pointed out that meeting Israel's requests and thus turning around a battle that the Egyptians were winning might "blight our relations with the Arabs."[4]

Admiral Moorer, the chairman of the JCS, who took the same stance, wanted a policy aimed more at containing Soviet influence and less with underwriting Israel's territorial expansion. On 11 October, he ordered a task force based on the carrier *John F. Kennedy* to steam from the North Sea to Gibraltar, but he held Vice Admiral Daniel Murphy's 6th Fleet in a dispersed pattern, stationing another task force built around the carrier *Independence* south of Crete. "It is hard to imagine a less forthcoming move to the plight of a friend who had just become the victim of a bloody surprise attack," Admiral Zumwalt, the CNO, angrily commented at this decision. Moorer rejected Murphy's request to move the carrier *Franklin D. Roosevelt* into the eastern Mediterranean and instructed him to maintain an "evenhanded approach toward the hostilities." Over the next several days Murphy asked Moorer several times to allow him to move "toward the east to make surveillance of the battle scene more effective," but each request was rejected. Meanwhile, Admiral Gorshkov was surging over 100 Russian naval vessels into the Mediterranean, while Soviet merchant marine and air transport commands continued their costly sea and air resupply effort to support Syria and Egypt.

Zumwalt believed that Israel's inability to mount a counteroffensive in the Sinai had "lost whatever chance they might have had to win a decisive victory fast," an apt description of the environment that Kissinger was trying to create. The CNO also realized that Nixon was "totally occupied" with the ongoing Watergate scandal and the resignation on 10 October of Vice President Spiro Agnew, who had just been convicted in a federal court of accepting bribes. Kissinger "simply did not want Israel to win decisively," Zumwalt believed. In his view, the secretary hoped instead that Israel would "bleed just enough to soften it up for the postwar diplomacy he was planning." Although Kissinger felt on the morning of the 9th that Israel's distress "had gone beyond logistic calculations," he still wanted to minimize the offense to the Arabs and preferred the "least conspicuous method of delivering supplies" to Israel. Zumwalt was "convinced that in the absence of U.S. resupply, Israel was going to lose," so he privately "told [Senator Henry] 'Scoop' Jackson that I was quite sure it was the White House, not the Pentagon, that was delaying the resupply of Israel." A rugged Democratic opponent of the Nixon administration, Jackson was a charter member of Capitol Hill's Israeli lobby. He immediately went to the head of the line of a chorus of Nixon's critics, most of whom were pressuring Kissinger to release new shipments of planes, tanks, and munitions to Tel Aviv.[5]

Kissinger shrewdly welcomed these calls for action. "There was some advantage in being seen to be pressed by Congress to do more for Israel" as "it might deflect some Arab resentment," he wrote. As it was, Nixon had already decided "to speed the delivery of consumables and aircraft" and to "guarantee to replace Israel's losses," thus freeing the Israelis from the need to worry about their stocks at the end of the war. After some bureaucratic bungling over the use of private charter companies, Nixon agreed on 13 October to employ Air Force C-5A jumbo transports to fly equipment in the Azores to Israel, and Kissinger decided to "present our massive resupply of Israel as a reaction to the Soviet airlift." A substantial sealift was also begun shortly thereafter. Admiral Murphy now positioned his ships to deter the Soviets from intervening and to support the resupply of the Israelis. From the guided missile frigate *Yarnell* off Gibraltar to the *Independence* task force south of Crete, the 6th Fleet provided a chain of support to the resupply aircraft and ships. Egypt announced that it was imposing a distant blockade on the Straits of Bab el Mandeb and an Egyptian destroyer fired on an American merchantman, but Admiral Moorer raced the carrier *Hancock* into the area and Cairo dropped the matter. Nixon's decision to resupply Israel caused Prime Minister Meir to instruct her chiefs of staff to take the offensive against Egypt, and the Israelis soon recovered the Sinai and established a bridgehead on the east bank of the Suez Canal. Egypt's air forces were destroyed, one Egyptian army was trapped on the Sinai, another Egyptian army was encircled on the west bank of the Suez Canal, and Cairo was exposed to a siege by an enraged foe.[6]

Kissinger used the Yom Kippur War to test his general concept of linkage, an attempt to connect détente to Soviet behavior outside of Europe. He flew to Moscow and on 20 October concluded a ceasefire agreement with Brezhnev that was approved by the UN Security Council. This arrangement collapsed when the

commanding general of the Egyptian 3rd Army tried to break
through Israeli lines on 22 October, an error that only persuaded
the Israelis to assault Suez City, which promptly surrendered the
next day. As midnight fell on Washington on the 23rd, Nixon received a message on the teletype hotline from Brezhnev, complaining about the renewed fighting, proposing a joint Russian-
American military intervention, and threatening unilateral Soviet
intervention unless Washington promised to restrain its clients. At
0025, Admiral Moorer was instructed by the president to order all
American forces to step up to Defense Condition Three alert so as
to warn Brezhnev that the United States would not allow unilateral Soviet military intervention in the Yom Kippur War. The Russians rather sheepishly backed down the next day. Nonetheless,
the buildup of American and Soviet naval forces in the Mediterranean continued apace. By the end of the month, eighty Russian
ships had been deployed to the region, confronting three American carrier task forces and an amphibious task force, which included the landing ship *Iwo Jima*. However, Admiral Murphy assured Moorer that Soviet naval activity was "confined to
maintaining one to three 'tattletales' on each carrier task group
and the amphibious group. Other combatants remained primarily in port or at anchorages." The real intent of Soviet naval operations was apparently to signal through the positioning of their
ships that they were unready to attack Murphy's fleet. Indeed,
Murphy estimated that his forces could sink most of the Soviet vessels within about fifteen minutes.[7]

The crisis proved to be illusory. In short order, Brezhnev
soothingly reassured Nixon that the Soviets would not send
forces onto the battlefield. A second UN ceasefire was agreed to
by Sadat and Golda Meir, and Admiral Murphy's fleet returned
to its normal routines after 27 October. Kissinger then undertook a brilliant series of negotiations among the warring parties.
In late December 1973, Kissinger had brought Egypt and Israel
to a peace conference in Geneva, and in May 1974 he secured an
agreement between Israel and Syria over the disputed Golan
Heights, which lasted for more than fifteen years. As part of these
arrangements, President Sadat further distanced Egypt from
Russia, drew closer to the United States, and promised to negotiate an end to the Egyptian-Israeli dispute in the near future.

The Yom Kippur War profoundly affected the American
strategic position in the eastern Mediterranean and the Middle
East. Sadat had withdrawn Egypt, the largest Arab nation, from

the Soviet orbit and had aligned his country with the United
States. In so doing, he crippled the expansion of Russian naval
power in the Mediterranean and reduced the Kremlin to seeking
friendly relations with an array of unstable, secondary clients,
none of whom could compensate for the loss of the Egyptian alliance. In 1976, Kissinger's successful diplomacy led Sadat to end
access rights for the Soviet Mediterranean Fleet to Egyptian
ports. For all practical purposes, this nearly ended the ability of
Soviet naval aviation to deploy in the Mediterranean and considerably reduced the Russian presence in the region. After being
ousted by Sadat from Egyptian ports in 1976, the Soviet Navy was
still welcome at a small repair base at Tartus, Syria. Two years earlier, the Soviets had signed a treaty of friendship with Somalia,
and they continued to develop small naval facilities in Iraq and
South Yemen, but these installations could support only a few
Russian ships in the area at a time. Meanwhile, relations between
Egypt and the United States were rapidly improving.

The Yom Kippur War also highlighted the dependence of
western Europe and Japan on Middle East oil. The Arab oil
states, led by Saudi Arabia, Iraq, and the Persian Gulf sheikdoms,
agreed in October 1973 to embargo the export of oil to the
United States and western Europe in retaliation for the American military airlift and sealift to Israel during the Yom Kippur
War. The Arab oil embargo forced up the price of gasoline and
lubricants throughout the West and made possible a temporarily
effective suppliers' cartel, under the aegis of the multinational
Organization of Petroleum Exporting Countries. OPEC's 1974
price fixing ignited an inflationary cycle in all the industrial
democracies that eventually infected the entire international
trading economy and highlighted the dependence of the NATO
powers on Middle East oil. Owing to the Arab oil embargo and
Jerusalem's truculent diplomacy after the Yom Kippur War, the
Israelis found themselves without any friends in Europe and totally dependent on the United States. "Allied help was unlikely to
be available [to the United States] in any real-world bilateral superpower crisis" in the Middle East, Admiral Zumwalt concluded.
On the other hand, in the decade following the 1973 Yom Kippur War, Soviet naval activity in the Mediterranean never again
reached the level seen during that crisis.[8]

Partly in reaction to Nixon's muscular posture during the
Yom Kippur War, but owing mostly to resentment over his Vietnam War policy, Democrats in Congress enacted—over the presi-

dent's veto—the 1974 War Powers Act. This measure required the president "to report" to Congress within forty-eight hours of engaging American military forces in hostile situations. Unless Congress voted to continue military operations within sixty days, the president was required to withdraw American forces from the battlefield. According to Nixon, the framers of the Constitution had deliberately decided to "draw a precise line of demarcation between [the] foreign policy powers of Congress and the President." He also argued that the measure would "strike from the President's hand a wide range of important peace-keeping tools by eliminating his ability to exercise quiet diplomacy backed by subtle shifts in military deployments." Nixon and his immediate successors claimed that the act was poorly drafted and denounced it as unconstitutional. The War Powers Act was, of course, irrelevant to a nuclear war. And, as a practical matter, concluded Secretary of State Rogers, even in a limited war "it might prove impossible to terminate those hostilities and to provide for the safety of our forces [during a withdrawal] within an arbitrary time period."[9]

During the final agony of the Nixon administration in the summer of 1974, the president and Secretary of State Kissinger flew to the Soviet Union for one last summit with Brezhnev in Moscow. It was during this conference that Kissinger achieved one of his major diplomatic triumphs, a treaty banning underground nuclear tests of warheads over 150 kilotons that included provisions for on-site inspections, something the Americans had demanded for two decades and the Soviets had theretofore always rejected. It was ironic that Nixon was, upon his return to Washington, denounced by Republicans for advancing arms control and by Democrats for not negotiating a complete test ban. As a result of this deadlock, the Senate ignored the treaty.

In August 1974, shortly after Nixon returned from his last summit, the House voted to impeach him over the Watergate scandal and he was forced to resign. He was succeeded by Vice President Gerald R. Ford. SALT I was to expire in October 1977, and Kissinger believed that a succeeding agreement had to be negotiated to keep up the momentum behind his policy of détente. Kissinger wanted a new ten-year pact; the Soviets pushed for a summit with President Ford, dropping hints that they were prepared to reach a compromise on the most divisive issues. The Soviets were clearly worried by the Americans' new MIRV vehicles, which allowed Minuteman silo-based and Poseidon sea-based missiles each to carry aloft a bus containing three to ten nuclear weapons, each of which might be delivered against a different target. Ford believed that the Soviets "were far behind us technologically and hadn't deployed any MIRVs of their own." On 23 November 1974, Ford met Brezhnev at a summit held in a seedy sanitorium in the small resort town of Okeanskaya in the suburbs of the port of Vladivostok. During the talks, Brezhnev quickly agreed to a mutual limit of 2,400 ballistic missiles, a figure that would force the Soviets to reduce their launchers by 300. In addition, the Soviets agreed not to include in these figures Western "forward-based systems" such as the Navy's nuclear-capable carrier attack aircraft or the Air Force's F-4 Phantoms and F-111s deployed in Europe. In return, Brezhnev asked Ford to cancel the Air Force's B-1 strategic bomber program and the Navy's Trident ballistic missile submarine program, but the new president rejected this ploy out of hand. How to handle rapidly developing new weapons always troubled arms controllers, and Ford and Brezhnev were unable to reach an accord covering either the American cruise missile program or the Soviet's very long-range Backfire strategic bomber. The final text mentioned cruise missiles but did not limit their development or production. The Vladivostok Agreement fixed a ceiling of 2,400 on the number of delivery ballistic or aircraft vehicles each power might possess, and of this number only 1,300 warheads could be MIRVed. Ford later described this summit as the "high-water mark" of his presidency, since over the next six months "everything that could go wrong did go wrong, and on almost every front the nation took quite a beating."[10]

A nasty, personal feud between Kissinger and Secretary of Defense James Schlesinger overshadowed military policy and national strategy during the Ford interregnum. When Schlesinger took office in 1973, he modified the longstanding American nuclear strategy of Mutual Assured Destruction in favor of a retaliatory counterforce strategy that targeted Soviet land-based ICBM silos rather than Russian cities and industries. Not only would a counterforce strategy thwart a Russian attempt to use their superiority in launchers and throwweight to blackmail the United States, but it also might partly rectify the traditional inferiority of NATO's conventional forces in Europe. Only about 800 one-megaton warheads were required to achieve Mutual Assured

Destruction, but at least 8,500 warheads of the same yield were needed to execute the counterforce strategy. This led Schlesinger to support an expensive program of strategic modernization, and he was surprisingly successful, despite his raspy personality, in persuading Congress to appropriate funds for the Trident ballistic missile submarine, the Air Force's B-1 manned bomber, the new MX ICBM, and programs to improve missile accuracy and warhead yields. Schlesinger, who resisted the program at first, also eventually supported the development of the Navy's Tomahawk cruise missile and persuaded Congress to appropriate funds for this ambitious program. And in 1975, Congress for the first time appropriated more than $100 billion for the military services, a peacetime threshold many liberal Democrats did not want to cross. "Détente without defense is delusion," Schlesinger warned, throwing down a gauntlet to Congress and to Kissinger and President Ford.

Ford, admitting that his personal relations with Schlesinger, a long-time Republican placeholder, "had never been good," recalled that they "slid downhill after I became president." He was angered that Schlesinger had told the press untruthfully that the secretary of defense had instructed the JCS and the unified commanders not to act on Nixon's orders during his last, fitful days in the White House. Schlesinger was also engaged in a simultaneous quarrel with Deputy Secretary of Defense William P. Clements, a crafty Texas oil tycoon whose involvement in Middle East policy matters appeared to Schlesinger to violate at least the spirit of the conflict-of-interest laws. More important was Schlesinger's two-year-old alliance with Senator Henry Jackson, a defense-minded Democrat who was demanding that the next SALT Treaty contain equal numerical limits on launchers and warheads, a policy Kissinger opposed. Schlesinger also resisted the Vladivostok Agreement, and publicly asked Kissinger not to undermine the cruise missile program in future arms control negotiations with Brezhnev.[11]

Kissinger did not wholly disagree with any of these policy positions, but he resented Schlesinger's intrusion into his area of expertise and doubted the willingness of Congress to match Soviet defense expenditures. In addition, Ford was unsuccessfully struggling with inflation and was unable to recapture the initiative from the Democrats on Capitol Hill. To achieve economies that he believed necessary to fight inflation, Ford slashed

Schlesinger's Defense Department budget in early 1975. In response, Schlesinger increased his requests for 1976, forcing the president to demand that that figure also be trimmed. When Schlesinger publicly refused to do this, Ford replaced him at the Pentagon with a more pliant figure, Donald Rumsfeld, who was then serving as White House chief of staff. Overnight the opponents of détente flocked to Schlesinger's defense, and the resulting political commotion destroyed Kissinger's last chance to negotiate another SALT Treaty.

Ford also had to deal with the detritus of Nixon's Vietnam War policy. After the Americans had withdrawn from Indochina under the terms of the 1973 Paris Peace Accords, South Vietnam faced a bleak future. The war had destroyed the country's rice economy, the government was bankrupt, the cities teemed with refugees, and the Communists occupied several provinces in the north. President Thieu, who did nothing to reduce corruption or broaden support for his venal regime, counted on Nixon's January 1973 promise to provide air and naval support for the South Vietnamese Army if the North Vietnamese violated the ceasefire. However, "Watergate had so weakened the President [Nixon] that he was not about to take a major military action, such as renewed bombings," claimed Vice President Ford. The scandal also emboldened liberal Democrats in Congress, who wanted to prevent Nixon from resuming military support for Saigon. In 1973, Congress cut off funds for Commando Bolt bombing operations against the Ho Chi Minh Trail in Cambodia, thus conferring on the Communists unhindered passage from North Vietnam to their army in South Vietnam. Next, in 1974, Democrats on Capitol Hill overrode Nixon's veto of the War Powers Act.[12]

Although Ford tried to distance his administration from Nixon, the two great crises of his presidency came as a result of the application of the Nixon Doctrine to Southeast Asia. Brezhnev had refused to allow North Vietnam to violate the Paris accords while Nixon remained in the White House, but soon after Ford became president the Kremlin substantially increased its shipments of trucks, tanks, and munitions to Haiphong. On 5 March 1975, the North Vietnamese Army launched armored attacks against South Vietnam's northern provinces. The South Vietnamese Army broke and fled, Thieu ordered a general retreat, and the setback degenerated into a countrywide rout.

The nuclear-powered carrier *Nimitz* (CVN-68) under way off the Norwegian coast during a 1986 NATO exercise, Northern Wedding, to test the Navy's new Maritime Strategy.

On 10 April, Ford addressed a joint session of Congress and asked for a quick appropriation of aid for South Vietnam, but Democratic Senators Frank Church and Joseph Biden of the Foreign Relations Committee told the president four days later that they had the votes to block further assistance to the Saigon government. Ford pressed the House for funds, but Majority Leader Thomas "Tip" O'Neill of Massachusetts rejected the president's entreaties. With South Vietnam collapsing, Defense Secretary Schlesinger started to ask Ford "almost daily" to approve the evacuation of all Americans from Saigon. Kissinger, on the other hand, "opposed so precipitous a withdrawal" on the grounds that it would provoke "even greater panic than already existed in the South Vietnamese capital" and might even induce the South Vietnamese troops to "turn their guns on Americans." Ambassador Graham Martin in Saigon also believed that an evacuation would hasten the collapse of Thieu's regime. Nonetheless, Admiral Noel Gayler, the commander in chief of the Pacific theater, instructed Vice Admiral George Steele of the 7th Fleet to move an immense task force, including the aircraft carriers *Enterprise*, *Coral Sea*, *Midway*, and *Hancock*, the flagship *Oklahoma City*, amphibious shipping, and a transport group, into the Gulf of

Tonkin. This task force was to take station off the coast and prepare to conduct Operation Frequent Wind, a plan to evacuate Americans and South Vietnamese from Saigon.[13]

When communist armor appeared in the outskirts of Saigon, Ambassador Martin reluctantly agreed to order all Americans to congregate at the Tan Son Nhut Airport, which served the capital. The communist siege of Saigon began on 25 April. At 1200 on the 27th, Ford approved a general evacuation plan, and over the next sixteen hours more than 6,500 Americans and South Vietnamese were rescued from Saigon. The following day, however, the Air Force was compelled to halt its evacuation flights out of Saigon when Tan Son Nhut came within range of the North Vietnamese artillery. On 29 April, Admiral Gayler ordered the commencement of Frequent Wind. Nearly 1,000 Marines were inserted to cover the operation, in which Navy and Marine helicopters from Admiral Steele's Tonkin Gulf Force rescued over 1,300 Americans and about 6,500 Vietnamese from Saigon over the next eighteen hours. Indeed, over the next several months, ships of the 7th Fleet rescued tens of thousands of Vietnamese and Cambodian "boat people," men, women, and children, plucked from the Tonkin Gulf and adjacent waters after they had made their escape from the bloody tyranny that North Vietnam unleashed throughout Indochina. The last Marines withdrew when they received news that the Communists had entered the city, and on 30 April 1975, Saigon surrendered to the North Vietnamese. The Vietnam War was over.

As a supplement to the last Spring Offensive, Hanoi had rearmed General Pol Pot's Khmer Rouge Army, which advanced toward the Cambodian capital of Phnom Penh in April. President Lon Nol's troops were unable to stop this offensive, and he fled the country on April Fool's Day. Under the command of Colonel S. H. Batchelder, Marine helicopters from the assault ship *Okinawa* landed on a soccer field near the American embassy in Phnom Penh, the troops established a landing zone, and 82 Americans and over 200 foreign nationals were evacuated during Operation Eagle Pull by Rear Admiral Donald Whitmire's Carrier Ready Group, consisting of the carrier *Hancock* and the helicopter carrier *Okinawa.*

President Ford's inability to prevent the North Vietnamese from overrunning South Vietnam—coupled with the spectacle of the last-minute American evacuation from Saigon—undermined the stature of the United States throughout Asia. At home, Ford was keenly aware that he was the nation's first appointed president and that liberal Democrats held commanding majorities in both houses of Congress. What came to be known as the *Mayaguez* incident was one result of the upheaval in Southeast Asia following the victory of the communist insurgencies in Laos and Cambodia. The *Mayaguez* affair was Ford's opportunity to demonstrate that he intended to exercise his powers as commander in chief and that his presidency was to be more than a footnote in history.

After entering Phnom Penh on 17 April 1975, Pol Pot's Khmer Rouge established a new government, undertook a vindictive campaign of eliminating all vestiges of the old order, and adopted a vituperative, isolationist foreign policy. Phnom Penh announced an extension of Cambodian territorial waters ninety miles out to sea, an area that included several offshore islands as well as a major shipping lane in the Gulf of Thailand. Several Thai fishing boats plying these waters were detained and released on 2 May. Two days later, Khmer Rouge gunboats opened fire on a South Korean cargo ship, the *Mansan Ho*, and attempted to board her before she escaped. On 8 May, the Cambodians seized a Panamanian ship, which they detained for thirty-six hours before allowing her to proceed. In spite of these provocations, the Defense Mapping Agency in Washington failed to issue a special warning to mariners, as the situation required.

Meanwhile, in Hong Kong, a cargo of paint, chemicals, and food was being loaded onto the American containership *Mayaguez*, which then stood out to sea and shaped a course for the port of Ban Sattahip on the southern coast of Thailand. Although the *Mayaguez* also may have carried a container of secret electronic equipment for the NSA listening post in Thailand, this apparently played no part in the events that transpired during the next week. After rounding the tip of Vietnam on 11 May, the *Mayaguez* entered the Gulf of Thailand and was steaming past the island of Poulo Way when a squadron of Cambodian gunboats brought her under fire and forced her to halt. An armed party boarded the merchantman and took her forty-man crew hostage. A distress call from the *Mayaguez* was relayed to Admiral Gayler, then in Washington, and he directed Commander J. A. Messagee of the Philippine Patrol Force to launch P-3 Orions from Utapao, Thailand, and Cubi Point in the Philippines to locate the

Mayaguez, which Gayler believed was heading toward the Cambodian port of Kompong Som, formerly Sihanoukville. The first P-3 Orion arrived over Poulo Way at 2130. She counted over sixty vessels large and small in the vicinity of the island but could not identify the *Mayaguez*, even with the aid of parachute-dropped flares.

This confusing picture confronted Ford in Washington when he met with his National Security Council at noon on the 12th, nine hours after the seizure. Complicating Ford's predicament was the severance of diplomatic relations between Phnom Penh and Washington and the reluctance of the Chinese, who had close ties to the Khmer Rouge, to mediate the dispute. Ford told Kissinger to have Ambassador George Bush in Beijing ask the Chinese to convey a protest to the Cambodians, and he also put in motion the first steps toward effecting a rescue of the ship and her crew. The carrier *Coral Sea*, then en route to Australia for a celebration of the World War II battle for which she was named, was ordered to change course and steam back into Southeast Asian waters. The carrier *Hancock*, then in the Philippines, was to reinforce the Rescue Force, while the destroyer *Henry B. Wilson* was to rendezvous with the *Coral Sea* off Koh Tang Island. At the same time, Commander Robert A. Peterson in the destroyer *Harold E. Holt*, which had just rescued a group of South Vietnamese boat people from the South China Sea, received orders to head toward the Gulf of Thailand. Admiral Gayler had already told the 3rd Marine Division on Okinawa to go on alert, and Ford now agreed that a Marine battalion landing unit should be airlifted from Okinawa to the American base at Utapao.

When dawn broke over the Gulf of Thailand on 13 May, a P-3 Orion descended and made a slow pass over a large vessel, which the pilot identified as the *Mayaguez*. She had been anchored seven miles off Poulo Way overnight but was now steaming slowly toward the mainland. Reflecting on Lyndon Johnson's difficulty in persuading the North Koreans to release the crew of the *Pueblo* in 1968, Ford directed that Air Force F-4 Phantoms based at Utapao try to turn back the *Mayaguez* by harassing and strafing her. Unbeknownst to the White House, at 0830 on the morning of the 13th, the Khmer Rouge boarding party had ordered Charles Miller, the master of the *Mayaguez*, to weigh anchor and head for Koh Tang, about thirty-four miles from the coast. That afternoon, Commander Messagee relayed to Washington a report from one of his P-3 Orion patrol planes that the *Mayaguez* had dropped anchor about one mile off Koh Tang and that a pair of Cambodian fishing vessels had been sighted carrying the hostages to the island. Although several conflicting reports confused Ford, nevertheless at noon on that day he decided that the American aircraft flying out of Utapao "should use whatever means they could to head off either ships going to the mainland or from the mainland of Koh Tang," thus effectively isolating the *Mayaguez* and her crew. Another message sent via the Chinese warned the Cambodians not to try to remove the *Mayaguez* to Kompong Som. At dawn on 14 May, however, a flight of Air Force fighters observed a large fishing vessel in company with two Cambodian gunboats heading from Koh Tang to the Cambodian coast. The American fighters dispersed the hostile escorts, then opened fire ahead of the fishing boat and drenched her with tear gas, but the attack was called off when one pilot realized that some of the hostages were on board.[14]

Thus, when Ford met with the NSC on the evening of 13 May, the Americans did not know exactly where all the hostages were being held. Kissinger, worried about the impact of the episode on eroding American prestige in Asia, was "emphatic on the use of force." Defense Secretary Schlesinger, on the other hand, was less concerned with sending signals and instead stressed the need to recover the ship and save the crew. "Even though the odds might be against us," Ford decided that a rescue operation coupled with punitive air strikes "was far better than doing nothing." He told the JCS to instruct Admiral Gayler to execute his rescue plan, while Kissinger was to press ahead on the diplomatic front.[15]

Gayler's rescue plan had three aspects. First, attack aircraft from the *Coral Sea* would hit four targets around Kompong Som. Ford reasoned that Cambodia was probably too disorganized to absorb a diplomatic signal delivered by tactical bombers, but he decided nonetheless to "make surgical strikes against military specific targets in the vicinity of Kompong Som" so as to confuse the Khmer Rouge and prevent them from reinforcing Koh Tang Island. Second, Air Force fighter-bombers from Utapao and attack aircraft from the *Coral Sea* would bomb Koh Tang Island in advance of a helicopter assault by Marines staged from Utapao. The Marines would overcome the garrison—estimated to be up to 100 men—and recover the hostages. Third, the *Harold B. Holt* would recover the *Mayaguez*.[16]

Things went awry from the start. For one thing, the Chinese refused to act as intermediaries. For another, "we knew by the time of this meeting how quickly the destroyer *Holt* would get there and how soon the destroyer *Wilson* would get there, but we didn't know whether the aircraft carrier *Coral Sea* would be close enough." For this reason, the rescue operation was postponed for twenty-four hours.

At 0609 on the morning of 15 May, five Air Force CH-53 helicopters approached Koh Tang, carrying an assault wave of 174 Marines who were supposed to land on the island and free the hostages. The unexpectedly strong Cambodian garrison there shot down two choppers on the western side of the island, however, killing fourteen Americans and leaving the small party of Marines who did land in unsupported isolation. On the eastern beach, the next three helicopters managed to land, but two were badly damaged on takeoff and a third had to ditch offshore. While the second wave of helicopters landed, only 131 Marines were put ashore, and 8 of 9 choppers either had to be ditched or were so badly damaged that they could no longer fly. With his men divided and pinned down by a determined enemy, Marine Lieutenant Colonel Randall W. Austin now called for his reserves. The move jeopardized the only 3 remaining CH-53s, which shortly after noon brought the total Marine strength on Koh Tang to 224. By then, however, everyone realized that the landing on Koh Tang had been a tragic mistake.

Three of the eleven CH-53 helicopters that took off from Utapao that morning headed for the destroyer *Holt*, which had entered the Gulf the previous evening and taken station about a mile to the east of Koh Tang. At dawn, the helicopters appeared overhead and forty-eight Marines descended to the deck of the *Holt*, which sped toward the *Mayaguez*, then riding at anchor to the north of the island. At 0650 Commander Peterson reported that six Khmer Rouge soldiers had been spotted on the deck of the *Mayaguez*, but when he came alongside and Marines boarded the vessel they found that she had been abandoned.

Until the morning of 15 May, Cambodia's government had said nothing through diplomatic channels or in public about the *Mayaguez*. When dawn arose in the Gulf of Thailand that day, however, evidence was plentiful that something was afoot. Suddenly, at 0609 Phnom Penh radio began to broadcast a long harangue about the *Mayaguez* affair, ending with the unexpected statement that the Khmer Rouge intended to release the ship im-

mediately. Ford received this news about ninety minutes later—
after the Marines had landed on Koh Tang, but before the first
Navy bombers reached their targets in Cambodia. Wondering if
the broadcast was authoritative, he recalled that it "made no
mention of the crew, and thus I decided that the [bombing] operation should proceed as planned." Only a few minutes earlier,
a flight of A-6 Intruders and A-7 Corsairs had been launched by
the *Coral Sea* and was en route to Kompong Som, but the White
House instructed these aircraft not to drop their ordnance while
the president was deciding what to do. A second wave of Navy aircraft hit the Ream airfield about 1000, damaging some aircraft
and destroying a few buildings, and an hour later a third wave
struck the Kompong Som naval base. Two warehouses, a fuel
storage depot, and a railway marshaling yard were damaged.
These strikes may have prevented the Khmer Rouge from supporting Koh Tang, although the enemy's purposes remained an
enigma throughout the crisis.[17]

Hardly had the first flight of strike aircraft been launched
when events took another strange turn. Shortly after 0900 American planes flying in the vicinity of Koh Tang sighted the
hostages standing on the deck of a Thai fishing vessel. The
Wilson rescued them at 0949, and the skipper learned that the
Mayaguez's entire crew had been held on Rong Som Lem Island
in Kompong Som harbor prior to their release earlier that
morning. Because the hostages were safe and the *Mayaguez* was
under tow, attention turned to extracting the Marines from Koh
Tang Island. The Khmer Rouge repulsed the first helicopter
that tried to descend on the eastern beach, but a second chop-
per managed to land and evacuate the Americans on that side of
the island. Since there were only three helicopters left, an Air
Force C-130 from Utapao was called upon to drop a 15,000-
pound BLU-82 bomb—the largest nonnuclear explosive in the
American arsenal—and this cleared a landing zone for the evacuation of the western side of Koh Tang. Then the *Wilson* closed
on the island and began to shell hostile positions, as did the
Holt, once free of her tow. Near sunset the *Coral Sea* appeared on
the horizon, and the remaining CH-53 choppers shuttled the
last Marines to the safety of the carrier. During this operation,
most of the American helicopters had been damaged or destroyed, fifteen men were killed, and fifty-three had been lost on
Koh Tang or were wounded.

The not altogether unambiguous success of the *Mayaguez* rescue inevitably led to conflicting interpretations, but Ford contended that his decisiveness "sort of turned the corner and changed the course" of his administration. The post-Vietnam mood of neoisolationism in Washington was nevertheless unmistakable. "In spite of détente and the end of U.S. fighting in the war in Southeast Asia," Admiral Holloway pointed out, the "United States has defense treaties with 43 other nations, and 41 of these [nations are] overseas. The validity of these arrangements depends upon our ability to maintain the integrity of our sea lines of communications." The revulsion against another Vietnam-style intervention was widespread, however. When the Soviets mounted a formidable air and sea lift to defend newly independent clients in Mozambique and Angola from insurrections and Ford hinted that he intended to respond, Congress cut off American military support to the anticommunist rebels in both of these countries in December 1975. "At some point," Ford warned resignedly, "the United States must draw the line."[18]

Chapter Thirty-four

The Days of Malaise
1977–1979

Governor Jimmy Carter of Georgia, a Naval Academy graduate and sometime peanut farmer, captured the Democratic Party nomination in 1976 and, after a close race, defeated Republican Gerald Ford in the presidential election. A moralist who denounced the often amoral pragmatism of his Republican predecessors, Carter believed that Woodrow Wilson's "call for national repentance . . . seemed appropriate" for the United States in the post-Vietnam era. To head the State Department, he named Cyrus Vance, a liberal attorney who viewed "Moscow's adventurism" as "founded more on capitalizing on targets of opportunity" than on advancing according to any overall plan. Neither Carter nor Vance, the president's closest adviser, possessed an overall, cohesive view of American foreign policy interests, global strategy, or military obligations. "Carter believes fifty things, but no one thing," commented a presidential assistant. "Values that others would find contradictory complement one another in his mind."[1]

Carter subscribed to the liberal dogma that intervening with American military power overseas—especially in Asia, Africa, and Latin America—had been since Truman's days a malevolent and mostly self-defeating policy. To contain this adventurist impulse, he turned to Europe in the hope of establishing a trilateral dialogue among the United States, NATO, and Japan, once more anchoring American foreign policy to frightened allies who were disinclined to take international risks. At the same time, he intended to pursue parallel policies of détente, nuclear nonproliferation, and a vigorous human rights test of the behavior of friends, nonaligned nations, and enemies alike. Soon, however, his European diplomacy was in shreds. NATO's leaders were unanimously contemptuous of Carter, fearful of Russia, unconcerned with Third World dialogues, and bitter about America's unconditional support for Israel. Within a year, Carter's plan for a new trilateralism had disintegrated. In the Middle East, where he could play a more independent hand, he scored a great coup in 1978 by arranging for peace talks at Camp David, Maryland, between Egypt's Anwar Sadat and Israel's Menachem Begin, who negotiated a bilateral treaty establishing diplomatic relations. Unfortunately, the Camp David Accords did not solve the Palestinian problem, which continued to fester.

Carter's overly trustful attitude toward the Soviets skirted disaster, however. In March 1977, he sent Vance to Moscow with a proposal for deep cuts in strategic nuclear forces, which was to serve as the basis for a SALT II treaty. Under this plan, only eight *Ohio*-class Trident missile submarines were to be built and the aging B-52 bomber wings would not be replaced. Simultaneously, the president announced his new human rights policy, under which he felt free to hector the Kremlin for persecuting Russian Jews and other dissidents, while insisting that there was no link between this diplomacy and the SALT II negotiations. Furious at this fumbling, inconsistent interpretation of détente, Brezhnev brusquely dismissed Vance's arms control scheme. Without really meaning it, Carter then hesitantly denounced Russian intervention in Africa and elsewhere just to "prove we weren't soft." To pressure Brezhnev to agree to a SALT II treaty, Carter next sent his national security adviser, Zbigniew Brzezinski, to China in March 1978 and established formal diplomatic relations with Beijing soon after. Carter also went back on his campaign pledge to reduce military spending; in early 1978, he proposed to increase the Defense Department budget by 3 percent above the inflation rate, with most of the additional funds earmarked for Army and Air Force support of NATO. These soft jabs apparently did little to impress the Soviets.[2]

Carter was facing complaints in Washington that the United States would confront in the next decade a "window of vulnerability" that would be open between the time the old triad of

B-52s, silo-based Minuteman missiles, and Polaris-Poseidon submarines were retired, and the succeeding triad of B-1 bombers,
mobile MX missiles, and *Ohio*-class Trident missile–bearing submarines were introduced. Although Carter canceled the B-1 project and unwittingly crippled the MX program by his inability to
decide on a basing mode, Brezhnev was clearly worried that the
long-term trend in strategic nuclear forces had now turned
against the Soviet Union. After both sides reverted to the framework of the Vladivostok Agreement, Carter and Brezhnev signed
the SALT II treaty during a summit meeting in Vienna in June
1979. Under this accord, each superpower was to be limited to
2,400 strategic nuclear delivery vehicles—including ICBMs, ballistic missile submarines, and manned bombers—until 1982,
when this figure was to drop to 2,250; launchers carrying MIRVs
were fixed at 1,200 apiece. SALT II was immediately denounced
by many conservative Republicans and moderate Democrats who
agreed with Senator Henry Jackson's charge that the treaty embodied Carter's general foreign policy of "appeasement." Even
Senator Frank Church, a liberal Democrat who chaired the Foreign Relations Committee, refused to support SALT II, aware of
the strength of the political opposition to the treaty and the president's general unpopularity. In the fall of 1979, Brzezinski confessed to the bankruptcy of Carter's diplomacy when he admitted
that with the refusal of the Senate to approve SALT II "there was
neither dialogue nor deterrence in our [remaining] relationship
with Moscow."[3]

Inasmuch as détente under Carter was intended to create an
environment in which both superpowers would possess no more
forces than necessary for Mutual Assured Destruction, second-
strike, retaliatory nuclear-weapons launchers assumed a greater
importance to American strategic planners. Thus, in 1978 Carter
announced that he was canceling the Air Force B-1 manned
bomber and would, instead, accelerate the development of air-,
land-, and sea-launched cruise missiles. On the other hand, Professor Francis West of the Naval War College pointed out in 1978
that "the national command authority does not take nuclear
warfighting seriously."[4]

The Navy was not unhappy with the temporary demise of
the B-1 bomber and favored the acceleration of the sea-launched
Tomahawk cruise missile program. This weapon promised a
means to increase the mix of targets a task force might hit during

a general war and would permit the deployment of missile-bearing ships to areas not normally covered by carriers and endow cruisers and destroyers with weapons capable of sinking Soviet ships or attacking land targets with conventional or nuclear payloads. The administration also restated the importance of continuing the Trident fleet ballistic missile submarine program, which Carter favored because it was unambiguously a retaliatory, second-strike system. By this time, however, the Trident program was in deep trouble, plagued by immense cost overruns and dispiriting delays. On 29 November 1977, Rear Admiral Donald Hall announced that the cost for each Trident-bearing *Ohio* class submarine had risen from $780 million to $1.2 billion. The builder, General Dynamics' Electric Boat Division, admitted that it could "not make the contract delivery date" for the lead boat. Electric Boat had agreed to deliver the *Ohio* in 1977 but would now promise only "to use its best efforts" to deliver the vessel two years later.[5]

Ford's secretary of defense, James Schlesinger, had been so discouraged about the long-delayed Trident program that he asked Admiral Holloway in 1975 about building a new, smaller submarine or more Poseidon-bearing submarines—a reasonable concept, which Admiral Rickover quickly smote like a snake in the grass. Rickover could not, on the other hand, argue against the need to deploy MIRV, multiple independently targeted re-entry vehicles, and several of the older Polaris submarines had been armed with the new Trident missiles, all of which carried MIRVs. Nonetheless, the *Ethan Allens* were so old that by 1980 about ten would have to be withdrawn from service, the first reduction in the fleet ballistic missile force since 1967. Mired in mismanagement, red ink, and claims and counterclaims, the $1.5 billion *Ohio* submarine did not enter the fleet until 1981, four years after the original contract date and nearly seven years after she was laid down. By this time, the American ballistic missile submarine fleet included only 31 vessels with 496 tubes, whereas the Soviets deployed 63 submarines with 950 missiles. Not only had the Soviets gained strategic superiority with their heavy land-based rockets, but their sea-based, second-strike, retaliatory throwweight now eclipsed the comparable American arsenal. This did not bother Carter, however; he believed that neither superpower would ever fire its nuclear weapons and thus saw no purpose in developing a counterforce strategy or in crafting a new nuclear warfighting strategy.

Carter's noninterventionist foreign policy and his emphasis on strengthening NATO's defenses on the central front in Germany lay at the root of his recurrent troubles with the Navy. He so wanted to believe that a NATO war would be localized to the central front, because then it could be waged with conventional ordnance, that he devised his strategy accordingly. "Our near-term objective is to assure that NATO could not be overwhelmed in the first few weeks of a blitzkrieg war, and we will spend our resources to that end," he told the JCS in April 1978. Inasmuch as the Navy could not play a decisive role in a short central front war, it was accorded a low priority in Carter's defense policy. One month earlier, his secretary of defense, Harold Brown, had instructed Admiral Holloway, the CNO, that the "prime wartime U.S. naval mission was to protect the sea lines of communications between Europe and America." By adopting a "defensive sea control" strategy, which aimed first and foremost at resupplying NATO, the Navy was to spare the president the need to revert to nuclear weapons to prevent the Red Army from overrunning Europe.

The Carter administration's "conventional wisdom," Undersecretary of the Navy R. James Woolsey wrote a few weeks later, was that resupplying NATO was really "the Navy's main, and only vital, mission." The "convoy escort navy posture" became the "vogue in the late 1970s," complained Vice Admiral Henry Mustin. Accordingly, Brown trimmed President Ford's last shipbuilding program by half, cutting to 70 the 159 ships the Republicans had intended to add to the fleet. Plagued by cost overruns, bloc obsolescence, raging inflation, and underfunded building programs, Holloway was discouraged about contesting this policy. The Navy was reduced to 459 ships in 1977, and Holloway even conceded that holding the Mediterranean in wartime—a longstanding obligation to NATO—would be "uncertain, at best." If the carrier task forces from the Pacific Fleet were to steam into the Atlantic when a global war began, he believed, then the Atlantic Fleet might defend the Greenland–Iceland–United Kingdom barriers and prevent Soviet attack submarines from debouching into the North Atlantic. "Control of the seas is required before the Navy can conduct other missions such as tactical air strike and amphibious operations," he told Congress. He had few reserves on which to call, however, and worried that attrition to the Atlantic Fleet from Soviet submarines and land-based naval air forces would be substantial.[6]

At the Naval War College in 1979, Office of Management and Budget analyst Randy Jayne outlined the priority of American ground defenses in Europe and argued that the new CNO, Admiral Thomas Hayward, had to provide a more impressive strategic rationale for maintaining a large fleet or watch it continue to shrink. This was difficult to do, given that NATO's supreme commander, General Alexander Haig, wanted to fight a war in Europe "come as you are." According to former Navy Secretary Nitze, "to move 10 million tons of American war supplies and 15 million tons of fuel to NATO ports within the first ninety days of hostilities to reinforce U.S. forces . . . would require 1,000 merchant vessels." If Soviet attack submarines attacked NATO-bound shipping during the first month of a general war, Navy planners estimated that over 600 freighters and tankers would be lost. Thinking the carriers could no longer survive in the Mediterranean against Soviet submarines and land-based air forces, Secretary Brown ruled that they were to defend Atlantic resupply convoys to Europe. He charged Navy Secretary W. Graham Claytor, a former railroad manager, with matching the Navy's shipbuilding policy with Carter's Swing Strategy, but Claytor disagreed with this formulation—which called for a large fraction of the Pacific Fleet to steam for the Atlantic at the outbreak of a general war—and characterized it as a "fundamental change in national strategy." That portion of the fleet not dedicated to NATO was about to become a mere "police force." It was ironic that Carter settled on the Swing Strategy because it provided no real counter to what was then known to be Russian naval strategy. Commerce raiding by indiscriminate attacks on enemy shipping was repeatedly condemned by the Red Navy's Admiral Gorshkov, who stressed the use of mines to defend Russia's ports and coastal waters, the protection of Soviet ballistic missile–bearing submarines, and antisubmarine operations against the American ballistic missile boats. Gorshkov clearly placed a low priority on antishipping operations in the North Atlantic, and when he did publicly discuss such attacks, he proposed using mines planted by aircraft or submarines rather than missile or torpedo attacks.[7]

The Navy's opposition to Carter's Swing Strategy was stiff. At bedrock was the conviction among Navy men that a NATO war would be global and could not be contained within Europe or the formal alliances. Instead of proving "support of the central

front in Europe," argued Admiral Robert Long, who commanded the Pacific theater, American "naval forces can be more effective against the Soviets in a global war if they are used elsewhere."
Admiral Harry Train of the Atlantic Fleet claimed to be confused
by the mechanics of the Carter-Brown strategy. "It was hard to en-
vision how the Swing Strategy would work," he admitted. "I knew
I was not really going to get carriers from the Pacific," Train
wrote, and the Pacific Fleet commander "knew he was not going
to send them, even though the Swing Strategy said this would
happen. So my warfighting strategies did not include those
things." Indeed, as early as 1977 the Atlantic Fleet had virtually
given up on plans to conduct barrier and escort operations, turning instead to a more vigorous antisubmarine strategy that relied
heavily on a combination of the fixed SOSUS hydrophone systems and more intensive use of the P-3 Orion patrol squadrons.
Under this new plan, the Atlantic Fleet intended to escort battle
groups and amphibious and replenishment groups across the
Atlantic but would at the same time accept some attrition against
allied cargo shipping while American antisubmarine forces
hunted down those Soviet submarines that had broken through
the barriers and entered the North Atlantic. According to
Admiral Hayward, "the prompt destruction of opposing naval
forces is the most economical and effective means to assure
control [of the seas]."[8]

Adopting a more offensive strategic outlook meant rebuild-
ing the carrier force, an issue first visited a decade earlier by
Admiral McDonald, who had persuaded President Johnson to inaugurate the *Nimitz*-class nuclear carrier program in 1966. Admiral Moorer wanted to order three of these ships under one contract, but the costs of the Vietnam War and liberal opposition in
Congress to defense spending compelled him to stretch out the
program, thus increasing the price of each vessel. After three
Nimitz-class carriers had been authorized by Congress, Admiral
Zumwalt in 1972 persuaded Defense Secretary Laird to request
funds to build a second, nonnuclear 55,000-ton *Kennedy*-class attack carrier. Although Secretary of Defense Schlesinger supported the plan, Admiral Rickover and most naval aviators so strongly
opposed it that Admiral Holloway killed it shortly after he became CNO in 1975. Holloway also inherited Zumwalt's plan to
lay down a class of antisubmarine Surface Control Ship, a very
small, 9,500-ton carrier that was to operate only Harrier VSTOL
aircraft and antisubmarine helicopters. Surface Control Ships

were intended to escort convoys, locate hostile submarines, and direct attacks against them by screening frigates and destroyers. The VSTOL jump-jet aircraft envisioned by Zumwalt was an expensive plane with a short operational radius, limited endurance, and low speed. The large attack carriers "had far too much offensive capability to waste on convoy duty," Zumwalt believed, but "in any real war situation there might be at sea [heading for Europe] as many as twenty convoys of merchantmen, troop transports, and naval auxiliaries in need of air protection from the time they left the reach of land-based air until they entered areas where the deployed [heavy] carriers were operating." The large amphibious ship *Guam* was altered for trials to test the concept, but after Zumwalt retired in 1974 the Surface Control Ship was bereft of supporters. "Both the nuclear folk and the aviators saw it as infringing on their turf," Zumwalt acknowledged.[9]

Reaching a consensus among Navy men on some new program gained greater urgency in the early 1970s when the last of the wartime *Essex*-class carriers was retired. The resolute opposition of Admiral Holloway to the Swing Strategy complicated Navy Secretary Claytor's dilemma. The CNO stood fast behind the traditional "balanced fleet" concept that the anti-interventionist Democrats in the administration and Congress so disliked. Secretary Claytor bridled at the implication that, because of what analyst Jayne termed the "benign environment" of the North Atlantic sea lines of communications, a larger fleet was unnecessary. Whereas the Americans could rely on the combination of attack submarines and the SOSUS hydrophone system in the eastern Atlantic, in the mid-Atlantic NATO antisubmarine defenses would be limited to maritime patrol aircraft and a handful of ocean escorts. Somehow the problem of Soviet attack submarines in the Atlantic had to be solved.[10]

Holloway decided that a strategy of attacking the Soviets on their northern European and Pacific flanks was preferable to the Swing and barrier and escort strategies, but neither Defense Secretary Brown nor Air Force General David Jones, the chairman of the JCS, took this seriously. Indeed, Brown brusquely told Holloway that building up Army and Air Force units dedicated to NATO's central front was Carter's overriding priority and that he intended the fleet to be prepared only for convoying and "localized contingencies outside Europe." Claytor responded that the Carter-Brown Swing Strategy was "the naval equivalent of the Maginot Line."[11]

Carter's most controversial step in naval policy was his unsuccessful attempt to end the *Nimitz*-class attack carrier program and force the Navy to lay down a new type of smaller, nonnuclear antisubmarine carrier instead. Given Carter's intention in 1977 to hold defense spending in check, the costs of the *Ohio*-class submarine program and improved antisubmarine forces had to be extracted from the *Nimitz*-class carrier program, the most expensive component of the shipbuilding schedule. The ensuing struggle was termed by wits the "great carrier war." The nuclear-powered *Nimitz* was commissioned on 3 May 1975, and her sister ship, the *Dwight D. Eisenhower*, joined the fleet two years later. A third *Nimitz*-class carrier was already under construction, the *Carl Vinson*, so the question faced by Carter in 1977 was whether to lay down a fourth large carrier of this class, or instead to turn to either the smaller antisubmarine carrier or the very austere escort carrier. Naval aviators had long criticized the escort carrier as being too small, vulnerable, and defenseless a ship with little purpose beyond the convoy mission. Whereas Zumwalt's proposed Surface Control Ship could only deal with local attacks on a convoy by Soviet submarines, the larger antisubmarine carrier could conduct hunting operations in either the Atlantic or the Pacific. However, neither of these vessels could deal with Soviet missile ships. Embarking an air group of only twenty-five VSTOL Harriers, the antisubmarine carrier would have to rely on her missile screen to defend her task force and could not be used to attack Soviet missile-bearing ship formations, air forces, bases, or other missile-defended targets. Because the antisubmarine carrier was oil-fired, Admiral Rickover opposed constructing it. President Ford had proposed as a compromise in 1974 to lay down one oil-fired 55,000-ton large escort carrier, but Rickover apparently persuaded congressional Democrats to ignore this plan.

In 1976 the Congressional Budget Office, directed by Alice Rivlin, published a study of American naval policy that urged a change in the basic missions of the fleet and promised corresponding savings in shipbuilding costs. In short, Rivlin suggested that the fleet be configured to escort resupply convoys to NATO ground and air forces during a central front war, support land-based air operations against Soviet targets in Europe, and not much else. Ironically, Michael Krepon, one of the authors, claimed that the VSTOL carrier was needed to execute the fleet's "secondary mission, which is the projection of power ashore in support of combat operations" on the periphery of Europe. Of course, this was exactly what the antisubmarine carrier was least capable of accomplishing.[12]

The CBO report profoundly influenced Carter's naval policy, although Secretary of Defense Brown made no secret of his opposition to building more carriers of any type. In a speech at Wake Forest University on 17 March 1978, Carter recognized the prevailing view "that this country somehow is pulling back from its interests and its friends around the world," a critique he labeled a "myth," but he nonetheless announced eleven days later that he was slashing the Navy's five-year building program from 159 to 70 ships. At Brown's urging, Carter also turned down Holloway's request for a fourth *Nimitz*-class carrier and asked Congress instead for funds to build the oil-fired antisubmarine carrier. Senators Robert Taft of Ohio and Gary Hart of Colorado, influenced by staffer William Lind, an eccentric gadfly, proposed that the Navy lay down one even smaller, less expensive, 20,000-ton escort carrier. As any antisubmarine or escort carrier could deal only with Soviet attack submarines and could not defend itself against hostile missile-bearing vessels, either Carter's or Hart's plan would leave the job of bottling up the Red Navy's striking ships to the few remaining heavy carrier battle groups and the overburdened attack submarines.[13]

Admiral Holloway recoiled at Carter's plan and responded to it near the end of his term as CNO with *Sea Plan 2000*, an analysis written by Professor West of the Naval War College. Rejecting the Swing Strategy, he argued instead that the fleet's primary mission should be "to maintain stability by forward deployment of carrier battle groups and Marines in . . . the Mediterranean, Northeast Asia, Southeast Asia, and the Indian Ocean." To do this the Navy needed at least 12 to 14 large carriers, 90 attack submarines, and a total fleet numbering between 535 and 585 ships. With this number of large carriers, Holloway explained, about five might be on station at any given time to "contain crises by U.S. superiority at sea." Since neither the escort carrier nor the antisubmarine carrier could execute this mission, Holloway and West dismissed constructing these vessels as a waste of money. "We retain a slim margin of superiority . . . in those scenarios involving our most vital interests," Holloway said on his retirement in July 1978, but without more carriers and other ships, that margin was not going to last long.[14]

Secretary Brown characterized this argument over carriers as a "red herring." Holloway's formulation defied any reasonable relationship to the president's foreign policy, which, after all, was founded on nonintervention, eschewed the use of force as a means to defend American interests in the Third World, and relied instead on moral suasion and economic sanctions. Carter showed no intention of using force to settle the dispute between Turkey and Greece over Cyprus, and his diplomacy toward Israel and Egypt stressed American good offices and economic aid, not military leverage. In spite of Carter's interest in NATO's central front, the number of ships assigned to the 6th Fleet declined during his presidency, but in 1981 Admiral Long, the commander of the Pacific theater, admitted that "the political consequences of drawing down the carrier forces in the Mediterranean have been nil." Since the Paris Peace Accords of 1973, nonintervention in Southeast Asia—regardless of the provocation—was an accepted staple of American grand strategy. Carter did nothing to prevent the communist Khmer Rouge regime in Laos from murdering nearly two million Laotians in a genocidal campaign, and he vigorously backed a plan to reduce the level of nonregional naval forces in the Indian Ocean. His main military concern, he told the JCS on several occasions, was to increase American support to NATO and to negotiate the SALT II treaty. Nonetheless, Admiral Holloway, who knew that "defending [North Atlantic] sea lanes" and "reinforcing U.S. allies" could not be accomplished without first dealing with the Red Navy, quietly pushed Congress to defeat the antisubmarine carrier plan and instead authorize a fourth *Nimitz*-class attack carrier on the grounds that the fleet needed a "balanced force."[15]

Carter's defeat in the "great carrier war" stemmed from his unwillingness or inability to exert leadership by imposing his will on his own subordinates. Carter easily mastered minutiae but lacked the intellectual depth to deal in large principles or the force of personality to convert or punish those who opposed him. Not only did he fail to convince Congress that his defense policy and shipbuilding plan were serious, but also he undercut his own case in 1978 by naming Admiral Thomas Hayward, the most outspoken advocate of the *Nimitz*-class carrier program and an early critic of the Swing Strategy, to succeed Holloway as the next CNO. In addition, Carter tolerated the near-public dissent of Navy Secretary Claytor, who announced on 28 May 1978 that he wanted Congress "to start building another carrier of some kind in the near future."[16]

Congressional Democrats who disliked Carter surprised many by their willingness to humble their party's president. The House voted to build a fourth *Nimitz*-class carrier, but Hart persuaded the Senate to pass a measure to lay down a second oil-fired, 60,000-ton *John F. Kennedy*-class antisubmarine carrier instead. After considerable wrangling, the House position was supported by a joint conference committee, and Congress sent the resulting bill to the White House. Brown told Carter not to accept this challenge to his authority as commander in chief, so the president took the unprecedented step of vetoing the entire Defense Department spending bill. The Democrats on the Hill backed down, revised the bill by omitting the carrier, and returned it to the White House for Carter's signature. The hostage crisis with Iran colored the resolution of the carrier issue in 1979. Admiral Hayward again asked Brown for funds to build a fourth *Nimitz*-class carrier, but the five-year shipbuilding program sent to Congress—which totaled only sixty-three ships—contained the earlier plan for the oil-fired, *Kennedy*-class antisubmarine carrier. With trouble brewing in the Middle East, the mood on the Hill had hardened against half measures, and both the responsible House and Senate committees voted to include a fourth *Nimitz*-class carrier in the Defense Department authorization bill. Crippled by his inability to resolve the Iranian crisis, Carter was faced by a certain override of a veto, so he meekly signed the act.

Defense Secretary Brown virtually ignored most of Zumwalt's High-Low Mix shipbuilding policy, but he did apply the concept to naval aircraft procurement. In 1968, Admiral Tom Connally had convinced Admiral Moorer and Congress to end the disastrous naval F-111B fighter-bomber program and to turn to the F-14 Tomcat to replace the aging F-4 Phantoms as the Navy's front-line fighter. Moorer thoroughly committed the Navy to the Tomcat as the replacement for the Phantoms, and even Zumwalt resisted a plan put forth by Nixon's first budget director, James Schlesinger, to jointly develop with the Air Force a low-cost light fighter. The Navy distrusted these schemes after the F-111 fiasco. As Schlesinger predicted, however, improvements to the F-14 Tomcat, inflation, and Grumman's mismanagement of the program vastly increased the cost of each plane. The Nixon and Ford administrations both scaled back the Navy's original procurement plan, and by 1977 it was evident that Congress would never appropriate enough money to buy all of the 1,300 Tomcats needed to fill out the fleet's fighter squadrons.

The Air Force, which found itself in much the same predicament because of the escalating cost of its front-line F-15 Eagle interceptor, chose to build a large number of cheaper light fighters intended to follow the radar-equipped F-15 flight leaders into battle. After competitive tests, the F-16 Falcon was selected for this role, but this left McDonnell Douglas, the manufacturer of the competing F-17 fighter, without any customers for its plane. McDonnell Douglas had, however, cleverly apportioned the subcontracts for the F-17 to as many congressional districts as possible, thus leading to irresistible pressure on the Carter administration from Capitol Hill to somehow save the aircraft. Defense Secretary Brown's response was to suspend the Marines' AV-8B Harrier VSTOL jump-jet program and use the money to pay for the F-17, which was redesigned to serve as a fighter-bomber and given a new name, the FA-18 Hornet. Brown also instructed Navy Secretary Claytor to buy FA-18 Hornets to succeed the A-7 Corsair II, although the Corsair was a superior attack aircraft in every respect and did not need to be replaced.

McDonnell Douglas FA-18A Hornet flies with VX-4, an air test and evaluation squadron of the Pacific Fleet. The Hornet is armed with Sidewinder air-to-air missiles on her wingtips and inboard Sparrow air-to-air missiles.

U.S. Navy Department

Brown insisted that the deployment of the FA-18 Hornets would endow each carrier with more fighters, but only the F-14 Tomcat armed with a Phoenix missile could deal at all with the greatest threat to the fleet—the new supersonic long-range Soviet missile-bearing Backfire bomber. Because the Backfire could reach into the mid-Atlantic and menace NATO's sea lines of communication with anti-ship missiles, countering this threat seemed especially important given Carter's dedication to a Europe-first escort and convoy strategy. Whereas the FA-18 Hornet might deal with the Soviet's older Badger bomber, defeating the Backfire would be difficult for the F-14 Tomcat but impossible for the FA-18 Hornet owing to its lack of sprint speed, limited combat radius, and inability to carry long-range, air-to-air missiles. Another effect of Brown's decision to buy the FA-18 Hornet was to considerably diminish the overall striking range and the payload of the fleet's attack squadrons.

Inasmuch as the Hornet met neither the Navy's requirements for a fighter equal to the Tomcat nor for a bomber equal to the Corsair II, Undersecretary of the Navy R. James Woolsey urged Brown to cancel the FA-18 program in December 1977, but Brown continued it, bowing to the interest of congressional Democrats. By reducing the number of F-14 Tomcats to be purchased by the Navy Department from 1,336 to about 400, Brown eliminated most of the savings on that plane from serial production, and the cost of each F-14 continued to climb. It was clear to the new CNO, Admiral Thomas Hayward, an aviator, that the Navy could never purchase enough Tomcats, so he lined up behind the FA-18 in 1979. McDonnell Douglas so badly managed the FA-18 program, however, that by 1982 either an F-14B Tomcat or an A-7 Corsair II cost less than the greatly inferior plane that Harold Brown had chosen to substitute for both of them. As a result, "our current ability to engage the Soviet fleet . . . will markedly diminish and the vulnerability of our [carrier] forces will be of major concern," reported the Navy's Operational Test and Evaluation Center in 1982. Brown's decision to buy the FA-18 Hornet measurably eroded the fleet's defenses against the Soviet air threat and its ability to deliver conventional ordnance against land targets.[17]

Harold Brown's demand that Admiral Holloway improve the fleet's escort force stemmed from the secretary's conviction that, during a crisis, NATO would have about two weeks warning be-

fore a central front war broke out and about four weeks to fight
and win it. Owing to the immense expenditure of munitions the
NATO armies expected during this time, escorting resupply convoys from the United States to western Europe seemed to be the
most essential mission for the Atlantic Fleet. The character of escort operations was changing dramatically, however. For one
thing, the new *Los Angeles*-class nuclear attack submarines were
expected to be effective standoff escorts for battle groups or
large convoys. Moreover, antisubmarine weapons and detection
systems had improved with the use of large supercomputers to
process data about narrow-band underwater sounds. On the other hand, the Soviet air threat to the Atlantic Fleet Striking Force
had increased substantially with the deployment of the missile-
armed Badger and long-range Backfire bombers.

To strengthen the fleet's escort force, Admiral Zumwalt had
accelerated work on the Navy's Aegis air defense system, originally designed for the nuclear-powered *California*-class cruisers and
their successors, the *Virginia*s. Congress had overridden
McNamara's opposition to the nuclear-powered *Virginia*-class
cruiser program in 1966 and provided funds over the next few
years to build four of these ships. Zumwalt preferred to lay down
a large number of Aegis destroyers, but Holloway disliked this
idea. The *Virginia*'s hull was too small to carry the Aegis system,
so Holloway turned his attention in 1974 to a design for a 17,000-
ton nuclear strike cruiser that he could arm with Tomahawk
cruise missiles, Harpoon anti-ship missiles, and an 8-inch gun to
support landing operations. Holloway wanted one Aegis-
equipped, nuclear-powered strike cruiser for every nuclear-powered carrier, an attempt to preserve the all-nuclear-powered task
force formation, but because the strike cruiser was to operate
VSTOL aircraft, she might also serve as a powerful escort or in
the lead of a surface battle group.

In 1976, President Ford had suspended the strike cruiser
program, however, and Carter canceled it one year after taking
office, at the same time that he propounded the flexibility of the
Tomahawk cruise missile as an alternative to the costly Air Force
B-1 bomber. Holloway then came up with a less expensive plan to
build an oil-fired Aegis cruiser using a large *Spruance*-class destroyer hull. To improve its offensive punch, he decided to arm
later versions of this new *Ticonderoga*-class cruiser with Harpoon
and Tomahawk missiles. The proposal to build ten *Ticonderoga*-

class cruisers was one of only two truly costly items found in Carter's shipbuilding program in 1978. Rickover opposed building the oil-fired *Ticonderogas*, but he lost the fight because neither the administration nor Congress favored building more nuclear-powered cruisers or destroyers, and Brown had ordered the Navy to delete all nuclear escorts from its budget and shipbuilding plans. As one observer sourly claimed, this move meant that the "nuclear surface fleet was dead."[18]

Chapter Thirty-five

Upholding the Carter Doctrine

1979–1980

Early in his presidency, Carter declared that he "wanted to work with the Soviet leaders to establish strict limits on the permanent deployment of naval forces in the Indian Ocean," a concept that the Russians and Indians had been propagandizing ever since Nixon dispatched the *Enterprise* task force to those waters during the 1971 Bangladesh War. Secretaries Vance and Brown agreed on a plan for interim bilateral talks with the Soviets to fix mutual limits on Indian Ocean deployments before negotiating an agreement on withdrawal and demilitarization. Admiral Holloway abhorred this plan, as it threatened to disrupt the Navy's ability to support American commitments in Southwest Asia and the Persian Gulf, but the CNO realized that outright opposition to the new administration's foreign policy might trigger revenge against the Navy Department by Carter and Brown on other issues. Acknowledging that "the administration had been elected on a platform of cutting defense" and a noninterventionist foreign policy, Holloway found it not surprising that advice from the JCS "was . . . too often not what the Secretary of Defense or the President wanted to hear." In the end, the Soviets would not agree to either interim limitations or total demilitarization of the Indian Ocean, Holloway reasoned, so he refrained from attacking the Vance-Brown plan with the thought that it would never come to pass.[1]

In June 1977, to Holloway's consternation, Brezhnev agreed to the Vance-Brown scheme, and Arms Control and Disarmament Agency chief Paul Warnke, another of McNamara's former "whiz kids," flew to Moscow, where he found the Kremlin willing to hold respective Indian Ocean naval forces to then-current levels. The agreement that Warnke initialed would have restricted the U.S. Navy to its long-established three-ship Middle East Force in the Persian Gulf and three separate, short-term carrier battle group deployments to the Indian Ocean each year, whereas the Red Navy was to be allowed to maintain a permanent squadron of ten warships and ten auxiliaries on station in those waters. Warnke also promised that the U.S. Navy would not convert Diego Garcia into a secondary fleet base and allowed the Soviets the continued use of their lavish network of support installations in India, South Yemen, Ethiopia, and the Seychelles.

Not satisfied with these remarkable concessions, the Soviet negotiators next demanded that the U.S. Navy's ballistic missile–bearing submarines be excluded from the Indian Ocean. Although Warnke was inclined to concede this issue, he realized that it would face ferocious opposition on several counts from Admiral Holloway and the rest of the JCS, the Navy, and Congress. Not only would verification of such a provision require the Navy Department to abandon its longstanding policy of neither confirming nor denying the presence of nuclear weapons on board American warships, but also it would violate the older national principle of the right of nonbelligerent vessels to unfettered freedom of navigation in international waters. Moreover, the Soviet strategic motive behind the move was transparent. With the U.S. Navy's ballistic missile–bearing submarines excluded from the Indian Ocean, the area of operations of the Soviet fleet's hard-pressed antisubmarine forces would be considerably reduced.

Alarmed by Moscow's stance on the American deterrent patrols, Warnke recessed the talks and returned to Washington to marshal support for his first set of concessions. Assuming that a "U.S.-Soviet force balance" was desirable, Leslie Gelb, Warnke's deputy, announced that "under a stabilization agreement neither the U.S. nor the Soviet Union could increase the size of its military presence in the Indian Ocean or significantly alter its pattern of deployments" regardless of political developments in Southwest Asia, the Persian Gulf, or the Middle East. This was a virtual prescription for Iraqi, Indian, and Soviet adventurism. Opposition in the Senate to Warnke's Indian Ocean Treaty caused Carter in early 1978 to suspend the talks. He was unwilling, nevertheless, to abandon this diplomacy entirely and supported a December 1978 UN resolution sponsored by India and Russia that endorsed the "zone of peace" concept, a step that led critics to charge that he was appeasing the Soviets. In spite of the ongoing East-West tension over Ethiopia—a crisis in which the Navy's ability to operate in the Indian Ocean was a concern—he was still willing to agree with Brezhnev at their 1979 Vienna summit to "meet promptly to discuss the resumption of talks on questions concerning arms limitations measures in the Indian Ocean." In short order, even Carter could not justify continuing this appeasing diplomacy while he was enlarging the Navy's presence in the area.[2]

Carter's Panama Canal policy reinforced the widely held view that he lacked the courage to defend historic American interests overseas. Since the 1914 opening of the canal, the terms of the original Hay–Bunau-Varilla Treaty of 1903 had caused recurrent discord between Republicans and Democrats—and between the United States and Panama. The canal was essential to American victory in World War II, but soon after the war the JCS judged it a "wasting asset" in the age of nuclear weapons. Revisions to the basic arrangement were negotiated by Roosevelt and LBJ, but these treaties left intact the American right to operate the canal, govern the Canal Zone, and defend Panama against outside aggression. Panamanian nationalists, who wanted to take over the canal and recover sovereignty over the zone, were unsatisfied. Responding to new tensions, Ford started talks with Panama in 1975 with the aim of revising the arrangement, and Carter accelerated the pace of the conversations when he took office two years later. Vance negotiated a new Panama Canal Treaty and Carter persuaded the Senate to approve it in 1978. The United States promised to turn over canal operations to the Panamanians and transfer sovereignty over the zone to Panama before the turn of the century, while retaining the right to defend the waterway against outside aggression. From a strategic standpoint, this was not a significant event, and the JCS testified in favor of the treaty when it came before the Senate. Nevertheless, the appearance of the United States truckling to Omar Torrijos Herrera, Panama's comic dictator, did little to enhance Carter's popularity at home.[3]

Carter's mishandling of Caribbean affairs also dealt his presidency a self-inflicted wound. Evidence of a more muscular Soviet hand there surfaced in 1979 when a U.S. Navy official leaked to the press a secret report that two Soviet attack submarines were operating in Cuban waters in violation of the 1962 Kennedy-Khrushchev agreement. This duplicated a similar Soviet deployment in 1970 that, when reported to President Nixon, had triggered such a menacing response that the submarines were quickly withdrawn. Although Carter sent a protest to Moscow in 1979, he preferred to ignore the issue and allow the crisis to die down. Later that year, however, the press disclosed that a Red Army brigade had landed in Cuba for training exercises. Vance untruthfully denied the report and urged Carter to pursue quiet diplomacy once again, but National Security Adviser Brzezinski at last persuaded the president to instruct the 2nd Fleet to conduct highly publicized landing exercises in Guantánamo Bay in mid-October to signal American concern. During each of these episodes, Carter was slow to perceive the latent threat to American political and strategic interests, and he utterly ignored the partisan volatility of the ensuing crises.

Carter's principled approach to foreign policy governed his reaction to Cold War tensions over the Horn of Africa. For over a century the Royal Navy had enforced regional stability at this gateway between Africa and Asia, but the onset of Britain's imperial decline led the United States, soon after the Korean War, to negotiate a vaguely constructed alliance with Emperor Haile Selassie of Ethiopia, then one of only three independent African nations. He agreed to the construction of a secret American communications post at Asmara, which supported the movement of Polaris ballistic missile submarines into the Indian Ocean in 1965. The Red Navy's Admiral Gorshkov was alarmed by this threat, and when Colonel Siad Barre seized power in neighboring Somalia four years later, the Russians negotiated an important military alliance with his pro-Soviet regime, allowing them to build an air base at Hargeisa and a naval base at the deep-water port of Berbera. The region was further disrupted by a devastating famine in Ethiopia in 1973, which set in motion events that ended with the overthrow of Haile Selassie by an army junta headed by Colonel Mengistu Haile Mariam. He launched a bloody campaign against his political opponents, while trying to fend off an offensive by rebels from the province of Eritrea who nearly severed the roadway between Addis Ababa and the Red Sea port of Aseb.

Although appalled by Mengistu's "Red Terror," President Ford had continued military assistance to Ethiopia. Carter, however, selected Mengitsu's regime as the first victim of his human rights policy and ended this aid, a move that led Addis Ababa to close the Asmara station and turn to Moscow for help. The Soviets adopted a two-track policy of friendship with both Ethiopia and Somalia, although they could not dissuade Somalia's Barre from sending his army into Ethiopia in January 1977 to annex the Ogaden Desert, where many ethnic Somalis lived. The Somalis and some Ogaden rebels mounted an offensive that cut the highway from Addis Ababa to Djibouti and imperiled the Ethiopian position in the province. The Soviets were frantic. Moscow mobilized its allies in the Organization of African Unity, who unsuccessfully called for a ceasefire in August, while Castro begged his friend Barre to withdraw from the Ogaden. When this diplomacy failed, Brezhnev decided to side with Addis Ababa, and Soviet advisers and an advance contingent of Cuban troops were shipped to the Ogaden, where they stiffened the Ethiopian lines in time to successfully defend the key fortress at Dire Dawa. In spite of this setback, the Somali advance continued. The Russians then initiated a massive air and sea lift to Ethiopia, which transported over 2,000 Russian advisers, 550 tanks, 80 MiG fighters, and 11,000 Cuban soldiers from the Soviet Union by way of Angola to the front lines in the Ogaden Desert. This was the first time the Russians had used armed force to defend a client in Africa. This policy predictably enraged Colonel Barre. He expelled his Soviet advisers and forced the Red Navy to abandon its naval base at Berbera, a large facility that had been the main supply base for the Soviet Indian Ocean Force.

Despite these Soviet provocations, Carter followed a noninterventionist policy in the Ogaden War, but Brzezinski was so unsettled by January 1978 that he proposed to signal American concern for Somalia by sending a carrier battle group into the Arabian Sea in the wake of the arrival of Cuban troops in Ethiopia. "Vance particularly was against any deployment of a carrier task force in the area of the horn" because it might disrupt the SALT talks and inject American forces into what he wrongly insisted was a purely regional dispute. Once it was clear that Carter had no intention of actually using force to stop an invasion, the JCS urged him not to deploy the carrier, as the move would be costly and ultimately useless. Defense Secretary Brown reasoned that if the Americans could be certain that the Ethiopians would not cross into Somalia, then Carter "might deploy the carrier and take credit for success in preventing an invasion." Should the Ethiopians and the Cubans overrun Somalia, however, the presence of American warships in nearby waters "would be viewed as a failure of the U.S. task force to do its job." Carter accepted this line of reasoning, rejected Brzezinski's arguments, and decided not to signal a level of determination that he patently did not possess.[4]

The Ogaden War, nonetheless, did compel Carter to take a few lesser steps. After 1970, 6th Fleet and 7th Fleet carriers and other ships had steamed into the Indian Ocean for only a few months at a time, but these deployments were random and the Navy's presence there impermanent. Soon after the Cubans arrived in Ethiopia, however, the Navy augmented the Middle East Force in the Persian Gulf, and in April 1978 the guided missile

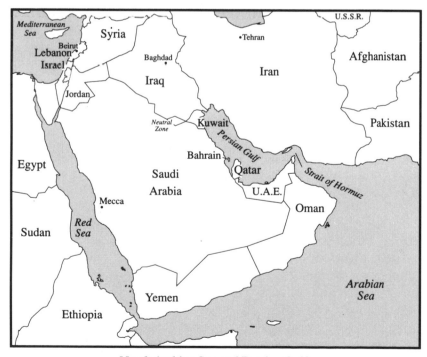

North Arabian Sea and Persian Gulf

cruiser *Fox* became the flagship for the new North Arabian Sea Force. After Somalia broke with Moscow and Colonel Barre mended his relations with Washington, the destroyer *Davis* became the first American warship to visit Berbera in May 1979. The Soviets matched this buildup, and by 1980 each side had deployed about twenty-five ships to the Indian Ocean, the Arabian Sea, and adjacent waters. Until the Iranian eruption in 1979, however, Carter refused to move a carrier battle group into the region, concerned that friction with the Soviets over their adventurism in Africa was endangering support in the United States for détente and SALT II. "All of them seem to me to be badly bitten by the Vietnam bug," Brzezinski observed sourly. In spite of Carter's refusal to back Somalia, the Soviets decided to consolidate their position in Ethiopia for the moment and not to risk an American response by overplaying their hand. Moscow instructed its Cuban proxies to evict the Somalis from the Ogaden but refused to allow Colonel Mengistu to invade Somalia. As an alternative, Mengistu launched another expensive, unsuccessful campaign to eliminate the Eritrean guerrillas, but this desperate move plunged his regime into a protracted struggle that led to a series of horrifying famines, decimating Ethiopia's population over the next decade. At long last, in 1991, Mengistu was overthrown and the heroic Eritreans were granted independence.[5]

Successive crises in Iran and Afghanistan forced Carter to thoroughly overhaul his foreign policy and military strategy in 1979. Two years earlier, after abandoning Nixon's Twin Pillars Policy, Carter had distanced himself from the shah of Iran, one of America's oldest clients, and permitted Vance's State Department to condemn the shah's regime for human rights abuses. This well-intentioned, yet maladroit diplomacy fueled the fires of a long-smoldering rebellion against the shah. Several rival factions opposed the shah, all of whom generally took their lead from the Ayatollah Khomeini, an aged fundamentalist cleric who directed the uprising from his Paris exile. By January 1978, when he visited Tehran, Carter had come to appreciate the dangers of uncorking the genie of Muslim fundamentalism, and he reassured the shah with a bearhug embrace and the promise that "no other nation on earth . . . is closer to us in planning for our national security." Soon after the president departed, riots and sabotage erupted throughout Iran, but the shah was too sick, tired, isolated, and indecisive to save his regime.[6]

On 15 November 1978, when the Iranian crisis reached a turning point, a battle group composed of the guided missile cruiser *Sterett*, the guided missile destroyer *Waddell*, the frigate *Bradley*, and an oiler entered the Indian Ocean, inaugurating an era of continuous American naval presence in the region. Brzezinski, who opposed appeasement, claimed that "once the crisis had become a contest of will and power, advocacy of compromise and conciliation simply played into the hands of those determined to effect a complete revolution." The shah's position continued to worsen, so on 27 December Defense Secretary Brown, without telling Carter, ordered the 7th Fleet commander to "position" a battle group built around the carrier *Constellation* "in the vicinity of Singapore . . . and make preparations for a possible deployment to the Arabian Sea if an augmented naval presence proved necessary." The next day the American press announced that this formation was about to enter the Indian Ocean, an inaccurate report that embarrassed Carter when he had to admit that this was not his intention. "The incident became enshrined as an example of President Carter's 'vacillation,'" wrote Navy Captain Gary Sick of the NSC staff. By this time, demonstrations of American support for the shah were too late. Broken by cancer and deserted by Carter, who rejected a last-minute plan to airlift the 82nd Airborne into Iran to prop up the monarchy, the shah conceded defeat. In January 1979, he asked Shahipur Bakhitar to take over as premier, an offer that Bakhitar accepted on the condition that the shah leave Iran and go into exile.[7]

Khomeini returned from Paris in early February and rallied the radicals to his cause from his new headquarters in the holy city of Qom. Riots gripped Tehran, and on the 14th a mob attacked the United States embassy, an unmistakable signal of the danger to those Americans still in Iran. Just a few weeks earlier, the JCS had reinforced the Middle East Force in the Persian Gulf with the addition of three destroyers and a replenishment oiler. On 21 February, the flagship *La Salle* led five destroyers in evacuating 200 Americans and 200 Europeans from the Iranian ports of Bandar Abbas and Bandar Shah. This move came none too soon. One month later, Khomeini backed a second coup in which his protégé Mehdi Bazargan assumed the premiership, established a Muslim republic ruled by a powerful religious parliament, and withdrew Iran from CENTO. Bazargan opposed

Khomeini's goal of establishing a Muslim theocracy, however, and he temporized, hoping to reestablish good relations with Washington, a line that ran counter to that of Khomeini's religious radicals. By now, the JCS was concerned that the Soviets intended to exploit the chaos in Tehran and might accept an invitation from Kurdish or Azerbaijani separatists to intervene in Iran on their behalf.

A related crisis on the Arabian peninsula erupted suddenly. Since 1977, Soviet influence with the communist regime of South Yemen had increased and the Red Navy had acquired anchorages at Socotra Island at the eastern end of the Gulf of Aden. Soviet warships frequently visited this station and the degree of land-based logistical support by the South Yemenis for Soviet naval forces increased alarmingly. Then, in February 1979, the South Yemenis renewed their war against North Yemen with the aim of overrunning the weak, pro-Western regime, which depended on Egypt and Saudi Arabia for support. Hardly had the embarrassing *Constellation* incident passed when it became evident that it was essential for the Navy to increase its presence in the area, and Rear Admiral Robert E. Kirksey, who commanded the 7th Fleet Strike Force, was assigned to coordinate naval operations between the Indian Ocean and the Persian Gulf. He thus became responsible for establishing most of the routines for subsequent deployments there. One of Kirksey's first decisions was to greatly increase the coverage of the eastern and western Indian Ocean by P-3 Orion maritime patrol aircraft flying out of the Philippines. Moscow moved quickly to match these steps, and in May 1979 the small Soviet carrier *Minsk*, the amphibious ship *Ivan Rogov*, and a *Kara*-class cruiser visited Aden.

Meanwhile, the radicalization of Iran proceeded apace, with Bazargan's government attempting to stay one step ahead of Khomeini's growing demands. Carter had at first refused to allow the shah to seek refuge in the United States, but when the president learned that his former ally had cancer, he relented and permitted the shah to seek treatment in New York. This infuriated Khomeini, who saw it as another American plot to thwart his revolution, and on 4 November 1979 a band of his religious hooligans stormed the United States embassy in Tehran and took hostage fifty-three Americans they found in the buildings. This act coincided with another coup in which Bazargan was replaced by Abolhassan Bani-Sadr. He was closer still to Khomeini but did

F-14A Tomcat fighter (*top*) shadows a Soviet TU-95 Bear maritime patrol bomber on 19 June 1979 about 1,600 miles east of Guam.

The *Ohio*-class, Trident-bearing fleet ballistic missile submarine *Georgia* (SSBN-729).

not share many of the ayatollah's goals. Carter demanded that
Iran release the hostages, and when Bani-Sadr refused, the president froze Iran's assets in the United States.

The Iranian hostage crisis resulted in the movement of two
carrier battle groups into the Indian Ocean, a strategy that continued for the next two years. The crisis also pointed to American
weakness in the Persian Gulf, to the Navy's inability to project
military power in the region, and to the reluctance of the Carter
administration to do so. In the last week of November, Carter ordered the carrier *Kitty Hawk* and her battle group, then in the
Philippines, to rendezvous in the North Arabian Sea with the carrier *Midway* and her five escorts, a belated attempt to pressure
Tehran and reassure the Saudis of American support. In January
1980, another battle group, which included the nuclear carrier
Nimitz and her nuclear-powered escorts, dashed from the
Mediterranean around the Cape of Good Hope and into the Arabian Sea to relieve the *Kitty Hawk.* These movements were in part
a reaction to the increased number of Russian ships deployed to
the region, and in part an attempt to reinforce Carter's secret
plan to declare war against Iran if Khomeini carried out his
threat to stage a show trial of the hostages in Tehran. Also, Carter
declared that "an attempt by an outside force to gain control of
the Persian Gulf region will be regarded as an assault on the vital
interests of the United States . . . and . . . will be repelled by . . .
military force."[8]

The families of the hostages publicly begged Carter to secure the freedom of their relatives. This gnawed at him, but in
January 1980 he told Congress that attempting to rescue the
hostages would likely fail and might even lead to their deaths. So
great was the heat of the political cauldron of a presidential election year, however, that just two months later he decided to stage
a rescue attempt anyway. As early as 29 November 1979, five days
before the second carrier battle group steamed into the Indian
Ocean, the JCS had taken under review Operation Eagle Claw, a
plan devised by the chairman, Air Force General David Jones, to
airlift the multiservice Delta Force commandos into Tehran and
rescue the hostages. Secretary of State Vance, who considered
Jones' scheme harebrained, recorded that the JCS were also decidedly "pessimistic" about its prospects of success. General Jones
had almost singlehandedly convinced Carter to press ahead and
refused to allow the JCS to thoroughly screen the plan.[9]

As a result of maladroit local commanders, Jones' incredibly poor planning, and unpredictable tragedy, Operation Eagle Claw ended in failure. CIA agents and their Iranian friends had located the Tehran site where most of the American hostages were being held. Jones, who knew nothing about combined operations, selected Army Colonel Charlie Beckwith to command the rescue, a shockingly poor choice inasmuch as Beckwith admitted his total ignorance of air transport operations. Jones planned that commandos from the streets would storm the building at the same time that a section of Navy RH-53 Sea Stallion helicopters from the *Nimitz* landed nearby. The minesweeping helicopters would then lift the hostages and the rescue teams out of the city and deposit them at a landing site in the hills on the outskirts of Tehran. F-14 Tomcats from the carriers *Nimitz* and *Coral Sea* were to rendezvous with the helicopters at the site and escort them back to Egypt. Overruling Vance, Carter agreed to the desperate plan.

On 24 April 1980, six Air Force C-130 Hercules transports laden with fuel and equipment took off from an Egyptian airbase, crossed over the Persian Gulf, and landed at a remote site 200 miles from Tehran known as Desert One. At dusk, eight Sea Stallions lifted off the *Nimitz* and began the 600-mile flight to Desert One, but by the time they rendezvoused with the transports, various mishaps and pilot errors meant that only five machines could continue. According to Lieutenant Commander M. G. Steen of the minesweeping squadron, one helicopter was disabled when "airflow to the . . . power supply was inadvertently blocked sometime during the flight. A second aircraft failure en route to Desert One resulted from a cracked hydraulic fitting." A third was disabled by "an impending main rotor blade failure" that threatened the "almost certain loss of the aircraft and its crew and passengers." And although they were well trained, the Marine pilots had little experience with very long-range flight operations. Beckwith, overly concerned with preserving his forces at the expense of the mission, now radioed Washington and persuaded Carter to cancel the operation.

"The U.S. military planner preparing an operation that relies heavily on secrecy for success begins with two strikes against him," according to Captain Sick, because the American press is eager to publish secret information. This need for excessive secrecy led directly to the "failure to conduct a full-scale rehearsal," with the resulting tragedy at Desert One. After Carter announced this fiasco on nationwide television, Secretary Vance, who had opposed the mission from the start, resigned in protest, abandoning Carter at the very moment that he came under stinging criticism from right and left for reversing his stand against a rescue attempt and then bungling the operation.[10]

At the height of the Iran imbroglio, the Soviet Union ignored American warnings and on Christmas Eve 1979 invaded Afghanistan, upsetting the very foundations of Jimmy Carter's foreign policy and grand strategy and dooming his reelection prospects. Utterly confounded, Carter confessed that his earlier benign assessment of Soviet aims had been tragically mistaken. Brzezinski stimulated this act of contrition by drawing for Carter "a parallel between the present crisis and the one faced by President Truman in regard to Greece and Turkey" in 1947. In his third State of the Union address on 23 January 1980, Carter declared that "any attempt by any outside force to gain control of the Persian Gulf region will be regarded as an assault on the vital interests of the United States," and threatened that "an assault will be repelled by any means necessary, including military force." Under this new formulation, quickly labeled the Carter Doctrine, the United States was to assume responsibility for the defense of the Persian Gulf states and their oil trade, although Carter refused to explain just which countries he would defend or whether his guarantee included protection from threats other than a Soviet movement into Iran. How all this was to be done without sapping American strength elsewhere was a question that Carter shunned. There was no question, however, that the adoption of the Carter Doctrine meant the downfall of the Swing Strategy, a watershed to which Secretary Brown alluded when he confessed that "although our emphasis has been on preparation to fight in Europe, recent events have made it clear that some of our forces must be configured for rapid deployment." Up to this point, Secretary Vance admitted, the Carter administration had been "preoccupied with strategic forces" and had largely ignored the "need to increase our ability to project conventional forces abroad, whether to maintain open sea lanes to Europe and Japan and to the vital Persian Gulf."[11]

The enunciation of the Carter Doctrine and the establishment of the Rapid Deployment Force compelled the JCS to reevaluate American naval strategy. "What is a doctrine without power?" asked former CIA director Richard Helms. In 1979, during the Iranian hostage crisis, all the carriers had been withdrawn for several months from the western Pacific for the first time in thirty years, thus reducing the 7th Fleet's ability to defend South Korea. And when the JCS moved the *Nimitz*'s all-nuclear battle group from the Mediterranean into the North Arabian Sea, the 6th Fleet was left with only one carrier, a violation of a thirty-year-old commitment to NATO. Admiral Zumwalt's decision ten years earlier to establish an advance base on Diego Garcia now proved fortuitous, as that station was essential to maintaining the Navy's growing Indian Ocean commitment. Still, the strain on the fleet was immense. The new nuclear-powered carrier *Eisenhower* deployed from Norfolk to the Indian Ocean for over eight months in 1980, with only one five-day liberty call at Singapore. These redeployments coincided with Carter's somewhat tardy recognition of the implausibility of the Swing Strategy, the reduced likelihood of a central front war in Europe, and a belated awareness that American weakness might occasion Soviet adventurism in the Middle East. In 1980, Undersecretary of Defense Robert W. Komer, recognizing the demands of Carter's new Indian Ocean commitments and the need to signal the NATO powers that they would have to increase their own spending on the alliance, released the Pacific Fleet from the Swing Strategy.[12]

In March 1980, to uphold the Carter Doctrine, the president established the Rapid Deployment Force, assigning to this new unified command responsibility for operations in the Persian Gulf, the Arabian Sea, and the Middle East. On 16 March, the 7th Fleet Amphibious Group, consisting of the helicopter assault ship *Okinawa*, the LSD *Alamo*, the attack cargo ship *Mobile*, and the LST *San Bernardino* carrying 1,800 Marines, steamed into the Indian Ocean, the first of four such formations to deploy there until the hostage crisis ended a year later. The Navy's sealift capacity had been so neglected by the Nixon and Carter administrations, however, that merely to transport a single Army division overseas would take fifty-nine of the fleet's sixty-three amphibious ships, which in peacetime were scattered at widely separated bases from Norfolk to Okinawa. One carrier battle group was withdrawn from the Mediterranean and another from the Pacific for the new Indian Ocean Force, which operated under the command of the 7th Fleet. The American base nearest to the Persian Gulf was at Diego Garcia, 2,000 miles away in the Indian Ocean.

Defense Secretary Brown sent teams into the region to lease bases for the Rapid Deployment Force, but only Oman, Somalia, and Kenya were willing to extend even limited, circumspect cooperation in the form of port, airfield, and storage facilities. This caused Carter to abandon his human rights policy, and in August 1980, he signed a treaty with Somalia allowing American naval forces to use Mogadishu and Berbera in return for economic aid.

The Carter Doctrine offered too little and came too late. Despite feverish activity, "we clearly do not have the assets for a three-ocean Navy," Captain James F. Kelly wrote in 1981. The Navy had to "emphasize in our ship-construction goals the procurement of battle-group capable forces," Admiral Hayward insisted. "This is essential to maintain fleet balance and to sustain our ability to conduct offensive operations in high-threat areas." After three years of slashing the Navy's shipbuilding program, Carter asked Congress in 1980 to increase the number of new ships to be built within five years from sixty-seven to ninety-five, although he added that most of these vessels were not to be laid down until 1983 or 1984. In short, he inaugurated naval rearmament but was utterly unwilling to pay for it. He also approved recommissioning one of the old *Iowa*-class battleships and converting her into a powerful missile-bearing command ship. On the other hand, Carter's five-year aircraft procurement plan for 1980, which proposed that the Navy buy only 66 F-14 Tomcats and 656 FA-18 Hornets, signaled that the administration was still very much committed to the inexpensive, low end of Admiral Zumwalt's old High-Low Mix.[13]

Although the NATO allies refused to align themselves unreservedly with American policy in the Middle East, Europe provided some reluctant support for the Carter Doctrine. Eight British ships had been deployed to the Gulf of Oman by September 1980, and within a year France's Indian Ocean fleet was increased to twenty-five ships, three of which constantly patrolled the Arabian Sea. Twenty-five American warships had deployed to the Arabian Sea by year's end, nearly matching the number the Soviets sent into the area. Australia and New Zealand also provided support for the Carter Doctrine in the Indian Ocean under the ANZUS Treaty. A combined battle group built around the Australian carrier *Melbourne* entered the Indian Ocean for an extended deployment in October. These Western naval forces frequently trained together, as in the four-day exercise known as

Harpoonex, meant to devise tactics to challenge the *La Combat-ante*-class ships of the now hostile Iranian fleet. The newly formed RDF command could call upon all services for forces, but as of mid-1983 it consisted of only seventeen supply ships riding at anchor at Diego Garcia and one California-based Marine division. If these troops were to be airlifted to the Arabian Peninsula, a Marine Corps study concluded, they "would run out of rations—and bullets, if committed—before the last of the division is landed" and before the Diego Garcia–based ships reached the Persian Gulf.[14]

The Carter Doctrine's new muscularity unsettled the Iranians, who had become international pariahs by violating the diplomatic immunity of some of their American hostages. With the approach of the American presidential elections in late 1980, Khomeini—perhaps fearing what a less restrained chief executive might do—offered to release the hostages in return for an agreement by Carter to unfreeze Iran's assets in the United States. While talks along these lines were reopened in October, the two carrier battle groups in the Indian Ocean were reduced to one. Scaling down the Navy's presence was intended to signal Tehran that Washington sought a reduction in tensions. As a result of this appeasement diplomacy, in January 1981 Carter consummated a deal with the Iranians, who released the hostages on the same day that he left office.

Chapter Thirty-six

The Maritime Strategy
1981–1988

Ronald Reagan not only evicted Carter from the White House in the 1980 elections but also brought with him enough Republicans to establish a majority in the Senate for the first time since 1954. His first-term foreign policy consisted of a renewed dedication to military containment, a lessened reliance on détente, and a new, muscular interventionism in the Middle East, Southwest Asia, and Latin America. Reagan capably enunciated broad principles and goals in foreign policy, but failed to keep abreast of many issues, often appeared to be ignorant of the complexities of others, and relied excessively on a parade of inexplicably maladroit national security advisers. As a result, his administration suffered from self-inflicted wounds arising out of petty personal and bureaucratic quarrels that he was ill suited by reason of a sunny temperament to mediate. These disputes tended to elevate the authority of the various cabinet secretaries, especially in the field of foreign policy and military affairs. As his first secretary of state, Reagan named General Alexander Haig, but Haig's combative manner alienated not only Reagan's White House staff but also Defense Secretary Caspar Weinberger, a longtime Reagan confidant. Haig resigned in mid-1982 and was replaced by George Shultz, a dogged, uninspiring placeholder whose main goal was to convince Reagan to resume the pursuit of détente.

Shultz' plan to resume serious arms control negotiations with the Soviets was irremediably complicated by turbulence and uncertainty in Moscow, the result of Brezhnev's death in 1981, the frail health of his two short-term successors, both of whom also died in office, and Mikhail Gorbachev's ascension to power in 1985. Reagan had, moreover, soon after his inauguration adopted the position that if the United States strengthened its strategic and theater nuclear forces, then the Soviets, unable to pay the price to compete, would agree to reasonable arms reductions. Reagan may have believed that the Soviet economy could not tolerate another round of arms competition, but he did not carefully articulate this view at the time. Finally, Reagan resurrected Kissinger's concept of linkage and attempted with little success until 1986 to tie progress in arms control to Soviet behavior in Afghanistan, Africa, and Central America.

Arms control was also complicated by Reagan's announcement on 23 March 1983 of his Strategic Defense Initiative, a controversial, expensive plan to develop, test, and construct several satellite-based laser and particle-beam antiballistic missile systems designed to create a shield over the United States against Soviet strategic rocket- and sea-launched ballistic missile attacks. Although the Russians had embarked on several smaller outer-space warfare projects, Gorbachev reckoned that the stagnating, backward Soviet economy could neither overcome nor outflank American high technology, so he demanded of Reagan at their first summit conference in Geneva in 1985 that the Americans abandon SDI in return for concessions on strategic arms control. Reagan rejected this proposal.

Late the following year, Reagan and Gorbachev met for a third summit at Reykjavik, Iceland, where a crude agreement in principle on a radical 50 percent mutual reduction of silo- and sea-based ballistic missiles came unglued at the last moment when the Soviets again demanded that the Americans forsake SDI. In spite of this setback, Gorbachev continued on an almost frenzied international campaign to promote arms control, while at the same time inaugurating sweeping political and economic reforms, labeled glasnost and perestroika, to reverse the economic decline of the Soviet Union and her Warsaw Pact satellites. To reignite the arms control process after the Reykjavik fiasco, Gorbachev suddenly agreed to an American plan to eliminate an entire class of European-based intermediate-range ballistic and land-based cruise missiles in the Intermediate Nuclear Forces Treaty, which was signed at the fourth summit in Washington in

1987. Still, Reagan's dedication to SDI obstructed a settlement on START when the two leaders met for their last negotiating session in Moscow in May 1988.

Reagan attributed the increasingly flexible Soviet attitude toward arms control almost entirely to the burden placed on Gorbachev and his predecessors of trying to keep up with the American rearmament program, an assessment encouraged by Secretary of Defense Weinberger. Agreeing with Reagan when the administration took office in 1981 that "in virtually every measure of military power the Soviet Union enjoys a decided advantage," Weinberger warned of "our collective failure to pursue an adequate balance of military strength" while the Soviets had engaged in "the greatest buildup of military power seen in modern times." During the previous decade, the Soviets had spent about $100 billion more than the United States on arms, producing six times as many ships, twice as many aircraft, and six times as many tanks. Assistant Secretary of Defense Lawrence Korb claimed that "at the beginning of the 1980s, the Soviets surpassed the United States in most quantitative indicators of military power." He asserted that an overall "rough equivalence best described the balance of power" in 1982. An articulate spokesman for rearmament, Weinberger persuaded Congress to approve enormous increases in defense appropriations during each of the four years of Reagan's first term, and then successfully defended this achievement against assaults by liberal Democrats in Congress until his retirement in 1987.[1]

Reagan intended not only to fulfill the historic American obligations to containment in Europe but also to develop a military capacity to execute several new missions. From 1981 to 1985, annual American defense spending increased by nearly one-third, from $199 billion to $264 billion, and the military's share of the gross national product rose from 5.2 percent in 1980 to about 6.6 percent four years later. Nuclear warfighting assumed an unprecedented importance in 1983 when Reagan announced the start of his SDI program. Reagan also sought to strengthen America's counterforce strategy by resuming production of 100 Air Force B-1 low-altitude manned bombers, temporarily deploying a handful of highly accurate but trouble-plagued Air Force MX ICBM missiles in old Titan ICBM missile silos, and developing the Lockheed B-2 Stealth manned bomber. A new guidance system and warhead for the old Minuteman III meant that these silo-based ICBMs alone could knock out over 40 percent of the Soviet ICBM force.

Defense Secretary Brown had convinced Carter in 1978 not to completely replace the 2,500-mile-range Poseidon C-3 ballistic missile with the Navy's new, more accurate Trident C-4 missile in nineteen Polaris submarines and instead to arm only a dozen older Polaris boats with the longer-range weapon. Reagan, soon after taking office, not only accelerated construction of the Trident-bearing *Ohio*-class ballistic missile submarines but also approved the rapid development of the very long-range, highly accurate Trident D-5 intercontinental missile. With navigational support from the Navy's Star navigation satellite, an *Ohio*-class submarine could now pinpoint her position at launch time as she could not do before, and this closed at last the longtime gap between sea- and land-based ballistic missiles. The Trident D-5 was designed to travel 7,000 miles and hit a target within a circle 100 feet in diameter. Developed to replace the Poseidon C-3 and Trident C-4 missiles, the Trident D-5 missile, first flight tested in January 1987, was scheduled for deployment in 1989. By the time Reagan left office, the ninth *Ohio*-class submarine had entered the fleet and the Trident D-5 missile, first sea launched in early 1989, was almost ready for serial production. Navy Secretary John Lehman planned to build twenty *Ohio*-class submarines at the rate of about one each year, so that when all these vessels were commissioned by the year 2000, the Navy would have a total of 4,800 submarine-launched warheads and a greater role in the nation's nuclear warfighting strategy.

Upgrading and increasing the size of the ballistic missile–bearing submarine force was especially urgent in the early 1980s, because Congress refused to approve either Carter's or Reagan's basing schemes for the MX mobile ICBM and because once the Soviets perfected the accuracy of their sea-based missile-launching system, their ballistic missile submarines could take station off the East and West Coasts and execute a quickdraw first strike by firing at America's ICBM silos and land-based bombers. This would in effect shift the entire retaliatory burden to the Navy's Poseidon-Trident ballistic missile–bearing submarines. The result was that the sea-based leg of the triad became proportionately more important in strategic planning in the 1980s. At the same time, however, the development of the Air Force's long-range, air-launched cruise missiles and the Navy's sea-based, 3,000-

pound, 18-foot-long Tomahawk made vulnerable the Soviets' land-based ICBMs. This was another signal that Reagan intended to create for the first time a sea-based, first-strike nuclear warfighting force. "This planned increase in U.S. hard-target capability would transform the ability of the United States [submarines] to conduct large-scale attacks on hardened targets in the Soviet Union," the Congressional Budget Office reported correctly in 1986.[2]

Reagan's defense buildup was based on his conviction that NATO's ground and air forces were "vastly outdistanced" by the corresponding forces of the Warsaw Pact, and that the Soviet fleet enjoyed "superiority at sea" as compared to the Western navies. Weinberger championed strengthening American military forces at every level, but the results of his rearmament program were nowhere more evident than in the Navy. After a few months in office, it was clear that Navy Secretary John Lehman had broken the chain of gray mediocrity, and often incompetence, that characterized the men who had held the office since the days of the last great secretary, James Forrestal. First, Lehman established his authority over the Navy, not only by doing his homework but also by eschewing many of the traditional ceremonial functions that had busied a long succession of civilian secretaries. Lehman also injected himself into the hitherto sacrosanct flag-selection process for admirals, punishing opponents, rewarding allies, and accumulating respect, if not always affection. The final step in Lehman's campaign to extend his writ over the Navy was his move to force into long overdue retirement the aging cleric of nuclear power, Admiral Hyman Rickover, who had been discredited by his underhanded and acrimonious dealings with shipyards and other contractors and whose most powerful supporters in Congress were passing from the scene. To replace Rickover, Lehman selected Admiral Kinnaird McKee, a narrow-minded reactor specialist who, unlike his mentor, commanded no patronage on the Hill. Just to be certain, Lehman had Congress limit McKee's term as director of Naval Nuclear Propulsion to eight years, and McKee retired gracefully in 1988.[3]

Lehman next turned on the Navy's major contractors in the belief that if he could not contain procurement costs, then Congress would refuse to support naval expansion. Since the halcyon days of the early Cold War and Kennedy's Apollo space program, these firms had fallen on hard times. Matters worsened when the Reagan administration ended a number of wasteful subsidies for the merchant marine and left the surviving private shipyards with no customers other than the Navy. Lehman first moved against General Dynamics, whose Electric Boat Division shipyard at Groton was mired in scandal and red ink resulting from its ludicrous mismanagement of several *Los Angeles*-class attack submarine contracts. At issue was a threat by General Dynamics president David Lewis to sue the Navy for enormous cost overruns, litigation that was wholly without merit but that menaced the entire shipbuilding program. Backed by Weinberger, Lehman so successfully browbeat Lewis that General Dynamics withdrew its lawsuit and negotiated a token settlement, and was then rewarded with a carefully drafted contract for another attack submarine. Lewis resigned in disgrace after the manager of Electric Boat fled to Greece to avoid prosecution and from exile fed the muckraking press a sordid tale of Lewis' corrupt behavior. Other Navy contractors were also roughly handled by Lehman's office.

Lehman not only established a coherent, expansionist shipbuilding policy, but he also devised a public relations strategy to promote his objectives, setting about "to restore the strength of the Navy, . . . not just in numbers of ships but [also] the self-confidence and sense of mission of the naval service itself." Naval expansion was furthered by Reagan's fondness for military ceremony and his need for, and effective use of, symbolic stage props—such as ships, warplanes, or Marines—to create the powerful images reinforcing the message of resurgent American strength that he so skillfully conveyed. Lehman worked to increase competition among Navy contractors, eliminate sole-source contracts for ships, weapons, and aircraft, reduce costly contract changes and Navy "gold-plating," and bring stability to the procurement process. After several procurement scandals were exposed in the early 1980s, he created a separate officer career path for Navy materiel managers. In the end, however, Lehman's herculean efforts failed to dent the larger wasteful, overly centralized, highly uncompetitive, and often corrupt Defense Department procurement process.[4]

"We set forth a program intended to recapture maritime superiority for the United States . . . based on a 600-ship Navy built around 15 [carrier] battle groups," Lehman declared. To "restore and maintain superiority over the Soviets," he asked

Congress to approve a shipbuilding program that was to lead to a 600-ship Navy—including 15 aircraft carriers and 100 attack submarines—by the end of the decade. By "frontloading" his shipbuilding program and exploiting the mandate on Capitol Hill for Reagan's military buildup, Lehman had in hand by December 1982 congressional approval to build more than 100 additional ships that, when added to the 500 already afloat, met his goal. The Navy's shipbuilding annual account increased from $7.5 billion in 1979 to $12.1 billion in 1985, and the fleet grew from 479 ships in 1981 to nearly 580 eight years later. When Congress refused to agree to additional increases in Defense Department spending after 1985, however, it was clear that the full 600-ship Navy would never put to sea. At a news conference on 24 February 1988, Reagan insisted that he was still "committed to a 600-ship Navy," but he nevertheless allowed Frank Carlucci, a colorless civil servant who succeeded Weinberger as secretary of defense in 1988, to slash the Navy's shipbuilding program and prematurely retire sixteen frigates.[5]

Lehman's entire Maritime Strategy, as it was known, was predicated on a strong peacetime forward-deployed heavy attack carrier force that could both take the offensive in a general war and provide the president with a quickdraw intervention option in a regional crisis. With fifteen carriers, the Navy might maintain one carrier battle group on each of the major stations—the Atlantic, the northern flank, the Mediterranean, the Indian Ocean, and the western Pacific—while the remaining ten were working up or being repaired or overhauled. Leading the list of new ships to enter the fleet during the Lehman era were the nuclear carriers *Theodore Roosevelt*, authorized in 1979 over Carter's objections, and the *Abraham Lincoln* and *George Washington*, which Congress authorized in 1982 as part of Reagan's rearmament program. Lehman decided not to ask Congress to authorize any more carriers for the rest of the decade, but he received a letter in 1986 from Virginia's congressional delegation recommending that the Navy lay down a seventh *Nimitz*-class carrier and modernize the *Enterprise*, the oldest nuclear-powered carrier. This unexpectedly strong support for his naval policy caused Lehman to suggest building two carriers as well as completing the *Enterprise* conversion work. At first Weinberger balked at this scheme, but he withdrew his opposition in December of that year at the request of Republican Senator John Warner, one of the Navy's more rugged supporters on the Hill, and Congress authorized both ships soon after. During the presidential campaign in 1988, Massachusetts Governor Michael Dukakis, the Democratic candidate, opposed the construction of these two carriers, the *John Stennis* and her sister ship, but Vice President George Bush, the successful Republican candidate, pledged to complete them so as to maintain a fifteen-carrier fleet into the twenty-first century. The reasonableness of this goal was brought into question in 1989 when Soviet hegemony over eastern Europe crumbled and the threat to NATO from the Warsaw Pact collapsed.

Lehman also revitalized naval air policy by initiating the development of a carrier-based Stealth fighter and the A-12 Avenger Stealth naval bomber and by browbeating the Navy's airframe contractors into considerably reducing their cost per plane. Lehman's success in persuading Congress to build four carriers was not matched by his efforts to increase the number of carrier air wings, however. Soon after he left office in 1986, the Navy decommissioned its fourteenth air wing, meaning that the fifteen-carrier fleet would be served by only thirteen air wings in the 1990s. This was especially worrisome because in wartime the numbered fleets might need two, three, or four carriers in each battle group to increase the ratio of attack aircraft to fighters and permit round-the-clock flight operations. Lehman's answer to this constant shortfall in air wings was to transfer a number of functions to the once-inert Naval Reserve squadrons and to equip them with FA-18 Hornets and A-7 Corsairs and nearly a dozen modern missile-bearing frigates. Finding successors to the F-14 Tomcat, the FA-18 Hornet, and the A-6 Intruder depended on work first undertaken by the Air Force to develop supersonic stealth bombers and fighters that would be considerably less visible to opposing radars.

The Air Force's ill-conceived B-2 Stealth bomber proved to be extremely costly, its Stealth fighter failed to live up to its proponents' claims, and the designs of both the Navy's Stealth fighter and its A-12 Avenger bomber ran into formidable obstacles. As a result, in 1988 the Navy asked for funds to purchase a new version of the A-6 Intruder all-weather bomber, but Congress turned this down, in part because Lehman had previously testified that the A-12 Avenger would eventually replace the aging Intruders. General Dynamics and McDonnell Douglas, who were to jointly manufacture the A-12 Avenger, encountered so many technical problems developing the vastly overweight plane, however, that William Ball III, Reagan's last secretary of the Navy, admitted in December 1988 that a decade might elapse before "the A-12 is fully developed and operational." Lehman had scheduled the Avenger to enter the fleet in the mid-1990s. The Navy needed at least 850 planes, costing over $100 million each, to provide for training and the thirteen carrier air wings, but Congress reduced this figure to 620 in April 1990 in the wake of the end of the Cold War. Soon after, the contractors admitted that they were far behind schedule and that the plane would not perform to specifications. When the Reagan administration left office, the fate of the once vaunted A-12 was in doubt.

A centerpiece in Lehman's program for a 600-ship Navy was the reactivation of all four *Iowa*-class battleships. Carter had agreed to reactivate the *New Jersey* and convert her into a cruise missile–bearing combatant, and Lehman greatly expanded and accelerated this program on the basis that the battleships were "tougher than any ship in anyone's navy. They were built to hold up against . . . 2,700-pound artillery shells from 18-inch naval guns fired at three times the speed of sound." The battleships' 16-inch guns could deliver 1,000 tons of ordnance an hour against targets more than twenty miles away. The *New Jersey* was withdrawn from mothballs at the Puget Sound Naval Shipyard in July 1981 and towed to Long Beach, where she was modernized by installing launchers for four variations of Tomahawk cruise missiles and sixteen shorter-range Harpoon anti-ship missiles, a Vulcan-Phalanx Gatling gun for close-in self-defense, a helicopter landing pad, and new radars and communications equipment. To win support in Congress for his battleship recommissioning program, Lehman wanted to deploy the *New Jersey* promptly, and she appeared off the coast of Lebanon in December 1982. The *Iowa* entered the fleet in 1984, and Lehman arranged for the battleships *Missouri* and *Wisconsin* to be recommissioned before Reagan left office. The cost of each conversion was about the price of a frigate. Lehman's other major contribution to the surface fleet was to accelerate the development of the new *Arleigh Burke*-class superdestroyer, designed to operate a small version of the complex Aegis air defense system. Phased-array radars linked to twenty high-speed computers would search the seas and airspace within a 200-mile radius of the ship, acquire multiple targets concurrently, and fire more than 100 surface-to-air missiles at them.[6]

To strengthen the offensive submarine force, Lehman established a goal of building up to 100 attack submarines by 1986, although this still left the Navy with only one-quarter of the number of submarines deployed by the Soviets and about two-thirds of the number needed to effectively defend the North Atlantic in a full-throttle war. Construction of the *Los Angeles*-class submarines was increased from one to three each year to replace the old *Sturgeon*-class boats, which were retiring. In 1983, Tomahawk cruise missile launchers were added to some *Los Angeles*-class submarines to endow them with the ability to attack over-the-horizon and inshore

The battleship *Iowa* (BB-61) is readied for recommissioning in April 1984. Four 49,000-ton *Iowas*, the U.S. Navy's first and only post–treaty-class battleships, were completed in 1943 and 1944. The early 1942 steel crisis forced the Navy to cancel two more *Iowas* and four 60,000-ton *Montana*-class superbattleships. Armed with nine 16-inch guns, each of which could fire a 2,700-pound shell twenty-three miles, and protected by a 12.1-inch armor belt, the graceful, flush-deck *Iowa* (BB-61) entered the fleet in December 1943, transported President Roosevelt and the Joint Chiefs to and from the Cairo-Tehran summit conferences, and then steamed into the Pacific where she spent the rest of the war screening the Fast Carrier Force. Decommissioned in 1949, she was brought back into service in 1951 for the Korean War but was retired again in 1958. Her sister ship, the *New Jersey*, saw action off Vietnam in 1968 but was decommissioned a year later. Under John Lehman's 600-ship Navy plan, all four *Iowas* were modernized in the early 1980s by the addition of drone planes, helicopters, and Tomahawk vertical missile launchers. Although the *Missouri* and the *Wisconsin* successfully launched barrages of Tomahawks at strategic targets in Baghdad and elsewhere in Iraq during the 1991 Persian Gulf War, the *Iowa* was already decommissioned and Secretary of Defense Dick Cheney had announced that the three remaining battleships would be withdrawn from service because of the cost of providing for the 1,500-member crews.

U.S. Navy Department

targets. To succeed the much-maligned *Los Angeles*-class attack submarines, Vice Admiral Ronald Thunman, the Deputy CNO for submarines, pressed for the construction of the new, fast, deep-diving *Seawolf*-class attack submarines, which were to be armed with a marginally improved fire-control system and upgraded long-range sonars. The *Los Angeles* had been designed primarily to escort task forces, but the new submarine had to be more flexible. The *Seawolf* was to be fitted with a vertical launching system for Tomahawk cruise missiles, a minelaying system, larger computers, and the means to hunt down Soviet ballistic missile submarines hiding under the Arctic ice pack. Congress approved the construction of the lead submarine in this class in 1986, and Admiral Bruce de Mars, who succeeded Admiral McKee in charge of the Navy's nuclear reactor program two years later, made them his first priority.

Lehman understood that the Navy's antisubmarine forces needed improvement so that the fleet could take the offensive against the Soviet Union. A widely recognized problem was that the aging SOSUS ocean hydrophone system, effective in the vicinity of the continental shelf, could not cover large midocean areas. An associated problem was reducing the time between acquiring hydrophone data and sending it to deployed antisubmarine hunting forces. Escorts trailing towed-array acoustic sensors, consisting of a long string of hydrophones towed hundreds of yards behind a ship, solved only part of the problem. Inasmuch as the listening devices operated clear of the noise of the ship, the escort could proceed at high speed and still detect submarines at relatively long ranges, pursue them with LAMPS III helicopters, and attack and sink them with homing torpedoes.

The U.S. Navy was traditionally short of antisubmarine escorts, however, and a Soviet submarine, moving at a speed of 25 knots, might reach any point inside a 50-square-mile area within ten minutes of a contact and any point inside a 500-square-mile area within half an hour. As an alternative to building more austere surface escorts, and to supplement the older SOSUS system, Lehman persuaded Congress to authorize the construction of the Surveillance Towed Array Sensor System. Each small, slow SURTASS vessel towed a 6,000-foot cable with a large passive hydrophone array at the end. The first of twelve SURTASS ships entered the fleet in 1984. One shore-based processing center on the East Coast and another on the West Coast gathered ocean sound signals and other target information from the SURTASS vessels, processed it, and transmitted the results back to the numbered fleets. The SURTASS ships improved the Navy's ability to locate Soviet submarines and to monitor their fleet bases, although the wartime effectiveness of these vessels would be limited to deep-ocean areas. However, the Navy planned to create long-lasting acoustic detection fields by using attack submarines or patrol aircraft to emplace command-activated sonobuoys quite near Soviet naval bases.

Technological breakthroughs that had been predicted for over a decade threatened even more profound changes in submarine and antisubmarine warfare. In 1980, William Perry, the Defense Department's director of research, reflected widespread concerns that the Soviets might be on the verge of a breakthrough in antisubmarine warfare technology, allowing them to "see through the water," a reference to advances in nonacoustic submarine detecting systems. "The risk is that the ocean may become transparent," argued Commander Walt Stephanson, a nuclear submariner. "The immutable laws of physics declare that the energy expended in moving a submarine will eventually be imparted to the medium through which it moves." One of the most promising new systems, satellite-borne synthetic aperture radar, observed changes in waves on the ocean's surface generated by the motion of objects below. In March 1984, an SAR set carried by a NASA Seasat A satellite unexpectedly located an American submarine in this manner, an event that reportedly caused the Navy to order the satellite's power to be disabled so as to prevent word leaking out about the discovery. That same year, the Soviets installed on the Salyut space station an SAR radar that was to operate in conjunction with aircraft below, and this team apparently located more than one *Delta*-class ballistic missile submarine operating at underwater depths of 200 to 300 feet. Nonacoustic systems were in their infancy, however. Most U.S. Navy submariners believed that their vessels were immune to underwater detection. "In the case of nuclear-powered ballistic missile submarines," insisted Rear Admiral J. W. Holland, the deputy director of the Navy's Space Command and Control Office, "there is neither an antisubmarine warfare threat to them in peace or in war."[7]

Naval aviation had more pressing problems. Lehman agreed with a fellow naval aviator's lament that, as a result of the paltry defense budgets of the 1970s, inflation, escalating weapons costs, misplaced priorities, and the increasing complexity of each weapon, the Navy had "improved our planes but not our weapons." For instance, Captain Ken Dickerson's Naval Weapons Center at China Lake, California, had designed the HARM missile to counter North Vietnam's radar-guided surface-to-air missiles. When it was first successfully test-fired in 1973, the Navy estimated that the mass-production cost of each missile would be about $20,000, but four years later Secretary Brown examined the program, decided that the HARM missile might be used against more complex Soviet radars, and insisted that Air Force requirements be superimposed on the Navy's project. As a result, the cost soared to over $600,000 for each missile by 1981 when the Navy took delivery of the first eighty HARMs.

The same fate nearly befell one of Lehman's pet projects, the 1,000-pound Skipper bomb, which had also been developed at China Lake by Burrell Hayes, the center's technical director. A cheap and simple weapon, the Skipper bomb contained a laser-guided seeker that allowed it to ride a radar beam to its target. In early tests, it hit targets as far away as six miles. However, Captain John J. Lahr, the Skipper's foremost proponent, could not get Navy support for the project because of the opposition of Texas' Senator John Tower, the powerful chairman of the Armed Services Committee, who wanted Texas Instruments, not the Navy, to develop the weapon. Lahr finally cornered Lehman and explained the problem in 1983. "It was a case of the best being the enemy of the good—the contractor's siren song, that they could produce what our lab had produced, and that it would be thicker, quicker, and slicker, by God—and do it for less cost," Lehman explained after he ordered the Skipper into production.[8]

Arming ships with cruise missiles constituted a "revolution at sea," according to Vice Admiral Joseph Metcalf, the Deputy CNO for surface warfare in 1986. Through his experience with arms control, Lehman understood the close relationship between weapons and strategy, especially in the field of cruise missiles, the "most effective weapons we have today." He planned to "add a family of cruise missiles" to the recommissioned *Iowa*-class battleships, "giving each 32 Tomahawks and 16 Harpoons that can attack on land or at sea." Several long-range, ship-launched air-breathing cruise missiles had been developed after World War II, but they were very inaccurate and so Defense Secretary McNamara had canceled the programs in 1962. The Air Force was indifferent or hostile to the cruise missile in the 1960s, and so Defense Secretary Laird, who was convinced that American forces had to overcome some of the limitations embodied in SALT I, agreed in 1972 to put the new Joint Cruise Missile Project under the supervision of Rear Admiral Walter M. Locke, a dynamic figure who was about to father a true revolution in naval warfare. Locke's work on the Tomahawk was given a boost in 1978 by Jimmy Carter, who used a decision to accelerate cruise missile development to justify his cancellation of the B-1 manned bomber. Locke's achievement was to integrate small, lightweight fission warheads; small, high-thrust, fuel-efficient turbofan engines; and the microchip-based, Tercom terrain map-matching system into a single weapon. One air-launched cruise missile was developed for the Air Force and three versions of the sea-launched Tomahawk cruise missile were developed for the Navy.[9]

In January 1984, a submarine-launched Tomahawk traveled over 1,500 miles and struck its target, and production of the short-range land attack version and its anti-ship counterpart soon began. Admiral Watkins ordered plans drawn up to install Tomahawk launchers in many of the destroyers and all of the attack submarines, battleships, and cruisers, a total of nearly 200 ships. In short, many antisubmarine or antimissile ships—hitherto single-purpose vessels—became powerful anti-ship killers, each as potentially lethal as a carrier's air wing. The perfection of efficient cruise missiles also permitted submarines and ships to conduct attacks on inland targets with conventional or nuclear ordnance. However, arming the fleet with Tomahawks threatened to blur the distinction between conventional and nuclear-tipped missiles, reduce the warning time available to either side in a crisis, and thereby destabilize the strategic balance of power. Rear Admiral Stephen Housetter, the director of the project, warned that inasmuch as Tomahawk missiles might deliver either conventional or nuclear payloads, the Soviets would thereafter have to "consider every battle group ship a potential threat" to their home territory.[10]

John Lehman crafted his Maritime Strategy not only to justify the creation of the 600-ship Navy but also to provide more muscle for Reagan's interventionist foreign policy and to put more starch into the president's threat to regain practical strategic nuclear superiority over the Soviets. Lehman believed that the Navy needed a strategy that was unique, was sufficiently controversial to generate debate—and, therefore, interest—in professional and public forums, and would serve as a benchmark against which new technology, ships, aircraft, weapons, and tactics might be measured. Because Reagan's military policy aimed to "ensure our preparedness to respond to, and if necessary, successfully fight either conventional or nuclear war," Lehman also decided that his Maritime Strategy had to transcend the widely accepted conviction that a firebreak existed between nuclear and conventional warfighting.[11]

The Maritime Strategy owed its origins to Admiral Holloway's opposition in 1977 to Carter's NATO-oriented Swing Strategy. Holloway's view was echoed by Admiral Thomas Hayward after he became CNO the following year. Contrasting the increasing geographical reach and operational tempo of Soviet naval activity with the decline of the American blue-water fleet during and after the Vietnam War, Hayward proposed to overcome this disparity not only by building more ships but also by adopting an offensive wartime strategy by which the Americans might seize the initiative in the earliest phase of a great-power conflict. Putting this strategy into effect posed several problems, not the least of which was that the United States' primary obligation was to defend NATO's central front in Germany. Given the supposed superiority of Soviet ground and air forces in Europe, reinforcements shipped from the East Coast to Europe were thought to be essential to NATO's capacity to resist a Red Army invasion of West Germany for more than a few weeks. As a result, American admirals had believed for years that the Navy's most important mission was to keep open the sea lines of communication with western Europe by defending the Greenland–Iceland–United Kingdom gap against Soviet submarines, attacking Soviet naval forces in the Mediterranean to obstruct their entry into the Atlantic, and escorting Europe-bound resupply and reinforcement convoys. Under these strategic plans, *Sturgeon-* and *Los Angeles*-class attack submarines and surface antisubmarine battle groups were to be stationed at chokepoints along the Greenland–Iceland–United Kingdom gap where, aided by the SOSUS hydrophone system, they could ambush enemy boats trying to debouch into the North Atlantic.

Admiral Zumwalt saw no alternative in the early 1970s to this barrier and escort strategy. Using the SOSUS hydrophone system, attack submarines, and the antisubmarine task forces to establish these barriers seemed a much more effective means of attriting Soviet submarines than risking ships in the Barents Sea. However, even at that time, according to Vice Admiral James Doyle, the Deputy CNO, there was a move afoot among Navy leaders to place "offensive operations in forward areas" above "barrier operations" and to assign the Navy's durable attack submarines "to conduct offensive operations in forward areas in the early stages of conflict." Admiral Isaac Kidd, the commander in chief of the Atlantic Fleet, pointed out in 1978 that a ground war in Europe would consume an unprecedented quantity of munitions and that the NATO powers did not possess enough readily available cargo shipping to absorb the losses that Soviet submarines might inflict if NATO strategy tied down the Atlantic Fleet to escort and barrier operations. If NATO-bound shipping were assembled in seventy-ship convoys, the Atlantic Fleet could protect only one-third of the required shipping. Although American troops would be airlifted to Europe, more than 3,000 freighters and tankers would be needed to support NATO forces on the central front, Kidd testified, predicting that losses to Soviet submarines would be a "staggering" 50 percent. Nor would a patrol strategy work. During a 1981 NATO naval exercise called Ocean Safari, the Atlantic Fleet attempted to protect a number of shipping lanes by aggressive patrolling, but the attacking submarines invariably breached these defenses. Under NATO's general war plan, nearly 1,000 ships carrying at least 10 million tons of weapons and equipment would be needed to resupply the Western armies and air forces during the early days of a central front war.

Much to the displeasure of the British, who still believed in the transatlantic escort-of-convoy strategy, admirals Holloway and Kidd agreed in 1975 to devise a more aggressive antisubmarine strategy to locate, hunt down, and sink any Soviet submarines that leached into the Atlantic through the traditional SOSUS barriers. This offensive antisubmarine strategy still relied heavily on the SOSUS system and the P-3 Orion maritime patrol squadrons based in Iceland and Britain to fix the positions and monitor the movements of enemy predators, and it also relied on the *Los Angeles*-class attack submarines to track down and sink them. Owing to the need to provide missile and antisubmarine screens for his carrier battle groups, amphibious task forces, and replenishment ships, however, Kidd now warned NATO that the alliance might have to accept tremendous attrition to its merchant shipping during the days or weeks it took to evict or sink Soviet submarines in the Atlantic. Convinced that this approach was an improvement over the escort strategy, he nonetheless realized its shortcomings. The Atlantic Fleet had no backup to the aging SOSUS system, which was thought to be highly vulnerable to a Soviet attack. And, while the large fixed underwater arrays and air-dropped sonobuoys could still locate most Soviet submarines entering the Atlantic, the Atlantic Fleet did not possess enough P-3 Orions to trail every trespasser even in peacetime, nor enough fast attack submarines or aircraft to sink them all quickly in wartime should the Soviets position their naval forces in the Atlantic before invading Germany.[12]

Neither Carter nor Brown took seriously the development of an offensive naval strategy, and Carter's emphasis on defending NATO's central front and implementing his Swing Strategy in 1977 alarmed Admiral Thomas Hayward, then commander in chief of the Pacific theater. Carter's attempt to reduce the number of American troops posted to South Korea imposed a proportionately greater burden on the 7th Fleet, with the growing Soviet naval presence in the Indian Ocean adding to this strain. And crises in Ethiopia, Yemen, Iran, and Afghanistan during the last two years of the Carter administration made the actual execution of the Swing Strategy seem increasingly remote. This problem was magnified by the increasing size of the Soviet fleet, as well as by a corresponding decline in the absolute number of deployable American warships. Nonetheless, Carter refused to consider an offensive global naval strategy aimed at endangering the Soviet's ballistic missile–bearing submarines, with the result that until 1980 the Navy did little to improve its surveillance of the Barents Sea and the Sea of Okhotsk.

Soon after becoming CNO in 1978, Admiral Hayward proposed to abandon the Swing Strategy and adopt instead an offensive naval strategy aimed at overcoming the disparity of numbers by seizing the opportunity early in a general war to attack deployed Soviet ships and submarines and their bases. The Navy should "seek out and destroy" Soviet warships "wherever they may be, even in coastal waters," Hayward declared. He planned a northern movement with four to six carriers steaming into the Norwegian and Barents seas so as to tie down enemy ships and submarines that would otherwise be attacking NATO-bound convoys in the mid-Atlantic. "Our current . . . carrier battle forces and their supporting units are well-suited for . . . this strategy," he told Congress in 1980. The administration revised its foreign policy that year by enunciating the Carter Doctrine and reluctantly accepted increases in the Navy's long-term shipbuilding plans. Navy strategists had convinced the administration in the meantime that the defense of Norway was vital to NATO and important to the security of the Atlantic sea lines of communication. A central front war might not be won in northern Norway, Carter at last confessed, but it might be lost by ignoring the region. However, Norway resisted Carter's proposal to study a northern strategy until late 1980 when Oslo finally agreed that the Marines might preposition stocks in the Trøndelag region of central Norway. Carter's defeat that November meant that little more was done during his administration on revising this aspect of American grand strategy.[13]

When he took office, Reagan had visions of a more muscular foreign policy and increased American military strength, but he had no strategy to put his concepts into practice, and, unlike Harold Brown, Caspar Weinberger was not dedicated to particular strategic formulas. To the public, Weinberger purveyed general rearmament, but when it came to advising the president, he usually resisted using military force to solve foreign policy problems. He did articulate one of Reagan's complaints about Carter's approach to defense policy, however. "For many years," he declared, "it has been U.S. policy to let the investment and planning for our conventional forces be determined by the requirement for fighting a war centered in Europe" in which "NATO forces would be attacked by the Warsaw Pact." Carter's central front and swing strategies ignored the fact that "the Soviet Union has enough active forces and reserves to conduct simultaneous campaigns in more than one theater."

A skilled practitioner of the strategic priesthood, Lehman stepped in to fill the resulting vacuum. He recognized the fallacy of treating naval strategy purely in the context of a conventional war. Whereas Admiral Zumwalt had argued that naval strategy was irrelevant once a general war crossed the thermonuclear threshold, Lehman believed that the two rival alliances might someday engage in either a general or limited war with both conventional and nuclear arms. He, therefore, worked on developing an offensive strategy that might enhance peacetime deterrence and contribute to victory in either a limited nuclear war or a conflict involving purely conventional arms. Lehman labeled the results of this work—which continued after a submariner, Admiral James Watkins, became CNO in 1982—the Maritime Strategy.

Lehman believed that the Navy had to operate at least fifteen heavy attack carriers to execute his Maritime Strategy and to provide the forces ready to deal with limited wars or peacetime overseas interventions or to fight a global war with conventional or nuclear arms. He was especially eager for the Navy to take the offensive against the Soviets' ballistic missile–bearing submarines. "If we try to draw a *cordon sanitaire* and declare that we are not going . . . above the GIUK [Greenland–Iceland–United Kingdom] gap or we are not going to go west of such and such a parallel, then obviously they [the Soviets] have the capability to use their attack submarines offensively against the SLOCs." To accommodate the asymmetry between the opposing forces in a general war, Lehman proposed that, when a conflict between the superpowers appeared likely, the Atlantic Fleet Striking Force send its attack submarines east of the North Cape to clear the way for the northward movement of three or more carrier battle groups into the Norwegian Sea and beyond. The carriers would rely on their aircraft and antiair missile–bearing ships to deal with nearby land-based enemy patrol bombers and on the U.S. Navy's superior escorting attack submarines and antisubmarine forces to overcome defending Soviet minefields. And the new Aegis-equipped cruisers could orchestrate the defense of the battle groups against saturation attacks by opposing land-based missile–bearing aircraft. Moreover, the recently invented Iliac 4 supercomputer, made available to the Navy in 1980, so greatly improved sound processing that the number of land- and carrier-based aircraft needed to locate and prosecute submarine contacts was considerably reduced.

In 1981, the carriers *Eisenhower* and *Forrestal* sailed up the Norwegian Sea and rounded the North Cape under radio silence, apparently without being located by the Soviets. Several *Los Angeles*-class attack submarines were already in position off key Soviet Northern Fleet naval bases. Murmansk was indeed the Soviets' only ice-free port to which access could not easily be blocked. This "aggressive forward movement" of attack submarines and allied land-based maritime patrol aircraft was intended to "force Soviet submarines to retreat to their defensive bastions to protect their ballistic missile submarines," according to Admiral Watkins. Menacing the bastions was the object of the northern movement. Most of the large Northern Fleet's strength was vested in ballistic missile and attack submarines. While fully 60 percent of Soviet ballistic missile submarines could strike American targets without leaving port, the Soviets deployed only about 15 percent of them at any time, and the Red Navy's new nuclear-powered *Typhoon*-class ballistic missile–bearing submarine, then being built at Severodvinsk, illustrated Moscow's commitment to maintaining a strong, modern submarine-launched missile force. "Given the survivability factor of the launch platform and the number of weapons available, about two such platforms are all the Soviets would need to obliterate the United States," observed Vice Admiral Gerald E. Miller.[14]

Lehman intended the northern movement to roll up enemy forces south of Iceland and the United Kingdom and to compel the Soviets' Northern Fleet to retire from the Norwegian and Barents seas and the Arctic Ocean. Meanwhile, escorting resupply convoys on the last leg of the voyage from the United States to western Europe would become the responsibility of the other NATO fleets. Without the northern movement, Lehman insisted, the Atlantic Fleet would be consigned to escorting convoys and defending the Greenland–Iceland–United Kingdom barrier, thus exposing northern Norway to a Soviet invasion and northern Britain to hostile air operations. The Atlantic Fleet would "have to move north of the GIUK gap," he told Congress in 1984. "We have to control the Norwegian Sea and force them back into the defensive further north, to use their attack submarines to protect their nuclear attack submarines, to use their attack submarines to protect the Kola and Murmansk coasts." Concurrently, the 6th Fleet battle groups would move forward into the Aegean to roll up the Soviets' Mediterranean Fleet, support Greece and Turkey, and attack Soviet targets on the Black Sea.

Lehman intended to create a "second front" by having the Pacific Fleet conduct a simultaneous northern movement during which the 7th Fleet carrier battle groups, preceded by attack submarines and maritime patrol bombers, were to drive the Red Fleet from its patrol areas in the Sea of Japan, the Sea of Okhotsk, and the North Pacific east of the Kamchatka Peninsula. This concept was tested when the new carrier *Carl Vinson* led her bat-

tle group into the Bering Sea and operated within striking distance of the Kamchatka Peninsula. "The Soviets didn't know
where we were for twelve days," boasted Admiral James Lyons,
the hot-tempered commander of the Pacific Fleet. On another
occasion, a battleship battle group operated under radio silence
with immunity in the Sea of Okhotsk, as did the carrier *Ranger*
when she was sent into those waters on an unscheduled fast
cruise across the Pacific to the Far East. Not only would such operations in wartime establish a fighting Far Eastern flank, but
also they might prevent Soviet attack submarines from slipping
into the Pacific and pouncing on allied shipping there with the
intention of disrupting NATO strategy.[15]

All approaches to Soviet bases were heavily mined, of course,
and Admiral Wesley McDonald admitted that his Atlantic Fleet
was "woefully inadequate" to counter mine warfare. The Maritime Strategy called for the fleet to sweep the minefields, and, to
prevent the Soviets from lunging into Norway, about 13,000
Marines, cooperating with the Norwegians, were to land on the
Kola Peninsula and establish an airbase there for 150 planes.
"Naval power can make the difference between winning and losing the land battle in northern Norway," insisted Vice Admiral
Henry Mustin of the 2nd Fleet, which he felt in turn meant winning or losing the Norwegian Sea "and hence the Battle of the
Atlantic and the land war in Europe." And if the North Pacific
minefields could be overcome, then the Soviets might be compelled to withdraw their ships and submarines to their naval
bases at Petropavlovsk and Vladivostok. Rear Admiral William
Pendley claimed that an offensive in the Northwest Pacific was
"directly relevant to a European war" because "the threat of U.S.
combat operations in the Pacific serves to tie down Soviet forces
. . . that could otherwise be committed to a European conflict."

Once the American battle groups had steamed within range
of the Soviet bastions, Lehman intended the carriers to launch
attacks with aircraft and missiles carrying conventional ordnance
against Soviet ballistic missile submarines and their bases. The
idea was "getting at the Soviet naval threat at its source." Because
the Soviets placed a high value on their ballistic missile fleet, they
were certain to react with alarm to this menace to their second-
strike nuclear retaliatory force. In doing so, Admiral Watkins argued, Moscow was likely to divert tactical aircraft from the central front to the northern flank, thus reducing Soviet superiority
in the air over Germany.[16]

Stressing the global character of conventional or nuclear war with the Soviets, Lehman pointed out that the Atlantic Fleet might contribute directly to the defense of the central front in a more immediate, effective way with the Maritime Strategy than it could by adopting a passive escort strategy. The Atlantic and Pacific fleets were to pin down Soviet air and ground forces on the edges of Russia, thus keeping them from joining the battle on the central front and ultimately forcing them to withdraw from Germany. Lehman offered this "horizontal escalation" as an alternative to a "vertical escalation" into nuclear war. "If they lose Kola," he argued, then the Soviets "would lose their whole strategic submarine fleet." It was "improbable," Watkins asserted, that the Atlantic Fleet's northern movement against the Red Fleet's ballistic missile submarines—cornering them in their bastions or hunting them down under the polar ice—would lead to escalation, because such an offensive would deny the Soviets the "attractiveness of nuclear escalation by changing the nuclear balance in our forces." Lehman, in a paroxysm of hyperbole, claimed that his Maritime Strategy represented "a change in the global military balance of power."[17]

The most daring aspect of the Maritime Strategy was Lehman's conviction that spreading land-attack nuclear-tipped missiles throughout the American fleet would broaden the base of the strategic deterrent force and thereby strengthen the restraints it imposed on the Soviets. This was to be accomplished by arming the *Los Angeles*-class attack submarines and Aegis-bearing cruisers with medium-range, nuclear-capable Tomahawk sea-launched cruise missiles. For the time being, however, the Atlantic Fleet Striking Force still depended for its offensive power merely on the heavy carriers, which embarked mostly fighters and A-6 Intruder attack bombers, and they possessed relatively little antisubmarine warfare capability.

The Maritime Strategy did not want for opponents. By early 1987, when Lehman resigned as secretary of the Navy, three secret versions of the Maritime Strategy had been promulgated and discussed. Critics charged that neither the Reagan Doctrine nor the Maritime Strategy betrayed any sense of priorities, a criticism echoed by the JCS in 1983 when they announced that "our current forces are insufficient to take on all tasks simultaneously," and that, as a result, "general strategic priorities [that is, Europe first] and specific circumstances . . . will govern force employment." As Commander of the Atlantic Fleet Admiral Harold

Train III pointed out, "the only problem with the Maritime Strategy is that it is a Navy maritime strategy; it is not yet embraced by all the other services nor by the secretary of defense." According to Lieutenant General Bernard E. Trainor, the former deputy Marine Corps commandant, "Weinberger and the Joint Chiefs of Staff and NATO have never formally approved the Lehman strategy."[18]

There were other problems. Lehman postulated that it was possible for NATO and the Warsaw Pact to wage war without bringing nuclear weapons into play, a point on which he and his critics differed totally. France's nuclear strategy of Instant Response might easily frustrate Washington's plan to control a European war with graduated response or horizontal escalation. Lehman also presumed that horizontal, or geographical, escalation would confer advantages on American forces, although they faced a supposedly powerful foe endowed with interior lines of communication. "If all Soviet ships were swept from the high seas and all Soviet home and overseas naval bases [were] put out of action," asked Robert Komer, Carter's undersecretary of defense, "could this prevent the U.S.S.R. from . . . overrunning Europe and the Middle East oil fields, emasculating or cowing China, or mounting a land-based missile and air threat to nearby Japan?" War gaming with specialists in Soviet strategy at the Naval War College in 1987 suggested that Komer was probably right. Even were the Atlantic Fleet carriers to attack the Soviet Northern Fleet and its bases and achieve "great success with acceptable losses," he asserted, "it would be like sticking pins in the hide of an elephant." He also charged Lehman with ignoring the Soviets' conservative habit of conducting aggression via clients, proxies, subversion, or surrogate forces and their historic refusal to send the Red Army or Air Force across noncontiguous frontiers. Komer reasoned wrongly, however, that an "overinvestment in a carrier-heavy Navy . . . could be tantamount to making it impossible to defend Europe, or the Persian Gulf, for that matter."[19]

Critics questioned the wisdom of sending carrier battle groups into the dangerous Norwegian and Barents seas and also argued that the Soviets would not expose their ballistic missile fleet to air and missile attacks without retaliating with nuclear weapons. The Northern Fleet's strategic submarines would try to escape into the Atlantic, and the handful of ballistic missile–bearing submarines already on deterrent patrol in the Barents Sea would race under the polar ice cap. Moreover, retired Admiral Stansfield Turner, Carter's CIA director, maintained that in a crisis "no president could possibly permit the Navy to attempt such a high risk effort" as the movement into the Norwegian Sea, inasmuch as they were needed in the Atlantic because the NATO navies were incapable of conducting independent escort operations.

Lehman believed that the Navy's carrier battle groups could reach positions in the Norwegian and Barents seas with acceptable losses in ships and aircraft, but many critics disagreed. It was clear, for instance, that the Soviets were well prepared to defend their flank in the Norwegian Sea. At Pechenga, eighteen miles from the Norwegian border, they had established a small advance naval base, and to defend the Kola Peninsula they had posted two motorized Red Army divisions supported by aircraft widely dispersed at approximately forty nearby military airfields. Although the Kola Peninsula was situated 125 miles above the Arctic Circle, an unusual current left the surrounding waters ice free throughout the year, but to approach the Soviet naval base at Polyarny, the home of the huge Northern Fleet, the Atlantic Fleet Striking Force would have to pass through the dangerous Bear Island gap off Norway's North Cape. "By the time the [American] carriers were within 1,600 miles of Soviet air bases, they would [also] be within range of over 90 percent of the U.S.S.R.'s land-based bombers," claimed Admiral Turner. "Yet, the Soviet bases would still be over 1,000 miles beyond the range of carrier aircraft." Indeed, some even charged that the Navy's leadership was fully aware of the carriers' vulnerability but were hiding that fact from Congress. In a review of Ocean Venture 81, an exercise that tested the Maritime Strategy, Lieutenant Commander Dean L. Knuth, a Navy analyst, wrote that he could not "accept the proposition that the *Eisenhower* and the *Forrestal* reached the Norwegian Sea from the North Atlantic without being attacked successfully, even though the Orange [Soviet submarine] threat was very low." And the Navy had not built enough support ships—fast oilers, ammunition ships, and combat stores ships—that could keep company with the fast battle groups. "Based on the . . . Maritime Strategy, we probably need twice the number of logistics ships we now have," argued Commander Michael Edwards.[20]

Indeed, the Soviet naval air force had deployed approximately 2,700 aircraft and 10,000 surface-to-air missiles to defend their bastions. Soviet assets were not inexhaustible, but penetrating these heavily defended positions posed a difficult challenge for the Navy. The effective operating radius of the F-14 Tomcat against missile-armed bombers was about 400 miles. Prior to 1985, the main threat to the northern movement stemmed from the cruise missile–armed Backfire bombers, whose 2,500-mile range would allow them to attack hostile early-warning radar aircraft such as the Navy's E-2C Hawkeyes, P-3 Orion antisubmarine patrol planes, or the Air Force's EA-3 AWACS. Moreover, the Soviets were quickly replacing their aging, short-range Kola-based Badger bombers with modern Backfires. And in 1986, to counter the threat from Tomahawk sea-launched cruise missiles, the Soviets stationed on the Kola Peninsula the first new Su-27 Flanker fighter, a plane with a refueled cruising radius of over 1,000 miles that was armed with a 1,130-mile-range look-down, shoot-down search radar, long-range radar-guided missiles, and short-range infrared-guided missiles. An obvious counter to the Maritime Strategy, the Flankers' basing was intended to thwart the Atlantic Fleet Striking Force's northern movement and to extend the Soviet air threat far south of the British Isles. Under the Maritime Strategy, the American fleets would have to invade the Norwegian and Barents seas and the Northwest Pacific, transit minefields leading to the Soviet bastions, destroy the defending Soviet Backfires and Flankers and sink the enemy's ballistic missile and attack submarines before they put to sea and raced under the icecap where they would be defended by undersea minefields, land-based missile-bearing patrol planes, and their own attack submarines. Air strikes against Soviet bases after their submarine fleet escaped would be of little strategic value. It would be "ill-advised to enter the Norwegian Sea and take losses," which "would be great in both aircraft and ships," Admiral Train concluded.

Also troubling was the supposition in the Maritime Strategy that most Soviet fleet ballistic missile submarines would remain in the vicinity of their bastions. "No one knowledgeable in antisubmarine warfare . . . believes we could come close to neutralizing even half of their deployed missile submarines before they could launch their payloads," asserted Lieutenant Commander Steven E. Mays. "Furthermore, the number of submarines in the antisubmarine mode necessary to do so would leave our surface combatants and convoys at the mercy of a very capable Soviet attack submarine force that outnumbers our fleet by more than three-to-one." In 1981, the first *Typhoon*-class strategic missile submarine was commissioned into the Soviet fleet. Armed with twenty tubes that could fire ballistic missiles able to reach targets 4,000 miles distant, she could remain in northern waters and still menace any city or military installation in the United States. Until 1983, about two-thirds of the Russian *Typhoon-*, *Delta-*, and *Yankee*-class ballistic missile submarines and the same fraction of their modern combat ships operated out of the Kola Peninsula and the White Sea ports. And, as Admiral Train pointed out, "the range of the missile on the *Delta* permits the submarine to be many other places."

Whereas Lehman believed that penetrating the bastions and sinking the Soviets' ballistic missile submarines would, by shifting the entire burden for nuclear warfighting to their Strategic Rocket Forces, cause the Kremlin to negotiate an end to the war, his critics contended that it would instead force the enemy to place his silo-based missiles on a hair-trigger launch-on-warning status. While these arguments were under way, it became clear that the Maritime Strategy was worrying the Russians. In June 1981, Brezhnev, reversing a longstanding Kremlin policy of trying to scare Norway out of NATO, urged the creation of a nuclear-free zone in Scandinavia guaranteed by both great powers. This diplomacy fell on deaf ears, however.[21]

Despite the emphasis on the northern movement in the Maritime Strategy, the Navy's carrier battle groups spent only about 100 days in the harsh environment of the Norwegian Sea in the 1980s. "Because of the press of other commitments . . . we haven't been able to get up there as often as we want," admitted Vice Admiral Henry Mustin in 1989. "That raises issues of readiness." Happily, the Maritime Strategy was never tested in war. It was put into place at the very time that the Warsaw Pact began to fracture and the Soviet Union started down a decade-long economic descent ending in political disintegration.

For Lehman's successor, Weinberger turned to one of his assistant secretaries of defense, James Webb, a Naval Academy graduate and sometime novelist, who told Congress that he supported Lehman's 600-ship Navy and the Maritime Strategy. Webb, although understanding the stakes at hand, proved to be uniquely inept in championing the policies he espoused. Owing to massive deficits accumulated by Reagan's budgets and tax cuts and the Democrats' opposition to Reagan's military policy, Congress, after 1985, refused to increase defense spending by much more than the rate of inflation. While Reagan's popularity and doggedness prevented defense cutbacks, the 1986 Gramm-Rudman Balanced Budget Act, enacted to reduce the bloated federal deficit, and the winding down of the Cold War near the end of Reagan's presidency prevented the Navy from reaching Lehman's goal of 600 deployable ships by the end of the decade. Weinberger skillfully sidestepped more serious reductions to the growth rate of military spending, but following his 1987 resignation his successor, former National Security Adviser Frank Carlucci, too readily agreed to major cuts in the 1989 Defense Department budget. On the morning that Webb learned that this would result in the early retirement of fifteen frigates, he submitted his resignation in an intemperate fit of pique and condemned Carlucci for being insensitive to the goal of a 600-ship fleet. Reagan quickly replaced Webb with William Ball III, a colorless White House figure who made no mark before the administration left office. By this time, the enormous economic and political pressure imposed on the Soviet Union by Reagan's defense policy, highlighted by John Lehman's 600-ship Navy and the Maritime Strategy, was convincing Moscow's leaders that their nation had lost the Cold War.[22]

Chapter Thirty-seven

The Reagan Doctrine
1982–1986

The Reagan Doctrine called on the United States to boldly confront the Soviet Union in the Third World. Some in the administration believed that the Kremlin's support of various terrorists was intended to discredit moderate, pro-Western regimes, radicalize politics, and exploit the resultant instability. The inspiration for most of the rising tide of terrorism, however, was the wave of Shiite Islamic fundamentalism that rolled over the Muslim world following the Iranian revolution of 1979. Carter eschewed reprisals against terrorists, but Reagan reversed this policy by announcing on 27 January 1981 that "when the rules of international behavior are violated, . . . our policy will be one of swift and effective retaliation." State Department diplomats often opposed this line because Reagan was clearly unwilling to disrupt relations with the Soviets over terrorism and because economic or military sanctions against Iran had little chance of succeeding. Moreover, Defense Secretary Caspar Weinberger and the JCS, overly sensitive to the residual trauma of Vietnam, argued that force should not be applied, even against terrorists, without the near-uniform consent of Congress and American public opinion.[1]

The first Gulf of Sidra incident came about when the Reagan administration, in the aftermath of several terrorist incidents, found itself unwilling to consider retaliation against the sponsors, the Soviet Union, Iran, or Syria, a willful Soviet client, and instead turned its attention to Libya, a diplomatic pariah

and the only nation to declare its unreserved support of interna-
tionalist terrorism of almost any coloration. In 1969, Colonel
Muammar al-Gaddafi, a young Muslim fanatic, staged a coup that
overthrew Libya's King Idris and put Gaddafi in power. He adopted a violently pro-Arab policy and attempted to lever the United
States into withdrawing support from Israel by closing Wheelus
Air Force Base in 1972, accepting military assistance from the Soviets, and providing training, arms, and sanctuary to a bewilder-
ing variety of terrorist gangs. Palestine Liberation Organization
commandos and other terrorists whom Gaddafi sponsored assassinated Israeli and moderate Arab diplomats in Europe, sky-
jacked or blew up commercial airliners in the Mediterranean,
and dynamited numerous public buildings in western Europe. By
1981, American diplomats serving in the Middle East were the
primary targets for these bloody operations.

Reagan decided early that year to match every Libyan provocation with an escalated response. A convenient playing field for
these confrontations already had been established by Gaddafi,
who unilaterally declared in 1973 that the entire Gulf of Sidra,
long an international waterway, was to be treated thereafter as
part of Libya's territorial waters. Gaddafi referred to the new maritime frontier, running across the Gulf from Tripoli to Benghazi,
as a "line of death" for those who trespassed without Libyan permission. At the time, the State Department had termed Gaddafi's
claim an "unacceptable . . . violation of international law" inasmuch as the 6th Fleet and other naval formations in the
Mediterranean had for many years exercised in the Gulf to avoid
overflying other Mediterranean countries or interfering with
commercial navigation. Nixon had refused to send the 6th Fleet
into the Gulf to challenge Gaddafi in 1973, for fear it would needlessly excite anti-American passions in the Middle East. These
conflicting American and Libyan positions over Libya's territorial
waters led to a succession of minor incidents that culminated in
1980 with an unsuccessful attack by a pair of Libyan MiG-23 Flogger fighters on a U.S. Air Force RC-135 tanker. Admiral Thomas
Hayward, the CNO, proposed that the 6th Fleet conduct a series
of Freedom of Navigation exercises in the Sidra Gulf to humiliate
Gaddafi by demonstrating his inability to enforce Libya's claims.
Carter had not only ignored Hayward's plan on the grounds that
a confrontation with Gaddafi would divert attention from the Iran
hostage crisis, but also ordered 6th Fleet aircraft to withdraw if

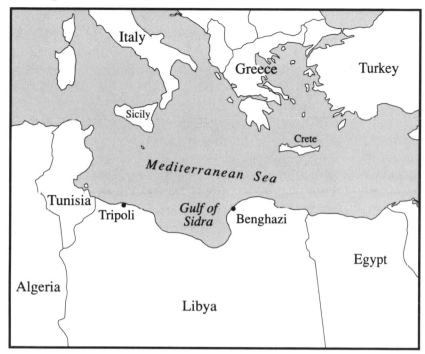

Gulf of Sidra

provoked by the Libyans and refused to sever diplomatic relations with Tripoli. On 6 May 1981, Reagan eagerly reversed this pusillanimous policy by breaking relations with Libya and putting Hayward's plan into effect.[2]

The JCS ordered Rear Admiral James Service to enter the Sidra Gulf with his 6th Fleet battle group and approved a change in Carter's rules of engagement so that Service's ships and aircraft would not have to allow an approaching enemy to take the first shot. The battle group, composed of the carriers *Nimitz* and *Forrestal*, eleven escorts, and a submarine screen, crossed the Tripoli-Benghazi line in the predawn hours of 18 August 1981. F-14 Tomcats flew out at 0600 to take station within forty miles of the Libyan coastline. A total of seventy-two Libyan Air Force French-built Mirage fighter-bombers and slow Soviet-built Su-22 Fitter attack aircraft, operating out of Benina to the east and Tripoli to the west, flew nearly 140 sorties in the vicinity of the battle group that day, but each intruder was intercepted and escorted back to and beyond the perimeter of the exercise area. At the end of the day, Service concluded that the Libyans had deployed the Fitters, which were unfit for aerial combat, in an attempt to make the Americans complacent, draw them south within range of Libya's land-based, surface-to-air missiles, and set them up for an easy shot.

Service launched his combat air patrol at dawn on 19 August while the battle group continued to exercise in the Gulf. E-2 Hawkeyes roamed overhead, providing radar surveillance for the fighters on combat air patrol. The F-14 Tomcats took station at 20,000 feet, flying a racetrack pattern at 220 knots, which kept at least one fighter's radar always pointed toward the Libyan coast. Shortly after 0700, a dozen Libyan Fitters flew toward the southernmost American air station, only to be located by a Hawkeye, which directed a section of nearby Tomcats to intercept them. When two hostile Fitters threatened to penetrate the American exercise area, they were picked up by Commander Hank Kleeman and his radar intercept officer, Lieutenant David Venlet, flying an F-14 Tomcat fighter. Kleeman and his wingman, Lieutenant Muczynski, also flying a Tomcat, accelerated and headed directly toward the Libyan aircraft. The opposing sections were less than 1,000 feet apart when one of the Libyan Fitters fired an Atoll air-to-air missile at Kleeman's aircraft. He broke left, eluded the missile, appeared over the enemy, waited ten seconds, and fired a Sidewinder at a range of about 1,300 yards that splashed its target. The second Fitter turned toward home, but Muczynski was on his tail within seconds and he too fired a Sidewinder. "There was a big explosion and fireball and debris," Muczynski said, and he was forced to turn straight up to avoid flying into it. The remaining Libyan aircraft were allowed to escape. An *Osa*-class missile patrol boat that had been operating within the American exercise perimeter also retired. The next day, its mission accomplished, Admiral Service's battle group steamed out of the Sidra Gulf.[3]

This first Sidra Gulf incident did nothing to moderate Gaddafi's support of international terrorism and, indeed, may have incited him to more violence. In October 1981, shortly after the Freedom of Navigation operations, Muslim fanatics assassinated Egyptian President Anwar Sadat, the foremost pro-American moderate in the Arab world. Although Gaddafi was not linked to Sadat's assassination, he publicly praised the killers and threatened to send gunmen to the United States to murder President Reagan. In response, Reagan imposed a trade embargo on Libya in December and ordered the 6,000 Americans who worked for oil companies doing business there to leave the country, ineffective gestures that had no effect on Libyan policy.

Israel's invasion of Lebanon in 1982 immeasurably complicated Reagan's antiterrorism policy. The Palestine Liberation Organization, founded by Yasir Arafat and other refugees from Palestine after the Suez War of 1956, served as a political umbrella for over a dozen groups dedicated to overthrowing the Jewish state and establishing an independent Palestine. When the Israelis overran the Gaza Strip and the West Bank of the Jordan River during the 1967 Six-Day War, they also drove the PLO eastward into Jordan, where the growing army of commandos made camp for three years. Arafat and Jordan's King Hussein fell out, and Hussein's army pushed the PLO into northern Lebanon in September 1970. Its presence in Lebanon upset that nation's fragile political coalition, undermined the Beirut government, and resulted in a civil war, which erupted when the Christian Falange militia moved against the Palestinians in 1975. Less than a year later, the Syrians invaded Lebanon to prevent the Falange from defeating the PLO, and in early 1978 the Israelis burst across the Lebanese border and advanced to the Litani River, ousting the Palestinians from artillery posts they had used for years to fire shells into Israeli territory. Washington and Moscow then arranged jointly to have the Israelis withdraw from Lebanon in April and inserted a UN peacekeeping force into southern Lebanon.

Carter had tried to maintain an even-handed policy between Israel and Arab moderates such as Sadat, but Reagan was less interested in expanding the Camp David Accords into a wider Middle East settlement than in reducing Soviet influence in the region. Secretary of State Haig hoped to subordinate the Middle East's passions to a higher "fear of the Soviet Union," a fear felt not only by Israel and moderate Muslim regimes such as Egypt, Jordan, Saudi Arabia, and Turkey, but also by radical-fundamentalist nations like Iran. However, Washington had lost all control over the Israelis, who became so frustrated with their inability to prevent PLO cross-border raids from Lebanon that on 6 June 1982 they launched Operation Peace for Galilee.

In this invasion, three Israeli divisions overran the PLO camps in southern Lebanon within six days, pushed the Syrian Army back up the Bekaa Valley, established an artillery position within range of Damascus, and forced Arafat's troops to retire to Beirut. Nearly 100 Syrian MiGs and a large fraction of Syria's Soviet-built SAM missile sites in the Bekaa Valley were destroyed by the Israeli air force. Linking arms with the Falange, the Israelis next cut the highway between Beirut and Damascus, laid siege to part of the Syrian Army and the PLO commandos who had taken refuge in the Lebanese capital, and shelled the city from the surrounding mountains with American-made weapons. Arafat was frantic. The PLO, abandoned by many of its sometime allies, was trapped and about to be destroyed.

Alarmed by the danger to the surprisingly large number of Americans who had remained in war-torn Beirut despite repeated State Department warnings, the JCS instructed Vice Admiral William H. Rowden to direct Captain Richard F. White's 6th Fleet Amphibious Squadron, then riding at anchor at the Navy's base at Rota, Spain, to steam into the eastern Mediterranean and take station about 100 miles off the Lebanese coast. On 24 June, White sent some Marines ashore at the small port of Juniyah, five miles south of the capital, where they boated nearly 600 American evacuees out to the landing ships *Nashville* and *Hermitage*.[4]

Reagan, furious with Israel, moved to prevent the dismemberment of Lebanon by sending Ambassador Philip Habib to Saudi Arabia where he persuaded King Fahd to help him arrange a ceasefire agreed to by Syria, its PLO allies, and Israel. This agreement provided for an ad hoc multinational Western peacekeeping force to go ashore and interpose itself between the 30,000-man Israeli army outside Beirut and the 13,000 Syrians and Palestinians trapped within the city. PLO troops would be transported to a friendly refuge in faraway Tunisia. To get the PLO to accept this arrangement, however, Habib foolishly promised that the United States would guarantee the safety of thousands of unarmed Palestinians who were to remain behind in Muslim West Beirut and in several outlying PLO refugee camps. "You're not going to get a multinational force if you're not prepared to put your own troops in," he insisted. The JCS were extremely skeptical about this logic and stiffly warned Weinberger that it would "be unwise for the U.S. to . . . put its military forces between the Israelis and the Arabs." It was ironic that Defense Secretary Weinberger, who usually resisted exposing American forces to hostilities, now sided with Habib and Reagan's newly appointed secretary of state, George Shultz. "We thought we could get some kind of peaceful conditions and return to previously existing borders," he recalled. Under the Habib Plan, 800 American Marines, 800 Frenchmen, and 400 Italians were to supervise the ceasefire and the subsequent evacuation of the PLO. In a message to the Marines, Reagan unwittingly revealed his own ambivalence about their mission by asserting that the multinational force "is crucial to achieving the peace that is so desperately needed in this long-tortured city."[5]

At 0500 on 25 August 1982, Habib met the LCU landing the first company of Marines, who were welcomed as saviors by the ragged PLO survivors and their Muslim allies. The French, already ashore, quickly turned the port area over to the Marines, and the evacuation of the PLO proceeded smoothly, highlighted by Arafat's noisy departure four days later. The Marines were boated out to their amphibious ships on 10 September, their mission seemingly accomplished, although Habib had petitioned Washington in vain to instruct them to remain ashore.

Events next took an almost predictable turn. While Commodore White's ships were steaming for Naples and preparing for an upcoming NATO exercise, the ceasefire in Beirut collapsed. On 14 September, the Israelis advanced into West Beirut to protect the Falange from the Shiite militia, thus violating Habib's arrangement. That same day, a Syrian agent assassinated the young, pro-American president-elect of Lebanon, Bashir Gemayel, whose family controlled the ruthless Falange militia. Two nights later, the Israelis and the Italians, whose base was nearby, allowed enraged Falange troops to enter the Sabra and Shatila refugee camps in West Beirut and take their revenge by murdering more than 700 unarmed Palestinians. "We had promised to protect the Palestinian civilians," said Geoffrey Kemp of the NSC, and "it was our allies, the Israelis, who permitted the massacre to happen, and it was our boy Bashir Gemayel's troops that did the killing." Under pressure from Reagan, the Israelis at long last withdrew from Beirut, but Gemayel's death and the massacres irrevocably alienated all three of Lebanon's armed religious factions.[6]

While the PLO was evacuating Beirut, Secretary Shultz announced his own Middle East peace plan, which aimed at expanding upon the Camp David Accords. He wanted the Arabs to recognize Israel in return for an Israeli promise to grant autonomy to the Palestinians on the West Bank and in the Gaza Strip.

The Arabs demanded that the Israelis withdraw from Lebanon, but the Israelis had announced that they would not leave until the Syrians did so first, a risky move Syrian President Assad refused to make. Shultz and Habib now concluded that reestablishing the multinational force and returning the Marines to Beirut might prevent a resumption of fighting among the Israelis, the Syrians, and the rival Muslim and Christian Lebanese militias. The French and Italians were willing to return, and Prime Minister Thatcher even agreed to send a small contingent of British troops. While Habib negotiated a mutual withdrawal plan, an American military mission was to reequip the Lebanese National Army so that it might reoccupy territory given up by the Syrian and Israeli forces. "Actually, there was no army to rebuild," reported Army Colonel Arthur Fintel, who directed the military assistance program. And, according to Weinberger, he and the JCS held that they "should not put people in on that kind of a mission that by definition could not be fulfilled unless you had an agreement to withdraw." With the exception of the CNO, Admiral James Watkins, none of the JCS thought much of the Shultz plan, which was, confessed Assistant Secretary of State Richard W. Murphy, "hard to condense into a few words." Its object "was to inject a measure of stability and confidence in the government of Lebanon" so that "it could begin the process of restoring its sovereignty and authority, its outreach across the country." Reagan overruled Weinberger and the JCS, however, and instructed Admiral Rowden to send Captain White's Amphibious Group and the Marines back to Beirut.[7]

At 1158 on 29 September 1982 the landing ship *Manitowoc* tied up at a Beirut dock and a company of Marines again walked ashore. Colonel James M. Mead had already established a support system at Green Beach—the same location where the Marines had chosen to land in 1958 to prop up the beleaguered Chamoun government—and the Marines were greeted by the new Lebanese president, Amin Gemayel, a brutal religious partisan and brother of slain Bashir. Inasmuch as the Beirut Airport was one of the few government functions still in Gemayel's hands, Habib had arranged for Mead's Marines to defend it by occupying the low, flat ground nearby, which was, unfortunately, dominated by the hills to the east. "It was a loser militarily," reflected Admiral Watkins soon after visiting the area.[8]

One month after the Marines occupied the Beirut Airport, the Shultz Plan ran into a stone wall of Arab-Israeli intransigence. Humiliated when the Israeli air force destroyed Syria's Soviet-built air and missile defenses, Moscow moved in October 1982 to rearm the Syrians by shipping them a large number of new, advanced SA-5 Gammon SAM batteries and radars. Although well equipped by a flood of communist arms, the rival factions in and around Beirut caused only minor problems for the first Marines ashore, who were relieved by Colonel Timothy J. Geraghty's Marine Amphibious Unit in February 1983. The whole atmosphere changed one month later, however, when someone pitched a grenade at Marines patrolling the airport's northern perimeter. Then, on 18 April 1983, a Shiite Muslim commando drove a delivery van carrying a 2,000-pound bomb into the center of the eight-story downtown Beirut building that housed the American embassy, killing sixty-three people. Among the dead was almost the entire CIA contingent in Lebanon, a calamity that was to blind American leaders to important events on the ground for at least a year. The embassy bombing was dismissed by the JCS as an isolated incident, but many Middle East analysts reckoned that it was a signal that the Muslim militias no longer viewed the American diplomats or the Marines as neutral peacekeepers. Soon thereafter, the Israelis, tired of the disadvantages attending the occupation of all of southern Lebanon, announced their intention to retire to a security zone north of the Litani that fall.

Upon learning that the Israelis intended to withdraw, the Muslim militias turned their attention to the multinational peacekeeping force. The artillery of both the Druze and Shiite religious factions shelled the airport in late July, and a few days later snipers fired on Marine patrols on the perimeter. "As soon as we start firing, we've lost our mission here," observed Captain Morgan France, who now commanded the amphibious task group offshore. On 29 August the violence ashore escalated when Druze artillery shelled the Marines' encampment, and Colonel Geraghty had no choice but to return fire and silence the hostile Muslim battery. Incoming rocket, mortar, and artillery fire intensified over the next week, prompting the commander of the twelve-ship battle group, Rear Admiral Jerry O. Tuttle, to instruct the frigate *Bowen* at 1130 on 8 September 1983

John F. Lehman, Jr.,
government official
and New York invest-
ment broker; Secre-
tary of the Navy,
1981–1987.

to open fire on the Muslim gun emplacements on the ridgeline
overlooking the airport.[9]

One day earlier, Tuttle had launched the first F-14 Tomcat
reconnaissance flight from the deck of the carrier *Dwight D.
Eisenhower*, a mission marking the first appearance of the Navy's
new Tactical Aerial Reconnaissance Pod System, which was designed to provide intelligence about the location and nature of
hostile gun and missile batteries and radar sites. These dangerous flights, the wisdom of which many questioned, disclosed the
positions of a number of highly sophisticated Soviet-built radars
and missiles in the hills around Beirut, but Tuttle was led to believe that the Syrians had installed them to defend against the Israeli air force and would not fire them at American aircraft.
Moreover, some of the artillery shells falling on the Marines were

the result of an ongoing Druze offensive aimed at overrunning a Lebanese Army stronghold at Suq-al-Gharb, just five miles from the Beirut Airport.

"We may well be at a turning point which will lead within a matter of days to a Syrian takeover of the country north of the Awali [River]," warned retired Marine Colonel Robert McFarlane, who had just become Reagan's third national security adviser. McFarlane had flown to Beirut to coordinate American policy in the region, but his witless behavior instead laid the groundwork for disaster. When the Syrians brought up artillery to support the Druze attack on Suq-al-Gharb, Colonel Fintel, among others, became convinced that the Lebanese Army would collapse if it lost the battle, and this caused him to call on Admiral Tuttle to provide the Lebanese with naval gunfire support. McFarlane also wanted the battle group and the Marines to assist the Lebanese Army, and Ambassador Robert Dillon supported him, but Weinberger and the JCS were reluctant to intervene. Reagan sided with the diplomats, however, so Weinberger stitched together an order that defined "direct support of the Lebanese Armed Forces . . . as an act of self-defense" but left the final decision about returning fire up to Marine Colonel Geraghty. Weinberger correctly predicted that Geraghty would be reluctant to call for naval gunfire because of the exposed position of his Marines and the fear of retaliation, but the secretary of defense's ploy was too clever by half. Geraghty manfully withstood six days of McFarlane's emotion-charged badgering before he relented and asked Tuttle to shell the Syrian and Druze positions. Tuttle responded by directing the nuclear cruiser *Virginia*, the destroyers *John Rodgers* and *Radford*, and the *Bowen* to bring the opposing forces under fire. Over the next five hours a fearsome barrage of 360 5-inch shells landed in the vicinity of the Muslim position. "It was really noisy and great," according to Fintel, "but it didn't cause any damage." Nonetheless, the sheer shock effect of the bombardment was probably the main cause of the Druze and Syrian retirement, which allowed the Lebanese Army to hold on to Suq-al-Gharb for the moment.[10]

"We were very cautious in our exchange of artillery and naval gunfire," claimed Marine Lieutenant Colonel Harold Slacum, but the Muslims and their rearmed PLO allies were incapable of appreciating this caution and angrily retaliated by shelling the American ambassador's residence in Beirut, then be-

ing used as a temporary embassy. Tuttle instructed the *Virginia*
and the *Bowen* to reply by engaging and suppressing the hostile
battery. After visiting Lebanon with McFarlane, Navy Captain
Philip Dur and Howard Teicher of the NSC staff had proposed
that the battleship *New Jersey* be deployed with Admiral Tuttle's
two-carrier battle group, a step that had been loudly advocated
for some time by Navy Secretary Lehman. Thinking that this
would reinforce the Marines and might humble the Muslim militias, the JCS agreed, and the ship rendezvoused with the battle
group off Beirut on 26 September, one day after the warring factions ashore agreed to another negotiated ceasefire. This lapse in
the fighting was highlighted by the establishment of a rival Shiite
government outside Beirut under the Muslim Amal militia, fruitless reconciliation talks in Geneva, and sporadic outbreaks of
shooting and shelling.

When the Marines had first arrived in Lebanon in 1982,
Colonel Mead's greatest concern was to defend his troops from
incoming Israeli artillery shells, and for this reason he selected as
his headquarters a four-story, reinforced concrete building near
the airport. That building, which also served as a communications center, observation post, and barracks, was inherited by
Colonel Geraghty, who moved another 150 Marines inside the
sturdy structure, reasoning that it had already survived repeated
shellfire. When the JCS extended permission to support the
Lebanese Army at Suq-al-Gharb, they had told Geraghty that
"nothing in this message shall be construed as changing the mission," but Geraghty's decision to have the ships fire on the
Muslim militias indisputably altered the Muslims' view of the
Marines' function.

Despite the embassy truck-bombing and frequent terrorist
attacks by rival factions against one another, neither Geraghty
nor his immediate superiors paid much heed to defending the
Marine compound against a suicide-style commando attack. Geraghty continued to house his Marines in the concrete building
near the airport, and this decision was unchallenged by a host of
high-ranking visitors, including Admiral Watkins and General
Paul X. Kelly, the commandant of the Marine Corps. There was
more concern with preventing the Marines from shooting at innocent Lebanese. For this reason, sentries at various guard posts
along the road leading to the compound were told not to chamber rounds in their weapons. Threats against the Marines were so

commonplace by now that American intelligence agencies, trying to cover their bets, issued overly broad warnings against any
and all contingencies. The Israelis, who possessed information
that something special was afoot, refused for their own reasons to
share their findings with the CIA.

At 0622 on 23 October 1983, a large yellow stake body truck
carrying explosives equivalent to six tons of TNT barreled up the
road alongside the Beirut Airport, turned toward the Marine barracks, and at 30 miles per hour drove over a five-foot-high roll of
concertina wire and into the lobby of the building where it exploded. The bomb, which carved an 8-foot crater in the reinforced concrete floor, killed 220 Marines and 21 Navy medical
personnel and soldiers assigned to the landing force. Americans
were shocked and outraged. Because the situation in Lebanon
was so complex, it was not surprising that Reagan could neither
easily articulate his policy nor satisfactorily explain why he had allowed the Marines to remain in such an utterly exposed position.
Admiral Tuttle and Vice Admiral James Lyons, the Deputy CNO
for plans, were quick to draft a scheme to retaliate. A flight of
twelve A-6 Intruders was to use precision-guided munitions to destroy the Sheik Abdullah barracks at Baalbek, where the Shiite
Muslim Hezbollah militia and its Iranian advisers were billeted.
"Those who directed this atrocity must be dealt justice and they
will be," Reagan promised solemnly, but he told the JCS at the
same time that he did not want them to attack targets in civilian
areas.

To immunize themselves from retaliation, members of the
Hezbollah militia were housing their families in the Baalbek barracks. Wanting to avoid killing women and children, the JCS recommended against retaliation. When Lyons' plan reached Air
Force General Richard Lawson, the deputy commander in chief
of the European theater in Germany, he also objected on the
grounds that bombing the barracks might endanger a nearby ancient temple. Admiral Watkins supported Lyons and Tuttle,
whereas General Kelly was against any retaliation that would expose his Marines to further reprisals. Weinberger also opposed
Lyons' plan owing to the lack of "the conclusive kind of target information that I think is essential," but Reagan decided that he
had to do something and on 14 November instructed the JCS to
proceed with the reprisal operation. Preparations were already
well in hand on board the carriers *John F. Kennedy* and *Eisenhower*,

which had been hurriedly recalled from Italy. According to Colonel McFarlane, however, Weinberger simply refused to convey Reagan's order to the 6th Fleet and the president was unaware of this or unwilling to direct him to do so. In the meantime, the admiral commanding the French task force off Lebanon proposed to Tuttle that they join forces and conduct a combined attack on the Baalbek barracks, and Tuttle had relayed this offer to Washington. "Before we could strike," wrote the president's press secretary, "the French beat us to the punch with an attack on the [Hezbollah] camp" the next day. This strike, however, resulted in little damage.[11]

A subsequent investigation of the bombing tragedy by a commission chaired by retired Admiral Robert Long not only found Colonel Geraghty at fault but also castigated the entire chain of command in the European theater. Both the Long Commission and a parallel investigation by the House Armed Services Committee condemned the policy that had brought the Marines to Lebanon in the first place and urged Reagan and Weinberger to clarify the mission of American forces there and to simplify the chain of command. Reagan shrank from retaliating against the most highly suspect Muslim militias. And Defense Secretary Weinberger allowed the wretchedly complex chain of command —forged over the decades by a series of interservice treaties—to remain intact.[12]

Although the Lyons plan was now scuttled, Admiral Tuttle still had to support the Marines at the airport, and their ranks increased with the arrival of reinforcements after the bombing. Tuttle's dilemma was further complicated during the first week in December 1983 when the tenuous ceasefire ended in a series of bloody clashes between the Lebanese Army and the Muslim militias. The Druze, Shiite, and Amal leaders were in agreement, however, that the Americans should leave.

On the morning of 3 December, a section of two F-14 Tomcats from the *Kennedy* flew inland on a routine reconnaissance mission, but when they appeared over the Bekaa Valley they were met not only by the usual harmless antiaircraft fire but also by corkscrews of smoke from heat-seeking SA-7 SAMs. The planes evaded the Syrian missiles and returned safely to the carrier, but Tuttle was now determined to retaliate. Up the ladder of the still-congested chain of command there was little opposition. "There was a feeling at the time that a response in kind was a legitimate thing," Admiral Watkins said. "If you're shot at, you shoot back." Tuttle proposed to bomb three Syrian missile sites. One target was a large white structure housing a French-built early warning radar system, a fixed target easy to hit. The other two targets consisted merely of coordinates where nearly thirty Syrian mobile missile launchers were thought to be located. The brown, creased eastern slope of the hills around Beirut camouflaged the opposing positions, so the Navy pilots would have to see the missile sites before they could bomb them. To give them the advantage of a midday sun, Admiral Tuttle decided to launch the strike at 1100 the next day, intending to put his planes over the targets about thirty minutes later.[13]

When the deputy commander of American naval forces in Europe, Vice Admiral M. Stasser Holcomb, examined this plan on the night of the 3rd in his London office, he concluded that only the white building housing the radar was a worthy target, and so he phoned General Lawson, the Stuttgart-based deputy European theater commander. Lawson's position in the ensuing fiasco was critical. General Bernard Rogers, the supreme commander of the European theater, lived at NATO headquarters in Mons, Belgium, but his time was so occupied by allied diplomacy that he had virtually abdicated his role as an American theater commander to Lawson in Stuttgart. Lawson was an Air Force bomber general who had no experience conducting naval air operations. Holcomb now suggested to Lawson that Tuttle employ the *New Jersey*'s 16-inch guns to shell the fixed target so as not to endanger any pilots or expensive aircraft. The *New Jersey*'s main batteries were notoriously inaccurate, however, and without forward observers on the ground or in the air over the targets there would be no way to spot the fall of the shells. "We had a very complex environment, a peacetime environment where collateral damage is a very big concern to us," Watkins later pointed out. The result was that Lawson turned down Holcomb's suggestion. This was an ironic turn of events. When the chairman of the JCS, General Vessey, had presented the air strike plan to Reagan just hours before, the president's sole question was about using the battleship. Whereas Admiral Tuttle was concentrating on the tactics of the operation, the JCS, trying to weigh the politics of retaliation, wanted the reaction to be swift and closely linked to the Syrian attack. Lawson, misinterpreting their intentions, instructed Tuttle to conduct an "early morning strike" at 0730 the next day.[14]

Tuttle was horrified when he received Lawson's order from Stuttgart at 0540 on the morning of 4 December. His plans called for a noontime strike and his planes were unready to attack at dawn. He appealed to Lawson three times for a delay, but the Air Force general rejected every appeal and agreed only to postpone the strike for one hour. "Someone up there doesn't understand this problem," complained Commander James Kidd, who was in charge of strike operations for the *Kennedy*'s air wing. Around midnight, Tuttle had told Kidd to be prepared to launch the strike the next day at 1100, not 0730. As a result, the carrier's ordnance crew waited until 0600 to begin loading bombs onto the strike aircraft's racks. Of the ten A-6 Intruders that flew off the *Kennedy* at dawn, only one carried a full load of Rockeye cluster bombs and 1,000-pound Mark 83 iron bombs; the other nine aircraft carried a total of four Mark 83s and fourteen Rockeyes.[15]

By 0800, twenty-three Intruders and A-7 Corsairs, the total launched by both carriers, were flying over the beach toward their targets, but several of the *Kennedy*'s pilots were so eager to attack the enemy that they did not bother to ascend to the assigned altitude of 12,000 feet before crossing over the ridgeline. An SA-7 SAM slammed into the lead plane from the *Independence*, but the pilot ejected over Beirut harbor and was rescued by a Lebanese fisherman. When Lieutenant Mark Lange saw another missile corkscrewing toward his aircraft, he pressed his chaff dispenser but it failed and the weapon collided with his plane and exploded. Both Lange and his radio intercept officer, Lieutenant Robert Goodman, ejected safely, but Lange's parachute malfunctioned and his seat pan amputated his leg when he hit the ground. Surrounded by Syrian gunners, he bled to death while they watched. Goodman was captured and taken to Damascus. A few weeks later, Jesse Jackson, a black Democratic politician, arrived in Syria and negotiated his release. The strike, which cost two aircraft, had damaged the radar site and knocked out two missile batteries, but the Syrians repaired the radar and it was operating two days later.

This attack reminded Navy Secretary Lehman that attack aircraft tactics had changed little since the Vietnam War. "Most of it was totally out of date; tactics built around dive bombing, daylight pop-up, lay-down maneuvers," he snorted. In addition, fighter tacticians, mostly concerned with defending their battle group, had virtually ignored the job of escorting naval bombers against land targets. Lehman was moved by the abysmal performance of the air wings over Beirut to establish the Strike Warfare Center at Fallon, Nevada, in April 1984. The center's first commanding officer, Captain Joseph Prueher, organized a curriculum to train Navy attack squadrons to hone their skills against modern Soviet-built missiles and radars before being deployed to the fleet.[16]

When the air strike failed to suppress continuing antiaircraft fire, Tuttle successfully appealed to the JCS for permission to allow the *New Jersey* to fire at the hostile gun emplacements. On 14 December, the battleship's 16-inch guns fired eleven 2,000-pound rounds preset for ground bursts against the Syrian positions. The following day, after the Marines came under a particularly violent mortar attack by the Amal militia, the *New Jersey* assisted with counterbattery naval gunfire. Owing to the absence of spotting, however, the effectiveness of all this was not known. By this time there was an alarming number of reports, many fantastic, warning of terrorist attacks on the battle group, and so the Navy sent out Army Stinger shoulder-held antiaircraft missiles to arm the ships against light, low-flying suicide planes, but the threat never materialized. "We are perceived as being allies of the Gemayel government," complained Senator Charles Percy, chairman of the Foreign Relations Committee, "and as long as we are not perceived as neutral, we will continue to be a target."[17]

By Christmas 1983, chaos had descended on Lebanon and on Reagan's Middle East policy, a condition for which he, Shultz, and Weinberger shared the blame. In September of that year, Admiral Watkins had told Congress that the JCS believed "that the withdrawal of the multinational force at this time probably would have a devastating effect and could plunge Lebanon into total anarchy," but within three months, anarchy ruled Beirut and the JCS now joined Secretary Weinberger's campaign to convince Reagan to withdraw the Marines. Liberal Democrats on the Hill were also pressuring him to abandon his policy. "America will never yield to terrorists," Senator Edward Kennedy exclaimed, but he and his fellow Democrats nonetheless tried to invoke the 1974 War Powers Act and force Reagan to extract the Marines from the Beirut Airport. "We can't cut and run," said Senator Alan J. Dixon, another Democrat, "but in a reasonable prudent time we should be out of there." Although Shultz and National Security Adviser McFarlane wanted to hold on, the pressure to withdraw was too great to resist. McFarlane did manage to cobble one last compromise, which directed the Marines to remain ashore until June 1984 but also called for increased naval gunfire support for their position. Watkins was horrified, as were the rest of the JCS, and they found excuses to avoid issuing the necessary instructions to the 6th Fleet. McFarlane reacted by forcing the JCS to provide him with a draft order that he then persuaded Reagan to sign, with the result that the ships fired regularly at the Muslim positions over the next month. McFarlane's compromise was based on wholly unrealistic assumptions about Lebanese affairs and so was bound to fail, although as late as 7 February 1984 Reagan was still convinced that withdrawing the multinational force "would mean the end of Lebanon." Owing to the disarray of Lebanese politics, however, the White House succumbed and announced that day that the Marines would retire to the amphibious ships offshore.[18]

The end of the Western peacekeeping effort was now in sight. On the day of Reagan's announcement, Shiite leaders called on their co-religionists to desert the Lebanese National Army, and it virtually disintegrated overnight, thus exposing the Marines at the airport to a vicious assault by the Druze militia. Brigadier General James Jay, who now commanded the Marines ashore, once again called on the battle group for assistance, and the American ships pounded the Muslim positions with 5-inch gunfire. The carriers also joined in, and one Druze target was the victim of two laser-guided bombs delivered by an Intruder flying off the *Kennedy*. Over the next four days, Jay supervised the evacuation of about 800 Seabees, Marine engineers, and embassy personnel from Beirut. During this evacuation, the Amal militia again brought the ambassador's residence under fire, but effective counterbattery shelling by the destroyer *Moosebrugger* and the *New Jersey* removed this threat. On 8 February, Beirut came under fire from Syrian batteries, which lobbed 5,000 artillery shells into the Christian half of the city, but the *New Jersey* was ready to reply with 300 rounds of 16-inch projectiles, silencing the Syrian guns. Unfortunately, this tremendous display of firepower was less a mark of American strength than a signal that the final chapter of the Beirut adventure was at hand.

Prime Minister Thatcher told Washington that she was ordering the British troops to withdraw, and the Italians followed suit on 19 February. Shultz and McFarlane made a last stand, urging Reagan to stay the course alone if necessary. At this critical point, Vice President George Bush intervened and at long last persuaded Reagan not to interrupt the withdrawal. The Marines turned over the airport to a ragtag force of Lebanese Army troops at 0600 on 26 February, but only six minutes after the last Marine left Beirut, Amal militia flags were raised over the watchtower. "Reagan was forced to admit that our attempts to keep peace in Lebanon were a failure," recalled White House spokesman Larry Speakes. Watching from the sidelines with apparent satisfaction, the Soviets did not respond to the concentration of four American carriers in the Mediterranean during the Lebanon crisis. Even the most charitable account held that the Reagan Doctrine in the Middle East was an abysmal failure.[19]

Chapter Thirty-eight

Defending the Reagan Doctrine

1985–1989

Nowhere did the administration apply the Reagan Doctrine so resolutely and with such mixed results as in the Caribbean and Central America. Soon after taking office, Reagan blocked Carter's quiet diplomatic opening to Cuba, provided long-term military and economic assistance to El Salvador that helped that unstable government resist a violent communist insurrection, and used covert action and an economic embargo to overthrow Daniel Ortega's communist regime in nearby Nicaragua. An embargo imposed in 1988 isolated Manuel Noriega, Panama's dictator and a violent drug runner, who would be overthrown and captured in December of the following year when troops from the Army's Southern Command invaded and occupied Panama in Operation Just Cause. Cuba still remained under Castro's bloody thumb at the end of the decade, however. On the other hand, the Reagan Doctrine was successfully applied during the Grenada crisis in 1982.

After gaining independence from the British Empire, the tiny, impoverished Caribbean island of Grenada had been governed by Sir Edward Gerry and a corrupt, inefficient oligarchy. Gerry was ousted in a coup by the communist New Jewel Movement led by Maurice Bishop, but President Carter resisted the temptation to intervene. Instead he tried to appease Bishop, but Bishop established a brutal police dictatorship, accepted Soviet arms and Cuban advisers, and hewed to Moscow's line in foreign policy. Reagan aligned the problem of Grenada with Cuban interventionism in Central America during a 1981 speech to the OAS, and Washington distanced itself from the Bishop government that year. Mindful of the drift of the president's views, the Atlantic Fleet's Ocean Venture 81 featured an exercise in which American troops landed on Vieques Island off Puerto Rico to rescue hostages seized by a fictitious communist government and remained ashore to supervise the installation of a new pro-American regime. For reasons that defy understanding, however, neither the JCS nor Admiral Wesley McDonald, the commander in chief of the Atlantic theater, prepared any contingency plans for an invasion of Grenada or acted to improve the primitive state of American intelligence about conditions on the island.

Sound military reasons were behind Reagan's concern for Grenada's future, one being that Cuban military aircraft might someday operate from that island. The Cuban Air Force consisted of about 200 older Soviet-built MiG fighters, but its operations were limited by the short flying radius of most of these aircraft. To establish a friendly air base at the southeastern end of the Caribbean, Castro sent Cuban construction workers and technicians to Grenada to build a 10,000-foot runway at Point Salinas that might handle fighters, transports, and patrol planes. In a speech on 10 March 1983, Reagan pointed out that should the Cuban Air Force ever operate from the Point Salinas airfield, then it could cover most targets in the Caribbean and menace shipping en route to the Panama Canal. Grenada replied that the Point Salinas airfield lacked many of the routine appurtenances of a military airbase, such as underground fuel tanks and radars. Nevertheless, Bishop mobilized his army to resist an American invasion, but Reagan, drowning in the Lebanese quagmire, was for the moment disenchanted with interventionism and did nothing to prevent work continuing on the Point Salinas runway.

Suddenly, in mid-October 1983, a struggle for power within the New Jewel Movement between Bishop and Bernard Coard, an extreme radical, climaxed with Bishop's arrest by the head of the army, General Hudson Austin. Riots in the capital followed and Bishop was shot and killed. Coard and Austin imposed a twenty-four-hour curfew to contain the chaos, threatening to shoot anyone who left his home, a measure that imperiled 600 Americans who attended St. George's University Medical School. Secretary Shultz urged Reagan to invade Grenada, but no one in

Washington knew much about what was transpiring on the island beyond the alarming news of the riots and a report that Austin refused to guarantee the safety of the American students. On 22 October, unnerved by the prospect of the extension of Cuban power into their region, the Organization of Eastern Caribbean States instructed the prime minister of Dominica, Eugenia Dominguez, to ask the United States to intervene in Grenada.

Despite this turmoil, the JCS reacted slowly. The NSC ordered Admiral McDonald in Norfolk to begin contingency planning on 14 October, but the JCS waited another full week before

Vice Admiral Joseph Metcalf III, Commander, 2nd Fleet, during the 1982 landing on Grenada.

Admiral Frank B. Kelso II. Commander, 6th Fleet, 1984–1986; Commander in Chief, Atlantic, 1986–1990; and Chief of Naval Operations, 1990–.

U.S. Navy Department   U.S. Navy Department

instructing him to plan to invade Grenada, rescue the students, and overthrow the New Jewel regime. To conduct this operation, codenamed Urgent Fury, McDonald decided to employ Captain Carl Eire's Amphibious Task Group, which consisted of the helicopter landing ship *Guam*, the LPD *Trenton*, the LSD *Fort Snelling*, and the LSTs *Manitowoc* and *Barnstable County*. Eire was to land a Marine battalion landing unit on the eastern side of the island to seize the Pearls Airport and the nearby port of Grenville. Army Rangers and elements of the 82nd Airborne were to drop onto the Point Salinas airfield, rescue the students at the nearby medical school, and occupy St. George's, the capital city. The Marines at Grenville would then converge on the Army position at St. George's. McDonald had initially thought of using only the amphibious force and the Marines, but he discarded this plan owing to the "importance of simultaneously seizing Pearls Airport on the east coast and multiple targets in the southern portion of the island." Navy Secretary Lehman later pointed out, however, that mixing joint forces and failing to concentrate at Point Salinas and St. George's "allowed the Grenadians and Cubans to hold off small U.S. forces before the main weight of the invasion could be brought to bear."[1]

Operational command of Urgent Fury fell to Vice Admiral Joseph Metcalf, the 2nd Fleet commander. He had little idea of what he would face. The latest aerial photographs of Grenada were five months old, and the CIA had not bothered to post an agent to the island. Metcalf had to rely, therefore, on Assistant Secretary of State Langhorne Motley's estimate that the Urgent Fury Force would face at most 700 Cuban guards and workers, 300 local police, and 1,200 poorly armed, ill-trained Grenadian troops. However, poor intelligence did not explain why McDonald and Metcalf failed entirely to take into account the need to protect the students should Austin decide to take them hostage. They assumed that the students would all be huddled near the Point Salinas Airport when the troops came ashore. With only six days left before the invasion, McDonald and Metcalf anticipated imperfect coordination among the American arms and so decided to compensate with overwhelmingly superior forces in the hope of demoralizing the enemy. Earlier that week, Eire's formation had put to sea en route to Lebanon, and the ships were steaming north of Bermuda at 2400 on 20 October when the commodore received an order from Metcalf directing him to turn south and take station 500 miles northeast of Grenada. Rear Admiral Richard Berry's task group, consisting of the carrier *Independence*, six escorts, and an oiler, was to provide air support for the landings and close ground support for the inland troop movements.

The early movements of the battle group and the amphibious force alerted Castro to what was afoot, and on 22 October he conveyed word to Washington that he would order the Cubans on Grenada not to resist, a promise he did not keep. Because of the need to minimize civilian casualties, Metcalf decided not to soften up the landing zones with air strikes or naval gunfire and not to employ naval gunfire against inland targets. Since the 82nd Airborne would constitute the largest part of his landing force, he named Army Major General H. Norman Schwarzkopf his deputy for Urgent Fury, but the Marines were unhappy with this chain of command and Metcalf did nothing to correct the situation. Another of Metcalf's problems was the presence of Marine Major General George Crist, a turbulent figure who had been sent down by the JCS to command the Caribbean Task Force, a multinational constabulary from OECS states hastily assembled to give Urgent Fury the gloss of regional collective security.

Word of the OECS request for American intervention and the chaos on Grenada led Reagan on 23 October to agree to the invasion plan. The following night, tragedy struck just as Operation Urgent Fury got under way. A Navy SEAL team, which was to reconnoitre St. George's, was lost in a helicopter crash off the island. A second SEAL team did manage to land that night and made its way at dawn to Government House and rescued British Governor General Sir Paul Scoon from Austin's soldiers. The plan was to evacuate him by helicopter to the *Guam*, but when Cuban and Grenadian soldiers surrounded the house, the SEALs settled for holding the building until more American troops arrived. Later that morning, Grenadian infantry used armored personnel carriers in an attempt to retake Government House, but Marine attack helicopters and A-6 Intruders drove them off. At 0200 on 25 October, a third SEAL team crept onto the beach near the Pearls Airport, investigated the area, and reported to Captain Eire that uncharted reefs nearby would probably prevent his landing craft from getting ashore. This news led Eire to decide to conduct the initial assault from the air. Launching at 0315 from the *Guam*, Marine AH-1 Cobra gunships covered a flight of

CH-46 transport helicopters that landed the Marine assault troops near the runway. The Cobras silenced two antiaircraft guns, while the infantry chased away a handful of Grenadian soldiers and secured the airport at 0730. Meanwhile, another SEAL team had used explosives to silence the radio station at Beausijour and called on the destroyer *Caron* to demolish the building.

On the other end of the island, an Army Delta Force commando team landed at dawn and tried but failed to take the Point Salinas runway. Army Rangers, who dropped around the airstrip at 0536, ran into unexpectedly determined resistance from antiaircraft guns in the surrounding hills and from small units of Cuban troops on the ground. Not until 1100 was Point Salinas sufficiently secure to allow Air Force C-5A cargo planes and C-130 transports from Barbados to land the Army's airborne troops and relieve the besieged Rangers. A few hours earlier, an Army patrol reached the medical school's True Blue campus and came upon some of the American students. More were rescued later that day at the Grand Anse campus, but the last of the students were not found until the third day of the invasion.

By this time the Army's advance on St. George's was bogged down, owing in part to the failure of the 2nd Fleet communicators to ensure that Admiral Metcalf could convey orders to his Army and Air Force components. Nor had they arranged for communications between the Army commanders on Grenada and the *Independence*'s A-7 Intruders, which were providing them with close ground support. The Army's air logistics plan had failed entirely to take into account the difficulties encountered on the Point Salinas runway, and the general commanding the airborne division acted as though he faced the Red Army rather than an ill-equipped gang of West Indian hooligans. Annoyed by the Army's lack of progress, Metcalf decided to outflank the enemy positions by using the *Guam*'s helicopters to land Marines on the beach at Grand Mal Bay just north of St. George's. The Marines and Army then converged and in doing so mopped up small pockets of resistance with the help of Navy aircraft attacking Fort Frederic, the communist redoubt in the hills overlooking the capital. These bloody encounters altogether took eighteen American lives. The multinational peacekeeping force under General Crist soon appeared on the scene, but Crist's prickly character and his presence in the Army's area of operations added immeasurably to the overall state of confusion.

Soon after Operation Urgent Fury, the 82nd Airborne's commanding general was forced to retire from the Army. "All four of the armed forces involved performed well," Navy Secretary Lehman recorded in a rare spirit of charity, "but faulty intelligence, planning haste, and the undue complications of jointness made the operation more difficult than it had to be." Austin, Coard, and their thugs were arrested by the invaders and later sentenced to death by a Grenadian court. American diplomats helped to restore democratic government, and the Marines and Army left Grenada in early November. "While it was far from a perfect military operation," admitted Rear Admiral Robert P. Hinton of the Joint Staff, "all military objectives were accomplished quickly with minimum casualties and collateral damage."[2]

The success of the Reagan Doctrine in Grenada, El Salvador, and Afghanistan, and Reagan's willingness to take an occasional risk to thwart international terrorism, reinforced his popularity at home and conveyed an image of a strong, determined chief executive. In 1984, the Republicans renominated Reagan for a second term, while the Democrats chose Carter's vice president, Walter Mondale. Mondale attacked Reagan's muscular foreign policy, advanced the cause of arms control, and assaulted the Republicans' domestic policies, but to no avail. Reagan crushed Mondale in a landslide in November, although the Democrats retained their hammerlock on the House and reduced the Republican majority in the Senate.

Partisan struggle attended the Reagan Doctrine in Latin America, whereas bipartisanship characterized American policy in the Middle East, especially when it came to support for Israel. Following the withdrawal of the Marines from Beirut in 1984, the forces supporting terrorist violence in the Middle East devoted themselves to establishing a new balance of power in war-torn Lebanon. As a result, there were only two hijackings of American airliners that year and no bombings. However, on 14 June 1985, commandos from a splinter group of the PLO boarded TWA Flight 847 in Athens, assumed control of the aircraft, and forced the pilot to fly to Beirut. Shortly before landing, the terrorists beat and shot one passenger, Navy Diver Robert D. Stethem, who was homeward bound after an assignment in Greece. After the plane landed, Stethem's body was dumped onto the runway. The hijackers demanded that the Israelis release over 700 Lebanese Shiite civilians who had been imprisoned without trial in Israel for nearly two years. The Israelis, who swore neither to dicker nor negotiate with the PLO, conveyed word to Washington that they would release these prisoners only if Reagan asked them to do so. Meanwhile, the JCS had instructed the 6th Fleet commander to send a battle group including the carrier *Nimitz*, the cruiser *South Carolina*, and the oiler *Kalamazoo* into the eastern Mediterranean. The destroyer *Kidd*, then visiting Tel Aviv, rendezvoused with the battle group off Beirut on 17 June. At the same time, a Delta Force commando team was flown to the Italian-American naval air station at Sigonella, Sicily.

Enraged by inaction, the hijackers forced the TWA pilot to take off, fly from Beirut to Algiers, and return to Beirut, movements that were tracked all the while by E-2 Hawkeyes from the *Nimitz*, Air Force AWACS aircraft, and Navy patrol planes from Sigonella. Soon after the plane was hijacked, the JCS had begun to study various rescue plans. Since the small, lightly armed Delta Force could not deal with the large body of Amal militiamen who surrounded the Beirut Airport, the chairman of the JCS, General Vessey told the president that the only alternatives were to put a Marine amphibious unit ashore nearby or to drop an Army airborne battalion around the airport. Either would deprive the Delta Force of the element of surprise. As a result, Reagan abandoned the idea of rescuing the hostages and instead instructed Secretary of State Shultz to ask the Israelis to release their prisoners. In the meantime, Syria's President Assad, who exerted some indirect influence over the hijackers, agreed to a negotiated end to the incident during talks with Hashemi Rafsanjani, the leader of Iran's parliament. The passengers were freed, the hijackers escaped, and the Israelis soon repatriated their Lebanese captives. Despite evidence that the terrorists were linked to Syria and Iran, Reagan—clearly influenced by Rafsanjani's role in the negotiations—refused to sanction punitive operations against either country.[3]

The second Gulf of Sidra incident stemmed directly from Reagan's unwillingness to retaliate against state-sponsored terrorism. His public hand wringing may have moved Gaddafi to more mischief. On 10 March 1982, Reagan imposed an embargo on Libyan oil and followed that with a second Freedom of Navigation operation in the Gulf, conducted by a battle group built around the carrier *Nimitz*, which crossed Gaddafi's line of death on 17 March. Gaddafi reacted by sending a pair of Libyan

MiG-23 fighters toward the American formation, but they were intercepted and turned back by a section of F-14 Tomcats. Gaddafi then became embroiled in a disastrous attempt to invade neighboring Chad, whose government was supported by the French and Americans. This turn of events caused Reagan to agree to the deployment of a battle group led by the carriers *Eisenhower* and *Coral Sea*, which took station about 150 miles off the Libyan coast. Naval aircraft provided combat air cover for Air Force AWACS surveillance planes monitoring the fighting in Chad. However, Reagan decided to let the French take the lead in defending their former colony, and after nearly two years of struggle, Chad was finally saved by the intervention of French paratroopers in August 1984. On the eve of this decisive action, Reagan again deployed a 6th Fleet battle group built around the carrier *Saratoga* to the edge of the Sidra Gulf, and her F-14 Tomcats on this occasion crossed over the line of death. Although Reagan wanted to support France's intervention in Chad, he was afraid, so close to the 1984 presidential elections, of provoking another crisis. Thus, the movement into the Gulf was conducted at night to avoid a confrontation with Libyan aircraft.

In spite of these warnings, Gaddafi continued to stir up the region. He next tried to overthrow the conservative regime of nearby Sudan and so alarmed Egypt's President Hosni Mubarak that he agreed to Operation Early Call, an American plan to discredit Gaddafi. Washington intended to lure Gaddafi into sending the Libyan Air Force across Egypt en route to the Sudan, where his planes were to launch air strikes on Khartoum in support of a pro-Libyan coup. On 14 February 1983, four Air Force AWACS airborne radar surveillance planes arrived in Egypt to begin training with Egyptian fighters for the proposed intercept operation. Simultaneously, Vice Admiral William Rowden, who commanded the 6th Fleet, positioned a battle group built around the carrier *Nimitz* at the edge of the Gulf of Sidra to distract Gaddafi from these preparations. Unfortunately, news of this top-secret operation appeared on American television two days later, and Gaddafi called off the attacks on Khartoum, although he retaliated by dispatching the cargo ferry *Ghat* into the Suez Canal, where she planted mines that damaged eighteen Egyptian vessels. In addition, Gaddafi offered the Red Navy's Mediterranean Fleet the use of the port of Tobruk, purchased a brace of new antiaircraft missile batteries from Moscow, and permitted the Soviets to begin constructing an airbase in the Libyan desert at Jufra. The Soviets, however, aware of Gaddafi's unpredictability and diplomatic isolation, were unwilling to extend unreserved support to Libya.

In October 1985, four Arab passengers armed with hand grenades and machine guns took over the Italian liner *Achille Lauro*, which was carrying ninety-seven elderly American and European vacationers from her home port of Genoa to Port Said, Egypt. The hijackers, agents of a PLO faction, demanded that the Israelis release fifty Palestinian commandos who were imprisoned in Israeli jails. Although the 6th Fleet went on alert, aircraft from the carrier *Saratoga*, then in the area conducting NATO exercises, could not locate the vessel. The *Achille Lauro* appeared unexpectedly the next day off the Syrian port of Taurus and requested permission to enter, but President Assad, hoping to discredit PLO leader Yasir Arafat, refused to allow her to drop anchor in the harbor. In an attempt to get Washington to pressure Assad, the terrorists shot Leon Klinghoeffer, a physically disabled American Jew, and threw his corpse overboard. Assad was unmoved. At this point the mastermind of the operation, Abu Abbas, one of Arafat's lieutenants, radioed the ship and instructed the hijackers to return to Port Said. When Reagan's sinister national security adviser, Vice Admiral John Poindexter, learned about the incident, he directed the newly organized Joint Special Operations Command to fly an Army Delta Force antiterrorist squad and a Navy SEAL team to Sigonella.

Israeli intelligence was intercepting radio communications between the *Achille Lauro*'s hijackers and Abu Abbas and relaying this intelligence to Washington on a continuing basis. Armed with this information, Rear Admiral David Jeremiah with the *Saratoga* battle group dispatched a handful of surveillance aircraft into the eastern Mediterranean, and they soon located the *Achille Lauro* off the coast of Israel. Next, he directed an attack submarine to the scene, carrying a SEAL team that was prepared to board the cruise ship and overcome the terrorists by force. Jeremiah was prepared to strike, but from the White House came no order to act. Instead, Jeremiah learned that Egypt's President Mubarak had permitted the *Achille Lauro* to drop anchor in Port Said, where the prisoners were released and the hijackers surrendered to Egyptian officials. Without informing Washington, however, Mubarak allowed Abu Abbas and his commandos to board

an Egyptian Air Lines Boeing 737 bound for Tunisia. When
Marine Lieutenant Colonel Oliver North of the National Security
Council staff heard that the Egyptians had freed the hijackers, he
and Navy Captain James Stark devised a daring plan to intercept
the Egypt Air 737 and capture the terrorists.

Admiral William Crowe, the new JCS chairman, agreed to
North's plan and sent an order to Jeremiah in the *Saratoga*, then
in the Adriatic, to head south and prepare to intercept the Egyptian airliner over the Mediterranean. Defense Secretary Weinberger, who was in Canada when he was apprised of the situation,
reflexively opposed the plan, but on this occasion he was overruled by Reagan, who told Crowe to proceed with the North
plan. By this time the *Saratoga*'s hardworking air wing staff had
put together an operational plan to intercept the airliner, and
Commander Ralph Zia in an E-2 Hawkeye was flying to a position
off Crete where he could begin to try to pick the plane out of the
busy air traffic corridor in the middle of the night. At about 2300
on 10 October, after three mistaken interceptions, Lieutenant
Commander Stephen Weatherspoon in an F-14 Tomcat found
the Egyptian 737 approximately eighty miles south of Crete. The
pilot had been denied landing rights by Tunisia and Athens and
was about to turn back for home, but two nearby Navy EA-6B
electronic warfare aircraft were jamming communications between the airliner and Cairo. Flying abreast of the airliner,
Weatherspoon confirmed her identification by reading her tail
number with his flashlight. He then radioed the airliner, informed the pilot that he was being escorted by two American
fighters—later joined by two others—and instructed him to head
for Sigonella.

Although the *Achille Lauro* was an Italian vessel, Italy's Prime
Minister Bettino Craxi had recently negotiated an unwritten
truce with the PLO, and he was reluctant to disrupt this arrangement. On 11 October, moments after the Egyptian 737 landed
on the Italian side of the Sigonella base at 0300, two Air Force
C-141 transports touched down right behind her and a Delta
Force team, including Navy SEAL Team Six, emerged and surrounded the airliner. At the same time, however, heavily armed
Italian troops surrounded the Delta Force and demanded that
the terrorists be surrendered to their custody. Unwilling to fire
on the Italians, the American commandos withdrew. Craxi had
four of the hijackers arrested—they were later imprisoned by an

Italian court—but he also arranged for Abu Abbas to escape surreptitiously. The 6th Fleet's spectacular capture of the hijackers offered Reagan an occasion for more hyperbole. The *Achille Lauro* incident "sent a message to terrorists everywhere," he claimed. "You can run but you can't hide."[4]

Gaddafi provided backing for another PLO terrorist, Abu Nidal, who plotted against Egypt from his Tripoli headquarters. In November 1985, Abu Nidal's commandos hijacked an Egypt Air flight en route from Athens to Cairo and forced the crew to fly to Malta. He struck again on 27 December 1985 with simultaneous commando attacks on the El Al Airline ticket counters at the Rome and Vienna airports, killing twenty bystanders, including five Americans. These attacks were applauded by Gaddafi. Reagan, now furious, responded on 7 January 1986 by cutting the few remaining economic ties with Libya and ordering the five American oil firms operating there, and their 1,500 employees, to leave the country. Secretary Shultz urged Reagan to retaliate, but Defense Secretary Weinberger and the JCS persuaded him to put off a decision, pointing out that the evidence linking Gaddafi with Abu Nidal was not incontrovertible. They also raised the possibility that Gaddafi might imprison some of the oil men if Libya were subjected to American air attacks. Consequently, when Reagan announced the economic sanctions, he merely issued another warning: "If these steps do not end Gaddafi's terrorism, I promise you that further steps will be taken."[5]

Admiral Crowe now devised a stairstep plan, codenamed Attain Document, that called for a series of incursions by the 6th Fleet battle force into the Gulf of Sidra. Attain Document was characterized by the old, discredited policy of graduated response as it sought to punish Gaddafi for each successive transgression. The first stage involved the destruction of the missile batteries at Sidra. The second was to be an attack on a number of Libyan military facilities and headquarters. The final stage was to apply more economic pressure on Gaddafi by using carrier air strikes or cruise missile attacks against Libya's main oil pipeline. Following the concentration of four carriers in the Mediterranean during the Lebanon crisis, the Navy had reverted to what was by now a normal peacetime strategy of five forward-deployed carriers: two in the Pacific, a third in the Atlantic, the fourth in the Mediterranean, and the fifth in the Indian Ocean. Because Reagan for the moment would agree only to another Freedom of

Navigation exercise, Crowe ordered the *Saratoga*, then on station near Diego Garcia, to transit the Suez Canal and steam into the Mediterranean, rendezvous with the 6th Fleet carrier *Coral Sea*, and prepare to execute the first stage of Attain Document. The *Saratoga*'s air wing was needed to provide both high- and low-altitude combat air patrols for the battle group.

At this point, the commander of the 6th Fleet, Vice Admiral Frank B. Kelso III, an inspirational leader, met with Weinberger in London and persuaded him to revise the rules of engagement so that if the Libyans attacked the battle group, Kelso might declare to be hostile all Libyan forces entering the Gulf and their supporting shore-based radars. The Libyans were alerted on 14 January that trouble was brewing when two MiG-25 Foxbat fighters made contact with an American EA-3 Hawkeye flight 140 miles off the Libyan coast, the farthest from land that the Libyan Air Force had ever operated. Three days later the *Saratoga* rendezvoused with the *Coral Sea* in the central Mediterranean, and the battle group began to train together for the upcoming operation. After a few days, Kelso steamed south to the northern edge of the Gulf of Sidra, determined "to show that we could operate in international waters and not be blackmailed by Gaddafi into thinking the Gulf of Sidra is his lake." Gaddafi, clad in a white designer jumpsuit, was photographed on the 25th on board a patrol boat in the Sidra Gulf issuing another threat to the Americans.[6]

That same day, the carriers *Coral Sea* and *Saratoga* steamed into the Gulf and launched FA-18 Hornet pickets to stations several hundred miles away from the battle group. To increase their time on station, these fighters were refueled in the air by A-6 Intruder tankers. One pair of FA-18 Hornets was approached by two Libyan Foxbats. Expecting combat, the Americans executed a stern intercept maneuver, thus bringing them up behind their opponents, who could only fire forward. Within an hour, several other patrols met up with Libyan aircraft, but nothing untoward happened. The Americans repeatedly maneuvered to prevent the Libyans from attaining firing positions, and after fuel ran low, both sides quit the joust and flew home. After four days of sending patrols to the edge of the line of death but not over it, Kelso's battle group retired on 30 January without having fired a shot.

This gesture produced no political effect as Gaddafi continued to extol terrorism, and NSA intercepts of Libyan diplomatic communications suggested that his agents were planning more operations. During the second Attain Document operation, which began on 12 February, Kelso sent out 160 patrols but, again, none flew beyond the line of death. Tomcat and Hornet pilots reported that Libyan radar correctly located the American patrols, but jamming and repositioning by E-2 Hawkeyes allowed the Navy's fighters to hide when the opposing sections closed to ten miles, and the American pilots repeatedly maneuvered to attain good firing positions behind the MiGs. The exhaust of the MiG-25 Foxbat, a front-line Soviet fighter, was so hot that the Sidewinder missile's infrared heat-seeking sensor detected the opposing aircraft ten miles away. During this operation, the Libyans tried to lure the Tomcats and Hornets into the missile belt south of the Benghazi-Misratah "line of death," but Kelso restrained his eager flyers, who thought the Libyan pilots were inept and stupidly led. This policy of restraint was extended to allow an overflight of the *Coral Sea* by a Libyan Il-76 Candid transport. Gaddafi kept one Candid in the air throughout the crisis, flying maritime reconnaissance patrols along the line of death, and Kelso provocatively badgered these planes with FA-18 Hornet or A-6 Intruder escorts. After operating within the Gulf of Sidra at a high state of alert for nearly four days, the battle group retired on 15 February. Gaddafi still gave no hint of a changed policy.

Shultz was still arguing for stronger action, but Weinberger resolutely opposed further escalation. To stall, Weinberger now insisted that the 6th Fleet battle group did not possess enough attack aircraft to conduct full-scale air strikes against the Libyan military targets, although neither Admiral Kelso nor Rear Admiral Jeremiah, the battle group commander, had asked for another carrier. Admiral Crowe, who favored retaliation, announced that Rear Admiral Henry H. Mauz in the carrier *America* could reach the Mediterranean in mid-March, an argument that further isolated the secretary of defense. Reagan still refused to countenance attacks on military installations that would result in collateral civilian casualties, although neither of the first two Attain Document operations had influenced Gaddafi's policy. Indeed, the arrival of the flagship of the Soviet Mediterranean Fleet at Tripoli seemed to increase Gaddafi's misplaced confidence in Libya's missile defenses and air and naval forces. Reagan chose the line of least resistance by agreeing on 14 March to a three-stage plan to increase the pressure on Gaddafi. The first part of this plan was to send the 6th Fleet back into the Gulf of Sidra where it would launch an attack on the Libyan missile battery at Sidra. Next would come the bombing of Libyan military installations at both ends of the Gulf. Finally, key junctions and pumping stations along the Libyan oil pipeline would be destroyed with the intent of shutting down oil exports and thereby crippling the economy.

The first stage of this new plan, codenamed Operation Prairie Fire, began to unfold at 1701 on 23 March when F-14 Tomcats from the three-carrier battle group flew over the line of death, followed at 0600 the next day by a surface action group composed of the Aegis cruiser *Ticonderoga* and the destroyers *Scott* and *Caron.* E-2 Hawkeyes and EA-6 Prowlers were launched to provide radar and signal intelligence on the batteries near Sidra on the coast and to control the ensuing air battle. At 0752, the Libyans launched two newly acquired Soviet-built SA-5 Gammon surface-to-air missiles from the Sidra battery at a section of FA-18 Hornet's fighter-bombers from the *Coral Sea* that were flying the southernmost combat air patrol, but the enemy had fired at extreme range and the projectiles splashed harmlessly in the ocean. Jeremiah believed that Gaddafi personally controlled the Sidra battery. "The decision to engage us was a national command decision as opposed to a pilot who might accidentally have reacted." Commander Robert Brodsky, who commanded the *Saratoga* air wing, was convinced that "the SA-5 site fired for the entire nation of Libya." Roughly five hours later, the Libyans fired three more SA-5 Gammons and old SA-2 Guideline surface-to-air missiles at the advancing American battle group, but they too fell short and dropped into the ocean. Later that morning, two Libyan MiG-25s approached the battle group's exercise area, but when a section of F-14 Tomcats flew out to meet them, the hostile aircraft turned back to the coast, thus marking the first and last appearance of the Libyan Air Force that day.[7]

At 1430, a Libyan *La Combatante*-class missile corvette stood out of Misratah and sped toward the American surface action group. Overhead a pair of A-7 Corsair bombers flying low-altitude surface air patrol from the *America* fired two Harpoon missiles, which badly damaged the enemy vessel. The second Intruder dropped Rockeye cluster bombs on the boat and it sank within minutes. Once darkness fell, Jeremiah was ready to attack the missile batteries. "It was basically a trap," Commander Bryon

Duff of the *Coral Sea* air group recalled. Flying one of two A-7 Corsairs at high altitude, Commander Brodsky closed on the Libyan port, exposing his section to the SA-5 radars. Below him, at an altitude of less than 500 feet, a second pair of A-7 Corsairs arrived unnoticed at a position approximately twenty miles off the Libyan coast. When the Sidra battery switched on its target acquisition radar and locked onto Duff's aircraft, the low-flying Corsairs sprang the trap by launching a pair of AGM-88 Harm antiradiation missiles that followed the enemy radar beam back to the missile site and put the radar dish out of commission. Within four hours, this Libyan radar was again in operation, however, but it went down for a second time after Admiral Jeremiah ordered another attack against it by A-7 Corsairs armed with Harm missiles.

Surprisingly, the Libyans did not desist. While the carriers were recovering their aircraft, a pair of *Nanucka*-class missile corvettes sped from the east toward the *Ticonderoga*, the southernmost ship with the surface group. Before these hostile vessels came within firing range, however, A-6 Intruders from the *Coral Sea* sank one with a Harpoon missile and Rockeye bombs while a second Intruder from the *Saratoga* badly damaged her companion. The confusion during this action was greater than usual. The cruiser *Yorktown* launched a Harpoon missile at a range of eight miles against a radar contact that was approaching the battle group at a speed of 37 knots, a ferocious response that disrupted the progress of a large flight of birds.

Admiral Mauz arranged for overlapping air operations so that the battle group was most heavily defended during the daytime when the Libyans were most likely to attack. The *America*'s air wing operated from midnight to noon, the *Saratoga*'s air wing flew in the afternoon and the evening. The *Coral Sea*'s aircraft worked from 0530 to 1830 daily. Kelso positioned the surface action group, led by the cruiser *Ticonderoga*, ahead of the carriers to provide them with a powerful missile screen. On 25 March, he sent more planes aloft and steamed south into the Gulf of Sidra, the arc of his air patrols often just skirting the twelve-mile limit of Libyan territorial waters. A few short electronic emissions from the radars at Sidra were detected by the battle group, but few Libyan aircraft took off and none of Gaddafi's missile boats dared to venture more than a few miles out to sea. After three more days, the Americans retired to the north, and on 29 March the battle group parted. The *Saratoga* steamed past Gibraltar, into the Atlantic, and back to Norfolk; the *Coral Sea* headed for Málaga, a liberty port on the southwest coast of Spain. In the wake of this successful mission, Washington still possessed no information that it had achieved any political results, and much evidence to the contrary.[8]

The climax of the American confrontation with Libya came when Gaddafi, reacting to Operation Prairie Fire, applauded the work of an obscure Arab terrorist faction that detonated a small bomb on board TWA Flight 840 just as the plane was about to land in Athens. Although Washington could not link Gaddafi with this act, British code breakers deciphered a message from the Libyan embassy in East Berlin to Tripoli, alerting Gaddafi to an unspecified but imminent terrorist incident. And then, at 0149 on the morning of Saturday, 5 April, a bomb exploded in La Belle Disco in West Berlin, a favorite spot for American soldiers. Two Army sergeants were killed and a large number of Americans were among the 229 wounded. Armed with "conclusive" evidence that Gaddafi had ordered the bombing, Reagan at last decided to strike back. This catalyst suspended the earlier debate about the wisdom of retaliation and moved Reagan, finally, to instruct Admiral Crowe to execute Operation Eldorado Canyon, the second phase of the stairstep plan.[9]

Planning for Eldorado Canyon had been under way since January under the direction of Stuttgart-based General Richard Lawson, who was determined to bring his Air Force into play in this operation. Vice Admiral Poindexter, the president's national security adviser, wanted to use sea-launched Tomahawk cruise missiles to strike Libya's oil pipeline while not endangering aircrews, but the 6th Fleet possessed too few Tomahawks to execute the mission, the missile's terrain-following computers could not be reprogrammed quickly to hit Libyan targets, and the Tomahawk's conventional warhead was too small to damage an industrial installation. The JCS opposed Poindexter's plan and argued instead for attacking specific targets associated with terrorist activities while minimizing civilian casualties. This view prevailed, and the chiefs agreed on Lawson's proposal to attack two sets of targets, three at Tripoli and two in the vicinity of Benghazi. Since the press was giving Gaddafi ample warning, the Americans would have to attack at night when Libya's defenses were the weakest. However, the 6th Fleet battle group carriers embarked only eighteen A-6 Intruders, the sole all-weather, night-flying naval aircraft capable of delivering laser-guided munitions. Since the two sets of targets were widely separated, Admiral Kelso's three-carrier battle group was incapable of attacking both, so the JCS assigned the Benghazi targets to the 6th Fleet and the Tripoli targets to two squadrons of Air Force F-111 fighter-bombers based at Royal Air Force airfields at Lakenheath and Upper Heyford, England.

On 10 April, General Vernon Walters, the American ambassador to the UN, flew to Paris to try to persuade President François Mitterrand to allow the Air Force fighter-bombers to overfly France en route to Libya, but the French, worried about provoking Gaddafi, turned down Walters' plea. On the other hand, Prime Minister Margaret Thatcher agreed to his request that British-based F-111s be used to attack Libya. News of this diplomacy and leaks of top-secret target lists and deployment schedules gave Gaddafi plenty of warning of what was afoot. A Soviet watchdog trawler in the Straits of Messina spotted the *Coral Sea* during her high-speed run into the Mediterranean and alerted a Soviet cruiser on station south of Sicily, but the American carrier had already escaped. Despite assistance from a pair of Soviet surveillance planes operating from a base near Tripoli, the Red Navy was thereafter unable to locate the American formation, which was operating under radio silence.

On 14 April, Kelso flew from Europe back to the carrier *America*, which was soon joined by the rest of the battle group prior to the movement toward the Gulf of Sidra. At 1750, the *Coral Sea*, on station 180 miles north of Benghazi, launched eight A-6 Intruders, six FA-18 Hornets, and a flight of F-14 Tomcats, radar suppression and combat air patrols. Five minutes earlier the *America* had begun to launch six A-6 Intruders and six A-7 Corsairs that also would support the operation. Altogether, seventy naval aircraft were in the air that moonlit night to conduct Eldorado Canyon.

At 1854, an Air Force EF-111 electronic warfare aircraft, flying from Lakenheath, made contact with an EA-6B Intruder from the battle group, and together they started to jam the opposing radars. Led by a pair of E-2 Hawkeyes, a section of FA-18 Hornets appeared over Benina Airfield outside Benghazi and at 1900 fired twenty Harm and four Shrike missiles, which disabled the nearby Libyan SA-5 missile batteries. The Libyans counter-

attacked by firing a few antiaircraft missiles, but the EA-6B
Prowlers successfully deceived or jammed their guidance systems.
Within seconds, the six A-6 Intruders from the *Coral Sea* arrived
over the Benina Airfield, surprised to find the runway lights
aglow. During three bombing runs, they pockmarked the runway, blew up a few buildings, and engulfed several parked aircraft
in flames. Some adjacent structures were damaged or destroyed.
The planners intended this attack to destroy the entire Libyan
fleet of Soviet-built Il-76 transports, but the press had so thoroughly alerted Gaddafi that he had taken the precaution of dispersing his air forces throughout the country. The A-6 Intruders
from the *America* "only got 10 percent of their weapons into the
target area," complained Rear Admiral Jerry Breast, who commanded the carrier division during Eldorado Canyon. Six A-6
Intruders also dropped MK-82 bombs on the Jamahariyah barracks complex, damaging a MiG assembly warehouse.[10]

At 1900, the very moment that the naval attack aircraft appeared over Benghazi, the F-111s arrived over Tripoli after a
1,500-mile flight from England during which they had refueled
in the air four times. When a flight of F-14 Tomcats from the
America arrived at a station twenty-five miles off the Libyan coast,
an EA-2 Hawkeye overhead switched on her equipment, thus
alerting the Libyan antiaircraft radars. In response, the A-7 Corsairs and FA-18 Hornets fired sixteen Harm and eight Shrike an-
tiradar missiles to silence the hostile defenses. Although these attacks disabled the SA-5 Gammon systems, the Libyans did fire a
handful of less lethal surface-to-air missiles, and their antiaircraft
gun batteries were active, but ultimately unsuccessful. Five F-111
bombers struck the Tripoli airport with BSU-49 high-drag bombs
that destroyed two Libyan transports and damaged several other
planes. At the Sidi Bilal naval complex, where terrorist frogmen
were trained, a swimming pool, dining hall, classroom, and a few
small craft were destroyed by 2,400-pound GBU-10 laser-guided
bombs dropped by three F-111 bombers.

The airfield and the frogman school were insignificant targets in comparison to the Azizayah barracks in downtown
Tripoli, where Gaddafi made his headquarters. Unfortunately,
General Lawson had imposed such restrictive target identification rules that the F-111 crews could not inflict much damage. Of
nine planes assigned to attack the Azizayah barracks, only three
reached the targets and dropped their GBU-10 bombs, demolish-

ing the headquarters building. A fourth F-111 bomber missed Gaddafi's complex entirely and struck Bin Ghashir, a residential neighborhood, killing and wounding about 100 civilians and damaging the French embassy, an inadvertent turn of events that did not cause much anguish in Washington. Gaddafi, one target of the raid, escaped injury. "We did have intelligence that Gaddafi was there [in his headquarters] some of the time," recalled a presidential aide, "but we did not know whether he would be there when we bombed them."[11]

By 0206, when the last bomb fell on Sidi Bilal, most of the American planes had retired from the scene, the naval aircraft to their carriers, the F-111 bombers—less one lost during the operation—to England. Admiral Kelso warned the battle group to brace for a counterattack by the Libyan Air Force, but only a few Libyan planes appeared over Benghazi that morning and none of them flew out to attack the American formation as it prepared to withdraw. On 18 April, the battle group steamed out of the Sidra Gulf and shaped a course for the 6th Fleet's base at Gaeta, Italy. Operation Eldorado Canyon was over.

Gaddafi struck back quickly by sending fast patrol boats into the Mediterranean to attack the U.S. Coast Guard station on Lampedusa, an Italian island 160 miles from the Libyan coast. Two missiles were fired prematurely and both splashed harmlessly into the sea. Gaddafi's agents also shot and wounded an American diplomat in Khartoum, killed an American hostage in Beirut, and mounted an unsuccessful grenade attack on a U.S. Air Force base in Turkey. In an unintended way, however, Eldorado Canyon led indirectly to a suspension of Gaddafi's operations. "The Reagan administration insisted that it had stopped terrorism cold—especially Gaddafi's role in it," wrote Assistant Secretary of Defense Noel Koch, an expert on terrorism. "That was nonsense. Gaddafi barely skipped a beat, changing the communications system that had led to the discovery of his involvement in the Berlin bombing and enlisting a more competent group of surrogates to continue his actions." However, the Europeans "did not want the U.S. conducting military operations on NATO's southern flank, with all the risks that entailed," Koch explained, so the Common Market imposed sanctions on Libya, over 100 Libyan diplomats were expelled from Europe, and the European intelligence services moved against Gaddafi's agents. The combination of Eldorado Canyon and stiffer European measures clearly influenced Libyan policy. Admiral Poindexter still wanted to complete the third stage of the stairstep plan, and Colonel North even drafted a proposal to deploy the cruiser *Atlanta* to the Gulf of Sidra where she was to fire Tomahawk cruise missiles against Libya's oil pumping stations, but Gaddafi's decision to curtail his terrorist operations caused an end to American retaliatory operations for the time being.[12]

The last round of Reagan's eight-year duel with Gaddafi started to unfold in late 1988 when the CIA learned that several West German firms had for many years been helping Libya to construct a chemical weapons plant in the desert. Gaddafi's disingenuous claim that the facility produced fertilizer was dismissed as frivolous by Secretary of State Shultz, who launched a diplomatic campaign to stop the Germans from providing the Libyans with technical assistance. While this was under way, Reagan responded ambiguously to a reporter's question about a preemptive bombing strike aimed at destroying the plant, and tensions between Washington and Tripoli again grew taut.

Closer to the scene, on the morning of 4 January 1989, the 6th Fleet carrier *Kennedy* was steaming eastward about 115 miles north of the Libyan port of Tobruk. Four F-14 Tomcats were flying routine combat air patrol just before 1200 when a supporting E-2C Hawkeye detected two Libyan MiG-23 Flogger fighters taking off from the Libyan airbase at Tobruk and heading out toward the battle group. About seventy miles from the carrier, a section of two Tomcats approached the hostile MiGs on an intercepting course. To avoid an incident, the Americans took five evasive maneuvers, but the Libyans continued to close on them, and one MiG pilot activated his fire-control radar. In response, the lead Tomcat fired a Sparrow air-to-air missile that splashed this MiG, and the second hostile Libyan Flogger was destroyed by a Sidewinder shot as she turned and tried to flee for home.

These recurrent crises with Libya exposed the difficulties of applying the Reagan Doctrine to the terrorist problem. The least that could be said for the new policy, however, was that Reagan, unlike Carter, had recognized that the United States could not uphold its position as a great power while standing by helplessly in the face of repeated provocations.

Chapter Thirty-nine

The Iran-Iraq War
1980–1989

Reagan's determined handling of Libya in 1986 increased confidence at home and abroad in his foreign policy—at least until the Iran-Contra scandal began to unfold in November— and helped to shape his decision two years later to intervene in the Iran-Iraq War. America's interest in Persian Gulf politics was the legacy of a confusing, tortured history. In the nineteenth century, to protect India's western flank against Russian expansion on the Caspian Sea, the British had employed diplomacy and naval power to establish their own hegemony over the Gulf, an enduring arrangement, owing to Britain's total dependence on imported oil from the region, that lasted long after India became independent in 1947. Iraq's 1958 radical revolution, Iran's postwar move into the American orbit, and the disintegration of the British Empire led to the end of this system in January 1968, when Prime Minister Harold Wilson announced that the Royal Navy was withdrawing its longtime strategic responsibilities "east of Suez." Washington, not eager to assume new military obligations in the midst of the Vietnam War, worked in vain to prevent or postpone Wilson's declaration, as it in effect challenged the United States to fill the upcoming vacuum of power in the Persian Gulf.[1]

For the most part, when American strategists turned to the Middle East during the Cold War, their gaze focused on the Arab-Israeli conflict or the northern-tier nations bordering on the Soviet Union, not on the Persian Gulf. American interests in the Gulf were limited to preventing the area from falling under Moscow's sway and safeguarding the oil trade with western Europe and Japan. The United States had no long-term political links to the Gulf sheiks and imported only a small fraction of its oil from their domains, although the continued flow of Gulf oil onto the world market stabilized prices and thereby benefitted the American economy. Until Britain withdrew after 1968, the most visible evidence of American interest in the Persian Gulf was the Navy's small Middle East Force, whose thankless task was to steam from port to port and show the flag. Rather than taking up Britain's heavy burden, however, Nixon adapted his doctrine to the Persian Gulf with the 1970 Twin Pillars Policy, under which the United States provided arms to Saudi Arabia and Iran so that they might share regional hegemony and peacekeeping duties.

Admiral Zumwalt, then CNO, backed this approach by deploying the newly constructed helicopter landing ship *LaSalle* to the Middle East Force to serve as its flagship in 1973 and by persuading the State Department to negotiate a new lease on the small American naval facility at Manama in the Bahrain Islands. Washington's influence in the region was still "tenuous," he realized. Then, soon after the 1973 Arab oil embargo, Secretary of State Kissinger issued a sharp warning that the United States would not tolerate further disruption to the oil trade, and President Ford added muscle to this threat by sending the carrier *Constellation* into the Persian Gulf on a "familiarization mission" in late November 1974. Less than three years later, however, America's prestige throughout the Middle East was eroding as a result of Carter's wild oscillations between his human rights policy and the established Twin Pillars approach. Defense Secretary Harold Brown might proclaim, as he did in February 1978, that "the U.S. will honor all of its commitments," but he had to confess that "this does not mean, however, that we must have the forces available to meet all of them simultaneously."[2]

The state of play in the Persian Gulf changed abruptly with Iran's revolution in 1979 and the enunciation of the Carter Doctrine the following year. The United States "will take any action . . . to safeguard production of oil and its transportation to consumer nations without interference from hostile powers," Brown declared, and this might include the use of "force if necessary." Secretary of State Vance, having previously supported disarmament negotiator Paul Warnke's efforts to abrogate the Navy's right to send ships into the Indian Ocean, reversed course and in August 1979 proposed "to increase moderately our permanent presence—mainly through naval deployments in the Indian Ocean." Carter established the Joint Rapid Deployment Force with this end in mind, but soon after the Republicans took office in 1981 Defense Secretary Weinberger admitted that American forces were still "incapable of stopping an assault [by the Soviets] on Western oil supplies" in the Gulf. The linkage between American interests in the Gulf and the Cold War competition was omnipresent.[3]

In part, then, Reagan's military and naval policy sought to correct this asymmetry. In 1983, Weinberger replaced the Rapid Deployment Force with a unified Central Command, a huge Florida-based headquarters whose mission was to beat any Soviet forces into the Persian Gulf with several carrier battle groups, an amphibious force, 7 Army and Marine divisions, and 7 Air Force tactical air wings totaling over 400 aircraft. The Navy was to acquire thirteen new maritime prepositioning supply ships and station them in the Indian Ocean. American depots were established at Masriah, Oman; Ras Banas, Egypt; and Dhahran and King Khalid Military City in Saudi Arabia. Weinberger also positioned at least one carrier battle group in the Indian Ocean or the North Arabian Sea, and during a crisis in 1983 he increased this number to three, while Reagan proclaimed his determination not to allow Saudi Arabia "to be[come] an[other] Iran.[4]

The Iran-Iraq War forced Reagan to reexamine his commitment to the Carter Doctrine. Historic territorial disputes, 240 cross-border clashes, and the Ayatollah Khomeini's attempt to export his Muslim fundamentalism to Iran's neighbors so strained relations between Baghdad and Tehran that Iraq's president, Saddam Hussein, ordered the Iraqi Army to invade Iran on 22 September 1980. He was bent on showing that Iraq was the dominant power in the Arab world and viewed a war with Iran as a means of achieving this end. He also expected a short, cheap victory since Iran was clearly unprepared for a major conflict, but the following spring Khomeini's troops counterattacked, crossed into Iraq, and established strong lines from which they punished Iraq in a grueling war of attrition. When Iran's counteroffensive ground to a halt in 1983, her small fleet blockaded Iraq's ports and caused Iraq to accelerate the construction of overland pipelines to Turkey and Kuwait in order to export her oil. Iraq retaliated by imposing its own blockade on Iran, in an attempt to shut down Iran's oil trade and so force Tehran to negotiate a ceasefire. Iraqi warplanes hit Iranian shipping in the northern Gulf, damaged one Greek tanker in October and sank another in November, and later that month issued a formal warning to neutral shipping to avoid a war zone in the northern Gulf and the waters surrounding Iran's oil terminal on Kharg Island. To enforce its blockade, Iraq relied exclusively on air attacks against oil facilities and shipping by missile-bearing French-built F-1 Mirage fighter-bombers and Soviet-built Badger bombers, the range of which enabled the Iraqi Air Force to hit Iran's Larak Island oil terminal in the Strait of Hormuz.

During the next four years, Iraq accounted for three-fourths of the antishipping attacks in the Persian Gulf, although these operations were mostly confined to the war zone. Arms sales and aid in the 1970s had placed sophisticated planes and weapons, including anti-ship, surface-to-air, air-to-surface, and cruise missiles and chemical weapons, in the hands of many volatile Third World nations, and the Iran-Iraq War belligerents tapped this arsenal. Iran responded to Iraq's antishipping campaign by ordering medium-range Silkworm surface-to-surface missiles from China and by launching its own mining campaign, which was aimed at tankers bound for Kuwait and Saudi Arabia, Iraq's principal allies. On 17 May 1985, the Soviet tanker *Marshal Chuykov* collided with an Iranian mine and became the first neutral vessel to be damaged. Moscow, which had backed Iran until 1982 when the Kremlin suddenly changed sides, inexplicably ignored this incident and downplayed its significance. Iran's army resumed its offensive in 1986, occupied the strategic Faw Peninsula—Iraq's only outlet to the sea—and threatened to overrun Basra, Iraq's second-largest city. Kuwait, alarmed by Iraq's weakened position and Iran's attacks on her small fleet of large tankers, turned to the Gulf Cooperation Council, a body formed in 1981 to thwart Iran by coordinating support for Iraq, and the council agreed to Kuwait's plan to ask both the Soviets and Americans to defend her tankers. Kuwait's objectives were to involve both superpowers in the Persian Gulf and thus prevent either one from dominating the region, more firmly range Moscow and Washington against Tehran, and give both superpowers more reasons to want to force Iran to end the war.

The United States, which did not enjoy diplomatic relations with either Iran or Iraq when the war erupted in 1980, remained officially neutral throughout the conflict but gradually inclined toward the Iraqis. Secretary of State Shultz worked to isolate Iran diplomatically and, through Project Staunch, to reduce Europe's arms sales to Tehran. Iran retaliated by ordering Islamic Jihad commandos to plant bombs that blew up the American and French embassies in Kuwait in December 1983. This, coupled with Iranian attacks on Saudi Arabian shipping, caused the Saudi ambassador in Washington to ask the State Department if Reagan might intervene to uphold the Carter Doctrine. The president responded by affirming American "support for Saudi Arabia and other Persian Gulf countries in any potential confrontation with Iran" and declared that he was "willing to help if requested to do so." Having just been humbled in Lebanon, however, Defense Secretary Weinberger and the JCS were in no mood for another entanglement, and they urged Reagan to retract his offer. Two days later he pulled back. "We have not volunteered to intervene," he told the press, "nor have we been asked to intervene." Increased military aid to Saudi Arabia was substituted for American forces for the moment. Reagan also restored diplomatic ties with Baghdad that year and provided Iraq with commercial credits and satellite-gathered intelligence about Iranian troop movements, although the bizarre Iran-Contra affair—in which the Reagan administration sold a small quantity of arms to Iran and used the profits to purchase weapons for the anti-communist Contras in Nicaragua—conflicted with this basic tilt of American policy.[5]

One problem with this approach was that the administration viewed all world events as somehow being related to the East-West conflict, and the Iran-Iraq War did not fit neatly into this cosmos. In his Maritime Strategy, Navy Secretary Lehman proposed to counter a Soviet advance toward the Gulf with a NATO move against the Warsaw Pact, and Weinberger pointed out that the American "deterrent capability in the Persian Gulf . . . is linked with our ability and willingness to shift or widen the war to other areas." The NATO powers, however, opposed extending their mutual obligations outside Europe, and did not take seriously this American strategy. The NATO allies and Japan were even less inclined to support collective Western intervention in the Iran-Iraq War, viewing it as a purely regional clash, so until

1987, Washington restricted itself to quiet support for Iraq and to statements pointing out the importance of the Gulf oil trade and denouncing the attacks on neutral shipping. "While we want no victory [by either side]," explained Assistant Secretary of Defense Richard Armitage, "we can't stand to see Iraq defeated." Because Iraq was conducting the more successful antishipping operations, moreover, it did not serve American ends to intervene. Reagan also reckoned that, after the aged Khomeini left the scene, his more "moderate" successors would want to bring Iran back into the Western sphere. American intervention in the Iran-Iraq War might delay and make more difficult this day of reconciliation.[6]

Kuwait's surprising request in late 1986 for American naval protection for her tanker fleet thus met with resistance in Washington until the administration realized the role the Soviets were to play in the Kuwaiti plan. In short, American strategy was about to be transfigured by Kuwait's diplomacy. Instead of having to fight its way to the Gulf, the Red Navy was now being invited to appear at the artery of Europe's oil supplies under the aegis of a multinational policing effort, a prospect that especially horrified Weinberger. On the other hand, Navy Secretary James Webb, a victim of what Lehman called the "Vietnam Syndrome," argued against defending Kuwaiti shipping on the grounds that it would be impossible to define when an operation with this object had succeeded, might entangle the United States in the Iran-Iraq War, and so risked losing public support. Weinberger disagreed, and his longstanding opposition to overseas military interventionism stood him in good stead when, at the White House on 4 March 1987, he urged Reagan to accept the Kuwaiti offer.

Reagan was loathe to incite Iran, but the new CNO, Admiral Carlisle Trost, reported that the Navy's already established Middle East Force could escort the Kuwaiti tankers without reinforcements. The CIA and State Department argued that this reduced the risk of Iranian retaliation, assessing the overall danger of a clash to be low. "If we don't do the job, the Soviets will," Reagan concluded. "That will jeopardize our own national security as well as our allies." He agreed to order the Middle East Force to escort the Kuwaiti tankers on condition that Kuwait withdraw its offer to the Soviets and deny the Red Fleet the use of Kuwait's port facilities. Although the Soviets showed no inclination to intervene, Kuwait's rejection of this condition further heightened

American fears that the Kremlin might change its mind and stiffened Reagan's determination to prevent this from coming to pass. In public, he disingenuously portrayed his policy as an attempt to forestall "the return to the days of . . . shortages . . . and international humiliation" for the United States.[7]

Kuwait's proposal was implemented by having a fictitious American firm purchase eleven Kuwaiti tankers that, after being inspected by the Coast Guard, were placed in American registry and reflagged. Inasmuch as few American-owned merchant ships sailed under the Stars and Stripes, Reagan's reflagging decision was to put the Navy in the awkward position of defending Kuwaiti-owned, American-flagged tankers while ignoring attacks on American-owned vessels flying foreign flags of convenience. On 4 April 1987, Weinberger ordered Admiral William Crowe, the chairman of the JCS, to prepare for Earnest Will, the codename for the escort-of-convoy operation.

Because Crowe was unwilling to violate an existing interservice treaty, the chain of command for Operation Earnest Will was unnecessarily complex. Moreover, many of the Navy's ships assigned to escort the convoys were poorly prepared for this work. The Middle East fell within the theater boundaries of Marine General George Crist's Florida-based Central Command, which supervised operations within the Persian Gulf and the North Arabian Sea. Rear Admiral Harold J. Bernsen's Middle East Force in the Gulf was to escort the tankers, while the North Arabian Sea Force, consisting of a carrier battle group, extra destroyers and frigates, and additional supply ships, was to operate "in support of" the Middle East Force by providing surface and combat air cover, airborne early warning, and replacements for Bernsen's escort groups. One of the ships scheduled to escort the Earnest Will convoys was the frigate *Harold R. Stark*, whose skipper, Captain Glenn R. Brindel, successfully put his vessel and her crew through a refresher training exercise in the Caribbean only weeks before she steamed for the Persian Gulf in February 1987.

When planning for the convoys began to take shape in April, naval intelligence compiled a formidable list of threats to American escorts operating in the Gulf from the belligerent air forces, the Iranian Navy, and the Chinese-built Silkworm surface-to-surface missiles that the Iranians had recently installed in a horseshoe pattern around Bandar Abbas, which guarded the mouth of the Strait of Hormuz. The Silkworms, capable of striking a target sixty miles distant, provided Iran with a lethal, quickdraw means of attack, and their appearance so menaced the Middle East Force that Washington warned Tehran that the North Arabian Sea Force would attack and destroy the sites and bomb Bandar Abbas "if it appears the missiles are about to be used."

In spite of the many dangers to the Middle East Force, Admiral Trost refused to freeze the crews of ships deploying to the Gulf, thus preventing excessive rotation. As a result, nine officers, including every department head, and one-third of the enlisted men, including many of the most senior petty officers, left the *Stark* between the time of her workup in the Caribbean and her arrival in the Gulf on 6 March 1987. Lieutenant Basil Montcrief, the *Stark*'s tactical action officer, did not join the crew until a month later and so did not hear an intelligence briefing given when the ship entered the Gulf. Admiral Bernsen, by contrast, was mindful of the menace faced by his command and alert to the dangers of an unwarranted attack by an American vessel against one of the many civilian or other friendly aircraft flying over the Gulf, an inadvertent attack by an Iraqi fighter, or an intentional attack by Iran against an American warship. To prevent an untoward incident, he ordered his ships to take special care in warning off approaching aircraft and in assessing their intent and to assume that all incoming Iraqi and Iranian aircraft were potentially hostile. "The probability of deliberate attack on U.S. warships was low," Bernsen's staff told Brindel on 28 February, but an "indiscriminate attack in the Persian Gulf" was thought to be "a significant danger." Such warnings were all too imprecise, claimed Commander David R. Carson of the frigate *Sides*, who charged that the "intelligence system . . . covered its six by forecasting every possible worst-case scenario." Bernsen was not entirely happy with his intelligence arrangements. All information was fed to the flagship *LaSalle* where a fourteen-officer detachment created a picture of the threat that was then transmitted to the ships. This hardworking unit, however, was clearly undermanned and inexperienced. Lamenting the lack of seasoned judgment that more senior men might have brought to the task, Bernsen complained, "I had lieutenants doing things that captains usually do." He also worked hard to improve the imperfect coordination among the Middle East Force, the North Arabian Sea Force, and the Omani-based Air Force AWACS surveillance aircraft and Navy P-3 Orions.[8]

The prospect of a more muscular American presence in the Persian Gulf failed to deter either Iran or Iraq from escalating their respective antishipping campaigns, and Iran even threatened in May to retaliate not only against the United States but also against Kuwait if she accepted American naval protection and consummated the reflagging arrangement. Iraq's fighter-bombers fired at least a dozen Exocet missiles at Iranian vessels in early May, while Iran's antishipping campaign continued apace, highlighted by attacks on three Kuwait-bound tankers during the first eleven days of the month. The Americans observed that the poorly trained Iraqi pilots were particularly dangerous, as they took no time to identify their targets and often fired blindly at radar contacts. Iraqi air strategy appeared to change on 13 May when her aircraft flew into the central Persian Gulf, well outside of the opposing war zones, for the first time in the campaign. An assessment by Bernsen's intelligence officers suggesting that this meant that Iraq intended to hit enemy targets in the central Gulf was conveyed to the American warships in the area. The next day, an Iraqi F-1 Mirage entered the central Gulf and approached the *Coontz*, and when it came within thirty-nine miles of his vessel—just short of the known range of the air-to-surface Exocet missile—Captain William Cobb was alarmed. He challenged the pilot, turned to bring his broadside weapons arc to bear on the target, put a Standard missile on its launching rail, armed the ship's chaff bloomer, and ordered the destroyer's target acquisition radar to lock onto the plane. Before the Mirage was "painted" by the radar, the Iraqi pilot turned away from Cobb's alert ship. At the time of this incident, the Earnest Will convoys had yet to get under way; liberal Democrats in Congress were trying to upset the plan by pressuring Reagan to implement the War Powers Act and so effectively cripple his policy.

At 0800 on 17 May 1987, the *Stark* stood out of Manama en route to the southern radar picket station, eighty-five miles northeast of Bahrain and twelve miles outside Iran's war zone. At about 2000 an Oman-based Air Force AWACS reported that an Iraqi Mirage was entering the Gulf, 200 miles to the north. The AWACS warned the *Stark* fifteen minutes later that the Iraqi plane—which was designated a "friendly aircraft"—was turning eastward and heading toward the general vicinity of the ship. The Mirage was located by the *Coontz'* radar, and Captian Cobb alerted the flagship and the *Stark*. Brindel, a former Naval Academy leadership instructor, was informed of this at 2015, but he paid it little heed. Aware that Iraq welcomed the reflagging policy and that most of Iraq's targets were within the Iranian war zone, he reasoned that the plane would not attack American ships. Moreover, Captain Brindel's attention that evening was diverted by the need to conduct a "full power run" engineering test mandated by Atlantic Fleet headquarters faraway in Norfolk. He began this test at 2024.

When the approaching Mirage was seventy miles away, the *Stark*'s radar picked it up, detected the plane's radar in the search mode, and tracked her progress as she streaked southward toward the frigate. Sailors in the ship's combat information center realized just before 2100 that only thirty miles separated the aircraft and the frigate and that the Iraqi pilot was turning again toward their position and was now within missile range. Two minutes later, the flagship *LaSalle* asked if the *Stark* was tracking the Iraqi plane and received a reassuring reply. Admiral Bernsen had ordered all Middle East Force ships to assume a wartime steaming alert status when operating in the Gulf, reasoning that "it is likely or possible that a ship may encounter [a] sudden enemy attack." He was unaware that Brindel was not now conforming to these orders. At about 2105 a technician in the combat information center detected radar emissions from the Mirage's air intercept radar and asked permission to transmit a warning to the Iraqi pilot. "No, wait," replied Lieutenant Montcrief, the tactical action officer. He recalled that he "had no reason to feel that we were under attack."[9]

At that moment Brindel could not be found, having left the bridge at 2058 for his cabin to answer nature's call. Montcrief refused on his own authority to activate the Standard missile's fire control radar on the incomprehensible grounds that this might precipitate an international incident. Indeed, not until 2108 did Montcrief allow the first warning to be broadcast. We had "given the same warning to [presumably hostile] Iranian aircraft," Brindel later pleaded. "They always answer or acknowledge those challenges and stay out of the general area." By this time, however, one of the *Stark*'s forward lookouts was already reporting a deadly bright light low on the horizon off the port bow. The Iraqi pilot, believing that he had trapped an Iranian vessel and having no means of distinguishing friend from foe at night, was within twelve miles of the *Stark* when he fired an Exocet missile at 2107, waited a few seconds, fired a second weapon, and turned for home. Montcrief, though now alarmed, still refused to switch the Phalanx antimissile Gatling gun system from standby to automatic or to activate the ship's defensive chaff bloomer.[10]

"Inbound missile, . . . all hands brace for shock," the *Stark*'s loudspeakers shrieked at 2109. Traveling at more than 575 knots, the first sea-skimming Exocet entered the frigate on the port side, punched through passageways, computer spaces, and crew quarters, and came to rest on the second deck. Her warhead did not explode, but she deposited 360 pounds of burning fuel along her trail through the *Stark*. About twenty-five seconds later the second Exocet slammed into the ship about eight feet forward of the first, penetrated five feet, and exploded, creating a huge hole in the hull and feeding fires already raging amidships. The temperature in these spaces reached over 3,000 degrees Fahrenheit, so hot that parts of the aluminum superstructure began to melt. Thirty-seven sailors died as a result of the attack. Only Lieutenant Art Conklin's heroic damage-control parties saved the ship, and, after emergency repairs, she limped back to Norfolk. When the Iraqis learned of the accident, they promptly issued an apology. A Navy board of inquiry headed by Rear Admiral Grant A. Sharp investigated the attack on the *Stark* and recommended that Brindel and Montcrief be court-martialed, a conclusion endorsed by General Crist, but Admiral Kelso, the commander in chief of the Atlantic Fleet, wisely allowed both men simply to resign from the Navy. The real tragedy of the *Stark*, said Admiral Bernsen sadly, was that "the crew . . . did not believe they were in any danger."[11]

The *Stark* incident alarmed Washington and led to changes, some ill considered, that were intended to strengthen the Middle East Force. Reagan, who wanted improved relations with Iraq and realized that the attack was inadvertent, simply announced that American forces would retaliate for any future attacks on their warships. Recalling that Reagan had resisted retaliating against terrorists, Admiral Crowe went up to the White House on 29 May and persuaded him to endorse a firm policy of proportional retaliation and to approve an increase in the Middle East Force to nine ships and the North Arabian Sea Force to about twenty ships. Reagan publicly ordered the Middle East Force to increase its alert status and liberalized the rules of engagement by declaring that the Earnest Will escorts were "to shoot immediately if they are threatened." All incoming aircraft were to be considered hostile, and the JCS required that radio warnings be broadcast and defensive measures be taken long before an incoming plane could fire on an American ship. In addition, the Aegis cruiser *Virginia* was deployed to the Gulf to improve the battle group's air defenses, and the frigates *Waddell* and *Conyngham* were hastily withdrawn from the Gulf and replaced by the destroyers *Kidd*, *Flatley*, and *Klarking*, which were armed with the Phalanx close-in antimissile system. Why Admiral Trost, the CNO, who was clearly responsible at the highest level in the chain of command for preparing ships for combat, allowed the poorly armed frigates to operate in the Persian Gulf's lethal air environment without adequate support in the first place was beyond understanding. Rear Admiral Anthony Less, commanding a ten-ship battle group built around the carrier *Ranger*, arrived on the scene on 20 August. A six-ship battle group built around the battleship *Missouri* moved into the North Arabian Sea to relieve the *Ranger* in September.

Less helpful was General Crist's decision to name Rear Admiral Dennis Brooks, the Philippines-based 7th Fleet battle group commander, to head a new joint command, the Middle East Task Force, and to place Admiral Bernsen's Middle East Force under his supervision. Brooks and Bernsen quarrelled and their staffs, who now performed essentially the same work, openly feuded. To get Brooks' fleet staff off their backs, at one point Bernsen's staff put a virtual "embargo" on the exchange of information, according to one admiral involved. Crist's move, in effect, further blurred responsibility for the success or failure of the convoy operations. Although the Atlantic and Pacific fleets supplied the ships for the escort forces, neither theater commander played any role in planning operations. "The chief absurdity results as usual from the Washington obsession with 'jointness,'" former Navy Secretary Lehman observed. "Throughout the spring and summer of 1987, the Pacific Fleet commander, Admiral [James] Lyons, protested that running a dangerous naval operation in the Gulf from a bureaucracy in Florida was unworkable and would lead to disaster." In September, "Lyons' dissent, sent through official channels, was so counter to sacred 'joint' orthodoxy that he was forced to retire" by Crowe and Trost.[12]

In July, after the Senate refused for the third time to pass a Democrat-sponsored resolution opposing the reflagging policy,

Reagan instructed Weinberger to begin Operation Earnest Will. It was by now evident, however, that Reagan's policy had not deterred Iran in the least. Swedish-built Iranian Boghammer armed speedboats attacked and damaged an unescorted Soviet freighter en route to Saudi Arabia on 6 May, and eleven days later a Soviet-leased Kuwaiti tanker struck an Iranian mine near the entrance to the Strait of Hormuz. These Iranian mines had been identified by the CIA as early as June 1987, and in May and June 1988 they damaged several ships in the Gulf. The CIA stubbornly insisted that Iran's mine inventory was low and that the Iranian Navy, wracked by Khomeini's religious purges and beset by shortages of skilled technicians and spare parts, lacked the means to conduct successful mine warfare in the wide passages and unpredictable currents of the Gulf. Admiral Trost also seemed not to heed this danger, although on 1 July Commander Francis Demast in the minesweeper *Inflict* discovered a dozen Iranian mines near one of the main shipping channels.

Preventing the Soviets from establishing a large naval task force in the Persian Gulf was behind Reagan's original reflagging decision, and in July this aim also drove an American effort to involve the NATO powers in the defense of shipping in the Persian Gulf, ham-fisted diplomacy that the British, Germans, Dutch, and Italians coldly rebuffed because they intended to avoid entangling the alliance outside of Europe. After an Iranian gunboat attacked a French tanker on 17 July 1987, however, France broke diplomatic relations with Iran and four days later announced that the French Navy would deploy a powerful task force to the Gulf to escort her merchant shipping there. Eventually, the British, Italians, Belgians, and Dutch sent warships into the Persian Gulf to defend their shipping.

The first Earnest Will convoy, consisting of the reflagged tankers *Gas Prince* and *Bridgeton*, rendezvoused the following day with Captain David P. Yonkers' three-ship escort group at the United Arab Emirates port of Khor Fakkan, passed through the Strait of Hormuz, and shaped a course for the Mina al-Ahmadi oil beacon forty miles off the Kuwaiti coast. The movement proceeded without incident until, eighteen miles west of Iran's Farsi Island, the 400,000-ton *Bridgeton* collided with a 1,000-pound Iranian mine that had been planted recently. The resulting blast punched a large hole in the hull and cracked an interior beam, but the tanker could still make way. Fearing more mines in the vicinity, Yonkers stationed his small, defenseless escorts behind the tankers, and ordered the *Bridgeton* to steam for a drydock in Dubai in the United Arab Emirates, while the *Gas Prince* and her escort continued on to Kuwaiti waters. "I do not have the capability to . . . defend against mines," Yonkers explained in his own defense shortly thereafter. Admiral Bernsen ordered Demast in the *Inflict* to investigate the area around Farsi Island, and on 26 July, he discovered a large minefield sown recently by the Iranian Navy.[13]

Critics of the administration and the Navy reacted with alarm to this news and congressional Democrats tried to exploit the *Bridgeton* incident to undermine Reagan's reflagging policy. Even Reagan's allies on the Hill were distressed. "[Admiral] Bernsen emphatically stated that he was equipped to deal with the threat [of mines], so we came away supporting the reflagging," complained Congressman Curt Weldon, a Republican who had backed Reagan's policy but now was uncomfortable with the results. The Middle East Force's inability to defend the *Bridgeton* could be laid at the doorsteps of General Crist, whose Central Command did not respond to Admiral Bernsen's earlier requests for more minesweepers, and to Admiral Trost, who failed to correctly assess the danger of Iranian mining operations and therefore apparently did nothing to see that the Middle East Force had the vessels or helicopters necessary to deal with that threat. "If you confine yourself to training to fight a war against the Soviets, you are going to go into an area like the Persian Gulf not very well equipped to operate," concluded Rear Admiral Raymond G. Zeller, who took command of a battle group in the Gulf of Oman a few months later. Shipboard sonars could not be used effectively to locate minefields in the Persian Gulf owing to the shallowness of those waters. Without minesweepers, commented Commander Daniel Murphy of the guided missile destroyer *Kidd,* "our capability to spot a moored mine is very poor." Trost in turn blamed Crist for this state of affairs and even sent Captain Thomas Triplett up to Capitol Hill to tell Congress that "it is not the U.S. Navy running the show in the Persian Gulf," but "the Central Command, which works through the Joint Chiefs." Inasmuch as Trost sat on the JCS, it was hard to see how he escaped responsibility.[14]

At the time, the entire American fleet contained only twenty-one Korean War–vintage, wooden-hulled minesweepers, and

Naval Reserves manned all but three of these vessels. Most of them suffered from dry rot and leaked badly. Although the Russians were proficient minelayers, the lack of American minesweepers seemed little cause for concern inasmuch as traditional Navy war plans counted on the NATO allies for this work. The Maritime Strategy called for both the Atlantic and Pacific fleets to advance into well-mined Soviet waters, and so Lehman asked Congress to authorize the construction of five *Avenger*-class minesweepers in 1982. Unlike most of the contracts let for Lehman's 600-ship Navy, however, this one was terribly mismanaged. The project manager decided to install some old engines already in inventory, but it was discovered too late that their shafts rotated in a direction opposite to that of the main gears. The cost overrun for the minesweepers was 50 percent, and the first vessel did not enter the fleet until 1986, two years late. Although it was clear before the Earnest Will convoys got under way that Iranian mines might endanger the operation, Trost, a nuclear submariner, failed to act to reinforce the Middle East Force with new minesweepers or minesweeping helicopters. In September, the *Missouri*'s battle group brought a few minesweepers and minehunting helicopters to the Gulf. The amphibious carrier *Guadalcanal* carrying eight Sea Stallion minehunting helicopters headed for the Gulf, while four small 30-ton minesweeping boats were loaded onto the amphibious transport *Raleigh* in Charleston and transported to the Middle East Force. Other minesweepers were shipped to the Gulf from Seattle, but Trost's failure to ready the fleet for the reflagging operations meant that they were not all on station until October. And it was not until January 1988 that two essential floating helicopter bases were positioned in the northern Gulf to support the minehunting effort.

Admiral Brooks' Middle East Task Force, enlarged to twenty-four ships, four minesweeping boats, minehunting helicopters, and several Navy SEAL teams, was ready to resume Operation Earnest Will in early August. Four American escorts defended the second convoy, composed of two tankers and one liquid natural gas carrier, which assembled in the North Arabian Sea on the 8th. When this formation entered the Strait of Hormuz, an Iranian F-4 Phantom streaked toward an American P-3 Orion patrol plane flying ahead of the convoy, but fighter aircraft from the nearby carrier *Constellation* drove her off with two Sparrow missile shots. The convoy and her escorts steamed northward, covered 550 miles, and arrived safely in Kuwaiti waters four days later. After the Middle East Force escorted another convoy through the Gulf safely, the Iranians decided to retaliate. On 21 September, a section of armed Army minehunting helicopters flying off the frigate *Jarret* caught the Iranian minelayer *Iran Ajr* planting contact mines near the Middle East Force's anchorage in the Bahrain Islands. The hostile vessel was captured, the mines confiscated, and the crew repatriated quickly. Later that month the Iranians fired three Chinese-built long-range surface-to-surface Silkworm missiles at Kuwaiti targets, one of which narrowly missed a coastal refinery.

On 4 October, to protect their mining operations, the Iranians sent out four patrol boats that attacked a section of American minehunting helicopters, but the Americans sank one of the attacking vessels and drove off the others. Then, on the 15th, an Iranian Silkworm fired from the Faw Peninsula traveled fifty miles and struck the American-owned, Liberian-flagged tanker *Sungari* while she was riding at anchor off Mina al-Ahmadi, Kuwait's main oil port. A few days earlier, the 81,000-ton reflagged tanker *Sea Isle City*, three other Kuwaiti tankers, and their American escorts had arrived safely at the Ahmadi anchorage at the end of the last leg of the eleventh successful Earnest Will convoy operation. The *Sea Isle City* was maneuvering into the Shuaiba oil terminal when she was hit by yet another Silkworm missile, which ripped through the tanker's superstructure, blinding the American master and causing considerable damage to the ship. Shortly after these attacks, the Naval Research Laboratory devised a means of spoofing a Silkworm attack by positioning barges carrying radar reflectors in the vicinity of obvious targets, a tactic that succeeded in December when a Silkworm homed in on one of these barges rather than a nearby oil terminal, its intended target.

These Silkworm attacks put great pressure on Reagan to retaliate, but again he selected the least provocative punitive option. In what he described as a "prudent yet restrained response," Reagan told Crowe to issue orders to admirals Brooks and Bernsen to attack and destroy an Iranian oil platform. The destroyers *Hoel, Leftwich,* and *Young* entered the Gulf on 19 October 1987, rendezvoused with the missile destroyer *Kidd* and the frigate *Thach,* and steamed toward Iran's Rostam oil platform. Earlier Iraqi attacks had disabled the platform's oil works, but

U.S. Navy Department

During Operation Earnest Will, an escort group consisting of the frigate *Hawes* (FFG-53) (*right*), the cruiser *William H. Standley* (CG-52), and the amphibious assault ship *Guadalcanal* (LPH-7) (*far left rear*) defended the movement of the reflagged Kuwaiti tanker *Gas King* (*center*) as she proceeded from the Strait of Hormuz to Kuwait in the northwestern Persian Gulf.

During Operation Praying Mantis in the Persian Gulf in 1988, the Iranian frigate *Sahand* is ablaze after being hit by two Harpoon anti-ship missiles, four laser-guided bombs launched by two A-6E Intruders, and a Harpoon fired by the guided missile destroyer *Strauss.*

U.S. Navy Department

the Iranians continued thereafter to use it as a communications and missile guidance site. Two F-14 Tomcat fighters and an E-2C Hawkeye surveillance plane from the carrier *Ranger* in the North Arabian Sea provided combat air cover for the destroyers, while the cruiser *Standley* took station to the northwest and established an antimissile screen for the destroyers. Beginning at 1400, the destroyer-frigate group fired 1,000 rounds at the target for eighty-five minutes. The shelling did not completely destroy the platform, however, so a Navy SEAL team had to land on it and finish the job with explosives. "We do not seek any further confrontation with Iran," Weinberger announced, but "we will . . . meet any escalation of military actions by Iran with stronger countermeasures"—the very policy of graduated response he had so often criticized in the past.[15]

The destruction of the Rostam platform and Weinberger's tough statement may have convinced the Iranians to turn their attention from the Earnest Will convoys and concentrate instead on attacking other neutral shipping that was still unprotected. Although Americans owned many of these flag-of-convenience vessels, Reagan still refused to allow the Middle East Force escorts to screen their movements. The twelfth Earnest Will convoy, consisting of the liquified petroleum tanker *Gas King* and the tanker *Ocean City*, escorted by the frigate *Ford*, left the Ahmadi beacon on the morning of 20 October and safely reached the Strait of Hormuz a few days later. During the next few months, several more Earnest Will convoys proceeded without incident, subject to only occasional Iranian harassment and the danger of a randomly planted Iranian mine. Following the American lead, the British and French strengthened their escort forces in the Persian Gulf, sent minesweepers to these stations, and quietly began to escort their own shipping. The success of these measures meant that the Middle East Task Force could be reduced from thirty-four ships at the onset of the campaign in the fall of 1987 to twenty-four ships by February 1988. Indeed, Frank Carlucci, the new Secretary of Defense, on a visit to Saudi Arabia one month earlier, rejected a Saudi request that the Middle East Force convoy its tankers and announced that he did not intend the Navy to be "the policeman of the high seas."[16]

These months also saw the tide of the war in the Persian Gulf turn against Iran. The conflict cost both belligerents hundreds of thousands of dead and wounded and exhausted their finances. Iraq was receiving aid and arms from the Saudis, Kuwait-is, Soviets, and western Europeans, but Iran's eccentric and unpredictable radicalism had left her friendless and isolated. Khomeini blamed the United States for this state of affairs, and the tempo of Iranian mining operations in the Gulf had increased in the spring of 1988. On the evening of 14 April, Commander Paul X. Rinn in the frigate *Samuel B. Roberts* was off Qatar returning to Kuwait when he discovered to his horror that he had unwittingly steamed into the middle of an Iranian minefield. He shut down one of his gas turbine engines, threw the other into reverse, and tried to back out of the minefield very slowly. Forty-five minutes later, Rinn's lookouts spotted three mines and he skillfully avoided them, but a fourth mine, pushed back and under the frigate by her wash, ascended and made contact with the bottom of the ship. The resulting explosion—the equivalent of 250 pounds of TNT—blew a 25-foot hole in the portside hull, threw the vessel up 10 feet, flexed her keel, and flung both engines off their mounts. Fuel spewed all over the engine room, fumes went up the stack, and a 150-foot fireball was seen shooting up into the air. Wasting no time, Rinn moved resolutely to save the *Samuel B. Roberts.* Using new fire-fighting devices—such as thermal imagers that located fires—one damage-control party fought the blazes while another wired and welded the damaged section of the hull together to prevent the stern from breaking away. By the end of the day, Commander Rinn and his well-trained crew had saved their ship.[17]

This time there was little debate in Washington over the need to retaliate swiftly. Weinberger had been the most consistent opponent of punitive measures, but Carlucci, his successor, took a much stiffer line. Because Reagan insisted on a policy of "measured response," Crowe selected as targets two functioning Iranian oil platforms and issued orders to conduct Operation Praying Mantis to Rear Admiral Anthony A. Less, who had relieved both admirals Bernsen and Brooks when the Middle East Force and the Middle East Task Force were finally consolidated. The true object of the operation, according to Less, was to sink an Iranian frigate. "If we didn't get the frigate," he observed soon after, "we'd go after another platform." At 0900 on 18 April, the largest surface naval battle the American fleet had fought since World War II began when the *Trenton,* in company with the destroyers *Merrill* and *Lynde D. McCormick,* converged on the Sassan oil platform, warned Iranian personnel to abandon the facility, and seventeen minutes later blasted the structure with 5-inch gunfire. A Marine demolition party boarded the platform an hour later and completed its destruction.[18]

Meanwhile, at 0932 a second surface action group, commanded by Captain James Chandler and composed of the destroyers *Simpson* and *Bagley* and the cruiser *Wainwright*, appeared off Iran's Sirri oil platform and opened fire. This barrage ignited fires that consumed the structure. The 275-ton Iranian missile boat *Joshan* had just finished escorting a convoy from Kharg Island to Lavan Island to the north when her skipper received orders that sent him steaming south to the Sirri platform. "It appeared to us the Iranians had lost the bubble," recalled Rear Admiral Zeller, who commanded the carrier battle group in the North Arabian Sea. "They knew there was some action going on but they weren't aware of what exactly it was." The *Joshan* closed on Chandler's ships at 1315. "Abandon ship or I will sink you," Chandler warned. The enemy ignored two warnings to stand off and fired one Harpoon surface-to-surface missile, which the *Wainwright* spoofed by using her chaff thrower. The *Wainwright* replied with her own Harpoon shot, which struck the *Joshan*, while the *Simpson* fired several missiles, scoring two direct hits. Within seconds, a fourth American missile slammed into the burning Iranian vessel, and she sank a short time later.[19]

The Iranians, now alert to the location of the American formation, sent two F-4 Phantoms into the Gulf, and they approached the *Wainwright* at 1352, but she fired two Standard surface-to-air missiles, damaging one plane and forcing both to return hastily to base. Earlier in the day, Iranian Boghammer armed speedboats, which had already attacked the American-owned tanker *Willi Tide*, sped toward the Panamanian supply ship *Scan Bay* and fired at her. Moments later, however, a section of A-6 Intruders from the carrier *Enterprise* appeared overhead, sank one hostile gunboat with a missile, and damaged two others. Earlier that day, the Iranians had brought their frigates into Bandar Abbas. Now the Iranian frigate *Sahand* rushed up to support the Boghammers, but her Sea Killer anti-ship missile missed. The American frigate *Strauss* responded with a successful Harpoon missile shot, while the A-6 Intruders hit the Iranian vessel with a pair of air-to-surface missiles and a laser-guided bomb.[20]

**Rear Admiral Anthony A. Less. Commander,
Joint Middle East Task Force, 1988–1989.**

Admiral Less barely had time to assess these events when, at 1817, the Iranian frigate *Sabalan* steamed into the Strait of Hormuz, closed on the frigate *Jack Williams*, launched Sea Killers against the ship, and then fired Sea Cat antiaircraft missiles at a section of A-6 Intruders flying combat air patrol nearby. The aircraft eluded the Iranian missiles and replied by delivering several laser-guided Skipper bombs onto the vessel. One bomb went directly into the stack and penetrated into the engineering spaces where her delayed fuse detonated the explosives. The ship "belched," according to witnesses; the stack erupted; and she went dead in the water, encased in smoke and flame. Admiral Less preferred to sink her, but Secretary Carlucci, who was following the battle in the Pentagon, ordered him not to do so unless she threatened American forces again, an unlikely circumstance. "We wish to close the incident and we urge maximum restraint upon the Iranian government," Carlucci announced, a foolish statement that tended to dilute the impact of the operation on Iranian politics. Operation Praying Mantis was proof that well-commanded missile-bearing ships, assisted by sophisticated aircraft, could operate in confined waters and that the Navy's investment in high technology paid off in combat.[21]

The administration's critics were now charging that Reagan, by implementing the reflagging policy, had foolishly blundered into the Iran-Iraq War without knowing the duration or likely outcome of the involvement and that he had no idea what to do next. Operation Praying Mantis may have persuaded the Iranians to stop attacking the Earnest Will convoys for the moment, but both Iran and Iraq continued their respective antishipping campaigns against other targets. Owing to Reagan's unexpected display of resolve in the wake of the Lebanon fiasco, "we are the big winners in the Gulf," General Crist told Congress in February 1988, but Democrats criticized Reagan for failing to establish milestones that would lead to an eventual withdrawal. However, they did not explain how shutting down the Earnest Will convoys might end the tanker war or protect the oil trade. More perceptive critics charged that defending freedom of navigation in the Gulf unwittingly assisted Iran, which depended on tankers to export its oil, rather than Iraq, which now relied on its pipelines to Turkey and Kuwait. The cost of Operation Earnest Will was also irksome. "The fundamental policy issue," observed Lehman, was "the hugely expensive force structure necessary to back up the Carter Doctrine and guarantee the security of the Gulf." Demanding that Japan and NATO help defend the oil trade, he favored creating a new regional alliance dedicated to that end. "That structure will involve some permanent Western presence because events since the British left have shown that a strictly local balance of power cannot be left to . . . regional ambitions." Although the British, French, Dutch, and West German flotillas in the Persian Gulf cooperated with the Middle East Force, a more formal allied arrangement was not possible, so Reagan vowed to stay the course.[22]

There was not long to wait, for the Iran-Iraq War ended suddenly—and in the wake of a great tragedy. The CIA learned in late June 1988 that Iran—perhaps reacting to an increasing number of Iraqi attacks on Iranian shuttle tankers and oil platforms in the upper Gulf—intended to make good several public threats against the United States by conducting a spectacular operation against the Navy's warships on or about the 4th of July. "Crews of ships reporting to the Middle East Force in the summer months were noticeably on edge," recalled Carson, skipper of the Sides, and one ship even fired at a hapless dhow when she ignored an English-language warning to stay clear of a Navy mobile sea base.

This "sense of imminent danger" was fed by new CIA reports of Iranian action, which were relayed to Admiral Less in the North Arabian Sea and to Captain Will Rogers, Jr., of the Aegis cruiser *Vincennes*. On the morning of 3 July, in company with the destroyer *Sides* and the frigate *Elmer Montgomery*, the *Vincennes* had just finished escorting a southbound convoy and was reentering the Gulf through the Strait of Hormuz. No convoys were at sea at the time and the carrier's pilots were exhausted, so Less saw no reason to provide the *Vincennes* formation with E-2 Hawkeye airborne early-warning coverage. The AWACS aircraft on duty in the northern Gulf could not monitor events far to the south. At about 0615, Rogers learned that a flotilla of Iranian Boghammers had fired in front of his Lamps III helicopter, perhaps to chase it off, and he asked Less for permission to shoot back. This "time-consuming request that . . . passed through two levels of the chain of command" was "not necessary if the action was required for self-defense," observed Carson, one of Rogers' vocal critics. When the *Vincennes* and *Montgomery* raced toward the Boghammers and maneuvered to engage at close range, the two speedboats bravely turned toward the American ships. Suddenly, an Iranian helicopter appeared on the horizon, her intent obviously hostile, and both the *Vincennes* and *Montgomery* brought the Boghammers under fire at 0642.[23]

When the Bandar Abbas air traffic control tower cleared for takeoff Iran Air Flight 655, an A300 Airbus carrying 290 passengers and crew, it was unaware of the ongoing battle in the Strait. Commercial jetliners had crisscrossed the Gulf throughout the war with immunity, owing to a long-established civilian air corridor linking Bandar Abbas with Dubai on the southern Gulf coast. This morning, however, that corridor led Flight 655 directly over the embattled *Vincennes*. When the Airbus took off, the cruiser's Aegis radar picked her up, but a confused radar operator misidentified the plane as an Iranian Tomcat fighter. Alarmed by this news, Rogers reasoned that she was racing to support the Iranian gunboats. American Tomcats did not carry anti-ship missiles or bombs, but the intelligence alert led Rogers to suspect that fanatical Iranians might have jerrybuilt one of their Tomcats to fire a Harpoon anti-ship missile, drop iron bombs, or conduct a kamikaze-style suicide attack. Moreover, Iranian F-4 Phantoms had scrambled from Bandar Abbas all day during Operation Praying Mantis and one had attacked the *Wainwright*.

Rogers broadcast repeated radio challenges to the plane, but the Iranian pilot did not respond. Moreover, the Airbus' identification transponder was issuing a confusing code. Rogers asked about civilian flights scheduled to cross the Gulf that morning, but the sailor who checked the roster inexplicably overlooked Flight 655. Radar operators in the *Vincennes'* combat information center, now convinced that the approaching aircraft was hostile, reported incorrectly to the captain that the plane was traveling at 450 knots and descending from an altitude of 9,000 feet, whereas the screens actually showed it to be at 12,000 feet and climbing at an airspeed of 350 knots. Carson in the *Sides* was eighteen miles away, and he too had picked up the Airbus, but because it "did not . . . react to the . . . fire control radar," he judged it to be "a nonthreat." Carson inexplicably failed to sound an alarm when Rogers reached the opposite conclusion, however. I "wondered aloud in disbelief," he wrote, "but I did not think to push for a reevaluation." Rogers was now certain that the plane was heading directly for the *Vincennes*, and the tragedy of the *Stark* could not have been far from his mind. Over a span of just seven minutes, he repeatedly queried Admiral Less, who rightly told him to use his own judgment. Only nine miles separated the *Vincennes* and the plane when Rogers reluctantly gave the order to fire two Standard surface-to-surface missiles. Within seconds the missiles slammed into the Airbus and knocked her out of the sky, killing all aboard.

Admiral Crowe appeared on national television within hours to defend the shootdown, but his ill-advised, misinformed explanation that the Airbus intended to attack the ship was soon discredited by news reports. "The rush to put a happy face on the entire affair" was bitterly criticized by many, including Commander Carson. Rear Admiral William A. Fogarty's subsequent investigation of the tragedy found that the *Vincennes'* Aegis system had functioned properly but that, after the operators mistook the airliner for a fighter, they overlooked or misinterpreted evidence that did not reinforce their original, erroneous conviction.[24]

The meaning of the Airbus shootdown was entirely misread by the outraged Tehran regime. Khomeini, long distrustful of American motives, rejected a formal apology delivered at the UN by Vice President George Bush and instead interpreted the event as a sign that the United States was abandoning all pretense of neutrality and would thereafter use its full resources to openly support Iraq. "Go to the war fronts and fight against America and its lackeys," he demanded. This order had little effect, however, inasmuch as Iran was by now bankrupt and burdened by enormous casualties, apathy at home for the war, and diplomatic isolation. Iraq had evicted the Iranian Army from the strategic Faw Peninsula earlier that year, and thereafter Iran's military effort almost ground to a halt. In short order, Tehran agreed to a ceasefire negotiation at the UN, which brought an end to the inconclusive Iran-Iraq War.[25]

Earnest Will probably reinforced the Soviet view of the United States as newly resolute, well armed, and unafraid to use force to protect its interests. Later events made it clear that this did not deter the Soviets from assisting the Kuwaitis, however. The reflagging policy played a role in bringing the Iran-Iraq War to an end on terms as favorable as Iraq might reasonably expect, and so helped to restore the uneasy balance of power in the Persian Gulf. Admiral Bernsen, who earned a place in the ranks of Struble, Zumwalt, and Kelso as one of the Navy's outstanding modern combat commanders, organized and conducted the first stage of Operation Earnest Will so successfully that none of the Kuwaiti tankers was lost and only the *Bridgeton* was damaged. Admiral Less, another dynamic figure, dealt Iran a dreadful blow with Operation Praying Mantis by knocking out 10 percent of her offshore oil production and virtually destroying the Iranian fleet. Iran soon extended peace feelers at the UN, but it took the tragedy of the *Vincennes* shootdown to convince Khomeini that the United States, the "Great Satan" of Iranian propaganda, was prepared to go to any length to support Iraq. In all likelihood the shock of this inadvertent tragedy made possible the critical last-minute negotiations that led to an end to the Iran-Iraq War, the bloodiest conflict since World War II.

Chapter Forty

The New World Order
1989–1991

There were hints aplenty that the Cold War was drawing to a dramatic close when Vice President George Bush accepted the 1988 Republican presidential nomination in July and then defeated his maladroit Democratic opponent, Massachusetts Governor Michael Dukakis, in November. Scarcely had Bush entered the White House the following January, however, when he faced a dizzying series of events, including the long awaited collapse of the Soviet-dominated communist regimes in Eastern Europe, the abandonment of the Warsaw Pact, the reunification of Germany, the disintegration of the Soviet Union, and a thorough revision of the global balance of power. "The world has changed at a fantastic pace, with each day writing a fresh page of history before yesterday's ink has even dried," Bush declared two years later.[1]

A decade of debt-ridden economic decline and political unrest in Eastern Europe climaxed with the collapse of the Warsaw Pact. In 1981, shipyard workers in Gdansk, Poland, led by a charismatic electrician, Lech Walesa, organized the Solidarity union and challenged Warsaw's hard-line communist government. Moscow insisted that the Brezhnev Doctrine—which required the communist regimes of Eastern Europe to adhere to Soviet leadership—be upheld, and the Soviets helped Polish Army General Wojciech Jaruzelski impose martial law and partly suppress the Solidarity uprising later that year. Soviet General Secretary Mikhail Gorbachev, who came to power in 1985, understood that reviving his nation's economy required reduced military spending and improved relations with the West. To bring this to pass, however, the Kremlin had to withdraw the Red Army from Afghanistan, abandon the Brezhnev Doctrine and its Eastern European clients, and negotiate strategic and conventional arms limitation agreements with the United States. Moreover, "glasnost," Gorbachev's term for allowing free speech and political discussion in the Soviet Union, and "perestroika," his concept that the Soviet government and economy needed restructuring, were patently incompatible with the Brezhnev Doctrine. As it was, Jaruzelski had never completely suppressed Solidarity, and when Poland's economic plight grew truly desperate in 1988 and the Soviets refused him more financial aid, he had no choice but to legalize Solidarity on 23 January 1989 and allow free elections that June. Polish voters gave Solidarity's candidates a thumping majority in the national parliament, and two years later Walesa replaced Jaruzelski as the country's president.

The tide of democracy spilled over into Czechoslovakia, Hungary, and East Germany. In 1991, East and West Germany were reunited. Even the rigid socialist dictatorships of Rumania, Albania, and Bulgaria were not immune. Three hundred and fifty thousand Red Army troops would be withdrawn from eastern Germany to Russia within four years, but because the Walesa government in Warsaw refused to allow the Red Army to operate in Poland, the Soviet troops in Germany no longer posed any threat to the West. In February 1991, Poland, Hungary, and Czechoslovakia, having long since suspended military cooperation with the Soviet Union, demanded that the Warsaw Pact be formally abandoned by April, and the Soviets agreed with nary a whimper.

Gorbachev was turning against Brezhnev's costly policy of supporting overseas clients. He directed Castro to withdraw the Cuban Army from Angola, Mozambique, and Ethiopia, where it had propped up brutal communist governments, and told him to end his support for the communist regime in Nicaragua and the rebels in El Salvador. Gorbachev reduced Soviet aid to Cuba so sharply that the Castro government started to breed rats to provide Cuban workers with meat. In 1991, the Red Army withdrew its last remaining troops from the beleaguered communist island.

The reverberations from eastern Europe were also felt in Asia. Increasingly isolated, North Korea's dictator, Kim Il Sung, opened talks on reunification with South Korea in 1991, which led to an agreement banning nuclear weapons from the peninsula. Few Koreans now doubted that the days of Kim's communist regime in Pyongyang were numbered. The upheaval in Europe also influenced politics in China, where students had occupied Beijing's main public area, Tiananmen Square, in May 1989, demanding an end to corruption and political reforms. Communist Party boss Deng Xiaoping was responsible for sweeping economic reforms in the 1980s, but his clique of aging autocrats was unwilling to relinquish political power. On 3 June 1989, Chinese army tanks rolled into Tiananmen Square and broke up the demonstrations. Soon after, many of the leaders were arrested or driven into exile. Bush, a former ambassador to China, was circumspect in dealing with the Tiananmen massacre on the grounds that the Beijing government rightly claimed a degree of political legitimacy its Warsaw Pact counterparts did not enjoy. While Bush condemned the use of force against the students and suspended arms sales to China two days after the massacre, he also dispatched his National Security Adviser, Lieutenant General Brent Scowcroft, and Undersecretary of State Lawrence Eagleburger to Beijing in mid-July and again in November to repair relations with Deng's villainous regime. Bush was rewarded the following year when China's envoy backed American diplomacy at the UN during the Persian Gulf War.

Gorbachev also slashed military spending, which he once claimed was consuming an astounding four-fifths of the Soviet Union's gross national product. "Our final goal is to have not a single Soviet soldier abroad by the year 2000," Soviet Deputy Foreign Minister Vladimir Petrosky told the UN in December 1989. The Red Navy, built largely to uphold Brezhnev's policy of international activism, was the first victim. Admiral Sergei Gorshkov, its aging patriarch, was retired, and funds for shipbuilding and steaming time were slashed. In 1991, Soviet warship construction nearly ground to a halt for want of materials. The Red Navy, which had developed a large naval base at Camranh Bay in Vietnam following the Chinese invasion of that country in 1979, began to withdraw ships and materiel from the facility in 1986 and dramatically cut back on overseas port visits soon after. Soviet submarine activity in the Atlantic and the Pacific was reduced by about 50 percent between 1984 and 1987. "There is no question that we have seen less forward naval deployments," Admiral William Crowe, the chairman of the JCS, declared. By 1991, the former Soviet fleet was virtually immobilized, and, with the Ukraine's declaration of independence, Moscow and Kiev argued about who owned the rusting Black Sea Fleet. "They have stripped the fleet of everything," complained the Red Navy minister on New Year's Eve. Within days, the CIA announced that the likelihood of a thermonuclear conflict with the former Soviet republics had "vanished." None of Gorbachev's cutbacks kept pace with the free-falling Soviet economy, which recorded an amazing 11 percent decline in gross national product in its last year. *Glasnost* and *perestroika* also exposed long suppressed ethnic and national passions among the various Soviet republics, and as early as 1989, Gorbachev had to rush to Lithuania in a fruitless bid to prevent the quarrelsome Baltic republics from declaring their independence from Moscow. "Soviet leaders will be preoccupied with domestic problems for years to come," CIA Director William Webster told Congress in 1990. "Gorbachev—and any successors—will have an even more pressing need than in the past few years to reduce the burden of defense spending and to transfer resources to civilian production."[2]

President Bush reacted cautiously to these stunning developments, uncertain how Gorbachev could withdraw the Red Army from Afghanistan, abandon the Eastern European empire, reform Soviet politics and the economy, and hold the Soviet Union together at the same time. Bush focused his European diplomacy on a series of arms control treaties and agreements that culminated in the summer of 1991 with a summit in Moscow where he and Gorbachev signed the historic START strategic arms reduction treaty.

In a dramatic announcement on 28 September 1991, Bush unilaterally ordered that nearly all medium- and short-range nuclear munitions be withdrawn from active service and destroyed. The Navy was to remove all nuclear ordnance and depth charges from the carriers and the nuclear warheads from its Tomahawk cruise missiles. "Under normal circumstances," Bush declared, "our ships will not carry nuclear weapons"—a policy first advanced by Admiral Frank B. Kelso II, who became CNO in 1990. The Air Force's B-52 bombers stood down, all tactical nuclear munitions and launchers were withdrawn from Europe, and the long debated, unpopular plan to erect a railroad-based MX strategic missile-launching system was scrapped. Insisting that "we can safely afford [these] steps," Bush nonetheless warned

Admiral Frank B. Kelso II.

An artist's concept of the controversial Boeing-Bell V-22 Osprey tilt-rotor aircraft.

that "the United States must maintain modern nuclear forces, including the strategic triad, and thus ensure the credibility of our deterrent."[3]

The end of the East-West strategic competition was symbolized when, on 9 November, the Poseidon missile–bearing submarine *Will Rogers* stood out of Holy Loch on her last deterrent patrol before returning to New London for decommissioning. Hers was the last patrol from the Navy base in western Scotland, which was about to be shut down. The culmination of a long-term American policy aimed at stabilizing and then ratcheting downward the level of the superpowers' nuclear arsenals, the START Treaty soon appeared to be an anachronistic icon of the Cold War, not a mainstay of what Bush labeled the "New World Order."

In August 1991, a coup against Gorbachev failed, and this led to the breakup of the Soviet Union, the downfall of socialism in Russia, and the close of the postwar East-West international competition. The dismemberment of the Soviet Union created an entirely new international politics for central Eurasia. Only China, North Korea, Cuba, and Vietnam remained under the thumb of traditional communist dictatorships. The disintegration of the Soviet Union and the end of the Warsaw Pact caused President Bush to redefine American foreign policy and national security interests. The NATO Alliance, originally aimed at checking Soviet aggression in Europe, was transfigured into a vehicle for more general European collective security with continued American and Canadian participation. NATO's unwillingness to use force to separate the opposing armies when war broke out in 1991 between newly independent Croatia and Serbia suggested the limits of this paradigm, however. Bush was eager to reiterate American support for its other traditional overseas security commitments, but the Soviet threat, which most of those obligations addressed, clearly no longer existed. How to articulate a new American foreign policy to deal with the New World Order and configure the military and naval forces to uphold it is one of the most vexing questions facing Americans in the last decade of the twentieth century.

Bush and the Democrats, who controlled Congress, agreed early in his presidency that defense spending should be cut, the differences separating them being more of degree than principle. Traditional Republicans were determined to reduce the national debt and the huge federal deficits of the Reagan years, whereas liberal Democrats, always on the lookout for ways to increase welfare spending, talked of a "peace dividend" being paid out of defense appropriations. The first round of post–Cold War cuts was announced soon after Bush met Gorbachev at sea off Malta in November 1989. Defense Secretary Dick Cheney proposed to reduce military spending by $180 billion over the next five years by trimming back the *Ohio*-class Trident ballistic missile–bearing submarine program, not building the Army's newest tank, limiting the scale of the SDI space-based early warning system, and retiring three *Forrestal*-class carriers and the last of the Navy's twenty-six old *Knox*-class frigates. The danger of this was, according to Admiral Carlisle Trost, the CNO, that "reducing carrier levels below fifteen without a concomitant reduction in our worldwide commitments will inevitably lead to a repetition of the descending readiness spiral of the 1970s. That period saw . . . the ships and aircraft upon which their effectiveness and our security depended were allowed to deteriorate to unsafe levels of readiness."[4]

It was unfortunate that the Navy was hamstrung by less than gifted leadership during these difficult years. Led by Admiral Trost, who became CNO in 1986, a clique of naval reactor engineers, whose training ill suited them to a broad view of events, occupied most of the Navy's important line billets. Trost foolishly responded to the winding down of the superpower rivalry by appearing to resist it. As late as December 1989, Rear Admiral Brent Baker, the Navy's chief of information, worried that "the Western world is reacting emotionally to the masterful public relations campaign of the Soviet Union" and urged fellow naval officers to "consider growing Soviet military capabilities." Indeed, many claimed that Trost was the last man in Washington to realize that the Cold War had ended. "None of the recent events in the political landscape of the world, including 'glasnost,' 'perestroika,' or 'new thinking' in the Soviet Union, and dramatic political transformation in Eastern Europe has in any way diminished or altered this nation's status as a maritime nation," he insisted in early 1990. The worst aspect of the end of the Cold War, he noted one year later, was that it was leading to "an effort to drive down the defense budget year after year." The crux of the problem was that Trost supported a naval policy bearing little relationship to the atomized international politics of the 1990s and beyond. Although confessing that "what we really need to do our job is a balanced force and a balance in capability," Trost allocated more than one-quarter of the Navy's 1990 five-year shipbuilding plan to laying down new *Seawolf*-class nuclear attack submarines and to completing the costly, poorly managed, largely unnecessary *Ohio*-class ballistic missile submarine program. Admiral Kelso, Trost's successor, inherited this unimaginative approach and early on evidenced little willingness to take charge of events by crafting an entirely new naval policy.[5]

Secretary Cheney's 1990 plan was to reduce military spending by one fourth within five years, although staving off even greater reductions hinged on both the White House and Congressional Democrats honoring a late-1990 federal budget agreement. The ink on this accord was barely dry when, reacting to the collapse of the Soviet Union, Senate Majority Leader George Mitchell proclaimed it no longer binding. Cheney asked for $278 billion for the Defense Department in 1992, a 25 percent reduction in spending in constant dollars as compared to 1985. The effect of this on the Navy was stunning. Bush and Cheney intended to reduce the fleet to the size President Carter had left it in 1981 by decommissioning nearly 100 vessels and building only 23 new ships and submarines. The 545 warships and major auxiliaries making up the fleet in 1990 would be reduced to 451 by 1994. This was to be accomplished by decreasing the number of attack carriers from fourteen to eleven, decommissioning all four *Iowa*-class battleships, and retiring sixty-six more ships and submarines by 1993 and another twenty-six a year later. The great battleship *Iowa*, one of the hallmarks of Navy Secretary John Lehman's 600-ship Navy program—modernized in 1984 at a cost of $435 million—was decommissioned on 25 October 1990. The *Iowa*, damaged by a mysterious explosion in her Number Two gun turret during a firing exercise, was retired early owing to the high cost of paying her 1,500-man crew.[6]

It was ironic that these drastic reductions in the number of ships in the fleet coincided with the appearance in 1991 of the 8,300-ton *Arleigh Burke*, the lead vessel in a new class of fleet air defense, guided missile–bearing superdestroyers. The *Burke* had a pad—but no hanger—for a Seahawk helicopter, a 5-inch gun, six torpedo tubes, and Tomahawk, Harpoon, and Standard missile launchers. She was a marked contrast to the 3,990-ton *Edson*, which was decommissioned in December 1988. This event marked the end of an era, inasmuch as the 30-year-old *Hull*-class destroyer was the last major U.S. Navy warship armed only with guns. The steel-hulled *Burkes*, centerpieces of the 600-ship Navy and first authorized in 1985, were to replace the *Knox*-class and the *Charles F. Adams*- and *Farragut*-class destroyers at a rate of five ships each year. Although originally advertised as costing less than a 1970s *Kidd*-class destroyer and two-thirds as much as a *Ticonderoga*-class cruiser, the *Burke* was the victim of so much mismanagement by the Navy and the Bath Iron Works that Congress would authorize only two ships in 1987. Three years later, the Bush administration, hoping to save money by mass production, asked for funds for ten *Burkes* in 1992 and another ten in 1994, but resistance on the Hill to the costly program was hardening and the Navy soon reduced the schedule to a total of fewer than thirty vessels. When the *Burke* was finally commissioned in 1991, after a two-year, multimillion-dollar delay, only a dozen ships of her class had been authorized and completing the entire program was in jeopardy.

Defense Secretary Cheney's budgets laid waste to Navy-Marine Corps aviation and the carrier force as well. He opposed acquiring the sea-based Boeing-Bell Osprey VSTOL assault amphibious transport plane and ordered that the venerable *Iwo Jima*-class helicopter assault ships, built between 1959 and 1970, be withdrawn from the fleet by 1994. As for the heavy carriers, the *Midway*, homeported in Yokasuka, Japan, since the mid-1970s, returned home in 1991 to be retired. The *Ranger* would be decommissioned the following year, and the *Saratoga* in 1995. Only the 1992 commissioning of the *George Washington*, the last of the *Nimitz*-class heavy, nuclear-powered carriers, partly offset this reduction in sea-based air strength.

The post–Cold War outlook for naval aviation was now bleak indeed, with a first-round reduction from thirteen to eleven carrier air wings. In 1989, Cheney also ordered an end to the acquisition of the F-14 Tomcat, although Congress forced the Navy to buy a few more fighters to keep Grumman Aircraft from bankruptcy. This meant that in the late 1990s, the Navy's fighter squadrons would be flying only the aging Tomcat, the controversial FA-18 Hornet, or the long promised, carrier-based version of the Air Force's Advanced Tactical Fighter, a trouble-plagued aircraft concept incorporating radar-evading stealth technology that was slow to get off the drawing boards. Owing to problems with the ATF fighter, Navy Secretary Lawrence Garrett proposed to order production of a new model of the F-14 Tomcat in December 1990, but Cheney vetoed this plan. Not only was a new generation of fighters not in sight, but also the Navy had to cancel the Lockheed P-7 patrol plane program, which had been scheduled to provide 130 aircraft to replace the 300 aging P-3 Orions. The evaporation of the Soviet submarine menace lessened the urgency of acquiring new antisubmarine patrol planes, but farsighted Navy men knew that the fleet would always need rugged land-based, long-range maritime bombers.

The Bush administration's January 1991 budget called for the abandonment of the Navy's A-12 stealth naval bomber program. Navy Secretary Lehman had ordered the purchase of this supposedly radar-immune bomber to replace the Navy's 300 aging A-6 Intruders after the loss of aircraft in the December 1982 attack on Lebanon's Bekka Valley and the 1986 Operation Eldorado Canyon against Libya. McDonnell Douglas and General Dynamics were awarded a $4.7 billion fixed-price contract to build 850 aircraft in January 1988, but they so badly handled the program that the first flight test date of 1990 had to be rescheduled to mid-1991. Although Vice Admiral Richard C. Gentz, the head of the Naval Air Systems Command, was aware of these troubles, he failed to explain them to Secretary Cheney when the issue came up in April 1990 at the Defense Department's Major Aircraft Review. Once Cheney learned what was afoot that December, he retired Gentz, sacked the equally culpable program managers, Rear Admiral John F. Calvert and Captain Lawrence G. Elberfield, and canceled the A-12 program altogether. "If we cannot spend the taxpayer's money wisely," Cheney told Congress, "we will not spend it." This stunning blow left the Navy with no prospects—other than the AD attack aircraft concept— for a new naval bomber to replace the A-6 Intruder, a plane designed in the early 1960s and already upgraded many times since. Both the F-14 Tomcat and the FA-18 Hornet might be used as bombers, but improving the Tomcat was very expensive and the Hornet's flying range was quite limited. Moreover, Congress had already rejected a 1988 plan to upgrade the Intruders with new engines, avionics, and radars in favor of building the A-12.[7]

Many of the troubles attending naval air policy in the late 1980s and 1990s might have been avoided, solved, or minimized had Reagan's last CNO, Admiral Trost, been more alert to the changing dimensions of national security and less parochial about the role of submarines in the reconfigured fleet. That Trost and his circle were immune to these new realities was demonstrated when he ignored aviators' objections and agreed with a 1989 JCS paper giving the Air Force the whiphand over military space policy by defining the Air Force as a "provider" and the Navy as a mere "user." Only a grand strategy embodying elements of flexible response and nuclear warfighting ever justified building the *Ohios* in the first place, but the logic behind such an approach receded quickly after 1985 and evaporated six years later. Nonetheless, Trost's clique insisted that the ballistic missile–bearing submarine program be completed. This meant that, in 1990, the Navy was planning to retire all sixteen of the older *Lafayette*-class Poseidon missile–bearing submarines and replace them with eighteen *Ohios*.[8]

Trost also initiated construction of the huge 9,150-ton reactor-powered *Seawolf* attack submarine, and Admiral Kelso continued that disastrous policy. Designed in the early 1980s to contribute to Lehman's Maritime Strategy by attacking Soviet ballistic missile–bearing submarines under the polar ice, the stealthy *Seawolf* had the most powerful reactor yet installed in a submarine and used British-designed jet pump propulsors to greatly increase her acoustic speed, the highest speed at which a submarine can steam and still operate her passive sonars. Defended by an immensely complex, fragile, computer-based sonar suite and armed with eight tubes amidships, the *Seawolf* was configured to fire Sea Lance antisubmarine torpedoes, Harpoon anti-ship missiles, or Tomahawk land-attack cruise missiles. The 600-ship Navy program envisioned a fleet containing 100 attack submarines, with the very fast *Seawolf* replacing the older, slower *Los Angeles*-class boats at a rate of three each year by the early 1990s. Congress, although unwilling to accept this level of construction while the Cold War was winding down, nonetheless authorized the first *Seawolf* in 1989, and a $726 million contract was signed with General Dynamics Electric Boat Division that December.

By that time, the program was already in trouble. Lehman had planned to divide the work between Electric Boat and the Newport News Shipyard—both to maintain the nation's shipbuilding industrial base and to reduce costs by competition. Newport News was scheduled to build the second boat in the class, but Navy Secretary Lawrence Garrett and Admiral Trost ended contract talks with Newport News in mid-1990, leaving Electric Boat with a virtual monopoly on Navy attack submarine construction. The *Seawolf* program was a model of such atrociously bad Navy and shipyard mismanagement that Admiral Bruce DeMars, a singleminded reactor engineer who headed the Naval Nuclear Reactor Command, confessed to Congress in July 1990 that he was unable to even estimate the cost overruns. A year later, informed speculation put the final price of the vessel at a stunning $4 billion. In mid-1991, for reasons that defy understanding, Secretary Garrett lobbied hard for the program on the Hill, and, with the bipartisan help of the Connecticut delegation, who needed the jobs for the state's depressed economy, persuaded Congress to allow the Navy to lay down a second submarine in 1993. Defense Secretary Cheney had already slashed the original program by half in August 1990, and he cut it again the following year. At best, Cheney's plan would leave the Navy with five or six *Seawolf*s and sixty *Los Angeles*-class attack submarines by the end of the decade. Mounting opposition within the Navy and on Capitol Hill to this debacle suggested that Congress would probably not continue the program, however, and Bush proposed to cancel it early the following year. By the end of 1991, it was apparent that both the *Ohio*-class and the *Seawolf*-class submarine programs constituted far too great an investment for a fleet whose only naval adversary had abandoned global adventurism and was allowing its ships and submarines to rust at anchor. In January 1992, Bush ordered an end to the production of the 475 kiloton W-88, the more advanced of two nuclear warheads carried by the Trident D-5 missile. This marked the first occasion since the onset of the Cold War that the Navy did not have nuclear munitions on order, a fitting end to the East-West strategic competition.

The evolution of Bush's New World Order policy occasioned by the end of the Cold War coincided with the adoption of the president's plans to dramatically reduce American military and naval strength. What was ironic was that Bush, more so than Reagan, wittingly implemented an interventionist foreign policy. In 1989, he ordered the Air Force at Clark Air Base in the Philippines to go on alert and prevent Philippine aircraft from assisting a coup against the newly elected democratic government of President Corazon Aquino. Three 7th Fleet Marine Amphibious Ready Groups were held offshore during the crisis to bolster

Bush's warning to the plotters that he would not allow them to topple the unsteady Aquino regime. Aquino repaid this debt by moderating her government's earlier, extreme demands for a renegotiated treaty leasing Clark Field and Subic Bay to the United States. The Air Force reluctantly decided to abandon the Philippines, however, when a volcanic eruption of nearby Mount Pinatubo virtually destroyed the air base and damaged the huge naval facility in 1991. Admiral Kelso wanted to rebuild the 7th Fleet base on Subic Bay and a new leasing arrangement was negotiated for that facility alone. In September, although the Philippine economy was in tatters and the Manila government desperately needed hard currency, mindless nationalists in the Manila Senate rejected the treaty embodying the lease. Several last-minute schemes to keep the facility open were suggested by Aquino, but the Navy announced before New Year's Day that the 7th Fleet would leave Subic Bay in 1992. Lacking a secure advance base in the Philippines, the 7th Fleet would have to pull back to Guam, greatly enlarge its facilities there, and lease berthing space at Singapore. Bush laid the diplomatic groundwork for this during a December 1991 trip to the Far East. Even with these adjustments, the loss of Subic Bay meant a reduced capacity to support naval operations in Asian waters and the Indian Ocean and also meant that deployments to the Arabian Sea–Persian Gulf area would be more dependent on the security of the vulnerable Suez Canal and the continuing friendship of America's sometime allies in the Middle East and East Africa.

Bush was also less reluctant than Reagan to use force to deal with Manuel Noriega, Panama's drug-dealing military dictator. Reagan had imposed economic sanctions on Panama in 1988 after Noriega ignored nationwide elections in which his hand-picked candidate was defeated. After several attempts to persuade him to go into exile or to kidnap him all failed, Bush instructed the U.S. Army's Southern Command to invade Panama in a police action in December 1989. In Operation Just Cause, 24,000 American troops spread out over the small country, overwhelmed and disarmed the poorly equipped Panamanian National Guard, and installed the previously elected government. Noriega was arrested and taken to a Florida jail to stand trial on charges of drug smuggling.

The American forces that intervened in the Philippines and Panama operated from long established bases adjacent to the scene of the action, but the United States would not often enjoy such a luxury. This was true in 1990 when the president ordered the Navy and Marine Corps into action in Operation Sharp Eagle during the Liberian Civil War. Sergeant Samuel Doe had seized power in Liberia in 1975 and established a military dictatorship, and under his bloody, autocratic rule, latent tribal and sectional rivalries intensified and the Liberian economy collapsed. Charles Taylor, whom Doe had ousted from his cabinet for corruption, organized an opposing coalition in neighboring Ivory Coast and invaded northern Liberia in December 1989. Doe's American-equipped army was thrashed by the rebels, and in fighting that ravaged the backward, impoverished country, Taylor's band forced the government's undisciplined troops to fall back on Monrovia, the capital.[9]

Alarmed by the savagery of both sides and the threat to foreign nationals in Liberia, President Bush ordered a task force built around the helicopter carrier *Saipan*, the LSD *Whidbey Island*, and the LST *Barnstable County* to a station off the Liberian coast in early June 1990. Over 2,800 American nationals, embassy personnel, and foreigners from thirty countries were rescued from the violent civil war. The generalized, unthinking brutality of the rebels' siege of Monrovia, Doe's rejection of an American offer to arrange for him to go into exile, and the advance of the rebel armies into the capital's suburbs now put the American embassy in danger. On 4 August, Captain A. M. Petruska in the *Saipan* was ordered to land the Marines, and at 0600 the small carrier turned into the wind and armed helicopter gunships lifted into the air to escort a flight of CH-46E Sea Knight helicopter transports, which were covered in turn by five Marine AV-8B Harrier jump jets. The choppers put ashore a 237-man Marine landing team that encircled the embassy and two Voice of America transmitter sites just outside the city and evacuated ninety-five American and foreign nationals to the ships offshore. Accomplishing this was dangerous and tricky because the Marines were under orders not to intervene in the bloody civil war.

Doe held out in the presidential palace until 9 September when he was captured by troops loyal to Prince Johnson, the leader of a second rebel band. Johnson had Doe brought before him, cut off his ears, nose, and other body parts, and had the dismembered corpse paraded through the streets of downtown Monrovia in a wheelbarrow. Soon after, the American ambassador arranged a shaky ceasefire between the two rival armed rebel bands. On 26 September, Marine helicopters transported more than a ton of emergency medical supplies from Freetown, Sierra Leone, to the embassy in Monrovia to assist in the reopening of a field hospital there that would treat some of the thousands of victims of the civil war. Some Liberian Army troops went over to Taylor's command while others aligned themselves with Prince Johnson, but the rivals maintained an uneasy truce until the Marines withdrew to their ships on 28 November. The Marines were replaced by an 8,000-man peacekeeping force organized by the 16-nation West African Economic Community, which imposed a second ceasefire. The West Africans, with American diplomatic support, arranged for Taylor and Johnson to share power in 1991 and write a new democratic constitution for their unhappy, war-torn land. Operation Sharp Eagle was a modern reminder of the historic need for naval forces to provide Americans overseas with some armed protection.

Bush's muscular foreign policy was nowhere more evident than in his handling of the Persian Gulf War, which erupted suddenly on 3 August 1990 when President Saddam Hussein ordered the Iraqi Army, which had massed on its southern border, to invade and occupy oil-rich Kuwait, Iraq's small, poorly defended neighbor. The dissolute Kuwaiti emir, Jabir al-Ahmad al-Sabah, had partly financed Iraq's eight-year war against Iran. When the fighting ended in 1988, the Baghdad regime was bankrupt and angry at Kuwait for insisting that OPEC hold down oil prices and that Iraq pay its war debts. The following year, Iraq disinterred a long-discredited claim to Kuwait's possession of oil-rich Bubiyan Island and began to menace Kuwait in early 1990. American Ambassador April Glaspie told Saddam Hussein in late July that the United States had no views on this issue. Clearly, it was not on the basis of her maladroit representation that Hussein decided to annex Kuwait, but Glaspie's obsequious, soft-spoken performance appeared at least to remove one obstacle to Iraq's adventure. On 18 July, Saddam Hussein publicly threatened to use force against Kuwait unless the emir reduced Kuwaiti oil production. Later that month, 100,000 Iraqi troops and 300 tanks were concentrated on the Kuwaiti border.[10]

Washington was now clearly concerned, and the White House announced on 25 July that ships of the Middle East Force—consisting of the 15,000-ton command ship *LaSalle*, the guided-missile cruiser *England*, the destroyer *David R. Ray*, and the frigates *Barbey, Reid, Vandergrift, Robert G. Bradley*, and *Taylor*—would exercise with vessels of the United Arab Emirates in the Persian Gulf. A day later, the Defense Department sent two Air Force aerial refueling tankers to the UAE. These diplomatic signals were entirely too weak and ambiguous, however, and to many it appeared that Saddam Hussein was bluffing so as to influence the ongoing OPEC price negotiations. The CIA reported that an invasion was "unlikely," but others in the American intelligence community thought that Baghdad's aims transcended purely financial concerns.

At 0300 on 3 August, the Iraqi Army crossed into Kuwait, an underpopulated country defended only by its poorly equipped, ill-trained 15,000-man National Guard. Iraqi artillery was shelling the capital, Kuwait City, three hours later, and the effete emir and his cowardly entourage fled to Saudi Arabia with unseemly haste. Within forty-eight hours, the fighting was effectively over, although a small, quickly-organized Kuwaiti resistance continued to harass the Iraqi occupiers for the next seven months. Baghdad annexed Kuwait in short order and referred to it thereafter as Iraq's nineteenth province. The exiled Kuwaiti regime and Saudi Arabia anxiously appealed to Washington for help.

Defending Kuwait's independence came under the rubric of the 1980 Carter Doctrine, a policy first enunciated at the time of the Soviet occupation of Afghanistan and the Iranian hostage crisis when Washington was fearful of a Red Army invasion of Iran. The Carter Doctrine had served as the basis of American support of Iraq during its eight-year war with Iran and of the defense of the reflagged Kuwaiti tankers in Operation Earnest Will in 1987 and 1988. Indeed, Bush had reaffirmed his administration's adherence to the Carter Doctrine in early 1989. That February, Moscow and Tehran proposed that the Red Navy's small flotilla and the U.S. Navy's Middle East Force—which now operated eight ships and six minesweepers—be simultaneously withdrawn from the Persian Gulf. This plan, intended to mask the collapse of Soviet global authority and diminish American influence in the Middle East, was promptly rejected by the new president. The Carter Doctrine assumed that the Cold War was ongoing and that the United States had a great stake in the Middle East oil supply. In mid-1990, however, American political and economic interests in Kuwait's fate were less unambiguous, and it

was thought that purely economic considerations provided no
clear justification for armed intervention. About 25 percent of
the oil imported by the United States came from the Persian
Gulf, and Iraq's annexation of Kuwait put Saddam Hussein in
control of a large fraction of the region's proven reserves and
placed his troops within 250 miles of the largest concentration of
Saudi oil fields. Nonetheless, oil was a fungible commodity
bought and sold freely on a world market, and the history of
OPEC proved that international price fixing seldom worked.
However, America's most important allies, Japan and the NATO
powers, were greatly dependent on Persian Gulf oil. Most European governments were reluctant, nonetheless, to become involved in defending Kuwait—the French agreed to provide
forces only after failing several times to arrange a compromise.
The Germans and Japanese bluntly refused to participate, although they helped finance the coalition buildup and operations. Furthermore, no treaty bound the United States to defend
either Kuwait or Saudi Arabia, the Bush administration had expressed no intention before 2 August of negotiating such agreements, and the recent record of American interventions in the
Middle East revealed something less than unalloyed success. To
some, the only immediate American concern was for the safety of
the hundreds of Americans trapped in Kuwait and the roughly
3,000 working in Saudi Arabia.

The prospects of success for American military intervention
in Kuwait were not encouraging. The Democrats, who had majorities on both sides of the Hill, reflexively opposed a muscular
foreign policy, and only one day earlier, on 1 August, Congressional Democrats had slashed the 1991 defense budget. Upon being told of the invasion on the 3rd, Georgia's Senator Sam Nunn,
the enigmatic chairman of the Armed Services Committee,
urged the president to use diplomatic and economic pressure,
not military action, to resolve the crisis. The Democrats were not
alone. On the day of the invasion, Bush delivered a prepared address at Aspen, Colorado, in which he called for a 25 percent reduction in American forces by 1995. It was not even clear that
Saudi Arabia or Kuwait's other Arab neighbors would welcome
the deployment of American forces to the Arabian peninsula.
The Arab League, called into session soon after the invasion, had
adjourned without condemning Iraq even though Iraq's action
violated the League charter, which forbade war by one Arab state

against another. Only Britain's formidable prime minister, Margaret Thatcher, was unshakable in support of an immediate movement of Western forces to the Persian Gulf.

Thatcher had no reason to be concerned about President Bush's stance. Although he would adduce secondary reasons for American actions in the Persian Gulf War, from the start Bush found a basis for his policy in the principle that resorting to force to redraw recognized international borders was an intolerable menace to the New World Order. He declared on the 5th that American forces would defend Saudi Arabia and that Iraq's annexation of Kuwait "will not stand." For the moment, informed observers characterized this as hyperbole, a gross underestimation of the commander in chief's grit. However, Bush was fully aware that most Americans supported a very stiff position on Iraq and overwhelmingly favored some military action.

A few years earlier, former Navy Secretary John Lehman had offered a model for a defensive military coalition to deal with such a situation, urging that the United States "begin at once the construction of a new framework for the coalition defense of the West, and the Persian Gulf should be its beginning point." Distressed over the uneven burden sharing during the 1987–1988 Earnest Will escort operations, Lehman admitted that only American naval and air forces were powerful enough to dominate the Gulf, but his model provided that the coalition partners contribute their own ships, aircraft, and divisions, and that "the financial burdens of maintaining this force structure should be borne on a basis proportional to the interests of the [oil] producing and consuming states." Making adjustments to fit the new international politics, Bush moved swiftly to put something not unlike Lehman's plan into place.[11]

Calling on carefully nurtured acquaintances with foreign leaders, Bush cobbled a twenty-eight-member international coalition bound by the common goal of compelling Iraq to withdraw from Kuwait by diplomacy, sanctions, and threats or, if that failed, by force. Secretary Baker, who had a close relationship with Foreign Minister Shevardnadze, convinced his friend that the Soviet Union should forsake Iraq, its longstanding ally, and give diplomatic backing to the United States. During the crisis, a heavy price was paid for holding the coalition together. When Red Army troops used gunfire in Vilnius to take over a building housing Lithuanian separatists, Washington complained but took no stiff action. Bush also looked the other way when, in October 1990, President Assad sent his army into Beirut to kill hundreds of anti-Syrian Lebanese and establish a pro-Syrian puppet government in Lebanon, thus ending the fifteen-year civil war there. Nonetheless, Assad held in check the Arab terrorists he controlled and provided a token force to the coalition army.

Conflicting interests and passions strained the coalition, but it remained intact throughout the Persian Gulf War. Bush first put it to use on 6 August, when coalition members and the Soviets and Chinese voted for a UN Security Council resolution condemning Iraqi aggression and calling on member nations to impose economic sanctions. That evening, Bush ordered General H. Norman Schwarzkopf, the commander in chief of the Central Command, which encompassed the Middle East and Southwest Asia, to implement Operation Desert Shield. Under this plan, Schwarzkopf was to shift his headquarters from Tampa, Florida, to Saudi Arabia and orchestrate the deployment of more than 1,000 aircraft and more than 200,000 soldiers and Marines to the Arabian peninsula. His first military objective was to defend Saudi Arabia from an Iraqi invasion. In the meantime, Defense Secretary Cheney had flown to Riyadh to negotiate an agreement with King Fahd under which American, British, and other coalition forces were to be deployed to his country.

On 13 August, in accord with the UN resolution, the president ordered Rear Admiral William A. Fogarty's Middle East Force to shut down all trade with Iraq in the Persian Gulf except for ships carrying food. To provide some muscle to deter Iraq from invading Saudi Arabia, the president again turned to the Navy. The carrier *Independence*, then exercising in the Indian Ocean with its six-ship battle group, was quickly ordered to the Gulf of Oman, and the guided-missile cruiser *Antietam*, which operated an Aegis air defense system, was detached and instructed to enter the Persian Gulf and operate there with Fogarty's growing force. The carrier *Eisenhower* and her consorts, the cruiser *Ticonderoga*, the destroyer *Scott*, the frigate *John Hall*, the ammunition ship *Suribachi*, and the oiler *Neosho*, were already in the Mediterranean, nearing the end of a six-month NATO deployment. On 8 August, these ships transited the Suez Canal and took station in the northern Red Sea, and the carrier began air operations over northern Saudi Arabia.

Once again, the vital margin was provided by the invaluable carriers. Captain Lyle G. Bien, who later served as the Navy's air liaison at Central Command Air Force headquarters, supposed that Saddam Hussein "had seen the Navy's carrier battle groups at work in the North Arabian Sea over enough years to have an appropriately high regard for their firepower." For the first two weeks of the Persian Gulf crisis, sea-based aircraft flying off the *Independence* and the *Eisenhower* provided the only serious military deterrent to an Iraqi invasion of Saudi Arabia. Meanwhile, on 3 August, the carrier *Saratoga*, her air wing reinforced with additional A-6 Intruder attack aircraft, put to sea with her escorts and the battleships *Wisconsin* and *Missouri* from Mayport, Florida, and shaped a course for the Red Sea. On the 15th, after receiving only a week's notice, another battle group, this one built around the carrier *Kennedy*, put out of Norfolk, her air wing including two squadrons of older A-7 Corsair heavy naval bombers rather than the newer, less capable FA-18 Hornets. The *Kennedy* steamed through the Strait of Gibraltar on the 22nd and reached the Red Sea in early September, relieving the *Eisenhower*, which returned home. In September, the carrier *Midway* and her reinforced cruiser-destroyer group, which had steamed from their home port of Yokosuka, Japan, through the Indian Ocean and into the North Arabian Sea, relieved the *Independence* in the Gulf of Oman. The Navy used ten of the eleven available carriers from August 1990 to March 1991 either in Desert Shield or as replacements for forward-deployed carriers. Two other carriers were in the shipyard being overhauled or improved. The Navy also ordered six nuclear-powered submarines to concentrate in the eastern Mediterranean and positioned the same number of submarines in the Indian Ocean.[12]

The Kuwaiti and Iraqi coasts seemed perfect sites for forced landings, but moving the necessary amphibious units from all over the world to the Persian Gulf theater was a herculean task. The Navy and Marine Corps already had plans on the shelf for such a rapid, large-scale deployment, however, and the JCS had studied the problem of countering Iraqi aggression in early 1990. On 5 August, the assault ship *Inchon*, carrying a Marine Expeditionary Group, the amphibious transport dock *Nashville*, the dock landing ship *Whidbey Island*, and the LSTs *Fairfax County* and *Newport* stood out of Norfolk en route to the Mediterranean. Led by the helicopter-Harrier carrier *Nassau,* one of five *Tarawa*-class stern-gate amphibious assault ships built during the 1970s, a task force of over twenty vessels—also including the dock landing ship *Gunston Hall* and the transport dock *Raleigh*—were called on in mid-August to transport the 40,000-man 1st Marine Expeditionary Force from three widely scattered bases at Kaneohe Bay, Hawaii; Camp Lejeune, North Carolina; and Twentynine Palms, California, to Saudi Arabia. The appearance of increasing numbers of Marines and amphibious ships in the Persian Gulf during Desert Shield caused Iraq's generals to concern themselves with coastal defense, and they positioned 50,000 troops, the equivalent of five divisions, just west of Kuwait City to repulse the Marines. By mid-January 1991, a 31-ship amphibious assault task force was on station in the Persian Gulf.

Schwarzkopf cleverly used the herd of 1,300 reporters in Saudi Arabia to deceive his Iraqi opponents. He encouraged them to publish stories about a 16,000-man Marine landing force that was supposed to be afloat in the Persian Gulf and to televise pictures of a mid-November 1990 landing exercise, Imminent Thunder, thus leading the Iraqis to believe that a landing was pending. Between 15 and 21 November, 1,000 Marines of the 1st Marine Expeditionary Brigade conducted field exercises ashore, 25 miles south of Kuwait. During that same week in the Persian Gulf, another 1,000 Marines conducted a well-publicized amphibious landing on the Saudi coast, 100 miles south of the Kuwaiti border, an exercise including mock air-to-air dogfights and close air support for the assault troops. This fixed the Iraqi's attention on defending the Kuwaiti coast and demonstrated that Schwarzkopf had no plans to send the Marines ashore in the first place.

The Navy's next problem was how to move the materiel necessary for the Desert Shield buildup to the faraway Persian Gulf. Concurrent with the passage of the infamous 1986 Goldwater-Nichols Act—which ennobled the Army–Air Force doctrine of "jointness" and gave the chairman of the JCS command authority over all unified commanders—Secretary of Defense Carlucci had approved an Army–Air Force scheme to create yet another huge unified bureaucracy. The Joint Transportation Command was to supervise the highly specialized work of the Navy's Military Sealift Command, the Army's Military Traffic Management Command, and the Air Force's Military Airlift Command. Despite the fact that Navy-managed shipping carried all but about 2 percent of the supplies and equipment transported by all the services, the Air Force prevailed in its demand that a four-star air general at Scott Air Force Base, Illinois, head this new, unwieldy establishment. Centralizing all American military logistics was an atrocious idea, made workable only by the expertise of Vice Admiral Francis R. Donovan, an astute, hard driving leader, who was the director of the Military Sealift Command during the Persian Gulf War.[13]

Donovan's problems were manifold. Lehman had launched a $7 billion sealift shipbuilding program in 1981 under which the Navy acquired thirteen maritime prepositioning ships to support three Marine expeditionary brigades, eight fast *Regulus*-class sealift ships, and two modern hospital ships. Moreover, the Navy had seventeen specially configured roll-on, roll-off cargo ships available on 2 August. Materiel, originally intended to support Carter's Rapid Deployment Force strategy, was stockpiled throughout the Persian Gulf and Indian Ocean areas. After Lehman left office in 1986 and Admiral Trost became CNO, however, little heed was paid to the sealift problem. Three years later, Congress appropriated $600 million for the Navy to buy sealift ships in 1990, but Defense Secretary Cheney chose to spend nearly half of this money on premiums for a military dependents' medical insurance program. Trost asked for no funds for sealift ships in 1990, preferring instead to build more *Ohio*-class and *Seawolf*-class submarines, but Congress appropriated $900 million for sealift anyway. Ten days after the Desert Shield emergency began, Donovan had four prepositioning ships in Saudi ports and, by 22 August, all eight *Regulus*-class fast sealift ships were en route to the Persian Gulf and both hospital ships were being made ready for deployment. By this time, Donovan had chartered nineteen more ships for Desert Shield. Within two weeks of the first sailing, more than 200,000 tons of materiel had been delivered to Saudi Arabia, and the Marines from Diego Garcia were ashore. Central Command's prewar plan supposed that some Army heavy forces would arrive in Saudi Arabia within three weeks and five divisions within two months, but by mid-September, only the Marines and the Army's light, highly mobile 82nd Airborne Division were in position. Moreover, of the forty-five Ready Reserve Force ships called up by the Department of Transportation's Maritime Administration for the Navy's use during crisis, only fourteen reached their loading ports on time. "Funding has been kept so low," complained Transportation Secretary Samuel Skinner, "that the readiness status of many Ready Reserve Force ships is not realistic." More than 100 Ready Reserve Force vessels were supposed to be available, but manning more than 42 proved to be impossible. The American merchant fleet had virtually collapsed in the 1970s, and Skinner claimed that "putting less than half of the emergency fleet in service has nearly exhausted the nation's supply of merchant mariners."[14]

The Navy's Military Sealift Command nevertheless delivered over three million tons of materiel to Saudi Arabia before the land battle began in February 1991, and at that time another 600,000 tons were en route. More than 100 different military and commercial transports were used to build up and support the American and coalition forces in Saudi Arabia, requiring a total of 179 cargo ships, including 38 tankers. Half of these were foreign vessels, but locating and chartering them proved to be one of Admiral Donovan's lesser problems. Saudi Arabia's fine, deep-water ports and a number of recently built airports facilitated the shipping of materiel, and her modern highways eased the Army's task of moving arms, troops, and stocks toward the Kuwaiti border. However, Vice Admiral Paul D. Butcher, the deputy commander of the new Illinois-based Joint Transportation Command, later warned, "It's dangerous to use Desert Shield and Desert Storm as a good example of what we can do in sealift because 47 percent of it came from foreign ships, which might not be available in the next emergency."[15]

Even as Donovan's impressive sealift plan was falling into place, Navy men were enforcing the UN blockade of Iraq. Owing to the ongoing tension between Iran and Iraq, Commander Kevin J. Cosgriff in the *Robert G. Bradley* had monitored the movements of American tankers in the Persian Gulf since his frigate had joined the Middle East Force. Soon after the UN resolution imposing economic sanctions was passed, Cosgriff was ordered to position his ship as the forwardmost element in the blockade operation. On 18 August, Cosgriff challenged the Iraqi tanker *Babr Gurgr*, fruitlessly negotiated with her master for two hours over the radio, and finally ordered that three shots be fired ahead of the vessel. On 4 September, Captain James A. Reid in the destroyer *Goldsborough* came upon the Iraqi cargo ship *Zanoobia* at dawn and received orders to board and search her. A six-man party, assisted by one of four Coast Guard teams working with ships on the blockade stations, inspected the freighter, found a cargo of tea, and demanded that the Iraqi, who was bound for Basra, head for another port. When he refused, Reid ordered his boarding party to take over the *Zanoobia*, and they escorted her to Muscat on the coast of Oman. When, ten days later, the *Al Fao* refused to allow a party from the frigate *Brewton* to board and inspect her cargo, Commander Craig Kennedy brought his crew to battle stations and ordered that shots be fired across the Iraqi tanker's bow. She still refused to stop, so the *Brewton* fired on her a second time, as did the accompanying blockade ship, the Australian frigate *Darwin*. The Iraqi master changed his mind. The American-Australian boarding party found the tanker empty, and Kennedy soon relayed an order allowing her to proceed to Basra. By the end of April 1991, coalition warships had challenged 9,800 merchantmen, boarded 1,370 of them, and forced 75 to divert to other ports. The commander of the 7th Fleet, Vice Admiral Stanley B. Arthur, who doubled as the Central Command's naval commander, was amazed that the Navy suffered no casualties during these interdiction operations. "Boarding ships is not an easy game at all," he said. "It's very dangerous, very risky."[16]

By the first week of November 1990, many reckoned that the UN sanctions and the naval blockade would probably not cause Saddam Hussein to withdraw his army from Kuwait. To enlist Arab support, he had attempted to confuse the issue by linking his aggression with the Arab-Israeli dispute over Palestine and by promising to restore Kuwaiti independence once Israel withdrew from the occupied Gaza Strip and the West Bank of the Jordan, an impossible condition. He made other conciliatory gestures, including the release of over 2,000 foreign nationals—among them about 900 Americans—trapped in Iraq and Kuwait at the time of the invasion. None of this overcame the hostility of those Arab and Muslim states courted by Bush and Baker: Egypt, Syria, Turkey, and the Gulf emirates. Their support for the American position, plus Iran's rigid neutrality, meant that Iraq was almost completely isolated. Jordan was the only exception. In violation of the UN sanctions, Jordan shipped food and arms to Iraq throughout the winter, although the quantities involved were not great enough to make much difference.

In late October, the president ordered General Colin Powell, the chairman of the JCS, to send more than 150,000 additional troops to Saudi Arabia to join the 230,000 already on the scene. "Everybody has done a superb job" in the Desert Shield buildup, noted Admiral Butcher, "but we ought to keep in perspective that we have the luxury of time . . . to land all that stuff with nobody firing a shot." Paralleling this move was the decision to send three new battle groups built around the carriers *Ranger, America,* and the recently commissioned *Theodore Roosevelt* to the Gulf in December. Georgia's Senator Nunn, the Democrat's spokesman on defense issues, objected, proposing instead a bizarre rotation scheme under which some troops, aircraft, and ships already in the theater would be brought home. The president ignored Nunn's complaints and turned again to the UN, urging the Security Council to pass a final resolution giving Iraq six weeks—or until 15 January—to withdraw from Kuwait. Once this deadline lapsed, member states might "use all necessary means" to compel the Iraqi Army to leave Kuwait. The resolution was passed on 29 November.[17]

The Desert Shield buildup continued in December, punctuated by a last-ditch attempt by Iraq to divide the coalition by ensnaring the United States in protracted negotiations beyond the UN deadline. On 9 January 1991, Baker flew to Geneva for a six-hour meeting with Iraqi Foreign Minister Tariq Aziz, but at the end of these talks the secretary of state announced resignedly, "I heard nothing today that suggested to me any Iraqi flexibility." This set the stage for a debate in Congress that began the following day. On 12 January, most Democrats, who opposed a muscular foreign policy and overseas military interventions, were led by Senator Nunn in voting against authorizing the president to go to war, but a handful of Israel's most devoted backers on the Hill and some Southern Democrats sided with the Republicans in support of the administration. Congress voted "to authorize the use of United States Armed Force pursuant to . . . [UN] Security Council Resolution 678" against Iraq under the terms of the controversial 1974 War Powers Act.[18]

The air campaign phase of Operation Desert Storm began on 17 January 1991 when Saddam Hussein, who might have prevented a war and divided the coalition by agreeing to a staged withdrawal and negotiations at the last minute, unaccountably allowed the UN deadline to lapse. Bush had directed that General Schwarzkopf be allowed to conduct the war without interference from Washington, with the result that the theater commanders selected the targets and decided when to strike and restrike them based on local conditions. The contrast between Secretary of Defense Dick Cheney's support of his commanders in the field and Robert McNamara's sorry handling of the halfhearted air war against North Vietnam could not have been sharper. In late 1990, Schwarzkopf had negotiated an agreement with the British, French, Egyptian, and other coalition commanders giving him effective strategic direction of the campaign. Air operations were planned and orchestrated by the Central Command air commander, Air Force Lieutenant General Charles Horner. During the Desert Shield buildup, the Air Force had organized a 1,000-man Riyadh-based headquarters, established an intricate satellite-based communications network linking the Air Staff in the Pentagon with its forces in Saudi Arabia, and brought in a mammoth air logistics command to service its many land-based aircraft. Horner had six months to devise and revise his copious air plan, and this "enabled Red Sea and Persian Gulf naval forces to learn to operate within this system," wrote Rear Admiral Riley D. Mixson, who commanded a Red Sea carrier battle group. "I do not know of a better way to orchestrate 2,000–3,000 sorties per day from the four services and the numerous allied air forces participating."[19]

Horner's first objective was to achieve absolute air control over Iraq by defeating the weak opposing air force and by silencing Saddam Hussein's air defenses, which consisted mostly of Soviet systems and some Western hardware. Because American forces trained to operate against Soviet radars and missiles and because the Soviets had recently provided Washington with information about their systems, Horner possessed an unusually rich assessment of his opponent. The air plan's second objective was to cripple Iraq's communications system and thereby sever Baghdad's ability to control and reinforce its armies. Lastly, coalition aircraft would turn their attention to isolating the Iraqi Army in southern Iraq and Kuwait by dropping nearly thirty bridges spanning the Tigris River and by destroying the adjacent rail network and then to bombing the enemy forces in southeastern Iraq and Kuwait. Even so formidable a figure as Rear Admiral Anthony Less, the Deputy CNO for Plans, greatly overestimated the Iraqi defenses. Drawing on his experience with Saddam Hussein's air

force when he commanded the Joint Middle East Task Force during the last year of the Iran-Iraq War, Less asserted that "Iraq is
clearly not a pushover." Few predictions of what was about to
happen were as far off the mark.

Sea- and air-launched land attack missiles played an important role in Horner's Desert Storm air plan. In March 1986, the
Navy had taken delivery of a new long-range, land-attack version
of the Tomahawk. With the onset of the Desert Shield buildup, a
rush order was placed for more missiles, and when the air battle
began the Navy had taken delivery of about 1,000 Tomahawks.
General Horner assigned the most important, best defended
fixed targets to the battle groups' Tomahawk sea-launched cruise
missiles. In the first few hours of the air battle, fifty-two Tomahawks were fired from battleships, cruisers, and destroyers. The
battleships had eight box launchers capable of firing thirty-two
Tomahawks. The *Ticonderoga*-class cruisers had two 61-tube vertical launchers, and a ship could carry anywhere from 25 to 122
missiles. Of the first fifty-two Tomahawks launched, all but one
hit their targets. The battleships *Missouri* and *Wisconsin* and ships
from their battle groups fired over 100 Tomahawks during the
first twenty-four hours. The first shots were aimed at the largest
generating plants of the enemy's electrical utility and succeeded
in disrupting Iraqi communications, shutting down several important defensive systems, and causing immense confusion within Saddam Hussein's higher command. So that the Navy's nuclear submariners might enjoy bragging rights to having been in the
fight, if only marginally, the *Louisville*, a submerged *Los Angeles*-
class attack submarine, fired a Tomahawk at a target in western
Iraq from her station in the eastern Mediterranean. Nuclear-
powered attack submarines in the Red Sea and Mediterranean
also fired undersea-launched Tomahawk missiles, probably the
most foolish, least cost-effective ordnance delivered in the modern history of naval warfare. Most of the Navy's Tomahawk missiles could not carry a conventional warhead large enough to seriously damage bunkered targets, however.

"The liberation of Kuwait has begun," the White House announced on nationwide television on the morning of 17 January.
A few hours earlier, the guided missile cruiser *San Jacinto* fired
the first wartime Tomahawk against hard command and control
targets in Baghdad, and soon after, the battleship *Wisconsin* fired
a Tomahawk barrage. Nine American warships fired cruise mis-

siles on the initial day of the air war, the first targets coming under attack by aircraft at about 0300. Coalition warplanes followed
the missiles into Iraqi airspace. Although they carried only two
small bombs, Air Force stealth F-117 fighter-bombers were the
only aircraft to attack targets in Baghdad on the first day of the
air war because they needed no escorting planes. While these
stealth aircraft were invisible to the inept Iraqis, the British
frigate *London* had no trouble detecting an outbound F-117 over
the Gulf and her older Sea Wolf ship-to-air missile system flaw-
lessly locked onto this target at a range of twelve miles, thus suggesting that U.S. Air Force hyperbole had greatly overrated the
plane's radar-evading technology. Early success in the air campaign was uniform, owing to superb air battle management, computer-based precision air navigation, guided bombs, night vision
equipment, electronic jamming, and the extraordinary skill of
the aircrews. Saddam Hussein's "air force isn't fighting," Captain
Bien concluded the next morning. "Maybe we aren't going to see
what he has." After only thirty-six air-to-air engagements with
coalition warplanes, the Iraqi Air Force quit the battle and hid on
the ground. With no planes aloft, the enemy had no means of
luring coalition fighters or bombers into land-based missile or
antiaircraft artillery gunfire traps. On 29 January, a flight of
Iraqi aircraft took off and, to the amazement of the coalition
commanders, sped to the east and landed at Iranian airfields.
American diplomats suspected that Saddam Hussein intended to
save his air force for postwar use or had arranged some sinister
deal with Tehran, but Iran interned the planes, eventually numbering over 150, for the remainder of the war.[20]

When Desert Storm erupted on the 17th, the *Midway* and
Ranger battle groups were on station in the Persian Gulf with the
battleships *Wisconsin* and *Missouri*, while the carriers *America*,
Kennedy, and *Saratoga* were in the Red Sea. The new nuclear-powered carrier *Theodore Roosevelt* was also in the Red Sea on 15 January, but Admiral Arthur held her in reserve for the moment.
On the first day of the air war, Lieutenant Commander Mark Fox
and Lieutenant Nick Mongillo, flying FA-18 Hornets off the
Saratoga, were streaking for their targets deep in Iraq when they
chanced upon two Iraqi Air Force MiGs. Dispatching the opposing aircraft with a combination of Sidewinder and Sparrow air-to-
air missiles, Fox and Mongillo continued on to their target, an
airfield, which they damaged with four 2,000-pound iron bombs.

Also flying off the *Saratoga* was Lieutenant Commander Michael S. Speicher, whose plane was splashed by an Iraqi surface-to-air missile during an early bombing raid, the first American combat casualty of Desert Storm. At 0120 on the 17th, ten A-7 Corsairs and six A-6E Intruders flew off the carrier *Kennedy* in the Red Sea, followed soon after by four F-14 Tomcats, four EA-6B Prowler jammers, four KA-6D tankers, and an E-2C Hawkeye electronic warfare aircraft. During the campaign, the Intruders often flew from the carriers to Saudi air bases where they were refueled and armed with a full load of twenty-eight 500-pound bombs. The need to land and refuel or to depend on airborne tankers worried Admiral Mixson. "The Navy is becoming hostage to land-based Air Force tanking for . . . [bombing missions] 200 miles from the battle force." Captain Bien admitted that "the Navy felt slighted in [land-based] tanker distribution," which, he added, "argues strongly for more capable carrier-based tankers, and ultimately U.S. Navy or Marine Corps KC-10 tankers."[21]

Laser-guided weapons constituted a majority of the guided bombs dropped on Iraq during Desert Storm, but the Navy was short of laser-guided bomb kits and so could not use them freely. However, the Navy's old lethal, electro-optical "fire-and-forget" Walleye bomb was available in large numbers. Navy attack airplanes dropped every bridge they attacked on the first try, with one exception; that bridge, shrouded by bad weather, had to be attacked again the next day. Bombing at low altitudes, between 3,500 and 5,000 feet, to evade enemy radars and fighters, one A-6 Intruder was splashed and another badly damaged by Iraqi anti-aircraft artillery on the first day of the air campaign. Inasmuch as the Iraqi Air Force was proving to be much less of a threat than predicted and the Iraqis possessed only unguided surface-to-air missiles, Arthur decided—against considerable opposition from his pilots—that most subsequent attacks would be flown at about 12,000 feet. Intruders from the *Kennedy* and the *Saratoga* were armed with the Navy's new laser-guided, stand-off SLAM missile, a land-attack version of the Harpoon, which carried a 488-pound payload over 100 miles to the target. When Desert Shield got under way, there were about 550 Harpoon-SLAM missiles in U.S. Navy's inventory. Tactics called for the A-6 Intruder to drop the SLAM and an accompanying A-7 Corsair to control the missile's flight to her target. Early on 18 January, aircraft from the *Kennedy* successfully launched the first two SLAMs at heavily defended targets well inside Iraq. Overall, however, about 95 percent of the ordnance delivered by the air forces during the entire conflict consisted of old-fashioned iron bombs. The Navy's role in the air campaign was significant. As of 30 January, Navy aircraft had flown about 10 percent of all coalition sorties, but by the end of Desert Storm, Navy planes, constituting about 16 percent of the total Allied combat air force, had flown over 20 percent of the total strike sorties.

Land-based Silkworm anti-ship missiles had been a U.S. Navy concern since the tense 1987 confrontation with Iran, and inasmuch as Iraq also possessed these Chinese-built weapons, they were one of the carriers' first targets when the air war began. Owing to the difficulty of locating these missiles' small mobile launchers—akin to the problem of finding the mobile Scud launchers—this phase of the air campaign was not wholly successful. On 30 January, A-6 Intruders had attacked and destroyed two Silkworm launchers that had been moved recently to the central Kuwaiti coast and were menacing the coalition warships in the Gulf. Not all the Silkworm sites were found, however, and on 24 February the Iraqis fired two Silkworms at the *Wisconsin* while she was shelling coastal installations. The first weapon fell short into the water, and the second was intercepted and destroyed in mid-air by a Sea Dart ship-to-air missile fired by the British destroyer *Gloucester*, then serving as the battleship's escort. Because this enemy launcher had exposed its position, it was easily attacked and destroyed by A-6 Intruder naval bombers from the nearby Persian Gulf carrier battle group.

Horner's air plan, issued daily in a volume that often exceeded 300 pages, was flawed in many respects. The prewar fear of the enemy air force was unreasonable. It was well known that for air defense Iraq did not rely on her fighters, which had performed poorly against Iran, but rather on her land-based mobile and fixed surface-to-air missiles and antiaircraft artillery. Clearly, Horner was careful to give the Air Force pride of place wherever possible. Early on, carrier-based fighters were not assigned to any of the major combat air patrol stations in Iraq, and Horner ignored Navy protests until the fifth week of combat when he relented and assigned the long inactive Basra station to the carrier air wings. The Air Force's overly centralized, rigid, inflexible system for managing the air war also made it difficult for the carriers to devote flights to highly mobile naval targets such as Iraqi minelayers. The minelayer *Aka*, a converted Iraqi salvage tug that laid several minefields, was located off the Faw Peninsula by an orbiting satellite, but days elapsed before this intelligence was relayed to the naval section of Horner's Riyadh headquarters and his Air Force planners agreed to put the ship on the Desert Storm target list. By this time, the *Aka* had steamed up the Shatt-al-Arab and was never hit.

Within twelve hours of the eruption of the air war, the Iraqis counterattacked in a wise attempt to alienate the Arab nations from the coalition by firing seven Scud medium-range ballistic missiles against Tel Aviv and Haifa. Saddam Hussein hoped that the Israelis would retaliate and that this would cause Egypt and Syria to turn against the coalition. Bush reacted quickly. On the 19th, U.S. Army Patriot missile batteries with American crews arrived in Israel and established a remarkably reliable antimissile defense system. They were followed by Undersecretary of State Eagleberger, who pointed out to Prime Minister Yitzhak Shamir that there were no targets in Iraq that the Israelis might attack that were not already being struck by the Desert Storm air campaign. To make certain that the Israelis did not enter the air war, the United States refused to share its aircraft recognition codes with them. Although the unreliable Scuds posed no military threat to coalition forces, their political value was considerable, with the result that Washington ordered General Horner to locate the fixed and mobile launchers and destroy them. Going after the Scuds met with only mixed success, reduced the level of bombing of Iraq, and lengthened the air phase of the offensive, but these missiles had no effect on the outcome of the war.

By the 23rd, coalition air forces had established complete "air superiority" over the Iraqi Army in the Kuwaiti Theater of Operations, an area that included Kuwait and the southeastern third of Iraq. On 21 January, Iraqi television broadcast pictures of several American and British POWs, including Lieutenant Jeffrey Zaun, a Naval Academy graduate whose A-6 Intruder from the *Saratoga* had been shot down during a bombing mission. Most were badly treated. Zaun's grotesquely disfigured image was televised constantly over the next few days and appeared on the cover of *Time* magazine. Americans were aghast. The nascent, homegrown antiwar movement, never strong, collapsed, and its liberal sympathizers in Congress were silent and contrite thereafter. As he had throughout the crisis, Bush both shared and shaped the national mood, reminding Iraq of its obligations under the Geneva Convention and pointing out to Americans and their coalition partners that Saddam Hussein's conduct of the war was unspeakably immoral.

At the start of the war, the Iraqi Navy consisted of about fifty *Osa*-class missile patrol boats, some converted mine-laying craft, and an assortment of other small vessels of miscellaneous pedigrees. On 17 January, the carriers *Ranger* and *Midway* launched A-6 Intruders, which attacked the Iraqi naval base at Umm Oasr and sank three Iraqi *Osas* with Harpoon antiship missiles. While the Iraqis might have used their missile boats against American warships in the northern Persian Gulf, their Navy instead occupied itself in mine-laying sorties until the 29th. On that day, however, an Iraqi formation consisting of a minesweeper, two captured Kuwaiti missile boats, and three *Polnochny* landing ships, each carrying about 175 soldiers, entered the northern Persian Gulf, possibly to effect a landing on the Saudi coast to support a concurrent Iraqi Army cross-border foray against the Saudi Arabian town of Kafji. Intruders sank all three amphibious craft off the Shatt-al-Arab. Then, the next day, more than twenty Iraqi ships and craft entered the Persian Gulf in an attempt to escape to Iran. All but one of the enemy vessels, an *Osa*-class missile patrol boat that got away, were sunk off Būbiyān Island by Intruders from the carriers *Midway* and *Ranger* and by Lynx and SH-60B helicopters from U.S. Navy and British ships in the Gulf. "They got one boat over," according to Arthur, "but it had a lot of holes in it by the time it got there." The British fired Sea Skua and Penguin air-to-surface missiles, and the Americans fired Harpoon anti-ship missiles and dropped laser-guided and free-falling bombs. The action puzzled Admiral Arthur, however, as he could find "no explanation why those [Iraqi] ships carrying Exocet and Styx anti-ship missiles went to the bottom, rather than try for a lucky hit."[22]

The Central Command now classified the Iraqi Navy as having been defeated. Twenty-three Iraqi naval vessels had been sunk and thirty-four damaged. Commander Mark Lawrence, the carrier *Theodore Roosevelt*'s intelligence officer, bragged, "We have done our job of clearing the coastline and now we are going to move in close." Contrary to the Navy's critics in Congress and the press, the narrow confines of the northern Persian Gulf proved to be an ideal environment for the capital ships. "We were tucked up into a corner of the Gulf," recalled Arthur, "and we knew where the threat had to come from." The result was that the battleships "were in their element."

On Friday, 18 January 1991, Commander Dennis G. Morral in the guided missile frigate *Nicholas* conducted a night attack on a complex of nine Iraqi-held oil platforms off the Kuwaiti coast being used to launch missiles and fire at Navy aircraft flying off the carriers in the Gulf. "We snuck in and surprised them," he said. The ship, her running lights off and radars shut down, closed on the site. Her helicopters ascended, fired guided rockets at two of the most well defended platforms, and destroyed the Iraqis' sandbag and plywood shelters. The choppers then landed and took the surrender of twenty-three frightened Iraqi soldiers. On 3 February, Morral in the *Nicholas* used her high-resolution sonars to evade nearby mines as he guided the battleship *Missouri* into position off the southern Kuwaiti coast. Recommissioned in 1986 at enormous cost, the *Missouri* fired her first shells of the war that day. Using a small, pilotless, radio-guided Pioneer drone for spotting, her 16-inch batteries destroyed Iraqi Army command bunkers on the northern edge of the Kuwait-Iraq border. She fired eleven shells at an Iraqi artillery battery and two radar sites. The next day, fifty-four rounds were expended on an enemy surface-to-air missile battery, artillery positions, and another radar site. Surely the most unusual incident of the entire war occurred when twenty-eight terrified Iraqi soldiers threw down their arms and surrendered to a Pioneer hovering overhead. Another target, just north of the Saudi-Kuwait border, was an Iraqi command bunker, which was located with the help of a Pioneer drone and then showered with seven 2,000-pound shells. The *Wisconsin* took over on the 7th, aiming at an artillery battery in southern Kuwait, which the Defense Intelligence Agency had identified as being capable of firing chemical-biological shells known to be in Saddam Hussein's inventory.[23]

Admiral Arthur, fearful of the danger of free-floating mines to the coalition warships, neutral merchantmen, and tankers in the Gulf, had recommended in mid-December 1990 that the Middle East Force be allowed to attack and sink Iraqi ships that were laying mines at the rate of forty to eighty each night in international waters off Kuwait. Schwarzkopf endorsed Arthur's plan, but General Powell in Washington rejected it on the grounds that Iraq would claim that her vessels were mining their own waters and that it might precipitate an unwanted Iraqi invasion of Saudi Arabia. Arthur was not surprised. Powell was the only administration official to oppose Desert Shield in the first place, and his orders to Arthur revealed the utter bankruptcy of the Army's "jointness" orthodoxy. "The only people who worry about mines are sailors," the admiral noted. "And everybody else had difficulty identifying with them." Arthur apparently understood Powell's reasoning but disagreed with the decision not to go after the enemy aircraft. Nations "laying mines in international waters are involved in an act of war," he snorted. "In my professional Navy career, we've never gone and sunk a guy laying mines the first shot out of the gun," he added. "We always sort of pace around the camp fire. So we sometimes buy ourselves into a problem by not exercising our right[s]." Moreover, Arthur was told by the generals to limit the northward movement of his air patrols in the northern Gulf so as not to appear overly provocative, and this prevented him from observing Iraqi mining operations and fixing the dimensions of the minefields. "We were trying to see the minefields from afar as best we could," he recalled. The fleet staff estimated the layout of the minefields, but their work was in error by about three miles, a miscalculation that contained the seeds of tragedy.[24]

The Navy's unhappy experience during Operation Earnest Will made Admiral Arthur especially aware when the Desert Shield buildup began that his ships would have to deal with mine warfare. Early in the buildup, the Dutch transport dock *Super Servant III* was contracted to ship the light, slow minesweepers *Avenger, Adroit, Impervious,* and *Leader* to the Gulf where they were joined by six MH-53E minesweeping helicopters, which towed sleds that dragged cutting wires through the water. The *Avenger*s used an unmanned miniature submarine with cutters to sever a mine's anchor cable and an explosive to destroy the mine. The other three older minesweepers operated wire sweeps to cut a mine's anchor cables. The NATO allies contributed sixteen minesweepers to the coalition's Persian Gulf Force. With the defeat of the Iraqi Navy, coalition warships closed on the Kuwaiti coast and appeared off the Faw Peninsula. "We knew that they were very, very near the mine fields, possibly in them," recalled Arthur. "We were taking a risk. We knew we had to get into that area to do the preparation for the possible amphibious landing and certainly for the gunfire support we wanted to do."[25]

On the morning of 18 February, Captain Bruce McEwen in the 18,000-ton helicopter carrier *Tripoli*, the flagship of the mine-clearing task group, was steaming in a shipping channel that McEwen had been told had been cleared of mines. The ship was operating her six Sea Stallion minehunting helicopters to hunt and sweep a minefield known to consist of three rows of mines, each separated by about one mile, but there were no minesweeping craft ahead of the vessel to protect her. At 0400, the *Tripoli* collided with a 300-pound moored contact mine designed to detonate when a ship sailed over it at low tide but not high tide. The resulting explosion tore a 20-foot hole in her hull about 10 feet below the waterline and left the carrier dead in the water for more than seven hours. The helicopter mine hunting in this area was discontinued indefinitely, and the *Tripoli* was towed to Bahrain for repairs. Oddly enough, many ships safely transited the area of this minefield before and after the *Tripoli* was damaged.[26]

A short time later, on the morning of the 18th, Captain Edward B. Hontz in the 9,600-ton *Princeton*, a two-year-old *Ticonderoga*-class Aegis cruiser costing over $1 billion, was operating in company with the British destroyer *Manchester* and the guided missile cruiser *Horne* about 50 miles off the Kuwaiti coast. "We received an intelligence report that indicated a possible Silkworm missile site was being activated along the coast of Kuwait," he recalled. "Our job at that time was to provide [missile screen] protection for the minesweeping and naval gunfire support forces" and "we took up a position that was . . . in a direct line between them and the Silkworm site." While fighters from the nearby attack carriers provided combat air cover against the Iraqi Air Force, British gun and missile–bearing helicopters defended the minesweeping vessels against sorties by enemy gunboats. Because the Iraqis had planted both surface contact mines and ocean floor pressure, magnetic, and acoustic mines, this force had to locate and detonate them one at a time. At 0716, Hontz was using the loudspeaker to warn his crew "to be on the lookout for mines because the *Tripoli* had hit a mine just hours earlier." At that very moment, the *Princeton* steamed over a 1,100-pound magnetic mine lying on the ocean floor, a weapon with a counter preventing it from being triggered by minesweeping sleds. Its detonation created a huge gas bubble that shot to the surface, struck the ship, and triggered a second mine, which exploded seconds later about 300 yards off the *Princeton*'s bow. The first weapon twisted the cruiser's hull aft and damaged half of her power plant, forcing Hontz to shut down one of her two gas turbine engines. While some would later point out that the ship's Aegis radars and missiles functioned after the attack, she was nonetheless badly damaged and three men were injured. The minesweeper *Adroit* soon arrived with the rescue craft *Beaufort*, which towed the *Princeton* to the port of Dubai for major repairs. "We can do our piece of the minesweeping business a lot better than we have," Arthur reflected sadly.[27]

The Navy was ready to land the Marines on the coast of Kuwait, Būbiyān Island, or the Faw Peninsula when the ground war began on 23 February 1991, even though that would mean risking more casualties from the lethal mines. "I had the lanes swept to put [the battleships] into positions, which was the first thing that I needed to do. . . . We also had that lane opened up to start the first amphibs in. And basically I had more minesweepers to do other lanes if we decided to go," Admiral Arthur recalled. Lieutenant General Walter Boomer, who commanded the Marines in the theater, favored a landing, but Schwarzkopf's Army-led headquarters did not, and so General Powell in Washington made the decision. Although Admiral Kelso, the CNO, and General Al Gray, the Marine Corps Commandant, wanted a landing, Powell ruled against it. Because the Iraqi Army put up little resistance to the coalition's ground offensive, the question of a landing soon lost its immediacy. When the ground war began, "the decision was we don't want to perform an amphibious landing unless General Boomer's Marines got into trouble," Arthur explained. "We had several landings and several feints all planned. And as time unfolded you had to say, 'OK, we're not going to do this one but to keep this option open.' "[28]

By mid-February, the Iraqi regime understood that its military position was perilous. The coalition air campaign—which was effectively unopposed soon after its inception—had isolated the Kuwaiti theater, destroyed most of Iraq's means of communication and resupply, demoralized the Iraqi Army, and greatly reduced its ability to maneuver in the open. American commandos, including Navy SEAL teams, now under another unwieldy, highly centralized, stateside, Army-dominated Joint Special Forces Command, were operating with near immunity behind Iraqi lines. Coalition warplanes had flown over 100,000 sorties as of 17 February, losing only 27 planes and 1 helicopter. Two days earlier, Saddam Hussein had offered to pull out of Kuwait, but Bush called this a "cruel hoax" because it was still linked to a concurrent Israeli withdrawal from occupied Palestine. Hussein turned in desperation to his sometime Soviet ally, sending Foreign Minister Aziz to Moscow for talks with Gorbachev on the 18th. Three days later, Gorbachev and Aziz announced a peace plan providing for an Iraqi withdrawal from Kuwait in three weeks, but Bush rejected the scheme on 22 February and demanded that Iraq accept the UN resolution, repatriate the coalition POWs within forty-eight hours, and complete its withdrawal from Kuwait within seven days. Upon learning that the Iraqis were setting fire to Kuwait's oil wells and massacring the residents of Kuwait City, Bush fixed a deadline of 2000 on 23 February for the withdrawal to start. This deadline came and went with no sign that the Iraqis intended to pull out.

"Our strategy [in the land battle]," General Powell announced in Washington, "to go after this army is very, very simple. First we're going to cut it off, and then we're going to kill it." Using laser-guided bombs, British and American aircraft had severed the bridge system connecting the northern and southern banks of the Tigris and Euphrates rivers, thus successfully obstructing the flow of supplies from the Baghdad area to the Kuwaiti theater. Intelligence reported that the Iraqi Army in Kuwait and southern Iraq consisted of roughly 550,000 troops spearheaded by Saddam Hussein's elite Republican Guard, but the air campaign had thoroughly isolated and demoralized these men. "We were pretty sure that nut was going to crack," Admiral David Jeremiah, the Vice Chairman of the JCS, told Congress on 12 March, "but we didn't know when." Nonetheless, when asked how long the war would last, the White House responded on 24 January, "probably months," and even Secretary Cheney claimed in early February that "this operation is likely to run for a long period of time." Clues as to the deteriorating condition of the Iraqi Army were fast accumulating, however. On 27 January, for instance, six FA-18 Hornets from the *Theodore Roosevelt* attacked Republican Guard positions inside Iraq and encountered almost no air defense opposition. "That pretty much surprised us," observed Commander Mark Lawrence. Thereafter, coalition bombers attacked the Iraqi Army almost at will.[29]

Bush and Cheney had given Schwarzkopf two missions: to evict the Iraqi Army from Kuwait and destroy as much of its equipment as possible. Coalition forces in the theater now included roughly 540,000 Americans of all services and another 200,000 British, French, Arab, and other allied troops. Schwarzkopf's strategy for the land battle had three main elements. First, while the amphibious task force in the northern Persian Gulf glued the enemy's attention on the Kuwaiti coast and the exposed Faw Peninsula and a small French force covered the westernmost desert flank, the Army's XVIII Corps, secretly repositioned to the west of the Kuwaiti border during the air campaign, crossed into Iraq and advanced rapidly north. Paratroopers of the 101st Airborne Division helicoptered 300 miles deep into Iraq, established a forward base to prevent any Iraqi forces from moving southwest, and raced up to the Euphrates. Second, the British 7th Armored Brigade and the U.S. Army's VII Corps simultaneously crossed into Iraq and moved north on a line roughly parallel to Kuwait's western border. Southwest of Basra, these troops crashed into and easily defeated the elite Republican Guard. The third prong of the land attack, consisting of General Boomer's 1st and 2nd Marine Divisions, burst into Kuwait at the same time, easily penetrating the poorly arranged minefields near the border and driving northward to Kuwait City. Advance elements of the Marines reached the outskirts of the capital on the evening of 24 February. The 2nd Marine Division circled north of Kuwait City to cut off an Iraqi retreat on the road from Mutlaa to Basra, while the 1st Marine Division—with the Arab forces on its flank—confronted and overran an Iraqi tank division south of the Kuwait Airport. Most Iraqi troops, numbed, starved, and isolated by the air campaign, resisted weakly, dropped their weapons and ran, or surrendered. The tank division near the Kuwait Airport stood and fought, but they were overpowered by a ruthless combination of close ground support aircraft, offshore naval gunfire, and Marine armor.

The Iraqi Army in and around Kuwait City had panicked, finished a last spree of looting, and headed north to Iraq on two highways, the six-lane Kuwait-Basra highway and the Subiya–Umm Qasr highway to the northeast running parallel with the coast. Moments after midnight on 26 February, Commander Frank Sweigart, leading a section of A-6 Intruders flying off the *Ranger*, emerged from low clouds just north of Kuwait City and unexpectedly came upon the escaping convoy, consisting of about 1,500 Iraqi tanks, trucks, armored personnel carriers, and stolen cars, on the Kuwait-Basra highway. Without antiair defenses, the vehicles below were "basically just sitting ducks," he recalled. Sweigart's bombers created a massive traffic jam by destroying or disabling vehicles at the head and tail of the long procession, and they then proceeded to strafe and drop 500-pound bombs along the length of the enemy convoy. Marine Harriers and FA-18 Hornets and Air Force fighter-bombers from Saudi airfields joined in; soon there were so many aircraft participating that the air traffic controllers had to divide the "killing box" on the highway in half so as to prevent mid-air collisions. Later that day, the second convoy on the Subiya–Umm Qasr highway was discovered, trapped, and destroyed in a like manner. Meanwhile, to the north in Iraq, between Safwan and Basra, an armored division of Saddam Hussein's vaunted Republican Guard, consisting of about 300 tanks, resisted the VII Corp's offensive, but without air cover its position was hopeless.[30]

On the 27th, with the land battle less than 100 hours old, Bush announced, "Kuwait is liberated," and declared a unilateral cessation of hostilities. Coalition forces had destroyed 3,700 of 4,280 Iraqi tanks and equivalent numbers of artillery pieces and other armored vehicles. Soon more than 60,000 Iraqi troops were in Saudi POW camps. There were fewer than 300 American dead and wounded. Bush and the Defense Department preferred to depict the war as relatively bloodless, which it was not, and Saddam Hussein was clearly uneasy about his army's collapse. As a result, neither Washington nor Baghdad had much interest in an accurate accounting of Iraqi military and civilian casualties. The Iraqi defeat was complete. On 3 March, Schwarzkopf met with the Iraqi Army chief of staff at Safwan in occupied southeastern Iraq and presented him with coalition demands: Saddam Hussein would agree to all UN resolutions, exchange POWs immediately, and provide maps of the thousands of land mines in Kuwait and sea mines in the northern Gulf. The Iraqis, faced with the prospect of renewed bombing if they rejected Schwarzkopf's terms, quickly agreed and soon released all of their POWs, repatriated thousands of Kuwaitis, and provided maps of the mined areas.

Within six months, American specialists had put out most of the 700 oil well fires set by the Iraqis in Kuwait. Later that year, UN inspection teams entered Iraq to assure that Saddam Hussein was dismantling his chemical-biological warfare installations and his advanced nuclear weapons program. A year later, Saddam Hussein and his Baath Party were still in power in Baghdad— soon after the war, they had crushed an uprising against the regime by pro-Iranian Muslim fundamentalists in Basra and temporarily accepted an American-imposed semi-autonomous Kurdish province on the border with Turkey. The UN sanctions, enforced by the Navy's Middle East Force in the northern Persian Gulf, were lifted slightly for humanitarian reasons and to allow Iraq to export some oil to pay reparations to Kuwait's emir.

The Persian Gulf War served as a reminder of the need for strong and ready American arms to uphold President Bush's New World Order foreign policy, but the consensus in Washington in early 1992 was that those forces should be considerably smaller than the administration had envisioned a year earlier. Army and Air Force generals, blind to the unique character of the Arabian campaign, were using the Desert Storm experience like a drill to implant their "jointness" orthodoxy in the cusp of American military policy. General Powell's first move came when Bush coupled his September 1991 announcement of the withdrawal of the Navy's tactical nuclear munitions with the news that the White House had agreed to an Air Force plan "to consolidate operational command of these forces into a U.S. Strategic Command . . . with participation from both services." This step, urged in the 1950s by the Air Force and opposed by Navy men since, effectively took the remaining *Lafayette-* and *Ohio*-class ballistic missile–bearing submarines—that had been under the direction of the Atlantic and Pacific fleets—and put them under an Air Force general based in Omaha. Powell also proposed to reorganize the overseas unified commands by keeping the joint Atlantic, Pacific, Central, and European commands and joining them with new Strategic Forces and Contingency Forces commands. This plan envisioned the Navy maintaining five carrier battle groups in the Atlantic Fleet, with two to three forward deployed in the Atlantic, Mediterranean, Red Sea, or Persian Gulf, and a Marine Readiness Group in the area. Six carrier battle groups and three Marine Expeditionary Forces would be attached to the Pacific Fleet. However, by the end of 1991, it was clear that Congress was no longer willing to provide for 11 carrier battle groups—Bush's shipbuilding schedule called for another *Nimitz*-class carrier to be laid down in 1996, but few believed Congress would agree to this—and the necessary air wings, and the Navy Department was drafting plans to reduce the fleet to about 350 ships and 8 or 9 carriers. Because the Army and Air Force exercised such unwarranted influence over naval policy as a result of unification, whether the Navy would operate the fleet necessary to police the New World Order was in doubt.[31]

Epilogue

As the century closes, the greatest problem American states-men and strategists face is how to configure American air, ground, and naval forces to meet a broad array of threats to the New World Order. The dismemberment of the Soviet Union paradoxically increases by default the relative obligation of the United States as the global bailiff. Despite recent claims to the contrary, the Persian Gulf War demonstrates that the United States remains, as she has since 1945, the only essentially "respon-sible" world power willing to dedicate force, however unevenly and inconsistently, to the often confusing and conflicting ends of order and peace. The collapse of the Soviet Union and the end of Soviet adventurism notwithstanding, in all too many regions, the law of an eye-for-an-eye still rules. The bases of most of these conflicts have little or no ideological component, bear little or no relationship to the older East-West alliance politics, and sug-gest no immediate solution. In southern Europe, Asia, the Middle East, North Africa, the Caribbean, and Central America, American military force—usually the naval forces that can be brought to bear in a crisis—may still play a major role in regional balance of power.

To deal with these problems, more attention might be paid to the elements of power needed to intervene quickly and deci-sively in regional conflicts with something less than unrestrained force. Naval strategists must configure forces for limited wars where politics and the local environment impose restrictions on the choice of military objectives as well as the means and timing of the use of force. And, in an atomized world, containing conflict will probably be as important or more important than defeating an enemy. Because the Army and Air Force can usually contribute almost nothing to timely overseas interventions except for military assistance to friendly local forces, modernizing American military assets must center on restructuring the Navy to meet these new, different, and dangerous responsibilities. The new fleet will have to respond promptly; insert itself and withdraw with unprecedented speed; defend itself and friendly forces against new, ubiquitous menaces; and strike quickly, surgically, sometimes gently, and often brutally—all the while protecting fragile local, bilateral, and regional political arrangements. It is difficult to imagine how this can be done until Navy leaders stop paying lipservice to "jointness" and mount a frontal attack on unification with the ultimate goal of dismembering the bloated, wasteful Defense Department edifice.

Some older concepts translated into new technologies appear to be shaping the Navy of the twenty-first century. The replacement of existing wiring and circuits in engines, machinery, sonars, radars, communications gear, weapons, and other systems with superconducting materials will result in vast improvements in speed, maintenance, fuel efficiency, endurance, reliability, and lethality. Steaming and flying costs should decline dramatically, as should the relative cost of delivering mass-produced, guided or remotely piloted missiles and various types of explosive or chemical-biological ordnance against hostile targets. Owing to the proliferation of launchers and munitions, the overall size of the fleet should increase if the new generation of Navy leaders chooses wisely between building fewer, more powerful multi-mission ships, planes, and weapons, or more numerous single-purpose vessels, aircraft, and projectiles. The basis for the first of these choices should be that carrier-based aircraft are useful means of policing the New World Order and attack submarines are not. While the Navy has maintained a remarkable record of nuclear reactor safety, at present, nuclear reactors are inherently dangerous and excessively costly sources of power generation for submarines and ships. Only a fraction of the present fleet consists of nuclear-powered vessels, but a safer, far cheaper second generation of reactors offers the promise of an affordable all-

nuclear-powered warship fleet. And the eventual marriage of su-
perconducting-wired engines and small, inexpensive supercomputers will reopen the way for the introduction of a second generation of heavy seaplanes, remotely piloted observation and
attack vehicles, and large, very long-range, land-based, missile-
bearing maritime patrol bombers.

Only mobility, endurance, and stealth ever justified the construction of large, reactor-powered fleet ballistic missile submarines in the first place. The very long ranges of new ballistic
and cruise bombardment missiles have already eliminated any
need for the continued construction or deployment of these very
expensive artifacts of the Cold War. One answer is the conversion
of the *Ohio*-class submarines into slow, short-range, diesel-driven
undersea missile barges for deployment on the floors of the
Great Lakes where such vessels would be immune to all known
non-space-based, antisubmarine warfare countermeasures. Effective, relatively inexpensive land-based and airborne anti-air and
antisatellite missile defenses of the Great Lakes can at present be
erected at relatively low costs. SDI would be an ideal system for
this purpose. Whether or not this step is taken, the upcoming
proliferation of inexpensive, powerful, long-life earth-orbiting
satellites, other nonacoustic sensors, supercomputer-based
sonars and sound processors, and speedy, powerful, very-long-
range air- or sea-launched homing torpedoes make it probable
that offensive antisubmarine warfare will, by the turn of the century, render unacceptably vulnerable the traditional ocean-going
ballistic missile submarine.

Defending traditional naval formations is bound to become
more difficult with the advent of chemical-biological-toxin–based
naval warfare. It has taken over four decades for weapons carrying materials derived from the discovery of DNA to arrive on the
battlefield, but that unhappy day is now on the horizon. Genetic
engineering technology may some day endow the leaders of willful, aggressive, inward-looking nations with the means to produce life-threatening biological organisms and the methods
needed to store, handle, and dispense these agents. The effects
on naval warfare should be profound and unsettling. Very small
air-burst missiles containing millions of tiny, sticky, nonsoluble
timed-release pellets dispensing DNA-engineered toxins may
more effectively disable a ship than any projectile-borne conventional explosives. Barrage-type missile launchers firing toxin-con-

tainer weapons may at first supplement, then replace, explosives in naval warfare as anti-ship weapons, thus necessitating the development of an entirely new and expensive set of close-in airborne and shipboard defensive systems. How to deal with these changes and still provide presidents with the iron fist of American foreign policy constitutes the Navy's most difficult challenge in the New World Order.

This book closes with the end of a remarkable year, which saw two heroic victories for American foreign policy and military force in Eurasia and the Persian Gulf. Navy warships still ply the dangerous Persian Gulf waters, enforcing the UN sanctions against Iraq, a vestige of that recent conflict and a reminder that the American policeman has not been relieved. For the foreseeable future, at the end of each day, Navy men, and now women, will be standing a similar watch, their ships ever on call to sail in harm's way. Not only American interests but also the world's body politic and humanity in general should welcome and share in the order, justice, and peace a strong United States Navy can help to create.

List of Abbreviations

AF: Air Force
AR: Annual Report of the Secretary of the Navy
ASC: Armed Services Committee
ASP: American State Papers
CNO: Chief of Naval Operations
FRUS: Foreign Relations of the United States
GenBd: General Board
GPO: U.S. Government Printing Office
HMSO: Her Majesty's Stationery Office
LC: Library of Congress
NA: National Archives
NHC: Operational Archives, Naval Historical Center,
    Washington Navy Yard
OH: Oral History
ONI: Office of Naval Intelligence
PRO: Public Records Office, Kew Gardens, London
RG: Record Group
USNA: Nimitz Library, U.S. Naval Academy, Annapolis, Maryland
WPD: War Plans Division

Notes

Chapter One

1. Churchill to Pound, 8 Jan 1942, Adm 205-13, PRO; William D. Leahy, *I Was There* (New York: Whittlesey House, 1950), p. 64; and Gordon Prange, *At Dawn We Slept* (New York: McGraw-Hill, 1981), pp. 543–47.

2. W. D. Puleston, *The Influence of Sea Power in World War II* (New Haven: Yale University Press, 1947).

3. Curtis Tarr, "The General Board Joint Staff Proposal of 1941," *Military Affairs* (Sum 1967), p. 89.

4. King to Flag Aide, 29 Apr 42, King Mss, OA, NHC.

5. James Leutze, *A Different Kind of Victory: A Biography of Admiral Thomas C. Hart* (Annapolis: Naval Institute Press, 1981), p. 231; and Edwin Hoyt, *How They Won the War in the Pacific: Nimitz and His Admirals* (New York: Weybright and Talley, 1970).

6. Leutze, *Hart*, pp. 232–42; and Walter G. Winslow, *The Fleet the Gods Forgot: The U.S. Asiatic Fleet in World War II* (Annapolis: Naval Institute Press, 1982).

7. John Mason, *The Pacific War: An Oral History* (Annapolis: Naval Institute Press, 1986), p. 33.

8. Leutze, *Hart*, p. 244.

9. D. Clayton James, *The Years of MacArthur* (Boston: Houghton Mifflin, 1970–85), Vol. II, pp. 19–23; and Entry, 27 Dec 1941, Stimson Diary, Yale University.

10. Robert W. Love, Jr., "Ernest J. King," in Love, ed., *The Chiefs of Naval Operations* (Annapolis: Naval Institute Press, 1980), p. 145.

11. Leutze, *Hart*, p. 269.

12. Leutze, *Hart*, p. 272.

13. Mason, *Pacific War*, p. 34.

14. Cooke to Captain Vincent R. Murphy, 4 Mar 1942, Box 9, Charles M. Cooke, Jr., Mss., Hoover Institution, Stanford, California.

Chapter Two

1. Love, "King," p. 149. See also Hoyt, *Nimitz and His Admirals*, Ch. 2; and Interview, Nimitz with Professor William Belote, 25 June 1964, William Belote Mss, Author's files.

2. John B. Lundstrom, *The First Team: Pacific Naval Air Power from Pearl Harbor to Midway* (Annapolis: Naval Institute Press, 1984), pp. 58–60.

3. Lundstrom, *First Team*, pp. 58–60; and Love, "King," p. 149.

4. Mason, *Pacific War*, p. 65.

5. George C. Dyer, *The Amphibians Came to Conquer: The Story of Admiral Richmond Kelly Turner* (Washington: GPO, 1971), Vol. I, p. 253.

6. John B. Lundstrom, *The First South Pacific Campaign: Pacific Fleet Strategy, December 1941–June 1942* (Annapolis: Naval Institute Press, 1976), p. 79.

7. Lundstrom, *First Team*, Chs. 9–13; Elias B. Mott, "Comment on 'Gross Sinner,'" *Naval War College Review* (Spr 1987), pp. 94–100; and Greenbacker to Author, 13 Aug 1986, Class of 1940 Archive, USNA.

8. Nimitz to King, 29 May 1942, Ernest J. King Mss; and Ernest J. King and Walter Muir Whitehill, *Fleet Admiral King: A Naval Record* (New York: Norton, 1952), p. 378.

9. Mitsuo Fuchida and Masatake Okumiya, *Midway: The Battle That Doomed Japan* (New York: Ballantine, 1958), pp. 54–72; and "Battle of Midway Symposium Issue," *Naval Aviation Museum Foundation* (Spr 1988).

10. Edwin Layton, John Costello, and Roger Pineau, *And I Was There* (New York: Morrow, 1985), pp. 338–469. Also see King to Marshall, 12 May 1942, CominCh Records, OA, NHC. (Note: The Naval Historical Center recently transferred the records of the Commander in Chief, U.S. Fleet, to the National Archives. A schedule for the transfer of other important World War II Navy Department records to the National Archives is available for the interested researcher at both locations.)

11. King, *Naval Record*, p. 379.

12. Mason, *Pacific War*, pp. 104–5.

13. William D. Owen, "The Japanese Attack on the *Yorktown*," *Naval Aviation Museum Foundation* (Spr 1988), p. 19; and Greenbacker to Clark Reynolds, c. 1964, Class of 1940 Archive, USNA.

Chapter Three

1. King to Tracy Kittredge, 1 Feb 50, Historical Section, JCS Organization, Pentagon; and King, *Naval Record*, p. 381.

2. Francis S. Low, "A Personal Narrative of Association with Fleet Admiral Ernest J. King," 1961, courtesy of the late Kenneth Knowles, Author's files; and King, *Naval Record*, p. 381.

3. M. E. Butcher, "Admiral Frank Jack Fletcher," *Naval War College Review* (May 1987), pp. 69–79.

4. Dyer, *Turner*, Vol. I, p. 371.

5. Ronald Spector, *Eagle Against the Sun: the American War with Japan* (New York: Free Press, 1985), p. 196.

6. Captain F. P. Sherman, "Action Report: Loss of the *Wasp*," 24 Sep 1942, OA, NHC; and Ben W. Blee, "Who Dunnit?" *Proceedings* (July 1982), pp. 42–49.

7. Love, "King," pp. 156–57; Entry, 21 Sept 1942, John W. Huston ed., "The Diary of General of the Air Force Henry H. Arnold," unpubl. manuscript; and Glen C. H. Perry, *"Dear Bart": Washington Views of World War II* (Westport, CT: Greenwood Press, 1982), p. 109.

8. Love, "King," pp. 156–57.

9. Spector, *Eagle*, p. 206.

10. Spector, *Eagle*, p. 207; and Samuel E. Morison, *The Two-Ocean War* (Boston: Atlantic, Little, Brown, 1963), p. 189.

11. William F. Halsey and J. Bryan III, *Admiral Halsey's Story* (New York: McGraw-Hill, 1947), p. 135.

12. Halsey, *Story*, p. 149.

13. Minutes, CominCh-CinCPac Conference, 23 Feb 1943, Cooke Mss.

Chapter Four

1. Pound to Ghormley, 22 Jan 1942, Adm 205-19, PRO; King and Marshall to FDR, 15 Jun 1942, King Mss; and Pound to Churchill, 18 Mar 1942, Adm 205-13, PRO.

2. Karl Dönitz, *Memoirs* (New York: Norden Publications, 1959), p. 33.

3. Entry, Eastern Sea Frontier War Diary, pp. 1–5, OA, NHC.

4. Norman Friedman, *U.S. Destroyers* (Annapolis: Naval Institute Press, 1982), p. 137.

5. Friedman, *Destroyers*, pp. 137–38.

6. Friedman, *Destroyers*, p. 138; and King, *Naval Record*, p. 447. A detailed British view of these events may be found in Rear Admiral Dorling, "BASR in BAD, Report, 1941–44," Adm 199-1236, PRO.

7. Dorling to Knox, 23 Jun 1941, PSF, FDR Mss, Hyde Park, New York; Friedman, *Destroyers*, p. 150; and King to JCS, 15 Jun 42, CominCh Records, OA, NHC.

8. Minutes, War Production Board Mtg XVII, 12 May 1942; and King to Douglas, 26 Jun 42, King Mss.

9. Andrews to King, 26 Feb 1942, in Eastern Sea Frontier War Diary, p. 175, OA, NHC; and Marc Milner, "RCN-USN, 1939–45: Some Reflections on the Origins of a New Alliance," in William B. Cogar, ed., *Naval History: The Seventh Symposium of the U. S. Naval Academy* (Annapolis: Naval Institute Press, 1989), p. 280.

10. Robert H. Freeman, ed., *The War Offshore: War Diary, Eastern Sea Frontier* (Ventnor, N.J.: Shellback Press, 1987), p. 67.

11. May 1942 Summary, Eastern Sea Frontier Diary, p. 247. Historians of the struggle in early 1942 against the U-boat off the East Coast would be wise to consult BAD (British Admiralty Delegation) to Admiralty, 18 Mar 42, Adm 205-13, PRO, for an assessment of the U.S. Navy's problem at the height of the campaign. A recent study of the U-boat campaign in early 1942, Michael Gannon, *Operation Drumbeat* (New York: Harper & Row, 1990), which its author claims to be "the dramatic true story of Germany's first U-boat attacks along the American coast in World War II," is quite unreliable. Gannon failed entirely to mention the dramatic decline in the volume and quality of Ultra intelligence between November 1941 and February 1942, ignored the effect on the Navy of the War Department's requests for emergency escorts for troop shipping after Pearl Harbor, and criticized Admiral King for holding ocean escorts on the great circle convoys—instead of positioning them off the East Coast—without pointing out that this would have merely induced Dönitz to shift his attacks back into the mid-Atlantic. Much of Gannon's argument rested on events he invented.

12. Wesley Frank Craven and James Lea Cate, eds., *The U. S. Army Air Force in World War II* (Chicago: University of Chicago Press, 1948–58), Vol. I, p. 539.

13. Smith and Lieutenant Colonel C. W. Bundy for JSPC to JPS, 7 May 1941, WPD Records, OA, NHC; and King, *Naval Record*, p. 371.

14. Walter Scott Dunn, Jr., *Second Front Now, 1943* (University: University of Alabama, 1980); and Mark A. Stoler, "The American Perception of British Mediterranean Strategy, 1941–45," in Craig Symonds, ed., *New Aspects of Naval History* (Annapolis: Naval Institute Press, 1981), pp. 325–39. Admiral King's suspicion that the British intended to exploit American resources to support their imperial policies was essentially correct. It was "in the Atlantic alone that the vital interests of ourselves and the United States are identical," the Admiralty believed. There the Royal Navy might "expect direct assistance . . . which may enable us to release our own forces for service in . . . the Eastern Mediterranean and the Indian Ocean." Admiral Charles Lambe to Pound, 8 Jan 1942, ADM 205-19, PRO.

15. King, *Naval Record*, p. 395; and FDR to King, 7 July 42, PSF, FDR Mss.

16. Vojtech Mastny, *Russia's Road to the Cold War* (New York: Columbia University Press, 1979), pp. 46–47; and Robert E. Sherwood, *Roosevelt and Hopkins* (New York: Harper and Bros., 1948), p. 556.

17. Minutes, JCS Mtg, 30 Jun 1942, JCS Records, Microfilm ed., USNA; and

Roosevelt Memorandum, 29 July 1942, Marshall File, PSF, FDR Mss.

18. King and Marshall to FDR, 12 Jun 1942, King Mss, LC; Dunn, *Second Front*, p. 16; and Thomas to Willson, 15 Oct 1942, Cooke Mss.

19. Theresa L. Kraus, "Joint Planning for Torch: The U.S. Navy," paper delivered at the Oct 1989 Naval History Symposium, USNA.

20. John Clagett, "Hewitt," *Naval War College Review* (Fall 1975), p. 72.

21. Clagett, "Hewitt," p. 76.

22. William F. Atwater, "U. S. Army and Navy Development of Joint Landing Operations" (Unpubl. Ph.D. Diss., Duke University, 1986), p. 184.

23. Clagett, "Hewitt," p. 80.

Chapter Five

1. Love, "King," p. 158.

2. Marshall and King to FDR, 12 Jun 1942, King Mss; and King to FDR, 7 July 42, PSF, FDR Mss.

3. Jurgen Rohwer, *The Critical Convoy Battles of March 1943* (Annapolis: Naval Institute Press, 1977), Ch. 4.

4. Kenneth A. Knowles, "Ultra and the Battle of the Atlantic," in Robert W. Love, Jr., ed., *Changing Interpretations and New Sources in Naval History* (New York: Garland Press, 1980), pp. 448–49; Ronald Lewin, *Ultra Goes to War* (New York: McGraw Hill, 1978); and Thomas Parrish, *The Ultra Americans* (New York: Stein and Day, 1986).

5. David Syrett, "German U-Boat Attacks on Convoy SC.118," *American Neptune* (Spr 1984), pp. 48–60.

6. "Allied Communications Intelligence and the Battle of the Atlantic," Pt. II, pp. 46–52, RG 457, NA.

7. Keith R. Tidman, *The Operations Evaluation Group* (Annapolis: Naval Institute Press, 1984), p. 55.

8. "Allied Communications . . . Atlantic," Pt. II, p. 101; and Morison, *Two-Ocean War*, p. 366.

9. William T. Y'Blood, *Hunter-Killer: U.S. Escort Carriers in the Battle of the Atlantic* (Annapolis: Naval Institute Press, 1983), pp. 285–86.

10. Y'Blood, *Hunter-Killer*, pp. 274–75. The Battle of the Atlantic has produced some of the best and much of the worst writing on World War II. Gannon's hyperbolic *Operation Drumbeat* must qualify as the foremost example of the latter category, but a more recent work by an Army colonel propounds an equally preposterous thesis. See Montgomery C. Meigs, *Slide Rules and Submarines* (Washington: National Defense University Press, 1990). Meigs argues that King opposed the creation of independent escort carrier hunter-killer task groups and had no understanding of the importance of aircraft in defeating the U-boat. He provided no evidence whatsoever—except from Army sources—to support his thesis, and often cited documents that do not uphold the argument put forth in the text. Incredibly, he asserted that Secretary of War Stimson "forced the Navy to accept many of his ideas" about the use of aircraft in anti-submarine operations. See Meigs, *Slide Rules*, p. 112.

Chapter Six

1. Cooke to King, 7 Nov 42, and Cooke to King, 28 Dec 1942, in CominCh Records; and King, *Naval Record*, p. 421.

2. Susan H. Godson, *Viking of Assault: Admiral John Leslie Hall, Jr., and Amphibious Warfare* (Washington: University Press of America, 1982), p. 74.

3. Godson, *Hall*, p. 93.

4. Robert Adelman and George Watson, *Rome Fell Today* (Boston: Little,

Brown, 1968), p. 141; and Mark W. Clark, *Calculated Risk* (New York: Harper and Bros., 1950), pp. 268–71.

5. Samuel E. Morison, *History of U.S. Naval Operations in World War* (Boston: Atlantic, Little, Brown, 1947–1962), Vol. IX, p. 349.

6. Winston S. Churchill *Closing the Ring* (Boston: Houghton Mifflin, 1950), pp. 488, 501.

Chapter Seven

1. Spector, *Eagle*, p. 179.

2. Lorelli, *Komandorski*, p. 72.

3. Entry, 25 Sep 1942, in Huston, "Arnold Diary"; and Mason, *Pacific War*, p. 36.

4. MacArthur to War Dept., 27 Jan 1943, CominCh Records.

5. John Brody, "Experiences in World War II," undated, Class of 1940 Archive, USNA.

6. King to Grace Pearson, 3 Jan 1949, Historical Section, JCS Organization, Pentagon.

7. Grace P. Hayes, *The History of the Joint Chiefs in World War II: The War Against Japan* (Annapolis: Naval Institute Press, 1982), p. 427.

8. Morison, *Two-Ocean War*, pp. 320–21; and George M. Elsey, "Naval Aspects of Normandy in Retrospect," in Eisenhower Foundation, *D-Day: The Normandy Invasion in Retrospect* (Lawrence: University Press of Kansas, 1971), p. 180.

Chapter Eight

1. Henry H. Adams, *Witness to Power: The Life of Fleet Admiral William D. Leahy* (Annapolis: Naval Institute Press, 1985), p. 234; and Keith Eubank, *Summit at Teheran* (New York: Morrow, 1987), p. 254.

2. King, *Naval Record*, p. 518; and Adams, *Witness*, p. 231.

3. Elsey, "Naval Aspects," p. 175.

4. Edward Ellsberg, *The Far Shore* (New York: Dodd, Mead, 1960), p. 160.

5. Ellsberg, *Shore*, p. 161.

6. Morison, *Naval Operations*, Vol. XI, p. 107; and Donald M. Weller, *Naval Gunfire Support of Amphibious Operations: Past, Present, and Future* (Dahlgren, Virginia: Naval Surface Weapons Center, October 1977), p. 24.

7. John Hall, OH, USNA.

8. Ellsberg, *Shore*, p. 201; and Weller, *Naval Gunfire*, p. 24.

9. Morison, *Naval Operations*, Vol. XI, p. 142.

10. Hall, OH.

11. Weller, *Naval Gunfire*, p. 34.

12. Weller, *Naval Gunfire*, pp. 34–35.

13. Hall, OH. See also Alan G. Kirk Mss, OA, NHC.

Chapter Nine

1. Carl Boyd, "The Japanese Submarine Force and the Legacy of Strategic and Operational Doctrine Developed between the World Wars," in Larry D. Addition, ed., *Selected Papers from the Citadel Conference on War and Diplomacy, 1978* (Charleston: Citadel Press, 1978), pp. 27–40; and Jerome B. Cohen, *Japan's Economy in War and Reconstruction* (Minneapolis: University of Minnesota Press, 1949), pp. 105–9, 266.

2. Stark to King, 16 May 1941, File: Signed Letters, Strategic Plans: 1940–1941 Records, OA, NHC.

3. Ben. D. Zevin, ed., *Nothing to Fear: The Selected Addresses of Franklin D. Roosevelt* (New York: Popular Library, 1961), p. 353.

4. Zevin, *Nothing*, p. 353; and Cooke to King, 21 Jun 1944, Cooke Mss.

5. Clay Blair, Jr., *Silent Victory: The U.S. Submarine War against Japan* (Philadelphia: J. B. Lippincott, 1975), p. 250.

6. Paul R. Schratz, *Submarine Commander* (Lexington: University Press of Kentucky, 1988), p. 52; and Richard Laning, "War Starts," undated, Class of 1940 Archive, USNA.

7. Blair, *Silent Victory*, p. 273.

8. Wilfred J. Holmes, *Double-Edged Secrets: U.S. Naval Intelligence Operations in the Pacific During World War II* (Annapolis: Naval Institute Press, 1979), p. 128; Blair, *Silent Victory*, p. 252; and J. J. Clark and Clark Reynolds, *Carrier Admiral* (New York: David McKay, 1967), p. 131.

9. Charles A. Lockwood, *Sink 'Em All* (New York: Bantam Books, 1984), pp. 101, 93.

10. Holmes, *Secrets*, p. 126; and Layton, *And I Was There*, pp. 471–72.

11. Holmes, *Secrets*, p. 129.

12. "The Role of Communications Intelligence in Submarine Warfare in the Pacific, January 1943–October 1943," SRH-001, RG 457, NA; Thomas J. Belke, "Intelligence in Perspective: [An Analysis of] 'The Role of Communications Intelligence in Submarine Warfare in the Pacific, Jan 1943–Oct 1943,'" (Unpubl. paper., May 1979, Author's Files, USNA); and Blair, *Silent Victory*, p. 751.

13. Holmes, *Secrets*, pp. 201–10.

14. Blair, *Silent Victory*, p. 853.

Chapter Ten

1. Zevin, *Nothing*, p. 353; Parry, *Dear Bart*, p. 109; and "Conference Notes, CominCh-CinCPac, 11–13 December 1942," King Mss. Admiral King unsuccessfully cautioned the U.S. Army's official historians against relying too heavily on the minutes of either the JCS meetings or the CominCh-CinCPac conferences. The secretaries who took the notes lacked any stenographic training and often misunderstood or missed what transpired. Moreover, he said, many of the most important JCS discussions occurred during "closed" sessions, when only generals Marshall and Handy and admirals King, Cooke, and occasionally, Leahy, were present. Only under these conditions of extreme secrecy and confidentiality might the principals articulate their political concerns and bring to bear all of the secret intelligence available. They could also discuss the strengths and weaknesses of their theater commanders somewhat more openly.

2. Pound to Churchill, 8 Mar 1942, Adm 205-13, PRO.

3. Love, "King," p. 164.

4. Holland M. Smith, *Coral and Brass* (New York: Scribners, 1949), p. 118.

5. Clark G. Reynolds, *The Fast Carriers: The Forging of an Air Navy* (New York: McGraw-Hill, 1968), pp. 54–57.

6. Reynolds, *Fast Carriers*, p. 96.

7. Smith, *Coral*, p. 121.

8. "Pacific Ocean Mobile Radio Intelligence Units," 1945, SHR-309, RG 457, NA; and Clark and Reynolds, *Carrier Admiral*, p. 131.

9. Smith, *Coral*, p. 141; and Layton, *And I Was There*, p. 480.

10. Clark and Reynolds, *Carrier Admiral* (New York: David McKay, 1967), p. 124.

11. Reynolds, *Fast Carriers*, p. 140.

Chapter Eleven

1. E. B. Potter, *Nimitz* (Annapolis: Naval Institute Press, 1976), p. 280; and

William T. Y'Blood, *Red Sun Setting: The Battle of the Philippine Sea* (Annapolis: Naval Institute Press, 1981), p. 11.

2. CinCPac Command Summary, p. 2323, OA, NHC.

3. Hoyt, *Nimitz and His Admirals*, Ch. 21.

4. Y'Blood, *Red Sun Setting*, p. 44.

5. Y'Blood, *Red Sun Setting*, p. 61.

6. Wilfred J. Homes, "Narrative, Combat Intelligence Center, Joint Intelligence Center, POA," SHR-20, RG 457, NA.

7. Morison, *Two-Ocean War*, p. 336.

8. Reynolds, *Fast Carriers*, p. 183; and Thomas B. Buell, *The Quiet Warrior: A Biography of Admiral Raymond A. Spruance* (Boston: Little, Brown, 1974), p. 270.

9. Blair, *Silent Victory*, p. 628.

10. Reynolds, *Fast Carriers*, p. 193.

11. Reynolds, *Fast Carriers*, p. 195.

12. Buell, *Warrior*, p. 275.

13. King, *Naval Record*, p. 559.

14. Reynolds, *Fast Carriers*, p. 205.

15. Reynolds, *Fast Carriers*, p. 206.

Chapter Twelve

1. King, *Naval Record*, p. 566; Buell, *Warrior*, p. 308; and Entry, 22 Jun 1944, Stimson Diary.

2. Halsey, *Story*, p. 195; and Minutes, JCS Mtg., 5 Sep 44, CCS 334, RG 218, NA.

3. A. Russell Buchanan, *The United States and World War II* (New York: Harper & Row, 1964), Vol. II, p. 535; and Ronald Lewin, *The American Magic* (New York: Farrar Straus Giroux, 1982), p. 268.

4. James, *MacArthur*, Vol. II, pp. 550–54.

5. Morison, *Two-Ocean War*, p. 451.

6. Robert M. Ancell, "Comment," *Proceedings* (Sep 1979), p. 89; and E. B. Potter, *Bull Halsey* (Annapolis: Naval Institute Press, 1985), p. 296.

7. Gerald Wheeler, "Thomas Kinkaid," in William M. Leary, ed., *We Shall Return! MacArthur's Commanders and the Defeat of Japan* (Lexington: University of Kentucky Press, 1988), p. 139; and Reynolds, *Fast Carriers*, p. 266.

8. Reynolds, *Fast Carriers*, p. 268.

9. Hoyt, *Nimitz and His Admirals*, p. 439.

10. Wheeler, "Kinkaid," p. 140; and Kinkaid OH, USNA.

11. Kinkaid OH. See also Potter, *Halsey*, Ch. 18.

12. Kinkaid OH.

13. The principals were well known to one another. For instance, King worked for Kinkaid's father and met the son before the younger Kinkaid entered the Naval Academy. Nonetheless, King was aware that Kinkaid "really hadn't much in the way of brains" and concluded that his problems in Leyte Gulf were caused because "he doesn't think through" problems. See Walter M. Whitehill, "Comments on Flag Officers of U.S. Navy [by Admiral King]," Whitehill-Buell Collection, NWC. Kinkaid was anguished when he learned that King held him partly responsible for the confusion on the night of 24 October, and he ably defended his conduct. "I very much want you to understand the actions taken by me at Leyte Gulf," he wrote. See Kinkaid to King, 2 Sep 1949, King Mss, LC. Admiral Cooke's somewhat broader perspective on the affair is in Cooke OH.

14. Deputy Chief of Naval Operations (Air), "The Navy's Air War," Vol. VIII: "The Mission Completed," OA, NHC.

15. Wheeler, "Kinkaid," p. 145.

Chapter Thirteen
1. Wheeler, "Kinkaid," p. 149.
2. Potter, *Nimitz*, p. 372.
3. Reynolds, *Fast Carriers*, p. 331.
4. King, *Naval Record*, p. 591; *FRUS: The Conferences at Malta and Yalta*, pp. 396–400; and Entry, 28 Feb 1945, Forrestal Diary, OA, NHC.
5. King, *Naval Record*, p. 591; *FRUS: Malta and Yalta*, p. 984; Russell D. Buhite, *Decisions At Yalta* (Wilmington: Scholarly Resources, 1986); and Zevin, *Nothing*, p. 453.
6. Zevin, *Nothing*, p. 461; "Conference Notes, CominCh-CinCPac, 11–13 Dec 1942," King Mss., OA, NHC.
7. Sherman, "Notes on Conference," 3–10 Nov 1944, Sherman Mss, OA, NHC.
8. William J. Sebald, *With MacArthur in Japan* (New York: Norton, 1965), pp. 21–22; and Michael S. Sherry, *Preparing for the Next War* (New Haven, Conn.: Yale University Press, 1977), p. 187.
9. Forrest C. Pogue, *George C. Marshall* (New York: Viking, 1963–1987), Vol. IV, pp. 17–18; Leahy to Marshall, 20 Jun 1945, Leahy Mss, OA, NHC; and Dennison OH, USNI.
10. Entry, 14 Jan 1944, Julius A. Furer Mss, LC.
11. Richard M. Leighton and Robert Coakley, *Global Logistics and Strategy* (Washington: GPO, 1955–68), Vol. II, p. 581.
12. Potter, *Nimitz*, p. 379.
13. Robert H. Ferrell, ed., *Off the Record: The Private Papers of Harry S. Truman* (New York: Harper & Row, 1980), p. 47; and Minutes, JCS Mtg with President, 18 Jun 1945, King Mss. In his memoir, *I Was There*, Admiral Leahy suggested that he had expressed moral objections to using atomic bombs against Japan, but no evidence survives to prove that he articulated this view prior to the bombings of Hiroshima and Nagasaki. At the 18 June White House meeting, he favored bombing Japan rather than invading Kyushu. For his part, Admiral King claimed after the war that he reluctantly went along with the Army's plans to invade Kyushu and Honshu, but believed that the naval and air blockade and conventional strategic bombing would bring about a Japanese surrender before American troops landed on Kyushu. See King and Whitehill, *Naval Record*, p. 605. The evidence to support this claim is slim. King advanced a contrary view when he explained the Navy's position on the invasion of Japan in King to JCS, "Pacific Strategy," 2 May 45, ABC 384, RG 165, NA. At the critical 18 June meeting with Truman, at least, he supported the invasion of Kyushu and did not make the argument that conventional bombing and the naval blockade would end the war. It was commonplace after the war for various other admirals to make the utterly unfounded claim that "the Navy" opposed the invasion of Japan and considered the use of the atomic bomb to be unnecessary. In the summer of 1945, however, only Admiral King, Admiral Cooke, and possibly Admiral Edwards, understood the tangled history of the question, the available political and military intelligence, and the wide-ranging political and military implications of the issue. Neither Admiral Nimitz nor General MacArthur, the Pacific theater commanders, was well informed about the state of play of surrender diplomacy, nor were they thought to be terribly astute politically, and the JCS did not solicit their views on this issue.
14. Robert J. C. Butow, *Japan's Decision to Surrender* (Stanford: Stanford University Press, 1954), p. 130.

15. Potter, *Nimitz*, p. 388.

16. Stuart Murray OH, USNI.

Chapter Fourteen

1. Walter Millis, ed., *The Forrestal Diaries* (New York: Viking, 1951), p. 14; and Roosevelt to Churchill, 6 Apr 1945, FDR Mss.

2. Donald White, "The Nature of World Power in American History: An Evaluation at the End of World War II," *Diplomatic History* (Wtr 1987), p. 184.

3. *FRUS: Europe, 1945*, Vol. V, pp. 96–97; Walter Poole, "From Conciliation to Containment," *Military Affairs* (Feb 1978), p. 15; and ONI, "Basic Factors in World Relations," 15 Dec 1945, Op-30 Files, OA, NHC.

4. *FRUS: 1946*, Vol. VIII, pp. 1215–19; JCS to SecWar and SecNav, 23 Aug 1946, Leahy Mss; Millis, *Forrestal*, p. 251; and Cato Glover, "Pincher," War Plans 1946, OA, NHC.

5. William C. Mott, "Comment: Barring the Door in the Med," *Proceedings* (Dec 1987), p. 110; and Bruce R. Kuniholm, *The Origins of the Cold War in the Near East* (Princeton: Princeton University Press, 1980).

6. Millis, *Forrestal*, p. 145.

7. "Letters . . . Voyage by *Missouri*," File EF-75, CNO Files, OA, NHC; Millis, *Forrestal*, p. 171; Stephen G. Xydis, "The Genesis of the Sixth Fleet," *Proceedings* (Aug 1958), pp. 41–50; and Thomas Bryson, *Tars, Turks, and Tankers* (Metuchen, New Jersey: Scarecrow Press, 1980), p. 98.

8. *New York Herald Tribune*, 2 Nov 1946; and Steven L. Rearden, *History of the Office of the Secretary of Defense, Vol I: The Formative Years, 1947–1950* (Washington: GPO, 1984), p. 393.

9. "Presentation to the President," 14 Jan 1947, CNO Chronological File, Sherman Mss, OA, NHC; *FRUS: 1947*, Vol. I, pp. 736–50; and Michael Palmer, *Origins of the Maritime Strategy: American Naval Strategy in the First Postwar Decade* (Washington: GPO, 1988), p. 28.

10. Harry S. Truman, *Memoirs* (New York: Doubleday, 1955–56), Vol I, pp. 522–23.

11. White, "Nature of Power," p. 182; Arthur W. Radford, *From Pearl Harbor to Vietnam*, ed. by Stephen Jurika, Jr., (Stanford: Hoover Institution Press, 1980), p. 127; and *FRUS: 1950*, Vol. I, p. 223.

12. Sherry, *Preparing*, p. 85; Lloyd J. Graybar, "Bikini Revisted," *Military Affairs* (Oct 1980), pp. 118–23; and Cato D. Glover, *On the Crest of the Wave* (New York: Vantage Press, 1974), p. 98.

13. JCS 1518, 19 Sep 1945, and Leahy to Lilienthal, 29 Oct 1947, JCS Records, RG 218, NA.

14. Vincent Davis, *Postwar Defense Policy and the United States Navy, 1943–1946* (Chapel Hill: University of North Carolina Press, 1966), p. 23; Millis, *Forrestal*, p. 513; and Mins, JCS Mtg, 2 Oct 1948, JCS Records, RG 218, NA.

15. *Army and Navy Register*, 17 Nov 1945, p. 17; JCS 1477-19, 13 Mar 1946, JCS Records, RG 218, NA; and Sherman to Nimitz, 7 Jun 1946, Conference with Op-30, Strategic Plans Files, 1946, OA, NHC.

16. Rearden, *Formative*, pp. 293–94; and Emile A. Nakhleh, *The Persian Gulf and American Policy* (New York: Praeger, 1982), pp. 97–98.

17. David A. Rosenberg, "The U.S. Navy and the Problem of Oil in a Future War: The Outline of a Strategic Dilemma, 1945–1950," *Naval War College Review* (Sum 1976), pp. 53–64.

18. Truman, *Memoirs*, Vol. I, p. 509; Sherry, *Preparing*, pp. 35, 220; "Report of Visit of Defence Planners to America," 13 Oct 1949, XC-A 028516, ADM 205-72, PRO; Arthur W. Radford, *From Pearl Harbor to Vietnam: Memoirs* (Stanford:

Hoover Institution Press, 1980), p. 75; and U.S. Senate, 79th Cong., 1st Sess., Hearings before the Committee on Naval Affairs, "Authorizing Permanent . . . Strength of the United States Navy . . . ," 13–14 Dec 1945, p. 5.

19. Millis, *Forrestal*, p. 196.

20. Millis, *Forrestal*, p. 139; and Glover, "Pincher."

21. *Public Papers of the Presidents: Harry S. Truman, 1947*, p. 179; and Memo, SWNCC, 18 Janaury 1947, State-War-Navy Coordinating Committee Records, Microfilm Copy, USNA.

22. Michael Petrovich, trans., Milovan Djilas, *Conversations with Stalin* (New York: Harcourt, Brace, and World, 1962), p. 182.

23. Rearden, *Formative*, p. 294.

24. Radford, *Memoirs*, p. 116; and Rearden, *Formative*, p. 463.

25. Timothy P. Ireland, *Creating the Entangling Alliance* (Westport, Conn.: Greenwood Press, 1981), p. 124.

26. Steven Ross, *American War Plans, 1945–1950* (New York: Garland Publ., 1988), Ch. 4; and Rosenberg, "Navy and Middle East Oil," p. 60.

27. Samuel Cox, "U.S. Naval Strategy and Foreign Policy in China, 1945–1950" (Trident Scholar Paper, 1980, USNA), p. 19. Cox argues persuasively that Admiral Cooke, Vice Admiral Badger, and other Americans who advised Chiang Kai-Shek that, in the end, Washington would not allow his regime to be defeated, may have contributed to his extreme reluctance to negotiate a power-sharing arrangement with the Communist Party. Material on Admiral Cooke's experiences in China and his later association with the Taiwan government may be found in the Cooke Mss.

28. Cox, "Navy in China," p. 45.

29. Cox, "Navy in China," p. 44. See also Pogue, *Marshall*, Vol. III, pp. 54–143.

30. Cox, "Navy in China," p. 61.

31. Radford, *Memoirs*, p. 250.

32. Cox, "Navy in China," pp. 67–68.

33. Cox, "Navy in China," p. 77.

34. Radford, *Memoirs*, p. 155.

35. Charles W. Moses, "China—1949—A Short Tour," *Shipmate* (May 1985), p. 21.

36. Cox, "Navy in China," p. 100.

37. Cox, "Navy in China," p. 98.

Chapter Fifteen

1. Prange, *At Dawn We Slept*, p. 722; and William A. Lucas and Raymond H. Dawson, *The Organizational Politics of Defense* (Pittsburgh: International Studies Assn., 1974), p. 31.

2. Millis, *Forrestal*, pp. 202, 88; and Robert J. Donovan, *Conflict and Crisis: The Presidency of Harry S. Truman, 1945–1948* (New York: Norton, 1977), p. 200. Also see Paolo E. Coletta, *The United States Navy and Defense Unification, 1947–1953* (Newark: University of Delaware Press, 1981); and Vincent Davis, *The Admirals' Lobby* (Chapel Hill: University of North Carolina Press, 1967).

3. Radford, *Memoirs*, pp. 90, 107.

4. Rearden, *Formative*, p. 19.

5. Millis, *Forrestal*, p. 161. A superb biography of Forrestal, by Townsend Hoopes and Douglas Brinkley, *Driven Patriot* (New York: Knopf, 1992), appeared too late for this book.

6. Radford, *Memoirs*, p. 91; and Millis, *Forrestal*, p. 540.

7. Rearden, *Formative*, p. 392.

8. Radford, *Memoirs*, p. 115; Rearden, *Formative*, p. 398; Millis, *Forrestal*, p. 222.

9. George B. Chafee, "Carrier Requirements for Future Naval Aircraft," *Naval Aviation Confidential Bulletin* (July 1947), p. 20; Radford, *Memoirs*, p. 95; and David A. Rosenberg, "American Postwar Air Doctrine and Organization: The Navy Experience," in Alfred F. Hurley and Robert C. Ehrhart, eds., *Air Power and Warfare* (Washington: Office of Air Force History, 1979), pp. 245–78. For Air Force views, see Larry D. O'Brien, "National Security and the New Warfare: Defense Policy, War Planning, and Nuclear Weapons, 1945–1950" (Unpubl. Ph.D. Diss., Ohio State University, 1981).

10. Radford, *Memoirs*, p. 121.

11. Dennison OH.

12. Stephen E. Ambrose, *Eisenhower* (New York: Simon and Schuster, 1983–90), Vol. I, pp. 486–87, Rearden, *Formative*, p. 411–12.

13. Paolo E. Coletta, "John L. Sullivan," in Paolo E. Coletta, ed., *American Secretaries of the Navy* (Annapolis: Naval Institute Press, 1980), Vol. II, p. 774.

14. Hanson Baldwin, "Review of Radford's *Memoirs*," *Proceedings* (Dec 1980), p. 89; and Rearden, *Formative*, p. 415; U.S. House, 81st Cong., 1st Sess., Committee on Armed Services, "Hearings on the National Defense Program: Unification and Strategy," 1949; and Paolo E. Coletta, "Francis P. Matthews," in Coletta, *Secretaries*, Vol. II, p. 794.

15. Rearden, *Formative*, pp. 415–17; Radford, *Memoirs*, p. 219; Omar Bradley and Clay Blair, *A General's Life* (New York: Simon and Schuster, 1983), pp. 509–13.

16. Rearden, *Formative*, p. 419.

17. Radford, *Memoirs*, p. 103; Coletta, "Sullivan," p. 777; and Ambrose, *Eisenhower*, Vol. II, p. 487.

18. Rearden, *Formative*, pp. 525–30.

19. Badger to Denfeld, 19 May 1949, Badger Mss, OA, NHC; and Joseph A. Sestak, Jr., "Balancing the Atlantic Tilt," *Proceedings* (Jan 1986), p. 68.

20. Rearden, *Formative*, p. 535.

Chapter Sixteen

1. Clay Blair, Jr., *The Forgotten War* (New York: Times Books, 1987); Glenn D. Paige, *The Korean Decision* (New York: Free Press, 1968); James A. Field, Jr., *History of U.S. Naval Operations: Korea* (Washington: GPO, 1962); and Chang-Il Ohn, "The Joint Chiefs of Staff and U.S. Policy and Strategy Regarding Korea, 1945–1953" (Unpubl. Ph.D. Diss, University of Kansas, 1983).

2. James F. Schnabel and Robert J. Watson, "The History of the Joint Chiefs of Staff," Vol. III: "The Korean War," pp. 13–14, USNA.

3. Radford, *Memoirs*, p. 219.

4. *FRUS: 1950*, Vol. I, p. 378; and Ferrell, *Off the Record*, p. 185.

5. U.S. Senate, 82nd Cong., 1st Sess., Committee on Armed Services and Committee on Foreign Relations, "Hearings to Conduct an Inquiry into the Military Situation in the Far East and the Facts Surrounding the Relief of General of the Army Douglas MacArthur," 1951, Pt. II, p. 1528.

6. Ferrell, *Off the Record*, p. 185; and Richard Morris, ed., *Great Presidential Decisions* (Philadelphia: Lippincott, 1960), p. 439.

7. Coletta, *Navy and Defense Unification*, p. 199.

8. Clark Reynolds, "Forrest P. Sherman," in Robert W. Love, Jr., ed., *The Chiefs of Naval Operations* (Annapolis: Naval Institute Press, 1980), pp. 223–24.

9. Radford, *Memoirs*, pp. 234–36.

10. Reynolds, "Sherman," p. 234.

11. Reynolds, "Sherman," p. 223; David Rees, *Korea: The Limited War* (New York: St. Martin's Press, 1964), Ch. 5; Victor H. Krulak, *First to Fight: An Inside View of the U.S. Marine Corps* (Annapolis: Naval Institute Press, 1984), p. 131; and Robert Smith, *MacArthur in Korea* (New York: Simon and Schuster, 1982), p. 78.

12. "Military Situation in the Far East", Pt. II, p. 1295; James, *MacArthur*, Vol. III, pp. 469–75; and Radford, *Memoirs*, p. 235.

13. James, *MacArthur*, Vol. III, p. 484; and Tidman, *Operations Evaluation*, p. 133.

14. Kenneth Veth OH, USNA.

15. Interview, Commander Rue O'Neill, 3 Nov 1987, Author's files. O'Neill commanded the destroyer *Collett* during the Inchon and Wŏnsan landings. Also see Edwin Simmons, "Mining at Wŏnsan—and in the Persian Gulf," *Fortitudine* (Sum 1987), pp. 3–7; and CinCPac to CNO, "Korean War: CinCPac Evaluation Report No. 1," pp. 9, 103–7, c. Dec 1950, Library, NHC. "Had the assault operations against Wŏnsan been of great tactical and military value on 20 Oct 1950," Struble later contended, "the landing would have been conducted on schedule." Malcolm W. Cagle and Frank A. Manson, *The Sea War in Korea* (Annapolis: Naval Institute Press, 1957), pp. 150–51.

16. John Edward Wiltz, "Truman and MacArthur: The Wake Island Meeting," *Military Affairs* (Dec 1978), pp. 169–76.

17. *FRUS: 1950*, Vol. VII, p. 1237.

18. Richard P. Hallion, *The Naval Air War in Korea* (Baltimore: Nautical and Aviation Publ., 1986), p. 75.

19. James, *MacArthur*, Vol. III, p. 553; and Radford, *Memoirs*, p. 248.

20. JCS 2118-5, 3 Jan 1951, JCS Records, University Publications Microfilm, USNA; and Radford, *Memoirs*, p. 231.

21. James, *MacArthur*, Vol. III, p. 549.

22. James, *MacArthur*, Vol. III, pp. 586–87.

23. James, *MacArthur*, Vol. III, p. 631; John Edward Wiltz, "The MacArthur Hearings of 1951: The Secret Testimony," *Military Affairs* (Dec 1975), pp. 167–73; and Roger Dingman, "Atomic Diplomacy During the Korean War," *International Security* (Wtr 1988), pp. 50–91.

Chapter Seventeen

1. Cagle and Manson, *Sea War*, p. 397.

2. C. Turner Joy, *How Communists Negotiate* (New York: Macmillan, 1955); and Weller, *Naval Gunfire*, p. 157.

3. Cagle and Manson, *Sea War*, p. 230. "The U.S. Air Force wasn't too interested in close air support," recalled Admiral John S. Thach, "so they were utterly unprepared to do close air support the way it had to be done if you were going to help the troops at the front lines. And it wasn't a matter of just curing a communications problem. It was a matter of education . . . and doctrine built up." John S. Thach, "Right on the Button: Marine Close Air Support in Korea," *Proceedings* (Nov 1975), pp. 54–56.

4. Cagle and Manson, *Sea War*, p. 230.

5. Cagle and Manson, *Sea War*, p. 252.

6. Interview, Vice Admiral Andrew Jackson, 26 Apr 1975, Author's files.

7. Walter G. Hermes, *The U. S. Army in the Korean War: Truce Tent and Fighting Front* (Washington: GPO, 1966), p. 319.

8. Cagle and Manson, *Sea War*, p. 270.

9. Hermes, *Truce Tent*, p. 265.

10. Hermes, *Truce Tent*, pp. 328–29.

11. Hermes, *Truce Tent*, p. 283.

12. Hermes, *Truce Tent*, pp. 328–29; and Cagle and Manson, *Sea War*, p. 396.

13. Daniel Gormley, "From Arcadia to Casablanca" (Unpubl. Ph.D. Diss., Georgetown, 1978), Appendix A. This appendix contains a revealing, wide-ranging interview with Clark on subjects well beyond the scope of the dissertation. Also see Richard K. Betts, *Soldiers, Statesmen, and Cold War Crises* (Cambridge: Harvard University Press, 1977), p. 106.

14. James F. Schnabel and Robert J. Watson, *The Joint Chiefs of Staff and National Policy*, Vol. III, pp. 953; and *FRUS: 1952–54, Korea*, Vol. 15, pp. 1061–62.

15. *FRUS: 1952–1954, Korea*, Vol 15, pp. 1012–17; Weller, *Naval Gunfire*, p. 160; Bevan Alexander, *Korea: The First War We Lost* (New York: Hippocrene Books, 1986), pp. 375, 474; Edward C. Keefer, "Eisenhower and the End of the Korean War," *Diplomatic History* (Sum 1986), pp. 267–89; and Samuel S. Stratton, "Korea: The Acid Test of Containment," *Proceedings* (Apr 1954), p. 371.

Chapter Eighteen

1. Robert J. Watson, *The JCS and National Policy, 1953–1954* (Washington: GPO, 1986), pp. 3–27; R. Gordon Hoxie, *Command Decision and the Presidency* (New York: Thomas Y. Crowell, 1977); Richard A. Aliano, *American Defense Policy from Eisenhower to Kennedy* (Athens: Ohio University Press, 1975); Laurel A. Mayer and Ronald J. Stupack, "The Evolution of Flexible Response in the Post-Vietnam Era," *Air University Review* (Nov 1975), p. 14; and William W. Kaufman, *The McNamara Strategy* (New York: Harper & Row, 1964), p. 25.

2. Betts, *Soldiers*, p. 107; Maxwell Taylor, *An Uncertain Trumpet* (New York: Harper & Row, 1960), pp. 58–59; and David N. Schwartz, *NATO's Nuclear Dilemmas* (Washington: Brookings Institution, 1983), pp. 75–79.

3. Radford, *Memoirs*, p. 319; and Watson, *JCS, 1953–54*, p. 43.

4. Robert Osgood, *NATO: The Entangling Alliance* (Chicago: University of Chicago Press, 1962), p. 24.

5. *New York Times*, 28 May 1954, p. 2; Radford, *Memoirs*, p. 327; and Betts, *Soldiers*, p. 123.

6. JCS 2101-112, 7 Dec 1953, JCS File, Strategic Plans Records, OA, NHC.

7. *FRUS: 1952–54*, Vol. II, pp. 514–34.

8. Sestak, "Balancing the Tilt," p. 66.

9. David A. Rosenberg and Floyd Kennedy, "U.S. Aircraft Carriers in the Strategic Role," Lulejian Co. Report, 1974, p. 165, Library, NHC.

10. Robert B. Pirie, "On My Watch," *Naval Aviation Museum Foundation* (Fall 1988), pp. 22–27.

11. U.S. House, 86th Cong., 1st Sess., Committee on Armed Services, "Hearings on Department of Defense Appropriations for 1958," Pt. 1, pp. 338, 415.

Chapter Nineteen

1. George Herring, *America's Longest War* (New York: Wiley, 1979), p. 18.

2. Radford, *Memoirs*, p. 233.

3. Edwin B. Hooper, Dean Allard, and Oscar Fitzgerald, *The United States Navy and the Vietnam Conflict: The Setting of the Stage to 1959* (Washington: GPO), Vol. I, p. 254.

4. Betts, *Soldiers*, p. 20.

5. Sherman Adams, *Firsthand Report* (New York: Harper and Bros., 1961), p. 120.

6. Herring, *Longest War*, pp. 35–37.

7. Paul Schratz, "Robert B. Carney," in Love, *Chiefs*, p. 250; and *Newsweek* (9 Feb 1953), p. 17.

8. Marc Trachtenberg, "A 'Wasting Asset': American Nuclear Strategy and the Nuclear Balance," *International Security* (Wtr 1988–89), p. 46; and Schratz, "Carney," p. 259.

9. Adams, *Report*, p. 129.

10. Adams, *Report*, pp. 118, 133.

11. Dept. of State, *Bulletin*, (15 Jun 1953), pp. 831–35.

12. Piers Brendon, *Ike* (New York: Harper & Row, 1986), p. 325.

13. Brendon, *Ike*, p. 325.

14. Brendon, *Ike*, p. 327.

15. Cato Glover, *Command Performance with Guts* (New York: Greenwich Books, 1969), p. 176; and Schratz, "Carney," p. 283.

Chapter Twenty

1. Richard G. Hewlett and Francis Duncan, *Nuclear Navy, 1946–1962* (Chicago: University of Chicago Press, 1974), p. 72; Harvey M. Sapolsky, *The Polaris System Development* (Cambridge: Harvard University Press, 1972); and James P. Craft, Jr., "The Role of Congress in the Determination of Naval Strategy in Support of U.S. Foreign Policy, 1956–1966" (Unpubl. Ph.D. Diss., University of Pennsylvania, 1969).

2. William M. Whitmore, "The Origins of Polaris," *Proceedings* (Mar 1980), pp. 55–59; and David A. Rosenberg, "Toward Armageddon: The Foundations of U.S. Nuclear Strategy, 1945–1961," (Unpubl. Ph.D. Diss., University of Chicago, 1983), p. 227.

3. Norman Polmar and Thomas B. Allen, *Rickover* (New York: Simon and Schuster, 1982), p. 542.

4. Taylor, *Uncertain Trumpet*, pp. 59–66; and U.S. House, 86th Cong., 1st Sess., Committee on Armed Services, "Hearings on United States Defense Policies in 1958," p. 14.

5. U.S. House, 85th Cong., 2nd Sess., Subcommittee of Committee on Appropriations, "Hearings on Department of Defense Appropriations for FY1959," 1958, pp. 378–79.

6. Kenneth R. Whiting, *Soviet Reactions to Changes in American Military Strategy* (Maxwell AFB: Air University Press, 1965), pp. 8–14.

7. U.S. Senate, 86th Cong., 2nd Sess., Committee on Foreign Relations, "Hearings on United States Foreign Policy," 1959, Pt. 1, p. 729; and Paul H. Backus, "Finite Deterrence," *Proceedings* (Mar 1959), pp. 23–29.

8. U.S. Senate, 86th Cong., 2nd Sess., Preparedness Investigating Subcommittee of the Committee on Armed Services in Conjunction with the Committee on Aeronautical and Space Sciences, "Hearings on Missile, Space, and Other Major Defense Matters," 1960, pp. 300–13.

9. U.S. House, 86th Cong., 2nd Sess., Committee on Armed Services, "Hearings, Department of Defense Appropriations for FY1961," 1959, Pt. 5, pp. 940–41; and David A. Rosenberg, "Arleigh Burke," in Love, ed., *Chiefs*, p. 294.

10. U.S. Senate, 86th Cong., 1st Sess., Preparedness Investigating Subcommittee of Committee on Armed Services, "Hearings on Major Defense Matters," 1959, pp. 33–34, 69–70; U.S. House, 84th Cong., 2nd Sess., Committee on Un-American Activites, "Hearings on Soviet Total War," 1956, Vol. I, p. 387; and U.S. House, 86th Cong., 1st Sess., Committee on Armed Services, "Hearings on United States Defense Policies in 1958," p. 15.

11. David A. Rosenberg, "U. S. Nuclear War Planning, 1945–1960," in Desmond Ball and Jeffrey Richelson, eds., *Strategic Nuclear Targeting* (Ithaca, N.Y.: Cornell University Press, 1986), p. 55.

12. U.S. House, 86th Cong., 2nd Sess., Committee on Armed Services,

"Hearings on Department of Defense Appropriations for FY1961," 1959, Pt. 7, pp. 118–21.

13. Hewlett and Duncan, *Nuclear Navy*, p. 196.

14. Jan Breemer, "A Few Good Ships," *Sea Power* (Oct 1987), p. 53.

Chapter Twenty-one

1. Dept. of State, *Bulletin*, 25 Mar 1957; Jonathan Trumbell Howe, *Multicrises: Sea Power and Global Politics in the Missile Age* (Cambridge: MIT Press, 1971); and Armin Rappaport, *A History of American Diplomacy* (New York: Macmillan, 1975), p. 438.

2. Bryson, *Tars, Turks, and Tankers*, p. 129.

3. Robert McClintock, "The American Landing in Lebanon," *Proceedings* (Oct 1962), pp. 71–76.

4 Adams, *Report*, p. 292.

5. Robert Murphy, *Diplomat Among Warriors* (New York: Doubleday, 1964), pp. 398–408; Adams, *Report*, p. 293; and Betts, *Soldiers*, p. 101.

6. Adams, *Report*, p. 293.

7. Norman A. Graebner, *America as a World Power* (Wilmington, Del.: Scholarly Resources, 1984), p. 203; and Hooper, Allard, and Fitzgerald, *Navy and Vietnam*, Vol. I, p. 357.

8. Lawrence Kuter, "Pacific Air Forces," *Air Force* (Sept 1959), pp. 124–30.

9. Betts, *Soldiers*, pp. 101, 123.

10. Dept. of State, *American Foreign Policy: Current Documents, 1958*, pp. 1149–52.

11. Dwight D. Eisenhower, *Mandate for Change* (New York: Doubleday, 1963), p. 459.

12. Thomas G. Patterson, J. Garry Clifford, and Kenneth J. Hagan, *American Foreign Policy* (Lexington, Mass.: D. C. Heath, 1988), Vol. II, p. 501.

13. U.S. Senate, 85th Cong., 1st Sess., Report of the Subcommittee on the Air Force of the Committee on Armed Services, *Air Power*, 1957, pp. 95–97; and *Public Papers of President Dwight D. Eisenhower, 1957*, pp. 7, 796.

14. Robert F. Futrell, *Ideas, Concepts, and Doctrine: A History of Basic Thinking in the United States Air Force, 1907–1964* (Maxwell AFB: Air University, 1971), Vol. II, pp. 515–24.

15. Adams, *Report*, p. 420.

Chapter Twenty-two

1. Kaufman, *McNamara Strategy*, pp. 40–43.

2. Frank Costigliola, "The Failed Design: Kennedy, de Gaulle, and the Struggle for Europe," *Diplomatic History* (Summer 1984), p. 241.

3. *The Public Papers of John F. Kennedy, 1961*, p. 385.

4. Costigliola, "Design," p. 237; and Arthur M. Schlesinger, Jr., *A Thousand Days: John F. Kennedy in the White House* (Boston: Houghton Mifflin, 1965), p. 874.

5. Costigliola, "Design," p. 248; and I. J. Galantin, "The Resolution of Polaris," *Proceedings* (Apr 1985), pp. 80–88.

6. *Public Papers . . . Kennedy, 1962*, pp. 908–10.

7. U.S. House, 88th Cong., 2nd Sess., Committee on Armed Services, "Hearings on Military Posture and H.R. 9637," 1963, pp. 6937–77.

8. Murphy, *Diplomat*, p. 569; and Trumbell Higgins, *The Perfect Failure: Kennedy, Eisenhower, and the CIA at the Bay of Pigs* (New York: Norton, 1987), p. 42.

9. Rosenberg, "Burke," pp. 314–16.

10. James Cable, *Gunboat Diplomacy, 1919–1979* (2nd ed.; New York: St. Martin's, 1981), p. 237.

11. Patterson, *Foreign Policy*, Vol. II, p. 540.

12. Peter Wyden, *Bay of Pigs: The Untold Story* (New York: Simon and Schuster, 1979), pp. 125–26.

13. Schlesinger, *Thousand Days*, pp. 200–201; Rosenberg, "Burke," p. 317; Jack Raymond, *Power at the Pentagon* (New York: Harper and Row, 1964), p. 284; and Theodore Sorensen, *Kennedy* (New York: Harper and Row, 1965).

14. The entire discussion of the Cuban Missile Crisis is based on Robert M. Beer, "The U.S. Navy and the Cuban Missile Crisis," Trident Scholar Report, May 1990, USNA. Beer's work draws on over fifty interviews and reinterviews with Navy men, Air Force officers, and other officials and is informed by thousands of recently declassified documents. See also Joseph Bouchard, "Use of Naval Force in Crises: A Theory of Stratified Crisis Intervention" (Unpubl. Ph.D. Diss., Stanford University, 1989); Forrest R. Johns, "Naval Quarantine of Cuba, 1962" (M.A. Thesis; University of California at San Diego, 1984); and Interviews, admirals Anderson, Ward, and Dennison, 14 and 22 Apr 1974, Author's files. Stage-managed conferences on the crisis in Moscow and Havana between 1989 and 1992 brought together some surviving participants from all three sides but produced few revelations and a good deal of misinformation. McNamara, for instance, claimed to be surprised by a Red Army general's assertion that the Soviet forces in Cuba possessed tactical nuclear weapons despite the fact that the 1962 OpPlans took this probability into account. Moreover, NcNamara claimed that he had rejected Admiral Dennison's request to send nuclear-armed forces into the Caribbean but did not point out that the attack carriers carried "special weapons" and that Air Force fighter-bombers in Florida had access to nuclear weapons. Dino Brugioni, *Eyeball to Eyeball: The Cuban Missile Crisis* (New York: Random House, 1991), contains some new material, but the author fails to examine the evidence available to Kennedy from NSA intercepts in July 1962.

15. Rowland Evans and Robert Novak, *Lyndon Johnson: The Exercise of Power* (New York: New American Library, 1966), p. 511.

16. James A. Dare, "Dominican Diary," *Proceedings* (Dec 1965), pp. 41–45.

17. Herbert G. Schoonmaker, "United States Military Forces in the Dominican Crisis of 1965" (Unpubl. Ph.D. Diss., University of Georgia, 1977), pp. 49–51; George W. Ball, *The Past Has Another Pattern* (New York: Norton, 1982), pp. 328–29. Also see John B. Martin, *Overtaken By Events* (New York: Doubleday, 1966); Abraham F. Lowenthal, *The Dominican Intervention* (Cambridge: Harvard University Press, 1972); and Lawrence A. Yates, *Power Pack: U.S. Intervention in the Dominican Republic, 1965–1966* (Leavenworth, Kansas: Combat Studies Institute, 1988).

18. Dare, "Diary," p. 45; Schoonmaker, "Dominican Crisis," p. 66; and Bruce Palmer, Jr., *Intervention in the Caribbean* (Lexington: University of Kentucky Press, 1989), p. 69.

Chapter Twenty-three

1. Allan Nevins, ed., *John F. Kennedy: The Strategy of Peace* (New York: Harper and Bros., 1960), p. 144; and Robert S. McNamara, *The Essence of Security* (New York: Harper and Row, 1968), p. 90.

2. Alain C. Enthoven, *How Much Is Enough? Shaping the Defense Program, 1961–1969* (New York: Harper and Row, 1971), p. 202; Pirie, "On My Watch," p. 25; and Jane E. Stromseth, *The Origins of Flexible Response* (New York: St. Martins, 1988), p. 70.

3. U.S. House, 88th Cong., 2nd Sess, Committee on Armed Services, "Hearings on Military Posture and H.R. 9637," 1963, p. 6951; and Paul Nitze, "Running the Navy," *Proceedings* (Sep 1989), p. 74.

4. Schlesinger, *Thousand Days*, pp. 727–28; U.S. House, 88th Cong., 2nd Sess, Committee on Armed Services, "Hearings on Military Posture and H.R. 9637," 1963, p. 6951; and U.S. Senate, 88th Cong., 1st Sess., Committee on Armed Services, "Hearings on Military Procurement Authorization, FY 1964," 1962, p. 317.

5. *New York Times* 7 May 1962; Floyd D. Kennedy, "David Lamar McDonald," in Love, *Chiefs*, p. 344; and Horacio Rivero OH, USNA.

6. David McDonald OH, USNA; and U. S. House, 88th Cong., 2nd Sess., "Hearings on Dept. of Defense Appropriations for 1965," 1963, Pt. 4, pp. 206–7.

7. Futrell, "Air Force," Vol. II, p. 621.

8. Enthoven, *How Much*, p. 214.

9. Breemer, "Good Ships," p. 53; Pirie, "On My Watch," p. 25; and Nitze, "Running the Navy," p. 74.

10. Breemer, "Good Ships," p. 53.

11. Polmar and Allen, *Rickover*, pp. 430–32.

12. U.S. Senate, 88th Cong., 1st Sess., Committee on Goverment Operations, Permanent Subcommittee on Investigations, "TFX Contract Investigation," 1963, Pt. 6, pp. 1513–14.

13. Gerald E. Miller, "The Crash of the TFX," *Naval Aviation Foundation Museum* (Fall 1988), p. 32; Kennedy, "McDonald," p. 342; and Roger Franklin, *The Defender* (New York: Harper, 1986), p. 207.

14. Franklin, *Defender*, p. 215. The nearly simultaneous Navy–Air Force development of the A-7 Corsair II is described in Richard G. Head, "Decision-Making on the A-7 Attack Aircraft" (Unpubl Ph.D. Diss., Syracuse University, 1971).

15. Miller, "Crash," p. 35.

Chapter Twenty-four

1. Dept. of Defense, *United States–Vietnam Relations, 1945–1967* [Pentagon Papers] (Washington: GPO, 1970), Book 10, p. 1362. Important official histories treating high policy and military strategy include John Schight, *The U. S. Air Force in Southeast Asia: The War in South Vietnam, The Years of the Offensive* (Washington: GPO, 1988); and Jeffrey Clarke, *The U. S. Army in Vietnam: Advice and Support, 1965–1973* (Washington: GPO, 1988).

2. Maxwell Taylor, *Swords and Plowshares* (New York: Morrow, 1972), p. 223; Schlesinger, *Thousand Days*, p. 324; and Edward J. Moralda and Oscar Fitzgerald, *The United States Navy and the Vietnam Conflict: From Military Assistance to Combat, 1959–1965* (Washington: GPO, 1984), Vol. II, p. 72.

3. Moralda and Fitzgerald, *Navy and Vietnam*, Vol. II, pp. 78–83; and Frederick Nolting, "The Turning Point," *Foreign Service Journal* (July 1968), p. 19.

4. Betts, *Soldiers*, p. 24.

5. Betts, *Soldiers*, p. 190.

6. Philip Bucklew OH, USNI.

7. Betts, *Soldiers*, p. 71.

8. Moralda and Fitzgerald, *Navy and Vietnam*, Vol. II, pp. 78–83.

9. The question of whether the North Vietnamese attacked the Desoto Patrol on the night of 4 August 1964 still interests naval historians. The opposing interpretations are outlined by Edward Moralda, "Tonkin Gulf: Fact and Fiction," in William B. Cogar, ed., *New Interpretations in Naval History: Selected Papers from the Eighth Naval History Symposium* (Annapolis: Naval Institute Press, 1989), pp. 281–303; and Edwin E. Moise, "Tonkin Gulf: Reconsidered," in Cogar, *New*

Interpretations, pp. 304–23. Moralda insisted that the attack took place; Moise built a case to prove that it did not. Moralda's thesis relied heavily on the testimony of Navy men who reviewed the evidence at the time or soon after. Moise pointed out that "the *Maddox* had been specially equipped to monitor enemy radio communications and enemy radar," but that she did not pick up either radio message traffic between the attacking North Vietnamese vessels or indications of North Vietnamese radar activity. "The idea that torpedo boats could have attempted to aim torpedoes without radar help at relatively maneuverable targets such as destroyers, on a dark night with poor visibility, strains credibility." Moreover, Moise contended that much of the evidence supporting Moralda's argument was cobbled together on the 6th or the 7th so as to support Johnson's and McNamara's representations to Congress regarding the Tonkin Gulf Resolution, and he attached overly sinister connotations to a message from the Joint Staff to the Pacific Fleet commands that asked for more proof of an attack. The delay in assembling the evidence in the theater probably had more to do with intervening operations than anything else. According to a confidential source, Admiral Roy Johnson's fury about Captain Herrick's handling of the engagement may account for the confusion. Also see Thomas D. Boettcher, *Vietnam: the Valor and the Sorrow* (Boston: Little, Brown, 1985), p. 199; Malcolm Cagle, "Task Force 77 in Action off Vietnam," in Frank Uhlig, ed., *Vietnam: The Naval Story* (Annapolis: Naval Institute Press, 1986), p. 22; and Herring, *Longest War*, p. 121.

    10. Moralda and Fitzgerald, *Navy and Vietnam*, Vol. II, pp. 420ff.

    11. Moralda and Fitzgerald, *Navy and Vietnam*, Vol. II, p. 420; and John Galloway, *The Gulf of Tonkin Resolution* (Cranbury, New Jersey: Farleigh Dickenson University Press, 1970), p. 262. Also see Andy Kerr, *A Journey Amongst the Good and the Great* (Annapolis: Naval Institute Press, 1987), pp. 177–78, 201–6.

    12. McDonald OH; and Ball, *Past*, p. 379.

    13. Moralda and Fitzgerald, *Navy and Vietnam*, Vol. II, pp. 438–42; Cagle, "Task Force 77," in Uhlig, *Naval Story*, p. 20; and U. S. Grant Sharp, *Strategy for Defeat* (San Rafael, Cal.: Presidio Press, 1978), p. 44. Also see U. S. Grant Sharp OH, USNI.

    14. Moralda and Fitzgerald, *Navy and Vietnam*, Vol. II, p. 442; Raphael Littauer, et al., *The Air War in Indochina* (Boston: Beacon Press, 1971); McDonald OH; and Ball, *Past*, p. 379.

    15. R. N. Livingston, "Comment and Discussion," *Proceedings* (July 1989), p. 74; James B. Stockdale, "The First Day of the War," *Proceedings* (Feb 1989), p. 12; and Norman Polmar and Peter Mersky, *Naval Air War in Vietnam* (Annapolis: Nautical and Aeronautical Pub., 1981).

    16. Boettcher, *Vietnam*, p. 203.

Chapter Twenty-five

    1. Interview, "The Ten Thousand Day War," TV program, Alan Enterprises, 1980; BDM Corporation, "A Study of Strategic Lessons Learned in Vietnam," Vol. VI: Conduct of the War, Book I: Operational Analysis, 1975, Defense Technical Information Center, Alexandria, Virginia; and McDonald OH.

    2. Cagle, "Task Force 77," in Uhlig, *Naval Story*, p. 22.

    3. Sharp, *Defeat*, p. 59.

    4. Herring, *Longest War*, p. 118; Clyde E. Pettit, ed., *The Experts* (Seacaucus, N.J.: Lyle Stuart, 1975), pp. 197–98; and Ball, *Past*, p. 397.

    5. Herring, *Longest War*, p. 137.

    6. Dept. of State, "The Evidence at Vung Ro Bay," 23 February 1965.

    7. Robert Salzer OH, USNA; Arthur Price OH, USNA; and "Ten Thousand

Day War."

8. Henry Graff, *The Tuesday Cabinet* (Englewood Cliffs, New Jersey: Prentice Hall, 1970).

9. Betts, *Soldiers*, p. 14; and Ball, *Past*, p. 394.

10. Philip L. Geylin, *LBJ and the World* (New York: Random House, 1978), pp. 213–14.

11. Dennis Chamberland, "Interview: Westmoreland," *Proceedings* (July 1986), pp. 45–48.

12. Charles E. Wunderlin, Jr., "The Paradox of Power: Infiltration, Coastal Surveillance, and the U.S. Navy in Vietnam, 1965–1968," *Journal of Military History* (July 1989), p. 286.

13. BDM, "Strategic Lessons," pp. 7–18; and R. L. Schreadley, "The Naval War in Vietnam, 1950–1970," in Uhlig, *Naval Story*, p. 191.

14. Wunderlin, "Infiltration," p. 286.

15. "Ten Thousand Day War."

16. Lyndon Johnson, *The Vantage Point* (New York: Holt, Rinehart, and Winston, 1971), p. 117; Enthoven, *How Much*, p. 194; Cagle, "Task Force 77," in Uhlig, *Naval Story*, p. 24; and Polmar and Mersky, *Naval Air War*, p. 56. Also see William C. Westmoreland, *A Soldier Reports* (New York: Doubleday, 1976).

Chapter Twenty-six

1. Polmar and Mersky, *Naval Air War*, p. 59; and René Francillon, *Tonkin Gulf Yacht Club* (Annapolis: Naval Institute Press, 1988).

2. Sharp, *Defeat*, p. 116.

3. Herring, *Longest War*, p. 178.

4. Thomas H. Moorer OH, Lyndon B. Johnson Library, Microfilm Copy, USNA; and Sharp, *Defeat*, p. 162.

5. Moorer OH.

6. William A. Momyer, *Airpower in Three Wars* (Washington: GPO, 1978), p. 303.

7. Sharp, *Defeat*, pp. 116, 178; and Betts, *Soldiers*, p. 207.

8. Sharp, *Defeat*, pp. 161, 145.

Chapter Twenty-seven

1. James A. Hodgman, "Market Time in the Gulf of Tonkin," in Uhlig, *Naval Story*, p. 329; Veth OH; Victor Croizat, *The Brown Water Navy* (Dorset, UK: Blandford Press, 1984); Thomas J. Cutler, *Brown Water, Black Berets: Coastal and Riverine Warfare in Vietnam* (Annapolis: Naval Institute Press, 1988); and Norman B. Hannah, *The Key to Failure: Laos and the Vietnam War* (New York: Madison Books, 1987).

2. Veth OH.

3. Veth OH.

4. Howard Kerr OH, USNA.

5. Veth OH.

6. Kerr OH.

7. Chamberland, "Westmoreland," pp. 45–48; and George C. Eckhardt, *Command and Control, 1950–1969* (Washington: GPO, 1974), pp. 77–80.

8. Kerr OH; William B. Fulton, *Riverine Operations, 1966–1969* (Washington: GPO, 1973), p. 87; and Price OH.

9. Fulton, *Riverine*, p. 85.

10. U.S. Naval Forces, Vietnam, "Monthly Summary, September 1968," copy at USNA.

11. John Albright, "Fight Along the Rach Ba Rai," in John Cash, et al., *Seven*

Firefights in Vietnam (Washington: Dept. of the Army, 1970), Ch. 4.

12. Fulton, *Riverine*, pp. 128–33. A recent treatment of the problem is in E. J. Megarre, "Doctrine for Navy-Marine Corps Joint Riverine Operations," May 1978, NWP-13, OA, NHC.

13. Charles Rauch OH, USNA; Veth OH; and Price OH.

14. Price OH; Veth OH; Fritz Steiner, "Forgotten Lessons of Riverine Warfare," *Proceedings* (May 1982), p. 208; and Elmo Zumwalt, et al., *My Father, My Son* (New York: Dell, 1986), p. 42.

15. David C. Humphrey, "Tuesday Lunch at the Johnson White House," *Diplomatic History* (Wtr 1984), p. 86; and Guenter Lewy, *America in Vietnam* (New York: Oxford University Press, 1978), p. 382.

16. Sharp, *Defeat*, pp. 122–23; Harry G. Summers, Jr., "Lessons: A Soldier's View," in Peter Braestrup, ed., *Vietnam as History* (Washington: University Press of America, 1984), p. 111; and Sayre A. Swartztrauber, "Review of L. J. Matthews, et al., *Assessing the Vietnam War*," *Naval War College Review* (Wtr 1988), p. 130.

17. Sharp, *Defeat*, pp. 122–23, 141, 145–50.

18. Neil Sheehan, *The Pentagon Papers* (New York: New York Times Books, 1971), pp. 565–66; and McDonald OH.

19. Veth OH.

20. Sharp, *Defeat*, p. 124.

21. Herring, *Longest War*, pp. 181, 159.

22. Westmoreland, *Soldier Reports*, p. 303; and "Ten Thousand Day War."

23. U.S. Senate, 90th Cong., 1st Sess., Preparedness Investigating Subcommittee of the Committee on Armed Services, "Hearings on the Air War in Vietnam," 9–10 Aug 1967, Pt. I, pp. 2, 334.

24. Herring, *Longest War*, p. 180.

Chapter Twenty-eight

1. Lloyd Bucher, "Bucher on the *Pueblo*," *Proceedings* (Feb 1989), p. 39.

2. Paul Schratz, "A Commentary on the *Pueblo* Affair," *Military Affairs* (Oct 1971), p. 94.

3. Bucher, "Bucher on the *Pueblo*," p. 39; Schratz, "Commentary," p. 94; Lloyd Bucher, *My Story* (New York: Doubleday, 1970), p. 192; and Lloyd Bucher, "The *Pueblo* Incident: Commander Bucher Replies," *Naval History* (Wtr 1989), pp. 44–50.

4. Horace H. Epes, Jr., "Comment on 'The Capture of the *Pueblo*,'" *Proceedings* (Mar 1990), p. 24; and Daniel V. Gallery, *The Pueblo Incident* (New York: Doubleday, 1970), p. 64.

5. Ball, *Past*, p. 437.

6. Gallery, *Pueblo*, p. 173.

7. Don Oberdorfer, *Tet: The Turning Point in the Vietnam War* (New York: Doubleday, 1971), p. 119.

8. Veth OH.

9. John Forbes and Robert Williams, *Riverine Force* (New York: Bantam, 1987), p. 107.

10. Veth OH; Patterson, *Foreign Policy*, Vol. II, p. 560; and Herring, *Longest War*, p. 193.

11. Strobe Talbot, *The Master of the Game* (New York: Knopf, 1988), p. 101.

12. Sharp, *Defeat*, p. 211.

13. Schreadley, "Naval War," in Uhlig, *Naval Story*, p. 302.

14. John Nichols and Barrett Tillman, *On Yankee Station: The Naval Air War over Vietnam* (Annapolis: Naval Institute Press, 1987), p. 16.

Chapter Twenty-nine

1. C. L. Sulzberger, *The World and Richard Nixon* (New York: Prentice Hall, 1987), p. 184.

2. Herring, *Longest War*, p. 223; and Pettit, *The Experts*, p. 372.

3. Herring, *Longest War*, p. 228; *New York Times*, 11 Apr 1988.

4. U.S. House, 92nd Cong., 2nd Sess., Committee on Foreign Affairs, Subcommittee on the Near East, "Hearings on U.S. Interests in and Policy Toward the Persian Gulf," Feb and June 1972, p. 95.

5. Elmo R. Zumwalt, Jr., *On Watch* (New York: Quadrangle/New York Times Books, 1976), pp. 126, 305, 330; and William Shawcross, *Sideshow* (New York: Simon and Schuster, 1979), p. 191.

6. Kerr OH; Zumwalt, *On Watch*, p. 41; and Price OH.

7. U.S. Naval Forces, Vietnam, "Monthly Summary, September 1968," USNA; and Robert Salzer OH, USNA.

8. Price OH.

9. Chamberland, "Westmoreland," p. 48; Veth OH; and Salzer OH.

10. Salzer OH.

11. Zumwalt, *On Watch*, pp. 35–42; and Kerr OH.

12. Salzer OH.

13. Salzer OH.

14. Veth OH; and Chamberland, "Westmoreland," p. 48.

Chapter Thirty

1. Dept. of State, News Release of Interview, 12 Apr 1975.

2. Futrell, "Air Force," Vol. II, p. 667; and Henry Kissinger, *Memoirs* (Boston: Little, Brown, 1979–), Vol. II, p. 257.

3. Enthoven, *How Much*, p. 208.

4. Kissinger, *Memoirs*, Vol. II, p. 1154.

5. Banning N. Garrett and Bonnie S. Glasser, "From Nixon to Reagan: China's Changing Role in American Strategy," in Kenneth A. Oye, et al., *Eagle Resurgent* (Boston: Little, Brown, 1987), p. 257; and Kissinger, *Memoirs*, Vol. I, p. 399.

6. U.S. Congress, 91st Cong., 2nd Sess., Joint Senate-House Committee on Armed Services, "Hearings on CVAN-70 Aircraft Carrier," 1970, p. 381; and Zumwalt, *On Watch*, p. 156. Also see Norman Friedman, "Elmo Zumwalt," in Love, *Chiefs*, pp. 365–80.

7. Harry D. Train II, "Commentary," in James L. George, ed., *The U. S. Navy: The View from the Mid-1980s* (Boulder, Colo.: Westview Press, 1985). p. 373.

8. Harold C. Hemmond, "The Flip Side of Rickover," *Proceedings* (July 1989), p. 46; and Kissinger, *Memoirs*, Vol. II, p. 1003.

9. Zumwalt, *On Watch*, p. 107.

10. Zumwalt, *On Watch*, p. 161.

11. Franklin, *Defender*, p. 304; and Polmar and Allen, *Rickover*, p. 569.

12. "Hearings on CVAN-70," pp. 176–77.

13. "Hearings on CVAN-70," pp. 176–77; and *Washington Post*, 14 Apr 1971.

14. John E. Lacoutre, "Comment," *Proceedings* (Sep 1979), p. 89.

15. Zumwalt, *On Watch*, 356.

16. Vice Admiral Philip A. Beshany, "As I Recall: Selling the *Los Angeles*," *Proceedings* (Oct 1967), pp. 109–10.

17. Patrick Tyler, *Running Critical* (New York: Harper and Row, 1986), p. 68; and Norman Friedman, "Review of *Running Critical*," *Proceedings* (Mar 1987), p. 27.

18. Zumwalt, *On Watch*, p. 106.

Chapter Thirty-one

1. Fred C. Parker, "Strategic History of the Vietnam War" (Unpubl. Ph.D. Diss., Georgetown University, 1987), Ch. 4.

2. Edward J. Moralda and G. Wesley Pryce III, "A Short History of the U.S. Navy and the Southeast Asian Conflict" (Washington: NHC, 1984), pp. 78–80, 84–86. Also see Gerald H. Turley, *Easter Offensive* (Novato, Calif.: Presidio Press, 1985).

3. Zumwalt, *On Watch*, p. 379; and Salzer OH.

4. Zumwalt, *On Watch*, pp. 384–85.

5. For a recent interpretation of Linebacker, see Mark Clodfelter, *The Limits of Air Power* (New York: Free Press, 1989).

6. Kissinger, *Memoirs*, Vol. I, Ch. 33.

7. Herring, *Longest War*, p. 254.

8. Herring, *Longest War*, p. 255; and Veth OH.

9. Al Santoli, ed., *Everything We Had: An Oral History of the Vietnam War* (New York: Ballantine, 1981), p. 226.

Chapter Thirty-two

1. Stephen J. Genco, "The Eisenhower Doctrine: Deterrence in the Middle East," in Alexander George and Richard Smoke, eds., *Deterrence in American Foreign Policy: Theory and Practice* (New York: Columbia University Press, 1974), pp. 309–62.

2. Kissinger, *Memoirs*, Vol. II, p. 849.

3. Zumwalt, *On Watch*, p. 458; and U.S. House, 93rd Cong., 2nd Sess., Committee on Foreign Affairs, Subcommittee on the Near East and South Asia, "Hearings on Proposed Expansion of U.S. Military Facilities in the Indian Ocean," Feb–Mar 1974.

4. Bruce R. Kuniholm, *The Persian Gulf and United States Policy* (Claremont, Calif.: Regina Books, 1974), p. 23; Francis West, Jr., "Planning for the Navy's Future," *Naval War College Review* (Oct 1979), p. 30.

5. Zumwalt, *On Watch*, p. 457.

6. Kissinger, *Memoirs*, Vol. II, pp. 848–49; and Zumwalt, *On Watch*, p. 363.

7. Zumwalt, *On Watch*, p. 364.

8. Zumwalt, *On Watch*, pp. 360–68.

9. Richard N. Haass, "Arms Control at Sea: the United States and the Soviet Union in the Indian Ocean, *Journal of Strategic Studies* (Jun 1987), p. 246.

10. Zumwalt, *On Watch*, p. 126; and Jan S. Breemer, *U.S. Naval Developments* (Annapolis: Nautical and Aviation Publ., 1983), p. 28.

11. Zumwalt, *On Watch*, p. 353.

12. U.S. House, 92nd Cong., 2nd Sess., Committee on Foreign Affairs, Subcommittee on the Near East, "Hearings on U.S. Interests in and Policy toward the Persian Gulf," Feb and June 1972, p. 109.

13. Elmo Zumwalt, "Total Force," *Proceedings* (May 1979), p. 104; and Friedman, *Destroyers*, p. 376.

14. Zumwalt, *On Watch*, p. 101.

15. Zumwalt, *On Watch*, p. 60.

16. "Holloway . . . Philosophy," *Navy Times*, 8 Mar 1975, p. 8.

17. Zumwalt, *On Watch*, p. 81.

18. Polmar and Allen, *Rickover*, p. 398.

19. Dov Zakheim, et al., *Shaping the General Purpose Navy* (Washington: Congressional Budget Office, 1980), pp. 87–93; and "Holloway . . . Philosophy," p. 8.

20. Zumwalt, *On Watch*, p. 82; and "Holloway . . . Philosophy," p. 8.

Chapter Thirty-three

1. James Ennes, *Assault on the* Liberty (New York: Random House, 1981), p. 96.

2. Ennes, *Assault*, p. 64.

3. Kissinger, *Memoirs*, Vol. II, p. 493.

4. Kissinger, *Memoirs*, Vol. II, pp. 490–93.

5. Zumwalt, *On Watch*, pp. 434–36.

6. Kissinger, *Memoirs*, Vol. II, p. 495.

7. Zumwalt, *On Watch*, pp. 435–38.

8. Zumwalt, *On Watch*, p. 300.

9. Richard P. Stebbins and Elaine P. Adam, *1972: American Foreign Relations, A Documentary Record* (New York: New York University Press, 1976), pp. 491, 483, 38; David L. Hall, "War Powers by the Clock," *Proceedings* (Sep 1987), pp. 36–40.

10. Gerald R. Ford, *A Time to Heal* (New York: Harper & Row, 1979), pp. 215–19.

11. Ford, *Time*, p. 321. On Schlesinger's counterforce strategy and his problems with Ford, see Joseph A. Cernik, "Strategy, Technology, and Diplomacy . . . James R. Schlesinger as Secretary of Defense" (Unpubl. Ph.D. Diss., New York University, 1982).

12. Ford, *Time*, pp. 285, 249.

13. Ford, *Time*, p. 253.

14. Richard G. Head, et al., *Crisis Resolution: Presidential Decision Making in the* Mayaguez *and Korean Confrontations* (Boulder, Col.: Westview Press, 1978), p. 118. Also see CinCPac Command History, "The SS *Mayaguez* Incident," 1975, copy in USNA; Christopher J. Lamb, "Belief Systems and Decision Making in the *Mayaguez* Crisis" (Unpubl. Ph.D. Diss., Georgetown University, 1986); and U.S. House, 94th Cong., 1st Sess., Subcommittee on International Political and Military Affairs, Committee on International Relations, "Hearings on the Seizure of the *Mayaguez*," Vols. I–IV, 14 May 1975–4 Oct 1976.

15. Roy Rowan, *The Four Days of* Mayaguez (New York: Norton, 1975), p. 142.

16. Ford, *Time*, p. 280.

17. Head, *Crisis*, p. 133.

18. Rowan, *Mayaguez*, p. 223; "Holloway Outines Naval Philosophy," *Navy Times*, 5 Mar 1975, p. 8; and Ford, *Time*, p. 276.

Chapter Thirty-four

1. Jimmy Carter, *Keeping Faith* (New York: Bantam Books, 1982), p. 19; Lawrence J. Korb, *The Fall and Rise of the Pentagon: American Defense Policies in the 1970s* (Westport, Conn.: Greenwood Press, 1979); Cyrus Vance, *Hard Choices* (New York: Simon and Schuster, 1983), p. 322; and James Fallows, "The Passionless Presidency," *Atlantic* (May 1979), pp. 33–46. Also see James Fallows, *National Defense* (New York: Random House, 1981).

2. Patterson, *Foreign Policy*, Vol. II, p. 639.

3. Patterson, *Foreign Policy*, Vol. II, p. 640; and Zbigniew Brzezinski, *Power and Principle* (New York: Farrar, Strauss, and Giroux, 1983), p. 353.

4. West, "Planning," p. 30; and James L. George, *Problems of Sea Power as We Approach the 21st Century* (Washington: American Enterprise Institute, 1977).

5. Polmar and Allen, *Rickover*, p. 570.

6. Floyd D. Kennedy, Jr., "National Maritime Strategy," in Kenneth J. Hagan, ed., *In Peace and War*, 2nd ed. (Westport, Conn.: Greenwood Press, 1984), p. 348; B. Gail, "Debating the Real Issues About the Future of the U.S. Navy,"

Armed Forces Journal (May 1978), pp. 28–30; John A. Williams, "U.S. Navy: Missions and Force Structure, A Critical Appraisal," *Armed Forces and Society* (Sum 1981), pp. 499–528; R. James Woolsey, "Planning a Navy: The Risks of Conventional Wisdom," *International Security* (Sum 1978), p. 19; Henry Mustin, "Maritime Strategy from the Deckplates," *Proceedings* (Sep 1986), pp. 33–37; and Paul B. Ryan, *First Line of Defense* (Stanford: Hoover Institution, 1981), pp. 91, 124.

7. Ryan, *First Line*, p. 91; Paul Nitze, et al., *Securing the Seas: The Soviet Naval Challenge and Western Alliance Options* (Boulder, Colo.: Westview Press, 1979), p. 380; and "Statement of Admiral James L. Holloway III before the Committee on Armed Services, U.S. Senate," *Navy Policy Briefs*, 1977, p. 2, USNA.

8. Robert L. J. Long, "Commentary," in George, *Navy*, p. 368; Train, "Commentary," in George, *Navy*, p. 371; and *CNO Report on the FY1980 Budget* (Washington: GPO, 1979), p. 15.

9. Zumwalt, *On Watch*, p. 76.

10. U.S. House, 95th Cong., 1st Sess., Committee on Armed Services, "U.S. Navy Analysis of Congressional Budget Office Issue Paper, General Purpose Forces: Navy," 12 Jan 1977; and Ryan, *First Line*, p. 109.

11. Breemer, *Naval Developments*, p. 29.

12. Ryan, *First Line*, pp. 113–14.

13. Congressional Quarterly, *U. S. Defense Policy* (Washington: Congressional Quarterly, 1978), p. 62-A.

14. Francis J. West, *Sea Plan 2000: Naval Force Planning Study* (Washington: Navy Dept., 1978); Ryan, *First Line*, p. 129; and Kennedy, "Strategy," p. 341.

15. Long, "Commentary," p. 369; and Ryan, *First Line*, p. 129.

16. *Washington Post*, 28 May 1978.

17. Richard A. Strubbing and Richard A. Mendel, *The Defense Game* (New York: Harper & Row, 1986), p. 196.

18. Polmar and Allen, *Rickover*, p. 399.

Chapter Thirty-five

1. Carter, *Faith*, p. 217; and J. L. Holloway III, "Inside the JCS: Decisions in Crisis," *Naval War College Review* (Oct 1985), p. 30.

2. Haass, "Arms Control at Sea," p. 246; Alvin J. Cottrell, et al., *Sea Power and Strategy in the Indian Ocean* (Beverly Hills, Calif.: Sage Publications, 1981); and Richard Best, Jr., "Commentary," *Proceedings* (Sep 1979), p. 21.

3. John Major, "Wasting Asset: The U.S. Re-Assessment of the Panama Canal, 1945–1949," *Journal of Strategic Studies* (Sep 1980), pp. 123–46.

4. Brzezinski, *Power*, pp. 182–83; and Vance, *Hard Choices*, pp. 156–57.

5. Brzezinski, *Power*, p. 183.

6. *Public Papers . . . Carter, 1977* (Washington: GPO, 1978), p. 2221.

7. Brzezinski, *Power*, p. 356; and Gary Sick, *All Fall Down: America's Tragic Encounter with Iran* (New York: Random House, 1985), pp. 147–49.

8. Brzezinski, *Power*, p. 444–50; Vance, *Hard Choices*, pp. 369–70; and Carter, *Faith*, pp. 471–72.

9. Vance, *Hard Choices*, p. 377.

10. M. G. Steen, Jr., "To Fly Safely," *Proceedings* (Mar 1987), p. 16; Sick, *All Fall Down*, pp. 354–55; Robert L. Earl, "A Matter of Principle," *Proceedings* (Feb 1983), pp. 30–36; Charlie A. Beckwith, *Delta Force* (New York: Harcourt Brace Jovanovich, 1983); and Paul B. Ryan, *The Iranian Rescue Mission* (Annapolis: Naval Institute Press, 1985).

11. Brzezinski, *Power*, p. 448; Robert J. Hanks, "The Indian Ocean," in George, *Navy*, p. 291; Breemer, *Naval Developments*, p. 30; and Vance, *Hard Choices*, p. 416.

12. Strubbing and Mendel, *Defense Game*, p. 31; and Robert P. Haffa, Jr., *The Half War: Planning U.S. Rapid Deployment Forces to Meet a Limited Contingency, 1960–1983* (Boulder, CO: Westview Press, 1984).

13. James F. Kelly, "Naval Deployments in the Indian Ocean," *Proceedings* (May 1983), p. 181; and *CNO Report, FY81*, p. 49.

14. Samuel F. Wells, Jr., "Limits on the Use of American Military Power," *Wilson Quarterly* (Wtr 1983), p. 129.

Chapter Thirty-six

1. Caspar Weinberger, *Fighting for Peace: Seven Critical Years in the Pentagon* (New York: Warner Books, 1990); *AR of the Secretary of Defense: 1982*, pp. 3–4; Stephen J. Cimbala, ed., *The Reagan Defense Program: An Interim Assessment* (Wilmington, Del.: Scholarly Resources, 1986); John Allen Williams, "The U.S. Navy under the Reagan Administration and Global Forward Strategy," in William P. Snyder and James Brown, eds., *Defense Policy in the Reagan Administration* (Washington: GPO, 1988), pp. 273–304; and Lawrence J. Korb, "The Defense Policy of the United States," in Douglas J. Murray and Paul R. Viotti, eds., *The Defense Policies of Nations* (Baltimore: Johns Hopkins Press, 1982), p. 52.

2. Congressional Budget Office, "Trident II Missiles: Capability, Costs, and Alternatives," (Washington: GPO, 1986), p. xi.

3. *New York Times*, 3 Oct 81.

4. Martin Linsky, "Threading the Shoals of the Media," *Government Executive* (May 1988), p. 30. Also see Anthony H. Cordesman, "The 600-Ship Navy: What Is It? Do We Need It? Can We Get It?", *AFJ* (Apr 1984), pp. 58–76.

5. John Lehman, "Where Do We Stand," *Shipmate* (June 1983), p. 26; Linsky, "Threading," p. 30; and *Defense Monitor* (No. 6, 1987), p. 1.

6. *U.S. News and World Report* (4 May 81), p. 37.

7. J. W. Holland, "Review of *Managing Nuclear Options*," *Proceedings* (Oct 1987), p. 202; and Walt Stephanson, "Comment on 'Acoustic Showdown for SSNs,'" *Proceedings* (Oct 1987), p. 22.

8. Strubbing and Mendel, *Defense Game*, p. 158.

9. Ken P. Werrell, "The Weapon the Military Did Not Want: The Modern Strategic Cruise Missile," *Journal of Military History* (Oct 1989), pp. 419–38; Joseph Metcalf, "Revolution at Sea," *Surface Warfare Magazine* (Nov 1986), p. 1; and *U.S. News and World Report* (4 May 1981), p. 37.

10. Jack Beatty, "In Harm's Way," *Atlantic Monthly* (May 1987), p. 41.

11. "First Strike Weapons at Sea," *Defense Monitor*, (1987), p. 2. For additional background, see John B. Hallendorf, "The Evolution of the Maritime Strategy: 1977 to 1987," *NWCR* (Sum 1988), pp. 7–28; and F. W. West, Jr., "Maritime Strategy and NATO Deterrence," *NWCR* (Oct 1985), pp. 5–19.

12. *Navy Times*, 23 Oct 1979, p. 29; and U.S. House, 90th Cong., 2nd Sess., Committee on Armed Services, "Hearings on Department of Defense Appropriations, for FY1970," 1969, Pt. 4, p. 227.

13. U.S. Senate, 95th Cong., 2nd Sess., Committee on Armed Services, "Hearings . . . on Department of Defense Appropriations for FY 1978," 1979, p. 1292; U.S. House, 96th Cong., 1st Sess., Committee on Armed Services, "Hearings on Department of Defense Appropriations for FY 1980," Jan–Feb 1979, p. 841; and Kenneth A. Myers, *North Atlantic Security: The Forgotten Flank?* (Beverly Hills, Calif.: Sage, 1979), p. 64.

14. U.S. Senate, 98th Cong., 2nd Sess., Committee on Armed Services, Subcommittee on Sea Power and Force Projection, "Hearings on Department of Defense . . . Appropriations for FY 1985," March–May 1984, Pt. 8, pp. 3870–71; and Gerald E. Miller, "Who Needs Arms Control?" *Proceedings* (Jan 1986), p. 40.

15. Frederick H. Hartmann, *Naval Renaissance: The U.S. Navy in the 1980s* (Annapolis: Naval Institute Press, 1989), p. 246.

16. "Global Maritime Strategy," *Proceedings* (Jan 1986), Suppl.; William Pendley, "The Maritime Strategy," *Proceedings* (Jun 1986), p. 84; "Lehman Seeks Superiority," *International Defense Review* (May 1982), p. 547; Tom Stefanick, *Strategic Antisubmarine Warfare and Naval Strategy* (Lexington, Mass.: D. C. Heath, 1987); and *U.S. Military Posture, FY1984* (Washington: Dept. of Defense, 1983), p. 6.

17. Donald C. Daniel and Philip D. Zelikow, "Superpower ASW Developments and the Survivability of Strategic Submarines," *Journal of Strategic Studies* (Mar 1987), pp. 5–35; and *U.S. Military Posture, FY1984*, p. 6.

18. Train, "Commentary," in George, *Navy*, p. 373.

19. *New York Times*, 23 Mar 1987; Robert Komer, "Maritime Strategy vs. Coalition Defense," *Foreign Affairs* (Sum 1982), pp. 1133–34; Beatty, "In Harm's Way," p. 46; Robert Komer, "Comment on 'Northern Flank Strategy,'" *Proceedings* (Jan 1986), p. 19; and Stephen P. Rosen, "Conventional Combat and Nuclear Balance," *Journal of Strategic Studies* (Mar 1987), pp. 36–61.

20. Stansfield Turner and George Thibault, "Preparing for the Unexpected: The Need for a New Military Strategy," *Foreign Affairs* (Fall 1982), p. 126; *Washington Post*, 4 May 1982; and Michael Edward, "Comments on 'Maritime Strategy from the Deckplates,'" *Proceedings* (Nov 1986), p. 14.

21. Steven E. Mays, "Letters," *Scientific American* (Mar 1981), p. 6; and Train, "Commentary," in George, *Navy*, p. 373.

22. Gerald O'Rourke, "Gulf Operations," *Proceedings* (May 1989), p. 50; and David Alan Rosenberg, "'It Is Hardly Possible to Imagine Anything Worse': Soviet Thoughts on the Maritime Strategy," *NWCR* (Sum 1988), pp. 69–105.

Chapter Thirty-seven

1. David C. Martin and John Walcott, *Best Laid Plans: The Inside Story of America's War Against Terrorism* (New York: Harper & Row, 1988), p. 43; John F. Lehman, *Command of the Seas: A Personal Story* (New York: Scribner's, 1988), pp. 307–8; and David P. Bolger, *Americans at War, 1975–1986: An Era of Violent Peace* (San Francisco: Presidio Press, 1988). Also see Barry Rubin, "The Reagan Administration and the Middle East," in Kenneth A. Oye et al., eds., *Eagle Resurgent: The Reagan Era in American Foreign Policy* (Boston: Little, Brown, 1987), Ch. 13; and James Cable, *Gunboat Diplomacy, 1919–1979* (2nd ed.; New York: St. Martins Press, 1981).

2. W. Hays Parks, "Crossing the Line," *Proceedings* (Nov 1986), p. 42.

3. Martin and Walcott, *Best*, p. 71; and L. MacFlenoe, "Comment on 'Sharpening the Claws of the Tomcat,'" *Proceedings* (Aug 1982), p. 86.

4. Alexander Haig, *Caveat: Realism, Reagan, and Foreign Policy* (New York: Macmillan, 1984), pp. 169–70.

5. Martin and Walcott, *Best*, p. 93; Benis M. Frank, *U.S. Marines in Lebanon, 1982–1984* (Washington: GPO, 1987), p. 13; and U.S. Senate, 98th Cong., 1st Sess., Committee on Foreign Relations, "Hearings on Authorization for U.S. Marines in Lebanon," 10 and 15 Nov 1983.

6. Martin and Walcott, *Best*, p. 95.

7. Martin and Walcott, *Best*, p. 114; and U.S. Senate, 98th Cong., 1st Sess., Committee on Foreign Relations, "Hearings on Authority for U.S. Marines in Lebanon," 1984, pp. 34–36.

8. Martin and Walcott, *Best*, p. 120.

9. Frank, *Lebanon*, p. 88.

10. *Report of the Department of Defense [Admiral Robert Long] Commission on*

Beirut International Airport Terrorist Act, October 23, 1983 (Washington: Dept. of Defense, 1983), p. 46; Martin and Walcott, *Best,* pp. 120–24; and Ralph A. Hallenbeck, "Force and Diplomacy" (Unpubl. Ph.D. Diss., Pennsylvania State University, 1986).

11. Roy Gutman, "Division at Top Meant Half-Measures, Mistakes," *Newsday,* 8 April 1984, p. 36; and Larry Speakes, *Speaking Out* (New York: Macmillan, 1988), p. 166.

12. Martin and Walcott, *Best,* p. 140.

13. Martin and Walcott, *Best,* p. 141.

14. George C. Wilson, *Supercarrier* (New York: Macmillan, 1986), pp. 110–55; and George C. Wilson, "Raid on Lebanon: What Went Wrong," *Navy Times,* 22 Sep 1986, p. 18.

15. Wilson, *Supercarrier,* p. 133.

16. Lehman, *Command,* pp. 326–38; and Hartmann, *Naval Renaissance,* p. 235. Also see R. James Woolsey, "Review of *Command of the Seas,*" in *Proceedings* (Feb 1989), p. 109.

17. U.S. Senate, 98th Cong., 1st Sess., Committee on Foreign Relations, "Hearings . . . on S. J. Res. 187 to Repeal the Multinational Force in Lebanon Resolution," 10 and 15 Nov 1983, p. 30.

18. U.S. Senate, 98th Cong., 1st Sess., Committee on Foreign Relations, "Hearings on Authority for U.S. Marines in Lebanon," 1984, pp. 19–20, 25.

19. Speakes, *Speaking Out,* p. 186.

Chapter Thirty-eight

1. Benjamin F. Schemmer, "JCS Reply . . . to Critique," *Armed Forces Journal* (July 1984), pp. 11–14; and Lehman, *Command,* p. 298. Also see Mark Adkin, *Urgent Fury* (Lexington, Mass.: D. C. Heath, 1989).

2. Lehman, *Command,* p. 301; Ronald H. Spector, *U.S. Marines in Grenada* (Washington: USMC, 1987); A. M. Leahy, "Grenada—In Retrospect," *Fortitudine* (Spr 1984), pp. 10–15; Anthony Payne et al., *Grenada: Revolution and Invasion* (New York: St. Martin's Press, 1984); Gregory Sandford and Richard Vigilante, *Grenada: The Untold Story* (Lanham, Md.: Madison Books, 1984); David P. Bolger, "Operation Urgent Fury and Its Critics," *Military Review* (July 1986), pp. 57–69; U.S. House, 98th Cong., 2nd Sess., Committee on Armed Services, "Hearings on Lessons Learned as a Result of the U.S. Military Operations in Grenada," 24 Jan 1984; and Robert P. Hinton, "Review of *Four Stars,*" *Proceedings* (Sept 1989), p. 123.

3. Martin and Walcott, *Best,* Ch. 7.

4. Scott Truver, "Maritime Terrorism," *Proceedings* (May 1986), p. 160; and Larry A. McCullough, "International and Domestic Criminal Law Issues in the *Achille Lauro* Incident," *Naval Law Review* (Wtr 1986), pp. 53–108.

5. Martin and Walcott, *Best,* p. 275.

6. Martin and Walcott, *Best,* p. 278.

7. Martin and Walcott, *Best,* p. 282.

8. Parks, "Crossing the Line," pp. 43–44.

9. Dept. of State, "International Terrorism," Selected Documents No. 24 (1986), pp. 1–2.

10. R. E. Stumpf, "Air War with Libya," *Proceedings* (Aug 1986), pp. 42–48; Martin and Walcott, *Best,* Ch. 10; and Vox Militaris, "The U.S. Strike Against Libya: Operation Eldorado Canyon," *The Army Quarterly and Defence Journal* (Apr 1986), pp. 134–48.

11. Speakes, *Speaking Out,* p. 181.

12. Lehman, *Command,* pp. 368–75; Stumpf, "Air War," pp. 42–48; Martin

and Walcott, *Best*, Ch. 10; Parks, "Crossing the Line," pp. 45–52; and Noel Koch, "But Our 'No-Negotiations' Policy May Not Have Helped," *Washington Post*, 18 Mar 1990.

Chapter Thirty-nine
1. Genco, "The Eisenhower Doctrine," pp. 309–62; and Janice G. Stein, "The Wrong Strategy in the Right Place: The United States in the Gulf," *International Security* (Wtr 1988), pp. 142–67.
2. Zumwalt, *On Watch*, p. 454.
3. John Lacouture, "Seapower in the Indian Ocean," *Proceedings* (Aug 1979), p. 30; and Vance, *Hard Choices*, p. 369.
4. *U.S. News and World Report*, 16 Feb 1981; and *Washington Post*, 17 July 1981.
5. *New York Times*, 22 and 23 May 1984.
6. *Washington Post*, 30 May 1987.
7. *Washington Post*, 26 and 28 July 1987; and *New York Times*, 21 July 1987.
8. *Navy Times*, 27 July 1987, p. 35; Grant A. Sharp, "Formal Investigation into the Circumstances Surrounding the Attack on the USS *Stark* (FFG 31) on 17 May 1987," 17 Jun 1987, Dept. of the Navy; David R. Carson, "The *Vincennes* Incident," *Proceedings* (Sep 1989), pp. 87–89; *New York Times*, 22 Jan 1989; and *Navy Times*, 1 June 1987, pp. 6–12. Also see Art Conklin, "We Gave 110% and Saved Our Ship," *Proceedings* (Dec 1988), p. 119.
9. Sharp, "Investigation . . . *Stark*;" *New York Times*, 6 July 1988; and *New York Times*, 4 July 1988.
10. *Navy Times*, 1 June 1987, p. 12. Triplett's statement, and Trost's position, were shrewdly crafted to avoid additional questions about the CNO's responsibility for the debacle. Title 10, U.S. Code, obligated the Navy "to be prepared to conduct prompt and sustained combat operations at sea in support of U.S. national interests." Dept. of Defense, "Functions of the Department of Defense and Its Major Components, Dir. No. 5100.1," (Washington: GPO, 1969), p. 1.
11. *Navy Times*, 1 June 1987, p. 12.
12. Lehman, *Command*, p. 395.
13. *Washington Post*, 26 July 1987.
14. *Navy Times*, 17 Aug 1987, pp. 33–34; "Operation Praying Mantis," *Surface Warfare* (Nov 1988), p. 18; J. B. Perkins III, "Operation Praying Mantis: The Surface View," *Proceedings* (May 1989), pp. 66–70; Bud Langston and Don Bringle, "Operation Praying Mantis," *Proceedings* (May 1989), pp. 54–56; O'Rourke, "Gulf Operations," pp. 42–50; *New York Times*, 29 July 1987, p. 3; and *Washington Post*, 1 May 1988. Murphy later claimed that the *New York Times* distorted his statement. Brent Baker, "Public Affairs Front," *Proceedings* (Sep 1988), p. 114.
15. *Washington Post*, 26 July 1987.
16. *Washington Post*, 1 May 1988.
17. Paul X. Rinn, "Comment and Discussion," *Proceedings* (May 1984), pp. 12–13.
18. Transcript, Anthony Less, "The Persian Gulf War," address at the Marine Corps Historical Center, Washington Navy Yard, 15 Jan 1990.
19. Less, "Persian Gulf War."
20. "Operation Praying Mantis," *Surface Warfare*, p. 18.
21. *Navy Times*, 2 May 1988, p. 25.
22. Lehman, *Command*, p. 400.
23. Carson, "*Vincennes*," pp. 87–89; Norman Friedman, "The *Vincennes* Inci-

dent," *Proceedings* (May 1989), pp. 72–79; and William M. Fogarty, "Formal Investigation into the Circumstances Surrounding the Downing of a Commercial Airliner by the USS *Vincennes* (CG49) on 3 July 1988," 28 July 1988, NHC.

24. Carson, "*Vincennes*," pp. 87–89; and Less, "Persian Gulf War."

25. *New York Times*, 5 July 1988.

Chapter Forty

1. "President Orders Sweeping Reductions in Strategic and Tactical Nuclear Arms," *Washington Post*, 28 Sep 1991.

2. *Washington Post*, 16 Dec 1989, p. 26; Michael R. Gordon, "Soviets Scale Back Naval Deployments and Large Exercises," *NYT*, 17 July 1988, p. 1; Interview, C-Span telecast of Soviet Television News, 31 Dec 1991; and Scott Truver, "Tommorrow's Fleet, *Proceedings* (July 1990), p. 83.

3. *Washington Post*, 28 Sep 1991.

4. "Trost Testimony," *AFJ* (April 1989), p. 66. Also see, John F. Morton, "The U.S. Navy in 1988," *Proceedings* (May 1989), pp. 154–57; and Edward J. Walsh, "U.S. Surface Navy Plans Ahead to 2020," *AFJ* (July 1989), p. 64. The Navy's addiction to the force levels embodied in the Cold War Maritime Strategy as late as 1990 may be viewed in Mark A. Randol and Wallace J. Thies, "The Opportunity Costs of Large-Deck Carriers: Naval Strategy for the 1990s and Beyond," *NWCR* (Sum 1990), pp. 9–31.

5. Brent Baker, "The War of Words," *Proceedings* (Dec 1989), pp. 35–39. The editors of *Proceedings* claimed in the subheading for the article that "our defense budget will suffer unless our military leaders learn to communicate with the press." John D. Morrocco, "Naval Air Warfare: Revolution in Jeopardy," *Proceedings* (June 1990), p. 58; Norman Polmar, "The U.S. Navy," *Proceedings* (June 1990), p. 71–72; and Norman Polmar, "The *Seawolf*: Crash Dive!", *Proceedings* (Oct 1990), pp. 133–34.

6. John Boatman et al., "Cuts to Continue Despite 'Storm,'" *Jane's Defence Weekly*, 9 Feb 91, p. 166.

7. *Navy Times*, 21 Jan 1991.

8. The lack of sophistication of the politico-strategic analysis supporting the *Seawolf* program was illustrated by an article by Commander Bruce Lemkin that appeared on the eve of the abortive August pro-communist coup in Moscow. While admitting that a "Second Russian Revolution" had taken place, Lemkin predicted with no supporting evidence that "the consequences of the social, economic, and political collapse in the Soviet Union are . . . more likely to be a repressive, totalitarian regime that seeks to assuage its internal troubles through the fabrication of an external threat." Bruce Lemkin, "The New Leader of the Pack," *Proceedings* (Jun 1991), pp. 42–45. As to Admiral Trost, in early 1986, Navy Secretary Lehman picked Admiral Kelso to succeed Admiral Watkins as CNO. Weinberger agreed, but when the nomination reached the White House, Vice Admiral John Poindexter, a submarine reactor engineer then serving as Reagan's national security adviser, persuaded the president to appoint Trost instead. Lehman, *Command*, p. 418. Poindexter's judgment must be considered suspect in light of his ongoing involvement in the malodorous Iran-Contra scandal for which he was dismissed from the White House, hastily retired from the Navy, and put on trial for various felonies.

9. Jonathan Wilde, "Liberian Rescue Mission," *All Hands* (Nov 1990), pp. 42–45.

10. Easily the most well-informed early history of the Persian Gulf War is Norman Friedman, *Desert Victory: The War for Kuwait* (Annapolis: Naval Institute Press, 1991). Peter Gilchrist, *Sea Power: The Coalition and Iraqi Navies* (London:

Osprey Publishing, 1991) is one of the better photography-text volumes show-ing the warships participating in the conflict. For an early impression of the buildup, see David Evans, "Desert Shield: From the Gulf," *Proceedings* (January 1991), pp. 77–84. "Desert Storm Special Issue," *All Hands* (July 1991), contains essential details about force levels and deployments. Harry G. Summers, Jr., "Strategy for Victory," *Military History's Desert War* (Mar 1991), p. 8–9, compares Iraqi strategy to Hitler's 1941 disastrous invasion of Russia.

11. Lehman, *Command*, p. 400.

12. Lyle G. Bien, "From the Strike Cell," *Proceedings* (June 1991), pp. 58–61.

13. Norman Friedman, "Lessons of the Gulf Crisis," *Proceedings* (Oct 1990), pp. 137–39.

14. Andrew E. Gibson and Jacob L. Shuford, "Desert Shield and Strategic Sealift," *NWCR* (Spr 1991), pp. 13–14.

15. *Washington Post*, 10 Feb 91.

16. John Burlage, "7th Fleet CO Denies Iraqi Targets Shifted to Air Force," *Navy Times*, 27 May 1991, p. 6.

17. *Washington Post*, 10 January 1991.

18. *Washington Post*, 28 Feb 1991.

19. William Matthews, "U.S. Military Strikes with Precision," *Navy Times*, 28 Jan 1991, pp. 3–4; David Steigman and Marc Zolton, "Navy, Marines Played Ma-jor Role in Attack," *Navy Times*, 28 Jan 1991, pp. 28–29; and Riley D. Mixson, "Where We Must Do Better," *Proceedings* (Aug 1991), p. 38.

20. "The Secret History of the War," *Newsweek*, 18 Mar 1991, p. 31.

21. Mixson, "Where We Must Do Better," p. 38 ; and Bien, "From the Strike Cell," p. 59.

22. Burlage, "7th Fleet CO," p. 6.; and Stanley R. Arthur and Marvin Pokrant, "Desert Storm at Sea," *Proceedings* (May 1991), p. 85.

23. Marc Zolton, "*Missouri, Wisconsin,* Open Up on Iraqi Positions," *Navy Times*, 5 Feb 1991, p. 10; Burlage, "7th Fleet CO," p. 6.

24. Tom Philpott, "Fleet Commander Recommended December Hits on Iraqi Minelayers," *Navy Times*, 27 May 1991, p. 4; and Edward J. Walsh, "Navy Struggles to Manage Mine Warfare Shipbuilding,"*AFJ* (Mar 1991), pp. 49–50. An article by David G. Clark, "The Surface Forces Are Ready," *Proceedings* (May 1988), pp. 78–93, suggests by omission some reasons why the Navy had so much difficulty with mines during the 1987–88 Earnest Will convoys and again in 1991.

25. Philpott, "Fleet Commander," p. 4.

26. J. M. Martin, "We Still Haven't Learned," *Proceedings* (July 1991), pp. 64–68; and Philpott, "Fleet Commander, p. 4.

27. Frank Evans, "*Princeton* Leaves the War," *Proceedings* (July 1991), p. 70; and Philpott, "Fleet Commander," p. 4.

28. Philpott, "Fleet Commander," p. 4.

29. William Matthews, "Allies Claim Air Superiority," *Navy Times*, 4 Feb 1991, p. 2; C-SPAN TV Program, 12 March 1991; and *Navy Times*, 11 Feb 1991, p. 2.

30. *Washington Post*, 11 March 1991.

31. *Washington Post*, 28 Sep 1991.

Index